Lecture Notes in Computer Science 16571

The series Lecture Notes in Computer Science (LNCS), including its subseries Lecture Notes in Artificial Intelligence (LNAI) and Lecture Notes in Bioinformatics (LNBI), has established itself as a medium for the publication of new developments in computer science and information technology research, teaching, and education.

LNCS enjoys close cooperation with the computer science R & D community, the series counts many renowned academics among its volume editors and paper authors, and collaborates with prestigious societies. Its mission is to serve this international community by providing an invaluable service, mainly focused on the publication of conference and workshop proceedings and postproceedings. LNCS commenced publication in 1973.

Kangkook Jee · Aniket Kate
Editors

Applied Cryptography and Network Security

24th International Conference, ACNS 2026
Stony Brook, NY, USA, June 22–25, 2026
Proceedings, Part I

Springer

Editors
Kangkook Jee
The University of Texas at Dallas
Richardson, TX, USA

Aniket Kate
Purdue University
West Lafayette, IN, USA

ISSN 0302-9743 ISSN 1611-3349 (electronic)
Lecture Notes in Computer Science
ISBN 978-3-032-32559-4 ISBN 978-3-032-32560-0 (eBook)
https://doi.org/10.1007/978-3-032-32560-0

This Springer imprint is published by the registered company Springer Nature Switzerland AG
The registered company address is: Gewerbestrasse 11, 6330 Cham, Switzerland

Preface

ACNS 2026, the 24th International Conference on Applied Cryptography and Network Security, was held in Stony Brook, NY, USA, on June 22–25, 2026. The conference covered all technical aspects of applied cryptography, network and computer security, and privacy, spanning academic research and developments at the industrial and technical frontiers. Authors were explicitly asked to address ethical considerations related to vulnerability disclosure where applicable. Continuing the initiative introduced in 2025, ACNS also solicited Systematization of Knowledge (SoK) papers aimed at placing complex research questions into a broader context.

The conference featured two submission cycles, one in September 2025 and one in January 2026. Across both cycles, 282 submissions were received: 129 in the first cycle and 153 in the second. The Program Committee selected 59 papers for publication in the conference proceedings, resulting in an overall acceptance rate of 20.9%.

The proceedings appear in three volumes collecting all 59 accepted papers. This volume, LNCS 16571, contains 20 papers organized into three topical sections: Post-Quantum Cryptography, Cryptographic Primitives and Proof Systems, and Secure Protocols and Multi-Party Computation.

In addition to the contributed paper presentations, ACNS 2026 hosted three distinguished keynote speakers: Elaine Shi (Carnegie Mellon University), Vitaly Shmatikov (Cornell Tech), and Dan Guido (Trail of Bits), whose talks spanned foundational theory and real-world security practice.

The Program Committee consisted of 98 leading experts in applied cryptography and security, supported by 40 external reviewers. The program was selected under a double-blind review model in which each submission received at least three reviews, with careful attention to conflicts of interest. After completing their evaluations, reviewers engaged in extensive discussions before final decisions were reached. In Cycle 2, the Program Chairs introduced a dedicated rebuttal phase—motivated by the strong engagement from both authors and reviewers observed during Cycle 1—which enriched deliberation and improved decision quality. The Program Chairs neither submitted papers nor handled submissions for which they had conflicts of interest. We would like to express our sincere gratitude to the Program Committee members and external reviewers for their dedication, thoughtful evaluations, and active participation throughout the review process.

In keeping with ACNS tradition, the Program Committee recognized outstanding student contributions through the Best Student Paper Award. This year, two papers were selected:

- *Photons Are Perfect, Protocols Are Not: Cracking QKD BBM92 via the Internet*—Kashyap Thimmaraju, Max Hiort, Darshit Suratwala, Elham Amini, and Jean-Pierre Seifert (TU Berlin)

- *(Partially) Blind Signatures from Cryptographic Group Actions*—Dung Duong, Xuan Thanh Khuc, and Willy Susilo (University of Wollongong), Youming Qiao (University of New South Wales/University of Technology Sydney), and Chuanqi Zhang (University of Technology Sydney)

This year, the ACNS leadership also organized the inaugural Test-of-Time Award. The selection committee—consisting of Lejla Batina, Marc Fischlin, Aniket Kate, Kangkook Jee, Veelasha Moonsamy, and Christina Pöpper—identified two influential papers published at ACNS between 2008 and 2010:

- *Attribute-Based Encryption with Partially Hidden Encryptor-Specified Access Structures* (ACNS 2008)—Takashi Nishide, Kazuki Yoneyama, and Kazuo Ohta
- *Homomorphic MACs: MAC-Based Integrity for Network Coding* (ACNS 2009)—Shweta Agrawal and Dan Boneh

Running a conference of this scale is a collective effort. We thank the ACNS Steering Committee, in particular Jianying Zhou and Moti Yung, for their continued guidance and support. We are grateful to the General Chairs, Omar Chowdhury and Nick Nikiforakis (Stony Brook University), for their excellent organization of the event, and to Rahul Chatterjee (Workshop Chair), Anrin Chakraborti (Poster Chair), and Josh Wiedemeier (Web Chair) for their valuable contributions to ACNS 2026. We thank our contacts at Springer for their support in ensuring a smooth publication process. We also gratefully acknowledge CACI for their generous sponsorship, which made this edition of ACNS possible. Finally, ACNS 2026 would not have been possible without the authors who submitted their work and the Program Committee members and reviewers who dedicated their time and expertise to evaluating it. We sincerely thank all contributors for making ACNS 2026 a success.

May 2026

Kangkook Jee
Aniket Kate

Organization

General Chairs

Omar Chowdhury	Stony Brook University, USA
Nick Nikiforakis	Stony Brook University, USA

Program Committee Chairs

Kangkook Jee	University of Texas at Dallas, USA
Aniket Kate	Supra Research/Purdue University, USA

Workshop Chair

Rahul Chatterjee	University of Wisconsin-Madison, USA

Poster Chair

Anrin Chakraborti	University of Illinois Chicago, USA

Web Chair

Josh Wiedemeier	University of Texas at Dallas, USA

Steering Committee

Moti Yung	Google; Columbia University, USA
Jianying Zhou	Singapore University of Technology and Design, Singapore

Program Committee

Adithya Bhat	Visa Research, USA
Alexander Block	University of Illinois Chicago, USA
Alishah Chator	Baruch College, USA
Alptekin Küpçü	Koç University, Turkey
Andre Kassis	University of Waterloo, Canada
Andrea Basso	IBM Research Europe, Switzerland
Aniket Kate	Supra Research/Purdue University, USA
Anna Lisa Ferrara	Università degli Studi del Molise, Italy
Antonin Leroux	Université de Rennes, France
Avishai Wool	Tel Aviv University, Israel
Barbara Masucci	University of Salerno, Italy
Bart Mennink	Maastricht University, The Netherlands
Chen-Da Liu-Zhang	Lucerne University of Applied Sciences and Arts, Switzerland
Chia-Mu Yu	National Yang Ming Chiao Tung University, Taiwan
Daniel Gibney	University of Texas at Dallas, USA
Daoyuan Wu	Lingnan University, China
David Jao	University of Waterloo, Canada
Davide Maiorca	University of Cagliari, Italy
Debajyoti Das	Lund University, Sweden
Donghang Lu	TikTok, USA
Doowon Kim	University of Tennessee, Knoxville, USA
Dung Duong	University of Wollongong, Australia
Elena Andreeva	TU Wien, Austria
Elizabeth Quaglia	Royal Holloway, University of London, UK
Eun-Sun Cho	Chungnam National University, South Korea
Fatemeh Ganji	Worcester Polytechnic Institute, USA
Frederik Armknecht	University of Mannheim, Germany
Geng Hong	Fudan University, China
George Theodorakopoulos	Cardiff University, UK
Giovanni Apruzzese	University of Liechtenstein, Liechtenstein
Hikaru Tsuchida	Saitama Institute of Technology, Japan
Hong Hu	Pennsylvania State University, USA
Hsu-Chun Hsiao	National Taiwan University, Taiwan
Huaming Chen	University of Sydney, Australia
Hyeonmin Lee	University of Virginia, USA
Hyoungshick Kim	Sungkyunkwan University, South Korea
Igors Stepanovs	Amazon, Spain
Imtiaz Karim	University of Texas at Dallas, USA

Jalaj Upadhyay	Rutgers University, USA
Jaspal Singh	Purdue University, Georgia Institute of Technology, USA
Jeremias Mechler	Karlsruhe Institute of Technology, KASTEL Security Research Labs, Germany
Jesko Dujmovic	Northeastern University, Boston University, USA
Jialong Zhang	Xi'an Jiaotong University, China
Jinwen Wang	University of Texas at Dallas, USA
Josh Wiedemeier	University of Texas at Dallas, USA
Julius Hermelink	Max Planck Institute for Security and Privacy, Germany
Kangkook Jee	University of Texas at Dallas, USA
Katerina Mitrokotsa	University of St. Gallen, Switzerland
Lukasz Chmielewski	Masaryk University, Czech Republic
Mainack Mondal	Indian Institute of Technology Kharagpur, India
Marcus Botacin	Texas A&M University, USA
Matthieu Rambaud	Télécom Paris, France
Maxwell Young	Mississippi State University, USA
Meng Hao	Singapore Management University, Singapore
Monosij Maitra	Indian Institute of Technology Kharagpur, India
Mu Zhang	University of Utah, USA
Murtuza Jadliwala	University of Texas at San Antonio, USA
Nesrine Kaaniche	Institut Polytechnique de Paris, France
Nicolas Alhaddad	Boston University, USA
Nirnimesh Ghose	University of Nebraska - Lincoln, USA
Omkant Pandey	Stony Brook University, USA
Peng Gao	Virginia Tech, USA
Pierre Parrend	EPITA; Université de Strasbourg, France
Poulami Das	Least Authority, Germany
Protik Kumar Paul	TU Darmstadt, Germany
Qingkai Shi	Nanjing University, China
Reihaneh Safavi-Naini	University of Calgary, Canada
Riccardo Lazzeretti	Sapienza University of Rome, Italy
Riccardo Spolaor	Shandong University, China
Ruoyu "Fish" Wang	Arizona State University, USA
Ryan Henry	University of Calgary, Canada
Samuel Jaques	University of Waterloo, Canada
Sanchuan Chen	Auburn University, USA
Saravanan Vijayakumaran	IIT Bombay, India
Sebastian Berndt	Technische Hochschule Lübeck, Germany
Seung Geol Choi	United States Naval Academy, USA
Shaileshh Bojja Venkatakrishnan	Ohio State University, USA

Shan Chen	Southern University of Science and Technology, China
Solmaz Salimi	Eurecom, France
Subhra Mazumdar	Indian Institute of Technology Indore, India
Sukarno Mertoguno	Georgia Institute of Technology, USA
Sushmita Ruj	University of New South Wales, Australia
Tamalika Mukherjee	Max Planck Institute for Security and Privacy, Germany
Thomas Peters	UCLouvain, Belgium
Toshinori Usui	NTT Social Informatics Laboratories, Japan
Vadim Safronov	University of Oxford, UK
Wen-jie Lu	TikTok Inc., China
Xiang Li	Nankai University, China
Xiangkun Jia	Institute of Software, Chinese Academy of Sciences, China
Xuejing Yuan	Beijing University of Posts and Telecommunications, China
Xusheng Xiao	Arizona State University, USA
Yanqi Gu	Meta, USA
Yanxue Jia	Purdue University & Illinois Institute of Technology, USA
Yingying Chen	Rutgers University, USA
Yuchen Yang	Pennsylvania State University, USA
Yue Duan	Singapore Management University, Singapore
Yuseok Jeon	Korea University, South Korea
Ziming Zhao	Northeastern University, USA

Additional Reviewers

Sven Argo
Adda-Akram Bendoukha
Robin Berger
Ritam Bhaumik
Arcangelo Castiglione
Anirban Chakrabarti
Nan Cheng
Stelvio Cimato
Ye Dong
Moumita Dutta
Tobias Fritz
Clemente Galdi
Jasmin Zalonis
Shreyas Gupta
Abir Islam
Aaron Kaiser
Vukašin Karadžić
Simon Klancher
Duc Le
Seunghoon Lee
Vikas Maurya
Erik Mårtensson
Anne Müller
Montassar Naghmouchi
Florias Papadopoulos
Shravani Patil

Kabir Peshawaria
Richard Petri
Lucas Piske
Eric Sageloli
A H M Nazmus Sakib
Samipa Samanta
Olga Sanina
Laltu Sardar
Joseph Spracklen
Wilson Tsuata
Mohit Vaid
Raveen Wijewickrama
Anshu Yadav
Ziling Yang

Contents

Post-quantum Cryptography

Cryptographic Primitives and Proof Systems

Efficient Post-quantum EPID Signatures From VOLE-in-the-Head

Zuming Liu[1], Yanhong Xu[1,2], Deng Tang[1(✉)], and Neng Zeng[3]

[1] School of Computer Science, Shanghai Jiao Tong University, Shanghai, China
dengtang@sjtu.eu.cn

[2] Key Laboratory of Intelligent Sensing System and Security (Ministry of Education), Hubei University, Wuhan, Hubei, China

[3] Department of Applied Mathematics, School of Mathematics and Physics, Xi'an Jiaotong-Liverpool University, Suzhou Industrial Park, Jiangsu, China

Abstract. Enhanced Privacy Identification (EPID) is a type of anonymous signature scheme. Due to its decentralized revocation procedure, EPID has been used in real-world systems for hardware enclave attestation and has been standardized in ISO/IEC. Recently, a prominent line of research has been contributing to the design of efficient EPID schemes based on post-quantum assumptions, including lattices and symmetric primitives. We observe that in this line of research, there is still room for improvement. In particular, Boneh et al. (CT-RSA 2019) proposed a new model for EPID signatures for attestation, which utilizes an accumulator to issue group credentials and enables group members to rejoin the system as needed. However, no formal security definitions were provided. In addition, all existing EPID schemes from symmetric primitives utilized the less efficient MPC-in-the-Head proof systems (Ishai et al., STOC 2007), resulting in large signature sizes.

In this work, we present an efficient hash-based EPID signature scheme derived from a recently developed VOLE-in-the-Head proof system (Baum et al., CRYPTO 2023). To this end, we first provide rigorous security requirements for EPID signatures that allow group members to rejoin the system. Next, we construct a hash-based accumulator accompanied by a zero-knowledge argument of knowledge of an accumulated value. Finally, we implement our EPID scheme and analyze its concrete efficiency. The results demonstrate the advantages of our scheme compared to other post-quantum constructions.

Keywords: Hash-based cryptography · EPID · VOLE-in-the-Head · Privacy-Preserving Primitives

1 Introduction

EPID. The enhanced privacy Identification (EPID), initially introduced by Brickell and Li [11,13], is an anonymous signature scheme that allows a group

Z. Liu and Y. Xu–Equal contribution.

K. Jee and A. Kate (Eds.): ACNS 2026, LNCS 16571, pp. 3–31, 2027.
https://doi.org/10.1007/978-3-032-32560-0_1

member to sign messages in the name of the group without revealing its identity. Compared to other anonymous signatures such as group signature (GS) [15] and Direct anonymous attestation (DAA) [14], EPID enables signature-based revocation. Particularly, a signature can be directly placed on a signature revocation list (SRL), and an EPID signature includes an additional proof demonstrating that none of the signatures on the revocation list were generated using the current signing key. This proof of non-revocation is the core component of EPID systems and largely dominates the complexity.

EPID signatures have received considerable attention since their inception. Brickell and Li [12] proposed a more efficient EPID scheme from bilinear maps. The security of their scheme is based on strong Diffie-Hellman and the decisional Diffie-Hellman assumptions. This scheme [12] has been deployed in hardware enclave attestation (e.g., Intel SGX), and has also been included in ISO/IEC standards [1]. Later, Dall et al. [22] proposed cache attacks on the Intel SGX EPID implementation. Faonio et al. [25] introduced a subversion-resilient EPID scheme, which provides the same functionality and security as the original EPID against potentially subverted hardware. Faonio et al. [25] also designed a practical construction based on the external Diffie-Hellman assumptions in the random oracle model. All the aforementioned schemes assumed that SRL is managed by some trusted entity, such as the group manager or honest verifiers. Sanders and Traoré [42] revisited the security notion of EPID and proposed a scheme supporting malicious revocation, in which a malicious entity generates the revocation lists. They [42] then designed very efficient schemes secure against such powerful adversaries. Sanders [41] further improved the efficiency of EPID by using a proof of non-revocation that is not zero-knowledge but whose combination with other parts of EPID systems yields an anonymous scheme. This line of research has reached high success. Remarkably, the signature size of the scheme [41] achieving 80-bit security is around 1 KB and 50 KB when the size of the signature revocation list is 0 and 1000, respectively. It is worth mentioning that the above constructions are not post-quantum secure.

Post-Quantum EPID. Solutions based on lattices or hash functions have recently appeared in the literature. The first post-quantum EPID schemes were constructed by Boneh et al. [10], and relied only on symmetric primitives. The signature size is around 200 MB and can be reduced to a few megabytes if frequent interaction with the group manager is allowed. However, the impact of the signature revocation list is never made explicit, and no implementation was provided. Shortly after [10], Kassem et al. [33] proposed the first lattice-based EPID scheme from structured lattices. The signature sizes are around 850 MB, and hundreds of seconds are required for signing and verification. Chen et al. [19] improved upon [33] in terms of computation and communication efficiency. Nevertheless, the core component of EPID systems, i.e., the proof of non-revocation, is not described. Recently, Chen et al. [17] improved over [10] by proposing a new hash-based EPID scheme. Their scheme [17] can handle large group sizes (up to 2^{60} group members) by employing F-SPHINCS+ [16,18] to issue group credentials. F-SPHINCS+ [16,18] is modified from SPHINCS+ [9] to have fewer hash evaluations. In particular, F-SPHINCS+ no longer utilizes the Winternitz one-time signature scheme and largely differs from the standardized SPHINCS+. More recently, Jeudy and Sanders [31] revisited the standard approach of non-revocation and proposed a novel technique to avoid heavy reliance on zero-knowledge proofs in proof of non-revocation. Their signature sizes [31] are the most compact to date. Unfortunately, they leave the implementation of their EPID scheme for future work. Nevertheless, we managed to provide an estimation of their runtimes. As commented by the authors [31], the signer is required to prove the knowledge of a group credential [3,29,30,38], and to generate one Falcon key and $|\mathsf{SRL}|$ Falcon signatures [40]. Here $|\mathsf{SRL}|$ is the cardinality of the revocation list SRL. We thus employ the numbers from [3,40] to estimate the runtime of [31]. However, since the experiments of [3,40] were conducted in different environments, the given estimations are for reference only. In Table 1, we provide a thorough comparison of existing post-quantum EPID constructions.

While existing schemes have made significant progress in terms of functionality, security, and efficiency, the state-of-the-art of EPID is still unsatisfactory. On the one hand, the most efficient lattice-based construction [31] lacks implementation, making its practical value unclear. On the other hand, the EPID constructions from symmetric primitives all utilize the Multi-Party-Computation-in-the-Head (MPCitH) proof systems [28,34], which are less efficient than the recently developed Vector-Oblivious-Linear-Evaluation-in-the-Head (VOLEitH) proof systems [5–7]. In this work, we aim to employ the most recent VOLEitH proof systems to construct more efficient EPID signatures from symmetric primitives.

Before introducing our contributions, let us first recall a generic approach adopted by previous EPID constructions. An EPID system consists of three types of entities, a group manager ($\mathcal{GM}$), group members, and verifiers. The $\mathcal{GM}$ is in charge of issuing group credentials/certificates to group members. This is typically accomplished by signing the public keys of group members, and the resulting signatures serve as the group credentials. In the process, group members also obtain secret keys that are only known to themselves. Later, a group member can prove membership to a verifier without revealing its identity by demonstrating the knowledge of the $\mathcal{GM}$'s signature on its public key, of which this member also knows the corresponding secret key. So far this is essentially GS [8,15]. The difference with GS lies in the mechanism for tracing and deterring malicious signing behaviors. Concretely, there is no opening procedure in EPID signatures. Instead, a group member signs a message with respect to a signature revocation list (SRL), and demonstrates that he did not produce any signature in SRL.

When it comes to concrete constructions, different techniques were proposed to achieve better efficiency. For instance, the proof of non-revocation proposed by Jeudy and Sanders [31] consists of generating one Falcon key and $|\mathsf{SRL}|$ Falcon signatures, which is supposed to be more efficient than the above generic method. Boneh et al. [10] proposed a new model that enables group members to rejoin the

Table 1. Comparison of existing post-quantum EPID schemes. The maximum number of group members allowed in the EPID system is given in (). The second construction by Boneh et al. [10] and our scheme allow group members to rejoin the system and employ an accumulator to issue group certificates. The schemes proposed by Chen et al. [17] can handle group sizes up to 2^{60}, no other scheme can compare to it. Reported runtimes of [17,33] are taken from the original publications.

Schemes	Sign	Verify	Sig size	|SRL|	Security	Type
KFM+19 [33] (2^{32})	361 s	114 s	836 MB	0	128	lattice
	371 s	117 s	838 MB	100	128	lattice
	372 s	119 s	845 MB	500	128	lattice
	374 s	121 s	854 MB	1000	128	lattice
JS25 [31] (2^{32}) ⋆⋆	350 ms	150 ms	0.12 MB	0	128	lattice
	360 ms	151 ms	0.17 MB	10	128	lattice
	375 ms	154 ms	0.64 MB	100	128	lattice
	442 ms	168 ms	2.71 MB	500	128	lattice
	526 ms	186 ms	5.31 MB	1000	128	lattice
BEF19-I [10] (2^{30})	–	–	216.82 MB	?	128	symm.
BEF19-II [10] (2^{20})	–	–	3.45 MB	?	128	symm.
CDK+24 [17] (2^{20})	12.9 s	6.3 s	0.83 MB	0	129	symm.
	13.6 s	6.6 s	0.95 MB	10	129	symm.
	19.6 s	9.5 s	1.83 MB	100	129	symm.
	47.2 s	22.6 s	6.03 MB	500	129	symm.
	80.4 s	38.8 s	11.23 MB	1000	129	symm.
Ours (2^{20}) non-optimized implementation	0.7 s	0.5 s	0.22 MB	0	128	symm.
	0.9 s	0.7 s	0.29 MB	10	128	symm.
	3.1 s	2.3 s	0.95 MB	100	128	symm.
	13.7 s	10.4 s	3.88 MB	500	128	symm.
	26.6 s	20.1 s	7.54 MB	1000	128	symm.
Ours (2^{20}) optimized implementation	58 ms	65 ms	0.22 MB	0	128	symm.
	71 ms	75 ms	0.29 MB	10	128	symm.
	101 ms	114 ms	0.95 MB	100	128	symm.
	331 ms	326 ms	3.88 MB	500	128	symm.
	593 ms	587 ms	7.54 MB	1000	128	symm.

⋆⋆ The runtimes are estimated based on the experiments of [3,40].
- No implementation is performed.
? No description of the cardinality of the signature revocation list (SRL) is given.

system and employs an accumulator to arrange group credentials. As a result, their second construction (secure in the new model) eliminates many expensive steps in the membership proof generation, leading to a significant reduction in signature size. However, security requirements are not formally defined for the new model.

Our Contributions. This work focuses on improving the state-of-the-art of EPID signatures. Our contributions are fourfold. First, we provide formal definitions for the new model proposed by Boneh et al. [10]. Particularly, definitions of unforgeability and anonymity of EPID signatures take into account the rejoining of group members and the impact of accumulator. Second, we construct a new Merkle tree accumulator based on the precursor of the standardized AES, namely, the Rijndael block cipher [21], rather than the less studied LowMC cipher [2]. In fact, many LowMC instances were broken (see, e.g., [36,37,43]). We then equip our accumulator with a companion zero-knowledge argument of knowledge of an accumulated value. Based on our accumulator, we present a new EPID signature scheme satisfying the stringent security requirements. Finally, we implement our EPID scheme and analyze its concrete efficiency. Table 1 shows that signature sizes of our scheme are comparable to those of the most efficient lattice-based construction [31], and are $1.5\times - 3.7\times$ more compact than the most efficient hash-based construction [17]. Signing times of our optimized implementation (see Sect. 4.3 for details) are $135\times - 222\times$ smaller than [17]. Since different configurations were employed, the experimental results might be biased. In particular, our optimized implementation is conducted on a workstation equipped with an AMD EPYC 9754 CPU @2.3 GHz and 512 GB RAM, leveraging AES-NI and OpenMP for parallelization. However, their programs [17] were executed on a laptop with Intel i7-8850H CPU @2.6 GHz and 32 GB RAM with the Ubuntu operating system. In addition, a single core was utilized. To make a (relatively) fair comparison, we provide a non-optimized implementation. This is conducted on a virtual machine configured with 16 GB RAM and an AMD Ryzen 7 4800H CPU running at 3 GHz. The results still demonstrate the advantages of our EPID scheme. Compared to the most efficient lattice-based construction [31], our scheme is advantageous when $|\mathsf{SRL}|$ is small while their scheme [31] scales better for larger $|\mathsf{SRL}|$.

We remark that the efficiency of our scheme stems from the employment of the more efficient VOLEitH proof system and the new EPID model. Specifically, the utilization of the accumulator shifts a substantial portion of tasks away from the zero-knowledge proof. However, this approach imposes a constraint on the group size, as it is impractical for the $\mathcal{GM}$ to manage a Merkle tree of 2^{30} leaves. Despite this limitation, the costs for signers and verifiers are logarithmic in the group size and hence manageable even for groups as large as 2^{30}, as also shown in Table 3 and Table 4. Nevertheless, we are investigating the construction of EPID signatures from the VOLEitH proof systems that can support an arbitrary number of group members.

Organizations. The rest of this paper is arranged as follows. Section 2 describes relevant preliminaries and our new security requirements of EPID signatures for attestation. Section 3 presents our hash-based accumulator and its companion zero-knowledge protocol. Section 4 provides the construction of our EPID signature scheme, as well as its efficiency analysis. Due to space limit, details of security proofs are deferred to the Appendix.

$\mathsf{Sign}(\mathsf{sk}_i, \mathsf{cert}_i, \Lambda, \sigma_\Lambda, m, \mathsf{SRL}) \rightarrow \Sigma/\bot$**.** This algorithm is run by a group member $\mathcal{P}_i$. It takes as input the secret key sk_i, a membership certificate cert_i, an accumulator value Λ, a signature σ_Λ, and a signature revocation list SRL, and outputs a signature Σ or $\bot$.

$\mathsf{Verify}(\mathsf{gpk}, m, \Sigma, \mathsf{KRL}, \mathsf{SRL})$**.** This algorithm verifies the validity of the signature Σ on message m with respect to the key revocation list KRL and the signature revocation list SRL. It returns 1 to accept the signature and 0 to reject it.

$\mathsf{KeyRevoke}(\mathsf{gpk}, \mathsf{KRL}, \mathsf{sk}) \rightarrow \mathsf{KRL}$**.** This algorithm adds sk to KRL, so signatures created with this key will no longer be accepted.

$\mathsf{SigRevoke}(\mathsf{gpk}, \mathsf{KRL}, \mathsf{SRL}, (m, \Sigma)) \rightarrow \mathsf{SRL}$**.** This algorithm adds Σ to SRL, so signatures created with the secret key underlying Σ will no longer be accepted.

An EPID signature must satisfy correctness, anonymity and unforgeability.

Correctness. Informally, correctness demands that any signature generated by a group member who has successfully obtained a membership certificate from joining or rejoining procedures is accepted by the verification algorithm, as long as its secret key and signatures have not been revoked. Let S_i be the set of signatures generated by group member $\mathcal{P}_i$. An EPID signature is correct if for any $(\mathsf{gsk}, \mathsf{gpk}) \leftarrow \mathsf{KeyGen}(1^\lambda)$, any $(\mathsf{sk}_i, \mathsf{cert}_i, \Lambda, \sigma_\Lambda)$ obtained from joining and rejoining protocols, and any $m \in \{0,1\}^*$, if $(\mathsf{sk}_i \notin \mathsf{KRL}) \wedge (S_i \cap \mathsf{SRL} = \emptyset)$, the following holds:

$$\Pr[\mathsf{Verify}(\mathsf{gpk},\ m,\ \mathsf{Sign}(\mathsf{sk}_i, \mathsf{cert}_i, \Lambda, \sigma_\Lambda, m, \mathsf{SRL}),\ \mathsf{KRL},\ \mathsf{SRL}) = 1] = 1 - \mathsf{negl}(\lambda).$$

Anonymity. Anonymity states that a signature does not reveal the identity of its signer. This is modeled in the following experiments $\mathsf{Exp}^{\mathsf{anony}-\mathsf{b}}_{\mathsf{EPID},\mathcal{A}}(1^\lambda)$ for $b \in \{0,1\}$ run between a challenger $\mathcal{C}$ and a PPT adversary $\mathcal{A}$.

Experiment: $\mathsf{Exp}^{\mathsf{anony}-\mathsf{b}}_{\mathsf{EPID},\mathcal{A}}(1^\lambda)$

The challenger $\mathcal{C}$ maintains a list $\mathcal{L}_{\mathsf{cert}}$ that contains user secret key sk_i, group member certificate cert_i together with $(\Lambda_i, \sigma_{\Lambda_i})$, a signature list $\mathcal{L}_{\mathsf{sig}}$, and a corrupted user list $\mathcal{L}_{\mathsf{CU}}$.

Setup. The adversary $\mathcal{A}$ computes $(\mathsf{gsk}, \mathsf{gpk}) \leftarrow \mathsf{KeyGen}(1^\lambda)$ and sends gpk to $\mathcal{C}$.

Unrestricted queries. $\mathcal{A}$ has access to the following queries.

Join. $\mathcal{A}$ requests for creating a new group member $\mathcal{P}_i$. $\mathcal{C}$ ensures that $\mathcal{P}_i$ has not been requested before. Then $\mathcal{C}$ acts as $\mathcal{P}_i$ and runs the interactive Join protocol with $\mathcal{A}$, who plays the role of the $\mathcal{GM}$. In the end, $\mathcal{C}$ obtains $(\mathsf{sk}_i, \mathsf{cert}_i, \Lambda, \sigma_\Lambda)$ and adds the tuple to $\mathcal{L}_{\mathsf{cert}}$.

Rejoin. $\mathcal{A}$ requests rejoining of a group member $\mathcal{P}_i$. $\mathcal{C}$ makes sure that $\mathcal{P}_i$ has joined or rejoined before. Then $\mathcal{C}$ and $\mathcal{A}$ run the interactive Rejoin protocol, in which $\mathcal{C}$ plays the role of user $\mathcal{P}_i$ and $\mathcal{A}$ plays the role of the $\mathcal{GM}$. In the end, $\mathcal{C}$ obtains updated $(\mathsf{cert}_i, \Lambda, \sigma_\Lambda)$ and updates $\mathcal{L}_{\mathsf{cert}}$ accordingly.

Sign. When $\mathcal{A}$ requests a signature on a message m from $\mathcal{P}_i$ with respect to SRL, $\mathcal{C}$ ensures that SRL is a subset of $\mathcal{L}_{\mathsf{sig}}$, and that $\mathcal{P}_i$ has been created. Then $\mathcal{C}$ retrieves $(\mathsf{sk}_i, \mathsf{cert}_i, \Lambda, \sigma_\Lambda)$ from $\mathcal{L}_{\mathsf{cert}}$, computes $\Sigma \leftarrow \mathsf{Sign}(\mathsf{sk}_i, \mathsf{cert}_i, \Lambda, \sigma_\Lambda, m, \mathsf{SRL})$, returns Σ to $\mathcal{A}$. $\mathcal{C}$ also adds Σ to $\mathcal{L}_{\mathsf{sig}}$.

Corrupt. When $\mathcal{A}$ requests the secret key of $\mathcal{P}_i$, $\mathcal{C}$ ensures that $\mathcal{P}_i$ has been created and $i \notin \mathcal{L}_{\mathsf{CU}}$. Then $\mathcal{C}$ retrieves sk_i from $\mathcal{L}_{\mathsf{cert}}$, returns sk_i to $\mathcal{A}$, and adds i to $\mathcal{L}_{\mathsf{CU}}$.

Challenge. In the challenge phase, $\mathcal{A}$ outputs a message m, a signature revocation list SRL, two indices i_0, i_1. $\mathcal{C}$ makes sure that $\mathcal{P}_{i_0}, \mathcal{P}_{i_1}$ have been created, $i_0 \notin \mathcal{L}_{\mathsf{CU}}$, $i_1 \notin \mathcal{L}_{\mathsf{CU}}$, and SRL does not contain signatures from either $\mathcal{P}_{i_0}$ or $\mathcal{P}_{i_1}$. Then, $\mathcal{C}$ retrieves $(\mathsf{sk}_{i_0}, \mathsf{cert}_{i_0}, \Lambda_{i_0}, \sigma_{\Lambda_{i_0}})$ and $(\mathsf{sk}_{i_1}, \mathsf{cert}_{i_1}, \Lambda_{i_1}, \sigma_{\Lambda_{i_1}})$ from $\mathcal{L}_{\mathsf{cert}}$. Particularly, $\mathcal{C}$ also makes sure $(\Lambda_{i_0}, \sigma_{\Lambda_{i_0}}) = (\Lambda_{i_1}, \sigma_{\Lambda_{i_1}})$. Finally, $\mathcal{C}$ computes $\Sigma^* \leftarrow \mathsf{Sign}(\mathsf{sk}_{i_b}, \mathsf{cert}_{i_b}, \Lambda_{i_b}, \sigma_{\Lambda_{i_b}}, m, \mathsf{SRL})$ and returns Σ^* to $\mathcal{A}$.

Restricted Queries. $\mathcal{A}$ can make queries as before except that (a) $\mathcal{A}$ cannot make **Corrupt** queries on $\mathcal{P}_{i_0}$ or $\mathcal{P}_{i_1}$ and (b) $\mathcal{A}$ cannot make **Sign** queries with respect to SRL such that $\Sigma^* \in \mathsf{SRL}$.

Output. This experiment outputs b', which is returned by $\mathcal{A}$ at the end of the experiment.

Definition 2 (Anonymity). *An EPID signature scheme for attestation is anonymous if* $|\Pr[\mathsf{Exp}^{\mathsf{anony}-0}_{\mathsf{EPID},\mathcal{A}}(1^\lambda) = 1] - \Pr[\mathsf{Exp}^{\mathsf{anony}-1}_{\mathsf{EPID},\mathcal{A}}(1^\lambda) = 1]|$, *the advantage of any PPT adversary* $\mathcal{A}$, *is negligible in* λ.

Unforgeability. Unforgeability demands that a revoked user, either through keys or signatures, could not produce valid signatures. This requirement is captured in the following experiment $\mathsf{Exp}^{\mathsf{unfor}}_{\mathsf{EPID},\mathcal{A}}(1^\lambda)$.

Experiment: $\mathsf{Exp}^{\mathsf{unfor}}_{\mathsf{EPID},\mathcal{A}}(1^\lambda)$

The challenger $\mathcal{C}$ maintains $\mathcal{L}_{\mathsf{cert}}$, $\mathcal{L}_{\mathsf{sig}}$, $\mathcal{L}_{\mathsf{CU}}$ as in experiment $\mathsf{Exp}^{\mathsf{anony}-b}_{\mathsf{EPID},\mathcal{A}}(1^\lambda)$.

Setup. $\mathcal{C}$ computes $(\mathsf{gsk}, \mathsf{gpk}) \leftarrow \mathsf{KeyGen}(1^\lambda)$, and sends gpk to $\mathcal{A}$.

Queries. $\mathcal{A}$ has access to the following queries.

Join. $\mathcal{A}$ requests creation of a new group member $\mathcal{P}_i$. $\mathcal{C}$ ensures that $\mathcal{P}_i$ has not been requested before. Then there are two cases, depending on the adversary's choice.

- $\mathcal{C}$ and $\mathcal{A}$ run the interactive Join protocol, with $\mathcal{C}$ playing the role of $\mathcal{GM}$ and $\mathcal{A}$ playing the role of $\mathcal{P}_i$. The challenger obtains $(\mathsf{cert}_i, \mathcal{X}, \Lambda, \sigma_\Lambda)$ and $\mathcal{A}$ obtains $(\mathsf{sk}_i, \mathsf{cert}_i, \Lambda, \sigma_\Lambda)$. $\mathcal{A}$ then sends sk_i to $\mathcal{C}$, who then adds i to $\mathcal{L}_{\mathsf{CU}}$ and adds $(\mathsf{sk}_i, \mathsf{cert}_i, \Lambda, \sigma_\Lambda)$ to $\mathcal{L}_{\mathsf{cert}}$.

- $\mathcal{C}$ runs the Join protocol internally, and adds $(\mathsf{sk}_i, \mathsf{cert}_i, \Lambda, \sigma_\Lambda)$ to $\mathcal{L}_{\mathsf{cert}}$. Also, $\mathcal{C}$ sends $(\mathsf{cert}_i, \Lambda, \sigma_\Lambda)$ to $\mathcal{A}$.

Rejoin. $\mathcal{A}$ requests rejoining of a group member $\mathcal{P}_i$. $\mathcal{C}$ ensures that $\mathcal{P}_i$ has joined or rejoined before. Then $\mathcal{C}$ and $\mathcal{A}$ run the interactive Rejoin with $\mathcal{C}$ acting as the $\mathcal{GM}$ and $\mathcal{A}$ acting as $\mathcal{P}_i$. Both parties obtain updated $(\mathsf{cert}_i, \Lambda, \sigma_\Lambda)$, and $\mathcal{C}$ updates $\mathcal{L}_{\mathsf{cert}}$ accordingly.

Sign. Same as in experiment $\mathsf{Exp}^{\mathsf{anony-b}}_{\mathsf{EPID},\mathcal{A}}(1^\lambda)$.

Corrupt. Same as in experiment $\mathsf{Exp}^{\mathsf{anony-b}}_{\mathsf{EPID},\mathcal{A}}(1^\lambda)$.

Forgery. Eventually, $\mathcal{A}$ outputs a message m^*, a signature revocation list SRL^*, a key revocation list KRL^*, a signature Σ^*.

Output. This experiment outputs 1 if (a) $\mathsf{Verify}(\mathsf{gpk}, m^*, \Sigma^*, \mathsf{KRL}^*, \mathsf{SRL}^*) = 1$, (b) for each $i \in \mathcal{L}_{\mathsf{CU}}$, either $\mathsf{sk}_i \in \mathsf{KRL}^*$ or one of the signatures created by $\mathcal{P}_i$ is in SRL^*, and (c) $\mathcal{A}$ did not obtain Σ^* by querying a signature on m^* with respect to SRL^*.

Definition 3 (Unforgeability). *An EPID signature scheme for attestation is unforgeable if the advantage* $\Pr[\mathsf{Exp}^{\mathsf{unfor}}_{\mathsf{EPID},\mathcal{A}}(1^\lambda) = 1]$ *of any PPT adversary $\mathcal{A}$ is negligible in λ.*

2.3 Zero-Knowledge from VOLE-in-the-Head

We now provide an introduction to the Vector-Oblivious-Linear-Evaluation-in-the-Head (VOLEitH) proof system [7]. A VOLE correlation defined over $\mathbb{F}_{2^k}$ allows the sender (often the prover) to obtain $\mathbf{u} \in \mathbb{F}_2^l$, $\mathbf{v} \in \mathbb{F}_{2^k}^l$ and the receiver (often the verifier) to obtain $\mathbf{q} \in \mathbb{F}_2^l$ and $\Delta \in \mathbb{F}_{2^k}$ satisfying:

$$\mathbf{q} = \Delta \cdot \mathbf{u} + \mathbf{v}.$$

Denote this correlation by $[\![\mathbf{u}]\!]$. A VOLE correlation can be viewed as a commitment scheme for the sender to commit to $\mathbf{u}$. The commitment scheme is hiding since $\mathbf{v}$ masks $\mathbf{u}$ and is binding since a cheating sender would need to guess the value of Δ to open $(\mathbf{u}, \mathbf{v})$ to different values. In addition, VOLE correlations are linearly homomorphic. Specifically, given public coefficients $c_0, c_1, \ldots, c_l \in \mathbb{F}_{2^k}$ and $[\![u_i]\!]$ for $i \in [1, l]$, the parties can compute $[\![u]\!] = c_0 + \sum_{i=1}^{l} c_i [\![u_i]\!]$, where prover computes $u = c_0 + \sum_{i=1}^{l} c_i \cdot u_i$ and $v = \sum_{i=1}^{l} c_i \cdot v_i$, and verifier computes $q = c_0 \cdot \Delta + \sum_{i=1}^{l} c_i \cdot q_i$.

Given random VOLE correlations, Yang et al. [44] proposed an efficient proof system named QuickSilver for arbitrary low-degree polynomial constraints. In this work, we focus on degree-2 constraints. Let $f_i(X_1, \ldots, X_{\hat{l}}) = \sum_{j=0}^{2} g_{i,j}(X_1, \ldots, X_{\hat{l}})$ be a degree-2 polynomial over $\mathbb{F}_{2^k}$ in the degree-separated form, i.e., all items of $g_{i,j}$ has degree j. Suppose both parties obtain VOLE relations for w_i such that $q_i = \Delta \cdot w_i + v_i$ for $i \in [1, \hat{l}]$. Yang et al. [44] observe that

$$\begin{aligned} B_i &= \underbrace{\sum_{j=0}^{2} g_{i,j}(q_1, \ldots, q_{\hat{l}}) \cdot \Delta^{2-j}}_{\text{computable by } \mathcal{V}} \\ &= \underbrace{f_i(w_1, \ldots, w_{\hat{l}})}_{0 \text{ if } \mathcal{P} \text{ is honest}} \cdot \Delta^2 + \underbrace{A_{0,i}}_{\text{computable by } \mathcal{P}} + \underbrace{A_{1,i}}_{\text{computable by } \mathcal{P}} \cdot \Delta. \end{aligned} \quad (1)$$

Therefore, to prove $f_i(w_1, \ldots, w_{\hat{l}}) = 0$, it suffices to prove $B_i = A_{0,i} + A_{1,i} \cdot \Delta$. In addition, t constraints can be checked once via a random linear combination. The details of the QuickSilver protocol are recalled below.

Protocol 1: π_{QS}

INPUTS. Both parties know t degree-2 constraints $\{f_i(X_1, \ldots, X_{\hat{l}}) : i \in [1, t]\}$ over $\mathbb{F}_{2^k}$. The prover additionally knows $\mathbf{w} = (w_1, \ldots, w_{\hat{l}}) \in \mathbb{F}_2^{\hat{l}}$ satisfying $f_i(\mathbf{w}) = 0$ for all $i \in [1, t]$. The parties are given $\hat{l} + k$ random VOLE correlations $\{[\![u_i]\!]\}_{i \in [1, \hat{l}+k]}$ over $\mathbb{F}_{2^k}$, with $u_i \in \mathbb{F}_2$. Then both parties can convert $\{[\![u_i]\!]\}_{i \in [\hat{l}+1, \hat{l}+k]}$ into a single VOLE correlation $Q^* = \Delta \cdot U^* + V^*$ with $U^* \in \mathbb{F}_{2^k}$.

1. For $i \in [1, \hat{l}]$, the prover sends $d_i = w_i - u_i$ to the verifier. Due to the linearity of VOLE correlations, both parties obtain $[\![w_i]\!] = [\![u_i]\!] + d_i$ for $i \in [1, \hat{l}]$.
2. The verifier samples random values $\chi_1, \ldots, \chi_t \in \mathbb{F}_{2^k}$ and sends them to the prover. Upon receiving $\{\chi_i\}_{i \in [1,t]}$, the prover computes $A_{0,i}$ and $A_{1,i}$ for $i \in [1, t]$ according to (1), and $U = \sum_{i=1}^{t} A_{0,i} \cdot \chi_i + U^*$, $V = \sum_{i=1}^{t} A_{1,i} \cdot \chi_i + V^*$, and then sends (U, V) to the verifier.
3. The verifier computes B_i for $i \in [1, t]$ according to (1), and $Q = \sum_{i=1}^{\ell} B_i \cdot \chi_i + Q^*$.

OUTPUT. The verifier outputs 1 if $U \cdot \Delta + V = Q$.

From the description, we see that π_{QS} is designated verifier, i.e., the protocol is verified against the party who knows Δ. Fortunately, this can be made publicly verifiable via the VOLEitH techniques [7]. The main building block of VOLEitH is all-but-one vector commitment (VC), which can be used to realize VOLE correlations. In an all-but-one VC scheme, the prover first commits to $\mathbf{r}_0, \ldots, \mathbf{r}_{N-1} \in \mathbb{F}_2^l$. When the verifier sends a random index $\Delta \in [0, N-1]$, the prover opens all messages except $\mathbf{r}_\Delta$ to the verifier. Define

$$\mathbf{u} = \sum_{i=0}^{N-1} \mathbf{r}_i \in \mathbb{F}_2^l, \quad \mathbf{v} = -\sum_{i=0}^{N-1} i \cdot \mathbf{r}_i \in \mathbb{F}_{2^k}^l, \quad \mathbf{q} = \sum_{i=0}^{N-1} (\Delta - i) \cdot \mathbf{r}_i \in \mathbb{F}_{2^k}^l. \quad (2)$$

In (2), we assume $N = 2^k$ and there is a correspondence between $[0, N-1]$ and $\mathbb{F}_{2^k}$. It is then verifiable that $\mathbf{q} = \Delta \cdot \mathbf{u} + \mathbf{v}$.

We now show how the VOLEitH proof system works. Let C be a circuit over $\mathbb{F}_2$ with t multiplication gates and l input bits. This can be seen as t degree-2 constraints with witness size $l + t$[1]. The prover and verifier proceed as follows.

1. The prover runs a GGM tree to generate N leaves $\mathbf{r}_0, \ldots, \mathbf{r}_{N-1} \in \mathbb{F}_2^{l+t+k}$, and then makes a commitment to these leaves. Next, the prover computes $\mathbf{u}, \mathbf{v}$ according to (2). The prover also computes $d_1, \ldots, d_l, d_{l+1}, \ldots, d_{l+t}$ as in π_{QS} and sends them to the verifier.
2. The verifier sends $\chi_1, \ldots, \chi_t$ to the prover.
3. The prover computes U, V as in π_{QS} and sends them to the verifier.
4. The verifier selects a random index $\Delta \in [0, N-1]$ and sends it to the prover.
5. The prover decommits all $\mathbf{r}_x$ except for $x = \Delta$ to the verifier. The verifier can now compute its $\mathbf{q}$ according to (2), and Q as in π_{QS}.

The above interactive protocol can be made non-interactive through the Fiat-Shamir transform [26] since it is public coin. As pointed out by Ouyang et al. [39], the resulting non-interactive protocol is also simulation-sound extractable [27].

For security level λ, however, the above protocol requires committing to $N = 2^\lambda$ values. In practice, the prover runs τ parallel GGM trees with $N = 2^k$ leaves such that $k\tau = \lambda$. Specifically, the prover and verifier obtain $\mathbf{q}_i = \Delta_i \cdot \mathbf{u}_i + \mathbf{v}_i$ for $i \in [0, \tau-1]$ from the τ runs, where $\Delta_i, \mathbf{q}_i, \mathbf{v}_i$ are over $\mathbb{F}_{2^k}$ and $\mathbf{u}_i$ is over $\mathbb{F}_2$. Then the prover sends correction values $\mathbf{c}_i = \mathbf{u}_0 - \mathbf{u}_i$ for $i \in [1, \tau-1]$ to the verifier. Due to the linearity of VOLE correlations, both parties obtain τ VOLE correlations (over $\mathbb{F}_{2^k}$) committing to $\mathbf{u}_0$ with respect to $\Delta_0, \ldots, \Delta_{\tau-1}$, respectively. These τ correlations are then lifted to a single VOLE correlation (over $\mathbb{F}_{2^{k\tau}}$) committing to $\mathbf{u}_0$. To ensure that correction values $\mathbf{c}_i$ are honestly generated, a consistency check is implemented with a linear hash [7].

To further improve the efficiency, Baum et al. [6] proposed batch all-but-one VC. In a nutshell, a single big tree is interpreted as embedding τ smaller trees. Then opening all but τ leaves of the big tree is more efficient than opening all but one leaf in each of the τ smaller trees, because with high probability some active paths in the big tree overlap. As a result, batch all-but-one opening causes variability in the number of internal nodes opened. Baum et al. [6] then fix a threshold number $\mathsf{T}_{\mathsf{open}}$ which cannot be exceeded during the opening phase.

The FAEST [5], a standard signature scheme constructed from applying VOLEitH protocols on AES one-way functions, also considers other optimizations. In this work, we will employ the optimized VOLEitH protocols as in [5] to implement our EPID signatures for attestation. In particular, the proof size is calculated as

$$\mathsf{size} = \tau \cdot (\hat{l} + 2 \cdot \lambda + 16) + \mathsf{T}_{\mathsf{open}} \cdot \lambda + 2 \cdot \lambda \cdot \tau + \lambda + 128 + 32, \tag{3}$$

[1] Witness includes the l input bits and the t output bits of multiplication gates. The t constraints are to verify the t multiplication gates.

where $\hat{l}$ is the size of witness in bits. We remark that to run the VOLEitH protocol [5] with small proof sizes, we need to convert the possibly complicate statements into degree-2 polynomial constraints with small witness size $\hat{l}$.

3 Hash-Based Merkle Tree Accumulator

In Sect. 3.1, we first present a Merkle tree accumulator from symmetric primitives. Next, Sect. 3.2 presents a zero-knowledge argument of knowledge (ZKAoK) of an accumulated value for the accumulator, which is crucial in designing our EPID signatures for attestation in Sect. 4.

3.1 Description of Our Accumulator

To build a Merkle tree accumulator [10,24,35] from symmetric primitives, we need a collision resistant hash function that compresses $2n$-bit strings into n-bit digests. While SHA families are efficient, they have high multiplicative complexity, making them unfriendly to privacy-preserving cryptographic protocols. Derler et al. [24] suggested using the LowMC round function in the sponge framework. Later, Boneh et al. [10] proposed applying the Davies-Meyer transformation to the LowMC cipher [2] as a collision resistant hash function on fixed-length inputs is required. The collision resistance of the Davies-Meyer transformation has been proven in the ideal cipher model. Note that LowMC cipher was initially proposed as an alternative to AES that has low multiplicative complexity. However, many instances of LowMC cipher have been broken (see, e.g., [36,37,43]). Thus, we propose applying the Davies-Meyer transformation to Rijndael [21], the precursor of the standardized AES. In particular, $H_{\mathsf{DM}}(m_1\|m_2) = \mathsf{Rijn}(m_1, m_2) \oplus m_2$, where m_1, m_2 are of equal length. To achieve 128-bit security, the output length of $H_{\mathsf{DM}}(m_1\|m_2)$ is required to be 256. Therefore, we resort to Rijndael-256. We note that achieving higher security requires a block cipher with a larger state. For instance, one can achieve 256-bit security by employing Vistrutah [4] with 512-bit keys and 512-bit block sizes. However, the security of such newly appeared ciphers requires further scrutiny from the community. For this reason, we focus on 128-bit security in this work.

Our hash-based Merkle tree accumulator $\mathsf{Acc}_{\mathsf{Rijn}}$ works as follows. The construction is adapted from the blueprint by previous works [10,24,35].

$\mathsf{ASetup}(1^\lambda)$. This algorithm chooses $n = 2\lambda$ and $H_{\mathsf{DM}} : \{0,1\}^n \times \{0,1\}^n \to \{0,1\}^n$ to be $H_{\mathsf{DM}}(m_1\|m_2) = \mathsf{Rijn}(m_1, m_2) \oplus m_2$. Let $\mathsf{pp} = \{n, H_{\mathsf{DM}}\}$.

$\mathsf{AEval}(\mathsf{pp}, \mathcal{X} = \{x_0, x_1, ..., x_{N-1} \in \{0,1\}^n\})$. Given a set of $N = 2^a$ strings, this algorithm builds a depth-a binary tree and outputs an accumulator value Λ as follows.

- Let $u_{i,j}$ denote the j-th (the leftmost node is indexed by 0) node value in the i-th layer (the leaf nodes are indexed by a).
- Let the leaf nodes be $u_{a,j} = x_j$ for $j \in [0, N-1]$.
- For $i \in \{a-1, \ldots, 0\}$, $j \in [0, 2^i - 1]$, compute $u_{i,j} = H_{\mathsf{DM}}(u_{i+1,2j}\|u_{i+1,2j+1})$.

- A hash-based accumulator constructed from Sect. 3.1. Denote $\mathsf{Acc}_{\mathsf{Rijn}} = (\mathsf{ASetup}, \mathsf{AEval}, \mathsf{AWitCreat}, \mathsf{AVerify})$. This is used by the group manager to create certificates for group members.
- A pseudorandom function (PRF) family $\mathcal{F}_{\mathsf{Rijn}} = \{f_\lambda : \{0,1\}^{n(\lambda)} \times \{0,1\}^{n(\lambda)} \to \{0,1\}^{n(\lambda)}\}$, constructed as $f(m_1, m_2) = \mathsf{Rijn}(m_1, m_2) \oplus m_2$. As we have seen in Sect. 3.1, this family is also collision resistant over its key space in the ideal cipher model.
- A standard signature scheme FAEST [5] that is strongly unforgeable under chosen message attacks in the random oracle model. Denote $\mathsf{FAEST} = (\mathsf{FAEST.Setup}, \mathsf{FAEST.Sign}, \mathsf{FAEST.Verify})$. This is utilized by the group manager to sign accumulator values.
- The optimized VOLEitH proof system as presented in [5]. Denote $\Pi = (\Pi.\mathsf{Setup}, \Pi.\mathsf{Prove}, \Pi.\mathsf{Verify})$. This efficient and versatile simulation-sound extractable ZK protocol is employed by the signer when signing messages.

We remark that any strongly unforgeability signature scheme and any simulation-sound extractable NIZK proof system that proves the satisfiability of degree-2 constraints can be directly plugged into our construction.

4.1 Description of Our EPID Scheme for Attestation

Our scheme works as follows.

$\mathsf{KeyGen}(1^\lambda)$. Given a security parameter 1^λ, the algorithm generates group key pair $(\mathsf{gpk}, \mathsf{gsk})$ as follows.

- Let $n(\lambda) = 2\lambda$. Specify a PRF family $\mathcal{F}_{\mathsf{Rijn}} = \{f_\lambda : \{0,1\}^n \times \{0,1\}^n \to \{0,1\}^n\}$, in which $f(m_1, m_2) = \mathsf{Rijn}(m_1, m_2) \oplus m_2$.
- Let $H_{\mathsf{DM}} : \{0,1\}^{2n} \to \{0,1\}^n$ be the collision resistant hash function, generated via $\mathsf{ASetup}(1^\lambda)$ from Sect. 3.1.
- Run the setup algorithm of the FAEST signature scheme, i.e., $(\mathsf{opk}, \mathsf{osk}) \leftarrow \mathsf{FAEST.Setup}(1^\lambda)$.
- Run the setup algorithm of the VOLEitH proof system [5], i.e., $\mathsf{crs} \leftarrow \Pi.\mathsf{Setup}(1^\lambda)$.

Set group public key as $\mathsf{gpk} = \{\mathcal{F}_{\mathsf{Rijn}}, H, \mathsf{opk}, \mathsf{crs}\}$ and group secret key as $\mathsf{gsk} = \{\mathsf{osk}\}$.

$\mathsf{Join}\langle \mathcal{GM}(\mathsf{gpk}, \mathsf{gsk}, \mathcal{X}_{\mathsf{current}}), \mathcal{P}_i(\mathsf{gpk})\rangle$. This is an interactive protocol between the $\mathcal{GM}$ and a potential group member.

- Upon receiving a joining request from a group member $\mathcal{P}_i$, the $\mathcal{GM}$ samples a challenge $c_i \in \{0,1\}^n$ and sends it to $\mathcal{P}_i$.
- Next, $\mathcal{P}_i$ chooses a random secret key $\mathsf{sk}_i \leftarrow \{0,1\}^n$, and computes $t_i^{\mathsf{join}} = f(\mathsf{sk}_i, c_i) \in \{0,1\}^n$. Then $\mathcal{P}_i$ sends t_i^{join} to $\mathcal{GM}$.
- Upon receiving t_i^{join}, $\mathcal{GM}$ defines $x_i = (t_i^{\mathsf{join}}, c_i)$, and updates $\mathcal{X}_{\mathsf{current}}$ to $\mathcal{X}_{\mathsf{new}} = \mathcal{X}_{\mathsf{current}} \cup \{x_i\}$. Next, the $\mathcal{GM}$ runs $\Lambda_{\mathsf{new}} \leftarrow \mathsf{AEval}(H_{\mathsf{DM}}, \mathcal{X}_{\mathsf{new}})$ and $\mathsf{wit}_{x_i,\mathsf{new}} \leftarrow \mathsf{AWitCreat}(H_{\mathsf{DM}}, \Lambda_{\mathsf{new}}, \mathcal{X}_{\mathsf{new}}, x_i)$. Finally, the $\mathcal{GM}$ produces a signature $\sigma_{\Lambda_{\mathsf{new}}} \leftarrow \mathsf{FAEST.Sign}(\mathsf{gsk}, \Lambda_{\mathsf{new}})$ on the accumulator value Λ_{new}.

Note that $x_i \in \{0,1\}^n \times \{0,1\}^n$ should be accumulated in the accumulator. However, our accumulator $\mathsf{Acc}_{\mathsf{Rijn}}$ from Sect. 3.1 only accepts n-bit leaf nodes. To this end, we propose applying H_{DM} on $(t_i^{\mathsf{join}}, c_i)$ to get an n-bit leaf value $H_{\mathsf{DM}}(t_i^{\mathsf{join}}, c_i) = \mathsf{Rijn}(t_i^{\mathsf{join}}, c_i) \oplus c_i$ and then running the accumulator $\mathsf{Acc}_{\mathsf{Rijn}}$.

- The $\mathcal{GM}$ sets $\mathsf{cert}_{i,\mathsf{new}} = (x_i, \mathsf{wit}_{x_i,\mathsf{new}})$ and sends a copy together with $(\Lambda_{\mathsf{new}}, \sigma_{\Lambda_{\mathsf{new}}})$ to $\mathcal{P}_i$.

$\mathsf{Rejoin}\langle \mathcal{GM}(\mathsf{gpk}, \mathsf{gsk}, \mathcal{X}_{\mathsf{current}}, \Lambda_{\mathsf{current}}, \sigma_{\Lambda_{\mathsf{current}}}), \mathcal{P}_i(\mathsf{sk}_i, \mathsf{cert}_{i,\mathsf{prev}}, \Lambda_{\mathsf{prev}}, \sigma_{\Lambda_{\mathsf{prev}}})\rangle$. When $\mathcal{P}_i$ with secret key sk_i, certificate $\mathsf{cert}_{i,\mathsf{prev}} = (x_i, \mathsf{wit}_{x_i,\mathsf{prev}})$, and $(\Lambda_{\mathsf{prev}}, \sigma_{\Lambda_{\mathsf{prev}}})$ requests to rejoin the group, if the $\mathcal{GM}$ accepts the request, the two parties proceed as follows.

- $\mathcal{P}_i$ sends $\mathsf{cert}_{i,\mathsf{prev}}$ and $(\Lambda_{\mathsf{prev}}, \sigma_{\Lambda_{\mathsf{prev}}})$ to the $\mathcal{GM}$.
- The $\mathcal{GM}$ runs $\mathsf{FAEST.Verify}(\mathsf{opk}, \Lambda_{\mathsf{prev}}, \sigma_{\Lambda_{\mathsf{prev}}})$ and $\mathsf{AVerify}(H, \Lambda_{\mathsf{prev}}, x_i, \mathsf{wit}_{x_i,\mathsf{prev}})$ to check the validity of $\mathcal{P}_i$'s membership. Abort if either check fails.
- Next, the $\mathcal{GM}$ checks if $x_i \in \mathcal{X}_{\mathsf{current}}$. Abort if this is not true.
- Else, the $\mathcal{GM}$ computes $\mathsf{wit}_{x_i,\mathsf{current}} \leftarrow \mathsf{AWitCreat}(H_{\mathsf{DM}}, \Lambda_{\mathsf{current}}, \mathcal{X}_{\mathsf{current}}, x_i)$ and then sends the updated certificate $\mathsf{cert}_{i,\mathsf{current}} = (x_i, \mathsf{wit}_{x_i,\mathsf{current}})$ and $(\Lambda_{\mathsf{current}}, \sigma_{\Lambda_{\mathsf{current}}})$ to $\mathcal{P}_i$.

$\mathsf{Sign}(\mathsf{sk}_i, \mathsf{cert}_i, \Lambda, \sigma_\Lambda, m, \mathsf{SRL})$. If $\mathsf{FAEST.Verify}(\mathsf{opk}, \Lambda, \sigma_\Lambda) = 0$ or there exists $\Sigma_j \in \mathsf{SRL}$ satisfying $t_{\Sigma_j} = f(\mathsf{sk}_i, r_{\Sigma_j})$, $\mathcal{P}_i$ aborts. Else, $\mathcal{P}_i$ performs the following steps. Let $\mathsf{cert}_i = ((t_i^{\mathsf{join}}, c_i), \mathsf{wit}_{x_i})$.

- Choose a random string $r_i \xleftarrow{\$} \{0,1\}^n \setminus \{c_i\}$ and compute tag $t_i = f(\mathsf{sk}_i, r_i) \in \{0,1\}^n$.
- Next, generate a VOLEitH proof of knowledge of $\eta = (\mathsf{sk}_i, t_i^{\mathsf{join}}, c_i, \mathsf{wit}_{x_i})$ such that the following conditions hold.
  (a) $t_i = f(\mathsf{sk}_i, r_i)$, i.e., the tag t_i is generated by the user's secret key sk_i and the randomnesses r_i.
  (b) $t_i^{\mathsf{join}} = f(\mathsf{sk}_i, c_i)$, i.e., t_i^{join} is generated by the user's secret key sk_i and the challenge c_i.
  (c) $r \neq c_i$.
  (d) $\mathsf{AVerify}(H_{\mathsf{DM}}, \Lambda, \mathsf{wit}_{x_i}, x_i) = 1$, i.e., $x_i = (t_i^{\mathsf{join}}, c_i)$ is honestly accumulated in Λ.
  (e) For each $\Sigma_j \in \mathsf{SRL}$, $t_{\Sigma_j} \neq f(\mathsf{sk}_i, r_{\Sigma_j})$, i.e., no signature generated by $\mathcal{P}_i$ has been placed into SRL.

  This is done by running $\pi \leftarrow \Pi.\mathsf{Prove}(\mathsf{crs}, \xi, \eta)$ presented in Sect. 4.2, where $\xi = (\mathsf{gpk}, t_i, r_i, m, \mathsf{SRL}, \Lambda, \sigma_\Lambda)$ are public inputs.
- Return signature $\Sigma = (t_i, r_i, \pi, \Lambda, \sigma_\Lambda)$.

$\mathsf{Verify}(\mathsf{gpk}, m, \Sigma, \mathsf{KRL}, \mathsf{SRL})$. Parse $\Sigma = (t, r, \pi, \Lambda, \sigma_\Lambda)$. This algorithm verifies the validity of Σ on message m with respect to the two revocation lists KRL, SRL as follows.

of memory. Our implementation is an architecture-specific C/C++ code optimized for x86-64 processors with AES-NI support, leveraging OpenMP for parallelization. Running times were averaged over 50 runs. Our implementation is publicly available[2] and open source. The benchmark results are shown in Table 4. When $(\tau, \mathsf{T}_{\mathsf{open}}) = (11, 103)$, the signing time and verification time are less than 280 ms for $|\mathsf{SRL}| = 0$, and increase to 3.4 seconds for $\mathsf{SRL} = 1000$. When $(\tau, \mathsf{T}_{\mathsf{open}}) = (16, 112)$, the times reduce to less than 100 ms for $|\mathsf{SRL}| = 0$ and less than 660 ms for $|\mathsf{SRL}| = 1000$. As we can see from Table 3 and Table 4,

Table 3. Proof sizes of our EPID signatures for different values of $|\mathsf{SRL}|$ and group size $N = 2^a$.

λ	a	τ	$\mathsf{T}_{\mathsf{open}}$	proof sizes (KB)				
				$\|\mathsf{SRL}\| = 0$	$\|\mathsf{SRL}\| = 10$	$\|\mathsf{SRL}\| = 100$	$\|\mathsf{SRL}\| = 500$	$\|\mathsf{SRL}\| = 1000$
128	5	11	103	53.1	104.6	568.5	2629.9	5206.7
		16	112	76.6	151.6	826.2	3824.7	7572.7
	10	11	103	86.6	138.2	602.0	2663.4	5240.2
		16	112	125.4	200.3	875.0	3873.4	7621.5
	15	11	103	120.1	171.7	635.5	2696.9	5273.7
		16	112	174.1	249.1	923.7	3922.2	7670.2
	20	11	103	153.7	205.2	669.0	2730.5	5307.2
		16	112	222.9	297.9	972.5	3970.9	7719.0
	30	11	103	220.7	272.2	736.0	2797.5	5374.2
		16	112	320.4	395.4	1070.0	4068.5	7816.5

Table 4. Running times of our EPID signatures for different values of $|\mathsf{SRL}|$ and group size $N = 2^a$.

λ	a	τ	$\mathsf{T}_{\mathsf{open}}$	(signing time, verification time) ms				
				$\|\mathsf{SRL}\| = 0$	$\|\mathsf{SRL}\| = 10$	$\|\mathsf{SRL}\| = 100$	$\|\mathsf{SRL}\| = 500$	$\|\mathsf{SRL}\| = 1000$
128	5	11	103	(143, 144)	(179, 175)	(419, 421)	(1554, 1549)	(2975, 2926)
		16	112	(53, 57)	(65, 69)	(94, 99)	(310, 311)	(569, 555)
	10	11	103	(164, 163)	(196, 197)	(452, 452)	(1583, 1580)	(2963, 2930)
		16	112	(55, 61)	(65, 70)	(95, 104)	(322, 312)	(573, 564)
	15	11	103	(192, 188)	(225, 223)	(484, 487)	(1645, 1644)	(3039, 3017)
		16	112	(57, 62)	(69, 73)	(97, 107)	(324, 322)	(585, 575)
	20	11	103	(207, 206)	(245, 251)	(511, 510)	(1666, 1660)	(3091, 3048)
		16	112	(58, 65)	(71, 75)	(101, 114)	(331, 326)	(593, 587)
	30	11	103	(275, 278)	(334, 332)	(584, 584)	(1752, 1724)	(3374, 3325)
		16	112	(97, 100)	(111, 116)	(154, 165)	(369, 372)	(655, 639)

[2] https://github.com/ddlfi/EPID2025.

increasing the signature sizes by around 50% leads to 60% – 80% reductions in running times. This shows the tradeoff between proof sizes and running times. In addition, the proof of non-revocation significantly contributes to the overall complexity. This phenomenon is consistent with previous works, e.g., [17,31].

4.4 Security Analysis of Our EPID Signatures

In this section, we prove the correctness, anonymity, and unforgeability of our EPID construction from Sect. 4.1. In Theorem 1–3, we aim to make the statements as general as possible without specifying the concrete choices of the proof system Π and signature scheme $\mathcal{SIG}$. These two ingredients can be easily replaced by more efficient choices as long as they satisfy the required properties.

Theorem 1. *Let Π be any complete proof system that accepts degree-2 polynomial constraints, and $\mathcal{SIG}$ be any correct signature scheme. Assume that the pseudorandom function family $\mathcal{F}_{\mathsf{Rijn}}$ is cryptographically secure and collision resistant over its key space, and that the hash-based accumulator $\mathsf{Acc}_{\mathsf{Rijn}}$ is correct, then our EPID scheme satisfies correctness.*

Proof. First, note that the employed VOLEitH proof system is complete and FAEST signature scheme is correct. Let S_i be the set of signatures generated by group member $\mathcal{P}_i$ who has joined the system successfully via the interactive Join and Rejoin algorithms. Let sk_i and $\mathsf{cert}_i = (t_i^{\mathsf{join}}, c_i, \mathsf{wit}_{x_i})$ be the obtained secret key and certificate of $\mathcal{P}_i$, respectively. The constructed EPID scheme is correct if $\mathsf{sk}_i \notin \mathsf{KRL}$, $S_i \cap \mathsf{SRL} = \emptyset$, and $\Sigma_i \leftarrow \mathsf{Sign}(\mathsf{gpk}, \mathsf{sk}_i, \mathsf{cert}_i, \Lambda, \sigma_\Lambda, m, \mathsf{SRL})$, the following holds:

$$\Pr\Big[\ \mathsf{Verify}(\ \mathsf{gpk},\ m, \Sigma_i,\ \mathsf{KRL},\ \mathsf{SRL}\ ) = 1\ \Big] = 1 - \mathsf{negl}(\lambda).$$

Denote $\Sigma_i = (t, r, \pi, \Lambda, \sigma_\Lambda)$. Since $\mathcal{P}_i$ is an honest member, then the tuple $(\Lambda, \sigma_\Lambda)$ is obtained from the group manager, and $t = f(\mathsf{sk}_i, r)$ is honestly computed from sk_i. Due to the correctness of the FAEST signature scheme, $\mathsf{FAEST.Verify}(\mathsf{opk}, \Lambda, \sigma_\Lambda) = 1$.

Next, we show that $\mathcal{P}_i$ possesses a valid witness $\eta = (\mathsf{sk}_i, t_i^{\mathsf{join}}, c_i, \mathsf{wit}_{x_i})$ such that the following constraints (13) hold with all but negligible probability.

$$\begin{cases} t_i^{\mathsf{join}} = f(\mathsf{sk}_i, c_i), \\ t = f(\mathsf{sk}_i, r), \quad r \neq c_i, \\ \mathsf{AVerify}(H_{\mathsf{DM}}, \Lambda, (t_i^{\mathsf{join}}, c_i), \mathsf{wit}_{x_i}) = 1 \\ \text{for each } \Sigma_j \in \mathsf{SRL}, t_{\Sigma_j} \neq f(\mathsf{sk}_i, r_{\Sigma_j}) \end{cases} \tag{13}$$

The exception is the event E_1, that some revoked signature Σ_j satisfies $t_{\Sigma_j} = f(\mathsf{sk}_i, r_{\Sigma_j})$, occurs. Since $S_i \cap \mathsf{SRL} = \emptyset$, those revoked signatures are not generated via the secret key sk_i. Particularly, $t_{\Sigma_j} = f(\mathsf{sk}_{\Sigma_j}, r_{\Sigma_j})$ with $\mathsf{sk}_{\Sigma_j} \neq \mathsf{sk}_i$. Therefore, the event E_1 happens with negligible probability due to the collision resistance of $\mathcal{F}_{\mathsf{Rijn}}$ over its key space. As a result, the completeness of the proof system Π implies that $\Pi.\mathsf{Verify}(\mathsf{crs}, \xi, \pi) = 1$, where $\xi = (\mathsf{gpk}, t, r, m, \mathsf{SRL}, \Lambda, \sigma_\Lambda)$.

$$\begin{aligned}|\Pr[\mathsf{Exp}^{\mathsf{anon}-0}_{\mathsf{EPID},\mathcal{A}}(1^\lambda)=1]-\Pr[\mathsf{Exp}^{\mathsf{anon}-1}_{\mathsf{EPID},\mathcal{A}}(1^\lambda)=1]| &= |\Pr[W_0]-\Pr[W_1]| \\ &= N^2|\Pr[W_0^{(1)}]-\Pr[W_1^{(1)}]| \\ &\le \mathsf{negl}(\lambda).\end{aligned}$$

This ends the proof.

A.2 Proof of Theorem 3

Proof. First, note that the employed VOLEitH proof system is simulation-sound extractable and zero-knowledge, and the FAEST signature scheme is strongly unforgeable.We prove the theorem via a series of hybrid games G_0, G_1, ..., G_7. Define W_i to be the event that Game G_i outputs 1.

Game G_0**.** This is the experiment $\mathsf{Exp}^{\mathsf{unfor}}_{\mathsf{EPID},\mathcal{A}}(1^\lambda)$. Let $\mathcal{C}$ be the challenger and $\mathcal{A}$ be a PPT adversary. In this experiment, $\mathcal{A}$ receivers gpk from the challenger $\mathcal{C}$ and has access to **Join**, **Rejoin**, **Sign**, **Corrupt** queries. $\mathcal{C}$ also maintains $\mathcal{L}_{\mathsf{cert}}$, $\mathcal{L}_{\mathsf{sig}}$, and a set $\mathcal{L}_{\mathsf{CU}}$ of corrupted group members as defined in $\mathsf{Exp}^{\mathsf{unfor}}_{\mathsf{EPID},\mathcal{A}}(1^\lambda)$. At some point, $\mathcal{A}$ outputs a forgery $(m^*, t^*, r^*, \pi^*, \Lambda^*, \sigma^*_\Lambda)$, together with two revocation lists: $\mathsf{KRL}^*, \mathsf{SRL}^*$. This game outputs 1, i.e., $\mathcal{A}$ wins the unforgeability game, if

$$\mathsf{Verify}(\mathsf{gpk}, m^*, (t^*, r^*, \pi^*, \Lambda^*, \sigma^*_\Lambda), \mathsf{KRL}^*, \mathsf{SRL}^*) = 1; \tag{14}$$

for any $i \in \mathcal{L}_{\mathsf{CU}}$, either $\mathsf{sk}_i \in \mathsf{KRL}^*$ or $S_i \cap \mathsf{SRL}^* \neq \emptyset$, and $(t^*, r^*, \pi^*, \Lambda^*, \sigma^*_\Lambda) \notin \mathcal{L}_{\mathsf{sig}}$. Here, S_i is the set of signatures generated by corrupted group member $\mathcal{P}_i$. In this game, $\mathcal{C}$ additionally maintains a list $\mathcal{L}_{\mathsf{join}}$, which contains each accumulated set $\mathcal{X}$, the corresponding accumulated value Λ and its signature σ_Λ from **Join** and **Rejoin** queries. By definition, $\Pr[W_0] = \Pr[\mathsf{Exp}^{\mathsf{unfor}}_{\mathsf{EPID},\mathcal{A}}(1^\lambda) = 1]$.

Game G_1**.** Let E_1 be the event that $(\Lambda,\ \sigma_\Lambda)$ among valid group membership $(t^{\mathsf{join}},\ c,\ \mathsf{wit},\ \Lambda,\ \sigma_\Lambda)$ received from the **Rejoin** queries is not from $\mathcal{L}_{\mathsf{join}}$. This game follows from Game G_0 except that it outputs 0 if event E_1 happens. However, E_1 violates the strong unforgeability of the employed signature scheme FAEST. Thus, Game G_1 and Game G_0 are computationally indistinguishable, indicating $|\Pr[W_1] - \Pr[W_0]| \le \mathsf{negl}(\lambda)$.

Game G_2**.** Let E_2 be the event that $(t^{\mathsf{join}},\ c)$ among valid group membership $(t^{\mathsf{join}},\ c,\ \mathsf{wit},\ \Lambda,\ \sigma_\Lambda)$ received from the **Rejoin** queries does not belong to the set $\mathcal{X}$ corresponding to $(\Lambda, \sigma_\Lambda)$. This game is identical to Game G_1 except that it outputs 0 if event E_2 occurs. It is not difficult to see that E_2 violates the collision freeness of the accumulator. Then Game G_2 and Game G_1 are computationally indistinguishable. Thus, $|\Pr[W_2] - \Pr[W_1]| \le \mathsf{negl}(\lambda)$.

Game G_3**.** This is Game G_2 except that this game outputs 0 if event E_3, that $(\Lambda^*, \sigma^*_\Lambda)$ in the forgery is not from $\mathcal{L}_{\mathsf{join}}$, occurs. Following from the indistinguishability of Game G_1 and G_0, Game G_3 and Game G_2 are computationally indistinguishable. Thus, $|\Pr[W_3] - \Pr[W_2]| \le \mathsf{negl}(\lambda)$.

Game G_4. This game follows Game G_3, but we run the simulated setup of the proof system Π. Also, for all signature queries, each proof π is produced via the simulator of the proof system Π. We then see that Game G_4 and Game G_3 are indistinguishable due to the zero-knowledge of the proof system Π. Therefore, $|\Pr[W_4] - \Pr[W_3]| \leq \mathsf{negl}(\lambda)$.

Game G_5. This game modifies Game G_4 as follows. Let $(m^*, t^*, r^*, \pi^*, \Lambda^*, \sigma_\Lambda^*)$ be a valid forgery output by the adversary $\mathcal{A}$, this game runs the extractor algorithm of the proof system Π and outputs 0 if extraction fails (E_5). Note that if $\mathcal{A}$ wins the unforgeability game, π^* is a valid proof for the statement $\xi^* = (\mathsf{gpk}, t^*, r^*, m^*, \mathsf{SRL}^*, \Lambda^*, \sigma_\Lambda^*)$. By the simulation-sound extractability of the proof system Π, extraction fails with negligible probability. We then obtain $|\Pr[W_5] - \Pr[W_4]| \leq \mathsf{negl}(\lambda)$. Let the extracted values be $(\mathsf{sk}^*, t^{\mathsf{join}*}, c^*, \mathsf{wit}^*)$. By the simulation-sound extractability, the following constraints hold.

$$t^{\mathsf{join}*} = f(\mathsf{sk}^*, c^*), \tag{15}$$
$$t^* = f(\mathsf{sk}^*, r^*), \quad r^* \neq c^*, \tag{16}$$
$$\mathsf{AVerify}(H_{\mathsf{DM}}, \Lambda^*, \sigma_\Lambda^*, (t^{\mathsf{join}*}, c^*), \mathsf{wit}^*) = 1, \tag{17}$$
$$\text{for each } \Sigma_j \in \mathsf{SRL}^*, t_{\Sigma_j} \neq f(\mathsf{sk}^*, r_{\Sigma_j}). \tag{18}$$

Game G_6. This game is identical to Game G_5, except that this game returns 0 if event E_6, that the extracted $(t^{\mathsf{join}*}, c^*)$ does not belong to the set $\mathcal{X}^*$ corresponding to $(\Lambda^*, \sigma_\Lambda^*)$, happens. However, due to the collision freeness of the employed accumulator, this event occurs with negligible probability. Therefore, $|\Pr[W_6] - \Pr[W_5]| \leq \mathsf{negl}(\lambda)$.

Game G_7. This game is the same as the previous game, but this game outputs 0 if event E_7, that there exists a corrupted member $j \in \mathcal{L}_{\mathsf{CU}}$ satisfying $t^{\mathsf{join}*} = f(\mathsf{sk}_j, c^*)$, happens. In other words, $t^{\mathsf{join}*} = f(\mathsf{sk}^*, c^*) = f(\mathsf{sk}_j, c^*)$. However, the facts that (14) holds and event E_7 occurs imply $\mathsf{sk}^* \neq \mathsf{sk}_j$. This then violates the collision resistance of $\mathcal{F}_{\mathsf{Rijn}}$ over its key space. Therefore, $|\Pr[W_7] - \Pr[W_6]| \leq \mathsf{negl}(\lambda)$.

Therefore, we have showed that G_7 and G_0 are indistinguishable, and hence $|\Pr[W_7] - \Pr[W_0]| = |\Pr[W_7] - \Pr[\mathsf{Exp}^{\mathsf{unfor}}_{\mathsf{EPID},\mathcal{A}}(1^\lambda) = 1]| \leq \mathsf{negl}(\lambda)$. We now show that Game G_7 outputs 1 with negligible probability, assuming the pseudorandomness of the function family $\mathcal{F}_{\mathsf{Rijn}}$.

Let $\mathcal{A}$ be a PPT adversary in Game G_7. We now construct an adversary $\mathcal{B}$, which has internal access to $\mathcal{A}$, to break the pseudorandomness of the function family $\mathcal{F}_{\mathsf{Rijn}}$. To begin with, $\mathcal{B}$ is interacting with a PRF challenger who has either a pseudorandom function or a truly random function. $\mathcal{B}$ utilizes $\mathcal{A}$ as follows.

First, $\mathcal{B}$ selects a random index $n^* \in [1, N]$, where N is an upper on the number of group members in the system. Then $\mathcal{B}$ acts as the challenger in Game G_7 except that any queries to $f(\mathsf{sk}_{n^*}, \cdot)$ are replaced by the responses from the PRF challenger. In more detail, when $\mathcal{A}$ requests creation of a new group member $\mathcal{P}_{n^*}$, there are two cases to consider. If $\mathcal{B}$ runs the Join internally, $\mathcal{B}$ samples c_{n^*} as in Game G_7 and forwards c_{n^*} to its PRF challenger. Denote the response by $t_{n^*}^{\mathsf{join}}$. $\mathcal{B}$ then performs the remaining steps of the **Join** queries as in Game G_7. If $\mathcal{B}$ and $\mathcal{A}$ runs the Join together, $\mathcal{B}$ aborts and returns 0. $\mathcal{B}$ also aborts if $\mathcal{A}$ makes a corruption query of group member $\mathcal{P}_{n^*}$. Suppose $\mathcal{B}$ does not abort. When $\mathcal{A}$ further requests a signature on a message from $\mathcal{P}_{n^*}$, $\mathcal{B}$ samples $r \neq c_{n^*}$ and forwards r to its PRF challenger. Let the response be t. $\mathcal{B}$ then generates a simulated proof as in Game G_7. We remark that $\mathcal{A}$ may make **Rejoin** queries for $\mathcal{P}_{n^*}$. This will only update $(\mathsf{wit}_{x_{n^*}}, \Lambda, \sigma_\Lambda)$ while maintaining $(t_{n^*}^{\mathsf{join}}, c_{n^*})$ unchanged.

At some point, $\mathcal{A}$ outputs a forgery $(m^*, t^*, r^*, \pi^*, \Lambda^*, \sigma_\Lambda^*)$. If $\mathcal{A}$ wins the unforgeability game, $\mathcal{B}$ runs the extractor algorithm of the proof system Π and obtains $(\mathsf{sk}^*, t^{\mathsf{join}*}, c^*, \mathsf{wit}^*)$. If $((t^{\mathsf{join}*}, c^*), \mathsf{wit}^*, \Lambda^*, \sigma_\Lambda^*)$ is not equal to the output of $\mathcal{P}_{n^*}$ in Join or Rejoin algorithms, $\mathcal{B}$ aborts. Otherwise, $\mathcal{B}$ sends r^* to its PRF challenger and receives $\widetilde{t}$ back. If $\widetilde{t} = f(\mathsf{sk}^*, r^*) = t^*$, $\mathcal{B}$ returns 1 (interacting with a pseudorandom function) to its PRF challenger. Otherwise, $\mathcal{B}$ returns 0 (interacting with a truly random function). We remark that this is why we need to check $r \neq c$ when running the Sign algorithm. If this check is omitted, an adversary could set $r^* = c^*$ and render the query of r^* to the PRF challenger useless since $\mathcal{B}$ already learns the response.

Let us now calculate the advantage of $\mathcal{B}$ that attacks the pseudorandomness of the function family $\mathcal{F}_{\mathsf{Rijn}}$.

First, with probability at least $1/N$, $\mathcal{B}$ will not abort before $\mathcal{A}$ outputs a forgery. Note that n^* is chosen independently of $\mathcal{A}$n's view. Also, due to the indistinguishability of the games $G_0, \ldots, G_7$, we assume that events $E_1, E_2, E_3, E_5, E_6, E_7$ do not occur and constraints (15)–(18) are satisfied. This then implies that $((t^{\mathsf{join}*}, c^*), \mathsf{wit}^*, \Lambda^*, \sigma_\Lambda^*)$ is equal to the output of an honest member in Join or Rejoin algorithms. Such honest group member is $\mathcal{P}_{n^*}$ with probability at least $1/N$. To summarize, $\mathcal{B}$ will not abort with probability at least $1/N$.

Next, we argue that $\mathcal{B}$ successfully distinguishes a pseudorandom function from a truly random function, assuming that $\mathcal{B}$ does not abort.

If $\mathcal{B}$ is interacting with a pseudorandom function, then $\mathcal{B}$ perfectly simulates the view of $\mathcal{A}$ as in Game G_7. We claim that key chosen by the PRF challenger, say sk, is exactly the extracted key sk^* with all but negligible probability. Suppose this is not true, then $f(\mathsf{sk}, c_{n^*}) = t_{n^*}^{\mathsf{join}}$ by the construction of $\mathcal{B}$. Also, $(t^{\mathsf{join}*}, c^*) = (t_{n^*}^{\mathsf{join}}, c_{n^*})$ with probability at least $1/N$. In addition, (15) is satisfied. As a result, $f(\mathsf{sk}, c_{n^*}) = f(\mathsf{sk}^*, c_{n^*})$, which then violates the collision resistance of $\mathcal{F}_{\mathsf{Rijn}}$ over its key space. Thus, $\mathsf{sk} = \mathsf{sk}^*$. This then implies that $\widetilde{t} = f(\mathsf{sk}, r^*) = f(\mathsf{sk}^*, r^*) = t^*$. $\mathcal{B}$ then always outputs 1 (interacting with a pseudorandom function).

If $\mathcal{B}$ is interacting with a truly random function, then $\widetilde{t}$ is a random string which collides with $t^* = f(\mathsf{sk}^*, r^*)$ with negligible probability. Then $\mathcal{B}$ returns 0 (interacting with a truly random function).

$$\begin{aligned}\mathsf{Adv}_{\mathsf{PRF},\mathcal{B}}(1^\lambda) &= |\Pr[\mathcal{B} \text{ returns } 1 \,|\mathrm{PRF}] - \Pr[\mathcal{B} \text{ returns } 1 | \text{truely random}]| \\ &\geq |\frac{1}{N}\Pr[W_7] - \mathsf{negl}(\lambda)|.\end{aligned}$$

Due to the security of the pseudorandomness of $\mathcal{F}_{\mathsf{Rijn}}$, $\mathsf{Adv}_{\mathsf{PRF},\mathcal{B}}(1^\lambda)$ is negligible, so is $\Pr[W_7]$. Recall that we also have $|\Pr[W_7]-\Pr[\mathsf{Exp}^{\mathsf{unfor}}_{\mathsf{EPID},\mathcal{A}}(1^\lambda)=1]| \leq \mathsf{negl}(\lambda)$. Hence, $\Pr[\mathsf{Exp}^{\mathsf{unfor}}_{\mathsf{EPID},\mathcal{A}}(1^\lambda)=1] \leq \mathsf{negl}(\lambda)$. This ends the proof.

References

1. ISO/IEC 20008-2:2013: Information technology - security techniques - anonymous digital signatures - part 2: Mechanisms using a group public key. Standard, International Organization for Standardization, Geneva, CH (2013). https://www.iso.org/standard/56916.html
2. Albrecht, M.R., Rechberger, C., Schneider, T., Tiessen, T., Zohner, M.: Ciphers for MPC and FHE. In: Oswald, E., Fischlin, M. (eds.) EUROCRYPT 2015. LNCS, vol. 9056, pp. 430–454. Springer, Heidelberg (2015). https://doi.org/10.1007/978-3-662-46800-5_17
3. Argo, S., Güneysu, T., Jeudy, C., Land, G., Roux-Langlois, A., Sanders, O.: Practical post-quantum signatures for privacy. In: CCS 2024, pp. 1523–1537. ACM (2024)
4. Avanzi, R., Chakraborty, B., List, E.: The large block cipher family vistrutah. IACR Cryptol. ePrint Arch. 976 (2025). To appear in ToSC 2026
5. Baum, C., et al.: Faest: algorithm specifications. Technical report, National Institute of Standards and Technology (2023). https://faest.info/faest-spec-v2.0.pdf
6. Baum, C., et al.: One tree to rule them all: optimizing GGM trees and owfs for post-quantum signatures. In: ASIACRYPT 2024. LNCS, vol. 15484, pp. 463–493. Springer, Heidelberg (2024). https://doi.org/10.1007/978-981-96-0875-1_15
7. Baum, C., et al.: Publicly verifiable zero-knowledge and post-quantum signatures from vole-in-the-head. In: CRYPTO 2023. LNCS, vol. 14085, pp. 581–615. Springer, Heidelberg (2023). https://doi.org/10.1007/978-3-031-38554-4_19
8. Bellare, M., Micciancio, D., Warinschi, B.: Foundations of group signatures: formal definitions, simplified requirements, and a construction based on general assumptions. In: Biham, E. (ed.) EUROCRYPT 2003. LNCS, vol. 2656, pp. 614–629. Springer, Heidelberg (2003). https://doi.org/10.1007/3-540-39200-9_38
9. Bernstein, D.J., Hülsing, A., Kölbl, S., Niederhagen, R., Rijneveld, J., Schwabe, P.: The sphincs$^+$ signature framework. In: ACM CCS 2019,, pp. 2129–2146. ACM (2019)
10. Boneh, D., Eskandarian, S., Fisch, B.: Post-quantum EPID signatures from symmetric primitives. In: Matsui, M. (ed.) CT-RSA 2019. LNCS, vol. 11405, pp. 251–271. Springer, Cham (2019). https://doi.org/10.1007/978-3-030-12612-4_13
11. Brickell, E., Li, J.: Enhanced privacy id: a direct anonymous attestation scheme with enhanced revocation capabilities. In: WPES 2007, pp. 21–30. ACM (2007)
12. Brickell, E., Li, J.: Enhanced privacy ID from bilinear pairing for hardware authentication and attestation. Int. J. Inf. Priv. Secur. Integr. **1**(1), 3–33 (2011)
13. Brickell, E., Li, J.: Enhanced privacy ID: a direct anonymous attestation scheme with enhanced revocation capabilities. IEEE Trans. Dependable Secur. Comput. **9**(3), 345–360 (2012)
14. Brickell, E.F., Camenisch, J., Chen, L.: Direct anonymous attestation. In: CCS 2004, pp. 132–145. ACM (2004)
15. Chaum, D., van Heyst, E.: Group signatures. In: Davies, D.W. (ed.) EUROCRYPT 1991. LNCS, vol. 547, pp. 257–265. Springer, Heidelberg (1991). https://doi.org/10.1007/3-540-46416-6_22

16. Chen, L., Dong, C., Kassem, N.E., Newton, C.J.P., Wang, Y.: Hash-based direct anonymous attestation. In: PQCrypto 2023. LNCS, vol. 14154, pp. 565–600. Springer, Heidelberg (2023). https://doi.org/10.1007/978-3-031-40003-2_21
17. Chen, L., Dong, C., Kassem, N.E., Newton, C.J.P., Wang, Y.: A new hash-based enhanced privacy ID signature scheme. In: PQCrypto 2024. LNCS, vol. 14771, pp. 37–71. Springer, Heidelberg (2024). https://doi.org/10.1007/978-3-031-62743-9_2
18. Chen, L., Dong, C., Newton, C.J.P., Wang, Y.: Sphinx-in-the-head: group signatures from symmetric primitives. ACM Trans. Priv. Secur. **27**(1), 11:1–11:35 (2024)
19. Chen, L., Xu, Z., Tu, T., Wang, Z.: Lattice-based privacy enhanced identity protocol for SDO services. In: ICSIP 2023, pp. 609–613. IEEE (2023)
20. Costan, V., Devadas, S.: Intel SGX explained. IACR Cryptol. ePrint Arch. 86 (2016)
21. Daemen, J., Rijmen, V.: The Design of Rijndael, vol. 2. Springer, Heidelberg (2002)
22. Dall, F., et al.: Cachequote: efficiently recovering long-term secrets of sgx epid via cache attacks. IACR Trans. Cryptogr. Hardware Embed. Syst. **2**, 2018 (2018)
23. Derler, D., Hanser, C., Slamanig, D.: Revisiting cryptographic accumulators, additional properties and relations to other primitives. In: Nyberg, K. (ed.) CT-RSA 2015. LNCS, vol. 9048, pp. 127–144. Springer, Cham (2015). https://doi.org/10.1007/978-3-319-16715-2_7
24. Derler, D., Ramacher, S., Slamanig, D.: Post-quantum zero-knowledge proofs for accumulators with applications to ring signatures from symmetric-key primitives. In: Lange, T., Steinwandt, R. (eds.) PQCrypto 2018. LNCS, vol. 10786, pp. 419–440. Springer, Cham (2018). https://doi.org/10.1007/978-3-319-79063-3_20
25. Faonio, A., Fiore, D., Nizzardo, L., Soriente, C.: Subversion-resilient enhanced privacy ID. In: Galbraith, S.D. (ed.) CT-RSA 2022. LNCS, vol. 13161, pp. 562–588. Springer, Cham (2022). https://doi.org/10.1007/978-3-030-95312-6_23
26. Fiat, A., Shamir, A.: How to prove yourself: practical solutions to identification and signature problems. In: Odlyzko, A.M. (ed.) CRYPTO 1986. LNCS, vol. 263, pp. 186–194. Springer, Heidelberg (1987). https://doi.org/10.1007/3-540-47721-7_12
27. Groth, J.: Simulation-sound NIZK proofs for a practical language and constant size group signatures. In: Lai, X., Chen, K. (eds.) ASIACRYPT 2006. LNCS, vol. 4284, pp. 444–459. Springer, Heidelberg (2006). https://doi.org/10.1007/11935230_29
28. Ishai, Y., Kushilevitz, E., Ostrovsky, R., Sahai, A.: Zero-knowledge from secure multiparty computation. In: STOC 2007, pp. 21–30. ACM (2007)
29. Jeudy, C., Sanders, O.: Worst-case lattice sampler with truncated gadgets and applications. IACR Cryptol. ePrint Arch. 1952 (2024)
30. Jeudy, C., Sanders, O.: Improved lattice blind signatures from recycled entropy. In: CRYPTO 2025. LNCS, vol. 16000, pp. 477–513. Springer, Heidelberg (2025). https://doi.org/10.1007/978-3-032-01855-7_16
31. Jeudy, C., Sanders, O.: Lattice epid with efficient revocation. IACR Cryptol. ePrint Arch. 1225 (2025)
32. Johnson, S., Scarlata, V., Rozas, C., Brickell, E., Mckeen, F., et al.: Intel software guard extensions: epid provisioning and attestation services. White Paper **1**(1–10), 119 (2016)
33. EL Kassem, N., Fiolhais, L., Martins, P., Chen, L., Sousa, L.: A lattice-based enhanced privacy ID. In: Laurent, M., Giannetsos, T. (eds.) WISTP 2019. LNCS, vol. 12024, pp. 15–31. Springer, Cham (2020). https://doi.org/10.1007/978-3-030-41702-4_2
34. Katz, J., Kolesnikov, V., Wang, X.: Improved non-interactive zero knowledge with applications to post-quantum signatures. In: CCS 2018, pp. 525–537. ACM (2018)

35. Libert, B., Ling, S., Nguyen, K., Wang, H.: Zero-knowledge arguments for lattice-based accumulators: logarithmic-size ring signatures and group signatures without trapdoors. J. Cryptol. **36**(3), 23 (2023)
36. Liu, F., Isobe, T., Meier, W.: Cryptanalysis of full LowMC and LowMC-M with algebraic techniques. In: Malkin, T., Peikert, C. (eds.) CRYPTO 2021. LNCS, vol. 12827, pp. 368–401. Springer, Cham (2021). https://doi.org/10.1007/978-3-030-84252-9_13
37. Liu, F., Sarkar, S., Wang, G., Meier, W., Isobe, T.: Algebraic meet-in-the-middle attack on lowmc. In: ASIACRYPT 2022. LNCS, vol. 13791, pp. 225–255. Springer, Heidelberg (2022). https://doi.org/10.1007/978-3-031-22963-3_8
38. Lyubashevsky, V., Seiler, G., Steuer, P.: The lazer library: lattice-based zero knowledge and succinct proofs for quantum-safe privacy. In: CCS 2024, pp. 3125–3137. ACM (2024)
39. Ouyang, Y., Tang, D., Xu, Y.: Code-based zero-knowledge from vole-in-the-head and their applications: simpler, faster, and smaller. In: ASIACRYPT 2024. LNCS, vol. 15488, pp. 436–470. Springer, Heidelberg (2024). https://doi.org/10.1007/978-981-96-0935-2_14
40. Prest, T., et al.: Falcon. Technical Report, NIST (2022)
41. Sanders, O.: EPID with efficient proof of non-revocation. In: ASIA CCS 2022, pp. 1126–1138. ACM (2022)
42. Sanders, O., Traoré, J.: EPID with malicious revocation. In: Paterson, K.G. (ed.) CT-RSA 2021. LNCS, vol. 12704, pp. 177–200. Springer, Cham (2021). https://doi.org/10.1007/978-3-030-75539-3_8
43. Sun, Y., Cui, J., Wang, M.: Improved attacks on lowmc with algebraic techniques. IACR Trans. Symm. Cryptol. **2023**(4), 143–165 (2023)
44. Yang, K., Sarkar, P., Weng, C., Wang, X.: Quicksilver: efficient and affordable zero-knowledge proofs for circuits and polynomials over any field. In: CCS 2021, pp. 2986–3001. ACM (2021)

The Best of Both KEMs: Securely Combining KEMs in Post-quantum Hybrid Schemes

Gorjan Alagic[1,2], Fahran Bajaj[3(✉)], and Aybars Kocoglu[3]

[1] QuICS, University of Maryland Institute for Advanced Computer Studies, College Park, MD 20742, USA
galagic@umd.edu
[2] National Institute of Standards and Technology, Gaithersburg, MD 20899, USA
[3] University of Maryland, College Park, MD 20742, USA
{fbajaj,akocoglu}@umd.edu

Abstract. Transitioning secure information systems to post-quantum cryptography (PQC) comes with certain risks, such as the potential for switching to PQC schemes with as yet undiscovered vulnerabilities. Such risks can be mitigated by combining multiple schemes in such a way that the resulting *hybrid* scheme is secure provided *at least one* of the ingredient schemes is secure. In the case of key encapsulation mechanisms (KEMs), this approach is already in use in practice, where the PQC scheme ML-KEM is combined with the "traditional" X25519 key exchange.

Combining multiple KEMs to construct a single hybrid KEM is largely straightforward, except for the crucial choice of how to derive the final shared secret key. A generic method for doing this in a manner that preserves IND-CCA security is to include the keys and ciphertexts of all ingredient KEMs in an appropriate key derivation step. In the specialized X-Wing construction, one instead relies on a special property of ML-KEM to avoid including its ciphertext in key derivation.

In this work, we show that this optimization can be done in a more general setting. Specifically, when combining multiple KEMs, one need not include the ciphertext of any KEM that satisfies ciphertext second preimage resistance (C2PRI)—provided the key combination step is performed using a split-key pseudorandom function. We also prove that any KEM constructed from a certain set of Fujisaki-Okamoto (FO) transforms satisfies C2PRI in the quantum random oracle model. This applies to KEMs such as BIKE, Classic McEliece, HQC, and ML-KEM.

Keywords: KEM · KEM Combiner · Hybrid KEM · Post-Quantum · IND-CCA

1 Introduction

The potential development of large-scale fault-tolerant quantum computers poses a dramatic threat to most public-key cryptographic schemes in use today. This

K. Jee and A. Kate (Eds.): ACNS 2026, LNCS 16571, pp. 32–74, 2027.
https://doi.org/10.1007/978-3-032-32560-0_2

threat has necessitated a transition to post-quantum cryptography (PQC). While most public-key schemes in widespread use today are still insecure against quantum adversaries, they (and their up-to-date implementations) have a long track record of security against classical attacks in the face of years of rigorous theoretical and empirical analysis. The same cannot necessarily be said for their proposed post-quantum replacements. Thus, there is an apparent tradeoff between present and future security guarantees.

In light of this, a popular strategy has been to combine schemes into hybrid constructions that are secure so long as one ingredient scheme remains unbroken. Combining well-established, "traditional" algorithms with newer post-quantum ones can then help with security in the face of both potential vulnerabilities in the new scheme and potential quantum attacks against the traditional one. One can also combine multiple post-quantum schemes to try to eliminate reliance on a single (perhaps not fully established) computational assumption. Using hybrid protocols is explicitly recommended by European agencies [25,26].

Due to the potential for "store-now, decrypt-later" attacks, key establishment has received significant focus in the post-quantum transition, and hence also in hybrid constructions. Hybrid post-quantum key-establishment has been incorporated into mainstream applications like Chrome [40] and Signal [17]. Hybrid key-establishment schemes typically take the form of a key-encapsulation mechanism (KEM), owing to the fact that all candidate post-quantum key-establishment protocols are KEMs. In fact, for most applications, it suffices to consider the case where all ingredients are KEMs[1]. The standard approach (and the one we consider here) is then to combine these ingredient KEMs in parallel. Specifically, given two KEMs Π_1 and Π_2, one creates a hybrid KEM Π whose encapsulation keys, decapsulation keys, and ciphertexts are concatenations of the corresponding elements of Π_1 and Π_2. What then remains is to choose how to generate the session key of Π.

As shown by Giacon, Heuer, and Poettering, generating the session key in a hybrid KEM is not as straightforward as one might expect [30]. For example, choosing $k = \mathsf{KDF}(k_1, k_2)$ as the session key corresponding to a ciphertext $c = (c_1, c_2)$ does not generically retain IND-CCA security—no matter what key derivation function KDF is used. Specifically, if Π_1 is broken to such an extent that an adversary can find a ciphertext $c_1' \neq c_1$ that also decapsulates to k_1, then they could perform a decapsulation query on (c_1', c_2) and recover the honest session key. As a result, the generic combiners in [30] include all relevant ciphertexts, computing the session key via

$$k = W(k_1, ..., k_n, c_1, ..., c_n) \tag{1}$$

for a certain *core function* W. They then prove that, provided W is *split-key pseudorandom*, the resulting hybrid KEM will preserve IND-CCA security. The split-key pseudorandom property ensures that W behaves like a PRF so long as at least one key k_j is sampled uniformly at random and hidden from the adversary. Several constructions of split-key PRFs are known [24,30].

[1] Hybrid protocols involving quantum key distribution are a notable exception.

For many KEMs, finding a colliding ciphertext as above yields a hash function collision, and is thus arguably much harder than breaking IND-CCA. For example, this appears to be the case for KEMs constructed via the Fujisaki-Okamoto (FO) transform [13,27,28]. The *Quantum Superiority Fighter* (QSF) framework of [13] takes advantage of this to argue that, for combining ML-KEM with X25519, one can use a more efficient combiner than (1), specifically

$$k = W(k_1, k_2, c_2) \tag{2}$$

where c_2 is the X25519 "ciphertext" and W is instantiated with SHA3-256. They prove that this construction preserves IND-CCA either when ML-KEM maintains its own IND-CCA security or when the strong Diffie-Hellman assumption holds in the X25519 nominal group, so long as ML-KEM satisfies a property they call *ciphertext second preimage resistance* (C2PRI). C2PRI requires an adversary, given an honestly generated public key, secret key, ciphertext, and session key, to find a new ciphertext decapsulating to the same session key. They prove that ML-KEM is C2PRI (against classical adversaries) if the underlying hash functions are modeled as random oracles. They then argue that, due to the significant size of the ML-KEM ciphertext, leaving it out of the core function leads to a notable improvement in performance.

In this work, we build upon the above results as follows. We show that combining two KEMs using (2) generically preserves IND-CCA provided the first KEM satisfies C2PRI and W is split-key pseudorandom. Additionally, we show that choosing the combiner $k = W(k_1, k_2)$, where W is a dual PRF, also preserves IND-CCA provided *both* KEMs satisfy C2PRI. In either case, a natural example is to simply choose W to be a hash function; a folklore result that we prove for completeness shows that this is secure in the (quantum-accessible) random oracle model (QROM). Finally, we show that a wide range of KEMs, including BIKE, Classic McEliece, HQC, and ML-KEM, satisfy the C2PRI property against quantum adversaries.

1.1 Summary of Results

We now briefly summarize our technical results.

Security of KEM Combiners. Let KEM_1 and KEM_2 be two δ-correct KEMs and Π be a KEM constructed from KEM_1 and KEM_2 using some "combiner" function family W. We are concerned with establishing IND-CCA security of Π against either classical probabilistic polynomial-time (PPT) adversaries or quantum polynomial-time (QPT) adversaries.

The combined KEM Π is constructed as follows. Key generation, encapsulation, and decapsulation run the corresponding algorithms of KEM_1 and KEM_2 in parallel and concatenate the results appropriately to form the encapsulation key, decapsulation key, and ciphertext of Π. At the end of encapsulation and decapsulation, the session key of Π is computed by $k = W(k_1, k_2, c_1, c_2)$. Our focus is on the security of Π in the setting where, for efficiency purposes, W ignores one or both of its ciphertext inputs.

We first instantiate W with a split-key PRF $F(k_1, k_2, c_2)$, ignoring the first ciphertext. The split-key property ensures that, provided either k_1 or k_2 is treated as the key, F is pseudorandom on the remaining two inputs. We show that the hybrid KEM Π is then CCA-secure provided (i.) KEM_1 is IND-CCA, or (ii.) KEM_2 is IND-CCA and KEM_1 is ciphertext second preimage resistant (C2PRI).

Theorem 1 (Informal). *Let $W(k_1, k_2, c_1, c_2) = F(k_1, k_2, c_2)$, and suppose $\mathcal{A}$ is a QPT adversary against the IND-CCA security of Π. Then there exist QPT adversaries $\mathcal{B}$, $\mathcal{C}$ and $\mathcal{D}$ such that*

$$\mathrm{Adv}_{\Pi,\mathcal{A}}^{\mathrm{IND\text{-}CCA}} \leq 2(\mathrm{Adv}_{\mathsf{KEM}_1,\mathcal{B}}^{\mathrm{C2PRI}} + \mathrm{Adv}_{\mathsf{KEM}_2,\mathcal{C}}^{\mathrm{IND\text{-}CCA}} + \mathrm{Adv}_{F,\mathcal{D}}^{\mathsf{split\text{-}key\text{-}PRF}} + \delta)\,. \tag{3}$$

Moreover, there also exist QPT adversaries $\mathcal{B}'$ and $\mathcal{C}'$ such that

$$\mathrm{Adv}_{\Pi,\mathcal{A}}^{\mathrm{IND\text{-}CCA}} \leq 2(\mathrm{Adv}_{\mathsf{KEM}_1,\mathcal{B}'}^{\mathrm{IND\text{-}CCA}} + \mathrm{Adv}_{F,\mathcal{C}'}^{\mathsf{split\text{-}key\text{-}PRF}} + \delta)\,. \tag{4}$$

Next, we instantiate W with a dual PRF $F(k_1, k_2)$, now ignoring both ciphertexts. The dual-PRF property ensures that, provided either k_1 or k_2 is treated as the key, F is pseudorandom on its remaining input. We show that the hybrid KEM Π is then CCA-secure provided KEM_1 is IND-CCA and KEM_2 is C2PRI, or vice-versa.

Theorem 2 (Informal). *Let $W(k_1, k_2, c_1, c_2) = F(k_1, k_2)$, and suppose $\mathcal{A}$ is a QPT adversary against the IND-CCA security of Π. Then there exist QPT adversaries $\mathcal{B}$, $\mathcal{C}$, and $\mathcal{D}$ such that*

$$\mathrm{Adv}_{\Pi,\mathcal{A}}^{\mathrm{IND\text{-}CCA}} \leq 2(\mathrm{Adv}_{\mathsf{KEM}_1,\mathcal{B}}^{\mathrm{C2PRI}} + \mathrm{Adv}_{\mathsf{KEM}_2,\mathcal{C}}^{\mathrm{IND\text{-}CCA}} + \mathrm{Adv}_{F,\mathcal{D}}^{\mathsf{dual\text{-}PRF}} + \delta)\,. \tag{5}$$

Together, these two theorems tell us that when one out of two ingredient KEMs is C2PRI, it is appropriate to omit the corresponding ciphertext from the key derivation function (Theorem 1), and when both are C2PRI, both ciphertexts can be omitted (Theorem 2). Theorems 1 and 2 are implied by two technical results stated in Sect. 3 and proved in Appendix A. In both theorems, all adversaries make only classical queries to their challenge oracles. This is the appropriate model for post-quantum security, as these oracles implement secretly-keyed functions, and (in practice) the secret key presumably resides only on an honest user's classical machine. In both theorems, the derived QPT adversaries $\mathcal{B}, \mathcal{C}, \mathcal{B}', \mathcal{C}'$ and $\mathcal{D}$ make at most one additional query to their oracles than the number of queries made by $\mathcal{A}$ to the decapsulation oracle of Π, and each adversary runs with at most constant-factor overhead compared to $\mathcal{A}$. As the reductions in our proofs are classical, these adversaries are PPT if $\mathcal{A}$ happens to be PPT. This case is important for settings in which one of the two ingredient KEMs is not post-quantum.

Further, we summarize how to extend our construction and security proofs to combine n different KEMs. Briefly put, one may continue running each ingredient

KEM in parallel and derive the hybrid session key by evaluating a split-key PRF over all ingredient session keys, as well as the ciphertexts of each KEM that is not believed to be C2PRI. In Appendix B, we sketch how the proof of Theorem 1 can be extended to this setting:

Theorem 3 (Informal).
Let $W(k_1, ..., k_n, c_1, ..., c_n) = F(k_1, ..., k_n, c_{\ell+1}, c_{\ell+2}, ..., c_n)$, and suppose $\mathcal{A}$ is a QPT adversary against the IND-CCA security of Π, and pick i between 1 and n. Then there exist QPT adversaries $\mathcal{B}_1, ..., \mathcal{B}_\ell$, $\mathcal{C}$ and $\mathcal{D}$ such that

$$\mathrm{Adv}_{\Pi,\mathcal{A}}^{\text{IND-CCA}} \leq 2\left(\left(\sum_{j=1,j\neq i}^{\ell} \mathrm{Adv}_{\mathsf{KEM}_j,\mathcal{B}_j}^{\text{C2PRI}}\right) + \mathrm{Adv}_{\mathsf{KEM}_i,\mathcal{C}}^{\text{IND-CCA}} + \mathrm{Adv}_{F,\mathcal{D}}^{\text{split-key-PRF}} + \delta\right). \qquad (6)$$

Again, each derived adversary makes at most one additional oracle query than $\mathcal{A}$ and runs with constant-factor overhead.

Post-quantum Split-Key PRFs. Several constructions of functions that are split-key pseudorandom against QPTs are known. These include the PRF-Then-XOR construction in [30] and the function $F(k_1, \ldots, k_n, x) = H(g(k_1, \ldots, k_n), x)$ for a function g with a certain "well-spread" property and a random oracle H [24]. In the special case where g is the identity function, a straightforward application of existing results shows that a random oracle is a split-key PRF, as follows.

Theorem 4. *Let H be a random oracle and let $\mathcal{A}$ be an adversary against the split-key pseudorandomness of $F(k_1, \ldots, k_n, x) := H(k_1 || \ldots || k_n || x)$ making at most q quantum queries to H, where $\mathcal{K}_i$ denotes the ith keyspace. Then,*

$$\mathrm{Adv}_{F,\mathcal{A}}^{\text{split-key-PRF}} \leq \max_{i=1,\ldots,n} 4\sqrt{\frac{q^2+q}{|\mathcal{K}_i|}} \qquad (7)$$

Specifically, this follows from the fact that $F_k(x) := H(k, x)$ is a PRF in the QROM. Although we are quite certain this has been shown before, we have been unable to find a reference. A proof using the O2H lemma is given in Appendix C. The adversary here is allowed quantum queries to H, since H is in practice instantiated with a public hash function. This adversary is also allowed to make queries to the (keyed) evaluation oracle that receives $n-1$ keys and one input, but the number of such queries does not enter into the bound. Indeed, a query to H with the incorrect missing key is equally useful to an adversary who has made one evaluation query as it is to an adversary who has the entire evaluation table. Using the above theorem, we outline how NIST's recommended key-derivation functions from [14], which include popular methods like HKDF, can be shown to be split-key PRFs in appropriate idealized models.

Classical and Quantum Bounds for C2PRI. Finally, we show that a class of post-quantum KEMs (constructed via a certain type of Fujisaki-Okamoto [FO] transform) satisfy ciphertext second preimage resistance (C2PRI) in the quantum random oracle model. Recall that, in the C2PRI experiment, an adversary is given an honestly generated public key, secret key, ciphertext, and session key, and then asked to find a new ciphertext decapsulating to the same session key.

Below we use the notation of [32] to refer to certain types of FO transforms, namely $\mathsf{U}^{\perp}, \mathsf{U}^{\not\perp}, \mathsf{U}^{\perp}_m$ and $\mathsf{U}^{\not\perp}_m$. These transforms involve the use of a single hash function, which we refer to below as H.

Theorem 5. *Let* KEM *be a* $\mathsf{U}^{\perp}$, $\mathsf{U}^{\not\perp}$, $\mathsf{U}^{\perp}_m$ *or* $\mathsf{U}^{\not\perp}_m$ *KEM with keyspace* $\mathcal{K}$ *and underlying hash function* H *modeled as a random oracle. Let* $\mathcal{C}$ *be an adversary against C2PRI for* KEM. *If* $\mathcal{C}$ *makes at most* q *classical queries to* H, *then*

$$\mathrm{Adv}^{\mathrm{C2PRI}}_{\mathsf{KEM},\mathcal{C}} \leq \frac{q+1}{|\mathcal{K}|} \tag{8}$$

If $\mathcal{C}$ *instead makes at most* q *quantum queries to* H, *then*

$$\mathrm{Adv}^{\mathrm{C2PRI}}_{\mathsf{KEM},\mathcal{C}} \leq 4\sqrt{\frac{q^2+q}{|\mathcal{K}|}} \tag{9}$$

The proof of Theorem 5 is given in Sects. 5 and 6. For the case of classical queries, our proof is a straightforward adaptation of the proof that ML-KEM is classically C2PRI [13]. This case is particularly relevant in the typical hybrid PQC construction, where security against classical adversaries is based on IND-CCA of a traditional KEM and (classical) C2PRI of a post-quantum KEM. For the case of quantum queries, our proof technique makes key use of the One-Way to Hiding Lemma [10].

Theorem 5 shows directly that some well-known KEMs (like BIKE and HQC) satisfy C2PRI. We also show how the proofs can be adapted to show C2PRI for other prominent KEMs, namely Classic McEliece, the fourth-round NIST PQC standardization submission of HQC, and ML-KEM [7]. The fourth-round submission of HQC is an interesting case, as it is known not to be ciphertext *collision-resistant* [38]. We provide specific advantage bounds for both classical queries and quantum queries.

Implications. As discussed by Barbosa et al. in [13], many post-quantum KEMs use large ciphertexts, allowing for noticeable improvements in performance when they are not unnecessarily included as an input to the hash function in session-key derivation. For their hybrid scheme X-Wing, they show that omitting ML-KEM-768 ciphertexts in key derivation empirically resulted in 8% and 9% performance gains in encapsulation and decapsulation, respectively. As the Quantum Superiority Fighter (QSF) framework which they used to construct X-Wing is similar in structure to our combiner, we expect similar performance gains when using our combiner with ML-KEM-768 as an ingredient. The standard parameter sets of Classic McEliece specified in [2] admit ciphertext sizes ranging from 96 to 208 bytes, suggesting more modest performance improvements when it is an ingredient of our combiner. However, several other notable post-quantum KEMs have ciphertext sizes close to or larger than that of ML-KEM-768, including ML-KEM-512 and ML-KEM-1024 with respective ciphertext sizes of 768 and 1568 bytes [5], BIKE with ciphertext sizes ranging from 1573 to 5154 bytes [3], and HQC with ciphertext sizes ranging from 4433 to 14421 bytes [6]. By establishing C2PRI security for Classic McEliece, BIKE, and HQC, we show that these KEMs can be used in QSF. Moreover, we demonstrate that one may efficiently combine two post-quantum KEMs with different underlying assumptions without including either ciphertext in the hash function. For example, one may be interested in combining ML-KEM and HQC to hedge against lattice- or code-based assumptions being broken. Creating hybrid schemes with C2PRI KEMs using our combiner is likely to yield substantial improvements over using a combiner that hashes the ciphertext(s) of the post-quantum ingredient KEM(s).

1.2 Related Work

Constructions for blackbox KEM combiners that make no assumptions on the ingredient KEMs are given in [18,19,30,42]. Most of these run each KEM in parallel and input each ciphertext into the final KDF, though the XOR-then-MAC approach of [18] and the construction from [42] use distinctive strategies. The authors of [21,34,39] present constructions that transform multiple IND-CPA secure public-key encryption schemes into a single IND-CCA secure robust hybrid KEM. These methods create a hybrid PKE scheme before applying the $\mathsf{U}^{\not\perp}$ transform, so our work implies that hybrid KEMs created in this way are ciphertext second preimage resistant. The Quantum Superiority Fighter (QSF) construction of [13] combines a nominal group with a C2PRI KEM and excludes the KEM's ciphertext from the core function. In particular, the authors highlight X-Wing, the instantiation of QSF with X25519 and ML-KEM-768. Alwen et al. consider the problem of combining multi-recipient KEMs (mKEMs) [9]. They note that the FO transform endows KEMs with a property they call *collision resistance* and construct an mKEM combiner with core function $F(k_1, k_2)$, where F is a dual-PRF. They prove that this construction is IND-CCA secure provided both ingredient mKEMs are collision-resistant and one is IND-CCA. Their requirement of collision resistance is strictly stronger than ours of ciphertext second preimage resistance because it allows an adversary, given a public/secret key pair, to output any two ciphertexts decapsulating to the same session key. This collision resistance property and when it holds are further explored as the LEAK-BIND-K,PK-CT property in [23,38]. Notably, [38] proves that the round-4 specification of HQC is not LEAK-BIND-K,PK-CT secure, but we prove that it is C2PRI, implying that the distinction between these two notions is practically relevant. Dual PRFs are studied in [11,12,15].

Recent Related Work. The present paper was submitted to a conference in Spring 2025, except for Sect. 4 and Appendix B, which were added shortly after. After that, the closely related independent work [22] appeared on eprint. Then, the present paper was also posted on eprint, with no modifications except the addition of this paragraph. Several minor changes were made after receiving comments from reviewers.

We now briefly describe the main differences between the present paper and [22] as we see them. The work [22] looks at binding and multi-user properties for their hybrid KEM constructions while our work does not. Our work looks at combining many KEMs (Appendix B) and various KDF choices (Sect. 4) while [22] does not. For KEM combiners that do not include any ciphertexts, the main results are the same. For combiners involving only one ciphertext, the results are incomparable (our result is proved in the standard model but relies on a KEM being IND-CCA, while theirs allows for the weaker OW-PCVA security notion but requires the classical ROM, the appropriate notion for their purposes). In terms of showing C2PRI for specific KEMs, [22] gives better bounds; they analyze ML-KEM, Classic McEliece, NTRU, FrodoKEM, and HQC, while we analyze ML-KEM, Classic McEliece, HQC (including the fourth-round submission of HQC, which does not include the salt in the key derivation), and BIKE. [22] also considers the salted and key confirmation variants of the FO transform, while we do not.

2 Preliminaries

2.1 Basic Notation

Below we list the notation that we use throughout this paper:

- $a||b$ denotes the concatenation of a and b
- $a \leftarrow b$ denotes deterministically assigning the value of b to the variable a.
- $a \leftarrow\$ A$ denotes sampling a uniformly at random from a set A.
- $a \leftarrow \mathcal{A}(I)$ denotes that the deterministic algorithm $\mathcal{A}$ is run with input I, resulting in output a. Similarly, $b \leftarrow\$ \mathcal{B}(I)$ denotes that the randomized algorithm $\mathcal{B}$ is run with input I, resulting in output b.
- $\mathcal{A}^{O(\cdot)}(I)$ denotes that algorithm $\mathcal{A}$ is run with input I and access to oracle O.
- $A[a]$ denotes accessing table A at position a. $A[\cdot]$ denotes all positions of table A.
- $\triangleright \mathrm{G}_1$ means that the relevant line of pseudocode is only executed in game G_1. Similarly, $\triangleright \mathrm{G}_1 - \mathrm{G}_3$ means that the relevant line is only executed in games G_1 through G_3.
- $b \leftarrow \mathrm{G}_0$ denotes the security game G_0 running and returning bit b.
- $\{\mathcal{X} \rightarrow \mathcal{Y}\}$ refers to the set of all functions from $\mathcal{X}$ to $\mathcal{Y}$.

2.2 Key-Encapsulation Mechanisms (KEMs)

Below, we list standard definitions for KEMs. For further reference, see, e.g., [35]. Many proposed post-quantum KEMs are constructed from variants of the Fujisaki-Okamoto transformation, described in [27,28,32].

A *key-encapsulation mechanism* (KEM) with session-key space $\mathcal{K}$, public-key space $\mathcal{PK}$, secret-key space $\mathcal{SK}$, and ciphertext space $\mathcal{C}$ is a triple

$$\mathsf{KEM} = (\mathsf{KEM.KeyGen}(1^n), \mathsf{KEM.Encaps}, \mathsf{KEM.Decaps}) \tag{10}$$

of algorithms called key generation, encapsulation, and decapsulation, respectively. These algorithms must satisfy the following.

- KeyGen is a randomized algorithm that, given a security parameter n in unary, outputs a public key $pk \in \mathcal{PK}$ and a secret key $sk \in \mathcal{SK}$. This is expressed as $(pk, sk) \leftarrow\$ \mathsf{KEM.KeyGen}(1^n)$.
- Encaps is a randomized algorithm that, given $pk \in \mathcal{PK}$, outputs a session key $k \in \mathcal{K}$ and a ciphertext $c \in \mathcal{C}$. This is expressed as $(k, c) \leftarrow\$ \mathsf{KEM.Encaps}(pk)$.
- Decaps is a deterministic algorithm that, given $c \in \mathcal{C}$ and $sk \in \mathcal{SK}$ either returns a session key $k \in \mathcal{K}$ or the reject symbol $\perp$. This is expressed as $y \leftarrow \mathsf{KEM.Decaps}(sk, c)$, where $y \in \mathcal{K} \cup \{\perp\}$.

A KEM is said to be δ-correct if the probability that an honestly-performed key establishment process results in Encaps and Decaps outputting different keys is at most δ. Specifically,

$$\Pr[k' \neq k \mid (pk, sk) \leftarrow\$ \mathsf{KEM.KeyGen}(1^n); (k, c) \leftarrow\$ \mathsf{KEM.Encaps}(pk); k' \leftarrow \mathsf{KEM.Decaps}(c)] \leq \delta\,. \tag{11}$$

Here, δ is implicitly a function of n.

Security. The prevailing notion of security for KEMs is that of session-key indistinguishability, i.e., whether an adversary can distinguish between session keys produced by the KEM and bitstrings sampled uniformly at random from the session-key space. In this work, we focus on IND-CCA security, which captures session-key indistinguishability against adversaries $\mathcal{A}$ who can make queries to a decapsulation oracle with any ciphertext $c \in \mathcal{C}$ except for the challenge ciphertext c^*. The security game is shown in Algorithm 1.

Algorithm 1 IND-CCA Security Games

Game $\text{IND-CCA}^b_{\mathsf{KEM},\mathcal{A}}$
$(pk, sk) \leftarrow\$ \mathsf{KEM.KeyGen}(1^n)$
$(k_0, c^*) \leftarrow\$ \mathsf{KEM.Encaps}(pk)$
$k_1 \leftarrow\$ \mathcal{K}$
$b' \leftarrow\$ \mathcal{A}^{\mathsf{Decaps}^{\perp c^*}_{sk}(\cdot)}(pk, c^*, k_b)$
return b'

Oracle $\mathsf{Decaps}^{\perp c^*}_{sk}(c)$
if $c = c^*$ **then**
  return $\perp$
$k \leftarrow \mathsf{KEM.Decaps}(sk, c)$
return k

The advantage of an adversary $\mathcal{A}$ against the IND-CCA security of KEM is defined by

$$\mathrm{Adv}^{\mathsf{KEM}}_{\text{IND-CCA},\mathcal{A}} := \left|\Pr[1 \leftarrow \text{IND-CCA}^0_{\mathsf{KEM},\mathcal{A}}] - \Pr[1 \leftarrow \text{IND-CCA}^1_{\mathsf{KEM},\mathcal{A}}]\right|. \tag{12}$$

We say that KEM is IND-CCA if, for all polynomial-time adversaries $\mathcal{A}$, $\mathrm{Adv}^{\mathsf{KEM}}_{\text{IND-CCA},\mathcal{A}}$ is a negligibly small function of the security parameter n. If we are concerned with post-quantum security, then we require that this holds for all quantum polynomial-time (QPT) adversaries making classical queries to the Decaps oracle.

Ciphertext Second Preimage Resistance. For certain KEMs, given a ciphertext c^*, it is difficult for an adversary to find a distinct ciphertext decapsulating to the same session key as c^*—under assumptions that are weaker than those required to prove IND-CCA. This notion was formalized as ciphertext second preimage resistance by [13]. Consider the game shown in Algorithm 2. Notice that by giving the adversary the secret key as input, the KEM is simulated as being completely broken.

For an adversary $\mathcal{A}$, we define their advantage against the ciphertext second preimage resistance of a KEM KEM as:

$$\mathrm{Adv}^{\mathsf{KEM}}_{\text{C2PRI},\mathcal{A}} = \Pr[1 \leftarrow \text{C2PRI}_{\mathsf{KEM},\mathcal{A}}] \tag{13}$$

In our C2PRI proofs, we distinguish between adversaries with access only to classical computation from those with access to quantum computation.

Algorithm 2 Ciphertext Second Preimage Resistance Game

Game $\text{C2PRI}_{\mathsf{KEM},\mathcal{A}}$
$(pk, sk) \leftarrow\$ \mathsf{KEM.KeyGen}(1^n)$
$(k^*, c^*) \leftarrow\$ \mathsf{KEM.Encaps}(pk)$
$c \leftarrow\$ \mathcal{A}(pk, sk, c^*, k^*)$
if $c \neq c^* \wedge \mathsf{KEM.Decaps}(sk, c) = k^*$ **then**
  return 1
return 0

2.3 Split-Key and Dual Pseudorandom Functions

Split-Key Pseudorandom Functions. A split-key pseudorandom function (PRF) is a function with multiple input keys that behaves like a truly random function as long as one key is obscured from an adversary. Split-key PRFs were introduced in [30] as an ingredient in hybrid KEM constructions. Split-key PRFs take n keys and are of the form $F : \mathcal{K}_1 \times \cdots \times \mathcal{K}_n \times \mathcal{X} \rightarrow \mathcal{Y}$ for key spaces $\mathcal{K}_1, \ldots, \mathcal{K}_n$, input space $\mathcal{X}$, and output space $\mathcal{Y}$. With respect to the security experiment outlined in Algorithm 3, for $1 \leq i \leq n$, we define the advantage of adversary $\mathcal{A}$ in distinguishing F from a random function F' when keyed on the ith key as:

$$\mathrm{Adv}^{\text{PR}_i}_{F,\mathcal{A}} = \left|\Pr\left[1 \leftarrow \text{PR}^0_{i,F,\mathcal{A}}\right] - \Pr\left[1 \leftarrow \text{PR}^1_{i,F,\mathcal{A}}\right]\right| \tag{14}$$

Algorithm 3 Split-Key Pseudorandom Function Game

Game $\mathrm{PR}^b_{i,F,\mathcal{A}}$

$F' \leftarrow\$ \{\mathcal{K}_1 \times \ldots \times \mathcal{K}_{i-1} \times \mathcal{K}_{i+1} \times \ldots \times \mathcal{K}_n \times \mathcal{X} \rightarrow \mathcal{Y}\}$
$k_i \leftarrow\$ \mathcal{K}_i$
$b' \leftarrow\$ \mathcal{A}^{\mathrm{Eval}^{k_i}_b(\cdot)}()$
return b'

Oracle $\mathrm{Eval}^{k_i}_b(k, x)$

$(k_1, \ldots, k_{i-1}, k_{i+1}, \ldots, k_n) \leftarrow k$
$y_0 \leftarrow F(k_1, \ldots, k_n, x)$
$y_1 \leftarrow F'(k_1, \ldots, k_{i-1}, k_{i+1}, \ldots, k_n, x)$
return y_b

When considering an arbitrary key, we define the advantage of adversary $\mathcal{A}$ in distinguishing F from a random function F' as:

$$\mathrm{Adv}^{\text{split-key-PRF}}_{F,\mathcal{A}} = \max_i \{\mathrm{Adv}^{\mathrm{PR}_i}_{F,\mathcal{A}}\} \quad (15)$$

Dual Pseudorandom Functions. The term dual PRF refers to a function of the form $F : \mathcal{K}_1 \times \mathcal{K}_2 \rightarrow \mathcal{Y}$ that behaves like a PRF when either input is hidden [15]. Dual PRFs can be thought of as split-key PRFs with two keys and $\mathcal{X} = \emptyset$. For this reason, we use the same notation and conventions for split-key and dual PRFs. In particular, for $i = 1, 2$, we still use the notation of $\mathrm{Adv}^{\mathrm{PR}_i}_{F,\mathcal{A}}$ to refer to adversary $\mathcal{A}$'s ability to distinguish between F and a random function when the ith key is obscured.

3 Security of Hybrid KEMs

3.1 Combiner Design

To combine two given KEMs, we follow the "Parallel KEM Combiner" approach of [30]. We will instantiate each KEM individually. The public key, secret key, and ciphertext of our hybrid mechanism will be the concatenation of each ingredient KEM's public key, secret key, and ciphertext respectively. The session key output will be the result of some *core function* W applied to the ciphertexts and session keys of each ingredient KEM. We denote this method of combining KEMs as $\Pi = \Pi(\mathsf{KEM}_1, \mathsf{KEM}_2, W)$ and outline pseudocode for it in Algorithm 4. Letting c_i and k_i be the ciphertext and session key returned from KEM_i, [30] proved that setting $W = F(k_1, k_2, c_1||c_2)$ for a split-key pseudorandom function F is sufficient to produce a robust hybrid KEM, where $c_1||c_2$ denotes the concatenation of c_1 and c_2. (A "robust hybrid KEM" retains its IND-CCA security so long as any single ingredient KEM does, see, e.g. [31].) In the case that the first KEM is ciphertext second preimage resistant, we will prove it is secure to output $W(k_1, k_2, c_1, c_2) = F(k_1, k_2, c_2)$ for a split-key pseudorandom function F. Similarly, we will show that when both KEMs are C2PRI, one can simply return the result of a dual PRF $W(k_1, k_2, c_1, c_2) = F(k_1, k_2)$. An outline of how to generalize this construction to combine n many KEMs is discussed in Appendix B.

Algorithm 4 Hybrid KEM design

$\Pi(\mathsf{KEM}_1, \mathsf{KEM}_2, W).\mathsf{KeyGen}(1^n)$:
$(sk_1, pk_1) \leftarrow\$ \mathsf{KEM}_1.\mathsf{KeyGen}(1^n)$
$(sk_2, pk_2) \leftarrow\$ \mathsf{KEM}_2.\mathsf{KeyGen}(1^n)$
$sk \leftarrow (sk_1, sk_2)$
$pk \leftarrow (pk_1, pk_2)$
return (sk, pk)

$\Pi(\mathsf{KEM}_1, \mathsf{KEM}_2, W).\mathsf{Encaps}(pk)$:
$(pk_1, pk_2) \leftarrow pk$
$(k_1, c_1) \leftarrow\$ \mathsf{KEM}_1.\mathsf{Encaps}(pk_1)$
$(k_2, c_2) \leftarrow\$ \mathsf{KEM}_2.\mathsf{Encaps}(pk_2)$
$c \leftarrow (c_1, c_2)$
return $W(k_1, k_2, c_1, c_2)$

$\Pi(\mathsf{KEM}_1, \mathsf{KEM}_2, W).\mathsf{Decaps}(sk, c)$:
$(sk_1, sk_2) \leftarrow sk$
$(c_1, c_2) \leftarrow c$
$k_1 \leftarrow \mathsf{KEM}_1.\mathsf{Decaps}(c_1, sk_1)$
$k_2 \leftarrow \mathsf{KEM}_2.\mathsf{Decaps}(c_2, sk_2)$
if $k_1 = \perp \vee k_2 = \perp$ **then**
  return $\perp$
return $W(k_1, k_2, c_1, c_2)$

3.2 Security Theorems

In Theorem 6, we show our construction is secure when KEM_1 is C2PRI and KEM_2 retains its IND-CCA security. This proof holds both when W is a split-key PRF taking c_2 as input and when W is a dual PRF receiving neither ciphertext. By symmetry, Theorem 6 shows that when both KEMs are C2PRI, setting $W = F(k_1, k_2)$ for a dual PRF F produces a robust hybrid KEM. Hence, Theorem 6 is sufficient to show Theorem 2. Notice this result is not enough to prove Theorem 1, where only the first KEM is C2PRI and we want to set $W = F(k_1, k_2, c_2)$ for a split-key PRF F. We need our hybrid to be as secure as either ingredient KEM, but in that setting, Theorem 6 only reduces the security of the hybrid KEM to that of KEM_2. Theorem 7 reduces the security of our construction to that of KEM_1 without relying on any properties of KEM_2, assuming that c_2 is given as input to the core function. Taken together, Theorems 6 and 7 imply Theorem 1, showing that when only KEM_1 is C2PRI, setting $W = F(k_1, k_2, c_2)$ produces a robust hybrid KEM.

Theorem 6. *Let* KEM_1 *be a C2PRI-secure KEM and* KEM_2 *be a* δ*-correct, IND-CCA KEM. Let* F *be a split-key (resp. dual) PRF, and set* $W(k_1, k_2, c_1, c_2) = F(k_1, k_2, c_2)$ *(resp.* $F(k_1, k_2)$*). Let* $\Pi = \Pi(\mathsf{KEM}_1, \mathsf{KEM}_2, W)$ *be the combination of these KEMs given in Algorithm 4. Then for all QPT adversaries* $\mathcal{A}$ *against the IND-CCA security of* Π *making at most* q *queries to their decapsulation oracle, there exist QPT adversaries* $\mathcal{B}$*,* $\mathcal{C}$*, and* $\mathcal{D}$ *such that:*

$$\mathrm{Adv}^{\text{IND-CCA}}_{\Pi,\mathcal{A}} \leq 2(\mathrm{Adv}^{\text{C2PRI}}_{\mathsf{KEM}_1,\mathcal{B}} + \mathrm{Adv}^{\text{IND-CCA}}_{\mathsf{KEM}_2,\mathcal{C}} + \mathrm{Adv}^{\text{PR}_2}_{F,\mathcal{D}} + \delta) \tag{16}$$

Moreover, $\mathcal{C}$ makes at most q classical queries to its own decapsulation oracle, $\mathcal{D}$ makes at most $q+1$ classical queries to its evaluation oracle, and all of $\mathcal{B}, \mathcal{C}$ and $\mathcal{D}$ run with constant-factor overhead compared to $\mathcal{A}$.

Theorem 7. *Let KEM_1 be a δ-correct, IND-CCA KEM and KEM_2 be a KEM. Let F be a split-key PRF and set $W(k_1, k_2, c_1, c_2) = F(k_1, k_2, c_2)$. Let $\Pi = \Pi(\mathsf{KEM}_1, \mathsf{KEM}_2, W)$ be the combination of these KEMs as described in Algorithm 4. Then for all QPT adversaries $\mathcal{A}$ against the IND-CCA security of Π making at most q classical queries to their decapsulation oracle, there exist QPT adversaries $\mathcal{B}$ and $\mathcal{C}$ such that:*

$$\mathrm{Adv}_{\Pi,\mathcal{A}}^{\text{IND-CCA}} \leq 2(\mathrm{Adv}_{\mathsf{KEM}_1,\mathcal{B}}^{\text{IND-CCA}} + \mathrm{Adv}_{F,\mathcal{C}}^{\text{PR}_1} + \delta) \tag{17}$$

Moreover, $\mathcal{B}$ makes at most q queries to its own decapsulation oracles, $\mathcal{C}$ makes at most $q+1$ queries to its evaluation oracle, and both run with at most constant-factor overhead compared to $\mathcal{A}$.

Proof. The proofs of these two theorems are in Appendix A. □

4 Common Key Derivation Functions are Split-Key PRFs

In this section, we provide an overview on how commonly used KDFs can be shown to be split-key PRFs, assuming idealized primitives. We begin with the assertion that a random oracle applied to concatenated keys and input constitutes a split-key PRF. While we are concerned with post-quantum secure split-key PRFs, the following theorem is stronger in the sense that it applies even when $\mathcal{A}$ is allowed to make quantum queries to its keyed evaluation oracle.

Theorem 8. *Let H be a random oracle and let $\mathcal{A}$ be an adversary against the split-key pseudorandomness of the function $F(k_1, \dots, k_n, x) = H(k_1 || \dots || k_n || x)$ making at most q quantum queries to H, where $\mathcal{K}_i$ denotes the ith keyspace. Then,*

$$\mathrm{Adv}_{F,\mathcal{A}}^{\text{PR}_i} \leq 4\sqrt{\frac{q^2+q}{|\mathcal{K}_i|}} \tag{18}$$

We believe this result is folklore, but we provide a proof in Appendix C for completeness. In what follows, we use this theorem to sketch arguments of split-key pseudorandomness for the key derivation functions recommended by NIST in [14].

KMAC. KMAC is a variable-length MAC/PRF scheme based on the customizable extendable output function cSHAKE. Both KMAC and cSHAKE are defined in [36]. In our context, we define KMAC as a split-key PRF to be:

$$\mathsf{KMAC}(k_1, ..., k_n, x) = \mathsf{cSHAKE}(salt||1||k_1||...||k_n||x, L, \text{“KMAC”}, \text{“KDF”}) \quad (19)$$

where *salt* is a fixed, previously agreed-upon, potentially secret string (having been pre-processed as outlined in [36]), L is the fixed desired output length, and 1, “KMAC”, and “KDF” are fixed byte strings acting as domain separators. cSHAKE is a sponge function, so it is known to be indifferentiable from a random oracle against classical [16] and quantum [8] adversaries when Keccak, the underlying permutation, is assumed to be random. Therefore, Theorem 8 can be clearly extended to give a bound on the split-key pseudorandomness of KMAC.

Hash Functions. Following NIST's recommendations in [14], to construct a split-key PRF from a hash function H, we consider the form:

$$F(k_1, \ldots, k_n, x) = H(1||k_1|| \ldots ||k_n||x)||H(2||k_1|| \ldots ||k_n||x)|| \ldots \quad (20)$$

continuing for as many hash evaluations as necessary to achieve the (fixed) desired output length. The counter at the beginning of each input is represented by a fixed-length byte string and acts as a domain separator, so when H is modeled as a random oracle, each hash output is an independent random value. Therefore, F also behaves like a random oracle, so Theorem 8 can again be used to bound split-key pseudorandomness in this setting.

HMAC (One-Step). HMAC is a message authentication code (MAC) defined in [1] over a hash function H as:

$$\mathsf{HMAC}(k, m) = H\left((k \oplus opad)||H((k \oplus ipad)||m)\right) \quad (21)$$

where *opad* and *ipad* are fixed byte strings. Again following from [14], we construct a split-key PRF from HMAC by using the form:

$$F(k_1, \ldots, k_n, x) = \mathsf{HMAC}(salt, 1||k_1|| \ldots ||k_n||x)||\mathsf{HMAC}(salt, 2||k_1|| \ldots ||k_n||x)|| \quad (22)$$

where *salt* is once again a fixed string. As above, the counter acts as a domain separator that creates distinct input messages for HMAC. HMAC is known to be indistinguishable from random against both classical [29] and quantum [33] adversaries, so again, Theorem 8 applies.

Two-Step Methods. In addition to the above, [14] also provides a two-step, extract-then-expand procedure. First, a key-derivation key K_{DK} is computed as a MAC of the initial shared secret, namely:

$$K_{DK} = \mathsf{MAC}(salt, k_1||...||k_n) \quad (23)$$

The allowable MAC algorithms are HMAC and CMAC. Next, K_{DK} is used to derive the final output key material using a PRF-based KDF constructed in [20], which presents options to construct KDFs based on an underlying PRF. (The algorithm used as the PRF in this step must match the MAC from the first step.) In each option, one fixes a length L and a label string and sets $F(k_1, ..., k_n, x) = K(1)||K(2)||...$ for some function K and as many rounds as necessary to produce a key of the desired length. The first option is *counter mode*, with

$$K(i) = \mathsf{PRF}(K_{DK}, i||Label||0||x||L) \tag{24}$$

In *feedback mode*, $K(0)$ is set to some initialization vector and

$$K(i) = \mathsf{PRF}(K_{DK}, K(i-1)||i||Label||0||x||L) \tag{25}$$

where the inclusion of i in the PRF is optional. Notably, the popular key derivation function HKDF is constructed with HMAC and a variant of feedback mode [37]. Finally, in *double pipeline mode*, two PRF evaluations are used in each step. Specifically, we have:

$$\begin{aligned} A(0) &= Label||0||x||L \\ A(i) &= \mathsf{PRF}(K_{DK}, A(i-1)) \\ K(i) &= \mathsf{PRF}(K_{DK}, A(i)||i||Label||0||x||L) \end{aligned}$$

where once again, the inclusion of i is optional. Each of these modes is shown to be indistinguishable from a random function in [41] when instantiated with either HMAC or CMAC, so Theorem 8 shows that they are valid constructions for split-key PRFs.

5 Ciphertext Second Preimage Resistance of $\mathsf{U}^{\perp}$ and $\mathsf{U}^{\not\perp}$ KEMs

5.1 $\mathsf{U}^{\perp}$ and $\mathsf{U}^{\not\perp}$ KEM Design

We define $\mathsf{U}^{\perp}$ and $\mathsf{U}^{\not\perp}$ KEMs to be the results of converting public-key encryption schemes into key-encapsulation mechanisms via the respective $\mathsf{U}^{\perp}$ and $\mathsf{U}^{\not\perp}$ transformations as defined in [32]. $\mathcal{M}$ consists of bitstrings of the same length, and no properties about the underlying PKE scheme are assumed in our C2PRI proofs. Some well-known KEMs encompassed by these definitions include the $\mathsf{U}^{\not\perp}$ KEMs BIKE and HQC, as respectively specified in [3,6]. Other popular KEMs such as Classic McEliece are similar in structure to these KEMs [2]. The pseudocode for these classes of KEMs is shown in Algorithm 5.

Algorithm 5 $\mathsf{U}^{\perp}$ and $\mathsf{U}^{\not\perp}$ KEMs

$\underline{\mathsf{KEM.KeyGen}(1^n)}$
$(pk', sk') \leftarrow\$ \mathsf{PKE.KeyGen}(1^n)$
$s \leftarrow\$ \mathcal{M}$
$sk \leftarrow (sk', s)$
return (pk', sk)

$\underline{\mathsf{KEM.Encaps}(pk)}$
$m \leftarrow\$ \mathcal{M}$
$c \leftarrow\$ \mathsf{PKE.Encrypt}(pk, m)$
$k \leftarrow H(m, c)$
return (k, c)

$\underline{\mathsf{KEM.Decaps}(sk, c)\ (\mathsf{U}^{\perp})}$
$(sk', s) \leftarrow sk$
$m' \leftarrow \mathsf{PKE.Decrypt}(sk', c)$
if $m' = \perp$ **then**
  return $\perp$
$k \leftarrow H(m', c)$
return k

$\underline{\mathsf{KEM.Decaps}(sk, c)\ (\mathsf{U}^{\not\perp})}$
$(sk', s) \leftarrow sk$
$m' \leftarrow \mathsf{PKE.Decrypt}(sk', c)$
if $m' = \perp$ **then**
  $k \leftarrow H(s, c)$
  return k
$k \leftarrow H(m', c)$
return k

5.2 Classical and Quantum C2PRI Proofs

Theorem 9. *Let* KEM *be a* $\mathsf{U}^{\perp}$ *or* $\mathsf{U}^{\not\perp}$ *KEM with keyspace* $\mathcal{K}$ *where the hash function* H *is modeled as a random oracle, and let* $\mathcal{C}$ *be an adversary against the ciphertext second preimage resistance of* KEM *making at most* q *classical queries to* H. *Then,*

$$\mathrm{Adv}^{\mathrm{C2PRI}}_{\mathsf{KEM},\mathcal{C}} \leq \frac{q+1}{|\mathcal{K}|} \tag{26}$$

Proof. There are two cases where there could be a collision: on inputs to H or on outputs of H. It is impossible for inputs to H to collide for distinct ciphertexts, as the ciphertext is an argument of H and messages are fixed-length. Hence, any collisions are limited to the output of H.

Without loss of generality (at a cost of one extra query) we can assume that the adversary only outputs a ciphertext that it has previously queried to H (along with some arbitrary m). We simulate the entire experiment by lazy sampling H. The first query occurs during the encapsulation step performed by the challenger, resulting in some session key k. The remaining queries are made by $\mathcal{C}$. For any fresh query x, the probability of $H(x) = k$ is $1/|\mathcal{K}|$. By a union bound over the $q+1$ queries made by $\mathcal{C}$, the probability of at least one query mapping to k is at most $(q+1)/|\mathcal{K}|$. □

Theorem 10. *Let* KEM *be a* $\mathsf{U}^{\perp}$ *or* $\mathsf{U}^{\not\perp}$ *KEM with keyspace* $\mathcal{K}$ *where the hash function* H *is modeled as a random oracle, and let* $\mathcal{C}$ *be an adversary against the ciphertext second preimage resistance of* KEM *making at most* q *quantum queries to* H. *Then,*

$$\mathrm{Adv}^{\mathrm{C2PRI}}_{\mathsf{KEM},\mathcal{C}} \leq 4\sqrt{\frac{q^2+q}{|\mathcal{K}|}} \tag{27}$$

Proof. First, let us generate a key $k \in \mathcal{K}$ using $\mathsf{KEM.KeyGen}$ and $\mathsf{KEM.Encaps}$. Consider random oracles H_0^0 and H_0^1, where H_0^0 is defined to be the random oracle modeling H and H_0^1 is defined to be H_0^0 punctured at inputs that map to k such that those inputs now map to keys sampled from $\mathcal{K}\backslash\{k\}$. In other words, if S is the set of $x \in X$ (where X is the input space of the random oracles) that map to $k \in \mathcal{K}$ under H_0^0, then $H_0^0(x) = H_0^1(x)$ for $x \in X\backslash S$ and $H_0^0(x) = k \neq H_0^1(x)$ for $x \in S$. In the random oracle model, S is random, H_0^0 and H_0^1 are random functions, and S and x are independent (i.e., any given input to H_0^0 has the same probability of being in S), so by Theorem 1 and Corollary 1 of [10] any adversary $\mathcal{D}$ has advantage:

$$\mathrm{Adv}_{H_0,\mathcal{D}}^{\mathrm{DIST}} \leq 2\sqrt{(d+1)\cdot P_{\mathrm{find}}} = 2\sqrt{(d+1)\cdot\frac{4q}{|\mathcal{K}|}} = 4\sqrt{\frac{q(d+1)}{|\mathcal{K}|}} \leq 4\sqrt{\frac{q^2+q}{|\mathcal{K}|}} \tag{28}$$

in Algorithm 6, shown below. The quantity d denotes the query depth of $\mathcal{D}$, for which $d \leq q$ holds by the definition of query depth, and P_{find} denotes the probability with which $\mathcal{D}$ can find an element of S.

Algorithm 6 H_0^0 and H_0^1 Distinguishing Game

Game $\mathrm{DIST}_{\mathcal{D}}^{H_0}$

Prepare random oracle H_0^0
$(pk, sk) \leftarrow\$ \mathsf{KEM.KeyGen}(1^n)$
$(k, c) \leftarrow\$ \mathsf{KEM.Encaps}(pk)$
Prepare H_0^1 as above
$b \leftarrow\$ \{0,1\}$
$b' \leftarrow\$ \mathcal{D}^{H_0^b(\cdot)}(k)$
return b'

The case where $b = 0$ corresponds to H_0^0 and the case where $b = 1$ corresponds to H_0^1. $\mathcal{D}$ attempts to output the value of b corresponding to the oracle to which it is given access, winning if and only if $b' = b$.

We now examine the game in Algorithm 7, where $\mathcal{D}$ calls on an adversary $\mathcal{A}$ against the ciphertext second preimage resistance of KEM^b, which is a modified version of KEM.

By construction, there is at least one preimage of k under H_0^0 and there are no preimages of k under H_0^1. The strategy that $\mathcal{D}$ employs in Algorithm 7 is to modify H_0^b to have an arbitrary honestly generated input to the hash function in KEM encapsulation map to k to create a random oracle H_1^b, then to construct KEM^b, which is a KEM with the same construction as KEM but uses H_1^b in place

Algorithm 7 H_0^0 and H_0^1 Distinguishing Game with Adversary $\mathcal{A}$

Game $\mathrm{DIST}_{\mathcal{D}}^{H_0}$
Prepare random oracle H_0^0
$(pk^*, sk^*) \leftarrow\$ \mathsf{KEM.KeyGen}(1^n)$
$(k, c^*) \leftarrow\$ \mathsf{KEM.Encaps}(pk^*)$
Prepare H_0^1 as above
$b \leftarrow\$ \{0,1\}$
$b' \leftarrow\$ \mathcal{D}^{H_0^b(\cdot)}(k)$
return b'

Adversary $\mathcal{D}^{H_0^b(\cdot)}(k)$
$(pk, sk) \leftarrow\$ \mathsf{KEM.KeyGen}(1^n)$
$m \leftarrow\$ \mathcal{M}$
$c \leftarrow\$ \mathsf{PKE.Encrypt}(pk, m)$
$x \leftarrow m||c$
if $H_0^b(x) = k$ **then**
  return 0
Prepare H_1^b
Prepare KEM^b
$c' \leftarrow\$ \mathcal{A}(pk, sk, c, k)$
if $c' \neq c \wedge \mathsf{KEM}'.\mathsf{Decaps}(sk, c') = k$ **then**
  return 0
return 1

of H everywhere H is used, and then finally to query $\mathcal{A}$ and post-process its output. $\mathcal{D}$ is allowed to prepare H_1^b as it does since H_1^b is modeled as a reversible quantum circuit. As H_1^b is constructed from H_0^b and has one input mapped to k, in the $b = 0$ setting there could be second preimages of k under H_1^b and in the $b = 1$ setting there can be none. Thus, if $\mathcal{A}$ finds a second preimage, then $\mathcal{D}$ can conclude that it has access to H_0^0. While it is clear that such a strategy is not optimal, as there could exist second preimages among hash inputs with different public and secret keys (or a secret string in the case of implicit rejection for a $\mathsf{U}^{\not\perp}$ KEM), $\mathcal{D}$ perfectly simulates the view of $\mathcal{A}$ in the ciphertext second preimage resistance game, yielding the result:

$$\mathrm{Adv}_{\mathsf{KEM}^0,\mathcal{A}}^{\mathrm{C2PRI}} = \Pr[1 \leftarrow \mathrm{C2PRI}_{\mathsf{KEM}^0,\mathcal{A}}] \leq \Pr[0 \leftarrow \mathrm{DIST}_{H_0,\mathcal{D}}^{H_0^0}] = \mathrm{Adv}_{H_0,\mathcal{D}}^{\mathrm{DIST}} \leq 4\sqrt{\frac{q^2+q}{|\mathcal{K}|}} \quad (29)$$

since $\Pr[0 \leftarrow \mathrm{DIST}_{H_0,\mathcal{D}}^{H_0^1}] = 0$ by the construction of H_0^1 and $\mathcal{D}$. An adversary $\mathcal{C}$ against the ciphertext second preimage resistance of KEM must have an advantage less than or equal to the advantage of $\mathcal{A}$ against the ciphertext second preimage resistance of KEM^0, as $H(x) = H_0^1(x)$ for all but one $x \in X$, and for the one $x \in X$ for which they could differ, it is known that $H_0^1(x) = k$ but nothing can be assumed about $H(x)$. Therefore, we obtain:

$$\mathrm{Adv}_{\mathsf{KEM},\mathcal{C}}^{\mathrm{C2PRI}} \leq \mathrm{Adv}_{\mathsf{KEM}^0,\mathcal{A}}^{\mathrm{C2PRI}} \leq 4\sqrt{\frac{q^2+q}{|\mathcal{K}|}} \quad (30)$$

as desired. □

5.3 Applications to BIKE, Classic McEliece, and HQC

BIKE [3] and HQC [?] are standard $\mathsf{U}^{\not\perp}$ KEMs at the time of writing, so our results can be applied directly. HQC was updated on August 22, 2025 to hash the full ciphertext (instead of a saltless version of the ciphertext) in key derivation. Previous versions of HQC, such as the fourth-round NIST PQC standardization submission of HQC, implemented a variant of the FO Transform that did not include the full ciphertext in key derivation (namely, excluding the salt), enabling attacks that make those versions of HQC not ciphertext collision resistant [38]. However, we will show that the fourth-round submission of HQC is C2PRI, demonstrating that there are relevant cases in which a KEM is not ciphertext collision resistant but still can be C2PRI.

Corollary 1. *Let* KEM *be an instantiation of BIKE [3] or HQC [6] with keyspace $\mathcal{K}$ and underlying hash function H modeled as a random oracle. Let $\mathcal{C}$ be an adversary against C2PRI for* KEM. *If $\mathcal{C}$ makes at most q classical queries to H, then*

$$\mathrm{Adv}^{\mathrm{C2PRI}}_{\mathsf{KEM},\mathcal{C}} \leq \frac{q+1}{|\mathcal{K}|} \tag{31}$$

If $\mathcal{C}$ instead makes at most q quantum queries to H, then

$$\mathrm{Adv}^{\mathrm{C2PRI}}_{\mathsf{KEM},\mathcal{C}} \leq 4\sqrt{\frac{q^2+q}{|\mathcal{K}|}} \tag{32}$$

Proof. Follows immediately from Theorems 9 and 10. □

Classic McEliece. Classic McEliece is another KEM designed with a slight modification of the $\mathsf{U}^{\not\perp}$ transformation, described in [2]. The notable difference is that Classic McEliece includes distinct domain separators in its hash function when outputting a session key via regular decapsulation versus implicit rejection. Additionally, it calls the subroutines FixedWeight (roughly corresponding to choosing a random message at the beginning of encapsulation), Encode (similar to encryption), and Decode (similar to decryption). Those algorithms are omitted here, as well as KeyGen, but the encapsulation and decapsulation algorithms for Classic McEliece are shown in Algorithm 8.

Corollary 2. *Let* KEM *be an instantiation of Classic McEliece [2] with keyspace $\mathcal{K}$ and underlying hash function H modeled as a random oracle. Let $\mathcal{C}$ be an adversary against C2PRI for* KEM. *If $\mathcal{C}$ makes at most q classical queries to H, then*

$$\mathrm{Adv}^{\mathrm{C2PRI}}_{\mathsf{KEM},\mathcal{C}} \leq \frac{q+1}{|\mathcal{K}|} \tag{33}$$

If $\mathcal{C}$ instead makes at most q quantum queries to H, then

$$\mathrm{Adv}^{\mathrm{C2PRI}}_{\mathsf{KEM},\mathcal{C}} \leq 4\sqrt{\frac{q^2+q}{|\mathcal{K}|}} \tag{34}$$

Proof. The domain separation used in session-key generation does not affect the proof of either Theorems 9 or 10 beyond prepending the inputs of the random oracles with a 0 or a 1 accordingly anywhere they are prepared or queried, so these results also hold for Classic McEliece. □

Algorithm 8 Classic McEliece KEM

$\underline{\mathsf{KEM.Encaps}(pk)}$	$\underline{\mathsf{KEM.Decaps}(sk, c)}$
$m \leftarrow\$ \mathsf{FixedWeight}()$	$(sk', s) \leftarrow sk$
$c = \mathsf{Encode}(m, pk)$	$b \leftarrow 1$
$k = H(1, m, c)$	$m \leftarrow \mathsf{Decode}(sk', c)$
return (k, c)	**if** $m = \perp$ **then**
	$\quad e \leftarrow s$
	$\quad b \leftarrow 0$
	$k \leftarrow H(b, m, c)$
	return k

HQC (Fourth-Round Submission). The fourth-round submission of the Hamming Quasi-Cyclic (HQC) KEM in the NIST Post-Quantum Cryptography Standardization Process is a KEM that is the result of converting the HQC public-key encryption scheme into a KEM via a variant of the FO Transform described in [4]. It has the same structure as a $\mathsf{U}^{\not\perp}$ KEM, but it derandomizes the underlying HQC PKE scheme in the KEM by using a function H_T and does not include part of the ciphertext in session-key derivation, posing important considerations in analyses of its ciphertext second preimage resistance (for simplicity, we consider the salt to be part of the ciphertext rather than separate from it, at no consequence to the applicability of our results). The pseudocode for this KEM in notation similar to that of [38] is shown in Algorithm 9. The parameters e, r_1, r_2, h, u, v, G, and ℓ are parameters of the HQC PKE scheme, and H_T derandomizes the scheme by using a random oracle G to generate a randomness parameter θ given arguments m, pk, and $salt$ and then using θ to generate e, r_1, and r_2 with prespecified Hamming weights. Henceforth, in this section, we will use "HQC" to exclusively refer to this particular version of HQC, and not the most recent version of HQC at the time of writing.

Corollary 3. *Let* HQC *be an instantiation of the fourth-round submission of HQC [4] with keyspace $\mathcal{K}$, message space $\mathcal{M}$, and underlying hash functions H and H_T modeled as random oracles. Let $\mathcal{C}$ be an adversary against C2PRI for* HQC. *If $\mathcal{C}$ makes at most q classical queries to H and q_{H_T} classical queries to H_T, then*

$$\mathrm{Adv}^{C2PRI}_{\mathsf{HQC},\mathcal{C}} \leq \frac{q+1}{|\mathcal{K}|} + \frac{q_{H_T}+1}{\binom{n}{w_r}} + \frac{1}{|\mathcal{M}|} \tag{35}$$

where n is the length of h, r_1, and r_2, and w_r is the Hamming weight of r_1 and r_2. If $\mathcal{C}$ instead makes at most q quantum queries to H and q_{H_T} quantum queries to H_T, then

$$\mathrm{Adv}^{C2PRI}_{\mathsf{HQC},\mathcal{C}} \leq 4\sqrt{\frac{q^2+q}{|\mathcal{K}|}} + 4\sqrt{\frac{q^2_{H_T}+q_{H_T}}{\binom{n}{w_r}}} + \frac{1}{|\mathcal{M}|} \tag{36}$$

Algorithm 9 HQC KEM (Fourth-Round Submission)

$\underline{\mathsf{KEM.KeyGen}(1^n)}$
$(pk', sk') \leftarrow\!\$\ \mathsf{PKE.KeyGen}(1^n)$
$s \leftarrow\!\$\ \mathcal{M}$
$sk \leftarrow (sk', s)$
return (pk', sk)

$\underline{\mathsf{KEM.Encaps}(pk)}$
$m \leftarrow\!\$\ \mathcal{M}$
$salt \leftarrow\!\$\ \mathcal{SL}$
$(e, r_1, r_2) \leftarrow H_T(m, \text{firstBytes}(pk, 32), salt)$
$u \leftarrow r_1 + hr_2$
$v \leftarrow \text{truncate}(mG + sr_2 + e, \ell)$
$c \leftarrow (u, v, salt)$
$k \leftarrow H(m, u, v)$
return (k, c)

$\underline{\mathsf{KEM.Decaps}(sk, c)}$
$(sk', s) \leftarrow sk$
$(u, v, salt) \leftarrow c$
$m' \leftarrow \mathsf{PKE.Decrypt}(sk', u, v)$
$(e', r_1', r_2') \leftarrow H_T(m', pk, salt)$
$u' \leftarrow r_1' + hr_2'$
$v' \leftarrow \text{truncate}(m'G + sr_2' + e', \ell)$
if $(u', v') \neq (u, v)$ **then**
  $k \leftarrow H(s, u, v)$
  return k
$k \leftarrow H(m', u, v)$
return k

Proof. HQC has a structure that introduces additional terms into the advantage bound. Both the classical and quantum C2PRI proofs rely on the fact that the entire ciphertext is used in key derivation to demonstrate that finding a second preimage entails finding a preimage of k under the hash function H. However, only part of the ciphertext is included in key derivation in HQC, which can be exploited by attacks like the one described in [38] against the ciphertext collision resistance of HQC. Fortunately, the implications are not nearly as drastic for the ciphertext second preimage resistance of HQC.

To adapt the C2PRI proofs to HQC, we must account for all cases where an adversary could find ciphertext second preimages that result in the same preimage of the hash function as the challenge hash preimage at the end of decapsulation. An adversary can only exploit implicit rejection in such a way that the adversary and challenge hash preimages are equal when $m = s$, in which case $\mathcal{A}$ could find a ciphertext with a salt such that implicit rejection is triggered but the parts of the ciphertext included in key derivation are equal to those of the challenge ciphertext. The probability that $m = s$ for any given instance of the C2PRI game is $\frac{1}{|\mathcal{M}|}$.

Analyzing the case where an adversary exploits normal key derivation in this way is slightly more involved. In normal key derivation during decapsulation of the challenge parameters, m, u, and v are hashed, and for the adversary hash preimage to be equal to the challenge hash preimage, for adversary preimage paramaters m', u', and v', we must have $m' = m, u' = u$, and $v' = v$. As a result of PKE decryption, $m' = m$ if $u' = u$ and $v' = v$ assuming the correctness of decryption, so it suffices for the adversary to find $c' = u||v||salt'$ where $c = u||v||salt$ and $salt' \neq salt$ such that rejection is not triggered in decapsulation for c' to fall in this case. For it to be true that $(u', v') = (u, v)$ in the rejection check, it must be true that $r_1' + hr_2' = u$ and that truncate$(m'G + sr_2' + e', \ell) = v$ in the decapsulation of c'. Moreover, such e', r_1', and r_2' must be generated by H_T given m', the first 32 bytes of pk, and $salt'$, where the adversary can only control the $salt'$ parameter. Thus, to quantify the probability of this case, we set up an adversary $\mathcal{B}$ against what we will denote as the salt second preimage resistance (S2PRI) of the process by which u' and v' are computed. The adversary $\mathcal{B}$ attempts to find a salt $salt'$ distinct from the challenge salt such that e', r_1', and r_2' by H_T with the property that $(r_1', r_2') \in U^{-1}(u)$ and $(e', r_2') \in V^{-1}(v)$, where $U(x_1, x_2) = x_1 + hx_2$ and $V(x_1, x_2) = \text{truncate}(m'G + sx_2 + x_1, \ell)$ for inputs x_1 and x_2. $\mathcal{B}$ has advantage $\Pr[1 \leftarrow \text{S2PRI}_{\mathsf{HQC},\mathcal{B}}]$ in the game shown in Algorithm 10.

Algorithm 10 Salt Second Preimage Resistance Game

Game $\text{S2PRI}_{\mathsf{HQC},\mathcal{B}}$
$(pk, sk') \leftarrow\$ \mathsf{PKE.KeyGen}(1^n)$
$s \leftarrow\$ \mathcal{M}$
$sk \leftarrow (sk', s)$
$m \leftarrow\$ \mathcal{M}$
$salt \leftarrow\$ \mathcal{SL}$
$(e, r_1, r_2) \leftarrow H_T(m, \text{firstBytes}(pk, 32), salt)$
$u \leftarrow U(r_1, r_2)$
$v \leftarrow V(e, r_2)$
$c \leftarrow (u, v, salt)$
$k \leftarrow H(m, u, v)$
$salt' \leftarrow\$ \mathcal{B}(pk, sk, c, k)$
$(e', r_1', r_2') \leftarrow H_T(m, pk, salt')$
if $salt' \neq salt \wedge (r_1', r_2') \in U^{-1}(u) \wedge (e', r_2') \in V^{-1}(v)$ **then**
  return 1
return 0

As $\mathcal{C}$ and thus $\mathcal{B}$ are computationally unbounded, $\mathcal{B}$ can compute the preimages of u and v with respect to e', r_1', and r_2' without any effects on advantage bounds. To account for all of the mentioned cases, we can model H_T as a random oracle and update the advantage bound for a classical adversary against the ciphertext second preimage resistance of HQC to be:

$$\text{Adv}^{\text{C2PRI}}_{\mathsf{HQC},\mathcal{C}} \leq \frac{q+1}{|\mathcal{K}|} + \text{Adv}^{\text{S2PRI}}_{\mathsf{HQC},\mathcal{B}} + \frac{1}{|\mathcal{M}|} \tag{37}$$

where $\mathcal{B}$ makes at most q_{H_T} classical queries to H_T, and the advantage bound for a quantum adversary against the ciphertext second preimage resistance of HQC to be:

$$\text{Adv}^{\text{C2PRI}}_{\mathsf{HQC},\mathcal{C}} \leq 4\sqrt{\frac{q^2+q}{|\mathcal{K}|}} + \text{Adv}^{\text{S2PRI}}_{\mathsf{HQC},\mathcal{B}} + \frac{1}{|\mathcal{M}|} \tag{38}$$

where $\mathcal{B}$ makes at most q_{H_T} quantum queries to H_T.

Now, it remains to bound the advantage of $\mathcal{B}$ in the S2PRI game. One way to do so is to bound the cardinalities of $U^{-1}(u)$ and/or $V^{-1}(v)$, after which a classical lazy sampling bound or a quantum search bound like that in the One-Way to Hiding Lemma in [10] can be applied. For simplicity, we consider only the cardinality of $U^{-1}(u)$. We know that $u = U(r_1, r_2) = r_1 + hr_2$, where $h, r_1, r_2 \in \mathbb{F}_2^n$ are bit vectors of length n, with r_1 and r_2 having Hamming weight w_r, and hr_2 is the vector representation of the product of the polynomials corresponding to h and r_2. If $h = 0$, then $u = r_1$ and so the cardinality of $U^{-1}(u)$ is $\binom{n}{w_r}$. As for $h \neq 0$, given an arbitrary r_2', we wish to quantify how many r_1' exist such that $r_1' + hr_2' = u$. Rearranging this equation, we obtain $r_1' = u - hr_2'$. The product hr_2' is unique for each r_2', as is the difference of u and hr_2'. Thus, for each r_2', if r_1' exists, then it is unique (alternatively, such an r_1' does not exist if $u - hr_2'$ does not have weight w_r). Since every r_2' has at most one r_1' such that $(r_1', r_2') \in U^{-1}(u)$, an upper bound on the cardinality of $U^{-1}(u)$ is the number of possible vectors r_2'. This number is $\binom{n}{w_r}$, so $|U^{-1}(u)| \leq \binom{n}{w_r}$. The total number of pairs is $\binom{n}{w_r}^2$, so the maximum probability of arbitrary parameters (r_1', r_2') being in $U^{-1}(u)$ is $\frac{\binom{n}{w_r}}{\binom{n}{w_r}^2} = \frac{1}{\binom{n}{w_r}}$. This probability allows us to apply bounds on finding a salt second preimage with respect to q_{H_T} according to classical lazy sampling bounds and the One-Way to Hiding Lemma. More specifically expressed, with n defined to be the length of h, r_1, and r_2 and w_r defined to be the Hamming weight of r_1 and r_2, the advantage bound for a classical adversary against the ciphertext second preimage resistance of HQC is:

$$\mathrm{Adv}_{\mathsf{HQC},\mathcal{C}}^{\mathrm{C2PRI}} \leq \frac{q+1}{|\mathcal{K}|} + \frac{q_{H_T}+1}{\binom{n}{w_r}} + \frac{1}{|\mathcal{M}|} \tag{39}$$

where $\mathcal{B}$ makes at most q_{H_T} classical queries to H_T, and the advantage bound for a quantum adversary against the ciphertext second preimage resistance of HQC is:

$$\mathrm{Adv}_{\mathsf{HQC},\mathcal{C}}^{\mathrm{C2PRI}} \leq 4\sqrt{\frac{q^2+q}{|\mathcal{K}|}} + 4\sqrt{\frac{q_{H_T}^2+q_{H_T}}{\binom{n}{w_r}}} + \frac{1}{|\mathcal{M}|} \tag{40}$$

where $\mathcal{B}$ makes at most q_{H_T} quantum queries to H_T. □

6 Ciphertext Second Preimage Resistance for $\mathsf{U}_m^{\perp}$ and $\mathsf{U}_m^{\not\perp}$ KEMs

6.1 $\mathsf{U}_m^{\perp}$ and $\mathsf{U}_m^{\not\perp}$ KEM Design

We define $\mathsf{U}_m^{\perp}$ and $\mathsf{U}_m^{\not\perp}$ KEMs to be the results of converting public-key encryption schemes into key-encapsulation mechanisms via the respective $\mathsf{U}_m^{\perp}$ and $\mathsf{U}_m^{\not\perp}$ transformations as defined in [32]. $\mathcal{M}$ consists of bitstrings of the same length, and no properties of the underlying PKE scheme are assumed except for (1) deterministic encryption and (2) rejection in decryption if re-encrypting the decrypted message does not yield the same ciphertext as the input ciphertext (i.e., if normal decryption before the re-encryption check returns m on inputs sk and c and if $m = \perp$ or $\mathsf{PKE.Encrypt}(pk, m) \neq c$, then $\mathsf{PKE.Decrypt}(sk, c) = \perp$). Together, these properties ensure that PKE.Decrypt does not output the same message for distinct ciphertexts and the same secret key, a fact which is used in the C2PRI proofs.

These properties are guaranteed for PKE schemes that are the result of the T transform in [32], where an initial PKE scheme PKE_0 is derandomized with a random oracle G and a re-encryption check. In [32], Hofheinz et al. use the T transform to transform OW-CPA secure PKE schemes into OW-PCA secure PKE schemes, which can then be transformed into IND-CCA KEMs, but PKE_0 can be an arbitrary PKE scheme with no assumed properties for our results to hold. The pseudocode for the T transform is shown in Algorithm 11.

Algorithm 11 The T Transform

$\mathsf{T}[\mathsf{PKE}_0, G].\mathsf{Encrypt}(pk, m)$	$\mathsf{T}[\mathsf{PKE}_0, G].\mathsf{Decrypt}(sk, c)$
$c \leftarrow \mathsf{PKE}_0.\mathsf{Encrypt}(pk, m; G(m))$	$m \leftarrow \mathsf{PKE}_0.\mathsf{Decrypt}(sk, c)$
return c	**if** $m = \perp \vee \mathsf{PKE}_0.\mathsf{Encrypt}(pk, m; G(m)) \neq c$
	return $\perp$
	return m

A well-known KEM which has a similar structure to a $\mathsf{U}^{\not\perp}_m$ KEM is ML-KEM. The pseudocode for these classes of KEMs is shown in Algorithm 12.

6.2 Classical and Quantum C2PRI Proofs

Theorem 11. *Let* KEM *be a* $\mathsf{U}^{\perp}_m$ *or* $\mathsf{U}^{\not\perp}_m$ *KEM with keyspace* $\mathcal{K}$ *where the hash function* H *is modeled as a random oracle, and let* $\mathcal{C}$ *be an adversary against the ciphertext second preimage resistance of* KEM *making at most* q *classical queries to* H. *Then,*

$$\mathrm{Adv}^{\mathrm{C2PRI}}_{\mathsf{KEM},\mathcal{C}} \leq \frac{q+1}{|\mathcal{K}|} \tag{41}$$

Proof. As in the proof that $\mathsf{U}^{\perp}$ and $\mathsf{U}^{\not\perp}$ KEMs are classically C2PRI, there can either be a collision on inputs to H or on outputs of H. PKE encryption is well-defined and deterministic, so for a given public key pk and message m it can only output one ciphertext c. It follows that during decapsulation, PKE.Decrypt cannot output the same message m' for distinct ciphertexts c_1 and c_2 and the

Algorithm 12 $\mathsf{U}^{\perp}_m$ and $\mathsf{U}^{\not\perp}_m$ KEMs

$\mathsf{KEM.KeyGen}(1^n)$
$(pk', sk') \leftarrow\$ \mathsf{PKE.KeyGen}(1^n)$
$s \leftarrow\$ \mathcal{M}$
$sk \leftarrow (sk', s)$
return (pk', sk)

$\mathsf{KEM.Encaps}(pk)$
$m \leftarrow\$ \mathcal{M}$
$c \leftarrow \mathsf{PKE.Encrypt}(pk, m)$
$k \leftarrow H(m)$
return (k, c)

$\mathsf{KEM.Decaps}(sk, c)$ $(\mathsf{U}^{\perp}_m)$
$(sk', s) \leftarrow sk$
$m' \leftarrow \mathsf{PKE.Decrypt}(sk', c)$
if $m' = \perp$ **then**
  return $\perp$
$k \leftarrow H(m')$
return k

$\mathsf{KEM.Decaps}(sk, c)$ $(\mathsf{U}^{\not\perp}_m)$
$(sk', s) \leftarrow sk$
$m' \leftarrow \mathsf{PKE.Decrypt}(sk', c)$
if $m' = \perp$ **then**
  $k \leftarrow H(s, c)$
  return k
$k \leftarrow H(m')$
return k

same secret key sk, so checking the result of PKE decryption with encryption will result in the rejection of at least one of these ciphertexts. Thus, the case where there is a collision on inputs to H during normal key derivation in decapsulation is impossible and can be reduced to the case where the output of H collides with the challenge key during implicit rejection, so the contribution of this specific case to the advantage bound is 0. Meanwhile, the case that there is a collision on inputs to H exploiting implicit rejection could result if $m' = s||c'$ for message m', secret s, and ciphertext c' in decapsulation. However, m' and s have the same length and c' must have a positive length by construction, so implicit rejection hash inputs are strictly longer than normal key derivation hash inputs and such a collision is impossible. Hence, the contribution of this case to the advantage bound is 0. As for collisions on outputs of H, by the same reasoning in the proof of Theorem 9, the probability of an adversary finding a second preimage of k is less than or equal to $\frac{q}{|\mathcal{K}|}$. Therefore, as in that proof, the advantage of a C2PRI adversary is bounded by $\frac{q+1}{|\mathcal{K}|}$. □

Theorem 12. *Let* KEM *be a* $\mathsf{U}^{\perp}_m$ *or* $\mathsf{U}^{\not\perp}_m$ *KEM with keyspace* $\mathcal{K}$ *where the hash function* H *is modeled as a random oracle, and let* $\mathcal{C}$ *be an adversary against the ciphertext second preimage resistance of* KEM *making at most* q *quantum queries to* H. *Then,*

$$\mathrm{Adv}^{\mathrm{C2PRI}}_{\mathsf{KEM},\mathcal{C}} \leq 4\sqrt{\frac{q^2+q}{|\mathcal{K}|}} \quad (42)$$

Proof. This proof proceeds much in the same manner as the proof of the quantum ciphertext second preimage resistance of $\mathsf{U}^{\perp}$ and $\mathsf{U}^{\not\perp}$ KEMs in Sect. 5.2. Let H^0_0

and H_0^1 be defined as they are in Sect. 5.2 so that by the same reasoning in that proof any adversary $\mathcal{D}$ has advantage:

$$\mathrm{Adv}_{H_0,\mathcal{D}}^{\mathrm{DIST}} \le 2\sqrt{(d+1)\cdot P_{\mathrm{find}}} = 2\sqrt{(d+1)\cdot\frac{4q}{|\mathcal{K}|}} = 4\sqrt{\frac{q(d+1)}{|\mathcal{K}|}} \le 4\sqrt{\frac{q^2+q}{|\mathcal{K}|}} \tag{43}$$

in the game depicted in Algorithm 13, where $b = 0$ corresponds to H_0^0 and $b = 1$ corresponds to H_0^1, and $\mathcal{D}$ attempts to output the value of b corresponding to the oracle to which it is given access, winning if and only if $b' = b$.

Algorithm 13 H_0^0 and H_0^1 Distinguishing Game

Game $\mathrm{DIST}_{\mathcal{D}}^{H_0}$

Prepare random oracle H_0^0
$(pk, sk) \leftarrow\$ \,\mathsf{KEM.KeyGen}(1^n)$
$(k, c) \leftarrow\$ \,\mathsf{KEM.Encaps}(pk)$
Prepare H_0^1 as above
$b \leftarrow\$ \{0, 1\}$
$b' \leftarrow\$ \,\mathcal{D}^{H_0^b(\cdot)}(k)$
return b'

As in the proof in Sect. 5.2, we now examine the game in Algorithm 14, where $\mathcal{D}$ calls on an adversary $\mathcal{A}$ against the ciphertext second preimage resistance of KEM^b, which is a modified version of KEM.

There is a notable difference between this game and the corresponding game in Sect. 5.2, namely that H_1^b maps m to k instead of $m||c$ to k. We claim that this difference does not affect the advantage bound of $\mathcal{A}$. Consider the ciphertext c' returned by $\mathcal{A}$. If c' truly constitutes a second preimage, then there are three possibilities for how such a second preimage exists: the inputs to $\mathsf{PKE.Decrypt}$ collide, the outputs of $\mathsf{PKE.Decrypt}$ collide, or the outputs of H_1^b collide. It is impossible for the inputs to $\mathsf{PKE.Decrypt}$ to collide, since $c' \neq c$. Meanwhile, $\mathsf{PKE.Decrypt}$ has an internal check to ensure that $\mathsf{PKE.Encrypt}$ returns c' given pk and the message m' it computes from sk and c', but if $m' = m$, as $\mathsf{PKE.Encrypt}(pk, m) = (k, c)$ and $c' \neq c$ this check will fail and $\mathsf{PKE.Decrypt}$ will return $\perp$, so it must be the case that $m' \neq m$. Thus, the only way there can be a second preimage is if there is a collision in the outputs of $H_1^b(\cdot)$ and it is still the case that if $\mathcal{A}$ finds a second preimage then $\mathcal{D}$ knows that it has access to H_0^0. It also still holds that $\Pr[0 \leftarrow \mathrm{DIST}_{H_0,\mathcal{D}}^{H_0^1}] = 0$ by the construction of H_0^1 and $\mathcal{D}$, so:

$$\mathrm{Adv}_{\mathsf{KEM}^0,\mathcal{A}}^{\mathrm{C2PRI}} = \Pr[1 \leftarrow \mathrm{C2PRI}_{\mathsf{KEM}^0,\mathcal{A}}] \le \Pr[0 \leftarrow \mathrm{DIST}_{H_0,\mathcal{D}}^{H_0^0}] = \mathrm{Adv}_{H_0,\mathcal{D}}^{\mathrm{DIST}} \le 4\sqrt{\frac{q^2+q}{|\mathcal{K}|}} \tag{44}$$

Algorithm 14 H_0^0 and H_0^1 Distinguishing Game with Adversary $\mathcal{A}$

Game $\underline{\text{DIST}_{\mathcal{D}}^{H_0}}$
Prepare random oracle H_0^0
$(pk^*, sk^*) \leftarrow\$ \mathsf{KEM.KeyGen}(1^n)$
$(k, c^*) \leftarrow\$ \mathsf{KEM.Encaps}(pk)$
Prepare H_0^1 as above
$b \leftarrow\$ \{0,1\}$
$b' \leftarrow\$ \mathcal{D}^{H_0^b(\cdot)}(k)$
return b'

Adversary $\underline{\mathcal{D}^{H_0^b(\cdot)}(k)}$
$(pk, sk) \leftarrow\$ \mathsf{KEM.KeyGen}(1^n)$
$m \leftarrow\$ \mathcal{M}$
$c \leftarrow\$ \mathsf{PKE.Encrypt}(pk, m)$
$x \leftarrow m$
if $H_0^b(x) = k$ **then**
  return 0
Prepare H_1^b
Prepare KEM^b
$c' \leftarrow\$ \mathcal{A}(pk, sk, c, k)$
if $c' \neq c \wedge \mathsf{KEM'.Decaps}(sk, c') = k$ **then**
  return 0
return 1

Again, as in the proof in Sect. 5.2, an adversary $\mathcal{C}$ against the ciphertext second preimage resistance of KEM must have an advantage less than or equal to the advantage of $\mathcal{A}$ against the ciphertext second preimage resistance of KEM^0. Therefore, we obtain:

$$\text{Adv}_{\mathsf{KEM},\mathcal{C}}^{\text{C2PRI}} \leq \text{Adv}_{\mathsf{KEM}^0,\mathcal{A}}^{\text{C2PRI}} \leq 4\sqrt{\frac{q^2+q}{|\mathcal{K}|}} \tag{45}$$

as desired. □

6.3 Application to ML-KEM

ML-KEM is designed with a slight modification of the $\mathsf{U}_m^{\not\perp}$ transform and is defined in [5]. Notably, it uses the key derivation function $G(m, H(pk))$ for hash functions G and H. In the case of implicit rejection, it outputs $J(s, c)$ for another hash function J. Additionally, it re-encrypts the message and checks if this equals the original ciphertext; if not, it implicitly rejects.

Corollary 4. *Let* KEM *be an instantiation of ML-KEM [5] with keyspace* $\mathcal{K}$ *and underlying hash functions* G *and* J *modeled as random oracles. Let* $\mathcal{C}$ *be an adversary against C2PRI for* KEM. *If* $\mathcal{C}$ *makes at most* q *total classical queries to* G *and* J, *then*

$$\text{Adv}_{\mathsf{KEM},\mathcal{C}}^{\text{C2PRI}} \leq \frac{q+2}{|\mathcal{K}|} \tag{46}$$

Algorithm 15 ML-KEM

$\mathsf{KEM.KeyGen}(1^n)$	$\mathsf{KEM.Encaps}(pk))$	$\mathsf{KEM.Decaps}(sk, c)$
$(pk, sk') \leftarrow\$ \mathsf{PKE.KeyGen}(1^n)$	$m \leftarrow\$ \mathcal{M}$	$(sk', pk, h, s) \leftarrow sk$
$s \leftarrow\$ \mathcal{M}$	$(k, r) \leftarrow G(m, H(pk))$	$m' \leftarrow \mathsf{PKE.Decrypt}(sk, c)$
$sk \leftarrow (sk', pk, H(pk), s)$	$c \leftarrow \mathsf{PKE.Encrypt}(pk, m, r)$	$(k, r') \leftarrow G(m', h)$
return (pk, sk)	**return** (k, c)	$c' \leftarrow \mathsf{PKE.Encrypt}(pk, m', r')$
		if $c \neq c'$ **then**
		return $J(s, c)$
		return k

If $\mathcal{C}$ instead makes at most q total quantum queries to G and H, then

$$\mathrm{Adv}^{\mathrm{C2PRI}}_{\mathsf{KEM},\mathcal{C}} \leq 4\sqrt{\frac{q^2 + q}{|\mathcal{K}|}} \tag{47}$$

Proof. The advantage of an adversary against the ciphertext second preimage resistance of ML-KEM making at most q_G classical queries to G and at most q_J classical queries to J was proved to be bounded above by $\frac{q_G+q_J+2}{|\mathcal{K}|}$ in [13]. As for its quantum second preimage resistance, the structure of ML-KEM is similar to that of $\mathsf{U}^{\not\perp}_m$ KEMs, but differs in that randomness generated as a byproduct of key derivation is included as a parameter in PKE encryption, a hash of the public key is included in normal key derivation, and distinct hash functions G and J are used for normal key derivation and implicit rejection, respectively. The first difference does not affect the quantum C2PRI proof beyond how $\mathcal{D}$ sets up the adversary $\mathcal{A}$, as the randomness does not affect session-key generation. The second difference also does not affect the bound, as $\mathcal{A}$ cannot change the challenge public key hashed and used in key derivation. Finally, to accommodate for G and J, we can use domain separation and adjust the oracles in the proof by prepending H^b_1 oracle inputs with 0 and 1 everywhere G and J would be respectively prepared and queried in KEM' and giving the oracle access to $G(\cdot) = H^b_1(0||\cdot)$ and $J(\cdot) = H^b_1(1||\cdot)$. These changes do not affect anything else in the proof, so the quantum C2PRI bound holds for adversaries against the ciphertext second preimage resistance of ML-KEM. □

Acknowledgments. The authors thank the University of Maryland MathQuantum Research Training Group, supported by NSF grant DMS-2231533, for making this work possible and for their continual support. FB and AK thank Mike Hamburg for his help with formulating the quantum second preimage resistance proofs, and GA's graduate students for their insights during weekly research discussions. GA's work is partly supported by NSF award CNS-21547.

Disclosure of Interests. The authors have no competing interests to declare that are relevant to the content of this article.

A Proofs of Theorems 6 and 7

Theorem 13 (Theorem 6 Restated). *Let* KEM_1 *be a C2PRI-secure KEM and* KEM_2 *be a* δ*-correct, IND-CCA KEM. Let* F *be a split-key (resp. dual) PRF, and set* $W(k_1, k_2, c_1, c_2) = F(k_1, k_2, c_2)$ *(resp.* $F(k_1, k_2)$*). Let* $\Pi = \Pi(\mathsf{KEM}_1, \mathsf{KEM}_2, W)$ *be the combination of these KEMs given in Algorithm 4. Then for all QPT adversaries* $\mathcal{A}$ *against the IND-CCA security of* Π *making at most* q *queries to their decapsulation oracle, there exist QPT adversaries* $\mathcal{B}$*,* $\mathcal{C}$*, and* $\mathcal{D}$ *such that:*

$$\mathrm{Adv}_{\Pi,\mathcal{A}}^{\text{IND-CCA}} \leq 2(\mathrm{Adv}_{\mathsf{KEM}_1,\mathcal{B}}^{\text{C2PRI}} + \mathrm{Adv}_{\mathsf{KEM}_2,\mathcal{C}}^{\text{IND-CCA}} + \mathrm{Adv}_{F,\mathcal{D}}^{\text{PR}_2} + \delta) \tag{48}$$

Moreover, $\mathcal{C}$ *makes at most* q *classical queries to its own decapsulation oracle,* $\mathcal{D}$ *makes at most* $q+1$ *classical queries to its evaluation oracle, and all of* $\mathcal{B}, \mathcal{C}$ *and* $\mathcal{D}$ *run with constant-factor overhead compared to* $\mathcal{A}$.

Proof. We will use a hybrid strategy similar to that in the proof of Theorem 1 of [30], as well as Theorems 1 and 2 of [13]. As an overview of the strategy, we start by considering the behavior of $\mathcal{A}$ when playing against the IND-CCA^0 game, labeling that game as hybrid G_0. We then consider the adversary playing against game G_1, where we slightly change in the decapsulation oracle, and argue that $\mathcal{A}$ can only detect this change with probability δ. In G_2, we have the decapsulation oracle abort when $\mathcal{A}$ inputs some KEM_1 ciphertext c_1 different from the challenge ciphertext c_1^* but decapsulating to the same session key. We show that noticing this change is as difficult as wining the C2PRI experiment for KEM_1. At this point, we can swap the KEM_1 session key used as input to F with a random key, bounding this change with the IND-CCA security of KEM_1. Once this key is generated uniformly at random, we may apply the security of F to replace the challenge key k^* that $\mathcal{A}$ receives with a random key. (Due to a small technical detail, this step requires two hybrid games.) Having achieved this, in G_5, we are nearly done with the proof. In game $\mathrm{G}_6 - \mathrm{G}_8$, we reverse the changes from the beginning of the proof, arguing in the same way as before that $\mathcal{A}$ cannot detect these modifications. G_8 is equivalent to the IND-CCA^1 game, so having shown it is difficult for $\mathcal{A}$ to notice any changes between G_0 and G_8, we conclude with our bound for $\mathrm{Adv}_{\Pi,\mathcal{A}}^{\text{IND-CCA}}$. We describe each individual hybrid below, and Algorithm 16 contains their pseudocode.

Game 0. Game G_0 represents $\mathcal{A}$ playing in the IND-CCA experiment for Π with the challenge bit set to 0. We run each KEM in parallel, just as Π does, and provide an honest session key to $\mathcal{A}$. Therefore:

$$\Pr[1 \leftarrow \text{IND-CCA}^0_{\Pi,\mathcal{A}}] = \Pr[1 \leftarrow \mathrm{G}_0^{\mathcal{A}}] \tag{49}$$

Algorithm 16 Hybrid games for the proof of Theorem 13

Games $G_0 - G_8$:

$W'[\cdot] \leftarrow \perp$ ▷ G_4
$pk_1, sk_1 \leftarrow\$ \mathsf{KEM}_1.\mathsf{KeyGen}(1^n)$
$pk_2, sk_2 \leftarrow\$ \mathsf{KEM}_2.\mathsf{KeyGen}(1^n)$
$pk \leftarrow (pk_1, pk_2)$
$k_1^*, c_1^* \leftarrow\$ \mathsf{KEM}_1.\mathsf{Encaps}(pk_1)$
$k_2^*, c_2^* \leftarrow\$ \mathsf{KEM}_2.\mathsf{Encaps}(pk_2)$
$k_2^* \leftarrow\$ \mathcal{K}_2$ ▷ $G_3 - G_5$
$c^* \leftarrow (c_1^*, c_2^*)$
$k^* \leftarrow W(k_1^*, k_2^*, c_1^*, c_2^*)$
$k^* \leftarrow\$ \mathcal{K}$ ▷ $G_4 - G_8$
$W'[k_1^*] \leftarrow k^*$ ▷ G_4
$b' \leftarrow\$ \mathcal{A}^{\mathsf{Decaps}(\cdot)}(pk, c^*, k^*)$

Oracle $\mathsf{Decaps}(c)$:

if $c = c^*$ **then**
  return $\perp$
$c_1, c_2 \leftarrow c$
$k_1 \leftarrow \mathsf{KEM}_1.\mathsf{Decaps}(sk_1, c_1)$
$k_2 \leftarrow \mathsf{KEM}_2.\mathsf{Decaps}(sk_2, c_2)$
if $c_2 = c_2^*$ **then** ▷ $G_1 - G_7$
  $k_2 \leftarrow k_2^*$ ▷ $G_1 - G_7$
if $k_1 = \perp \vee k_2 = \perp$ **then**
  return $\perp$
if $k_1 = k_1^* \wedge c_1 \neq c_1^*$ **then** ▷ $G_2 - G_6$
  abort$_1$ ▷ $G_2 - G_6$
if $c_2 = c_2^*$ **then** ▷ G_4
  if $W'[k_1] = \perp$: ▷ G_4
    $W'[k_1] \leftarrow\$ \mathcal{K}$ ▷ G_4
  return $W'[k_1]$ ▷ G_4
return $W(k_1, k_2, c_1, c_2)$

Game 1. In game G_1, we make a small modification to the decapsulation oracle. When receiving (c_1, c_2) as input such that $c_2 = c_2^*$, it sets k_2 as k_2^* instead of performing $k_2 \leftarrow \mathsf{KEM}_2.\mathsf{Decaps}(sk_2, c_2)$ (The notation used here is the same as in Algorithm 16). Games 0 and 1 should nearly always be identical, and they only differ when KEM_2 would incorrectly decapsulate c_2^*. Decapsulation is deterministic, and we are only changing how the oracle decapsulates c_2^* (not other KEM_2 ciphertexts), so this G_0 and G_1 are different with probability at most δ regardless of how many times $\mathcal{A}$ queries the oracle. Therefore, we have:

$$\left|\Pr[1 \leftarrow G_0^{\mathcal{A}}] - \Pr[1 \leftarrow G_1^{\mathcal{A}}]\right| \leq \delta \tag{50}$$

Game 2. In game G_2, we again modify the decapsulation oracle. Now, it aborts when it receives an input (c_1, c_2) such that $c_1 \neq c_1^*$ but $\mathsf{KEM}_1.\mathsf{Decaps}(sk_1, c_1) = k_1^*$. Notice this abort condition precisely matches the win condition for KEM_1's ciphertext second preimage resistance game, so we claim there exists a QPT adversary $\mathcal{B}_1$ such that:

$$\left|\Pr[1 \leftarrow G_1^{\mathcal{A}}] - \Pr[1 \leftarrow G_2^{\mathcal{A}}]\right| \leq \Pr[\text{abort}_1] = \mathrm{Adv}^{\mathrm{C2PRI}}_{\mathsf{KEM}_1, \mathcal{B}_1} \tag{51}$$

The pseudocode for adversary $\mathcal{B}_1$ is shown in Algorithm 17. When starting its challenge, $\mathcal{B}_1$ receives a public/secret key pair, ciphertext, and session key for KEM_1. It runs key generation and encapsulation for KEM_2, then uses these to instantiate $\mathcal{A}$. Because $\mathcal{B}_1$ has access to both secret keys, it can easily answer $\mathcal{A}$'s decapsulation queries. It perfectly simulates games 1 and 2 for $\mathcal{A}$ right until the abort condition would be triggered in game G_2, and $\mathcal{B}_1$ wins its C2PRI challenge exactly when this abort would occur. (Note if the abort never occurs, $\mathcal{B}_1$ returns c_1^* and loses its challenge.) This justifies the claim.

Algorithm 17 Adversaries $\mathcal{B}_1$ and $\mathcal{B}_2$ against the ciphertext second preimage resistance of KEM_1. The commented line is only executed for $\mathcal{B}_2$.

Adversary $\mathcal{B}_1(pk_1, sk_1, c_1^*, k_1^*)$
$pk_2, sk_2 \leftarrow\$ \mathsf{KEM}_2.\mathsf{KeyGen}(1^n)$
$pk \leftarrow (pk_1, pk_2)$
$k_2^*, c_2^* \leftarrow\$ \mathsf{KEM}_2.\mathsf{Encaps}(pk_2)$
$c^* \leftarrow (c_1^*, c_2^*)$
$k^* \leftarrow W(k_1^*, k_2^*, c_1^*, c_2^*)$
$k^* \leftarrow\$ \mathcal{K}$
$b' \leftarrow\$ \mathcal{A}^{\mathsf{Decaps}(\cdot)}(pk, c^*, k^*)$
return c_1^*

If $\mathcal{A}$ **Calls** $\mathsf{Decaps}(c)$**:**
if $c = c^*$ **then**
  return $\perp$
$c_1, c_2 \leftarrow c$
$k_1 \leftarrow \mathsf{KEM}_1.\mathsf{Decaps}(sk_1, c_1)$
$k_2 \leftarrow \mathsf{KEM}_2.\mathsf{Decaps}(sk_2, c_2)$
if $c_2 = c_2^*$ **then** $\triangleright\ \mathcal{B}_2$
  $k_2 \leftarrow k_2^*$
if $k_1 = \perp \vee k_2 = \perp$ **then**
  return $\perp$
if $k_1 = k_1^* \wedge c_1 \neq c_1^*$ **then**
  stop with c_1
return $W(k_1, k_2, c_1, c_2)$

Game 3. In game 3, we replace k_2^*, the session key for KEM_2, with a key generated uniformly at random. This should be difficult for $\mathcal{A}$ to detect so long at KEM_2 retains IND-CCA security. Indeed, we claim there exists a QPT adversary $\mathcal{C}_1$ such that:

$$\left|\Pr[1 \leftarrow \mathrm{G}_2^{\mathcal{A}}] - \Pr[1 \leftarrow \mathrm{G}_3^{\mathcal{A}}]\right| \leq \mathrm{Adv}_{\mathsf{KEM}_2,\mathcal{C}_1}^{\text{IND-CCA}} \tag{52}$$

The pseudocode to construct $\mathcal{C}_1$ is shown in Algorithm 18. $\mathcal{C}_1$ receives a public key, ciphertext, and session key for KEM_2. It creates keys and a ciphertext for KEM_1 and uses these to call $\mathcal{A}$. Adversary $\mathcal{C}_1$ can answer most of $\mathcal{A}$'s decapsulation queries by decapsulating c_1 with its own secret key and c_2 with its oracle. However, it cannot call its decapsulation oracle on c_2^*, so in that case, it uses the session key k_2^* it was given. (Notice due to the change in G_1, this is the correct way of simulating games G_2 and G_3 for $\mathcal{A}$.) When $\mathcal{C}$ is instantiated on the IND-CCA^0 game, the session key k_2^* was honestly generated, so $\mathcal{C}_1$ perfectly simulates G_2 for $\mathcal{A}$. When instantiated on the IND-CCA^1 game, it receives a random key and therefore simulates G_3 for $\mathcal{A}$. $\mathcal{C}_1$ returns the same output as $\mathcal{A}$, so the claim follows.

Game 4. Now that k_2^* is generated uniformly at random, we can apply the split-key pseudorandom property of F to replace k^* with a random session key. In this game, on decapsulation queries that include c_2^*, we return a random element

Algorithm 18 IND-CCA adversaries $\mathcal{C}_1$ and $\mathcal{C}_2$ against KEM_2. The commented line is only executed for $\mathcal{C}_2$.

Adversary $\mathcal{C}_1^{\mathsf{Decaps}^{\mathcal{O}}(\cdot)}(pk_2, c_2^*, k_2^*)$
$pk_1, sk_1 \leftarrow\$ \mathsf{KEM}_1.\mathsf{KeyGen}(1^n)$
$pk \leftarrow (pk_1, pk_2)$
$c_1^*, k_1^* \leftarrow\$ \mathsf{KEM}_1.\mathsf{Encaps}(pk_1)$
$c \leftarrow (c_1^*, c_2^*)$
$k^* \leftarrow W(k_1^*, k_2^*, c_1^*, c_2^*)$
$k^* \leftarrow\$ \mathcal{K}$ $\triangleright \mathcal{C}_2$
$b' \leftarrow\$ \mathcal{A}^{\mathsf{Decaps}(\cdot)}(pk, c^*, k^*)$
return b'

If $\mathcal{A}$ **Calls** $\mathsf{Decaps}(c)$:
if $c = c^*$ **then**
  return $\perp$
$c_1, c_2 \leftarrow c$
$k_1 \leftarrow \mathsf{KEM}_1.\mathsf{Decaps}(sk_1, c_1)$
if $c_2 = c_2^*$ **then**
  $k_2 \leftarrow k_2^*$
else
  $k_2 \leftarrow \mathsf{Decaps}^{\mathcal{O}}(c_2)$
if $k_1 = \perp \vee k_2 = \perp$ **then**
  return $\perp$
if $k_1 = k_1^* \wedge c_1 \neq c_1^*$ **then**
  abort_1
return $W(k_1, k_2, c_1, c_2)$

of $\mathcal{K}$, using the table W' to maintain consistency across queries. We need to do this to accommodate the PRF adversary we will construct, which does not have access to k_2^* in its challenge. We will reverse this change in game G_5. We claim there exists a QPT adversary $\mathcal{D}_1$ such that:

$$\left|\Pr[1 \leftarrow \mathrm{G}_3^{\mathcal{A}}] - \Pr[1 \leftarrow \mathrm{G}_4^{\mathcal{A}}]\right| \leq \mathrm{Adv}_{F,\mathcal{D}_1}^{\mathrm{PR}_2} \tag{53}$$

We construct adversary $\mathcal{D}_1$ in Algorithm 19. (That algorithm shows $\mathcal{D}_1$ in the case that F is a split-key PRF taking a ciphertext as input. The dual PRF case is the same, except we don't include a ciphertext on queries to Eval.) $\mathcal{D}_1$ receives no input and runs key generation and encapsulation for both KEMs. When instantiated with game PR_2^0, $\mathcal{D}_1$ makes evaluation queries to F keyed with k_1^* and a random element of $\mathcal{K}_2$, so k^* is computed exactly as in G_3. However, $\mathcal{D}_1$ does not have access to the element of $\mathcal{K}_2$ used to compute k^*, so on decapsulation queries including c_2^*, $\mathcal{D}_1$ must make queries to Eval instead of computing the session key with F. Notice in the PR_2^0 setting, $\mathcal{D}_1$ generates k_2^* but never uses it, instead using the randomly-generated PRF key for its challenge. Since G_3 samples k_2^* at random, $\mathcal{D}_1$ is perfectly simulating G_3 for $\mathcal{A}$ in this setting. When $\mathcal{D}_1$ is instantiated on PR_2^1, all of its evaluation queries return random elements of $\mathcal{K}$. In the split-key pseudorandomness experiment, the evaluation oracle always returns consistent results across multiple queries with the same input; this is why we use the table W' in game G_4 instead of returning a randomly sampled element of $\mathcal{K}$ whenever $\mathcal{A}$ queries the decapsulation oracle with c_2^*. In the PR_2^1 case, $\mathcal{D}_1$ is perfectly simulating game G_4 for $\mathcal{A}$, so the claim follows.

Algorithm 19 Adversaries $\mathcal{D}_1$ and $\mathcal{D}_2$ against the split-key pseudorandomness of F, keyed on the second input. The commented line is only executed for $\mathcal{D}_2$.

Adversary $\mathcal{D}_1^{\mathsf{Eval}(\cdot,\cdot)}$
$pk_1, sk_1 \leftarrow\$ \mathsf{KEM}_1.\mathsf{KeyGen}(1^n)$
$pk_2, sk_2 \leftarrow\$ \mathsf{KEM}_2.\mathsf{KeyGen}(1^n)$
$pk \leftarrow (pk_1, pk_2)$
$c_1^*, k_1^* \leftarrow\$ \mathsf{KEM}_1.\mathsf{Encaps}(pk_1)$
$c_2^*, k_2^* \leftarrow\$ \mathsf{KEM}_2.\mathsf{Encaps}(pk_2)$
$c \leftarrow (c_1^*, c_2^*)$
$k^* \leftarrow \mathsf{Eval}(k_1^*, c_2^*)$
$k^* \leftarrow\$ \mathcal{K}$ ▷ $\mathcal{D}_2$
$b' \leftarrow\$ \mathcal{A}^{\mathsf{Decaps}(\cdot)}(pk, c^*, k^*)$
return b'

If $\mathcal{A}$ Calls $\mathsf{Decaps}(c)$:
if $c = c^*$ **then**
  return $\perp$
$c_1, c_2 \leftarrow c$
$k_1 \leftarrow \mathsf{KEM}_1.\mathsf{Decaps}(sk_1, c_1)$
$k_2 \leftarrow \mathsf{KEM}_2.\mathsf{Decaps}(sk_2, c_2)$
if $k_1 = \perp \vee (k_2 = \perp \wedge c_2 \neq c_2^*)$ **then**
  return $\perp$
if $k_1 = k_1^* \wedge c_1 \neq c_1^*$ **then**
  abort_1
if $c_2 = c_2^*$ **then**
  return $\mathsf{Eval}(k_1, c_2)$
return $W(k_1, k_2, c_1, c_2)$

Game 5. In game 5, we remove the table W' used in G_4 and answer decapsulation queries as in game 3. We claim there exists a QPT adversary $\mathcal{D}_2$ such that:

$$\left|\Pr[1 \leftarrow G_4^{\mathcal{A}}] - \Pr[1 \leftarrow G_5^{\mathcal{A}}]\right| \leq \mathrm{Adv}_{F,\mathcal{D}_2}^{\mathrm{PR}_2} \tag{54}$$

The pseudocode for $\mathcal{D}_2$ is also shown in Algorithm 19 (as in the previous game, Algorithm 19 shows the case that F is a split-key PRF, but the dual PRF case is very similar). It behaves nearly identically to $\mathcal{D}_1$, but it always samples k^* randomly from $\mathcal{K}$. Similar to $\mathcal{D}_1$, when $\mathcal{D}_2$ is instantiated on PR_2^1, it returns random elements of $\mathcal{K}$ on decapsulation queries including c_2^*, simulating G_4 for $\mathcal{A}$. $\mathcal{D}_2$ does differ slightly from G_4: in G_4, $k^* = F'[k_1^*]$, but $\mathcal{D}_2$ choses k^* randomly with no relation to $\mathsf{Eval}(k_1^*, c_2^*)$. This would be a problem if $\mathcal{A}$ could query its decapsulation oracle in such a way as to recover $\mathsf{Eval}(k_1^*, c_2^*)$ and compare this to k^*. The decapsulation oracle only returns Eval queries when $c_2 = c_2^*$, and due to our abort condition, we cannot have $k_1 = k_1^*$ and $c_2 = c_2^*$ unless $c_1 = c_1^*$ and $c_2 = c_2^*$. But the decapsulation oracle always returns $\perp$ on that specific query. Therefore, when $\mathcal{D}_2$ playing against PR_2^1, it is still simulating G_4 for $\mathcal{A}$. When $\mathcal{D}_2$ is instantiated on PR_2^0, its evaluation queries are once again honest evaluations of F keyed on a random element of $\mathcal{K}_2$. Therefore, $\mathcal{D}_2$ perfectly simulates G_5 for $\mathcal{A}$ in this case, justifying our claim.

In the rest of the proof, we undo the changes made in games 1, 2, and 3. Now that k^* is sampled randomly from $\mathcal{K}$, this will yield the IND-CCA[1] game.

Game 6. In game 6, we undo the change from game G_3 and once again generate k_2^* honestly. Similar to game 3, we claim there exists a QPT adversary $\mathcal{C}_2$ such that:

$$\left|\Pr[1 \leftarrow G_5^{\mathcal{A}}] - \Pr[1 \leftarrow G_6^{\mathcal{A}}]\right| \leq \mathrm{Adv}_{\mathsf{KEM}_2,\mathcal{C}_2}^{\mathrm{IND\text{-}CCA}} \tag{55}$$

$\mathcal{C}_2$ is very similar to $\mathcal{C}_1$ and is shown in Algorithm 18. When instantiated on IND-CCA^1, $\mathcal{C}_2$ uses a random element of $\mathcal{K}_2$ as k_2^* and as such, simulates G_5 for $\mathcal{A}$. When playing against IND-CCA^0, $\mathcal{C}_2$ is using the output of $\mathsf{KEM}_2.\mathsf{Encaps}(pk_2)$ as k_2^* and simulating G_6. Therefore, the claim holds.

Game 7. In game 7, we undo the change from G_2 and no longer abort on decapsulation queries with $k_1 = k_1^*$ and $c_1 \neq c_1^*$. We claim there exists a QPT adversary $\mathcal{B}_2$ such that:

$$\left|\Pr[1 \leftarrow G_6^{\mathcal{A}}] - \Pr[1 \leftarrow G_7^{\mathcal{A}}]\right| \leq \Pr[\text{abort}_1] = \text{Adv}_{\mathsf{KEM}_1,\mathcal{B}_2}^{\text{C2PRI}} \tag{56}$$

Once again, $\mathcal{B}_2$ is similar to $\mathcal{B}_1$ and is shown in Algorithm 17. $\mathcal{B}_2$ receives a public/secret key pair, ciphertext, and session key for KEM_1 and creates the same for KEM_2. As in games 6 and 7, it samples k^* randomly from $\mathcal{K}$ and runs $\mathcal{A}$, answering decapsulation queries using its two secret keys. Games 6 and 7 are identical except for the abort condition, and $\mathcal{B}_2$ perfectly simulates both of them to $\mathcal{A}$ until the abort is triggered, at which time it wins its own C2PRI challenge. This justifies the claim.

Game 8. In game 8, we undo the change from G_1. On queries including c_2^*, instead of setting $k_2 = k_2^*$, we once again decapsulate c_2^* using sk_2. Similar to game 1, we have:

$$\left|\Pr[1 \leftarrow G_7^{\mathcal{A}}] - \Pr[1 \leftarrow G_8^{\mathcal{A}}]\right| \leq \delta \tag{57}$$

Now, we have that k^* is sampled uniformly at random from $\mathcal{K}$, and we have undone our other changes. Therefore, G_8 is equivalent to the IND-CCA^1 game, and:

$$\Pr[1 \leftarrow G_8^{\mathcal{A}}] = \Pr[1 \leftarrow \text{IND-CCA}_{\mathcal{A}}^1] \tag{58}$$

The theorem follows by setting $\mathcal{B}$ (respectively $\mathcal{C}$, $\mathcal{D}$) to whichever of $\mathcal{B}_1$ or $\mathcal{B}_2$ (respectively $\mathcal{C}_1$ or $\mathcal{C}_2$, $\mathcal{D}_1$ or $\mathcal{D}_2$) attains a greater advantage and summing the terms in each claim. □

Theorem 14 (Theorem 7 Restated). *Let KEM_1 be a δ-correct, IND-CCA KEM and KEM_2 be a KEM. Let F be a split-key PRF and set $W(k_1, k_2, c_1, c_2) = F(k_1, k_2, c_2)$. Let $\Pi = \Pi(\mathsf{KEM}_1, \mathsf{KEM}_2, W)$ be the combination of these KEMs as described in Algorithm 4. Then for all QPT adversaries $\mathcal{A}$ against the IND-CCA security of Π making at most q classical queries to their decapsulation oracle, there exist QPT adversaries $\mathcal{B}$ and $\mathcal{C}$ such that:*

$$\text{Adv}_{\Pi,\mathcal{A}}^{\text{IND-CCA}} \leq 2(\text{Adv}_{\mathsf{KEM}_1,\mathcal{B}}^{\text{IND-CCA}} + \text{Adv}_{F,\mathcal{C}}^{\text{PR}_1} + \delta) \tag{59}$$

Moreover, $\mathcal{B}$ makes at most q queries to its own decapsulation oracles, $\mathcal{C}$ makes at most $q+1$ queries to its evaluation oracle, and both run with at most constant-factor overhead compared to $\mathcal{A}$.

Proof. The proof of this theorem follows in much the same way as Theorem 13 and is once again similar to Theorem 1 of [30] and Theorems 1–2 of [13]. The largest difference is that because c_2 is part of the input to F, we don't need to rely on ciphertext second preimage resistance. This changes how we analyze adversary $\mathcal{D}$, which plays the same role that $\mathcal{E}$ did in the above proof. We refer to the previous proof for many other details and omit explicit constructions of $\mathcal{B}$, $\mathcal{C}$, and $\mathcal{E}$ here. Once again, we use hybrid games, described in Algorithm 20.

Algorithm 20 Hybrid games for the proof of Theorem 14

Games $\mathrm{G}_0 - \mathrm{G}_6$:		Oracle Decaps(c):	
$W'[\cdot] \leftarrow \perp$	$\triangleright$ G_3	**if** $c = c^*$ **then**	
$pk_1, sk_1 \leftarrow\$ \mathsf{KEM}_1.\mathsf{KeyGen}(1^n)$		**return** $\perp$	
$pk_2, sk_2 \leftarrow\$ \mathsf{KEM}_2.\mathsf{KeyGen}(1^n)$		$c_1, c_2 \leftarrow c$	
$pk \leftarrow (pk_1, pk_2)$		$k_1 \leftarrow \mathsf{KEM}_1.\mathsf{Decaps}(sk_1, c_1)$	
$k_1^*, c_1^* \leftarrow\$ \mathsf{KEM}_1.\mathsf{Encaps}(pk_1)$		$k_2 \leftarrow \mathsf{KEM}_2.\mathsf{Decaps}(sk_2, c_2)$	
$k_2^*, c_2^* \leftarrow\$ \mathsf{KEM}_2.\mathsf{Encaps}(pk_2)$		**if** $c_1 = c_1^*$ **then**	$\triangleright$ $\mathrm{G}_1 - \mathrm{G}_5$
$k_1^* \leftarrow\$ \mathcal{K}_1$	$\triangleright$ $\mathrm{G}_2 - \mathrm{G}_4$	$k_1 \leftarrow k_1^*$	$\triangleright$ $\mathrm{G}_1 - \mathrm{G}_5$
$c^* \leftarrow (c_1^*, c_2^*)$		**if** $k_1 = \perp \vee k_2 = \perp$ **then**	
$k^* \leftarrow W(k_1^*, k_2^*, c_1^*, c_2^*)$		**return** $\perp$	
$k^* \leftarrow\$ \mathcal{K}$	$\triangleright$ $\mathrm{G}_3 - \mathrm{G}_6$	**if** $c_1 = c_1^*$ **then**	$\triangleright$ G_3
$W'[k_2^*, c_2^*] \leftarrow k^*$	$\triangleright$ G_3	**if** $W'[k_2, c_2] = \perp$:	$\triangleright$ G_3
$b' \leftarrow\$ \mathcal{A}^{\mathsf{Decaps}(\cdot)}(pk, c^*, k^*)$		$W'[k_2, c_2] \leftarrow\$ \mathcal{K}$	$\triangleright$ G_3
		return $W'[k_2, c_2]$	$\triangleright$ G_3
		return $W(k_1, k_2, c_1, c_2)$	

Games 0 3. Games 0, 1, 2, and 3 of this proof play the same roles as games 0, 1, 3, and 4 respectively in the proof of Theorem 13. Game 0 is equivalent to the IND-CCA game with challenge bit set to 0. In G_1, we set $k_1 \leftarrow k_1^*$ for decapsulation queries with $c_1 = c_1^*$, bounding the difference between these two games with δ. In game 2, we sample k_1^* randomly from $\mathcal{K}_1$, justifying this change with the IND-CCA security of KEM_1. In game 3, we choose k^* uniformly at random. Additionally, just like in G_4 of Theorem 13, on decapsulation queries with $c_1 = c_1^*$, we return random elements of $\mathcal{K}$, using the table W' to maintain consistency across queries. None of these changes relied on the abort condition we introduced in game 2 of the previous theorem, so similarly to before, we have that there exist QPT adversaries $\mathcal{B}_1$ and $\mathcal{C}_1$ such that:

$$\left|\Pr[1 \leftarrow \text{IND-CCA}_{\mathcal{A}}^0] - \Pr[1 \leftarrow \mathrm{G}_3^{\mathcal{A}}]\right| \leq \delta + \mathrm{Adv}_{\mathsf{KEM}_1,\mathcal{B}_1}^{\text{IND-CCA}} + \mathrm{Adv}_{F,\mathcal{C}_1}^{\mathrm{PR}_1} \tag{60}$$

Game 4. Game 4 is analogous to game 5 of the previous proof, where we remove the table W'. This time, W' is being used to answer decapsulation queries containing c_1^*. We claim there exists a QPT adversary $\mathcal{C}_2$ such that:

$$\left|\Pr[1 \leftarrow \mathrm{G}_3^{\mathcal{A}}] - \Pr[1 \leftarrow \mathrm{G}_4^{\mathcal{A}}]\right| \leq \mathrm{Adv}_{F,\mathcal{C}_2}^{\mathrm{PR}_1} \tag{61}$$

The pseudocode to construct $\mathcal{C}_2$ is shown in Algorithm 21. It generates public/secret key pairs, ciphertexts, and session keys for each KEM and selects k^* randomly from $\mathcal{K}$ so as to simulate games 3 and 4. When $\mathcal{C}_2$ is playing against PR_1^0, the Eval queries return honest evaluations of F keyed on a random element of $\mathcal{K}_1$, so $\mathcal{D}$ is properly simulating G_4 for $\mathcal{A}$. In the PR_1^1 setting, the evaluation queries return random elements of $\mathcal{K}$. This nearly simulates G_3, except that in G_3, $k^* = F'[k_2^*, c_2^*]$, but $\mathcal{C}_2$ does not guarantee that $k^* = \mathsf{Eval}(k_2^*, c_2^*)$. This means that $\mathcal{C}_2$ only replicates G_3 so long as $\mathcal{A}$ cannot recover $\mathsf{Eval}(k_2^*, c_2^*)$ from the decapsulation oracle. However, the oracle only returns Eval queries on inputs with $c_1 = c_1^*$. We would also need $c_2 = c_2^*$ for the decapsulation oracle to return an Eval query containing c_2^*, but if $c_1 = c_1^*$ and $c_2 = c_2^*$ then Decaps returns $\perp$. Therefore, when $\mathcal{C}_2$ is instantiated on PR_1^1, it can perfectly simulate G_3 for $\mathcal{A}$, justifying the claim.

Algorithm 21 Adversary $\mathcal{C}_2$ against the split-key pseudorandomness of F, keyed on the first input.

Adversary $\mathcal{C}_2^{\mathsf{Eval}(\cdot,\cdot)}$
```
pk_1, sk_1 <-$ KEM_1.KeyGen(1^n)
pk_2, sk_2 <-$ KEM_2.KeyGen(1^n)
pk <- (pk_1, pk_2)
c_1^*, k_1^* <-$ KEM_1.Encaps(pk_1)
c_2^*, k_2^* <-$ KEM_2.Encaps(pk_2)
c <- (c_1^*, c_2^*)
k^* <- Eval(k_2^*, c_2^*)
k^* <-$ K
b' <-$ A^{Decaps(·)}(pk, c^*, k^*)
return b'
```

If $\mathcal{A}$ **Calls** Decaps(c):
```
if c = c^* then
  return ⊥
c_1, c_2 <- c
k_1 <- KEM_1.Decaps(sk_1, c_1)
k_2 <- KEM_2.Decaps(sk_2, c_2)
if (k_1 = ⊥ ∧ c_1 ≠ c_1^*) ∨ k_2 = ⊥ then
  return ⊥
if c_1 = c_1^* then
  return Eval(k_2, c_2)
return W(k_1, k_2, c_1, c_2)
```

Games 5-6. Once again, games 5 and 6 are similar to games 6 and 8 of the previous proof. In game 5, we return to generating k_1^* honestly, bounding this difference with the IND-CCA security of KEM_1. In game 6, we stop setting $k_1 \leftarrow k_1^*$ on queries $c_1 \leftarrow c_1^*$, justifying this with the correctness of KEM_1. Therefore, there exists a QPT advesary $\mathcal{B}_2$ such that:

$$\left|\Pr[1 \leftarrow \mathrm{G}_4^{\mathcal{A}}] - \Pr[1 \leftarrow \mathrm{G}_6^{\mathcal{A}}]\right| \leq \mathrm{Adv}_{\mathsf{KEM}_1,\mathcal{C}_2}^{\mathrm{IND\text{-}CCA}} \tag{62}$$

But G_6 is equivalent to the IND-CCA game with challenge bit set to 1, so:

$$\Pr[1 \leftarrow G_6^{\mathcal{A}}] = \Pr[1 \leftarrow \text{IND-CCA}_{\mathcal{A}}^1] \tag{63}$$

Once again, the theorem follows by setting $\mathcal{B}/\mathcal{C}$ to whichever of $\mathcal{B}_1$ or $\mathcal{B}_2/\mathcal{C}_1$ or $\mathcal{C}_2$ attains a greater advantage and summing each inequality. □

B Extension to Many KEMs

In this section, we briefly outline how our construction and proofs can be generalized to combine n different KEMs. A natural extension of our two-KEM construction to combine n KEMs is to concatenate the n public keys, secret keys, and ciphertexts of the ingredient KEMs whenever those of the two KEMs in the two-KEM construction are concatenated and adapt everything accordingly, as shown in Algorithm 22. Supposing KEMs 1 through ℓ are ciphertext second preimage resistant, one can compute the hybrid session key by applying a split-key PRF to each ingredient session key, as well as the ciphertexts from KEMs $\ell + 1$ through n. We will continue referring to this construction as Π.

Algorithm 22 n-KEM Hybrid design

$\Pi(\mathsf{KEM}_1, \ldots, \mathsf{KEM}_n, W).\mathsf{KeyGen}(1^m)$:
$(sk_1, pk_1) \leftarrow\$ \mathsf{KEM}_1.\mathsf{KeyGen}(1^m)$
...
$(sk_n, pk_n) \leftarrow\$ \mathsf{KEM}_n.\mathsf{KeyGen}(1^m)$
$sk \leftarrow (sk_1, \ldots, sk_n)$
$pk \leftarrow (pk_1, \ldots, pk_n)$
return (sk, pk)

$\Pi(\mathsf{KEM}_1, \ldots, \mathsf{KEM}_n, b).\mathsf{Encaps}(pk)$:
$(pk_1, \ldots, pk_n) \leftarrow pk$
$(k_1, c_1) \leftarrow\$ \mathsf{KEM}_1.\mathsf{Encaps}(pk_1)$
...
$(k_n, c_n) \leftarrow\$ \mathsf{KEM}_n.\mathsf{Encaps}(pk_n)$
$c \leftarrow (c_1, \ldots, c_n)$
return $W(k_1, \ldots, k_n, c_1, \ldots, c_n)$

$\Pi(\mathsf{KEM}_1, \ldots, \mathsf{KEM}_n, b).\mathsf{Decaps}(sk, c)$:
$(sk_1, \ldots, sk_n) \leftarrow sk$
$(c_1, \ldots, c_n) \leftarrow c$
$k_1 \leftarrow \mathsf{KEM}_1.\mathsf{Decaps}(c_1, sk_1)$
...
$k_n \leftarrow \mathsf{KEM}_n.\mathsf{Decaps}(c_n, sk_n)$
if $k_1 = \perp \vee \ldots \vee k_n = \perp$ **then**
  return $\perp$
return $W(k_1, \ldots, k_n, c_1, \ldots, c_n)$

Theorem 15. *Let* $\mathsf{KEM}_1, \ldots, \mathsf{KEM}_n$ *be KEMs, where* KEM_i *is* δ*-correct. Let* F *be a split-key PRF, and set* $W(k_1, \ldots, k_n, c_1, \ldots, c_n) = F(k_1, \ldots, k_n, c_{\ell+1}, c_{\ell+2}, \ldots, c_n)$. *Let* $\Pi = \Pi(\mathsf{KEM}_1, \ldots, \mathsf{KEM}_n, W)$ *be the combination of these KEMs given in Algorithm 22. Then for all QPT adversaries* $\mathcal{A}$ *against the* IND-CCA *security* *of Π making at most q queries to their decapsulation oracle, there exist QPT adversaries $\mathcal{B}_1, ..., \mathcal{B}_\ell, \mathcal{C}$, and $\mathcal{D}$ such that:*

$$\mathrm{Adv}_{\Pi,\mathcal{A}}^{\text{IND-CCA}} \leq 2\left(\left(\sum_{j=1,j\neq i}^{\ell} \mathrm{Adv}_{\mathsf{KEM}_j,\mathcal{B}_j}^{\text{C2PRI}}\right) + \mathrm{Adv}_{\mathsf{KEM}_i,\mathcal{C}}^{\text{IND-CCA}} + \mathrm{Adv}_{F,\mathcal{D}}^{\text{PR}_i} + \delta\right) \quad (64)$$

Moreover, $\mathcal{C}$ makes at most q classical queries to its own decapsulation oracle, $\mathcal{D}$ makes at most $q+1$ classical queries to its evaluation oracle, and each adversary runs with constant-factor overhead compared to $\mathcal{A}$.

Proof Sketch. This theorem can be proved using the same structure as Theorem 13, and we only highlight the main differences here. Game 2 is replaced with a series of games $2.1, ..., 2.\ell$. (We exclude $2.i$ if $1 \leq i \leq \ell$.) In game $2.j$, we prohibit $\mathcal{A}$ from making decapsulation queries where the jth coordinate c_j is different from the jth challenge ciphertext c_j^* but decapsulates to k_j^*, the jth challenge session key. We bound the difference between each of these game hops with $\mathrm{Adv}_{\mathsf{KEM}_j,\mathcal{B}_{1,j}}^{\text{C2PRI}}$ and construct $\mathcal{B}_{1,j}$ similarly to adversary $\mathcal{B}_1$ of Theorem 13. In game 4, we once again select the challenge session key k^* randomly and answer decapsulation queries randomly when $c_i = c_i^*$, using the table W to maintain consistency. W takes as input a session key from each KEM except KEM_i, as well as a ciphertext from each of $\mathsf{KEM}_{\ell+1}, ..., \mathsf{KEM}_n$, again except KEM_i (if applicable). In game 5, we continue selecting k^* randomly but remove the other changes of game 4, bounding this difference with the advantage of a adversary $\mathcal{D}_2$ against the split-key pseudorandomness of F. Similar to game 5 of Theorem 13, $\mathcal{D}_2$ would fail to properly simulate game 5 to $\mathcal{A}$ if $\mathcal{A}$ could query the decapsulation oracle in a way that creates the same preimage of F as was used to initially compute k^*. However, just like in the previous proofs, due to the changes from games $2.1, ..., 2.\ell$, it is impossible to make such a query without submitting the challenge ciphertext, which is always prohibited. So $\mathcal{D}_2$ can properly simulate game 5 for $\mathcal{A}$. To complete the proof, games 6, 7, and 8 once again undo the changes of games 1, 2, and 3.

C A Proof of Theorem 4

Theorem 16 (Theorem 4/Theorem 8 Restated). *Let H be a random oracle and let $\mathcal{A}$ be an adversary against the split-key pseudorandomness of the function $F(k_1, \ldots, k_n, x) = H(k_1||\ldots||k_n||x)$ making at most q quantum queries to H, where $\mathcal{K}_i$ denotes the ith keyspace. Then,*

$$\mathrm{Adv}_{F,\mathcal{A}}^{\text{PR}_i} \leq 4\sqrt{\frac{q^2+q}{|\mathcal{K}_i|}} \quad (65)$$

Proof. Denote H by H_0. We start by considering the game in Algorithm 23, where an adversary $\mathcal{D}$ is tasked with distinguishing whether it has access to H_0 or a reprogrammed version denoted by H_1. Specifically, H_1 is defined such that $H_1(x) = H_0(x)$ for $x \in X \setminus S$, where X is the input space of H and S is the set of inputs that include the k_i uniformly randomly sampled from $\mathcal{K}_i$ by the challenger, and such that $H_1(x)$ is sampled from $\mathcal{Y}$ for $x \in S$ and output space $\mathcal{Y}$. The adversary has access to an Eval oracle with which it can query H_0 with k_i fixed in the ith key position in the argument of H_0.

Algorithm 23 Random Oracle Distinguishing Game

Game $\text{DIST}_{\mathcal{D}}^{b}$
$k_i \leftarrow\$ \mathcal{K}_i$
Prepare Eval as above
$b' \leftarrow\$ \mathcal{D}^{H_b(\cdot),\text{Eval}^{k_i}(\cdot)}$
return b'

Oracle $\text{Eval}^{k_i}(k', x)$
$k_1 ... k_{i-1} k_{i+1} ... k \leftarrow k'$
$y \leftarrow H_0(k_1, ..., k_i, ..., k_n, x)$
return y

The case where $b = 0$ corresponds to H_0, and the case where $b = 1$ corresponds to H_1. The adversary $\mathcal{D}$ attempts to output the value of b corresponding to the version of the H_b oracle to which it is given access. By Theorem 1 and Corollary 1 of [10], any adversary $\mathcal{D}$ has a bounded advantage:

$$\text{Adv}_{H_b,\mathcal{D}}^{\text{DIST}} \leq 2\sqrt{(d+1) \cdot P_{\text{find}}} = 2\sqrt{(d+1) \cdot \frac{4q}{|\mathcal{K}_i|}} = 4\sqrt{\frac{q(d+1)}{|\mathcal{K}_i|}} \leq 4\sqrt{\frac{q^2+q}{|\mathcal{K}_i|}} \tag{66}$$

in this game. We now consider a modified version of this game, as shown in Algorithm 24, where instead of distinguishing whether it has access to H_0 or H_1, the adversary is tasked with distinguishing whether it has access to $\text{Eval}_0^{k_i}$ or $\text{Eval}_1^{k_i}$, with $\text{Eval}_0^{k_i}$ being the Eval oracle in Algorithm 23 and $\text{Eval}_1^{k_i}$ having the same construction as Eval_0 but using H_1 rather than H_0. The adversary is also given access to H_0.

As in the previous game, the adversary $\mathcal{E}$ attempts to output the value of b corresponding to the version of the H_b oracle to which it is given access, winning if and only if $b' = b$. We claim that these games are distributionally identical. It is clear that the adversaries in both games have equivalent tasks: determining whether the Eval oracle is instantiated with the same version of H to which it has access, with the $b = 0$ case being that they are the same and the $b = 1$ case being that they are different. When $b = 0$, the adversaries in both games both have access to H_0 and Eval_0^i, so when $b = 0$ the two games are equivalent. Meanwhile, when $b = 1$, the adversary in the H_b distinguishing game has access to H_1 and

Algorithm 24 Eval Oracle Distinguishing Game

Game $\text{DIST}^b_{\mathcal{E}}$
$k_i \leftarrow\$ \mathcal{K}_i$
Prepare $\text{Eval}^{k_i}_b$ as above
$b' \leftarrow\$ \mathcal{E}^{H_0(\cdot),\text{Eval}^{k_i}_b(\cdot)}$
return b'

Oracle $\text{Eval}^{k_i}_b(k', x)$
$k_1...k_{i-1}k_{i+1}...k \leftarrow k'$
$y \leftarrow H_b(k_1, ..., k_i, ..., k_n, x)$
return y

$\text{Eval}^{k_i}_0$ while the adversary in the Eval_b distinguishing game has access to H_0 and Eval_1. By the fact that H_0 and H_1 are random oracles that can differ only when k_i is in the ith key position in the argument, the setting where the adversary has access to H_1 and $\text{Eval}^{k_i}_0$ and the setting where the adversary has access to H_0 and $\text{Eval}^{k_i}_1$ are identical from the perspective of the adversary up to labeling the oracles, since in both settings the adversary is given access to a random oracle and an Eval oracle that is constructed to return random outputs that are independent of the random oracle. Hence, when $b = 1$ the two games are also equivalent, so the games are distributionally identical and the advantage of an adversary in the Eval^i_b distinguishing game must be bounded by the advantage of an adversary in the H_b distinguishing game:

$$\text{Adv}^{\text{DIST}}_{\text{Eval}_b,\mathcal{E}} \leq \text{Adv}^{\text{DIST}}_{H_b,\mathcal{D}} \tag{67}$$

We now claim that the $\text{Eval}^{k_i}_b$ distinguishing game is identical to the split-key pseudorandom function game instantiated with the split-key construction with H_0, as when $b = 0$, the two games are the same, and when $b = 1$, returning $H_1(k_1, \ldots, k_i, \ldots, k_n, x)$ is equivalent to returning a random value from the output space $\mathcal{Y}$ by the construction of H_1. Therefore, we obtain the following bound for an adversary $\mathcal{A}$ in the split-key pseudorandom function game:

$$\text{Adv}^{\text{PR}_i}_{F,\mathcal{A}} = \text{Adv}^{\text{DIST}}_{\text{Eval}_b,\mathcal{E}} \leq \text{Adv}^{\text{DIST}}_{H_b,\mathcal{D}} \leq 4\sqrt{\frac{q^2 + q}{|\mathcal{K}_i|}} \tag{68}$$

as desired. □

References

1. The keyed-hash message authentication code (HMAC). FIPS PUB 198-1 (2008). https://nvlpubs.nist.gov/nistpubs/fips/nist.fips.198-1.pdf
2. Classic McEliece: conservative code-based cryptography: cryptosystem specification (2022). https://classic.mceliece.org/mceliece-spec-20221023.pdf
3. BIKE: Bit flipping key encapsulation (2024). https://bikesuite.org/files/v5.2/BIKE_Spec.2024.10.10.1.pdf
4. Hamming quasi-cyclic (HQC) (2024). https://pqc-hqc.org/doc/archive_submissions.zip

5. Module-lattice-based key-encapsulation mechanism standard. FIPS 203 (2024). https://nvlpubs.nist.gov/nistpubs/FIPS/NIST.FIPS.203.pdf
6. Hamming quasi-cyclic (HQC) (2025). https://pqc-hqc.org/doc/hqc_specifications_2025_08_22.pdf
7. Alagic, G., et al.: Status report on the fourth round of the NIST post-quantum cryptography standardization process (2025). https://doi.org/10.6028/NIST.IR.8545, https://tsapps.nist.gov/publication/get_pdf.cfm?pub_id=959556
8. Alagic, G., Carolan, J., Majenz, C., Tokat, S.: The sponge is quantum indifferentiable. arXiv:2504.16887 (2025)
9. Alwen, J., Hartmann, D., Kiltz, E., Mularczyk, M., Schwabe, P.: Post-quantum multi-recipient public key encryption. In: CCS '23, Proceedings of the 2023 ACM SIGSAC Conference on Computer and Communications Security, pp. 1108–1122. Association for Computing Machinery, New York, NY, USA (2023). https://doi.org/10.1145/3576915.3623185
10. Ambainis, A., Hamburg, M., Unruh, D.: Quantum security proofs using semi-classical oracles. In: Advances in Cryptology – CRYPTO 2019 (2021)
11. Aviram, N., Dowling, B., Komargodski, I., Paterson, K.G., Ronen, E., Yogev, E.: Practical (post-quantum) key combiners from one-wayness and applications to TLS. Cryptology ePrint Archive, Paper 2022/065 (2022). https://eprint.iacr.org/2022/065
12. Backendal, M., Bellare, M., Günther, F., Scarlata, M.: When messages are keys: is hmac a dual-prf? In: Handschuh, H., Lysyanskaya, A. (eds.) Advances in Cryptology – CRYPTO 2023, pp. 661–693. Springer Nature Switzerland, Cham (2023). https://doi.org/10.1007/978-3-031-38548-3_22
13. Barbosa, M., et al.: X-wing. IACR Commun. Cryptology **1**(1) (2024). https://doi.org/10.62056/a3qj89n4e
14. Barker, E., Chen, L., Davis, R.: Recommendation for key-derivation methods in key-establishment schemes. NIST SP 800-56C Rev. 2 (2020). https://doi.org/10.6028/NIST.SP.800-56Cr2
15. Bellare, M.: New proofs for NMAC and HMAC: security without collision-resistance. In: Dwork, C. (ed.) Advances in Cryptology - CRYPTO 2006, pp. 602–619. Springer, Berlin Heidelberg, Berlin, Heidelberg (2006). https://doi.org/10.1007/11818175_36
16. Bertoni, G., Daemen, J., Peeters, M., Van Assche, G.: On the indifferentiability of the sponge construction. In: Smart, N. (ed.) Advances in Cryptology - EUROCRYPT 2008, pp. 181–197. Springer, Berlin Heidelberg, Berlin, Heidelberg (2008). https://doi.org/10.1007/978-3-540-78967-3_11
17. Bhargavan, K., Jacomme, C., Kiefer, F., Schmidt, R.: Formal verification of the PQXDH post-quantum key agreement protocol for end-to-end secure messaging. In: 33rd USENIX Security Symposium (USENIX Security 24), pp. 469–486. USENIX Association, Philadelphia, PA (2024). https://www.usenix.org/conference/usenixsecurity24/presentation/bhargavan
18. Bindel, N., Brendel, J., Fischlin, M., Goncalves, B., Stebila, D.: Hybrid key encapsulation mechanisms and authenticated key exchange. In: Ding, J., Steinwandt, R. (eds.) PQCrypto 2019. LNCS, vol. 11505, pp. 206–226. Springer, Cham (2019). https://doi.org/10.1007/978-3-030-25510-7_12
19. Campagna, M., Petcher, A.: Security of hybrid key encapsulation. Cryptology ePrint Archive, Paper 2020/1364 (2020). https://eprint.iacr.org/2020/1364
20. Chen, L.: Recommendation for key derivation using pseudorandom functions. NIST SP 800-108r1-upd1 (2022). https://nvlpubs.nist.gov/nistpubs/SpecialPublications/NIST.SP.800-108r1-upd1.pdf

21. Chevalier, C., Lebrun, G., Martinelli, A.: Spilling-cascade: an optimal PKE combiner for KEM hybridization. In: 23rd International Conference on Applied Cryptography and Network Security (ACNS'25). Munich, Germany (2025). https://hal.science/hal-05027882
22. Connolly, D., Hövelmanns, K., Hülsing, A., Kousidis, S., Meijers, M.: Starfighters — on the general applicability of x-wing. Cryptology ePrint Archive, Paper 2025/1397 (2025). https://eprint.iacr.org/2025/1397
23. Cremers, C., Dax, A., Medinger, N.: Keeping up with the KEMs: stronger security notions for KEMs and automated analysis of KEM-based protocols. In: CCS '24, Proceedings of the 2024 on ACM SIGSAC Conference on Computer and Communications Security, pp. 1046–1060. Association for Computing Machinery, New York, NY, USA (2024). https://doi.org/10.1145/3658644.3670283
24. Don, J., Fehr, S., Huang, Y.H.: Adaptive versus static multi-oracle algorithms, and quantum security of a split-key PRF. In: Theory of Cryptography: 20th International Conference, TCC 2022, Chicago, IL, USA, November 7–10, 2022, Proceedings, Part I, pp. 33–51. Springer-Verlag, Berlin, Heidelberg (2022). https://doi.org/10.1007/978-3-031-22318-1_2
25. Federal Office for Information Security (BSI): Quantum-safe cryptography - fundamentals, current developments and recommendations (2022). https://www.bsi.bund.de/SharedDocs/Downloads/EN/BSI/Publications/Brochure/quantum-safe-cryptography.pdf?__blob=publicationFile&v=6
26. French Cybersecurity Agency (ANSSI) and Federal Office for Information Security (BSI) and Netherlands National Communications Security Agency (NLNCSA) and Swedish National Communications Security Authority, Swedish Armed Forces: Position paper on quantum key distribution (2024). https://cyber.gouv.fr/sites/default/files/document/Quantum_Key_Distribution_Position_Paper.pdf
27. Fujisaki, E., Okamoto, T.: Secure integration of asymmetric and symmetric encryption schemes. In: Wiener, M. (ed.) CRYPTO 1999. LNCS, vol. 1666, pp. 537–554. Springer, Heidelberg (1999). https://doi.org/10.1007/3-540-48405-1_34
28. Fujisaki, E., Okamoto, T.: Secure integration of asymmetric and symmetric encryption schemes. J. Cryptol. **26**(1), 80–101 (2013). https://doi.org/10.1007/s00145-011-9114-1
29. Gaži, P., Pietrzak, K., Rybár, M.: The exact PRF-security of NMAC and HMAC. In: Garay, J.A., Gennaro, R. (eds.) CRYPTO 2014. LNCS, vol. 8616, pp. 113–130. Springer, Heidelberg (2014). https://doi.org/10.1007/978-3-662-44371-2_7
30. Giacon, F., Heuer, F., Poettering, B.: KEM combiners. In: Abdalla, M., Dahab, R. (eds.) PKC 2018. LNCS, vol. 10769, pp. 190–218. Springer, Cham (2018). https://doi.org/10.1007/978-3-319-76578-5_7
31. Harnik, D., Kilian, J., Naor, M., Reingold, O., Rosen, A.: On robust combiners for oblivious transfer and other primitives. In: Cramer, R. (ed.) EUROCRYPT 2005. LNCS, vol. 3494, pp. 96–113. Springer, Heidelberg (2005). https://doi.org/10.1007/11426639_6
32. Hofheinz, D., Hövelmanns, K., Kiltz, E.: A modular analysis of the Fujisaki-Okamoto transformation. In: Kalai, Y., Reyzin, L. (eds.) TCC 2017. LNCS, vol. 10677, pp. 341–371. Springer, Cham (2017). https://doi.org/10.1007/978-3-319-70500-2_12
33. Hosoyamada, A., Iwata, T.: On tight quantum security of HMAC and NMAC in the quantum random oracle model. In: Malkin, T., Peikert, C. (eds.) CRYPTO 2021. LNCS, vol. 12825, pp. 585–615. Springer, Cham (2021). https://doi.org/10.1007/978-3-030-84242-0_21

34. Huguenin-Dumittan, L., Vaudenay, S.: FO-like combiners and hybrid post-quantum cryptography. In: Conti, M., Stevens, M., Krenn, S. (eds.) CANS 2021. LNCS, vol. 13099, pp. 225–244. Springer, Cham (2021). https://doi.org/10.1007/978-3-030-92548-2_12
35. Katz, J., Lindell, Y.: Introduction to Modern Cryptography, Third edn. CRC Press (2021)
36. Kelsey, J., Chang, S.j., Perlner, R.: SHA-3 derived functions: cSHAKE, KMAC, TupleHash, and ParallelHash . NIST SP 800-185 (2016). https://nvlpubs.nist.gov/nistpubs/SpecialPublications/NIST.SP.800-185.pdf
37. Krawczyk, H., Eronen, P.: HMAC-based extract-and-expand key derivation function (HKDF). RFC 5869 (2010). https://doi.org/10.17487/RFC5869, https://www.rfc-editor.org/info/rfc5869
38. Krämer, J., Struck, P., Weishäupl, M.: Binding security of implicitly-rejecting KEMs and application to BIKE and HQC. Cryptology ePrint Archive, Paper 2024/1233 (2024). https://eprint.iacr.org/2024/1233
39. Liu, Y., Zhou, B., Jiang, H.: CuKEM: a concise and unified hybrid key encapsulation mechanism. Cryptology ePrint Archive, Paper 2025/1862 (2025). https://doi.org/10.1145/3719027.3744863, https://eprint.iacr.org/2025/1862
40. O'Brien, D.: Protecting chrome traffic with hybrid kyber KEM. Chromium blog (2023). https://blog.chromium.org/2023/08/protecting-chrome-traffic-with-hybrid.html
41. Shen, Y., Wang, L., Gu, D.: Security analysis of NIST key derivation using pseudorandom functions. Cryptology ePrint Archive, Paper 2025/815 (2025). https://eprint.iacr.org/2025/815
42. Xu, J., Gao, Y., Lim, H.W., Wang, H., Chang, E.C.: Stateful KEM: towards optimal robust combiner for key encapsulation mechanism. Cryptology ePrint Archive, Paper 2021/989 (2021). https://eprint.iacr.org/2021/989

Towards More Efficient Registration-Based Encryption from LWE

Toi Tomita[1,2](✉)

[1] Organization for the Promotion of Education, Yokohama National University, Yokohama, Japan
tomita-toi-sk@ynu.ac.jp
[2] Institute of Advanced Sciences, Yokohama National University, Yokohama, Japan

Abstract. Registration-based encryption (RBE) effectively addresses the key escrow problem in identity-based encryption. However, existing post-quantum RBE schemes suffer from prohibitive ciphertext sizes in the gigabyte range for systems with 2^{10} registered users. This poor scalability is a major obstacle to the large-scale implementation of RBE in society. In this work, we propose a framework for constructing efficient RBE schemes that can be instantiated from the learning with errors (LWE) assumption. Specifically, the ciphertext size remains around 221 MB even as the number of registered users increases. The core techniques involve introducing decomposable laconic encryption and integrating it with a refined snapshotting trick. Our work represents an important milestone towards achieving practical post-quantum RBEs.

Keywords: Registration-based encryption · Post-quantum cryptography · Learning with errors

1 Introduction

1.1 Background

Registration-based encryption (RBE), introduced by Garg et al. [19], is a novel primitive that bridges the gap between traditional public-key encryption (PKE) and identity-based encryption (IBE). The core appeal of RBE is its ability to eliminate the key escrow problem inherent in IBE. In an IBE system, a trusted key generation center (KGC) possesses a master secret key that can decrypt any message. This vulnerability has long hindered the adoption of IBE in privacy-critical environments [6,32]. RBE modifies the conventional trust model in which users generate their own key pairs locally and then register their public keys and their identities with a semi-trusted key curator (KC). The KC maintains a succinct digest (called a public parameter) of all registered users, enabling any sender to encrypt messages using only the recipient's identity and the current system parameters. The public parameter is updated each time a user registers. Therefore, registered users must obtain the helper decryption key used in the decryption process from the KC. Importantly, the RBE definition requires that

K. Jee and A. Kate (Eds.): ACNS 2026, LNCS 16571, pp. 75–98, 2027.
https://doi.org/10.1007/978-3-032-32560-0_3

the number of updates increase logarithmically with the number of users. It is not feasible to update all users' keys each time a new public key is registered, which is why this requirement is necessary. Since the initial works [19,20], rapid interest in RBEs has emerged, and they have advanced on many fronts, including efficiency [11,13,15,21], security [10,22], and theoretical lower bounds [14,23,29, 30].

Despite its theoretical elegance, constructing efficient RBE schemes, especially those secure against quantum adversaries, has proven exceptionally challenging. Early RBE constructions [19,20] relied on highly theoretical and prohibitively inefficient cryptographic primitives, with estimated ciphertext sizes in the terabyte range [11], rendering them completely un-deployable. While pairing-based RBE schemes [15,21] have reached practical efficiency (with ciphertexts under 1 KB), they lack post-quantum resistance. On the other hand, existing post-quantum RBE schemes based on the learning with errors (LWE) assumption [13,15] have ciphertext sizes exceeding gigabytes for systems with 2^{10} registered users. This pervasive issue presents a fundamental obstacle to their adoption. Thus, we pose the following pressing question, which forms the central motivation of our work:

Can we construct more efficient post-quantum RBE schemes?

1.2 Our Contribution

In this work, we answer this question in the affirmative. We propose a framework for constructing efficient RBE schemes that can be instantiated from the LWE assumption. Specifically, the ciphertext size remains around 221 MB even as the number of registered users increases. Compared to existing works [13,15], our results significantly improve the concrete efficiency of the post-quantum RBE scheme. The core techniques are summarized as follows:

- We introduce *decomposable laconic encryption (dLE)*, a novel primitive inspired by the decomposability found in multi-recipient encryption. The key insight of dLE is that a ciphertext can be decomposed into two constituent parts. Through this decomposition, our framework achieves remarkable compactness and scalability.
- Moving beyond the traditional approach to construct RBEs, we implement a *refined snapshotting trick*. As a result of this, our ciphertext size scales only by $O(\mathsf{hw}(N))$, a significant improvement over $O(\ell \cdot \log N)$ for [13] and $O(\log N_{\max} \cdot \log N)$ for [15]. Here, $\mathsf{hw}(N)$ denotes the Hamming weight of the binary representation of N, ℓ is the length of the identity, and $N_{\max}$ is the maximum number of registered users.

We compare our scheme with the state-of-the-art post-quantum RBE schemes in Table 1. This table shows that our scheme achieves a significantly smaller ciphertext size and superior scalability compared with prior schemes. Furthermore, the limitations inherent in [15]'s scheme are not present in our scheme. Although our ciphertext size is still large at 221 MB, our work represents an important milestone towards achieving practical post-quantum RBEs.

Table 1. A comparison of the concrete ciphertext sizes of LWE-based RBE schemes. $N_{\max}$ is the maximum number of registered users. N is the number of current registered users. "Unbounded users" means the maximum number of users is not bounded in advance. "Adaptive compactness" implies that it satisfies the standard definition of compactness.

	$N_{\max}$	Ciphertext size [MB]			Unbounded users	Adaptive compactness
		$N = 2^{10}$	$N = 2^{20}$	$N = 2^{30}$		
[13]	∞	4428.38	8856.76	13285.14	✓	✓
[15]	2^{20}	1523.03	3046.07	-	-	-
	2^{30}	2211.98	4423.96	6635.94		
Ours	∞	221.43	221.45	221.47	✓	✓

1.3 Technical Overview

Here, we provide an overview of our techniques for obtaining efficient RBEs.

The Bottleneck of the Previous Approach. Most existing RBE constructions [13,15,19–22] rely on the *powers-of-two* approach [25] or its variant, the *snapshotting trick* [22]. These allow an RBE scheme without update frequency requirements to be converted into an RBE scheme with a low update frequency. Especially in the snapshotting trick, the KC maintains a logarithmic number of snapshots of the registration state (represented as a digest of the base scheme). These snapshots divide the registered user space into disjoint groups of sizes 2^j (e.g., $1, 2, 4, \ldots, 2^\lambda$). A snapshot is only replaced or merged when a new registration completes a group of a specific size. This ensures that the size of public parameters and the total number of updates per user all scale logarithmically with N. However, these approaches increase the ciphertext size by a factor of $O(\log N)$ because the encryption process must generate a ciphertext for each of the $\log N$ active digests of the base scheme. In the post-quantum setting (e.g., LWE-based schemes [13,15]), the ciphertext size of the base scheme already reaches several hundred megabytes. Consequently, even when $\log N = 10$, the resulting overhead leads to impractical ciphertext sizes of several gigabytes.

Our Key Insight: Leveraging Decomposability. To overcome this issue, our framework transitioned from a paradigm of simple repetition to one of effective repetition via *decomposability*. Inspired by recent advancements of post-quantum multi-recipient encryption (mPKE) [3,24,26], we introduce a novel primitive: Decomposable Laconic Encryption (dLE) is a decomposable variant of laconic encryption that was introduced in [13]. It can be considered a form of RBE without requiring an update frequency. While (d)LE can be converted to RBE using the previous approaches, it incurs multiplicative overhead. The key insight of dLE is that a ciphertext can be decomposed into two constituent parts: a relatively large, *digest-independent* part ($\mathsf{ct}^{\mathsf{ind}}$) and a very compact, *digest-dependent* part ($\mathsf{ct}^{\mathsf{dep}}$). This allows the encryptor to generate only a single digest-independent part, regardless of the number of active digests. The only additional cost associated with an increase in active digests is the compact digest-dependent part. To utilize dLE securely as described above, dLE must have a slightly stronger security requirement. That is to say, the message is hidden, even given one digest-independent part and multiple digest-dependent parts generated by different digests and *shared randomness.* We call such security *multi-digest security.* For more details, we give the formal definition of dLE in Sect. 3.

Fortunately, the LWE-based laconic encryption scheme proposed in [13] is already decomposable since the ciphertext can be decomposed into $\mathsf{ct}^{\mathsf{ind}}$ and $\mathsf{ct}^{\mathsf{dep}}$, where $\mathbf{A}_{\mathsf{id}}$ is a matrix determined by the identity id, $\mathbf{y}$ is the digest, $\mathbf{r}_0, \ldots, \mathbf{r}_\ell$ are the LWE secrets, and $\mathbf{e}$ and e are the LWE noises. That is, $\mathsf{ct}^{\mathsf{dep}}$ is only one LWE ciphertext and is significantly compact. However, simply applying the security proof in [13] repeatedly to each digest is insufficient to prove the security of a multi-digest. The original proof assumes that each ciphertext is generated with independent randomness. In contrast, multi-digest security involves multiple $\mathsf{ct}^{\mathsf{dep}}$ that are strongly correlated with a single $\mathsf{ct}^{\mathsf{ind}}$ through shared randomness $\mathbf{r}_0$. Therefore, when randomizing $\mathsf{ct}^{\mathsf{dep}}$ for a specific digest, the simulation must be performed without compromising the consistency of $\mathsf{ct}^{\mathsf{dep}}$ for the other digests or $\mathsf{ct}^{\mathsf{ind}}$. For more details, we refer the reader to Sect. 5.

Our Generic Transformation. Rather than a naive application of previous approaches, our RBE construction employs a refined snapshotting trick tailored to dLE. In our transformation, the public parameter pp consists of a set of digests $(\tilde{\mathsf{dig}}_1, \ldots, \tilde{\mathsf{dig}}_{\mathsf{hw}(N)})$, where each digest represents a snapshot of the registration state. The number of these snapshots is strictly limited to $\mathsf{hw}(N)$. Upon the registration of a new user, snapshots are merged in a manner analogous to a binary counter, ensuring that older snapshots are only replaced when a new snapshot can cover an equivalent power-of-two number of users. To encrypt a message, the encryptor does not generate multiple full ciphertexts. Instead, the encryptor produces a single digest-independent part $(\tilde{\mathsf{ct}}^{\mathsf{ind}})$ and then attaches multiple digest-dependent parts $(\tilde{\mathsf{ct}}_i^{\mathsf{dep}})$ corresponding to each active snapshot. The resulting ciphertext is $\mathsf{ct} = (\tilde{\mathsf{ct}}^{\mathsf{ind}}, \tilde{\mathsf{ct}}_1^{\mathsf{dep}}, \ldots, \tilde{\mathsf{ct}}_{\mathsf{hw}(N)}^{\mathsf{dep}})$. The size of ct is computed as $|\mathsf{ct}| = |\tilde{\mathsf{ct}}^{\mathsf{ind}}| + \mathsf{hw}(N) \cdot |\tilde{\mathsf{ct}}_i^{\mathsf{dep}}|$ instead of $O(\log N) \cdot (|\tilde{\mathsf{ct}}^{\mathsf{ind}}| + |\tilde{\mathsf{ct}}_i^{\mathsf{dep}}|)$.

In particular, when instantiated with the above dLE scheme, the ciphertext size only scales with $\mathsf{hw}(N)$ LWE ciphertexts. The concrete breakdown of the ciphertext size is $|\tilde{\mathsf{ct}}^{\mathsf{ind}}| = 221.41$ MB and $|\tilde{\mathsf{ct}}_i^{\mathsf{dep}}| = 1.86$ KB. Consequently, while the ciphertext size in previous LWE-based RBE schemes doubled from 2^{10} to 2^{20} users, our ciphertext size grows only by a few tens of kilobytes. This remarkable efficiency can be attributed to the fact that a substantial portion of the ciphertext is shared across all snapshots. At the same time, the growth part is confined to the compact digest-dependent components. The synergy between dLE and snapshotting enables the scheme to achieve a more efficient post-quantum RBE, yielding an order-of-magnitude reduction in ciphertext size. A more detailed description of our transformation is provided in Sect. 4. We believe that our techniques could be useful for more advanced applications.

1.4 Related Works

In recent years, there has been growing interest in generalizing RBEs to registered fine-grained encryption, such as registered attribute-based encryption (RABE) [25] and registered function-based encryption (RFE) [16]. Most proposals are based on indistinguishability obfuscation [12,16,25,28] or pairing-based assumptions [4,5,8,12,16,18,25,28,35,36,38]. Very recently, we have had some lattice-based RABE constructions from private/public-coin evasive LWE [17,34,35,37], succinct LWE [9,33], or decomposed LWE [1] assumptions, which are significantly stronger variants of the LWE assumption.

2 Preliminaries

Notations. The basic notations used in this paper are summarized here. For $n, m \in \mathbb{N}$ with $n \leq m$, we write $[n, m] := \{n, \ldots, m\}$ and $[m] := \{1, \ldots, m\}$. For $b \in \{0, 1\}$, we write $\bar{b} := 1 - b$. For $x \in \{0, 1\}^n$, let $\mathsf{hw}(x)$ denote its Hamming weight. When $x \in \mathbb{N}$, $\mathsf{hw}(x)$ denotes the Hamming weight of the binary representation of x. For $x \in \{0, 1\}^n$ and $1 \leq \ell \leq n$, let $x_{1:\ell}$ denote the length-ℓ prefix of x. We write $x \leftarrow_\$ \mathcal{S}$ to denote that x is sampled uniformly from a finite set $\mathcal{S}$. We write $x \leftarrow \mathcal{D}$ to denote that x is sampled from the distribution $\mathcal{D}$.

Throughout this work, we write λ to denote the security parameter. We write $\mathsf{poly}(\lambda)$ to denote a function that is $O(\lambda^c)$ for some constant $c \in \mathbb{N}$ and $\mathsf{negl}(\lambda)$ to denote a function that is $o(\lambda^{-c})$ for all $c \in \mathbb{N}$. We say that two families of distributions $\mathcal{D}_0 := \{\mathcal{D}_{0,\lambda}\}_{\lambda \in \mathbb{N}}$ and $\mathcal{D}_1 = \{\mathcal{D}_{1,\lambda}\}_{\lambda \in \mathbb{N}}$ are computationally indistinguishable, denoted as $\mathcal{D}_0 \approx_c \mathcal{D}_1$ if no probabilistic polynomial time (PPT) algorithm can distinguish them with non-negligible probability. We say that they are statistically indistinguishable, denote as $\mathcal{D}_0 \approx_s \mathcal{D}_1$, if the statistical distance between $\mathcal{D}_0$ and $\mathcal{D}_1$ is bounded by $\mathsf{negl}(\lambda)$. We use bold uppercase letters (e.g., $\mathbf{M}$) to denote matrices and bold lowercase letters (e.g., $\mathbf{v}$) to denote vectors. For an algorithm A and data x, A^x (resp., $\mathsf{A}^{[x]}$) denotes a read (resp., read/write) random access operation performed by A on x.

2.1 Registration-Based Encryption

Here, we define registration-based encryption (RBE) [19].

Definition 1 (Registration-Based Encryption). *Let $\mathcal{ID} = \{\mathcal{ID}_\lambda\}_{\lambda \in \mathbb{N}}$ be the identity space and $\mathcal{M} = \{\mathcal{M}_\lambda\}_{\lambda \in \mathbb{N}}$ be the message space. A registration-based encryption (RBE) scheme with identity space $\mathcal{ID}$ and message space $\mathcal{M}$ is a tuple of PPT algorithms with the following syntax:*

- $\mathsf{Setup}(1^\lambda) \to \mathsf{crs}$*: On input the security parameter λ, the setup algorithm outputs a common reference string* crs.
- $\mathsf{KGen}(\mathsf{crs}) \to (\mathsf{sk}, \mathsf{pk})$*: On input* crs*, the key-generation algorithm outputs a key pair* $(\mathsf{sk}, \mathsf{pk})$.

- $\mathsf{Reg}^{[\mathsf{aux}]}(\mathsf{crs},\mathsf{pp},\mathsf{id},\mathsf{pk}) \to \mathsf{pp}'$: *On input* crs, *the current public parameter* pp, *an identity* $\mathsf{id} \in \mathcal{ID}$ *to be registered, and a corresponding public key* pk, *the registration algorithm* deterministically *outputs the updated public parameter* pp′ *via (read/write) random access to the auxiliary information* aux. *(The system is initialized with public parameters* pp *and auxiliary information* aux *set to* $\perp$.*)*
- $\mathsf{Enc}(\mathsf{crs},\mathsf{pp},\mathsf{id},\mathsf{m}) \to \mathsf{ct}$: *On input* crs, pp, *a recipient identity* $\mathsf{id} \in \mathcal{ID}$, *and a message* $\mathsf{m} \in \mathcal{M}$, *the encryption algorithm outputs a ciphertext* ct.
- $\mathsf{Upd}^{\mathsf{aux}}(\mathsf{pp},\mathsf{id}) \to \mathsf{hsk}$: *On input* pp *and an identity* $\mathsf{id} \in \mathcal{ID}$, *the update algorithm* deterministically *outputs a helper decryption key* hsk *via (read) random access to* aux.
- $\mathsf{Dec}(\mathsf{sk},\mathsf{hsk},\mathsf{ct}) \to \mathsf{m} \in \mathcal{M} \cup \{\mathsf{GetUpd},\perp\}$: *On input a secret key* sk, *a helper decryption key* hsk, *and* ct, *the decryption algorithm outputs either a message* $\mathsf{m} \in \mathcal{M}$, *or a special symbol in* $\{\mathsf{GetUpd},\perp\}$. *(Here,* GetUpd *indicates that a key update might be needed for decryption.)*

Definition 2 (Correctness, Compactness, and Efficiency). *Let* Π *be an RBE scheme. For a security parameter* $\lambda \in \mathbb{N}$ *and an adversary* $\mathcal{A}$, *we define the following game* $\mathsf{Cor}_{\Pi,\mathcal{A}}(1^\lambda)$ *between* $\mathcal{A}$ *and a challenger* Chal*:*

- ***Initialization:*** Chal *sets* $(\mathsf{pp},\mathsf{aux},\mathsf{hsk},\mathcal{S},\mathsf{id}^*,t) := (\perp,\perp,\perp,\emptyset,\perp,0)$ *and* $\mathsf{crs} \leftarrow \mathsf{Setup}(1^\lambda)$, *and sends* crs *to* $\mathcal{A}$.
- *Every round* $\mathcal{A}$ *does one of these actions:*
  (a) *Registering a new (non-target) identity:* $\mathcal{A}$ *sends a new identity* $\mathsf{id} \notin \mathcal{S}$ *and a public key* pk *to* Chal, *which registers and updates* $\mathsf{pp} := \mathsf{Reg}^{\mathsf{aux}}(\mathsf{crs},\mathsf{pp},\mathsf{id},\mathsf{pk})$. Chal *also updates* $\mathcal{S} := \mathcal{S} \cup \{\mathsf{id}\}$.
  (b) *Registering the target identity: If the target identity* id^* *is already chosen, then do nothing. Otherwise,* $\mathcal{A}$ *sends a target identity* id^* *to* Chal. *If* $\mathsf{id}^* \notin \mathcal{S}$ *then* Chal *samples an honest key pair* $(\mathsf{sk}^*,\mathsf{pk}^*) \leftarrow \mathsf{KGen}(\mathsf{crs})$ *and registers and updates* $\mathsf{pp} := \mathsf{Reg}^{[\mathsf{aux}]}(\mathsf{crs},\mathsf{pp},\mathsf{id},\mathsf{pk}^*)$, $\mathcal{S} := \mathcal{S} \cup \{\mathsf{id}^*\}$, *and sends* pk^* *to* $\mathcal{A}$.
  (c) *Encrypting to the target identity: If the target identity* id^* *is not yet chosen, then do nothing. Otherwise,* Chal *sets* $t := t+1$*and receives a message* m_t *from* $\mathcal{A}$. Chal *sends a ciphertext* $\mathsf{ct}_t \leftarrow \mathsf{Enc}(\mathsf{crs},\mathsf{pp},\mathsf{id}^*,\mathsf{m}_t)$ *to* $\mathcal{A}$.
  (d) *Decrypting for target identity:* $\mathcal{A}$ *sends* $i \in [t]$ *to* Chal, *which computes* $\mathsf{m}'_i := \mathsf{Dec}(\mathsf{sk}^*,\mathsf{hsk},\mathsf{ct}_i)$. *If* $\mathsf{m}'_i = \mathsf{GetUpd}$, *then* Chal *computes the helper decryption key* $\mathsf{hsk} := \mathsf{Upd}^{\mathsf{aux}}(\mathsf{pp},\mathsf{id}^*)$ *and computes* $\mathsf{m}'_i := \mathsf{Dec}(\mathsf{sk}^*,\mathsf{hsk},\mathsf{ct}_i)$. *If* $\mathsf{m}'_j \neq \mathsf{m}_j$, *the game halts with outputs* $b = 1$.

  If $\mathcal{A}$ *finished making queries and the game has not halted (as a result of a decryption query), then the game outputs* $b = 0$.

Let $N = |\mathcal{S}|$. *We say that* Π *is correct and efficient if for all security parameters* $\lambda \in \mathbb{N}$ *and all (possibly unbounded) adversaries* $\mathcal{A}$ *making at most a polynomial number of queries, the following properties hold:*

- ***Correctness:*** *It holds that* $\Pr\left[\mathsf{Cor}_{\Pi,\mathcal{A}}(1^\lambda) = 1\right] = \mathsf{negl}(\lambda)$.

- ***(Adaptive) compactness:*** *It holds that* $|\mathsf{pp}| = \mathsf{poly}(\lambda, \log N)$ *and* $|\mathsf{hsk}^*| = \mathsf{poly}(\lambda, \log N)$ *(at all points in the game).*
- ***(Weakly) efficiency:*** *Then, in the course of the above game,* Chal *invokes the update algorithm* Upd *at most* $O(\log N)$ *times, where each invocation runs in* $\mathsf{poly}(\lambda, \log N)$ *time in the RAM model of computation.*

Definition 3 (Security). *Let* Π *be an RBE scheme. For a security parameter* $\lambda \in \mathbb{N}$ *and an adversary* $\mathcal{A}$*, we define the following game* $\mathsf{Sec}_{\Pi,\mathcal{A}}(1^\lambda)$ *between* $\mathcal{A}$ *and a challenger* Chal.

- ***Initialization:*** Chal *sets* $(\mathsf{pp}, \mathsf{aux}, \mathsf{hsk}, \mathcal{S}, \mathsf{id}^*) := (\perp, \perp, \perp, \emptyset, \perp)$ *and* $\mathsf{crs} \leftarrow \mathsf{Setup}(1^\lambda)$*, and sends* crs *to* $\mathcal{A}$.
- *Every round* $\mathcal{A}$ *does one of these actions:*
  (a) *<u>Registering a new (non-target) identity:</u>* $\mathcal{A}$ *sends a new identity* $\mathsf{id} \notin \mathcal{S}$ *and a public key* pk *to* Chal*, which registers and updates* $\mathsf{pp} := \mathsf{Reg}^{\mathsf{aux}}(\mathsf{crs}, \mathsf{pp}, \mathsf{id}, \mathsf{pk})$. Chal *also updates* $\mathcal{S} := \mathcal{S} \cup \{\mathsf{id}\}$.
  (b) *<u>Registering the target identity:</u> If the target identity* id^* *is already chosen, then do nothing. Otherwise,* $\mathcal{A}$ *sends a target identity* id^* *to* Chal*. If* $\mathsf{id}^* \notin \mathcal{S}$ *then* Chal *samples an honest key pair* $(\mathsf{sk}^*, \mathsf{pk}^*) \leftarrow \mathsf{KGen}(\mathsf{crs})$ *and registers and updates* $\mathsf{pp} := \mathsf{Reg}^{[\mathsf{aux}]}(\mathsf{crs}, \mathsf{pp}, \mathsf{id}, \mathsf{pk}^*)$*,* $\mathcal{S} := \mathcal{S} \cup \{\mathsf{id}^*\}$*, and sends* pk^* *to* $\mathcal{A}$.
- ***Encrypting for target identity:*** $\mathcal{A}$ *sends* $\mathsf{m}_0, \mathsf{m}_1 \in \mathcal{M}$*. If no target identity* id^* *is chosen,* $\mathcal{A}$ *sends* id^* *to* Chal*. Then,* Chal *samples a random bit* $b \leftarrow_{\$} \{0,1\}$*, generates an encryption to the target identity* $\mathsf{ct}^* \leftarrow \mathsf{Enc}(\mathsf{crs}, \mathsf{pp}, \mathsf{id}^*, \mathsf{m}_b)$*, and sends* ct^* *to* $\mathcal{A}$.
- $\mathcal{A}$ *outputs a bit* $b' \in \{0,1\}$*. The game outputs* 1 *if* $b = b'$ *and* 0 *otherwise.*

We say that Π *is secure if for all security parameter* $\lambda \in \mathbb{N}$ *and all PPT adversaries* $\mathcal{A}$*, it holds that* $\Pr[\mathsf{Sec}_{\Pi,\mathcal{A}}(1^\lambda) = 1] \leq 1/2 + \mathsf{negl}(\lambda)$.

3 Decomposable Laconic Encryption

In this section, we formally introduce *decomposable* laconic encryption (dLE), which is a generalization of the standard laconic encryption in [13] with modifications described in Remark 1.

Definition 4 (Decomposable Laconic Encryption). *Let* $\mathcal{M} = \{\mathcal{M}_\lambda\}_{\lambda \in \mathbb{N}}$ *be the message space. A decomposable laconic encryption (dLE) scheme with message space* $\mathcal{M}$ *is a tuple of PPT algorithms with the following syntax:*

- $\mathsf{Setup}(1^\lambda, 1^\ell) \rightarrow (\mathsf{crs}, \mathsf{dig}, \mathsf{st})$*: On input a security parameter* λ *and an index-length parameter* ℓ*, the setup algorithm outputs a common reference string* crs*, an initial digest* dig*, and an initial state* st*. We assume that* crs *implicitly defines a randomness space* $\mathcal{R} = (\mathcal{R}^{\mathsf{ind}}, \mathcal{R}^{\mathsf{dep}})$*, where* $\mathcal{R}^{\mathsf{ind}}$ *is the randomness space for digest-independent encryption and* $\mathcal{R}^{\mathsf{dep}}$ *is the randomness space for digest-dependent encryption.*

- $\mathsf{KGen}(\mathsf{crs}) \to (\mathsf{sk}, \mathsf{pk})$: *On input* crs, *the key-generation algorithm outputs a key pair* $(\mathsf{sk}, \mathsf{pk})$.
- $\mathsf{IsValid}(\mathsf{crs}, \mathsf{pk}) \to b$: *On input* crs *and a public key* pk, *the key-validation algorithm* deterministically *outputs a bit* $b \in \{0,1\}$ *indicating whether* pk *is valid or not.*
- $\mathsf{MemUpd}^{[\mathsf{st}]}(\mathsf{crs}, \mathsf{dig}, \mathsf{id}, \mathsf{pk}) \to \mathsf{dig}'$: *On input* crs, *the current digest* dig, *an index* $\mathsf{id} \in \{0,1\}^{\ell}$, *and* pk, *the membership update algorithm* deterministically *outputs the updated digest* dig' *via (read/write) random access to the state* st.
- $\mathsf{Enc}(\mathsf{crs}, \mathsf{dig}, \mathsf{id}, \mathsf{m}; \mathsf{r}^{\mathsf{ind}}, \mathsf{r}^{\mathsf{dep}}) \to \mathsf{ct} = (\mathsf{ct}^{\mathsf{ind}}, \mathsf{ct}^{\mathsf{dep}})$: *The* decomposable *encryption algorithm, runs with randomness* $(\mathsf{r}^{\mathsf{ind}}, \mathsf{r}^{\mathsf{dep}}) \in \mathcal{R}^{\mathsf{ind}} \times \mathcal{R}^{\mathsf{dep}}$, *splits into the following two algorithms:*
  - $\mathsf{Enc}^{\mathsf{ind}}(\mathsf{crs}, \mathsf{id}; \mathsf{r}^{\mathsf{ind}}) \to \mathsf{ct}^{\mathsf{ind}}$: *On input* crs, $\mathsf{id} \in \{0,1\}^{\ell}$, *and* $\mathsf{r}^{\mathsf{ind}} \in \mathcal{R}^{\mathsf{ind}}$, *the digest-independent encryption algorithm outputs a digest-independent ciphertext* $\mathsf{ct}^{\mathsf{ind}}$.
  - $\mathsf{Enc}^{\mathsf{dep}}(\mathsf{crs}, \mathsf{dig}, \mathsf{id}, \mathsf{m}; \mathsf{r}^{\mathsf{ind}}, \mathsf{r}^{\mathsf{dep}}) \to \mathsf{ct}^{\mathsf{dep}}$: *On input* crs, dig, $\mathsf{id} \in \{0,1\}^{\ell}$, *a message* $\mathsf{m} \in \mathcal{M}$, *and* $(\mathsf{r}^{\mathsf{ind}}, \mathsf{r}^{\mathsf{dep}}) \in \mathcal{R}^{\mathsf{ind}} \times \mathcal{R}^{\mathsf{dep}}$, *the digest-dependent encryption algorithm outputs a digest-dependent ciphertext* $\mathsf{ct}^{\mathsf{dep}}$.
- $\mathsf{WGen}^{\mathsf{st}}(\mathsf{crs}, \mathsf{dig}, \mathsf{id}, \mathsf{pk}) \to \mathsf{wit}$: *On input* crs, dig, $\mathsf{id} \in \{0,1\}^{\ell}$, *and* pk, *the witness generation algorithm* deterministically *outputs a membership witness* wit *via (read) random access to* st.
- $\mathsf{Dec}(\mathsf{sk}, \mathsf{wit}, \mathsf{ct}) \to \mathsf{m} \in \mathcal{M} \cup \{\bot\}$: *On input* sk, wit, *and* ct, *the decryption algorithm outputs either a message* $\mathsf{m} \in \mathcal{M}$ *or a special symbol* $\bot$.

Furthermore, all the above algorithms run in time at most $\mathsf{poly}(\lambda, \ell)$.

Remark 1 (Differences from standard laconic encryption). Below, we summarize the difference between decomposable and standard laconic encryption [13].

- The most important modification is *decomposability*, which allows the encryption algorithm to be split into two parts: a digest-independent and a digest-dependent part. We also introduce *ciphertext compactness* (Definition 6) and *multi-digest security* (Definition 7). Ciphertext compactness requires that a digest-dependent ciphertext be sufficiently compact. Multi-digest security requires that the message is hidden from the challenge ciphertext, which consists of one digest-independent part and *multiple digest-dependent parts* generated by different digests and shared randomness.
- Inspired by [25], we make a minor change by adding a key-validation algorithm. The algorithm verifies the validity of the public key. We define completeness (Definition 5) to require that public keys generated by a key-generation algorithm pass verification by the key-validation algorithm.
- In the correctness game (Definition 6), we modify the challenge ciphertext to be generated from *the time-specific digest chosen by the adversary instead of the most recent one.*

We define the completeness requirement of a dLE scheme. Completeness requires that the public key generated by KGen be valid.

Definition 5 (Completeness). *We say that a dLE scheme Π is complete if for all $\lambda, \ell \in \mathbb{N}$, all* $(\mathsf{crs}, \mathsf{dig}, \mathsf{st}) \leftarrow \mathsf{Setup}(1^\lambda, 1^\ell)$*, and all* $(\mathsf{sk}, \mathsf{pk}) \leftarrow \mathsf{KGen}(\mathsf{crs})$*, it holds that* $\mathsf{IsValid}(\mathsf{crs}, \mathsf{pk}) = 1$.

We define the correctness and compactness requirements of a dLE scheme. The correctness requirement is essentially the same as in [13], except that the challenge ciphertext is generated from the time-specific digest chosen by the adversary instead of the most recent one. The compactness requires that a digest, a witness, and a digest-dependent ciphertext are sufficiently compact.

Definition 6 (Correctness and Compactness). *Let Π be a dLE scheme. For parameters $\lambda, \ell \in \mathbb{N}$ and an adversary $\mathcal{A}$, we define the following game* $\mathsf{Cor}_{\Pi,\mathcal{A}}(1^\lambda, 1^\ell)$ *between $\mathcal{A}$ and a challenger* Chal*:*

- ***Setup phase:*** Chal *samples* $(\mathsf{crs}, \mathsf{dig}, \mathsf{st}) \leftarrow \mathsf{Setup}(1^\lambda, 1^\ell)$ *and gives them to $\mathcal{A}$.* Chal *also initializes a counter* $\mathsf{ctr} := 0$ *and an (initially-empty) dictionary mapping indices to key-pair* $\mathsf{Dict_H} = \emptyset$*. Finally, it gives* $(\mathsf{crs}, \mathsf{dig}, \mathsf{st})$ *to $\mathcal{A}$.*
- ***Query phase:*** *$\mathcal{A}$ can now issue the following queries:*
  - *Honest query: In this query, $\mathcal{A}$ specifies an index* $\mathsf{id} \in \{0,1\}^\ell$*. In response,* Chal *increments* $\mathsf{ctr} := \mathsf{ctr} + 1$*, generates* $(\mathsf{sk}, \mathsf{pk}) \leftarrow \mathsf{KGen}(\mathsf{crs})$*, runs* $\mathsf{dig} := \mathsf{MemUpd}^{[\mathsf{st}]}(\mathsf{crs}, \mathsf{dig}, \mathsf{id}, \mathsf{pk})$*, and replies to $\mathcal{A}$ with* $(\mathsf{dig}, \mathsf{st}, \mathsf{sk}, \mathsf{pk})$*. In addition,* Chal *adds the mapping* $\mathsf{id} \mapsto (\mathsf{sk}, \mathsf{pk})$ *to the dictionary* $\mathsf{Dict_H}$ *and stores* $(\mathsf{dig}_{\mathsf{ctr}}, \mathsf{st}_{\mathsf{ctr}}) := (\mathsf{dig}, \mathsf{st})$.
  - *Malicious query: In this query, $\mathcal{A}$ specifies an index* $\mathsf{id} \in \{0,1\}^\ell$ *and a public key* pk*. In response,* Chal *first checks that* $\mathsf{IsValid}(\mathsf{crs}, \mathsf{pk}) = 1$*. If the check fails, it outputs $\perp$. Otherwise,* Chal *increments* $\mathsf{ctr} := \mathsf{ctr} + 1$ *and runs* $\mathsf{dig} := \mathsf{MemUpd}^{[\mathsf{st}]}(\mathsf{crs}, \mathsf{dig}, \mathsf{id}, \mathsf{pk})$*. Then,* Chal *replies to $\mathcal{A}$ with* $(\mathsf{dig}, \mathsf{st})$*. In addition,* Chal *stores* $(\mathsf{dig}_{\mathsf{ctr}}, \mathsf{st}_{\mathsf{ctr}}) := (\mathsf{dig}, \mathsf{st})$.
- ***Challenge phase:*** *At some point, $\mathcal{A}$ specifies an index* $\mathsf{id}^* \in \{0,1\}^\ell$*, a message* $\mathsf{m}^* \in \mathcal{M}$*, and a time index* $t \in [\mathsf{ctr}]$*,* Chal *outputs $b = 1$ if* $\mathsf{id}^* \notin \mathsf{Dict_H}$*. Otherwise,* Chal *computes* $\mathsf{ct}^* = (\mathsf{ct}^{\mathsf{ind}}, \mathsf{ct}^{\mathsf{dep}}) \leftarrow \mathsf{Enc}(\mathsf{crs}, \mathsf{dig}_t, \mathsf{id}^*, \mathsf{m}^*)$*. Then, it retrieves* $(\mathsf{sk}^*, \mathsf{pk}^*) \leftarrow \mathsf{Dict_H}[\mathsf{id}^*]$*, generates* $\mathsf{wit}^* := \mathsf{WGen}^{\mathsf{st}_t}(\mathsf{crs}, \mathsf{dig}, \mathsf{id}^*, \mathsf{pk}^*)$*, and computes* $\mathsf{m} := \mathsf{Dec}(\mathsf{sk}^*, \mathsf{wit}^*, \mathsf{ct}^*)$*. Finally,* Chal *outputs $b = 1$ if* $\mathsf{m} \neq \mathsf{m}^*$*, $b = 0$ otherwise.*

We say that a dLE scheme Π is correct and compact if for all $\lambda, \ell \in \mathbb{N}$ and all (possibly unbounded) adversaries $\mathcal{A}$, the following properties holds:

- ***Correctness:*** *It holds that* $\Pr\left[\mathsf{Cor}_{\Pi,\mathcal{A}}(1^\lambda, 1^\ell) = 1\right] = \mathsf{negl}(\lambda)$.
- ***Compactness:*** *It holds that* $|\mathsf{dig}| = \mathsf{poly}(\lambda, \ell)$ *(at all points in the game),* $|\mathsf{wit}^*| = \mathsf{poly}(\lambda, \ell)$*,* $|\mathsf{ct}^{\mathsf{ind}}| = \mathsf{poly}(\lambda, \ell)$*, and* $|\mathsf{ct}^{\mathsf{dep}}| = \mathsf{poly}(\lambda, \log \ell)$.

We define the *multi-digest* security requirements of a dLE scheme. The security requirement is essentially the same as in [13], except that the challenge ciphertext is generated from the time-specific digest chosen by the adversary instead of the most recent one.

Definition 7 (L-Digest Security). *Let Π be a dLE scheme. For parameters $\lambda, \ell, L \in \mathbb{N}$ and an adversary $\mathcal{A}$, define the following game $\mathsf{Sec}_{\Pi,\mathcal{A}}(1^\lambda, 1^\ell)$ between $\mathcal{A}$ and a challenger Chal:*

- ***Setup phase:*** *Chal samples $(\mathsf{crs}, \mathsf{dig}, \mathsf{st}) \leftarrow \mathsf{Setup}(1^\lambda, 1^\ell)$. Chal also initializes a counter $\mathsf{ctr} := 0$ and a set $C_\mathsf{M} := \emptyset$. Finally, it gives $(\mathsf{crs}, \mathsf{dig}, \mathsf{st})$ to $\mathcal{A}$.*
- ***Query phase:*** *$\mathcal{A}$ can now issue the following queries:*
  - *Honest query: In this query, $\mathcal{A}$ specifies an index $\mathsf{id} \in \{0,1\}^\ell$. In response, Chal increments $\mathsf{ctr} := \mathsf{ctr} + 1$, generates $(\mathsf{sk}, \mathsf{pk}) \leftarrow \mathsf{KGen}(\mathsf{crs})$, and runs $\mathsf{dig} := \mathsf{MemUpd}^{[\mathsf{st}]}(\mathsf{crs}, \mathsf{dig}, \mathsf{id}, \mathsf{pk})$. Then, Chal replies to $\mathcal{A}$ with $(\mathsf{dig}, \mathsf{st}, \mathsf{pk})$. In addition, Chal stores $(\mathsf{dig}_\mathsf{ctr}, \mathsf{st}_\mathsf{ctr}) := (\mathsf{dig}, \mathsf{st})$.*
  - *Malicious query: In this query, $\mathcal{A}$ specifies an index $\mathsf{id} \in \{0,1\}^\ell$ and a public key pk. In response, Chal first checks that $\mathsf{IsValid}(\mathsf{crs}, \mathsf{pk}) = 1$. If the check fails, it outputs $\perp$. Otherwise, Chal increments $\mathsf{ctr} := \mathsf{ctr} + 1$ and runs $\mathsf{dig} \leftarrow \mathsf{MemUpd}^{[\mathsf{st}]}(\mathsf{crs}, \mathsf{dig}, \mathsf{id}, \mathsf{pk})$ if $\mathsf{IsValid}(\mathsf{crs}, \mathsf{pk}) = 1$. Then, Chal replies to $\mathcal{A}$ with $(\mathsf{dig}, \mathsf{st})$. In addition, Chal adds id to the set C_M and stores $(\mathsf{dig}_\mathsf{ctr}, \mathsf{st}_\mathsf{ctr}) := (\mathsf{dig}, \mathsf{st})$.*
- ***Challenge phase:*** *At some point, $\mathcal{A}$ specifies an index $\mathsf{id}^* \in \{0,1\}^\ell$, two messages $\mathsf{m}_0, \mathsf{m}_1 \in \mathcal{M}$, and L distinct time indices $t_1, \ldots, t_L \in [\mathsf{ctr}]$. Chal outputs 0 if $\mathsf{id}^* \in C_\mathsf{M}$. Otherwise, Chal samples $\mathsf{r}^\mathsf{ind} \leftarrow_\$ \mathcal{R}^\mathsf{ind}$ and $\mathsf{r}_1^\mathsf{dep}, \ldots, \mathsf{r}_L^\mathsf{dep} \leftarrow_\$ \mathcal{R}^\mathsf{dep}$, computes $\mathsf{ct}^\mathsf{ind} := \mathsf{Enc}^\mathsf{ind}(\mathsf{crs}, \mathsf{id}^*; \mathsf{r}^\mathsf{ind})$ and $\mathsf{ct}_i^\mathsf{dep} := \mathsf{Enc}^\mathsf{dep}(\mathsf{crs}, \mathsf{dig}_{t_i}, \mathsf{id}^*, \mathsf{m}_b; \mathsf{r}^\mathsf{ind}, \mathsf{r}_i^\mathsf{dep})$ for all $i \in [L]$, and replies to $\mathcal{A}$ with $(\mathsf{ct}^\mathsf{ind}, \mathsf{ct}_1^\mathsf{dep}, \ldots, \mathsf{ct}_L^\mathsf{dep})$.*
- ***Output phase:*** *$\mathcal{A}$ outputs a bit $b' \in \{0,1\}$. The game outputs 1 if $b = b'$ and 0 otherwise.*

We say that a dLE scheme Π is L-digest secure if for all security parameters $\lambda \in \mathbb{N}$, all polynomials $\ell = \ell(\lambda)$ and $L = L(\lambda)$, and all PPT adversaries $\mathcal{A}$, it holds that $\Pr[\mathsf{Sec}_{\Pi,\mathcal{A}}(1^\lambda, 1^\ell) = 1] \leq 1/2 + \mathsf{negl}(\lambda)$.

4 Efficient RBE from dLE

In this section, we present our generic transformation from a dLE scheme to an efficient RBE scheme.

4.1 Construction

Let $\Pi_\mathsf{dLE} = (\widetilde{\mathsf{Setup}}, \widetilde{\mathsf{KGen}}, \widetilde{\mathsf{IsValid}}, \widetilde{\mathsf{MemUpd}}, \widetilde{\mathsf{Enc}} = (\widetilde{\mathsf{Enc}}^\mathsf{ind}, \widetilde{\mathsf{Enc}}^\mathsf{dep}), \widetilde{\mathsf{WGen}}, \widetilde{\mathsf{Dec}})$ be a dLE scheme with message space $\mathcal{M} = \{\mathcal{M}_\lambda\}_{\lambda \in \mathbb{N}}$. In Fig. 1, we describe our construction of RBE scheme $\Pi_\mathsf{RBE} = (\mathsf{Setup}, \mathsf{KGen}, \mathsf{Reg}, \mathsf{Enc}, \mathsf{Upd}, \mathsf{Dec})$ with identity space $\mathcal{ID} = \{0,1\}^\ell$ and the same message space $\mathcal{M}$, where $\ell = O(\lambda)$ is the index-length parameter for Π_dLE. If a collision-resistant hash function $\mathsf{H} : \{0,1\}^* \rightarrow \{0,1\}^\ell$ is available, one can use an arbitrary string as an identity. In the description, we adopt the following conventions:

- The auxiliary information $\mathsf{aux} = (\mathsf{ctr}, \mathsf{Dict}_1, \mathsf{Dict}_2, \mathsf{pp}, \tilde{\mathsf{st}})$ consists of the following components:
  - A counter $\mathsf{ctr} \geq 0$ is the current number of registered users in the system.
  - A dictionary Dict_1 mapping a counter ctr to the ctr-th registered identity/key pair $(\mathsf{id}, \mathsf{pk})$.
  - A dictionary Dict_2 mapping an identity id to a collection of the helper decryption keys $\mathsf{hsk} = \{(\mathsf{ctr}, \tilde{\mathsf{wit}})\}$ associated with id, where $\tilde{\mathsf{wit}}$ is a membership witness generated upon the ctr-th registration.
  - The current public parameter $\mathsf{pp} = (\mathsf{ctr}, \tilde{\mathsf{dig}}_1, \ldots, \tilde{\mathsf{dig}}_{\mathsf{hw}(\mathsf{ctr})})$, where ctr is the current counter and $\tilde{\mathsf{dig}}_1, \ldots, \tilde{\mathsf{dig}}_{\mathsf{hw}(\mathsf{ctr})}$ are the digests of Π_{dLE}. Of the digests, $\tilde{\mathsf{dig}}_1$ is the oldest version and $\tilde{\mathsf{dig}}_{\mathsf{hw}(\mathsf{ctr})}$ is the newest version.
  - The state $\tilde{\mathsf{st}}$ corresponding to the newest digest $\tilde{\mathsf{dig}}_{\mathsf{hw}(\mathsf{ctr})}$.
- We use a function $\delta : \mathbb{N} \to \mathbb{N}$ that, for an input $x \in \mathbb{N}$, outputs the position where the least significant bit is 1 in the binary representation of x.

4.2 Correctness, Compactness, and Efficiency

Here, we will show that the correctness, compactness, and efficiency of Π_{RBE} are implied by the correctness and compactness of Π_{dLE}.

Theorem 1 (Correctness). *If Π_{dLE} is complete and correct, Π_{RBE} is correct.*

Proof. Consider the correctness game for Π_{RBE} (Definition 2) played by an adversary $\mathcal{A}_{\mathsf{RBE}}$ and a challenger Chal. Let $\mathsf{crs} = \tilde{\mathsf{crs}} \leftarrow \widetilde{\mathsf{Setup}}(1^\lambda, 1^\ell)$ be the common reference string, let $(\mathsf{sk}^*, \mathsf{pk}^*) := (\tilde{\mathsf{sk}}^*, \tilde{\mathsf{pk}}^*) \leftarrow \widetilde{\mathsf{KGen}}(\tilde{\mathsf{crs}})$ be the target-key sampled by Chal in response to a target-identity registration query on the challenge identity id^*, and let ctr^* be the counter when $(\mathsf{id}^*, \mathsf{pk}^*)$ is registered. Further, let $\mathsf{aux} = (\mathsf{ctr}, \mathsf{Dict}_1, \mathsf{Dict}_2, \mathsf{pp}, \tilde{\mathsf{st}})$ be the auxiliary information (maintained by Chal) at any point in the correctness game *after* $\mathcal{A}_{\mathsf{RBE}}$ has made a target-identity registration query. We can write $\mathsf{pp} = (\mathsf{ctr}, \tilde{\mathsf{dig}}_1, \ldots, \tilde{\mathsf{dig}}_{\mathsf{hw}(\mathsf{ctr})})$ with $\mathsf{ctr} \geq \mathsf{ctr}^*$.

We need to show that in the correctness game, for any (possibly unbounded) adversary $\mathcal{A}_{\mathsf{RBE}}$, the probability that $b = 1$ (indicating decryption failure) is negligible. Let $\mathsf{m}_t \in \mathcal{M}$ be the t-th encryption query made by $\mathcal{A}_{\mathsf{RBE}}$, and let $\mathsf{ct}_t \leftarrow \mathsf{Enc}(\mathsf{crs}, \mathsf{pp}, \mathsf{id}^*, \mathsf{m}_t)$ be the resulting ciphertext. Consider a decryption query on any index $j \in [t]$. Here, Chal computes $\mathsf{m}'_j \leftarrow \mathsf{Dec}(\mathsf{sk}^*, \mathsf{hsk}^*, \mathsf{ct}_j)$.

- By construction, we can write $\mathsf{ct}_j = (\mathsf{ctr}_{\mathsf{enc}}, \tilde{\mathsf{ct}}_j^{\mathsf{ind}}, \tilde{\mathsf{ct}}_{j,1}^{\mathsf{dep}}, \ldots, \tilde{\mathsf{ct}}_{j,\mathsf{hw}(\mathsf{ctr}_{\mathsf{enc}})}^{\mathsf{dep}})$ and $\mathsf{hsk}^* = \{(\mathsf{ctr}_i, \tilde{\mathsf{wit}}_i)\}_{i \in [d]}$.
- If $\mathsf{ctr}_{\mathsf{enc}} < \mathsf{ctr}_1$, Chal replies with $\perp$.
- If there is no counter such that $(\mathsf{ctr}_{\mathsf{enc}} \oplus \mathsf{ctr}_i) < 2^{\delta(\mathsf{ctr}_i)}$, Chal updates $\mathsf{hsk}^* := \mathsf{Upd}^{\mathsf{aux}}(\mathsf{pp}, \mathsf{id}^*)$ (As will be shown later, the updated helper decryption key hsk^* always includes the counter ctr_i that satisfies the above).
- Chal replies with $\mathsf{m}'_j \leftarrow \widetilde{\mathsf{Dec}}(\tilde{\mathsf{sk}}^*, \tilde{\mathsf{wit}}_i, (\tilde{\mathsf{ct}}_j^{\mathsf{ind}}, \tilde{\mathsf{ct}}_{j,\mathsf{hw}(\mathsf{ctr}_i)}^{\mathsf{dep}}))$.

We now examine three failure cases.

$\mathsf{Setup}(1^\lambda) \to \mathsf{crs}$:

1: $(\widetilde{\mathsf{crs}}, \widetilde{\mathsf{dig}}, \widetilde{\mathsf{st}}) \leftarrow \widetilde{\mathsf{Setup}}(1^\lambda, 1^\ell)$
2: $\mathsf{aux} := (0, \emptyset, \emptyset, (0, \widetilde{\mathsf{dig}}), \widetilde{\mathsf{st}})$
3: **return** $\mathsf{crs} := \widetilde{\mathsf{crs}}$

$\mathsf{KGen}(\mathsf{crs}) \to (\mathsf{sk}, \mathsf{pk})$:

1: $(\widetilde{\mathsf{sk}}, \widetilde{\mathsf{pk}}) \leftarrow \widetilde{\mathsf{KGen}}(\widetilde{\mathsf{crs}})$
2: **return** $(\mathsf{sk}, \mathsf{pk}) := (\widetilde{\mathsf{sk}}, \widetilde{\mathsf{pk}})$

$\mathsf{Upd}^{\mathsf{aux}}(\mathsf{pp}, \mathsf{id}) \to \mathsf{hsk}$:

1: $\{(\mathsf{ctr}_i, \widetilde{\mathsf{wit}}_i)\}_{i \in [d]} \leftarrow \mathsf{Dict}_2[\mathsf{id}]$
2: **return** $\mathsf{hsk} := \{(\mathsf{ctr}_i, \widetilde{\mathsf{wit}}_i)\}_{i \in [d]}$

$\mathsf{Reg}^{[\mathsf{aux}]}(\mathsf{crs}, \mathsf{pp}, \mathsf{id}, \mathsf{pk}) \to \mathsf{pp}$:

1: **if** $\widetilde{\mathsf{IsValid}}(\widetilde{\mathsf{crs}}, \widetilde{\mathsf{pk}}) = 0$ **then**
2:     **return** pp
3: $\mathsf{ctr} := \mathsf{ctr} + 1, \mathsf{Dict}_1[\mathsf{ctr}] := (\mathsf{id}, \mathsf{pk})$
4: $\widetilde{\mathsf{dig}} := \widetilde{\mathsf{MemUpd}}^{[\widetilde{\mathsf{st}}]}(\widetilde{\mathsf{crs}}, \mathsf{dig}, \mathsf{id}, \widetilde{\mathsf{pk}})$
5: **for** $i = 1, \ldots, 2^{\delta(\mathsf{ctr})}$ **do**
6:     $(\mathsf{id}, \widetilde{\mathsf{pk}}) \leftarrow \mathsf{Dict}_1[\mathsf{ctr} + 1 - i]$
7:     $\widetilde{\mathsf{wit}} := \widetilde{\mathsf{WGen}}^{\widetilde{\mathsf{st}}}(\widetilde{\mathsf{crs}}, \widetilde{\mathsf{dig}}, \mathsf{id}, \widetilde{\mathsf{pk}})$
8:     $\mathsf{Dict}_2[\mathsf{id}] := \mathsf{Dict}_2[\mathsf{id}] \cup \{(\mathsf{ctr}, \widetilde{\mathsf{wit}})\}$
9: $\mathsf{pp} := (\mathsf{ctr}, \widetilde{\mathsf{dig}}_1, \ldots, \widetilde{\mathsf{dig}}_{\mathsf{hw}(\mathsf{ctr})-1}, \widetilde{\mathsf{dig}})$
10: **return** pp

$\mathsf{Enc}(\mathsf{crs}, \mathsf{pp}, \mathsf{id}, \mathsf{m}) \to \mathsf{ct}$:

1: $\tilde{\mathsf{r}}^{\mathsf{ind}} \leftarrow\$ \tilde{\mathcal{R}}^{\mathsf{ind}}, \tilde{\mathsf{r}}_1^{\mathsf{dep}}, \ldots, \tilde{\mathsf{r}}_{\mathsf{hw}(\mathsf{ctr})}^{\mathsf{dep}} \leftarrow\$ \tilde{\mathcal{R}}^{\mathsf{dep}}$
2: $\tilde{\mathsf{ct}}^{\mathsf{ind}} := \widetilde{\mathsf{Enc}}^{\mathsf{ind}}(\widetilde{\mathsf{crs}}, \mathsf{id}; \tilde{\mathsf{r}}^{\mathsf{ind}})$
3: **for** $i = 1, \ldots, \mathsf{hw}(\mathsf{ctr})$ **do**: $\tilde{\mathsf{ct}}_i^{\mathsf{dep}} := \widetilde{\mathsf{Enc}}^{\mathsf{dep}}(\widetilde{\mathsf{crs}}, \widetilde{\mathsf{dig}}_i, \mathsf{id}, \mathsf{m}; \tilde{\mathsf{r}}^{\mathsf{ind}}, \tilde{\mathsf{r}}_i^{\mathsf{dep}})$
4: **return** $\mathsf{ct} := (\mathsf{ctr}, \tilde{\mathsf{ct}}^{\mathsf{ind}}, \tilde{\mathsf{ct}}_1^{\mathsf{dep}}, \ldots, \tilde{\mathsf{ct}}_{\mathsf{hw}(\mathsf{ctr})}^{\mathsf{dep}})$

$\mathsf{Dec}(\mathsf{sk}, \mathsf{hsk}, \mathsf{ct}) \to \mathsf{m}$:

1: **parse** $\mathsf{ct} := (\mathsf{ctr}_{\mathsf{enc}}, \tilde{\mathsf{ct}}^{\mathsf{ind}}, \tilde{\mathsf{ct}}_1^{\mathsf{dep}}, \ldots, \tilde{\mathsf{ct}}_{\mathsf{hw}(\mathsf{ctr}_{\mathsf{enc}})}^{\mathsf{dep}})$
2: **if** $\mathsf{ctr}_{\mathsf{enc}} < \mathsf{ctr}_1$ **then return** $\perp$
3: **if** $\nexists \mathsf{ctr}_i$ s.t. $(\mathsf{ctr}_{\mathsf{enc}} \oplus \mathsf{ctr}_i) < 2^{\delta(\mathsf{ctr}_i)}$ **then return** GetUpd
4: **return** $\mathsf{m} := \widetilde{\mathsf{Dec}}(\widetilde{\mathsf{sk}}, \widetilde{\mathsf{wit}}_i, (\tilde{\mathsf{ct}}^{\mathsf{ind}}, \tilde{\mathsf{ct}}_{\mathsf{hw}(\mathsf{ctr}_i)}^{\mathsf{dep}}))$

Fig. 1. An RBE scheme Π_{RBE} from a dLE scheme Π_{dLE}.

- Case 1: $\mathsf{ctr}_{\mathsf{enc}} < \mathsf{ctr}_1$. By construction, we have $\mathsf{ctr}_1 = \mathsf{ctr}^*$. In the correctness game, Chal only encrypts messages after the target identity id^* is registered. Thus, $\mathsf{ctr}_{\mathsf{enc}} \geq \mathsf{ctr}^* = \mathsf{ctr}_1$ always holds. Therefore, this case never occurs.
- Case 2: No suitable counter ctr_i exists. For any $\mathsf{ctr}_{\mathsf{enc}} \geq \mathsf{ctr}^*$, let the binary representation of $\mathsf{ctr}_{\mathsf{enc}}$ be $\sum_{j=1}^{\mathsf{hw}(\mathsf{ctr}_{\mathsf{enc}})} 2^{d_j}$ with $d_1 > d_2 > \cdots > d_{\mathsf{hw}(\mathsf{ctr}_{\mathsf{enc}})}$. This defines a canonical partition of $[1, \mathsf{ctr}_{\mathsf{enc}}]$ into $\mathsf{hw}(\mathsf{ctr}_{\mathsf{enc}})$ intervals $\mathcal{B}_i := [T_i - 2^{d_i} + 1, T_i]$, where $T_i = \sum_{j=1}^{i} 2^{d_j}$. Since $\mathsf{ctr}^* \in [1, \mathsf{ctr}_{\mathsf{enc}}]$, there exists $i \in [\mathsf{hw}(\mathsf{ctr}_{\mathsf{enc}})]$ such that $\mathsf{ctr}^* \in \mathcal{B}_i$. By the Reg algorithm, when the global counter ctr reached T_i, the loop in step 5 added the tuple $(T_i, \widetilde{\mathsf{wit}})$ to $\mathsf{Dict}_2[\mathsf{id}^*]$ because id^* was within the $2^{\delta(T_i)}$ most recent registrations. Furthermore, the condition $(\mathsf{ctr}_{\mathsf{enc}} \oplus T_i) \leq 2^{\delta(T_i)}$ is satisfied because $\mathsf{ctr}_{\mathsf{enc}}$ and T_i share the

same bits of all positions higher than $d_i = \delta(T_i)$, and $\mathsf{ctr}_{\mathsf{enc}} \geq T_i$. This means that there exists a suitable counter $\mathsf{ctr}_i = T_i$. Therefore, this failure case is resolved by obtaining the latest hsk^*.

- Case 3: Π_{dLE} decryption fails. Finally, we consider the case that $\mathsf{m}_j \neq \mathsf{m}'_j$. By the correctness of Π_{dLE}, this would occur with only negligible probability if the witness $\widetilde{\mathsf{wit}}_i$ and the digest $\widetilde{\mathsf{dig}}_{\mathsf{hw}(\mathsf{ctr}_i)}$ behind $\widetilde{\mathsf{ct}}^{\mathsf{dep}}_{j,\mathsf{hw}(\mathsf{ctr}_i)}$ were *synchronized.* Here, $\widetilde{\mathsf{wit}}_i$ is the witness for the id^* generated through the execution of $\widetilde{\mathsf{WGen}}^{\mathsf{st}}(\widetilde{\mathsf{crs}}, \widetilde{\mathsf{dig}}, \mathsf{id}^*, \widetilde{\mathsf{pk}}^*)$ during the ctr_i-th registration. Hence, it is sufficient to show that $\widetilde{\mathsf{dig}}_{\mathsf{hw}(\mathsf{ctr}_i)}$ is generated by the execution of $\widetilde{\mathsf{MemUpd}}$ in the ctr_i-th registration. The condition $(\mathsf{ctr}_{\mathsf{enc}} \oplus \mathsf{ctr}_i) < 2^{\delta(\mathsf{ctr}_i)}$ ensures $\mathsf{ctr}_{\mathsf{enc}}$ and ctr_i share the same prefix beyond the $\delta(\mathsf{ctr}_i)$-th bit. By the description of the Reg algorithm, this guarantees that $\widetilde{\mathsf{dig}}_{\mathsf{hw}(\mathsf{ctr}_i)}$ is generated by the execution of $\widetilde{\mathsf{MemUpd}}$ in the ctr_i-th registration.

Therefore, the overall probability of decryption failure is negligible. This completes the proof. □

Theorem 2 (Compactness). *If Π_{dLE} is compact, Π_{RBE} is compact.*

Proof. We consider each requirement separately:

Compactness of the Public Parameter: By construction, the public parameter pp simply consists of a counter ctr indicating the current number of registered users, along with $\mathsf{hw}(\mathsf{ctr})$ digests $\widetilde{\mathsf{dig}}_1, \ldots, \widetilde{\mathsf{dig}}_{\mathsf{hw}(\mathsf{ctr})}$ for the underlying dLE scheme Π_{dLE}. By compactness of Π_{dLE} and $\ell = O(\lambda)$, we have $|\widetilde{\mathsf{dig}}_i| = \mathsf{poly}(\lambda, \ell) = \mathsf{poly}(\lambda)$ for all $i \in [\mathsf{hw}(\mathsf{ctr})]$. Since $\mathsf{hw}(\mathsf{ctr}) \leq \log(\mathsf{ctr})$, we have $|\mathsf{pp}| \leq |\mathsf{ctr}| + \log(\mathsf{ctr}) \cdot |\widetilde{\mathsf{dig}}_i| = \mathsf{poly}(\lambda, \log(\mathsf{ctr}))$.

Compactness of the Helper Decryption Key: Let $\mathsf{hsk} = \{(\mathsf{ctr}_i, \widetilde{\mathsf{wit}}_i)\}_{i\in[d]}$ be a helper decryption key for some id. By construction, we have $\mathsf{ctr}_i < \mathsf{ctr}_{i+1}$ and $\mathsf{ctr}_{i+1} - 2^{\delta(\mathsf{ctr}_{i+1})} + 1 \leq \mathsf{ctr}_i$ for all $i \in [d-1]$. The latter is because $(\mathsf{ctr}_{i+1}, \widetilde{\mathsf{wit}}_{i+1})$ is added to $\mathsf{Dict}_2[\mathsf{id}]$ when $\mathsf{ctr}_{i+1} - 2^{\delta(\mathsf{ctr}_{i+1})} + 1 \leq \mathsf{ctr}_i$ occurs.

Then, we show that

$$\mathsf{ctr}_{i+1} - 2^{\delta(\mathsf{ctr}_{i+1})} + 1 \leq \mathsf{ctr}_i < \mathsf{ctr}_{i+1} \tag{1}$$

implies $\delta(\mathsf{ctr}_i) < \delta(\mathsf{ctr}_{i+1})$. By definition of δ, we can write $\mathsf{ctr}_{i+1} = k_{i+1} \cdot 2^{\delta(\mathsf{ctr}_{i+1})}$ for some odd integer k_i. Thus, the inequality (1) can be written

$$(k_{i+1} - 1) \cdot 2^{\delta(\mathsf{ctr}_{i+1})} + 1 \leq \mathsf{ctr}_i \leq k_{i+1} \cdot 2^{\delta(\mathsf{ctr}_{i+1})} - 1.$$

This means that $\mathsf{ctr}_i \equiv 1 \mod 2^{\delta(\mathsf{ctr}_{i+1})}$. If $\delta(\mathsf{ctr}_i) \geq \delta(\mathsf{ctr}_{i+1})$, then ctr_i must be divisible by $2^{\delta(\mathsf{ctr}_i)}$, which contradicts the above. Therefore, we have $\delta(\mathsf{ctr}_i) < \delta(\mathsf{ctr}_{i+1})$. From the above argument, we have $\delta(\mathsf{ctr}_1) < \delta(\mathsf{ctr}_2) < \cdots < \delta(\mathsf{ctr}_d) \leq \log N$. and then $d \leq \log N$. Hence, hsk consists of at most $\log N$ pairs of counters and witnesses. By compactness of Π_{dLE}, we have $|\widetilde{\mathsf{wit}}_i| = \mathsf{poly}(\lambda, \ell) = \mathsf{poly}(\lambda)$ since $\ell = O(\lambda)$. Therefore, $|\mathsf{hsk}| = \mathsf{poly}(\lambda, \log N)$. □

Furthermore, by the (ciphertext) compactness of Π_{dLE}, Π_{RBE} satisfies:

$$|\mathsf{ct}| = |\mathsf{ctr}| + |\tilde{\mathsf{ct}}^{\mathsf{ind}}| + \sum_{i=1}^{\mathsf{hw}(\mathsf{ctr})} |\tilde{\mathsf{ct}}_i^{\mathsf{dep}}| \leq |\tilde{\mathsf{ct}}^{\mathsf{ind}}| + O(\log N) \cdot \mathsf{poly}(\lambda, \log \ell). \quad (2)$$

Theorem 3 (Efficiency). *If Π_{dLE} is compact, Π_{RBE} is (weakly) efficient.*

Proof. We consider each requirement separately:

Running Time of Update: By construction, the GetUpd operation simply looks up the helper decryption key hsk. By Theorem 2, we have $|\mathsf{hsk}| = \mathsf{poly}(\lambda, \log N)$. Since the auxiliary information maintains a dictionary Dict_2 mapping each identity to its helper decryption key, the update operation can be implemented in $\mathsf{poly}(\lambda, \log N)$ time in the RAM model of computation.

Number of Updates: Let $\mathsf{hsk} = \{(\mathsf{ctr}_i, \tilde{\mathsf{wit}}_i)\}_{i \in [d]}$ be a helper decryption key for some id. By construction and Theorem 2, a new element is added to $\mathsf{Dict}_2[\mathsf{id}]$ whenever $\delta(\mathsf{ctr}_i) < \delta(\mathsf{ctr}_{i+1})$, so a registered identity id must invoke the Upd algorithm. Therefore, for any identity, its i-th update occurs when 2^i new identities are registered after its $(i-1)$-th update. Since there are at most N registrations, the number of updates received by any identity is at most $\log N$. □

4.3 Security

We will show that the security of Π_{RBE} is implied by the multi-digest security of Π_{dLE}. Recall the security game from Definition 3.

Theorem 4 (Security). *If Π_{dLE} is $\lceil \log N \rceil$-digest secure, Π_{RBE} is secure.*

Proof. Let $\mathcal{A}_{\mathsf{RBE}}$ be an adversary for Π_{RBE}, Let $\mathsf{ctr}_{\mathsf{enc}}$ be the counter used for encrypting the target identity, and let ct^* be the challenge ciphertext. By construction, we can write $\mathsf{ct}^* = (\mathsf{ctr}_{\mathsf{enc}}, \tilde{\mathsf{ct}}^{\mathsf{ind}}, \tilde{\mathsf{ct}}_1^{\mathsf{dep}}, \ldots, \tilde{\mathsf{ct}}_{\mathsf{hw}(\mathsf{ctr}_{\mathsf{enc}})}^{\mathsf{dep}})$. Here, $\mathsf{hw}(\mathsf{ctr}_{\mathsf{enc}}) \leq \log N$. We use $\mathcal{A}_{\mathsf{RBE}}$ to construct a PPT algorithm $\mathcal{B}_{\mathsf{dLE}}$ for the security of Π_{dLE}:

- **Setup phase:** Given $(\tilde{\mathsf{crs}}, \tilde{\mathsf{dig}}, \tilde{\mathsf{st}})$, $\mathcal{B}_{\mathsf{dLE}}$ proceeds as follows:
  1. $\mathcal{B}_{\mathsf{dLE}}$ initializes a counter $\mathsf{ctr} := 0$ and dictionaries $\mathsf{Dict}_1, \mathsf{Dict}_2 := \emptyset$.
  2. $\mathcal{B}_{\mathsf{dLE}}$ also initializes $\mathsf{pp} := (0, \tilde{\mathsf{dig}})$, $\mathsf{aux} = (\mathsf{ctr}, \mathsf{Dict}_1, \mathsf{Dict}_2, \mathsf{pp}, \tilde{\mathsf{st}})$, $\mathcal{S} := \emptyset$, $\mathsf{id}^* := \perp$.
  3. In addition, $\mathcal{B}_{\mathsf{dLE}}$ internally maintains an ordered list $\mathsf{List} := \perp$ which will track the digests and states generated during Reg algorithm execution.
  4. Finally, $\mathcal{B}_{\mathsf{dLE}}$ gives $\mathsf{crs} := \tilde{\mathsf{crs}}$ to $\mathcal{A}_{\mathsf{RBE}}$.
- **Query phase:** $\mathcal{B}_{\mathsf{dLE}}$ simulates responses to actions made by $\mathcal{A}_{\mathsf{RBE}}$ as follows:
  - Registering a new (non-target) identity: When $\mathcal{A}_{\mathsf{RBE}}$ specifies an identity id and a public key $\mathsf{pk} = \tilde{\mathsf{pk}}$, $\mathcal{B}_{\mathsf{dLE}}$ outputs the current public parameter pp if $\tilde{\mathsf{IsValid}}(\tilde{\mathsf{crs}}, \tilde{\mathsf{pk}}) = 0$. Otherwise, it proceeds as follows:
    1. $\mathcal{B}_{\mathsf{dLE}}$ obtains $(\tilde{\mathsf{dig}}, \tilde{\mathsf{st}})$ by making a malicious query on $(\mathsf{id}, \tilde{\mathsf{pk}})$.

2. $\mathcal{B}_{\mathsf{dLE}}$ updates $\mathsf{ctr} := \mathsf{ctr} + 1$, $\mathsf{pp} := (\mathsf{ctr}, \tilde{\mathsf{dig}}_1, \ldots, \tilde{\mathsf{dig}}_{\mathsf{hw(ctr)}-1}, \tilde{\mathsf{dig}})$, $\mathsf{Dict}_1[\mathsf{ctr}] := (\mathsf{id}, \tilde{\mathsf{pk}})$, $\mathsf{aux} = (\mathsf{ctr}, \mathsf{Dict}_1, \mathsf{Dict}_2, \mathsf{pp}, \tilde{\mathsf{st}})$, $\mathcal{S} := \mathcal{S} \cup \{\mathsf{id}\}$, and $\mathsf{List}[\mathsf{ctr}] := (\tilde{\mathsf{dig}}, \tilde{\mathsf{st}})$.

- Registering the target identity: When $\mathcal{A}_{\mathsf{RBE}}$ specifies an identity id^*, $\mathcal{B}_{\mathsf{dLE}}$ proceeds as follows:
  1. $\mathcal{B}_{\mathsf{dLE}}$ obtains $(\tilde{\mathsf{dig}}, \tilde{\mathsf{st}}, \tilde{\mathsf{pk}})$ by making an honest query on id.
  2. $\mathcal{B}_{\mathsf{dLE}}$ updates $\mathsf{ctr} := \mathsf{ctr} + 1$, $\mathsf{pp} := (\mathsf{ctr}, \tilde{\mathsf{dig}}_1, \ldots, \tilde{\mathsf{dig}}_{\mathsf{hw(ctr)}-1}, \tilde{\mathsf{dig}})$, $\mathsf{Dict}_1[\mathsf{ctr}] := (\mathsf{id}^*, \tilde{\mathsf{pk}})$, $\mathsf{aux} = (\mathsf{ctr}, \mathsf{Dict}_1, \mathsf{Dict}_2, \mathsf{pp}, \tilde{\mathsf{st}})$, $\mathcal{S} := \mathcal{S} \cup \{\mathsf{id}^*\}$, and $\mathsf{List}[\mathsf{ctr}] := (\tilde{\mathsf{dig}}, \tilde{\mathsf{st}})$.
  3. $\mathcal{B}_{\mathsf{dLE}}$ replies to $\mathcal{A}_{\mathsf{RBE}}$ with $\mathsf{pk}^* := \tilde{\mathsf{pk}}$.

– **Challenge phase:** After $\mathcal{A}_{\mathsf{RBE}}$ outputs a pair of messages $\mathsf{m}_0, \mathsf{m}_1$ and id^* (if no target identity id^* is chosen), $\mathcal{B}_{\mathsf{dLE}}$ proceeds as follows: $\mathcal{B}_{\mathsf{dLE}}$ constructs $\mathsf{ct}^* = (\mathsf{ctr}_{\mathsf{enc}}, \tilde{\mathsf{ct}}^{\mathsf{ind}}, \tilde{\mathsf{ct}}_1^{\mathsf{dep}}, \ldots, \tilde{\mathsf{ct}}_{\mathsf{hw}(\mathsf{ctr}_{\mathsf{enc}})}^{\mathsf{dep}})$ as follows:
  1. Let $\mathsf{pp} = (\mathsf{ctr}_{\mathsf{enc}}, \tilde{\mathsf{dig}}_1, \ldots, \tilde{\mathsf{dig}}_{\mathsf{hw}(\mathsf{ctr}_{\mathsf{enc}})})$ be the current public parameter.
  2. For $j \in [\mathsf{hw}(\mathsf{ctr}_{\mathsf{enc}})]$, let $t_j \in [\mathsf{ctr}_{\mathsf{enc}}]$ be the time index at which $\tilde{\mathsf{dig}}_j$ were generated, respectively.
  3. $\mathcal{B}_{\mathsf{dLE}}$ makes a challenge query on $(t_1, \ldots, t_{\mathsf{hw}(\mathsf{ctr}_{\mathsf{enc}})}, \mathsf{id}^*, \mathsf{m}_0^*, \mathsf{m}_1^*)$ to obtain $\tilde{\mathsf{ct}}^* = (\tilde{\mathsf{ct}}^{\mathsf{ind}}, \tilde{\mathsf{ct}}_1^{\mathsf{dep}}, \ldots, \tilde{\mathsf{ct}}_{\mathsf{hw}(\mathsf{ctr}_{\mathsf{enc}})}^{\mathsf{dep}})$.
  4. $\mathcal{B}_{\mathsf{dLE}}$ finally gives $\mathsf{ct}^* = (\mathsf{ctr}_{\mathsf{enc}}, \tilde{\mathsf{ct}}^{\mathsf{ind}}, \tilde{\mathsf{ct}}_1^{\mathsf{dep}}, \ldots, \tilde{\mathsf{ct}}_{\mathsf{hw}(\mathsf{ctr}_{\mathsf{enc}})}^{\mathsf{dep}})$ to $\mathcal{A}_{\mathsf{RBE}}$.

– **Output phase:** $\mathcal{A}_{\mathsf{RBE}}$ outputs a bit $b' \in \{0,1\}$, which $\mathcal{B}_{\mathsf{dLE}}$ also outputs.

According to the above simulation, if id^* is registered as a non-target identity, then $\mathcal{B}_{\mathsf{dLE}}$ also does not make a malicious query on id^*. Therefore, the game will not end due to the challenge query made by $\mathcal{B}_{\mathsf{dLE}}$. Then, we show that $\mathcal{B}_{\mathsf{dLE}}$ perfectly simulates an execution of the RBE security game for $\mathcal{A}_{\mathsf{RBE}}$. In the case where $\tilde{\mathsf{ct}}_j^{\mathsf{dep}} \leftarrow \tilde{\mathsf{Enc}}^{\mathsf{dep}}(\tilde{\mathsf{crs}}, \tilde{\mathsf{dig}}_j, \mathsf{id}^*, \mathsf{m}_0)$, $\mathcal{B}_{\mathsf{dLE}}$ simulates the challenger in the security game of RBE when $b = 0$ whereas in the another case, $\mathcal{B}_{\mathsf{dLE}}$ simulates the challenger in the security game of RBE when $b = 1$. Correspondingly, $\mathcal{B}_{\mathsf{dLE}}$ wins the dLE security game with the same probability. □

5 Instantiation from Lattice

In this section, we present a lattice-based RBE construction obtained by instantiating the transformation from the previous section.

5.1 Preliminaries on Lattices

Here, we give preliminaries on lattices necessary to describe our dLE scheme.

Cyclotomic Rings. Let $\mathcal{K} = \mathbb{Q}(\zeta)$ be a cyclotomic field and $\mathcal{R} = \mathbb{Z}[\zeta]$ its ring of integers, where $\zeta \in \mathbb{C}$ is a root of unity. Write $\deg_{\mathcal{R}}$ for the degree of $\mathcal{R}$. The (infinity) norm $\|a\|$ of an element $a = \sum_{i \in [0, \deg_{\mathcal{R}}-1]} a_i \zeta^i \in \mathcal{R}$ is defined as the infinity norm of its coefficient vector $(a_0, \ldots, a_{\deg_{\mathcal{R}}-1})^\top$, i.e. $\|a\| := \max_i \|a_i\|_\infty$. For a vector $\mathbf{x} = (x_1, \ldots, x_m)^\top \in \mathcal{R}^m$, its norm is defined as $\|\mathbf{x}\| := \max_{i \in [m]} \|x_i\|$. For $q \in \mathbb{N}$, we write $\mathcal{R}_q := \mathcal{R}/q\mathcal{R}$.

We then recall the ring expansion factor and its property.

Definition 8 (Expansion Factor). *The expansion factor of $\mathcal{R}$, denoted by $\gamma_{\mathcal{R}}$, is $\gamma_{\mathcal{R}} := \max_{a,b\in\mathcal{R}\setminus\{0\}} \frac{\|a\cdot b\|}{\|a\|\cdot\|b\|}$.*

Lemma 1 ([2]). *If $\mathcal{R}$ is a prime-power cyclotomic ring, then $\gamma_{\mathcal{R}} \leq 2\deg_{\mathcal{R}}$. If $\mathcal{R}$ is a power-of-2 cyclotomic ring, then $\gamma_{\mathcal{R}} \leq \deg_{\mathcal{R}}$.*

We also recall a version of the leftover hash lemma over cyclotomic rings.

Lemma 2 (Adapted from [7, Lemma 7]**).** *Let $n = \mathsf{poly}(\lambda)$, $q \in \mathbb{N}$, and $m \geq n \cdot \lceil \log q \rceil + \omega(\log \lambda)$. Then, it holds that*

$$\left\{(\mathbf{B},\mathbf{y}) : \begin{matrix} \mathbf{B} \leftarrow_{\$} \mathcal{R}_q^{n\times m}, \mathbf{x} \leftarrow_{\$} \mathcal{R}_2^m \\ \mathbf{y} := \mathbf{B}\mathbf{x} \bmod q \end{matrix}\right\} \approx_s \left\{(\mathbf{B},\mathbf{y}) : \begin{matrix} \mathbf{B} \leftarrow_{\$} \mathcal{R}_q^{n\times m} \\ \mathbf{y} \leftarrow_{\$} \mathcal{R}_q^n \end{matrix}\right\}.$$

Gadget Matrix. Let $q, n, m \in \mathbb{N}$ with $m = n \cdot \lceil \log q \rceil$. The gadget matrix [31] is defined as $\mathbf{G} := \mathbf{I}_n \otimes \left(1\ 2 \cdots 2^{\lfloor \log q \rfloor}\right) \in \mathcal{R}_q^{n\times m}$. Further, we write $\mathbf{G}^{-1}(\cdot)$ to denote the binary decomposition.

Discrete Gaussian Distribution. For a positive real σ, the Gaussian function over $\mathbb{R}$ with parameter σ is defined as $\rho_\sigma(x) := \exp(-\pi|x|^2/\sigma^2)$ with support $\mathbb{R}$. Then, we define discrete Gaussian distributions over $\mathbb{Z}$ and $\mathcal{R}$.

Definition 9 (Discrete Gaussian Distribution). *The discrete Gaussian distribution over $\mathbb{Z}$ with parameter σ is defined as $\mathcal{D}_{\mathbb{Z},\sigma}(x) := \rho_\sigma(x)/\rho_\sigma(\mathbb{Z})$ with support $\mathbb{Z}$, where $\rho_\sigma(\mathbb{Z}) := \sum_{y\in\mathbb{Z}} \rho_\sigma(y)$ The discrete Gaussian distribution over $\mathcal{R}$ with parameter σ, denoted by $\mathcal{D}_{\mathcal{R},\sigma}$, is defined by independently sampling* $\deg_{\mathcal{R}}$ *coefficients x_i from $\mathcal{D}_{\mathbb{Z},\sigma}$, and setting $x := \sum_{i\in[0,\deg_{\mathcal{R}}-1]} x_i \cdot \zeta^i \in \mathcal{R}$.*

We will use the following properties of discrete Gaussian distributions.

Lemma 3 (Derived from [31, Lemma 7]**).** *For any $k > 0$, it holds that* $\Pr_{x\leftarrow\mathcal{D}_{\mathcal{R},\sigma}}[\|x\| > k\cdot\sigma] < 2\cdot\deg_{\mathcal{R}}\cdot\exp(-\pi\cdot k^2)$.

Learning with Errors and Variants. We define the (module) learning with errors (LWE) problem and its leaky variant as follows.

Definition 10 (LWE) *Let* $\mathsf{params} = (\mathcal{R}, n, m, q, \mathcal{E})$ *be parametrised by λ, where $\mathcal{R}$ is a ring, $n, m, q \in \mathbb{N}$, $\mathcal{E}$ is distributions over $\mathcal{R}^m$. For a bit $b \in \{0,1\}$ and an adversary $\mathcal{A}$, we define the experiment* $\mathsf{Exp\text{-}LWE}^b_{\mathsf{params},\mathcal{A}}(1^\lambda)$ *as in Fig. 2. The* $\mathsf{LWE}_{\mathsf{params}}$ *assumption states that for any PPT $\mathcal{A}$, it holds that*

$$\left|\Pr[\mathsf{Exp\text{-}LWE}^0_{\mathsf{params},\mathcal{A}}(1^\lambda) = 1] - \Pr[\mathsf{Exp\text{-}LWE}^1_{\mathsf{params},\mathcal{A}}(1^\lambda) = 1]\right| \leq \mathsf{negl}(\lambda).$$

Definition 11 (Leaky LWE [27, Definition 3]**).** *Let* $\mathsf{params} = (\mathcal{R}, n, m, q, Q, \mathcal{E}, \mathcal{F}, \mathcal{L})$ *be parametrized by λ, where $\mathcal{R}$ is a ring, $n, m, q, Q \in \mathbb{N}$, $\mathcal{E}$ and $\mathcal{F}$ are distributions over $\mathcal{R}^m$ and $\mathbb{Z}^Q$, respectively, and $\mathcal{L} \subseteq \mathcal{R}^{m\times Q}$ is a polynomial-time decidable family of tuple of matrices. For $b \in \{0,1\}$ and an adversary $\mathcal{A} = (\mathcal{A}_0, \mathcal{A}_1)$, we define the experiment* $\mathsf{Exp\text{-}LLWE}^b_{\mathsf{params},\mathcal{A}}(1^\lambda)$ *as in Fig. 2. The* $\mathsf{LLWE}_{\mathsf{params}}$ *assumption states that for any PPT $\mathcal{A}$, it holds that*

$$\left|\Pr[\mathsf{Exp\text{-}LLWE}^0_{\mathsf{params},\mathcal{A}}(1^\lambda) = 1] - \Pr[\mathsf{Exp\text{-}LLWE}^1_{\mathsf{params},\mathcal{A}}(1^\lambda) = 1]\right| \leq \mathsf{negl}(\lambda).$$

$\mathsf{Exp\text{-}LWE}^b_{\mathsf{params},\mathcal{A}}(1^\lambda)$	$\mathsf{Exp\text{-}LLWE}^b_{\mathsf{params},\mathcal{A}}(1^\lambda)$
$\mathbf{A} \leftarrow\$ \mathcal{R}_q^{n\times m}$	$\mathbf{A} \leftarrow\$ \mathcal{R}_q^{n\times m}$
$\mathbf{s} \leftarrow\$ \mathcal{R}_q^n, \mathbf{e} \leftarrow \mathcal{E}$	$(\mathbf{L}, \mathsf{state}) \leftarrow \mathcal{A}_0(\mathbf{A})$ // assert $\mathbf{L} \in \mathcal{L}$
if $b = 0$ **then** $\mathbf{b}^\top := \mathbf{s}^\top\mathbf{A} + \mathbf{e}^\top \bmod q$	$\mathbf{s} \leftarrow\$ \mathcal{R}_q^n, \mathbf{e} \leftarrow \mathcal{E}, \mathbf{f} \leftarrow \mathcal{F}$
if $b = 1$ **then** $\mathbf{b} \leftarrow\$ \mathcal{R}_q^m$	**if** $b = 0$ **then** $\mathbf{b}^\top := \mathbf{s}^\top\mathbf{A} + \mathbf{e}^\top \bmod q$
return $b' \leftarrow \mathcal{A}(\mathbf{A}, \mathbf{b})$	**if** $b = 1$ **then** $\mathbf{b} \leftarrow\$ \mathcal{R}_q^m$
	$\mathbf{l}^\top := \mathbf{e}^\top\mathbf{L} + \mathbf{f}^\top$
	return $b' \leftarrow \mathcal{A}_1(\mathbf{b}, \mathbf{l}, \mathsf{state})$

Fig. 2. The security experiments $\mathsf{Exp\text{-}LWE}^b_{\mathsf{params},\mathcal{A}}(1^\lambda)$ and $\mathsf{Exp\text{-}LLWE}^b_{\mathsf{params},\mathcal{A}}(1^\lambda)$.

Lemma 4 (Hardness of LLWE [27, Theorem 3]). *Let* $\mathsf{params}^* = (\mathcal{R}, n, m, q, \mathcal{E}^*)$, $\mathsf{params} = (\mathcal{R}, n, m, q, Q, \mathcal{E}, \mathcal{F}, \mathcal{L})$, *and* ϵ *be such that all constraints in the following condition are satisfied:*

- $\mathcal{E}^* = \mathcal{D}^m_{\mathcal{R},\sigma^*}$, $\mathcal{E} = \mathcal{D}^m_{\mathcal{R},\sigma}$, *and* $\mathcal{F} = \mathcal{D}_{\mathcal{R},\sigma'}$, *where* $\sigma^*, \sigma, \sigma' \in \mathbb{R}$,
- $\sigma^* \geq \sqrt{2}\eta_\epsilon(\mathcal{R}^m)$,
- $\mathcal{L} :- \left\{\mathbf{L} \in \mathcal{R}^{m\times Q} : \|\mathbf{L}^\top\mathbf{L}\| \leq \sigma'^2 \cdot \left((2\eta_\epsilon(\mathcal{R}^{n+m})^2 + (\sigma^*)^2)^{-1} - \sigma^{-2}\right)\right\}$.

Then, for any PPT adversary $\mathcal{A}$, *there exists a PPT adversary* $\mathcal{B}$ *such that*

$$\mathsf{Adv}^{\mathsf{LWE}}_{\mathsf{params}^*,\mathcal{B}}(\lambda) \geq \mathsf{Adv}^{\mathsf{LLWE}}_{\mathsf{params},\mathcal{A}}(\lambda) - 4\epsilon/(1-\epsilon).$$

5.2 Lattice-Based dLE Scheme

Our dLE scheme is syntactically built upon the laconic encryption scheme of Döttling et al. [13]. Let $n, m, \bar{m}, q \in \mathbb{N}$ and $\sigma, \sigma', \bar{\sigma} \in \mathbb{R}$ be parametrized by λ (Fig. 3).

Correctness, Completeness, and Compactness. Our dLE scheme inherits correctness directly from the LE scheme in [13].

Theorem 5 (Correctness). *If* $q > 2\sqrt{\lambda}(\sigma' + 2\ell m\gamma_{\mathcal{R}}\sigma + \bar{m}\gamma_{\mathcal{R}}\bar{\sigma}) + 1$, *our dLE scheme is correct.*

Proof. Observe that the decryption is correct whenever

$$\mathsf{noise} := \left| e' - \sum_{j=0}^{\ell-1} \mathbf{e}_j^\top \begin{pmatrix} \mathbf{u}_{\mathsf{id}_{1:j}\|0} \\ \mathbf{u}_{\mathsf{id}_{1:j}\|1} \end{pmatrix} - \mathbf{e}_\ell^\top \mathbf{x} \right| < \frac{q-1}{4}.$$

By Lemma 3, with probability $1 - \mathsf{negl}(\lambda)$, we have $|e'| \leq \frac{\sqrt{\lambda}}{2}\sigma'$, $\|\mathbf{e}_j\| \leq \frac{\sqrt{\lambda}}{2}\sigma$ for all $j \in [0, \ell-1]$, and $\|\mathbf{e}_\ell\| \leq \frac{\sqrt{\lambda}}{2}\bar{\sigma}$. Since $\|\mathbf{x}\| \leq 1$ and $\left\|\mathbf{u}_{\mathsf{id}_{1:j}\|b}\right\| \leq 1$ for all $j \in [\ell-1]$ and $b \in \{0,1\}$, we have $\mathsf{noise} \leq \frac{\sqrt{\lambda}}{2}(\sigma' + 2\ell m\gamma_{\mathcal{R}}\sigma + \bar{m}\gamma_{\mathcal{R}}\bar{\sigma}) < \frac{q-1}{4}$ with probability $1 - \mathsf{negl}(\lambda)$. □

$\mathsf{Setup}(1^\lambda, 1^\ell) \to (\mathsf{crs}, \mathsf{dig}, \mathsf{st})$:

$\mathbf{A}_0, \mathbf{A}_1 \leftarrow\$ \mathcal{R}_q^{n\times m}$, $\mathbf{B} \leftarrow\$ \mathcal{R}_q^{n\times \bar{m}}$
$\mathbf{y}_\epsilon := \mathbf{y}^* \leftarrow\$ \mathcal{R}_q^n$
$\mathsf{crs} := (\ell, \mathbf{A}_0, \mathbf{A}_1, \mathbf{B}, \mathbf{y}^*)$, $\mathsf{dig} := \mathbf{y}_\epsilon$
$\mathsf{st} := (\mathcal{T} := \{\epsilon\}, \{\mathbf{y}_v\}_{v\in\mathcal{T}})$
return $(\mathsf{crs}, \mathsf{dig}, \mathsf{st})$

$\mathsf{KGen}(\mathsf{crs}) \to (\mathsf{sk}, \mathsf{pk})$:

$\mathbf{x} \leftarrow\$ \mathcal{R}_2^{\bar{m}}$, $\mathbf{y} := \mathbf{B}\mathbf{x} \bmod q$
return $(\mathsf{sk}, \mathsf{pk}) := (\mathbf{x}, \mathbf{y})$

$\mathsf{IsValid}(\mathsf{crs}, \mathsf{pk}) \to b$:

if $\mathbf{y} \in \mathcal{R}_q^n$ **then return** 1
else return 0

$\mathsf{MemUpd}^{[\mathsf{st}]}(\mathsf{crs}, \mathsf{dig}, \mathsf{id}, \mathsf{pk}) \to \mathsf{dig}$:

$\mathcal{T} := \mathcal{T} \cup \{\mathsf{id}\}$
for $j = \ell-1, \ldots, 0$ **do**
  if $(\mathsf{id}_{1:j}\|0) \notin \mathcal{T} \wedge (\mathsf{id}_{1:j}\|1) \notin \mathcal{T}$ **then** $\mathcal{T} := \mathcal{T} \setminus \{\mathsf{id}_{1:j}\}$
  else
    if $(\mathsf{id}_{1:j}\|\bar{\mathsf{id}}_{j+1}) \notin \mathcal{T}$ **then** $\mathbf{y}_{\mathsf{id}_{1:j}\|\bar{\mathsf{id}}_{j+1}} := \mathbf{y}^*$
    $\mathbf{u}_{\mathsf{id}_{1:j}\|0} := -\mathbf{G}^{-1}(\mathbf{y}_{\mathsf{id}_{1:j}\|0})$, $\mathbf{u}_{\mathsf{id}_{1:j}\|1} := -\mathbf{G}^{-1}(\mathbf{y}_{\mathsf{id}_{1:j}\|1})$
    $\mathcal{T} := \mathcal{T} \cup \{\mathsf{id}_{1:j}\}$
    $\mathbf{y}_{\mathsf{id}_{1:j}} := \mathbf{A}_0\mathbf{u}_{\mathsf{id}_{1:j}\|0} + \mathbf{A}_1\mathbf{u}_{\mathsf{id}_{1:j}\|1} \bmod q$
return $\mathsf{dig} := \mathbf{y}_\epsilon$

$\mathsf{Enc}(\mathsf{crs}, \mathsf{dig}, \mathsf{id}, \mathsf{m}) \to \mathsf{ct} = (\mathsf{ct}^{\mathsf{ind}}, \mathsf{ct}^{\mathsf{dep}})$:

$\mathbf{r}_0, \ldots, \mathbf{r}_\ell \leftarrow\$ \mathcal{R}_q^n$
$\mathbf{e}_0, \ldots, \mathbf{e}_{\ell-1} \leftarrow \mathcal{D}_{\mathcal{R},\sigma}^{2m}$
$\mathbf{e}_\ell \leftarrow \mathcal{D}_{\bar{\sigma}}^{\bar{m}}$
$\mathsf{r}^{\mathsf{ind}} := (\mathbf{r}_0, \ldots, \mathbf{r}_\ell, \mathbf{e}_0, \ldots, \mathbf{e}_\ell)$
$\mathsf{ct}^{\mathsf{ind}} := \mathsf{Enc}^{\mathsf{ind}}(\mathsf{crs}, \mathsf{id}; \mathsf{r}^{\mathsf{ind}})$
$\mathsf{r}^{\mathsf{dep}} := e' \leftarrow \mathcal{D}_{\mathcal{R},\sigma'}$
$\mathsf{ct}^{\mathsf{dep}} := \mathsf{Enc}^{\mathsf{dep}}(\mathsf{crs}, \mathsf{dig}, \mathsf{id}, \mathsf{m}; \mathsf{r}^{\mathsf{ind}}, \mathsf{r}^{\mathsf{dep}})$
return $\mathsf{ct} := (\mathsf{ct}^{\mathsf{ind}}, \mathsf{ct}^{\mathsf{dep}})$

$\mathsf{Enc}^{\mathsf{ind}}(\mathsf{crs}, \mathsf{id}; \mathsf{r}^{\mathsf{ind}})$

for $j = 0, \ldots, \ell-1$ **do**
  $\mathbf{B}_j := \begin{pmatrix} \mathbf{A}_0 & \mathbf{A}_1 \\ \bar{\mathsf{id}}_{j+1}\cdot\mathbf{G} & \mathsf{id}_{j+1}\cdot\mathbf{G} \end{pmatrix}$
  $\mathbf{c}_j^\top := (\mathbf{r}_j^\top, \mathbf{r}_{j+1}^\top)\mathbf{B}_j + \mathbf{e}_j^\top \bmod q$
$\mathbf{c}_\ell^\top := \mathbf{r}_\ell^\top\mathbf{B} + \mathbf{e}_\ell^\top \bmod q$
return $\mathsf{ct}^{\mathsf{ind}} := (\mathbf{c}_0, \ldots, \mathbf{c}_\ell)$

$\mathsf{Enc}^{\mathsf{dep}}(\mathsf{crs}, \mathsf{dig}, \mathsf{id}, \mathsf{m}; \mathsf{r}^{\mathsf{ind}}, \mathsf{r}^{\mathsf{dep}})$

$d := \mathbf{r}_0^\top\mathbf{y}_\epsilon + e' + \lfloor q/2 \rfloor \cdot \mathsf{m} \bmod q$
return $\mathsf{ct}^{\mathsf{ind}} := d$

$\mathsf{WGen}^{\mathsf{st}}(\mathsf{crs}, \mathsf{dig}, \mathsf{id}, \mathsf{pk}) \to \mathsf{wit}$:

for $j = \ell-1, \ldots, 0$ **do**
  $\mathbf{u}_{\mathsf{id}_{1:j}\|0} := -\mathbf{G}^{-1}(\mathbf{y}_{\mathsf{id}_{1:j}\|0})$
  $\mathbf{u}_{\mathsf{id}_{1:j}\|1} := -\mathbf{G}^{-1}(\mathbf{y}_{\mathsf{id}_{1:j}\|1})$
return $\mathsf{wit} := (\mathbf{u}_{\mathsf{id}_{1:j}\|0}, \mathbf{u}_{\mathsf{id}_{1:j}\|1})_{j=0}^{\ell-1}$

$\mathsf{Dec}(\mathsf{sk}, \mathsf{wit}, \mathsf{ct}) \to \mathsf{m}'$:

$\mathbf{c}_{\mathsf{id}}^\top := \sum_{j=0}^{\ell-1} \mathbf{c}_j^\top \begin{pmatrix} \mathbf{u}_{\mathsf{id}_{1:j}\|0} \\ \mathbf{u}_{\mathsf{id}_{1:j}\|1} \end{pmatrix}$
$\mu := d - \mathbf{c}_{\mathsf{id}}^\top - \mathbf{c}_\ell^\top\mathbf{x} \bmod q$
return $\mathsf{m}' := \mathsf{Decode}(\mu)$

Fig. 3. Construction of lattice-based dLE.

We then show the completeness and compactness of our dLE scheme.

Theorem 6 (Completeness). *Our dLE scheme is complete.*

Proof. Completeness holds since $\mathsf{IsValid}$ always outputs 1 on all public keys $\mathsf{pk} \in \mathcal{R}_q^n$. By construction, the public keys output by KGen are in $\mathcal{R}_q^n$. □

Theorem 7 (Compactness). *If $q = O(\ell)$, our dLE scheme is compact.*

Proof. By construction, we have $\mathsf{dig} \in \mathcal{R}_q^n$, $\mathsf{wit} \in (\mathcal{R}_2^m)^{2\ell}$, $\mathsf{ct}^{\mathsf{ind}} \in \mathcal{R}_q^{2m\ell+\bar{m}}$, and $\mathsf{ct}^{\mathsf{dep}} \in \mathcal{R}_q$. If $q = O(\ell)$, then we have $|\mathsf{dig}| = \mathsf{poly}(\lambda, \log \ell)$, $|\mathsf{wit}| = \mathsf{poly}(\lambda, \ell)$, $|\mathsf{ct}^{\mathsf{ind}}| = \mathsf{poly}(\lambda, \ell)$, and $|\mathsf{ct}^{\mathsf{dep}}| = \mathsf{poly}(\lambda, \log \ell)$. Thus, our dLE scheme is compact. □

Multi-digest Security. We show the multi-digest security of our dLE scheme.

Theorem 8 (Multi-Digest Security). *Let $\bar{m} \geq n \cdot \lceil \log q \rceil + \omega(\log \lambda)$ and $L = \mathsf{poly}(\lambda)$. Further let $\mathsf{params} = (\mathcal{R}, n, 2m, q, 1, \mathcal{D}_{\mathcal{R},\sigma}^{2m}, \mathcal{D}_{\mathcal{R},\sigma'}, \mathcal{L})$ and $\mathsf{params}' = (\mathcal{R}, n, \bar{m} + L, q, \mathcal{D}_{\mathcal{R},\bar{\sigma}}^{\bar{m}})$ be parametrized by λ, where $\mathcal{L} = \{\mathbf{l} \in \mathcal{R}^{2mm} : \|\mathbf{l}\|_2 \leq \sqrt{(2\ell m + \bar{m}) \deg_{\mathcal{R}}}\}$. If the $\mathsf{LLWE}_{\mathsf{params}}$ and $\mathsf{LWE}_{\mathsf{params}'}$ assumptions hold, our dLE scheme is L-digest secure.*

Proof. First, we will briefly explain the difference in the proof in [13]. Unlike the proof for a single digest, we introduce sets of time indices, $\{\mathcal{H}_i\}$, and adopt a method that sequentially isolates multiple $\mathsf{ct}^{\mathsf{dep}} = d$ from the outside in according to the path's branching depth. This allows us to sequentially randomize each digest-dependent part while maintaining correlation with $\mathbf{r}_0$.

Let $\mathsf{ctr} \in \mathbb{N}$ be the counter when the adversary $\mathcal{A}$ makes the challenge query. We assume that $\mathcal{A}$ specifies an index $\mathsf{id}^* = (\mathsf{id}_1^*, \ldots, \mathsf{id}_\ell^*) \in \{0,1\}^\ell$, a pair of messages $\mathsf{m}_0^*, \mathsf{m}_1^* \in \mathcal{M}$, and L time indices $t_1, \ldots, t_L \in [\mathsf{ctr}]$. For $l \in [L]$, let $\mathsf{dig}_{t_l} = \mathbf{y}_{\epsilon,l}$ be the t_l-th root node, let $\mathsf{st}_{t_l} = (\mathcal{T}_l, \{\mathbf{y}_{v,l}\}_{v \in \mathcal{T}_l})$ be the t_l-th tree, and let $k_l \in [0, \ell]$ be such that $\mathsf{id}_{1:k_l}^*$ is a leaf node in the t_l-th tree for which $\mathcal{A}$ does not have a corresponding preimage. Furthermore, we denote $\mathbf{y}_{i,l}^* = \mathbf{y}_{\mathsf{id}_{1:i}^*,l}$ at the nodes $\mathsf{id}_{1:1}^*, \ldots, \mathsf{id}_{1:i}^*$ in t_l-th tree. Finally, we consider $L' (\leq L)$ sets $\mathcal{H}_1, \ldots, \mathcal{H}_{L'} \subseteq [L]$ satisfying the following conditions:

1. For any $i \subset [L']$ and any $h, h' \in \mathcal{H}_i$, we have $k_h - k_{h'}$.
2. For any $i, i' \subset [L']$ with $i < i'$, any $h \in \mathcal{H}_i$, and any $h' \in \mathcal{H}_{i'}$, we have $k_h < k_{h'}$.

In the following, let $\mathsf{ct}^* = (\mathbf{c}_0, \ldots, \mathbf{c}_{\ell-1}, \mathbf{c}_\ell, d_1, \ldots, d_L)$ be the challenge ciphertext. Consider the following hybrids:

– $\mathsf{Hyb}_0 (= \mathsf{Sec}_{\Pi,\mathcal{A}}^0(1^\lambda, 1^\ell))$: In this hybrid, ct^* is computed as follows:

$$\mathbf{c}_j^\top = \mathbf{r}_j^\top (\mathbf{A}_0 \; \mathbf{A}_1) + \mathbf{r}_{j+1}^\top (\bar{\mathsf{id}}_{j+1}^* \cdot \mathbf{G} \; \mathsf{id}_{j+1}^* \cdot \mathbf{G}) + \mathbf{e}_j^\top, \quad \forall j \in [0, \ell-1], \quad (3)$$
$$\mathbf{c}_\ell^\top = \mathbf{r}_\ell^\top \mathbf{B} + \mathbf{e}_\ell^\top,$$
$$d_l = \mathbf{r}_0^\top \mathbf{y}_{\epsilon,l} + e_l' + \lfloor q/2 \rfloor \cdot \mathsf{m}_0^*, \; \forall l \in [L].$$

- $\mathsf{Hyb}_{1,i}$ for $i = 1, \ldots, L'$: Let $k = k_h$ for some $h \in \mathcal{H}_i$. In this hybrid, we sample $\mathbf{c}_0, \ldots, \mathbf{c}_{k-1} \leftarrow_{\$} \mathcal{R}_q^{2m}$ and $\mathbf{e}_0, \ldots, \mathbf{e}_{k-1} \leftarrow \mathcal{D}_{\mathcal{R},\sigma}^{2m}$ and set

$$d_l = \begin{cases} d \leftarrow_{\$} \mathcal{R}_q, & \text{if } l \in \bigcup_{j=1}^{i-1} \mathcal{H}_j \\ \sum_{j=0}^{k-1} (\mathbf{c}_j - \mathbf{e}_j)^\top \mathbf{z}_{j,l} + \mathbf{r}_k^\top \mathbf{y}_{k,l}^* + e_l' + \lfloor q/2 \rfloor \cdot \mathsf{m}_0^*, & \text{if } l \in \mathcal{H}_i, \\ \sum_{j=0}^{k} (\mathbf{c}_j - \mathbf{e}_j)^\top \mathbf{z}_{j,l} + \mathbf{r}_{k+1}^\top \mathbf{y}_{k+1,l}^* + e_l' + \lfloor q/2 \rfloor \cdot \mathsf{m}_0^*, & \text{if } l \in \bigcup_{j=i+1}^{L'} \mathcal{H}_j, \end{cases}$$

where $\mathbf{z}_{j,l} = \begin{pmatrix} \mathbf{u}_{\mathsf{id}_{1:j}^* \| 0, l} \\ \mathbf{u}_{\mathsf{id}_{1:j}^* \| 1, l} \end{pmatrix} \in \mathcal{R}_2^{2m}$. Then, we compute $\mathbf{c}_k, \ldots, \mathbf{c}_\ell$ as in Eq. 3.

  In this hybrid, d_l for $l \in \bigcup_{j=1}^{i-1} \mathcal{H}_j$ has already randomized, whereas d_l for $l \in \bigcup_{j=i+1}^{L'} \mathcal{H}_j$ are still calculated to maintains consistency with the common $\mathbf{c}_0, \ldots, \mathbf{c}_k$. This structure enables the elimination of the influence of the shared randomness $\mathbf{r}_0$ one by one.
- $\mathsf{Hyb}_{2,i}$ for $i = 1, \ldots, L'$: Let $k = k_h$ for some $h \in \mathcal{H}_i$. In this hybrid, we uniformly randomly sample $\mathbf{c}_k$ from $\mathcal{R}_q^{2m}$ if $k \neq \ell$, and from $\mathcal{R}_q^{\bar{m}}$ if $k = \ell$, and $d_l \leftarrow_{\$} \mathcal{R}_q$ for all $l \in \mathcal{H}_i$.
- $\mathsf{Hyb}_3 (= \mathsf{Sec}_{\Pi,\mathcal{A}}^1(1^\lambda, 1^\ell))$: This hybrid is the same as Hyb_0 except that d_l for all $l \in [L]$ is computed as $d_l = \mathbf{r}_0^\top \mathbf{y}_{\epsilon,l} + e_l' + \lfloor q/2 \rfloor \cdot \mathsf{m}_1^*$.

To complete the proof, we prove the following lemmas. □

Lemma 5. *If the* $\mathsf{LLWE}_{\mathsf{params}}$ *assumption holds, it holds that* $\mathsf{Hyb}_0 \approx_c \mathsf{Hyb}_{1,1}$.

Proof. This can be proved in the same way as the proof of [13, Lemma 3]. □

Lemma 6. *Let* $\bar{m} \geq n \cdot \lceil \log q \rceil + \omega(\log \lambda)$. *If the* $\mathsf{LWE}_{\mathsf{params}'}$ *assumption holds, it holds that* $\mathsf{Hyb}_{1,i} \approx_c \mathsf{Hyb}_{2,i}$ *for all* $i \in [L']$.

Proof. This can be proved in the same way as the proof of [13, Lemma 4]. □

Lemma 7. *If the* $\mathsf{LLWE}_{\mathsf{params}}$ *assumption holds, it holds that* $\mathsf{Hyb}_{2,i} \approx_c \mathsf{Hyb}_{1,i+1}$ *for all* $i \in [L']$.

Proof. This can be proved in the same way as the proof of [13, Lemma 3]. □

Lemma 8. *Let* $\bar{m} \geq n \cdot \lceil \log q \rceil + \omega(\log \lambda)$. *If the* $\mathsf{LLWE}_{\mathsf{params}}$ *and* $\mathsf{LWE}_{\mathsf{params}'}$ *assumptions hold, it holds that* $\mathsf{Hyb}_{2,L'} \approx_c \mathsf{Hyb}_3$.

Proof. This can be proved by applying Lemmata 5 to 7 in reverse order. □

5.3 Efficiency and Comparison

Our RBE construction of Sect. 4.1 can be instantiated with our dLE scheme of Sect. 5.2. Here, we discuss the efficiency of this concrete instantiation and compare it to existing schemes.

The ciphertext size of our dLE scheme is $|\mathsf{ct}^{\mathsf{ind}}| = (2m\ell + \bar{m}) \cdot |\mathcal{R}_q|$ and $|\mathsf{ct}^{\mathsf{dep}}| = |\mathcal{R}_q|$. Combined with Eq. 2, we achieve the following ciphertext size:

$$|\mathsf{ct}| = \lceil \log N \rceil + |\mathsf{ct}^{\mathsf{ind}}| + \mathsf{hw}(N) \cdot |\mathsf{ct}^{\mathsf{dep}}| = \lceil \log N \rceil + (2\,m\ell + \bar{m} + \mathsf{hw}(N)) \cdot |\mathcal{R}_q|$$

where N is the number of currently registered users. The last inequality is an equality if and only if $N = 2^{\kappa} - 1$ for some $\kappa \in \mathbb{N}$. In most cases, $\mathsf{hw}(N)$ is strictly less than $\lceil \log N \rceil$. The case $N = 2^{\kappa}$ is of particular note. In this case, $\mathsf{hw}(N) = 1$ and the ciphertext size achieves $|\mathsf{ct}| = \kappa + (2m\ell + \bar{m} + 1) \cdot |\mathcal{R}_q|$ This is the same size as the dLE ciphertext except for the overhead of κ bits.

We provide a comparison of ciphertext sizes for (M)LWE-based RBE schemes in Table 2. For the concrete comparison in Table 1, we chose the following parameters with reference to [13]: $\mathcal{R}_q = \mathbb{Z}_q[X]/(X^{256} + 1)$ and $(\log q, n, m, \bar{m}, \ell) = (58, 4, 232, 512, 256)$.

Table 2. A comparison of ciphertext sizes for (M)LWE-based RBE schemes.

	Ciphertext size
[13]	$(n + 4m\ell + 2\bar{m} + 2) \cdot \lceil \log N \rceil \cdot |\mathcal{R}_q|$
[15]	$(n + 8(2m(\log N_{\max} + 1)) + \bar{m} + 1) \cdot \lceil \log N \rceil \cdot |\mathcal{R}_q|$
Ours	$\lceil \log N \rceil + (2m\ell + \bar{m} + \mathsf{hw}(N)) \cdot |\mathcal{R}_q|$

Acknowledgments. This work was supported by JSPS KAKENHI Grant Number JP25K21197 and JST K Program Grant Number JPMJKP24U2, Japan.

References

1. Abram, D., Malavolta, G., Roy, L.: Key-homomorphic computations for RAM: fully succinct randomised encodings and more. In: Kalai, Y.T., Kamara, S.F. (eds.) CRYPTO 2025, Part III. LNCS, vol. 16002, pp. 236–268. Springer, Cham (2025). https://doi.org/10.1007/978-3-032-01881-6_8
2. Albrecht, M.R., Lai, R.W.F.: Subtractive sets over cyclotomic rings - limits of Schnorr-like arguments over lattices. In: Malkin, T., Peikert, C. (eds.) CRYPTO 2021, Part II. LNCS, vol. 12826, pp. 519–548. Springer, Cham (2021). https://doi.org/10.1007/978-3-030-84245-1_18
3. Alwen, J., Hartmann, D., Kiltz, E., Mularczyk, M., Schwabe, P.: Post-quantum multi-recipient public key encryption. In: Meng, W., Jensen, C.D., Cremers, C., Kirda, E. (eds.) ACM CCS 2023, pp. 1108–1122. ACM Press (2023). https://doi.org/10.1145/3576915.3623185

4. Asano, K., Attrapadung, N., Hara, K., Hashimoto, K., Watanabe, Y.: Key revocation in registered attribute-based encryption. In: Jager, T., Pan, J. (eds.) PKC 2025, Part III. LNCS, vol. 15676, pp. 102–133. Springer, Cham (2025). https://doi.org/10.1007/978-3-031-91826-1_4
5. Attrapadung, N., Tomida, J.: A modular approach to registered ABE for unbounded predicates. In: Reyzin, L., Stebila, D. (eds.) CRYPTO 2024, Part III. LNCS, vol. 14922, pp. 280–316. Springer, Cham (2024). https://doi.org/10.1007/978-3-031-68382-4_9
6. Boneh, D., Franklin, M.K.: Identity-based encryption from the Weil pairing. In: Kilian, J. (ed.) CRYPTO 2001. LNCS, vol. 2139, pp. 213–229. Springer, Heidelberg (2001). https://doi.org/10.1007/3-540-44647-8_13
7. Boudgoust, K., Jeudy, C., Roux-Langlois, A., Wen, W.: Towards classical hardness of module-LWE: the linear rank case. In: Moriai, S., Wang, H. (eds.) ASIACRYPT 2020, Part II. LNCS, vol. 12492, pp. 289–317. Springer, Cham (2020). https://doi.org/10.1007/978-3-030-64834-3_10
8. Branco, P., Lai, R.W.F., Maitra, M., Malavolta, G., Rahimi, A., Woo, I.K.Y.: Traitor tracing without trusted authority from registered functional encryption. In: Chung, K.M., Sasaki, Y. (eds.) ASIACRYPT 2024, Part III. LNCS, vol. 15486, pp. 33–66. Springer, Singapore (2024). https://doi.org/10.1007/978-981-96-0891-1_2
9. Champion, J., Hsieh, Y.C., Wu, D.J.: Registered ABE and adaptively-secure broadcast encryption from succinct LWE. In: Kalai, Y.T., Kamara, S.F. (eds.) CRYPTO 2025, Part III, LNCS, vol. 16002, pp. 3–34. Springer, Cham (2025). https://doi.org/10.1007/978-3-032-01881-6_1
10. Chiku, S., Hara, K., Hashimoto, K., Tomita, T., Shikata, J.: How to apply Fujisaki-Okamoto transformation to registration-based encryption. In: Kohlweiss, M., Di Pietro, R., Beresford, A.R. (eds.) CANS 2024, Part II. LNCS, vol. 14906, pp. 145–165. Springer, Singapore (2024). https://doi.org/10.1007/978-981-97-8016-7_7
11. Cong, K., Eldefrawy, K., Smart, N.P.: Optimizing registration based encryption. In: Paterson, M.B. (ed.) 18th IMA International Conference on Cryptography and Coding. LNCS, vol. 13129, pp. 129–157. Springer, Cham (2021). https://doi.org/10.1007/978-3-030-92641-0_7
12. Datta, P., Pal, T., Yamada, S.: Registered FE beyond predicates: (attribute-based) linear functions and more. In: Chung, K.M., Sasaki, Y. (eds.) ASIACRYPT 2024, Part I. LNCS, vol. 15484, pp. 65–104. Springer, Singapore (2024). https://doi.org/10.1007/978-981-96-0875-1_3
13. Döttling, N., Kolonelos, D., Lai, R.W.F., Lin, C., Malavolta, G., Rahimi, A.: Efficient laconic cryptography from learning with errors. In: Hazay, C., Stam, M. (eds.) EUROCRYPT 2023, Part III. LNCS, vol. 14006, pp. 417–446. Springer, Cham (2023). https://doi.org/10.1007/978-3-031-30620-4_14
14. Dujmovic, J., Malavolta, G., Qi, W.: Registration-based encryption in the plain model. In: Jager, T., Pan, J. (eds.) PKC 2025, Part I. LNCS, vol. 15674, pp. 194–226. Springer, Cham (2025). https://doi.org/10.1007/978-3-031-91820-9_7
15. Fiore, D., Kolonelos, D., de Perthuis, P.: Cuckoo commitments: registration-based encryption and key-value map commitments for large spaces. In: Guo, J., Steinfeld, R. (eds.) ASIACRYPT 2023, Part V. LNCS, vol. 14442, pp. 166–200. Springer, Singapore (2023). https://doi.org/10.1007/978-981-99-8733-7_6
16. Francati, D., Friolo, D., Maitra, M., Malavolta, G., Rahimi, A., Venturi, D.: Registered (inner-product) functional encryption. In: Guo, J., Steinfeld, R. (eds.) ASIACRYPT 2023, Part V. LNCS, vol. 14442, pp. 98–133. Springer, Singapore (2023). https://doi.org/10.1007/978-981-99-8733-7_4

17. Freitag, C., Waters, B., Wu, D.J.: How to use (plain) witness encryption: registered ABE, flexible broadcast, and more. In: Handschuh, H., Lysyanskaya, A. (eds.) CRYPTO 2023, Part IV. LNCS, vol. 14084, pp. 498–531. Springer, Cham (2023). https://doi.org/10.1007/978-3-031-38551-3_16
18. Garg, R., Lu, G., Waters, B., Wu, D.J.: Reducing the CRS size in registered ABE systems. In: Reyzin, L., Stebila, D. (eds.) CRYPTO 2024, Part III. LNCS, vol. 14922, pp. 143–177. Springer, Cham (2024). https://doi.org/10.1007/978-3-031-68382-4_5
19. Garg, S., Hajiabadi, M., Mahmoody, M., Rahimi, A.: Registration-based encryption: removing private-key generator from IBE. In: Beimel, A., Dziembowski, S. (eds.) TCC 2018, Part I. LNCS, vol. 11239, pp. 689–718. Springer, Cham (2018). https://doi.org/10.1007/978-3-030-03807-6_25
20. Garg, S., Hajiabadi, M., Mahmoody, M., Rahimi, A., Sekar, S.: Registration-based encryption from standard assumptions. In: Lin, D., Sako, K. (eds.) PKC 2019, Part II. LNCS, vol. 11443, pp. 63–93. Springer, Cham (2019). https://doi.org/10.1007/978-3-030-17259-6_3
21. Glaeser, N., Kolonelos, D., Malavolta, G., Rahimi, A.: Efficient registration-based encryption. In: Meng, W., Jensen, C.D., Cremers, C., Kirda, E. (eds.) ACM CCS 2023, pp. 1065–1079. ACM Press (2023). https://doi.org/10.1145/3576915.3616596
22. Goyal, R., Vusirikala, S.: Verifiable registration-based encryption. In: Micciancio, D., Ristenpart, T. (eds.) CRYPTO 2020. LNCS, vol. 12170, pp. 621–651. Springer, Cham (2020). https://doi.org/10.1007/978-3-030-56784-2_21
23. Hajiabadi, M., Mahmoody, M., Qi, W., Sarfaraz, S.: Lower bounds on assumptions behind registration-based encryption. In: Rothblum, G.N., Wee, H. (eds.) TCC 2023, Part II. LNCS, vol. 14370, pp. 306–334. Springer, Cham (2023). https://doi.org/10.1007/978-3-031-48618-0_11
24. Hashimoto, K., Katsumata, S., Postlethwaite, E., Prest, T., Westerbaan, B.: A concrete treatment of efficient continuous group key agreement via multi-recipient PKEs. In: Vigna, G., Shi, E. (eds.) ACM CCS 2021, pp. 1441–1462. ACM Press (2021). https://doi.org/10.1145/3460120.3484817
25. Hohenberger, S., Lu, G., Waters, B., Wu, D.J.: Registered attribute-based encryption. In: Hazay, C., Stam, M. (eds.) EUROCRYPT 2023, Part III. LNCS, vol. 14006, pp. 511–542. Springer, Cham (2023). https://doi.org/10.1007/978-3-031-30620-4_17
26. Katsumata, S., Kwiatkowski, K., Pintore, F., Prest, T.: Scalable ciphertext compression techniques for post-quantum KEMs and their applications. In: Moriai, S., Wang, H. (eds.) ASIACRYPT 2020, Part I. LNCS, vol. 12491, pp. 289–320. Springer, Cham (2020). https://doi.org/10.1007/978-3-030-64837-4_10
27. Lai, R.W.F., Swarnakar, M., Woo, I.K.Y.: Leaky LWE: learning with errors with semi-adaptive secret- and error-leakage. IACR Commun. Cryptol. **2**(3) (2025). https://doi.org/10.62056/ah89ksuc2
28. Lu, G., Waters, B., Wu, D.J.: Multi-authority registered attribute-based encryption. In: Fehr, S., Fouque, P.A. (eds.) EUROCRYPT 2025, Part III. LNCS, vol. 15603, pp. 3–33. Springer, Cham (2025). https://doi.org/10.1007/978-3-031-91131-6_1
29. Mahmoody, M., Qi, W.: Online mergers and applications to registration-based encryption and accumulators. In: Chung, K.M. (ed.) ITC 2023. LIPIcs, vol. 267, pp. 15:1–15:23. Schloss Dagstuhl (2023). https://doi.org/10.4230/LIPIcs.ITC.2023.15
30. Mahmoody, M., Qi, W., Rahimi, A.: Lower bounds for the number of decryption updates in registration-based encryption. In: Kiltz, E., Vaikuntanathan, V. (eds.)

TCC 2022, Part I. LNCS, vol. 13747, pp. 559–587. Springer, Cham (2022). https://doi.org/10.1007/978-3-031-22318-1_20
31. Micciancio, D., Peikert, C.: Trapdoors for lattices: simpler, tighter, faster, smaller. In: Pointcheval, D., Johansson, T. (eds.) EUROCRYPT 2012. LNCS, vol. 7237, pp. 700–718. Springer, Heidelberg (2012). https://doi.org/10.1007/978-3-642-29011-4_41
32. Rogaway, P.: The moral character of cryptographic work. Cryptology ePrint Archive, Report 2015/1162 (2015). https://eprint.iacr.org/2015/1162
33. Wee, H., Wu, D.J.: Unbounded distributed broadcast encryption and registered ABE from succinct LWE. In: Kalai, Y.T., Kamara, S.F. (eds.) CRYPTO 2025, Part III, LNCS, vol. 16002. pp. 204–235. Springer, Cham (2025). https://doi.org/10.1007/978-3-032-01881-6_7
34. Yang, X., Zhang, Y., Gao, Y., Chen, J.: Registered ABE for circuits from evasive lattice assumptions. Cryptology ePrint Archive (2025)
35. Zhang, Y., Chen, J., He, D., Zhang, Y.: Bounded collusion-resistant registered functional encryption for circuits. In: Chung, K.M., Sasaki, Y. (eds.) ASIACRYPT 2024, Part I, LNCS, vol. 15484, pp. 32–64. Springer, Singapore (2024). https://doi.org/10.1007/978-981-96-0875-1_2
36. Zhu, Z., Li, J., Zhang, K., Gong, J., Qian, H.: Registered functional encryptions from pairings. In: Joye, M., Leander, G. (eds.) EUROCRYPT 2024, Part II. LNCS, vol. 14652, pp. 373–402. Springer, Cham (2024). https://doi.org/10.1007/978-3-031-58723-8_13
37. Zhu, Z., Zhang, K., Chen, Z., Gong, J., Qian, H.: Black-box registered ABE from lattices. Cryptology ePrint Archive, Report 2025/051 (2025). https://eprint.iacr.org/2025/051
38. Zhu, Z., Zhang, K., Gong, J., Qian, H.: Registered ABE via predicate encodings. In: Guo, J., Steinfeld, R. (eds.) ASIACRYPT 2023, Part V. LNCS, vol. 14442, pp. 66–97. Springer, Singapore (2023). https://doi.org/10.1007/978-981-99-8733-7_3

Dynamic Puncturable Encryption

Priyanka Dutta(✉), Willy Susilo, Fuchun Guo, and Dung Hoang Duong

Institute of Cybersecurity and Cryptology, School of Computing and Information Technology, University of Wollongong, Northfields Avenue, Wollongong 2522, Australia
{pdutta,wsusilo,fuchun,hduong}@uow.edu.au

Abstract. Dynamic access control is a central requirement in modern encrypted data storage, where decryption privileges must evolve as credentials and permissions change over time. In practice, such changes are routine: users join or leave projects, roles shift, devices are replaced or lost, keys expire or are rotated, and security incidents may necessitate immediate revocation or later restoration of access. Motivated by the need for dynamic access control in encrypted data storage, we explore how to implement puncturable encryption (PE) in environments where user credentials and permissions evolve over time. PE offers a powerful fine-grained revocation functionality. By "puncturing" a secret key, one can revoke decryption capability for specific ciphertexts, enabling fine-grained access control over who can get access to which data. This capability has driven strong theoretical and practical interest since the introduction of PE. However, the existing PE and its variants fall short in dynamic environments where revocation is not always permanent. Specifically, many deployments require the ability to restore access, or to lawfully delegate decryption rights for specific ciphertexts that were previously revoked.

In this work, we bridge this gap by introducing a novel primitive Dynamic Puncturable Encryption (DPE). By "dynamicity", we mean that the system simultaneously supports user-controlled revocation of decryption, trusted authority-controlled revocation or granting of access to data, and delegation of decryption rights based on requirements, all at a finer level. Such a feature further broadens the practical applicability of the PE paradigm and allows dynamic access control. We formalize the concept of DPE, and realize it through a lattice-based construction in the standard model that ensures quantum safety.

Keywords: Updatable Ciphertext · Access Control · Revoke or Restore Decryption Capability · Learning with Errors

1 Introduction

Encryption has become the default mechanism for securing modern data storage systems. It prevents unintended disclosure of data while allowing intended

K. Jee and A. Kate (Eds.): ACNS 2026, LNCS 16571, pp. 99–130, 2027.
https://doi.org/10.1007/978-3-032-32560-0_4

users to obtain decryption capabilities to access it. In practice, decryption eligibility is governed by a trusted authority, which may be a data owner, a security administrator, or an organizational controller responsible for defining and enforcing policies or restrictions. However, such decryption rights are inherently dynamic rather than static. In real deployments, user accounts and credentials must be provisioned, updated, suspended, and revoked as individuals join or leave projects, change roles, replace or lose devices, or security incidents may require emergency revocation of access. Further, many deployments also require the ability to restore access or to lawfully delegate decryption rights for specific ciphertexts that were previously revoked. NIST[1] explicitly emphasizes these, specifically restricting access when individuals are transferred or terminated and administering accounts in a dynamic, ongoing manner. It creates a practical demand for dynamic access control over encrypted data.

In terms of access control, puncturable encryption (PE) [16], offers a compelling primitive for fine-grained revocation of decryption capabilities. By "puncturing" a secret key with a tag, one can disable decryption of ciphertexts associated with that tag, yielding a fine-grained mechanism to revoke access to selected messages without any interaction with the sender. This core functionality has proven essential for enabling forward secrecy in practical applications, most notably as a building block for forward-secret 0-RTT key exchange [8,17], a critical component in modern TLS protocols [17], secure group messaging [23], cloud email [26], secure deletion [16], etc. To broaden the applications of PE in the distributed storage systems, Derler et al. [9,11] introduced fully PE and dual-form PE, respectively. Additionally, to remove certificate repositories, Wei *et al.* [26] introduced puncturable identity-based encryption (PIBE), in which a secret key corresponding to each identity can be extracted from the master secret key, and recipients may puncture the extracted keys arbitrarily many times. Derler *et al.* [10] later formulated identity-based puncturable encryption, extending PIBE, where secret keys can be extracted not only from the master secret key but also from previously punctured secret keys. Additionally, key puncturing and key extraction can occur in any order. Further, hierarchical identity-based puncturable encryption [12], puncturable attribute-based encryption [14,22] have been introduced. To broaden the applicability of PE, puncturable proxy re-encryption [23] and puncturable identity-based proxy re-encryption [18] combine the functionalities of proxy re-encryption and PE, enabling delegation of decryption rights. However, neither approach provides a mechanism to regain decryption rights for specific ciphertexts after those rights have been revoked through puncturing.

The above limitations of variants of PE create a significant research gap. However, addressing this gap is challenging. The main hindrance to crafting this solution arises from the fundamental conflict between the fine-grained forward secrecy offered by PE and the restoration of decryption capabilities over the same encrypted data. These two features are inherently at odds because the presence of a restoration mechanism could be exploited by an attacker, thereby

[1] https://nvlpubs.nist.gov/nistpubs/SpecialPublications/NIST.SP.800-53r5.pdf.

compromising fine-grained forward secrecy. This dichotomy leads to the following challenging question: "*Can we construct a new primitive in the paradigm of* PE *for multi-user systems that supports dynamic access control for users without compromising fine-grained forward secrecy?*"

1.1 Our Contributions and Technical Overview

In this work, we answer the above question assertively by introducing Dynamic Puncturable Encryption (DPE), a novel primitive that simultaneously supports dynamic access control and provides fine-grained forward secrecy for users. Specifically, it enables controlled revocation or granting of re-access over encrypted data, and lawful delegation of decryption rights based on requirements, controlled by a trusted authority. It also supports user-controlled revocation of decryption rights at a finer level, while ensuring fine-grained forward secrecy, thereby significantly enhancing prior ideas on PE. We provide a qualitative comparison of DPE with PE schemes and their variants in Table 1.

Table 1. Qualitative Comparison with DPE

Schemes	Revocation of decryption capability	Delegation of decryption rights	Restoration of decryption capability	Dynamic Access Control
PE [16]	✓	×	×	×
PIBE, IBPE [10,13,14]	✓	×	×	×
FuPE, DFPE [9,11]	✓	×	×	×
PPRE [23]	✓	✓	×	×
PIBPRE [18]	✓	✓	×	×
DPE (Sect. 4)	✓	✓	✓	✓

PE: Puncturable Encryption; PIBE: Puncturable Identity-based Encryption; IBPE: Identity-based Puncturable Encryption; FuPE: Fully Puncturable Encryption; DFPE: Dual-form Puncturable Encryption; PPRE: Puncturable Proxy Re-encryption; PIBPRE: Puncturable Identity-based Proxy Re-encryption; DPE: Dynamic Puncturable Encryption.

To formalize DPE, we introduce a *two-layer revocation mechanism* as one of the main technical ingredients. In this approach, decryption rights are revoked through two coordinated layers of key puncturing under the control of a trusted authority, enabling selective access restoration without undermining the overall system's forward secrecy. We further introduce *dynamic tag updates* to enhance these controls by allowing ciphertexts to be re-tagged, without altering the underlying message. These enable the restoration or lawful delegation of decryption rights through information (tokens) issued by the trusted authority. In a nutshell, we define the syntax and security of DPE, and to realize it, we provide a novel construction from standard lattices that ensures quantum safety.

Formalization of Dynamic Puncturable Encryption
Formalizing DPE is subtle because it must reconcile two goals that naturally pull in opposite directions: fine-grained forward secrecy and controlled restoration of decryption capability. The technical challenge is then to let access evolve across both dimensions without creating loopholes that undo puncturing. To capture this dynamicity, we divide the lifetime of a DPE system into a polynomial number of discrete time periods and endow ciphertexts with a time period, and two types of tags, positive and negative, where a positive tag indicates permission, and a negative tag indicates denial of decryption. We resolve this tension by introducing two core technical ingredients: a *two-layer revocation mechanism* and *dynamic tag updates.*

In the *two-layer revocation mechanism*, revocation is realized via two layers of key puncturing. In the first layer, the trusted authority issues each user a secret key tied to a unique positive tag and punctured on an initial set of negative tags, enabling decryption only for ciphertexts matching the user's positive tag and negative tags distinct from those on which the key was punctured. To realize the first layer of key puncturing, we devise the KeyGen algorithm. Users may further self-revoke their access by puncturing their key on additional negative tags, as in standard PE, via the Punc algorithm. In the second layer, the trusted authority periodically publishes a time-specific period key punctured on selected positive tags, which disables decryption for those users during that period even if they retain their user keys. To realize the second layer of key puncturing, we formulate the RevAccK algorithm. We assume this time-dependent information is publicly available at the start of each period. Conceptually, we divide the power of decryption ability of the user into two key components: one key is generated for each user, and another key is generated for each time period. This key generation is carried out in a dual component-wise fashion, meaning that to decrypt or access data, a user needs both keys, provided that the user still has decryption rights after both layers of revocation.

To go beyond these revocations and to enable selective restoration and lawful delegation, we introduce *dynamic tag updates.* This allows ciphertexts to be re-tagged and/or advanced to later times without altering the underlying plaintext. These transformations are driven by time and tag-specific tokens issued by the trusted authority. We implement this mechanism by designing the Token algorithm. By updating ciphertexts using these tokens, users can regain access or get decryption rights while preserving message confidentiality. These update mechanisms are implemented by devising the UpdateCT algorithm.

Defining security for DPE, we consider the concept of indistinguishability against chosen plaintext attack (IND-CPA), and extend the selective-tag framework by having the adversary declare the challenge positive tag, negative tags, and a time period upfront. Consistent with the standard selective-tag security definition, the adversary retains the ability to learn the user keys. Furthermore, we permit the adversary to revoke positive tags of their choice, including the challenge positive tag, at any time. Notably, we permit the adversary to learn the secret key for the challenge positive tag, but only if it was revoked at the designated challenge time. As the ability to update ciphertexts and the associated concept of update tokens are not inherent to standard PE, we need to consider additional measures to ensure security guarantees. In particular, we recognize the potential risks of misuse of update tokens, such as updating ciphertexts in the reverse direction or re-updating ciphertexts that have already been updated. To protect against these risks, a secure DPE scheme must enforce that the update token can be applied to a non-updated ciphertext with a matching positive tag, thereby transforming it into an updated ciphertext. It must not allow reverse updates or repeated updates, as the ability to update an already updated ciphertext would compromise DPE security. Together, these considerations lead to our notion of IND-sDPE-CPA, providing a unified security foundation for DPE.

Lattice-Based Construction of Dynamic Puncturable Encryption
As an effort to instantiate DPE scheme, we design a lattice-based construction that is proven secure in the standard model, assuming the hardness of the Learning With Errors (LWE) problem [25]. At a high level, the design faces three intertwined challenges: (i) supporting two independent revocation mechanisms without giving any single artifact full decryption power, (ii) supporting user-side puncturing, which necessitates delegatable trapdoor structure, and (iii) enabling token-based ciphertext updates for restoration or delegation of decryption rights while preventing token misuse and related attacks. We meet these requirements through a component-wise key architecture: user keys retain a trapdoor form to enable further puncturing, yet remain insufficient on their own for decryption, while the authority publishes time-specific revocation key. This key is publicly accessible and must not possess any decryption power alone. Making these components interoperate securely is the main technical hurdle and the heart of the construction.

Our construction uses a binary tree (BT) with N leaves to manage up to N users/positive tags. Each user is assigned a leaf (positive tag) ρ, and each node θ carries an identifier $\mathbf{V}_\theta$, a user key embeds secrets for the nodes on $\mathsf{Path}(\rho)$, enabling efficient time-dependent revocation via Subset-Cover techniques. The public key include matrices $\mathbf{A}, \mathbf{D}$, while the master secret key holds trapdoors $\mathbf{T}_\mathbf{A}, \mathbf{T}_\mathbf{D}$. For each user tag ρ, we derive positive tag-specific matrices $\mathbf{A}_\rho, \mathbf{D}_\rho$ together with trapdoors. The user's secret key consists of two components. The first component relates to $\mathbf{A}_\rho$ and supports negative-tag puncturing through a key delegation technique from [4]. Importantly, it retains a trapdoor matrix form, allowing the user to puncture further later on. The second component pertains to $\mathbf{D}_\rho$, which binds the user to the tree path using the complete subtree method described in [20]. This involves sampling short vectors for the identifiers along $\mathsf{Path}(\rho)$ while linking $\mathbf{D}_\rho$ with $\mathbf{A}_\rho$. For the second revocation layer, the trusted authority periodically publishes a public revoke-access key for each time period t, and the revoked list of positive tags P_t, derived from a matrix $\mathbf{D}_t$ and the cover set $\mathsf{KUNodes}(\mathsf{BT}, \mathsf{P}_t)$. This update must be public and carry no standalone decryption power, yet must "plug into" the user's key to enable decryption, thereby capturing exactly the separation of power required by DPE.

Ciphertexts are encrypted under a positive tag ρ, a fixed-size set of negative tags, and a time period t, and consist of three components $ct = (\mathbf{c}, \mathbf{c}_{out}, \tilde{\mathbf{c}})$ that share the same randomness $\mathbf{s} \in \mathbb{Z}_q^n$. The first component binds the negative tags and time, the second component is associated with a common random matrix $\mathbf{U}$ and the message, and the third component links the positive tag with time, enabling it to interact with both revocation layers. Decryption is successful only if the user survives both revocation layers. When $\rho \notin \mathsf{P}_t$, the user combines the node in $\mathsf{Path}(\rho) \cap \mathsf{KUNodes}(\mathsf{BT}, \mathsf{P}_t)$ with the second key component to derive a transformation key. This key partially decrypts $\tilde{\mathbf{c}}$ down to an $\mathbf{A}_\rho$-bound ciphertext, which can then be fully decrypted using the first key component, provided that the user has not self-punctured the relevant negative tags.

Restoration and delegation are realized via ciphertext updates driven by the trusted authority issued tokens that are time-and-tag specific. A token can push a ciphertext from time t to $t'(> t)$ and optionally change its tags (changing the positive tag enables delegation of decryption rights; changing negative tags enables selective restoration of access). The core difficulty here is that a valid update must maintain ciphertext well-formedness while preserving the underlying plaintext and the shared randomness and without excessive noise growth. We address this with a two-part token (Δ_1, Δ_2). The first component Δ_1 updates the first part of the ciphertext to reflect the intended time and negative tags, resulting in the first part of the updated ciphertext. To generate the third part of the updated ciphertext incorporating the intended positive tag and time, we use Δ_2, which creates the third part of the updated ciphertext by taking the first and the third components of the original ciphertext as input. This process leaves the second component unchanged during the update. It is important to note that this update process maintains the common randomness. Additionally, since the randomness is represented by a uniform vector in $\mathbb{Z}_q^n$ and the encryption scheme is additively homomorphic, updated ciphertexts can be easily re-randomized.

Finally, the security reduction blends oracle-simulation ideas from lattice-based identity-based encryption [1] and key delegation technique from delegatable attribute-based encryption [4], with subtle adjustments needed to handle the two-layer revocation and token-based updates.

Organization. The rest of this paper is organized as follows. In Sect. 2, we present the formal definitions and security model of DPE. In Sect. 3, we briefly recall some background about lattices. Our lattice-based construction of DPE is described in Sect. 4 and analyzed in Sect. 5. Due to space limitations, the detailed correctness and security analysis of our lattice-based construction are deferred to the Appendix.

2 Dynamic Puncturable Encryption

We now define the syntax and security properties of DPE. As discussed in the technical overview in Sect. 1.1, formalizing DPE is subtle because it must reconcile two goals that naturally pull in opposite directions: fine-grained forward secrecy and controlled restoration of decryption capability. We address this challenge through two core components: a *two-layer revocation mechanism*, realized through the KeyGen and RevAccK algorithms, and *dynamic tag updates*, realized through the Token and UpdateCT algorithms. In addition, users may self-revoke access via the Punc algorithm. Together, these components capture the dynamic nature of the system. In this section, we make these ideas precise by defining the syntax of DPE, its correctness, and introducing the security notion IND-sDPE-CPA.

Definition 1 (DPE). *A Dynamic Puncturable Encryption scheme with a message space $\mathcal{M}$, a time space $\mathcal{T}$, a positive tag space $\mathcal{P}$, and a negative tag space $\mathcal{N}$, is a tuple of algorithms* (SetUp, KeyGen, Punc, Encrypt, RevAccK, Decrypt, Token, UpdateCT) :

- $(\mathsf{pk}, \mathsf{msk}) \leftarrow \mathsf{SetUp}(1^\lambda, d)$: *On input a security parameter λ and a maximum number of negative tags d, it outputs a public key* pk *and a master secret key* msk.
- $\mathsf{sk}_\mathsf{N}^\rho \leftarrow \mathsf{KeyGen}(\mathsf{pk}, \mathsf{msk}, \rho, \mathsf{N})$: *On input the public key* pk*, the master secret key* msk*, a positive tag $\rho \in \mathcal{P}$ and a negative tag set* N*, it outputs a punctured secret key* $\mathsf{sk}_\mathsf{N}^\rho$.[2]
- $\mathsf{sk}_{\mathsf{N}\cup\{\eta\}}^\rho \leftarrow \mathsf{Punc}(\mathsf{pk}, \mathsf{sk}_\mathsf{N}^\rho, \eta)$: *On input the public key* pk*, a punctured secret key* $\mathsf{sk}_\mathsf{N}^\rho$ *and a negative tag $\eta \in \mathcal{N}$, it outputs a new punctured secret key* $\mathsf{sk}_{\mathsf{N}\cup\{\eta\}}^\rho$.
- $ct \leftarrow \mathsf{Encrypt}(\mathsf{pk}, m, \rho, \boldsymbol{\eta}, t)$: *On input the public key* pk*, a message $m \in \mathcal{M}$, a positive tag $\rho \in \mathcal{P}$, a d-tuple of negative tags $\boldsymbol{\eta} = (\eta_1, \cdots, \eta_d) \in \mathcal{N}^d$, and a time period $t \in \mathcal{T}$, it outputs a ciphertext ct. For simplicity and wlog, we assume that $\rho, \boldsymbol{\eta}$ and t are efficiently computable from ct.*
- $\mathsf{rk}_\mathsf{P}^t \leftarrow \mathsf{RevAccK}(\mathsf{pk}, \mathsf{msk}, \mathsf{P}, t)$: *On input the public key* pk*, the master secret key* msk*, a time period t, a set of revoked positive tags* P *on time t, it outputs a revoke access key* rk_P^t.[3]
- $m/\bot \leftarrow \mathsf{Decrypt}(\mathsf{pk}, \mathsf{sk}_\mathsf{N}^{\rho'}, \mathsf{rk}_\mathsf{P}^t, ct, \rho, \boldsymbol{\eta}, t)$: *On input the public key* pk*, a secret key* $\mathsf{sk}_\mathsf{N}^{\rho'}$*, a revoke access key* rk_P^t *on time t, and a ciphertext ct with tags $\rho, \boldsymbol{\eta}$ on time t, it outputs a plaintext m or $\bot$ if decryption fails.*
- $\mathsf{tk}_{\mathcal{E}_1\to\mathcal{E}_2} \leftarrow \mathsf{Token}(\mathsf{pk}, \mathsf{msk}, \mathcal{E}_1, \mathcal{E}_2)$: *On input the public key* pk*, the master secret key* msk*, and two tuples $\mathcal{E}_1 = (\rho_1, \boldsymbol{\eta}_1, t_1)$, $\mathcal{E}_2 = (\rho_2, \boldsymbol{\eta}_2, t_2(> t_1))$ consisting of a positive tag, a d-tuple of negative tags and a time, it outputs a token* $\mathsf{tk}_{\mathcal{E}_1\to\mathcal{E}_2}$ *or $\bot$.*
- $ct' \leftarrow \mathsf{UpdateCT}(\mathsf{pk}, \mathsf{tk}_{\mathcal{E}_1\to\mathcal{E}_2}, ct, \rho_1, \boldsymbol{\eta}_1, t_1)$: *On input the public key* pk*, a token* $\mathsf{tk}_{\mathcal{E}_1\to\mathcal{E}_2}$ *with $\mathcal{E}_1 = (\rho_1, \boldsymbol{\eta}_1, t_1)$, $\mathcal{E}_2 = (\rho_2, \boldsymbol{\eta}_2, t_2(> t_1))$, and a ciphertext ct with tags ρ_1 and $\boldsymbol{\eta}_1 = (\eta_1, \cdots, \eta_d)$ on time t_1, it outputs the updated ciphertext ct' with tags ρ_2, $\boldsymbol{\eta}_2 = (\eta_1', \cdots, \eta_d')$ for time t_2 or $\bot$ indicating ct is invalid.*

---

[2] Note that we sometimes use N_ρ for $\mathsf{sk}_{\mathsf{N}_\rho}^\rho$ to specify a set of ρ-specific punctured negative tags.

[3] Note that we sometimes use P_t for $\mathsf{rk}_{\mathsf{P}_t}^t$ to specify a set of t-specific punctured positive tags.

Definition 2 (DPE Correctness). *A Dynamic Puncturable Encryption scheme* (SetUp, KeyGen, Punc, Encrypt, RevAccK, Decrypt, Token, UpdateCT) *with a message space* $\mathcal{M}$*, a time space* $\mathcal{T}$ *and a positive tag space* $\mathcal{P}$*, a negative tag space* $\mathcal{N}$*, respectively, is said to be correct if for any security parameter* $\lambda \in \mathbb{N}$*, for any* $(\mathsf{pk}, \mathsf{msk}) \leftarrow \mathsf{SetUp}(1^\lambda, d)$*, for any* $\rho' \in \mathcal{P}$*, for any* $\mathsf{N}, \mathsf{N}' \subset \mathcal{N}$*, for any* $\mathsf{sk}_{\mathsf{N}}^{\rho'} \leftarrow \mathsf{KeyGen}(\mathsf{pk}, \mathsf{msk}, \rho')$*, for any* $\eta \in \mathcal{N}$*, for any* $\mathsf{sk}_{\mathsf{N}'}^{\rho'} \leftarrow \mathsf{Punc}(\mathsf{pk}, \mathsf{sk}_{\mathsf{N}}^{\rho'}, \eta)$*, where* $\mathsf{N}' = \mathsf{N} \cup \{\eta\}$*, we require that*

1. *For any message* $m \in \mathcal{M}$*, for any* $\rho \in \mathcal{P}$*, for any d-tuple of negative tags* $\boldsymbol{\eta} = (\eta_1, \cdots, \eta_d) \in \mathcal{N}^d$*, for any time* $t \in \mathcal{T}$*, for any* $\mathsf{rk}_{\mathsf{P}}^t \leftarrow \mathsf{RevAccK}(\mathsf{pk}, \mathsf{msk}, \mathsf{P}, t)$*, the following holds.*
   - *If* $\rho \notin \mathsf{P} \ \wedge \ \rho' = \rho \ \wedge \ \mathsf{N}' \cap \{\eta_1, \cdots, \eta_d\} = \phi$,

$$\Pr\left[\begin{array}{c|c} \mathsf{Decrypt}(\mathsf{pk}, \mathsf{sk}_{\mathsf{N}'}^{\rho'}, \mathsf{rk}_{\mathsf{P}}^t, & \\ ct, \rho, \boldsymbol{\eta}, t) = m & ct \leftarrow \mathsf{Encrypt}(\mathsf{pk}, m, \rho, \boldsymbol{\eta}, t) \end{array}\right] = 1 - \mathsf{negl}(\lambda);$$

   - *If* $\rho \in \mathsf{P} \ \vee \ \rho' \neq \rho \ \vee \ \mathsf{N}' \cap \{\eta_1, \cdots, \eta_d\} \neq \phi$,

$$\Pr\left[\begin{array}{c|c} \mathsf{Decrypt}(\mathsf{pk}, \mathsf{sk}_{\mathsf{N}'}^{\rho'}, \mathsf{rk}_{\mathsf{P}}^t, & \\ ct, \rho, \boldsymbol{\eta}, t) = \perp & ct \leftarrow \mathsf{Encrypt}(\mathsf{pk}, m, \rho, \boldsymbol{\eta}, t) \end{array}\right] = 1 - \mathsf{negl}(\lambda);$$

   where $\mathsf{negl}(\cdot)$ *is a negligible function, and the probabilities are taken over the random coins of the algorithms.*
2. *For any message* $m \in \mathcal{M}$*, for any* $\rho_1, \rho_2 \in \mathcal{P}$*, for any d-tuple of negative tags* $\boldsymbol{\eta}_1 \in \mathcal{N}^d$*, and* $\boldsymbol{\eta}_2 = (\eta_1', \cdots, \eta_d') \in \mathcal{N}^d$*, for any time* $t_1, t_2 \in \mathcal{T}$*, for any* $ct \leftarrow \mathsf{Encrypt}(\mathsf{pk}, m, \rho_1, \boldsymbol{\eta}_1, t_1)$*, for any* $\mathsf{rk}_{\mathsf{P}_{t_2}}^{t_2} \leftarrow \mathsf{RevAccK}(\mathsf{pk}, \mathsf{msk}, \mathsf{P}_{t_2}, t_2)$*, the following holds.*
   - *If* $\rho_2 \notin \mathsf{P}_{t_2} \ \wedge \ \rho' = \rho_2 \ \wedge \mathsf{N}' \cap \{\eta_1', \cdots, \eta_d'\} = \phi$,

$$\Pr\left[\begin{array}{c|c} & \mathsf{tk}_{\mathcal{E}_1 \to \mathcal{E}_2} \leftarrow \mathsf{Token}(\mathsf{pk}, \mathsf{msk}, \mathcal{E}_1, \mathcal{E}_2), \\ \mathsf{Decrypt}(\mathsf{pk}, \mathsf{sk}_{\mathsf{N}'}^{\rho'}, \mathsf{rk}_{\mathsf{P}_{t_2}}^{t_2}, & \text{where } \mathcal{E}_1 = (\rho_1, \boldsymbol{\eta}_1, t_1), \\ ct', \rho_2, \boldsymbol{\eta}_2, t_2) = m & \mathcal{E}_2 = (\rho_2, \boldsymbol{\eta}_2, t_2 (> t_1)); \\ & ct' \leftarrow \mathsf{UpdateCT}(\mathsf{pk}, \mathsf{tk}_{\mathcal{E}_1 \to \mathcal{E}_2}, ct, \rho_1, \boldsymbol{\eta}_1, t_1) \end{array}\right]$$
$$= 1 - \mathsf{negl}(\lambda);$$

   - *If* $\rho_2 \in \mathsf{P}_{t_2} \ \vee \ \rho' \neq \rho_2 \ \vee \mathsf{N}' \cap \{\eta_1', \cdots, \eta_d'\} \neq \phi$,

$$\Pr\left[\begin{array}{c|c} & \mathsf{tk}_{\mathcal{E}_1 \to \mathcal{E}_2} \leftarrow \mathsf{Token}(\mathsf{pk}, \mathsf{msk}, \mathcal{E}_1, \mathcal{E}_2), \\ \mathsf{Decrypt}(\mathsf{pk}, \mathsf{sk}_{\mathsf{N}'}^{\rho'}, \mathsf{rk}_{\mathsf{P}_{t_2}}^{t_2}, & \text{where } \mathcal{E}_1 = (\rho_1, \boldsymbol{\eta}_1, t_1), \\ ct', \rho_2, \boldsymbol{\eta}_2, t_2) = \perp & \mathcal{E}_2 = (\rho_2, \boldsymbol{\eta}_2, t_2 (> t_1)); \\ & ct' \leftarrow \mathsf{UpdateCT}(\mathsf{pk}, \mathsf{tk}_{\mathcal{E}_1 \to \mathcal{E}_2}, ct, \rho_1, \boldsymbol{\eta}_1, t_1) \end{array}\right]$$
$$= 1 - \mathsf{negl}(\lambda);$$

where $\mathsf{negl}(\cdot)$ *is a negligible function, and the probabilities are taken over the random coins of the algorithms.*

Security Game of DPE for Selective Tags against Chosen Plaintext Attack (IND-sDPE-CPA): Let $\mathcal{A}$ be the PPT adversary and $\Pi =$ (SetUp, KeyGen, Punc, Encrypt, RevAccK, Decrypt, Token, UpdateCT) be a DPE scheme with a message space $\mathcal{M}$, time space $\mathcal{T}$, a positive tag space $\mathcal{P}$ and a negative tag space $\mathcal{N}$. Security game is defined according to the following game $\mathsf{Exp}_{\mathcal{A}}^{\mathsf{IND\text{-}sDPE\text{-}CPA}}(1^\lambda)$:

1. **Initial**: $\mathcal{A}$ sends the target positive tag $\rho^* \in \mathcal{P}$, the target d-tuple of negative tags $\boldsymbol{\eta}^* = (\eta_1^*, \cdots, \eta_d^*) \in \mathcal{N}^d$, and time $t^* \in \mathcal{T}$ to the challenger. Let P^* be the set of revoked positive tags at time t^*.
2. **Set Up**: The challenger runs $\mathsf{SetUp}(1^\lambda, d)$ to get $(\mathsf{pk}, \mathsf{msk})$ and give pk to $\mathcal{A}$. It initializes three empty sets $P, C, \overline{C}$ to record puncture key queries, corrupt key queries, and token queries. Also, the challenger introduces a counter numCT to 0, a key-value store $\mathcal{H}$ to be empty, and a set Derive to be empty.
3. **Query Phase 1**: The adversary $\mathcal{A}$ may make following queries polynomially many times:

- $\mathcal{Q}_{Puncture}(\rho, \eta)$: Given a positive tag $\rho \in \mathcal{P}$, a negative tag $\eta \in \mathcal{N}$, the challenger updated the negative tag set N_ρ, on which the secret key has been punctured, as $\mathsf{N}_\rho := \mathsf{N}_\rho \cup \{\eta\}$, and computes $\mathsf{sk}_{\mathsf{N}_\rho}^{\rho}$ by running $\mathsf{KeyGen}, \mathsf{Punc}$ algorithms accordingly. Update the tuple $(\rho, \mathsf{sk}_{\mathsf{N}_\rho}^{\rho}, \mathsf{N}_\rho)$ from the set P.
- $\mathcal{Q}_{Corrupt}(\rho)$: The challenger consider the following cases.

Case-1: $\rho \neq \rho^*$

- The first time the adversary issues this query for ρ, the challenger do as follows:
  - It returns $\perp$, if there was a query to $\mathcal{Q}_{RevAccK}(t, \mathsf{P}_t)$ with $\rho \notin \mathsf{P}_t$ and a token query $\mathcal{Q}_{Token}(\rho^*, \boldsymbol{\eta}^*, t^* \rightarrow \rho, \boldsymbol{\eta}, t)$, where $\boldsymbol{\eta} \cap \mathsf{N}_\rho = \phi$. Add $(\rho, \perp, \mathsf{N}_\rho)$ to the set C.
  - Otherwise, it returns the most recent secret key $\mathsf{sk}_{\mathsf{N}_\rho}^{\rho}$. Add $(\rho, \mathsf{sk}_{\mathsf{N}_\rho}^{\rho}, \mathsf{N}_\rho)$ to the set C.
- All subsequent queries for this positive tag ρ return $\perp$.

Case-2: $\rho = \rho^*$

- The first time the adversary issues this query for ρ^*, the challenger do as follows:
  - It returns $\perp$, if any of the following holds and add $(\rho^*, \perp, \mathsf{N}_{\rho^*})$ to C.
    1. $\mathsf{N}_{\rho^*} \cap \{\eta_1^*, \cdots, \eta_d^*\} = \emptyset$ and there was a query to $\mathcal{Q}_{RevAccK}(t^*, \mathsf{P}_{t^*})$ with $\rho^* \notin \mathsf{P}_{t^*}$.
    2. If there was a query to $\mathcal{Q}_{RevAccK}(t, \mathsf{P}_t)$ with $\rho^* \notin \mathsf{P}_t$ and a token query $\mathcal{Q}_{Token}(\rho^*, \boldsymbol{\eta}^*, t^* \rightarrow \rho^*, \boldsymbol{\eta}, t)$, where $\boldsymbol{\eta} \cap \mathsf{N}_{\rho^*} = \phi$.
  - Otherwise, it returns the most recent secret key $\mathsf{sk}_{\mathsf{N}_{\rho^*}}^{\rho^*}$ to the adversary. Add $(\rho^*, \mathsf{sk}_{\mathsf{N}_{\rho^*}}^{\rho^*}, \mathsf{N}_{\rho^*})$ to the set C.
- All subsequent queries for this positive tag ρ^* return $\perp$.

- $\mathcal{Q}_{RevAccK}(t, \mathsf{P}_t)$: On input time t, a list of revoked positive tags P_t, the challenger outputs the revoke access key $\mathsf{rk}_{\mathsf{P}_t}^{t}$ for time t satisfying the following.

- If there was a query to $\mathcal{Q}_{Corrupt}(\rho^*)$ with $\mathsf{N}_{\rho^*} \cap \{\eta_1^*, \cdots, \eta_d^*\} = \emptyset$, then ρ^* must be in P_{t^*}.
- If there was a query to $\mathcal{Q}_{Token}(\rho^*, \boldsymbol{\eta}^*, t^* \rightarrow \rho, \boldsymbol{\eta}, t(> t^*))$ and a corrupt query on ρ with $\mathsf{N}_\rho \cap \boldsymbol{\eta} = \phi$, then ρ must be in P_t.

Note that the adversary is allowed to query only one revoked access key at each time t. If $t = t^*$, then P^* must be a subset of the P_{t^*} at t^*.

- $\mathcal{Q}_{Token}(\mathcal{E}_1 = (\rho_1, \boldsymbol{\eta}_1, t_1) \rightarrow \mathcal{E}_2 = (\rho_2, \boldsymbol{\eta}_2, t_2))$: Given two positive tags $\rho_1, \rho_2 \in \mathcal{P}$, and two d-tuple of negative tags $\boldsymbol{\eta}_1, \boldsymbol{\eta}_2 \in \mathcal{N}^d$, and time periods $t_1, t_2(> t_1)$, the challenger consider the following two cases:
  - For $(\rho_1, \boldsymbol{\eta}_1, t_1) \neq (\rho^*, \boldsymbol{\eta}^*, t^*)$, it returns a token $\mathsf{tk}_{\mathcal{E}_1 \rightarrow \mathcal{E}_2}$ and add it to $\overline{C}$.
  - For $(\rho_1, \boldsymbol{\eta}_1, t_1) = (\rho^*, \boldsymbol{\eta}^*, t^*)$, it returns a token if there was no query to $\mathcal{Q}_{Corrupt}(\rho_2)$ with $\boldsymbol{\eta}_2 \cap \mathsf{N}_{\rho_2} = \phi$ and no $\mathcal{Q}_{RevAccK}(t_2, \mathsf{P}_{t_2})$ with $\rho_2 \notin \mathsf{P}_{t_2}$. Add token $\mathsf{tk}_{\mathcal{E}_1 \rightarrow \mathcal{E}_2}$ to $\overline{C}$. Otherwise, it returns $\perp$.

- $\mathcal{Q}_{\mathsf{Enc}}(\rho, \boldsymbol{\eta}, m, t)$: Given a positive tag ρ, a d-tuple of negative tags $\boldsymbol{\eta} = (\eta_1, \cdots, \eta_d)$, and message m, time period t, outputs ciphertext ct by running $\mathsf{Encrypt}(\cdot)$. Increment $numCt$ and add ct to the set $\mathcal{H}$ with key $(\rho, \boldsymbol{\eta}, t, numCt)$.
- $\mathcal{Q}_{\mathsf{Update}}$: Given two positive tags ρ_1, ρ_2, two d-tuple of negative tags $\boldsymbol{\eta}_1 = \{\eta_1, \cdots, \eta_d\}, \boldsymbol{\eta}_2 = \{\eta_1', \cdots, \eta_d'\}$ and key $(\rho_1, \boldsymbol{\eta}_1, t, k)$, where $k \leq numCt$, outputs $\perp$ if there is no value in $\mathcal{H}$ with key $(\rho_1, \boldsymbol{\eta}_1, t, k)$. Otherwise, let ct be that value in $\mathcal{H}$ and outputs updated ciphertext ct' by running $\mathsf{UpdateCT}(\cdot)$.

4. **Challenge**: $\mathcal{A}$ submits two messages $m_0, m_1 \in \mathcal{M}$ to the challenger. The challenger outputs a challenge ciphertext $ct_\beta \leftarrow \mathsf{Encrypt}(\mathsf{pk}, m_\beta, \rho^*, \boldsymbol{\eta}^*, t^*)$ for either $\beta = 0$ or $\beta = 1$, by choosing a random bit $\beta \in \{0, 1\}$. Increment $numCt$ and add $numCt$ to the set $Derive$. Store the value ct_β^* to the set $\mathcal{H}$ with key $(\rho^*, \boldsymbol{\eta}^*, t^*, numCt)$.
5. **Query Phase 2**: This phase is identical to **Query Phase 1**. After receiving the challenge ciphertext, $\mathcal{A}$ continues to have access to the $\mathcal{Q}_{\mathsf{Puncture}}$, $\mathcal{Q}_{\mathsf{Corrupt}}$, $\mathcal{Q}_{\mathsf{RevAccK}}$, $\mathcal{Q}_{\mathsf{Token}}$, $\mathcal{Q}_{\mathsf{Enc}}$, and $\mathcal{Q}_{\mathsf{Update}}$ as in **Query Phase 1** except the following constraints for $\mathcal{Q}_{\mathsf{Update}}$ oracle: Outputs $\perp$ if $k \in Derive$.
6. **Guess**: On input β' from $\mathcal{A}$, this oracle outputs 1 if $\beta = \beta'$ and 0 otherwise.

The advantage of an adversary in the above experiment $\mathsf{Exp}_{\mathcal{A}}^{\mathsf{IND\text{-}sDPE\text{-}CPA}}(1^\lambda)$ is defined as $|\Pr[\beta' = \beta] - \frac{1}{2}|$.

Definition 3. *A* DPE *scheme is* IND-sDPE-CPA *secure if all* PPT *adversaries* $\mathcal{A}$ *have at most a negligible advantage in experiment* $\mathsf{Exp}_{\mathcal{A}}^{\mathsf{IND\text{-}sDPE\text{-}CPA}}(1^\lambda)$.

Remark 1. To prevent the adversary $\mathcal{A}$ from trivially winning the security game, the above game has some restrictions on the corrupt queries, the revoke access key queries, and the token queries, respectively. Here, we discuss the rationale behind the conditions adopted in the security model above. Intuitively, for a

tuple $(m_0, m_1, \rho^*, \boldsymbol{\eta}^*, t^*)$ such that $m_0 \neq m_1$, issued by $\mathcal{A}$ at challenge phase to obtain the ct_β, and $\mathcal{A}$ issues some specific queries to $\mathcal{Q}_{Corrupt}$, $\mathcal{Q}_{RevAccK}$, $\mathcal{Q}_{Token}$. Then, $\mathcal{A}$ could trivially know the challenge bit β in the following two cases.
Case-1: $\mathcal{A}$ issues the query $\mathcal{Q}_{Corrupt}(\rho^*)$ and get $\mathsf{sk}^{\rho^*}_{\mathsf{N}_{\rho^*}}$ such that $\mathsf{N}_{\rho^*} \cap \boldsymbol{\eta}^* = \phi$, and the query $\mathcal{Q}_{RevAccK}(t^*, \mathsf{P}_{t^*})$, where $\rho^* \notin \mathsf{P}_{t^*}$.
Case-2: $\mathcal{A}$ issues a token query $\mathcal{Q}_{Token}(\rho^*, \boldsymbol{\eta}^*, t^* \rightarrow \rho, \boldsymbol{\eta}, t)$ and a query $\mathcal{Q}_{Corrupt}(\rho)$ and get $\mathsf{sk}^{\rho}_{\mathsf{N}_\rho}$ such that $\mathsf{N}_\rho \cap \boldsymbol{\eta} = \phi$ and the query $\mathcal{Q}_{RevAccK}(t, \mathsf{P}_t)$, where $\rho \notin \mathsf{P}_t$.

In case-1, since $\rho^* \notin \mathsf{P}_{t^*}$ and $\mathsf{N}_{\rho^*} \cap \boldsymbol{\eta}^* = \phi$, with the revoke access key for time t^* and the secret key of ρ^*, $\mathcal{A}$ can correctly decrypt the message m_β and get to know about the challenge bit β.

In case-2, since $\mathcal{A}$ has a token $\mathsf{tk} \leftarrow \mathcal{Q}_{Token}(\rho^*, \boldsymbol{\eta}^*, t^* \rightarrow \rho, \boldsymbol{\eta}, t)$, with this token tk, $\mathcal{A}$ can update the challenge ciphertext ct_β to ct'_β. Note that ct'_β is with tags $\rho, \boldsymbol{\eta}$ and time t. Since, $\mathcal{A}$ has the revoke access key for time t and the secret key of ρ satisfying $\rho \notin \mathsf{P}_t$ and $\mathsf{N}_\rho \cap \boldsymbol{\eta} = \phi$, $\mathcal{A}$ can correctly decrypt ct'_β with the revoke access key for time t and the secret key of ρ, and get to know about the message m_β, so about the challenge bit β.

In order to avoid these trivial wins, we enforced the restrictions in $\mathcal{Q}_{Corrupt}$, $\mathcal{Q}_{RevAccK}$, and $\mathcal{Q}_{Token}$.

3 Prerequisites for the Construction

We denote the real numbers and the integers by $\mathbb{R}, \mathbb{Z}$, respectively. We denote column-vectors by lower-case bold letters (e.g. $\mathbf{b}$), so row-vectors are represented via transposition (e.g. $\mathbf{b}^t$). Matrices are denoted by upper-case bold letters and treat a matrix $\mathbf{X}$ interchangeably with its ordered set $\{\mathbf{x}_1, \mathbf{x}_2, \ldots\}$ of column vectors. We use $\mathbf{I}$ for the identity matrix and $\mathbf{0}$ for the zero matrix, where the dimension will be clear from context. We use $[*|*]$ to denote the concatenation of vectors or matrices. The *statistical distance* between two distributions $\mathbf{X}$ and $\mathbf{Y}$ over a countable domain Ω defined as $\frac{1}{2}\sum_{w \in \Omega} |\Pr[\mathbf{X} = w] - \Pr[\mathbf{Y} = w]|$. We say that a distribution over Ω is ϵ-far if its statistical distance from the uniform distribution is at most ϵ.

Lattices: A *lattice* Λ is a discrete additive subgroup of $\mathbb{R}^m$. Specially, a lattice Λ in $\mathbb{R}^m$ with basis $\mathbf{B} = [\mathbf{b}_1 | \cdots | \mathbf{b}_n] \in \mathbb{R}^{m \times n}$ is defined as $\Lambda := \{\sum_{i=1}^{n} \mathbf{b}_i x_i | x_i \in \mathbb{Z}\ \forall i = 1, \ldots, n\} \subseteq \mathbb{R}^m$. We call n the rank of Λ, and if $n = m$, we say that Λ is a full rank lattice. In this paper, we mainly consider full rank lattices containing $q\mathbb{Z}^m$, called q-ary lattices, defined as: for a given matrix $\mathbf{A} \in \mathbb{Z}_q^{n \times m}$ and $\mathbf{u} \in \mathbb{Z}_q^n$, $\Lambda_q^\perp(\mathbf{A}) := \{\mathbf{z} \in \mathbb{Z}^m : \mathbf{A}\mathbf{z} = 0 \bmod q\}$; $\Lambda_q(\mathbf{A}) := \{\mathbf{z} \in \mathbb{Z}^m : \exists\ \mathbf{s} \in \mathbb{Z}_q^n\ s.t.\ \mathbf{z} = \mathbf{A}^\top \mathbf{s} \bmod q\}$; $\Lambda_q^{\mathbf{u}}(\mathbf{A}) := \{\mathbf{z} \in \mathbb{Z}^m : \mathbf{A}\mathbf{z} = \mathbf{u} \bmod q\} = \Lambda_q^\perp(\mathbf{A}) + \mathbf{x}\ for\ \mathbf{x} \in \Lambda_q^{\mathbf{u}}(\mathbf{A})\}$.

Matrix Norms: For a vector $\mathbf{u}$, we let $\|\mathbf{u}\|$ denotes its ℓ_2 norm. For a matrix $\mathbf{R} \in \mathbb{Z}^{k \times m}$, let $\widetilde{\mathbf{R}}$ be the result of applying Gram-Schmidt (GS) orthogonalization to the columns of $\mathbf{R}$. We denote three matrix norms as: $\|\mathbf{R}\|$ denotes the ℓ_2 length of the longest column of $\mathbf{R}$; $\|\mathbf{R}\|_{\text{GS}} = \|\widetilde{\mathbf{R}}\|$, where $\widetilde{\mathbf{R}}$ is the GS orthogonalization of $\mathbf{R}$; $\|\mathbf{R}\|_2$ is the operator norm of $\mathbf{R}$ defined as $\|\mathbf{R}\|_2 = \sup_{\|\mathbf{x}\|=1} \|\mathbf{R}\mathbf{x}\|$.

Gaussian on Lattices: Let $\Lambda \subseteq \mathbb{Z}^m$ be a lattice. For a vector $\mathbf{c} \in \mathbb{R}^m$ and a positive parameter $\sigma \in \mathbb{R}$, define: $\rho_{\mathbf{c},\sigma}(\mathbf{x}) = \exp\left(\pi \frac{\|\mathbf{x}-\mathbf{c}\|^2}{\sigma^2}\right)$ and $\rho_{\mathbf{c},\sigma}(\Lambda) = \sum_{\mathbf{x}\in\Lambda} \rho_{\mathbf{c},\sigma}(\mathbf{x})$. The discrete Gaussian distribution over Λ with center $\mathbf{c}$ and parameter σ is $\mathcal{D}_{\mathbf{c},\sigma}(\Lambda)(\mathbf{y}) = \frac{\rho_{\mathbf{c},\sigma}(\mathbf{y})}{\rho_{\mathbf{c},\sigma}(\Lambda)}, \forall \mathbf{y} \in \Lambda$.

Lemma 1 **([4], Lemma 2.5).** *Let $n, m, k, q, \sigma > 0$ and $\mathbf{A} \in \mathbb{Z}_q^{n\times m}, \mathbf{U} \in \mathbb{Z}_q^{n\times k}$. If $\mathbf{R} \in \mathbb{Z}^{m\times k}$ is sampled from $\mathcal{D}_\sigma(\Lambda_q^{\mathbf{U}}(\mathbf{A}))$ and $\mathbf{S}$ is sampled uniformly in $\{+1,-1\}^{m\times m}$, the followings hold with overwhelming probability in m:*

$$\|\mathbf{R}^\top\|_2 \leq \sigma\sqrt{mk}, \quad \|\mathbf{R}\|_2 \leq \sigma\sqrt{mk} \quad \textit{and} \quad \|\mathbf{S}\|_2 \leq 20\sqrt{m}.$$

Learning With Errors (LWE) **[24]:** The Learning with Errors (LWE) problem was introduced by Regev [24]. Here, we define the decisional version of LWE. The security of our scheme is based on this hardness assumption.

Definition 4 (Decisional LWE (dLWE)**).** *Consider a prime integer q, positive integers n, m, and a noise distribution χ over $\mathbb{Z}_q$. The $\mathsf{dLWE}_{n,m,q,\chi}$ problem is to distinguish the two distributions $(\mathbf{A}, \mathbf{A}^\top\mathbf{s}+\mathbf{e})$ and $(\mathbf{A}, \mathbf{u})$, where $\mathbf{A} \xleftarrow{\$} \mathbb{Z}_q^{n\times m}$, $\mathbf{s} \xleftarrow{\$} \mathbb{Z}_q^n$, $\mathbf{u} \xleftarrow{\$} \mathbb{Z}_q^m$ and $\mathbf{e} \xleftarrow{\$} \chi^m$ are sampled.*

Let the noise distribution χ is B- bounded if its support is in $[-B, B]$. For any constant $d > 0$ and sufficiently large q, Regev [24] through a quantum reduction showed that taking χ as a q/n^d-bounded discretized Gaussian distribution, the $\mathsf{dLWE}_{n,m,q,\chi}$ problem is as hard as approximating the worst-case $GapSVP$ to $n^{O(d)}$ factors, which is believed to be hard. In subsequent works, (partial) dequantization of Regev's reduction was achieved [5,21]. More generally, let $\chi_{max} < q$ be the bound on the noise distribution. The difficulty of the problem is measured by the ratio q/χ_{max}. The problem appears to remain hard even when $q/\chi_{max} < 2n^\epsilon$ for some fixed ϵ that is $0 < \epsilon < 1/2$. We refer the reader to [4,6,21,24] for more information.

Trapdoor Generators and Related Algorithms: Here, we briefly describe the properties of algorithms for generating a short basis of lattices and algorithms for finding a low-norm matrix $\mathbf{X} \in \mathbb{Z}^{m\times k}$ such that $\mathbf{AX} = \mathbf{U}$.

Lemma 2. *Let $n, m, q > 0$ be integers with q prime. There are polynomial time algorithms as follows:*

1. $(\mathbf{A}, \mathbf{T_A}) \leftarrow \mathsf{TrapGen}(1^n, 1^m, q)$ *[2,3,19]: A randomized algorithm that, when $m = \Theta(n \log q)$, outputs a full-rank matrix $\mathbf{A} \in \mathbb{Z}_q^{n\times m}$, and a basis $\mathbf{T_A} \in \mathbb{Z}^{m\times m}$ for $\Lambda_q^\perp(\mathbf{A})$ such that $\mathbf{A}$ is $\mathsf{negl}(\lambda)$-close to uniform and $\|\mathbf{T}\|_{GS} = O(\sqrt{n\log q})$ with all but negligible probability in n.*
2. $\mathbf{T}_{(\mathbf{A}|\mathbf{B})} \leftarrow \mathsf{ExtendRight}(\mathbf{A}, \mathbf{T_A}, \mathbf{B})$ *[7]: A deterministic algorithm that given full-rank matrices $\mathbf{A}, \mathbf{B} \in \mathbb{Z}_q^{n\times m}$, and a basis $\mathbf{T_A}$ of $\Lambda_q^\perp(\mathbf{A})$ outputs a basis $\mathbf{T}_{(\mathbf{A}|\mathbf{B})}$ of $\Lambda_q^\perp(\mathbf{A}|\mathbf{B})$ such that $\|\mathbf{T_A}\|_{GS} = \|\mathbf{T}_{(\mathbf{A}|\mathbf{B})}\|_{GS}$.*

3. $\mathbf{T_M} \leftarrow \mathsf{ExtendLeft}(\mathbf{A}, \mathbf{G}, \mathbf{T_G}, \mathbf{R})$, *where* $\mathbf{M} = [\mathbf{A} | \mathbf{G} + \mathbf{AR}]$ *[1]: A deterministic algorithm that given full-rank matrices* $\mathbf{A}, \mathbf{G} \in \mathbb{Z}_q^{n \times m}$, *and a basis* $\mathbf{T_G}$ *of* $\Lambda_q^{\perp}(\mathbf{G})$ *outputs a basis* $\mathbf{T_M}$ *of* $\Lambda_q^{\perp}(\mathbf{M})$ *such that* $\|\mathbf{T_M}\|_{GS} \leq \|\mathbf{T_G}\|_{GS} \cdot (1 + \|\mathbf{R}\|_2)$.

Lemma 3 ([4], Lemma 2.6). *Let* $\mathbf{A} \in \mathbb{Z}_q^{n \times m}$, $\mathbf{T_A} \in \mathbb{Z}^{m \times m}$ *be a basis for* $\Lambda_q^{\perp}(\mathbf{A})$ *and* $\mathbf{U} \in \mathbb{Z}_q^{n \times k}$. *There are polynomial time algorithms that output* $\mathbf{X} \in \mathbb{Z}^{m \times k}$ *satisfying* $\mathbf{AX} = \mathbf{U}$ *with the properties below:*

1. $\mathbf{X} \leftarrow \mathsf{SampleD}(\mathbf{A}, \mathbf{T_A}, \mathbf{U}, \sigma)$ *[15]: A randomized algorithm that, when* $\sigma = \|\mathbf{T_A}\|_{GS} \cdot \omega(\sqrt{\log m})$, *outputs a random sample* $\mathbf{X}$ *from a distribution that is statistically close to* $\mathcal{D}_\sigma(\Lambda_q^{\mathbf{U}}(\mathbf{A}))$.
2. $\mathbf{T}'_{\mathbf{A}} \leftarrow \mathsf{RandBasis}(\mathbf{A}, \mathbf{T_A}, \sigma)$ *[7]: A randomized algorithm that, when* $\sigma = \|\mathbf{T_A}\|_{GS} \cdot \omega(\sqrt{\log m})$, *outputs a basis* $\mathbf{T}'_{\mathbf{A}}$ *of* $\Lambda_q^{\perp}(\mathbf{A})$ *sampled from a distribution that is statistically close to* $(\mathcal{D}_\sigma(\Lambda_q^{\perp}(\mathbf{A})))^m$. *Here* $\|\mathbf{T}'_{\mathbf{A}}\|_{GS} < \sigma\sqrt{m}$ *with all but negligible probability.*

Lemma 4 ([4], Lemma 2.8).

1. $\mathbf{X} \leftarrow \mathsf{SampleRight}(\mathbf{A}, \mathbf{T_A}, \mathbf{B}, \mathbf{U}, \sigma)$*: A randomized algorithm that given full-rank matrices* $\mathbf{A}, \mathbf{B} \in \mathbb{Z}_q^{n \times m}$, *and a matrix* $\mathbf{U} \in \mathbb{Z}_q^{n \times m}$, *a basis* $\mathbf{T_A}$ *of* $\Lambda_q^{\perp}(\mathbf{A})$ *and* $\sigma = \|\mathbf{T_A}\|_{GS} \cdot \omega(\sqrt{\log m})$, *outputs a random sample* $\mathbf{X} \in \mathbb{Z}^{2m \times m}$ *from a distribution that is statistically close to* $\mathcal{D}_\sigma(\Lambda_q^{\mathbf{U}}((\mathbf{A}|\mathbf{B})))$. *This algorithm is the composition of two algorithms:* $\mathbf{T}_{(\mathbf{A}|\mathbf{B})} \leftarrow \mathsf{ExtendRight}(\mathbf{A}, \mathbf{T_A}, \mathbf{B})$ *and* $\mathbf{X} \leftarrow \mathsf{SampleD}((\mathbf{A}|\mathbf{B}), \mathbf{T}_{(\mathbf{A}|\mathbf{B})}, \mathbf{U}, \sigma)$.
2. $\mathbf{X} \leftarrow \mathsf{SampleLeft}(\mathbf{A}, \mathbf{S}, y, \mathbf{U}, \sigma)$*: A randomized algorithm that given full-rank matrix* $\mathbf{A} \in \mathbb{Z}_q^{n \times m}$, *and matrices* $\mathbf{S}, \mathbf{U} \in \mathbb{Z}_q^{n \times m}$, $y \neq 0 \in \mathbb{Z}_q$ *and* $\sigma = \sqrt{5} \cdot (1 + \|\mathbf{S}\|_2) \cdot \omega(\sqrt{\log m})$, *outputs a random sample* $\mathbf{X} \in \mathbb{Z}^{2m \times m}$ *from a distribution that is statistically close to* $\mathcal{D}_\sigma(\Lambda_q^{\mathbf{U}}((\mathbf{A}|y\mathbf{G} + \mathbf{AS})))$. *This algorithm is the composition of two algorithms:* $\mathbf{T}_{(\mathbf{A}|y\mathbf{G}+\mathbf{AS})} \leftarrow \mathsf{ExtendLeft}(\mathbf{A}, y\mathbf{G}, \mathbf{T_G}, \mathbf{S})$ *and* $\mathbf{X} \leftarrow \mathsf{SampleD}((\mathbf{A}|y\mathbf{G} + \mathbf{AS}), \mathbf{T}_{(\mathbf{A}|y\mathbf{G}+\mathbf{AS})}, \mathbf{U}, \sigma)$.

Next, we define three types of evaluation algorithms from [4]. Let n and $q = q(n)$, and $m = \Theta(n \log q)$ be positive integers. Let $\mathbf{G} \in \mathbb{Z}_q^{n \times m}$ be the fixed matrix. For $x \in \mathbb{Z}_q, \mathbf{B} \in \mathbb{Z}_q^{n \times m}, \mathbf{s} \in \mathbb{Z}_q^n$, and $\delta > 0$ define the set $E_{\mathbf{s},\delta}(x, \mathbf{B}) = \{(x\mathbf{G} + \mathbf{B})^\top \mathbf{s} + \mathbf{e} \in \mathbb{Z}_q^m, \text{where} \|\mathbf{e}\| < \delta\}$.

Lemma 5 (Evaluation Algorithms [4]). *The three efficient deterministic evaluation algorithms* $\mathsf{Eval_{pk}}, \mathsf{Eval}_{ct}, \mathsf{Eval}_{sim}$ *satisfy the following properties with respect to the family of functions* $\mathcal{F} = \{f : (\mathbb{Z}_q)^\ell \to \mathbb{Z}_q\}$, *in which each function can be computed by some circuit of a family of depth d, polynomial-size arithmetic circuits* $(\mathcal{C}_\lambda)_{\lambda \in \mathbb{N}}$ *and a positive integer-valued function* $\alpha_{\mathcal{F}} : \mathbb{Z} \to \mathbb{Z}$:

1. $\mathbf{B}_f \leftarrow \mathsf{Eval_{pk}}(f \in \mathcal{F}, \{\mathbf{B}_i\}_{i=1}^\ell)$, *where* $\mathbf{B}_f$ *and each* $\mathbf{B}_i \in \mathbb{Z}_q^{n \times m}$.
2. $\mathbf{c}_f \leftarrow \mathsf{Eval}_{ct}(f \in \mathcal{F}, \{x_i, \mathbf{B}_i, \mathbf{c}_i\}_{i=1}^\ell)$, *where* $\mathbf{c}_f \in \mathbb{Z}_q^m$, *and each* $x_i \in \mathbb{Z}_q, \mathbf{B}_i \in \mathbb{Z}_q^{n \times m}$, *and* $\mathbf{c}_i \in E_{\mathbf{s},\delta}(x_i, \mathbf{B}_i)$ *for some* $\mathbf{s} \in \mathbb{Z}_q^n$ *and* $\delta > 0$. *The output* $\mathbf{c}_f$ *must satisfy* $\mathbf{c}_f \in E_{\mathbf{s},\Delta}(f(\mathbf{x}), \mathbf{B}_f)$, *where* $\mathbf{B}_f \leftarrow \mathsf{Eval_{pk}}(f \in \mathcal{F}, \{\mathbf{B}_i\}_{i=1}^\ell)$, $\mathbf{x} = (x_1, \cdots, x_\ell)$, *and* $\Delta < \delta \cdot \alpha_{\mathcal{F}}(n)$, *where* $\alpha_{\mathcal{F}}(n)$ *measures the increase in the noise magnitude in* $\mathbf{c}_f$ *compared to the input ciphertext.*

3. $\mathbf{R}_f \leftarrow \mathsf{Eval}_{sim}(f \in \mathcal{F}, \{x_i^*, \mathbf{R}_i\}_{i=1}^{\ell}, \mathbf{A})$, *where* $\mathbf{R}_f$ *and each* $\mathbf{R}_i \in \mathbb{Z}_q^{m\times m}$, *each* $x_i^* \in \mathbb{Z}_q$. *For* $\mathbf{x}^* = (x_1^*, \cdots, x_\ell^*)$, $\mathbf{R}_f$ *satisfies* $\mathbf{A}\mathbf{R}_f - f(\mathbf{x}^*)\mathbf{G} = \mathbf{B}_f$, *where* $\mathbf{B}_f \leftarrow \mathsf{Eval}_{\mathsf{pk}}(f \in \mathcal{F}, \{\mathbf{A}\mathbf{R}_i - x_i^*\mathbf{G}\}_{i=1}^{\ell})$. *For all* $f \in \mathcal{F}$, *and for* $\mathbf{R}_1, \cdots, \mathbf{R}_\ell \xleftarrow{\$} \{+1, -1\}^{m\times m}$, $\|\mathbf{R}_f\|_2 < \alpha_{\mathcal{F}}(n)$ *with all but negligible probability.*

The Complete Subtree Method: The complete subtree (CS) method, proposed by Naor, Naor, and Lotspiech [20], is commonly used in revocation systems. This method utilizes a node selection algorithm known as KUNodes. In this algorithm, we construct a complete binary tree (BT) with at least N leaf nodes, where N represents the maximum number of positive tags in the system. Each positive tag corresponds to a leaf node in the binary tree. We use the following notation: if θ is a non-leaf node, θ_l and θ_r represent the left and right children of θ, respectively. Whenever ρ is a leaf node, the set $\mathsf{Path}(\rho)$ denotes the collection of nodes from θ to the root, including both θ and the root node. The KUNodes algorithm takes two inputs: the binary tree BT and a revocation list P_t, which contains the revoked positive tags at time t. The algorithm outputs a set of nodes $\mathbf{Y}$, which is the smallest subset of nodes containing an ancestor for all the leaf nodes corresponding to the non-revoked active positive tags. It is known that the size of the set $\mathbf{Y}$, generated by $\mathsf{KUNodes}(\mathsf{BT}, \mathsf{P}_t)$, is at most $r \log \frac{N}{r}$, where r is the number of positive tags in P_t. A detailed description of the KUNodes algorithm is provided below.

$\mathsf{KUNodes}(\mathsf{BT}, \mathsf{P}_t)$

$$\mathbf{X}, \mathbf{Y} \leftarrow \emptyset$$

$$\forall \rho_i \in \mathsf{P}_t : \quad \text{add } \mathsf{Path}(\rho_i) \text{ to } \mathbf{X}$$

$$\forall \theta \in \mathbf{X} : \quad \text{if } \theta_l \notin \mathbf{X}, \text{ then add } \theta_l \text{ to } \mathbf{Y}; \quad \text{if } \theta_r \notin \mathbf{X}, \text{ then add } \theta_r \text{ to } \mathbf{Y}$$

If $\mathbf{Y} = \emptyset$, &then add root to $\mathbf{Y}$

Return $\mathbf{Y}$.

4 The Proposed Construction of Dynamic Puncturable Encryption (DPE)

In this section, we present our lattice-based construction of DPE. As discussed in the technical overview in Sect. 1.1, the main challenge in instantiating DPE is to support two independent revocation mechanisms and user-side puncturing without granting any single artifact full decryption power, while also enabling token-based ciphertext updates without misuse. At a high level, KeyGen outputs a two-component user secret key: the first component is a trapdoor-based key that supports user-side negative-tag puncturing via Punc, while the second binds the user's positive tag to a binary-tree path, enabling efficient time-dependent access control. RevAccK periodically publishes a public revoke-access key, derived from $\mathsf{KUNodes}(\cdot)$. This public information has no standalone decryption power, but is required by Dec, so that decryption succeeds only when both revocation layers permit it. To support controlled restoration and delegation of decryption rights via ciphertext updates, Token issues time and tag specific update tokens, and $\mathsf{UpdateCT}$ uses these tokens to re-tag ciphertexts or/and advance them to later times. The main challenge is to perform these updates while preserving ciphertext well-formedness, the underlying plaintext, and the shared randomness, without incurring excessive noise growth. We address this using a two-part token (Δ_1, Δ_2) that updates the ciphertext component-wise while preserving the plaintext and controlling noise growth.

We begin the construction by setting the parameters as follows.

- $\mathbf{G} \in \mathbb{Z}_q^{n\times m}$ is a gadget matrix for integer n, large enough prime power $q = poly(n)$, $m = \Theta(n \log q)$ and $k = \lceil \log q \rceil$.
- Let $d(< q)$ be the maximum number of tags per ciphertext.
- Consider the message space is $\mathcal{M} = \{0,1\}^m$, the time space is $\mathcal{T} \subset \mathbb{Z}_q^n$ and the positive tag space is $\mathcal{P} = \mathbb{Z}_q^n$, the negative tag space is $\mathcal{N} = \mathbb{Z}_q$.
- Choose $N = poly(\lambda)$ as the maximum number of positive tags that the system will support. Obtain a binary tree BT with at least N leaf nodes.
- Full-Rank Difference (FRD) map [1]: In the following construction, we use an encoding function with *full-rank difference*, defined as FRD: $\mathbb{Z}_q^n \to \mathbb{Z}_q^{n\times n}$, mapping $\rho \mapsto \mathbf{H}_\rho$. FRD satisfies the following properties:
  1. $\forall$ *distinct* $\rho_1, \rho_2 \in \mathbb{Z}_q^n$, the matrix $\mathbf{H}_{\rho_1} - \mathbf{H}_{\rho_2} \in \mathbb{Z}_q^{n\times n}$ is full rank;
  2. $\forall\ \rho \in \mathbb{Z}_q^n \setminus \{\mathbf{0}\}$, the matrix $\mathbf{H}_\rho \in \mathbb{Z}_q^{n\times n}$ is full rank;
  3. FRD is computable in polynomial time (in $n \log q$).
- Let χ be a χ_{max}-bounded distribution for which $\mathsf{dLWE}_{n,3m,q,\chi}$ is hard.
- Initially, set $\sigma_0 = \omega(\alpha_{\mathcal{F}} \cdot \sqrt{\log m})$.
- Let $\boldsymbol{\eta} = (\eta_1, \cdots, \eta_d)$. We define the family of functions $\mathcal{F} = \{f_\eta \mid f_\eta : \mathbb{Z}_q^d \to \mathbb{Z}_q, \forall \eta \in \mathbb{Z}_q\}$, where $f_\eta(\boldsymbol{\eta}) \neq 0 \mod q$ if $\eta \in \{\eta_1, \cdots, \eta_d\}$, otherwise $f_\eta(\boldsymbol{\eta}) = 0 \mod q$.

The proposed DPE consists of the following algorithms:

$\mathsf{SetUp}(1^\lambda, d)$: On input a security parameter λ, the maximum number of tags d with each ciphertext, do as follows:

1. Generate two independent pairs $(\mathbf{A}, \mathbf{T}_\mathbf{A}), (\mathbf{D}, \mathbf{T}_\mathbf{D})$ by using $\mathsf{TrapGen}(1^n, 1^m, q)$, where $\mathbf{A}, \mathbf{D} \leftarrow \mathbb{Z}_q^{n\times m}$, and $\mathbf{T}_\mathbf{A}, \mathbf{T}_\mathbf{D} \in \mathbb{Z}_q^{m\times m}$, bases of $\Lambda_q^\perp(\mathbf{A})$, $\Lambda_q^\perp(\mathbf{D})$, respectively.
2. Choose $d+5$ uniformly random matrices $\mathbf{A}_0, \mathbf{A}_1, \mathbf{B}_1, \cdots, \mathbf{B}_d, \mathbf{D}_0, \mathbf{D}_1, \mathbf{U} \in \mathbb{Z}_q^{n\times m}$.
3. Outputs a public key $\mathsf{pk} = \{\mathbf{A}, \mathbf{D}, \mathbf{A}_0, \mathbf{A}_1, \mathbf{B}_1, \cdots, \mathbf{B}_d, \mathbf{D}_0, \mathbf{D}_1, \mathbf{U}, \mathbf{G}\}$, a master secret key $\mathsf{msk} = \{\mathbf{T}_\mathbf{A}, \mathbf{T}_\mathbf{D}\}$.

$\mathsf{KeyGen}(\mathsf{pk}, \mathsf{msk}, \rho, \mathsf{N})$: On input the public key pk, the master secret key msk, a positive tag $\rho \in \mathcal{P}$ and a negative tag set $\mathsf{N} = \{\eta_1, \cdots, \eta_\ell\}$, where each $\eta_i \in \mathbb{Z}_q$, and a positive tag $\rho \in \mathbb{Z}_q^n$, do as follows:

1. Let $\mathbf{H}_\rho$ be the encoding of ρ. Set $\mathbf{A}_\rho = \mathbf{A}_0 + \mathbf{H}_\rho \mathbf{G}$, $\mathbf{D}_\rho = \mathbf{D}_0 + \mathbf{H}_\rho \mathbf{G}$.
2. For a negative tag set $\mathsf{N} = \{\eta_1, \cdots, \eta_\ell\}$, evaluate $\mathbf{B}_{f_\eta} \leftarrow \mathsf{Eval}_{\mathsf{pk}}(\{\mathbf{B}_i\}_{i=1}^d, f_\eta)$ for each $\eta_i \in \mathbb{Z}_q$. Compute $\mathbf{T}_{\mathsf{N}}^{\rho,\mathrm{ER}} \leftarrow \mathsf{ExtendRight}\left(\mathbf{A}, \mathbf{T}_{\mathbf{A}}, \left[\mathbf{A}_\rho \middle| \mathbf{B}_{f_{\eta_1}} \middle| \cdots \middle| \mathbf{B}_{f_{\eta_\ell}}\right]\right)$. Compute the re-randomized trapdoor $\mathbf{T}_{\mathsf{N}}^\rho$ for $\left[\mathbf{A} \middle| \mathbf{A}_\rho \middle| \mathbf{B}_{f_{\eta_1}} \middle| \cdots \middle| \mathbf{B}_{f_{\eta_\ell}}\right]$ as $\mathbf{T}_{\mathsf{N}}^\rho \leftarrow \mathsf{RandBasis}\left(\left[\mathbf{A} \middle| \mathbf{A}_\rho \middle| \mathbf{B}_{f_{\eta_1}} \middle| \cdots \middle| \mathbf{B}_{f_{\eta_\ell}}\right], \mathbf{T}_{\mathsf{N}}^{\rho,\mathrm{ER}}, \sigma_{\ell+1}\right)$, where $\sigma_{\ell+1} = \sigma_0 \cdot (\sqrt{m \log m})^\ell$.
   Set $\mathsf{sk}_{1,\mathsf{N}}^\rho = \mathbf{T}_{\mathsf{N}}^\rho$.
3. $\forall\, \theta \in Path(\rho)$, if $\mathbf{V}_\theta$ is undefined, then pick $\mathbf{V}_\theta \xleftarrow{\$} \mathbb{Z}_q^{n\times m}$ and store it on θ.
   Sample $\mathbf{E}_{1,\theta} \leftarrow \mathsf{SampleRight}(\mathbf{D}, \mathbf{D}_\rho, \mathbf{T}_{\mathbf{D}}, \mathbf{A}_\rho - \mathbf{V}_\theta, \sigma_0)$ for each $\theta \in Path(\rho)$. Note that $\mathbf{E}_{1,\theta} \in \mathbb{Z}^{2m\times m}$, $[\mathbf{D}|\mathbf{D}_\rho] \cdot \mathbf{E}_{1,\theta} = \mathbf{A}_\rho - \mathbf{V}_\theta$. Set $\mathsf{sk}_2^\rho = (\theta, \mathbf{E}_{1,\theta})_{\theta \in Path(\rho)}$.
4. Output the punctured secret key $\mathsf{sk}_{\mathsf{N}}^\rho = \{\mathsf{sk}_{1,\mathsf{N}}^\rho, \mathsf{sk}_2^\rho\}$.

$\mathsf{Punc}(\mathsf{pk}, \mathsf{sk}_{\mathsf{N}}^\rho, \eta)$: On input the public key pk, a secret key $\mathsf{sk}_{\mathsf{N}}^\rho = \{\mathsf{sk}_{1,\mathsf{N}}^\rho, \mathsf{sk}_2^\rho\}$, where $\mathsf{sk}_{1,\mathsf{N}}^\rho = \mathbf{T}_{\mathsf{N}}^\rho$ is punctured on a positive tag ρ and the negative tag set $\mathsf{N} = \{\eta_1, \cdots, \eta_\ell\}$, and a negative tag $\eta \in \mathcal{N}$, do as follows:

1. Evaluate $\mathbf{B}_{f_\eta} \leftarrow \mathsf{Eval}_{\mathsf{pk}}(\{\mathbf{B}_i\}_{i=1}^d, f_\eta)$.
2. Compute $\mathbf{T}_{\mathsf{N}\cup\{\eta\}}^{\rho,\mathrm{ER}} \leftarrow \mathsf{ExtendRight}\left(\left[\mathbf{A} \middle| \mathbf{A}_\rho \middle| \mathbf{B}_{f_{\eta_1}} \middle| \cdots \middle| \mathbf{B}_{f_{\eta_\ell}}\right], \mathbf{T}_{\mathsf{N}}^\rho, \mathbf{B}_{f_\eta}\right)$.
3. Finally, compute the re-randomized trapdoor as
   $\mathbf{T}_{\mathsf{N}\cup\{\eta\}}^\rho \leftarrow \mathsf{RandBasis}\left(\left[\mathbf{A} \middle| \mathbf{A}_\rho \middle| \mathbf{B}_{f_{\eta_1}} \middle| \cdots \middle| \mathbf{B}_{f_{\eta_\ell}} \middle| \mathbf{B}_{f_\eta}\right], \mathbf{T}_{\mathsf{N}\cup\{\eta\}}^{\rho,\mathrm{ER}}, \sigma_{\ell+2}\right)$,
   where $\sigma_{\ell+2} = \sigma_0 \cdot (\sqrt{m \log m})^{\ell+1}$. Set $\mathsf{sk}_{1,\mathsf{N}\cup\{\eta\}}^\rho = \mathbf{T}_{\mathsf{N}\cup\{\eta\}}^\rho \in \mathbb{Z}_q^{(\ell+3)m\times(\ell+3)m}$.
4. Output the punctured secret key $\mathsf{sk}_{\mathsf{N}\cup\{\eta\}}^\rho = \{\mathsf{sk}_{1,\mathsf{N}\cup\{\eta\}}^\rho, \mathsf{sk}_2^\rho\}$.

$\mathsf{Encrypt}(\mathsf{pk}, \mathbf{m}, \rho, \boldsymbol{\eta}, t)$: On input the public key pk, a message $\mathbf{m} \in \{0,1\}^m$, a positive tag $\rho \in \mathbb{Z}_q^n$, a d-tuple of negative tags $\boldsymbol{\eta} = (\eta_1, \cdots, \eta_d) \in \mathbb{Z}_q^d$, where each $\eta_i \in \mathbb{Z}_q$, and a time period $t \in \mathcal{T}$, do as follows:

1. Choose a uniformly random vector $\mathbf{s} \leftarrow \mathbb{Z}_q^n$, error vectors $\mathbf{e}_0, \mathbf{e}_{out}, \mathbf{e}_0' \in \chi^m$; and $d+3$ uniformly random matrices $\mathbf{R}_0, \mathbf{R}_1, \cdots, \mathbf{R}_d, \mathbf{S}_1, \mathbf{S}_2 \in \{+1, -1\}^{m\times m}$.
2. Evaluate the encoding of ρ, t as $\mathbf{H}_\rho, \mathbf{H}_t$ and set $\mathbf{A}_t = \mathbf{A}_1 + \mathbf{H}_t \mathbf{G}$, $\mathbf{D}_\rho = \mathbf{D}_0 + \mathbf{H}_\rho \mathbf{G}$, $\mathbf{D}_t = \mathbf{D}_1 + \mathbf{H}_t \mathbf{G}$.
3. Set $\mathbf{H}_1 = \left[\mathbf{A} \middle| \mathbf{A}_t \middle| \eta_1 \mathbf{G} + \mathbf{B}_1 \middle| \cdots \middle| \eta_d \mathbf{G} + \mathbf{B}_d\right] \in \mathbb{Z}_q^{n\times(d+2)m}$, and an error vector $\mathbf{e} = \left[\mathbf{I}_m \middle| \mathbf{R}_0 \middle| \mathbf{R}_1 \middle| \cdots \middle| \mathbf{R}_d\right]^\top \cdot \mathbf{e}_0$.
   Compute $\mathbf{c} = \left[\mathbf{c}_{in} \middle| \bar{\mathbf{c}}_1 \middle| \mathbf{c}_1 \middle| \cdots \middle| \mathbf{c}_d\right] = \mathbf{H}_1^\top \mathbf{s} + \mathbf{e} \in \mathbb{Z}_q^{(d+2)m}$, where $\mathbf{c}_{in} = \mathbf{A}^\top \mathbf{s} + \mathbf{e}_0$, $\bar{\mathbf{c}}_1 = \mathbf{A}_t^\top \mathbf{s} + \mathbf{R}_0^\top \mathbf{e}_0$, and $\mathbf{c}_i = (\eta_i \mathbf{G} + \mathbf{B}_i)^\top \mathbf{s} + \mathbf{R}_i^\top \mathbf{e}_0$ $\forall\, i \in \{1, \cdots, d\}$.
4. Compute $\mathbf{c}_{out} = \mathbf{U}^\top \mathbf{s} + \mathbf{e}_{out} + \lfloor q/2 \rfloor \cdot \mathbf{m} \in \mathbb{Z}_q^m$.
5. Set $\mathbf{H}_2 = \left[\mathbf{D} \middle| \mathbf{D}_\rho \middle| \mathbf{D}_t\right] \in \mathbb{Z}_q^{n\times 3m}$ and an error vector $\mathbf{e}' = \left[\mathbf{I}_m \middle| \mathbf{S}_1 \middle| \mathbf{S}_2\right]^\top \cdot \mathbf{e}_0'$.
   Compute $\tilde{\mathbf{c}} = [\tilde{\mathbf{c}}_0 | \tilde{\mathbf{c}}_1 | \tilde{\mathbf{c}}_2] = \mathbf{H}_2^\top \mathbf{s} + \mathbf{e}' \in \mathbb{Z}_q^{3m}$, where $\tilde{\mathbf{c}}_0 = \mathbf{D}^\top \mathbf{s} + \mathbf{e}_0'$, $\tilde{\mathbf{c}}_1 = \mathbf{D}_\rho^\top \mathbf{s} + \mathbf{S}_1^\top \mathbf{e}_0'$, and $\tilde{\mathbf{c}}_2 = \mathbf{D}_t^\top \mathbf{s} + \mathbf{S}_2^\top \mathbf{e}_0'$.

6. Output the ciphertext $ct = (\mathbf{c}, \mathbf{c}_{out}, \tilde{\mathbf{c}}) \in \mathbb{Z}_q^{(d+6)m}$.

$\mathsf{RevAccK}(\mathsf{pk}, \mathsf{msk}, \mathsf{P}, t)$: On input the public key pk, the master secret key msk, a time period t, a set of revoked positive tags P on time t, do as follows:

1. Compute $\mathbf{D}_t = \mathbf{D}_1 + \mathbf{H}_t\mathbf{G} \in \mathbb{Z}_q^{n\times m}$.
2. For each $\theta \in \mathsf{KUNodes}(\mathsf{BT}, \mathsf{P})$, retrieve $\mathbf{V}_\theta$ (which is always pre-defined in algorithm **KeyGen**), and sample $\mathbf{E}_{2,\theta} \leftarrow \mathsf{SampleRight}(\mathbf{D}, \mathbf{T}_\mathbf{D}, \mathbf{D}_t, \mathbf{V}_\theta, \sigma_0)$. Note that $\mathbf{E}_{2,\theta} \in \mathbb{Z}^{2m\times m}$ and $[\mathbf{D}|\mathbf{D}_t] \cdot \mathbf{E}_{2,\theta} = \mathbf{V}_\theta$.
3. Output the revoke access key for time t as $\mathsf{rk}_\mathsf{P}^t = (\theta, \mathbf{E}_{2,\theta})_{\theta\in\mathsf{KUNodes}(\mathsf{BT},\mathsf{P})}$.

$\mathsf{Decrypt}(\mathsf{pk}, \mathsf{sk}_\mathsf{N}^{\rho'}, \mathsf{rk}_\mathsf{P}^t, ct, \rho, \boldsymbol{\eta}, t)$: On input the public key pk, the punctured secret key $\mathsf{sk}_\mathsf{N}^{\rho'} = \{\mathsf{sk}_{1,\mathsf{N}}^{\rho'}, \mathsf{sk}_2^{\rho'}\}$, where $\mathsf{sk}_{1,\mathsf{N}}^{\rho'} = \mathbf{T}_\mathsf{N}^{\rho'}$, punctured on the negative tag set $\mathsf{N} = \{\eta_1', \cdots, \eta_\ell'\}$, a positive tag ρ' and $\mathsf{sk}_2^{\rho'} = (\theta, \mathbf{E}_{1,\theta})_{\theta\in I)}$, a revoke access key $\mathsf{rk}_\mathsf{P}^t = (\theta, \mathbf{E}_{2,\theta})_{\theta\in J}$ for some set of nodes I, J, for time t and a ciphertext $ct = (\mathbf{c}, \mathbf{c}_{out}, \tilde{\mathbf{c}})$ with a positive tag $\rho \in \mathbb{Z}_q^n$, a d-tuple of negative tags $\boldsymbol{\eta} = (\eta_1, \cdots, \eta_d) \in \mathbb{Z}_q^d$, and a time period $t \in \mathcal{T}$, do as follows:

1. If $I \cap J = \emptyset$, or $\rho \neq \rho'$, or $\exists$ some $j \in \{1, \cdots, \ell\}$ such that $f_{\eta_j'}(\boldsymbol{\eta}) \neq 0$, outputs $\perp$. Otherwise, proceed as below:
   - As $I \cap J \neq \phi$, choose $\theta \in I \cap J$, and set $\mathbf{E}_1 = \mathbf{E}_{1,\theta}$, and $\mathbf{E}_2 = \mathbf{E}_{2,\theta}$. Note that $[\mathbf{D}|\mathbf{D}_\rho] \cdot \mathbf{E}_1 + [\mathbf{D}|\mathbf{D}_t] \cdot \mathbf{E}_2 = \mathbf{A}_\rho$.
   - Parse $\tilde{\mathbf{c}} = [\tilde{\mathbf{c}}_0|\tilde{\mathbf{c}}_1|\tilde{\mathbf{c}}_2]$, where $\tilde{\mathbf{c}}_i \in \mathbb{Z}_q^m$, for $i \in \{0, 1, 2\}$. Compute $\bar{\mathbf{c}}_0 = \mathbf{E}_1^\top[\tilde{\mathbf{c}}_0|\tilde{\mathbf{c}}_1] + \mathbf{E}_2^\top[\tilde{\mathbf{c}}_0|\tilde{\mathbf{c}}_2] \in \mathbb{Z}_q^m$.
   - Evaluate the encoding of ρ, t as $\mathbf{H}_\rho, \mathbf{H}_t$ and set $\mathbf{A}_t = \mathbf{A}_1 + \mathbf{H}_t\mathbf{G}$, $\mathbf{A}_\rho = \mathbf{A}_0 + \mathbf{H}_\rho\mathbf{G}$. Set $\mathbf{H}' = \left[\mathbf{A}\middle|\mathbf{A}_\rho\middle|\mathbf{A}_t\middle|\eta_1\mathbf{G} + \mathbf{B}_1\middle|\cdots\middle|\eta_d\mathbf{G} + \mathbf{B}_d\right]$.
   - Since $\rho' = \rho$, $\mathbf{T}_\mathsf{N}^{\rho'} = \mathbf{T}_\mathsf{N}^\rho$ is a trapdoor for $\left[\mathbf{A}\middle|\mathbf{A}_\rho\middle|\mathbf{B}_{f_{\eta_1'}}\middle|\cdots\middle|\mathbf{B}_{f_{\eta_\ell'}}\right]$. Compute $\mathbf{T}_\mathsf{N}^{\rho,\mathrm{ER}} \leftarrow \mathsf{ExtendRight}\left(\left[\mathbf{A}\middle|\mathbf{A}_\rho\middle|\mathbf{B}_{f_{\eta_1'}}\middle|\cdots\middle|\mathbf{B}_{f_{\eta_\ell'}}\right], \mathbf{T}_\mathsf{N}^\rho, \mathbf{A}_t\right)$. We switch the rows of $\mathbf{T}_\mathsf{N}^{\rho,\mathrm{ER}}$ to get a matrix $\mathbf{T}_{\mathbf{H}'}$, a trapdoor for $\mathbf{H}'$. This operation does not change the Gram-Schmidt norm of the basis.
   - Sample $\mathbf{R} \leftarrow \mathsf{SampleD}\left(\left[\mathbf{A}\middle|\mathbf{A}_\rho\middle|\mathbf{A}_t\middle|\mathbf{B}_{f_{\eta_1'}}\middle|\cdots\middle|\mathbf{B}_{f_{\eta_\ell'}}\right], \mathbf{T}_{\mathbf{H}'}, \mathbf{U}, \sigma_{\ell+1}\right)$.
   - Parse $\mathbf{c} = \left[\mathbf{c}_{in}\middle|\bar{\mathbf{c}}_1\middle|\mathbf{c}_1\middle|\cdots\middle|\mathbf{c}_d\right]$. Evaluate $c_{f_{\eta_j'}} \leftarrow \mathsf{Eval}_{ct}(\{\eta_i', \mathbf{B}_i, \mathbf{c}_i\}_{i=1}^d, f_{\eta_j'})$ for each $j \in \{1, \cdots, \ell\}$. Set $\mathbf{c}' = \left[\mathbf{c}_{in}\middle|\bar{\mathbf{c}}_0\middle|\bar{\mathbf{c}}_1\middle|\mathbf{c}_{f_{\eta_1'}}\middle|\cdots\middle|\mathbf{c}_{f_{\eta_\ell'}}\right]$.
   - Compute $(m_1, \cdots, m_m) = \mathbf{c}_{out} - \mathbf{R}^\top\mathbf{c}'$. For each i, if $|m_i| < q/4$, take $m_i = 0$, otherwise take $m_i = 1$. Output $\mathbf{m} = (m_1, \cdots, m_m)$.

$\mathsf{Token}(\mathsf{pk}, \mathsf{msk}, \mathcal{E}_1, \mathcal{E}_2)$: On input the public key pk, the master secret key msk, and two tuples $\mathcal{E}_1 = (\rho_1, \boldsymbol{\eta}_1, t_1)$, $\mathcal{E}_2 = (\rho_2, \boldsymbol{\eta}_2, t_2(> t_1))$ consisting of a positive tag, a d-tuple of negative tags and a time, do as follows:

1. Let $\mathbf{A}_{\rho_1} = \mathbf{A}_0 + \mathbf{H}_{\rho_1}\mathbf{G}$, $\mathbf{A}_{\rho_2} = \mathbf{A}_0 + \mathbf{H}_{\rho_2}\mathbf{G}$, $\mathbf{A}_{t_1} = \mathbf{A}_1 + \mathbf{H}_{t_1}\mathbf{G}, \mathbf{A}_{t_2} = \mathbf{A}_1 + \mathbf{H}_{t_2}\mathbf{G}, \mathbf{D}_{\rho_1} = \mathbf{D}_0 + \mathbf{H}_{\rho_1}\mathbf{G}, \mathbf{D}_{\rho_2} = \mathbf{D}_0 + \mathbf{H}_{\rho_2}\mathbf{G}, \mathbf{D}_{t_1} = \mathbf{D}_1 + \mathbf{H}_{t_1}\mathbf{G}, \mathbf{D}_{t_2} = \mathbf{D}_1 + \mathbf{H}_{t_2}\mathbf{G}$, where $\mathbf{H}_{\rho_1}, \mathbf{H}_{\rho_2}, \mathbf{H}_{t_1}, \mathbf{H}_{t_2}$ are the encoding of ρ_1, ρ_2, t_1, t_2, respectively. Let $\boldsymbol{\eta}_1 = (\eta_1, \cdots, \eta_d), \boldsymbol{\eta}_2 = (\eta'_1, \cdots, \eta'_d)$.
2. If $\boldsymbol{\eta}_1 = \boldsymbol{\eta}_2$, proceed as follows:
   - Let $\mathsf{L} = \left[\eta_1\mathbf{G} + \mathbf{B}_1 \middle| \cdots \middle| \eta_d\mathbf{G} + \mathbf{B}_d\right] \in \mathbb{Z}_q^{n\times dm}$.
   - Choose $\mathbf{Y} \leftarrow \chi^{m\times m}$. Sample $\mathbf{X} \leftarrow \mathsf{SampleRight}\left(\mathbf{A}, \mathbf{T}_{\mathbf{A}}, \mathsf{L}, \mathbf{A}_{t_2} - \mathbf{A}_{t_1}\mathbf{Y}, \sigma_0\right)$.

$$\begin{cases} \text{Note that } \mathbf{X} \in \mathbb{Z}^{(d+1)m\times m} \text{ and } \left[\mathbf{A}\middle|\mathsf{L}\right]\cdot\mathbf{X} = \mathbf{A}_{t_2} - \mathbf{A}_{t_1}\mathbf{Y}; \\ \text{Parse } \mathbf{X} \text{ as } (\mathbf{X}^{(0)}, \mathbf{X}^{(1)}) \in \mathbb{Z}^{m\times m} \times \mathbb{Z}^{dm\times m}; \\ \text{Observe that } \mathbf{A}\cdot\mathbf{X}^{(0)} + \mathsf{L}\cdot\mathbf{X}^{(1)} = \mathbf{A}_{t_2} - \mathbf{A}_{t_1}\mathbf{Y}. \end{cases}$$

   - Set $\Delta_1 = \begin{bmatrix} \mathbf{I}_{m\times m} & \mathbf{X}^{(0)} & \mathbf{0} \\ \mathbf{0} & \mathbf{Y} & \mathbf{0} \\ \mathbf{0} & \mathbf{X}^{(1)} & \mathbf{I}_{dm\times dm} \end{bmatrix} \in \mathbb{Z}^{(d+2)m\times(d+2)m}$.

   If $\boldsymbol{\eta}_1 \neq \boldsymbol{\eta}_2$, proceed as follows:
   - Without loss of generality, we assume that first $j(\leq d)$ components of $\boldsymbol{\eta}_1, \boldsymbol{\eta}_2$ are different. We have $\eta_1 \neq \eta'_1, \cdots, \eta_j \neq \eta'_j$, and $\eta_{j+1} = \eta'_{j+1}, \cdots, \eta_d = \eta'_d$. Let $\mathsf{M} = \left[\eta_{j+1}\mathbf{G} + \mathbf{B}_{j+1} \middle| \cdots \middle| \eta_d\mathbf{G} + \mathbf{B}_d\right] \in \mathbb{Z}_q^{n\times(d-j)m}$.
   - Choose $\mathbf{Y}_0, \mathbf{Y}_1, \cdots, \mathbf{Y}_j \leftarrow \chi^{m\times m}$ and sample $\mathbf{X}_0 \leftarrow \mathsf{SampleRight}\left(\mathbf{A}, \mathbf{T}_{\mathbf{A}}, \mathsf{M}, \mathbf{A}_{t_2} - \mathbf{A}_{t_1}\mathbf{Y}_0, \sigma_0\right)$ and $\forall\, i \in \{1, \cdots, j\}$, $\mathbf{X}_i \leftarrow \mathsf{SampleRight}\left(\mathbf{A}, \mathbf{T}_{\mathbf{A}}, \mathsf{M}, (\eta'_{d_i}\mathbf{G} + \mathbf{B}_{d_i}) - (\eta_{d_i}\mathbf{G} + \mathbf{B}_{d_i})\mathbf{Y}_i, \sigma_0\right)$.

$$\begin{cases} \text{Note that } \mathbf{X}_0 \in \mathbb{Z}^{(d-j+1)m\times m} \text{ and } \left[\mathbf{A}\middle|\mathsf{M}\right]\cdot\mathbf{X}_0 = \mathbf{A}_{t_2} - \mathbf{A}_{t_1}\mathbf{Y}_0; \\ \text{Parse } \mathbf{X}_0 \text{ as } (\mathbf{X}_0^{(0)}, \mathbf{X}_0^{(j+1)}, \cdots, \mathbf{X}_0^{(d)}) \in \underbrace{\mathbb{Z}^{m\times m} \times \cdots \times \mathbb{Z}^{m\times m}}_{(d-j+1)\text{ times}}; \\ \text{Observe that} \\ \mathbf{A}\cdot\mathbf{X}_0^{(0)} + (\eta_{j+1}\mathbf{G} + \mathbf{B}_{j+1})\cdot\mathbf{X}_0^{(j+1)} + \cdots + (\eta_d\mathbf{G} + \mathbf{B}_d)\cdot\mathbf{X}_0^{(d)} \\ \qquad = \mathbf{A}_{t_2} - \mathbf{A}_{t_1}\mathbf{Y}. \end{cases}$$

   For each $i = \{1, \cdots, j\}$, the following holds:

$$\begin{cases} \mathbf{X}_i \in \mathbb{Z}^{(d-j+1)m\times m} \text{ and } \left[\mathbf{A}\middle|\mathsf{M}\right]\cdot\mathbf{X}_i = (\eta'_{d_i}\mathbf{G} + \mathbf{B}_{d_i}) - (\eta_{d_i}\mathbf{G} + \mathbf{B}_{d_i})\mathbf{Y}_i; \\ \text{Parse } \mathbf{X}_i \text{ as } (\mathbf{X}_i^{(0)}, \mathbf{X}_i^{(j+1)}, \cdots, \mathbf{X}_i^{(d)}) \in \underbrace{\mathbb{Z}^{m\times m} \times \cdots \times \mathbb{Z}^{m\times m}}_{(d-j+1)\text{ times}}; \\ \text{Observe that} \\ \mathbf{A}\cdot\mathbf{X}_i^{(0)} + (\eta_{j+1}\mathbf{G} + \mathbf{B}_{j+1})\cdot\mathbf{X}_i^{(j+1)} + \cdots + (\eta_d\mathbf{G} + \mathbf{B}_d)\cdot\mathbf{X}_0^{(d)} \\ \qquad = (\eta'_{d_i}\mathbf{G} + \mathbf{B}_{d_i}) - (\eta_{d_i}\mathbf{G} + \mathbf{B}_{d_i})\mathbf{Y}_i. \end{cases}$$

- Set

$$\Delta_1 = \begin{bmatrix} \mathbf{I}_{m\times m} & \mathbf{X}_0^{(0)} & \mathbf{X}_1^{(0)} & \cdots & \mathbf{X}_j^{(0)} & \mathbf{0} & \cdots & \mathbf{0} \\ \mathbf{0} & \mathbf{Y}_0 & \mathbf{0} & \cdots & \mathbf{0} & \mathbf{0} & \cdots & \mathbf{0} \\ \mathbf{0} & \mathbf{0} & \mathbf{Y}_1 & \cdots & \mathbf{0} & \mathbf{0} & \cdots & \mathbf{0} \\ \cdots & \cdots & \cdots & \cdots & \cdots & \mathbf{0} & \cdots & \mathbf{0} \\ \mathbf{0} & \mathbf{0} & \mathbf{0} & \cdots & \mathbf{Y}_j & \mathbf{0} & \cdots & \mathbf{0} \\ \mathbf{0} & \mathbf{X}_0^{(j+1)} & \mathbf{X}_1^{(j+1)} & \cdots & \mathbf{X}_j^{(j+1)} & \mathbf{I}_{m\times m} & \cdots & \mathbf{0} \\ \cdots & \cdots & \cdots & \cdots & \cdots & \cdots & \cdots & \cdots \\ \mathbf{0} & \mathbf{X}_0^{(d)} & \mathbf{X}_1^{(d)} & \cdots & \mathbf{X}_j^{(d)} & \mathbf{0} & \cdots & \mathbf{I}_{m\times m} \end{bmatrix}.$$

Using basic algebra, it is easy to form the matrix $\Delta_1 \in \mathbb{Z}^{(d+2)m\times(d+2)m}$ containing $\mathbf{X}_0, \mathbf{X}_1, \cdots, \mathbf{X}_j$ and $\mathbf{Y}_0, \mathbf{Y}_1, \cdots, \mathbf{Y}_j$, satisfying $\left[\mathbf{A}\middle|\mathbf{A}_{t_1}\middle|\eta_1\mathbf{G}+\mathbf{B}_1\middle|\cdots\middle|\eta_d\mathbf{G}+\mathbf{B}_d\right] \cdot \Delta_1 = \left[\mathbf{A}\middle|\mathbf{A}_{t_2}\middle|\eta_1'\mathbf{G}+\mathbf{B}_1\middle|\cdots\middle|\eta_d'\mathbf{G}+\mathbf{B}_d\right]$.

3. Let $\mathsf{N} = \left[\mathbf{A}_{t_1}\middle|\eta_1\mathbf{G}+\mathbf{B}_1\middle|\cdots\middle|\eta_d\mathbf{G}+\mathbf{B}_d\right] \in \mathbb{Z}_q^{n\times(d+1)m}$. If $\rho_1 = \rho_2$, proceed as follows:
   - Choose $\mathbf{Y}' \leftarrow \chi^{m\times m}$ and sample $\mathbf{X}' \leftarrow \mathsf{SampleRight}(\mathbf{A}, \mathbf{T}_\mathbf{A}, [\mathsf{N}|\mathbf{D}_{\rho_1}], \mathbf{D}_{t_2} - \mathbf{D}_{t_1}\mathbf{Y}', \sigma_0)$.

$$\begin{cases} \text{Note that } \mathbf{X}' \in \mathbb{Z}^{(d+3)m\times m} \text{ and } \left[\mathbf{A}\middle|\mathsf{N}\middle|\mathbf{D}_{\rho_1}\right] \cdot \mathbf{X}' = \mathbf{D}_{t_2} - \mathbf{D}_{t_1}\mathbf{Y}'; \\ \text{Parse } \mathbf{X}' \text{ as } (\mathbf{X}'^{(0)}, \mathbf{X}'^{(1)}) \in \mathbb{Z}^{(d+2)m\times m} \times \mathbb{Z}^{m\times m}; \\ \text{Observe that } [\mathbf{A}|\mathsf{N}] \cdot \mathbf{X}'^{(0)} + \mathbf{D}_{\rho_1} \cdot \mathbf{X}'^{(1)} = \mathbf{D}_{t_2} - \mathbf{D}_{t_1}\mathbf{Y}'. \end{cases}$$

   - Set $\Delta_2 = \begin{bmatrix} \mathbf{0}_{(d+2)m\times m} & \mathbf{0}_{(d+2)m\times m} & \mathbf{X}'^{(0)} \\ \mathbf{I}_{m\times m} & \mathbf{0}_{m\times m} & \mathbf{0}_{m\times m} \\ \mathbf{0}_{m\times m} & \mathbf{I}_{m\times m} & \mathbf{X}'^{(1)} \\ \mathbf{0}_{m\times m} & \mathbf{0}_{m\times m} & \mathbf{Y}' \end{bmatrix} \in \mathbb{Z}^{(d+5)m\times 3m}$.

   If $\rho_1 \neq \rho_2$, proceed as follows:
   - Choose $\mathbf{Y}_1, \mathbf{Y}_2 \leftarrow \chi^{m\times m}$ and sample $\mathbf{X}_1 \leftarrow \mathsf{SampleRight}(\mathbf{A}, \mathbf{T}_\mathbf{A}, \mathsf{N}, \mathbf{D}_{\rho_2} - \mathbf{D}_{\rho_1}\mathbf{Y}_1, \sigma_0)$ and $\mathbf{X}_2 \leftarrow \mathsf{SampleRight}(\mathbf{A}, \mathbf{T}_\mathbf{A}, \mathsf{N}, \mathbf{D}_{t'} - \mathbf{D}_t\mathbf{Y}_2, \sigma_0)$.

$$\begin{cases} \text{Note that } \mathbf{X}_1', \mathbf{X}_2' \in \mathbb{Z}^{(d+2)m\times m} \text{ and} \\ \left[\mathbf{A}\middle|\mathsf{N}\right] \cdot \mathbf{X}_1' = \mathbf{D}_{\rho_2} - \mathbf{D}_{\rho_1}\mathbf{Y}_1', \; \left[\mathbf{A}\middle|\mathsf{N}\right] \cdot \mathbf{X}_2' = \mathbf{D}_{t_2} - \mathbf{D}_{t_1}\mathbf{Y}_2'. \end{cases}$$

   - Set $\Delta_2 = \begin{bmatrix} \mathbf{0}_{(d+2)m\times m} & \mathbf{X}_1' & \mathbf{X}_2' \\ \mathbf{I}_{m\times m} & \mathbf{0}_{m\times m} & \mathbf{0}_{m\times m} \\ \mathbf{0}_{m\times m} & \mathbf{Y}_1' & \mathbf{0}_{m\times m} \\ \mathbf{0}_{m\times m} & \mathbf{0}_{m\times m} & \mathbf{Y}_2' \end{bmatrix} \in \mathbb{Z}^{(d+5)m\times 3m}$.

4. Output the update token $\mathsf{tk}_{\mathcal{E}_1\rightarrow\mathcal{E}_2} = \{\Delta_1, \Delta_2\}$.

$\mathsf{UpdateCT}(\mathsf{pk}, \mathsf{tk}_{\mathcal{E}_1 \to \mathcal{E}_2}, ct, \rho_1, \boldsymbol{\eta}_1, t_1)$: On input the public key pk, a ciphertext ct with tags ρ_1, $\boldsymbol{\eta}_1$ and a token $\mathsf{tk}_{\mathcal{E}_1 \to \mathcal{E}_2} = \{\Delta_1, \Delta_2\}$ for $\mathcal{E}_1 = (\rho_1, \boldsymbol{\eta}_1, t_1)$, $\mathcal{E}_2 = (\rho_2, \boldsymbol{\eta}_2, t_2(> t_1))$, do as follows:

1. Parse $ct = (\mathbf{c}, \mathbf{c}_{out}, \tilde{\mathbf{c}})$, where $\mathbf{c} = [\mathbf{c}_{in}|\bar{\mathbf{c}}_1|\mathbf{c}_1|\cdots|\mathbf{c}_d]$, $\tilde{\mathbf{c}} = [\tilde{\mathbf{c}}_0|\tilde{\mathbf{c}}_1|\tilde{\mathbf{c}}_2]$.
2. Choose a uniformly random vector $\mathbf{r} \leftarrow \mathbb{Z}_q^n$ and error vectors $\tilde{\mathbf{e}}_1 \in \chi^{(d+2)m}$, $\tilde{\mathbf{e}}_2 \in \chi^m, \tilde{\mathbf{e}}_3 \in \chi^{3m}$.
3. Let $\boldsymbol{\eta}_2 = (\eta_1', \cdots, \eta_d')$. Set $\mathbf{H}_1' = \left[\mathbf{A}|\mathbf{A}_{t_2}|\eta_1'\mathbf{G} + \mathbf{B}_1|\cdots|\eta_d'\mathbf{G} + \mathbf{B}_d\right]$ and $\mathbf{H}_2' = \left[\mathbf{D}|\mathbf{D}_{\rho_2}|\mathbf{D}_{t_2}\mathbf{G}\right]$.
4. Compute $ct' = (\mathbf{c}', \mathbf{c}'_{out}, \tilde{\mathbf{c}}')$ as $\mathbf{c}' = \Delta_1^\top \cdot \mathbf{c} + \mathbf{H}_1'^\top \mathbf{r} + \tilde{\mathbf{e}}_1$, $\mathbf{c}'_{out} = \mathbf{c}_{out} + \mathbf{U}^\top \mathbf{r} + \tilde{\mathbf{e}}_2$, and $\tilde{\mathbf{c}}' = \Delta_2^\top \cdot [\mathbf{c}|\tilde{\mathbf{c}}] + \mathbf{H}_2'^\top \mathbf{r} + \tilde{\mathbf{e}}_3$.
5. Output the updated ciphertext $ct' \in \mathbb{Z}_q^{(d+6)m}$.

5 Analysis of the Proposed Construction

In this section, we analyzed the correctness, efficiency, and securityof the proposed construction. Due to page restrictions, we provide the proof sketches here, and the full proofs of correctness and security are deferred to Appendix B and Appendix C, respectively.

Theorem 1 (Correctness). *The* DPE *scheme is correct if the following condition holds:* $3\alpha_{\mathcal{F}}^3 \cdot \chi_{max}^2 \cdot (d+3)^2(\ell+3)^2 \cdot m^{\frac{\ell+1}{2}+3} < q/4$.

Proof Sketch. We argue that Dec outputs the correct message with all but negligible probability for both honestly generated and correctly updated ciphertexts. Let $ct = (\mathbf{c}, \mathbf{c}_{out}, \tilde{\mathbf{c}})$ be an honestly computed ciphertext of $\mathbf{m}$ under positive tag ρ, negative tag set $\boldsymbol{\eta} = \{\eta_1, \ldots, \eta_d\}$ on time t. If the user's access has not been revoked in either of the two revocation layers, then by using its secret key $\mathsf{sk}_{\mathsf{N}}^{\rho}$ and the public revoke-access key $\mathsf{rk}_{\mathsf{P}}^{t}$, the user computes $\bar{\mathbf{c}}_0 = \mathbf{A}_\rho^\top \mathbf{s} + \mathsf{error}_1$. Moreover, for every punctured negative tag, evaluation yields $\mathbf{c}_{f_{\eta_j}} = \mathbf{B}_{f_{\eta_j}}^\top \mathbf{s} + \mathbf{e}$ with $\|\mathbf{e}\| < \Delta$. Finally, it evaluates $\mathbf{c}_{out} - \mathbf{R}^\top[\mathbf{c}_{in} \mid \bar{\mathbf{c}}_0 \mid \cdots |\mathbf{c}_{f_{\eta_\ell}}] = \lfloor q/2 \rfloor \cdot \mathbf{m} + \mathsf{error}_2$, where error_2 aggregates error_1, and some other noises. By Lemma 1 and the tail bounds of the discrete Gaussian sampling, $\|\mathsf{error}_1\|$ is small with overwhelming probability. Using the norm bounds on $\mathbf{R}$ (by Lemma 1), error_1 and the other noises, we obtain $\|\mathsf{error}_2\| \leq \beta_1$ with overwhelming probability; choosing parameters so that $\beta_1 < q/4$ implies correct output of the original message $\mathbf{m}$.

Let $ct' = (\mathbf{c}', \mathbf{c}'_{out}, \tilde{\mathbf{c}}')$ be an updated ciphertexts obtained from ct using a valid token $\mathsf{tk}_{\mathcal{E}_1 \to \mathcal{E}_2} = (\Delta_1, \Delta_2)$ for $\mathcal{E}_1 = (\rho_1, \boldsymbol{\eta}_1, t_1)$ and $\mathcal{E}_2 = (\rho_2, \boldsymbol{\eta}_2, t_2)$ with $t_2 > t_1$. This update preserves the message and maintains consistency of the shared randomness by effectively shifting $\mathbf{s}$ to $\mathbf{s}+\mathbf{r}$ for uniform $\mathbf{r} \leftarrow \mathbb{Z}_q^n$, i.e., $\mathbf{c}' = \mathbf{H}_1'^\top(\mathbf{s}+\mathbf{r}) + \text{noise}$, $\tilde{\mathbf{c}}' = \mathbf{H}_2'^\top(\mathbf{s}+\mathbf{r}) + \text{noise}$, and $\mathbf{c}'_{out} = \mathbf{U}^\top(\mathbf{s}+\mathbf{r}) + \lfloor q/2 \rfloor \mathbf{m} + \text{noise}$. If $\rho_2 \notin \mathsf{P}_{t_2}$, the same transform-and-decrypt procedure yields $\lfloor q/2 \rfloor \mathbf{m} + \mathsf{error}_2'$. Bounding $\|\Delta_1\|, \|\Delta_2\|$ (by Lemma 1 and the structure of SampleRight) and the additional update noises gives $\|\mathsf{error}_2'\| \leq \beta_2$ with overwhelming probability. Hence, for $\beta = \max\{\beta_1, \beta_2\} < q/4$, decryption is correct for both original and updated ciphertexts. We set $\beta = 3\alpha_{\mathcal{F}}^3 \cdot \chi_{max}^2 \cdot (d+3)^2(\ell+3)^2 \cdot m^{\frac{\ell+1}{2}+3} < q/4$.

Efficiency

Table 2 summarizes the asymptotic bit-size of public parameter, secret key, revoke access key, ciphertext, token, and updated ciphertext in DPE scheme.

Table 2. Data Sizes of Proposed DPE

Public parameter size	$O(d \cdot n^2 \log^2 q)$
Secret key size	$O(\eta^2 \cdot n^2 \log^3 q)$
punctured (with tags $\{t_1, \cdots, t_\eta\}$)	
Revoke access Key size	$O(r \log(N/r) \cdot n^2 \log^2 q)$
Ciphertext size	$O(d \cdot n \log^2 q))$
Token size	$O(d^2 \cdot n^2 \log^3 q)$
Updated Ciphertext size	$O(d \cdot n \log^2 q))$

d is the maximum number of negative tags per ciphertext; N is the maximal number of positive tags the system will support; ℓ is the punctured times; above secret key sizes and ciphertext size, updated ciphertext size are given with respect to the maximum number of negative tags per ciphertext d; r is the number of revoked positive tags; n is an integer; q is a prime.

Theorem 2 (Security). *The above scheme is* IND-sDPE-CPA *secure assuming the hardness of* $\mathsf{dLWE}_{n,3m,q,\chi}$.

Proof Sketch. We prove IND-sDPE-CPA security via a sequence of games. The adversary $\mathcal{A}$ commits upfront to the challenge tuple $(\rho^*, \boldsymbol{\eta}^*, t^*)$, and the challenger answers the puncture, corruption, revoke-access key queries, and token, encryption, update queries, subject to the experiment's restrictions. Game 0 is the original IND-sDPE-CPA experiment. In Game 1, we differently set $\mathbf{A}_0, \mathbf{A}_1, \mathbf{B}_1, \cdots, \mathbf{B}_d$,
$\mathbf{D}_0, \mathbf{D}_1$ from the public key pk to embed the challenge tags and time $(\rho^*, \boldsymbol{\eta}^*, t^*)$. The remainder of this game is unchanged. Game 0 is statistically indistinguishable from Game 1 due to the left-over hash lemma. In Game 2, we change how $\mathbf{A}, \mathbf{D}$ in pk are chosen. Here, the challenger chooses random $\mathbf{A}, \mathbf{D}$ from $\mathbb{Z}_q^{n\times m}$ instead of using the TrapGen algorithm. We then simulate all key and revocation oracles using trapdoor delegation and sampling techniques. For example, in the real scheme, the keys $\mathsf{sk}^{\rho}_{1,\mathsf{N}_\rho}$ are generated using the algorithm ExtendRight, RandBasis for every ρ. In contrast, during the simulation, they are drawn from ExtendLeft, ExtendRight, RandBasis. The properties of these sampling algorithms (see Sect. 3) ensure that the resulting distributions are statistically indistinguishable. In particular, tokens for non-challenge tuples are generated using the trapdoor, while for the challenge tuple, we return tokens sampled from the correct distribution without revealing any trapdoor information, and

updates are only permitted in a one-way manner. Besides, the way we embed the challenge tags and time in the public parameter, we can respond to the queries using the trapdoor $\mathbf{T_G}$. Game 2 is otherwise same as Game 1. Since the keys and responses to the queries are statistically close to those in Game 1, Game 2 and Game 1 are statistically indistinguishable. Game 3 is identical to Game 2 except that the challenge ciphertext ct^* is chosen randomly from $\mathbb{Z}_q^{(d+6)m}$. Finally, we show that Game 2 and Game 3 are computationally indistinguishable for a PPT adversary, by giving a reduction from the dLWE problem.

Acknowledgements. This work is supported by Australian Research Council (ARC) Discovery Project under Grant DP220100003. The work of Willy Susilo is supported by the ARC Laureate Fellowship under Grant FL230100033. The work of Fuchun Guo is partially supported by ARC Future Fellowship under Grant FT220100046.

A Deferred Prerequisites

Lemma 6 ([19]). $\mathbf{R}' \leftarrow \mathsf{DelTrap}(\mathbf{A}' = [\mathbf{A}|\mathbf{A}_1], \mathbf{R}, \mathbf{H}', \mathbf{s})$: *On input an oracle $\mathcal{O}$ for discrete Gaussian sampling over cosets of $\Lambda = \Lambda^{\perp}(\mathbf{A})$ with parameter $s \geq \eta_{\epsilon}(\Lambda^{\perp}(\mathbf{A})$, an extended matrix $\mathbf{A}'$ of $\mathbf{A}$, an invertible matrix $\mathbf{H}'$, the algorithm will sample (using $\mathcal{O}$) each column of $\mathbf{R}'$ independently from a discrete Gaussian with parameter s over the appropriate coset of $\Lambda^{\perp}(\mathbf{A})$, so that $\mathbf{AR}' = \mathbf{H}'\mathbf{G} - \mathbf{A}_1$. The algorithm outputs a trapdoor $\mathbf{R}'$ for $\mathbf{A}'$ with tag $\mathbf{H}'$.*

Lemma 7 ([19]). *Let $q \geq 2, \overline{m} \geq 1$, $k = \lceil \log_2 q \rceil$, and $m = \overline{m} + nk = O(n \log q)$. $(\mathbf{s}, \mathbf{e}) \leftarrow \mathsf{Invert}(\mathbf{R}, \mathbf{A}, \mathbf{b}^t = \mathbf{s}^t\mathbf{A} + \mathbf{e}^t)$: On input a uniform matrix $\mathbf{A}$ and its $\mathbf{G}$-trapdoor $\mathbf{R}$, and a vector $\mathbf{b}$ such that $\mathbf{b}^t = \mathbf{s}^t\mathbf{A} + \mathbf{e}^t$,* Invert *returns* $(\mathbf{s}$ *and* $\mathbf{e})$. *Note that if $\mathbf{e} \leftarrow D_{\mathbb{Z}^m, \alpha q}$ and $1/\alpha \geq 2\sqrt{5(s_1(\mathbf{R})^2 + 1)} \cdot \omega(\sqrt{\log n})$ then* Invert *succeeds with overwhelming probability over the choice of* $\mathbf{e}$.

Lemma 8 (Left-over Hash Lemma ([1], **Lemma 13).** *Suppose that $m > (n+1)\log_2 q + \omega(\log n)$ and that $q > 2$ is prime. Let $\mathbf{R}$ be an $m \times k$ matrix chosen uniformly in $\{1, -1\}^{m \times k} \mod q$, where $k = k(n)$ is polynomial in n. Let $\mathbf{A}$ and $\mathbf{B}$ be matrices chosen uniformly in $\mathbb{Z}^{n \times m}$ and $\mathbb{Z}^{n \times k}$ respectively. Then, for all vectors $\mathbf{e} \in \mathbb{Z}_q^m$, the distribution $(\mathbf{A}, \mathbf{AR}, \mathbf{R}^{\top}\mathbf{e})$ is statistically close to the distribution $(\mathbf{A}, \mathbf{B}, \mathbf{R}^{\top}\mathbf{e})$.*

B Proof of Theorem 1

Proof. We will demonstrate that the scheme satisfies the correctness requirements with all but negligible probability. Suppose that $ct = (\mathbf{c}, \mathbf{c}_{out}, \tilde{\mathbf{c}})$ is an honestly computed ciphertext of message $\mathbf{m}$ with respect to a positive tag ρ, a negative tag set $\boldsymbol{\eta} = \{\eta_1, \cdots, \eta_d\}$ on time t. Let the secret key for the positive tag ρ is $\mathsf{sk}_{\mathsf{N}}^{\rho} = \{\mathsf{sk}_{1,\mathsf{N}}^{\rho}, \mathsf{sk}_2^{\rho}\}$, where $\mathsf{sk}_{1,\mathsf{N}}^{\rho} = \mathbf{T}_{\mathsf{N}}^{\rho}$ on negative tag set $\mathsf{N} = \{\eta_1, \cdots, \eta_\ell\}$, a positive tag ρ and $\mathsf{sk}_1^{\rho} = (\theta, \mathbf{E}_{1,\theta})_{\theta \in I)}$. If ρ is not revoked at time t, then from secret key $\mathsf{sk}_{\mathsf{N}}^{\rho}$ and the revoke access key $\mathsf{rk}_{\mathsf{P}}^t$ on time t, we have $(\mathbf{E}_{1,\theta}, \mathbf{E}_{2,\theta})$, which satisfies $[\mathbf{D}|\mathbf{D}_\rho] \cdot \mathbf{E}_{1,\theta} + [\mathbf{D}|\mathbf{D}_t] \cdot \mathbf{E}_{2,\theta} = \mathbf{A}_\rho$.

To show that the decryption algorithm outputs the correct $\mathbf{m}$, it is required for Eval_{ct} that for $f_{\eta_j}(\boldsymbol{\eta}) = 0$, the resulting ciphertext $\mathbf{c}_{f_{\eta_j}} \in \mathbf{E}_{\mathbf{s},\Delta}(0, \mathbf{B}_{f_{\eta_j}})$ for all $j \in \{1, \cdots, \ell\}$. So that $\mathbf{c}_{f_{\eta_j}} = \mathbf{B}_{f_{\eta_j}}^\top \mathbf{s} + \mathbf{e}$ with $\|\mathbf{e}\| < \boldsymbol{\Delta} < \chi_{\mathbf{max}} \cdot \alpha_{\mathcal{F}}$.

Parse $\tilde{\mathbf{c}} = [\tilde{\mathbf{c}}_0|\tilde{\mathbf{c}}_1|\tilde{\mathbf{c}}_2]$, where $\tilde{c}_i \in \mathbb{Z}_q^m$, for $i \in \{0, 1, 2\}$. Compute

$$\begin{aligned}
\bar{\mathbf{c}}_0 &= \mathbf{E}_{1,\theta}^\top[\tilde{\mathbf{c}}_0|\tilde{\mathbf{c}}_1] + \mathbf{E}_{2,\theta}^\top[\tilde{\mathbf{c}}_0|\tilde{\mathbf{c}}_2] \\
&= \mathbf{E}_{1,\theta}^\top\left([\mathbf{D}|\mathbf{D}_\rho]^\top \mathbf{s} + \begin{bmatrix} \mathbf{e}_0' \\ \mathbf{S}_1^\top \mathbf{e}_0' \end{bmatrix}\right) + \mathbf{E}_{2,\theta}^\top\left([\mathbf{D}|\mathbf{D}_t]^\top \mathbf{s} + \begin{bmatrix} \mathbf{e}_0' \\ \mathbf{S}_2^\top \mathbf{e}_0' \end{bmatrix}\right) \\
&= \mathbf{A}_\rho^\top \mathbf{s} + \underbrace{\mathbf{E}_{1,\theta}^\top \begin{bmatrix} \mathbf{e}_0' \\ \mathbf{S}_1^\top \mathbf{e}_0' \end{bmatrix} + \mathbf{E}_{2,\theta}^\top \begin{bmatrix} \mathbf{e}_0' \\ \mathbf{S}_2^\top \mathbf{e}_0' \end{bmatrix}}_{\mathsf{error}_1}.
\end{aligned}$$

The following holds

$$\begin{aligned}
\mathbf{m} &= \mathbf{c}_{out} - \mathbf{R}^\top \left[\mathbf{c}_{in} \middle| \bar{\mathbf{c}}_0 \middle| \bar{\mathbf{c}}_1 \middle| \mathbf{c}_{f_{\eta_1}} \middle| \cdots \middle| \mathbf{c}_{f_{\eta_\ell}}\right] \\
&= \mathbf{c}_{out} - \mathbf{R}^\top\left(\left[\mathbf{A}|\mathbf{A}_\rho|\mathbf{A}_t|\cdots|\mathbf{B}_{f_{\eta_\ell}}\right]^\top \mathbf{s} + \left[\mathbf{e}_0| \ \mathsf{error}_1 \ |\mathbf{R}_0^\top \mathbf{e}_0|\cdots|\mathbf{e}_{f_{\eta_\ell}}\right]\right) \\
&= \mathbf{U}^\top \mathbf{s} + \mathbf{e}_{out} + \lfloor q/2 \rfloor \cdot \mathbf{m} - \mathbf{U}^\top \mathbf{s} - \mathbf{R}^\top \left[\mathbf{e}_0| \ \mathsf{error}_1 \ |\mathbf{R}_0^\top \mathbf{e}_0|\cdots|\mathbf{e}_{f_{\eta_\ell}}\right] \\
&= \lfloor q/2 \rfloor \cdot \mathbf{m} + \underbrace{\mathbf{e}_{out} - \mathbf{R}^\top \left[\mathbf{e}_0| \ \mathsf{error}_1 \ |\mathbf{R}_0^\top \mathbf{e}_0|\cdots|\mathbf{e}_{f_{\eta_\ell}}\right]}_{\mathsf{error}_2}.
\end{aligned}$$

To get a correct decryption of the original ciphertext ct, the norm of the above error term "error_2" should be less than $q/4$, i.e. it requires to satisfy $\|\mathbf{e}_{out} - \mathbf{R}^\top \cdot \left[\mathbf{e}_{in}|\mathbf{e}_0|\mathbf{e}_0'|\mathbf{e}_{f_{\eta_1}}|\cdots|\mathbf{e}_{f_{\eta_\ell}}\right]\| < q/4$. Since, $\mathbf{E}_{1,\theta}, \mathbf{E}_{2,\theta} \in \mathbb{Z}^{2m \times m}$ are sampled from the distribution $\mathcal{D}_\sigma\left(\Lambda_q^{(\mathbf{A}_\rho - \mathbf{V}_\theta)}(\mathbf{D}|\mathbf{D}_\rho)\right)$, $\mathcal{D}_\sigma\left(\Lambda_q^{\mathbf{V}_\theta}(\mathbf{D}|\mathbf{D}_t)\right)$, respectively, we know that $[\mathbf{D}|\mathbf{D}_\rho] \cdot \mathbf{E}_{1,\theta} = \mathbf{A}_\rho - \mathbf{V}_\theta$, $[\mathbf{D}|\mathbf{D}_t] \cdot \mathbf{E}_{2,\theta} = \mathbf{V}_\theta$, and by Lemma 1, $\|\mathbf{E}_{1,\theta}^\top\|_2, \|\mathbf{E}_{2,\theta}^\top\|_2 < 2m\sigma$ with overwhelming probability. Since $\mathbf{S}_1, \mathbf{S}_2$ are random matrices in $\{+1, -1\}^{m \times m}$, by Lemma 1, $\|\mathbf{S}_1^\top\|_2, \|\mathbf{S}_2^\top\|_2 < 20\sqrt{m}$. Since $\mathbf{e}_0' \in \chi^m$, we know $\|\mathbf{e}_0'\| \leq \chi_{max}$. Finally, we have $\|\mathsf{error}_1\| < 2(1 + 20\sqrt{m})m\sigma\chi_{max}$ with overwhelming probability.

Since $\mathbf{e}_{out} \in \chi^m$, we know $\|\mathbf{e}_{out}\| \leq \chi_{max}$. Since $\mathbf{R} \in \mathbb{Z}^{(\ell+3)m \times n}$ is sampled from the distribution $\mathcal{D}_{\sigma_{\ell+1}}\left(\Lambda_q^{\mathbf{U}}(\mathbf{A}|\mathbf{A}_\rho|\mathbf{A}_t|\mathbf{B}_{f_{\eta_1'}}|\cdots|\mathbf{B}_{f_{\eta_\ell'}})\right)$, we know that $[\mathbf{A}|\mathbf{A}_\rho|\mathbf{A}_t|\mathbf{B}_{f_{\eta_1'}}|\cdots|\mathbf{B}_{f_{\eta_\ell'}}] \cdot \mathbf{R} = \mathbf{U}$ and by Lemma 1, $\|\mathbf{R}^\top\| < (\ell+3)m\sigma_{\ell+1}$ with overwhelming probability. Since $\mathbf{R}_0$ is random in $\{+1, -1\}^{m \times m}$, by Lemma 1, we have that $\|\mathbf{R}_0^\top\|_2 < 20\sqrt{m}$. So we have $\|\left[\mathbf{e}_0| \ \mathsf{error}_1 \ |\mathbf{R}_0^\top \mathbf{e}_0|\mathbf{e}_{f_{\eta_1}}|\cdots|\mathbf{e}_{f_{\eta_\ell}}\right]\| < \chi_{max} + 2(1+20\sqrt{m})m\sigma\chi_{max} + 20\sqrt{m}\chi_{max} + \ell\Delta < (\ell\alpha_{\mathcal{F}} + m\sqrt{m}\sigma + \sqrt{m} + 1)\chi_{max}$. Finally, using $\sigma_{\ell+1} = \sigma_0 \cdot (\sqrt{m \log m})^{\ell+1}$, $\sigma = \omega(\alpha_{\mathcal{F}} \cdot \sqrt{\log m})$, we have $\|\mathsf{error}_2\| = \|\mathbf{e}_{out} - \mathbf{R}^\top \cdot \left[\mathbf{e}_0| \ \mathsf{error}_1 \ |\mathbf{R}_0^\top \mathbf{e}_0|\mathbf{e}_{f_{\eta_1}}|\cdots|\mathbf{e}_{f_{\eta_\ell}}\right]\| \leq \chi_{max} + (\ell+3)m\sigma_{\ell+1} \cdot (\ell\alpha_{\mathcal{F}} + m\sqrt{m}\sigma + \sqrt{m} + 1)\chi_{max} \leq 3\alpha_{\mathcal{F}}^2 \cdot \chi_{max} \cdot (\ell+3)^2 \cdot m^{\frac{\ell}{2}+3}$ with overwhelming probability. Let $\beta_1 = 3\alpha_{\mathcal{F}}^2 \cdot \chi_{max} \cdot (\ell+3)^2 \cdot m^{\frac{\ell}{2}+3}$. By choosing the parameters such that $\beta_1 < q/4$, the decryption will be correct.

To show the correct decryption of an updated ciphertext, we proceed as follows. Let $ct = (\mathbf{c}, \mathbf{c}_{out}, \tilde{\mathbf{c}})$ has been updated to $ct' = (\mathbf{c}', \mathbf{c}_{out}', \tilde{\mathbf{c}}')$ with the update token $\mathsf{tk}_{\mathcal{E}_1 \to \mathcal{E}_2} = \{\Delta_1, \Delta_2\}$, where $\mathcal{E}_1 = (\rho_1, \boldsymbol{\eta}_1, t_1), \mathcal{E}_2 = (\rho_2, \boldsymbol{\eta}_2, t_2)$. Let $\mathbf{r} \leftarrow \mathbb{Z}_q^n$ be a uniformly random vector and $\tilde{\mathbf{e}}_1 \in \chi^{(d+2)m}$, $\tilde{\mathbf{e}}_2 \in \chi^m, \tilde{\mathbf{e}}_3 \in \chi^{3m}$ are error vectors. Let $\boldsymbol{\eta}_2 = (\eta_1', \cdots, \eta_d')$. Set $\mathbf{H}_1' = \left[\mathbf{A} \middle| \mathbf{A}_{t_2} \middle| \eta_1'\mathbf{G} + \mathbf{B}_1 \middle| \cdots \middle| \eta_d'\mathbf{G} + \mathbf{B}_d\right] \in \mathbb{Z}_q^{n \times (d+2)m}$ and $\mathbf{H}_2' = \left[\mathbf{D} \middle| \mathbf{D}_{\rho_2} \middle| \mathbf{D}_{t_2}\right] \in \mathbb{Z}_q^{n \times 3m}$. The updated ciphertext $ct' = (\mathbf{c}', \mathbf{c}'_{out}, \tilde{\mathbf{c}}')$ has the following form:

$$\mathbf{c}' = [\mathbf{c}'_{in}, \bar{\mathbf{c}}'_1, \mathbf{c}'_1, \cdots, \mathbf{c}'_d] = \Delta_1^\top \cdot [(\mathbf{c}_{in}, \bar{\mathbf{c}}_1, \mathbf{c}_1, \cdots, \mathbf{c}_d)] + \mathbf{H}_1'^\top \mathbf{r} + \tilde{\mathbf{e}}_1$$
$$= \mathbf{H}_1'^\top (\mathbf{s} + \mathbf{r}) + \underbrace{\Delta_1^\top \mathbf{e} + \tilde{\mathbf{e}}_1}_{\mathbf{p}}. \quad \left(\text{Parse } \mathbf{p} \text{ as } [e'_{in} | \mathbf{e}'_0 | \mathbf{e}'_{f_{\eta_1}} | \cdots | \mathbf{e}'_{f_{\eta_\ell}}]\right)$$

$$\mathbf{c}'_{out} = \mathbf{c}_{out} + \mathbf{U}^\top \mathbf{r} + \tilde{\mathbf{e}}_2 = \mathbf{U}^\top (\mathbf{s} + \mathbf{r}) + \mathbf{e}_{out} + \tilde{\mathbf{e}}_2 + \lfloor q/2 \rfloor \cdot \mathbf{m}.$$
$$\tilde{\mathbf{c}}' = [\tilde{\mathbf{c}}'_0 | \tilde{\mathbf{c}}'_1 | \tilde{\mathbf{c}}'_2] = \Delta_2^\top \cdot [\mathbf{c} | \tilde{\mathbf{c}}] + \mathbf{H}_2'^\top \mathbf{r} + \tilde{\mathbf{e}}_3 = \mathbf{H}_2'^\top (\mathbf{s} + \mathbf{r}) + \Delta_2^\top \begin{bmatrix} \mathbf{e} \\ \mathbf{e}' \end{bmatrix} + \tilde{\mathbf{e}}_3.$$

If ρ_2 is not revoked at time t', then there are $(\mathbf{E}'_{1,\theta}, \mathbf{E}'_{2,\theta})$, which satisfies $[\mathbf{D} | \mathbf{D}_{\rho_2}] \cdot \mathbf{E}'_{1,\theta} + [\mathbf{D} | \mathbf{D}_{t'}] \cdot \mathbf{E}'_{2,\theta} = \mathbf{A}_{\rho_2}$. For $\tilde{\mathbf{c}}' = [\tilde{\mathbf{c}}'_0 | \tilde{\mathbf{c}}'_1 | \tilde{\mathbf{c}}'_2]$, it holds $\bar{\mathbf{c}}'_0 = \mathbf{E'}_{1,\theta}^\top [\tilde{\mathbf{c}}'_0 | \tilde{\mathbf{c}}'_1] + \mathbf{E'}_{2,\theta}^\top [\tilde{\mathbf{c}}'_0 | \tilde{\mathbf{c}}'_2]$. Parse $\mathbf{E}'_{i,\theta} = (\mathbf{E}'^{(0)}_{i,\theta}, \mathbf{E}'^{(1)}_{i,\theta})$ for $i \in \{1, 2\}$. We can form a matrix $\mathbf{E} = \begin{bmatrix} \mathbf{E}'^{(0)}_{1,\theta} + \mathbf{E}'^{(0)}_{2,\theta} \\ \mathbf{E}'^{(1)}_{1,\theta} \\ \mathbf{E}'^{(1)}_{2,\theta} \end{bmatrix} \in \mathbb{Z}^{3m \times m}$, which satisfies $\bar{\mathbf{c}}'_0 = \mathbf{E}^\top \cdot \tilde{\mathbf{c}}'$.

$$\text{We have } \bar{\mathbf{c}}'_0 = \mathbf{E}^\top \cdot \tilde{\mathbf{c}}' = \mathbf{E}^\top \cdot \left([\mathbf{D} | \mathbf{D}_{\rho_2} | \mathbf{D}_{t'}]^\top (\mathbf{s} + \mathbf{r}) + \Delta_2^\top \begin{bmatrix} \mathbf{e} \\ \mathbf{e}' \end{bmatrix} + \tilde{\mathbf{e}}_3 \right)$$
$$= \mathbf{A}_{\rho_2}^\top (\mathbf{s} + \mathbf{r}) + \underbrace{\mathbf{E}^\top \cdot (\Delta_2^\top \begin{bmatrix} \mathbf{e} \\ \mathbf{e}' \end{bmatrix} + \tilde{\mathbf{e}}_3)}_{\mathsf{error}'_1}.$$

After evaluating $\mathbf{c}'_{f_{\eta_j}} \leftarrow \mathsf{Eval}_{ct}(\{\eta_i, \mathbf{B}_i, \mathbf{c}'_i\}_{i=1}^d, f_{\eta_j})$ for all $j \in \{1, \cdots, \ell\}$, we have the magnitude of the noise in $\mathbf{c}'_{f_{\eta_j}}$, i.e., $\|\mathbf{e}'_{f_{\eta_j}}\| < \Delta$. Therefore, during decryption of updated ciphertexts, one obtains:

$$\mathbf{m} = \mathbf{c}'_{out} - \mathbf{R}'^\top \left[\mathbf{c}'_{in} \middle| \bar{\mathbf{c}}'_0 \middle| \bar{\mathbf{c}}'_1 \middle| \mathbf{c}'_{f_{\eta_1}} \middle| \cdots \middle| \mathbf{c}'_{f_{\eta_\ell}}\right]$$
$$= \mathbf{c}'_{out} - \mathbf{R}'^\top \left(\left[\mathbf{A}_0 | \mathbf{A}_{\rho_2} | \mathbf{A}_{t'} | \cdots | \mathbf{B}_{f_{\eta_\ell}}\right]^\top (\mathbf{s} + \mathbf{r}) + \left[\mathbf{e}'_{in} | \ \mathsf{error}'_1 \ | \mathbf{e}'_0 | \cdots | \mathbf{e}'_{f_{\eta_\ell}}\right] \right)$$
$$= \lfloor q/2 \rfloor \cdot \mathbf{m} + \underbrace{\mathbf{e}_{out} + \tilde{\mathbf{e}}_3 - \mathbf{R}'^\top \left[\mathbf{e}'_{in} | \ \mathsf{error}'_1 \ | \mathbf{e}'_0 | \cdots | \mathbf{e}'_{f_{\eta_\ell}}\right]}_{\mathsf{error}'_2}.$$

Note that the tokens Δ_1, Δ_2 are formed with the matrices sampled via the SampleRight algorithm, matrices chosen from χ, the identity matrix, and the zero matrix. The structure depends on the number of changes in tags required. To find the norm of Δ_1 and Δ_2, we consider the form for which the norm will be maximum from all the possible cases. Following Lemma 1 and the property of χ-distribution, we have $\|\Delta_1^\top\|_2 < (d+1)m\sigma + \chi_{max}$ and $\|\Delta_2^\top\|_2 < (d+3)m\sigma + \chi_{max}$. Since $\mathbf{E}'_{1,\theta}, \mathbf{E}'_{2,\theta} \in \mathbb{Z}^{2m \times m}$ are sampled from the distribution $\mathcal{D}_\sigma(\Lambda_q^{(\mathbf{A}_{\rho_2} - \mathbf{V}_\theta)}(\mathbf{D} | \mathbf{D}_{\rho_2}))$, $\mathcal{D}_\sigma(\Lambda_q^{\mathbf{V}_\theta}(\mathbf{D} | \mathbf{D}_{t_2}))$, respectively, we know that $[\mathbf{D}|\mathbf{D}_{\rho_2}] \cdot \mathbf{E}_{1,\theta} = \mathbf{A}_{\rho_2} - \mathbf{V}_\theta$, $[\mathbf{D}|\mathbf{D}_{t_2}] \cdot \mathbf{E}_{2,\theta} = \mathbf{V}_\theta$, and by Lemma 1, $\|\mathbf{E}^\top\|_2 < 3m\sigma$ with overwhelming probability. Since, $\tilde{e}_3 \in \chi^{3m}$, we know $\|\tilde{e}_3\| \le \chi_{max}$. We have $\mathbf{e} = \left[\mathbf{I}_m|\mathbf{R}_0|\mathbf{R}_1|\cdots|\mathbf{R}_d\right]^\top \cdot \mathbf{e}_0 \in \mathbb{Z}_q^{(d+2)m}$ and $\mathbf{e}' = \left[\mathbf{I}_m|\mathbf{S}_1|\mathbf{S}_2\right]^\top \cdot \mathbf{e}'_0 \in \mathbb{Z}_q^{3m}$, where $\mathbf{R}_0, \mathbf{R}_1, \cdots, \mathbf{R}_d, \mathbf{S}_1, \mathbf{S}_2$ are random in $\{+1,-1\}^{m\times m}$, by Lemma 1, $\|\mathbf{R}_i^\top\|_2 < 20\sqrt{m}$ for $i \in \{0, 1, \cdots, d\}$ and $\|\mathbf{S}_1^\top\|_2, \|\mathbf{S}_2^\top\|_2 < 20\sqrt{m}$ with overwhelming probability. Also, $\mathbf{e}_0, \mathbf{e}'_0 \in \chi^m$, we know $\|\mathbf{e}_0\|, \|\mathbf{e}'_0\| \le \chi_{max}$. We have $\|\begin{bmatrix}\mathbf{e}\\ \mathbf{e}'\end{bmatrix}\| < 2\chi_{max} + 20\sqrt{m}(d+3)\chi_{max}$. So, we have $\|\mathsf{error}'_1\| = \|\mathbf{E}^\top \cdot \left(\Delta_2^\top \begin{bmatrix}\mathbf{e}\\ \mathbf{e}'\end{bmatrix} + \tilde{\mathbf{e}}_3\right)\| < 20\sqrt{m}((d+3)m\sigma\chi_{max})^2$ with overwhelming probability.

Since, $\mathbf{e}_{out} \in \chi^m$, we know $\|\mathbf{e}_{out}\| \le \chi_{max}$. Since $\mathbf{R}' \in \mathbb{Z}^{(\ell+3)m\times n}$ is sampled from the distribution $\mathcal{D}_{\sigma_{\ell+1}}\left(\Lambda_q^{\mathbf{U}}(\mathbf{A}|\mathbf{A}_{\rho_2}|\mathbf{A}_{t_2}|\mathbf{B}_{f_{\eta'_1}}|\cdots|\mathbf{B}_{f_{\eta'_\ell}})\right)$, we know that $[\mathbf{A}|\mathbf{A}_{\rho_2}|\mathbf{A}_{t_2}|\mathbf{B}_{f_{\eta'_1}}|\cdots|\mathbf{B}_{f_{\eta'_\ell}}] \cdot \mathbf{R}' = \mathbf{U}$ and by Lemma 1, $\|\mathbf{R}'^\top\| < (\ell+3)m\sigma_{\ell+1}$ with overwhelming probability. So we have $\|\mathsf{error}'_2\| \le 3\alpha_{\mathcal{F}}^3 \cdot \chi_{max}^2 \cdot (d+3)^2(\ell+3)^2 \cdot m^{\frac{\ell+1}{2}+3}$ with overwhelming probability. Let $\beta_2 = 3\alpha_{\mathcal{F}}^3 \cdot \chi_{max}^2 \cdot (d+3)^2(\ell+3)^2 \cdot m^{\frac{\ell+1}{2}+3}$. By choosing the parameters such that $\beta_2 < q/4$, the decryption of the updated ciphertext will be correct. For the correctness of the scheme, choose $\beta = max\{\beta_1, \beta_2\}$ and set the parameters such that, $\beta < q/4$, i.e., $3\alpha_{\mathcal{F}}^3 \cdot \chi_{max}^2 \cdot (d+3)^2(\ell+3)^2 \cdot m^{\frac{\ell+1}{2}+3} < q/4$.

□

C Proof of Theorem 2

Proof. We build an dLWE algorithm $\mathcal{B}$ that uses a selective DPE attacker $\mathcal{A}$ to solve dLWE. We will demonstrate that if there is a PPT adversary $\mathcal{A}$ succeeding in breaking the IND-sDPE-CPA security of our DPE scheme, then we can use it to construct a PPT algorithm $\mathcal{B}$ to solve $\mathsf{dLWE}_{n,3m,q,\chi}$. $\mathcal{A}$ sends the target positive tag $\rho^* \in \mathcal{P}$, the target d-tuple of negative tags $\boldsymbol{\eta}^* = (\eta_1^*, \cdots, \eta_d^*) \in \mathcal{N}^d$, and time $t^* \in \mathcal{T}$ to the challenger. Let P^* be the set of revoked positive tags at t^*. The challenger initializes three empty sets $P, C, \overline{C}$ to record puncture key queries, corrupt key queries, and token queries. Also, the challenger introduces a counter numCI to 0, a key-value store $\mathcal{H}$ to be empty, and a set Derive to be empty. It sets a binary tree BT with at least N leaf nodes. The proof proceeds in a sequence of games. The first game is identical to the original IND-sDPE-CPA game from the Definition 3. The last two games are indistinguishable due to the hardness of the dLWE problem.

***Game* 0**: This is the original IND-sDPE-CPA game from definition between an adversary $\mathcal{A}$ against scheme and an IND-sDPE-CPA challenger.

***G*Game 1**: This game is same as Game 0, except the generation of $\mathbf{A}_0, \mathbf{A}_1, \mathbf{B}_1, \cdots, \mathbf{B}_d, \mathbf{D}_0, \mathbf{D}_1$ in the public key pk during Set up phase. The challenger chooses $(d+4)$ uniformly random matrices $\bar{\mathbf{R}}_0^*, \mathbf{R}_0^*, \mathbf{R}_1^*, \cdots, \mathbf{R}_d^*$ and $\mathbf{S}_1'^*, \mathbf{S}_2'^*$ from $\{+1,-1\}^{m\times m}$. Set $\mathbf{A}_0, \mathbf{A}_1, \mathbf{B}_1, \cdots, \mathbf{B}_d$ and $\mathbf{D}_0, \mathbf{D}_1$ as follows:

$\mathbf{A}_0 = \mathbf{A}\bar{\mathbf{R}}_0^*$, $\mathbf{A}_1 = \mathbf{A}\mathbf{R}_0^* - \mathbf{H}_{t^*}\mathbf{G}$, $\mathbf{B}_i = \mathbf{A}\mathbf{R}_i^* - \eta_i^*\mathbf{G}$ for $i \in \{1, \cdots, d\}$, $\mathbf{D}_0 = \mathbf{D}\mathbf{S}_1^{'*} - \mathbf{H}_{\rho^*}\mathbf{G}$, and $\mathbf{D}_1 = \mathbf{D}\mathbf{S}_2^{'*} - \mathbf{H}_{t^*}\mathbf{G}$.

The challenger generate $\mathbf{A}, \mathbf{D}, \mathbf{U}, \mathbf{G}$ same as Game 0, and sends $\mathsf{pk} = \{\mathbf{A}, \mathbf{D}, \mathbf{A}_0, \mathbf{A}_1, \mathbf{B}_1, \cdots, \mathbf{B}_d, \mathbf{D}_0, \mathbf{D}_1, \mathbf{U}, \mathbf{G}\}$ to the adversary $\mathcal{A}$. The remainder of the game is same as Game 0. Due to Lemma 8 (Left-over Hash Lemma), $\mathbf{A}\bar{\mathbf{R}}_0^*, \mathbf{A}\mathbf{R}_0^*$ and $\mathbf{A}\mathbf{R}_1^*, \cdots, \mathbf{A}\mathbf{R}_d^*$, and $\mathbf{D}\mathbf{S}_1^{'*}, \mathbf{D}\mathbf{S}_2^{'*}$ are statistically indistinguishable with uniform distribution. So, $\mathbf{A}_0, \mathbf{A}_1, \mathbf{B}_1, \cdots, \mathbf{B}_d, \mathbf{D}_0, \mathbf{D}_1$ as defined above, are close to uniform. Hence, Game 0 and Game 1 are statistically indistinguishable.

***G*Game 2**: Here, the challenger chooses random $\mathbf{A}, \mathbf{D}$ from $\mathbb{Z}_q^{n\times m}$ instead of having from TrapGen algorithm and the construction of $\mathbf{A}_0, \mathbf{A}_1, \mathbf{B}_1, \cdots, \mathbf{B}_d, \mathbf{D}_0, \mathbf{D}_1, \mathbf{U}, \mathbf{G}$ in pk remain same as Game 1. The adversary issues following queries adaptively and the challenger does as follows:
$\mathcal{Q}_{Puncture}(\rho, \eta)$: Here, the challenger first defines $\mathbf{V}_\theta$ for each $\theta \in \mathsf{BT}$ as follows:

- If $\theta \in Path(\rho^*)$, pick $\mathbf{E}_{1,\theta}^* \leftarrow \mathcal{D}_{\mathbb{Z}^{2m\times m},s}$ and $\mathbf{V}_\theta = \mathbf{A}_{\rho^*} - [\mathbf{D}|\mathbf{D}_{\rho^*}] \cdot \mathbf{E}_{\mathbf{1},\theta}^*$.
- If $\theta \notin Path(\rho^*)$, pick $\mathbf{E}_{2,\theta}^* \leftarrow \mathcal{D}_{\mathbb{Z}^{2m\times m},s}$ and $\mathbf{V}_\theta = [\mathbf{D}|\mathbf{D}_{\mathbf{t}^*}] \cdot \mathbf{E}_{\mathbf{2},\theta}^*$.

Given a positive tag ρ and a negative tag η, consider following two cases:

1. *Query for* $\rho (\neq \rho^*)$:
   - When $\mathcal{A}$ issues the first puncture query under ρ, the challenger compute $\mathsf{sk}_{\mathsf{N}_\rho}^\rho$, where $\mathsf{N}_\rho = \{\eta\}$ as follows:
   Construct $\mathbf{A}_\rho = \mathbf{A}_0 + \mathbf{H}_\rho\mathbf{G} = \mathbf{A}\bar{\mathbf{R}}_0^* + (\mathbf{H}_\rho - \mathbf{H}_{\rho^*})\mathbf{G}$. Since, $\mathbf{T}_\mathbf{G}$ is a trapdoor for $\mathbf{G}$, so it's also a trapdoor for $(\mathbf{H}_\rho - \mathbf{H}_{\rho^*})\mathbf{G}$, as $(\mathbf{H}_\rho - \mathbf{H}_{\rho^*}) \neq 0$ by definition of FRD. Then obtain $\mathbf{T}_{(\mathbf{A}|\mathbf{A}_\rho)}^{\mathrm{EL}} \leftarrow \mathsf{ExtendLeft}(\mathbf{A}, (\mathbf{H}_\rho - \mathbf{H}_{\rho^*})\mathbf{G}, \mathbf{T}_\mathbf{G}, \bar{\mathbf{R}}_0^*)$. Evaluate $\mathbf{B}_{f_\eta} \leftarrow \mathsf{Eval}_{\mathsf{pk}}(\{\mathbf{B}_i\}_{i=1}^d, f_\eta)$. Compute $\mathbf{T}_{\{\eta\}}^{\rho,\mathrm{ER}} \leftarrow \mathsf{ExtendRight}\left([\mathbf{A}|\mathbf{A}_\rho|\mathbf{B}_{f_\eta}], \mathbf{T}_{(\mathbf{A}|\mathbf{A}_\rho)}^{\mathrm{EL}}, \mathbf{B}_{f_\eta}\right)$. Finally, compute a randomized trapdoor $\mathbf{T}_{\{\eta\}}^\rho \leftarrow \mathsf{RandBasis}((\mathbf{A}|\mathbf{A}_\rho|\mathbf{B}_{f_\eta}), \mathbf{T}_{\{\eta\}}^{\rho,\mathrm{ER}}, \sigma_0)$. Set this as the punctured secret key $\mathsf{sk}_{1,\mathsf{N}_\rho}^\rho = \mathbf{T}_{(\mathbf{A}|\mathbf{A}_\rho)}$ for positive tag ρ, where $\mathsf{N}_\rho = \{\eta\}$, the set of containing negative tags.
   - To compute sk_2^ρ, the challenger proceeds as follows:
   Construct $\mathbf{D}_\rho = \mathbf{D} + \mathbf{H}_\rho\mathbf{G} = \mathbf{D}\mathbf{S}_1^{'*} + (\mathbf{H}_\rho - \mathbf{H}_{\rho^*})\mathbf{G}$. Since, $T_\mathbf{G}$ is a trapdoor for $\mathbf{G}$, so it's also a trapdoor for $(\mathbf{H}_\rho - \mathbf{H}_{\rho^*})\mathbf{G}$, as $(\mathbf{H}_\rho - \mathbf{H}_{\rho^*}) \neq 0$ by definition of FRD.
   Then sample $\mathbf{E}_{1,\theta} \leftarrow \mathsf{SampleLeft}\left(\mathbf{D}, \mathbf{S}_1^{'*}, (\mathbf{H}_\rho - \mathbf{H}_{\rho^*}), \mathbf{A}_\rho - \mathbf{V}_\theta, \sigma\right)$ for each $\theta \in Path(\rho)$. Note that $\mathbf{E}_{1,\theta} \in \mathbb{Z}^{2m\times m}$ and $[\mathbf{D}|\mathbf{D}_\rho] \cdot \mathbf{E}_{1,\theta} = \mathbf{A}_\rho - \mathbf{V}_\theta$. Set $\mathsf{sk}_2^\rho = (\theta, \mathbf{E}_{1,\theta})_{\theta \in Path(\rho)}$.
   - Set $\mathsf{sk}_{\mathsf{N}_\rho}^\rho = \{\mathsf{sk}_{1,\mathsf{N}_\rho}^\rho, \mathsf{sk}_2^\rho\}$, where $\mathsf{N}_\rho = \{\eta\}$ is the set of containing negative tags and add $(\rho, \mathsf{sk}_{\mathsf{N}_\rho}^\rho, \mathsf{N}_\rho)$ to P. For further queries on ρ, use Punc algorithm accordingly and update the N_ρ and $\mathsf{sk}_{1,\mathsf{N}_\rho}^\rho$ in the tuple $(\rho, \mathsf{sk}_{\mathsf{N}_\rho}^\rho, \mathsf{N}_\rho)$.
2. *Query for* $\rho = \rho^*$:

- The challenger add η to T_{ρ^*}, set $\mathsf{sk}_2^{\rho^*} = (\theta, \mathbf{E}_{1,\theta}^*)_{\theta \in Path(\rho^*)}$. Observe that $\mathbf{E}_{1,\theta}^* \in \mathbb{Z}^{2m \times m}$ and $[\mathbf{D}|\mathbf{D}_{\rho^*}] \cdot \mathbf{E}_{1,\theta}^* = \mathbf{A}_{\rho^*} - \mathbf{V}_\theta$. Set $\mathsf{sk}_{\mathsf{N}_{\rho^*}}^{\rho^*} = \{-, \mathsf{sk}_2^{\rho^*}\}$. Construct a tuple $(\rho^*, \mathsf{sk}_{\mathsf{N}_{\rho^*}}^{\rho^*}, \mathsf{N}_{\rho^*})$ and add it to P. For further puncture queries on ρ^*, update the N_{ρ^*} in P.

$\mathcal{Q}_{Corrupt}(\rho)$: The first time $\mathcal{A}$ makes a corruption query for ρ, challenger responses as the follows, and for all subsequent queries for ρ, returns $\perp$.

1. *Query for* ρ $(\neq \rho^*)$: Based on the restrictions, defined in Definition 3, it returns either $\perp$ or the most recent key $\mathsf{sk}_{\mathsf{N}_\rho}^{\rho}$ from the table P. Add $(\rho, \perp/\mathsf{sk}_{\mathsf{N}_\rho}^{\rho}, \mathsf{N}_\rho)$ to C.
2. *Query for* ρ^*: For the tuple $(\rho^*, \mathsf{sk}_{\mathsf{N}_{\rho^*}}^{\rho^*} = \{-, \mathsf{sk}_2^{\rho^*}\}, \mathsf{N}_{\rho^*})$ in P, where N_{ρ^*} is the set $\{\eta_1, \cdots, \eta_k\}$, evaluate $\mathbf{B}_{f_{\eta_j}} \leftarrow \mathsf{Eval}_{\mathsf{pk}}(\{\mathbf{B}_i\}_{i=1}^d, f_{\eta_j})$, $\forall\, j \in \{1, \cdots, k\}$. Let $\mathsf{L} = [\mathbf{A}|\mathbf{A}_{\rho^*}|\mathbf{B}_{f_{\eta_1}}|\cdots|\mathbf{B}_{f_{\eta_k}}]$. To compute $\mathsf{sk}_{1,\mathsf{N}_{\rho^*}}^{\rho^*}$, it proceeds as follows:
   - If $\mathsf{N}_\rho^* \cap \{\eta_1^*, \cdots, \eta_d^*\} = \emptyset$: Observe that $[\mathbf{A}|\mathbf{A}_{\rho^*}] = [\mathbf{A}|\mathbf{A}\bar{\mathbf{R}}_0^* + \mathbf{H}_{\rho^*}\mathbf{G}]$. Since, $T_{\mathbf{G}}$ is a trapdoor for $\mathbf{G}$, so it's also a trapdoor for $\mathbf{H}_{\rho^*}\mathbf{G}$, as $\mathbf{H}_{\rho^*} \neq 0$. Compute $\mathbf{T}_{[\mathbf{A}|\mathbf{A}_{\rho^*}]}^{\mathrm{EL}} \leftarrow \mathsf{ExtendLeft}(\mathbf{A}, \mathbf{H}_{\rho^*}\mathbf{G}, \mathbf{T}_{\mathbf{G}}, \bar{\mathbf{R}}_0^*)$.
     Compute $\mathbf{T}_{\mathsf{N}_{\rho^*}}^{\rho^*,\mathrm{ER}} \leftarrow \mathsf{ExtendRight}\left([\mathbf{A}|\mathbf{A}_{\rho^*}], \mathbf{T}_{[\mathbf{A}|\mathbf{A}_{\rho^*}]}^{\mathrm{EL}}, [\mathbf{B}_{f_{\eta_1}}|\cdots|\mathbf{B}_{f_{\eta_k}}]\right)$.
     Observe that $\mathbf{T}_{\mathsf{N}_{\rho^*}}^{\rho^*,\mathrm{ER}}$ is a trapdoor for L. Compute a randomized trapdoor $\mathbf{T}_{\mathsf{N}_{\rho^*}}^{\rho^*} \leftarrow \mathsf{RandBasis}(\mathsf{L}, \mathbf{T}_{\mathsf{N}_{\rho^*}}^{\rho^*,\mathrm{ER}}, \sigma_0)$. Set $\mathsf{sk}_{1,\mathsf{N}_{\rho^*}}^{\rho^*} = \mathbf{T}_{\mathsf{N}_{\rho^*}}^{\rho^*}$. Update the tuple from $(\rho^*, \mathsf{sk}_{\mathsf{N}_{\rho^*}}^{\rho^*} = \{-, \mathsf{sk}_2^{\rho^*}\}, \mathsf{N}_{\rho^*})$ to $(\rho^*, \mathsf{sk}_{\mathsf{N}_{\rho^*}}^{\rho^*} = \{\mathsf{sk}_{1,\mathsf{N}_{\rho^*}}^{\rho^*}, \mathsf{sk}_2^{\rho^*}\}, \mathsf{N}_{\rho^*})$.
   - If $\mathsf{N}_\rho^* \cap \{\eta_1^*, \cdots, \eta_d^*\} \neq \emptyset$: It implies that there exist at least one $\eta_i \in \mathsf{N}_\rho^*$ such that $f_{\eta_i}(\boldsymbol{\eta}^*) \neq 0$. Without loss of generality, we assume that $f_{\eta_k}(\boldsymbol{\eta}^*) \neq 0$. Compute $\mathbf{S}_{f_{\eta_k}}^* \leftarrow \mathsf{Eval}_{sim}(f_{\eta_k}, \{\eta_j^*, \mathbf{R}_j^*\}_{j=1}^d, \mathbf{A})$, and let $\mathbf{B}_{f_{\eta_k}} = \mathbf{A}\mathbf{S}_{f_{\eta_k}}^* - f_{\eta_k}(\boldsymbol{\eta}^*)\mathbf{G}$, where, $\|\mathbf{S}_{f_{\eta_k}}^*\|_2 \leq \alpha_{\mathcal{F}}$.
     Compute $\mathbf{T}_{[\mathbf{A}|\mathbf{B}_{f_{\eta_k}}]}^{\mathrm{EL}} \leftarrow \mathsf{ExtendLeft}\left(\mathbf{A}, f_{\eta_k}(\boldsymbol{\eta}^*)\mathbf{G}, \mathbf{T}_{\mathbf{G}}, \mathbf{S}_{f_{\eta_k}}^*\right)$. Compute a trapdoor $\mathbf{T}_{[\mathbf{A}|\mathbf{B}_{f_{\eta_k}}|\mathbf{A}_{\rho^*}|\mathbf{B}_{f_{\eta_1}}|\cdots|\mathbf{B}_{f_{\eta_{k-1}}}]}^{\mathrm{ER}}$ by running $\mathsf{ExtendRight}\left([\mathbf{A}|\mathbf{B}_{f_{\eta_k}}], \mathbf{T}_{(\mathbf{A}|\mathbf{B}_{f_{\eta_k}})}^{\mathrm{EL}}, (\mathbf{A}_{\rho^*}|\mathbf{B}_{f_{\eta_1}}|\cdots|\mathbf{B}_{f_{\eta_{k-1}}})\right)$. By switching the rows of the matrix $\mathbf{T}_{(\mathbf{A}|\mathbf{B}_{f_{\eta_k}}|\mathbf{A}_{\rho^*}|\mathbf{B}_{f_{\eta_1}}|\cdots|\mathbf{B}_{f_{\eta_{k-1}}})}^{\mathrm{ER}}$, we get a trapdoor $\mathbf{T}_{\mathsf{L}}^{\mathrm{ER}}$ for L. Set $\mathbf{T}_{\mathsf{N}_{\rho^*}}^{\rho^*,\mathrm{ER}} = \mathbf{T}_{\mathsf{L}}^{\mathrm{ER}}$ and by Lemma 2, $\|\mathbf{T}_{\mathsf{N}_{\rho^*}}^{\rho^*,\mathrm{ER}}\|_{\mathrm{GS}} \leq \sqrt{5}\alpha_{\mathcal{F}}$.
     Compute a randomized trapdoor $\mathbf{T}_{\mathsf{N}_{\rho^*}}^{\rho^*} \leftarrow \mathsf{RandBasis}(\mathsf{L}, \mathbf{T}_{\mathsf{N}_{\rho^*}}^{\rho^*,\mathrm{ER}}, \sigma_0)$.
     Set $\mathsf{sk}_{1,\mathsf{N}_{\rho^*}}^{\rho^*} = \mathbf{T}_{\mathsf{N}_{\rho^*}}^{\rho^*}$ and update the tuple $(\rho^*, \mathsf{sk}_{\mathsf{N}_{\rho^*}}^{\rho^*} = (-, \mathsf{sk}_2^{\rho^*}), \mathsf{N}_{\rho^*})$ to $(\rho^*, \mathsf{sk}_{\mathsf{N}_{\rho^*}}^{\rho^*} = \{\mathsf{sk}_{1,\mathsf{N}_{\rho^*}}^{\rho^*}, \mathsf{sk}_2^{\rho^*}\}, \mathsf{N}_{\rho^*})$ in P.

   Based on the restrictions, defined in Definition 3, it returns either $\perp$ or the secret key $\mathsf{sk}_{\mathsf{N}_{\rho^*}}^{\rho^*}$ from P. Add the tuple $(\rho^*, \perp/\mathsf{sk}_{\mathsf{N}_{\rho^*}}^{\rho^*}, \mathsf{N}_{\rho^*})$ to C accordingly.

Observe that in the real scheme, the key $\mathsf{sk}^{\rho}_{1,\mathsf{N}_\rho}$ are generated using the algorithm ExtendRight, RandBasis for every ρ. In contrast, during the simulation, they are drawn from ExtendLeft, ExtendRight, RandBasis. Also, the matrices $\mathbf{E}_{1,\theta}$ are generated using SampleRight for every ρ in the real scheme. In contrast, during the simulation in , they are drawn from $\mathcal{D}_{\mathbb{Z}^{2m\times m},s}$ when $\rho = \rho^*$, and sampled using SampleLeft when $\rho \neq \rho^*$. The properties of these algorithms (see Sect. 3) ensure that the resulting distributions are statistically indistinguishable.
$\mathcal{Q}_{RevAccK}(t, \mathsf{P}_t)$: On input time t, the challenger first update the revoke list P_t based on the restriction provided in Definition 3, and it returns $\mathsf{rk}^t_{\mathsf{P}_t}$ as follows.

1. *Query for* $t(\neq t^*)$: the challenger construct $\mathbf{D}_t = \mathbf{D} + \mathbf{H}_t\mathbf{G} = \mathbf{D}\mathbf{S}_1^{'*} + (\mathbf{H}_t - \mathbf{H}_{t^*})\mathbf{G}$. Since, $\mathbf{T_G}$ is a trapdoor for $\mathbf{G}$, so it's also a trapdoor for $(\mathbf{H}_t - \mathbf{H}_{t^*})\mathbf{G}$, as $(\mathbf{H}_t - \mathbf{H}_{t^*}) \neq 0$ by definition of FRD.
   Then sample $\mathbf{E}_{2,\theta} \leftarrow \mathsf{SampleLeft}\left(\mathbf{D}, \mathbf{S}_1^{'*}, (\mathbf{H}_t - \mathbf{H}_{t^*}), \mathbf{V}_\theta, \sigma\right)$ for each $\theta \in \mathsf{KUNodes}(\mathsf{BT}, \mathsf{P}_t)$. Note that $\mathbf{E}_{2,\theta} \in \mathbb{Z}^{2m\times m}$ and $[\mathbf{D}|\mathbf{D}_t] \cdot \mathbf{E}_{2,\theta} = \mathbf{V}_\theta$.
   Set $\mathsf{rk}_t = (\theta, \mathbf{E}_{2,\theta})_{\theta\in\mathsf{KUNodes}(\mathsf{BT},\mathsf{P}_t)}$ and returns $\mathsf{rk}^t_{\mathsf{P}_t}$.
2. *Query for* $t = t^*$: for the challenge time period t^*, the challenger returns $(\theta, \mathbf{E}^*_{2,\theta})_{\theta\in\mathsf{KUNodes}(\mathsf{BT},\mathsf{P}_{t^*},t^*)}$. (Defined in $\mathcal{Q}_{Puncture}$). Note that $\mathbf{E}^*_{2,\theta} \in \mathbb{Z}^{2m\times m}$ and $[\mathbf{D}|\mathbf{D}_{t^*}] \cdot \mathbf{E}^*_{2,\theta} = \mathbf{V}_\theta$. Set $\mathsf{rk}_{t^*} = (\theta, \mathbf{E}^*_{2,\theta})_{\theta\in\mathsf{KUNodes}(\mathsf{BT},\mathsf{P}_t)}$ and returns $\mathsf{rk}^t_{\mathsf{P}_t}$.

Observe that in the real scheme, the matrices $\mathbf{E}_{2,\theta}$ are generated using the algorithm SampleRight for every t. In contrast, during the simulation, they are drawn from $\mathcal{D}_{\mathbb{Z}^{2m\times m},s}$ when $t = t^*$, and sampled using SampleLeft when $t \neq t^*$. The properties of these sampling algorithms (see Sect. 3) ensure that the resulting distributions are statistically indistinguishable.
$\mathcal{Q}_{Token}(\rho_1, \boldsymbol{\eta}_1, t_1 \rightarrow \rho_2, \boldsymbol{\eta}_2, t_2)$: The challenger consider the following two cases: If $(\rho_1, \boldsymbol{\eta}_1, t_1) = (\rho^*, \boldsymbol{\eta}^*, t^*)$, it proceeds as follows.

- If $\boldsymbol{\eta}_1 = \boldsymbol{\eta}_2$: the challenger uniformly samples $\mathbf{X}^{(0)}, \mathbf{X}^{(1)}$ from $\mathbb{Z}^{m\times m} \times \mathbb{Z}^{dm\times m}$, and $\mathbf{Y} \leftarrow \chi^{m\times m}$, respectively. Set

$$\Delta_1 = \begin{bmatrix} \mathbf{I}_{m\times m} & \mathbf{X}^{(0)} & \mathbf{0} \\ \mathbf{0} & \mathbf{Y} & \mathbf{0} \\ \mathbf{0} & \mathbf{X}^{(1)} & \mathbf{I}_{dm\times dm} \end{bmatrix} \in \mathbb{Z}^{(d+2)m\times(d+2)m}$$

.

If $\boldsymbol{\eta}_1 \neq \boldsymbol{\eta}_2$: let $\boldsymbol{\eta}_1 = (\eta_1, \cdots, \eta_d), \boldsymbol{\eta}_2 = (\eta'_1, \cdots, \eta'_d)$. Without loss of generality, we assume that first $j(\leq d)$ components of $\boldsymbol{\eta}_1, \boldsymbol{\eta}_2$ are different. We have $\eta_1 \neq \eta'_1, \cdots, \eta_j \neq \eta'_j$, and $\eta_{j+1} = \eta'_{j+1}, \cdots, \eta_d = \eta'_d$. Choose $\mathbf{Y}_0, \mathbf{Y}_1, \cdots, \mathbf{Y}_j \leftarrow \chi^{m\times m}$, and uniformly samples
$\mathbf{X}_0 = (\mathbf{X}_0^{(0)}, \mathbf{X}_0^{(j+1)}, \cdots, \mathbf{X}_0^{(d)}) \in \underbrace{\mathbb{Z}^{m\times m} \times \cdots \times \mathbb{Z}^{m\times m}}_{(d-j+1)\text{ times}}$, and

$\mathbf{X}_i = (\mathbf{X}_i^{(0)}, \mathbf{X}_i^{(j+1)}, \cdots, \mathbf{X}_i^{(d)}) \in \underbrace{\mathbb{Z}^{m\times m} \times \cdots \times \mathbb{Z}^{m\times m}}_{(d-j+1)\text{ times}}$ for each $i = \{1, \cdots, j\}$. Set

$$\Delta_1 = \begin{bmatrix} \mathbf{I}_{m\times m} & \mathbf{X}_0^{(0)} & \mathbf{X}_1^{(0)} & \cdots & \mathbf{X}_j^{(0)} & \mathbf{0} & \cdots & \mathbf{0} \\ \mathbf{0} & \mathbf{Y}_0 & \mathbf{0} & \cdots & \mathbf{0} & \mathbf{0} & \cdots & \mathbf{0} \\ \mathbf{0} & \mathbf{0} & \mathbf{Y}_1 & \cdots & \mathbf{0} & \mathbf{0} & \cdots & \mathbf{0} \\ \cdots & \cdots & \cdots & \cdots & \cdots & \mathbf{0} & \cdots & \mathbf{0} \\ \mathbf{0} & \mathbf{0} & \mathbf{0} & \cdots & \mathbf{Y}_j & \mathbf{0} & \cdots & \mathbf{0} \\ \mathbf{0} & \mathbf{X}_0^{(j+1)} & \mathbf{X}_1^{(j+1)} & \cdots & \mathbf{X}_j^{(j+1)} & \mathbf{I}_{m\times m} & \cdots & \mathbf{0} \\ \cdots & \cdots & \cdots & \cdots & \cdots & \cdots & \cdots & \cdots \\ \mathbf{0} & \mathbf{X}_0^{(d)} & \mathbf{X}_1^{(d)} & \cdots & \mathbf{X}_j^{(d)} & \mathbf{0} & \cdots & \mathbf{I}_{m\times m} \end{bmatrix} \in \mathbb{Z}^{(d+2)m\times(d+2)m}.$$

- If $\rho_1 = \rho_2$: the challenger uniformly samples $(\mathbf{X}'^{(0)}, \mathbf{X}'^{(1)})$ from $\mathbb{Z}^{(d+2)m\times m} \times \mathbb{Z}^{m\times m}$ and $\mathbf{Y}' \leftarrow \chi^{m\times m}$, respectively.

$$\text{Set } \Delta_2 = \begin{bmatrix} \mathbf{0}_{(d+2)m\times m} & \mathbf{0}_{(d+2)m\times m} & \mathbf{X}'^{(0)} \\ \mathbf{I}_{m\times m} & \mathbf{0}_{m\times m} & \mathbf{0}_{m\times m} \\ \mathbf{0}_{m\times m} & \mathbf{I}_{m\times m} & \mathbf{X}'^{(1)} \\ \mathbf{0}_{m\times m} & \mathbf{0}_{m\times m} & \mathbf{Y}' \end{bmatrix} \in \mathbb{Z}^{(d+5)m\times 3m}.$$

  If $\rho_1 \neq \rho_2$: the challenger uniformly samples $\mathbf{X}'_1, \mathbf{X}'_2$ from $\mathbb{Z}^{(d+2)m\times m}$, and $\mathbf{Y}_1, \mathbf{Y}_2 \leftarrow \chi^{m\times m}$.

$$\text{Set } \Delta_2 = \begin{bmatrix} \mathbf{0}_{(d+2)m\times m} & \mathbf{X}'_1 & \mathbf{X}'_2 \\ \mathbf{I}_{m\times m} & \mathbf{0}_{m\times m} & \mathbf{0}_{m\times m} \\ \mathbf{0}_{m\times m} & \mathbf{Y}'_1 & \mathbf{0}_{m\times m} \\ \mathbf{0}_{m\times m} & \mathbf{0}_{m\times m} & \mathbf{Y}'_2 \end{bmatrix} \in \mathbb{Z}^{(d+5)m\times 3m}.$$

If $(\rho_1, \boldsymbol{\eta}_1, t_1) \neq (\rho^*, \boldsymbol{\eta}^*, t^*)$, then challenger can use $\mathbf{T_G}$ to compute the token. Send $\mathsf{tk}^{t_1\to t_2}_{\rho_1,\boldsymbol{\eta}_1\to\rho_2,\boldsymbol{\eta}_2} = \{\Delta_1, \Delta_2\}$ or $\perp$ to the adversary $\mathcal{A}$ following the restriction defined in Definition 3. The challenger adds this the token to the set $\overline{C}$.
$\mathcal{Q}_{\mathsf{Enc}}(\rho, \boldsymbol{\eta}, \mathbf{m}, t)$: Given a positive tag ρ, a d-tuple of negative tags $\boldsymbol{\eta} = (\eta_1, \cdots, \eta_d)$, and message $\mathbf{m}$, time t, outputs ciphertext ct by running $\mathsf{Encrypt}(\cdot)$. Increment $numCt$ and add ct to the set $\mathcal{H}$ with key $(\rho, \boldsymbol{\eta}, t, numCt)$.

$\mathcal{Q}_{\mathsf{Update}}$: Given $\rho', \boldsymbol{\eta}', t'(> t)$ and a key $(\rho, \boldsymbol{\eta}, t, numCt)$, where $k \leq numCt$, outputs $\perp$ if there is no value in $\mathcal{H}$ with key $(\rho, \boldsymbol{\eta}, t, k)$. Otherwise, let ct be that value in $\mathcal{H}$ and it computes the updated ciphertext ct' by proceeding as follows:

- If there is a token $\mathsf{tk}^{t\to t'}_{\rho,\boldsymbol{\eta}\to\rho',\boldsymbol{\eta}'}$ in the set $\overline{C}$, it computes the updated ciphertext ct' using this key by running the algorithm $\mathsf{UpdateCT}$. Sends ct' to $\mathcal{A}$.
- If there is no token $\mathsf{tk}^{t\to t'}_{\rho,\boldsymbol{\eta}\to\rho',\boldsymbol{\eta}'}$ in the set $\overline{C}$, it first computes the key as in $\mathcal{Q}_{Token}(\rho, \boldsymbol{\eta}, t \to \rho', \boldsymbol{\eta}', t')$. Then, it computes the updated ciphertext ct' using this key by running the algorithm $\mathsf{UpdateCT}$ and sends ct' to $\mathcal{A}$. If $\mathcal{Q}_{Token}$ returns $\perp$, then challenger also returns $\perp$ to $\mathcal{A}$.

Game 2 is otherwise same as Game 1. Since the Keys and responses to the queries are statistically close to those in Game 1, the adversary $\mathcal{A}$'s advantage in Game 2 is at most negligibly different from its advantage in Game 1.

Game 3: Game 3 is identical to Game 2 except that the challenge ciphertext $ct^* = (\mathbf{c}^*, \mathbf{c}^*_{out}, \tilde{\mathbf{c}}^*)$ chosen randomly from $\mathbb{Z}_q^{(d+6)m}$. We show that Game 2 and

Game 3 are computationally indistinguishable for a PPT adversary, by giving a reduction from the dLWE problem.

Reduction from dLWE: Suppose $\mathcal{A}$ has non-negligible advantage in distinguishing Game 2 and Game 3. Using $\mathcal{A}$, we construct a dLWE solver $\mathcal{B}$.

- **dLWE instance:** $\mathcal{B}$ begins by obtaining an dLWE challenge consisting of three random matrices $\mathbf{A}, \mathbf{D}, \mathbf{U} \in \mathbb{Z}_q^{n \times m}$ and three vectors $\mathbf{c}'_{in}, \mathbf{c}'_{out}, \tilde{\mathbf{c}}'_0 \in \mathbb{Z}_q^m$. Here, $\mathbf{c}'_{in}$, $\mathbf{c}'_{out}$, $\tilde{\mathbf{c}}'_0$ are either random in $\mathbb{Z}_q^m$ or $\mathbf{c}'_{in} = \mathbf{A}^\top \mathbf{s} + \mathbf{e}_0$, $\mathbf{c}'_{out} = \mathbf{U}^\top \mathbf{s} + \mathbf{e}_{out}$ and $\tilde{\mathbf{c}}'_0 = \mathbf{D}^\top \mathbf{s} + \mathbf{e}'_0$ for some random vector $\mathbf{s} \in \mathbb{Z}_q^n$ and some small noise vectors $\mathbf{e}_0$, $\mathbf{e}_{out}$, $\mathbf{e}'_0, \in \chi^m$. The goal of $\mathcal{B}$ is to distinguish these two cases with non-negligible advantage by using $\mathcal{A}$.
- **Initial:** $\mathcal{A}$ begins by announcing the target positive tag $\rho^* \in \mathcal{P}$, the target d-tuple of negative tags $\boldsymbol{\eta}^* = (\eta_1^*, \cdots, \eta_d^*) \in \mathcal{N}^d$, and time $t^* \in \mathcal{T}$.
- **SetUp:** $\mathcal{B}$ constructs the public key as in Game 2. Note that $\mathbf{A}_1 = \mathbf{A}\mathbf{R}_0^* - \mathbf{H}_{t^*}\mathbf{G}$, and $\mathbf{B}_i = \mathbf{A}\mathbf{R}_i^* - \eta_i^* \mathbf{G}$ for $i \in \{1, \cdots, d\}$, and $\mathbf{D}_0 = \mathbf{D}\mathbf{S}_1'^* - \mathbf{H}_{\rho^*}\mathbf{G}, \mathbf{D}_1 = \mathbf{D}\mathbf{S}_2'^* - \mathbf{H}_{t^*}\mathbf{G}$, where $\mathbf{R}_i^*$ for $i \in \{0, 1, \cdots, d\}$ and $\mathbf{S}_1'^*, \mathbf{S}_2'^*$ are uniformly random matrices from $\{+1, -1\}^{m \times m}$. It gives pk to $\mathcal{A}$.
- **Query Phase 1:** $\mathcal{B}$ answers $\mathcal{A}$'s all key queries as in Game 2.
- **Challenge:** $\mathcal{A}$ sends two messages $\mathbf{m}_0, \mathbf{m}_1 \in \{0,1\}^m$ to $\mathcal{B}$. $\mathcal{B}$ chooses a random bit $\beta \in \{0,1\}$ and compute $ct^* = (\mathbf{c}^*, \mathbf{c}^*_{out}, \tilde{\mathbf{c}}^*) \in \mathbb{Z}_q^{(d+6)m}$, where $\mathbf{c}^* = [\mathbf{c}^*_{in} | \bar{\mathbf{c}}^*_1 | \mathbf{c}^*_1 | \cdots | \mathbf{c}^*_d]$ and $\tilde{\mathbf{c}}^* = [\tilde{\mathbf{c}}^*_0 | \tilde{\mathbf{c}}^*_1 | \tilde{\mathbf{c}}^*_2]$, as follows:

$$\begin{cases} \mathbf{c}^*_{in} = \mathbf{c}'_{in},\ \bar{\mathbf{c}}^*_1 = (\mathbf{R}_0^*)^\top \cdot \mathbf{c}^*_{in},\ \mathbf{c}^*_i = (\mathbf{R}_i^*)^\top \cdot \mathbf{c}^*_{in} \text{ for } i \in \{1, \cdots, d\}, \\ \mathbf{c}^*_{out} = \mathbf{c}'_{out} + \lfloor q/2 \rfloor \cdot \mathbf{m}_\beta \in \mathbb{Z}_q^m, \\ \tilde{\mathbf{c}}^*_0 = \tilde{\mathbf{c}}'_0,\ \tilde{\mathbf{c}}^*_1 = (\mathbf{S}_1'^*)^\top \cdot \tilde{\mathbf{c}}'_0,\ \tilde{\mathbf{c}}^*_2 = (\mathbf{S}_2'^*)^\top \cdot \tilde{\mathbf{c}}'_0. \end{cases}$$

  $\mathcal{B}$ sends ct^* to $\mathcal{A}$ as the challenge ciphertext. Increment $numCt$ and add $numCt$ to the set $Derive$. Store ct^*_β to the set $\mathcal{H}$ with key $(\rho^*, \boldsymbol{\eta}^*, t^*, numCt)$.

  - Suppose $\mathbf{c}'_{in}, \mathbf{c}'_{out}, \tilde{\mathbf{c}}'_0$ are generated by dLWE i.e. $\mathbf{c}'_{in} = \mathbf{A}^\top \mathbf{s} + \mathbf{e}_0$, $\mathbf{c}'_{out} = \mathbf{U}^\top \mathbf{s} + \mathbf{e}_{out}$ and $\tilde{\mathbf{c}}'_0 = \mathbf{D}^\top \mathbf{s} + \mathbf{e}'_0$. From the Encrypt algorithm, we have,

$$\begin{aligned} \mathbf{c}^* &= \left[\mathbf{c}^*_{in} \middle| \bar{\mathbf{c}}^*_1 \middle| \mathbf{c}^*_1 \middle| \cdots \middle| \mathbf{c}^*_d\right] = \left[\mathbf{I}_m \middle| \mathbf{R}_0^* \middle| \mathbf{R}_1^* \middle| \cdots \middle| \mathbf{R}_d^*\right]^\top \cdot (\mathbf{A}^\top \mathbf{s} + \mathbf{e}_0) \\ &= \left[\mathbf{A} \middle| \mathbf{A}_{t^*} \middle| \mathbf{B}_1 + \eta_1^* \mathbf{G} \middle| \cdots \middle| \mathbf{B}_d + \eta_d^* \mathbf{G}\right]^\top \mathbf{s} + \left[\mathbf{I}_m \middle| \mathbf{R}_0^* \middle| \mathbf{R}_1^* \middle| \cdots \middle| \mathbf{R}_d^*\right]^\top \cdot \mathbf{e}_0. \\ \tilde{\mathbf{c}}^* &= [\tilde{\mathbf{c}}^*_0 | \tilde{\mathbf{c}}^*_1 | \tilde{\mathbf{c}}^*_2] = \left[\mathbf{I}_m \middle| \mathbf{S}_1'^* \middle| \mathbf{S}_2'^*\right]^\top \cdot (\mathbf{D}^\top \mathbf{s} + \mathbf{e}'_0) \\ &= \left[\mathbf{D} \middle| \mathbf{D}_{\rho^*} \middle| \mathbf{D}_{t^*}\right]^\top \mathbf{s} + \left[\mathbf{I}_m \middle| \mathbf{S}_1'^* \middle| \mathbf{S}_2'^*\right]^\top \cdot \mathbf{e}'_0. \end{aligned}$$

    It is easy to see that $\mathbf{c}^*, \tilde{\mathbf{c}}^*$ are computed as in Game 2. Also, $\mathbf{c}^*_{out} = \mathbf{U}^\top \mathbf{s} + \mathbf{e}_{out} + \lfloor q/2 \rfloor \cdot \mathbf{m}_\beta$. Then ct^* is a valid ciphertext of $\mathbf{m}_\beta$ with the positive tag ρ^*, negative tag set $\boldsymbol{\eta}^*$, and time t^*.
  - When $\mathbf{c}'_{in}, \mathbf{c}'_{out}, \tilde{\mathbf{c}}'_0$ are random in $\mathbb{Z}_q^m$, by left-over hash lemma, $\bar{\mathbf{c}}^*_1, \mathbf{c}^*_1, \cdots, \mathbf{c}^*_d, \tilde{\mathbf{c}}'_1, \tilde{\mathbf{c}}'_2$ are statistically indistinguishable with uniform. Also, $\mathbf{c}^*_{out}$ is uniform. So, $ct^* = (\mathbf{c}^*, \mathbf{c}^*_{out}, \tilde{\mathbf{c}}^*)$ are uniform in $\mathbb{Z}_q^{(d+6)m}$, as in Game 3.
- **Query Phase 2:** As in Game 2 except the following constraints for $\mathcal{Q}_{\mathsf{Update}}$ oracle: Outputs $\perp$ if $k \in Derive$.

- **Guess**: $\mathcal{A}$ guesses if it is interacting with a Game 2 or Game 3 challenger. $\mathcal{B}$ outputs $\mathcal{A}$'s guess as the answer to the dLWE challenge it is trying to solve.

Hence, $\mathcal{B}$'s advantage in solving dLWE is the same as $\mathcal{A}$'s advantage in distinguishing Game 2 and Game 3, as required. This completes the proof. □

References

1. Agrawal, S., Boneh, D., Boyen, X.: Efficient lattice (H) IBE in the standard model. In: EUROCRYPT 2010, pp. 553–572. Springer (2010)
2. Ajtai, M.: Generating hard instances of the short basis problem. In: ICALP 1999, pp. 1–9. Springer (1999)
3. Alwen, J., Peikert, C.: Generating shorter bases for hard random lattices. In: STACS 2009, pp. 75–86 (2009)
4. Boneh, D., et al.: Fully key-homomorphic encryption, arithmetic circuit ABE and compact garbled circuits. In: Nguyen, P.Q., Oswald, E. (eds.) EUROCRYPT 2014. LNCS, vol. 8441, pp. 533–556. Springer, Heidelberg (2014). https://doi.org/10.1007/978-3-642-55220-5_30
5. Brakerski, Z., Langlois, A., Peikert, C., Regev, O., Stehle, D.: Classical hardness of learning with errors. In: STOC 2013, pp. 575–584 (2013)
6. Brakerski, Z., Vaikuntanathan, V.: Circuit-ABE from LWE: unbounded attributes and semi-adaptive security. In: Robshaw, M., Katz, J. (eds.) CRYPTO 2016. LNCS, vol. 9816, pp. 363–384. Springer, Heidelberg (2016). https://doi.org/10.1007/978-3-662-53015-3_13
7. Cash, D., Hofheinz, D., Kiltz, E., Peikert, C.: Bonsai trees, or how to delegate a lattice basis. In: Gilbert, H. (ed.) EUROCRYPT 2010. LNCS, vol. 6110, pp. 523–552. Springer, Heidelberg (2010). https://doi.org/10.1007/978-3-642-13190-5_27
8. Derler, D., Jager, T., Slamanig, D., Striecks, C.: Bloom filter encryption and applications to efficient forward-secret 0-RTT key exchange. In: Nielsen, J.B., Rijmen, V. (eds.) EUROCRYPT 2018. LNCS, vol. 10822, pp. 425–455. Springer, Cham (2018). https://doi.org/10.1007/978-3-319-78372-7_14
9. Derler, D., Krenn, S., Lorünser, T., Ramacher, S., Slamanig, D., Striecks, C.: Revisiting proxy re-encryption: forward secrecy, improved security, and applications. In: Abdalla, M., Dahab, R. (eds.) PKC 2018. LNCS, vol. 10769, pp. 219–250. Springer, Cham (2018). https://doi.org/10.1007/978-3-319-76578-5_8
10. Derler, D., Ramacher, S., Slamanig, D., Striecks, C.: I want to forget: fine-grained encryption with full forward secrecy in the distributed setting. IACR Cryptol. ePrint Arch. **2019**, 912 (2019)
11. Derler, D., Ramacher, S., Slamanig, D., Striecks, C.: Fine-grained forward secrecy: allow-list/deny-list encryption and applications. In: International Conference on Financial Cryptography and Data Security, pp. 499–519. Springer (2021)
12. Dutta, P., Jiang, M., Duong, D.H., Susilo, W., Fukushima, K., Kiyomoto, S.: Hierarchical identity-based puncturable encryption from lattices with application to forward security. In: ACM AsiaCCS 2022, pp. 408–422 (2022)
13. Dutta, P., Susilo, W., Duong, D.H., Roy, P.S.: Puncturable identity-based encryption from lattices. In: Baek, J., Ruj, S. (eds.) ACISP 2021. LNCS, vol. 13083, pp. 571–589. Springer, Cham (2021). https://doi.org/10.1007/978-3-030-90567-5_29
14. Dutta, P., Susilo, W., Duong, D.H., Roy, P.S.: Puncturable identity-based and attribute-based encryption from lattices. Theoret. Comput. Sci. **929**, 18–38 (2022)

15. Gentry, C., Peikert, C., Vaikuntanathan, V.: Trapdoors for hard lattices and new cryptographic constructions. In: STOC 2008, pp. 197–206 (2008)
16. Green, M.D., Miers, I.: Forward secure asynchronous messaging from puncturable encryption. In: 2015 IEEE S&P, pp. 305–320. IEEE (2015)
17. Günther, F., Hale, B., Jager, T., Lauer, S.: 0-RTT key exchange with full forward secrecy. In: Coron, J.-S., Nielsen, J.B. (eds.) EUROCRYPT 2017. LNCS, vol. 10212, pp. 519–548. Springer, Cham (2017). https://doi.org/10.1007/978-3-319-56617-7_18
18. Liu, H., Ming, Y., Wang, C., Zhao, Y.: Flexible selective data sharing with fine-grained erasure in vanets. IEEE TIFS (2024)
19. Micciancio, D., Peikert, C.: Trapdoors for lattices: simpler, tighter, faster, smaller. In: Pointcheval, D., Johansson, T. (eds.) EUROCRYPT 2012. LNCS, vol. 7237, pp. 700–718. Springer, Heidelberg (2012). https://doi.org/10.1007/978-3-642-29011-4_41
20. Naor, D., Naor, M., Lotspiech, J.: Revocation and tracing schemes for stateless receivers. In: Kilian, J. (ed.) CRYPTO 2001. LNCS, vol. 2139, pp. 41–62. Springer, Heidelberg (2001). https://doi.org/10.1007/3-540-44647-8_3
21. Peikert, C.: Public-key cryptosystems from the worst-case shortest vector problem. In: STOC 2009, pp. 333–342 (2009)
22. Phuong, T.V.X., Ning, R., Xin, C.,Wu, H.: Puncturable attribute-based encryption for secure data delivery in internet of things. In: INFOCOM 2018, pp. 1511–1519. IEEE (2018)
23. Phuong, T.V.X., Susilo, W., Kim, J., Yang, G., Liu, D.: Puncturable proxy re-encryption supporting to group messaging service. In: Sako, K., Schneider, S., Ryan, P.Y.A. (eds.) ESORICS 2019. LNCS, vol. 11735, pp. 215–233. Springer, Cham (2019). https://doi.org/10.1007/978-3-030-29959-0_11
24. Regev, O.: On lattices, learning with errors, random linear codes, and cryptography. In: STOC 2005, pp. 84–93 (2005)
25. Regev, O.: On lattices, learning with errors, random linear codes, and cryptography. J. ACM (JACM) **56**(6), 1–40 (2009)
26. Wei, J., Chen, X., Wang, J., Hu, X., Ma, J.: Forward-secure puncturable identity-based encryption for securing cloud emails. In: Sako, K., Schneider, S., Ryan, P.Y.A. (eds.) ESORICS 2019. LNCS, vol. 11736, pp. 134–150. Springer, Cham (2019). https://doi.org/10.1007/978-3-030-29962-0_7

A Post Quantum Vector Commitment Scheme with Efficient Insertions and Deletions

Vir Pathak[1] and Sushmita Ruj[2(✉)]

[1] Department of Computer Science, Stony Brook University, New York, USA
vir.pathak@stonybrook.edu
[2] School of Computer Science and Engineering, University of New South Wales, Sydney, Australia
sushmita.ruj@unsw.edu.au

Abstract. Vector Commitments (VCs) are a cryptographic primitive that allows users to commit to a tuple and later provide proofs about entries of the committed tuple. Literature on VCs provides many secure constructions with properties attractive for decentralized applications. These include fast commitment/proof update algorithms after a value in the committed vector changes, algorithms to aggregate position proofs, generating proofs for subvectors, commitment hiding, and many more. However, these works assume a static setting, where only vector values change and the length of the committed vector never changes. We initiate the study of designing VCs which support efficient updates to commitments and proofs after a change in vector length occurs (i.e. an insertion or a deletion of a vector value at an *arbitrary* position). In order to construct such a primitive, we formalize a VC framework implicitly considered in VC based verifiable decentralized storage constructions. Parties control a subset of positions in the committed vector. A proof for an inserted vector value at a given position may only be generated via participation from enough honest parties. We call such primitives *Multiparty Dynamic Vector Commitments*. Our work provides formal definitions for multiparty dynamic VC functionality and security. In particular, standard VC binding does not extend to our dynamic setting. This motivates us to define the *dynamic multiparty binding* security notion. We also comment on how multiparty dynamic VCs can be applied to extend existing VC based instantiations of verifiable storage. Finally, we provide a vector commitment construction and show that it possesses multiparty dynamic binding under standard lattice assumptions.

Keywords: Vector Commitment · Dynamic · Lattice-based

1 Introduction

Vector commitments were proposed by Catalano and Fiore [7] and Libert and Yung [14]. We use VCs to generate a commitment $\mathbf{c}$ to a vector $\mathbf{x} \in \mathcal{M}^\ell$ in some

K. Jee and A. Kate (Eds.): ACNS 2026, LNCS 16571, pp. 131–157, 2027.
https://doi.org/10.1007/978-3-032-32560-0_5

space $\mathcal{M}$. Later, a user who knows the value x_i of the ith entry of $\mathbf{x}$ can generate a proof convincing a verifier that the ith entry of the vector $\mathbf{x}$ committed in $\mathbf{c}$ is indeed x_i. VCs come with a security guarantee known as *position binding*, which informally guarantees that a malicious prover cannot produce two proofs π_i and π_i' convincing a verifier that the ith position in $\mathbf{x}$ is x_i and x_i' respectively (with $x_i \neq x_i'$).

In recent years, VCs have generated a great deal of attention. New functionalities have been proposed, such as subvector proofs [13], aggregating position proofs [25], efficiently updating all proofs after an entry changes [23], cross-aggregating proofs [11], and many more. These properties were introduced as a way to seamlessly instantiate applications such as SNARK construction, stateless blockchain design, or verifiable databases. Our work is motivated by this last use case. Instantiating a verifiable database via VCs has been long been studied in a large body of VC constructions [4,7]. The main idea is as follows: assume a client has a large file which can be modeled as a vector. The file is to be stored in a storage node. The client will keep a commitment to this file and the storage node will store the actual file contents along with the corresponding position proofs. When the client queries for a certain portion of the file, the node presents it to the client, along with the position proofs or a corresponding subvector proof. To make sure the storage node presented the correct values, the client can run the VC verification algorithm on these values and proofs against the commitment which the client stores. A related notion is verifiable decentralized storage via VC, [4], where multiple storage nodes store different chunks of the file. This corresponds to a large vector being distributed into subvectors for each node in the network to store. A client again stores a commitment to the entire vector. When queried for contents in a node's designated subvector, the node can provide those contents, along with proofs establishing their veracity.

Unfortunately, VC designs for these use cases assume a static model, where information cannot be added or deleted. In all of the aforementioned use cases, we can envision a dynamic situation where new content can be added and old content can be removed from the committed vector. Therefore, we would like to design vector commitment schemes which can work in a such a setting. Namely, we would like to design schemes that can support efficient commitment/proof updates in the case of an insertion/deletion of a value to the committed vector.

Adding *stateless* insertion to most constructions is difficult. To see why, consider the problem of inserting a value at position i and updating the commitment/existing position proofs. Since all values after position i get pushed 1 position over, we must know all values in the vector after position i. Furthermore, it is not clear how to insert securely. In particular, we demonstrate a construction that satisfies standard VC binding (assuming standard worst case lattice problems) and proceed to add insertion/deletion algorithms which compromise the scheme's security.

Our construction works in a new *multiparty* based VC model we propose. Briefly, we assume that various parties will control different subvectors of the committed vector v. We further assume that no pair of parties P_i, P_j will have an entry in common in the subvectors they control. In our multiparty model, we propose a threshold version of standard VC binding (in addition to modifications needed to capture binding in a dynamic setting). For security reasons, it seems the multiparty model is necessary for our construction. Parties generate partial proofs which can be reconstructed to generate a full position proof. In the Appendix (see Appendix A), we show why the analogous single party version of our scheme is insecure. In this way, we are able to show a separation between standard binding VCs and VCs which are binding in a dynamic setting.

Apart from the security reasons, multi-party setting is required in many applications. For example, in decentralized verifiable database protocols parties store parts of the database and insert or delete content from the database. Such cases require parties to communicate about values getting inserted or deleted, thus maintaining the updated state of the database. Therefore requiring participation from multiple nodes in the protocol for a valid insertion is not a huge cost. We have worked in a multiparty model that provides a reasonable security claim for our construction. However, we do understand that for some applications requiring the participation of multiple parties to do insertion is clearly an unsatisfactory solution.

1.1 Our Results

This work presents the following contributions:

1. We introduce multiparty dynamic vector commitments. We provide formal definitions describing the new functionalities.
2. We show that the standard VC binding security notion is not sufficient for this new dynamic setting. Therefore, we introduce *multiparty dynamic binding*, which captures the security notion for VCs in the setting we consider.
3. We design a novel multiparty dynamic VC and prove security under standard lattice assumptions. Our scheme supports updates after insertions/deletions, as well as modifications to existing entries.
4. We discuss how such a VC design can be leveraged in improving existing VC based verifiable storage protocols.

While our VC design allows clients to perform insertion/deletion updates, we note that insertion requires multiple parties to participate due to the partial lattice trapdoor techniques we use. Existing instantiations of verifiable storage via VC cannot handle requests to enlarge or shrink the file via insertions or deletions, as the underlying VCs do not possess such functionality. One exception is the verifiable decentralized storage solution proposed by Campanelli et al. [4], which does allow for insertions and deletions. However, their solution does not allow for insertions or deletions at arbitrary positions in the vector. Furthermore, their VC security is based on groups of unknown order. In contrast, ours is lattice based and therefore enjoys *post quantum* security in the random oracle model. Our construction only requires modifying proofs' indexing for positions affected after insertion/deletion. Nontrivially modifying all position proofs after such an update is costly. Since we are also able to trivially modify an existing entry by deleting it and subsequently inserting the modified value, our scheme also achieves *maintainability* [23] (i.e. the ability to update *all* position proofs in time sublinear in vector length after an entry change). We surpass the maintainable state-of-the-art [5,23].

Our scheme's main drawback is that requires the participation of multiple parties for insertion. However, the multiparty protocol only requires a single round of communication. We consider designing VCs supporting updates of entry values, insertions, and deletions without requiring the participation of multiple parties as an important open problem.

Let us briefly clarify on our usage of the word "dynamic". We emphasize that dynamism previously referred to notions only involving updates to commitments/proofs after *updating existing vector values.* That is, to the best of our knowledge, existing dynamic vector commitment schemes like [24] only support fast updates to commitments and proofs following an alteration of one of the existing vector entries. Our notion of dynamism significantly differs from this, since we require fast updates to commitments and proofs after insertions/deletions of vector values at arbitrary positions instead of after modifications of existing entries. To the best of our knowledge, designing VC schemes which support such changes in the vector length have not been explored. Campanelli et al. [4] modify a VC scheme in order to support this functionality for a decentralized storage construction. However, one can only insert/delete at certain spots in the vector. Moreover, our work is done in the lattice setting, while their security is based on computational problems in groups of unknown order, showing that dynamism can be achieved from multiple assumptions.

We note that this notion of "dynamism" appears in the context of proofs of retrievability [21,22] and proofs of data possession in [9,20].

1.2 Technical Overview

A Multiparty Model. The decentralized storage framework serves as a blueprint for ours. In our setting, we allow a fixed set of parties $\{P_1, \ldots, P_k\}$ to control values at designated positions in the vector. A party P_i will be responsible for the values at the indices in S_{P_i}, and $S_{P_i} \cap S_{P_j} = \emptyset$ for $i \neq j$. Under this setting, we are able to construct a scheme with secure insertion and deletion functionalities. We note that if a party P_i requests insertion of a value a, at a position j, that results in all entries at or after j getting pushed forward by one. Moreover, S_{P_i} gets updated to $S_{P_i} \cup \{j\}$. Similarly, if P_i requests for a deletion at j, values after j get pushed back by one and S_{P_i} gets updated to $S_{P_i} \setminus \{j\}$. Therefore we must take care to update all parties' index sets, in addition to the commitment and existing position proofs after such an update. Finally, if a party P_i wants to update or delete a value at position j, we must first check that P_i actually controls this position (namely $j \in S_{P_i}$).

When designing a VC scheme, we imagine a global commitment available to all parties. When a party wants to insert or delete an entry, it may require help from a sufficient number of other parties. Consider a VC scheme which initially commits to vectors in $\mathbb{Z}_q^\ell$ for a prime q. Let $\mathbf{x}$ be such a vector and let $\mathbf{c}$ be a commitment to $\mathbf{x} = (x_1, \ldots, x_\ell)$. The goal of this work is to introduce the notion of multiparty *dynamic* vector commitments. To accomplish this, we define the following algorithms: `Add, Del, AddPfs, DelPfs`. A party P_i invokes the `Add` algorithm in order to insert a new value a at a position j. If a sufficient number of other parties are willing to participate, the algorithm generates a new proof for the inserted value and updates the commitment $\mathbf{c}$ to $\mathbf{c}'$ which is a commitment to $\mathbf{x}' = (x_1, \ldots, x_{i-1}, a, x_i, x_{i+1}, \ldots, x_\ell) \in \mathbb{Z}_q^{\ell+1}$. The `AddPfs` algorithm efficiently updates all position proofs after such an insertion occurs. The `Del` and `DelPfs` algorithms are analogous to `Add` and `AddPfs` respectively in the case of a deletion of an entry, rather than an insertion.

We acknowledge that a multiparty model is not an ideal solution for achieving a VC scheme with efficient insertions and deletions. However we believe it is useful for instantiating decentralized verifiable database solutions. Assume a party in a decentralized network wants the help of other nodes in the network to store a large file. We assume the file can be modeled as a vector v. As with the decentralized verifiable database setting, these nodes will store subvectors of the file. Let us also stipulate that no two nodes can store a common portion of the file. That is, no two nodes can store a common subvector of v. Furthermore, assume that the file can be changed by modifying/inserting/deleting arbitrary entries. Then multiparty dynamic VCs present a natural solution: the party owning the large file initially can generate a commitment to it and distribute subvectors to participating nodes, who store the subvectors and their corresponding position proofs. Any node may propose an insertion/deletion, and others may help generating a proof for the inserted element and updating the commitment/ existing position proofs after these operations. An insertion protocol requiring the participation of multiple nodes is a drawback. However communication between nodes during insertion is inevitable, as all nodes must be in agreement on the positions they control in any real world deployment of the scheme.

Construction. Adding efficient `Add, Del, AddPfs`, and `DelPfs` algorithms is seemingly challenging due to the following observation: after an insertion or deletion at some index i, all vector entries at or after/before i get shifted by one position. Therefore, after an insertion/deletion, we need to update all position proofs after i. If a vector has length ℓ, updating all the proofs after an insertion/deletion will take $O(\ell)$ time in the worst case if we just use naive proof update functionalities which already exist. In this work, we show how to improve upon this naive upper bound (Table 1).

Our scheme builds on top of a scheme due to Wee and Wu [27]. The Wee-Wu scheme can be thought of as follows: it begins by generating ℓ statistically close to random matrices $(A_i)_{i\in\{1,\ldots\ell\}}$ with each $A_i \in \mathbb{Z}_q^{n\times m}$ along with corresponding trapdoors. Using the trapdoors, a user can jointly sample a statistically close to random commitment $\mathbf{c} \in \mathbb{Z}_q^m$ for $\mathbf{x} \in \mathbb{Z}_q^\ell$ along with ℓ "short" position proofs $(\mathbf{v}_1, \ldots \mathbf{v}_\ell)$. The position proofs are sampled in a way relating A_i, $\mathbf{c}$, x_i, and $\mathbf{v}_i$

Table 1. Comparison of selected VC schemes. p is short for *poly*, λ is the security parameter, and ℓ is the length of vectors being committed. The scheme due to Campanelli et al. [4] can support updates after insertions/deletions to the committed but only at certain positions. Our construction supports insertion/deletion at arbitrary positions.

Scheme	Security	Ins/Del	$\lvert pp\rvert$	$\lvert\pi\rvert$	$\lvert c\rvert$
Tomescu et al. [25]	classical	no	$O(\ell)$	$\lvert\mathbb{G}\rvert$	$\lvert\mathbb{G}\rvert$
Lai et al. (LMC) [13]	classical	no	$O(\ell^2)$	$\lvert\mathbb{G}\rvert$	$\lvert\mathbb{G}\rvert$
Wee et al. [26]	post quantum	no	$O(p(\lambda,\ell))$	$O(p(\lambda,\log\ell))$	$O(p(\lambda,\log^2\ell))$
Campanelli [4]	classical	yes*	$\lvert\mathbb{G}\rvert$	$O(1)\lvert\mathbb{G}\rvert$	$4\lvert\mathbb{G}\rvert+2\lvert\mathbb{Z}_{2^{2\lambda}}\rvert$
Our Construction	post quantum	**yes**	$O(p(\lambda,\ell))$	$O(p(\lambda,\log\ell))$	$O(p(\lambda,\log^2\ell))$

in a matrix-vector equation for each i. Verification of a position proof amounts to checking $\mathbf{v}_i$ is short and certain conditions hold.

If we want to insert a value a at the ith position we can sample a new random verification key A'. Using lattice trapdoor preimage sampling techniques, we can obtain a preimage which can be used as a short proof in the verification equation. In this way, the old commitment c along with the old position proofs do not have to be modified. However the existing verification keys must be reordered to accommodate the insertion. Deleting a value at a position i simply amounts to deleting a verification key A_i and reordering the remaining verification keys.

The key property about the Wee-Wu scheme is that commitments and position proof are not tied to value-position pairs (x_i, i). This is in contrast to many existing vector commitment schemes. For example in Hyperproofs [23], computing a commitment to a vector $\mathbf{x} = (x_1, \ldots, x_\ell) \in \mathbb{Z}_q^\ell$ means computing $g^{\sum_{i=1}^{\ell} x_i \cdot S_i(\tau)}$, where S_i is a multilinear Lagrange basis polynomial. We are given commitments $g^{S_i(\tau)}$ as public parameters. To compute the above value, we must take each $g^{S_i(\tau)}$ and raise it to the value x_i. Then we must combine all of these quantities using group multiplication. Trying to insert a new value x_i' at position i means we must now compute $g^{S_j(\tau)^{x_{j-1}}}$ for all $j \geq i$. In the worst case, this will take $O(\ell)$ group exponentiations and group multiplications. The source of this slowdown was that the process to generate the commitment to x implicitly depends on the position i along with the vector value x_i. This is why we suspect VC schemes based on polynomial commitments are unlikely to support efficient updates after entries are inserted to/deleted from committed vectors.

One issue with our framework is that allowing anyone to generate the new verification key and proof is insecure because this process introduces a lattice trapdoor which can be used to break the binding of the scheme. In this way, we show that standard VC binding does not immediately imply binding in a dynamic setting. In order to address this and present a scheme allowing for reasonably secure insertion and deletion, we introduce our multiparty dynamic framework. We call the corresponding security notion *multiparty dynamic binding*. This notion captures essentially the same concept as standard binding, except now the adversary can make queries for insertions and deletions before presenting a commitment and two conflicting values/proofs which pass verification. Additionally, our scheme operates in a multiparty setting where we assume that an adversary cannot corrupt more than a certain threshold number of parties controlling positions in the vector.

We make use of the recent lattice trapdoor splitting techniques developed by Albrecht et al. [3]. A *partial lattice trapdoor scheme* allows a user to take a standard lattice preimage sampling trapdoor with respect to an input matrix A and "split" it among multiple parties. Each party receives a partial trapdoor. When the parties want to compute a short preimage for some target y with respect to the matrix A, they can use their partial trapdoors to compute a partial preimage. Subsequently, they can recombine all their preimages to get a short, random preimage x for the target y with respect to A. The scheme guarantees that an adversary cannot generate such a preimage if it cannot corrupt at least a threshold number of parties. Our strategy for secure insertion is the following: we sample extra matrices $\{A'_1, \ldots, A'_n\}$ to be used as verification keys when a party wants to insert a value. For each A'_i, we give party P_j a partial trapdoor ptd_{i_j}. If P_j wants to insert some x', it, along with enough other participating parties, generates partial preimages with respect to some insertion key A'_i and target $H(x')$, where H is a random oracle. At verification time, these partial preimages are recombined into a short preimage h such that $A'_i \cdot h = H(x')$ and h is short. Batch insertions/deletions are also possible without increasing the number of rounds. Deletion is straightforward. For insertion, we execute the same process with a sufficient number of the desired insertion matrices. Parties would compute all the partial preimages locally at once.

A Note on Real World Deployment. We now consider how deploying a scheme matching our framework would work in a real world decentralized system. While our public parameter size is linear in the initial vector length plus the number of possible insertions, the advantage of our work is that modifying the actual commitment or all of the existing proofs is as cheap as possible during insertions or deletions.

We must treat the set of verification keys and their indices at any given time as part of the *state* of the system. Note that a possible attack vector for an adversary of the system is to convince network participants into believing conflicting states. For example, assume the current state's verification keys are (A_1, A_2, A_3). Then after an insertion at position two, they become (A_1, A'_2, A_2, A_3). If a participant is made aware of the insertion, the position of insertion, the new key A'_2 for the second index, as well as the previous state's verification keys (A_1, A_2, A_3) they will be able to correctly verify a position proof. However, if one of these pieces of information are not known after an insertion, then a participant is prone to incorrectly verifying proofs with respect to the current state of the system. Therefore a real world deployment must modify the underlying consensus algorithm the participants use to agree on the condition of the state. The consensus must now include agreement upon the set of the verification keys as well as their indices.

We must also note that while our VC captures *binding* in a traditional sense, it is not robust. That is, if some party P_1 wants to insert a value x' at some position and parties $P_2, \ldots, P_k$ are willing to participate, then an incorrect proof for x' can be generated if one of these parties is malicious and deviates from the protocol. Moreover, all parties must know the value x' that P_1 wants to insert in order to generate the correct local preimages. This will incur a communication overhead, although there is only a single round of communication.

1.3 Related Work

Vector commitments were proposed by Catalano and Fiore [7]. Along with formally defining the primitive, they showed how VCs could be applied to applications such as verifiable databases and zero knowledge elementary databases.

An important property is the ability to generate proofs for arbitrary *subvectors* in the committed vector. Subvector openings were first introduced by Lai and Malavolta [13], who proposed a new SNARK design technique with VCs with subvector openings along with PCPs as the underlying mechanisms. This was a direct improvement of the classical "CS Proofs" (Computationally Sound Proofs) [15] paradigm due to Killian [12]. Knowledge of subvector openings along with proof aggregation/disaggregation techniques are instrumental building blocks in the decentralized storage protocol in [4].

Classical constructions geared towards other decentralized applications quickly emerged, such as stateless blockchains [8] and verifiable decentralized storage [4]. In order to efficiently instantiate such applications via VCs, it is critical to build VCs which could support efficient updates after a specific *vector value* was altered. The authors of the Hyperproofs VC scheme [23] defined maintainability, which was the property of being able to update all position proofs in *sublinear* time after a change in one of the committed vector entries. By noticing a tree structure in PST polynomial commitments [18], Hyperproofs achieves maintainability with $O(\log \ell)$ update time, where ℓ is the length of the committed vector. Their technique was generalized and shown to apply for any pairing based VC scheme with various algebraic properties [5]. Surveys on VC appear in [17, 19].

Designing lattice based VCs is a topic currently receiving increased interest. Albrecht et al. design a scheme which opens to low degree polynomials as a way to design a lattice based SNARK [2]. However, their scheme relies on a nonstandard knowledge assumption, which was later shown to be insecure in a work by Wee and Wu [26]. De Castro and Peikert design transparent functional commitments [6], which can be efficiently specialized to VCs. Finally, Wee and Wu [27] design a VC whose security reduces to SIS. Our work uses this construction as a building block. We keep the same commit and prove functionalities and augment the original `Setup` procedure to allow for efficient updates after insertions or deletions.

2 Preliminaries

2.1 Notation

We use λ for the security parameter. The letter q denotes a prime and $\mathbb{Z}_q$ denotes the integers modulo q. A capital letter such as A or B will denote a matrix, whereas a lowercase letter like x or a will denote a value (usually a value in $\mathbb{Z}_q$). A bolded letter (like $\mathbf{x}$) denotes a vector.

Definition 1 (Negligible Function). *A function $f : \mathbb{N} \to \mathbb{R}$ is said to be in the class of negligible functions (written as $f \in negl(\lambda)$) if for all $c \geq 0$ there exists $n_0 \in \mathbb{N}$ such that for all integers $n \geq n_0$, we have $|f(n)| < \frac{1}{n^c}$.*

That is, a negligible function is a function which decreases faster than the inverse of any polynomial.

Definition 2. *Let λ be a parameter. The class $poly(\lambda)$ denotes the functions which are bounded from above by a polynomial in λ.*

Definition 3. *We say a probabilistic algorithm is in the class Probabilistic Polynomial Time (PPT) if its expected running time is bounded from above by a polynomial in its input size.*

Definition 4. *We say that two families of distributions $\{D_1\}_{\lambda \in \mathbb{N}}$ and $\{D_2\}_{\lambda \in \mathbb{N}}$ are statistically close if their statistical distance is bounded by a negligible function in λ.*

For a matrix or a vector, we denote $||\cdot||$ as its infinity norm.

2.2 Lattice Preliminaries

Definition 5 (Lattice). *Let B be a full rank matrix in $\mathbb{R}^{k\times k}$. The lattice $\mathcal{L}(B)$ generated by B is the set of all integer linear combinations of the columns in B. That is, $\mathcal{L}(B) = \{B\mathbf{x} : \mathbf{x} \in \mathbb{Z}^k\}$.*

Definition 6 (SIS Assumption). *Let $n, m \in \mathbb{Z}_{>0}, \beta \in \mathbb{R}_{>0}, q \in \mathbb{Z}_{>0}$ be functions in the security parameter λ. The $SIS_{n,m,q,\beta}$ assumption states that a for any efficient adversary $\mathcal{A}$, the probability of $\mathcal{A}$ winning the following game with a challenger is negligible in λ: (1). The challenger samples $A \leftarrow \mathbb{Z}_q^{n\times m}$ and sends it to $\mathcal{A}$. (2). $\mathcal{A}$ outputs a vector $\mathbf{x} \in \mathbb{Z}_q^m$.*
$\mathcal{A}$ wins if $A\mathbf{x} = 0 \pmod q$ and $||\mathbf{x}|| \leq \beta$.

The Shortest Integer Solution (SIS) problem has been shown [1] to be at least as hard as standard problems in the worst case related to finding short vectors in lattices. We recall the definition of a discrete Gaussian, following Wee and Wu's [27] exposition.

Definition 7 (Discrete Gaussian). *Let $s \in \mathbb{R}_+$ and $n \in \mathbb{Z}_{>0}$. We define the Gaussian function of width s to be*

$$\rho_s(\mathbf{x}) = exp(-\pi||\mathbf{x}||_2^2/s^2).$$

We can define a probability distribution on lattice cosets. For a coset $\mathbf{c} + \mathcal{L}$, we define the mass function to be

$$\rho_s(\mathbf{c} + \mathcal{L}) = \sum_{\mathbf{x} \in \mathcal{L}} \rho(\mathbf{c} + \mathbf{x}).$$

Define the discrete Gaussian distribution on $\mathbb{Z}^n$ by

$$D_{\mathbb{Z}^n,s}(\mathbf{x}) = \rho_s(\mathbf{x})/\rho_s(\mathbb{Z}^n).$$

For $s > 0$, $A \in \mathbb{Z}_q^{n\times m}$, and $\mathbf{v} \in \mathbb{Z}_q^n$ we write $A_s^{-1}(\mathbf{v})$ to denote a random variable $\mathbf{x}$, where $\mathbf{x} \leftarrow D_{\mathbb{Z}^m,s}$ conditioned on $A\mathbf{x} = \mathbf{v} \pmod q$. We sample matrices in an analogous way by applying A_s^{-1} to all the columns of the input matrix.

Definition 8 (Gadget Matrix). *Let $n, q \in \mathbb{Z}_{>0}$. Let $m' = n\lfloor \log q \rfloor + 1$. The corresponding gadget matrix is defined as $G = I_n \otimes g^T \in \mathbb{Z}_q^{n\times m'}$. Here, $g^T = [1, 2, \ldots, 2^{\log q}]$.*

Next, we recall the trapdoor and preimage sampling algorithms due to Micciancio and Peikert [16]. We again follow Wee and Wu's exposition.

Theorem 1 (Trapdoor Preimage Sampling). *Let n, m, q, m' be as before. There exists efficient algorithms (TrapGen, SamplePre) which work as follows:*

1. *TrapGen$(1^n, q, m) \to (A, td)$: Takes matrix dimensions n and m along with the modulus q as input. The algorithm generates an $n \times m$ matrix over $\mathbb{Z}_q$ along with a trapdoor $td \in \mathbb{Z}_q^{m\times m'}$.*
2. *SamplePre$(A, td, \mathbf{v}, s) \to x$: Takes a matrix $A \in \mathbb{Z}_q^{n\times m}$ along with its trapdoor $td \in \mathbb{Z}_q^{m\times m'}$, an image $\mathbf{v} \in \mathbb{Z}_q^n$ and a Gaussian width parameter s as input. The algorithm outputs a vector $\mathbf{u} \in \mathbb{Z}_q^m$.*

For $m \geq O(n \log q)$, these tuple of algorithms have the following properties:

1. *The output (A, td) of the TrapGen algorithm is such that $A{\cdot}td = G$, $||td|| = 1$, and the statistical distance between A and a uniformly sampled matrix A' over $\mathbb{Z}_q^{n\times m}$ is less than or equal to 2^{-n}.*
2. *For all $td \in \mathbb{Z}_q^{m\times m'}$, all $\mathbf{v}$ in the column span of A, the vector $\mathbf{x}$ is such that $A\mathbf{x} = \mathbf{v}$.*
3. *If td is a gadget trapdoor for A (e.g. if (A, td) is the output of TrapGen), then for all $s \geq \sqrt{mm'} \cdot ||td|| \cdot \omega(\sqrt{\log n})$, the statistical distance between*

$$\{\mathbf{x} \leftarrow \textit{SamplePre}(A, td, v, s)\} \quad \text{and } \{\mathbf{x} \leftarrow A_s^{-1}(\mathbf{v})\}$$

less than or equal to 2^{-n}.

We can extend the SamplePre targets to include matrices $V \in \mathbb{Z}_q^{n\times k}$ in the following way: We define SamplePre(A, td, V, s) to be the matrix whose ith column is SamplePre$(A, td, \mathbf{v_i}, s)$, where $\mathbf{v_i}$ is the ith column of V.

We now proceed to state the $\text{BASIS}_{\text{rand}}$ assumption [27].

Definition 9 (BASIS). *Let n, m, q, s be as before chosen with respect to the security parameter λ. Let Samp be an efficient sampling algorithm that takes λ and $A \in \mathbb{Z}_q^{n\times m}$ as input. The algorithm outputs a matrix $B \in \mathbb{Z}_q^{n'\times m'}$ along with some auxiliary information aux. We say the $BASIS_{rand}$ Assumption holds if all efficient adversaries $\mathcal{A}$ win the following game between $\mathcal{A}$ and a challenger Chal with negligible probability:*

1. *Chal selects $A \leftarrow \mathbb{Z}_q^{n\times m}$, and runs $(B, aux) \leftarrow Samp(\lambda, A), T \leftarrow B_s^{-1}(G_{n'})$. He sends (A, B, T, aux) to $\mathcal{A}$.*
2. *$\mathcal{A}$ outputs a vector $\mathbf{x}$.*

$\mathcal{A}$ wins if $A\mathbf{x} = 0 \pmod q$ and $0 < ||\mathbf{x}|| \leq \beta$.

Definition 10 ($\text{BASIS}_{\text{rand}}$). *Let n, m, q, s, β be as before. Let $\ell \in \mathbb{Z}_{>0}$. When Samp is instantiated in the following way, we refer to the corresponding assumption as the $BASIS_{rand}$ assumption parameterized by n, m, q, s, β, and ℓ:*

Given the input matrix A and the security parameter, the algorithm samples $i^* \leftarrow \{1, \ldots, \ell\}$. For all $i \in \{1, \ldots \ell\}$ with $i \neq i^*$, the algorithm samples $A_i \leftarrow \mathbb{Z}_q^{(n+1)\times m}$. Next, it chooses $\mathbf{a} \leftarrow \mathbb{Z}_q^m$ and sets $A_i^* = \begin{bmatrix} \mathbf{a}^{\mathrm{T}} \\ A \end{bmatrix}$.

Finally, it sets

$$B = \left[\begin{array}{ccccc|c} A_1 & & & & & -G_{n+1} \\ & A_2 & & & & -G_{n+1} \\ & & \cdot & & & -G_{n+1} \\ & & & \cdot & & -G_{n+1} \\ & & & & A_\ell & -G_{n+1} \end{array}\right]$$

with $aux = i^*$.

Wee and Wu provide a tight reduction showing $\text{BASIS}_{\text{rand}}$ is at least as hard as the SIS problem. We conclude this section by defining a partial lattice trapdoor scheme. We follow the exposition due to Albrecht et al. [3].

Definition 11 (Partial Lattice Trapdoor). *A (t, k)-threshold partial lattice trapdoor scheme over $\mathbb{Z}_q$ is an extension of a (full) lattice trapdoor scheme (TrapGen, SamplePre) over $\mathbb{Z}_q$ with the PPT algorithms (PTrapGen, PSampPre, Rec):*

1. *$ptd_j \leftarrow PTrapGen(A, td, j)$: The partial trapdoor generation algorithm inputs a matrix A, its (full) trapdoor td, and an index $j \in [k]$ and generates a partial trapdoor ptd_j of A for j.*
2. *$x_j \leftarrow PSampPre(A, ptd_j, T, y, \sigma)$: The partial preimage sampling algorithm, given a partial trapdoor ptd_j for index j, a set $T \subseteq [k]$, a target image y, and a Gaussian parameter σ, samples a partial preimage x_j for j.*

3. $x \leftarrow Rec((x_j)_{j\in T})$: *The reconstruction algorithm, given a tuple of partial preimages* $(x_j)_{j\in T}$ *reconstructs a preimage* x.

Let $k, t \in \mathbb{N}$ *be such that* $t \leq k$ *and* n, m, m', β *be as before. Let* s *be a Gaussian width parameter for* $(TrapGen, SamplePre)$ *(i.e. the parameter from point (3) in Theorem 1) and let* $\sigma > 0$ *be the Gaussian width parameter from above. A* (t,k)*-threshold partial lattice trapdoor scheme is said to be* (n, m, s, β, σ)*-correct with respect to* $(TrapGen, SamplePre)$ *if for any* t*-subset* $T \subseteq_t [k]$ *and vector* $y \in \mathbb{Z}_q^n$, *it holds*

$$Pr\left[\begin{array}{c|c} A\cdot x=y & (A,td)\leftarrow TrapGen(1^\lambda,1^n,1^m) \\ \wedge\|x\|\leq\beta & ptd_j\leftarrow PTrapGen(A,td,j)\forall j\in[k] \\ & x_j\leftarrow PSampPre(A,ptd_j,T,y,\sigma)\forall j\in T \\ & x\leftarrow Rec((x_j)_{j\in T}) \end{array}\right] \geq 1 - negl(\lambda).$$

That is, the reconstructed preimage x *is a correct preimage if it was reconstructed using partial preimages* x_j, *where all the* x_j *were obtained by running the PTrapGen algorithm.*

Albrecht et al. [3] develop a partial lattice trapdoor scheme over R_q, where R_q is the ring of integers over a cyclotomic field modulo some prime ideal q. However, their scheme naturally translates to one over $\mathbb{Z}_q$. Similar to the methods developed by Gentry et al. [10], the distribution of reconstructed preimages satisfy the following property: for fixed (A, v_j) and pairs (x_j, z_j) of images and partial preimages respectively, we have that the two distributions

1. Sample z_j uniformly at random. Then, use ptd_j to sample short x_j such that $A \cdot x_j = v_j \otimes z_j \pmod q$.
2. independently sample a Gaussian x_j from an ambient lattice. Compute z_j satisfying $A \cdot x_j = v_j \otimes z_j \pmod q$

This guarantee allows Albrecht et al. to construct a threshold signature scheme using GPV signatures [10] as a natural blueprint. In GPV, signing a message m, constitutes sampling a short, random preimage x such that $A \cdot x = H(m) \pmod q$. In the threshold version, the partial signatures are the partial preimages x_j. We use the reconstruction algorithm to obtain the short preimage x from the x_j's. In the context of our scheme, we will keep an extra insertion matrix A'_i. When a party wants to insert some $x' \in \mathbb{Z}_q$ at position i, it will obtain partial preimages $(x_j)_{j\in T}$ from other participating parties. A verifier can use these partial preimages to reconstruct a short h such that $A_i \cdot h = x' \pmod q$. In this way, we can reduce security to forging threshold signatures.

3 Multiparty Dynamic VC

We refer to the setting in Sect. 1.2. We say a party is *honest* if it generates the correct partial preimages when participating in an insertion and keeps its private parameters secret (see our definition below). Our scheme only requires participation of multiple parties for the insertion of new entries. However, our definition of multiparty dynamic VCs allows participation of other parties when deleting or updating an entry.

Definition 12 (Multiparty Dynamic Vector Commitment). *Let $P = \{P_1, \dots, P_r\}$ be a set of r parties. We say an r-Party Dynamic Vector Commitment is a tuple of the following algorithms:*

$\texttt{Setup}(\lambda, \ell) \to (pp, pp_1, \dots pp_r)$: *Given the security parameter λ and the initial length $\ell = poly(\lambda)$ of the vector being committed, output public parameters pp, as well as private parameters $pp_1, \dots, pp_r$. The private parameters pp_j are sent to party P_j through a secure channel. Note that this inherently requires the setup process to be trusted. The* `Setup` *algorithm also outputs index sets $S_{P_1}, \dots S_{P_r}$ such that $\bigcup_{i=1}^{r} S_{p_i} = [\ell]$ and $S_{P_i} \cap S_{P_j} = \emptyset$ for $i \neq j$.*

The next three algorithms are **public***: meaning that anyone can run them and that they may implicitly use public parameters generated at Setup time.*

$\texttt{Commit}(\mathbf{x}) \to (\mathbf{c}, aux)$: *Outputs a commitment $\mathbf{c}$ for a vector $\mathbf{x}$ of length ℓ. Some auxiliary information aux may also be generated.*

$\texttt{Open}(x_i, i, aux) \to \pi_i$: *Possibly using the auxiliary information aux, the opening algorithm generates a proof π_i convincing a verifier that x_i is the value at the ith position in the committed vector $\mathbf{x}$.*

$\texttt{Verify}(\mathbf{c}, y, i, \pi_i) \to 0/1$: *Given a commitment $\mathbf{c}$, a value y, a position i, and a proof π_i, a verifier outputs 1 or 0, respectively indicating an acceptance or rejection of the proof that y is the ith value in the committed vector (i.e., $y = x_i$).*

The following algorithms can only be initiated by one of the parties. They may require the joint participation of multiple parties. These protocols may require parties to implicitly perform computations locally using their private parameters.

$\texttt{Add}(\mathbf{c}, x', i, P_j, P) \to (\mathbf{c}', u, pp')$: *At least $d+1$ parties (denote the set of parties by P) may jointly run this algorithm. Let $P_j \in P$ be a chosen party in this set who wants to initiate an insertion. The algorithm updates the commitment $\mathbf{c}$ corresponding to vector $[x_1, \dots, x_\ell]$ to a commitment $\mathbf{c}'$ corresponding to the vector $[x_1, \dots, x_{i-1}, x', x_i, x_{i+1}, \dots, x_\ell]$.*

Assume P_j controls positions in the index set S_{P_j}. Then S_{P_j} gets updated to $S_{P_j} \cup \{i\}$.

Some update information u and updated public parameters pp' may also be released. Finally, the algorithm outputs a new proof π_i that verifies with respect to the updated commitment, the new inserted value, and the ith position.

$\texttt{AddPfs}(\mathbf{c}', i, x', \{\pi_j\}_{j \in [\ell']}, u)$: *Once the commitment to a vector $\mathbf{x}$ (currently of length ℓ') has been modified to $\mathbf{c}'$ after an insertion, this algorithm modifies all existing position proofs for the other entries using public update information u.*

Note that an entry at position $k > i$ in the vector will now be at position $k+1$. Parties whose index sets are affected must locally update them accordingly during such an insertion.

$\texttt{Del}(\mathbf{c}, i, P_j, P) \to (\mathbf{c}', u, pp')$: *At least $d+1$ parties P may jointly run this algorithm. Assume position i is an index controlled by exactly one of these parties $P_j \in P$. The algorithm first checks if $i \in S_{P_j}$. If not, it aborts. Otherwise, it updates the commitment $\mathbf{c}$ corresponding to vector $[x_1, \dots, x_\ell]$ to a commitment*

$\mathbf{c}'$ *corresponding to the vector* $[x_1, \dots, x_{i-1}, x_{i+1}, \dots, x_\ell]$. *Some update information* u *and updated public parameters* pp' *may also be outputted.*

Assume party P_j *controls positions in index set* S_{P_j}. *Then* S_{P_j} *gets updated to* $S_{P_j} \setminus \{i\}$.

$\texttt{DelPfs}(\mathbf{c}', i, x_i, \{\pi_j\}_{j \in [\ell']}, u)$: *Once a commitment to a vector* $\mathbf{x}$ *(currently of length* ℓ'*) has been modified to* $\mathbf{c}'$ *after a deletion of the* i*th entry* x_i*, this algorithm modifies all existing position proofs for the other entries using public update information* u.

Note that an entry at position $k > i$ *in the vector will now be at position* $k-1$. *The algorithm updates all other parties' index sets accordingly during such a deletion.*

$\texttt{Update}(\mathbf{c}, i, x_i, x_i', P_j, P) \leftarrow (\mathbf{c}', u, pp')$: *At least* $d+1$ *parties* P *may jointly run this algorithm. Assume position* i *is an index controlled by exactly one of these parties* $P_j \in P$. *The algorithm first checks if* $i \in S_{P_j}$. *If not, it aborts. Otherwise, it updates the commitment* $\mathbf{c}$ *corresponding to vector* $[x_1, \dots, x_i, \dots, x_\ell]$ *to a commitment* $\mathbf{c}'$ *corresponding to the vector* $[x_1, \dots, x_i', \dots, x_\ell]$. *Some update information* u *and updated public parameters* pp' *may also be outputted.*

$\texttt{UpdatePfs}(\mathbf{c}', i, x_i', \{\pi_j\}_{j \in [\ell']}, u)$: *Once a commitment to a vector* $\mathbf{x}$ *(currently of length* ℓ'*) has been modified to* $\mathbf{c}'$ *after the* i*th entry* x_i *gets modified to* x_i'*, this algorithm modifies all existing position proofs for the other entries using public update information* u.

In our definition above, we assume the following:

1. By "jointly", we mean that a set of parties must engage in the multiparty protocol described. We assume that parties can communicate with each other and with the Trusted Setup through secure and authenticated channels.
2. A party P_j can insert in any position it wants to. To insert in position i, it does not have to control position i beforehand. After the insertion occurs, the index sets of the other parties increment (or stay the same) accordingly.
3. On the other hand, we require P_j to control position i if they want to delete the ith value. Once P_j runs `Del`, the other parties check if P_j controls position i in order to determine if the deletion is valid. If it is not, they reject the `Del` update and/or the modified public parameters which P_j returns after the Del operation. Note that all parties keep a copy of the index sets which they control as well as the index sets which other parties control.
4. Recall in the decentralized verifiable database setting, we envision a party initially holding a large file. Using the public parameters already generated, it may generate a commitment to the file and distribute corresponding subvectors to nodes participating in storing it. Therefore, we opted to designate committing as a public operation.

Next, correctness is similar to standard VC correctness, except we modify it to accommodate insertions and deletions of elements into the committed vector.

Definition 13 (Dynamic VC Correctness). *Let* ℓ *be the length of the initial vector being committed to. Let* $pp \leftarrow \texttt{Setup}(1^\lambda, \ell)$ *and* $\mathbf{c}$ *be a commitment to a* *vector of length ℓ possibly using pp. Possibly after a sequence of updates, insertions, or deletions, assume the resulting commitment changes to $\mathbf{c}'$ and the public parameters change to pp'. Moreover, assume the length of the vector committed to is now some ℓ'.*

Then a position proof for an entry x_i with $i \in \ell'$ can be generated in one of the following ways:

1. *x_i was an entry in the vector initially committed. Possibly, x_i was at position j in the initial vector. A proof π was generated using $\texttt{Open}(x_i, j, aux)$. After the possible sequence of insertions or deletions to existing entries, x_i went from being the jth entry in the vector to the ith. Moreover $\mathbf{c}$ got updated to $\mathbf{c}'$ and π got modified to π' after applying the corresponding sequence of algorithms to update it. Then we require $\texttt{Verify}(c', x_i, i, \pi') = 1$ with all but negligible probability in the security parameter.*
2. *x_i was an entry inserted after the initial vector was committed. Let $\overline{\mathbf{c}}$ be the commitment to this vector before x_i was inserted. Possibly, x_i was inserted at position j. A proof π was generated by at least $d+1$ parties denoted by P (i.e. using $\texttt{Add}(\overline{\mathbf{c}}, x_i, j, P_k, P)$). After the possible sequence of insertions or deletions to existing entries, x_i went from being the jth entry in the vector to the ith. Moreover $\overline{\mathbf{c}}$ got updated to $\mathbf{c}'$ and π got modified to π' after applying the corresponding sequence of algorithms to update it. Then we require $\texttt{Verify}(\mathbf{c}', x_i, i, \pi') = 1$ with all but negligible probability in the security parameter.*

Security is similar to standard VC security, except now we require infeasibility for a fixed number $d > 0$ or less parties to generate conflicting proofs for inserted values. In what follows, let $\mathcal{C} = \{C_1, \ldots C_k\}$ be a set of corrupt parties. Each corrupt party C_i controls positions in the index set S_{C_i} with $S_{C_i} \cap S_{C_j} = \emptyset$ for $i \neq j$.

Definition 14 (d out of r Dynamic Binding). *Let VC_{dyn} be a Multiparty Dyamic Vector Commitment scheme. We say VC_{dyn} is d out of r Dynamic Binding if a polynomially bounded adversary $\mathcal{A}$ wins the following game with negligible probability:*

1. *The adversary outputs a set of corrupt parties $\mathcal{C}$ and the positions each party controls. The challenger will control the rest of the $r-k$ honest parties.*
2. *The challenger first checks $k < d+1$, if $\bigcup_{i=1}^{k} S_{C_i} \subset [\ell]$, and if $S_{C_i} \cap S_{C_j} = \emptyset$ for $i \neq j$. Next, the challenger runs $(pp, pp_1, \ldots, pp_r) \leftarrow VC_{dyn}.\texttt{Setup}(1^\lambda, 1^\ell)$. The challenger proceeds to send $(pp, \{pp_i\}_{i=1}^{k})$ to $\mathcal{A}$ (without loss of generality, assume the first k out of r parties are the corrupt ones and assume pp_i is meant for party C_i for $i = 1, \ldots, k$).*
3. *$\mathcal{A}$ generates a commitment $\mathbf{c}$ and sends it to the challenger.*
4. *$\mathcal{A}$ can query the challenger for an insertion of a value x_i' at any position i. Alternatively, it can query for a deletion at some position i in the vector (where $i \in S_{C_j}$ for $j = 1, \ldots, k$). The challenger will run $\texttt{Add}$ or $\texttt{Del}$ to modify the commitment, obtain updated public parameters pp' as well as update*

information u, and a new position proof π_i (in the case of an insertion). This will be run simulating any set parties of $\mathcal{A}$'s choosing. Note that the challenger will have to be involved, as $\mathcal{A}$ controls less than d+1 positions. The challenger will additionally send $\mathcal{A}$ any communication between the chosen $d+1$ parties when simulating the `Add` *or* `Del` *algorithms. Lastly, the challenger sends pp' and u so that $\mathcal{A}$ can run VC_{dyn}.*`AddPfs` *or VC_{dyn}.*`DelPfs` *depending on if an insertion or deletion was queried. If an insertion was queried, the challenger will also send the new proof π_i.*

5. *$\mathcal{A}$ finally outputs a commitment $\mathbf{c}'$, a position proofs π_j and π'_j corresponding to values x_j, x'_j. $\mathcal{A}$ wins the game if $x_j \neq x'_j$ but $VC_{dyn}.\mathtt{Verify}(\mathbf{c}', x_j, j, \pi_j) = VC_{dyn}.\mathtt{Verify}(\mathbf{c}', x'_j, j, \pi'_j) = 1$.*

If $\mathcal{A}$ makes at most Q queries, we say $\mathcal{A}$ is a Q-Query dynamic binding adversary.

4 Lattice Based Construction

4.1 Starting Point: The Wee-Wu VC Scheme

We begin by reviewing the Wee-Wu VC design, which our scheme builds on. Let λ be the security parameter. The construction is parameterized by the following values in λ: n, m, q, s_0, s_1, and B. Set $m' = n\lceil \log q \rceil + 1$. The values n and m are matrix dimensions, q is a prime, s_0, s_1 are Gaussian width values, and B is the SIS bound. We now describe the scheme. Assume we are committing to a vector $\mathbf{x} \in \mathbb{Z}_q^\ell$. As of now, this scheme does not support efficient insertions/deletions.

`Setup`(λ, ℓ) : For $i = 1, \ldots, \ell$, sample

$$(A_i, td_i) \leftarrow TrapGen(1^n, q, m)$$

with $A_i \in \mathbb{Z}_q^{n \times m}$. Next, form the matrix

$$B_\ell = \left[\begin{array}{ccccc|c} A_1 & & & & & -G \\ & A_2 & & & & -G \\ & & \cdot & & & -G \\ & & & \cdot & & -G \\ & & & & A_\ell & -G \end{array}\right] \in \mathbb{Z}_q^{n\ell \times (\ell m + m')}$$

Then, note that we have $B_\ell R = G_{n\ell}$, where $R = \left(\frac{diag(td_1, \ldots td_\ell)}{0}\right)$. To obtain a (statistically close to) random trapdoor for B_ℓ, we run

$$T \leftarrow SamplePre(B_\ell, R, G_{n\ell}, s_0).$$

We finish the `Setup` Process by outputting $pp := (A_1, \ldots A_\ell, T)$.

Note that the `Setup` process is *trusted*: if an untrusted party runs `Setup`, they have access to all the trapdoors for the A_i public parameters. This can be used to break scheme's binding.

`Commit`$(pp, \mathbf{x})$: Use the trapdoor T to run

$$(\mathbf{v}_1, \ldots \mathbf{v}_\ell, \hat{\mathbf{c}}) \leftarrow SamplePre(B_\ell, T, -\mathbf{x} \otimes \mathbf{e}_1, s_1)$$

where $\mathbf{e}_1$ is the first standard basis vector in $\mathbb{Z}_q^m$. We set the commitment to be $\mathbf{c} = G\hat{\mathbf{c}} \in \mathbb{Z}_q^n$. A position proof π_i for index i is simply the vector $\mathbf{v_i} \in \mathbb{Z}_q^m$. In this way, the commitment and proofs are sampled *jointly*. We output the commitment $\mathbf{c} = G\hat{\mathbf{c}}$ and auxiliary information $(\mathbf{v_1}, \ldots, \mathbf{v}_\ell)$.

`Open`(x_i, i, aux): Output $\pi_i = \mathbf{v}_i \in \mathbb{Z}_q^m$.

`Verify`$(\mathbf{c}, x_i, i, \pi)$: Parse the proof π as the vector $\mathbf{v}_i \in \mathbb{Z}_q^m$. By construction of how we sampled our commitment/proofs, we must have $A_i \cdot \mathbf{v}_i = \mathbf{c} - x_i e_1$. To verify, we therefore check the following: $||\mathbf{v}_i|| \leq B$ and $A_i \cdot \mathbf{v}_i = \mathbf{c} - x_i \mathbf{e}_1$.

Before presenting our scheme, we present a first attempt in Appendix A. We also show why this attempt is not secure. The reader is encouraged to read this to understand why our construction works.

4.2 Scheme Description

In this section, we present a secure d out of ℓ multiparty dynamic VC scheme. While our scheme supports updates after insertion/deletion, it is not endowed with a natural update mechanism which the original Wee-Wu scheme had due to its homomorphic properties. We also note that the participation of multiple parties are only truly necessary for insertion.

Our protocol makes use of a random oracle $H : \mathbb{Z}_q \to \mathbb{Z}_q^n$. The security of our scheme will reduce to the standard binding of the Wee-Wu scheme or the existential unforgeability of the threshold GPV [10] signature scheme presented by Albrecht et al. in [3]. Assume that the initial vector we commit to is of length ℓ as before. Let $k < d < \ell$ be a threshold. For simplicity, we will assume every party can control at most k positions and controls exactly one of the ℓ positions at the intial commit time (so there are ℓ parties). Therefore, the vector can be stretched to a length of at most $k\ell$. Assuming $PT = (PTrapGen, PSampPre, Rec)$ is d out of ℓ, our construction will be d out of ℓ dynamic binding.

`Setup`$(1^\lambda, 1^\ell)$: First we describe how to generate the initial public parameters pp. For $i = 1, \ldots, \ell$, sample

$$(A_i, td_i) \leftarrow TrapGen(1^n, q, m)$$

with $A_i \in \mathbb{Z}_q^{n\times m}$. Next, form the matrix

$$B_\ell = \left[\begin{array}{ccccc|c} A_1 & & & & & -G \\ & A_2 & & & & -G \\ & & \cdot & & & -G \\ & & & \cdot & & -G \\ & & & & A_\ell & -G \end{array}\right] \in \mathbb{Z}_q^{n\ell\times(\ell m+m')}$$

Then, note that we have $B_\ell R = G_{n\ell}$, where $R = \left(\frac{diag(td_1,\ldots td_\ell)}{0}\right)$. To obtain a (close to) random trapdoor for B_ℓ, we run

$$T \leftarrow SamplePre(B_\ell, R, G_{n\ell}, s_0).$$

Choose new Gaussian width parameters s_1, s_1'.

Next, we describe how to generate the private parameters $pp_1, \dots pp_\ell$. For $j = 1, \dots, k\ell$, run $(A'_j, td'_j) \leftarrow TrapGen(1^n, q, m)$. Next, for $k = 1, \dots, \ell$, run $ptd_{j_k} \leftarrow PTrapGen(A'_j, td'_j, k)$. Then for the nth party define $pp_n = (ptd_{1_n}, \dots, ptd_{k\ell_n})$.

Set $pp := (A_1, \dots A_\ell, T, A'_1, \dots A'_{k\ell})$. Securely send the mth private parameter pp_m to the mth party for $m = 1 \dots \ell$.

Denote all the parties by $P_1, \dots P_\ell$. For each P_i, output their initial set S_{P_i} of indices they control (at Setup time recall that this set consists of a single position).

`Commit`$(pp, \mathbf{x})$: Let $\mathbf{x} = (x_1, \dots, x_\ell) \in \mathbb{Z}_q^\ell$ Compute

$$\mathbf{a} = \mathbf{a}_1 || \mathbf{a}_2 || \dots || \mathbf{a}_\ell = H(x_1) || H(x_2) || \dots || H(x_\ell).$$

Use the trapdoor T and the matrix B_ℓ from `Setup` to run

$$(\mathbf{v}_1, \dots \mathbf{v}_\ell, \hat{\mathbf{c}}) \leftarrow SamplePre(B_\ell, T, \mathbf{a}, s_1).$$

Output $\mathbf{c} = G\hat{\mathbf{c}}$ as the commitment and $aux = (\mathbf{v}_1, \dots \mathbf{v}_\ell)$.

`Open`(x_i, i, aux) : Output $\pi = \mathbf{v}_i$.

`Add`$(\mathbf{c}, x', i, p, P)$: This algorithm is invoked by some set of parties P controlling positions in the vector. After this algorithm terminates, position i will hold the value x' and will be controlled by party $p \in P$. Without loss of generality, let $P = \{P_1, \dots P_k\}$ and let $p = P_1$. Their respective private parameters are denoted by $pp_1, \dots, pp_k$.

Leave the commitment $\mathbf{c}$ unchanged.

Take an A'_j in the current set of public parameters. Each party running the algorithm does the following

1. Recall that a party P_i will have a partial trapdoor ptd_{j_i} for the matrix A'_j. Party P_i takes their partial trapdoor and computes a partial preimage by running

$$\mathbf{x}_i \leftarrow PSampPre(A'_j, ptd_{j_i}, \{1, \dots, k\}, c - H(x'), s'_1).$$

2. Publicly post the partial preimage $\mathbf{x}_i$.

Update the public parameters to $pp' = (A_1, A_2, \dots A_{i-1}, A'_j, A_i, \dots A_\ell, A'_1, \dots A'_{j-1}, A'_{j+1}, \dots A'_{k\ell})$. Let $p = P_1$'s index set be S_{P_1}. Update this set to $S_{P_1} \cup \{i\}$. Output the insertion position, p's updated index set, the updated public parameters, and the set of partial preimages. That is, output (i, S_{P_1}, pp', v'), where $v' = \{\mathbf{x}_h\}_{h=1}^k$.

`AddPfs`$(\mathbf{c}, i, x', \{\pi_j\}_{j \in [\ell']}, (i, pp', v'))$: Output $\mathbf{v}' = (\mathbf{v}_1, \dots \mathbf{v}_{i-1}, v', \mathbf{v}_i, \dots, \mathbf{v}_{\ell'})$. Additionally, use the fact that the insertion occurred at position i to modify all parties' index sets accordingly.

`Del`$(\mathbf{c}, i, p, P)$: Without loss of generality, assume $p = P_1 \in P$ controls the position i.

Leave the commitment $\mathbf{c}$ unchanged. Set the updated public parameters pp' to $pp' = (A_1, A_2, \dots, A_{i-1}, A_{i+1}, \dots A_\ell, A'_1, \dots A'_{k\ell})$. Take $p = P_1$'s index set S_{P_1} and update it to $S_{P_1} \setminus \{i\}$. Output (pp', S_{P_1})

DelPfs$(\mathbf{c}, i, x_i, \{\pi_j\}_{j\in[\ell']}, (pp')$: Output $\mathbf{v}' = (\mathbf{v}_1, \ldots, \mathbf{v}_{i-1}, \mathbf{v}_{i+1}, \ldots \mathbf{v}'_\ell)$. Update all other parties' index sets using the fact that the deletion occurred at position i.

Verify$(\mathbf{c}, y, i, \pi_i)$: Parse π as $\mathbf{v_i} \in \mathbb{Z}_q^m$. Check if $||\mathbf{v}_i|| \leq B$ and $A_i \cdot \mathbf{v}_i = \mathbf{c} - H(x_i) \pmod q$.

5 Security

In this section, we prove the security of the scheme presented in the previous section in the random oracle model. Breaking dynamic binding reduces to either breaking standard binding in the Wee-Wu scheme, or forging the threshold-GPV signature [3] in the multi user setting.

We present the security of d out of ℓ Threshold GPV game in Appendix B. Next we present the security of d out of ℓ Threshold GPV with commitments game which is used to prove the security of our scheme.

d out of ℓ Threshold GPV With Commitments: We make a slight modification to the d out of ℓ Threshold GPV security game. The game now is as follows:

1. The adversary $\mathcal{A}$ outputs a set of corrupt parties $\mathcal{C} = \{C_1, \ldots, C_k\}$
2. The challenger first checks $k < d+1$, if $\bigcup_{i=1}^k S_{C_i} \subset [\ell]$, and if $S_{C_i} \cap S_{C_j} = \emptyset$ for $i \neq j$.
3. Next, for $i = 1, \ldots, k\ell$, the challenger runs

$$(A_i, td_i) \leftarrow TrapGen(1^n, 1^m, q).$$

For $j = 1, \ldots, k\ell$
For $h = 1, \ldots, \ell$, the challenger runs

$$ptd_{j_h} \leftarrow PT.PTrapGen(A_j, td_j, h).$$

The challenger sends ptd_{j_h} for $h \in \{1, \ldots, k\}$ to $\mathcal{A}$.
4. $\mathcal{A}$ fixes a value $\mathbf{c} \in \mathbb{Z}_q^n$ and sends it to the challenger.
5. $\mathcal{A}$ can make at most Q queries. On the ith query, $\mathcal{A}$ asks for an index j_i, positions T_i, and a value μ_i. It sends (j_i, T_i, μ_i) to the challenger.
6. If j_i has already been queried, the challenger outputs $\perp$. Otherwise, it does the following:

For $h \in T_i$ run

$$\pi_{i_h} \leftarrow PT.PSampPre(A_{j_i}, ptd_{j_{i_h}}, T_i, \mathbf{c} - H(\mu_i), \sigma)$$

Send $\{\pi_{i_h}\}_{h\in T_i}$ to $\mathcal{A}$.
7. At the end of the querying, $\mathcal{A}$ outputs an index w, a value x, and a vector v. $\mathcal{A}$ wins if x was not the query it made with respect to A_w, v is short, and $A_w \cdot v = \mathbf{c} - H(x)$.

Lemma 1 (*d* **out of** ℓ **Threshold GPV with Commitments is Secure).**

Proof. The only difference between d out of ℓ GPV and d out of ℓ Threshold GPV with Commitments is that in d out of ℓ Threshold GPV with Commitments, the target which we find a preimage for is $\mathbf{c} - H(x)$ rather than just $H(x)$. Since $\mathbf{c}$ is fixed and $H(x)$ is modeled as a random oracle, the distribution of the target in d out of ℓ Threshold GPV with Commitments is exactly the same as it is in d out of ℓ Threshold GPV.

Theorem 2. *Let $\mathcal{A}$ be a d out of ℓ dynamic binding adversary. Let ϵ be the probability $\mathcal{A}$ wins conditioned on its output being with respect to a verification key that existed since committing time. Then there exists a standard VC binding adversary $\mathcal{B}$ and a d out of ℓ Threshold GPV with Commitments adversary $\mathcal{C}$ such that*

$$\begin{aligned}&Pr[\mathcal{A} \text{ wins the dynamic VC binding game}] \leq \\ &Pr[\mathcal{B} \text{ wins the standard VC binding game}] + \\ &Pr[\mathcal{C} \text{ wins the } d \text{ out of } \ell \text{ Threshold GPV with Commitments game}]\end{aligned}$$

Proof. We first condition on $\mathcal{A}$'s output being with respect to a verification key which existed since committing time. Then our standard binding adversary $\mathcal{B}$ works as follows: it receives $(A_1, \dots A_\ell, T, A'_1, \dots A'_{k\ell})$ from its (standard VC binding) challenger. $\mathcal{B}$ passes the public parameters *pp* onto the dynamic binding adversary $\mathcal{A}$ and acts as the dynamic binding challenger. $\mathcal{A}$ will output some commitment $\mathbf{c}$ and query for insertions/deletions. $\mathcal{B}$ will generate new verification keys for insertions and perform the necessary reorderings of the public parameters.

$\mathcal{A}$ finally outputs $i, \mathbf{c}', x, x', \mathbf{v}, \mathbf{v}'$. $\mathcal{B}$ outputs the same values, except possibly the position i, as $\mathcal{B}$ must break VC binding with respect to the original public parameters. Since insertion/deletion reshuffles the indices for the (original) public A_i matrices, $\mathcal{B}$, will need to keep track of this as it answers $\mathcal{A}$'s queries and output the original position which i corresponded to at the beginning of the game. Then we clearly see that $\mathcal{B}$ wins its game with the same probability $\mathcal{A}$ wins the dynamic binding game.

Next, we condition on $\mathcal{A}$'s output being with respect to an inserted verification key. We construct an algorithm $\mathcal{C}$ which solves d out of ℓ GPV with Commitments.

In the d out of ℓ with Commitments game, the challenger sends $k\ell$ many instances $A'_1 \dots A'_{k\ell}$ to $\mathcal{C}$. Next, $\mathcal{C}$ plays the role of the dynamic VC binding challenger to $\mathcal{A}$. $\mathcal{C}$ generates $(A_1, \dots A_\ell, T)$ and sends $crs = (A_1, \dots A_\ell, T, A'_1 \dots A'_{k\ell})$ to $\mathcal{A}$. $\mathcal{A}$ responds with some commitment $\mathbf{c}$.

$\mathcal{A}$ and $\mathcal{C}$ engage in the dynamic binding game. For an insertion query with respect to a set of indices T, position i for some value x', $\mathcal{C}$ and $\mathcal{A}$ locally generate partial preimages with respect to one of matrices A'_j left in the public parameters. $\mathcal{A}$ will generate partial preimages for positions in T which it controls, while $\mathcal{C}$ will generate partial preimages for the other positions in T. The set of partial preimages can be reconstructed into a short proof $\mathbf{h}'$ such that $A'_j \cdot \mathbf{h}' = \mathbf{c} - H(x')$. $\mathcal{A}$ gets access to all these partial preimages.

At the end of the querying, $\mathcal{A}$ outputs an index j, a value x_j, and a short proof $\mathbf{h}$ which are supposed to break binding with respect to one of the (new) verification keys A'_j. $\mathcal{C}$ checks that x_j is not the value $\mathcal{A}$ queried to be inserted with respect to the matrix A'_j, aborting if this is the case. Otherwise, $\mathcal{C}$ sends x_j and $\mathbf{h}'$ to the d out of ℓ Threshold GPV challenger, where $\mathbf{h}'$ acts as a forged signature for x_j. Moreover, $\mathcal{C}$ wins its game with the same probability $\mathcal{A}$ wins the dynamic binding game. This completes the proof.

5.1 Parameter Instantiation and Complexity Analysis

Let λ be the security parameter and ℓ be the length of the initial vector to be committed. We can take the same parameters as done in the Wee-Wu scheme. That is,

1. Set $n = \lambda$, $m = O(n \log q)$.
2. Set $s_0 = O(\ell m \log(n\ell))$, $s_1 = O(\ell^{3/2} m^{3/2} \log(n\ell)) = O(\ell^{5/2} m^{5/2} \log^2(n\ell))$, and $s'_1 = \omega(\sqrt{\log m})$.
3. Set the SIS bound $B = \sqrt{\ell m + m' \cdot s_1} = O(\ell^3 n^3 \log^2(n\ell) \log^3 q)$.
4. Set $q = B \cdot poly(n)$. In this way, the VC binding reduces to the $\mathrm{SIS}_{n,m,2B,q}$ assumption, while forging a GPV signature (i.e. breaking binding with respect to an inserted verification key) reduces to the $\mathrm{SIS}_{n,m,B,q}$ assumption.

We have $\log q = O(\log \lambda + \log \ell)$. Then the commitment $\mathbf{c}$ to a message of length ℓ is an element in $\mathbb{Z}_q^n$. The commitment size is therefore

$$|\mathbf{c}| = O(n \log q) = O(\lambda(\log q + \log \ell)).$$

A position proof existing since commitment time π is a vector $\mathbf{v} \in \mathbb{Z}_q^m$ whose norm is bounded by B. Therefore we have

$$|\pi| = O(m \log B) = O(\lambda \cdot (\log^2 \lambda + \log^2 \ell)).$$

A verification key is of dimension $m \times n$ with $m = n \log q$. If the initial length is ℓ, and we do r insertions, the size of all the verification keys is

$$O(l + r)(nm \log q) = O(l + r)(n^2 \log^2 q) = O(l + r)(\lambda^2 log^2 q).$$

Next, r insertions constitute $r(d+1)$ vectors. They contribute

$$r(d+1)(m) = r(d+1)(\log q)$$

bits to the size. Totally,

$$|pp| = O((\ell + r)(\lambda^2 log^2 q) + r(d+1)(\lambda \log q))$$

For our scheme, insertion of Q new elements corresponds to an instantiation of the threshold GPV signature scheme in the Q user setting. Therefore, we can allow Q to take a value of $poly(\lambda)$. That is, we can allow $poly(\lambda)$ many insertions at any given time.

Next we expand upon the complexity of inserting, deleting, and updating entries. A deletion's complexity is independent of the vector size and therefore takes $O(1)$ time.

Insertion is also independent of the vector size. We conduct our analysis in terms of the length of the committed vector. Assume an instantiation of our scheme is d out of ℓ multiparty dynamic. Then running `Add` amounts to each participating party sampling a partial preimage for a public parameter $A'_j \in \mathbb{Z}_q^{n\times m}$. Each party can run the sampling procedure independently. Therefore the insertion complexity is not dependent on the vector size and runs in time $O(1)$.

Note that modifying all existing proofs after an insertion or deletion (i.e. running `AddPfs` or `DelPfs` also runs in $O(1)$ time, since these algorithms do not need to examine existing proofs and we delegate reconstructing a partial proof to verification time. Updating index sets is a task we delegate to the parties. Therefore updating the proofs also runs in $O(1)$ time.

Since a modification is a deletion followed by an insertion, it also runs in $O(1)$ to modify an entry in the committed vector, as well as update all the existing position proofs. Therefore, our scheme presents a new method for achieving *maintainability*, which is the ability to update all existing position proofs after a modification of an entry in sublinear time in the vector length.

6 Conclusion

In this paper, we defined multiparty dynamic vector commitments. A multiparty dynamic VC works in a framework where multiple parties control the entry values of designated positions in a committed vector. If a party controls some position i, they have the power to modify or delete the entry value in that position. Multiparty dynamic VCs also support efficient updates after the length of the committed vector changes via insertion or deletion. By naively trying to extend the Wee and Wu VC scheme, we saw that binding in the static setting does not necessarily imply security in our dynamic setting. This motivated the notion of multiparty dynamic binding, which captures security for dynamic VCs. We proceeded to present a multiparty dynamic VC using lattice trapdoor splitting techniques. However, our scheme does not natural, homomorphic updates after modifications to existing entries in the committed vector. We believe an important further step is to design dynamic VCs which support natural updates after modifications to entries and do not require other parties to participate during insertions. Another important open problem is to design a multiparty dynamic VC where the public parameters' size remains small even after many insertions.

Acknowledgement. The authors would like to thank the anonymous reviewers whose comments and suggestions were very helpful to improve the quality of the paper.

Appendix A: A First Attempt

The crucial property of the Wee-Wu scheme which we use in our construction is that a position proof for index i is not dependent on i itself, unlike a number of other VC schemes. Rather, it is only dependent on its verification key A_i. Therefore, insertion/deletion of a value and position proof corresponds to an insertion/deletion of a verification key. In this way, we will show that no modifications to the prior commitment or position proofs are necessary when inserting or deleting values.

We will now add (single-party) insertion and deletion mechanisms to Wee-Wu. Unfortunately, we will see that these modifications in their current state compromise the security of the scheme. However, this exercise motivates the ultimate multiparty construction we propose. Assume we commit to an initial vector of length ℓ. After deletions/insertions of this value, this length can change. `Setup`(λ, ℓ) : Same as in the Wee-Wu scheme. That is, for $i = 1, \ldots, \ell$, sample

$$(A_i, td_i) \leftarrow TrapGen(1^n, q, m)$$

with $A_i \in \mathbb{Z}_q^{n \times m}$. Next, form the matrix

$$B_\ell = \left[\begin{array}{ccccc|c} A_1 & & & & & -G \\ & A_2 & & & & -G \\ & & \cdot & & & -G \\ & & & \cdot & & -G \\ & & & & A_\ell & -G \end{array}\right] \in \mathbb{Z}_q^{n\ell \times (\ell m + m')}$$

Then, note that we have $B_\ell R = G_{n\ell}$, where $R = \left(\frac{diag(td_1, \ldots td_\ell)}{0}\right)$. To obtain a (close to) random trapdoor for B_ℓ, we run

$$T \leftarrow SamplePre(B_\ell, R, G_{n\ell}, s_0).$$

Additionally, choose a new Gaussian width parameter s_1'.

Output $pp := (A_1, \ldots A_\ell, T)$.

`Commit`$(pp, \mathbf{x})$: Same as before. That is, use the trapdoor T to run

$$(\mathbf{v}_1, \ldots \mathbf{v}_\ell, \hat{\mathbf{c}}) \leftarrow SamplePre(B_\ell, T, \quad \mathbf{x} \otimes \mathbf{e}_1, s_1)$$

where $\mathbf{e}_1$ is the first standard basis vector in $\mathbb{Z}_q^n$. Output the commitment $\mathbf{c} = G\hat{\mathbf{c}}$ and auxiliary information $(\mathbf{v}_1, \ldots, \mathbf{v}_\ell)$.

`Open`(x_i, i, aux) : Output $\pi_i = \mathbf{v}_i \in \mathbb{Z}_q^m$.

`Verify`$(pp, \mathbf{c}, i, x_i, \pi)$: Check if $||\mathbf{v}_i|| \leq B$ and if $A_i \cdot \mathbf{v}_i = \mathbf{c} - x_i \mathbf{e}_1 \pmod q$.

`Add`$(i, \mathbf{c}, x')$: Keep the commitment $\mathbf{c}$ unchanged.

`AddPf`$(pp, \mathbf{c}, i, x', \{\pi_j\}_{j=1,\ldots,\ell})$: Run

$$(A_i', td_i') \leftarrow TrapGen(1^n, q, m).$$

Next, run

$$\mathbf{v}' \leftarrow SamplePre(A_i', td_i', \mathbf{c} - x'\mathbf{e}_1, s_1')$$

where $\mathbf{c}$ is the commitment generated to the initial vector before any insertions/deletions. Take the (ordered) verification keys $(A_1, \ldots, A_\ell)$, and modify them to be $(A_1, \ldots, A_{i-1}, A_i', A_i, \ldots, A_\ell)$. Output $\mathbf{v}'$, which is the new verification proof for x' with respect to position i. The previous verification proofs for position $j > i$ verifies for position $j+1$, as the jth verification key has now become the $j+1$th verification key.

`Del`(i, c) : Keep the commitment $\mathbf{c}$ unchanged

`DelPf`$(i, \mathbf{c}, \{\pi_j\}_{j=1,\ldots,\ell})$: Rearrange the verification keys to be $(A_1, \ldots, A_{i-1}, A_{i+1}, \ldots, A_\ell)$.

This scheme is correct, but it is not secure because the user generating the new verification key also now has access to the corresponding trapdoor. They can use this trapdoor to submit false proofs. Therefore, extending Wee-Wu in this way does not guarantee binding, which means that standard VC binding does not extend to the insertion/deletion setting. A trivial method to circumvent this issue is to make a user send their desired insertion value x' to a trusted party and request it to sample a random matrix and a random short preimage for x' with respect to the random matrix sampled. The preimage would serve as the new proof with respect to the new verification key. The trusted party would present this new proof along with the verification key, as well as reorder the public parameters.

The construction we present takes the above approach, except we use a partial lattice trapdoor scheme to get rid of the trusted party and decentralize the process of generating a random short preimage for an inserted value.

Appendix B: *d* out of *ℓ* Threshold GPV

We first define a variant of SIS and prove its hardness. It is essentially a multi-user version of forging threshold GPV signatures [3] (where an adversary only gets to ask a single signing query). This variant will be used in the security analysis of our dynamic option for insertions/deletions.

Security Game: The security game takes place between an adversary $\mathcal{A}$ and a challenger. Let PT be a d out of ℓ partial lattice trapdoor scheme. The game is as follows:

1. The adversary $\mathcal{A}$ outputs a set of corrupt parties $\mathcal{C} = \{C_1, \ldots, C_k\}$
2. The challenger first checks $k < d+1$, if $\bigcup_{i=1}^{k} S_{C_i} \subset [\ell]$, and if $S_{C_i} \cap S_{C_j} = \emptyset$ for $i \neq j$.
3. Next, for $i = 1, \ldots, k\ell$, the challenger runs

$$(A_i, td_i) \leftarrow TrapGen(1^n, 1^m, q).$$

For $j = 1, \ldots, k\ell$
For $h = 1, \ldots, \ell$, the challenger runs

$$ptd_{j_h} \leftarrow PT.PTrapGen(A_j, td_j, h).$$

The challenger sends ptd_{j_h} for $h \in \{1, \ldots, k\}$ to $\mathcal{A}$.

4. $\mathcal{A}$ can make at most Q queries. On the ith query, $\mathcal{A}$ asks for an index j_i, positions T_i, and a value μ_i. It sends (j_i, T_i, μ_i) to the challenger.
5. If j_i has already been queried, the challenger outputs $\perp$. Otherwise, it does the following:

   For $h \in T_i$ run

$$\pi_{i_h} \leftarrow PT.PSampPre(A_{j_i}, ptd_{j_{i_h}}, T_i, H(\mu_i), \sigma)$$

   Send $\{\pi_{i_h}\}_{h \in T_i}$ to $\mathcal{A}$
6. At the end of the querying, $\mathcal{A}$ outputs an index w, a value x, and a vector v. $\mathcal{A}$ wins if x was not the query it made with respect to A_w, v is short, and $A_w \cdot v = H(x)$.

Lemma 2 (d out of ℓ Threshold GPV is Secure). *Let $\ell = poly(\lambda)$ and let $\mathcal{A}$ be an adversary for d out of ℓ Threshold GPV. Then $\mathcal{A}$'s winning probability is negligible.*

Proof. Let $\epsilon_{threshold}$ denote the advantage a PPT adversary has in breaking the existential unforgery of a threshold GPV signature with respect to some public key. Then under standard lattice assumptions, we know that $\epsilon_{threshold}$ is negligible. Next, let $\epsilon_{d/\ell}$ denote the winning probability for a PPT adversary for the d out of ℓ threshold GPV game. Note that the d out of ℓ GPV game is exactly the same as the game of trying to forge a threshold GPV signature [2] with respect to one of $k\ell = poly(\lambda)$ public keys. Then by a standard complexity leveraging argument, we know

$$\epsilon_{d/\ell} \leq (k\ell) \cdot \epsilon_{threshold}.$$

Since $\epsilon_{threshold}$ is negligible in λ and $k\ell$ is polynomial in λ, we must have that $\epsilon_{d/\ell}$ is negligible in λ.

References

1. Ajtai, M.: Generating hard instances of lattice problems. In: Proceedings of the Twenty-Eighth Annual ACM Symposium on Theory of Computing, pp. 99–108 (1996)
2. Albrecht, M.R., Cini, V., Lai, R.W., Malavolta, G., Thyagarajan, S.A.: Lattice based snarks: publicly verifiable, preprocessing, and recursively composable. In: Annual International Cryptology Conference, pp. 102–132. Springer (2022)
3. Albrecht, M.R., Lai, R.W.F., Lapiha, O., Woo, I.K.Y.: Partial lattice trapdoors: how to split lattice trapdoors, literally. In: Hanaoka, G., Yang, B. (eds.) Advances in Cryptology - ASIACRYPT 2025, Part III. LNCS, vol. 16247, pp. 265–296. Springer (2025). https://doi.org/10.1007/978-981-95-5099-9_9
4. Campanelli, M., Fiore, D., Greco, N., Kolonelos, D., Nizzardo, L.: Incrementally aggregatable vector commitments and applications to verifiable decentralized storage. In: Moriai, S., Wang, H. (eds.) ASIACRYPT 2020. LNCS, vol. 12492, pp. 3–35. Springer, Cham (2020). https://doi.org/10.1007/978-3-030-64834-3_1

5. Campanelli, M., Nitulescu, A., Ràfols, C., Zacharakis, A., Zapico, A.: Linear-map vector commitments and their practical applications. In: International Conference on the Theory and Application of Cryptology and Information Security, pp. 189–219. Springer (2022)
6. de Castro, L., Peikert, C.: Functional commitments for all functions, with transparent setup and from sis. In: Annual International Conference on the Theory and Applications of Cryptographic Techniques, pp. 287–320. Springer (2023)
7. Catalano, D., Fiore, D.: Vector commitments and their applications. In: Kurosawa, K., Hanaoka, G. (eds.) PKC 2013. LNCS, vol. 7778, pp. 55–72. Springer, Heidelberg (2013). https://doi.org/10.1007/978-3-642-36362-7_5
8. Chepurnoy, A., Papamanthou, C., Srinivasan, S., Zhang, Y.: Edrax: a cryptocurrency with stateless transaction validation. Cryptology ePrint Archive (2018)
9. Erway, C.C., Küpçü, A., Papamanthou, C., Tamassia, R.: Dynamic provable data possession. ACM Trans. Inf. Syst. Secur. **17**(4), 15:1–15:29 (2015). https://doi.org/10.1145/2699909
10. Gentry, C., Peikert, C., Vaikuntanathan, V.: Trapdoors for hard lattices and new cryptographic constructions. In: Proceedings of the Fortieth Annual ACM Symposium on Theory of Computing, pp. 197–206 (2008)
11. Gorbunov, S., Reyzin, L., Wee, H., Zhang, Z.: Pointproofs: aggregating proofs for multiple vector commitments. In: Proceedings of the 2020 ACM SIGSAC Conference on Computer and Communications Security, pp. 2007–2023 (2020)
12. Kilian, J.: A note on efficient zero-knowledge proofs and arguments. In: Proceedings of the Twenty-Fourth Annual ACM Symposium on Theory of Computing, pp. 723–732 (1992)
13. Lai, R.W.F., Malavolta, G.: Subvector commitments with application to succinct arguments. In: Boldyreva, A., Micciancio, D. (eds.) CRYPTO 2019. LNCS, vol. 11692, pp. 530–560. Springer, Cham (2019). https://doi.org/10.1007/978-3-030-26948-7_19
14. Libert, B., Yung, M.: Concise mercurial vector commitments and independent zero-knowledge sets with short proofs. In: Micciancio, D. (ed.) TCC 2010. LNCS, vol. 5978, pp. 499–517. Springer, Heidelberg (2010). https://doi.org/10.1007/978-3-642-11799-2_30
15. Micali, S.: CS proofs (extended abstracts). In: 35th Annual Symposium on Foundations of Computer Science, Santa Fe, New Mexico, USA, 20–22 November 1994, pp. 436–453. IEEE Computer Society (1994). https://doi.org/10.1109/SFCS.1994.365746
16. Micciancio, D., Peikert, C.: Trapdoors for lattices: simpler, tighter, faster, smaller. In: Annual International Conference on the Theory and Applications of Cryptographic Techniques, pp. 700–718. Springer (2012)
17. Nitulescu, A.: SoK: vector commitments. https://www.di.ens.fr/~nitulesc/files/vc-sok.pdf
18. Papamanthou, C., Shi, E., Tamassia, R.: Signatures of correct computation. In: Theory of Cryptography Conference, pp. 222–242. Springer (2013)
19. Pathak, V.N., Ruj, S., van der Meyden, R.: Vector commitment design, analysis, and applications: a survey. ACM Comput. Surv. (2026, to appear). https://eprint.iacr.org/2025/667
20. Sengupta, B., Ruj, S.: Publicly verifiable secure cloud storage for dynamic data using secure network coding. In: Chen, X., Wang, X., Huang, X. (eds.) Proceedings of the 11th ACM on Asia Conference on Computer and Communications Security, AsiaCCS 2016, Xi'an, China, May 30 - June 3, 2016, pp. 107–118. ACM (2016). https://doi.org/10.1145/2897845.2897915

21. Sengupta, B., Ruj, S.: Efficient proofs of retrievability with public verifiability for dynamic cloud storage. IEEE Trans. Cloud Comput. **8**(1), 138–151 (2020). https://doi.org/10.1109/TCC.2017.2767584
22. Shi, E., Stefanov, E., Papamanthou, C.: Practical dynamic proofs of retrievability. In: Sadeghi, A., Gligor, V.D., Yung, M. (eds.) 2013 ACM SIGSAC Conference on Computer and Communications Security, CCS'13, Berlin, Germany, 4–8 November 2013, pp. 325–336. ACM (2013). https://doi.org/10.1145/2508859.2516669
23. Srinivasan, S., Chepurnoy, A., Papamanthou, C., Tomescu, A., Zhang, Y.: Hyperproofs: aggregating and maintaining proofs in vector commitments. In: 31st USENIX Security Symposium (USENIX Security 2022), pp. 3001–3018 (2022)
24. Tas, E.N., Boneh, D.: Vector commitments with efficient updates. In: Bonneau, J., Weinberg, S.M. (eds.) 5th Conference on Advances in Financial Technologies, AFT 2023, Princeton, NJ, USA, 23–25 October 2023. LIPIcs, vol. 282, pp. 29:1–29:23. Schloss Dagstuhl - Leibniz-Zentrum für Informatik (2023). https://doi.org/10.4230/LIPICS.AFT.2023.29
25. Tomescu, A., Abraham, I., Buterin, V., Drake, J., Feist, D., Khovratovich, D.: Aggregatable subvector commitments for stateless cryptocurrencies. In: International Conference on Security and Cryptography for Networks, pp. 45–64. Springer (2020)
26. Wee, H., Wu, D.J.: Lattice-based functional commitments: fast verification and cryptanalysis. In: International Conference on the Theory and Application of Cryptology and Information Security, pp. 201–235. Springer (2023)
27. Wee, H., Wu, D.J.: Succinct vector, polynomial, and functional commitments from lattices. In: Annual International Conference on the Theory and Applications of Cryptographic Techniques, pp. 385–416. Springer (2023)

(Partially) Blind Signatures from Cryptographic Group Actions

Dung Hoang Duong[1(✉)], Xuan Thanh Khuc[1], Youming Qiao[2], Willy Susilo[1], and Chuanqi Zhang[3]

[1] Institute of Cybersecurity and Cryptology, School of Computing and Information Technology, University of Wollongong, Wollongong, Australia
{hduong,xtkhuc,wsusilo}@uow.edu.au

[2] School of Computer Science and Engineering, The University of New South Wales, Sydney, Australia

[3] Department of Software Systems and Cybersecurity, Faculty of Information Technology, Monash University, Melbourne, Australia
chuanqi.zhang@monash.edu

Abstract. Blind and partially blind signatures are important tools in building privacy-preserving systems such as electronic cash, anonymous authentication, and credential schemes. Blind signatures allow a user to obtain a valid signature without revealing the message to the signer, protecting user privacy. Partially blind signatures extend this idea by letting both parties agree on some public information—like validity periods or conditions—while still hiding the rest of the message, balancing privacy with accountability.

In this paper, we provide a generic construction of (partially) blind signatures from cryptographic group actions following the framework of the blind signature CSI-Otter introduced by Katsumata et al. (CRYPTO'23) in the context of isogeny (commutative group action). We adapt and modify that framework to make it work even for non-commutative group actions. As a result, we obtain a (partially) blind signature from abstract group actions which are proven to be secure in the random oracle model (ROM). We also propose an instantiation based on a variant of linear code equivalence, interpreted as a symmetric group action.

Keywords: (Partially) Blind Signatures · Group Actions · Canonical Forms

1 Introduction

Blind signatures, introduced by Chaum [28] in 1982, are interactive protocols between a signer, who holds a secret key, and a user, who holds a message, to jointly create a signature on a message in such a way that the message is oblivious to the signer at the signing time. Blind signatures have found many applications such as in e-cash [28,30], in e-voting [29,60], and in blockchains [26,52,75], and

K. Jee and A. Kate (Eds.): ACNS 2026, LNCS 16571, pp. 158–186, 2027.
https://doi.org/10.1007/978-3-032-32560-0_6

much more; see [44] and references therein for a rich list of applications and references.

One approach to construct a blind signature is to design a Schnorr-like sigma protocol [31] (or identification scheme) which has *module* structures [49] enabling the randomization of the interaction. The Schnorr blind signature was generalized by Pointcheval and Stern [70] and Abe and Okamoto [1]. The security proof of Abe and Okamoto contained a bug that has recently been fixed by Kastner, Loss and Xu [55] who provided a generic proof for Abe-Okamoto style blind signature. At CRYPTO'23, Katsumata et al. [57] proposed the first isogeny-based blind signature in the context of *cryptographic group actions*, called CSI-Otter, inspired by the Abe-Okamoto's construction in which Katsumata et al. utilized the *quadratic twist* of an elliptic curve in a clever way to endow isogenies with richer structure than abstract group actions, but still weaker than module structures, that enables the blindness. The security proofs are obtained by adapting the framework by Kastner et al. [55] into their setting.

Cryptographic group actions were first introduced by Brassard and Yung [22] in the context of *one-way* group actions. It was then considered independently by Couveignes [35] in the context of *hard homogeneous spaces* and by Rostovsev and Stolbunov [72] in the context of isogenous elliptic curves. This line of research was largely ignored until the proposal of CSIDH by Castryck et al. [27] in which the authors considered supersingular elliptic curves defined over a large prime field, rather than to ordinary elliptic curves as in the previous work of Couveignes [35] and Rostovsev-Stolbunov [72], on which many efficient isogeny-based constructions are based, such as CSI-FiSh signature [15], threshold signature [43], ring signatures [14], group signature [13] and blind signature CSI-Otter [57].

In the context of non-commutative group actions, there have been several proposals that submitted to NIST's recent call for additional post-quantum signatures[1], including LESS [17], MEDS [33], ALTEQ [74], and HAWK [39]. There have been several analogous cryptographic constructions to the case of isogenies in this context, such as (inefficient) threshold signature [8] and ring signatures [7,18]. However, due to the non-commutativity of the underlying groups, the cryptographic constructions in this setting are still limited. For example, pub lic key encryptions based on non-commutative group actions are only recently shown with *quantum ciphertexts* [53].

Even though non-commutative group action constructions are less efficient than the isogeny counterparts in terms of key/signature sizes, those schemes however enjoy efficiency in terms of implementation. Furthermore, actions by "highly non-commutative" groups, such as symmetric and general linear groups, enjoy the property that most known quantum algorithmic techniques do not work for hidden subgroup problems for such groups [47]. These make non-commutative group actions an appealing candidate for post-quantum cryptography, so it is desirable to develop more advanced cryptographic schemes to increase cryptographic functionalities based on them. In particular, it brings to us the following question:

[1] https://csrc.nist.gov/news/2023/additional-pqc-digital-signature-candidates.

Can we construct a (partially) blind signature from non-commutative group actions?

1.1 Our Contribution

In this paper, we provide an affirmative answer to the above question. Our contribution in this paper is two-fold and can be summarized as follows.

- We provide a framework to construct a Schnorr-type blind signature from abstract group actions. Our framework follows closely with the construction of CSI-Otter [57] with modifications to adjust for the case of generic groups. In particular, because we do not have *twists* as in the case of elliptic curves, we need to *double* the public key, compared to that of CSI-Otter, in such a way that the *additional* public key element plays a twist role in our context; see Sect. 1.2 for more detail. Another contribution in this fold is a zero-knowledge proof for well-formed public key. In contrast to the case of isogenies, one can easily verify that the public key is valid, i.e., the public key is indeed a valid supersingular elliptic curve. In our setting, we need a zero-knowledge protocol allowing one to validate the public key. In addition, we also extend our blind signature into a *partially* blind signature.
- We provide an efficient instantiation from non-commutative group actions.[2] In order to provide an instantiation for non-commutative group actions, we require several conditions for the underlying group. If the group is non-commutative, to ensure the soundness of our protocol, we need a group with an efficient square-root algorithm. This is because in our protocol, given two accepted transcripts with the same commitment, an extractor can obtain only g^2, where g is the secret key. Hence, we need an efficient algorithm to compute g given g^2 in the group. In order to enable an efficient instantiation inherited from existing efficient schemes, we proposed a variant of LESS that instead of having monomial matrix $\mathrm{Mon}(n, q)$ action as in LESS, we have a permutation group action which fulfils our purpose; see details in Sect. 1.2.

1.2 Technique Overview

In this section, we present in detail our contributions. We will first describe the core in the construction of CSI-Otter [57], on which our framework is based. We then present a variant of linear code equivalence problem in LESS from which we provide an instantiation for a blind signature following our framework.

Construction Framework. In CSI-Otter [57], the authors consider the CSIDH group action $* : G \times \mathcal{E} \to \mathcal{E}$ where G is an ideal class group and $\mathcal{E}$ is a set of elliptic curves. It can be assumed that the structure of G is known and we can express G as $G = \langle \mathfrak{g} \rangle \cong \mathbb{Z}_N$ for some positive integer $N \in \mathbb{N}$ and generator

[2] We note that our framework can be instantiated for generic groups, both commutative and non-commutative.

$\mathfrak{g} \in G$. In isogeny settings, an elliptic curve $E_0 \in \mathcal{E}$ is fixed and the public key is of the form $A = [\mathfrak{g}^a] * E_0$ for a random $a \leftarrow_{\$} \mathbb{Z}_N$, and the first-sender message (i.e., commitment) is computed similarly as $Y = [\mathfrak{g}^y] * E_0$ for a random $y \leftarrow_{\$} \mathbb{Z}_N$. In order to enable a Schnorr-type blind signature, the normal procedure for the user in blinding the message M would be: (i) randomize the commitment, which can be done by computing $[\mathfrak{g}^z] * Y$ for $z \leftarrow_{\$} \mathbb{Z}_N$; (ii) randomize the public key A and public parameter E_0, which can be done by computing $[\mathfrak{g}^b] * A$ and $[\mathfrak{g}^d] * E_0$ for $d, b \leftarrow_{\$} \mathbb{Z}_N$; (iii) associate $[\mathfrak{g}^z] * Y$, $[\mathfrak{g}^b] * A$ and $[\mathfrak{g}^d] * E_0$ into one element, say X; (iv) compute the hash value $c = H(X \| M)$; and lastly (v) use z, d, b to randomize c to obtain a randomized challenge c' and send to the signer. In the discrete logarithm setting [31], all steps (i)–(v) can be done easily, especially step (iii) since $[\mathfrak{g}^z] * Y$, $[\mathfrak{g}^b] * A$ and $[\mathfrak{g}^d] * E_0$ are all group elements on which we can do operation to create a group element X. However, it is not the case for isogeny setting since $[\mathfrak{g}^z] * Y$, $[\mathfrak{g}^b] * A$ and $[\mathfrak{g}^d] * E_0$ are all elliptic curves and we do not have operations on elliptic curves.

In order to overcome that problem, Katsumata et al. [57] have cleverly used *quadratic twist* in elliptic curves. Briefly speaking, given $A = [\mathfrak{g}^a] * E_0$ for an unknown $a \in \mathbb{Z}$, every one can easily compute its quadratic twist $[\mathfrak{g}^{-a}] * E_0$, which was denoted by A^{-1} in [57]. Now step (i)–(iii) above can be done together in [57] as follows: choose $(d, z) \leftarrow_{\$} \{-1, 1\} \times \mathbb{Z}_N$ and set $X := [\mathfrak{g}^z] * Y^d$. For the proof to work, following the proof by Kastner-Loss-Xu [55] for Abe-Okamoto blind signature [1], Katsumata et al. [57] modified the above idea to use the OR composition of the underlying sigma protocol. Specifically, CSI-Otter uses two public key $A_0 = [\mathfrak{g}^a] * E_0, A_1 = [\mathfrak{g}^b] * E_0$ where $a, b \leftarrow_{\$} \mathbb{Z}_N$, and the secret key is one of the a_0 or a_1; see [57] for the details.

Since quadratic twists exist only in the isogeny setting, to enable a construction analogous to CSI-Otter for abstract group actions, what we do is to *double* the public key. To be more precise, consider a group G acting on a set S by $* : G \times S \to S$ and fix an element $E_0 \in S$.[3] Our public key will consist of $A_b^{(c)} = g_b^c * E_0$ for $b \in \{0, 1\}, c \in \{-1, 1\}$ and the secret key is either $g_0 \in G$ or $g_1 \in G$. Here $A_b^{(-1)}$ will play the role for quadratic twists of $A_b^{(1)}$ as in the case of CSI-Otter. We also construct a protocol for an OR relation (cf. [40, Fig. 7]) as in CSI-Otter as the underlying sigma protocol for the blind signature. Our blind signature follows the same route as in CSI-Otter but with modifications; see Sect. 4 for the detail. We highlight below two noteworthy differences between our scheme with CSI-Otter:

- Firstly, in our scheme, one of the responses is of the form $r = hg_\delta^{-1} \in G$ where g_δ with $\delta \in \{0, 1\}$ is the secret key. For the verification, we need to compute the action on $A_\delta^{(-1)} = g_\delta^{-1} * E_0$ and expect the outcome to be one of the commitments $Y := h^{-1} * E_0$.

  In this case, if we use $r^{-1} = g_\delta h^{-1}$ then we need g and h^{-1} commute. However, requiring h^{-1} to commute with g would break the HVZK property of the

[3] We use the same notation as in CSI-Otter to make readers easily follow the flows of the construction.

underlying sigma protocol.
Therefore, instead of having one response hg_δ^{-1}, we send two responses hg_δ^{-1} and $h^{-1}g_\delta$. This turns out to be useful in restoring HVZK.
- Secondly, in order to ensure the soundness of the underlying sigma protocol in our scheme, the extractor can obtain, from two given accepted transcripts with the same commitment, the square g_δ^2 of the secret key g_δ. Hence, we need an efficient square-root algorithm in the group G to compute g_δ from g_δ^2, which we provide in Sect. 6.

Another contribution is a zero-knowledge protocol to validate the public key. In contrast to the case of isogeny-based cryptography in which everyone can easily validate the public key – a valid supersingular elliptic curve, it is not the case for abstract group actions. Our protocol is presented in Fig. 1.

Extending to Partially Blind. We also extend our construction to obtain a partially blind signature from abstract (non-commutative) group actions, also following the framework by Katsumata et al. [57] in the isogeny setting. The idea is to keep the public key as in the blind signature consisting of $(A_b^{(c)})$ with $b \in \{0,1\}$ and $c \in \{-1,1\}$ as before, and add two more elements $A_2^{(1)} = g_2 * E_0$ and $A_2^{(-1)} := g_2^{-1} * E_0$ where $g_2 = \mathsf{G}(\mathsf{info})$ with G a function $\{0,1\}^* \to G$. We then modify the signer to prove that it knows at least two of the three secrets (g_0, g_1, g_2) generating $(A_b^{(c)})$ with $b \in \{0,1,2\}$ and $c \in \{-1,1\}$. Our first step is to provide a sigma protocol for a 2-out-of-3 relation in which the prover convinces the verifier that he knows two of the secrets, say g_0, g_2, among three g_0, g_1, g_2. Then we turn this protocol into a partially blind signature. Because of the 'extra' secret g_2 and hence the extra public key, which is associated with the tag info, the resulting transcript and hence signature size of the partially blind signature is increased by 50% compared to that of the blind signature, which happens similarly in the case of $\mathsf{CSI\text{-}Otter}$ [57].

Instantiation. As mentioned above, to instantiate our blind signatures with non-commutative group actions, we require the corresponding group G to satisfy the following:

- Given g^2, there exists an efficient algorithm to compute g.
- Reusing $g \in G$ twice still gives a secure protocol (see Definition 4 for a more precise requirement).

To identify a non-commutative group action satisfying the above seems like a tricky business. We will make further discussions in Sect. 6.1. To address the issues, we interpret the monomial code equivalence problem as a group action of the symmetric group. This is made possible by a canonical form algorithm ([40, Appendix B]). In contrast to LESS, where the group action is by the monomial group, our group actions avoid the attacks on reusing group elements as in [23,25] (Sect. 6.2). We also show that by selecting a family of permutations that satisfy the square-root requirement ([40, Appendix B]).

1.3 Related Work

Most of the existing post-quantum blind signatures are constructed from lattices. The first post-quantum blind signature was proposed by Rückert [73] following the design paradigm by Pointcheval and Stern [70]. However, Hauck et al. [50] discovered a flaw in Rückert's security argument which results in many blind signatures [5,21,63,65] following the design and security arguments of Rückert [73] being insecure. Hauck et al. [50] also introduced a new blind signature from linear hash functions [49] but it is impractical. Lyubashevsky et al. [64], del Pino-Katsumata [69], and Agrawal et al. [2] respectively proposed efficient two-round lattice-based blind signatures, which was further improved by Beullens et al. [16] with a two-round blind signature from standard lattice problems with signature size around 22 KB.

In another context, Petzoldt et al. [67] constructed a blind signature from multivariate quadratic equations. However, it has been recently broken by Beullens [12]. Blazy et al. [20] proposed a blind signature from codes but it had a flaw in the security proof, which was later fixed [19].

At CRYPTO 2023, Katsumata et al. [57] proposed the first construction of a (partially) blind signature from isogenies. Kuchta, LeGrow and Persichetti proposed a construction of blind signatures from matrix code equivalence [61] following the framework in [57], with a focus on matrix code equivalence. To resolve issues caused by non-commutativity, the authors of [61] make use of the actions of both A and its inverse transpose A^{-T} for an invertible matrix A, and require A to be (anti)symmetric. The security of the scheme relies on the hardness assumption of the Modified Inverse Matrix Code Equivalence Problem (MIMCE), which is a variant of the Inverse Matrix Code Equivalence Problem (IMCE). However, there have been some recent attacks [32,45] on MIMCE, breaking the claimed bit security of the blind signature scheme proposed in [61]. Separately, Katsumata et al. [58] and Do et al. [38] independently propose a polynomial-time attack against the l-concurrent unforgeability of Schnorr-type blind signatures. Hence such attack is applicable to both [61] and our scheme in this paper, which means the security of our construction is limited to the sequential setting.

More recently, Hanzlik et al. [48] proposed a novel framework for efficient blind signatures from group actions which also achieves polynomially concurrent security. Their frameworks can be instantiated in both commutative and non-commutative group action settings. In a following work [62], Lai and Persichetti provided a compact and efficient instantiation of Tanuki from code equivalence. However, we note that neither [61] nor [48] discusses whether or how their blind signature can be made partially blind, so it is still open to construct a partially blind signature from non-commutative group actions, which we will resolve in this paper.

In this paper, we generalize those results in [57] to abstract group actions. Our framework is applicable for general (non-commutative) group actions, with security based on assumptions such as in Definition 9. One requirement for instantiating our scheme is the reuse of secret keys, which leads us to propose the use of symmetric group action to equivalence classes of linear codes under the action of the general linear group and the diagonal group. This viewpoint helps to thwart the attack of reusing keys as in [23,25]; see Sect. 6 for the details.

Table 1. Efficiency comparison of blind and partially blind signature schemes. Here, $\mathsf{size}(G)$ and $\mathsf{size}(S)$ denote the size of a single element in the acting group G and the acted set S, respectively, and n is the challenge dimension (security parameter). All computational costs are measured in terms of the number of group actions. The (partially) blind signature schemes of CSI-Otter [57] correspond to the basic versions without optimization, while Tanuki [48] corresponds to Framework 1 with log-concurrent and sequential one-more unforgeability.

Scheme	**Size**			**Computational Cost**		
	$\lvert\mathsf{sk}\rvert$	$\lvert\mathsf{pk}\rvert$	$\lvert\sigma\rvert$	Signer	User	Verifier
CSI-Otter [57]	$\mathsf{size}(G)+1$	$2\cdot\mathsf{size}(S)$	$2n\cdot\mathsf{size}(S)+4n$	$2n$	$4n$	$2n$
CSI-Otter (Partially Blind) [57]	$\mathsf{size}(G)+1$	$2\cdot\mathsf{size}(S)$	$6n\cdot\mathsf{size}(S)+6n$	$6n$	$13n$	$6n$
Tanuki [48]	$\mathsf{size}(G)$	$\mathsf{size}(S)$	$n\cdot\mathsf{size}(S)+n\cdot\mathsf{size}(G)$	n	$2n$	n
Our Blind Signature	$\mathsf{size}(G)+1$	$4\cdot\mathsf{size}(S)$	$4n\cdot\mathsf{size}(S)+2n$	$4n$	$8n$	$4n$
Our Partially Blind Signature	$\mathsf{size}(G)+1$	$6\cdot\mathsf{size}(S)$	$6n\cdot\mathsf{size}(S)+2n$	$6n$	$12n$	$6n$

A natural question is whether one can simply add tags to obtain PBS. We do not think this is immediate. Binding the agreed public information info into the verification relation changes what is committed and hashed, so one would need to re-establish the transcript-balance and indistinguishability arguments used in Tanuki. Moreover, Tanuki's concurrent-security proofs are sensitive to random-oracle programming and transcript distributions across many interleavings, so making the relation tag-dependent appears to require revisiting the concurrent simulation and extraction arguments. Thus, concurrently secure PBS from group actions in the sense of Tanuki seems to be a non-trivial extension.

A related question is whether our CSI-Otter-like framework can be strengthened to achieve concurrent security in the sense of Tanuki [48]. Our setting has an additional constraint: the challenge space must carry a compatible group structure, since the proof relies on algebraic manipulations over challenges. Since Tanuki does not require this, adapting its concurrency techniques to our setting does not seem straightforward and would likely require substantial redesign. We therefore view Tanuki as the appropriate reference for stronger concurrent-security guarantees, while our work focuses on a simpler CSI-Otter-like construction tailored to our setting.

In Table 1, we provide a comparison between our construction with CSI-Otter[57] and Tanuki [48]. Since we do not have yet the concrete parameters for the modified group actions, we hence provide the comparison in terms of the size of the group and the set as well as the number of group actions.

2 Preliminaries

2.1 Notations

For a prime power q, let $\mathbb{F}_q$ be the field consisting of q elements. Denote by $\mathbb{F}_q^n$ the linear space of length-n row vectors over $\mathbb{F}_q$. Denote by $\mathrm{Mat}(m \times n, q)$ the linear space of $m \times n$ matrices over $\mathbb{F}_q$, and $\mathrm{Mat}(n, q) := \mathrm{Mat}(n \times n, q)$. We use $\mathrm{GL}(n, q)$ to denote the group of $n \times n$ invertible matrices over $\mathbb{F}_q$, and $\mathrm{D}(n, q)$ to denote the group of $n \times n$ invertible diagonal matrices over $\mathbb{F}_q$. The symmetric group on $\{1, \ldots, n\}$ is denoted by S_n. By encoding each $\sigma \in \mathrm{S}_n$ as a $n \times n$ permutation matrix over $\mathbb{F}_q$, we can embed S_n as a subgroup of $\mathrm{GL}(n, q)$. A matrix in $\mathrm{Mat}(n, q)$ is said to be monomial, if it is the product between a diagonal and a permutation matrix. The group of monomial matrices is denoted by $\mathrm{Mon}(n, q)$.

For a positive integer k, we denote $[k]$ to be the set $\{1, \ldots, k\}$. For integers a, b we denote by $[a : b]$ the set $\{a, a+1, \ldots, b\}$. For a vector $\overrightarrow{h}$, denote by h_i the i-th entry of $\overrightarrow{h}$. We will also denote a vector by bold characters, e.g., $\mathbf{h}$. For a finite set S, we write $x \leftarrow\!\!\$\, S$ to denote x is sampled randomly from S. We use $\odot$ to denote the component-wise multiplication of vectors in $\mathbb{R}$. In particular, for $c \in \mathbb{R}$ and vectors $\mathbf{a} = (a_1, \cdots, a_k), \mathbf{b} = (b_1, \ldots, b_k)$, we write $c \odot \mathbf{a}$ for $(ca_1, \ldots, ca_k)$ and $\mathbf{a} \odot \mathbf{b} = (a_1 b_1, \ldots, a_k b_k)$. If $\mathbf{g}, \mathbf{h}$ are group element vectors, we also write $\mathbf{gh}$ for $(g_1 h_1, \ldots, g_k h_k)$. We also extend this component-wise notation for exponentiation, e.g., we write $\mathbf{a}^c$ for $(a_1^c, \ldots, a_k^c)$, $\mathbf{a}^{\mathbf{b}}$ for $(a_1^{b_1}, \ldots, a_k^{b_k})$, and for group action, e.g., we write the action of vector $\mathbf{a}$ on $\mathbf{s} \in S^k$ as $\mathbf{a} * \mathbf{s}$ for $(a_1 * s_1, \ldots, a_k * s_k)$ (here $*$ indicates the action operation - see Sect. 2.3 for group action definition).

2.2 Sigma Protocols

Definition 1 (Sigma Protocol). *A sigma protocol for an NP relation $R \subseteq \{0,1\}^* \times \{0,1\}^*$ is a public-coin three-move interactive protocol between a prover $\mathcal{P} = (\mathcal{P}_1, \mathcal{P}_2)$ and a verifier $\mathcal{V}$ as follows.*

- *The prover on input a statement X and a witness W such that $(\mathsf{X}, \mathsf{W}) \in R$, runs $(\mathsf{com}, \mathsf{state}) \leftarrow \mathcal{P}_1(\mathsf{X}, \mathsf{W})$ and sents a commitment com to the verifier.*
- *The verifier samples a random challenge $\mathsf{ch} \leftarrow\!\!\$\, \mathcal{C}$ from the challenge space $\mathcal{C}$ and sends ch to the prover.*
- *Upon receiving the challenge ch, the prover $\mathcal{P}_2$ generates a response rsp and sents rsp to the verifier.*
- *The verifier runs $\mathcal{V}(\mathsf{X}, \mathsf{com}, \mathsf{ch}, \mathsf{rsp})$ and outputs 1 to indicate acceptance, and 0 otherwise.*

A sigma protocol must satisfy correctness, honest-verifier zero-knowledge (HVZK), and special soundness defined as the following.

Correctness. It is required that if the prover $\mathcal{P}$ and the verifier $\mathcal{V}$ follow the sigma protocol honestly, then the verifier would output 1 with probability 1.

Honest Verifier Zero-Knowledge (HVZK). There exists a PPT simulator Sim that given a statement X, a challenge $\mathsf{ch} \in \mathcal{C}$, outputs a valid transcipt $(\mathsf{com}, \mathsf{ch}, \mathsf{rsp})$ that is indistinguishable from a real transcript.

Special Soundness. There exists a determinsitic polynomial time extractor Ext that given two accepted transcripts $(\mathsf{com}, \mathsf{ch}, \mathsf{rsp})$ and $(\mathsf{com}, \mathsf{ch}', \mathsf{rsp}')$ with the same commitment com and different challenges $\mathsf{ch} \neq \mathsf{ch}'$, outputs W such that $(\mathsf{X}, \mathsf{W}) \in R$.

We also provide a definition for a hard instance generator for the NP relation R as follows.

Definition 2 (Hard Instance Generator). *An NP relation R is associated with an instance generator (IG) if IG, given as input the security parameter 1^n, outputs a statement-witness pair $(\mathsf{X}, \mathsf{W}) \in R$. Moreover, we say that the instance generator is hard if the following holds for any* PPT *adversary $\mathcal{A}$:*

$$\Pr[(\mathsf{X}, \mathsf{W}) \leftarrow \mathsf{IG}(1^n), \mathsf{W}' \leftarrow \mathcal{A}(\mathsf{X}) : (\mathsf{X}, \mathsf{W}') \in R] = \mathrm{negl}(n).$$

2.3 Cryptographic Group Actions

Let G be a group and S a set. An action of G on S is a map $* : G \times S \to S$ satisfying the following properties: (i) $\mathrm{id} * s = s$ for all $s \in S$ and the identity element $\mathrm{id} \in G$; and (ii) $g * (h * s) = gh * s$ for all $g, h \in G$ and $s \in S$. A group action is said to be [3]:

- *transitive* if for all $s, t \in S$, there exists $g \in G$ such that $g * s = t$;
- *faithful* if there does not exist $g \in G \setminus \{\mathrm{id}\}$ such that $g * s = s$ for all $s \in S$, i.e., if $g * s = s$ for all $s \in S$ then $g = \mathrm{id}$;
- *free* if whenever there exists $s \in S$ such that $g * s = s$ then $g = id$; and
- *regular* if it is free and transitive.

Given a group action $*$ of G on S, the orbit of an element $s \in S$ is defined as $\mathsf{Orb}(s) := \{g * s : \forall g \in G\}$. Note that if the group action is transitive, then $\mathsf{Orb}(s) = S$. The stabilizer of s is defined by $\mathsf{Stab}(s) := \{g \in G : g * s = s)\}$ which is a subgroup of G. The Orbit-Stabilizer theorem says that, if G is finite then $|G| = |\mathsf{Stab}(s)| \cdot |\mathsf{Orb}(s)|$.

In this paper, we shall mostly consider finite groups acting on finite sets. To use group actions in algorithms, we assume that group and set elements have natural encodings, as well as group operations, group actions, and random samplings of group and set elements can be efficiently computed; see [3,22,54] for more details and certain variations. In particular, we assume that uniform random samplings from the group G and the set S are efficient.

A group action is *one-way*, if for a random s, the function $f_s : G \to S$ defined by $f_s(g) := g * s$ is one-way. The one-way assumption is formulated as the *Group Action Inverse Problem* (GAIP) defined in the following.

Definition 3 (Group Action Inverse Problem (*GAIP*)). *Given a group action* $* : G \times S \to S$*, uniformly random* $s \in S$*, and uniformly random* $t \in \mathsf{Orb}(s)$*, find* $g \in G$ *such that* $g * s = t$*.*

Here we restrict to the case of transitive group actions, as in the isogeny-based setting [27,35,42], or we can restrict the element g to be in the orbit $\mathsf{Orb(s)}$ of s as in the case of non-commutative group actions [17,33,74].

For the purpose of our paper, we define what we call the *Inverse Group Action Problem* (IGAP), as follows.

Definition 4 (Inverse Group Action Problem (IGAP)). *Given a group action* $* : G \times S \to S$*, uniformly random* $s \in S$*, and a pair* $(g * s, g^{-1} * s)$*, find* g*.*

IGAP was called the *Inverse Linear Code Equivalence* (ILCE) problem [7] in the context of linear code equivalence underlying LESS, and called the *Inverse Matrix Code Equivalence* (IMCE) problem [33] in the context of matrix code equivalence underlying MEDS. Recently, [23,25] introduced heuristic efficient algorithms for the ILCE problem, while it remains unclear whether similar efficient algorithms exist for the IMCE problem.

Note that the lattice isomorphism problems used in HAWK [39] and the alternating trilinear form equivalence problems used in ALTEQ [74] also admit formulations as group actions and corresponding IGAP. However, [24] gave a heuristic efficient algorithm to solve the corresponding IGAP for lattice isomorphism problems. The hardness of the corresponding IGAP for the alternating trilinear form equivalence problems is still unclear. We will discuss this again to justify our choice of instantiation in Sect. 6.1.

In this paper, we provide a generic framework of a blind signature for abstract group actions. For the framework to work, an instantiated group G needs to satisfy the following assumptions.

Assumption 1 (Square-root assumption)**.** Given an element $h \in G$ promised to be a square (i.e., $h = g^2$ for $g \in G$), there exists an efficient algorithm that outputs all $g \in G$ such that $g^2 = h$.

Assumption 1 is needed in the soundness proof of the underlying protocol. In the extraction argument, given two accepting transcripts with the same commitment, our extractor recovers an element of the form g^2, where g is the signer's secret. To complete extraction, we therefore require an efficient procedure that, given g^2, recovers the secret g, as stated in Assumption 1.

We note that square roots are not necessarily unique, i.e., it could be the case that $g^2 = (g')^2$ for some $g \neq g'$. Two standard ways to deal with this are: either requiring the square-root procedure to return all roots, or restricting it to a domain in which square roots are unique. Our instantiation follows the second approach; see [40, Remark 6]. In Sect. 6.1, we also discuss the applicability of Assumption 1 for MEDS, ALTEQ, LESS, and HAWK.

2.4 (Partially) Blind Signatures

We follow [1,55–57] to define a three-move blind signature.

Definition 5 (Partially Blind Signature). *A three-move partially blind signature* PBS *with efficient decidable public key space* $\mathcal{PK}$ *consists of the following* PPT *algorithms.*

- $\mathsf{PBS.KGen}(1^n) \to (\mathsf{pk}, \mathsf{sk})$: *On input the security parameter* 1^n, *the key generation algorithm outputs a pair of public and secret keys* $(\mathsf{pk}, \mathsf{sk})$.
- $\mathsf{PBS.S} = (\mathsf{PBS.S}_1, \mathsf{PBS.S}_2)$: *The signer consists of two phases:*
  - $\mathsf{PBS.S}_1(\mathsf{sk}, \mathsf{info}) \to (\mathsf{state}_S, \rho_{S,1})$: *On input the secret key* sk *and a tag* info, *it outputs an internal signer state* state_S *and the first-sender message* $\rho_{S,1}$.
  - $\mathsf{PBS.S}_2(\mathsf{state}_S, \rho_U) \to \rho_{S,2}$: *On input the signer state* state_S *and a user message* ρ_U, *it outputs a second-sender message* $\rho_{S,2}$.
- $\mathsf{PBS.U} = (\mathsf{PBS.U}_1, \mathsf{PBS.U}_2)$: *The user consists of two phases:*
  - $\mathsf{PBS.U}_1(\mathsf{pk}, \mathsf{info}, M, \rho_{S,1}) \to (\mathsf{state}_U, \rho_U)$: *On input the public key* $\mathsf{pk} \in \mathcal{PK}$, *a tag* info, *a message* M *and the first-sender message* $\rho_{S,1}$, *it outputs an internal user state* state_U *and a user message* ρ_U.
  - $\mathsf{PBS.U}_2(\mathsf{state}_U, \rho_{S,2})$: *On input a user state* state_U *and a second-signer message* $\rho_{S,2}$, *outputs a signature* σ
- $\mathsf{PBS.Verify}(\mathsf{pk}, \mathsf{info}, M, \sigma)$: *On input the public key* pk, *a tag* info, *a message* M *and a signature* σ, *it outputs* 1 *to indicate the signature is valid, and* 0 *otherwise.*

If the partially blind signature scheme only accepts a unique tag info, it is referred to as a blind signature (BS), and info is omitted from the scheme's syntax.

A valid partially blind signature must satisfy three essential properties: *correctness, partial blindness under chosen keys,* and *one-more unforgeability,* as formally defined below.

Definition 6 (Correctness). *A three-move partial blind signature scheme* PBS *is correct if for all public and secret key pair* $(\mathsf{pk}, \mathsf{sk}) \leftarrow \mathsf{PBS.KGen}(1^n)$, *we have*

$$\Pr\left[\mathsf{PBS.Verify}(\mathsf{pk}, \mathsf{info}, M, \sigma) = 1 \;\middle|\; \begin{array}{c} (\mathsf{state}_S, \rho_{S,1}) \leftarrow \mathsf{PBS.S}_1(\mathsf{sk}, \mathsf{info}) \\ (\mathsf{state}_U, \rho_U) \leftarrow \mathsf{PBS.U}_1(\mathsf{pk}, \mathsf{info}, M, \rho_{S,1}) \\ \rho_{S,2} \leftarrow \mathsf{PBS.S}_2(\mathsf{state}_S, \rho_U) \\ \sigma \leftarrow \mathsf{PBS.U}_2(\mathsf{state}_U, \rho_{S,2}) \end{array}\right] = 1.$$

Definition 7 (Partial Blindness under Chosen Keys). *For a partial blind signature* PBS, *define the following game* $\mathsf{Blind}_{\mathsf{PBS}}$ *with an adversary* $\mathcal{A}$ *(playing the signer) as follows.*

Setup. *The challenger samples a bit* $\mathsf{coin} \leftarrow_\$ \{0,1\}$ *and runs* $\mathcal{A}$ *on input* 1^n.

Online Phase. $\mathcal{A}$ *outputs a tag* info, *two message* M_0^* *and* M_1^*, *a public key* $\mathsf{pk} \in \mathcal{PK}$, *the game checks if* pk *is valid and if so, it assigns* $(M_0, M_1) = (M^*_{\mathsf{coin}}, M^*_{1-\mathsf{coin}})$. *If* pk *is not valid, the game aborts and outputs* 0. *The adversary* $\mathcal{A}$ *is given access to oracles* $\mathsf{U}_1, \mathsf{U}_2$ *which behave as follows*

- **Oracle** U_1. *On input* $b \in \{0,1\}$ *and a first-signer message* $\rho_{S,1,b}$, *if the session* b *is not yet open, the oracle marks session* b *as* opened *and generates a state and a challenge as* $(\mathsf{state}_{U,b}, \rho_{U,b}) \leftarrow_{\$} \mathsf{PBS.U}_1(\mathsf{pk}, \mathsf{info}, M_b, \rho_{S,1})$. *It returns* $\rho_{U,b}$ *to* $\mathcal{A}$.
- **Oracle** U_2. *On input* $b \in \{0,1\}$ *and a second-signer message* $\rho_{S,2,b}$, *if the session* b *is* opened, *the oracle creates a signature* $\sigma_b \leftarrow \mathsf{PBS.U}_2(\mathsf{state}_{U,b}, \rho_{S,2,b})$. *It marks session* b *as* closed. *Oracle* U_2 *does not output anything.*

Output Determination. *When both sessions are closed and for* $b \in \{0,1\}$ *we have that* $\mathsf{PBS.Verify}(\mathsf{pk}, \mathsf{info}, M_b, \sigma_b) = 1$, *the oracle returns the two signatures* $(\sigma_{\mathsf{coin}}, \sigma_{1-\mathsf{coin}})$ *to* $\mathcal{A}$, *where note that* σ_{coin} *(resp.* $\sigma_{1-\mathsf{coin}}$*) is a valid signature for* M_0^* *(resp.* M_1^**) regardless of the choice of* coin. $\mathcal{A}$ *outputs a guess* coin^* *for* coin. *We say that* $\mathcal{A}$ *wins if* $\mathsf{coin}^* = \mathsf{coin}$.

We say that PBS *is partial blind under chosen keys if the probability that* $\mathcal{A}$ *wins is negligible.*

Definition 8 (One-More Unforgeability). *For a partial blind signature* PBS *and* $l \in \mathbb{N}$, *we define* l*-one-more unforgeability via the following game between a challenger and an adversary* $\mathcal{A}$*:*

Setup. *The challenger samples* $(\mathsf{pk}, \mathsf{sk}) \leftarrow \mathsf{PBS.KGen}(1^n)$ *and runs* $\mathcal{A}$ *on input* pk. *It initializes* $l_{\mathsf{closed}} = 0$ *and* $\mathsf{opened}_{\mathsf{sid}} = \mathsf{false}$ *for all* $\mathsf{sid} \in \mathbb{N}$.

Online Phase. $\mathcal{A}$ *is given access to two oracle* S_1 *and* S_2 *as follows.*

- **Oracle** S_1*: The oracle samples a fresh session identifier* sid. *It sets* $\mathsf{opened}_{\mathsf{sid}} \leftarrow \mathsf{true}$ *and generates* $(\mathsf{state}_{S,\mathsf{sid}}, \rho_{S,1}) \leftarrow \mathsf{PBS.S}_1(\mathsf{sk}, \mathsf{info})$. *It then returns* sid *and the first-sender message* $\rho_{S,1}$ *to* $\mathcal{A}$.
- **Oracle** S_2*: On input a user message* ρ_U *and a session identifier* sid, *if* $l_{\mathsf{closed}} \geq l$ *or* $\mathsf{opened}_{\mathsf{sid}} = \mathsf{false}$, *then it returns* $\perp$. *Otherwise, it increments* l_{closed} *and* $\mathsf{opened}_{\mathsf{sid}} = \mathsf{false}$. *It then computes the second-signer message* $\rho_{S,2} \leftarrow \mathsf{PBS.S}_2(\mathsf{state}_{S,\mathsf{sid}}, \rho_U)$ *and returns* $\rho_{S,2}$ *to* $\mathcal{A}$.

Output Determination. *When* $\mathcal{A}$ *outputs distinct tuples of message-signature pairs* $(M_1, \sigma_1, \mathsf{info}), \ldots, (M_k, \sigma_k, \mathsf{info})$, *we say that* $\mathcal{A}$ *wins if* $k \geq l_{\mathsf{closed}} + 1$ *and for all* $i \in [k]$, $\mathsf{PBS.Verify}(\mathsf{pk}, \mathsf{info}, M_i, \sigma_i) = 1$.

We say that the blind signature PBS *is* l*-one-more unforgeable if the probability that* $\mathcal{A}$ *wins is negligible.*

3 Sigma Protocol for Validating Public Key

Unlike the isogeny setting of CSI-Otter [57], public-key validity is not immediate for generic group actions. In this section, we give a sigma protocol for proving that a public key is well formed, namely for the relation

$$R = \{(\mathsf{X} = (A^{(1)}, A^{(-1)}), \mathsf{W} = g) \mid A^{(b)} = g^b * E,\ \forall b \in \{-1,1\}\}. \tag{1}$$

$\mathcal{P}(\mathsf{X} = (A^{(1)}, A^{(-1)}), \mathsf{W} = g)$ $\qquad\qquad$ $\mathcal{V}(\mathsf{X} = (A^{(1)}, A^{(-1)})$

$h \leftarrow\!\$\; G$

$Y^{(1)} = h * E, Y^{(-1)} = h^{-1} * E$

$A := h * A^{(-1)}$ $\qquad \xrightarrow{(Y^{(1)}, Y^{(-1)}, A)}$

$\qquad \xleftarrow{c}$ $\qquad c \leftarrow\!\$\; \{0, 1\}$

$r = hg^{-c}$ $\qquad \xrightarrow{r}$ $\qquad$ if $c = 0$ check whether

$$r^b * E = Y^{(b)} \text{ for } b \in \{-1, 1\}$$
$$\wedge\, r * A^{(-1)} = A$$

if $c = 1$ check whether

$$r * A^{(1)} = Y^{(1)} \wedge r * E = A$$

Fig. 1. Sigma Protocol for Validating Public Key

Here, G acts on S and $E \in S$ is fixed. The protocol is shown in Fig. 1. It is a variant of the GMW-type protocol for generic group actions; see, e.g., [18]. Proofs are given in [40, Appendix C].

For this protocol, we assume the hardness of the following *Group Action Strong Decisional Diffie–Hellman* (GASDDH) problem, analogous to the strong decisional Diffie–Hellman assumption in [68, Assumption 2].

Definition 9 (Group Action Strong Decisional Diffie–Hellman (*GA-SDDH*)). *Given a group action* $* : G \times S \to S$ *and* $s \in S$, *distinguish the distributions between* $(s,\, g * s,\, g^{-1} * s,\, h * s,\, (hg^{-1}) * s,\, h^{-1} * s)$ *and* $(s,\, \alpha(g, s),\, \alpha(g^{-1}, s),\, \alpha(h, s),\, \alpha(hg^{-1}, s),\, \alpha(f, s))$ *for uniformly random* $g, h, f \in G$.

If no PPT adversary can distinguish the two distributions above, then the simulated and real transcripts for $c = 1$ are clearly indistinguishable as well. In particular, this problem is at least as hard as the following problem of *Group Action Inverse Decisional Diffie-Hellman* (GAIDDH), in analogy to the inverse decisional Diffie-Hellman assumption first studied in [68].

Definition 10 (Group Action Inverse Decisional Diffie–Hellman (*GA-IDDH*)). *Given a group action* $* : G \times S \to S$ *and* $s \in S$, *distinguish the distributions between* $(s,\, h * s,\, h^{-1} * s)$ *and* $(s,\, h * s,\, f * s)$ *for uniformly random* $h, f \in G$.

We observe that there is a worst-case reduction from the problem of GAIDDH to the problem of GASDDH. Indeed, suppose we have a PPT algorithm to solve GASDDH, then given a group action $\alpha : G \times S \to S$, $s \in S$, and two distributions $(s,\, \alpha(h, s),\, \alpha(h^{-1}, s))$ and $(s,\, \alpha(h, s),\, \alpha(f, s))$ for some uniformly random $h, f \in$

G, we can treat it as an instance applicable to the algorithm for GASDDH by taking $g = \mathrm{id} = g^{-1}$, where id is the identity element in G. It follows that GAIDDH can also be solved efficiently in this case.

4 Our Blind Signature Scheme

In this section, we present our blind-signature construction for generic group actions, following the CSI-Otter-style framework of Katsumata et al. [57]. Our construction is obtained by applying the blinding transformation to the underlying OR sigma protocol (see [40, Fig. 7]); the full proofs are given in [40, Appendix E]. Let G be a group acting on a set S, and fix an element $E \in S$. We assume that square roots in G can be computed efficiently. Let $H : \{0,1\}^* \to \{-1,1\}^n$ be a hash function modeled as a random oracle. The blind signature BS consists of the following algorithms, which are summarized in Fig. 2.

$\mathsf{BS.KGen}(1^n)$: On input the security parameter 1^n, it samples a bit $\delta \in \{0,1\}$, $(g_0, g_1) \in G^2$ and computes $A_b^{(c)} = g_b^c * E$ for $b \in \{0,1\}$ and $c \in \{-1,1\}$. It outputs a public key $\mathsf{pk} = (A_0^{(1)}, A_0^{(-1)}, A_1^{(1)}, A_1^{(-1)})$ and a secret key $\mathsf{sk} = (\delta, g_\delta)$. Before any signing interaction starts, the public key is verified once at setup/registration time using the sigma protocol in Fig. 1; accordingly, the online algorithms are defined only for valid public keys.

$\mathsf{BS.S_1}(\mathsf{sk})$: On input the secret key $\mathsf{sk} = (\delta, g_\delta)$, the signer first samples $\mathbf{h}_\delta \leftarrow_\$ G^n$, and sets $\mathbf{Y}_\delta = \{\mathbf{h}_{\delta,k}^c * E\}$ for $c \in \{-1,1\}, k \in [n]$. Here given a vector $\mathbf{c} = (c_1, \ldots, c_n) \in \{-1,1\}^n$, we write $\mathbf{Y}_\delta^{(\mathbf{c})}$ for the vector $(\mathbf{h}_{\delta,k}^{c_k} * E)_{k \in [n]}$. We will extend this convenience accordingly in the scheme.
Then it samples $(\mathbf{c}_{1-\delta}^*, \mathbf{r}_{1-\delta}^{*(1)}, \mathbf{r}_{1-\delta}^{*(-1)}) \leftarrow_\$ \{-1,1\}^n \times G^n \times G^n$ and set $\mathbf{r}_{1-\delta}^* := \{\mathbf{r}_{1-\delta,k}^{*(c)}\}_{c \in \{-1,1\}, k \in [n]}$. Next it computes $\mathbf{Y}_{1-\delta} = \{\mathbf{r}_{1-\delta,k}^{*(c)} * A_{1-\delta}^{(c \odot \mathbf{c}_{1-\delta,k}^*)}\}_{c \in \{-1,1\}, k \in [n]}$. It outputs the signer state $\mathsf{state}_S = (\mathbf{h}_\delta, \mathbf{c}_{1-\delta}^*, \mathbf{r}_{1-\delta}^*)$ and the first-sender message $\rho_{S,1} = (\mathbf{Y}_0, \mathbf{Y}_1)$.

$\mathsf{BS.U_1}(\mathsf{pk}, M, \rho_{S,1})$: On input the public key $\mathsf{pk} = (A_0^{(1)}, A_0^{(-1)}, A_1^{(1)}, A_1^{(-1)})$, a message M, and the first-sender message $\rho_{S,1} = (\mathbf{Y}_0, \mathbf{Y}_1)$, it samples, for $b \in \{0,1\}$, $(\mathbf{d}_b, \mathbf{z}_b) \leftarrow_\$ \{-1,1\}^n \times G^n$ and sets $\mathbf{Z}_b = \mathbf{z}_b * \mathbf{Y}_b^{(\mathbf{d}_b)}$. Then it computes $\mathbf{c} = H(\mathbf{Z}_0 \| \mathbf{Z}_1 \| M)$ and sets $\mathbf{c}^* = \mathbf{c} \odot \mathbf{d}_0 \odot \mathbf{d}_1 \in \{-1,1\}^n$. It outputs the internal user state $\mathsf{state}_U = (\mathbf{d}_b, \mathbf{z}_b)_{b \in \{0,1\}}$ and a user message $\rho_U = \mathbf{c}^*$.

$\mathsf{BS.S_2}(\mathsf{state}_S, \rho_U)$: On input the internal state $\rho_S = (\mathbf{h}_\delta, \mathbf{c}_{1-\delta}^*, \mathbf{r}_{1-\delta}^*)$ and a user message $\rho_U = \mathbf{c}^*$, it computes $\mathbf{c}_\delta^* = \mathbf{c}^* \odot \mathbf{c}_{1-\delta}^* \in \{-1,1\}^n$ and $\mathbf{r}_\delta^* = \{\mathbf{h}_{\delta,k}^c g_\delta^{-c \odot \mathbf{c}_{\delta,k}^*}\}_{c \in \{-1,1\}, k \in [n]}$. It outputs the second-sender message $\rho_{S,2} = (\mathbf{c}_b^*, \mathbf{r}_b^*)_{b \in \{0,1\}}$.

$\mathsf{BS.U_2}(\mathsf{state}_U, \rho_{S,2})$: On input the internal user state $\mathsf{state}_U = (\mathbf{d}_b, \mathbf{z}_b)_{b \in \{0,1\}})$ and $\rho_{S,2} = (\mathbf{c}_b^*, \mathbf{r}_b^*)_{b \in \{0,1\}}$, it sets $\mathbf{c}_b = \mathbf{c}_b^* \odot \mathbf{d}_b, \mathbf{r}_b^{(\mathbf{d}_b)} = \mathbf{z}_b(\mathbf{r}_b^{*(\mathbf{d}_b)})$ for $b \in \{0,1\}$. Then it checks if

$$\mathbf{c}_0 \odot \mathbf{c}_1 = H(\mathbf{r}_0^{(\mathbf{d}_0)} * \mathbf{A}_0^{(\mathbf{c}_0)} \| \mathbf{r}_1^{(\mathbf{d}_1)} * A_1^{(\mathbf{c}_1)} \| M). \tag{2}$$

If it holds then it outputs a signature $\sigma = (\mathbf{c}_b, \mathbf{r}_b^{(1)}, \mathbf{r}_b^{(-1)})_{b \in \{0,1\}}$.

$\mathsf{BS.Verify}(\mathsf{pk}, M, \sigma)$: On input the public key $\mathsf{pk} = (A_0^{(1)}, A_0^{(-1)}, A_1^{(1)}, A_1^{(-1)})$, a message M and a signature $\sigma = (\mathbf{c}_b, \mathbf{r}_b^{(1)}, \mathbf{r}_b^{(-1)})_{b\in\{0,1\}}$, it outputs 1 if the Eq. (2) holds, and 0 otherwise.

$\mathsf{BS.KGen}(1^n)$

$\delta \leftarrow\$ \{0,1\}$
$(g_0, g_1) \leftarrow\$ G^2$
$(A_0^{(1)}, A_0^{(-1)}) \leftarrow (g_0 * E, g_0^{-1} * E)$
$(A_1^{(1)}, A_1^{(-1)}) \leftarrow (g_1 * E, g_1^{-1} * E)$
$\textbf{return } \mathsf{pk} = (A_0^{(1)}, A_0^{(-1)}, A_1^{(1)}, A_1^{(-1)})$
$\qquad\qquad \mathsf{sk} = (\delta, g_\delta)$

$\mathsf{BS.S_1}(\mathsf{sk})$

$\textbf{parse } (\delta, g_\delta) \leftarrow \mathsf{sk}$
$\mathbf{h}_\delta \leftarrow\$ G^n$
$\mathbf{Y}_\delta = \{\mathbf{h}_{\delta,k}^c * E\}_{c\in\{-1,1\},k\in[n]}$
$(\mathbf{c}_{1-\delta}^*, \mathbf{r}_{1-\delta}^{*(1)}, \mathbf{r}_{1-\delta}^{*(-1)}) \leftarrow\$ \{-1,1\}^n \times G^n \times G^n$
$\text{set } \mathbf{r}_{1-\delta}^* := \{\mathbf{r}_{1-\delta,k}^{*(c)}\}_{c\in\{-1,1\},k\in[n]}$
$\mathbf{Y}_{1-\delta} = \{\mathbf{r}_{1-\delta,k}^{*(c)} * A_{1-\delta}^{(c\odot \mathbf{c}_{1-\delta,k}^*)}\}_{c\in\{-1,1\},k\in[n]}$
$\mathsf{state}_S \leftarrow (\mathbf{h}_\delta, \mathbf{c}_{1-\delta}^*, \mathbf{r}_{1-\delta}^*)$
$\rho_{S,1} = (\mathbf{Y}_0, \mathbf{Y}_1)$
$\textbf{return } (\mathsf{state}_S, \rho_{S,1})$

$\mathsf{BS.U_1}(\mathsf{pk}, M, \rho_{S,1})$

$\textbf{parse } (\mathbf{Y}_0, \mathbf{Y}_1) \leftarrow \rho_{S,1}$
$\textbf{for } b \in \{0,1\}$
$\quad (\mathbf{d}_b, \mathbf{z}_b) \leftarrow\$ \{-1,1\}^n \times G^n$
$\quad \mathbf{Z}_b^{(1)} \leftarrow \mathbf{z}_b * \mathbf{Y}_b^{(\mathbf{d}_b)}$
$\quad \mathbf{Z}_b^{(-1)} \leftarrow \mathbf{z}_b^{-1} * \mathbf{Y}_b^{(-\mathbf{d}_b)}$
$\mathbf{c} \leftarrow H(\mathbf{Z}_0^{(1)} \| \mathbf{Z}_0^{(-1)} \| \mathbf{Z}_1^{(1)} \| \mathbf{Z}_1^{(-1)} \| M)$
$\mathbf{c}^* \leftarrow \mathbf{c} \odot \mathbf{d}_0 \odot \mathbf{d}_1 \in \{-1,1\}^n$
$\mathsf{state}_U \leftarrow (\mathbf{d}_b, \mathbf{z}_b)_{b\in\{0,1\}}$
$\textbf{return } (\mathsf{state}_U, \rho_U = \mathbf{c}^*)$

$\mathsf{BS.S_2}(\mathsf{state}_S, \rho_U)$

$\textbf{parse } (\mathbf{h}_\delta, \mathbf{c}_{1-\delta}^*, \mathbf{r}_{1-\delta}^*) \leftarrow \mathsf{state}_S$
$\textbf{parse } \mathbf{c}^* \leftarrow \rho_U$
$\mathbf{c}_\delta^* \leftarrow \mathbf{c}^* \odot \mathbf{c}_{1-\delta}^* \in \{-1,1\}^n$
$\mathbf{r}_\delta^* = \{\mathbf{h}_{\delta,k}^c g_\delta^{-c\cdot \mathbf{c}_{\delta,k}^*}\}_{c\in\{-1,1\},k\in[n]}$
$\textbf{return } \rho_{S,2} = (\mathbf{c}_b^*, \mathbf{r}_b^*)_{b\in\{0,1\}}$

$\mathsf{BS.U_2}(\mathsf{state}_U, \rho_{S,2})$

$\textbf{parse } (\mathbf{d}_b, \mathbf{z}_b)_{b\in\{0,1\}} \leftarrow \mathsf{state}_U$
$\textbf{parse } (\mathbf{c}_b^*, \mathbf{r}_b^*)_{b\in\{0,1\}} \leftarrow \rho_{S,2}$
$\textbf{for } b \in \{0,1\}$
$\quad \mathbf{c}_b \leftarrow \mathbf{c}_b^* \odot \mathbf{d}_b$
$\quad \mathbf{r}_b^{(1)} \leftarrow \mathbf{z}_b(\mathbf{r}_b^{*(\mathbf{d}_b)})$
$\quad \mathbf{r}_b^{(-1)} \leftarrow \mathbf{z}_b^{-1}(\mathbf{r}_b^{*(-\mathbf{d}_b)})$
$\mathbf{c}' \leftarrow H(\mathbf{r}_0^{(1)} * A_0^{(\mathbf{c}_0)} \| \mathbf{r}_0^{(-1)} * A_0^{(-\mathbf{c}_0)} \|$
$\qquad \mathbf{r}_1^{(1)} * A_1^{(\mathbf{c}_1)} \| \mathbf{r}_1^{(-1)} * A_1^{(-\mathbf{c}_1)} \| M)$
$\textbf{if } \mathbf{c}_0 \odot \mathbf{c}_1 = \mathbf{c}'$
$\quad \textbf{return } \sigma = (\mathbf{c}_b, \mathbf{r}_b^{(1)}, \mathbf{r}_b^{(-1)})_{b\in\{0,1\}}$
$\textbf{return } \sigma = \perp$

$\mathsf{BS.Verify}(\mathsf{pk}, M, \sigma)$

$\textbf{parse } (\mathbf{c}_b, \mathbf{r}_b^{(1)}, \mathbf{r}_b^{(-1)})_{b\in\{0,1\}} \leftarrow \sigma$
$\mathbf{c}' \leftarrow H(\mathbf{r}_0^{(1)} * A_0^{(\mathbf{c}_0)} \| \mathbf{r}_0^{(-1)} * A_0^{(-\mathbf{c}_0)} \|$
$\qquad \mathbf{r}_1^{(1)} * A_1^{(\mathbf{c}_1)} \| \mathbf{r}_1^{(-1)} * A_1^{(-\mathbf{c}_1)} \| M)$
$\textbf{if } \mathbf{c}_0 \odot \mathbf{c}_1 = \mathbf{c}'$
$\quad \textbf{return } 1$
$\textbf{return } 0$

Fig. 2. Blind Signature from Cryptographic Group Action. Here for example, given a vector $\mathbf{c} = (c_1, \ldots, c_n) \in \{-1,1\}^n$, we write $\mathbf{Y}_\delta^{(\mathbf{c})}$ for the vector $(\mathbf{h}_{\delta,k}^{c_k} * E)_{k\in[n]}$, and extend to others similarly to $\mathbf{Y}_{1-\delta}, \mathbf{r}_\delta^*, \mathbf{r}_{1-\delta}^*$ accordingly.

Due to page limit, we present the proofs in [40, Appendix E]. In order to prove the one-more unforgeability, we use the techniques developed in [56] and [57] that we summarize in [40, Appendix D]. We summarize the main result in the following Theorem.

Theorem 1. *Our blind signature is correct and blind under chosen keys. In addition, our blind signature satisfies the one-more unforgeability property under Assumption 1 and the hardness of* IGAP *problem. To be more precise, for* $l \in \mathbb{N}$, *if there exist an adversary* $\mathcal{A}$ *that makes* Q *hash queries to the random oracle and breaks the* l*-one-more unforgeability of* BS *with advantage* $\epsilon_{\mathcal{A}} \geq \frac{C_1}{|\mathcal{C}|}\binom{Q}{l+1}$, *then there exists an efficient algorithm* $\mathcal{B}$ *that breaks the* IGAP *problem with advantage* $\epsilon_{\mathcal{B}} \geq C_2 \cdot \frac{\epsilon_{\mathcal{A}}^2}{\binom{Q}{l+1}^2 \cdot (l+1)^3}$ *for some universal positive constants* C_1 *and* C_2.

5 Our Partially Blind Signature Scheme

In this section, we present our partially blind-signature construction for generic group actions, also following the framework of Katsumata et al. [57]. As in the blind-signature case, this construction is obtained from the corresponding base sigma protocol for the 2-out-of-3 relation, which extends the OR-proof idea used above; the full protocol and proofs are given in [40, Appendix F]. Let G be a group acting on a set S, and fix an element $E \in S$. We assume that square roots in G can be computed efficiently. Let $H : \{0,1\}^* \to \{-1,1\}^n$ be a hash function modeled as a random oracle. The partially blind signature PBS consists of the following algorithms:

$\mathsf{PBS.KGen}(1^n)$: On input the security parameter 1^n, it samples a bit $\delta \in \{0,1\}$, $(g_0, g_1) \in G^2$ and computes $A_b^{(c)} = g_b^c * E$ for $b \in \{0,1\}$ and $c \in \{-1,1\}$. It outputs a public key $\mathsf{pk} = (A_0^{(1)}, A_0^{(-1)}, A_1^{(1)}, A_1^{(-1)}, A_2^{(1)}, A_2^{(-1)})$ and a secret key $\mathsf{sk} = (\delta, g_\delta)$.
Before any signing interaction starts, the public key is verified once at setup/registration time using the sigma protocol in Fig. 1; accordingly, the online algorithms are defined only for valid public keys.

$\mathsf{PBS.S_1}(\mathsf{sk}, \mathsf{info})$: On input the secret key $\mathsf{sk} = (\delta, g_\delta)$ and a tag info, for each $j \in \{0,1\}$, the signer first samples $(\mathbf{h}_{\delta,j}, \mathbf{h}_{2,j}) \leftarrow_{\$} G^{2n}$. Then, it sets $\mathbf{Y}_{\delta,j} = \{\mathbf{h}_{\delta,j,k}^c * E\}$ for $c \in \{-1,1\}, k \in [n]$ and $\mathbf{Y}_{2,j} = \{\mathbf{h}_{2,j,k}^c * E\}$ for $c \in \{-1,1\}, k \in [n]$. Given a vector $\mathbf{c} = (c_1, \ldots, c_n) \in \{-1,1\}^n$, we write $\mathbf{Y}_{\delta,j}^{(\mathbf{c})}, \mathbf{Y}_{2,j}^{(\mathbf{c})}$ for the vectors $(\mathbf{h}_{\delta,j,k}^{c_k} * E)_{k\in[n]}$ and $(\mathbf{h}_{2,j,k}^{c_k} * E)_{k\in[n]}$. We will extend this convenience accordingly in the scheme. Then it samples $(\mathbf{c}_{[1-\delta+j]_3}^*, \mathbf{r}_{1-\delta,j}^{*(1)}, \mathbf{r}_{1-\delta,j}^{*(-1)}) \leftarrow_{\$} \{-1,1\}^n \times G^n \times G^n$ and set $\mathbf{r}_{1-\delta,j}^* := \{\mathbf{r}_{1-\delta,j,k}^{*(c)}\}_{c\in\{-1,1\},k\in[n]}$. Next it computes $\mathbf{Y}_{1-\delta,j} = \{\mathbf{r}_{1-\delta,j,k}^{*(c)} * A_{1-\delta}^{(c\odot \mathbf{c}_{[1-\delta+j]_3,k}^*)}\}_{c\in\{-1,1\},k\in[n]}$. It outputs the signer state $\mathsf{state}_S = (\mathbf{h}_{\delta,j}, \mathbf{c}_{[1-\delta+j]_3}^*, \mathbf{r}_{1-\delta,j}^*)$ for each $j \in \{0,1\}$ and the first-sender message $\rho_{S,1} = (\mathbf{Y}_{k,j})$ for all $(k,j) \in [0:2] \times \{0,1\}$.

$\mathsf{PBS.U_1}(\mathsf{pk}, \mathsf{info}, M, \rho_{S,1})$: On input the public key $\mathsf{pk} = (A_0^{(1)}, A_0^{(-1)}, A_1^{(1)}, A_1^{(-1)})$, a tag info, a message M, and the first-sender message $\rho_{S,1} = (\mathbf{Y}_{k,j})$ for all $(k,j) \in [0:2] \times \{0,1\}$, it samples $\mathbf{d}_k \leftarrow_{\$} \{-1,1\}^n$ for $k \in [0:2]$. Then, for each $j \in \{0,1\}$, it samples $\mathbf{z}_{k,j} \leftarrow_{\$} G^n$ and sets $\mathbf{Z}_{k,j}^{(1)} = \mathbf{z}_{k,j} * \mathbf{Y}_{k,j}^{(\mathbf{d}_{[k+j]_3})}$ and $\mathbf{Z}_{k,j}^{(-1)} = \mathbf{z}_{k,j}^{-1} * \mathbf{Y}_{k,j}^{(-\mathbf{d}_{[k+j]_3})}$. Next, it computes

$\mathbf{c} = H((\mathbf{Z}_{k,j}^{(1)} \| \mathbf{Z}_{k,j}^{(-1)})_{(k,j)\in[0:2]\times\{0,1\}} \|\mathsf{info}\| M)$ and sets $\mathbf{c}^* = \mathbf{c} \odot \mathbf{d}_0 \odot \mathbf{d}_1 \odot \mathbf{d}_2 \in \{-1,1\}^n$. It outputs the internal user state $\mathsf{state}_U = (\mathbf{d}_k, (\mathbf{z}_{k,j})_{j\in\{0,1\}})_{k\in[0:2]}$ and a user message $\rho_U = \mathbf{c}^*$.

$\mathsf{PBS.S}_2(\mathsf{state}_S, \rho_U)$: On input the internal state $\mathsf{state}_S = (\mathbf{h}_{\delta,j}, \mathbf{c}^*_{[1-\delta+j]_3}, \mathbf{r}^*_{1-\delta,j})$ for each $j \in \{0,1\}$ and a user message $\rho_U = \mathbf{c}^*$, it computes $\mathbf{c}^*_{[3-\delta]_3} = \mathbf{c}^* \odot \mathbf{c}^*_{[1-\delta]_3} \odot \mathbf{c}^*_{[2-\delta]_3} \in \{-1,1\}^n$. Next, for each $j \in \{0,1\}$, it computes $\mathbf{r}^*_{\delta,j} = \{\mathbf{h}^c_{\delta,j,k} g_\delta^{-c\odot\mathbf{c}^*_{[\delta+j]_3,k}}\}_{c\in\{-1,1\},k\in[n]}$ and $\mathbf{r}^*_{2,j} = \{\mathbf{h}^c_{2,j,k} g_2^{-c\odot\mathbf{c}^*_{[2+j]_3,k}}\}_{c\in\{-1,1\},k\in[n]}$. It outputs the second-sender message $\rho_{S,2} = (\mathbf{c}^*_k, (\mathbf{r}^*_{k,j})_{j\in\{0,1\}})_{kk\in[0:2]}$.

$\mathsf{PBS.U}_2(\mathsf{state}_U, \rho_{S,2})$: On input the internal user state $\mathsf{state}_U = (\mathbf{d}_k, (\mathbf{z}_{k,j})_{j\in\{0,1\}})_{k\in[0:2]}$ and $\rho_{S,2} = (\mathbf{c}^*_k, (\mathbf{r}^*_{k,j})_{j\in\{0,1\}})_{k\in[0:2]}$, it computes $g_2 = \mathsf{G}(\mathsf{info})$. Next, for each $k \in [0:2]$, it sets $\mathbf{c}_k = \mathbf{c}^*_k \odot \mathbf{d}_k$. Then, for each $j \in \{0,1\}$, it computes $\mathbf{r}^{(1)}_{k,j} = \mathbf{z}_{k,j}(\mathbf{r}_{k,j}^{*(\mathbf{d}_{[k+j]_3})})$ and $\mathbf{r}^{(-1)}_{k,j} = \mathbf{z}^{-1}_{k,j}(\mathbf{r}_{k,j}^{*(-\mathbf{d}_{[k+j]_3})})$. Then it checks if

$$\mathbf{c}_0 \odot \mathbf{c}_1 \odot \mathbf{c}_2 = H((\mathbf{r}^{(1)}_{k,j} * A_k^{(\mathbf{c}_{[k+j]_3})}, \mathbf{r}^{(-1)}_{k,j} * A_k^{(-\mathbf{c}_{[k+j]_3})})_{(k,j)\in[0:2]\times\{0,1\}} \|\mathsf{info}\| M). \tag{3}$$

If it holds then it outputs a signature $\sigma = (\mathbf{c}_k, (\mathbf{r}^{(1)}_{k,j}, \mathbf{r}^{(-1)}_{k,j})_{j\in\{0,1\}})_{k\in[0:2]}$.

$\mathsf{PBS.Verify}(\mathsf{pk}, \mathsf{info}, M, \sigma)$: On input the public key $\mathsf{pk} = (A_0^{(1)}, A_0^{(-1)}, A_1^{(1)}, A_1^{(-1)})$, a tag info, a message M and a signature $\sigma = (\mathbf{c}_k, (\mathbf{r}^{(1)}_{k,j}, \mathbf{r}^{(-1)}_{k,j})_{j\in\{0,1\}})_{k\in[0:2]}$, it outputs 1 if the Eq. (3) holds, and 0 otherwise.

Due to page limit, we present the proofs in [40, Appendix F]. We summarize the main result in the following Theorem.

Theorem 2. *Our partially blind signature is perfectly correct and perfectly blind under chosen keys. In addition, our partially blind signature satisfies the one-more unforgeability property under Assumption 1 and the hardness of* IGAP *problem. Concretely, for* $l \in \mathbb{N}$*, if there exist an adversary* $\mathcal{A}$ *that makes* Q *hash queries to the random oracle and breaks the* l*-one-more unforgeability of* PBS *with advantage* $\epsilon_\mathcal{A} \geq \frac{C_1}{|\mathcal{C}|}\binom{Q}{l+1}$*, then there exists an efficient algorithm* $\mathcal{B}$ *that breaks the* IGAP *problem with advantage* $\epsilon_\mathcal{B} \geq C_2 \cdot \frac{\epsilon_\mathcal{A}^2}{\binom{Q}{l+1}^2 \cdot (l+1)^3}$ *for some universal positive constants* C_1 *and* C_2.

6 Instantiation Based on Monomial Code Equivalence

In this section, we present a concrete blind signature protocol based on monomial code equivalence for our (partially) blind signatures. Before delving into the details of our instantiation, we outline the requirements for the underlying group G and explain how they guide our choice of instantiation in this paper.

6.1 Instantiation Requirements

To instantiate the generic framework proposed in Sect. 5, we need to specify the underlying group G and set S. The basic requirements are that the group operations and element sampling in G are efficient and that the set S is sufficiently large and also allows efficient sampling. Besides, we have three more specific requirements corresponding to the framework, which are:

1. There is an efficient algorithm that can compute all the square roots of any given group element in G.
2. The underlying group action $* : G \times S \to S$ satisfies that IGAP is hard, i.e., given a random $s \in S$, and a pair $(g * s, g^{-1} * s)$, computing g is hard.
3. For public key validation using the sigma protocol in Fig. 1, it is also required that the hardness of GASDDH holds for the underlying group action $* : G \times S \to S$. That is, given a random $s \in S$, it is hard to distinguish the distributions between $(s, g*s, g^{-1}*s, h*s, (hg^{-1})*s, h^{-1}*s)$ and $(s, \alpha(g,s), \alpha(g^{-1},s), \alpha(h,s), \alpha(hg^{-1},s), \alpha(f,s))$ for uniformly random $g, h, f \in G$.

Remark 1. The necessity of an efficient square-root algorithm arises directly from the special soundness proof of our protocol. In the witness extraction phase, the extractor combines responses from two distinct challenges to recover the secret key. However, due to the dual nature of our public key structure, which means both forward and inverse group actions are simultaneously used, this algebraic combination could yield the square of the secret key rather than the key itself. Thus, an efficient algorithm that can compute every square root is required to allow the extractor to recover the valid witness and thereby complete the security reduction, establishing that the honest prover does possess the secret key.

In the context of non-commutative cryptographic group actions, there are mainly three lines of problems that have been intensively studied: linear code equivalence [11,17] as used in LESS, tensor isomorphism and its variations [33, 46,54,74] as used in MEDS and ALTEQ, and lattice isomorphism [9,39,51] as used in HAWK.

For MEDS and ALTEQ, the underlying group is $\mathrm{GL}(n,q)$. For $\mathrm{GL}(n,q)$, the matrix square-root problem was addressed in [10], but the algorithm there requires going to an extension field.[4] So, it is an interesting problem to devise a matrix square-root algorithm without going to the extension field. This seems to be the only bottleneck for using the group actions underlying MEDS and ALTEQ, because the IGAP for these actions seem still hard. For LESS, the underlying group is the monomial group $\mathrm{Mon}(n,q)$, consisting of matrices in $\mathrm{GL}(n,q)$ with each row and each column having exactly one non-zero entry. Although square-root search can be performed efficiently in this group, reusing group elements

[4] Although the square-root algorithm for $\mathrm{GL}(n,q)$ in [10] runs in poly-time, the entries of the output square-root matrix could go to an extension field of the original field $\mathbb{F}_q$. Thus, the proof for special soundness that extracts the secret key would fail if the algorithm cannot produce square-root solutions over $\mathbb{F}_q$.

there is risky, and for certain parameters, using the same group element twice can result in an insecure protocol according to attacks in [23,25]. For HAWK, the underlying group is the group $\mathrm{GL}(n, \mathbb{Z})/\{\pm I_n\}$, which also fails to meet the IGAP hardness requirement by a similar attack in [24]. We will continue to discuss these attacks in Sect. 6.2.

The first requirement motivates us to consider the symmetric group S_n, where square-root search can be done even more efficiently than group operations (see Proposition 2). In particular, $1/n$ of permutations are full cycles, whose square root is unique. This imposes an additional constraint on the permutations sampled as the secret key, to avoid complications in analyzing the number of square roots.[5]

Accordingly, a main task for us is to find a problem satisfying the hardness assumption of IGAP with symmetric group actions. We achieve this by proposing a new interpretation of monomial code equivalence problems in Sect. 6.2. We also provide the hardness evidence in Sect. 6.2 (see Corollary 1) and [40, Appendix A].

Remark 2. For public key validation using the sigma protocol in Fig. 1, we need to assume the hardness of GASDDH (defined in Definition 9) under the choices of G and S in our instantiation. Recall that there is a worst-case reduction from GAIDDH (as defined in Definition 10) to GASDDH, and DmILCE is the computational search version of GAIDDH in the instantiated case. So, we also leave open for further investigation whether a search-to-distinguish reduction exists; if it does, it would strengthen the justification for our current instantiation choice.

Note that our main goal is to show that the framework can be instantiated from a non-commutative group action satisfying the required properties. Since concrete parameter selections for the proposed instantiation would require a more detailed cryptanalytic study of the underlying hardness assumptions, we limit ourselves to structural efficiency comparisons and operation counts rather than concrete size estimates.

6.2 A New Interpretation of Monomial Code Equivalence

A linear code over $\mathbb{F}_q$ is a subspace of $\mathbb{F}_q^n$. An m-dimensional code in $\mathbb{F}_q^n$ is represented by $C \in \mathrm{Mat}(m \times n, q)$, whose rows form a basis of the code. The monomial code equivalence problem is the following.

Problem 1 (Monomial code equivalence (LCE)). For $n \in \mathbb{N}$, let $m \in [n]$. Let $C, C' \in \mathrm{Mat}(m \times n, q)$ be of rank m. Decide if there exist $A \in \mathrm{GL}(m, q)$, $D \in \mathrm{D}(n, q)$, and $P \in \mathrm{S}_n$, such that $ACDP = C'$. If yes, compute such A, D, and P.

[5] In general, we only need an efficient algorithm that can compute all square roots. This implies that the number of square roots is polynomially bounded, since otherwise merely outputting them would already be inefficient. In other words, uniqueness of square roots is not a necessary condition, but it is a sufficient one.

Equivalently, we can formulate monomial code equivalence as asking if there exist $A \in \mathrm{GL}(m,q)$ and $M \in \mathrm{Mon}(n,q)$, such that $ACM = C'$. By writing $M \in \mathrm{Mon}(n,q)$ as DP where $D \in \mathrm{D}(n,q)$ and $P \in \mathrm{S}_n$, we can define a symmetric group action as below.

Monomial code equivalence as a symmetric group action. Let $C, C' \in \mathrm{Mat}(m \times n, q)$. In Definition 1, three matrices, $A \in \mathrm{GL}(m,q)$, $D \in \mathrm{D}(n,q)$, and $P \in \mathrm{S}_n$, are used to define equivalence between C and C'. As a result, there is more than one way to interpret the group action behind monomial code equivalence.

The first, most straightforward, way is to consider the action of the group $\mathrm{GL}(m,q) \times (\mathrm{D}(n,q) \rtimes \mathrm{S}_n) = \mathrm{GL}(m,q) \times \mathrm{Mon}(n,q)$[6] on the set $\mathrm{Mat}(m \times n, q)$ that consists of all generator matrices of m-dimensional codes in $\mathbb{F}_q^n$.

The second approach is to consider the monomial group $\mathrm{Mon}(n,q)$ acting on the set of m-dimensional codes in $\mathbb{F}_q^n$. This is the natural action from the viewpoint of coding theory, as seen in [17,23,25,36,66]. This group-theoretic perspective is further developed in [34] through a general framework that partitions the set of m-dimensional codes in $\mathbb{F}_q^n$ into orbits under subgroups of $\mathrm{Mon}(n,q)$, and thus the equivalence testing can be reframed as comparing canonical representatives within those subgroup-induced orbits. In this setting, the LCE problem corresponds to the finest partition induced by the trivial subgroup.

We take the third approach by formulating it as the symmetric group S_n acting on a set S. In particular, this set S is the set of equivalence classes of m-dimensional codes in $\mathbb{F}_q^n$ under scalar multiplications on the coordinates. Note that this is actually in line with the second approach in the sense that the monomial group $\mathrm{Mon}(n,q)$ can be seen to act on the equivalence classes of $\mathrm{Mat}(m \times n, q)$ under left multiplication by $\mathrm{GL}(m,q)$. Nevertheless, what sets this perspective apart is that the objects of the group action are the equivalence classes of codes, in contrast to the generator matrices or codes themselves as in other approaches.

Let us examine this set S in more detail. Recall that $m \in [n]$. For $C_1, C_2 \in \mathrm{Mat}(m \times n, q)$, we define an equivalence relation $\sim$ as $C_1 \sim C_2$ if and only if there exists some $A \in \mathrm{GL}(m,q)$ and $D \in \mathrm{D}(n,q)$ such that $C_1 = AC_2D$. Note that this equivalence relation partitions $\mathrm{Mat}(m \times n, q)$ into orbits of $\mathrm{Mat}(m \times n, q)$ under the action of $\mathrm{GL}(m,q) \times \mathrm{D}(n,q)$. Denote by $[C]_\sim := \{ACD : A \in \mathrm{GL}(m,q), D \in \mathrm{D}(n,q)\}$ the equivalence class determined by $\sim$ and corresponding to $C \in \mathrm{Mat}(m \times n, q)$. Let $\mathrm{Mat}(m \times n, q)/\!\sim\, = \{[C]_\sim : C \in \mathrm{Mat}(m \times n, q)\}$ be the set of equivalence classes under $\sim$. This is the set S to be acted on.

We wish to define an action of S_n on $\mathrm{Mat}(m \times n, q)/\!\sim$. For $P \in \mathrm{S}_n$, since $[C]_\sim := \{ACD : A \in \mathrm{GL}(m,q), D \in \mathrm{D}(n,q)\}$ is a set of matrices, a natural map is to send $[C]_\sim$ to $[C]_\sim P := \{ACDP : A \in \mathrm{GL}(m,q), D \in \mathrm{D}(n,q)\}$. For S_n to act on $\mathrm{Mat}(m \times n, q)/\!\sim$, we need to show that $[C]_\sim P$ is an element in $\mathrm{Mat}(m \times n, q)/\!\sim$ by the following proposition.

Proposition 1. *Let* $[C]_\sim \in \mathrm{Mat}(m \times n, q)/\!\sim$, $P \in \mathrm{S}_n$, *and* $[C]_\sim P$ *be as above. Then* $[C]_\sim P = [CP]_\sim$.

[6] Here $\rtimes$ denotes semidirect product of groups.

Proof. Recall that $C \in \mathrm{Mat}(m \times n, q)$. Let $A \in \mathrm{GL}(m, q)$, and $D \in \mathrm{D}(n, q)$. Note that for any $P \in \mathrm{S}_n$, we have $\mathrm{D}(n,q) = P^{-1}\mathrm{D}(n,q)P = \{P^{-1}DP : D \in \mathrm{D}(n,q)\}$. This is because one can verify that $P^{-1}DP$ is a diagonal matrix with ith diagonal entry being the $P(i)$th entry of D. Therefore, $[C]_{\sim}P := \{ACDP : A \in \mathrm{GL}(m,q), D \in \mathrm{D}(n,q)\} = \{ACPP^{-1}DP : A \in \mathrm{GL}(m,q), D \in \mathrm{D}(n,q)\} = \{ACPD' : A \in \mathrm{GL}(m,q), D' \in \mathrm{D}(n,q)\} = [CP]_{\sim}$.

This ensures that the map $\alpha : \mathrm{S}_n \times \mathrm{Mat}(m \times n, q)/{\sim} \to \mathrm{Mat}(m \times n, q)/{\sim}$ by $P \in \mathrm{S}_n$ sending $[C]_{\sim}$ to $[C]_{\sim}P = [CP]_{\sim}$ is a well-defined group action. Now we can state our security problem in this instantiated case as follows:

Problem 2 (Diagonal-masked inverse linear code equivalence (DmILCE)). For $n \in \mathbb{N}$, let $m \in [n]$. Let $\{C_0, C_1, C_2\} \subseteq \mathrm{Mat}(m \times n, q)$. Decide if there exist $A_1, A_2 \in \mathrm{GL}(m, q)$, $D_1, D_2 \in \mathrm{D}(n, q)$, and $P \in \mathrm{S}_n$, such that $C_1 = A_1C_0D_1P$ and $C_2 = A_2C_0D_2P^{-1}$. If yes, find the secret permutation P.

As preliminary evidence for the hardness of Problem 2, we refer to the Gröbner-basis experiments reported in [40, Appendix A].

Comparison with Reusing the Monomial Matrix. Our instantiation has two main ingredients. First, we choose the group G to be the symmetric group, since square-root computation is efficient there (for the class of elements we use). Second, we hide elements of the acted set S inside suitable equivalence classes, since a direct symmetric-group action is not secure enough. In a related setting, recent works [23,25] have considered the following relaxed monomial code equivalence problem with multiple samples.

Problem 3 (Inverse linear code equivalence (ILCE)). For $n \in \mathbb{N}$, let $m \in [n]$. Let $\{C_0, C_1, C_2\} \subseteq \mathrm{Mat}(m \times n, q)$. Decide if there exist $A \in \mathrm{GL}(m, q)$ and $M \in \mathrm{Mon}(n, q)$, such that $C_1 = AC_0M$ and $C_2 = A^{-1}C_0M^{-1}$. If yes, find the secret monomial matrix M.

From the group action viewpoint, this problem corresponds to reusing monomial group actions (compared to our symmetric group actions) and there is only a single general linear group $\mathrm{GL}(m, q)$ acting on the left of the generator matrices (compared to our equivalence classes under a composite group $\mathrm{GL}(m, q) \times \mathrm{D}(n, q)$) used to hide secret information during communication. Therefore, by applying the parity-check matrices of the linear codes, one can get rid of the left general group actions A and A^{-1} and leave the monomial matrix M as the only variable matrix. In this way, Problem 3 reduces to solving a homogeneous linear system, and therefore [23] managed to give a heuristic algorithm to tackle it for $m = n/2$ and [25] further refined it to solve the cases for any code rate. We also note that the subsequent attacks [24,32,45] on other secret-reuse problems all rely on this crucial linearization technique.

However, their techniques does not help in attacking our Problem 2, whether experimentally or theoretically. The main reason is that in an equivalence class, the way to scale the columns of the generator matrices can vary, so treating these scalars as additional variables and combining them with the common permutation as another variable matrix would make a quadratic equation system instead of a linear system, which makes the heuristic analysis dedicated to linear systems in [23–25, 32, 45] completely inapplicable to our case. Furthermore, the linearization techniques for solving quadratic polynomial systems in [59] also cannot apply due to the insufficient number of equations. Besides, a key step of the algorithms in [23, 25] is to guess the entries of the common monomial matrix and check whether setting one of them to 1 can lead to the system having a solution. This is because in a homogeneous system, if M is a solution, and cM is also a solution for all $c \in \mathbb{F}_q$. Again, since the scalars for the commitment and keys keep updating in our protocol, guessing the diagonal values is more costly, and checking the existence of solutions to a system of quadratic equations is harder. These essential gaps differentiate our use of monomial code equivalence from those broken in [23, 25], which is also supported by our experimental results in [40, Appendix A]; see [40, Remark 4].

We now relate our problem to a recently introduced problem that underpins the hardness assumption used in the key exchange protocol of [41].

Problem 4 General diagonal-masked linear code equivalence (DmLCE) [41]). For $n \in \mathbb{N}$, let $m \in [n]$. Let $\{C_i : i \in [n]\} \subseteq \mathrm{Mat}(m \times n, q)$. Decide if there exist $\{A_i : i \in [n-1]\} \subseteq \mathrm{GL}(m, q)$, $\{D_i : i \in [n-1]\} \subseteq \mathrm{D}(n, q)$, and an $n \times n$ permutation matrix P, such that $A_i C_i D_i P = C_{i+1}$ for all $i \in [n-1]$. If yes, find the secret permutation matrix P.

By [41, Fact 2], DmLCE reduces to the following 2-DmLCE problem.

Problem 5 (2-samples diagonal-masked linear code equivalence (2-DmLCE) [41]). For odd prime $n \in \mathbb{N}$, let $m \in [n]$. Let $C_1, C_2, C_3 \in \mathrm{Mat}(m \times n, q)$. Decide if there exist $A_1, A_2 \in \mathrm{GL}(m, q)$, $D_1, D_2 \in \mathrm{D}(n, q)$, and an $n \times n$ permutation matrix P, such that $A_1 C_1 D_1 P = C_2$ and $A_2 C_2 D_2 P = C_3$. If yes, compute all instances of such a common permutation matrix P.

We note that Problem 5 (2-DmLCE) is exactly equivalent to our Problem 2 (DmILCE), by moving P^{-1} in $C_2 = A_2 C_0 D_2 P^{-1}$ to the left-hand side.

Corollary 1. *Problem 4 (DmLCE) $\leq_p$ Problem 2 (DmILCE).*

This ensures that our underlying computational problem, DmILCE, of the IGAP assumption for this instantiation, is as hard as a known conjectured hard problem, DmLCE [41]. We leave further cryptanalysis of DmILCE as an intriguing open question, and we believe that research on this problem is inherently meaningful and could be beneficial to the entire community, as it is a natural variant of the standard code-based assumptions.

Remark 3. A very recent work by Alecci and D'Alconzo [4] has investigated an equivalent algebraic formulation of the DmILCE problem. Using tools from algebraic geometry, including Plücker coordinates and fields of invariant rational functions, they construct polynomial equations whose roots are the entries of the common permutation matrix. However, the resulting equations are not practical for cryptographic parameters. Specifically, the polynomials have a degree of $2k$

and contain $2(k!)^2$ monomials, which grow exponentially. Thus, their work provides a theoretical algebraic model for stripping away the diagonal mask, but also shows that this direct invariant-theoretic approach is infeasible at cryptographic sizes. This offers indirect support for the hardness of the DmILCE problem, while not a formal proof of hardness.

6.3 Square-Root and Canonical Form Algorithms

To achieve the soundness of the underlying sigma protocol for our blind signature, we need an algorithm to efficiently compute a certain square root of $g_\delta^2 \in \mathrm{S}_n$. Note that finding g_δ costs less than a group operation which corresponds to matrix multiplication in our instantiation. The proof can be found in [40, Appendix B].

Proposition 2. *There is an $O(n)$-time square-root algorithm that inputs $\sigma \in \mathrm{S}_n$ and outputs a square root of σ if it exists.*

When blinding the message concatenated with the set elements (e.g., $\mathbf{Z}_0^{(1)}$, $\mathbf{Z}_0^{(-1)}$, $\mathbf{Z}_1^{(1)}$, $\mathbf{Z}_1^{(-1)} \in S^n$) under a hash function H, it is less practical to feed the entire equivalence class into H. By contrast, we can efficiently compute the *canonical forms* that can uniquely represent the underlying equivalence classes. Specifically, for an authentic signature, to ensure that the resulting hash values c and c' are the same, the user (and other verifiers) need to perform a canonical form algorithm for the equivalence classes. Canonical forms are a well-studied topic for graphs and matrix tuples [6,71]. Given a group G acting on a set S, a canonical form algorithm for this group action takes $s \in S$ and outputs $s^* \in \mathsf{Orb}(s) := \{g * s : \forall g \in G\}$. Furthermore, for another $s' \in \mathsf{Orb}(s)$, the algorithm should output the same s^*. In our case, G and S can be interpreted as $\mathrm{GL}(m,q) \times \mathrm{D}(n,q)$ and $\mathrm{Mat}(m \times n, q)$, respectively. Accordingly, we establish the following proposition, which strengthens the result in [37, Proposition 4] by eliminating the failure probability. Again, the proof can be found in [40, Appendix B].

Proposition 3. *There is an $O(m^2n)$-time canonical form algorithm for the action of $\mathrm{GL}(m,q) \times \mathrm{D}(n,q)$ on $\mathrm{Mat}(m \times n, q)$.*

Acknowledgement. We would like to thank the anonymous reviewers for their careful reading and constructive feedback, which helped us improve the paper. We also thank Lucjan Hanzlik, Jesús-Javier Chi-Domínguez, Edoardo Persichetti, Veronika Kuchta, and Jason LeGrow for their insightful comments and helpful discussions. This work is partially supported by the ARC Linkage Project LP220100332, the ARC Discovery Project DP200100950, and the Sydney Quantum Academy, Sydney, NSW, Australia. Part of this work was done when Chuanqi was a PhD student and Youming was an associate professor at the Centre for Quantum Software and Information, University of Technology Sydney, Australia.

References

1. Abe, M., Okamoto, T.: Provably secure partially blind signatures. In: Advances in Cryptology - CRYPTO 2000. Lecture Notes in Computer Science, vol. 1880, pp. 271–286. Springer (2000). https://doi.org/10.1007/3-540-44598-6_17
2. Agrawal, S., Kirshanova, E., Stehlé, D., Yadav, A.: Practical, round-optimal lattice-based blind signatures. In: Proceedings of the 2022 ACM SIGSAC Conference on Computer and Communications Security, CCS 2022, Los Angeles, CA, USA, 7–11 November 2022, pp. 39–53. ACM (2022). https://doi.org/10.1145/3548606.3560650
3. Alamati, N., Feo, L.D., Montgomery, H., Patranabis, S.: Cryptographic group actions and applications. In: Advances in Cryptology - ASIACRYPT 2020 - 26th International Conference on the Theory and Application of Cryptology and Information Security, Daejeon, South Korea, 7–11 December 2020, Proceedings, Part II. Lecture Notes in Computer Science, vol. 12492, pp. 411–439. Springer (2020). https://doi.org/10.1007/978-3-030-64834-3_14
4. Alecci, G., D'Alconzo, G.: Linear code equivalence via plücker coordinates. arXiv preprint arXiv:2603.09869 (2026)
5. Alkadri, N.A., Bansarkhani, R.E., Buchmann, J.: BLAZE: practical lattice-based blind signatures for privacy-preserving applications. In: Bonneau, J., Heninger, N. (eds.) Financial Cryptography and Data Security - 24th International Conference, FC 2020, Kota Kinabalu, Malaysia, 10–14 February 2020 Revised Selected Papers. Lecture Notes in Computer Science, vol. 12059, pp. 484–502. Springer (2020). https://doi.org/10.1007/978-3-030-51280-4_26
6. Babai, L.: Canonical form for graphs in quasipolynomial time: preliminary report. In: Charikar, M., Cohen, E. (eds.) Proceedings of the 51st Annual ACM SIGACT Symposium on Theory of Computing, STOC 2019, Phoenix, AZ, USA, 23–26 June 2019, pp. 1237–1246. ACM (2019). https://doi.org/10.1145/3313276.3316356
7. Barenghi, A., Biasse, J., Ngo, T., Persichetti, E., Santini, P.: Advanced signature functionalities from the code equivalence problem. Int. J. Comput. Math. Comput. Syst. Theory **7**(2), 112–128 (2022). https://doi.org/10.1080/23799927.2022.2048206
8. Battagliola, M., Borin, G., Meneghetti, A., Persichetti, E.: Cutting the GRASS: threshold group action signature schemes. In: Oswald, E. (ed.) Topics in Cryptology - CT-RSA 2024 - Cryptographers' Track at the RSA Conference 2024, San Francisco, CA, USA, 6–9 May 2024, Proceedings. Lecture Notes in Computer Science, vol. 14643, pp. 460–489. Springer (2024). https://doi.org/10.1007/978-3-031-58868-6_18
9. Benčina, B., Budroni, A., Chi-Domínguez, J.J., Kulkarni, M.: Properties of lattice isomorphism as a cryptographic group action. In: International Conference on Post-Quantum Cryptography, pp. 170–201. Springer (2024)
10. Berthomieu, J., Faugere, J.C., Perret, L.: Polynomial-time algorithms for quadratic isomorphism of polynomials: the regular case. J. Complex. **31**(4), 590–616 (2015). https://doi.org/10.1016/j.jco.2015.04.001
11. Beullens, W.: Not enough LESS: an improved algorithm for solving code equivalence problems over $\mathbb{F}_q$. In: Dunkelman, O., Jacobson, Jr., M.J., O'Flynn, C. (eds.) SAC 2020. LNCS, vol. 12804, pp. 387–403. Springer, Cham (2021). https://doi.org/10.1007/978-3-030-81652-0_15
12. Beullens, W.: Multivariate blind signatures revisited. IACR Cryptol. ePrint Arch. 720 (2024). https://eprint.iacr.org/2024/720

13. Beullens, W., Dobson, S., Katsumata, S., Lai, Y., Pintore, F.: Group signatures and more from isogenies and lattices: generic, simple, and efficient. In: Dunkelman, O., Dziembowski, S. (eds.) Advances in Cryptology - EUROCRYPT 2022 - 41st Annual International Conference on the Theory and Applications of Cryptographic Techniques, Trondheim, Norway, May 30 - June 3, 2022, Proceedings, Part II. Lecture Notes in Computer Science, vol. 13276, pp. 95–126. Springer (2022). https://doi.org/10.1007/978-3-031-07085-3_4
14. Beullens, W., Katsumata, S., Pintore, F.: Calamari and Falafl: logarithmic (linkable) ring signatures from isogenies and lattices. In: Moriai, S., Wang, H. (eds.) ASIACRYPT 2020. LNCS, vol. 12492, pp. 464–492. Springer, Cham (2020). https://doi.org/10.1007/978-3-030-64834-3_16
15. Beullens, W., Kleinjung, T., Vercauteren, F.: CSI-FiSh: efficient isogeny based signatures through class group computations. In: Galbraith, S.D., Moriai, S. (eds.) ASIACRYPT 2019. LNCS, vol. 11921, pp. 227–247. Springer, Cham (2019). https://doi.org/10.1007/978-3-030-34578-5_9
16. Beullens, W., Lyubashevsky, V., Nguyen, N.K., Seiler, G.: Lattice-based blind signatures: short, efficient, and round-optimal. In: Proceedings of the 2023 ACM SIGSAC Conference on Computer and Communications Security, CCS 2023, Copenhagen, Denmark, 26–30 November 2023, pp. 16–29. ACM (2023). https://doi.org/10.1145/3576915.3616613
17. Biasse, J.-F., Micheli, G., Persichetti, E., Santini, P.: LESS is more: code-based signatures without syndromes. In: Nitaj, A., Youssef, A. (eds.) AFRICACRYPT 2020. LNCS, vol. 12174, pp. 45–65. Springer, Cham (2020). https://doi.org/10.1007/978-3-030-51938-4_3
18. Bläser, M., et al.: On digital signatures based on group actions: QROM security and ring signatures. In: Saarinen, M.O., Smith-Tone, D. (eds.) Post-Quantum Cryptography - 15th International Workshop, PQCrypto 2024, Oxford, UK, 12–14 June 2024, Proceedings, Part I. Lecture Notes in Computer Science, vol. 14771, pp. 227–261. Springer (2024). https://doi.org/10.1007/978-3-031-62743-9_8
19. Blazy, O., Gaborit, P., Mac, D.T.: A correction to a code-based blind signature scheme. In: Code-Based Cryptography - 9th International Workshop, CBCrypto 2021, Munich, Germany, 21–22 June 2021 Revised Selected Papers. Lecture Notes in Computer Science, vol. 13150, pp. 84–94. Springer (2021). https://doi.org/10.1007/978-3-030-98365-9_5
20. Blazy, O., Gaborit, P., Schrek, J., Sendrier, N.: A code-based blind signature. In: 2017 IEEE International Symposium on Information Theory, ISIT 2017, Aachen, Germany, 25–30 June 2017, pp. 2718–2722. IEEE (2017). https://doi.org/10.1109/ISIT.2017.8007023
21. Bouaziz-Ermann, S., Canard, S., Eberhart, G., Kaim, G., Roux-Langlois, A., Traoré, J.: Lattice-based (partially) blind signature without restart. IACR Cryptol. ePrint Arch. 260 (2020). https://eprint.iacr.org/2020/260
22. Brassard, G., Yung, M.: One-way group actions. In: Advances in Cryptology - CRYPTO 1990, pp. 94–107 (1990). https://doi.org/10.1007/3-540-38424-3_7
23. Budroni, A., Chi-Domínguez, J., D'Alconzo, G., Di Scala, A.J., Kulkarni, M.: Don't use it twice! solving relaxed linear equivalence problems, vol. 15491, pp. 35–65 (2024). https://doi.org/10.1007/978-981-96-0944-4_2
24. Budroni, A., Chi-Domínguez, J.J., Franch, E.: Don't use it twice: reloaded! on the lattice isomorphism group action. Cryptology ePrint Archive (2025)
25. Budroni, A., Natale, A.: On the sample complexity of linear code equivalence for all code rates. Cryptography and Communications, pp. 1–23 (2025)

26. Buser, M., et al.: A survey on exotic signatures for post-quantum blockchain: challenges and research directions. ACM Comput. Surv. **55**(12), 251:1–251:32 (2023). https://doi.org/10.1145/3572771
27. Castryck, W., Lange, T., Martindale, C., Panny, L., Renes, J.: CSIDH: an efficient post-quantum commutative group action. In: Peyrin, T., Galbraith, S. (eds.) ASIACRYPT 2018. LNCS, vol. 11274, pp. 395–427. Springer, Cham (2018). https://doi.org/10.1007/978-3-030-03332-3_15
28. Chaum, D.: Blind signatures for untraceable payments. In: Chaum, D., Rivest, R.L., Sherman, A.T. (eds.) Advances in Cryptology: Proceedings of CRYPTO 1982, Santa Barbara, California, USA, 23–25 August 1982, pp. 199–203. Plenum Press, New York (1982). https://doi.org/10.1007/978-1-4757-0602-4_18
29. Chaum, D.: Elections with unconditionally-secret ballots and disruption equivalent to breaking RSA. In: Günther, C.G. (ed.) Advances in Cryptology - EUROCRYPT 1988. LNCS, vol. 330, pp. 177–182. Springer (1988). https://doi.org/10.1007/3-540-45961-8_15
30. Chaum, D., Fiat, A., Naor, M.: Untraceable electronic cash. In: Goldwasser, S. (ed.) CRYPTO 1988. LNCS, vol. 403, pp. 319–327. Springer, New York (1990). https://doi.org/10.1007/0-387-34799-2_25
31. Chaum, D., Pedersen, T.P.: Wallet databases with observers. In: Brickell, E.F. (ed.) CRYPTO 1992. LNCS, vol. 740, pp. 89–105. Springer, Heidelberg (1993). https://doi.org/10.1007/3-540-48071-4_7
32. Chi-Domínguez, J.J.: Weak instances of the inverse matrix code equivalence problem. Cryptology ePrint Archive (2025). https://eprint.iacr.org/2025/1909
33. Chou, T., et al.: Take your meds: digital signatures from matrix code equivalence. In: Progress in Cryptology - AFRICACRYPT 2023 (2023). https://doi.org/10.1007/978-3-031-37679-5_2
34. Chou, T., Persichetti, E., Santini, P.: On linear equivalence, canonical forms, and digital signatures. Des. Codes Cryptogr. 1–43 (2025). https://doi.org/10.1007/s10623-025-01576-1
35. Couveignes, J.M.: Hard homogeneous spaces. IACR Cryptology ePrint Archive (2006). http://eprint.iacr.org/2006/291
36. D'Alconzo, G., Di Scala, A.J.: Representations of group actions and their applications in cryptography. Finite Fields Appl. **99**, 102476 (2024). https://doi.org/10.1016/j.ffa.2024.102476
37. D'Alconzo, G., Meneghetti, A., Signorini, E.: Group factorisation for smaller signatures from cryptographic group actions. Des. Codes Crypt. **94**(2), 42 (2026). https://doi.org/10.1007/s10623-025-01787-6
38. Do, K., Hanzlik, L., Paracucchi, E.: M&m's: mix and match attacks on schnorr-type blind signatures with repetition. In: Advances in Cryptology - EUROCRYPT 2024 - 43rd Annual International Conference on the Theory and Applications of Cryptographic Techniques, Zurich, Switzerland, 26–30 May 2024, Proceedings, Part VI. Lecture Notes in Computer Science, vol. 14656, pp. 363–387. Springer (2024). https://doi.org/10.1007/978-3-031-58751-1_13
39. Ducas, L., Postlethwaite, E.W., Pulles, L.N., Woerden, W.V.: Hawk: module lip makes lattice signatures fast, compact and simple. In: International Conference on the Theory and Application of Cryptology and Information Security, pp. 65–94. Springer (2022). https://doi.org/10.1007/978-3-031-22972-5_3
40. Duong, D.H., Khuc, X.T., Qiao, Y., Susilo, W., Zhang, C.: Blind signatures from cryptographic group actions. Cryptology ePrint Archive, Paper 2025/397 (2025). https://eprint.iacr.org/2025/397

41. Duong, D.H., Qiao, Y., Zhang, C.: Diffie-Hellman key exchange from commutativity to group laws. In: 17th Innovations in Theoretical Computer Science Conference (ITCS 2026). Leibniz International Proceedings in Informatics (LIPIcs), vol. 362, pp. 52:1–52:20. Schloss Dagstuhl – Leibniz-Zentrum für Informatik, Dagstuhl, Germany (2026). https://doi.org/10.4230/LIPIcs.ITCS.2026.52. https://eprint.iacr.org/2025/1677
42. De Feo, L., Galbraith, S.D.: SeaSign: compact isogeny signatures from class group actions. In: Ishai, Y., Rijmen, V. (eds.) EUROCRYPT 2019. LNCS, vol. 11478, pp. 759–789. Springer, Cham (2019). https://doi.org/10.1007/978-3-030-17659-4_26
43. De Feo, L., Meyer, M.: Threshold schemes from isogeny assumptions. In: Kiayias, A., Kohlweiss, M., Wallden, P., Zikas, V. (eds.) PKC 2020. LNCS, vol. 12111, pp. 187–212. Springer, Cham (2020). https://doi.org/10.1007/978-3-030-45388-6_7
44. Fuchsbauer, G., Wolf, M.: Concurrently secure blind schnorr signatures. In: Joye, M., Leander, G. (eds.) Advances in Cryptology - EUROCRYPT 2024 - Part II. LNCS, vol. 14652, pp. 124–160. Springer (2024). https://doi.org/10.1007/978-3-031-58723-8_5
45. Gilchrist, V., Marco, L., Petit, C., Tang, G.: On the security of two blind signatures from code equivalence problems. IACR Commun. Cryptol. **2**(4) (2026). https://doi.org/10.62056/aesg893y6
46. Grochow, J.A., Qiao, Y.: Isomorphism problems for tensors, groups, and cubic forms: completeness and reductions (2019). arXiv:1907.00309
47. Hallgren, S., Moore, C., Rötteler, M., Russell, A., Sen, P.: Limitations of quantum coset states for graph isomorphism. J. ACM **57**(6), 34:1–34:33 (2010). https://doi.org/10.1145/1857914.1857918
48. Hanzlik, L., Lai, Y., Mula, M., Paracucchi, E., Slamanig, D., Tang, G.: Tanuki: new frameworks for (concurrently secure) blind signatures from post-quantum groups actions. In: Advances in Cryptology – ASIACRYPT 2025, pp. 35–69. Springer, Singapore (2026). https://doi.org/10.1007/978-981-95-5113-2_2
49. Hauck, E., Kiltz, E., Loss, J.: A modular treatment of blind signatures from identification schemes. In: Ishai, Y., Rijmen, V. (eds.) EUROCRYPT 2019. LNCS, vol. 11478, pp. 345–375. Springer, Cham (2019). https://doi.org/10.1007/978-3-030-17659-4_12
50. Hauck, E., Kiltz, E., Loss, J., Nguyen, N.K.: Lattice-based blind signatures, revisited. In: Micciancio, D., Ristenpart, T. (eds.) CRYPTO 2020. LNCS, vol. 12171, pp. 500–529. Springer, Cham (2020). https://doi.org/10.1007/978-3-030-56880-1_18
51. Haviv, I., Regev, O.: On the lattice isomorphism problem. In: Proceedings of the Twenty-Fifth Annual ACM-SIAM Symposium on Discrete Algorithms, SODA 2014, Portland, Oregon, USA, 5–7 January 2014, pp. 391–404 (2014)
52. Heilman, E., Baldimtsi, F., Goldberg, S.: Blindly signed contracts: anonymous on-blockchain and off-blockchain bitcoin transactions. In: Clark, J., Meiklejohn, S., Ryan, P.Y.A., Wallach, D., Brenner, M., Rohloff, K. (eds.) FC 2016. LNCS, vol. 9604, pp. 43–60. Springer, Heidelberg (2016). https://doi.org/10.1007/978-3-662-53357-4_4
53. Hhan, M., Morimae, T., Yamakawa, T.: From the hardness of detecting superpositions to cryptography: quantum public key encryption and commitments. In: Annual International Conference on the Theory and Applications of Cryptographic Techniques, pp. 639–667. Springer (2023). https://doi.org/10.1007/978-3-031-30545-0_22
54. Ji, Z., Qiao, Y., Song, F., Yun, A.: General linear group action on tensors: a candidate for post-quantum cryptography. In: Theory of Cryptography Conference, pp. 251–281. Springer (2019). https://doi.org/10.1007/978-3-030-36030-6_11

55. Kastner, J., Loss, J., Xu, J.: On pairing-free blind signature schemes in the algebraic group model. In: Hanaoka, G., Shikata, J., Watanabe, Y. (eds.) Public-Key Cryptography - PKC 2022 - 25th IACR International Conference on Practice and Theory of Public-Key Cryptography, Virtual Event, 8–11 March 2022, Proceedings, Part II. Lecture Notes in Computer Science, vol. 13178, pp. 468–497. Springer (2022). https://doi.org/10.1007/978-3-030-97131-1_16
56. Kastner, J., Loss, J., Xu, J.: The Abe-Okamoto partially blind signature scheme revisited. In: Agrawal, S., Lin, D. (eds.) Advances in Cryptology - ASIACRYPT 2022 - 28th International Conference on the Theory and Application of Cryptology and Information Security, Taipei, Taiwan, 5–9 December 2022, Proceedings, Part IV. Lecture Notes in Computer Science, vol. 13794, pp. 279–309. Springer (2022). https://doi.org/10.1007/978-3-031-22972-5_10
57. Katsumata, S., Lai, Y., LeGrow, J.T., Qin, L.: CSI-Otter: isogeny-based (partially) blind signatures from the class group action with a twist. In: Handschuh, H., Lysyanskaya, A. (eds.) Advances in Cryptology - CRYPTO 2023 - 43rd Annual International Cryptology Conference, CRYPTO 2023, Santa Barbara, CA, USA, 20–24 August 2023, Proceedings, Part III. Lecture Notes in Computer Science, vol. 14083, pp. 729–761. Springer (2023). https://doi.org/10.1007/978-3-031-38548-3_24
58. Katsumata, S., Lai, Y., Reichle, M.: Breaking parallel ROS: implication for isogeny and lattice-based blind signatures. In: Public-Key Cryptography - PKC 2024 - 27th IACR International Conference on Practice and Theory of Public-Key Cryptography, Sydney, NSW, Australia, 15–17 April 2024, Proceedings, Part I. Lecture Notes in Computer Science, vol. 14601, pp. 319–351. Springer (2024). https://doi.org/10.1007/978-3-031-57718-5_11
59. Kipnis, A., Shamir, A.: Cryptanalysis of the HFE public key cryptosystem by relinearization. In: Wiener, M. (ed.) CRYPTO 1999. LNCS, vol. 1666, pp. 19–30. Springer, Heidelberg (1999). https://doi.org/10.1007/3-540-48405-1_2
60. Kucharczyk, M.: Blind signatures in electronic voting systems. In: Kwiecień, A., Gaj, P., Stera, P. (eds.) CN 2010. CCIS, vol. 79, pp. 349–358. Springer, Heidelberg (2010). https://doi.org/10.1007/978-3-642-13861-4_37
61. Kuchta, V., LeGrow, J.T., Persichetti, E.: Post-quantum blind signatures from matrix code equivalence. IACR Cryptol. ePrint Arch. 274 (2025). https://eprint.iacr.org/2025/274
62. Lai, Y.F., Persichetti, E.: LEAF: compact and efficient blind signature from code-based assumptions. Cryptology ePrint Archive, Paper 2025/1585 (2025). https://eprint.iacr.org/2025/1585
63. Le, H.Q., Susilo, W., Khuc, T.X., Bui, M.K., Duong, D.H.: A blind signature from module latices. In: 2019 IEEE Conference on Dependable and Secure Computing, DSC 2019, Hangzhou, China, 18–20 November 2019, pp. 1–8. IEEE (2019). https://doi.org/10.1109/DSC47296.2019.8937613
64. Lyubashevsky, V., Nguyen, N.K., Plançon, M.: Efficient lattice-based blind signatures via gaussian one-time signatures. In: Hanaoka, G., Shikata, J., Watanabe, Y. (eds.) Public-Key Cryptography - PKC 2022 - 25th IACR International Conference on Practice and Theory of Public-Key Cryptography, Virtual Event, 8–11 March 2022, Proceedings, Part II. Lecture Notes in Computer Science, vol. 13178, pp. 498–527. Springer (2022). https://doi.org/10.1007/978-3-030-97131-1_17
65. Papachristoudis, D., Hristu-Varsakelis, D., Baldimtsi, F., Stephanides, G.: Leakage-resilient lattice-based partially blind signatures. IET Inf. Secur. **13**(6), 670–684 (2019). https://doi.org/10.1049/IET-IFS.2019.0156

66. Persichetti, E., Santini, P.: A new formulation of the linear equivalence problem and shorter less signatures. In: International Conference on the Theory and Application of Cryptology and Information Security, pp. 351–378. Springer (2023). https://doi.org/10.1007/978-981-99-8739-9_12
67. Petzoldt, A., Szepieniec, A., Mohamed, M.S.E.: A practical multivariate blind signature scheme. In: Kiayias, A. (ed.) FC 2017. LNCS, vol. 10322, pp. 437–454. Springer, Cham (2017). https://doi.org/10.1007/978-3-319-70972-7_25
68. Pfitzmann, B.P., Sadeghi, A.-R.: Anonymous fingerprinting with direct non-repudiation. In: Okamoto, T. (ed.) ASIACRYPT 2000. LNCS, vol. 1976, pp. 401–414. Springer, Heidelberg (2000). https://doi.org/10.1007/3-540-44448-3_31
69. del Pino, R., Katsumata, S.: A new framework for more efficient round-optimal lattice-based (partially) blind signature via trapdoor sampling. In: Advances in Cryptology - CRYPTO 2022 - 42nd Annual International Cryptology Conference, CRYPTO 2022, Santa Barbara, CA, USA, 15–18 August 2022, Proceedings, Part II. Lecture Notes in Computer Science, vol. 13508, pp. 306–336. Springer (2022). https://doi.org/10.1007/978-3-031-15979-4_11
70. Pointcheval, D., Stern, J.: Security arguments for digital signatures and blind signatures. J. Cryptol. **13**(3), 361–396 (2000). https://doi.org/10.1007/s001450010003
71. Qiao, Y., Sun, X.: Canonical forms for matrix tuples in polynomial time. In: 2024 IEEE 65th Annual Symposium on Foundations of Computer Science (FOCS), pp. 780–789. IEEE (2024). https://doi.org/10.1109/FOCS61266.2024.00054
72. Rostovtsev, A., Stolbunov, A.: Public-key cryptosystem based on isogenies. IACR Cryptol. ePrint Arch. 145 (2006). http://eprint.iacr.org/2006/145
73. Rückert, M.: Lattice-based blind signatures. In: Abe, M. (ed.) ASIACRYPT 2010. LNCS, vol. 6477, pp. 413–430. Springer, Heidelberg (2010). https://doi.org/10.1007/978-3-642-17373-8_24
74. Tang, G., Duong, D.H., Joux, A., Plantard, T., Qiao, Y., Susilo, W.: Practical post-quantum signature schemes from isomorphism problems of trilinear forms. In: Advances in Cryptology - EUROCRYPT 2022 - 41st Annual International Conference on the Theory and Applications of Cryptographic Techniques, Trondheim, Norway, May 30 - June 3, 2022, Proceedings, Part III. Lecture Notes in Computer Science, vol. 13277, pp. 582–612. Springer (2022). https://doi.org/10.1007/978-3-031-07082-2_21
75. Yi, X., Lam, K.: A new blind ECDSA scheme for bitcoin transaction anonymity. In: Proceedings of AsiaCCS 2019, pp. 613–620. ACM (2019). https://doi.org/10.1145/3321705.3329816

Protecting Quantum Circuits Through Compiler-Resistant Obfuscation

Pradyun Parayil[1(✉)], Amal Raj[2], and Vivek Balachandran[2]

[1] Department of Electronics and Communication Engineering, Amrita School of Engineering, Coimbatore Amrita Vishwa Vidyapeetham, Coimbatore 641112, India
cb.en.u4cce23067@cb.students.amrita.edu
[2] Singapore Institute of Technology, Singapore, Singapore
{amal.raj,vivek.b}@singaporetech.edu.sg

Abstract. Quantum circuit obfuscation is becoming increasingly important to prevent theft and reverse engineering of quantum algorithms. As quantum computing advances, the need to protect the intellectual property contained in quantum circuits continues to grow. Existing methods often provide limited defense against structural and statistical analysis or introduce considerable overhead. In this paper, we propose a novel quantum obfuscation method that uses randomized U3 transformations to conceal circuit structure while preserving functionality. We implement and assess our approach on QASM circuits using Qiskit AER, achieving over 93% semantic accuracy with minimal runtime overhead. The method demonstrates strong resistance to reverse engineering and structural inference, making it a practical and effective approach for quantum software protection.

Keywords: Quantum Obfuscation · Basis Conjugation · Randomized Basis Transformation · QASM Compatibility · Compiler-Resistant Quantum Security · Quantum Circuit Security

1 Introduction

Quantum computing leverages the principles of quantum mechanics, such as superposition, entanglement, and quantum interference, to perform computations that are infeasible for classical computers. It is poised to revolutionize fields like cryptography, where it can break conventional encryption schemes, optimization, where it tackles complex combinatorial problems, and quantum simulation, where it models molecular and material properties for drug discovery and materials science [1]. Quantum computers are used in research labs, cloud-based quantum platforms, and increasingly in industrial applications to solve specialized problems that require massive parallelism and probabilistic computation [2]. As quantum software development accelerates, protecting intellectual property (IP) and securing quantum circuits against reverse engineering and

P. Parayil and A. Raj—Both authors contributed equally to the work.

K. Jee and A. Kate (Eds.): ACNS 2026, LNCS 16571, pp. 187–208, 2027.
https://doi.org/10.1007/978-3-032-32560-0_7

structural analysis has become a critical concern. Quantum programs, typically expressed in gate-level formats like QASM, reveal their underlying structure, making it easier for adversaries to extract proprietary logic or algorithmic optimizations. Developing robust obfuscation techniques that preserve functionality while concealing the circuit's logical structure is essential for ensuring the security and commercial viability of quantum software in practical applications.

1.1 Proposed Idea

This work introduces a quantum circuit protection technique that resists critical scrutiny and ensures operational functionality. The obfuscation of quantum circuit topology is accomplished by applying random `U3` gate transformations. The main idea is to perform a full circuit transformation by enclosing it with a random basis transformation and its dual. Each internal gate is transformed as well with this same transformation, thereby masking their identity while maintaining functionality. All the gates in the circuit are transformed through single-qubit `U3` matrices, which hide the circuit's inner workings without affecting its primary function.

This method makes sure the circuit's output stays the same because the changes cancel each other out. Traditional ways of doing obfuscation add more gates or make the circuit hard to understand, but our method adds only negligible extra overhead. This keeps the circuit quick and efficient on quantum hardware [2]. It fits right in with any quantum program, does not require modifications to the original algorithm, and is simple to deploy across different quantum setups. Due to these merits, our method is a flexible and practical approach for safeguarding quantum software in real-world scenarios. The overall workflow is illustrated in Fig. 1.

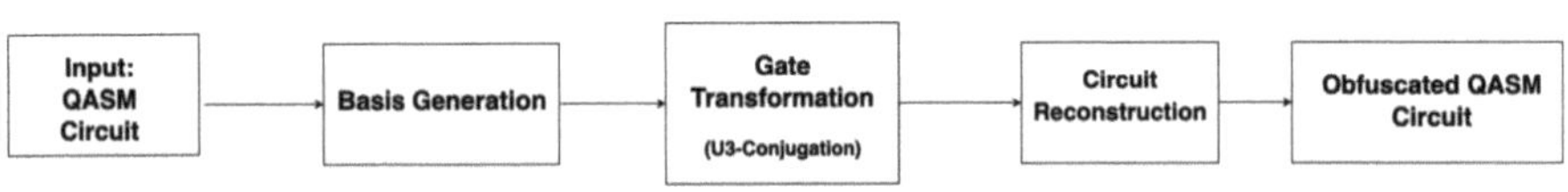

Fig. 1. Workflow of the proposed quantum circuit obfuscation using U3-conjugation. The process begins with a QASM circuit, applies a randomized basis transformation, transforms each gate, and restores the original basis to produce an obfuscated circuit with preserved functionality.

Paper Organization

The rest of this paper is structured as follows. Section 2 provides background on quantum computing, including qubits, quantum gates, compilation, and measurement operations. It also reviews existing work on quantum circuit obfuscation, highlighting current techniques and their limitations. Section 3 outlines the proposed methodology and presents our obfuscation technique. Section 4 illustrates the methodology through the obfuscation of a QAOA circuit. Section 5 presents evaluation metrics and results, demonstrating the effectiveness of the proposed technique. Section 6 details the security guarantees provided by our approach, formalizing the threat model and the protections achieved. Section 7 discusses the limitations of our approach and proposes directions for future research. Section 8 concludes the paper by summarizing the key contributions and their implications for secure quantum software development.

2 Background

2.1 Quantum Computing Fundamentals

Quantum computing diverges from classical computing by employing quantum bits, or qubits, which leverage quantum mechanics to process information. Unlike classical bits, restricted to a binary state of 0 or 1, qubits can exist in a superposition, embodying multiple states simultaneously. This capability enables quantum computers to perform parallel computations, vastly exceeding classical systems for certain tasks. Additionally, qubits can be entangled, meaning the state of one qubit is directly tied to another, allowing instant correlations across distances. Such properties enable quantum algorithms to tackle complex problems in cryptography, optimization, and beyond with remarkable efficiency [1]. Quantum gates, the core of quantum computation, manipulate qubit states through reversible operations, represented as unitary matrices. For instance, the Hadamard gate creates superposition, while the controlled-NOT gate fosters entanglement, enabling intricate quantum interactions [3].

Quantum circuits, composed of sequences of quantum gates, orchestrate computations by evolving qubit states toward a desired outcome. A single measurement yields one classical outcome, whereas repeated executions of the circuit generate a probability distribution over possible results. Quantum Assembly Language (QASM), particularly its evolution from `OPENQASM 2.0` to `OPENQASM 3.0`, standardizes circuit descriptions, supporting classical control flow and dynamic operations [4]. This facilitates circuit portability across quantum platforms but also raises concerns about protecting intellectual property embedded in these circuits. Compilation, a vital step for executing circuits on physical hardware, translates high-level designs into hardware-specific instructions. Tools like Qiskit's transpiler optimize gate sequences and map qubits to physical hardware, minimizing circuit depth to enhance performance on Noisy Intermediate-Scale Quantum (NISQ) devices. Yet, this process exposes circuits to potential reverse-engineering, as adversaries could analyze gate structures to extract proprietary algorithms [5].

2.2 Related Works

Several approaches have been proposed to secure quantum circuits through obfuscation, each with distinct trade-offs. Suresh et al. introduced a method that inserts a dummy gate at a specific circuit location to obscure its functionality, intentionally disrupting results during execution [6]. Post-compilation, this gate is removed to restore the original computation. To prevent optimization, barriers are placed around the dummy gate, and additional barriers are inserted around other gates to mask its identity from adversaries. However, this reliance on barriers compromises circuit optimization, increasing depth and degrading performance on NISQ hardware [6]. Similarly, Rehman, Langford and Liu proposed an obfuscation technique that modifies gate parameters using secret keys to conceal circuit logic [7]. While effective in hiding structure, this method requires significant classical processing for key management, complicating deployment and scalability, particularly for resource-constrained quantum systems. Another approach by Bartake et al. uses redundant gate insertion to obscure the intent of the circuit. This improves security, but the added gates significantly increase the depth of the circuit, making it more prone to errors on NISQ devices and limiting practical applicability [5]. These methods highlight the challenge of balancing security with performance, as increased complexity often undermines execution fidelity on current quantum hardware [2,6].

3 Methodology

Our quantum circuit obfuscation technique leverages basis transformations via U3 conjugation to obscure gate identities while preserving functional correctness. For clarity, the formulation presented in this paper adopts the weakest variant of the obfuscation framework, where a single random basis transformation is applied uniformly across the circuit. This setting intentionally models the worst case for security analysis and served as the baseline design during development. A strictly stronger variant assigns an independently sampled U3 basis to a randomly selected subset of gates, which removes global structural correlations and drives an adversary's inference probability to negligible values. A detailed discussion of the resulting security guarantees is presented in Sect. 6.

The technique proceeds in four phases: input parsing, basis generation, gate transformation, and circuit reconstruction. Together, these stages preserve QASM compatibility, maintain semantic equivalence, and enhance resistance to reverse engineering.

3.1 QASM Input Parsing

The first step in our quantum circuit obfuscation process is to accurately interpret the user-provided quantum circuit, which is specified in Quantum Assembly Language (QASM). QASM serves as a standardized, platform-independent format for describing quantum circuits, including gate operations, qubit allocations, and measurement instructions [4]. To ensure compatibility with a wide range of quantum circuits, our system is designed to parse input strings written in either `OPENQASM 2.0` or the more advanced `OPENQASM 3.0` specification, accommodating both legacy and modern quantum programming workflows.

The input QASM string is first trimmed to remove any extra whitespace. Based on its prefix, the QASM version is identified: Qiskit uses *qiskit.qasm2.loads()* for OPENQASM 2.0 and *qiskit.qasm3.loads()* for OPENQASM 3.0, which supports advanced features like control flow and custom gate definitions [4,8]. If the version is unrecognized, an error is raised. This process produces a QuantumCircuit object with the circuit's gates, qubits, and measurements.

3.2 Basis Generation

The core of our obfuscation relies on a randomized basis transformation applied across all qubits. We generate random parameters ($\theta \in [0, \pi]$, $\phi \in [0, 2\pi]$, $\lambda \in [0, 2\pi]$) for a U3 gate using a uniform random distribution. The U3 gate is a universal single-qubit gate that can represent any unitary operation by tuning its parameters, making it well-suited for implementing a wide range of basis transformations. Randomization ensures that each circuit instantiation produces a unique basis, enhancing obfuscation by preventing predictable patterns that could be exploited in reverse engineering. As shown in Eq. 1, the gate's matrix representation is defined by these parameters.

$$U3(\theta, \phi, \lambda) = \begin{bmatrix} \cos\left(\frac{\theta}{2}\right) & -e^{i\lambda}\sin\left(\frac{\theta}{2}\right) \\ e^{i\phi}\sin\left(\frac{\theta}{2}\right) & e^{i(\phi+\lambda)}\cos\left(\frac{\theta}{2}\right) \end{bmatrix} \tag{1}$$

3.3 Gate Transformation

To obfuscate a quantum circuit, each gate G in the original circuit is transformed using unitary conjugation, expressed as $U^\dagger \cdot G \cdot U$, where U is the unitary matrix of a `U3` gate with randomly chosen parameters (θ, ϕ, λ). Measurements and resets are left unchanged because the obfuscation method applies only to unitary operations. Since measurement is non-unitary, conjugating it with $U^\dagger$ and U would rotate the measurement basis and alter the circuit's behavior. For circuits containing mid-circuit measurements, we simply treat the computation as a sequence of unitary segments separated by measurement boundaries and obfuscate each unitary segment independently.

Using Qiskit's `Operator` class, the gate G is first converted into its matrix representation to facilitate this transformation. For multi-qubit gates, the basis matrix U is constructed by computing the Kronecker product of single-qubit `U3` matrices for each qubit. The Kronecker product, a tensor operation that combines matrices to form a larger matrix, ensures that the transformation scales appropriately for systems with multiple qubits, preserving the gate's functionality across the circuit's qubit register [9]. The resulting matrix $U^\dagger \cdot G \cdot U$ is then encapsulated as a `UnitaryGate` with a unique label, such as `Obf_H_0` for a Hadamard gate, effectively concealing the original gate's identity. This process is applied to all gates, as detailed in Algorithm 1.

Algorithm 1. Gate Transformation via U3-Conjugation

Require: Gate G, `qubits`, `U3` parameters (θ, ϕ, λ)
Convert G to matrix using `Operator(G)`
Compute $U = U3(\theta, \phi, \lambda)^{\otimes n}$ for n qubits
Compute $U^\dagger = U3(-\theta, -\lambda, -\phi)^{\otimes n}$
Compute transformed matrix $U^\dagger \cdot G \cdot U$
Encapsulate as `UnitaryGate` with label `Obf_G_id`
Replace original gate G with the transformed `UnitaryGate` in the circuit

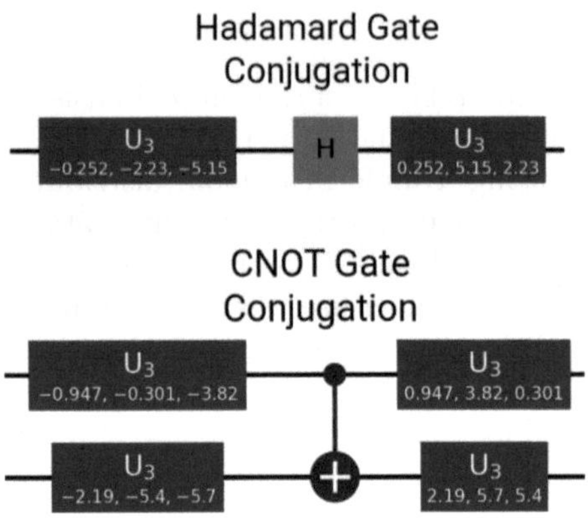

Fig. 2. Diagram of the conjugation process $U^\dagger \cdot G \cdot U$ for a single-qubit gate (Hadamard) and a multi-qubit gate (CNOT). This figure illustrates the underlying matrix operations and does not imply additional quantum gates or circuit depth. The result of this matrix multiplication ($U^\dagger \cdot G \cdot U$) is encapsulated as a single, opaque `UnitaryGate` object, thereby incurring no space overhead in the quantum circuit.

3.4 Basis Transformation and Obfuscation

For a circuit with n qubits, a global basis transformation $U = U3(\theta, \phi, \lambda)^{\otimes n}$ is applied to all qubits at the circuit's start, with its inverse $U^\dagger = U3(-\theta, -\lambda, -\phi)^{\otimes n}$ applied at the end. The parameters θ, ϕ, and λ are randomly sampled from a uniform distribution to maximize obfuscation. For each gate G, a local basis transformation is applied, replacing G with its conjugated form $G' = U3(-\theta, -\lambda, -\phi) \cdot G \cdot U3(\theta, \phi, \lambda)$, which encapsulates the original gate in a new basis while preserving its functionality. This transformation is implemented using Qiskit's circuit manipulation tools, where each gate is directly replaced with its transformed version $U^\dagger G U$. To ensure the circuit's original functionality, the inverse basis transformation $U^\dagger$ is applied across all qubits as a single instruction labeled `InvBasis` after all gates are processed. Barriers from the original circuit are retained to maintain structural hints for hardware compatibility. The reconstructed circuit is then transpiled and executed using the Qiskit AER simulator, producing results statistically equivalent to the original circuit. Figure 2 illustrates this process with examples of Hadamard and CNOT gate transformations. The implementation code is available in the GitHub repository in [10].

3.5 Preservation of Functionality: Hadamard and CNOT Gate Examples

To illustrate how our obfuscation technique preserves the functionality of quantum circuits, we examine the transformation of two fundamental quantum gates: the single-qubit Hadamard (H) gate and the two-qubit controlled-NOT (CNOT) gate. These gates are critical building blocks in quantum algorithms, with the H gate creating superposition and the CNOT gate introducing entanglement [1]. By applying our basis conjugation approach to each gate individually, we demonstrate that their computational behavior remains unchanged despite structural obfuscation.

For the Hadamard gate, represented by the 2×2 unitary matrix $H = \frac{1}{\sqrt{2}}\begin{bmatrix} 1 & 1 \\ 1 & -1 \end{bmatrix}$, we apply a basis transformation using a `U3` gate with randomly chosen parameters (θ, ϕ, λ). The transformation is defined as $U = U3(\theta, \phi, \lambda)$, and the obfuscated gate is computed as:

$$H_{\text{obf}} = U^{\dagger} \cdot H \cdot U \tag{2}$$

To verify preservation of functionality, we apply the inverse transformation:

$$U \cdot H_{\text{obf}} \cdot U^{\dagger} = U \cdot (U^{\dagger} \cdot H \cdot U) \cdot U^{\dagger} = (UU^{\dagger}) \cdot H \cdot (UU^{\dagger}) = H \tag{3}$$

This confirms that the obfuscated Hadamard gate, when wrapped by the basis transformation and its inverse, behaves identically to the original H gate, preserving its ability to create superposition. The matrix-level transformation of the Hadamard gate is shown in Fig. 3.

For the two-qubit CNOT gate, represented by a 4×4 unitary matrix, we use a basis transformation $U = U3(\theta, \phi, \lambda)^{\otimes 2}$, formed by the Kronecker product of two single-qubit `U3` matrices to scale the transformation across both qubits [9]. The obfuscated CNOT gate is:

$$\text{CNOT}_{\text{obf}} = U^{\dagger} \cdot \text{CNOT} \cdot U \tag{4}$$

Applying the inverse transformation yields:

$$\begin{aligned} U \cdot \text{CNOT}_{\text{obf}} \cdot U^{\dagger} &= U \cdot (U^{\dagger} \cdot \text{CNOT} \cdot U) \cdot U^{\dagger} \\ &= (UU^{\dagger}) \cdot \text{CNOT} \cdot (UU^{\dagger}) \\ &= \text{CNOT} \end{aligned} \tag{5}$$

This demonstrates that the CNOT gate's entanglement-generating functionality is fully preserved, as the basis transformations cancel out, leaving the original gate's behavior intact. This process, applied to individual gates, ensures that the circuit's overall semantics remain unchanged, as the global basis shift and its inverse cancel out during execution. The corresponding matrix-level transformation for the CNOT gate is shown in Fig. 4.

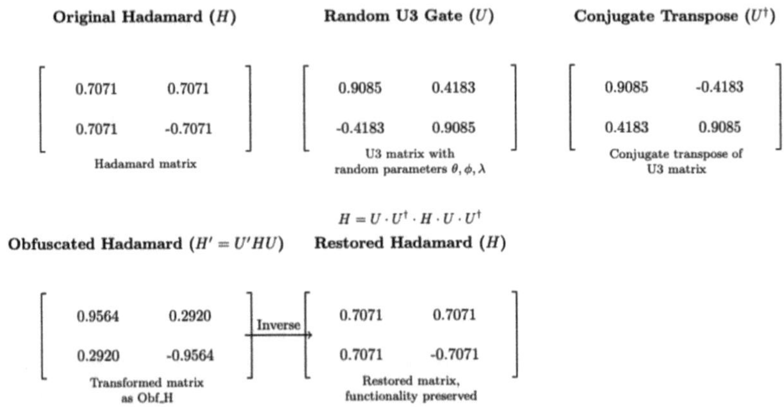

Fig. 3. Matrix-level transformation of a Hadamard gate using U3 conjugation. The functionality remains unchanged due to the inverse transformation restoring the original gate.

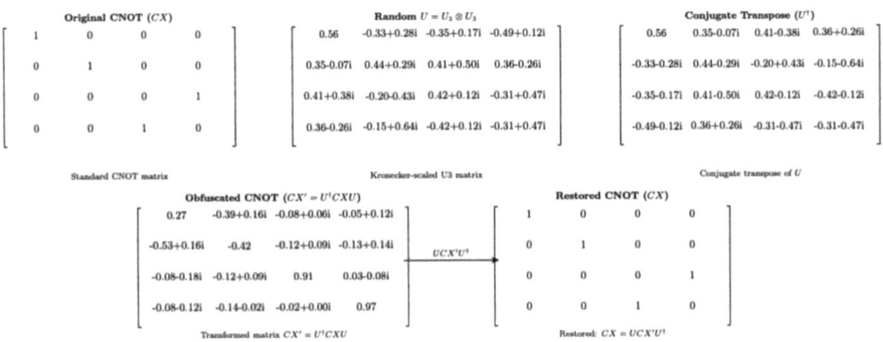

Fig. 4. Matrix-level transformation of a CNOT gate using U3 conjugation, with the Kronecker product scaling the basis for two qubits.

4 Case Study: Quantum Approximate Optimization Algorithm (QAOA)

4.1 Overview of QAOA

The Quantum Approximate Optimization Algorithm (QAOA) is a hybrid quantum-classical algorithm designed for solving combinatorial optimization problems such as MaxCut and Max3SAT [11]. It combines parameterized quantum circuits with classical optimization to approximate the solution to a given cost function. QAOA is particularly relevant due to its practical applicability on near-term quantum devices and its structured circuit layout, making it a suitable candidate for testing circuit obfuscation techniques.

In this case study, we focus on a QAOA circuit targeting the MaxCut problem on a 5-node graph. The circuit involves alternating applications of the problem (cost) unitary and a mixing unitary, parameterized by angles γ and β, respectively. We implement this circuit in `OPENQASM 2.0`, simulate its behavior before and after obfuscation, and evaluate functional correctness and performance overhead.

4.2 Circuit Description

The QAOA circuit is constructed with five qubits representing the five graph nodes in the MaxCut problem, where the edges are $(0,1)$, $(1,2)$, $(1,3)$, $(2,4)$ and $(3,4)$, as shown in Fig. 5. The initial state is prepared using Hadamard gates to create a uniform superposition over all possible bitstrings. The cost unitary is implemented using two-qubit R_{ZZ} rotations (decomposed into `CX-RZ-CX`) corresponding to the edges in the graph. Each edge contributes a term in the cost Hamiltonian, and the circuit applies these terms with an optimized parameter γ. This is followed by a layer of R_X gates applied to each qubit, representing the mixer Hamiltonian and controlled by the parameter β.

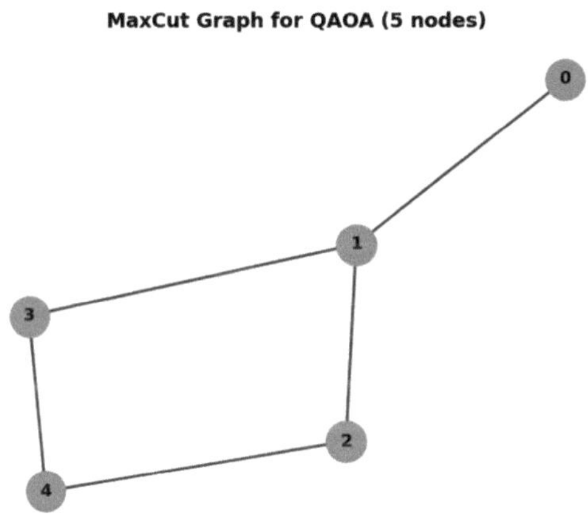

Fig. 5. MaxCut graph corresponding to the 5-node QAOA circuit.

In this implementation, the QAOA depth is $p = 1$, meaning one alternating layer of cost and mixer unitaries is applied. The parameters were optimized via classical simulation to $\gamma \approx 0.865$ and $\beta \approx 0.457$, producing a strong probability concentration on the optimal MaxCut solutions. The corresponding QAOA circuit structure for this problem is illustrated in Fig. 6. The two optimal MaxCut bitstrings for this graph are `01001` and `10110`.

4.3 Circuit Obfuscation

To apply our obfuscation methodology (Sect. 3) to the QAOA circuit, we generated a random single-qubit basis transformation using $U3(\theta, \phi, \lambda)$ with

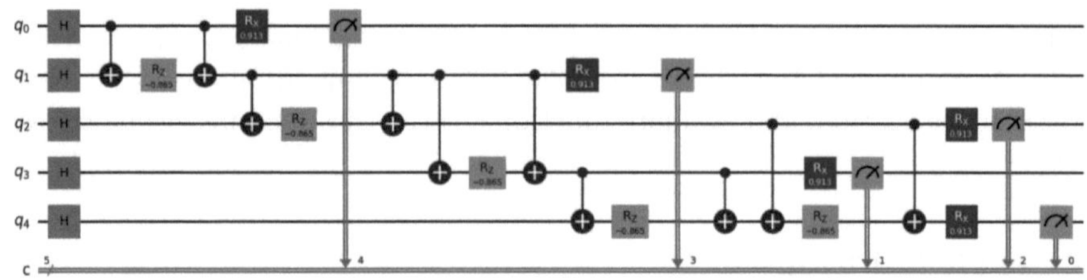

Fig. 6. QAOA circuit diagram for MaxCut on a 5-node graph, depth $p = 1$ with optimized parameters.

parameters $\theta = 2.86$, $\phi = 2.33$, and $\lambda = 0.762$. This unitary was then extended to the five-qubit system as a global basis $U = U3(2.86, 2.33, 0.762)^{\otimes 5}$ applied across all qubits at the beginning of the circuit, with its inverse $U^\dagger = U3(-2.86, -0.762, -2.33)^{\otimes 5}$ appended at the end to preserve the circuit's overall functionality. Each gate G in the QAOA layers was obfuscated using the conjugation $G' = U^\dagger G U$ and encapsulated as an opaque `UnitaryGate` with a unique label (e.g., `Obf_H_0`). The transformed structure of the obfuscated QAOA circuit is illustrated in Fig. 7.

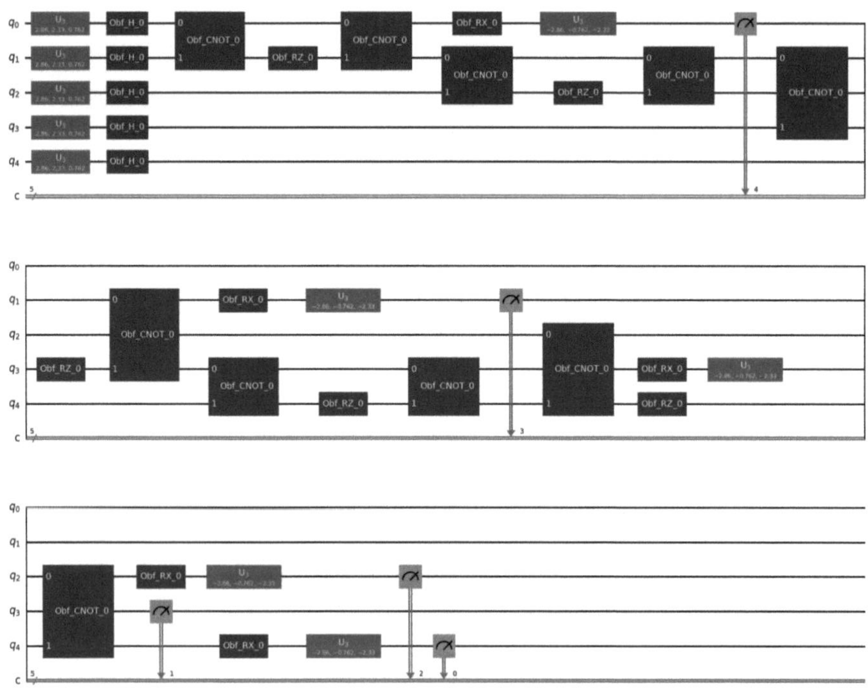

Fig. 7. Obfuscated QAOA circuit diagram, showing the transformed gate structure.

The resulting obfuscated circuit is functionally equivalent to the original but structurally unreadable, providing resistance against reverse engineering. Both the original and obfuscated circuits were then tested under identical simulation settings. The measurement outcomes for both the original and obfuscated QAOA circuits are shown in Fig. 8.

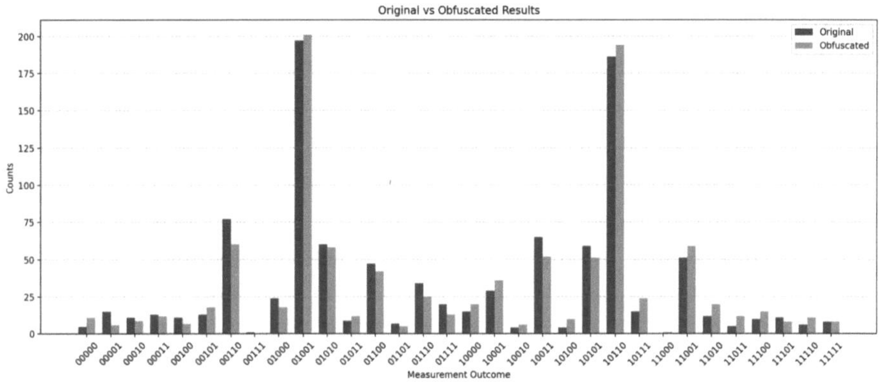

Fig. 8. Histogram of measurement outcomes for the original and obfuscated QAOA circuits. Optimal solutions are highlighted.

4.4 Testing Process

To evaluate the obfuscation technique, both the original and obfuscated QAOA circuits were executed using Qiskit's `AerSimulator` (version 0.36.0). Each configuration was run with 1,024 shots to ensure sufficient sampling. The output distributions were recorded and plotted using histograms. Execution times were also measured to detect any latency introduced by obfuscation.

The comparison focused on:

i. **Semantic accuracy**—probability assigned to each bitstring in the obfuscated circuit compared to the original.
ii. **Total Variation Distance (TVD)**—quantifying statistical difference between distributions.
iii. **Functional equivalence**—whether optimal solutions remain present with comparable probability.
iv. **Execution time**—runtime overhead introduced by the obfuscation process

4.5 Results

Both circuits produce highly similar output distributions, with only minor statistical variation due to sampling noise. The semantic accuracy of the obfuscated circuit reached **93.30%**, and the TVD was calculated to be **0.0840**, indicating strong fidelity to the original behavior. The two optimal MaxCut bitstrings (`01001` and `10110`) emerged as the two highest-probability peaks in both runs, dominating the output distributions with comparable counts. Execution time measurements showed negligible overhead introduced by the obfuscation process.

These results confirm that the obfuscation strategy preserves the computational intent and functional output of the original circuit, with the chosen optimized QAOA parameters successfully amplifying the probability of the optimal solutions.

4.6 Implementation Setup

The simulations were conducted on a standard Macbook Air M1 with 16 GB RAM and MacOS 18.6. To provide a comprehensive evaluation of our obfuscation technique, Quantum Approximate Optimization Algorithm (QAOA) for combinatorial optimization was tested alongside nine other quantum circuits, representing a diverse set of quantum algorithms: Shor's algorithm for integer factorization [12], the Bernstein-Vazirani (BV) algorithm for learning hidden linear functions [13], Grover's algorithm for unstructured search [14], the Variational Quantum Eigensolver (VQE) for quantum chemistry simulations [15], the Phase Kickback Circuit [16], the Deutsch-Jozsa (DJ) algorithm for classifying balanced or constant functions [17], the Quantum Fourier Transform (QFT) for periodicity analysis [18], and Simon's algorithm for finding periods in functions [19]. These algorithms, spanning applications from cryptography to quantum simulations, provide a robust testbed for assessing the obfuscation method's versatility.

Each circuit, including QAOA, was executed 100 times with 1,024 shots per execution under noise-free conditions using Qiskit's AerSimulator. The Toffoli circuit used three qubits, while the other algorithms ranged from 4 to 12 qubits, depending on their complexity.

5 Evaluation Metrics

These circuits were executed under noise-free conditions using Qiskit's AerSimulator to ensure consistent and reproducible results. The evaluation focuses on three primary metrics: *semantic accuracy*, *Total Variation Distance (TVD)*, and *execution time*, which together assess functional fidelity, statistical similarity, and computational overhead.

Semantic Accuracy

Semantic accuracy counts the overlapping probability mass between the two distributions, expressed as a percentage of the total probability in the original circuit's output. It quantifies whether the obfuscated circuit preserves the functional behavior of the original circuit under realistic, finite-shot quantum execution. This metric was used by Bartake et al. to quantify preservation of circuit behavior after their circuit-level transformations [5]. Given two measurement distributions `original` and `obfuscated`, the semantic accuracy is calculated as:

$$\text{Semantic Accuracy} = \frac{\sum_{x \in X} \min(\text{original}[x], \text{obfuscated}[x])}{\sum_{x \in X} \text{original[x]}} \times 100\% \tag{6}$$

where X is the union of all bitstrings observed in either distribution.

Since quantum measurements are inherently probabilistic, two runs of the same circuit will exhibit slight differences in their empirical output distributions unless an infinite number of shots is used. Semantic accuracy captures this agreement by computing the fraction of output bitstrings whose measured probabilities in the obfuscated circuit fall within the statistical variation of those from the original circuit.

Values slightly below 100% are therefore expected even for functionally identical circuits and do not indicate any semantic deviation introduced by the obfuscation. Instead, they reflect natural run-to-run statistical fluctuations. In the idealized infinite-shot limit, the empirical distributions of equivalent circuits would converge exactly, and semantic accuracy would approach 100%. High semantic accuracy in our experiments (typically above 90%) demonstrates that the obfuscated circuits remain consistent with the intended computation within the limits of finite-shot quantum sampling.

Total Variation Distance (TVD)

Total Variation Distance (TVD) is a statistical measure of the difference between two probability distributions [20]. In this work, TVD is used to quantify the effect of gate additions introduced during obfuscation. TVD is also a standard and widely used metric for comparing output distributions of quantum circuits, and it has been adopted in several prior works on quantum obfuscation [21,22]. It is computed as the sum of the absolute differences between the measurement counts of the original and obfuscated circuits, normalized by the total number of shots, as given by:

$$\text{TVD} = \frac{\sum_{i} |x_{i,\text{obfus}} - x_{i,\text{orig}}|}{2 \times \text{Number of shots}} \tag{7}$$

where $x_{i,\text{orig}}$ and $x_{i,\text{obfus}}$ denote the counts of the ith measurement outcome for the original and obfuscated circuits, respectively. A TVD of 0 means the two output distributions are exactly the same, showing no statistical difference at all, while a TVD of 1 means the distributions are completely distinct with no overlap, representing the maximum possible statistical difference.

Execution Time

Execution time refers to the duration required by the simulator to execute the circuit for a fixed number of shots (1024 in our case), excluding compilation time. It serves as a practical measure of the computational overhead introduced by circuit-level transformations, and its use is consistent with prior work in both quantum and classical settings. Studies on quantum program performance explicitly analyze execution time as a key metric to evaluate runtime and performance overhead in simulators and hardware [23], while recent work in binary obfuscation likewise evaluates execution time overhead to quantify the performance cost of structural code transformations [24]. Our results show that the overhead is minimal (typically < 1 ms), making the approach practical for real-world quantum workloads.

5.1 Obfuscation's Compiler Resistance: A Key Advantage

A core strength of our `U3`-conjugation technique lies in its ability to effectively conceal the original gate identities from quantum compilers and reverse-engineering tools. As demonstrated in our QAOA case study, when the obfuscated circuit is passed to a transpiler or compiler (such as Qiskit's transpiler), the individual original gates (e.g., Hadamard, CNOT) are no longer recognizable as their standard forms. Instead, they appear as opaque `UnitaryGate` objects, each representing the complex, randomized matrix resulting from the $U^{\dagger} \cdot G \cdot U$ transformation. Our method's compiler resistance stems from this deliberate lack of identifiable internal structure. Adversaries are forced to treat each transformed gate as an unknown unitary operation, greatly hindering reverse engineering of the proprietary quantum logic. Figure 9 visually exemplifies this transformation from a recognizable gate to an opaque block.

5.2 Overhead Analysis

To make the overhead of the obfuscation explicit, we summarize both the empirical execution-time overhead and the formal structural overhead introduced by the transformation. The execution-time results in Table 1 and Fig. 12 show that the runtime increase introduced by obfuscation is extremely small, typically well under one millisecond.

Consider an original circuit with m gates acting on n qubits. For each gate, we insert two single-qubit U_3 operations, resulting in an additional

$$G_m = 2m$$

single-qubit gates surrounding the original operations.

We further apply n single-qubit U_3 gates at the beginning and n at the end of the circuit, contributing:

$$G_n = 2n$$

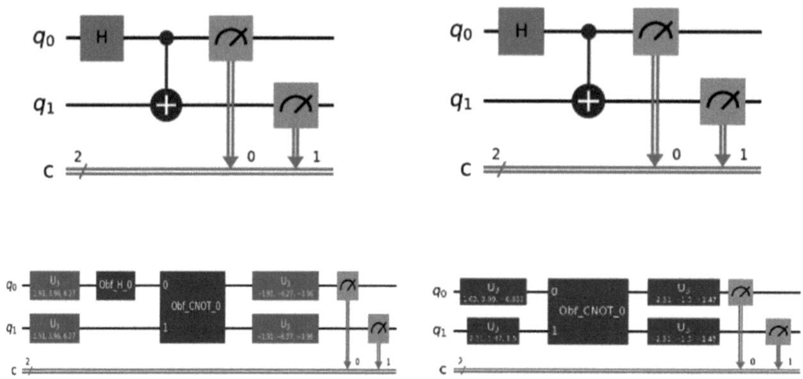

Fig. 9. Illustration of compiler resistance: On the left, the original Bell state circuit and its obfuscated counterpart. On the right, their respective compiled forms. While the original circuit structure is preserved after compilation, the obfuscated circuit appears as a single opaque UnitaryGate, concealing its functionality from quantum compilers and analysis tools.

additional gates.
Before fusion, the total number of gates is therefore

$$G_{\text{total, pre-fuse}} = m + 2m + 2n = 3m + 2n$$

The $3m$ gates surrounding the original m positions are fused into m effective gates by multiplying the three matrices acting at each position:

$$3m \longrightarrow m,$$

yielding a final structural gate count of

$$G_{\text{final}} = m + 2n$$

The two global boundary layers contribute a fixed depth increase:

$$\Delta D = 2$$

For example, in the QAOA case study, the computational overhead was negligible because each transformed operation is represented as a single opaque unitary during simulation, contributing no additional internal cost. Because the structural additions are constant and independent of circuit size, the empirical overhead remains negligible even for large workloads.

5.3 Results Summary

Table 1 presents the evaluation metrics for all tested circuits, including QAOA. The results show high semantic accuracy ($> 93\%$) and low TVD (≈ 0) across all circuits, confirming that the obfuscation preserves functionality. Execution times remain comparable, with minimal overhead, highlighting the method's efficiency. Visualizations in Fig. 10, 11, and 12 further illustrate the consistency of TVD, accuracy, and execution times, reinforcing the robustness of the obfuscation technique across diverse quantum algorithms.

Table 1. Evaluation metrics across quantum circuits.

Circuit	Original Time (s)	Obfuscated Time (s)	Semantic Accuracy (%)	TVD
BV (1011)	0.00309	0.00390	100.00	0.0000
DJ	0.00141	0.00147	100.00	0.0000
Grover (101)	0.00148	0.00148	97.17	0.0302
Phase Kickback	0.00165	0.00151	100.00	0.0000
QAOA	0.00156	0.00166	93.30	0.0840
QFT	0.00147	0.00178	94.73	0.0770
Shor	0.00179	0.00201	96.68	0.0146
Simon	0.00266	0.00183	94.24	0.0380
Toffoli	0.00167	0.00168	100.00	0.0000
VQE	0.00125	0.00132	99.51	0.0048

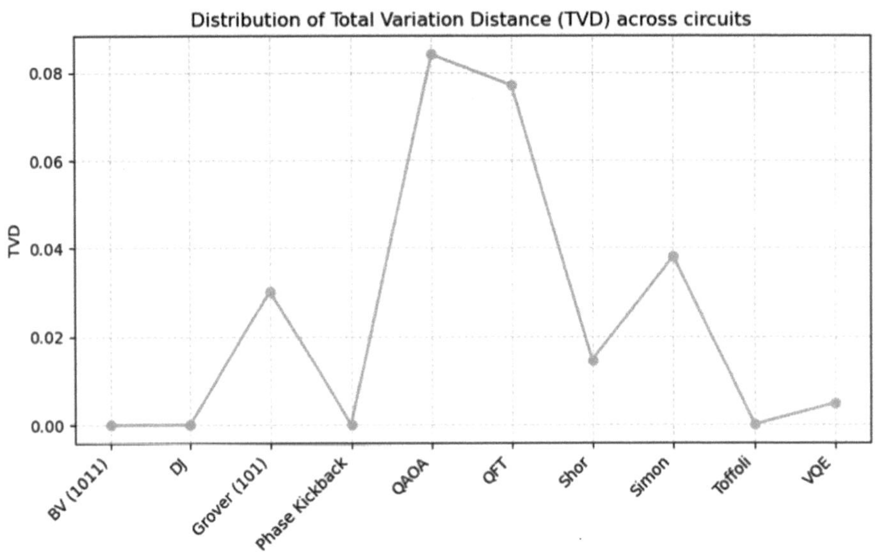

Fig. 10. Distribution of Total Variation Distance (TVD) across circuits, with low values indicating strong statistical similarity between original and obfuscated outputs.

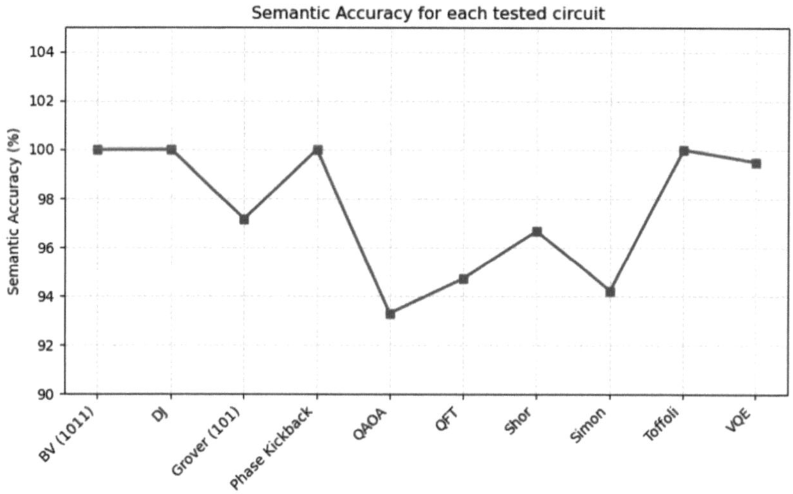

Fig. 11. Semantic accuracy for each tested circuit, with high values demonstrating functional correctness of obfuscated versions.

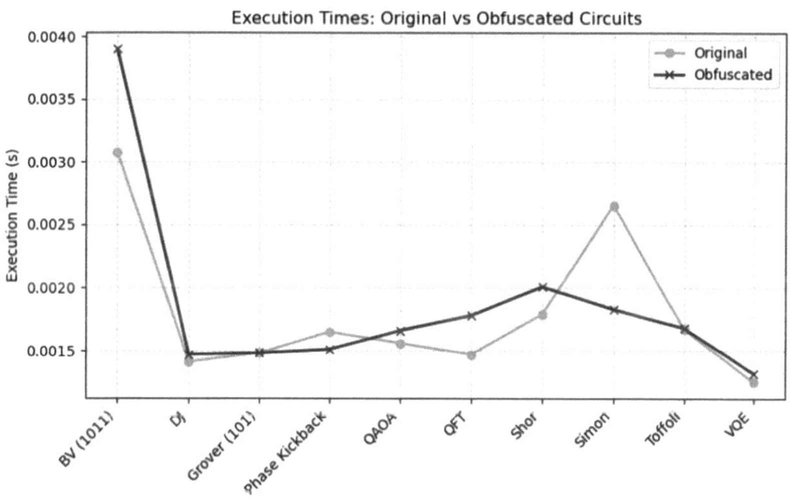

Fig. 12. Comparison of execution times between original and obfuscated quantum circuits, showing minimal overhead.

6 Security Guarantee

We quantify the difficulty of deobfuscation under two natural cases:

6.1 Black-Box Adversary (No Circuit Access)

In this model, the adversary does not see the obfuscated circuit description. Instead, they have only black-box access to its input-output behavior (e.g., they can prepare input states and observe measurement statistics). Our obfuscation replaces each protected single-qubit gate G by a basis-conjugated form $U^\dagger \cdot G' \cdot U$, where $G' = U \cdot G \cdot U^\dagger$ and the basis rotation U is sampled from the continuous $U3$ parameter domain $(\theta, \phi, \lambda) \in [0, \pi] \times [0, 2\pi) \times [0, 2\pi)$. An adversary who does not see the circuit would need to determine these continuous parameters solely from observed input-output statistics. Because the parameter space is uncountable, the probability of exactly guessing the correct triplet (θ, ϕ, λ) approaches 0.

Under a practical finite-precision discretization of step size δ (that is, each angle quantized in increments of δ), the number of possible basis rotations is on the order of

$$\left(\frac{2\pi}{\delta}\right)^3$$

and therefore a random-guessing adversary succeeds with probability at most

$$\left(\frac{\delta}{2\pi}\right)^3$$

which is negligible for realistic values of δ. Thus, in the black-box setting, both full and partial obfuscation lead to a difficult continuous parameter-recovery problem.

6.2 White-Box Adversary (Circuit Access)

In this stronger model, the adversary has access to the full obfuscated circuit (e.g., QASM or a Qiskit circuit) and can directly observe the explicit gates $U_i^\dagger$, G_i', and U_i inserted around protected gates. If all n gates in the circuit are obfuscated, the obfuscation pattern is trivial: the adversary may assume every gate is protected and straightforwardly recover the original gate as

$$G_i = U_i^\dagger \cdot G_i' \cdot U_i,$$

thus succeeding with probability 1.

The problem becomes non-trivial when only a selected subset of gates is obfuscated. Let the original circuit contain n gates, and let the obfuscator randomly choose a hidden subset $S \subseteq \{1, \ldots, n\}$ of size $|S| = x$. Only positions in S are replaced by basis-conjugated blocks $(U_i^\dagger \cdot G_i' \cdot U_i)$; the remaining gates stay unchanged. A white-box adversary must therefore first determine which gate positions belong to S before applying the algebraic simplification above.

If S is sampled uniformly from all $\binom{n}{x}$ choices of size x, then any adversary who attempts to guess the full obfuscation pattern in one shot succeeds with probability

$$p_{\text{succ}}(n, x) = \Pr[\widehat{S} = S] = \frac{1}{\binom{n}{x}}$$

The corresponding min-entropy of the obfuscation pattern is

$$H_\infty(S) = -\log_2 p_{\text{succ}}(n, x) = \log_2 \binom{n}{x}$$

This value is 0 in the trivial cases $x = 0$ (no obfuscation) and $x = n$ (all gates obfuscated), but strictly positive for $1 \le x \le n-1$, and maximised when $x \approx n/2$, where $H_\infty(S) \approx n$ bits. Thus:

1. When all gates are obfuscated ($x = n$), a white-box adversary can de-obfuscate by simplifying every block.
2. When only a randomly selected subset of gates is obfuscated ($1 \le x \le n-1$), the adversary must identify which gates are protected; this requires distinguishing among $\binom{n}{x}$ possible obfuscation patterns. The success probability $\frac{1}{\binom{n}{x}}$ is exponentially small when $x \approx n/2$.

7 Limitations and Future Work

While the proposed U3-based basis conjugation technique effectively preserves functional correctness and provides strong resistance to compiler-level reverse engineering, it introduces structural overhead that impacts scalability on near-term quantum hardware.

7.1 Limitations

The obfuscation process can be computationally intensive, especially when applying basis transformations to multi-qubit gates. Constructing these transformations using Kronecker products, as outlined in [9], involves manipulating high-dimensional matrices (such as 8×8 for three-qubit gates), which is feasible for small circuits (e.g., Toffoli). However, for deeper circuits, the large number of gates leads to significant computational costs from repeated matrix operations, limiting scalability [25]. Generating new random $U3$ parameters for each gate further increases time and memory usage, posing challenges for algorithms with high depth or width.

As analyzed in Sect. 5.2, the obfuscation process replaces each protected gate with a conjugated form that introduces additional single-qubit basis rotations, together with two global basis transformation layers applied at the circuit boundaries. Under ideal, noise-free simulation, these additional operations are algebraically fused into opaque unitary blocks, resulting in negligible execution-time overhead and no loss of functional equivalence. Consequently, ideal simulation masks the practical impact of this added structure.

When deployed on NISQ hardware, the additional basis operations introduced by conjugation must be realized as physical gate executions with nonzero error probabilities. Each single-qubit rotation corresponds to a calibrated control pulse whose imperfections accumulate as circuit depth increases, imposing a practical scalability limit even when individual gate fidelities are relatively high. For example, a two-qubit CNOT gate in a depth-D circuit is transformed under basis conjugation into $U^\dagger \cdot \mathrm{CNOT} \cdot U$, introducing single-qubit basis rotations on both qubits before and after the entangling operation. While these rotations are algebraically fused into a single opaque unitary during simulation, on physical hardware they must be executed as separate calibrated pulses. Consequently, a circuit containing m such entangling gates incurs $O(m)$ additional single-qubit operations, causing errors to accumulate with depth and limiting scalability for deep circuits such as the Quantum Fourier Transform (QFT) or Variational Quantum Eigensolvers (VQE), despite preserved functional correctness in ideal execution.

Finally, the current implementation does not exploit hardware-specific gate sets or connectivity constraints, which could mitigate some of the depth overhead through optimized decompositions. Incorporating hardware-aware synthesis and calibration-informed transformations remains an important direction for improving scalability on NISQ platforms.

7.2 Future Work

To overcome these challenges, we plan to pursue several targeted improvements to enhance the technique's scalability, hardware compatibility, and security. First, to reduce the computational burden of matrix calculations for deep circuits like QFT, or VQE, we will cache precomputed U3-transformed gates (e.g., $U^\dagger \cdot G \cdot U$ for Hadamard or CNOT), minimizing repetitive Kronecker product operations. Second, we will investigate methods to reduce the fidelity losses introduced by the extra single-qubit rotations in the conjugated form $U \cdot G \cdot U^\dagger$, including hardware-calibrated decompositions and approximation-aware synthesis to limit error accumulation. In addition, to better support NISQ devices, we will tailor U3 transformations to match the native gate sets and connectivity of specific quantum hardware, reducing circuit depth and errors. Finally, we also plan to add special gates that trigger errors if tampered with, helping detect unauthorized analysis attempts. These enhancements will make the technique more efficient and secure, supporting applications like protecting intellectual property in cloud-based quantum computing to visualize secure quantum circuits.

8 Conclusion

Our quantum circuit obfuscation method, built on `U3` gate conjugation, hides the structure of quantum circuits while preserving functionality. By applying randomized basis transformations, it ensures compatibility with `OPENQASM 2.0` and `OPENQASM 3.0`. The evaluation presented in this work uses the conservative single-basis variant, while the per-gate randomized variant provides strictly stronger security without altering the functional behavior of the circuit.

We tested the method on a diverse set of circuits—Shor's algorithm, QAOA, Bernstein-Vazirani, Grover's algorithm, VQE, Phase Kickback, Deutsch-Jozsa, QFT, Toffoli, and Simon's algorithm—covering applications from cryptography to quantum chemistry. The obfuscated circuits achieve an average semantic accuracy of at least 93% and a Total Variation Distance (TVD) below 0.035, indicating minimal changes in output distributions. Using Qiskit's `UnitaryGate` to implement transformed gates ($U^\dagger \cdot G \cdot U$) enables seamless integration into quantum circuits, with runtime overhead typically under 1 ms.

These results demonstrate that the method is both practical and versatile, spanning circuits from small Toffoli gates to complex algorithms like QFT and Shor. Future enhancements will focus on improving scalability for larger algorithms, optimizing transformations for NISQ hardware. These advances will strengthen the method's utility for protecting commercial quantum software, enabling secure cloud execution in quantum computing.

Declaration of Competing Interests. The authors have no competing interests to declare relevant to this article.

References

1. Nielsen, M.A., Chuang, I.L.: Quantum Computation and Quantum Information. Cambridge University Press, Cambridge (2010)
2. Preskill, J.: Quantum computing in the nisq era and beyond. Quantum **2**, 79 (2018). https://doi.org/10.22331/q-2018-08-06-79
3. Rieffel, E.G., Polak, W.H.: Quantum Computing: A Gentle Introduction. MIT Press (2011)
4. Cross, A.W., Bishop, L.S., Smolin, J.A., Gambetta, J.M.: Open quantum assembly language (2017). https://arxiv.org/abs/1707.03429
5. Bartake, N., Jie, S.T.Z., Jiawen, C.W., Ren, D.F.Y., Kasper, M., Balachandran, V.: Obfusqate: unveiling the first quantum program obfuscation framework. In: Proceedings of the 2025 Workshop on Research on Offensive and Defensive Techniques in the Context of Man At The End (MATE) Attacks, CheckMATE 2025, pp. 10–19. Association for Computing Machinery, New York, NY, USA (2025). https://doi.org/10.1145/3733817.3762700
6. Suresh, A., Saki, A.A., Alam, M., o Topalaglu, R., Ghosh, S.: A quantum circuit obfuscation methodology for security and privacy (2021). https://arxiv.org/abs/2104.05943
7. Rehman, A., Langford, V., Liu, Y.: Opaque: obfuscating phase in quantum circuit compilation for efficient IP protection (2025). https://arxiv.org/abs/2502.16605
8. Cross, A., et al.: Openqasm3: a broader and deeper quantum assembly language. ACM Trans. Quantum Comput. **3**(3), 1–50 (2022). https://doi.org/10.1145/3505636
9. Laub, A.J.: Matrix Analysis for Scientists and Engineers. SIAM, Philadelphia (2005)

10. Parayil, P., Raj, A., Balachandran, V.: Basis Transformation. https://github.com/vivekianity/Basis-Transformation
11. Farhi, E., Goldstone, J., Gutmann, S.: A quantum approximate optimization algorithm (2014). https://arxiv.org/abs/1411.4028
12. Shor, P.W.: Polynomial-time algorithms for prime factorization and discrete logarithms on a quantum computer. SIAM J. Comput. **26**(5), 1484–1509 (1997). https://doi.org/10.1137/S0097539795293172
13. Bernstein, E., Vazirani, U.: Quantum complexity theory. SIAM J. Comput. **26**(5), 1411–1473 (1997). https://doi.org/10.1137/S0097539796300921
14. Grover, L.K.: A fast quantum mechanical algorithm for database search. In: Proceedings of the 28th Annual ACM Symposium on Theory of Computing, pp. 212–219 (1996). https://doi.org/10.1145/237814.237866
15. Peruzzo, A., et al.: A variational eigenvalue solver on a photonic quantum processor. Nat. Commun. **5**, 4213 (2014). https://doi.org/10.1038/ncomms5213
16. Cleve, R., Ekert, A., Macchiavello, C., Mosca, M.: Quantum algorithms revisited. Proc. Roy. Soc. London Ser. A Math. Phys. Eng. Sci. **454**(1969), 339–354 (1998). https://doi.org/10.1098/rspa.1998.0164
17. Deutsch, D., Jozsa, R.: Rapid solution of problems by quantum computation. Proc. Roy. Soc. London Ser. A **439**(1907), 553–558 (1992). https://doi.org/10.1098/rspa.1992.0167
18. Coppersmith, D.: An approximate fourier transform useful in quantum factoring (2002). https://arxiv.org/abs/quant-ph/0201067
19. Simon, D.R.: On the power of quantum computation. SIAM J. Comput. **26**(5), 1474–1483 (1997). https://doi.org/10.1137/S0097539796298637
20. Verdú, S.: Total variation distance and the distribution of relative information. In: 2014 Information Theory and Applications Workshop (ITA), pp. 1–6. San Diego, CA, USA (2014). https://doi.org/10.1109/ITA.2014.6804281
21. Wang, Q., John, J., Dong, B., Liu, Y.: Tetrislock: quantum circuit split compilation with interlocking patterns (2025). https://arxiv.org/abs/2503.11982
22. Liu, Y., John, J., Wang, Q.: E-loq: enhanced locking for quantum circuit IP protection. In: 2025 IEEE International Symposium on Hardware Oriented Security and Trust (HOST), pp. 67–77. IEEE (2025). https://doi.org/10.1109/host64725.2025.11050014
23. Ma, N., Li, H.: Understanding and estimating the execution time of quantum circuits (2025). https://arxiv.org/abs/2411.15631
24. Zhang, P., et al.: Shining light on the inter-procedural code obfuscation: keep pace with progress in binary diffing. ACM Trans. Archit. Code Optim. **22**(1) (2025). https://doi.org/10.1145/3701992
25. Zhou, Y., Stoudenmire, E.M., Waintal, X.: What limits the simulation of quantum computers? Phys. Rev. X **10**, 041038 (2020). https://doi.org/10.1103/PhysRevX.10.041038

Cryptographic Primitives and Proof Systems

Tight Multi-user Security of CCM and Enhancement by Tag-Based Key Derivation

Yusuke Naito[1(✉)], Yu Sasaki[2,3], and Takeshi Sugawara[4]

[1] Mitsubishi Electric Corporation, Kanagawa, Japan
Naito.Yusuke@ce.MitsubishiElectric.co.jp
[2] NTT Social Informatics Laboratories, NTT Corporation, Tokyo, Japan
yusk.sasaki@ntt.com
[3] Associate of National Institute of Standards and Technology, Gaithersburg, USA
[4] The University of Electro-Communications, Tokyo, Japan
sugawara@uec.ac.jp

Abstract. This paper studies the multi-user (mu) bound of Counter with CBC-MAC (CCM), the authenticated encryption mode for block ciphers (BCs). Galois/Counter Mode (GCM) is more advanced in the study of mu security, and Hoang et al. achieved the tight mu-security bound of $\frac{\sigma_u \sigma}{2^n} + \frac{up+u^2}{2^k}$, where k and n are respectively the key and block sizes, u is the number of users, p is the number of offline queries. Here, σ and σ_u are the crucial factors that represent the total number of BC invocations by all users and the maximum number of BC invocations per user, respectively. In contrast, while there are two known mu bounds for CCM, $\frac{u\sigma_u^2}{2^n} + \frac{up+u^2}{2^k}$ by Luykx et al. (Asiacrypt 2017) and $\frac{\sigma^2}{2^n} + \frac{up+u\sigma}{2^k}$ by Zhang et al. (CCS 2024), both of which are not tight and worse than the bound for GCM. Another line of research studies methods to enhance mu-security without disruptive changes, such as nonce randomization (NR) and nonce-based key derivation (NKD) to improve offline and online security, respectively, but their applicability to CCM has never been discussed. Filling these gaps, this paper first proves an improved mu-security bound of CCM, which is tight, and reaches the GCM's bound. We also prove that CCM combined with NR and NKD achieves the same bound as GCM. With these results, CCM is now proved to be as secure as GCM. Furthermore, we propose a new enhancement method called nonce-based and tag-based key derivation (NTKD) and apply it to GCM and CCM. NTKD achieves a better bound beyond NR and NKD, and the resulting schemes satisfy the needs of real-world applications that demand massive data.

Keywords: CCM · Multi-user Security · Security Proof · Improved Bound · Nonce Randomization · Nonce/Tag-based Key Derivation

K. Jee and A. Kate (Eds.): ACNS 2026, LNCS 16571, pp. 211–240, 2027.
https://doi.org/10.1007/978-3-032-32560-0_8

1 Introduction

Privacy and message authenticity are two fundamental properties required for secure and reliable information systems. Real-world systems widely deploy authenticated encryption (AE), a symmetric-key cryptosystem that provides both privacy and authenticity, and researchers are actively studying their provable security bounds to provide theoretical foundation for determining their operational parameters, such as the frequency of changing a key.

Galois/Counter Mode (GCM) and Counter with CBC-MAC (CCM) are popular ways of constructing AE schemes based on a block cipher (BC) and a message authentication code (MAC). GCM uses the counter (CTR) mode for encryption and a polynomial hash function for MAC. GCM is standardized as ISO/IEC 19772 [15] and NIST SP800-38D [9] and widely used in many practical protocols, including Ethernet security [30], WPA3 Wifi security protocol [35], IPSec [32], and TLS [29]. CCM, on the other hand, uses the CTR mode for encryption and the cipher block chaining MAC (CBC-MAC) for MAC. It is standardized in IEEE 802.11 standard for wireless LANs [28,33], RFC 3610 [34], and NIST SP800-38C [8] and widely deployed in ZigBee [38], IPSec [4,14], Bluetooth [36], and TLS 1.3 defined in 2018 [20,26].

Conventionally, the security of AE schemes has been proved and analyzed based on the single-user (su) model that considers a single user with a fixed key. Missing consideration of an attack targeting a service with many users is a considerable gap, and there is a demand for rigorous security evaluation with the multi-user (mu) model, which considers an attacker who tries to compromise any of multiple users. Addressing the issue, researchers have evaluated several AE schemes in the last few years, including AES-GCM [2,13,19], AES-GCM-SIV [5], and ChaCha20-Poly1305 [7]. Based on those results, major protocols, such as TLS, DTLS, and QUIC, determine the rekeying intervals of AES-GCM according to the mu-security limit [26,27,31]. Moreover, the ongoing discussion on the usage limit of AEs, published as Internet-Draft [12], considers mu-security for other schemes, including AES-CCM.

Hoang et al. [13] proved that GCM's mu-security bound is $\frac{\sigma_\mathsf{u}\sigma}{2^n}+\frac{q_\mathsf{d}}{2^t}+\mathbf{Adv}_E^{\mathsf{muprp}}$, where E is the underlying BC, n and k are the block and key lengths of E, t is the tag length, and $\mathbf{Adv}_E^{\mathsf{muprp}}$ is the mu-pseudorandom-permutation (mu-PRP) advantage of E. σ is the total BC invocations in online queries, i.e., the queries to the encryption and decryption oracles, and σ_u is the upper bound of the number of BC invocations in online queries for each user, and q_d is the number of decryption queries. Note that Table 1 summarizes the parameters included in the bounds that appear throughout the paper. Assuming that $\frac{q_\mathsf{d}}{2^t} \leq \frac{\sigma_\mathsf{u}\sigma}{2^n}$, the bound matches the collision finding attack on CTR and is tight regarding online security.[1]

---

[1] The adversary has access to u users and makes encryption queries such that all plaintexts are zero strings and the number of plaintext blocks per user is σ_u, thus $\sigma = u\sigma_\mathsf{u}$. Since no collision occurs in the BC's outputs within the same user, the birthday analysis offers the distinguishing probability $\Omega(\frac{u\sigma_\mathsf{u}^2}{2^n}) = \Omega(\frac{\sigma_\mathsf{u}\sigma}{2^n})$.

Table 1. Parameters that appear in the bounds.

Parameter	Description
E	Underlying block cipher
n	Block length of E
k	Key length of E
t	Tag length
u	Number of users
p	Number of offline queries to an ideal cipher
d	The number of the same nonces across distinct keys
σ	Total number of BC invocations in online queries
σ_{u}	The number of BC invocations for each user
σ_{n}	The number of BC invocations for each nonce in a single user
q_{d}	Number of decryption queries
v	Threshold by implementing lockdown with failed decryption attempts

In contrast, mu-security of CCM is relatively unclear compared to GCM. Jonsson [17] proved that CCM's su-security bound in the ideal cipher (IC) model is $\frac{\sigma^2}{2^n} + \frac{q_{\mathsf{d}}}{2^t} + \frac{p}{2^k}$, wherein p is the number of offline queries to IC. The aforementioned Internet-Draft document [12] evaluates mu-security of AES-CCM with a generic bound, i.e., an mu-bound obtained from an su-bound with a hybrid argument, given by $\frac{u\sigma^2}{2^n} + \frac{uq_{\mathsf{d}}}{2^t} + \frac{up+u\sigma}{2^k}$. Such a generic bounds degrades with the number of users u, and further improvement with dedicated proofs is a significant research challenge [19,37]. Luykx et al. [19] showed a condition on deriving an mu-bound from an su-bound without security degradation, providing the improved mu-bound of CCM, given by $\frac{u\sigma_{\mathsf{u}}^2}{2^n} + \frac{q_{\mathsf{d}}}{2^t} + \mathbf{Adv}_E^{\mathsf{muprp}}$ wherein $\mathbf{Adv}_E^{\mathsf{muprp}}$ is bounded by $\frac{up+u^2}{2^k}$ in the IC model.

Table 2. Mu-bounds of GCM, CCM, and their enhancements with NR and NKD. For NKD, the mu-PRF advantage of KDF is omitted in this table, since it can be negligible by choosing a KDF and its key length appropriately.

Target	Bound	Ref.	Target	Bound	Ref.
GCM	$\frac{\sigma_{\mathsf{u}}\sigma}{2^n} + \frac{q_{\mathsf{d}}}{2^t} + \frac{up+u^2}{2^k}$	[13]	CCM	$\frac{\sigma_{\mathsf{u}}\sigma}{2^n} + \frac{q_{\mathsf{d}}}{2^t} + \frac{up+u^2}{2^k}$	Ours
+NR	$\frac{\sigma_{\mathsf{u}}\sigma}{2^n} + \frac{q_{\mathsf{d}}}{2^t} + \frac{dp}{2^k}$	[13]	+NR	$\frac{\sigma_{\mathsf{u}}\sigma}{2^n} + \frac{q_{\mathsf{d}}}{2^t} + \frac{dp}{2^k}$	Ours
+NR, NKD	$\frac{\sigma_{\mathsf{n}}\sigma}{2^n} + \frac{q_{\mathsf{d}}}{2^t} + \frac{dp}{2^k}$	[13]	+NR, NKD	$\frac{\sigma_{\mathsf{n}}\sigma}{2^n} + \frac{q_{\mathsf{d}}}{2^t} + \frac{dp}{2^k}$	Ours
CCM	$\frac{u\sigma^2}{2^n} + \frac{uq_{\mathsf{d}}}{2^t} + \frac{up+u\sigma}{2^k}$	Generic	Tag-based AE	$\frac{\sqrt{\sigma_{\mathsf{n}}}\sigma}{2^n} + \frac{q_{\mathsf{d}}}{2^t} + \frac{dp}{2^k}$	Ours
CCM	$\frac{u\sigma_{\mathsf{u}}^2}{2^n} + \frac{q_{\mathsf{d}}}{2^t} + \frac{up+u^2}{2^k}$	[19]	+NR, NTKD		
CCM	$\frac{\sigma^2}{2^n} + \frac{q_{\mathsf{d}}}{2^t} + \frac{up+u\sigma}{2^k}$	[37]			

Zhang et al. [37] showed another mu-bound of CCM, which is $\frac{\sigma^2}{2^n} + \frac{q_{\mathsf{d}}}{2^t} + \frac{up+u\sigma}{2^k}$. They showed the tightness of the bound under some conditions. The second term $\frac{q_{\mathsf{d}}}{2^t}$ is tight with generic forgery attacks that exhaustively guess the tags. The third term $\frac{up+u\sigma}{2^k}$ corresponds to attacks with offline queries, and this is tight when the offline query overwhelms the online query, i.e., $\sigma \le p$. In contrast, the first term $\frac{\sigma^2}{2^n}$ is proved to be tight only in the extreme case with $\sigma_{\mathsf{u}} \approx \sigma$, i.e., an adversary sends all online queries to a single user. This case is essentially equivalent that the adversary performs an su-attack even the access to multi-users is given, thus it does not demonstrate truly meaningful tightness w.r.t. mu-security.

Significance between $\frac{u\sigma_{\mathsf{u}}^2}{2^n}$ and $\frac{\sigma^2}{2^n}$ depends on the parameters u, σ_{u}, and σ; Zhang et al.'s $\frac{\sigma^2}{2^n}$ is better than Luykx et al.'s $\frac{u\sigma_{\mathsf{u}}^2}{2^n}$ in the extreme cases with $u \approx \sigma$ (e.g., $\sigma_{\mathsf{u}} = \sigma^{3/4}$ and $u \approx \sigma$), but Zhang et al.'s bound is worse in other cases, such as $\sigma \approx u\sigma_{\mathsf{u}}$, i.e. each of u users is queried with σ_{u} BC invocations. However, both bounds have critical problems. Zhang et al.'s $\frac{\sigma^2}{2^n}$ indicates that CCM's security is broken when σ reaches the birthday bound, and this cannot be avoided no matter how strong limitations are imposed on each user. Luykx et al.'s $\frac{u\sigma_{\mathsf{u}}^2}{2^n}$ only considers the maximum BC invocation per user, and thus non-tight when data from some users do not reach the maximum. Moreover, both bounds are worse than GCM's mu-bound of $\frac{\sigma_{\mathsf{u}}\sigma}{2^n}$ [13].

Another line of research work aims to enhance the security without disruptive changes in the scheme. For example, both GCM's and CCM's mu-offline security is already tight bounded by Biham's attack [3], which lowers the amount of offline queries to $\frac{2^k}{u}$, and there is no room for improvement as long as GCM's and CCM's specification are maintained. GCM in TLS 1.3 implements a countermeasure called nonce randomization (NR) that preprocesses the nonce without changing the GCM's implementation interface. NR uses a randomized nonce $N_{\mathsf{rand}} = N_{\mathsf{orig}} \oplus R$ with the original ν-bit nonce N_{orig} and a user-specific random mask $R \in \{0,1\}^\nu$. With this modification, Biham's attack additionally requires a collision in N_{rand} and the offline security is improved from $\frac{2^k}{u}$ to 2^k.

Bellare and Tackmann [2] proved confidentiality of NR, but the analysis is merely non-tight and did not consider integrity. Hoang et al. [13] formalized NR by introducing the d-bound model, where the number of the same randomized nonces across distinct users is bounded by d;[2] in the d-bound and the IC models, the new mu-bound of GCM with NR becomes $\frac{\sigma_{\mathsf{u}}\sigma}{2^n} + \frac{q_{\mathsf{d}}}{2^t} + \frac{dp}{2^k}$, as summarized in Table 2.

Nonce-based key derivation (NKD) [11] is another method that enhances online (cf. offline) security. Note that NKD is a meaningful technique for real-world applications, and in fact, NIST recently announced their interest in revising NIST SP800-38D to standardize the combination of GCM and NKD [23]. In NKD, each pair of a randomized nonce and a key for key derivation function (KDF) generates a fresh key of an AE scheme, and combining it with the mu-

[2] As a principle of nonce respect, the same (randomized) nonce is never repeated with the same key. However, the same nonce may appear between different users, and it is necessary to evaluate the number of nonce repetitions across distinct users.

bound in the d-bound model provides the following mu-bound of GCM with NKD, $\frac{\sigma_{\mathsf{n}}\sigma}{2^n} + \frac{q_{\mathsf{d}}}{2^t} + \frac{dp}{2^k} + \mathbf{Adv}_{\mathsf{F}}^{\mathsf{muprf}}$, where σ_{n} is the maximum number of BC invocations per nonce in a single user and $\mathbf{Adv}_{\mathsf{F}}^{\mathsf{muprf}}$ is an mu-pseudorandom-function (mu-PRF) advantage of the KDF F. Note that $\mathbf{Adv}_{\mathsf{F}}^{\mathsf{muprf}}$ can be negligible by choosing a KDF and its key length appropriately. Since $\sigma_{\mathsf{n}} \leq \sigma_{\mathsf{u}}$, NKD enhances the security of GCM. In particular, we can significantly improve security by limiting the number of decryption failures to some constant, i.e., $\sigma_{\mathsf{n}} \ll \sigma_{\mathsf{u}}$.

So far, enhancing methods such as NR and NKD have only been discussed for GCM, but their applicability to CCM has never been discussed. CCM is far behind GCM also in this respect.

It is also necessary to consider whether the enhanced security by NR and NKD is sufficient. The offline security term $\frac{dp}{2^k}$ is almost tight, because $k - \log_2 d \approx k$. Hence, possible concerns are on online security. Amazon AWS showed that AE schemes should allow to encrypt 2^{92} messages [18]. By combining it with the limitation of TLS 1.3 [26] that the maximum size of each message, ℓ, is 2^{10} blocks, AE schemes must be secure for $\sigma = 2^{102}$ BC invocations. Let us assume that the BC is AES having $n = 128$. With the original GCM and only with NR, the online term is $\frac{\sigma_{\mathsf{u}}\sigma}{2^{128}}$. TLS 1.3 [26] limits $\sigma_{\mathsf{u}} = 2^{34.5}$ BC invocations in AES-GCM,[3] and the aforementioned Internet Draft document [12] is establishing similar limits for other schemes. NIST standards have the same kind of limits: NIST SP800-38B for CMAC [10] recommends $\sigma_{\mathsf{u}} = 2^{48}$ BC invocations when $n = 128$, and NIST SP800-38D for AES-GCM [9] limits $\sigma_{\mathsf{u}} = 2^{53}$ BC invocations.[4] Even with the strongest limitation of $\sigma_{\mathsf{u}} = 2^{34.5}$ by TLS 1.3, the maximum σ is $2^{93.5}$ as shown in Table 3, which does not reach the goal of 2^{102}. When NKD is used, the online term is $\frac{\sigma_{\mathsf{n}}\sigma}{2^{128}}$. Adversaries can make queries under the same nonce up to v, the number of acceptable verification failures in decryption, hence σ_{n} is upper-bounded by about $v\ell$. To ensure security for $\sigma = 2^{102}$ with $\ell = 2^{24}$ coming from the maximum counter size of CCM, v can be at most 4. Practical systems can limit v to a constant threshold by implementing lockdown with failed decryption attempts, however $v = 4$ is too strong limitation, which significantly lowers usability.

In summary, mu-security of CCM still falls short compared to GCM in online security and the existing enhancements, as summarized in Table 2. Moreover, the existing enhancements may not be sufficient for some practical use cases. This paper aims to fill the gaps between CCM and GCM, and to present a new enhancement method to reach an ideal mu-security level. In particular, we address the following research questions: (1) What is the tight online mu-bound of CCM? Is it better or worse compared to GCM? (2) Do conventional enhancing methods, i.e., NR and NKD, improve mu-security of CCM? If yes, how much? (3) Is it possible to further enhance mu-security beyond NR and NKD, which works for both GCM and CCM?

---

[3] $2^{34.5}$ is derived from the maximum number of messages ($2^{24.5}$) and $\ell = 2^{10}$ blocks.

[4] NIST SP800-38D [9] tolerates 2^{21} messages for each key with 96-bit IV and 2^{32} blocks per message restricted by the counter length, totaling 2^{53} blocks for each key.

Table 3. Upper-bounds of BC invocations for online mu-security with concrete parameters: $n = 128$ and several per-user usage limits, (i) $\sigma_\mathsf{u} = 2^{34.5}$, (ii) $\sigma_\mathsf{u} = 2^{48}$, and (iii) $\sigma_\mathsf{u} = 2^{53}$, from practical standards. σ_n is upper-bounded by about $v\ell$ and this table evaluates σ for $v = 2^{10}$ and $\ell = 2^{24}$. We approximate that $k - \log_2 d \approx k$.

Target	Online				Offline
	Generic	$\sigma_\mathsf{u} = 2^{34.5}$	$\sigma_\mathsf{u} = 2^{48}$	$\sigma_\mathsf{u} = 2^{53}$	Generic
CCM [37]	$\sigma \le 2^{n/2}$	$\sigma \le 2^{64}$	$\sigma \le 2^{64}$	$\sigma \le 2^{64}$	$k - \log_2 u$
CCM	$\sigma \le \frac{2^n}{\sigma_\mathsf{u}}$	$\sigma \le 2^{93.5}$	$\sigma \le 2^{80}$	$\sigma \le 2^{75}$	$k - \log_2 u$
CCM w/ NR	$\sigma \le \frac{2^n}{\sigma_\mathsf{u}}$	$\sigma \le 2^{93.5}$	$\sigma \le 2^{80}$	$\sigma \le 2^{75}$	k
CCM w/ NR + NKD	$\sigma \le \frac{2^n}{\sigma_\mathsf{n}}$	$\sigma \le 2^{94}$			k
GCM/CCM w/ NR + NTKD	$\sigma \le \frac{2^n}{\sqrt{\sigma_\mathsf{n}}}$	$\sigma \le 2^{111}$			k

Contributions

In the first part of this paper, we prove that CCM is as good as GCM with respect to mu-security for the standard model, NR, and NKD, with the following contributions. The generation methods of key and nonce for these schemes are summarized in Table 4.

Table 4. Key generation methods and nonce generation methods of CCM/GCM, NKD, NTKD, and NR. K_AE and N_AE are a key and nonce of CCM/GCM, respectively. N_orig is an original nonce input to the target AE. $K_\mathsf{AE} \xleftarrow{\$} \{0,1\}^n$ means that K_AE is chosen uniformly at random from $\{0,1\}^k$. F_K is a KDF with a key K. For NR, R is a per-user fixed random value with the same length as N_AE. For NTKD, i is the sector number and T_{i-1} is a tag of the previous AE call.

Target	AE's Key Generation	Target	AE's Nonce Generation
CCM/GCM	$K_\mathsf{AE} \xleftarrow{\$} \{0,1\}^n$	CCM/GCM	$N_\mathsf{AE} \leftarrow N_\mathrm{orig}$
+NKD	$K_\mathsf{AE} \leftarrow \mathsf{F}_K(N_\mathrm{orig})$	+NR	$N_\mathsf{AE} \leftarrow N_\mathrm{orig} \oplus R$
+NTKD	$(K_\mathsf{AE}, *) \leftarrow \mathsf{F}_K(N_\mathrm{orig}, T_{i-1})$	+NTKD	$(*, \hat{N}) \leftarrow \mathsf{F}_K(N_\mathrm{orig}, 0^t)$; $N_\mathsf{AE} \leftarrow \hat{N} + (i-1)$

Tight Mu-bound in the Standard Model (Sect. 5**).** We first improve the mu-bound of CCM in the standard model to $\frac{\sigma_\mathsf{u}\sigma}{2^n} + \frac{q_\mathsf{d}}{2^t} + \mathbf{Adv}_E^{\mathsf{muprp}}$. The first two terms $\frac{\sigma_\mathsf{u}\sigma}{2^n} + \frac{q_\mathsf{d}}{2^t}$ represent the online security, which are better than the corresponding terms in the previous work, i.e., $\frac{\sigma^2}{2^n} + \frac{q_\mathsf{d}}{2^t}$ and $\frac{u\sigma_\mathsf{u}^2}{2^n} + \frac{q_\mathsf{d}}{2^t}$, for any adversary since $\sigma \le u\sigma_\mathsf{u}$ and $\sigma_\mathsf{u} \le \sigma$. The new online terms are tight, i.e. match the generic bounds of the distinguishing attack on CTR and a generic forgery attack. Furthermore, with condition $\sigma_\mathsf{u} \ll 2^{n/2}$, which can be ensured by adequate rekeying, CCM achieves beyond-birthday-bound online security. The offline security of

CCM, on the other hand, is derived from the last term $\mathbf{Adv}_E^{\mathsf{muprp}}$. This mu-PRP term offers the bound $\frac{up+u^2}{2^k}$ in the IC model, which is also tight, matching the bounds of the generic attacks [3]. In summary, the entire bound is tight, and CCM achieves the same level of mu security as GCM, as summarized in Table 2.

Enhancing Offline Security with NR (Sect. 6). Next, we prove that the mu-bound of CCM with NR in the d-bound and IC models is $\frac{\sigma_{\mathsf{u}}\sigma}{2^n} + \frac{q_{\mathsf{d}}}{2^t} + \frac{dp}{2^k}$. The last term $\frac{dp}{2^k}$ represents offline security, where d is $\approx \frac{n}{\log_2 n}$ and negligible. Thus, NR enhances offline security from $\frac{k}{u}$ to k bits, making it independent of the number of users. The online security represented by the first two terms, on the other hand, is identical to that of bare CCM in the standard model, which is tight. The bound is again the same as that of GCM in the d-bound and IC models, as shown in Table 2.

Enhancing Online Security with NKD (Sect. 7). While NR enhances the offline security of CCM, the online security remains unchanged with the term $\frac{\sigma_{\mathsf{u}}\sigma}{2^n}$. We improve it using NKD, following the previous approach for GCM [13]. The mu-security of CCM with NKD in the d-bound and IC models is $\frac{\sigma_{\mathsf{n}}\sigma}{2^n} + \frac{q_{\mathsf{d}}}{2^t} + \frac{dp}{2^k} + \mathbf{Adv}_{\mathsf{F}}^{\mathsf{muprf}}$, obtained by replacing σ_{u} with σ_{n} and adding the mu-PRF advantage of F in the above mu-bound of CCM with NR. Although the mu-PRF advantage is added as a new offline term, it becomes negligible by choosing an appropriate KDF with sufficient key length, and the overall offline security is k bits.

The online security is enhanced under the condition that $\frac{\sigma_{\mathsf{n}}\sigma}{2^n} \geq \frac{q_{\mathsf{d}}}{2^t}$ and $\sigma_{\mathsf{n}} \ll \sigma_{\mathsf{u}}$. Because σ_{n} is upper-bounded by about $v\ell$, the online term is improved to about $\frac{v\ell\sigma}{2^n}$. The bound is the same as the one of GCM with NKD in the IC and d-bound models, thus CCM achieves the same level of mu security as GCM.

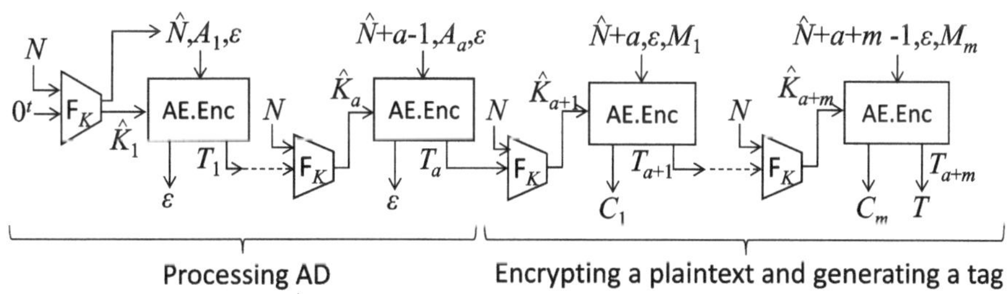

Fig. 1. Encryption of AE_NTKD. AE.Enc is the underlying tag-based AE encryption. F_K is the KDF that takes nonce and a tag and generates a key of AE.Enc (and a nonce-based IV $\hat{N}$ for the first AE.Enc call). $A_1, \ldots, A_a$ are AD sectors, $M_1, \ldots, M_m$ are plaintext sectors, $C_1, \ldots, C_m$ are ciphertext sectors, $T_1, \ldots, T_{a+m}$ are tags of AE.Enc, T is a tag of AE_NTKD. $\hat{N}$ with a counter addition is used as nonce of AE.Enc.

Nonce-Based and Tag-Based Key Derivation (NTKD) (Sect. 8). In the second part of this paper, we present a new method called NTKD to further enhance online mu-security. NTKD can be applied to both GCM and CCM, and can be applied in generic for any tag-based AE: an AE such that (i) encryption generates a ciphertext C and a tag T and (ii) decryption generates T' without using T and authenticates the data by matching T and T'. The basic idea of NTKD is to separate the input data into multiple *sectors*, an appropriately parameterized number of data blocks, and apply AE to each sector by setting the key for the ith sector to an output of KDF that is computed from the nonce and the tag for $(i-1)$-th sector. The encryption of NTKD is depicted in Fig. 1 and the key generation method is given in Table 4. This has the effect of rekeying in every sector and improves security. By setting the sector length to $\sqrt{\sigma_{\mathsf{n}}}$, the mu-bound becomes $\frac{\sqrt{\sigma_{\mathsf{n}}}\sigma}{2^n} + \frac{q_{\mathsf{d}}}{2^t} + \frac{dp}{2^k}$. Because σ_{n} is upper-bounded by about $v\ell$, with $n = 128$, $\ell = 2^{24}$, and $\sigma = 2^{102}$, security is ensured as long as $v \leq 2^{28}$, which is significantly higher than $v \leq 4$ for NKD with the same setting. Also we evaluate the value of σ that can be securely processed for some v. with $n = 128$, $v = 2^{10}$, and $\ell = 2^{24}$, NTKD ensures security up to $\sigma = 2^{111}$, while NKD ensures security up to $\sigma = 2^{94}$, which does not reach $\sigma = 2^{102}$, as shown in Table 3.

Regarding the speed, the performance of NTKD depends on the plaintext length and the chosen sector length. The overhead may become significant with short plaintexts or small sector sizes; however, it becomes negligible for long plaintexts and appropriately chosen sector lengths, and NTKD achieves performance comparable to that of the original scheme.

2 Notations

Let ε be the empty string, $\emptyset$ the empty set, and $\{0,1\}^*$ the set of all bit strings. For integers $i \leq j$, let $[i,j] := \{i, i+1, \ldots, j\}$ and $[j] := [1,j]$. If $i > j$ then $[i,j] := \emptyset$. For an integer $n \geq 0$, let $\{0,1\}^n$ be the set of all n-bit strings, $\{0,1\}^0 := \{\varepsilon\}$, $\{0,1\}^{\leq n} := \cup_{i\in[0,n]}\{0,1\}^i$, and $\{0,1\}^{n*} := \{X \in \{0,1\}^* \mid |X| > 0, |X| \bmod n = 0\}$. Let 0^i be the bit string of i-bit zeros. For a bit-string $D \in \{0,1\}^*$ and a positive integer n, let $|D|_n := \lceil |D|/n \rceil$ be the n-bit block length of D. For $X \in \{0,1\}^j$, let $|X| := j$. The concatenation of two bit strings X and Y is written as $X\|Y$ or XY when no confusion is possible. For integers $0 \leq j \leq i$ and $X \in \{0,1\}^i$, let $\mathsf{msb}_j(X)$ (resp. $\mathsf{lsb}_j(X)$) be the most (resp. least) significant j bits of X. For a non-empty set $\mathcal{S}$, $S \xleftarrow{\$} \mathcal{S}$ means that an element is chosen uniformly at random from $\mathcal{S}$ and assigned to S. For two sets $\mathcal{S}$ and $\mathcal{S}'$, $\mathcal{S} \xleftarrow{\cup} \mathcal{S}'$ means $\mathcal{S} \leftarrow \mathcal{S} \cup \mathcal{S}'$. For an integer $l \geq 0$ and $X \in \{0,1\}^*$, $X_1, \ldots, X_\ell \xleftarrow{l} X$ means parsing of X into fixed-length l-bit strings, where if $X \neq \varepsilon$ then $X = X_1\|\cdots\|X_\ell$, $|X_i| = l$ for $i \in [\ell - 1]$, and $0 < |X_\ell| \leq l$; if $X = \varepsilon$ then $\ell = 1$ and $X_1 = \varepsilon$. For integers $m, n \geq 0$, let $\mathsf{Func}(m,n)$ be the set of all functions from $\{0,1\}^m$ to $\{0,1\}^n$. For an integer $n \geq 0$, let $\mathsf{Perm}(n)$ be the set of all n-bit permutations. For a set $\mathcal{S}$ and $j \in [l]$, let $(y_1, \ldots, y_{j-1}, *, y_{j+1}, \ldots, y_l) \in \mathcal{S}$ be a condition that $\exists y$ s.t. $(y_1, \ldots, y_{j-1}, y, y_{j+1}, \ldots, y_l) \in \mathcal{S}$.

Algorithm 1 CTR

Encryption/Decryption $\mathsf{CTR}[E_K](N, D)$

$m \leftarrow |D|_n$; **for** $i = 1, \ldots, m$ **do** $X_{2,i} \leftarrow \mathsf{add}(N, i)$; $Y_{2,i} \leftarrow E_K(X_{2,i})$ **end for**

$KS \leftarrow \mathsf{msb}_{|D|}(Y_{2,1} \| \cdots \| Y_{2,m})$; $D' \leftarrow D \oplus KS$; **return** D'

Algorithm 2 CBC

MAC $\mathsf{CBC}[E_K](B)$

$b \leftarrow |B|_n$; $B_1, \ldots, B_b \xleftarrow{n} B$; $Y_{1,0} \leftarrow 0^n$

for $i = 1, \ldots, b$ **do** $X_{1,i} \leftarrow B_i \oplus Y_{1,i-1}$; $Y_{1,i} \leftarrow E_K(X_{1,i})$ **end for**

return $Y_{1,b}$

Algorithm 3 CCM

Encryption $\mathsf{CCM.Enc}[E_K](N, A, M)$

$B \leftarrow \mathsf{f}_{\mathsf{CCM}}(N, A, M)$; $S \leftarrow \mathsf{CBC}[E_K](B)$; $X_{2,0} \leftarrow \mathsf{add}(N, 0)$; $Y_{2,0} \leftarrow E_K(X_{2,0})$

$T \leftarrow \mathsf{lsb}_t(S \oplus Y_{2,0})$; $C \leftarrow \mathsf{CTR}[E_K](N, M)$; **return** (C, T)

Decryption $\mathsf{CCM.Dec}[E_K](N, A, C, \widetilde{T})$

$M \leftarrow \mathsf{CTR}[E_K](N, C)$; $B \leftarrow \mathsf{f}_{\mathsf{CCM}}(N, A, M)$; $S \leftarrow \mathsf{CBC}[E_K](B)$

$X_{2,0} \leftarrow \mathsf{add}(N, 0)$; $Y_{2,0} \leftarrow E_K(X_{2,0})$; $T \leftarrow \mathsf{lsb}_t(S \oplus Y_{2,0})$

if $T = \widetilde{T}$ **then return** M **else return reject end if**

3 Specification of CCM

CCM is a block-cipher(BC)-based and nonce-based AE scheme with the Encrypt-and-MAC structure. The encryption part is the CTR mode and the MAC part is CBC-MAC, which is simply denoted by CBC throughout the paper.

3.1 Block Cipher (BC)

A BC is a set of permutations indexed by a key. For positive integers k and n, let $E : \{0,1\}^k \times \{0,1\}^n \rightarrow \{0,1\}^n$ be an encryption of a BC with k-bit keys and n-bit blocks. Let $E^{-1} : \{0,1\}^k \times \{0,1\}^n \rightarrow \{0,1\}^n$ be its decryption. Let $E^{\pm} := (E, E^{-1})$. E with a key K is denoted by E_K or $E(K, \cdot)$. Similarly, E^{-1} with a key K is denoted by E_K^{-1} or $E\ ^{1}(K, \cdot)$.

3.2 CTR Mode

CTR is a parallelizable encryption scheme with a BC E_K. The specification of CTR is given in Algorithm 1 and Fig. 2(right). Let c be a parameter for the counters. $\mathsf{CTR}[E_K] : \{0,1\}^\nu \times \{0,1\}^{\leq n(2^c-2)} \rightarrow \{0,1\}^{\leq n(2^c-2)}$ takes a tuple of a key K, a nonce N, and a plaintext/ciphertext D, and returns its ciphertext/plaintext D' such that $|D| = |D'|$. If D is a plaintext (resp. ciphertext), then D' is the ciphertext (resp. plaintext). KS is a key stream with which a ciphertext (resp. plaintext) is defined by XORing a plaintext (resp. ciphertext). $\mathsf{add} : \{0,1\}^\nu \times [0, 2^c] \rightarrow \{0,1\}^n$ is a function that on an input pair of a nonce

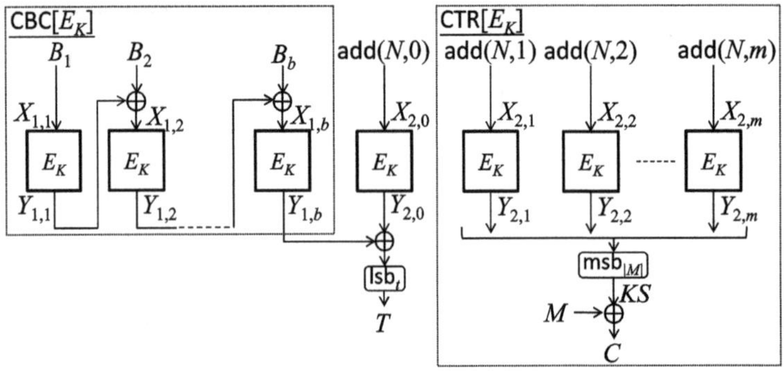

Fig. 2. The encryption of CCM, where $B \leftarrow \mathsf{f}_{\mathsf{CCM}}(N, A, M)$ and $B_1, \ldots, B_b \xleftarrow{n} B$.

and a counter, returns an input block of E such that for any $N \in \{0,1\}^\nu$ and distinct values $i, j \in [0, 2^c]$, $\mathsf{add}(N, i) \neq \mathsf{add}(N, j)$. Note that "$2^c$" is reserved for the first block of CBC and "0" is reserved for masking CBC outputs.

3.3 CBC Mode

CBC is a BC-based MAC that is an iterated construction of E_K. $\mathsf{CBC}[E_K] : \{0,1\}^{n*} \to \{0,1\}^n$ takes a message B of length multiple of n, and returns an n-bit tag $Y_{1,b}$. The specification of CBC is given in Algorithm 2 and Fig. 2(left).

3.4 CCM Mode

CCM is a nonce-based AE scheme with E_K. Let ν be the nonce size such that $\nu \leq n$. Let $\mathcal{M} = \{0,1\}^{\leq n(2^c-2)}$ be plaintext/ciphertext spaces and $\mathcal{A} \subset \{0,1\}^*$ an associated data (AD) space. Let t be the tag size of CCM such that $t \leq n$. The specification of CCM is given in Algorithm 3 and Fig. 2. Let $\mathsf{f}_{\mathsf{CCM}} : \{0,1\}^\nu \times \mathcal{A} \times \mathcal{M} \to \{0,1\}^*$ be an injective formatting function that takes a nonce N, an AD A, and a plaintext M, and returns an encoded message $B = \mathsf{f}_{\mathsf{CCM}}(N, A, M)$ such that its first n-bit block $B_1 = \mathsf{add}(N, 2^c)$, meaning that all first input blocks of CBC are distinct from all input blocks of CTR. The input blocks defined by add, namely $X_{1,1}, X_{2,0}, X_{2,1}, \ldots, X_{2,m}$, are called the nonce-dependent input blocks, and the other input blocks, $X_{1,2}, \ldots, X_{1,b}$, are called the nonce-independent input blocks.

$\mathsf{CCM.Enc}[E_K] : \{0,1\}^\nu \times \mathcal{A} \times \mathcal{M} \to \mathcal{M} \times \{0,1\}^t$ is the encryption of CCM with E_K. It accepts a nonce $N \in \{0,1\}^\nu$, an AD $A \in \mathcal{A}$, and a plaintext $M \in \mathcal{M}$, and returns a ciphertext $C \in \mathcal{M}$ such that $|C| = |M|$.

$\mathsf{CCM.Dec}[E_K] : \{0,1\}^\nu \times \mathcal{A} \times \mathcal{M} \times \{0,1\}^t \to \mathcal{M} \cup \{\mathbf{reject}\}$ is the decryption of CCM with E_K. It accepts a nonce $N \in \{0,1\}^\nu$, an AD $A \in \mathcal{A}$, a cipher $C \in \mathcal{M}$, and a tag $\widetilde{T} \in \{0,1\}^t$ and returns, deterministically, either the distinguished invalid symbol **reject** $\notin \mathcal{M}$ or a valid plaintext $M \in \mathcal{M}$.

We define a nonce extracting function $\mathsf{ext}_{\mathsf{nonce}} : \{0,1\}^n \rightarrow \{0,1\}^\nu$ that takes an n-bit input block $X \in \{0,1\}^n$ and returns a ν-bit value such that for an input block X, if $\exists N \in \{0,1\}^\nu, i \in [0, 2^c]$ s.t. $X = \mathsf{add}(N, i)$, then $\mathsf{ext}_{\mathsf{nonce}}(X) = N$.

4 Security Definitions and Proof Tools

4.1 Distinguishing Advantage

We consider distinguishing-type security notions for BCs and AEs. We thus define the following distinguishing advantage of an adversary $\mathbf{A}$ that has access to either $\mathcal{O}_1$ or $\mathcal{O}_2$ and returns a decision bit. For $i \in [2]$, let $\mathbf{A}^{\mathcal{O}_i} = 1$ be an event that $\mathbf{A}$ with $\mathcal{O}_i$ returns 1. Then, the distinguishing advantage of $\mathbf{A}$ is defined as

$$\mathbf{Adv}^{\mathsf{dist}}_{\mathcal{O}_1,\mathcal{O}_2}(\mathbf{A}) := \Pr\left[\mathbf{A}^{\mathcal{O}_1} = 1\right] - \Pr\left[\mathbf{A}^{\mathcal{O}_2} = 1\right].$$

4.2 Security Models for BCs

In the mu-security proofs of CCM, we consider two models for BCs: the standard multi-user-pseudorandom-permutation (mu-PRP) security and the ideal cipher (IC) models.

Standard Model. In this model, the underlying BCs are assumed to be mu-PRP secure, where BC instantiations with independent keys are securely replaced with independent random permutations (RPs). Let u be the number of users. In the mu-PRP game, an adversary interacts with either the real-world oracles $(E_{K_1}, \ldots, E_{K_u})$ or the ideal-world oracles $(P_1, \ldots, P_u)$, where $\forall \omega \in [u] : K_\omega \xleftarrow{\$} \{0,1\}^k$ and RPs are defined as $\forall \omega \in [u] : P_\omega \xleftarrow{\$} \mathsf{Perm}(n)$. At the end of this game, $\mathbf{A}$ returns a decision bit in $\{0,1\}$. The mu-PRP advantage function of $\mathbf{A}$ is defined as

$$\mathbf{Adv}^{\mathsf{muprp}}_{E}(\mathbf{A}) := \mathbf{Adv}^{\mathsf{dist}}_{(E_{K_1},\ldots,E_{K_u}),(P_1,\ldots,P_u)}(\mathbf{A}).$$

For all possible adversaries $\mathbf{A}$ that have access to u users, make at most q queries, and run in time τ, the maximum advantage is defined as

$$\mathbf{Adv}^{\mathsf{muprp}}_{E}(u, q, \tau) := \max_{\mathbf{A}} \mathbf{Adv}^{\mathsf{muprp}}_{E}(\mathbf{A}).$$

Ideal Cipher (IC) Model. Let $\mathcal{BC}$ be the set of all encryptions of k-bit key and n-bit block BCs. An IC is an ideal BC and defined as $E \xleftarrow{\$} \mathcal{BC}$. In the IC model, all parties including CCM oracles and adversaries obtain IC's outputs by accessing an IC $E^{\pm} = (E, E^{-1})$.

4.3 Security Models for CCM

Multi-user-AE (mu-AE) security is the indistinguishability between the real and ideal worlds. Let u be the number of users. Let $\$_\omega$ be a random-bit oracle of the ω-th user that takes an input tuple (N, A, M) of a nonce, an AD, and a plaintext, and returns a pair of a random ciphertext and a tag defined as $(C, T) \xleftarrow{\$} \{0,1\}^{|\mathsf{CCM.Enc}[E_K](N,A,M)|}$. Let $\perp_\omega$ be a reject oracle that returns **reject** for any query. Let $K_1, \ldots, K_u$ be users' keys defined as $\forall \omega \in [u] : K_\omega \xleftarrow{\$} \{0,1\}^k$. In the this game, an adversary $\mathbf{A}$ has access to either real-world oracles $\mathcal{O}_{\mathsf{real}}$ or ideal-world oracles $\mathcal{O}_{\mathsf{ideal}}$ defined as follows.

$$\textbf{Standard}: \mathcal{O}_{\mathsf{real}}^{\mathsf{sm}} := (\mathsf{CCM}[E_{K_\omega}])_{\omega \in [u]};\ \mathcal{O}_{\mathsf{ideal}}^{\mathsf{sm}} := (\$_\omega, \perp_\omega)_{\omega \in [u]},$$
$$\textbf{IC}: \mathcal{O}_{\mathsf{real}}^{\mathsf{icm}} := ((\mathsf{CCM}[E_{K_\omega}])_{\omega \in [u]}, E^{\pm});\ \mathcal{O}_{\mathsf{ideal}}^{\mathsf{icm}} := ((\$_\omega, \perp_\omega)_{\omega \in [u]}, E^{\pm}).$$

At the end of this game, $\mathbf{A}$ return a decision bit in $\{0,1\}$. The mu-AE-security advantage functions of $\mathbf{A}$ are defined as

$$\textbf{Standard}: \mathbf{Adv}_{\mathsf{CCM}}^{\mathsf{muae,sm}}(\mathbf{A}) := \mathbf{Adv}_{\mathcal{O}_{\mathsf{real}}^{\mathsf{sm}}, \mathcal{O}_{\mathsf{ideal}}^{\mathsf{sm}}}^{\mathsf{dist}}(\mathbf{A}),$$
$$\textbf{IC}: \mathbf{Adv}_{\mathsf{CCM}}^{\mathsf{muae,icm}}(\mathbf{A}) := \mathbf{Adv}_{\mathcal{O}_{\mathsf{real}}^{\mathsf{icm}}, \mathcal{O}_{\mathsf{ideal}}^{\mathsf{icm}}}^{\mathsf{dist}}(\mathbf{A}).$$

Queries to each user are called online queries. Queries to encryption oracles $\mathsf{CCM.Enc}[E_{K_\omega}]$ or $\$_\omega$ (resp. decryption oracles $\mathsf{CCM.Dec}[E_{K_\omega}]$ or $\perp_\omega$) are called encryption (resp. decryption) queries. In the IC model, Queries to an IC are called offline queries, and offline queries to E (resp. E^{-1}) are called forward (resp. inverse) queries.

We consider nonce-respecting adversaries where for each user, all nonces in encryption queries are distinct. Moreover, making a repeated or trivial decryption query is forbidden, where the trivial query $(N, A, C, \widetilde{T})$ is such that the query tuple was obtained by some previous encryption query to the same user.

4.4 Adversaries and Its Resources

In our proofs, we consider computationally-bounded and/or computationally-unbounded adversaries. Queries to encryption oracles $\mathsf{CCM.Enc}[E_{K_\omega}]$ or $\$_\omega$ (resp. decryption oracles $\mathsf{CCM.Dec}[E_{K_\omega}]$ or $\perp_\omega$) are called encryption (resp. decryption) queries. Let q_{e} be the number of encryption queries, q_{d} be the number of decryption queries, and σ be the number of BC invocations in online queries. and σ_ω the number of BC invocations in online queries to the ω-th user such that $\sum_{\omega \in [u]} \sigma_\omega = \sigma$. For computationally-bounded (resp. computationally-unbounded) adversaries, the time resources are expressed by its running time τ (resp. the number of offline queries to an IC denoted by p). Let σ_{u} be the maximum number of BC invocations per user, i.e., $\forall \omega \in [u] : \sigma_\omega \leq \sigma_{\mathsf{u}}$. Let $\mathcal{A}_{\mathsf{sm}}$ (resp. $\mathcal{A}_{\mathsf{icm}}$) be the set of all possible adversaries in the standard (resp. IC) model with the above resources.

4.5 Definitions for Proofs

In our proofs, we use the following notations and definitions.

- For $\alpha \in [p]$, let $(\hat{K}^{(\alpha)}, \hat{X}^{(\alpha)}, \hat{Y}^{(\alpha)})$ be the α-th offline query-response tuples such that $\hat{Y}^{(\alpha)} = E(\hat{K}^{(\alpha)}, \hat{X}^{(\alpha)})$.
- For $\omega \in [u]$ and $\alpha \in [q]$, ω is called "user index" and α is called "query index."
- For $\alpha \in [q]$, values corresponding with the α-th online query are denoted by using the superscript symbol of (α) such as $M^{(\alpha)}$, $C^{(\alpha)}$, $N^{(\alpha)}$, $A^{(\alpha)}$, etc. The lengths b and m for the α-th online query are denoted by b_α and m_α, respectively. Let $\mathsf{u}_\alpha \in [u]$ be the user index for the α-th online query. If an α-th online query is to an ω-th user, then $\mathsf{u}_\alpha = \omega$.
- Let $\mathcal{Q}_{\mathsf{Enc}} \subseteq [q]$ (resp. $\mathcal{Q}_{\mathsf{Dec}} \subseteq [q]$) be the set of encryption (resp. decryption) query indexes. Let $\mathcal{Q}^{[\omega]}_{\mathsf{Enc}} \subseteq \mathcal{Q}_{\mathsf{Enc}}$ (resp. $\mathcal{Q}^{[\omega]}_{\mathsf{Dec}} \subseteq \mathcal{Q}_{\mathsf{Dec}}$) be the set of encryption (resp. decryption) query indexes of the ω-th user. Let $\mathcal{Q}^{[\omega]} := \mathcal{Q}^{[\omega]}_{\mathsf{Enc}} \cup \mathcal{Q}^{[\omega]}_{\mathsf{Dec}}$ be the set of online query indexes of the ω-th user.
- For $\alpha \in [q]$, let $\mathsf{Index}^{(\alpha)} := (\{1\} \times [b_\alpha]) \cup (\{2\} \times [0, m_\alpha])$ be the set of indexes of input-output pairs in the α-th online query.
- Let $\mathcal{X}^{[\omega]} := \{X^{(\alpha)}_{i,j} \mid \alpha \in \mathcal{Q}^{[\omega]}, (i,j) \in \mathsf{Index}^{(\alpha)}\}$ be all input blocks for the ω-th user. Let $\mathcal{X}^{[\omega]}_{\mathsf{Enc}} := \{X^{(\alpha)}_{i,j} \mid \alpha \in \mathcal{Q}^{[\omega]}_{\mathsf{Enc}}, (i,j) \in \mathsf{Index}^{(\alpha)}\}$ be all input blocks for encryption queries to the ω-th user. Let $\mathcal{X}^{[\omega]}_2 := \{(X^{(\gamma)}_{2,j}, Y^{(\gamma)}_{2,j}) \mid \gamma \in \mathcal{Q}^{[\omega]}, j \in [0, m_\gamma]\}$ be all input-output pairs defined in CTR and the tag generation of the ω-th user. Let $\mathcal{X}^{[\omega]}_{\mathsf{N}} := \{X^{(\alpha)}_{1,1}, X^{(\alpha)}_{2,1}, \ldots, X^{(\alpha)}_{2,m_\alpha} \mid \alpha \in \mathcal{Q}^{[\omega]}\}$ be the set of nonce-dependent input blocks for the ω-th user. Let $\mathcal{X}^{[\omega]}_{\neq\mathsf{N}} := \{X^{(\alpha)}_{1,2}, \ldots, X^{(\alpha)}_{1,b_\alpha} \mid \alpha \in \mathcal{Q}^{[\omega]}\}$ be the set of nonce-independent input blocks for the ω-th user.
- Let $\mathcal{Y}^{[\omega]} := \{Y^{(\alpha)}_{i,j} \mid \alpha \in \mathcal{Q}^{[\omega]}, (i,j) \in \mathsf{Index}^{(\alpha)}\}$ be the set of output blocks for the ω-th user.
- We call "a query phase" a phase that an adversary makes queries to its oracles and "a decision phase" a phase after finishing all queries and before outputting a decision bit.

5 Mu-Security of CCM in the Standard Model

We give an mu-bound of CCM in the standard model and the security proof.

5.1 Security Bound

Theorem 1 (Mu-Security of CCM in the Standard Model). *$\forall \mathbf{A} \in \mathcal{A}_{\mathsf{sm}}$:*

$$\mathbf{Adv}^{\mathsf{muae,sm}}_{\mathsf{CCM}}(\mathbf{A}) \leq \mathbf{Adv}^{\mathsf{muprp}}_{E}(u, \sigma, \tau + O(\sigma)) + \left(\sum_{\omega \in [u]} \frac{\sigma_\omega^2}{2^n}\right) + \frac{q_{\mathsf{d}}}{2^t}.$$

With the parameters σ and σ_{u}, $\forall \mathbf{A} \in \mathcal{A}_{\mathsf{sm}}$:

$$\mathbf{Adv}^{\mathsf{muae,sm}}_{\mathsf{CCM}}(\mathbf{A}) \leq \mathbf{Adv}^{\mathsf{muprp}}_{E}(u, \sigma, \tau + O(\sigma)) + \frac{\sigma_{\mathsf{u}}\sigma}{2^n} + \frac{q_{\mathsf{d}}}{2^t}.$$

5.2 Proof of Theorem 1

Without loss of generality, assume that **A** is deterministic. Let σ_ω be the number of BC calls in online queries to the ω-th user, where $\sigma_\omega \leq \sigma_{\mathsf{u}}$. In this proof, we consider four games.

Real World → Game 2. We start the proof from the real world, followed by Game 2. In the real world, **A** has access to $\mathcal{O}_{\mathsf{real}}$. From the real world to Game 2, the u BCs $(E_{K_\omega})_{\omega\in[u]}$ are replaced with u RPs $(P_\omega)_{\omega\in[u]}$, where $\forall\omega \in [u] : P_\omega \xleftarrow{\$} \mathsf{Perm}(n)$. Hence, in Game 2, **A** has access to the modified oracles $\mathcal{O}_2 := (\mathsf{CCM}[P_\omega])_{\omega\in[u]}$. The BC-RP switch yields the following bound.

$$\mathbf{Adv}^{\mathsf{dist}}_{\mathcal{O}_{\mathsf{real}},\mathcal{O}_2}(\mathbf{A}) \leq \mathbf{Adv}^{\mathsf{muprp}}_{E}(\sigma, \tau + O(\sigma)).$$

Game 2 → Game 3. We next consider Game 3. Hereafter, we consider a computationally-unbounded adversary **A**. From Game 2 to Game 3, the RPs $(P_\omega)_{\omega\in[u]}$ are replaced with random functions (RFs) $(\mathcal{R}_\omega)_{\omega\in[u]}$, where $\forall\omega \in [u] : \mathcal{R}_\omega \xleftarrow{\$} \mathsf{Func}(n, n)$. Hence, in Game 3, **A** has access to the modified oracles $\mathcal{O}_3 := (\mathsf{CCM}[\mathcal{R}_\omega])_{\omega\in[u]}$. For each $\omega \in [u]$, a RF $\mathcal{R}_\omega$ is the same as a RP as long as no output collision occurs, and the collision probability is $\binom{\sigma_\omega}{2} \cdot \frac{1}{2^n} \leq \frac{0.5\sigma_\omega^2}{2^n}$. Hence, by the RP-RF switch, we have

$$\mathbf{Adv}^{\mathsf{dist}}_{\mathcal{O}_2,\mathcal{O}_3}(\mathbf{A}) \leq \sum_{\omega\in[u]} \frac{0.5\sigma_\omega}{2^n}.$$

Game 3 → Ideal World. Finally, we evaluate the difference between Game 3 and the ideal world. We derive the following bound.

Lemma 1. *For any computationally-unbounded adversary* **A**,

$$\mathbf{Adv}^{\mathsf{dist}}_{\mathcal{O}_3,\mathcal{O}_{\mathsf{ideal}}}(\mathbf{A}) \leq \frac{q_{\mathsf{d}}}{2^t} + \sum_{\omega\in[u]} \frac{0.5\sigma_\omega^2}{2^n},$$

where $\mathcal{O}_3 = (\mathsf{CCM}[\mathcal{R}_\omega])_{\omega\in[u]}$ *and* $\mathcal{O}_{\mathsf{ideal}} = (\$_\omega, \perp_\omega)_{\omega\in[u]}$.

Hereafter, we provide a high-level overview of the proof of Lemma 1, and the formal proof is given in the full version of this paper [22].

Proof of Lemma 1 (Overview). We first consider encryption queries in Game 3. For each user, all input blocks $X_{2,i}^{(\alpha)}$ in CTR are distinct, and the outputs $Y_{2,i}^{(\alpha)}$ are chosen independently and uniformly at random from $\{0,1\}^n$. Hence, the responses $(C^{(\alpha)}, T^{(\alpha)})$ to the encryption queries are indistinguishable from those defined by $\$_\omega$ in the ideal world.

The remaining work is to evaluate the difference of responses to decryption queries between Game 3 and the ideal world. In Game 3, for some response of the decryption query, a valid plaintext ($\neq$ **reject**) is probabilistically returned, and we have

$$\mathbf{Adv}^{\mathsf{dist}}_{\mathcal{O}_3,\mathcal{O}_{\mathsf{ideal}}}(\mathbf{A}) \leq \Pr[\exists\beta \in \mathcal{Q}_{\mathsf{Dec}} \text{ s.t. } T^{(\beta)} = \widetilde{T}^{(\beta)}].$$

We evaluate the probability by using the following event:

$$\mathsf{coll}_{X_{1,b}} \Leftrightarrow \exists\beta \in \mathcal{Q}_{\mathsf{Dec}} \text{ s.t. } X^{(\beta)}_{1,b_\beta} \in \mathcal{X}^{[\mathsf{u}_\beta]}_{\mathsf{Enc}}.$$

The event means that for some decryption query, the last input block in CBC collides with some input block defined by the encryption query. In other worlds, if the event does not occur, then all tags $T^{(\beta)}$ are defined independently of the responses of the encryption queries. Thus,

$$\Pr[\exists\beta \in \mathcal{Q}_{\mathsf{Dec}} \text{ s.t. } T^{(\beta)} = \widetilde{T}^{(\beta)} \mid \neg\mathsf{coll}_{X_{1,b}}] \leq \frac{q_{\mathsf{d}}}{2^t},$$

and

$$\begin{aligned}\mathbf{Adv}^{\mathsf{dist}}_{\mathcal{O}_3,\mathcal{O}_{\mathsf{ideal}}}(\mathbf{A}) &\leq \Pr[\exists\beta \in \mathcal{Q}_{\mathsf{Dec}} \text{ s.t. } T^{(\beta)} = \widetilde{T}^{(\beta)} \mid \neg\mathsf{coll}_{X_{1,b}}] + \Pr[\mathsf{coll}_{X_{1,b}}] \\ &\leq \frac{q_{\mathsf{d}}}{2^t} + \Pr[\mathsf{coll}_{X_{1,b}}].\end{aligned}$$

We evaluate the probability $\Pr[\mathsf{coll}_{X_{1,b}}]$. By the iterated structure of CBC and the property of add,[5] the event $\mathsf{coll}_{X_{1,b}}$ implies that there exists $\beta \in \mathcal{Q}_{\mathsf{Dec}}$, and $j \in [b_\beta]$ such that the j-th CBC input block is $X^{(\beta)}_{1,j} \in \mathcal{X}^{[\mathsf{u}_\beta]}_{\mathsf{Enc}}$ but the previous input block is $X^{(\beta)}_{1,j-1} \notin \mathcal{X}^{[\mathsf{u}_\beta]}_{\mathsf{Enc}}$. The j-th input block has the form of $X^{(\beta)}_{1,j} = B^{(\beta)}_j \oplus Y^{(\beta)}_{1,j-1}$ and $Y^{(\beta)}_{1,j-1}$ is chosen independently of all output blocks for the encryption queries. Using the randomness of $Y^{(\beta)}_{1,j-1}$, we have the following birthday bound:

$$\Pr[\mathsf{coll}_{X_{1,b}}] \leq \sum_{\omega\in[u]} \binom{\sigma_\omega}{2} \cdot \frac{1}{2^n} \leq \sum_{\omega\in[u]} \frac{0.5\sigma_\omega^2}{2^n}.$$

By using the above bounds, we obtain the bound in Lemma 1.

■ (Lemma 1 (Overview))

Conclusion of the Proof. By using these bounds, we have

$$\begin{aligned}\mathbf{Adv}^{\mathsf{muae,sm}}_{\mathsf{CCM}}(\mathbf{A}) &\leq \mathbf{Adv}^{\mathsf{dist}}_{\mathcal{O}_{\mathsf{real}},\mathcal{O}_2}(\mathbf{A}) + \mathbf{Adv}^{\mathsf{dist}}_{\mathcal{O}_2,\mathcal{O}_3}(\mathbf{A}) + \mathbf{Adv}^{\mathsf{dist}}_{\mathcal{O}_3,\mathcal{O}_{\mathsf{ideal}}}(\mathbf{A}) \\ &\leq \mathbf{Adv}^{\mathsf{muprp}}_{E}(u,\sigma,\tau+O(\sigma)) + \sum_{\omega\in[u]} \frac{0.5\sigma_\omega^2}{2^n} + \frac{q_{\mathsf{d}}}{2^t}.\end{aligned}$$

■ (Theorem 1)

[5] The property of add ensures that for each $\omega \in [u]$, $\alpha \in \mathcal{Q}^{[\omega]}_{\mathsf{Enc}}$, and $\beta \in \mathcal{Q}^{[\omega]}_{\mathsf{Dec}}$, the messages $B^{(\alpha)}$ and $B^{(\beta)}$ of CBC are distinct and the first input block $B^{(\beta)}_1$ is distinct from all input blocks in CTR, offering the condition $\exists\beta, j$ s.t. $(X^{(\beta)}_{1,j-1} \notin \mathcal{X}^{[\mathsf{u}_\beta]}_{\mathsf{Enc}}) \wedge (X^{(\beta)}_{1,j} \in \mathcal{X}^{[\mathsf{u}_\beta]}_{\mathsf{Enc}})$.

6 Mu-Security of CCM with NR

We evaluate the security of CCM with randomized nonce in the IC model. We use the d-bound model by Hoang and Tessaro [13], which is a generalization of the randomized nonce.

6.1 d-Bound Adversaries

In the d-bound model, the number of collisions of nonces in encryption queries across users is bounded by d. Note that there is no collision in nonces in encryption queries within the same user.

Definition 1 (d-bound model). *For $\omega \in [u]$, let $\mathcal{N}^{[\omega]}$ be the set of nonces in encryption queries to the ω-th user. A d-bound adversary is such that for any $N \in \{0,1\}^\nu$, $|\{\omega \in [u] \mid N \in \mathcal{N}^{[\omega]}\}| \leq d$.*

The parameter d can be small by using a random nonce: each original nonce N_{orig} is defined by incrementing 1, i.e., $N_{\text{orig}} \leftarrow N_{\text{orig}} + 1$ (initially $N_{\text{orig}} = 0^n$), and a randomized nonce N is defined as $N = N_{\text{orig}} \oplus R$ with the ν-bit original nonce N_{orig} and a user-specific random mask $R \in \{0,1\}^\nu$.

We study the bound d. We consider the following randomized nonce: each original nonce N_{orig} is defined by incrementing 1, i.e., $N_{\text{orig}} \leftarrow N_{\text{orig}}+1$ (initially $N_{\text{orig}} = 0^n$), and a randomized nonce N is defined as $N = N_{\text{orig}} \oplus R$ with the ν-bit original nonce N_{orig} and a user-specific random mask $R \in \{0,1\}^\nu$. Then, for each of d randomized nonces $N^{(\alpha_1)}, \ldots, N^{(\alpha_d)}$ such that the user indexes $\mathsf{u}_{\alpha_1}, \ldots, \mathsf{u}_{\alpha_d}$ are all distinct, we have $\Pr[N^{(\alpha_1)} = \ldots = N^{(\alpha_d)}] \leq \left(\frac{1}{2^\nu}\right)^{d-1}$. Using the bound with $d := \frac{\nu}{\log_2 \nu}$, we have

$$\begin{aligned}
\Pr[\exists \alpha_1, \ldots, \alpha_d \text{ s.t. } N^{(\alpha_1)} = \ldots = N^{(\alpha_d)}] &\leq \binom{q_{\mathsf{e}}}{d} \cdot \left(\frac{1}{2^\nu}\right)^{d-1} \\
&\leq 2^\nu \left(\frac{eq_{\mathsf{e}}}{d2^\nu}\right)^d = 2^\nu \left(\frac{eq_{\mathsf{e}}}{\frac{\nu}{\log_2 \nu} \cdot 2^\nu}\right)^{\frac{\nu}{\log_2 \nu}} \\
&\leq \left((2^\nu)^{\frac{\log_2 \nu}{\nu}} \cdot \frac{eq_{\mathsf{e}}}{\frac{\nu}{\log_2 \nu} \cdot 2^\nu}\right)^{\frac{\nu}{\log_2 \nu}} \\
&\leq \left(\frac{3(\log_2 \nu) q_{\mathsf{e}}}{2^\nu}\right)^{\frac{\nu}{\log_2 \nu}},
\end{aligned}$$

using Stirling's approximation ($d! \geq (d/e)^d$ for any d). We then consider for the common parameter for CCM: the nonce size is $\nu = 3n/4$ ($\nu = 96$ when using the AES parameter $n = 128$). In this case, $d = \frac{3n/4}{\log_2(3n/4)}$ and the bound of d can be ensured up to $q_{\mathsf{e}} \approx 2^{3n/4}$ encryption queries.

6.2 Security Bound

The mu-security bound of CCM with NR is given below.

Theorem 2 (Mu-Security of CCM with NR in the IC Model). $\forall \mathbf{A} \in \mathcal{A}_{\mathsf{icm}}$ *such that* $\mathbf{A}$ *is a d-bound adversary:*

$$\mathbf{Adv}^{\mathsf{muae,icm}}_{\mathsf{CCM}}(\mathbf{A}) \leq \frac{q_{\mathsf{d}}}{2^t} + \sum_{\omega \in [u]} \frac{\sigma_\omega^2}{2^n} + \frac{\left(d + \frac{n}{\log_2 n}\right)(p+\sigma)}{2^k} + \left(\frac{3(\log_2 n)\sigma}{2^n}\right)^{\frac{n}{\log_2 n}} + \frac{\sigma(p+\sigma)}{2^{k+n}}.$$

With the parameters σ *and* σ_{u}, $\forall \mathbf{A} \in \mathcal{A}_{\mathsf{icm}}$ *such that* $\mathbf{A}$ *is a d-bound adversary:*

$$\mathbf{Adv}^{\mathsf{muae,icm}}_{\mathsf{CCM}}(\mathbf{A}) \leq \frac{q_{\mathsf{d}}}{2^t} + \frac{\sigma_{\mathsf{u}}\sigma}{2^n} + \frac{\left(d + \frac{n}{\log_2 n}\right)(p+\sigma)}{2^k} + \left(\frac{3(\log_2 n)\sigma}{2^n}\right)^{\frac{n}{\log_2 n}} + \frac{\sigma(p+\sigma)}{2^{k+n}}.$$

Assume that $n \leq k$. The last three terms excluding p are of online security and become a constant if σ is about 2^n. On the other hand, the second term becomes a constant if σ is about $\frac{2^n}{\sigma_{\mathsf{u}}}$. Hence, the first two terms are dominant online terms. The last term excluding σ is of offline security and becomes a constant if $p = \frac{2^{k+n}}{\sigma}$. Since $\sigma \leq 2^n$, the third term excluding σ is a dominant offline term. Since d is about $\frac{n}{\log_2 n}$, dominant terms in the bound is $\frac{q_{\mathsf{d}}}{2^t} + \frac{\sigma_{\mathsf{u}}\sigma}{2^n} + \frac{dp}{2^k}$.

6.3 Proof of Theorem 2

Without loss of generality, we assume that $\mathbf{A}$ is deterministic. In this evaluation, we consider three games.

Real World $\rightarrow$ Game 2. We start the proof from the real world, followed by Game 2. In the real world, $\mathbf{A}$ has access to $\mathcal{O}_{\mathsf{real}}$. From the real world to Game 2, the u BCs $(E_{K_\omega})_{\omega \in [u]}$ are replaced with u RFs $(\mathcal{R}_\omega)_{\omega \in [u]}$. Hence, in Game 2, $\mathbf{A}$ has access to the modified oracles $\mathcal{O}_2 := ((\mathsf{CCM}[\mathcal{R}_\omega])_{\omega \in [u]}, E^{\pm})$, where $E \xleftarrow{\$} \mathcal{BC}$ and $\forall \omega \in [u] : \mathcal{R}_\omega \xleftarrow{\$} \mathsf{Func}(n, n)$. The following lemma shows an upper-bound of the difference between the real world and Game 2.

Lemma 2. *For any computationally-unbounded adversary* $\mathbf{A}$,

$$\mathbf{Adv}^{\mathsf{dist}}_{\mathcal{O}_{\mathsf{real}},\mathcal{O}_2}(\mathbf{A}) \leq \frac{\left(d + \frac{n}{\log_2 n}\right)(p+\sigma)}{2^k} + \frac{\sigma(p+\sigma)}{2^{k+n}} + \left(\frac{3(\log_2 n)\sigma}{2^n}\right)^{\frac{n}{\log_2 n}} + \sum_{\omega \in [u]} \frac{0.5\sigma_\omega^2}{2^n},$$

where $\mathcal{O}_{\mathsf{real}} = ((\mathsf{CCM}[E_{K_\omega}])_{\omega \in [u]}, E^{\pm})$ *and* $\mathcal{O}_2 = ((\mathsf{CCM}[\mathcal{R}_\omega])_{\omega \in [u]}, E^{\pm})$.

Hereafter, we provide a high-level overview of the proof, and the formal proof is given in the full version of this paper [22].

Proof of Lemma 2 (Overview). From the real world to Game 2, the underlying primitives are replaced from an IC E (with independent keys) to independent RFs $(\mathcal{R}_\omega)_{\omega\in[u]}$. We thus define the following three events that are taken into account the difference.

EVENT $\mathsf{coll}_{\mathsf{on},\neq\mathsf{u}}$. We first define the following event:

$$\mathsf{coll}_{\mathsf{on},\neq\mathsf{u}} \Leftrightarrow \exists\omega_1,\omega_2 \in [u] \text{ s.t. } \omega_1 \neq \omega_2 \wedge K^{[\omega_1]} = K^{[\omega_2]} \wedge (\mathcal{X}^{[\omega_1]} \cap \mathcal{X}^{[\omega_2]} \neq \emptyset \vee \mathcal{Y}^{[\omega_1]} \cap \mathcal{Y}^{[\omega_2]} \neq \emptyset),$$

which considers a collision of pairs of key and input/output block between distinct users. If it does not occur in the real world, for each user, the underlying primitive can be independent of those of the other users as Game 2. $\mathcal{X}^{[\omega_1]}\cap\mathcal{X}^{[\omega_2]} \neq \emptyset$ is the condition on the input-block collision and $\mathcal{Y}^{[\omega_1]}\cap\mathcal{Y}^{[\omega_2]} \neq \emptyset$ is the one on the output-block collision.

We consider the collisions $K^{[\omega_1]} = K^{[\omega_2]} \wedge \mathcal{X}^{[\omega_1]} \cap \mathcal{X}^{[\omega_2]} \neq \emptyset$.

- If $\mathcal{X}_{\mathsf{N}}^{[\omega_1]} \cap \mathcal{X}_{\mathsf{N}}^{[\omega_2]} \neq \emptyset$, i.e., a collision occurs in nonce-dependent input blocks, then a collision of nonces between distinct users occurs. In the d-bound model, for each nonce $N^{(\alpha)}$ of the ω_1-th user, the number of the other different users with the same nonce is at most d. Hence, for each pair of key and nonce, the probability that the pair collides with one of the pairs of the other different users is at most $\frac{d}{2^k}$. Thus, we have

$$\Pr[K^{[\omega_1]} = K^{[\omega_2]} \wedge \mathcal{X}_{\mathsf{N}}^{[\omega_1]} \cap \mathcal{X}_{\mathsf{N}}^{[\omega_2]} \neq \emptyset] \leq \sum_{\alpha\in[q]} \frac{d}{2^k} = \frac{dq}{2^k}.$$

- If $\mathcal{X}_{\neq\mathsf{N}}^{[\omega_1]} \cap \mathcal{X}^{[\omega_2]} \neq \emptyset$, i.e., a collision with nonce-independent input blocks occurs, then each input block $X_{1,j}^{(\alpha)} \in \mathcal{X}_{\neq\mathsf{N}}^{[\omega_1]}$ is defined as $X_{1,j}^{(\alpha)} = B_{1,j}^{(\alpha)} \oplus Y_{1,j-1}^{(\alpha)}$ where $Y_{1,j-1}^{(\alpha)}$ is an n-bit random value. Hence, we can use the n-bit randomness, providing the bound

$$\Pr[K^{[\omega_1]} = K^{[\omega_2]} \wedge \mathcal{X}_{\neq\mathsf{N}}^{[\omega_1]} \cap \mathcal{X}^{[\omega_2]} \neq \emptyset] \leq \binom{\sigma}{2} \cdot \frac{1}{2^{k+n}} \leq \frac{\sigma^2}{2^{k+n}}.$$

We next consider the collisions $K^{[\omega_1]} = K^{[\omega_2]} \wedge \mathcal{Y}^{[\omega_1]} \cap \mathcal{Y}^{[\omega_2]} \neq \emptyset$. The evaluation is the same as the one for the collisions $K^{[\omega_1]} = K^{[\omega_2]} \wedge \mathcal{X}_{\mathsf{N}}^{[\omega_1]} \cap \mathcal{X}_{\mathsf{N}}^{[\omega_2]} \neq \emptyset$. In this case, instead of the multi-collision bound d for input blocks, we use a multi-collision event for output blocks $\cup_{\omega\in[u]}\mathcal{Y}^{[\omega]}$. By using the randomness of the output blocks, the probability that $(\frac{n}{\log_2 n})$-multi-collision occurs in the output blocks can be bounded by $(\frac{3(\log_2 n)\sigma}{2^n})^{\frac{n}{\log_2 n}}$. Assuming that the multi-collision does not occur, by the same evaluation (but d is replaced with the bound $\frac{n}{\log_2 n}$), we have

$$\Pr[K^{[\omega_1]} = K^{[\omega_2]} \wedge \mathcal{Y}^{[\omega_1]} \cap \mathcal{Y}^{[\omega_2]} \neq \emptyset] \leq \frac{\frac{n}{\log_2 n} \cdot \sigma}{2^k}.$$

Summing these bounds, we have the following bound:

$$\Pr[\mathsf{coll}_{\mathsf{on},\neq\mathsf{u}}] \leq \frac{\left(d + \frac{n}{\log_2 n}\right)\sigma}{2^k} + \left(\frac{3(\log_2 n)\sigma}{2^n}\right)^{\frac{n}{\log_2 n}} + \frac{\sigma^2}{2^{k+n}}.$$

Event $\mathsf{coll}_{\mathsf{on},\mathsf{off}}$. In Game 2, the underlying primitives $(\mathcal{R}_\omega)_{\omega\in[u]}$ are independent of $E^{\pm}$. On the other hand, in the real world, all underlying primitives are E (with independent keys). We thus define the following event for the difference:

$$\mathsf{coll}_{\mathsf{on},\mathsf{off}} \Leftrightarrow \alpha \in [q], (i,j) \in \mathsf{Index}^{(\alpha)}, \beta \in [p] \text{ s.t.}$$
$$K^{[\mathsf{u}_\alpha]} = \hat{K}^{(\beta)} \wedge (X_{i,j}^{(\alpha)} = \hat{X}^{(\beta)} \vee Y_{i,j}^{(\alpha)} = \hat{Y}^{(\beta)}).$$

The event considers a collision of pairs of key and input/output block between online and offline queries. If it does not occur, outputs of user's primitives can be independent of offline query-response tuples. The evaluation is similar to the evaluation for the event $\mathsf{coll}_{\mathsf{on},\neq\mathsf{u}}$. By using the d-bound model for the input-block collision and the $(\frac{n}{\log_2 n})$-multi-collision event for the output-block collision, we can obtain

$$\Pr[\mathsf{coll}_{\mathsf{on},\mathsf{off}}] \leq \frac{\left(d + \frac{n}{\log_2 n}\right)p}{2^k} + \frac{\sigma p}{2^{k+n}}.$$

Event $\mathsf{coll}_{\mathsf{on},=\mathsf{u}}$. In Game 2, for each $\omega \in [u]$, each output of the underlying primitive $\mathcal{R}_\omega$ is chosen with replacement. On the other hand, in the real world, all underlying primitives are E (with independent keys) and for each $\omega \in [u]$, each output of the underlying primitive is chosen without replacement. We thus define the following event for the RP-RF difference:

$$\mathsf{coll}_{\mathsf{on},=\mathsf{u}} \Leftrightarrow \exists\omega \in [u], X_{i_1,j_1}^{(\alpha_1)}, X_{i_2,j_2}^{(\alpha_2)} \in \mathcal{X}^{[\omega]} \text{ s.t.}$$
$$X_{i_1,j_1}^{(\alpha_1)} \neq X_{i_2,j_2}^{(\alpha_2)} \wedge Y_{i_1,j_1}^{(\alpha_1)} = Y_{i_2,j_2}^{(\alpha_2)},$$

where $Y_{i_1,j_1}^{(\alpha_1)}$ and $Y_{i_2,j_2}^{(\alpha_2)}$ are independently chosen. By the birthday analysis, we have

$$\Pr[\mathsf{coll}_{\mathsf{on},=\mathsf{u}}] \leq \sum_{\omega\in[u]} \binom{\sigma_\omega}{2} \cdot \frac{1}{2^n} \leq \sum_{\omega\subset[u]} \frac{0.5\sigma_\omega^2}{2^n}.$$

Deriving the Bound in Lemma 2. These events cover the differences from the replacements of the underlying primitives from $(E_{K_\omega})_{\omega\in[u]}$ to $(\mathcal{R}_\omega)_{\omega\in[u]}$, thus by the above bounds,

$$\begin{aligned}\mathbf{Adv}^{\mathsf{dist}}_{\mathcal{O}_{\mathsf{real}},\mathcal{O}_2}(\mathbf{A}) &\leq \Pr[\mathsf{coll}_{\mathsf{on},\neq\mathsf{u}}] + \Pr[\mathsf{coll}_{\mathsf{on},\mathsf{off}}] + \Pr[\mathsf{coll}_{\mathsf{on},=\mathsf{u}}]\\ &\leq \frac{\left(d + \frac{n}{\log_2 n}\right)(p+\sigma)}{2^k} + \frac{\sigma(p+\sigma)}{2^{k+n}}\\ &\quad + \left(\frac{3(\log_2 n)\sigma}{2^n}\right)^{\frac{n}{\log_2 n}} + \sum_{\omega\in[u]} \frac{0.5\sigma_\omega^2}{2^n}.\end{aligned}$$

■ (Lemma 2 (Overview))

Game 2 → Ideal World. For the difference between Game 2 and the ideal world, we use Lemma 1 in the proof of Theorem 1. In Lemma 1, an IC is absent, whereas in this evaluation, an IC is available. However, the responses of online queries are independent of the IC, thus an adversary can simulate an IC. Hence, the difference between Game 2 and the ideal world can be bounded by the bound in Lemma 1, and we have

$$\mathbf{Adv}^{\mathsf{dist}}_{\mathcal{O}_2,\mathcal{O}_{\mathsf{ideal}}}(\mathbf{A}) \leq \left(\sum_{\omega \in [u]} \frac{0.5\sigma_\omega^2}{2^n} \right) + \frac{q_{\mathsf{d}}}{2^t}.$$

Conclusion of the Proof. Using the above bounds, we have

$$\begin{aligned}\mathbf{Adv}^{\mathsf{muae,icm}}_{\mathsf{CCM}}(\mathbf{A}) &\leq \mathbf{Adv}^{\mathsf{dist}}_{\mathcal{O}_{\mathsf{real}},\mathcal{O}_2}(\mathbf{A}) + \mathbf{Adv}^{\mathsf{dist}}_{\mathcal{O}_2,\mathcal{O}_{\mathsf{ideal}}}(\mathbf{A}) \\ &\leq \frac{q_{\mathsf{d}}}{2^t} + \sum_{\omega \in [u]} \frac{\sigma_\omega^2}{2^n} + \frac{\left(d + \frac{n}{\log_2 n}\right)(p+\sigma)}{2^k} \\ &\quad + \left(\frac{3(\log_2 n)\sigma}{2^n}\right)^{\frac{n}{\log_2 n}} + \frac{\sigma(p+\sigma)}{2^{k+n}}.\end{aligned}$$

■ (Theorem 2)

7 Mu-Security of CCM with NKD

In this section, we consider the mu-security of CCM_NKD, CCM with the nonce-based key derivation NKD, following the previous application to GCM [11]. Compared to CCM with NR, CCM_NKD replaces the dominant term $\frac{\sigma_{\mathsf{u}}\sigma}{2^n}$ to $\frac{\sigma_{\mathsf{n}}\sigma}{2^n}$, wherein σ_{n} is the maximum number of BC invocations within the same nonce and user's key, thus its online security becomes independent of σ_{u}.

7.1 Specification of CCM_NKD

Let $\mathsf{F}_K : \{0,1\}^\nu \to \{0,1\}^k$ be a KDF with a κ-bit key K that accepts a nonce and returns a nonce-based key of CCM. The encryption and decryption algorithms of CCM_NKD are defined in the following.

- For an input tuple $(N, A, M) \in \{0,1\}^\nu \times \mathcal{A} \times \mathcal{M}$, the encryption is defined as

$$\mathsf{CCM\_NKD.Enc}[E, \mathsf{F}_K](N, A, M) := \mathsf{CCM.Enc}[E_{\mathsf{F}_K(N)}](N, A, M).$$

- For an input tuple $(N, A, C, \widetilde{T}) \in \{0,1\}^\nu \times \mathcal{A} \times \mathcal{M} \times \{0,1\}^t$, the decryption is defined as

$$\mathsf{CCM\_NKD.Dec}[E, \mathsf{F}_K](N, A, C, \widetilde{T}) := \mathsf{CCM.Dec}[E_{\mathsf{F}_K(N)}](N, A, C, \widetilde{T}).$$

7.2 Multi-user PRF Security

In our proof, we assume that the KDF is mu-pseudorandom function (mu-PRF) secure. Let u be the number of users. In the mu-PRF-security game, an adversary **A** has access to either real-world oracles $(\mathsf{F}_{K_1}, \ldots, \mathsf{F}_{K_u})$ or ideal-world ones $(\mathcal{R}_1, \ldots, \mathcal{R}_u)$, where K_i is the i-th user's key defined as $K_i \xleftarrow{\$} \{0,1\}^\kappa$ and $\mathcal{R}_i$ is a random function of the i-th user defined as $\mathcal{R}_i \xleftarrow{\$} \mathsf{Func}(\nu, k)$. At the end of this game, **A** return a decision bit. Then, the mu-PRF-security advantage function of **A** is defined as

$$\mathbf{Adv}_{\mathsf{F}}^{\mathsf{muprf}}(\mathbf{A}) := \mathbf{Adv}^{\mathsf{dist}}_{(\mathsf{F}_{K_\omega})_{\omega\in[u]},(\mathcal{R}_\omega)_{\omega\in[u]}}(\mathbf{A}).$$

For all possible adversaries **A** that have access to u users, make at most q queries, and run in time τ, the maximum advantage is defined as

$$\mathbf{Adv}_{\mathsf{F}}^{\mathsf{muprf}}(u, q, \tau) := \max_{\mathbf{A}} \mathbf{Adv}_{\mathsf{F}}^{\mathsf{muprf}}(\mathbf{A}).$$

7.3 Mu-Security of CCM_NKD

For each nonce, the KDF in CCM_NKD provides a fresh key of CCM under the assumption that F_K is a secure PRF. Hence, in the mu-setting, there are at most q keys of CCM via the KDF in CCM_NKD. By using the bounds in Theorems 1 and 2, we obtain the following bounds of the mu-AE security of CCM_NKD. Let σ_{n} be the maximum number of BC invocations whose keys are defined by CCM_NKD with the same nonce and user's key.

Corollary 1 (Mu-Security of CCM_NKD in the Standard Model). *For any computationally-bounded adversary* **A**,

$$\mathbf{Adv}_{\mathsf{CCM\_NKD}}^{\mathsf{muae,sm}}(\mathbf{A}) \leq \frac{\sigma_{\mathsf{n}}\sigma}{2^n} + \frac{q_{\mathsf{d}}}{2^t} + \mathbf{Adv}_{\mathsf{F}}^{\mathsf{muprf}}(u, q, \tau + O(\sigma)) + \mathbf{Adv}_{E}^{\mathsf{muprp}}(q, \sigma, \tau + O(\sigma)).$$

Corollary 2 (Mu-Security of CCM_NKD in the d-bound and IC Models). *For any computationally-bounded adversary* **A**,

$$\mathbf{Adv}_{\mathsf{CCM\_NKD}}^{\mathsf{muae,icm}}(\mathbf{A}) \leq \mathbf{Adv}_{\mathsf{F}}^{\mathsf{muprf}}(u, q, \tau + O(\sigma)) + \frac{q_{\mathsf{d}}}{2^t} + \frac{\sigma_{\mathsf{n}}\sigma}{2^n} + \frac{\left(d + \frac{n}{\log_2 n}\right)(p+\sigma)}{2^k} + \left(\frac{3(\log_2 n)\sigma}{2^n}\right)^{\frac{n}{\log_2 n}} + \frac{\sigma(p+\sigma)}{2^{k+n}}.$$

With a discussion similar to Sect. 6, dominant terms in the bounds are $\frac{q_{\mathsf{d}}}{2^t} + \frac{\sigma_{\mathsf{n}}\sigma}{2^n} + \frac{dp}{2^k}$.

7.4 Choices for PRF

As mentioned in [5,11,21], the concatenation of truncated BCs and CENC [16] are nice choices for the KDF in CCM_NKD. Particularly, when implementing AES with AES-NI, the KDF can be efficiently performed.

8 Authenticated Encryption with NTKD

We present an AE mode AE_NTKD that enhances the mu-security of tag-based and BC-based AE schemes including CCM and GCM by respecting its interfaces. AE_NTKD equips a nonce- and tag-based key derivation NTKD.

8.1 Parameters of AE_NTKD

Let κ, ν, and t be lengths of keys, nonce, and tags of AE_NTKD such that $t \leq n$. In AE_NTKD, AD and a plaintext/ciphertext are divided into data blocks called *sectors*. Each sector is processed by using the underlying AE. Let s be the length of each sector.

8.2 The Underlying AE of AE_NTKD

Let AE be a tag-based AE scheme that is a pair of encryption and decryption algorithms $(\mathsf{AE.Enc}, \mathsf{AE.Dec})$. Let $\mathcal{K}$, $\mathcal{N}$, $\mathcal{A}$, $\mathcal{M}$, $\mathcal{C}$, and $\mathcal{T}$ be the sets of keys, nonce, AD, plaintexts, ciphertexts, and tags of AE, respectively. We define the set of tags as $\mathcal{T} := \{0,1\}^t$.

- The encryption algorithm $\mathsf{AE.Enc} : \mathcal{K} \times \mathcal{N} \times \mathcal{A} \times \mathcal{M} \rightarrow \mathcal{C} \times \mathcal{T}$ takes (K, N, A, M), and returns, deterministically, a pair (C, T).
- The decryption algorithm $\mathsf{AE.Dec} : \mathcal{K} \times \mathcal{N} \times \mathcal{A} \times \mathcal{C} \times \mathcal{T} \rightarrow \{\mathbf{reject}\} \cup \mathcal{M}$ takes a tuple $(K, N, A, C, \widetilde{T})$ and returns, deterministically, either the distinguished invalid symbol $\mathbf{reject} \notin \mathcal{M}$ or a plaintext $M \in \mathcal{M}$.

We require that

$$\begin{aligned} &\forall (K, N, A, M), (K', N', A', M') \text{ s.t.} \\ &\qquad |M| = |M'| : |\mathsf{AE.Enc}(K, A, M)| = |\mathsf{AE.Enc}(K', A', M')|, \\ &\forall K, N, A, M : \mathsf{AE.Dec}(K, A, \mathsf{AE.Enc}(K, N, A, M)) = M. \end{aligned}$$

$\mathsf{AE.Enc}$ and $\mathsf{AE.Dec}$ with a key $K \in \mathcal{K}$ are denoted by $\mathsf{AE.Enc}_K$ and $\mathsf{AE.Dec}_K$. Let $\mathsf{AE}_K := (\mathsf{AE.Enc}_K, \mathsf{AE.Dec}_K)$.

We extract a tag generation function and a core function of AE.Dec. Let $\mathsf{TagGen} : \mathcal{K} \times \mathcal{N} \times \mathcal{A} \times \mathcal{C} \rightarrow \mathcal{T}$ be the tag generation function such that for any $(K, N, A, M) \in \mathcal{K} \times \mathcal{N} \times \mathcal{A} \times \mathcal{M}$, $(C, \mathsf{TagGen}(K, N, A, C)) = \mathsf{AE.Enc}(K, N, A, M)$ holds. TagGen with a key K is denoted by TagGen_K. Let $\mathsf{AE.Dec}^* : \mathcal{K} \times \mathcal{N} \times \mathcal{A} \times \mathcal{C} \times \mathcal{T} \rightarrow \mathcal{M} \times \mathcal{T}$ be the core function of AE.Dec that produces an unverified plaintext M and a tag T, i.e., for an input $(K, N, A, C, \widetilde{T}) \in \mathcal{K} \times \mathcal{N} \times \mathcal{A} \times \mathcal{C} \times \mathcal{T}$ to AE.Dec, the output is defined as follows: $(M, T) \leftarrow \mathsf{AE.Dec}^*(K, N, A, C)$ and the output is M if $T = \widetilde{T}$; **reject** otherwise.

8.3 The Underlying KDF of AE_NTKD

Let $\mathsf{F} : \{0,1\}^\kappa \times \{0,1\}^\nu \times \{0,1\}^t \rightarrow \mathcal{K} \times \mathcal{N}$ be the KDF that takes a κ-bit key, nonce, and tag, and based on nonce and a tag, returns a pair of key and IV. F with a key K is denoted by F_K. For $(K, N, T) \in \{0,1\}^\kappa \times \{0,1\}^\nu \times \{0,1\}^t$, let $\mathsf{F}^1_K(N, T) := \hat{K}$ and $\mathsf{F}^2_K(N, T) := \hat{N}$ such that $\mathsf{F}_K(N, T) = (\hat{K}, \hat{N})$.

Algorithm 4 AE_NTKD

Encryption AE_NTKD.Enc(K, N, A, M)

$T_0 \leftarrow 0^t$; $\hat{N} \leftarrow \mathsf{F}^2_K(N, 0^t)$; $A_1, \ldots, A_a \overset{s}{\leftarrow} A$; $M_1, \ldots, M_m \overset{s}{\leftarrow} M$
for $i \in [a+m]$ **do**
  $\hat{K}_i \leftarrow \mathsf{F}^1_K(N, T_{i-1})$; $\hat{N}_i \leftarrow \mathsf{add}_{\mathsf{ntk}}(\hat{N}, i)$
  if $i \le a$ **then** $(C_i, T_i) \leftarrow \mathsf{AE.Enc}(\hat{K}_i, \hat{N}_i, A_i, \varepsilon)$
    else $(C_{i-a}, T_i) \leftarrow \mathsf{AE.Enc}(\hat{K}_i, \hat{N}_i, \varepsilon, M_{i-a})$ **end if**
end for
$C \leftarrow C_1 \| \cdots \| C_m$; $T \leftarrow T_{a+m}$; **return** (C, T)

Decryption AE_NTKD.Dec$(K, N, A, C, \widetilde{T})$

$T_0 \leftarrow 0^t$; $\hat{N} \leftarrow \mathsf{F}^2_K(N, 0^t)$; $A_1, \ldots, A_a \overset{s}{\leftarrow} A$; $C_1, \ldots, C_m \overset{sn}{\longleftarrow} C$
for $i \in [a+m]$ **do**
  $\hat{K}_i \leftarrow \mathsf{F}^1_K(N, T_{i-1})$; $\hat{N}_i \leftarrow \mathsf{add}_{\mathsf{ntk}}(\hat{N}, i)$
  if $i \le a$ **then** $(M_i, T_i) \leftarrow \mathsf{AE.Enc}(\hat{K}_i, \hat{N}_i, A_i, \varepsilon)$
    else $(M_{i-a}, T_i) \leftarrow \mathsf{AE.Dec}^*(\hat{K}_i, \hat{N}_i, \varepsilon, C_{i-a})$ **end if**
end for
$M \leftarrow M_1 \| \cdots \| M_m$; $T \leftarrow T_{a+m}$
if $T = \widetilde{T}$ **then return** M **else return reject end if**

8.4 Specification of AE_NTKD

The specification is given in Algorithm 4 and Fig. 1. For l_{max} which is a maximum number of sectors in AD or a plaintext, let $\mathsf{add}_{\mathsf{ntk}} : \{0,1\}^\nu \times [l_{\mathsf{max}}] \to \mathcal{N}$ be a nonce-updating function that takes nonce $\hat{N}$ and a counter i, and returns nonce of the underlying AE such that $\forall \hat{N} \in \{0,1\}^\nu, i, j \in [l_{\mathsf{max}}]$ s.t. $i \ne j$: $\mathsf{add}_{\mathsf{ntk}}(\hat{N}, i) \ne \mathsf{add}_{\mathsf{ntk}}(\hat{N}, j)$. Note that in Fig. 1, $\mathsf{add}_{\mathsf{ntk}}(\hat{N}, i) = \hat{N} + (i-1)$.

AE_NTKD.Enc$_K$: $\{0,1\}^\nu \times \{0,1\}^* \times \{0,1\}^* \to \{0,1\}^* \times \{0,1\}^t$ is the encryption algorithm with a key $K \in \{0,1\}^\kappa$ that takes a tuple of nonce, AD, and a plaintext, and returns a pair of a ciphertext and a tag. In AE_NTKD.Enc, AD and plaintext are respectively divided into sectors of s bits $A_1, \ldots, A_a$ and $M_1, \ldots, M_m$. Note that if $A = \varepsilon$, then $a = 0$. First, a nonce-based key $\hat{K}_1$ and a nonce-based IV $\hat{N}$ are defined by using the KDF F_K. Then, by iterating AE.Enc and F_K, AD sectors are processed, followed by the process of plaintext sectors. The KDF takes nonce N and a tag of the previous AE.Enc call, and returns a key of the next AE.Enc call.

AE_NTKD.Dec$_K$: $\{0,1\}^\nu \times \{0,1\}^* \times \{0,1\}^* \times \{0,1\}^t \to \{0,1\}^* \times \{0,1\}^t$ is the decryption algorithm with a key $K \in \{0,1\}^\kappa$ that takes a tuple of nonce, AD, a ciphertext, and a tag, and returns a valid plaintext if the inputs are authenticated; the reject symbol **reject** otherwise. In AE_NTKD.Dec$_K$, AD and a ciphertext are respectively divided into sectors $A_1, \ldots, A_a$ and $C_1, \ldots, C_m$. Then, similarly to AE_NTKD.Enc$_K$, the AD sector blocks are processed by iterating AE.Enc and F_K, and then the ciphertext sector blocks are processed by iterating AE.Dec* (instead of AE.Enc) and F_K.

8.5 Security Definition for AE_NTKD

We consider the mu-AE security of AE_NTKD in the IC model. Let u be the number of users. We use the security definition in Sect. 4 with the real-world oracles $\mathcal{O}_{\mathsf{real}} := ((\mathsf{AE\_NTKD}_{K^{[\omega]}})_{\omega \in [u]}, E^{\pm})$ and the ideal-world oracles $\mathcal{O}_{\mathsf{ideal}} := ((\$_{\omega}, \perp_{\omega})_{\omega \in [u]}, E^{\pm})$, where $\forall \omega \in [u] : K^{[\omega]} \xleftarrow{\$} \{0,1\}^{\kappa}$ and $E^{\pm}$ is an IC. The advantage function of an adversary $\mathbf{A}$ is defined as

$$\mathbf{Adv}^{\mathsf{muae}}_{\mathsf{AE\_NTKD}}(\mathbf{A}) := \mathbf{Adv}^{\mathsf{dist}}_{\mathcal{O}_{\mathsf{real}}, \mathcal{O}_{\mathsf{ideal}}}(\mathbf{A}).$$

Let p (resp. σ) be the number of offline queries (resp. BC calls of AE_NTKD in online queries). Let q_{d} be the number of decryption queries. Let $\mathcal{A}$ be the set of all possible nonce-respecting computationally-unbounded adversaries with the resources.

8.6 Assumption

Regarding the KDF, we assume that F is mu-PRF secure. The definition of mu-PRF security is given in Sect. 7.

Regarding the underlying AE, we assume that AE is mu-AE secure in the IC model. Let u_1 be the number of users. We use the security definition given in Sect. 4. In this case, we consider the following real-world and ideal-world oracles:

$$\mathcal{O}_{\mathsf{real}} := ((\mathsf{AE}_{K^{[w]}})_{w \in [u_1]}, E^{\pm}), \qquad \mathcal{O}_{\mathsf{ideal}} := ((\$_{\omega}, \perp_{\omega})_{\omega \in [u_1]}, E^{\pm}),$$

where $\forall w \in [u_1] : K^{[w]} \xleftarrow{\$} \mathcal{K}$ and $E^{\pm}$ is an IC. Then, the advantage function of an adversary $\mathbf{B}$ is defined as

$$\mathbf{Adv}^{\mathsf{muae}}_{\mathsf{AE}}(\mathbf{B}) := \mathbf{Adv}^{\mathsf{dist}}_{\mathcal{O}_{\mathsf{real}}, \mathcal{O}_{\mathsf{ideal}}}(\mathbf{B}).$$

Let ℓ_1 be the maximum number of primitive calls of AE per online query. Let $q_{\mathsf{d},1}$ be the number of decryption queries. Let σ_1 be the number of primitive calls of AE in all queries made by $\mathbf{B}$. Let p_1 be the number of offline queries. Let $\mathcal{Q}_1 := (u_1, \sigma_1, q_{\mathsf{d},1}, \ell_1, p_1)$ be the query resources of adversaries. Then, for all possible computationally-unbounded adversaries with the resource $\mathcal{Q}_1$, the maximum of the advantage function is denoted by

$$\mathbf{Adv}^{\mathsf{muae}}_{\mathsf{AE}}(\mathcal{Q}_1) := \max_{\mathbf{B}} \mathbf{Adv}^{\mathsf{muae}}_{\mathsf{AE}}(\mathbf{B}).$$

In addition to the mu-AE assumption, we assume that TagGen is regular and almost universal. The definitions are given below.

Definition 2 (Regular and Almost Universal (AU)). *For an input tuple $\mathcal{D}$ to TagGen_K, let $N_{\mathcal{D}}$ be the number of primitive calls (such as BC calls and n-bit field multiplications) of $\mathsf{TagGen}_K(\mathcal{D})$. Let δ be a function that takes the number of primitive calls of TagGen_K with $\mathcal{D}_1$ and returns a probability for regular and AU.* TagGen *is said to be δ-regular if for any $Y \in \{0,1\}^t$ and any input tuple $\mathcal{D}$,*

$$\Pr[K \xleftarrow{\$} \mathcal{K}; \mathsf{TagGen}_K(\mathcal{D}) = Y] \leq \delta(N_{\mathcal{D}}, 0).$$

TagGen *is said to be δ-AU if for any distinct tuples $\mathcal{D}_1, \mathcal{D}_2$,*

$$\Pr[K \xleftarrow{\$} \mathcal{K}; \mathsf{TagGen}_K(\mathcal{D}_1) = \mathsf{TagGen}_K(\mathcal{D}_2)] \leq \delta(N_{\mathcal{D}_1}, N_{\mathcal{D}_2}).$$

8.7 mu-AE Security of AE_NTKD

The following theorem shows the mu-AE-security bound of AE_NTKD with the assumptions that F is mu-PRF secure, AE is mu-AE secure, and TagGen is regular and AU.

Theorem 3. *Let b_s be the maximum number of BC calls in* AE.Enc *with a pair of s-bit AD and the empty plaintext or a pair of empty AD and an s-bit plaintext. Let* TagGen *be δ-regular and δ-AU such that for the numbers of primitive calls N_1, N_2 and a positive integer c, $\delta(N_1, N_2) = \frac{c(N_1+N_2)}{2^t}$. Then, $\forall \mathbf{A} \in \mathcal{A}$:*

$$\mathbf{Adv}^{\mathsf{muae}}_{\mathsf{AE\_NTKD}}(\mathbf{A}) \leq \mathbf{Adv}^{\mathsf{muprf}}_{\mathsf{F}}(u, \sigma, \tau + O(\sigma)) + \frac{c\sigma_{\mathsf{n}}\sigma}{b_s 2^t} + \mathbf{Adv}^{\mathsf{muae}}_{\mathsf{AE}}(\mathcal{Q}_1),$$

where $\mathcal{Q}_1$ $(= (u_1, \sigma_1, q_{\mathsf{d},1}, \ell_1, p_1)) = (\lfloor \sigma/b_s \rfloor + q, \sigma, q_{\mathsf{d}}, b_s, p)$.

Intuitively, assuming that F is mu-PRF secure and no collision occurs on the tags, we can ensure that each AE call has a fresh random key. Thus, the mu-AE security of AE_NTKD can be reduced to that of AE. The term $\frac{c\sigma_{\mathsf{n}}\sigma}{b_s 2^t}$ is the probability of the tag collision. The proof is given in Sect. 8.9.

8.8 Applications to CCM and GCM

We first consider AE_NTKD with CCM in the IC model, i.e., AE = CCM. Note that the parameter c of CCM is a constant [1]. Assume that $\mathbf{Adv}^{\mathsf{muprf}}_{\mathsf{F}}(u, \sigma, \tau + O(\sigma))$ is negligible compared with the other terms, which can be realized by using highly secure KDFs, such as BC-based PRFs [5,6,11,21] and SHA-2/3-based KDFs [24,25].

We evaluate the term $\mathbf{Adv}^{\mathsf{muae}}_{\mathsf{CCM}}(\mathcal{Q}_1)$ with Theorem 2. Let $\mathbf{B}$ be an adversary with the resource $\mathcal{Q}_1$. Let v be the maximum number of decryption queries per user. For $w \in [u_1]$, let σ_w be the number of BC calls in queries to the w-th user. Hence, $\sigma = \sum_{w \in [u_1]} \sigma_w$. By Theorem 2, for any adversary $\mathbf{B}$, we have

$$\mathbf{Adv}^{\mathsf{muae,icm}}_{\mathsf{CCM}}(\mathbf{B}) \leq \frac{q_{\mathsf{d}}}{2^t} + \sum_{w \in [u_1]} \frac{\sigma_w^2}{2^n} + \frac{\left(d + \frac{n}{\log_2 n}\right)(p + \sigma)}{2^k} + \left(\frac{3(\log_2 n)\sigma}{2^n}\right)^{\frac{n}{\log_2 n}} + \frac{\sigma(p+\sigma)}{2^{k+n}}.$$

Regarding the term $\sum_{w \in [u_1]} \frac{\sigma_w^2}{2^n}$, since the number of encryption queries to each user is at most 1 and the number of BC calls in each query is at most b_s, the term is maximum when for each of some $\lfloor q_{\mathsf{d}}/v \rfloor + 1$ users, $\mathbf{B}$ makes v decryption queries that require b_s BC calls per user. Without loss of generality, assume that the user indexes with the decryption queries is from 1 to $\lfloor q_\mathsf{d}/v \rfloor + 1$. In this case, for $w_1 \in [\lfloor q_\mathsf{d}/v \rfloor + 1]$, $\sigma_{w_1} = b_s + b_s v$, and for $w_2 \in [\lfloor q_\mathsf{d}/v \rfloor + 2, u_1]$, $\sigma_{w_2} \leq b_s$. We thus have

$$\sum_{w \in [u_1]} \frac{\sigma_w^2}{2^n} \leq (\lfloor q_\mathsf{d}/v \rfloor + 1) \cdot \frac{(b_s + b_s v)^2}{2^n} + \sum_{w_2 \in [\lfloor q_\mathsf{d}/v \rfloor + 2, u_1]} \frac{b_s \sigma_{w_2}}{2^n} \leq \frac{8 b_s^2 v q_\mathsf{d}}{2^n} + \frac{b_s \sigma}{2^n}.$$

Regarding the number of forgery attempts v, it can be limited by rekeying. We thus assume that $v q_\mathsf{d} \leq \sigma$, and the above bound is at most $\frac{9 b_s \sigma}{2^n}$. We then use the parameter $b_s = \sqrt{2^{n-t} \sigma_\mathsf{n}}$ that ensures $\frac{b_s \sigma}{2^n} = \frac{\sigma_\mathsf{n} \sigma}{b_s 2^t}$. Putting the bound of $\mathbf{Adv}^{\mathsf{muae}}_{\mathsf{CCM}}(\mathbf{B})$ with $b_s = \sqrt{2^{n-t} \sigma_\mathsf{n}}$ into Theorem 3, the mu-AE-security bound is about

$$\frac{q_\mathsf{d}}{2^t} + \frac{\sqrt{2^{n-t} \sigma_\mathsf{n}} \sigma}{2^n} + \frac{dp}{2^k}.$$

When $t = n$, the bound ensures that AE_NTKD with CCM is mu-AE secure as long as $\sigma \leq 2^n / \sqrt{\sigma_\mathsf{n}}$ and $p \leq 2^k$.

Regarding GCM [9], Hoang et al. [13] derive the same bound for $\mathbf{Adv}^{\mathsf{muae}}_{\mathsf{GCM}}(\mathcal{Q}_1)$ as our CCM's bound in the d-bound model. Note that GCM uses the MAC algorithm GMAC and the parameter c of GMAC is a constant. Hence, AE_NTKD with GCM is as secure as AE_NTKD with CCM regarding mu-AE security. By using $b_s = \sqrt{\sigma_\mathsf{n}}$ and assuming that $\mathbf{Adv}^{\mathsf{muprf}}_{\mathsf{F}}(u, \sigma, \tau + O(\sigma))$ is negligible and $v q_\mathsf{d} \leq \sigma$, the mu-AE-security bound is about

$$\frac{q_\mathsf{d}}{2^t} + \frac{\sqrt{2^{n-t} \sigma_\mathsf{n}} \sigma}{2^n} + \frac{dp}{2^k}.$$

When $t = n$, AE_NTKD with GCM is mu-AE secure as long as $\sigma \leq 2^n / \sqrt{\sigma_\mathsf{n}}$ and $p \leq 2^k$.

8.9 Proof of Theorem 3

We first modify the real world, where $\mathcal{R}_\omega$ is replaced with $\mathsf{F}_{K[\omega]}$ for each $\omega \in [u]$. The modified world is called "middle world." Hence, an adversary $\mathbf{A}$ interacts with the middle-world oracles $\mathcal{O}_{\mathsf{middle}} :- ((\mathsf{AE\_NTKD}[\mathcal{R}_\omega])_{\omega \in [u]}, E^{\pm})$, where $E^{\pm}$ is an IC and AE_NTKD$[\mathcal{R}_\omega]$ is AE_NTKD$_{K[\omega]}$ with $\mathcal{R}_\omega$. We then have

$$\begin{aligned}\mathbf{Adv}^{\mathsf{muae}}_{\mathsf{AE\_NTKD}}(\mathbf{A}) = &\left(\Pr\left[\mathbf{A}^{\mathcal{O}_{\mathsf{real}}} = 1\right] - \Pr\left[\mathbf{A}^{\mathcal{O}_{\mathsf{middle}}} = 1\right]\right) \\ &+ \left(\Pr\left[\mathbf{A}^{\mathcal{O}_{\mathsf{middle}}} = 1\right] - \Pr\left[\mathbf{A}^{\mathcal{O}_{\mathsf{ideal}}} = 1\right]\right).\end{aligned}$$

We evaluate each difference in the followings.

Upper-Bounding $\Pr\left[\mathbf{A}^{\mathcal{O}_{\mathsf{real}}} = 1\right] - \Pr\left[\mathbf{A}^{\mathcal{O}_{\mathsf{middle}}} = 1\right]$. By the replacement from $\mathcal{O}_{\mathsf{real}}$ to $\mathcal{O}_{\mathsf{middle}}$, the difference is bounded by the mu-PRF advantage, i.e.,

$$\Pr[\mathbf{A}^{\mathcal{O}_{\mathsf{real}}} = 1] - \Pr[\mathbf{A}^{\mathcal{O}_{\mathsf{middle}}} = 1] \leq \mathbf{Adv}^{\mathsf{muprf}}_{\mathsf{F}}(u, \sigma, \tau + O(\sigma)).$$

Upper-Bounding $\mathbf{Pr}\left[\mathbf{A}^{\mathcal{O}_{\mathsf{middle}}} = 1\right] - \mathbf{Pr}\left[\mathbf{A}^{\mathcal{O}_{\mathsf{ideal}}} = 1\right]$**.** We use the following notations. For $\alpha \in [q]$, let m_α and a_α be the lengths m and a of the plaintext and AD in the α-th online query. For $\alpha \in [q]$, values regarding the α-th online query are denoted by using the superscript symbol of (α), e.g., $M^{(\alpha)}, C^{(\alpha)}$, etc. Let u_α be the user index of the α-th online query.

We next define the following collision events in the middle world. For $\alpha \in [q]$ and $i \in [a_\alpha + m_\alpha]$, let $\mathcal{D}_i^{(\alpha)}$ be a pair of an AD sector and a ciphertext sector at the i-th AE call of the α-th online query. If $i \le a_\alpha$, then $\mathcal{D}_i^{(\alpha)} = (A_i^{(\alpha)}, \varepsilon)$; if $i > a_\alpha$, then $\mathcal{D}_i^{(\alpha)} = (\varepsilon, M_{i-a_\alpha}^{(\alpha)})$.

$$\begin{aligned}\mathsf{coll} \Leftrightarrow \exists \alpha, \beta \in [q], i \in [a_\alpha + m_\alpha], j \in [a_\beta + m_\beta] \text{ s.t. } (\alpha, i) \ne (\beta, j)\\ \wedge\, \mathsf{u}_\alpha = \mathsf{u}_\beta \wedge N^{(\alpha)} = N^{(\beta)}\\ \wedge\, (T_{i-1}^{(\alpha)}, \mathcal{D}_i^{(\alpha)}) \ne (T_{j-1}^{(\beta)}, \mathcal{D}_j^{(\beta)}) \wedge T_i^{(\alpha)} = T_j^{(\beta)}.\end{aligned}$$

The collision event considers a tag collision of some two distinct sectors or keys, yielding a key collision of the underlying AE. In other worlds, each key of the AE is independently chosen as long as coll does not occur. With the event, we have

$$\begin{aligned}\Pr\left[\mathbf{A}^{\mathcal{O}_{\mathsf{middle}}} = 1\right] - \Pr\left[\mathbf{A}^{\mathcal{O}_{\mathsf{ideal}}} = 1\right] \le \Pr\left[\mathbf{A}^{\mathcal{O}_{\mathsf{middle}}} = 1 \mid \neg\mathsf{coll}\right]\\ - \Pr\left[\mathbf{A}^{\mathcal{O}_{\mathsf{ideal}}} = 1\right] + \Pr[\mathsf{coll}].\end{aligned}$$

Upper-Bounding $\mathbf{Pr}\left[\mathbf{A}^{\mathcal{O}_{\mathsf{middle}}} = 1 \mid \neg\mathsf{coll}\right] - \mathbf{Pr}\left[\mathbf{A}^{\mathcal{O}_{\mathsf{ideal}}} = 1\right]$**.** We give an overview of the evaluation. The detail evaluation is given in the full version of this paper [22].

Assume that coll does not occur. In the nonce-respecting setting, all keys of $\mathsf{AE.Enc}$ in the middle world are independently chosen by RFs $(\mathcal{R}_\omega)_{\omega \in [u]}$. Hence, $\{\mathsf{AE\_NTKD.Enc}[\mathcal{R}_\omega]\}_{\omega \in [u]}$ behave as random-bit oracle up to the advantage $\mathbf{Adv}_{\mathsf{AE}}^{\mathsf{muae}}(\mathcal{Q}_1)$, where $\mathcal{Q}_1 = (\lceil \sigma / b_s \rceil + q, \sigma, q_{\mathsf{d}}, b_s, p)$. Moreover, each tag of $\mathsf{AE\_NTKD.Dec}$ in the middle world is defined by using $\mathsf{AE.Dec}$. Hence, the probability of forging a tag of $\mathsf{AE\_NTKD.Dec}[\mathcal{R}_\omega]$ is bounded by the advantage $\mathbf{Adv}_{\mathsf{AE}}^{\mathsf{muae}}(\mathcal{Q}_1)$. We thus have

$$\Pr\left[\mathbf{A}^{\mathcal{O}_{\mathsf{middle}}} = 1 \mid \neg\mathsf{coll}\right] - \Pr\left[\mathbf{A}^{\mathcal{O}_{\mathsf{ideal}}} = 1\right] \le \mathbf{Adv}_{\mathsf{AE}}^{\mathsf{muae}}(\mathcal{Q}_1).$$

Upper-Bounding $\mathbf{Pr}[\mathsf{coll}]$**.** For each $\alpha, \beta \in [q], i \in [a_\alpha + m_\alpha], j \in [a_\beta + m_\beta]$ such that $(\alpha, i) \ne (\beta, j)$, $\mathsf{u}_\alpha = \mathsf{u}_\beta$ and $N^{(\alpha)} = N^{(\beta)}$, if $T_{i-1}^{(\alpha)} \ne T_{j-1}^{(\beta)}$, then the keys $\hat{K}_i^{(\alpha)}$ and $\hat{K}_j^{(\beta)}$ are independently chosen, and thus by the regular property of TagGen, the probability of the tag collision $T_i^{(\alpha)} = T_j^{(\beta)}$ is at most $\frac{cb_s}{2^n}$. If $T_{i-1}^{(\alpha)} = T_{j-1}^{(\beta)}$ and $\mathcal{D}_i^{(\alpha)} \ne \mathcal{D}_j^{(\beta)}$, then by the AXU or regular property of TagGen, the probability of the tag collision is at most $\frac{2cb_s}{2^n}$.

For $\omega \in [u]$, let N_ω be the number of distinct nonces in queries to the ω-th user. For $i \in [N_\omega]$, let $\sigma_{\omega,i}$ be the number of BC calls in online queries with the

i-th nonce to the ω-th user. Then, for each $i \in [N_\omega]$, there are at most $\lceil \frac{\sigma_{\omega,i}}{b_s} \rceil$ keys of AE. By using the above bounds, we have

$$\begin{aligned}
\Pr[\mathsf{coll}] &\le \sum_{\omega\in[u], i\in[N_\omega]} \binom{\lceil \frac{\sigma_{\omega,i}}{b_s} \rceil}{2} \cdot \frac{2cb_s}{2^t} \\
&\le \sum_{\omega\in[u], i\in[N_\omega]} \frac{0.5(\lceil \frac{\sigma_{\omega,i}}{b_s} \rceil)^2 \cdot 2cb_s}{2^t} \\
&\le \sum_{\omega\in[u], i\in[N_\omega]} \frac{4c(\sigma_{\omega,i}/b_s)^2 \cdot b_s}{2^t} \\
&\le \frac{4c\sigma_{\mathsf{n}}\sigma}{b_s 2^t}.
\end{aligned}$$

Conclusion of the Proof. Combining the above bounds, we obtain the bound in Theorem 3.

■ (Theorem 3)

References

1. Bellare, M., Pietrzak, K., Rogaway, P.: Improved security analyses for CBC MACs. In: CRYPTO 2005. LNCS, vol. 3621, pp. 527–545. Springer (2005)
2. Bellare, M., Tackmann, B.: The multi-user security of authenticated encryption: AES-GCM in TLS 1.3. In: CRYPTO 2016. LNCS, vol. 9814, pp. 247–276. Springer (2016)
3. Biham, E.: How to decrypt or even substitute DES-encrypted messages in 2^{28} steps. Inf. Process. Lett. **84**(3), 117–124 (2002)
4. Black, D.L., McGrew, D.A.: Using authenticated encryption algorithms with the encrypted payload of the internet key exchange version 2 (IKEv2) protocol. RFC **5282**, 1–19 (2008)
5. Bose, P., Hoang, V.T., Tessaro, S.: Revisiting AES-GCM-SIV: multi-user security, faster key derivation, and better bounds. In: EUROCRYPT 2018. LNCS, vol. 10820, pp. 468–499 (2018)
6. Cogliati, B., Jha, A., Nandi, M.: How to build optimally secure PRFs using block ciphers. In: Moriai, S., Wang, H. (eds.) ASIACRYPT 2020. LNCS, vol. 12491, pp. 754–784. Springer, Cham (2020). https://doi.org/10.1007/978-3-030-64837-4_25
7. Degabriele, J.P., Govinden, J., Günther, F., Paterson, K.G.: The security of ChaCha20-Poly1305 in the multi-user setting. In: CCS 2021, pp. 1981–2003. ACM (2021)
8. Dworkin, M.: NIST Special Publication 800-38C: Recommendation for Block Cipher Modes of Operation: the CCM Mode for Authentication and Confidentiality (2007). https://csrc.nist.gov/pubs/sp/800/38/c/upd1/final
9. Dworkin, M.: NIST Special Publication 800-38D: Recommendation for Block Cipher Modes of Operation: Galois/Counter Mode (GCM) and GMAC (2007). https://csrc.nist.gov/pubs/sp/800/38/d/final

10. Dworkin, M.: NIST Special Publication 800-38B: Recommendation for Block Cipher Modes of Operation: The CMAC Mode for Authentication (2016). https://csrc.nist.gov/pubs/sp/800/38/b/upd1/final
11. Gueron, S., Lindell, Y.: Better bounds for block cipher modes of operation via nonce-based key derivation. In: CCS 2017, pp. 1019–1036. ACM (2017)
12. Günther, F., Thomson, M., Wood, C.A.: Usage Limits on AEAD Algorithms (2023). https://datatracker.ietf.org/doc/html/draft-irtf-cfrg-aead-limits-07
13. Hoang, V.T., Tessaro, S., Thiruvengadam, A.: The multi-user security of GCM, revisited: tight bounds for nonce randomization. In: CCS 2018, pp. 1429–1440. ACM (2018)
14. Housley, R.: Using advanced encryption standard (AES) CCM mode with IPSec encapsulating security payload (ESP). RFC **4309**, 1–13 (2005)
15. ISO: ISO/IEC 19772:2020 information security—authenticated encryption (2020)
16. Iwata, T.: New blockcipher modes of operation with beyond the birthday bound security. In: Robshaw, M. (ed.) FSE 2006. LNCS, vol. 4047, pp. 310–327. Springer, Heidelberg (2006). https://doi.org/10.1007/11799313_20
17. Jonsson, J.: On the security of CTR + CBC-MAC. In: Selected Areas in Cryptography, SAC 2002. LNCS, vol. 2595, pp. 76–93. Springer (2002)
18. Kampanakis, P., Campagna, M., Crocket, E., Petcher, A.: Practical challenges with AES-GCM and the need for a new mode and wide-block cipher. Presented at NIST The Third NIST Workshop on Block Cipher Modes of Operation 2023 (2023). https://csrc.nist.gov/Presentations/2023/practical-challenges-with-aes-gcm
19. Luykx, A., Mennink, B., Paterson, K.G.: Analyzing multi-key security degradation. In: Takagi, T., Peyrin, T. (eds.) ASIACRYPT 2017. LNCS, vol. 10625, pp. 575–605. Springer, Cham (2017). https://doi.org/10.1007/978-3-319-70697-9_20
20. McGrew, D.A., Bailey, D.V.: AES-CCM cipher suites for transport layer security (TLS). RFC **6655**, 1–8 (2012)
21. Naito, Y.: Tweakable blockciphers for efficient authenticated encryptions with beyond the birthday-bound security. IACR Trans. Symmetric Cryptol. **2017**(2), 1–26 (2017)
22. Naito, Y., Sasaki, Y., Sugawara, T.: Tight multi-user security of CCM and enhancement by tag-based key derivation applied to GCM and CCM. IACR Cryptol. ePrint Arch. 953 (2025)
23. National Institute of Standards and Technology: Pre-Draft Call for Comments: GCM and CMAC Block Cipher Modes of Operation (2025). https://csrc.nist.gov/pubs/sp/800/38/d/r1/iprd
24. NIST: Fips pub. 198-1: The keyed-hash message authentication code (HMAC) (2008). https://nvlpubs.nist.gov/nistpubs/FIPS/NIST.FIPS.198-1.pdf
25. NIST: Fips pub. 202: Sha-3 standard: Permutation-based hash and extendable-output functions) (2015). https://nvlpubs.nist.gov/nistpubs/FIPS/NIST.FIPS.202.pdf
26. Rescorla, E.: The Transport Layer Security (TLS) Protocol Version 1.3. RFC, vol. 8446, pp. 1–160 (2018)
27. Rescorla, E., Tschofenig, H., Modadugu, N.: The Datagram Transport Layer Security (DTLS) Protocol Version 1.3 – draft-ietf-tls-dtls13-43 (2021). https://tools.ietf.org/html/draft-ietf-tls-dtls13-43
28. Rogaway, P., Wagner, D.A.: A Critique of CCM. Cryptology ePrint Archive, Paper 2003/070 (2003)
29. Salowey, J.A., McGrew, D., Choudhury, A.: AES Galois counter mode (GCM) cipher suites for TLS. RFC **5288**, 1–8 (2008)

30. Seaman, M.: IEEE Standard for Local and Metropolitan Area Networks—Media Access Control (MAC) Security (2018). https://ieeexplore.ieee.org/document/8585421
31. Thomson, M., Turner, S.: Using TLS to secure QUIC. RFC **9001**, 1–52 (2021)
32. Viega, J., McGrew, D.: The use of galois message authentication code (GMAC) in IPsec ESP and AH. RFC **4543**, 1–14 (2006)
33. Whiting, D., Housley, R., Ferguson, N.: IEEE P802.11 Wireless LANs: AES Encryption & Authentication Using CTR Mode & CBC-MAC (2002). https://mentor.ieee.org/802.11/dcn/02/11-02-0001-02-000i-aes-encryption-authentication-using-ctr-mode-with-cbc-mac.doc
34. Whiting, D., Housley, R., Ferguson, N.: Counter with CBC-MAC (CCM). RFC **3610**, 1–26 (2003)
35. Wi-Fi Alliance: WPA3 Specification Version 3.2 (2023). https://www.wi-fi.org/system/files/WPA3%20Specification%20v3.2.pdf
36. Woolley, M.: Bluetooth core specification version, vol. 5, p. 4 (2023)
37. Zhang, X., Shen, Y., Wang, L.: Multi-user security of CCM authenticated encryption mode. In: CCS 2024, pp. 4331–4345. ACM (2024)
38. ZigBee Alliance, Inc.: Zigbee specification (2015). https://zigbeealliance.org/wp-content/uploads/2019/11/docs-05-3474-21-0csg-zigbee-specification.pdf

FlexProofs: A Vector Commitment with Flexible Linear Time for Computing All Proofs

Jing Liu and Liang Feng Zhang(✉)

ShanghaiTech University, Shanghai, China
{liujing1,zhanglf}@shanghaitech.edu.cn

Abstract. In this paper, we introduce FlexProofs, a new *vector commitment (VC)* scheme that achieves two key properties: (1) the prover can generate all individual opening proofs for a vector of size N in optimal time $\mathcal{O}(N)$, and there is a flexible batch size parameter b that can be increased to further reduce the time to generate all proofs; and (2) the scheme is directly compatible with a family of zkSNARKs that encode their input as a multi-linear polynomial. As a critical building block, we propose the first *functional commitment (FC)* scheme for multi-exponentiations with batch opening. Compared with HydraProofs, the only existing VC scheme that computes all proofs in optimal time $\mathcal{O}(N)$ and is directly compatible with zkSNARKs, FlexProofs may speed up the process of generating all proofs, if the parameter is properly chosen. Our experiments show that for $N = 2^{16}$ and $b = \log^2 N$, FlexProofs can be $6\times$ faster than HydraProofs. Moreover, when combined with suitable zkSNARKs, FlexProofs enable practical applications such as verifiable secret sharing and verifiable robust aggregation.

Keywords: Vector Commitment · Functional Commitment · zkSNARKs

1 Introduction

Zero-knowledge succinct non-interactive arguments of knowledge (zkSNARKs) [30,36] allow a prover to convince a verifier with input $\mathbf{m}$ that $\mathbf{y}$ is the output of a computation $\mathcal{C}(\mathbf{m}, \mathbf{w})$, where $\mathcal{C}$ is typically represented as an arithmetic circuit and $\mathbf{w}$ may be a private input held by the prover. While zkSNARKs have been widely used to secure real-world applications [1,31,45,46,56] and are well known for enabling efficient verification by end-users, it is less clear how to apply them in a *multi-user* setting where N participants $\{\mathcal{V}_i\}_{i=0}^{N-1}$, each holding a private input m_i, delegate the computation of $\mathcal{C}((m_0, \ldots, m_{N-1}), \mathbf{w})$ to a service provider. Such multi-user settings underlie numerous applications such as distributed machine learning [50], crowdsourcing [32], secret sharing [61], and

K. Jee and A. Kate (Eds.): ACNS 2026, LNCS 16571, pp. 241–271, 2027.
https://doi.org/10.1007/978-3-032-32560-0_9

collaborative filtering [57], where it may be crucial to address the risk of a dishonest service provider [24,47]. The traditional zkSNARKs are not directly suitable for this setting because they assume each verifier knows the entire input $\mathbf{m} = (m_0, \ldots, m_{N-1})$, which however is not true in the multi-user setting.

Recently, Pappas, Papadopoulos, and Papamanthou [54] proposed a method of adapting zkSNARKs to the multi-user setting by combining them with *vector commitment (VC)* [17]. In their solution, the prover uses a VC scheme to commit to the input vector $\mathbf{m} = (m_0, \ldots, m_{N-1})$ and runs a zkSNARK for $\mathcal{C}(\mathbf{m}, \mathbf{w})$ (similar to commit-and-prove zkSNARKs [13,25]). Since VCs support openings of the vector at chosen indices, the prover can additionally provide each verifier $\mathcal{V}_i$ with a proof that its input m_i is indeed the i-th element of the committed vector used in the zkSNARK, ensuring both computation correctness and individual data inclusion. This scenario requires a VC scheme that can *efficiently generate all proofs* and is *directly compatible with zkSNARKs.*

Among the existing VC schemes, the Merkle trees [51] support generating all proofs in $\mathcal{O}(N)$ time, but are inefficient when integrated into zkSNARKs. Some modern VC schemes, e.g., those based on elliptic curves [28,44,62,65,67] or error-correcting codes [74,76], are directly compatible with many zkSNARKs [27,59,71], yet require $\mathcal{O}(N^2)$ time to naively produce all proofs. Some constructions [44,62,65,74,76] may reduce the time cost to $\mathcal{O}(N \log N)$. To the best of our knowledge, HydraProofs [54] is the only existing VC scheme that can generate all opening proofs in $\mathcal{O}(N)$ time and is directly compatible with zkSNARKs based on multi-linear polynomials [19,59,71]. In particular, the $\mathcal{O}(N)$ time cost is incurred by $\mathcal{O}(N)$ field operations and $\mathcal{O}(N)$ cryptographic operations (e.g., group exponentiations or pairings). In this paper, we propose FlexProofs, a new VC scheme that preserves zkSNARK compatibility and generates all proofs using only $\mathcal{O}(N)$ field operations and $\mathcal{O}(N/b + \sqrt{N} \log N)$ heavy cryptographic operations, where b is the batch size (ranging from 1 to $\sqrt{N}$). Compared with HydraProofs, FlexProofs requires fewer heavy cryptographic operations for larger b, enabling more efficient generation of all proofs.

1.1 Our Contributions

Functional Commitment Scheme for Multi-Exponentiations with Batch Opening. To construct FlexProofs, we propose the first *functional commitment (FC)* scheme for multi-exponentiations with batch opening. In the scheme, the prover commits to a vector and later generates a batch proof for multiple computations over the vector; any verifier can check computation results against the commitment. The scheme achieves constant-size commitments and logarithmic-size proofs, and is proven secure in the algebraic group model (AGM) and the random oracle model (ROM) under the n-ASDBP and q-SDH assumptions; our implementation confirms the high efficiency of batch opening.

FlexProofs. We introduce FlexProofs, a new *vector commitment (VC)* scheme that achieves two key properties. First, the prover can generate all proofs for a vector of size N in optimal time $\mathcal{O}(N)$, which is incurred by $\mathcal{O}(N)$ field operations and $\mathcal{O}(N/b + \sqrt{N} \log N)$ cryptographic operations, where batch size b

ranges from 1 to $\sqrt{N}$. Second, the scheme is directly compatible with a family of zkSNARKs that encode their input as a multi-linear polynomial [19,59,71]. FlexProofs builds on the proposed FC scheme and an existing polynomial commitment (PC) scheme, and is proven correct and secure (see below for the detailed design rationale). Compared with HydraProofs, the only existing VC scheme that computes all proofs in time $\mathcal{O}(N)$ (incurred by $\mathcal{O}(N)$ field operations and $\mathcal{O}(N)$ cryptographic operations) and is directly compatible with zkSNARKs, FlexProofs requires fewer cryptographic operations for larger b, enabling more efficient proof generation. Our experiments show that for $N = 2^{16}$ and $b = \log^2 N$, FlexProofs generates all proofs about 6× faster than HydraProofs, while achieving similar verification time and slightly larger proofs. Finally, combining our VC scheme with suitable zkSNARKs enables practical applications such as verifiable secret sharing and verifiable robust aggregation.

Design Rationale for FlexProofs. FlexProofs adopts a clear two-layer structure: each sub-vector is first committed using an existing PC scheme, and the resulting PC commitments are then committed with our proposed FC scheme. Correspondingly, the proof generation process also naturally splits into an FC layer and a PC layer, which allow us to do optimization independently: the FC layer employs our batch-opening FC scheme to lower the cost, while the PC layer applies ideas similar to HydraProofs to further reduce the cost. Overall, the two-layer structure combining FC and PC, together with our batch-opening FC scheme, enables FlexProofs to outperform purely PC-based HydraProofs.

1.2 Applications

Verifiable Secret Sharing. A real-world application involving multiple users' data is *verifiable secret sharing (VSS)*. At a high level, a secret sharing scheme [61] allows a dealer to split a secret value s into N shares such that any $t+1$ of them can reconstruct s, while any subset of at most t reveals nothing about it. Verifiability protects the receivers of shares against a dishonest dealer who may issue malformed or inconsistent shares [21,24]. The combination of VCs and zkSNARKs yields a VSS scheme where each receiver can verify that all shares form a valid sharing of s and that its own share is consistent with this sharing.

Verifiable Robust Aggregation. Another application is *federated learning (FL)* [4,37,50], where multiple clients train local models and send gradients to an *aggregator*, who combines them into a global model. This process is repeated iteratively until the model converges. Due to its decentralized nature, FL is vulnerable to misbehaving clients that submit poisoned or low-quality gradients, motivating a long line of work on *robust aggregation* to mitigate the impact of such adversarial inputs [8,15,26,34,49]. However, the security of robust aggregation relies on an honest aggregator, and these guarantees collapse when the aggregator is untrusted. In practice, aggregators often have strong incentives to misuse their power for personal benefit. For instance, in federated recommendation systems [63,73], an aggregator can tamper with the model to promote its products, influence markets, or push its political agendas [23,33,64]; in FL-as-a-Service [38], it may delay convergence for monetary gain [72]. To safeguard FL against both a misbehaving aggregator and malicious clients, Pappas et al. [54] introduce the notion of *verifiable robust aggregation (VRA)*. And by applying the combination of VCs and zkSNARKs to existing robust aggregation algorithms such as FLTrust [15], one can obtain such a VRA scheme.

1.3 Related Work

Functional Commitments. Existing FC schemes target polynomials [18,69], linear functions [14,22,39,41,48], monotone span programs [18], or semi-sparse polynomials [43]. Prior FC schemes for Boolean or arithmetic circuits cannot handle multi-exponentiation $\prod_{i=0}^{n-1} \mathbf{A}[i]^{\mathbf{b}[i]} (\mathbf{A} \in \mathbb{G}_1^n, \mathbf{b} \in \mathbb{F}_p^n)$, where $\mathbb{G}_1$ is the source group of a bilinear group. Some schemes fail because they cannot commit to vectors over $\mathbb{G}_1$: for instance, [16,55] commit to vectors over $\mathbb{Z}_q$; [3] commits to vectors over a commutative ring; [70] commits to vectors over finite rings; and [11] commits to arithmetic circuits in a field. Other schemes fail for a different reason: FC schemes [60,68,69] targeting Boolean functions $f : \{0,1\}^l \rightarrow \{0,1\}$ operate over bitstrings and fixed Boolean predicates, which cannot represent or efficiently compute exponentiations over $\mathbb{G}_1$.

Vector Commitments. Merkle trees [51] support generating all proofs in $\mathcal{O}(N)$ time. However, they are not well suited for zkSNARKs, since incorporating this VC pre-image into existing zkSNARKs would essentially require reconstructing the entire tree within the zkSNARK arithmetic circuit, which is highly inefficient even with SNARK-friendly hash functions [29]. Some modern VC schemes, such as those based on elliptic curves [28,44,62,65,67] or error-correcting codes [74, 76], are directly compatible with many zkSNARKs [27,59,71] since they use the same data encoding. However, unlike Merkle trees, generating all N proofs is inefficient: the naive cost is $\mathcal{O}(N^2)$, and even improved constructions [44,62,65, 74,76] require $\mathcal{O}(N \log N)$ time. To the best of our knowledge, HydraProofs [54] is the only existing VC scheme that can generate all proofs in $\mathcal{O}(N)$ time while being directly compatible with zkSNARKs based on multi-linear polynomials [19,59,71]. We do not consider lattice-based VC techniques [53,55,69], as the corresponding lattice-based zkSNARKs remain largely impractical.

2 Preliminaries

Notation. For any integer $n > 0$, let $[0, n) = \{0, 1, \ldots, n-1\}$. Let $\mathbf{m}$ be a vector of length n. For any $i \in [0, n)$, we denote by $\mathbf{m}[i]$ the i-th element of $\mathbf{m}$. For any $I \subseteq [0, n)$, we denote $\mathbf{m}[I] = (\mathbf{m}[i])_{i \in I}$. Besides, we denote

$$\mathbf{m}_L = (\mathbf{m}[0], \ldots, \mathbf{m}[n/2-1]), \quad \mathbf{m}_R = (\mathbf{m}[n/2], \ldots, \mathbf{m}[n-1]),$$

We denote by $\mathbb{G}$ a multiplicative group, and by $\mathbb{F}_p$ the finite field of prime order p. For a vector $\mathbf{A} \in \mathbb{G}^n$, a vector $\mathbf{b} \in \mathbb{F}_p^n$ and a scalar $x \in \mathbb{F}_p$, we denote

$$\mathbf{A}^x = (\mathbf{A}[0]^x, \ldots, \mathbf{A}[n-1]^x), x\mathbf{b} = (x\mathbf{b}[0], \ldots, x\mathbf{b}[n-1]), \langle \mathbf{A}, \mathbf{b} \rangle = \prod_{i \in [0,n)} \mathbf{A}[i]^{\mathbf{b}[i]}.$$

Here, $\langle \mathbf{A}, \mathbf{b} \rangle$ compactly denotes the multi-exponentiation of $\mathbf{A}$ by $\mathbf{b}$, which our FC scheme is designed to support. For two vectors $\mathbf{A}, \mathbf{A}' \in \mathbb{G}^n$, we denote $\mathbf{A} \circ \mathbf{A}' = (\mathbf{A}[0]\mathbf{A}'[0], \ldots, \mathbf{A}[n-1]\mathbf{A}'[n-1])$. Let $\mathbf{u}_i$ be the i-th unit vector, with 1 at the i-th position and zeros elsewhere. We define $\mathsf{Bin}(i) = (i_{\ell-1}, \ldots, i_0)$ as the *bit decomposition* of an ℓ-bit integer i if $i = \sum_{k \in [0,\ell)} i_k 2^k$. Any vector $\mathbf{m} \in \mathbb{F}_p^n$ can be encoded as a multilinear polynomial $f_{\mathbf{m}} : \mathbb{F}_p^{\log n} \to \mathbb{F}_p$ as below:

$$f_{\mathbf{m}}(\mathbf{x}) = \sum_{i \in [0,n)} \mathbf{m}[i] \prod_{k \in [0, \log n)} (i_k x_k + (1 - i_k)(1 - x_k)), \tag{1}$$

where $\mathbf{x} = (x_{\log n - 1}, \ldots, x_0)$, $\mathsf{Bin}(i) = (i_{\log n - 1}, \ldots, i_0)$. We refer to $f_{\mathbf{m}}$ as the *multi-linear extension* of $\mathbf{m}$. For any finite set S, we denote by $s \leftarrow S$ the process of choosing s uniformly from S. We denote by $y \leftarrow \mathsf{Alg}(x)$ the process of running an algorithm Alg on an input x and assigning the output to y. We say that a function $\epsilon(\lambda)$ is *negligible* in λ and denote $\epsilon(\lambda) = \mathsf{negl}(\lambda)$, if $\epsilon(\lambda) = o(\lambda^{-c})$ for all $c > 0$. Our security proofs are in the *random oracle model* (ROM), formalized in [5]: we model a cryptographic hash function as a truly random function, accessible to all parties only via oracle queries. Specifically, we use two random oracles $H, H' : \{0,1\}^* \to \mathbb{F}_p$.

Bilinear Group. We denote by $\mathsf{BG}(1^\lambda)$ a bilinear group generator that takes a security parameter λ as input and outputs a bilinear group context $\mathbf{bg} = (p, \mathbb{G}_1, \mathbb{G}_2, \mathbb{G}_T, e, g_1, g_2)$, where $\mathbb{G}_1 = \langle g_1 \rangle, \mathbb{G}_2 = \langle g_2 \rangle$ and $\mathbb{G}_T$ are groups of prime order p, and $e : \mathbb{G}_1 \times \mathbb{G}_2 \to \mathbb{G}_T$ is a *pairing* such that $e(u^\alpha, v^\beta) = e(u, v)^{\alpha\beta}$ for all $u \in \mathbb{G}_1, v \in \mathbb{G}_2$ and $\alpha, \beta \in \mathbb{Z}_p$. We assume *Type-3* bilinear groups where *no* efficiently computable homomorphisms exist between $\mathbb{G}_1$ and $\mathbb{G}_2$. For any $\mathbf{A} \in \mathbb{G}_1^n, \mathbf{B} \in \mathbb{G}_2^n$, we denote $\mathbf{A} * \mathbf{B} = \prod_{i \in [0,n)} e(\mathbf{A}[i], \mathbf{B}[i])$.

2.1 Functional Commitments with Batch Openings

Libert et al. [41] introduced a *functional commitment* (FC) model for linear functions over finite fields. Multi-exponentiations over bilinear groups naturally extends these linear functions: for $\mathbf{A} \in \mathbb{G}_1^n$ and $\mathbf{b} \in \mathbb{F}_p^n$, $\langle \mathbf{A}, \mathbf{b} \rangle = \prod_{i=0}^{n-1} \mathbf{A}[i]^{\mathbf{b}[i]}$. We extend the FC model of [41] to support multi-exponentiations and batched evaluations on multiple field vectors. An FC scheme $\mathsf{FC} = (\mathsf{Setup}, \mathsf{Commit}, \mathsf{BOpen}, \mathsf{BVerify})$ in our model consists of four algorithms:

- $\mathsf{FC.Setup}(1^\lambda, 1^n) \to \mathsf{pp}$: *Given the security parameter* λ *and the vector size* n, *outputs public parameters* pp, *an implicit input to all remaining algorithms.*
- $\mathsf{FC.Commit}(\mathbf{A}) \to C$: *Given a vector* $\mathbf{A} \in \mathbb{G}_1^n$, *outputs a commitment* C.

- $\mathsf{FC.BOpen}(C, \mathbf{A}, \{\mathbf{b}^{(i)}\}_{i\in[0,t)}, \{y_i\}_{i\in[0,t)}) \to \pi_y$: *Given a commitment* C (to $\mathbf{A}$), *a vector* $\mathbf{A}$, *and vectors* $\mathbf{b}^{(0)}, \ldots, \mathbf{b}^{(t-1)} \in \mathbb{F}_p^n$, *outputs a batch proof* π_y for $\{y_i = \langle \mathbf{A}, \mathbf{b}^{(i)} \rangle\}_{i\in[0,t)}$.
- $\mathsf{FC.BVerify}(C, \{\mathbf{b}^{(i)}\}_{i\in[0,t)}, \{y_i\}_{i\in[0,t)}, \pi_y) \to \{0,1\}$: *Verifies the batch proof* π_y for $\{y_i = \langle \mathbf{A}, \mathbf{b}^{(i)} \rangle\}_{i\in[0,t)}$ *against* C *and outputs 1 (accept) or 0 (reject).*

An FC scheme is *correct* if FC.BVerify always outputs 1, provided that all algorithms are correctly executed.

Definition 1 (Correctness). *For any security parameter* λ, *any integer* $n > 0$, *any vector* $\mathbf{A} \in \mathbb{G}_1^n$, *any integer* $t > 0$, *any vectors* $\mathbf{b}^{(0)}, \ldots, \mathbf{b}^{(t-1)} \in \mathbb{F}_p^n$, *define* $y_i = \langle \mathbf{A}, \mathbf{b}^{(i)} \rangle$ *for all* $i \in [0,t)$, *then*

$$\Pr\left[\begin{array}{c} \mathsf{pp} \leftarrow \mathsf{FC.Setup}(1^\lambda, 1^n), C \leftarrow \mathsf{FC.Commit}(\mathbf{A}), \\ \pi_y \leftarrow \mathsf{FC.BOpen}(C, \mathbf{A}, \{\mathbf{b}^{(i)}\}_{i\in[0,t)}, \{y_i\}_{i\in[0,t)}) : \\ \mathsf{FC.BVerify}(C, \{\mathbf{b}^{(i)}\}_{i\in[0,t)}, \{y_i\}_{i\in[0,t)}, \pi_y) = 1 \end{array}\right] = 1.$$

Referring to [69], an FC scheme is *function binding* if no probabilistic polynomial time (PPT) adversary can open the commitment C to two distinct values for the same field vector.

Definition 2 (Function binding). *For any security parameter* λ, *any integer* $n > 0$, *and any PPT adversary* $\mathcal{A}$,

$$\Pr\left[\begin{array}{c} \mathsf{pp} \leftarrow \mathsf{FC.Setup}(1^\lambda, 1^n), (C, \{\mathbf{b}^{(i)}, y_i, \hat{y}_i\}_{i\in[0,t)}, \pi_y, \pi_{\hat{y}}) \leftarrow \mathcal{A}(\mathsf{pp}) : \\ (\mathsf{FC.BVerify}(C, \{\mathbf{b}^{(i)}\}_{i\in[0,t)}, \{y_i\}_{i\in[0,t)}, \pi_y) = 1) \wedge \\ (\mathsf{FC.BVerify}(C, \{\mathbf{b}^{(i)}\}_{i=0}^{t-1}, \{\hat{y}_i\}_{i=0}^{t-1}, \pi_{\hat{y}}) = 1) \wedge (\exists j \in [0,t) : y_j \neq \hat{y}_j) \end{array}\right] \leq \mathsf{negl}(\lambda).$$

2.2 Polynomial Commitments

A *polynomial commitment* (PC) scheme [7,35,52,66,75] enables a prover to commit to an n-variate polynomial of maximum degree d (per variable), and later open its evaluation at any point by generating an evaluation proof. A PC scheme $\mathsf{PC} = (\mathsf{Setup}, \mathsf{Commit}, \mathsf{Eval}, \mathsf{Verify})$ consists of four algorithms:

- $\mathsf{PC.Setup}(1^\lambda, 1^d, 1^n) \to \mathsf{pp}$: *Given the security parameter* λ, *the maximum degree per variable* d *and the number of variables* n, *outputs the public parameters* pp, *an implicit input to all remaining algorithms.*
- $\mathsf{PC.Commit}(f) \to C$: *Outputs the commitment of* f.
- $\mathsf{PC.Eval}(f, \mathbf{r}) \to (y, \pi)$: *Generates a proof* π *showing that* $f(\mathbf{r}) = y$.
- $\mathsf{PC.Verify}(C, \mathbf{r}, y, \pi) \to \{0,1\}$: *Returns 1 if for the committed polynomial* f *it holds that* $f(\mathbf{r}) = y$.

Informally, a PC scheme is *complete* if the verifier always accepts the proof for a correctly evaluated point.

Definition 3 (Completeness). *A PC scheme is complete if for any* λ, n, d,

$$\Pr\left[\begin{array}{l} \mathsf{pp} \leftarrow \mathsf{PC.Setup}(1^\lambda, 1^d, 1^n), C \leftarrow \mathsf{PC.Commit}(f), \\ (y, \pi) \leftarrow \mathsf{PC.Eval}(f, \mathbf{r}) : \mathsf{PC.Verify}(C, \mathbf{r}, y, \pi) = 1 \end{array}\right] = 1.$$

A PC scheme is *knowledge sound* if for any PPT adversary that produces an accepting proof, there exists an extractor $\mathcal{E}_{PC}$ that extracts the committed polynomial f, such that the probability that $f(\mathbf{r}) \neq y$ is negligible.

Definition 4 (Knowledge Soundness). *A PC scheme is knowledge sound, if for any λ, n, d and PPT adversary $\mathcal{A}_{PC}$ there exists an extractor $\mathcal{E}_{PC}$ having access to $\mathcal{A}_{PC}$ such that:*

$$\Pr\left[\begin{array}{c}\mathsf{pp} \leftarrow \mathsf{PC.Setup}(1^\lambda, 1^d, 1^n), (C, y, \pi, \mathbf{r}) \leftarrow \mathcal{A}_{PC}(\mathsf{pp}),\\ f \leftarrow \mathcal{E}_{PC}^{\mathcal{A}_{PC}}(\mathsf{pp}) : (\mathsf{PC.Verify}(C, \mathbf{r}, y, \pi) = 1) \wedge \\ ((f(\mathbf{r}) \neq y) \vee (C \neq \mathsf{PC.Commit}(f)))\end{array}\right] \leq \mathsf{negl}(\lambda).$$

For our construction, we use the PST multivariate polynomial commitment scheme [52], which has commitment and evaluation complexities *linear* in the size of the polynomial, and proof size and verification time logarithmic in it.

HyperEval Algorithm. In some scenarios, the prover needs to generate 2^n evaluation proofs of a multi-linear polynomial $f : \mathbb{F}_p^n \to \mathbb{F}_p$ at all hypercube points $\mathbf{i} \in \{0,1\}^n$. This is formalized by the PC.HyperEval [54]:

- $\mathsf{PC.HyperEval}(f) \to \{y_i, \pi_i\}_{i \in [0, 2^n)}$: *Generate 2^n evaluation proofs showing that $y_i = f(\mathsf{Bin}(i))$ for all $i \in [0, 2^n)$.*

The HyperEval algorithm for the PST scheme achieves $\mathcal{O}(n2^n)$ complexity [62].

2.3 Vector Commitments

A *vector commitment* (VC) scheme [17,42] enables a prover to commit to a vector $\mathbf{m} \in \mathbb{F}_p^N$ and later prove that an element m_i is the i-th element of the committed vector. A VC scheme $\mathsf{VC} = (\mathsf{Setup}, \mathsf{Commit}, \mathsf{Open}, \mathsf{Verify})$ consists of the following algorithms:

- $\mathsf{VC.Setup}(1^\lambda, 1^N) \to \mathsf{pp}$: *Given the security parameter λ and vector size N, outputs the public parameters, an implicit input to all remaining algorithms.*
- $\mathsf{VC.Commit}(\mathbf{m}) \to (C, \mathsf{aux})$: *Outputs the vector commitment of $\mathbf{m}$ and an auxiliary information* aux.
- $\mathsf{VC.Open}(\mathsf{aux}, i, \mathbf{m}) \to \pi_i$: Outputs an opening proof π_i showing that m_i is the i-th element of $\mathbf{m}$.
- $\mathsf{VC.Verify}(C, i, m_i, \pi_i) \to \{0,1\}$: *Returns 1 if m_i is the i-th element of the committed vector.*

A VC scheme is *correct* if VC.Verify always outputs 1, provided that all algorithms are correctly executed.

Definition 5 (Correctness). *For any security parameter λ, any integer $N > 0$, any vector $\mathbf{m} \in \mathbb{F}_p^N$ and any index $i \in [0, N)$, a VC scheme is correct if*

$$\Pr\left[\begin{array}{c}\mathsf{pp} \leftarrow \mathsf{VC.Setup}(1^\lambda, 1^N), (C, \mathsf{aux}) \leftarrow \mathsf{VC.Commit}(\mathbf{m}),\\ \pi_i \leftarrow \mathsf{VC.Open}(\mathsf{aux}, i, \mathbf{m}) : \mathsf{VC.Verify}(C, i, \mathbf{m}[i], \pi_i) = 1\end{array}\right] = 1.$$

A VC scheme is *position binding* if the probability that a PPT adversary generates valid proofs for two different elements at the same index i is negligible.

Definition 6 (Position binding). *For any security parameter λ, any integer $N > 0$, and any PPT adversary $\mathcal{A}$,*

$$\Pr\left[\begin{matrix}\mathsf{pp} \leftarrow \mathsf{VC.Setup}(1^\lambda, 1^N), (C, i, m_i, m_i', \pi_i, \pi_i') \leftarrow \mathcal{A}(\mathsf{pp}) : \\ (\mathsf{VC.Verify}(C, i, m_i, \pi_i) = 1) \wedge \\ (\mathsf{VC.Verify}(C, i, m_i', \pi_i') = 1) \wedge (m_i \neq m_i')\end{matrix}\right] \leq \mathsf{negl}(\lambda).$$

OpenAll Algorithm. Recent VC schemes [44,54,62,65,67] support an $\mathsf{OpenAll}$ algorithm that *efficiently* generates all opening proofs in an offline pre-processing phase and later reply to open queries with no additional computation. The formal definition of the $\mathsf{VC.OpenAll}$ algorithm is as follows.

- $\mathsf{VC.OpenAll}(\mathsf{aux}, \mathbf{m}) \rightarrow \{\pi_i\}_{i \in [0,N)}$: Generate N opening proofs, one for each element of the vector.

3 A Functional Commitment with Batch Opening

Bünz et al. [12] proposed a known-exponent *multi-exponentiation inner product argument* (MIPA) which employs structured-key variants of the commitment in [2] to commit to $(\mathbf{A}, \mathbf{b})$ and allows one to prove that a value $U \in \mathbb{G}_1$ is equal to $\langle \mathbf{A}, \mathbf{b} \rangle$ against this commitment, where $\mathbf{A} \in \mathbb{G}_1^n$ is hidden and $\mathbf{b} \in \mathbb{F}_p^n$ is publicly known and structured of the form $(1, b, \ldots, b^{n-1})$ for some $b \in \mathbb{F}_p$.

We observe that in the MIPA, the vector $\mathbf{b}$ can be any vector in $\mathbb{F}_p^n$ and extend the argument to the *first* FC scheme with batch openings for multi-exponentiations. To develop the final FC scheme, we first transform the MIPA (which originally verified $\langle \mathbf{A}, \mathbf{b} \rangle$ for fixed $\mathbf{A}$ and $\mathbf{b}$) into an FC scheme that commits to $\mathbf{A}$, enabling verification of $\langle \mathbf{A}, \mathbf{b} \rangle$ for *any* $\mathbf{b}$. Opening the commitment of vector $\mathbf{A}$ to $y_0 = \langle \mathbf{A}, \mathbf{b}^{(0)} \rangle, \ldots, y_{t-1} = \langle \mathbf{A}, \mathbf{b}^{(t-1)} \rangle$ is equivalent to proving:

$$\{\langle \mathbf{A}, \mathbf{b}^{(i)} \rangle = y_i\}_{i \in [0,t)}. \tag{2}$$

As shown in Lemma 1 (Appendix B), this task can be reduced to showing that a randomized linear combination of these equations holds:

$$\langle \mathbf{A}, \sum_{i \in [0,t)} r_i \mathbf{b}^{(i)} \rangle = \prod_{i \in [0,t)} y_i^{r_i}, \tag{3}$$

where each r_i is random and may be computed with a hash function. We then show that this FC scheme gives a VC scheme in which $\mathsf{VC.OpenAll}$ algorithm runs in linear time (Sect. 4). Below we give a formal description of our FC scheme, assuming without loss of generality that the vector length n is a power of 2, i.e., $n = 2^\ell$ for some integer ℓ.

- $\mathsf{FC.Setup}(1^\lambda, 1^n)$: *Choose* $(p, \mathbb{G}_1, \mathbb{G}_2, \mathbb{G}_T, e, g_1, g_2) \leftarrow \mathsf{BG}(1^\lambda)$ *and* $\beta \leftarrow \mathbb{F}_p$. *Compute* $\mathbf{v} = \left((g_2)^{\beta^{2i}}\right)_{i\in[0,n)}$ *and output* $\mathsf{pp} = \mathbf{v}$. *Note that* β *must never be known to the adversary, and thus our scheme requires a trusted setup.*
- $\mathsf{FC.Commit}(\mathbf{A})$: *Given the implicit input* $\mathsf{pp} = \mathbf{v} \in \mathbb{G}_2^n$ *and a vector* $\mathbf{A} \in \mathbb{G}_1^n$, *output a commitment* $C = \mathbf{A} * \mathbf{v}$.
- $\mathsf{FC.BOpen}(C, \mathbf{A}, \{\mathbf{b}^{(i)}\}_{i\in[0,t)}, \{y_i\}_{i\in[0,t)})$: *Parse the implicit input* pp *as* $\mathbf{v}$. *Set*
$$\mathbf{b} = \sum_{i\in[0,t)} r_i \mathbf{b}^{(i)}, \tag{4}$$
where $r_i = H(\mathbf{b}^{(i)}, C, \{\mathbf{b}^{(k)}\}_{k\in[0,t)}, \{y_k\}_{k\in[0,t)}), \forall i \in [0,t)$, *and* $H : \{0,1\}^* \rightarrow \mathbb{F}_p$ *is a hash function. Set* $\mathbf{A}_0 = \mathbf{A}, \mathbf{v}_0 = \mathbf{v}, \mathbf{b}_0 = \mathbf{b}$, *and let* x_0 *be the empty string. For* $j = 1, 2, \ldots, \ell$, *compute*
$$\begin{aligned}
\mathbf{L}_j &= ((\mathbf{A}_{j-1})_R * (\mathbf{v}_{j-1})_L, \langle(\mathbf{A}_{j-1})_R, (\mathbf{b}_{j-1})_L\rangle),\\
\mathbf{R}_j &= ((\mathbf{A}_{j-1})_L * (\mathbf{v}_{j-1})_R, \langle(\mathbf{A}_{j-1})_L, (\mathbf{b}_{j-1})_R\rangle),\\
x_j &= H'(x_{j-1}, \mathbf{L}_j, \mathbf{R}_j),\\
\mathbf{A}_j &= (\mathbf{A}_{j-1})_L \circ ((\mathbf{A}_{j-1})_R)^{x_j},\\
\mathbf{v}_j &= (\mathbf{v}_{j-1})_L \circ ((\mathbf{v}_{j-1})_R)^{1/x_j},\\
\mathbf{b}_j &= (\mathbf{b}_{j-1})_L + (1/x_j)\cdot(\mathbf{b}_{j-1})_R,
\end{aligned} \tag{5}$$
where $H' : \{0,1\}^* \rightarrow \mathbb{F}_p$ *is a hash function. Output* $\pi_y = \left\{\{\mathbf{L}_j, \mathbf{R}_j\}_{j=1}^{\ell}, \mathbf{A}_\ell\right\}$.
- $\mathsf{FC.BVerify}(C, \{\mathbf{b}^{(i)}\}_{i\in[0,t)}, \{y_i\}_{i\in[0,t)}, \pi_y)$: *Parse the implicit input* pp *as* $\mathbf{v}$. *Compute* $\{r_i\}_{i\in[0,t)}$ *and* $\mathbf{b}$ *as in algorithm* $\mathsf{FC.BOpen}$, *and then compute*
$$y = \prod_{i\in[0,t)} y_i^{r_i}. \tag{6}$$
Let $\mathbf{C}_0 = (C, y)$ *and let* x_0 *be the empty string. Parse* π_y *as* $\{\{\mathbf{L}_j, \mathbf{R}_j\}_{j=1}^{\ell}, \mathbf{A}_\ell\}$. *For* $j = 1, 2, \ldots, \ell$, *compute* $x_j, \mathbf{v}_j$ *and* $\mathbf{b}_j$ *as per Eq. (5), and compute*
$$\mathbf{C}_j = \mathbf{L}_j^{x_j} \circ \mathbf{C}_{j-1} \circ (\mathbf{R}_j)^{1/x_j}.$$
Finally, if $\mathbf{C}_\ell = (\mathbf{A}_\ell * \mathbf{v}_\ell, \langle\mathbf{A}_\ell, \mathbf{b}_\ell\rangle)$, *output 1; otherwise, output 0.*

Correctness and Security. The correctness of our FC scheme is proven below, while its security (function binding) is proven in Appendix B.1.

Theorem 1. *The FC scheme satisfies the correctness property (Definition 1).*

Proof. To prove the correctness of the FC scheme, it suffices to show that for all $k \in \{0, 1, \ldots, \ell\}$, $\mathbf{C}_i = (\mathbf{A}_i * \mathbf{v}_i, \langle\mathbf{A}_i, \mathbf{b}_i\rangle)$. We begin by proving this statement for the base case $k = 0$. Since for each $i \in [0,t)$, $y_i = \langle\mathbf{A}, \mathbf{b}^{(i)}\rangle$ and r_i is computed as in algorithm $\mathsf{FC.BOpen}$, we obtain
$$\prod_{i\in[0,t)} y_i^{r_i} = \prod_{i\in[0,t)} \langle\mathbf{A}, \mathbf{b}^{(i)}\rangle^{r_i} = \left\langle \mathbf{A}, \sum_{i\in[0,t)} r_i \mathbf{b}^{(i)} \right\rangle.$$

By equations (4) and (6), it follows that $y = \langle \mathbf{A}, \mathbf{b} \rangle$. Hence, it is evident that $\mathbf{C}_0 = (C, y) = (\mathbf{A}_0 * \mathbf{v}_0, \langle \mathbf{A}_0, \mathbf{b}_0 \rangle)$, as required.

By mathematical induction, it remains to show the statement is true for $k = j$ when it is true for $k = j-1$. For simplicity, we denote $\bar{\mathbf{A}} = \mathbf{A}_{j-1}, \bar{\mathbf{v}} = \mathbf{v}_{j-1}$, and $\bar{\mathbf{b}} = \mathbf{b}_{j-1}$. According to the algorithm FC.BVerify, $\mathbf{C}_j = \mathbf{L}_j^{x_j} \circ \mathbf{C}_{j-1} \circ (\mathbf{R}_j)^{1/x_j}$. By Eq. (5) and the induction hypothesis,

$$\begin{aligned}\mathbf{C}_j &= (\bar{\mathbf{A}}_R * \bar{\mathbf{v}}_L, \langle \bar{\mathbf{A}}_R, \bar{\mathbf{b}}_L \rangle)^{x_j} \circ (\bar{\mathbf{A}} * \bar{\mathbf{v}}, \langle \bar{\mathbf{A}}, \bar{\mathbf{b}} \rangle) \circ (\bar{\mathbf{A}}_L * \bar{\mathbf{v}}_R, \langle \bar{\mathbf{A}}_L, \bar{\mathbf{b}}_R \rangle)^{1/x_j} \\ &= ((\bar{\mathbf{A}}_R^{x_j} * \bar{\mathbf{v}}_L) \cdot (\bar{\mathbf{A}} * \bar{\mathbf{v}}) \cdot (\bar{\mathbf{A}}_L^{1/x_j} * \bar{\mathbf{v}}_R), \langle \bar{\mathbf{A}}_R^{x_j}, \bar{\mathbf{b}}_L \rangle \cdot \langle \bar{\mathbf{A}}, \bar{\mathbf{b}} \rangle \cdot \langle \bar{\mathbf{A}}_L^{1/x_j}, \bar{\mathbf{b}}_R \rangle).\end{aligned}$$

Since $\bar{\mathbf{A}} * \bar{\mathbf{v}} = (\bar{\mathbf{A}}_L * \bar{\mathbf{v}}_L) \cdot (\bar{\mathbf{A}}_R * \bar{\mathbf{v}}_R)$ and $\langle \bar{\mathbf{A}}, \bar{\mathbf{b}} \rangle = \langle \bar{\mathbf{A}}_L, \bar{\mathbf{b}}_L \rangle \cdot \langle \bar{\mathbf{A}}_R, \bar{\mathbf{b}}_R \rangle$, we have

$$\mathbf{C}_j = (((\bar{\mathbf{A}}_R^{x_j} \circ \bar{\mathbf{A}}_L) * \bar{\mathbf{v}}_L) \cdot ((\bar{\mathbf{A}}_R \circ \bar{\mathbf{A}}_L^{1/x_j}) * \bar{\mathbf{v}}_R), \langle \bar{\mathbf{A}}_R^{x_j} \circ \bar{\mathbf{A}}_L, \bar{\mathbf{b}}_L \rangle \cdot \langle \bar{\mathbf{A}}_R \circ \bar{\mathbf{A}}_L^{1/x_j}, \bar{\mathbf{b}}_R \rangle).$$

Since $\bar{\mathbf{A}}_R \circ \bar{\mathbf{A}}_L^{1/x_j} = (\bar{\mathbf{A}}_R^{x_j} \circ \bar{\mathbf{A}}_L)^{1/x_j}$, by replacing the left-hand side of this equality with the right-hand side in $\mathbf{C}_j$, we have

$$\mathbf{C}_j = ((\bar{\mathbf{A}}_R^{x_j} \circ \bar{\mathbf{A}}_L) * (\bar{\mathbf{v}}_L \circ \bar{\mathbf{v}}_R^{1/x_j}), \langle \bar{\mathbf{A}}_R^{x_j} \circ \bar{\mathbf{A}}_L, \bar{\mathbf{b}}_L + 1/x_j \cdot \bar{\mathbf{b}}_R \rangle).$$

According to Eq. (5), $\mathbf{C}_j = (\mathbf{A}_j * \mathbf{v}_j, \langle \mathbf{A}_j, \mathbf{b}_j \rangle)$. □

Faster Verification. The FC scheme uses the same approach as the known-exponent MIPA in Bünz et al. [12], which allows the verifier to outsource the computation of $\mathbf{v}_\ell$ to the untrusted prover and reduces verification time. However, this comes at the cost of additionally relying on the n-SDH assumption (**Assumption** 1). We implicitly assume the faster verifier.

Efficiency. The efficiency of the FC scheme with faster verification is analyzed below and summarized in Table 1. In our analysis of group operations, we focus on pairings and exponentiations, ignoring the cheaper multiplications.

- *Proof size.* The original proof contains $2\log n$ elements in $\mathbb{G}_T$ and $2\log n + 1$ elements in $\mathbb{G}_1$. To enable faster verification, two additional elements in $\mathbb{G}_2$ (i.e., $\mathbf{v}_\ell$ and its proof) were included. Hence, the proof size is $\mathcal{O}(\log n)$.
- *Commit.* Committing to an n-sized vector requires n pairings.
- *Batch opening.* Computing vector $\mathbf{b}$ requires tn field operations. Computing $\{\mathbf{L}_j, \mathbf{R}_j\}_{j=1}^{\ell}$ requires $2n$ pairings and $2n$ exponentiations in $\mathbb{G}_1$. Rescaling $\mathbf{A}, \mathbf{v}, \mathbf{b}$ requires n exponentiations in $\mathbb{G}_1$ and $\mathbb{G}_2$, n field operations. Moreover, to achieve faster verification, the proof of $\mathbf{v}_\ell$ must be computed, and this computation requires performing $2n$ exponentiations in $\mathbb{G}_2$.
- *Batch Verification.* Computing $\mathbf{b}$ requires tn field operations, and computing y requires t exponentiations in $\mathbb{G}_1$. Rescaling the commitments and $\mathbf{b}$ requires $2\log n$ exponentiations in $\mathbb{G}_T$ and $\mathbb{G}_1$, and n field operations. The final check equation requires 1 pairing and an exponentiation in $\mathbb{G}_1$. With faster verification, the verifier no longer needs to compute $\mathbf{v}_l$, but needs to verify its correctness; this requires two pairings and $\log n$ field operations.

Table 1. The efficiency of our FC scheme with faster verification.

Algorithms	Field operations	Exponentiations	Pairings
FC.Commit	-	-	$\mathcal{O}(n)$
FC.BOpen	$\mathcal{O}(tn)$	$\mathcal{O}(n)$	$\mathcal{O}(n)$
FC.BVerify	$\mathcal{O}(tn)$	$\mathcal{O}(\log n + t)$	$\mathcal{O}(1)$

4 A VC Scheme with Linear-Time OpenAll

Based on the scheme FC from Sect. 3, we construct FlexProofs (denoted by VC), a VC scheme that achieves linear-time VC.OpenAll with a flexible batch size parameter b, where b provides a tradeoff and the running time of VC.OpenAll can be continuously reduced by increasing b. Our scheme is directly compatible with the zkSNARKs based on multi-linear polynomials.

4.1 FlexProofs

FlexProofs is structured in two layers. We set $\mu = \sqrt{N}$ and partition the vector $\mathbf{m} \in \mathbb{F}_p^N$ into μ subvectors of length μ:

$$\mathbf{m} = \big(\mathbf{m}_0, \mathbf{m}_1, \ldots, \mathbf{m}_{\mu-1}\big).$$

In the first layer, each $\mathbf{m}_j$ $(j \in [0, \mu))$ is encoded using its multilinear extension $f_j : \mathbb{F}_p^{\log \mu} \to \mathbb{F}_p$ and committed via a commitment scheme PC [52] for multilinear polynomials. In the second layer, the vector of the commitments of all $\mathbf{m}_j (j \in [0, \mu))$ is committed using the scheme FC from Sect. 3. Specifically, the algorithms VC.Setup and VC.Commit in our VC scheme are as follows.

- $\mathsf{VC.Setup}(1^\lambda, 1^N)$: *Generate public parameters for* PC *and* FC *by invkoing*

$$\mathsf{pp}_{PC} \leftarrow \mathsf{PC.Setup}(1^\lambda, 1, \log \mu), \ \mathsf{pp}_{FC} \leftarrow \mathsf{FC.Setup}(1^\lambda, 1^\mu). \tag{7}$$

  Output the public parameters $\mathsf{pp} = \{\mathsf{pp}_{PC}, \mathsf{pp}_{FC}\}$.
- $\mathsf{VC.Commit}(\mathbf{m})$: *For each* $j \in [0, \mu)$, *the subvector* $\mathbf{m}_j$ *is encoded using its multilinear extension* f_j *and then committed as*

$$C_j \leftarrow \mathsf{PC.Commit}(f_j). \tag{8}$$

  For the vector $\mathbf{C} = (C_0, \ldots, C_{\mu-1})$ *of* μ *polynomial commitments, generate a functional commitment*

$$C \leftarrow \mathsf{FC.Commit}(\mathbf{C}). \tag{9}$$

  Output the commitment C *and an auxiliary information string* $\mathsf{aux} = \mathbf{C}$.

Given the commitment process defined by (8) and (9), there is a *two-step* method of proving the correctness of $\mathbf{m}[i]$ for each $i \in [0, N)$. First, use our FC scheme to prove the correctness of $C_{\lfloor i/\mu \rfloor}$ with respect to C, i.e., $C_{\lfloor i/\mu \rfloor} = \langle \mathbf{C}, \mathbf{u}_{\lfloor i/\mu \rfloor} \rangle$. Second, use the PC scheme to prove the correctness of $\mathbf{m}[i]$ with respect to $C_{\lfloor i/\mu \rfloor}$, i.e., $f_{\lfloor i/\mu \rfloor}(\mathsf{Bin}(i \bmod \mu)) = \mathbf{m}[i]$. Since both steps have time complexity $\mathcal{O}(\sqrt{N})$, the computational cost of the two-step method is $\mathcal{O}(\sqrt{N})$. Consequently, proving the correctness of all elements of $\mathbf{m}$ one after the other with the two-step method requires $\mathcal{O}(N\sqrt{N})$ time. By examining the two-step proving process, we observe that: (1) proving the correctness of C_j with respect to C takes place μ times and can be done only once for all elements in $\mathbf{m}_j$; (2) for all $j \in [0, \mu)$, the μ processes of proving the correctness of all elements in $\mathbf{m}_j$ with respect to C_j share a similar structure and thus can be combined. Based on these observations, we propose an *OpenAll* protocol, in which the prover can prove the correctness of all elements in $\mathbf{m}$ in $\mathcal{O}(N)$ time.

4.2 Linear-Time OpenAll

In this section, we first present *OpenAll* as an interactive protocol and then make it non-interactive with the Fiat-Shamir variant of [74], yielding the algorithms VC.OpenAll and VC.Verify. In the non-interactive version of our VC scheme, the executions of the algorithms VC.Commit and VC.OpenAll form a *pre-processing* phase and the latter algorithm generates N opening proofs for any vector $\mathbf{m}$ of length N. In particular, the N opening proofs can be used to directly reply any query to VC.Open, which is an algorithm different from VC.OpenAll and every time generates an opening proof for any *single* element of the vector.

The interactive protocol *OpenAll* is a protocol between a prover holding a vector $\mathbf{m}$ and N verifiers $\{\mathcal{V}_i\}_{i \in [0,N)}$, where each verifier $\mathcal{V}_i$ holds a commitment C (to $\mathbf{m}$) and a value m_i, and verifies that m_i is the i-th element of the vector committed in C by interacting with the prover.

Intuition of Our Protocol. Our *OpenAll* protocol consists of two steps: (1) proving the correctness of C_j with respect to C for all $j \in [0, \mu)$, and (2) combining the μ processes of proving the correctness of all elements in $\mathbf{m}_j$ with respect to C_j. For the first step, if the prover uses the scheme FC from Sect. 3 to generate a proof for each C_j, then it needs to generate μ proofs and thus performs $\mathcal{O}(N)$ field operations and $\mathcal{O}(N)$ cryptographic operations (e.g., group exponentiations or pairings) according to Table 1. To reduce this cost, the prover partitions the vector $\mathbf{C}$ into blocks and uses FC to generate one batch proof per block. With a batch size of b, the prover only needs to generate $\lceil \mu/b \rceil$ batch proofs, which require $\mathcal{O}(N)$ field operations and $\mathcal{O}(N/b)$ cryptographic operations. For the second step, we combine the μ processes by folding μ polynomials into a single polynomial [10,27], called *folded* polynomial, which is essentially a linear combination of the μ polynomials, such that if an evaluation claim at a hypercube point is wrong in one of the μ polynomials, then it will be wrong for the folded polynomial with overwhelming probability. For the folded polynomial, we invoke PC.HyperEval.

Protocol 1: Efficient OpenAll. We assume a prover holding a vector $\mathbf{m} \in \mathbb{F}_p^N$, the commitment C and an auxiliary information string $\mathsf{aux}(=\mathbf{C})$. We assume N verifiers $\{\mathcal{V}_i\}_{i\in[0,N)}$, where each verifier $\mathcal{V}_i$ holds the commitment C and an element m_i and wants to verify whether m_i is the i-th element of $\mathbf{m}$.

- **Step 1: Prove the correctness of $\mathbf{C}_k$ for all $k \in [0, \lceil \mu/b \rceil)$.**
  1) For each $k \in [0, \lceil \mu/b \rceil)$, the prover sets $S_k = [kb, (k+1)b)$, generates a batch proof
  $$\pi_{\mathbf{C}_k} \leftarrow \mathsf{FC.BOpen}(C, \mathbf{C}, \{\mathbf{u}_a\}_{a\in S_k}, \{C_a\}_{a\in S_k}), \tag{10}$$
  and sends $(\mathbf{C}_k, \pi_{\mathbf{C}_k})$ to the verifiers $\{\mathcal{V}_i\}_{i\in[k\mu b,(k+1)\mu b)}$.
  2) The verifier $\mathcal{V}_i$ sets $k = \lfloor i/(\mu b) \rfloor$ and $S_k = [kb, (k+1)b)$, and checks the correctness of $\mathbf{C}_k$ by executing
  $$\mathsf{FC.BVerify}(C, \{\mathbf{u}_a\}_{a\in S_k}, \{C_a\}_{a\in S_k}, \pi_{\mathbf{C}_k}).$$

- **Step 2: Fold all μ polynomials $\{f_j\}_{j=0}^{\mu-1}$ into a single polynomial g^* and then invoke $\mathsf{PC.HyperEval}$ on the folded polynomial g^*.**
  1) The prover receives random values $\{r_j\}_{j\in[0,\mu)}$ from the verifiers and computes
  $$g_j = r_j f_j, \qquad D_j = C_j^{r_j}. \tag{11}$$
  For each $i \in [0, N)$, the verifier $\mathcal{V}_i$, holding m_i and $C_{\lfloor i/\mu \rfloor}$, computes
  $$y_{\lfloor i/\mu \rfloor, (i \bmod \mu)} = r_{\lfloor i/\mu \rfloor} m_i, \qquad D_{\lfloor i/\mu \rfloor} = C_{\lfloor i/\mu \rfloor}^{r_{\lfloor i/\mu \rfloor}} \tag{12}$$
  The prover folds the randomized polynomials $\{g_j\}_{j\in[0,\mu)}$ into a single polynomial in a tree-like, bottom-up fashion. At the leaf level, the state of the j-th leaf is initialized as $\big(\mathcal{P} : \{g_j\},\ \boldsymbol{\mathcal{V}}_j : \{(y_{j,a}, D_j)\}_{a\in[0,\mu)}\big)$, where the prover $\mathcal{P}$ holds only the polynomial g_j, and $\boldsymbol{\mathcal{V}}_j = (\mathcal{V}_{j\mu}, \ldots, \mathcal{V}_{(j+1)\mu-1})$ is the vector of verifiers, with each $\boldsymbol{\mathcal{V}}_j[a]$ holding $y_{j,a}$ claimed to be $g_j(\mathsf{Bin}(a))$ together with the commitment D_j. For each internal node w, the state $\mathcal{S}_w = (\mathcal{P} : \{g_w\},\ \boldsymbol{\mathcal{V}}_w : \{(y_{w,a}, D_w)\}_{a\in[0,\mu)})$ is computed from its left child $\mathcal{S}_{w_l}$ and right child $\mathcal{S}_{w_r}$ using the **Sub-protocol**. This process is repeated recursively up the tree until the root.
  2) At the root, the final state is $\mathcal{S}^* = \big(\mathcal{P} : \{g^*\},\ \boldsymbol{\mathcal{V}}^* : \{(y_a^*, D^*)\}_{a\in[0,\mu)}\big)$. The prover follows the $\mathsf{PC.HyperEval}$ algorithm to generate μ proofs $\{\pi_a^*\}_{a\in[0,\mu)}$ proving that each $y_a^* = g^*(\mathsf{Bin}(a))$, and sends π_a^* to verifiers $\{\mathcal{V}_{j\mu+a}\}_{j\in[0,\mu)}$. Verifiers $\{\mathcal{V}_{j\mu+a}\}_{j\in[0,\mu)}$ validates by running $\mathsf{PC.Verify}(D^*, \mathsf{Bin}(a), y_a^*, \pi_a^*)$.

Protocol Description. Formally our interactive *OpenAll* protocol is shown in **Protocol 1** and consists of the following two steps.

- The first step: The prover partitions the vector $\mathbf{C}$ into $\lceil \mu/b \rceil$ blocks of size b such that
$$\mathbf{C} = (\mathbf{C}_0, \ldots, \mathbf{C}_{\lceil \mu/b \rceil - 1}),$$

where $\mathbf{C}_i = (C_{ib}, \ldots, C_{(i+1)b-1})$. For each $k \in [0, \lceil \mu/b \rceil)$, the prover invokes $\mathsf{FC.BOpen}$ to generate a batch proof for the correctness of $\mathbf{C}_k$, and sends $\mathbf{C}_k$ together with this proof to the verifiers $\{\mathcal{V}_i\}_{i \in [kb\mu,(k+1)b\mu)}$. These verifiers then validate using $\mathsf{FC.BVerify}$.

- *The second step:* At this point, $\mathcal{V}_i$ assures that $C_{\lfloor i/\mu \rfloor}$ is the $\lfloor i/\mu \rfloor$-th element of the vector committed in C. It remains to verify that $f_{\lfloor i/\mu \rfloor}(\mathsf{Bin}(i \bmod \mu)) = \mathbf{m}[i]$. The prover has to prove this identity for all $i \in [0, N)$ or equivalently generate proofs for the evaluations of the μ polynomials $\{f_j\}_{j=0}^{\mu-1}$ at all boolean hypercube points in $\{0,1\}^{\log \mu}$. If the prover invokes $\mathsf{PC.HyperEval}$ on the μ polynomials one by one, the total time complexity will be $\mathcal{O}(N \log \sqrt{N})$. To be more efficient, we first fold the μ polynomials into a single polynomial g^* and then invoke $\mathsf{PC.HyperEval}$ on the folded polynomial g^*.
  Next, for clarity, each verifier step is presented immediately after its corresponding prover step to illustrate all participants' actions. To efficiently compute the folded polynomial g^*, the verifiers send a set $\{r_j\}_{j \in [0,\mu)}$ of random values to the prover. The prover then uses each random value r_j to compute a randomized polynomial $g_j = r_j f_j$ and a commitment $D_j = C_j^{r_j}$. Meanwhile, for each $i \in [0, N)$, the verifier $\mathcal{V}_i$, holding m_i and $C_{\lfloor i/\mu \rfloor}$, computes $y_{\lfloor i/\mu \rfloor, (i \bmod \mu)} = r_{\lfloor i/\mu \rfloor} m_i$ and $D_{\lfloor i/\mu \rfloor} = C_{\lfloor i/\mu \rfloor}^{r_{\lfloor i/\mu \rfloor}}$. The prover folds the randomized polynomials $\{g_j\}_{j \in [0,\mu)}$ into a single polynomial in a tree-like, bottom-up fashion. At the leaf level, the state of the j-th leaf is initialized as $\left(\mathcal{P} : \{g_j\},\ \boldsymbol{\mathcal{V}}_j : \{(y_{j,a}, D_j)\}_{a \in [0,\mu)}\right)$, where the prover $\mathcal{P}$ holds only the polynomial g_j, and $\boldsymbol{\mathcal{V}}_j = (\mathcal{V}_{j\mu}, \ldots, \mathcal{V}_{(j+1)\mu-1})$ is the vector of verifiers, with each $\boldsymbol{\mathcal{V}}_j[a]$ holding $y_{j,a}$ claimed to be $g_j(\mathsf{Bin}(a))$ together with the commitment D_j. For each internal node w, the state

$$\mathcal{S}_w = (\mathcal{P} : \{g_w\},\ \boldsymbol{\mathcal{V}}_w : \{(y_{w,a}, D_w)\}_{a \in [0,\mu)})$$

  is computed from its left child $\mathcal{S}_{w_l}$ and right child $\mathcal{S}_{w_r}$ using the **Subprotocol**. This process is repeated recursively up the tree until the root.
  At the root, the final state is $\mathcal{S}^* = \left(\mathcal{P} : \{g^*\},\ \boldsymbol{\mathcal{V}}^* : \{(y_a^*, D^*)\}_{a \in [0,\mu)}\right)$, where the prover holds the final folded polynomial g^*, and each verifier $\mathcal{V}_{j\mu+a}$ (for $j \in [0,\mu), a \in [0,\mu)$) holds the claimed evaluation $y_a^* = g^*(\mathsf{Bin}(a))$ together with the commitment D^*. Finally, the prover runs the $\mathsf{PC.HyperEval}$ algorithm for g^* to generate proofs $\{\pi_a^*\}_{a \in [0,\mu)}$ proving that each $y_a^* = g^*(\mathsf{Bin}(a))$, and sends π_a^* to verifiers $\{\mathcal{V}_{j\mu+a}\}_{j \in [0,\mu)}$. Verifiers $\{\mathcal{V}_{j\mu+a}\}_{j \in [0,\mu)}$ validates by running $\mathsf{PC.Verify}(D^*, \mathsf{Bin}(a), y_a^*, \pi_a^*)$.

Making Our Protocol Non-interactive. Up to this point, our protocol has been presented in the interactive setting: in *Step 1*, the prover sends a message to the verifiers; in *Step 2*, the prover receives their challenges and responds accordingly. To make it non-interactive, we adopt the Fiat-Shamir variant of [74], which is designed for the multi-verifier setting and proven secure in ROM. Our protocol becomes non-interactive as follows. For *Step 2*, the prover builds a Merkle tree by hashing the coefficients of all polynomials to be folded and their corresponding commitments. Each verifier then receives a proof that includes a Merkle tree membership path, showing that its data is correctly included.

Sub-protocol: Computing the parent state from the two child states. For each $z \in \{l, r\}$, the child node w_z is associated with a state

$$\mathcal{S}_{w_z} = (\mathcal{P} : \{g_{w_z}\},\ \boldsymbol{\mathcal{V}}_{w_z} : \{(y_{w_z,a}, D_{w_z})\}_{a \in [0,\mu)}),$$

where the prover $\mathcal{P}$ holds the polynomial g_{w_z}, and for each $a \in [0, \mu)$, the verifiers $\boldsymbol{\mathcal{V}}_{w_z}[a]$ hold a point $y_{w_z,a}$ claimed to be $g_{w_z}(\mathsf{Bin}(a))$ together with the commitment D_{w_z}. At the end of the folding, the parent node w has a state

$$\mathcal{S}_w = (\mathcal{P} : \{g_w\},\ \boldsymbol{\mathcal{V}}_w : \{(y_{w,a}, D_w)\}_{a \in [0,\mu)}),$$

where the prover holds the polynomial g_w, and $\boldsymbol{\mathcal{V}}_w = \big(\boldsymbol{\mathcal{V}}_{w_l}[0] \cup \boldsymbol{\mathcal{V}}_{w_r}[0],\ \ldots,\ \boldsymbol{\mathcal{V}}_{w_l}[\mu - 1] \cup \boldsymbol{\mathcal{V}}_{w_r}[\mu - 1]\big)$ collects the verifier vectors. For each $a \in [0, \mu)$, both $\boldsymbol{\mathcal{V}}_{w_l}[a]$ and $\boldsymbol{\mathcal{V}}_{w_r}[a]$ now hold the same claimed evaluation $y_{w,a}$ and the commitment D_w. Our protocol works as follows.

1. The prover computes the folded polynomial $g_w(\mathbf{x}) = g_{w_l}(\mathbf{x}) + g_{w_r}(\mathbf{x})$.
2. For every $\boldsymbol{\mathcal{V}}_{w_l}[a]$, the prover provides D_{w_r} and $y_{w_r,a}$ and for every $\boldsymbol{\mathcal{V}}_{w_r}[a]$, the prover provides D_{w_l} and $y_{w_l,a}$.
3. Next, every $\boldsymbol{\mathcal{V}}_w[a]$ computes $y_{w,a} = y_{w_l,a} + y_{w_r,a}$ and $D_w = D_{w_l} D_{w_r}$.

The correctness and security of FlexProofs are proven in Appendix C. A zero-knowledge variant of *OpenAll* can also be obtained using standard techniques [20, 40] (see Appendix A for the formal definition). In this case, the PC scheme is replaced with its zero-knowledge version, whereas the FC scheme does not require zero-knowledge since it only operates on already hidden commitments.

4.3 Efficiency

Efficiency Improvements in the First Step of Protocol 1. Note that the working process of the first step in the protocol implies the *first* subvector commitment scheme over group elements. Below, we describe some efficiency improvements for this scheme. In the FC model, the vector length is denoted by n; in our setting this length is μ, so we set $\ell = \log \mu$. As a starting point, we consider the case where $\mathbf{b}$ in Eq. (5) is the i-th *unit vector* $\mathbf{u}_i$. Note that $\mathsf{Bin}(i) = (i_{\ell-1}, \ldots, i_0)$. In the first folding round:

$$(\mathbf{u}_i)_1 = (\mathbf{u}_i)_L + 1/x_1 \cdot (\mathbf{u}_i)_R.$$

If $i_{\ell-1} = 0$, the only non-zero entry 1 appears in $(\mathbf{u}_i)_L$, resulting in a single non-zero entry of 1 in $(\mathbf{u}_i)_1$. Conversely, if $i_{\ell-1} = 1$, the only non-zero 1 entry appears in $(\mathbf{u}_i)_R$, which leads to a single non-zero entry of $1/x_1$ in $(\mathbf{u}_i)_1$. In summary, the only non-zero entry in $(\mathbf{u}_i)_1$ is $(1/x_1)^{i_{\ell-1}}$, located at the index $(i_{\ell-2}, \ldots, i_0)$. In general, at the j-th round, the only non-zero entry in $(\mathbf{u}_i)_j$ is $\prod_{k=1}^{j} (1/x_k)^{i_{\ell-k}}$, with index $(i_{\ell-j-1}, \ldots, i_0)$. Hence, after ℓ rounds, we have:

$$(\mathbf{u}_i)_\ell = \prod_{k=1}^{\ell} (1/x_k)^{i_{\ell-k}}. \tag{13}$$

Let $I \subseteq [0, \mu)$ be a set of indices. For batch opening over I, $\mathbf{b} = \sum_{i \in I} r_i \mathbf{u}_i$. Let $\hat{\mathbf{u}}_i = r_i \mathbf{u}_i (i \in I)$, thus $\mathbf{b} = \sum_{i \in I} \hat{\mathbf{u}}_i$. According to the folding of $\mathbf{b}$ in Eq. (5), at the first round: $\mathbf{b}_1 = \mathbf{b}_L + 1/x_1 \mathbf{b}_R = (\sum_{i \in I} \hat{\mathbf{u}}_i)_L + 1/x_1 (\sum_{i \in I} \hat{\mathbf{u}}_i)_R = \sum_{i \in I} (\hat{\mathbf{u}}_i)_L + 1/x_1 (\hat{\mathbf{u}}_i)_R = \sum_{i \in I} (\hat{\mathbf{u}}_i)_1$; at the j-th round: $\mathbf{b}_j = \sum_{i \in I} ((\hat{\mathbf{u}}_i)_{j-1})_L + 1/x_j ((\hat{\mathbf{u}}_i)_{j-1})_R = \sum_{i \in I} (\hat{\mathbf{u}}_i)_j$. After ℓ rounds and by Eq. (13):

$$\mathbf{b}_\ell = \sum_{i \in I} (\hat{\mathbf{u}}_i)_\ell \text{ and } (\hat{\mathbf{u}}_i)_\ell = r_i \prod_{k=1}^{\ell} (1/x_k)^{i_{\ell-k}}.$$

Therefore, FC.BOpen can run faster, and FC.BVerify can run in $\mathcal{O}(|I| \log \mu)$ time.

Complexity Analysis of FlexProofs. The underlying homomorphic PC scheme for multi-linear polynomials achieves commitment and evaluation complexity of $\mathcal{O}(N)$, proof size of $\mathcal{O}(\log N)$, verification time of $\mathcal{O}(\log N)$, and PC.HyperEval complexity of $\mathcal{O}(N \log N)$. Next, we analyze the complexity of FlexProofs.

- *Commitment complexity.* Algorithm VC.Commit makes μ calls to PC.Commit, each on a polynomial of size μ, and then makes one call to FC.Commit on a vector of size μ. Due to the linear commit complexity of both the PC scheme and our FC scheme, the overall commitment complexity is $\mathcal{O}(N)$.
- *Prover complexity.* In *Step 1*, the prover creates proofs for $\lceil \mu/b \rceil$ batches, each containing b elements. According to Table 1, this step takes $\mathcal{O}(N)$ field operations and $\mathcal{O}(N/b)$ cryptographic operations. In *Step 2*, the prover has to (1) randomize polynomials and their commitments, (2) fold polynomials in a tree-like structure, (3) call PC.HyperEval. Due to the underlying PC scheme achieves PC.HyperEval complexity of $\mathcal{O}(N \log N)$, both (1) and (2) require $\mathcal{O}(N)$ field operations and $\mathcal{O}(\mu)$ cryptographic operations, (3) has a complexity of $\mathcal{O}(\sqrt{N} \log N)$. Overall, the prover runs in time $\mathcal{O}(N)$, with $\mathcal{O}(N)$ field operations and $\mathcal{O}(N/b + \sqrt{N} \log N)$ cryptographic operations.
- *Proof size.* In *Step 1*, each $\mathcal{V}_i$ receives $\mathbf{C}_{\lfloor i/\mu b \rfloor}$ of size $\mathcal{O}(b)$ and the batch proof $\pi_{\mathbf{C}_{\lfloor i/\mu b \rfloor}}$ of size $\mathcal{O}(\log N)$. In *Step 2*, it receives $\log N$ commitments, $\log N$ claimed evaluations and an opening proof of the PC scheme. Since the PC scheme has a proof size of $\mathcal{O}(\log N)$, the proof size would be $\mathcal{O}(\log N + b)$ for the interactive version and $\mathcal{O}(\log N + b)$ for the non-interactive version.
- *Verification time.* In *Step 1*, each $\mathcal{V}_i$ runs the FC.BVerify algorithm to verify the correctness of $\mathbf{C}_{\lfloor i/\mu b \rfloor}$, which takes $\mathcal{O}(b \log \mu)$ time. In *Step 2*, it needs to (1) compute the final evaluation and commitment, and (2) verify the final evaluation. Since the underlying PC scheme has a verification time of $\mathcal{O}(\log N)$, the complexities of (1) and (2) are $\mathcal{O}(\log \mu)$ and $\mathcal{O}(\log N)$, respectively. Thus, the verification time would be $\mathcal{O}(b \log N)$ for both the interactive and non-interactive versions.

In conclusion, FlexProofs is a VC scheme with $\mathcal{O}(N)$ Commit and OpenAll complexity, $\mathcal{O}(\log N + b)$ proof size and $\mathcal{O}(b \log N)$ verification time.

4.4 Compatible with a Family of ZkSNARKs

Paper [54] proposes a construction that combines a VC scheme with a zkSNARK in order to prove the correctness of computations over data originating from multiple sources. To adapt FlexProofs to this construction, we first extend our *OpenAll* for sub-arrays and then show how FlexProofs is directly compatible with a family of zkSNARKs.

Extending *OpenAll* for Sub-arrays. The above *OpenAll* protocol proves the correctness of all individual elements of $\mathbf{m}$. We now extend this to proving the correctness of all *consecutive sub-arrays*. More formally, for each verifier $\mathcal{V}_j$ with $j \in [0, M)$, we aim to prove that its array $\mathbf{m}_j \in \mathbb{F}^{N/M}$ is indeed the j-th sub-array of the committed vector $\mathbf{m} \in \mathbb{F}^N$. This can be achieved by showing that the commitment C_j of $\mathbf{m}_j$ is the j-th element of the committed vector $\mathbf{C}$, as established in *Step 1* of *OpenAll*. To generate all opening proofs in this setting, all parties follow the $\mathsf{VC.Commit}$ algorithm and *Step 1*, with the following modifications. In the $\mathsf{VC.Commit}$ algorithm, partition $\mathbf{m}$ into M segments of size N/M such that $\mathbf{m} = (\mathbf{m}_0, \ldots, \mathbf{m}_{M-1})$; for each $\mathbf{m}_j$, compute its multi-linear extension commitment C_j; then compute the commitment of the vector $\mathbf{C} = (C_0, \ldots, C_{M-1})$. Upon receiving C_j, verifier $\mathcal{V}_j$ checks whether the polynomial committed in C_j corresponds to the multi-linear extension of $\mathbf{m}_j$.

Compatibility with a family of zkSNARKs. According to [54], if a VC scheme encodes the committed vector $\mathbf{m}$ as a multi-linear polynomial and supports generation of an evaluation proof for the polynomial at a random point, it is directly compatible with a family of zkSNARKs that encode inputs as multi-linear polynomials [19,59,71]. Since FlexProofs is built on PC and FC schemes, it can be viewed as encoding the committed vector $\mathbf{m}$ into a multi-linear polynomial and supports generating an evaluation proof for the committed polynomial at a random point. We next show how FlexProofs produces such a proof. By Eq. (1), the multi-linear extension of a vector $\mathbf{m} \in \mathbb{F}_p^N$ is

$$f_{\mathbf{m}}(\mathbf{x}) = \sum_{i \in [0,N)} \mathbf{m}[i] \prod_{k \in [0,\log N)} \left(i_k x_k + (1-i_k)(1-x_k)\right), \tag{14}$$

where $\mathbf{x} = (x_{\log N-1}, \ldots, x_0)$ and $\mathsf{Bin}(i) = (i_{\log N-1}, \ldots, i_0)$; and for $j \in [0, \mu)$, the multi-linear extension of $\mathbf{m}_j \in \mathbb{F}_p^{\mu}$ is

$$f_j(\mathbf{x}_R) = \sum_{a \in [0,\mu)} \mathbf{m}_j[a] \prod_{k \in [0,\log \mu)} \left(a_k x_k + (1-a_k)(1-x_k)\right), \tag{15}$$

where $\mathsf{Bin}(a) = (a_{\log \mu - 1}, \ldots, a_0)$. From Eq. (14) and (15), we have

$$f_{\mathbf{m}}(\mathbf{x}) = \sum\nolimits_{j \in [0,\mu)} f_j(\mathbf{x}_R) \mathcal{T}_{j,\log \mu}(\mathbf{x}_L), \tag{16}$$

where $\mathcal{T}_{j,\log \mu}(\mathbf{x}_L) = \prod_{a \in [0,\log \mu)} (j_a x_{a+\log \mu} + (1-j_a)(1-x_{a+\log \mu}))$ and $\mathsf{Bin}(j) = (j_{\log \mu - 1}, \ldots, j_0)$. To prove the evaluation of $f_{\mathbf{m}}(\mathbf{x})$ at $\mathbf{r} = (r_{\log N-1}, \ldots, r_0) \in$

$\mathbb{F}_p^{\log N}$, it suffices to prove the evaluation of $f_{\mathbf{m}}(\mathbf{r}_L, \mathbf{x}_R)$ at $\mathbf{r}_R$. Let us first define $F(\mathbf{x}_R) = f_{\mathbf{m}}(\mathbf{r}_L, \mathbf{x}_R)$; using Eq. (16), we then obtain the expression:

$$F(\mathbf{x}_R) = \sum\nolimits_{j \in [0,\mu)} f_j(\mathbf{x}_R) \mathcal{T}_{j,\log \mu}(\mathbf{r}_L).$$

Thus, the original problem reduces to proving the evaluation of $F(\mathbf{x}_R)$ at $\mathbf{r}_R$, which can be accomplished through the following steps:

1. Compute the commitment to $F(\mathbf{x}_R)$ as $C_F = \prod_{j \in [0,\mu)} C_j^{\mathcal{T}_{j,\log \mu}(\mathbf{r}_L)}$.
2. Prove the correctness of C_F using our FC scheme as C_F can be expressed as $\langle \mathbf{C}, (\mathcal{T}_{0,\log \mu}(\mathbf{r}_L), \dots, \mathcal{T}_{\mu-1,\log \mu}(\mathbf{r}_L)) \rangle$, where $\mathbf{C}$ is already committed in C.
3. Generate a proof for the evaluation of F at $\mathbf{r}_R$ with the PC scheme.

Therefore, to prove the evaluation of $f(\mathbf{x})$ at a random point $\mathbf{r}$, the prover sends C_F along with proofs generated by the FC and PC schemes to the verifier, who then checks both proofs. The above process can be adapted into a zero-knowledge version via standard techniques [20,40]. Here, the underlying PC is replaced with its zero-knowledge variant, while the FC component does not require zero-knowledge, as it only operates on hidden commitments.

5 Performance Evaluation

In this section, we implement the non-interactive variants of FlexProofs[1] in the single-thread and evaluate their performance. For field and group operations, we use the mcl library and choose BN_SNARK1 elliptic curve to achieve approximately 100 bits of security. Our codes are run on an Intel(R) Xeon(R) E-2286G CPU @ 4.0GHz with 6 cores and 64GB memory. Unless otherwise stated, we run each experiment 3 times and report their average.

5.1 Evaluation of Our FC Scheme

We evaluate our FC scheme for $n \in \{2^8, 2^9, 2^{10}, 2^{11}, 2^{12}\}$, and show the results in Table 2.

Proof Size. The proof size grows with $\log n$, and is about 9.91 KiB for $n = 2^{12}$.

Commit. As shown in Table 2, the time costs of FC.Commit are roughly proportional to n. For $n = 2^{12}$, committing needs 0.54s.

Batch Opening. For $n = 2^{12}$, the running time of FC.BOpen$(t = 32)$ is approximately 1.73 s, which is only 3% of the total time required to run FC.BOpen$(t = 1)$ 32 times. Fig. 2 compares the running time of a single FC.BOpen call with batch size t (denoted FC.BOpen-t) against t sequential calls with batch size 1 (denoted $t \times$ FC.BOpen-1), for $n = 2^{12}$ and $t \in \{16, 32, 64, 128, 256, 512\}$. And it shows that the efficiency gain of batching increases with the batch size t.

[1] https://github.com/FlexProofs.

Table 2. Single-threaded running time of our FC scheme.

n	2^8	2^9	2^{10}	2^{11}	2^{12}
$\|\pi_y\|$ (KiB)	6.66	7.47	8.28	9.09	9.91
FC.Commit (s)	0.03	0.07	0.14	0.27	0.54
FC.BOpen($t = 1$) (s)	0.12	0.23	0.45	0.88	1.70
FC.BVerify($t = 1$) (s)	0.004	0.005	0.005	0.006	0.007
FC.BOpen($t = 32$) (s)	0.13	0.23	0.46	0.89	1.73
FC.BVerify($t = 32$) (s)	0.007	0.01	0.02	0.03	0.05

Batch Verification. For $n = 2^{12}$, the running time of FC.BVerify($t = 32$) is approximately 0.05 s, which is only 22% of the total time required to run FC.BVerify($t = 1$) 32 times. This demonstrates the high efficiency of our proposed batching technique. Fig. 3 compares the running time of a single FC.BVerify call with batch size t (denoted FC.BVerify-t) against t sequential calls with batch size 1 (denoted $t \times$ FC.BVerify-1), for $n = 2^{12}$ and $t \in \{16, 32, 64, 128, 256, 512\}$.

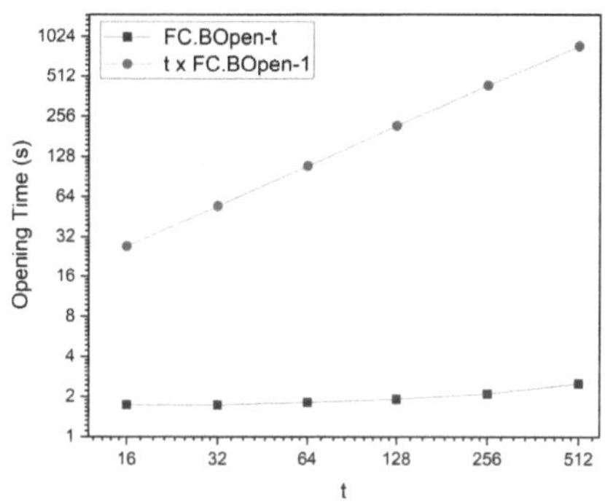

Fig. 2. Opening time. Both axes use logarithmic scales.

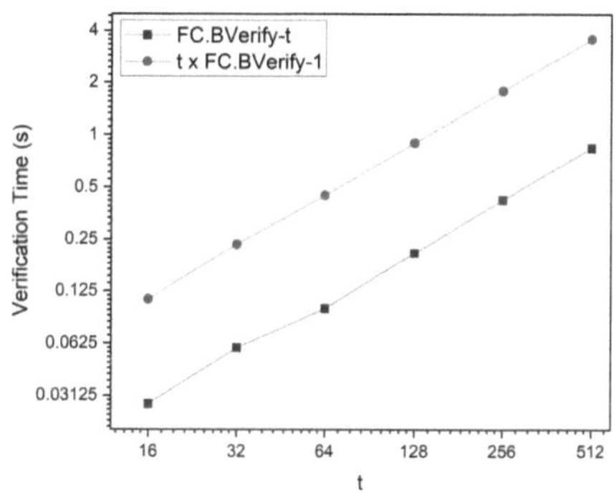

Fig. 3. Verification time. Both axes use logarithmic scales.

5.2 Evaluation of FlexProofs and Comparison with HydraProofs

We microbenchmark FlexProofs with batch sizes $b \in \{2 \log N, \log^2 N\}$. We also compared it with HydraProofs [54], the state-of-the-art vector commitment scheme. HydraProofs is the only known VC construction that achieves $\mathcal{O}(N)$ time to generate all opening proofs for a vector of size N, while also being directly compatible with a family of zkSNARKs. For fairness, we implement both schemes in C++ using the same elliptic curve and techniques for $N \in \{2^{16}, 2^{18}, 2^{20}, 2^{22}, 2^{24}\}$. The experimental results are shown in Table 3.

Table 3. The comparison between FlexProofs (FP) and HydraProofs.

N		2^{16}	2^{18}	2^{20}	2^{22}	2^{24}
Commit (s)	FP ($b = 2\log N$)	0.83	3.02	8.81	31.87	116.61
	FP ($b = \log^2 N$)	0.82	3.01	8.70	31.53	116.41
	HydraProofs	0.82	3.01	8.66	31.71	116.64
Compute all proofs (s)	FP ($b = 2\log N$)	1.03	3.58	12.17	43.64	159.30
	FP ($b = \log^2 N$)	**0.23**	**0.82**	**2.61**	**9.24**	**32.71**
	HydraProofs	1.42	4.82	17.15	58.66	210.07
Verify a proof (s)	FP ($b = 2\log N$)	**0.006**	**0.007**	**0.008**	**0.009**	**0.011**
	FP ($b = \log^2 N$)	0.01	0.012	0.013	0.015	0.017
	HydraProofs	0.01	0.011	0.012	0.013	0.014
Proof size (KiB)	FP ($b = 2\log N$)	8.91	10	11.09	12.19	13.28
	FP ($b = \log^2 N$)	15.91	19	22.34	25.94	29.78
	HydraProofs	**5.53**	**6.63**	**7.81**	**9.09**	**10.47**

Commit. In FlexProofs, the commitment time grows roughly linearly with N, taking about 0.82 seconds when $N = 2^{16}$. HydraProofs shows a similar linear growth in commitment time.

Computing all Proofs. In FlexProofs, computing all proofs requires $\mathcal{O}(N)$ field operations and $\mathcal{O}(N/b+\sqrt{N}\log N)$ cryptographic operations, so the proving time decreases as b grows. Experiments confirm this: when $N = 2^{16}$, computing all proofs takes 1.03 seconds for $b = 2\log N$, but only 0.23 seconds for $b = \log^2 N$. In HydraProofs, computing all proofs requires $\mathcal{O}(N)$ field operations and $\mathcal{O}(N)$ cryptographic operations. Thus, FlexProofs requires fewer cryptographic operations as b increases. Consequently, when $N = 2^{16}$, FlexProofs is about 1.3× faster than HydraProofs with $b = 2\log N$, and about 6× faster with $b = \log^2 N$.

Verifying a Proof. When $b = 2\log N$, the verification complexity in FlexProofs is $\mathcal{O}(\log^2 N)$, whereas for $b = \log^2 N$ it increases to $\mathcal{O}(\log^3 N)$. Experimental results confirm this: when $N = 2^{16}$, verifying a proof takes 0.006 seconds for $b = 2\log N$, and 0.01 seconds for $b = \log^2 N$. In HydraProofs, the verification complexity is also $\mathcal{O}(\log^2 N)$. And the experimental results show that when $b = 2\log N$, FlexProofs verifies proofs slightly faster than HydraProofs.

Proof Size. When $b = 2\log N$, the proof size in FlexProofs is $\mathcal{O}(\log N)$, while for $b = \log^2 N$ it grows to $\mathcal{O}(\log^2 N)$. In HydraProofs, the proof size has complexity $\mathcal{O}(\log^2 N)$. For the values of N shown in Table 3, HydraProofs yields smaller proofs; for instance, when $N = 2^{16}$ it requires only 5.53 KiB compared to 8.91 KiB in our scheme. This gap arises because asymptotic bounds capture only the growth trend as N increases, while for moderate N the hidden constants dominate the concrete size. As N becomes larger, the slower asymptotic growth of FlexProofs is expected to eventually result in smaller proofs.

6 Conclusions

We first propose an FC scheme for multi-exponentiations with batch opening. Based on this, we construct FlexProofs, a VC scheme that can generate all proofs for a vector of size N in optimal time $\mathcal{O}(N)$ (incurred by $\mathcal{O}(N)$ field operations and $\mathcal{O}(N/b + \sqrt{N}\log N)$ cryptographic operations) and is directly compatible with zkSNARKs, where batch size b ranges from 1 to $\sqrt{N}$. Finally, FlexProofs, combined with suitable zkSNARKs, enables applications such as VSS and VRA.

Acknowledgments. The authors would like to thank the anonymous shepherd and reviewers for their insightful comments. The corresponding author Liang Feng Zhang's research is partially supported by the National Natural Science Foundation of China (Grant No. 62372299).

A Definitions

Definition 7 (Zero-Knowledge of Polynomial Commitment). *A polynomial commitment (PC) scheme is zero-knowledge if for any λ, n, d, adversary $\mathcal{A}$, and simulator $\mathcal{S}$, we have:*

$$\Pr\left(Real_{\mathcal{A},f}(1^\lambda) = 1\right) \approx \Pr\left(Ideal_{\mathcal{A},\mathcal{S}}(1^\lambda) = 1\right).$$

$\mathbf{Real}_{\mathcal{A},f}(1^\lambda)$:	$\boldsymbol{Ideal}_{\mathcal{A},\mathcal{S}}(1^\lambda)$:
1. $\mathsf{pp} \leftarrow \mathsf{PC.Setup}(1^\lambda, 1^n, 1^d)$ 2. $C_f \leftarrow \mathsf{PC.Commit}(f, r_f)$ 3. $m \leftarrow \mathcal{A}(1^\lambda, \mathsf{pp}, C_f)$ 4. For each step $j \in \{2, 3, \ldots, m\}$: (a) $\mathbf{x}_j \leftarrow \mathcal{A}(1^\lambda, C_f, y_1, \ldots, y_{j-1}, \pi_1, \ldots, \pi_{j-1}, \mathsf{pp})$ (b) $y_j, \pi_j \leftarrow \mathsf{PC.Eval}(f, x_j)$ 5. Output $b \leftarrow \mathcal{A}(1^\lambda, C_f, y_1, \ldots, y_m, \pi_1, \ldots, \pi_m, \mathsf{pp})$	*1.* $(C_f, \mathsf{pp}, t) \leftarrow \mathcal{S}(1^\lambda, 1^n)$ *2.* $m \leftarrow \mathcal{A}(1^\lambda, \mathsf{pp}, C_f)$ *3. For each step* $j \in \{2, 3, \ldots, m\}$*:* *(a)* $\mathbf{x}_j \leftarrow \mathcal{A}(1^\lambda, C_f, y_1, \ldots, y_{j-1}, \pi_1, \ldots, \pi_{j-1}, \mathsf{pp})$ *(b)* $y_j, \pi_j \leftarrow \mathcal{S}(\mathsf{pp}, f, \mathbf{x}_j)$ *4. Output* $b \leftarrow \mathcal{A}(1^\lambda, C_f, y_1, \ldots, y_m, \pi_1, \ldots, \pi_m, \mathsf{pp})$

Definition 8 (Position Hiding of Vector Commitment). *A vector commitment (VC) scheme is position hiding if for any PPT adversary $\mathcal{A}$ and simulator $\mathcal{S}$, the following holds:*

$$\Pr\left(Real_{\mathcal{A},\mathbf{m}}(1^\lambda) = 1\right) \approx \Pr\left(Ideal_{\mathcal{A},\mathcal{S}}(1^\lambda) = 1\right).$$

$\mathbf{Real}_{\mathcal{A},\mathbf{m}}(1^\lambda)$:	$\textit{Ideal}_{\mathcal{A},\mathcal{S}}(1^\lambda)$:
1. $\mathsf{pp} \leftarrow \mathsf{VC.Setup}(1^\lambda, 1^N)$	1. $(C, \mathsf{pp}, \mathit{trap}) \leftarrow \mathcal{S}(1^\lambda, N)$
2. $C \leftarrow \mathsf{VC.Commit}(\mathbf{m})$	2. $i_1, \ldots, i_n, m_{i_1}, \ldots, m_{i_n} \leftarrow \mathcal{A}(1^\lambda, \mathsf{pp}, C)$ (for $n < N$)
3. $i_1, \ldots, i_n, m_{i_1}, \ldots, m_{i_n} \leftarrow \mathcal{A}(1^\lambda, \mathsf{pp}, C)$ (for $n < N$)	3. $\{\pi_{i_1}, \ldots, \pi_{i_n}\} \leftarrow \mathcal{S}(i_1, \ldots, i_n, m_{i_1}, \ldots, m_{i_n}, \mathit{trap}, \mathsf{pp})$
4. $\{\pi_i\}_{i=1}^N \leftarrow \mathsf{VC.OpenAll}(\mathbf{m})$. Send $\{\pi_{i_1}, \ldots, \pi_{i_n}\}$ to $\mathcal{A}$	4. Output $b \leftarrow \mathcal{A}(1^\lambda, C, m_{i_1}, \ldots, m_{i_n}, \pi_{i_1}, \ldots, \pi_{i_n}, \mathsf{pp})$
5. Output $b \leftarrow \mathcal{A}(1^\lambda, C, m_{i_1}, \ldots, m_{i_n}, \pi_{i_1}, \ldots, \pi_{i_n}, \mathsf{pp})$	

B Our FC Scheme

Assumption 1 **(q-Strong Diffie-Hellman assumption (q-SDH)[9]).** *Given a security parameter λ, algorithm* BG *outputs* $\mathbf{bg} = (p, \mathbb{G}_1, \mathbb{G}_2, \mathbb{G}_T, e, g_1, g_2)$. *The q-SDH assumption holds relative to* BG *if for any efficient algorithm $\mathcal{A}$,*

$$\Pr\left[\begin{array}{c}\mathbf{bg} \leftarrow \mathsf{BG}(1^\lambda), \gamma \xleftarrow{\$} \mathbb{F}_p, \mathsf{pp} = (\mathbf{bg}, g_1^\gamma, \ldots, g_1^{\gamma^q}, g_2^\gamma) : \\ (a, g_1^{1/(\gamma+a)}) \leftarrow \mathcal{A}(1^\lambda, \mathsf{pp})\end{array}\right] \leq \mathsf{negl}(\lambda).$$

Assumption 2 **(q-Auxiliary Structured Double Pairing assumption)(q-ASDBP).** *Given a security parameter λ,* BG *output* $\mathbf{bg} = (p, \mathbb{G}_1, \mathbb{G}_2, \mathbb{G}_T, e, g_1, g_2)$. *The q-ASDBP assumption holds relative to* BG *if for any efficient algorithm $\mathcal{A}$,*

$$\Pr\left[\begin{array}{c}\mathbf{bg} \leftarrow \mathsf{BG}(1^\lambda),\ \beta \xleftarrow{\$} \mathbb{F}_p, (A_0, \ldots, A_{q-1}) \leftarrow \mathcal{A}(\mathbf{bg}, g_1^\beta, \{g_2^{\beta^{2i}}\}_{i=1}^{q-1}) : \\ ((A_0, \ldots, A_{q-1}) \neq \mathbf{1}_{\mathbb{G}_1}) \wedge (1_{\mathbb{G}_T} = \prod_{i=0}^{q-1} e(A_i, g_2^{\beta^{2i}}))\end{array}\right] \leq \mathsf{negl}(\lambda).$$

Lemma 1. *Let $\mathbf{A} \in \mathbb{G}_1^n$. Let $\mathbf{b}^{(i)} \in \mathbb{F}_p^n$ and $y_i \in \mathbb{G}_1$ for $i \in [0, t)$. Assume each $r_i (i \in [0, t))$ is chosen uniformly at random from $\mathbb{F}_p$. Then with probability at least $1 - 1/p$, all Eq. (2) are satisfied iff Eq. (3) is satisfied.*

Proof. Clearly, if Eq. (2) holds, then Eq. (3) holds. For the other direction, assume the correct value of $\mathbf{A}^{\mathbf{b}^{(i)}}$ is $\hat{y}_i$ for $i \in [0, t)$, then there exists at least one j such that $y_j \neq \hat{y}_j$ and $\prod_{i \in [0,t)} y_i^{r_i} = \prod_{i \in [0,t)} \hat{y}_i^{r_i}$. Define the $a_i = \log_{g_1} y_i / \hat{y}_i$, then there will be at least one j for which $a_j \neq 0$ and $\sum_{i \in [0,t)} a_i r_i = 0 \mod p$. By the Schwartz-Zippel lemma [58,77], this occurs with probability $\leq 1/p$. Therefore, if Eq. (2) is not fully satisfied, Eq. (3) holds with probability at most $1/p$. □

Non-interactive Argument of Knowledge in the ROM. Bünz et al. [12] define a non-interactive argument of knowledge in the random oracle model (ROM). In ROM, a hash function is replaced by a random function which is sampled from the space of all random functions $\rho \leftarrow \mathcal{U}(1^\lambda)$. The non-interactive argument is an argument system where the prover sends a single message π, and the verifier using the proof accepts or rejects. Both the prover and verifier have access to a random oracle ρ. An argument of knowledge in the ROM has the property that for each convincing prover there exists an extractor which can rewind the prover and reinitialize the random oracle with new randomness.

Definition 9. (Non-interactive argument of knowledge in the ROM, from [12]). *A non-interactive argument is an argument of knowledge for a relation $\mathcal{R}$ with knowledge error $\kappa(\lambda)$ if for every adversary $\widetilde{\mathcal{P}}$ there exists an extractor $\mathcal{E}$ such that*

$$\Pr\left[\begin{array}{c}\rho \leftarrow \mathcal{U}(1^\lambda),\ \mathsf{crs} \leftarrow \mathsf{Setup}(1^\lambda), (\mathbb{x}, \pi) \leftarrow \widetilde{\mathcal{P}}^\rho(\mathsf{crs}), \\ \mathbb{w} \leftarrow \mathcal{E}^{\widetilde{\mathcal{P}},\rho}(\mathsf{crs}, \mathbb{x}, \pi) : (\mathcal{V}^\rho(\mathsf{crs}, \mathbb{x}, \pi) = 1) \wedge ((\mathbb{x}, \mathbb{w}) \notin \mathcal{R})\end{array}\right] \leq \kappa(\lambda).$$

The $\mathcal{E}$ can rewind the prover and reinitialize (but not program) the random oracle.

B.1 Function Binding

Before proving the function binding of our FC scheme, we first show that our FC scheme is a non-interactive argument of knowledge in the ROM for the relation $\mathcal{R}_B = \{(C \in \mathbb{G}_T, \{\mathbf{b}^{(i)}\}_{i\in[0,t)} \subset \mathbb{F}_p^n, \{y_i\}_{i\in[0,t)} \subset \mathbb{G}_1, \mathbf{v} \in \mathbb{G}_2^n; \mathbf{A} \in \mathbb{G}_1^n) : (C = \mathbf{A}*\mathbf{v}) \wedge (\forall i \in [0,t), y_i = \langle \mathbf{A}, \mathbf{b}^{(i)} \rangle)\}$. That is, we show that for any PPT adversary $\mathcal{A}_B$, we can construct a PPT extractor $\mathcal{E}_B$ that extracts the vector $\mathbf{A}$ such that

$$\Pr\left[\begin{array}{c}\rho \leftarrow \mathcal{U}(1^\lambda),\ \mathsf{pp}(=\mathbf{v}) \leftarrow \mathsf{FC.Setup}(1^\lambda, 1^n), \\ (C, \{\mathbf{b}^{(i)}\}_{i\in[0,t)}, \{y_i\}_{i\in[0,t)}, \pi_y) \leftarrow \mathcal{A}_B^\rho(\mathsf{pp}), \\ \mathbf{A} \leftarrow \mathcal{E}_B^{\mathcal{A}_B,\rho}(\mathsf{pp}, C, \{\mathbf{b}^{(i)}\}_{i\in[0,t)}, \{y_i\}_{i\in[0,t)}, \pi_y) : \\ (\mathsf{FC.BVerify}^\rho(C, \{\mathbf{b}^{(i)}\}_{i\in[0,t)}, \{y_i\}_{i\in[0,t)}, \pi_y) = 1) \wedge \\ ((C, \{\mathbf{b}^{(i)}\}_{i\in[0,t)}, \{y_i\}_{i\in[0,t)}, \mathbf{v}; \mathbf{A}) \notin \mathcal{R}_B)\end{array}\right] \leq \mathsf{negl}(\lambda).$$

To prove this, we first prove the knowledge soundness of the FC.BOpen and FC.BVerify algorithms in the single-instance case (specifically, $t = 1$) and without the random value r_0.

Knowledge Soundness in the Single-Instance Case and Without the Random Value. For simplicity, we denote the FC.BOpen and FC.BVerify algorithms in the single-instance case (specifically, $t = 1$) and without the random value r_0 as FC.Open and FC.Verify. Note that in FC.Open and FC.Verify, $\mathbf{b} = \mathbf{b}^{(0)}$ and $y = y_0$. We will show that the scheme consisting of algorithms FC.Setup, FC.Commit, FC.Open and FC.Verify is a non-interactive argument of knowledge in the ROM for the relation $\mathcal{R}_S = \{(C \in \mathbb{G}_T, \mathbf{b} \in \mathbb{F}_p^n, y \in \mathbb{G}_1, \mathbf{v} \in \mathbb{G}_2^n; \mathbf{A} \in \mathbb{G}_1^n) : C = \mathbf{A} * \mathbf{v} \wedge y = \langle \mathbf{A}, \mathbf{b} \rangle\}$. That is, we show that for any PPT adversary $\mathcal{A}_S$, we can construct a PPT extractor $\mathcal{E}_S$ that extracts the vector $\mathbf{A}$ such that

$$\Pr\left[\begin{array}{c}\rho \leftarrow \mathcal{U}(1^\lambda),\ \mathsf{pp}(=\mathbf{v}) \leftarrow \mathsf{FC.Setup}(1^\lambda, 1^n), \\ (C, \mathbf{b}, y, \pi_y) \leftarrow \mathcal{A}_S^\rho(\mathsf{pp}),\ \mathbf{A} \leftarrow \mathcal{E}_S^{\mathcal{A}_S,\rho}(\mathsf{pp}, C, \mathbf{b}, y, \pi_y) : \\ (\mathsf{FC.Verify}^\rho(C, \mathbf{b}, y, \pi_y) = 1) \wedge ((C, \mathbf{b}, y, \mathbf{v}; \mathbf{A}) \notin \mathcal{R}_S)\end{array}\right] \leq \mathsf{negl}(\lambda).$$

The existence of $\mathcal{E}_S$ is guaranteed by [12].

Constructing $\mathcal{E}_B$. $\mathcal{E}_B$ builds a adversary $\mathcal{A}_S$ against the extractability game of algorithms $\mathsf{FC.Verify}$. $\mathcal{A}_S$ is given $(\mathsf{pp}, C, \{\mathbf{b}^{(i)}\}_{i\in[0,t)}, \{y_i\}_{i\in[0,t)}, \pi_y)$, computes $\mathbf{b} = \sum_{i\in[0,t)} r_i\mathbf{b}^{(i)}$ and $y = \prod_{i\in[0,t)} y_i^{r_i}$, and output $(C, \mathbf{b}, y, \pi_y)$. Then $\mathcal{E}_B$ invokes $\mathcal{E}_S$ which outputs the vector $\mathbf{A}$ such that $C = \mathbf{A} * \mathbf{v}$ and $y = \langle \mathbf{A}, \mathbf{b}\rangle$. The equation $y = \langle \mathbf{A}, \mathbf{b}\rangle$ means that $\prod_{i\in[0,t)} y_i^{r_i} = \langle \mathbf{A}, \sum_{i\in[0,t)} r_i\mathbf{b}^{(i)}\rangle$. According to Lemma 1, with overwhelming probability, all $\{\langle \mathbf{A}, \mathbf{b}^{(i)}\rangle = y_i\}_{i\in[0,t)}$ are satisfied. Therefore, $\mathcal{E}_B$ can output vector $\mathbf{A}$ such that $(C, \{\mathbf{b}^{(i)}\}_{i\in[0,t)}, \{y_i\}_{i\in[0,t)}, \mathbf{v}; \mathbf{A}) \in \mathcal{R}_B$ with overwhelming probability. The probability $\mathcal{E}_B$ fails is only negligible to the security parameter.

Proving Function Binding. From the above, we prove the function binding of our FC scheme as follows. Assuming that an adversary $\mathcal{A}$ outputs C, $\{\mathbf{b}^{(i)}, y_i, \hat{y}_i\}_{i\in[0,t)}, \pi_y, \pi_{\hat{y}}$ such that (1) $\mathsf{FC.BVerify}(C, \{\mathbf{b}^{(i)}\}_{i\in[0,t)}, \{y_i\}_{i\in[0,t)}, \pi_y) = 1$ and (2) $\mathsf{FC.BVerify}(C, \{\mathbf{b}^{(i)}\}_{i\in[0,t)}, \{\hat{y}_i\}_{i\in[0,t)}, \pi_{\hat{y}}){=}1$ with non-negligible probability. By the knowledge soundness of our FC scheme, equation (1) means that we can extract a vector $\mathbf{A}$ such that $C = \mathbf{A} * \mathbf{v}$ and $\{y_i = \langle \mathbf{A}, \mathbf{b}^{(i)}\rangle)\}_{i\in[0,t)}$, equation (2) means that we can extract a vector $\mathbf{A}'$ such that $C = \mathbf{A}' * \mathbf{v}$ and $\{\hat{y}_i = \langle \mathbf{A}', \mathbf{b}^{(i)}\rangle)\}_{i\in[0,t)}$. Since there exists $j \in [0, t)$ such that $y_j \neq \hat{y}_j$, we have $\mathbf{A} \neq \mathbf{A}'$. Since $\mathbf{A} \neq \mathbf{A}'$ and $\mathbf{A} * \mathbf{v} = \mathbf{A}' * \mathbf{v}$, we construct another adversary $\mathcal{B}$ which outputs $(\mathbf{A}[i]/\mathbf{A}'[i])_{i\in[0,n)}$ which satisfy $(\mathbf{A}[0]/\mathbf{A}'[0], \ldots, \mathbf{A}[n-1]/\mathbf{A}'[n-1]) \neq 1_{\mathbb{G}_1} \wedge 1_{\mathbb{G}_T} = \prod_{i=0}^{n-1} e(\mathbf{A}[i]/\mathbf{A}'[i], h^{\beta^{2i}})$ with non-negligible probability, breaking n-ASDBP assumption.

C Correctness and Security Analysis of FlexProofs

Theorem 2. *FlexProofs satisfies the correctness property (Definition 5).*

Proof. We first prove that the interactive version of FlexProofs satisfies the correctness property. Specifically, we show that for any security parameter λ, any integer $N > 0$, any vector $\mathbf{m} \in \mathbb{F}_p^N$, and any index $i \in [0, N)$, it holds that:

$$\Pr\left[\begin{array}{c}\mathsf{pp} \leftarrow \mathsf{VC.Setup}(1^\lambda, 1^N), (C, \mathsf{aux}) \leftarrow \mathsf{VC.Commit}(\mathbf{m}),\\ \langle \mathcal{P}_{OpenAll}(\mathsf{pp}, \mathsf{aux}, i, \mathbf{m}),\ \mathcal{V}_i(\mathsf{pp}, C, i, \mathbf{m}[i])\rangle = 1\end{array}\right] = 1.$$

By Eq. (8) and (9), C is a commitment to a vector $\mathbf{C}(= (C_0, \ldots, C_{\mu-1}))$ under the FC scheme. Let $k = \lfloor i/(\mu b)\rfloor$ and $K = [kb, (k+1)b)$. According to Eq. (10), the proof $\pi_{\mathbf{C}_k}$ is a batch proof for $\{C_a = \langle \mathbf{C}, \mathbf{u}_a\rangle\}_{a\in K}$ (i.e., C_a is the a-th element of $\mathbf{C}$). By Definition 1, the correctness property of the FC scheme ensures that $\mathsf{FC.BVerify}(C, \{\mathbf{u}_a\}_{a\in K}, \{C_a\}_{a\in K}, \pi_{\mathbf{C}_k}) = 1$.

As per Eq. (11), the prover $\mathcal{P}_{OpenAll}$ random its values. For convenience, let $[i]_\mu = i \bmod \mu$. As per Eq. (12), the verifier $\mathcal{V}_i$ computes $D_{\lfloor i/\mu\rfloor}$ and $y_{\lfloor i/\mu\rfloor, [i]_\mu}$. As described in Step 2.2, the verifier also receives $\{D_w, y_{w,[i]_\mu}\}_{w\in\mathsf{sib}(\lfloor i/\mu\rfloor)}$, where $\mathsf{sib}(\lfloor i/\mu\rfloor)$ is the set of sibling nodes along the path from the root to the $\lfloor i/\mu\rfloor$-th leaf in the folding tree. Then, the verifier computes:

$$D^* = \sum_{w\in\mathsf{sib}(\lfloor i/\mu\rfloor)} D_w + D_{\lfloor i/\mu\rfloor},\quad y^*_{[i]_\mu} = \sum_{w\in\mathsf{sib}(\lfloor i/\mu\rfloor)} y_{w,[i]_\mu} + y_{\lfloor i/\mu\rfloor,[i]_\mu}.$$

By the construction of the folding scheme, we have: $D^* = \prod_{j=0}^{\mu-1} C_j^{r_j}$ and $g^* = \sum_{j=0}^{\mu-1} r_j f_j$, so that D^* is a commitment to the folded polynomial g^*, and $y^*_{[i]_\mu} = g^*(\mathsf{Bin}([i]_\mu))$. As per Step 2.3, the proof $\pi^*_{[i]_\mu}$ proves $y^*_{[i]_\mu} = g^*(\mathsf{Bin}([i]_\mu))$. Then, by Definition 3, the correctness property of the underlying PC scheme implies that $\mathsf{PC.Verify}(D^*, \mathsf{Bin}([i]_\mu), y^*_{[i]_\mu}, \pi^*_{[i]_\mu}) = 1$.

Thus, the verifier accepts the proof with probability 1, confirming the correctness of the interactive protocol. And under the random oracle model, the correctness of the non-interactive protocol resulting from the Fiat-Shamir transformation [74] follows directly from the established correctness of the underlying interactive scheme.

Theorem 3. *FlexProofs satisfies the position binding property (Definition 6) in the ROM.*

Proof. We first prove that the interactive version of FlexProofs satisfies the position binding property. Concretely, we show that for any security parameter λ, any integer $N > 0$, and any PPT adversary $\mathcal{A}_{OpenAll}$,

$$\Pr\left[\begin{matrix}\mathsf{pp} \leftarrow \mathsf{VC.Setup}(1^\lambda, 1^N) : (\langle \mathcal{A}_{OpenAll}, \mathcal{V}_i\rangle(\mathsf{pp}, C, i, m_i) = 1)\wedge \\ (\langle \mathcal{A}_{OpenAll}, \mathcal{V}_i\rangle(\mathsf{pp}, C, i, m_i') = 1) \wedge (m_i \neq m_i')\end{matrix}\right] \leq \mathsf{negl}(\lambda).$$

Suppose there is a PPT adversary $\mathcal{A}_{OpenAll}$ that breaks the position binding property of the interactive version with a non-negligible probability ϵ. To distinguish the messages, denote all messages and proofs during the second acceptance (for m_i') with primes.

Let $k = \lfloor i/(\mu b) \rfloor$ and $K = [kb, (k+1)b)$. Then either

$$\exists a \in K : C_a \neq C_a', \text{ or} \tag{17}$$
$$\forall a \in K : C_a = C_a'. \tag{18}$$

For the remaining part of the proof, we discuss two cases. In the first case, $\mathcal{A}_{OpenAll}$ breaks the position binding property of the interactive version with two accepting proof transcripts that satisfies (17). In the second case, $\mathcal{A}$ breaks the position binding property of the interactive version with two accepting proof transcripts that satisfies (18). For $\ell \in \{1, 2\}$, let ϵ_ℓ be the probability that case ℓ occurs. Then $\epsilon = \epsilon_1 + \epsilon_2$. We will show that ϵ is negligible by showing that both ϵ_1 and ϵ_2 are negligible.

ϵ_1 is negligible. If ϵ_1 is non-negligible, we construct an adversary $\mathcal{B}_{FC}$ that breaks the function binding of the FC scheme with probability at least ϵ_1 and thus give a contradiction. Given the pp_{FC} in Eq. (7), $\mathcal{B}_{FC}$ generates pp_{PC} as per Eq. (7), and invokes $\mathcal{A}_{OpenAll}$ with $\mathsf{pp} = \{\mathsf{pp}_{FC}, \mathsf{pp}_{PC}\}$. Upon receiving $\mathcal{A}_{OpenAll}$'s two accepting proof transcripts that satisfies (17), $\mathcal{B}_{FC}$ outputs

$$(C, \{\mathbf{u}_a, C_a, C_a'\}_{a\in K}, \pi_{\mathbf{C}_k}, \pi_{\mathbf{C}_k}').$$

Note that these values satisfies the following properties:

(1) $\mathsf{FC.BVerify}(C, \{\mathbf{u}_a\}_{a\in K}, \{C_a\}_{a\in K}, \pi_{\mathbf{C}_k}) = 1$; (by the transcript for m_i)
(2) $\mathsf{FC.BVerify}(C, \{\mathbf{u}_a\}_{a\in K}, \{C'_a\}_{a\in K}, \pi'_{\mathbf{C}_k}) = 1$; (by the transcript for m'_i)
(3) $\exists a \in K : C_a \neq C'_a$. (by Eq. (17))

Therefore, $\mathcal{B}_{FC}$ breaks the function binding property of the FC scheme with probability $\geq \epsilon_1$, which gives a contradiction.

$\epsilon_2$is negligible. The soundness of the folding scheme for PC.HyperEval is guaranteed by [10,27]. If ϵ_2 is non-negligible, we construct an adversary $\mathcal{B}_{FH}$ that breaks the soundness of the folding scheme with probability at least ϵ_2 and thus give a contradiction.

For convenience, let $j = \lfloor i/\mu \rfloor$ and $[i]_\mu = i \bmod \mu$. First, recall that the accepting proof transcript contains the following: (1) a random value r_j, (2) $\{D_w, y_{w,[i]_\mu}\}_{w\in \mathsf{sib}(j)}$, where $\mathsf{sib}(j)$ denotes the set of sibling nodes along the path from the root to the j-th leaf node in the folding tree and (3) an opening proof $\pi^*_{[i]_\mu}$ of the final folded polynomial.

Given the pp_{PC} in Eq. (7), $\mathcal{B}_{FH}$ generates pp_{FC} as per Eq. (7), and invokes $\mathcal{A}_{OpenAll}$ with $\mathsf{pp} = \{\mathsf{pp}_{FC}, \mathsf{pp}_{PC}\}$. Upon receiving $\mathcal{A}_{OpenAll}$'s two accepting proof transcripts that satisfies (17), $\mathcal{B}_{FH}$ computes

$$D_c = \sum_{w\in \mathsf{sib}(j)} D_w,\ y_{[i]_\mu} = \sum_{w\in \mathsf{sib}(j)} y_{w,[i]_\mu},\ D'_c = \sum_{w\in \mathsf{sib}(j)} D'_w,\ y'_{[i]_\mu} = \sum_{w\in \mathsf{sib}(j)} y'_{w,[i]_\mu}.$$

Then it outputs two folding transcripts

$$\rho_1 = (D_c, C_j, [i]_\mu, y_{[i]_\mu}, m_i, r_j, \pi^*_{[i]_\mu}), \rho_2 = (D'_c, C'_j, [i]_\mu, y'_{[i]_\mu}, m'_i, r'_j, \pi^{*\prime}_{[i]_\mu}).$$

Note that these values satisfies the following properties:

(1) ρ_1 passes the verification of the folding scheme; (by the transcript for m_i)
(2) ρ_2 passes the verification of the folding scheme; (by the transcript for m'_i)
(3) $C_j = C'_j$; (by Eq. (18))
(4) $m_i \neq m'_i$.

Therefore, $\mathcal{B}_{FH}$ breaks the soundness of the folding scheme for PC.HyperEval with probability $\geq \epsilon_2$, which gives a contradiction.

We have shown that the interactive version of FlexProofs satisfies soundness, captured by the *position binding* property. Next, we show that the interactive version of FlexProofs satisfies a stronger notion of soundness called *state restoration soundness* [6]. To prove state restoration soundness, we consider adversaries that are allowed to reset or rewind the verifier, potentially reusing the verifier's randomness or internal state. We note that the above soundness proof is robust to such behaviors. In particular, the reductions used in both cases (function binding and folding soundness) remain valid even if the verifier's challenge randomness is reused across different transcripts. Hence, the soundness proof already implies that the interactive protocol satisfies state restoration soundness.

The work [74] formally proves that as long as an interactive proof protocol is secure against state restoration attacks, then the non-interactive protocol by applying their Fiat-Shamir transformation is sound in the random oracle model. Therefore, we conclude that our non-interactive scheme satisfies soundness (i.e., position binding) in the random oracle model. □

References

1. Abbaszadeh, K., Pappas, C., Katz, J., Papadopoulos, D.: Zero-knowledge proofs of training for deep neural networks. In: Proceedings of the 2024 on ACM SIGSAC Conference on Computer and Communications Security, pp. 4316–4330 (2024)
2. Abe, M., Fuchsbauer, G., Groth, J., Haralambiev, K., Ohkubo, M.: Structure-preserving signatures and commitments to group elements. J. Cryptol. **29**(2), 363–421 (2016)
3. Balbás, D., Catalano, D., Fiore, D., Lai, R.W.: Functional commitments for circuits from falsifiable assumptions. IACR Cryptol. ePrint Arch. **2022**, 1365 (2022)
4. Bekkerman, R., Bilenko, M., Langford, J.: Scaling Up Machine Learning: Parallel and Distributed Approaches. Cambridge University Press (2011)
5. Bellare, M., Rogaway, P.: Random oracles are practical: a paradigm for designing efficient protocols. In: Proceedings of the 1st ACM Conference on Computer and Communications Security, pp. 62–73 (1993)
6. Ben-Sasson, E., Chiesa, A., Spooner, N.: Interactive oracle proofs. In: Hirt, M., Smith, A. (eds.) Theory of Cryptography Conference, pp. 31–60. Springer (2016). https://doi.org/10.1007/978-3-662-53644-5_2
7. Benabbas, S., Gennaro, R., Vahlis, Y.: Verifiable delegation of computation over large datasets. In: Rogaway, P. (eds.) Annual Cryptology Conference, pp. 111–131. Springer (2011). https://doi.org/10.1007/978-3-642-22792-9_7
8. Biggio, B., Nelson, B., Laskov, P.: Poisoning attacks against support vector machines. arXiv preprint arXiv:1206.6389 (2012)
9. Boneh, D., Boyen, X.: Short signatures without random oracles and the SDH assumption in bilinear groups. J. Cryptol. **21**(2), 149–177 (2008)
10. Boneh, D., Drake, J., Fisch, B., Gabizon, A.: Halo infinite: proof-carrying data from additive polynomial commitments. In: Malkin, T., Peikert, C. (eds.) Annual International Cryptology Conference, pp. 649–680. Springer (2021). https://doi.org/10.1007/978-3-030-84242-0_23
11. Boneh, D., Nguyen, W., Ozdemir, A.: Efficient functional commitments: How to commit to a private function. Cryptology ePrint Archive (2021)
12. Bünz, B., Maller, M., Mishra, P., Tyagi, N., Vesely, P.: Proofs for inner pairing products and applications. In: Tibouchi, M., Wang, H. (eds.) ASIACRYPT 2021, pp. 65–97. Springer (2021). https://doi.org/10.1007/978-3-030-92078-4_3
13. Campanelli, M., Fiore, D., Querol, A.: LegoSnark: modular design and composition of succinct zero-knowledge proofs. In: Proceedings of the 2019 ACM SIGSAC Conference on Computer and Communications Security, pp. 2075–2092 (2019)
14. Campanelli, M., Nitulescu, A., Ràfols, C., Zacharakis, A., Zapico, A.: Linear-map vector commitments and their practical applications. In: Agrawal, S., Lin, D. (eds.) ASIACRYPT 2022, pp. 189–219. Springer (2022). https://doi.org/10.1007/978-3-031-22972-5_7
15. Cao, X., Fang, M., Liu, J., Gong, N.Z.: FLTRUST: byzantine-robust federated learning via trust bootstrapping. arXiv preprint arXiv:2012.13995 (2020)

16. de Castro, L., Peikert, C.: Functional commitments for all functions, with transparent setup and from sis. In: Hazay, C., Stam, M. (eds.) EUROCRYPT 2023. pp. 287–320. Springer (2023). https://doi.org/10.1007/978-3-031-30620-4_10
17. Catalano, D., Fiore, D.: Vector commitments and their applications. In: Kurosawa, K., Hanaoka, G. (eds.) PKC 2013. LNCS, vol. 7778, pp. 55–72. Springer, Heidelberg (2013). https://doi.org/10.1007/978-3-642-36362-7_5
18. Catalano, D., Fiore, D., Tucker, I.: Additive-homomorphic functional commitments and applications to homomorphic signatures. In: Agrawal, S., Lin, D. (eds.) ASIACRYPT 2022, pp. 159–188. Springer (2022). https://doi.org/10.1007/978-3-031-22972-5_6
19. Chen, B., Bünz, B., Boneh, D., Zhang, Z.: HyperPlonk: plonk with linear-time prover and high-degree custom gates. In: Hazay, C., Stam, M. (eds.) Annual International Conference on the Theory and Applications of Cryptographic Techniques, pp. 499–530. Springer (2023). https://doi.org/10.1007/978-3-031-30617-4_17
20. Chiesa, A., Forbes, M.A., Spooner, N.: A zero knowledge sumcheck and its applications. arXiv preprintarXiv:1704.02086 (2017)
21. Chor, B., Goldwasser, S., Micali, S., Awerbuch, B.: Verifiable secret sharing and achieving simultaneity in the presence of faults. In: 26th Annual Symposium on Foundations of Computer Science (SFCS 1985), pp. 383–395. IEEE (1985)
22. Chu, H., Fiore, D., Kolonelos, D., Schröder, D.: Inner product functional commitments with constant-size public parameters and openings. In: Galdi, C., Jarecki, S. (eds.) SCN 2022, pp. 639–662. Springer (2022). https://doi.org/10.1007/978-3-031-14791-3_28
23. CNBC: Amazon has been promoting its own products at the bottom of competitors' listings (2018). https://www.cnbc.com/2018/10/02/amazon-is-testing-a-new-feature-that-promotes-its-private-label-brands-inside-a-competitors-product-listing.html
24. Feldman, P.: A practical scheme for non-interactive verifiable secret sharing. In: 28th Annual Symposium on Foundations of Computer Science (SFCS 1987), pp. 427–438. IEEE (1987)
25. Fiore, D., Fournet, C., Ghosh, E., Kohlweiss, M., Ohrimenko, O., Parno, B.: Hash first, argue later: adaptive verifiable computations on outsourced data. In: Proceedings of the 2016 ACM SIGSAC Conference on Computer and Communications Security, pp. 1304–1316 (2016)
26. Fung, C., Yoon, C.J., Beschastnikh, I.: Mitigating sybils in federated learning poisoning. arXiv preprint arXiv:1808.04866 (2018)
27. Gabizon, A., Williamson, Z.J., Ciobotaru, O.: Plonk: Permutations over Lagrange-bases for Oecumenical noninteractive arguments of knowledge. Cryptology ePrint Archive (2019)
28. Gorbunov, S., Reyzin, L., Wee, H., Zhang, Z.: PointProofs: aggregating proofs for multiple vector commitments. In: CCS 2020, pp. 2007–2023 (2020)
29. Grassi, L., Khovratovich, D., Rechberger, C., Roy, A., Schofnegger, M.: Poseidon: a new hash function for {Zero-Knowledge} proof systems. In: 30th USENIX Security Symposium (USENIX Security 21), pp. 519–535 (2021)
30. Groth, J.: On the size of pairing-based non-interactive arguments. In: Fischlin, M., Coron, JS. (eds.) Annual International Conference on the Theory and Applications of Cryptographic Techniques, pp. 305–326. Springer (2016). https://doi.org/10.1007/978-3-662-49896-5_11
31. Grubbs, P., Arun, A., Zhang, Y., Bonneau, J., Walfish, M.: {Zero-Knowledge} middleboxes. In: 31st USENIX Security Symposium (USENIX Security 22), pp. 4255–4272 (2022)

32. Howe, J., et al.: The rise of crowdsourcing. Wired Mag. **14**(6), 176–183 (2006)
33. Hu, R., Guo, Y., Pan, M., Gong, Y.: Targeted poisoning attacks on social recommender systems. In: 2019 IEEE Global Communications Conference (GLOBECOM), pp. 1–6. IEEE (2019)
34. Kasyap, H., Tripathy, S.: Hidden vulnerabilities in cosine similarity based poisoning defense. In: 2022 56th Annual Conference on Information Sciences and Systems (CISS), pp. 263–268. IEEE (2022)
35. Kate, A., Zaverucha, G.M., Goldberg, I.: Constant-size commitments to polynomials and their applications. In: Abe, M. (ed.) ASIACRYPT 2010. LNCS, vol. 6477, pp. 177–194. Springer, Heidelberg (2010). https://doi.org/10.1007/978-3-642-17373-8_11
36. Kilian, J.: A note on efficient zero-knowledge proofs and arguments. In: Proceedings of the Twenty-Fourth Annual ACM Symposium on Theory of Computing, pp. 723–732 (1992)
37. Konečný, J., McMahan, H.B., Yu, F.X., Richtárik, P., Suresh, A.T., Bacon, D.: Federated learning: strategies for improving communication efficiency. arXiv preprint arXiv:1610.05492 (2016)
38. Kourtellis, N., Katevas, K., Perino, D.: FLAAS: federated learning as a service. In: Proceedings of the 1st Workshop on Distributed Machine Learning, pp. 7–13 (2020)
39. Lai, R.W.F., Malavolta, G.: Subvector commitments with application to succinct arguments. In: Boldyreva, A., Micciancio, D. (eds.) CRYPTO 2019. LNCS, vol. 11692, pp. 530–560. Springer, Cham (2019). https://doi.org/10.1007/978-3-030-26948-7_19
40. Lee, J.: Dory: Efficient, transparent arguments for generalised inner products and polynomial commitments. In: Nissim, K., Waters, B. (eds.) Theory of Cryptography Conference, pp. 1–34. Springer (2021). https://doi.org/10.1007/978-3-030-90453-1_1
41. Libert, B., Ramanna, S.C., Yung, M.: Functional commitment schemes: from polynomial commitments to pairing-based accumulators from simple assumptions. In: ICALP 2016 (2016)
42. Libert, B., Yung, M.: Concise mercurial vector commitments and independent zero-knowledge sets with short proofs. In: Micciancio, D. (ed.) TCC 2010. LNCS, vol. 5978, pp. 499–517. Springer, Heidelberg (2010). https://doi.org/10.1007/978-3-642-11799-2_30
43. Lipmaa, H., Pavlyk, K.: Succinct functional commitment for a large class of arithmetic circuits. In: Moriai, S., Wang, H. (eds.) ASIACRYPT 2020. LNCS, vol. 12493, pp. 686–716. Springer, Cham (2020). https://doi.org/10.1007/978-3-030-64840-4_23
44. Liu, J., Zhang, L.F.: Matproofs: maintainable matrix commitment with efficient aggregation. In: CCS 2022, pp. 2041–2054 (2022)
45. Liu, T., Xie, T., Zhang, J., Song, D., Zhang, Y.: Pianist: Scalable ZKROLLUPS via fully distributed zero-knowledge proofs. In: 2024 IEEE Symposium on Security and Privacy (SP), pp. 1777–1793. IEEE (2024)
46. Liu, T., Xie, X., Zhang, Y.: ZKCNN: zero knowledge proofs for convolutional neural network predictions and accuracy. In: Proceedings of the 2021 ACM SIGSAC Conference on Computer and Communications Security, pp. 2968–2985 (2021)
47. Liu, X., Yang, X., Wang, Y., Zhang, X., Yang, X.: Evaluate and guard the wisdom of crowds: zero knowledge proofs for crowdsourcing truth inference. arXiv preprint arXiv:2308.00985 (2023)

48. Luo, G., Fu, S., Gong, G.: Updatable linear map commitments and their applications in elementary databases. In: PST 2021, pp. 1–6. IEEE (2021)
49. Ma, Z., Ma, J., Miao, Y., Li, Y., Deng, R.H.: SHIELDFL: mitigating model poisoning attacks in privacy-preserving federated learning. IEEE Trans. Inf. Forensics Secur. **17**, 1639–1654 (2022)
50. McMahan, B., Moore, E., Ramage, D., Hampson, S., y Arcas, B.A.: Communication-efficient learning of deep networks from decentralized data. In: Artificial Intelligence and Statistics, pp. 1273–1282. PMLR (2017)
51. Merkle, R.C.: A digital signature based on a conventional encryption function. In: Pomerance, C. (eds.) CRYPTO 1987, pp. 369–378. Springer (1987). https://doi.org/10.1007/3-540-48184-2_32
52. Papamanthou, C., Shi, E., Tamassia, R.: Signatures of correct computation. In: Sahai, A. (ed.) TCC 2013. LNCS, vol. 7785, pp. 222–242. Springer, Heidelberg (2013). https://doi.org/10.1007/978-3-642-36594-2_13
53. Papamanthou, C., Shi, E., Tamassia, R., Yi, K.: Streaming authenticated data structures. In: Johansson, T., Nguyen, P.Q. (eds.) Annual International Conference on the Theory and Applications of Cryptographic Techniques, pp. 353–370. Springer (2013). https://doi.org/10.1007/978-3-642-38348-9_22
54. Pappas, C., Papadopoulos, D., Papamanthou, C.: HydraProofs: optimally computing all proofs in a vector commitment (with applications to efficient ZKSNARKS over data from multiple users). In: 2025 IEEE Symposium on Security and Privacy (SP), pp. 3421–3439. IEEE (2025)
55. Peikert, C., Pepin, Z., Sharp, C.: Vector and functional commitments from lattices. In: Nissim, K., Waters, B. (eds.) TCC 2021. LNCS, vol. 13044, pp. 480–511. Springer, Cham (2021). https://doi.org/10.1007/978-3-030-90456-2_16
56. Sasson, E.B., et al.: ZeroCash: decentralized anonymous payments from bitcoin. In: 2014 IEEE Symposium on Security and Privacy, pp. 459–474. IEEE (2014)
57. Schafer, J.B., Frankowski, D., Herlocker, J., Sen, S.: Collaborative filtering recommender systems. In: The adaptive web: methods and strategies of web personalization, pp. 291–324. Springer (2007). https://doi.org/10.1007/978-3-540-72079-9_9
58. Schwartz, J.T.: Fast probabilistic algorithms for verification of polynomial identities. J. ACM **27**(4), 701–717 (1980)
59. Setty, S.: Spartan: Efficient and general-purpose ZKSNARKS without trusted setup. In: Micciancio, D., Ristenpart, T. (eds.) Annual International Cryptology Conference, pp. 704–737. Springer (2020). https://doi.org/10.1007/978-3-030-56877-1_25
60. Sha, J., Liu, S., Han, S.: Functional commitments for arbitrary circuits of bounded sizes. In: Designs, Codes and Cryptography, pp. 1–35 (2024)
61. Shamir, A.: How to share a secret. Commun. ACM **22**(11), 612–613 (1979)
62. Srinivasan, S., Chepurnoy, A., Papamanthou, C., Tomescu, A., Zhang, Y.: Hyperproofs: aggregating and maintaining proofs in vector commitments. In: USENIX Security 22, pp. 3001–3018 (2022)
63. Tan, B., Liu, B., Zheng, V., Yang, Q.: A federated recommender system for online services. In: Proceedings of the 14th ACM Conference on Recommender Systems, pp. 579–581 (2020)
64. The guardian: revealed: the Facebook loophole that lets world leaders deceive and harass their citizens (2021). https://www.theguardian.com/technology/2021/apr/12/facebook-loophole-state-backed-manipulation

65. Tomescu, A., Abraham, I., Buterin, V., Drake, J., Feist, D., Khovratovich, D.: Aggregatable Subvector commitments for stateless cryptocurrencies. In: Galdi, C., Kolesnikov, V. (eds.) SCN 2020. LNCS, vol. 12238, pp. 45–64. Springer, Cham (2020). https://doi.org/10.1007/978-3-030-57990-6_3
66. Wahby, R.S., Tzialla, I., Shelat, A., Thaler, J., Walfish, M.: Doubly-efficient ZKSNARKS without trusted setup. In: 2018 IEEE Symposium on Security and Privacy (SP), pp. 926–943. IEEE (2018)
67. Wang, W., Ulichney, A., Papamanthou, C.: {BalanceProofs}: maintainable vector commitments with fast aggregation. In: USENIX Security 23, pp. 4409–4426 (2023)
68. Wee, H., Wu, D.J.: Lattice-based functional commitments: Fast verification and cryptanalysis. In: Guo, J., Steinfeld, R. (eds.) ASIACRYPT 2023, pp. 201–235. Springer (2023). https://doi.org/10.1007/978-981-99-8733-7_7
69. Wee, H., Wu, D.J.: Succinct vector, polynomial, and functional commitments from lattices. In: Hazay, C., Stam, M. (eds.) EUROCRYPT 2023, pp. 385–416. Springer (2023). https://doi.org/10.1007/978-3-031-30620-4_13
70. Wee, H., Wu, D.J.: Succinct functional commitments for circuits from k-lin. In: Joye, M., Leander, G. (eds.) EUROCRYPT 2024, pp. 280–310. Springer (2024). https://doi.org/10.1007/978-3-031-58723-8_10
71. Xie, T., Zhang, J., Zhang, Y., Papamanthou, C., Song, D.: Libra: succinct zero-knowledge proofs with optimal prover computation. In: Boldyreva, A., Micciancio, D. (eds.) Annual International Cryptology Conference, pp. 733–764. Springer (2019). https://doi.org/10.1007/978-3-030-26954-8_24
72. Xu, G., Li, H., Liu, S., Yang, K., Lin, X.: VerifyNet: secure and verifiable federated learning. IEEE Trans. Inf. Forensics Secur. **15**, 911–926 (2019)
73. Yang, L., Tan, B., Zheng, V.W., Chen, K., Yang, Q.: Federated recommendation systems. In: Yang, Q., Fan, L., Yu, H. (eds.) Federated Learning: Privacy and Incentive, pp. 225–239. Springer (2020). https://doi.org/10.1007/978-3-030-63076-8_16
74. Zhang, J., Xie, T., Hoang, T., Shi, E., Zhang, Y.: Polynomial commitment with a {One-to-Many} prover and applications. In: 31st USENIX Security Symposium (USENIX Security 22), pp. 2965–2982 (2022)
75. Zhang, J., Xie, T., Zhang, Y., Song, D.: Transparent polynomial delegation and its applications to zero knowledge proof. In: 2020 IEEE Symposium on Security and Privacy (SP), pp. 859–876. IEEE (2020)
76. Zhang, Z., Li, W., Guo, Y., Shi, K., Chow, S.S., Liu, X., Dong, J.: Fast {RS IOP} multivariate polynomial commitments and verifiable secret sharing. In: 33rd USENIX Security Symposium (USENIX Security 24), pp. 3187–3204 (2024)
77. Zippel, R.: Probabilistic algorithms for sparse polynomials. In: Ng, E.W. (eds.) EUROSAM 1979, pp. 216–226. Springer (1979). https://doi.org/10.1007/3-540-09519-5_73

Faster Signature Verification with 3-Dimensional Decomposition

Vojtěch Suchánek(✉), Marek Sýs, and Łukasz Chmielewski

Masaryk University, Brno, Czech Republic
{vojtechsu,syso}@mail.muni.cz, chmiel@fi.muni.cz

Abstract. We introduce a novel technique that accelerates verification of Schnorr signatures using fast endomorphisms. Traditionally, fast endomorphisms over prime field curves are used to decompose a scalar into two scalars of half the size. We show that signature verification allows decomposition into three scalars of a third of the size. Our technique applies to single Schnorr signature verification, batch verification, and BLS signature verification in the Blind Diffie-Hellman key exchange. Our experiments on AMD x86 and ARM Cortex-M4 platforms show performance improvements of approximately 20%, 13%, and 27%, respectively. The technique can also be used to accelerate the verification of ECDSA signatures, provided that one additional bit is appended to the signature.

We analyze the performance of 3-dimensional lattice reduction algorithms, which are critical for multi-scalar decompositions. To identify the most efficient approach, we experimentally compare Semaev's algorithm—known for its best asymptotic complexity—with the simpler Lagrange's algorithm. Our results reveal that, despite its simplicity, Lagrange's algorithm is nearly twice as fast as Semaev's in practice.

Keywords: elliptic curve · Schnorr · verification · GLV · endomorphism

1 Introduction

Classical elliptic curve signatures, including ECDSA or Schnorr signature, are the key components of modern cryptographic systems. Their importance grew even further with their adoption into the Bitcoin cryptocurrency [26], where each transaction contains a signature that is later verified as proof of ownership. In systems like Bitcoin, where nodes frequently process and validate large volumes of transactions, the efficiency of signature verification becomes a critical performance factor. The need for efficiency was one of the key motivations behind the introduction of Schnorr signatures to Bitcoin, as they offer improved verification speed compared to traditional ECDSA signatures, along with other benefits such as linearity and smaller signature sizes.

K. Jee and A. Kate (Eds.): ACNS 2026, LNCS 16571, pp. 272–296, 2027.
https://doi.org/10.1007/978-3-032-32560-0_10

To verify a Schnorr signature[1], one needs to perform a (multi-)scalar multiplication on an elliptic curve to verify an equality $uG + vQ = R$, where Q is the public key point, G is a generator on the curve and the scalars u, v with the point R are derived from the signature. An equivalent equation is checked in the ECDSA verification, where only the x-coordinates of both sides are checked.

The literature contains numerous techniques to speed up scalar multiplication to compute vQ or $uG+vQ$, in particular [19,37]. Generally, the cost of these techniques is proportional to the sizes of the scalars u and v, which motivated several methods to lower their size [17,18]. One of them is the Gallant-Lambert-Vanstone (GLV) method [18] that decomposes vQ into the multi-scalar multiplication $v_0Q + v_1\varphi(Q)$ with smaller scalars v_0, v_1 using an efficiently computable endomorphism φ. Brumley [10] reports 50% acceleration using the GLV curves, making them the fastest elliptic curves in the OpenSSL library. More recently, the GLV decomposition has been used for the acceleration of scalar multiplication on pairing-friendly curves [9,24] such as BLS12-381 used in Zcash or Ethereum.

In principle, decomposing the scalar v into more than two smaller scalars can lead to greater speed-ups [17]. However, existing methods that support such decompositions rely on curves defined over extension fields. As a result, prime field curves have, so far, been limited to 2-dimensional decompositions. This work introduces a 3-dimensional decomposition for the signature verification over prime field curves. More precisely, we present the following **contributions:**

1. We present a new technique, called GLV-3, for the verification $uG + vQ = R$ using a fast endomorphism that applies to all Schnorr-like signatures, including modified ECDSA signatures (Sect. 3). The technique brings a 20% speed-up for a single signature verification, 13% speed-up for batch verification, and a 27% speed-up for the Blind Diffie-Hellman protocol [36].
2. The results are experimentally verified on a 64-bit AMD x86 processor and on a 32-bit ARM Cortex-M4 STM32F407 microcontroller over 384-bit and 521-bit curves[2]. This demonstrates that the approach applies not only to modern CPUs, which are commonly used in server applications, but also to embedded architectures found in secure elements, such as smartcards.
3. We experimentally compare Semaev's algorithm [32] with the naive Lagrange's 3-dimensional algorithm for scalar decomposition. Despite Semaev's better asymptotic complexity (quadratic vs. cubic), Lagrange's is up to 45% faster on both the x86 processor and the microcontroller (Sect. 3.1).

Our method reduces the size of the used scalars. The application of this reduction goes beyond the acceleration of signature verification as we show in our final contribution to the area of side-channel attacks. The zero-value point attack and the exceptional procedure attack are powerful side-channel attacks that can recover a static ECDH key [1,31] or, more recently, can be used for reverse-engineering [21]. However, the amount of information these attacks recover is limited by

[1] More variants of the verification exist. We use the one usually considered in recent works, including the Bitcoin protocol [39].

[2] The source code is available at github.com/vojtechsu/glv3.

the underlying mathematical problem called the dependent coordinates problem (DCP). As an additional fourth contribution, we prove that the 4-dimensional variant of our technique (GLV-4) reduces the complexity of DCP from $O(n)$ to $O(\sqrt{n}\log^3 n)$ (Sect. 4). This is the first general and non-trivial reduction of DCP, previously solvable only via brute force.

2 Background

We focus on elliptic curves in the short Weierstrass form $E/\mathbb{F}_p : y^2z = x^3 + axz^2 + bz^3$, where $a, b \in \mathbb{F}_p$ and $p \geq 5$ is a prime. The set of projective points $(x : y : z)$ over $\mathbb{F}_p$, which forms a finite abelian group with a neutral point $\infty = (0 : 1 : 0)$, is denoted $E(\mathbb{F}_p)$. As usual in elliptic curve cryptography, we assume that there is a large subgroup of prime order $n \approx p$ and h is the cofactor, i.e., $\#E(\mathbb{F}_p) = nh$. Denote t the bit-length of n.

For any point $P \in E(\mathbb{F}_p)$, denote its coordinates by x_P, y_P, z_P. Apart from these standard projective coordinates, we also use Jacobian coordinates [7] and the affine coordinates $(x_P, y_P) = (x_P : y_P : 1)$. The addition of two points P_1+P_2 can be defined using polynomial functions in their coordinates $x_{P_i}, y_{P_i}, z_{P_i}$ [37]. The case $P_1 = P_2$ is often treated separately using a more efficient doubling formula, though this depends on the used coordinate system.

We can define scalar multiplication kP as the k-fold addition $P+\cdots+P$. This can be effectively computed using several algorithms that generally iterate over the digits of k in an appropriate representation, computing point doublings and additions in each iteration. A standard example is the double-and-add algorithm (Algorithm 4 in the Appendix or Algorithm 3.26 in [19]) which performs, on average, t doublings, one for each bit of k, and $t/2$ additions, one for each bit equal to 1.

2.1 GLV Method

Gallant, Lambert, and Vanstone [18] introduced a technique to accelerate scalar multiplication using *fast endomorphisms*—the GLV method. An endomorphism $\varphi : E \to E$ is a group homomorphism defined by rational maps. Any such endomorphism naturally acts as a scalar multiplication by $\lambda_\varphi \in \mathbb{Z}$ on the (cyclic) subgroup of prime order n. Any scalar $k \in \mathbb{Z}$ can be then decomposed using the extended Euclidean algorithm as

$$k = k_0 + k_1\lambda_\varphi \pmod{n}, \quad k_0, k_1 \approx \sqrt{n}.$$

The benefit of this decomposition is that k_0, k_1 have half the bit-length of k, and so the number of iterations in the scalar multiplication is also halved if the Straus-Shamir trick [4] is used: Instead of computing kP, we can compute $k_0P + k_1\varphi(P)$ by iterating through the bits of k_0, k_1 at the same time. In each iteration, we add P, $\varphi(P)$, or $P + \varphi(P)$ depending on the bits. The points $\varphi(P)$, $P+\varphi(P)$ are precomputed at the beginning. The cost of this multiscalar multiplication is roughly $t/2$ doublings and $3t/8$ additions—half the amount of doublings and $t/8$ fewer additions than the double-and-add.

The Joint Sparse Form (JSF) [30,34] can be used to reduce the number of additions. In general, JSF is a joint representation of two or more scalars that represents each pair of bits (one bit for each scalar) using $0, 1$ or -1 such that the number of non-zero pairs is minimal. The joint Hamming weight (the number of non-zero pairs) then equals the number of additions during the Straus-Shamir trick. The size of the JSF form is larger than the binary form by at most one (signed) bit and so the number of additions only increases by at most one. The expected joint Hamming weight of two s-bit scalars in JSF is $0.5s$, whereas, in simple binary, it would be $0.75s$. We will also consider the JSF of three and four scalars for which the expected weight is $0.59s$ and $0.64s$, respectively.

In the case of GLV, the two $t/2$-bit scalars k_0, k_1 have joint Hamming weight $t/4$ resulting in $t/2$ doublings and $t/4$ additions (Algorithm 5 in the Appendix). For comparison, the simple double-and-add with the non-adjacent form (NAF) representation [19] performs t doublings and $t/3$ additions, i.e., twice as many doublings and $t/12$ more additions.

Naturally, the GLV method makes sense only if $\varphi(P)$ can be computed much more efficiently than the scalar multiplication by λ_φ. Elliptic curves in the form $y^2 = x^3 + b$ (i.e., $a = 0$), where $p = 1 \pmod 3$, are equipped with an endomorphism which can be computed using only one multiplication in $\mathbb{F}_p$. More precisely, they have an endomorphism $\varphi : (x, y) \mapsto (\beta x, y)$, where $\beta \in \mathbb{F}_p^\times$. The corresponding scalar λ_φ satisfies the quadratic equation $\lambda_\varphi^2 + \lambda_\varphi + 1 = 0 \pmod n$. Popular examples of such curves are the secp256k1 curve used in Bitcoin and the pairing-friendly curve BLS12-381 [9].

2.2 Scalar Decomposition

The usual use case (e.g., ECDSA) assumes that decomposed scalar $k = k_0 + k_1\lambda_\varphi \pmod n$ is not fixed and so the scalar decomposition needs to be done efficiently on the fly. The common approach is to consider the lattice

$$\mathcal{L} = \langle (z_0, z_1) \mid z_0 + z_1\lambda_\varphi = 0 \pmod n \rangle$$

and find a close vector $v \in \mathcal{L}$ to the vector $(k, 0)$. The decomposition (k_0, k_1) is the short vector $(k, 0) - v$. Assuming we have a short basis of $\mathcal{L}$, with vector norms $\approx n^{1/2}$, Babai's technique finds v resulting in $k_0, k_1 \approx n^{1/2}$ [3].

The bottleneck is finding the short basis for $\mathcal{L}$, but this can be done once for the curve using the following early abort version of the Extended Euclidean Algorithm (EEA): Recall that for any two integers, (n, λ_φ) in our case, EEA produces a sequence of equations

$$s_i n + t_i \lambda_\varphi = r_i, \quad \text{where } s_0 = 1,\ t_0 = 0,\ r_0 = n,\ s_1 = 0,\ t_1 = 1,\ r_1 = \lambda_\varphi,\ r_i \geq 0.$$

The sequence r_i is strictly decreasing, starting from n until it reaches the greatest common divisor of λ_φ and n. The sequence $|t_i|$ is strictly increasing, starting from 0. Heuristically, the sequences are expected to meet in the middle when

$r_i \approx |t_i| \approx n^{1/2}$, in which case the algorithm is aborted, and two smallest vectors $(r_i, -t_i)$ are taken as the basis of $\mathcal{L}$. This does not work in general. For example, when $\lambda_\varphi < n^{1/2}$, then no short basis is found since the algorithm terminates at $i = 1$ with $(\lambda_\varphi, -1)$, $(n, 0)$.

Since one endomorphism enables us to decompose k into two smaller scalars, one would like to use more endomorphisms for larger decompositions. This is the idea of the GLS method [17,23], which uses curves over extension fields that are equipped with two fast endomorphisms φ and ψ:

$$k = k_0 + k_1\lambda_\varphi + k_2\lambda_\psi + k_3\lambda_\varphi\lambda_\psi \pmod{n}, \quad k_i \approx \sqrt[4]{n}.$$

Similarly to the 2-dimensional case, the decomposition (k_0, k_1, k_2, k_3) is the vector $(k, 0, 0, 0) - v$, where v is the closest vector to $(k, 0, 0, 0)$ in the lattice

$$\mathcal{L} = \langle (z_0, z_1, z_2, z_3) \mid z_0 + z_1\lambda_\varphi + z_2\lambda_\psi + z_3\lambda_\varphi\lambda_\psi = 0 \pmod{n} \rangle.$$

The part that does not generalize easily is the search for the short basis of $\mathcal{L}$. Usually, the short basis is found by applying some reduction algorithm (e.g., LLL [22]) to the (long) basis: $(\lambda_\varphi, -1, 0, 0), (\lambda_\psi, 0, -1, 0), (\lambda_\varphi\lambda_\psi, 0, 0, -1), (n, 0, 0, 0)$. The short basis can be precomputed again once for the given curve, so this does not have any effect on the performance. Several optimizations have been then developed [12,15,20] including the 3-dimensional variant [40]. The main limitation of the GLS method and its variants is that it is only supported by curves over extension fields. Our work focuses on prime field curves that are used in cryptographic protocols.

2.3 Signatures

This part summarizes the signature schemes considered in this paper. Let E be an elliptic curve as defined above. Denote G, the generator of the prime subgroup of order n, and H, a cryptographic hash function. For all the signature schemes denote $d \in [1, n]$ the private key, $P = dG$ the public key, and m any message.

Schnorr Signature. Schnorr signature over E is a pair (R, s), where $R = rG$ for a random $r \in [1, n]$ and $s = r + H(R, m)d \pmod{n}$ Here, R is encoded using only x_R for the hash function. To verify (R, s) anyone can then check the equation $sG = R + H(R, m)P$. To save space, the signature (R, s) can contain only the coordinate x_R and one additional bit signaling the parity of y_R, which is then used for the recovery of $y_R = \sqrt{x_R^3 + ax_R + b}$ (another option is to force the bit during the generation of $R = rG$). Note that there is another variant of the Schnorr signature defined as (e, s), where $e = H(sG - eP, m)$. We only focus on the first, and more popular variant that supports batch verification and is part of the Bitcoin improvement proposal (BIP) 340 [39].

Modified ECDSA. The classical ECDSA signature is the pair (r, s), where $r = x_{kG} \pmod{n}$ for a random $k \in [1, n]$ and $s = k^{-1}(H(m) + rd) \pmod{n}$. Anyone can then verify (r, s) by computing $R = H(m)s^{-1}G + rs^{-1}P$ and checking that $x_R \pmod{n} = r$. ECDSA signatures can be verified in a similar way as

Schnorr signatures, i.e., checking that $R = H(m)s^{-1}G + rs^{-1}P$, assuming we have the point R (and not merely r). Antipa et al. [2] considered two versions of ECDSA which include the coordinates of R in the signature or append enough information for the reconstruction of the coordinates. For prime order curves, including the popular NIST curves or secp256k1, one bit is enough. This work will focus on these Schnorr-like versions of ECDSA (denoted ECDSA*) as well.

BLS Signature. The BLS signature [8] is the point $\sigma = dH_E(m)$, where H_E is an appropriate hash-to-curve function, i.e., $H_E(m)$ is a point on E. The verification equation is $e(\sigma, G) = e(H_E(m), P)$. Here, e is a bilinear pairing. Hence, only pairing-friendly curves (with efficiently computable pairing) can be used in practice. While the signing itself is simple and fast, the computation of the pairing can be a limiting factor, especially for resource-constrained devices.

BDHKE. The Blind Diffie-Hellman Key Exchange (BDHKE) protocol [36] is not a classical signature algorithm, but uses the idea of the BLS signature and serves as another target of our work. The goal of this protocol is to make the signer sign a blinded value for a second party (user) so that when the unblinded value is revealed, the signer can verify it but cannot trace it back to the user. The exact steps of the protocol between a user and a signer are the following:

- User computes the point $h(m)$ as in the BLS signature and blinds it by adding a factor rG for a random r: $C = H_E(m) + rG$. The user sends C to the signer.
- The signer computes $T' = dC$ and sends it back to the user.
- The user unblinds the point T' using the signer's public key: $T = T' - rP$.
- Later, when the signer is provided (m, T), they verify that $dH_E(m) = T$.

The protocol has been used for Cashu – an e-cash system backed by Bitcoin [28]. One of the key properties of this protocol is that the verification is done only by the owner of the private key. This means that the costly pairing-based verification can be replaced by a simple signature reconstruction.

Remark 1. The verification equation in the popular EdDSA signature scheme [6] is the same as in the Schnorr signature. Yet, we exclude it from this work for the following reasons. EdDSA is designed for Edwards curves with complete addition formulas. More precisely, EdDSA uses a curve of the form $-x^2 + y^2 = 1 + dx^2y^2$ over $\mathbb{F}_p$, where $d \in \mathbb{F}_p$ is a non-square and $p = 1 \pmod 4$ (implying that -1 is a square in $\mathbb{F}_p$). Our work uses GLV curves that have an efficient endomorphism of degree 1 that are of the form $y^2 = x^3 + b$ or $y^2 = x^3 + ax$; these curves are precisely the ones with endomorphism ring with nontrivial units that correspond to endomorphisms with their rational maps of degree 1. Such GLV curves cannot be transformed to the Edwards curve. The reason follows from the birational equivalence between Weierstrass curves $y^2 = x^3 + ax + b$ and twisted Edwards curves [5]. It can be shown that the Edwards d coefficient must be equal to $3\alpha^2 + a$ for the equivalence to exist, where α is a root of $x^3 + ax + b$. For both considered forms of GLV curves, simple expression manipulation shows that d is always a square, breaking the EdDSA assumption. Nevertheless, curves with less efficient endomorphisms (of higher degree) could be considered, but we leave this as a future work.

2.4 Verification of Signatures

The focus of this work is the verification of Schnorr signatures (VSS), ECDSA* signatures, and the verification of scalar multiplication (VSM) in BDHKE. These can be generalized by the following two problems:

(VSM) Given two affine points P, R and a scalar $k \in \mathbb{Z}$, decide:

$$kP \stackrel{?}{=} R.$$

(VSS) Let G be a fixed generator. Given two affine points Q, R and two scalars $u, v \in \mathbb{Z}$, decide:

$$uG + vQ \stackrel{?}{=} R.$$

The first and obvious approach to both problems is to recompute kP or $uG + vQ$ and compare with the other side of the equation—the point R. The ECC literature contains a plethora of techniques for (multi-)scalar multiplication [11,19]. The overall principle is to iterate over the digits or windows of the scalars in some representation. Depending on the context, the techniques might assume that one of the points is fixed and leverage some precomputation. Additionally, the threat of side-channel attacks is also often considered in the literature.

In our context, we assume that only the point G is fixed in VSS. Furthermore, we do not consider side-channel attacks, as only public data are verified. Our work follows the observation that the cost of (multi-)scalar multiplication is proportional to the bit-lengths of the involved scalars. Two notable techniques that are based on this idea can be summarized in the following way.

First, the GLV method (Sect. 2.5) decomposes the scalar k (or v for VSS) into $k = k_0 + k_1\lambda_\varphi \pmod{n}$ using a scalar λ_φ and then applies Straus-Shamir trick to check whether $k_0P + k_1\lambda_\varphi P = R$. It works with the assumption that $\lambda_\varphi P$ can be efficiently computed as $\varphi(P)$.

$$kP \stackrel{?}{=} R \quad \rightarrow \quad k = k_0 + k_1\lambda_\varphi \pmod{n} \quad \rightarrow \quad k_0P + k_1\varphi(P) \stackrel{?}{=} R \qquad \text{(GLV)}$$

The second method by Antipa et al. [2] (Sect. 2.6) similarly splits the scalar k by decomposing 0 into $0 = k_0 - k_1k \pmod{n}$ using the scalar k. Then it applies the Straus-Shamir trick to check $k_0P - k_1kP = \infty$. The assumption here is that the equation to be verified $kP = R$ holds and kP can be efficiently 'computed' by simply taking $kP = R$.

$$kP \stackrel{?}{=} R \quad \rightarrow \quad 0 = k_0 - k_1k \pmod{n} \quad \rightarrow \quad k_0P - k_1R \stackrel{?}{=} \infty \qquad \text{([2])}$$

We will explain the full details of the above ideas in Sect. 2.5 and Sect. 2.6. To express the cost of the described algorithms, we use the following notation: A and D denote the cost of point addition and doubling, respectively. Also, recall that we work with points of order n, where n has t bits.

2.5 Verification with GLV

Sect. 2.1 described the GLV method that can be used for VSM (Algorithm 5). We will now compute the cost in terms of the number of point additions A and doublings D, as well as the number of field multiplications M, i.e., the cost in the form $c_1A+c_2D+c_3M$. We will also use the standard Jacobian formulas [7] with $A=11M$, $D=7M$, to express the cost purely in the number of multiplications, i.e., cM. We have selected these formulas as they are generally the fastest for Weierstrass curves with $a=0$ (in terms of the number of field multiplications), and they are also implemented in the Mbed TLS library that we used for experiments. Furthermore, we assume that the curve admits an endomorphism φ with the cost of its application equal to one finite field multiplication.

For the precomputation (Step 1 of Algorithm 5), it is helpful to use the fact that opposite points differ only by a sign in the y-coordinate and so we can compute and store only half the points. This amounts to the input point P and three points $\varphi(P)$, $P+\varphi(P)=-\varphi(\varphi(P))$, $P-\varphi(P)$ that can be computed with the cost M, M, A, respectively. The evaluation part uses $t/2$ doublings. The number of additions is given by the joint Hamming weight of the two $t/2$-bit scalars in JSF, which is $\frac{t}{4}$ on average. The total cost is then

$$\left(\frac{t}{4}+1\right)A+\frac{t}{2}D+2M=(6.25t+13)M.$$

The idea can be adapted to the VSS problem (as in the libsecp256k1 library [38]) by decomposing both the scalars u,v and computing $u_0G+u_1\varphi(G)+v_0Q+v_1\varphi(Q)$ using two simultaneous Straus-Shamir tricks. We precompute the points for $u_0G+u_1\varphi(G)$ and $v_0+v_1\varphi(Q)$ separately and then run the evaluation at the same time. The combined Hamming weight of the two pairs of scalars in JSF is $2\frac{t}{4}=\frac{t}{2}$. The overall cost is then

$$\left(\frac{t}{2}+2\right)A+\frac{t}{2}D+4M=(9t+26)M.$$

2.6 Verification by Antipa Et Al

Antipa et al. [2] do not apply the simple recomputation of the (multi-)scalar multiplication to the VSS and VSM problems. Instead of using the point R just for the final comparison, they use it for the computation of the scalar multiplication. The idea is to express k as a fraction $k=\frac{k_0}{k_1}$ of two smaller scalars of half the bit-length of k. Or from another point of view, we decompose 0 as $0=k_0-k_1k$ using k. The pair (k_0,k_1) is a short vector in the lattice

$$\langle(z_0,z_1)\mid z_0-z_1k=0\pmod n\rangle$$

and can be found using EEA as described in Sect. 2.2. To solve VSM, we then use the Straus-Shamir trick to compute k_0P-k_1R and check if the result is ∞.

Applying this method to VSS is a bit more tricky and needs to use the fact that G is fixed: We can decompose $0 = v_0 - v_1 v \pmod{n}$, $v_0, v_1 \approx n^{1/2}$, which gets us $uv_1 G + v_0 Q - v_1 R = \infty$. The only scalar bigger than $n^{1/2}$ is uv_1, but we can use the fact that G is a fixed point and the multiple $G' = 2^{t/2} G$ can be precomputed once and stored. Using G', we can split uv_1 into the upper and lower binary halves u_U, v_L which gets us the following verification equation:

$$u_L G + u_U G' + v_0 Q - v_1 R = \infty.$$

The left side is then computed as in Sect. 2.5 with a similar overall cost (slightly worse since the endomorphism cannot be used in the precomputation). Antipa et al. [2] report a speed-up of 36% on the ARM7TDMI platform when compared to the simple Straus-Shamir trick on $uG + vQ$.

Compared to the GLV approach (Sect. 2.5), this method has the advantage that no endomorphisms are necessary. One could get the idea of using both methods to reduce the size of the scalars even further. Unfortunately, they are not compatible in any trivial way. For instance, we could try to decompose $v = v_0 + v_1 \lambda_\varphi$ using λ_φ and then try to express v_0, v_1 as fractions of smaller scalars. The problem is that since already $v_i \approx n^{1/2}$, they are not likely to be fractions of much smaller scalars. The EEA would most likely give us trivial equality $v_0 = \frac{v_0}{1}$. Trying the opposite way (decomposition and then fractions) suffers from the same problem. The decompositions of v_0, v_1 using λ_φ for $v = \frac{v_0}{v_1}$ are most likely to be trivial as well. Hence, a simple application of one method after the other does not work.

Antipa et al. [2] extended their idea of 4 half-size scalar multiplications to 6 third-size scalar multiplications, but assume that a multiple Q' must be precomputed and available for verification. One option is to append it to the signature, and another is to include it in the public key certificate as it depends on the public key only. Either way, this cannot be used for the current signature schemes, and so we will not discuss this further. In the following section, we present a new method with 6 third-size scalar multiplications without this assumption.

3 Verification Using 3-Dimensional GLV

This section presents the contribution of our work: a 3-dimensional GLV method that accelerates the verification of signatures (VSS) and scalar multiplication (VSM) using a fast endomorphism. The section contains theoretical analysis and results of experiments.

The two presented approaches (Sect. 2.5 and Sect. 2.6) to VSM and VSS reduced the size of the involved scalars using an appropriate decomposition. The GLV method decomposes $k = k_0 + k_1 \lambda_\varphi \pmod{n}$ using λ_φ, with the assumption that we have an efficient endomorphism such that $\varphi(P) = \lambda_\varphi P$. The second method by Antipa et al. [2] decomposes $0 = k_0 - k_1 k \pmod{n}$ using k, assuming that the equality $kP = R$ is true. As explained in Sect. 2.6, naively applying these two methods in sequence (using two separate 2-dimensional reductions) does not lead to a better reduction.

Our method (that we call *3-dimensional GLV* or GLV-3 for short) merges both of the methods described above using a simultaneous 3-dimensional decomposition. More precisely, we consider the decomposition of 0 by k and λ_φ at the same time: $0 = l_0 + l_1\lambda_\varphi + l_2 k \pmod{n}$. It essentially imitates the GLS method that uses two endomorphisms for a decomposition by taking λ_φ and k as the endomorphisms. For VSM, we verify the following equation:

$$(l_0 + l_1\lambda_\varphi + l_2 k)P = l_0 P + l_1\varphi(P) + l_2 R = \infty,$$

assuming the equality $kP = R$ is true. To find an appropriate triple (l_0, l_1, l_2), we follow the GLS method and consider the lattice generated by the vectors $(k, 0, -1), (\lambda_\varphi, -1, 0)$, and $(n, 0, 0)$. Assuming k is a large random scalar, which is the case for signature schemes specified above, we should expect a short vector (l_0, l_1, l_2) in the lattice of norm $\approx n^{1/3}$. As we will see in Sect. 3.1, the introduction of a 3-dimensional lattice causes a technical challenge since we cannot use the EEA as in the GLV or the Antipa et al. [2] method.

Note that the correctness of the new verification equation $l_0 P + l_1\varphi(P) + l_2 R = \infty$ takes a little care. If we subtract $(l_0 + l_1\lambda_\varphi + l_2 k)P$, we get $l_2 kP = l_2 R$. This is equivalent to the original VSM $kP = R$ as long as $l_2 \neq 0 \pmod{n}$. While this condition needs to be checked, it can be done only once for the curve since it is determined purely by the endomorphism: $l_2 = 0$ means that $0 = l_0 + l_1\lambda_\phi \pmod{n}$ and λ_ϕ is a ratio of two small numbers $l_0, l_1 \approx n^{1/3}$. This is extremely unlikely to happen on accident (with probability $n^{-1/3}$). Nevertheless, it has to be done when a new curve is chosen. The same condition applies to VSS.

In Sect. 3.1, we select an appropriate lattice reduction technique for finding the short vector (l_0, l_1, l_2). Section 3.2 and Sect. 3.3 apply GLV-3 to VSM and VSS in full detail and present experimental results. Section 3.4 presents how the technique can be easily modified for batch signatures.

Remark 2. All of our algorithms were implemented in the Mbed TLS library [16] and tested on a 64-bit AMD x86 processor and on a 32-bit ARM Cortex-M4 STM32F407 microcontroller (MC). We ran each experiment 1000 times on the AMD processor and 10 times on the MC[3] . We used elliptic curves over three different bit-lengths: 256, 384, and 521. For the 256-bit case, we used the popular secp256k1 curve $y = x^3 + 7$ over $\mathbb{F}_p$ with $p = 2^{256} - 2^{32} - 977$. For the remaining two bit-lengths, we generated two curves of the same form $y^2 = x^3 + 7$ as secp256k1 for easier implementation. The base field $\mathbb{F}_p$ is of the size $p = 2^{384} - 170937$ and $p = 2^{521} - 503629$, respectively (the bit-length 521 was chosen based on the NIST P-521 curve). Finally, the experiments for batch verification were only simulated in Python, and the cost was approximated based on the previous experiments on both platforms. We have to emphasize that the goal of the experiments is not to break the records for signature verification on the platforms. Rather, our goal is a fair comparison between individual algorithms and so we are interested in the relative performance.

[3] This is a reasonable number since, for the MC, we measure execution time in clock cycles. We expect to obtain always the same number since our algorithms are not randomized.

3.1 Reducing 3-Dimensional Lattices

This part describes our choice of a lattice reduction algorithm for the lattice given by the vectors

$$(k, 0, -1), (\lambda_\varphi, -1, 0), (n, 0, 0).$$

Recall that the classical 2-dimensional GLV (or 4-dimensional GLS) decomposition precomputes the reduced basis (e.g., using the LLL algorithm) once and then uses it to decompose each scalar efficiently. The situation with the method by Antipa et al. [2] is slightly more complicated since the lattice is defined by the given scalar, and the reduction cannot be precomputed. However, the dimension is only 2, and the efficient EEA can be used, which makes the cost of the reduction negligible when compared to the scalar multiplication. Our GLV-3 method inherits the worst of both worlds as we have a 3-dimensional lattice defined per each scalar. Our goal is to accelerate signature verification, and so the choice of the reduction algorithm is crucial.

Our strategy is to follow the work by Semaev [32] on the reduction of 3-dimensional lattices. However, rather than selecting the lattice reduction algorithm with the best asymptotical complexity that always finds a good basis, we take the experimental approach. We select the algorithm that experimentally worked best for the typical sizes of input values in our context.

Algorithm 1: Lagrange's lattice reduction

Input: Basis b_1, b_2 of a lattice $\mathcal{L} \subset \mathbb{R}^2$
Output: Basis b_1, b_2 of $\mathcal{L}$ satisfying $|b_1| \leq |b_2|$, $2|\langle b_1, b_2\rangle| < |b_1|^2$

1 **do**
2   **if** $|b_1| > |b_2|$ **then** swap b_1, b_2
3     $m \leftarrow \lfloor \langle b_1, b_2\rangle / |b_1|^2 \rceil$
4     $b_2 \leftarrow b_2 - m b_1$
5 **while** $m \neq 0$
6 **return** b_1, b_2

Semaev [32] builds up on the basic reduction algorithm for a general 2-dimensional lattice—the Lagrange's algorithm (Algorithm 1). The idea of Lagrange's algorithm for given vectors b_1, b_2 is to iteratively reduce the bigger vector, say b_2, by subtracting a multiple of the other vector, i.e., replace b_2 with $b_2 - mb_1$. The optimal choice for m is to approximate the orthogonal projection of b_2 to the orthogonal complement of b_1: $m = \lfloor \langle b_1, b_2\rangle / |b_1|^2 \rceil$. Here, $|\cdot|$ is the Euclidean norm and $\langle \cdot, \cdot \rangle$ is the scalar product. The output of the algorithm is a *reduced pair* b_1', b_2' satisfying $|b_1'| \leq |b_2'|$, $2|\langle b_1', b_2'\rangle| < |b_1'|^2$, which we denote $(b_1', b_2') = G(b_1, b_2)$ as in [32]. The reduced pair forms the so-called Minkowski reduced basis and always contains the shortest vector in the lattice. Note that the costly division in Step 3 in Algorithm 1 can be computed with low precision since the result is then rounded to the closest integer. As a further optimization, the scalar products $\langle b_i, b_j \rangle$ are computed once at the beginning and stored in the Gram matrix. With each replacement in Step 4, we only update the Gram matrix, store m, and reconstruct the final vectors at the end.

Algorithm 2: Lagrange's 3-dimensional lattice reduction

Input: Basis b_1, b_2, b_3 of a lattice $\mathcal{L} \subset \mathbb{R}^3$
Output: A 2-reduced basis b_1, b_2, b_3 of $\mathcal{L}$

```
do
    2-reduced ← True
    foreach i, j ∈ {1, 2, 3} do
        if b_i, b_j not reduced then
            b_i, b_j ← G(b_i, b_j)                // Using Algorithm 1
            2-reduced ← False
while not 2-reduced
return b_1, b_2
```

As Semaev [32] further shows, Algorithm 1 can be naively extended to 3 dimensions by iteratively applying Algorithm 1 to every pair until we get a basis in which each pair is reduced (see Algorithm 2). We call such basis *2-reduced*. As Semaev explains, one can easily construct basis vectors that are 2-reduced but do not contain the shortest vector, and thus the algorithm is not guaranteed to find it. Luckily, this can be solved by appending one quick computation at the end of the algorithm (see Algorithm 2 in [32]). The algorithm then outputs the Minkowski reduced basis containing the shortest vector. Regarding asymptotic complexity, this can take as many $O(\log^3 M)$ operations to find the 2-reduced basis, where $|b_1|, |b_2|, |b_3| \leq M$. As an example supporting this lower bound on the complexity, Semaev presents a specially constructed lattice with vectors $(1, 1, 0), (M, 0, 0), (0, M^2, 1)$ with significantly different sizes. However, as we will see, this is not the typical case.

Finally, Semaev presents an algorithm that finds the Minkowski reduced basis with quadratic asymptotic complexity (Algorithm 3). The idea is to minimize the quadratic form $|b_3 - x_1 b_1 - x_2 b_2|$ in x_1, x_2, where $|b_1| \leq |b_2| \leq |b_3|$ and b_1, b_2 is a reduced pair. The optimal values for x_1, x_2 are found in real numbers, and the four possible combinations of the nearest integers are then checked. This is done repeatedly until the biggest vector cannot be reduced.

Table 1 presents our experimental results of Lagrange's 3-dimensional algorithm and Semaev's algorithm (Algorithm 3). The column 'Bits' shows the average bit-length of the shortest found vector norm. While Lagrange's algorithm is theoretically not guaranteed to find the shortest vector, it found it every time except for 4 out of 3000 cases (across the three bit-lengths). In these 4 cases, the sizes of the norms of the shortest found vectors for Semaev's and Lagrange's algorithms differed only by at most one bit. Surprisingly, Lagrange's algorithm was roughly 45% faster than Semaev's on the AMD. It was also much faster on the microcontroller, though it depended on the bit-length: 35%, 45%, 21% for

Algorithm 3: Semaev's lattice reduction

Input: Basis b_1, b_2, b_3 of a lattice $\mathcal{L} \subset \mathbb{R}^3$, s.t. $|b_1| \leq |b_2| \leq |b_3|$
Output: A reduced basis b_1, b_2, b_3 of $\mathcal{L}$

while True **do**
- $b_1, b_2 \leftarrow G(b_1, b_2)$
- $D \leftarrow 1 - \frac{\langle b_1, b_2 \rangle}{|b_1|^2} \cdot \frac{\langle b_1, b_2 \rangle}{|b_2|^2}$
- $y_1, y_2 \leftarrow -\frac{1}{D} \cdot \left(\frac{\langle b_1, b_3 \rangle}{|b_1|^2} - \frac{\langle b_1, b_2 \rangle}{|b_1|^2} \cdot \frac{\langle b_2, b_3 \rangle}{|b_2|^2} \right), -\frac{1}{D} \cdot \left(\frac{\langle b_2, b_3 \rangle}{|b_2|^2} - \frac{\langle b_1, b_2 \rangle}{|b_2|^2} \cdot \frac{\langle b_1, b_3 \rangle}{|b_1|^2} \right)$
- Select integers $x_1 \in [y_1 - 1, y_1 + 1], x_2 \in [y_2 - 1, y_2 + 1]$ such that $|b_3 + x_2 b_2 + x_1 b_1|$ is minimal
- $b_3' \leftarrow b_3 + x_2 b_2 + x_1 b_1$
- **if** $|b_3'| \geq |b_3|$ **then return** b_1, b_2, b_3
- $b_3 \leftarrow b_3'$
- Order b_1, b_2, b_3 by their norms.

the bit-lengths 256, 384, 521, respectively. This is in contrast with the theoretical comparison of the asymptotical complexities. As a result, we select Lagrange's algorithm for lattice reductions in the following sections.

Table 1. Comparison of implementations of Lagrange's 3-dimensional Algorithm and Semaev's Algorithm on a 64-bit AMD x86 processor and on a 32-bit ARM Cortex-M4 STM32F407 microcontroller. The columns show the asymptotic complexity, bit-lengths of inputs k and n, average bit-length of the shortest vector norm, the runtime in milliseconds (AMD), and cycle count on the MC.

	Complexity	$\log n$	Avg. bits	Time (AMD)	Cycles (MC)
Lagrange	$\Omega(\log^3 n)$	256	84.813	0.062 ms	937211
		384	127.593	0.097 ms	1738715
		521	173.215	0.139 ms	2782500
Semaev	$O(\log^2 n)$	256	84.811	0.110 ms	1449521
		384	127.593	0.176 ms	3077910
		521	173.214	0.257 ms	3538717

Remark 3. Experimentally, we have found that in Algorithm 1, it is enough to perform the division on only the most significant byte of the numerator $\langle b_1, b_2 \rangle$ and denominator $|b_1|^2$. Similarly, in Algorithm 3, y_1, y_2 can be computed as

$$y_1 = -\frac{\langle b_1, b_3 \rangle - \langle b_1, b_2 \rangle \cdot \langle b_2, b_3 \rangle}{|b_1||b_2|^2 - \langle b_1, b_2 \rangle^2}, \quad y_2 = -\frac{\langle b_2, b_3 \rangle - \langle b_1, b_2 \rangle \cdot \langle b_1, b_3 \rangle}{|b_1||b_2|^2 - \langle b_1, b_2 \rangle^2},$$

where only the two most significant bytes of each term $\langle b_i, b_j \rangle$, or $|b_i|^2$ are considered. This differs from the original approach in [33], which we found to be slightly slower for the selected bit-lengths. Other approximations could be used as in [29] but this might depend on the platform. Furthermore, since the second and third vector of the initial basis $(k, 0, -1), (\lambda_\varphi, -1, 0), (n, 0, 0)$ are fixed for the given curve, we compute the reduction $b_1, b_2 \leftarrow G((\lambda_\varphi, -1, 0), (n, 0, 0))$ using Algorithm 1 once and store u_1, u_2. Finally, at the beginning we also decompose k into k_0, k_1 as described in Sect. 2.2 and replace $(k, 0, -1)$ with $u_3 = (k_0, k_1, -1)$. Hence, the input vectors to both algorithms are the three vectors u_1, u_2, and u_3.

3.2 Scalar Multiplication Verification with GLV-3

We assume that the curve admits an endomorphism φ with the cost of its application equal to one finite field multiplication. This section explains how our GLV-3 can be used to solve VSM faster than the previous methods (Sect. 2.5 and Sect. 2.6). As explained at the beginning of this section, we can transform the equation $kP = R$ (VSM) to $l_0P + l_1\varphi(P) + l_2R = \infty$, where $l_i \approx n^{1/3}$ are found using the Lagrange's 3-dimensional algorithm.

To verify $l_0P + l_1\varphi(P) + l_2R = \infty$, we compute the left-hand side using the classical Straus-Shamir trick with JSF for three scalars. We iterate through the signed bits of l_0, l_1, l_2 and add one of the 26 points $j_0P + j_1\varphi(P) + j_2R$, $j_i \in \{\pm 1, 0\}$, which are precomputed at the beginning. If we leverage the fast sign switch of points, it is enough to precompute 13 points (including the input points) with the cost of $9A + 2M$. The cost of the Straus-Shamir trick is then given by the number of additions and doublings. The number of doublings is equal to the maximum of the bit-lengths of l_0, l_1, l_2, which is $\approx \frac{t}{3}$, where t is the bit-length of n. The number of additions is given by the compound Hamming weight of l_0, l_1, l_2 which is $\approx 0.59 \cdot \frac{t}{3} \approx \frac{t}{5}$ in the JSF form. The overall cost is

$$\left(9 + \frac{t}{5}\right) A + \frac{t}{3} D + 2M \approx (4.53t + 101)M.$$

Compared to the GLV method Sect. 2.5 with $(6.25t + 13)M$ complexity, this is a $\approx$ 22-25% speed-up for the typical values of t (between 256 and 521).

We have to emphasize that this 25% speed-up only considers the complexity of the Straus-Shamir trick in terms of additions and doublings, and the actual speed-up will be lower. The computation usually also involves, for example, a transformation of the precomputed points into an affine form. More importantly, we did not include the cost of Lagrange's algorithm to find l_0, l_1, l_2, which is a significant burden that the GLV does not have. Rather than theoretically assessing the complexities of the GLV and our GLV-3, we experimentally compare them. Table 2 shows the comparison for the common curve bit-lengths and the timing on our two platforms. For 384 and 521-bit curves, we measured the speed-up to be 23 – 24% on the AMD and 25 – 26% on the MC. For the 256-bit curves, it is only 5% on the AMD and 13% on the MC. This is mainly because of Lagrange's algorithm, whose cost grows with the bit-length (see Table 1), but not as rapidly as with the whole scalar multiplication.

Table 2. Comparison of the GLV method and our GLV-3 for solving VSM. The first column shows the theoretical cost in the number of point additions, doublings, and field multiplications. The third column contains equivalent cost purely in the number of field multiplications for common bit-lengths. The last two columns show the speed in milliseconds (on a 64-bit AMD x86) and the cycle count (32-bit ARM Cortex-M4 MC).

	Cost	t	Mult.	Time (AMD)	Cycles (MC)
GLV	$(\frac{t}{4}+1)A+\frac{t}{2}D+2M$	256	1613M	0.50 ms	12 668 727
		384	2413M	4.6 ms	226 492 679
		521	3269M	10.67 ms	539 123 262
GLV-3	$(9+\frac{t}{5})A+\frac{t}{3}D+2M$	256	1261M	0.48 ms	11 048 969
		384	1841M	3.56 ms	170 030 994
		521	2461M	8.13 ms	400 341 296

Remark 4. We note that a similar idea for verifying scalar multiplication was recently introduced in the context of the SNARK protocol [14]. While in this work the scalar decomposition is part of the running time, the verification in the SNARK circuit works with already precomputed decomposition. Moreover, the authors use the half extended Euclidean algorithm for the scalar decomposition.

3.3 Signature Verification with GLV-3

This section applies GLV-3 to the verification of signatures (VSS). Let $uG+vQ=R$ be the verification equation. Using Lagrange's algorithm, we can find scalars $l_0, l_1, l_2 \approx n^{1/3}$ such that $l_0+l_1\lambda_\varphi+l_2v=0 \pmod{n}$. We multiply the verification equation by l_2, and after the substitution, we get $l_2uG-l_0Q-l_1\varphi(Q)-l_2R=\infty$. Now we split the scalar $l_2u \pmod{n}$ into three scalars of a third of the bit-length, i.e., $l_2u = u_0 + 2^{t/3}u_1 + 2^{2t/3}u_2 \pmod{n}$. Denote $G_1 = 2^{t/3}G$, $G_2 = 2^{2t/3}G$. Putting this all together, we get:

$$u_0G_0 + u_1G_1 + u_2G_2 - l_0Q - l_1\varphi(Q) - l_2R = \infty.$$

All of the scalars have $\approx t/3$ bits. To evaluate the left-hand side, we run two simultaneous Straus-Shamir tricks for u_0, u_1, u_2 and for l_0, l_1, l_2, both with JSF (see Algorithm 6 in the appendix). More precisely, at the beginning, we precompute two sets of points: $h_0G_0 + h_1G_1 + h_2G_2$ and $j_0Q + j_1\varphi(Q) + j_2R$, $h_i, j_i \in \{\pm1, 0\}$, where we exclude points with opposite signs. This amounts to 26 points computed with the cost $19A+2M$. During the Straus-Shamir tricks, we iterate through $t/3$ bits of the scalars u_i, l_i and make two additions, one for each precomputed set. Since the compound weight of all the scalars is $2\cdot 0.59\cdot\frac{t}{3}\approx\frac{2t}{5}$, the total cost is

$$\left(19+\frac{2t}{5}\right)A+\frac{t}{3}D+2M \approx (6.73t+211)M.$$

Compared to the GLV method with the cost $(9t + 26)M$, this is a 17-21% speed-up for t between 256 and 521 bits. Table 3 presents the experimental results. For 256 bits, the overhead of Lagrange's algorithm and the precomputation is too large, and GLV-3 is only 2% faster than GLV on the MC and even 2% worse on AMD. However, for 384 and 521 bits, the speed-up is 18-20% on both platforms.

Table 3. Comparison of the GLV method and our GLV-3 for solving VSS. The first column shows the theoretical cost in the number of point additions, doublings, and field multiplications. The third column contains equivalent cost purely in the number of field multiplications for common bit-lengths. The last two columns show the speed in milliseconds (on a 64-bit AMD x86) and the cycle count (32-bit ARM Cortex-M4 MC).

	Cost	t	Mult.	Time (AMD)	Cycles (MC)
GLV	$(\frac{t}{2} + 2)A + \frac{t}{2}D + 4M$	256	2330M	0.81 ms	19 341 897
		384	3482M	7.13 ms	328 380 849
		521	4715M	15.72 ms	772 028 416
GLV-3	$\frac{t}{3}D + (19 + \frac{2t}{5})A + 2M$	256	1934M	0.82 ms	18 902 318
		384	2795M	5.79 ms	268 629 338
		521	3717M	12.80 ms	615 912 490

3.4 Batch Verification

Previous sections discussed accelerations of the verification of a single signature. Systems often need to verify a *batch* of signatures, so we will now modify the GLV-3 method for batch verification. The signatures in a batch might all correspond to one public key Q or, more generally, to several Q_i. We will first assume that the public key is fixed and focus on the general case afterward. The usual approach for batch signatures, proposed in [25] and since then adopted for EdDSA [6] and Schnorr signatures [39], is to verify a random linear combination of the verification equations. Let $u_iG + v_iQ - R_i$ be the set of B equations. The idea is to multiply each equation by a random integer z_i and verify their sum:

$$\left(\sum_{i=1}^{B} z_i u_i\right) G + \left(\sum_{i=1}^{B} z_i v_i\right) Q - \sum_{i=1}^{B} z_i R_i = \infty.$$

The left side, containing $B + 2$ scalars and points, is then computed and checked with the neutral point on the right side. One of the state-of-the-art multiplication methods for multi-scalar multiplication, also used for batch signatures in [6], is the Bos-Coster method [13]. To compute the general expression $k_1P_1 + k_2P_2 + \cdots + k_sP_s$, where $k_1 \geq k_2 \geq \cdots \geq k_s$, the Bos-Coster method recursively computes $(k_1 - k_2)P_1 + k_2(P_1 + P_2) + k_3P_3 \cdots + k_sP_s$.

The complexity of the Bost-Coster method is determined by the number of iterations, which equals the number of point additions. In general, it is difficult to find a closed formula for the number of iterations. Hence, we simulated the execution for the usually considered batch of size 64 signatures. The average number of iterations turned out to be, on average, 3352, 5012, and 6788 for scalars of bit-length 256, 384, and 521, respectively.

The GLV method can be used to decompose each of the $B+2$ scalars, resulting in twice the amount $(2B+4)$ of scalars, but half the size. For a batch of size 64, the average number of iterations was then reduced to 2958, 4400, and 5925 for the individual bit-lengths in our simulation. This resulted in roughly 12% speed-up when compared to simple Bos-Coster for all three bit-lengths.

Our GLV-3 method can be adapted to batch signatures as well. For each equation $z_iu_iG + z_iv_iQ = z_iR_i$, we find $l_{i,0}, l_{i,1}, l_{i,2}$ such that $l_{i,0} + l_{i,1}\lambda_\varphi + l_{i,2}z_i = 0 \pmod{n}$ using Lagrange's algorithm. Substituting into the verification equation, we get

$$l_{i,2}z_iu_iG + l_{i,2}z_iv_iQ + l_{i,0}R_i + l_{i,1}\varphi(R_i) = \infty,$$

with the following sum to be verified:

$$\left(\sum_{i=1}^{B} l_{i,2}z_iu_i\right)G + \left(\sum_{i=1}^{B} l_{i,2}z_iv_i\right)Q + \sum_{i=1}^{B} l_{i,0}R_i + \sum_{i=1}^{B} l_{i,1}\varphi(R_i) = 0.$$

The scalar corresponding to G can be further split into three parts as in the previous sections assuming that we have two precomputed multiples of G. We can do the same trick for the point Q and the corresponding scalar, but here we have to compute the multiples of Q for each batch corresponding to Q, and so the cost of this must be included as well. The left side contains $2B+6$ scalars of size similar to $n^{1/3}$.

For a batch of size 64, we found that the average number of additions (including the precomputation for Q) is then reduced to 2192, 3260, and 4376 for the individual bit lengths. We can use the measurements on both platforms to compare these batch versions of GLV-3 and GLV. If we multiply the number of iterations with the average measured cost of point addition, we get the approximate cost of GLV in Table 4 (columns 'Fixed key'). The cost of GLV-3 can be approximated in the same way with the addition of the cost of the lattice reduction measured in Table 1. The speed-up of GLV-3 for batch signatures is similar to the single-signature case. For 256 bits, the speed-up is negligible on the MC (2%) and even negative on AMD, but for 384 and 521 bits, it reaches 20-23% on both platforms.

Now, we will remove the assumption of a fixed key Q. Consider a public key Q_i for every verification equation. The linear combination of the equations is

$$\left(\sum_{i=1}^{B} z_iu_i\right)G + \sum_{i=1}^{B} z_iv_iQ_i - \sum_{i=1}^{B} z_iR_i = \infty.$$

Table 4. The cost of the GLV method and our 3-dimensional GLV for batch verification on two platforms (64-bit AMD x86 and 32-bit ARM Cortex-M4 MC) for three bit-lengths. The duration and the clock cycles are approximated based on the number of iterations and the cost of individual operations. Two cases are considered: all signatures in the batch share the same public key and the general case of multiple keys.

		Time (AMD)		Cycles (MC)	
	t	Fixed key	Multiple keys	Fixed key	Multiple keys
GLV	256	0.22 ms	0.38 ms	3 919 026	6 666 850
	384	2.03 ms	3.49 ms	39 809 138	67 946 960
	521	4.71 ms	8.10 ms	92 734 489	159 409 414
GLV-3	256	0.23 ms	0.39 ms	3 841 371	6 697 835
	384	1.61 ms	3.10 ms	31 233 667	60 285 290
	521	3.62 ms	7.08 ms	71 272 985	139 403 489

Experiments showed that Bos-Coster takes approximately 5705, 8532, and 11556 iterations to compute the left side with $2B+1$ scalars for individual bit-lengths. The GLV method doubles the number of scalars (with half the size), resulting in 5108, 7588, and 10229 iterations, i.e., 10-11% speed-up.

Applying the GLV-3 method is not as straightforward as with the fixed public key. Using the same substitution with $l_{i,0} + l_{i,1}\lambda_\varphi + l_{i,2}z_i = 0 \pmod{n}$, we get

$$\left(\sum_{i=1}^{B} l_{i,2}z_i u_i\right) G + \sum_{i=1}^{B} l_{i,2}z_i v_i Q_i + \sum_{i=1}^{B} l_{i,0}R_i + \sum_{i=1}^{B} l_{i,1}\varphi(R_i) = \infty,$$

where $l_{i,0}$ and $l_{i,1}$ are small scalars ($\approx n^{1/3}$), but $l_{i,2}z_i v_i \approx n$. We can, however, decompose each $l_{i,2}z_i v_i$ using λ_φ to two scalars of half the size ($\approx n^{1/2}$). As a result, we have $2B+3$ scalars of similar size as $n^{1/3}$ (corresponding to $R_i, \varphi(R_i)$ and G) and $2B$ scalars of similar size as $n^{1/2}$ (corresponding to Q_i). Because of this gap between the two sets of the scalars, in one iteration of the Bos-Coster, the largest scalar $k_1 \approx n^{1/2}$ can be much bigger than the second largest $k_2 \approx n^{1/3}$. Hence, a simple scalar multiplication by k_2 might be needed to reduce k_1. Otherwise, the technique works the same as with scalars of the same size.

Table 4 (columns 'Multiple keys') summarizes the cost approximated in the same way as for the case with fixed Q. On both platforms, there is no speed-up for 256 bits and 11-13% speed-up for the higher bit-lengths.

We remind the reader that the experiments for the batch verification were only simulated. The lattice reductions and individual additions on curve were measured, but the overall cost was only summed up based on the measured number of iterations. Implementing the Bos-Coster method with a fast heap structure would require non-trivial effort that we considered out of scope for this work. Our aim was the comparison of different verification strategies that would all use the Bos-Coster method.

3.5 4-Dimensional GLV

The GLS method described in Sect. 2.2 uses two endomorphisms for the 4-dimensional decomposition. While our GLV-3 method uses only one fast endomorphism, it imitates the GLS method by considering the scalar multiplication to be verified as a second endomorphism (recall the beginning of Sect. 3). This section describes why we did not focus on the 4-dimensional decomposition as used in the GLS method.

For the VSM equality $kQ = R$ on a curve with endomorphism φ, we have considered k as an endomorphism for which kQ has been computed for us. Similarly, we can consider $k\varphi(Q) = \varphi(R)$ and find $l_0, l_1, l_2, l_3 \approx n^{1/4}$ satisfying:

$$l_0 + l_l\lambda_\varphi + l_2 k + l_3 k\lambda\varphi = 0 \pmod{n}$$
$$l_0 Q + l_1\varphi(Q) + l_2 R + l_3\varphi(R) = \infty$$

with the assumption that $kQ = R$. In principle, this gives us a verification equation[4] with smaller scalars than GLV-3. Using two Straus-Shamir tricks with two pairs of scalars l_0, l_1 and l_2, l_3 in the JSF form, we can compute the left side with the cost $(\frac{t}{4} + 2)A + \frac{t}{4}D + 4M = (4.5t + 26)M$. Compared to the GLV-3 method, this brings only $4-7\%$ speed-up. We can also precompute all possible combinations $j_0 Q + j_1\varphi(Q) + j_2 R + j_3\varphi(R)$, $j_i \in \{0, \pm 1\}$ and consider all four scalars in the JSF form with the join Hamming weight $0.64 \cdot \frac{t}{4} = \frac{4t}{25}$. The precomputation then costs $34A + 4M$ and the overall cost is $\approx (3.51t + 378)M$, which is actually worse than GLV-3 for $t = 256$ and 10% better for $t = 521$.

The main issue of this 4-dimensional approach is the search for the short vector (l_0, l_1, l_2, l_3) in a 4-dimensional lattice. Our experiments showed that Lagrange's algorithm adapted to 4 dimensions very often does not find a short vector of norm $\approx n^{1/4}$. Other algorithms could be used, e.g., [27], but we leave this as a future work. We could also apply this idea to VSS, resulting in eight scalars. Based on the observations with VSM, we decided that the overhead of the precomputation and the lattice reduction is too troublesome and most likely not worth the speed-up.

4 The Dependent Coordinates Problem

The GLV-3 method uses a fast endomorphism and a precomputed equality $kP = R$ to decompose the scalar k into three smaller scalars. Smaller scalars imply faster scalar multiplication, which increases the presented speed. Beyond fast scalar multiplication, this decomposition also finds another application. This section completely changes the context and moves away from the verification of signatures into the field of side-channel attacks. We show that the GLV-3 technique can be used to significantly reduce the complexity of a specific type of side-channel attack.

[4] It should be noted that if the second equation holds, then $kQ = R$ is true (and gets correctly verified) as long as $l_2 + l_3\lambda_\varphi \neq 0 \pmod{n}$, but this is expected.

Side-channel attacks are a common threat to ECC protocols implemented on embedded systems. We will consider certain types of side-channel attacks called zero-value point (ZVP) attacks [1]. ZVP attacks target a static private key during scalar multiplication where the attacker has control over the input point for the multiplication (c.g., ECDH). The attack works with the assumption that operations involving zero values are distinguishable from general random operations using power or EM analysis. The full context and the details can be found in the original paper [1].

We are interested in only one step of the attack—solving the dependent coordinates problem (DCP)[5] defined as follows:

(DCP) Given a scalar $k \in \mathbb{Z}$ and a polynomial $f \in \mathbb{F}_p[x_1, x_2]$, find two points P, Q, such that $f(x_P, x_Q) = 0$ and $Q = kP$.

Solving DCP efficiently is an open problem, but there are two cases, in which the problem can be efficiently solved. Firstly, for small scalars k (at most 20 bits), one can generate the multiplication-by-k map and substitute it into f, which results in a univariate polynomial equation in x_P with a degree $\approx k^2 \deg f$ that is then solved for x_P. Secondly, the problem is also easy when f is already a univariate polynomial (in either x_P or x_Q). Nevertheless, for general k and f, the best approach is to guess the point P with the complexity $O(n)$. As a result, the ZVP attack is very limited by the difficulty of DCP, and only a few bits of the private key can be recovered.

Suchánek, Sedláček, and Sýs [35] realized that an implementation that uses the GLV method for scalar multiplication exposes more bits of the private. The DCP is, in that case, defined for $k = k_0 + k_1\lambda_\varphi$, where k_0, k_1 are small for the first several iterations. This allows the attacker to target both k_0 and k_1 at the same time, recovering almost twice as many bits as the original ZVP. While this result increases the number of recovered bits, the complexity of the general DCP remains to be $O(n)$. The method uses multiplication-by-k_i maps of degree k_i^2. Since for general k we should expect $k_i^2 \approx n$, the complexity is at best $O(n)$.

We will show how the 4-dimensional GLV method described in Sect. 3.5 can be used to reduce the complexity of DCP on a GLV curve to $O(\sqrt{n}\log^3 n)$. Let Q, P be the DCP solution points and $l_0, l_1, l_2, l_3 \approx n^{1/4}$ such that

$$l_0 + l_1\lambda_\varphi + l_2 k + l_3\lambda_\varphi k = 0 \pmod{n}.$$

These can be found using, e.g., the LLL algorithm. The idea is to follow the symbolical approach described above, but instead of using a multiplication-by-k map of degree n^2, we use the multiplication-by-l_i maps of degree $\sqrt{n}$. Specifically, as in [35], we use the Semaev polynomial [33] that satisfies $S_4(x_{P_1}, x_{P_2}, x_{P_3}, x_{P_4}) = 0$ for any $P_1 \pm P_2 \pm P_3 \pm P_4 = \infty$. In our case with $l_0P + l_1\varphi(P) + l_2Q + l_3\varphi(Q) = \infty$:

$$S(x_P, x_Q) = S_4(r_0(x_P), r_1(x_{\varphi(P)}), r_2(x_Q), r_3(x_{\varphi(Q)})) = 0,$$

[5] The problem was formalized and named in [31].

where r_0, r_1, r_2, r_3 are the x-coordinates of the multiplication maps for l_0, l_1, l_2, l_3, respectively. The degree of S is given by $\deg S_4 = 16$ and by the degrees of the r_i maps, which is $\approx \sqrt{n}$. Together with $f(x_P, x_Q) = 0$, we have two polynomial equations with two unknowns x_P, x_Q. It remains to compute the resultant, a univariate polynomial in x_P, and find its roots. Assuming fast integer arithmetic, this can be done in $O(\sqrt{n}\log^3 n)$ operations—a significant reduction from the original $O(n)$ complexity.

5 Conclusions and Future Work

Our work shows that endomorphisms that have been used so far for 2-dimensional decomposition can also be used for higher dimensions in the right context. This improves the verification of Schnorr-like signature schemes. Specifically, experiments demonstrate a $\approx 20\%$ speed-up for single signature verification and 13% speed-up for batch verification. The improvement is mainly relevant for curves with higher bit-lengths with endomorphisms, including the classical pairing-friendly curves, such as BLS12-381 [9]. In addition, the technique applies to any protocol involving the verification of scalar multiplication, such as the Blind Diffie-Hellman protocol, where we show 27% speed up.

The three dimensions in our GLV-3 technique came with the price of reducing 3-dimensional lattices. We analyzed 3-dimensional lattice reduction algorithms and concluded that the simple adaptation of Lagrange's algorithm for 3 dimensions is efficient enough and even faster than Semaev's algorithm with the state-of-the-art complexity. Finally, to demonstrate that the idea of the GLV-3 extends beyond a signature verification, we lower the asymptotic complexity of the hard DCP problem that is hindering the so-called Zero-value point attack.

This work considered Schnorr signatures, modified ECDSA signatures, and the BDHKE protocol. Other schemes, not necessarily signatures, could also benefit from the GLV-3 method. There are only two requirements for the method: 1) the curve must admit an efficient endomorphism, and 2) scalar multiplication is verified in the scheme. As discussed in Remark 1, the EdDSA scheme over an Edwards curve with complete formulas could take advantage of the method as long as an appropriate curve with an efficient endomorphism would be found.

Acknowledgements. This paper is supported by the European Union under Grant Agreement No. 101087529 (CHESS).

Appendix

Algorithm 4: double-and-add

Input: Point P, t-bit scalar $k = (k_{t-1}, k_{t-2}, \dots, k_0)$
Output: kP

$Q \leftarrow \infty$
for $i = t - 1$ down to 0 **do**
    $Q \leftarrow 2Q$
    if $k_i = 1$ **then** $Q \leftarrow Q + P$;
return Q

Algorithm 5: GLV method with Straus-Shamir trick

Input: Point P, $t/2$-bit scalars k_0, k_1, endomorphism φ
Output: $k_0 P + k_1 \varphi(P)$

$T[j_0, j_1] \leftarrow j_0 P + j_1 \varphi(P)$ for all $(j_0, j_1) \in \{0, 1, -1\}^2$
$Q \leftarrow \infty$
for $(j_0, j_1) \in \mathrm{JSF}(k_0, k_1)$ **do**
    $Q \leftarrow 2Q$
    $Q \leftarrow Q + T[j_0, j_1]$
return Q

Algorithm 6: Signature verification using GLV-3

Input: $u, v \in \mathbb{Z}$, points G, Q, R, $G_1 = 2^{t/3}G$, $G_2 = 2^{2t/3}G$ on a curve with order n and endomorphism φ
Output: $uG + vQ \stackrel{?}{=} R$

$l_0, l_1, l_2 \leftarrow$ Algorithm 2 on $(v, 0, -1), (\lambda_\varphi, -1, 0), (n, 0, 0)$
Find u_0, u_1, u_2, s.t. $ul_2 \pmod{n} = u_2 | u_1 | u_0$, where $|$ is conc. of bits.
Compute $h_0 G + h_1 G_1 + h_2 G_2$ and $j_0 Q + j_1 \varphi(Q) + j_2 R$ for $j_i, h_i \in \{\pm 1, 0\}$
$T \leftarrow \infty$
for $(h_0, h_1, h_2), (j_0, j_1, j_2) \in \mathrm{JSF}(u_0, u_1, u_2), \mathrm{JSF}(l_0, l_1, l_2)$ **do**
    $T \leftarrow 2T$
    $T \leftarrow T + h_0 G + h_1 G_1 + h_2 G_2$
    $T \leftarrow T - j_0 Q - j_1 \varphi(Q) - j_2 R$
return $T \stackrel{?}{=} \infty$

References

1. Akishita, T., Takagi, T.: Zero-value point attacks on elliptic curve cryptosystem. In: Boyd, C., Mao, W. (eds.) Information Security, pp. 218–233. Springer, Berlin, Heidelberg (2003). https://doi.org/10.1007/10958513_17
2. Antipa, A., Brown, D., Gallant, R., Lambert, R., Struik, R., Vanstone, S.: Accelerated verification of ECDSA signatures. In: Preneel, B., Tavares, S. (eds.) International Workshop on Selected Areas in Cryptography, pp. 307–318. Springer (2005). https://doi.org/10.1007/11693383_21

3. Babai, L.: On Lovász' lattice reduction and the nearest lattice point problem. Combinatorica **6**, 1–13 (1986)
4. Bellman, R., Straus, E.: Addition chains of vectors (problem 5125). Am. Math. Monthly **71**(7), 806–808 (1964)
5. Bernstein, D.J., Birkner, P., Joye, M., Lange, T., Peters, C.: Twisted Edwards curves. In: Vaudenay, S. (ed.) AFRICACRYPT 2008. LNCS, vol. 5023, pp. 389–405. Springer, Heidelberg (2008). https://doi.org/10.1007/978-3-540-68164-9_26
6. Bernstein, D.J., Duif, N., Lange, T., Schwabe, P., Yang, B.-Y.: Highspeed high-security signatures. J. Cryptogr. Eng. **2**(2), 77–89 (2012)
7. Bernstein, D.J., Lange, T.: Explicit-formulas database (2007). http://hyperelliptic.org/EFD
8. Boneh, D., Lynn, B., Shacham, H.: Short signatures from the Weil pairing. In: Boyd, C. (eds.) International Conference on the Theory and Application of Cryptology and Information Security, pp. 514–532. Springer (2001). https://doi.org/10.1007/3-540-45682-1_30
9. Bowe, S.: BLS12-381 for the rest of us (2025). https://hackmd.io/@benjaminion/bls12-381. Visited on 07/16/2025
10. Brumley, B.B.: Faster software for fast endomorphisms. In: Mangard, S., Poschmann, A.Y. (eds.) COSADE 2014. LNCS, vol. 9064, pp. 127–140. Springer, Cham (2015). https://doi.org/10.1007/978-3-319-21476-4_9
11. Cohen, H., et al.: Handbook of Elliptic and Hyperelliptic Curve Cryptography, 2nd edn. Chapman & Hall/CRC (2012). ISBN: 1439840008
12. Costello, C., Longa, P.: Four: four-dimensional decompositions on ACURVE over the MERSENNE prime. In: Iwata, T., Cheon, J. (eds.) International Conference on the Theory and Application of Cryptology and Information Security. Springer, pp. 214–235 (2015). https://doi.org/10.1007/978-3-662-48797-6_10
13. De Rooij, P.: Efficient exponentiation using precomputation and vector addition chains. In: Workshop on the Theory and Application of of Cryptographic Techniques. Springer, pp. 389–399 (1994). https://doi.org/10.1007/BFb0053453
14. Eagen, L., Housni, Y.E., Masson, S., Piellard, T.: Fast elliptic curve scalar multiplications in SN(T)ARK circuits. Cryptology ePrint Archive, Paper 2025/933 (2025). https://eprint.iacr.org/2025/933
15. Faz-Hernández, A., Longa, P., Sánchez, A.H.: Efficient and secure algorithms for GLV-based scalar multiplication and their implementation on GLV-GLS curves. In: Benaloh, J. (ed.) CT-RSA 2014. LNCS, vol. 8366, pp. 1–27. Springer, Cham (2014). https://doi.org/10.1007/978-3-319-04852-9_1
16. Firmware, T.: MBED TLS (2024). https://github.com/Mbed-TLS/mbedtls
17. Galbraith, S.D., Lin, X., Scott, M.: Endomorphisms for faster elliptic curve cryptography on a large class of curves. In: Joux, A. (ed.) EUROCRYPT 2009. LNCS, vol. 5479, pp. 518–535. Springer, Heidelberg (2009). https://doi.org/10.1007/978-3-642-01001-9_30
18. Gallant, R.P., Lambert, R.J., Vanstone, S.A.: Faster point multiplication on elliptic curves with efficient endomorphisms. In: Kilian, J. (ed.) CRYPTO 2001. LNCS, vol. 2139, pp. 190–200. Springer, Heidelberg (2001). https://doi.org/10.1007/3-540-44647-8_11
19. Hankerson, D., Menezes, A.J., Vanstone, S.: Guide to Elliptic Curve Cryptography. Springer-Verlag, Berlin, Heidelberg (2003). ISBN: 038795273X
20. Hu, Z., Longa, P., Xu, M.: Implementing the 4-dimensional GLV method on GLS elliptic curves with J-invariant . Des. Codes Cryptogr. **63**(3), 331–343 (2012)

21. Jancar, J., Suchanek, V., Svenda, P., Sedlacek, V., Chmielewski, L.: PYECSCA: reverse engineering black-box elliptic curve cryptography via side-channel analysis. In: IACR Transactions on Cryptographic Hardware and Embedded Systems, pp. 355–381 (2024). https://doi.org/10.46586/tches.v2024.i4.355-381. https://tches.iacr.org/index.php/TCHES/ article/view/11796
22. Lenstra, A.K., Lenstra, H.W., Lovász, L.: Factoring polynomials with rational coefficients. Mathematische annalen **261**, 515–534 (1982)
23. Longa, P., Sica, F.: Four-dimensional gallant-lambert-Vanstone scalar multiplication. In: Wang, X., Sako, K. (eds.) ASIACRYPT 2012. LNCS, vol. 7658, pp. 718–739. Springer, Heidelberg (2012). https://doi.org/10.1007/978-3-642-34961-4_43
24. Masson, S., Sanso, A., Zhang, Z.: Bandersnatch: a fast elliptic curve built over the BLS12-381 scalar field. Des. Codes Cryptogr. **92**(12), 4131–4143 (2024). ISSN: 0925-1022. https://doi.org/10.1007/s10623-024-01472-0
25. Naccache, D., M'RaÏhi, D., Vaudenay, S., Raphaeli, D.: Can DSA be improved?—complexity trade-offs with the digital signature standard. In: Advances in Cryptology—EUROCRYPT 1994: Workshop on the Theory and Application of Cryptographic Techniques Perugia, Italy, May 9–12, 1994 Proceedings 13, pp. 77–85. Springer (1995)
26. Nakamoto, S.: Bitcoin: a peer-to-peer electronic cash system. In: Satoshi Nakamoto (2008)
27. Nguyen, P.Q., Stehlé, D.: Low-dimensional lattice basis reduction revisited. ACM Trans. Algorithms (TALG) **5**(4) (2009)
28. OpenCash: Cashu. https://cashu.space/
29. Pornin, T.: Optimized lattice basis reduction in dimension 2, and fast SCHNORR and EdDSA signature verification. Cryptology ePrint Archive, Paper 2020/454 (2020). https://eprint.iacr.org/2020/454
30. Proos, J.: Joint sparse forms and generating zero columns when combing. Tech. rep. Technical Report CORR 2003-23, Department of Combinatorics and Optimization (2003)
31. Sedlacek, V., Chi-Domínguez, J.-J., Jancar, J., Brumley, B.B.: A formula for disaster: a unified approach to elliptic curve special-point-based attacks. In: Tibouchi, M., Wang, H. (eds.) ASIACRYPT 2021. LNCS, vol. 13090, pp. 130–159. Springer, Cham (2021). https://doi.org/10.1007/978-3-030-92062-3_5
32. Semaev, I.: A 3-dimensional lattice reduction algorithm. In: Silverman, J.H. (eds.) Cryptography and Lattices: International Conference, CaLC 2001 Providence, RI, USA, March 29–30, 2001 Revised Papers. Springer, pp. 181–193 (2001). https://doi.org/10.1007/3-540-44670-2_13
33. Semaev, I.: Summation polynomials and the discrete logarithm problem on elliptic curves. Cryptology ePrint Archive. Paper 2004/031. eprint.iacr. org/2004/031 (2004). eprint.iacr.org/2004/031
34. Solinas, J.A.: Low-weight binary representation for pairs of integers. In: Centre for Applied Cryptographic Research, University of Waterloo, Combinatorics and Optimization Research Report CORR 2001-41 (2001)
35. Suchánek, V., Sedláček, V., Sýs, M.: Decompose and conquer: ZVP attacks on GLV curves. Cryptology ePrint Archive, Paper 2025/076 (2025). https://eprint.iacr.org/2025/076
36. Wagner, D.: Chaumian ecash without RSA (1996). https://cypherpunks.venona.com/date/1996/03/msg01848.html
37. Washington, L.C.: Elliptic Curves: Number Theory and Cryptography. CRC Press (2008)

38. Wuille, P.: libsecp256k1 (2013). https://github.com/bitcoin-core/secp256k1
39. Wuille, P., Nick, J., Ruffing, T.: SCHNORR signatures for secp256k1 (2020). https://github.com/bitcoin/bips/blob/master/bip-0340.mediawiki
40. Zhou, Z., Hu, Z., Xu, M., Song, W.: Efficient 3-dimensional GLV method for faster point multiplication on some GLS elliptic curves. Inf. Process. Lett. **110**(22), 1003–1006 (2010)

Efficient Sum-Check for High-Degree Polynomials

Yu Wang[1,2,3], Yuncong Zhang[1,2,3], and Yu Chen[1,2,3,4](✉)

[1] School of Cyber Science and Technology, Shandong University, Qingdao 266237, China
ywang21@mail.sdu.edu.cn,
{yuncong,yuchen}@sdu.edu.cn

[2] State Key Laboratory of Cryptography and Digital Economy Security, Shandong University, Qingdao 266237, China

[3] Key Laboratory of Cryptologic Technology and Information Security of Ministry of Education, Shandong University, Qingdao 266237, China

[4] State Key Laboratory of Cryptology, P.O. Box 5159, Beijing 100878, China

Abstract. This paper presents a new framework for constructing efficient sum-check protocols for high-degree virtual multivariate polynomials. Existing approaches, such as HyperPlonk, suffer from an inherent bottleneck: polynomial multiplications inside the sum-check protocol lead to quasi-linear prover overhead in the polynomial degree d. To address this issue, we introduce doubly efficient sum-check (DESC) PIOP, which achieves linear prover time by integrating a generalized GKR protocol for general arithmetic circuits. The key insight is to reformulate virtual polynomial evaluation as a data-parallel circuit execution, thereby avoiding explicit polynomial multiplications.

Building on the DESC framework, we derive two concrete applications. First, for customizable constraint systems (CCS), we reduce prover time complexity from $O(qmd\log^2 d)$ to $O(qmd)$, where q denotes the number of constraint multisets, m the number of constraints, and d the maximum degree of any variable across all polynomials. Second, we propose SPARK PIOP, an improved polynomial IOP for sparse multilinear commitments, which reduces the total commitment size by nearly a quarter compared to the Lasso construction.

Finally, as a conceptual consolidation, we emphasize that the efficiency of sum-check–based proof systems is fundamentally determined by how algebraic constraints are organized. By reorganizing circuit layers into low-degree polynomial relations, we reduce communication complexity while preserving the doubly efficient properties of GKR for both the prover and the verifier.

Keywords: Sum-Check · High-Degree Polynomial · GKR Protocol

1 Introduction

Zero-knowledge succinct non-interactive arguments of knowledge (zkSNARKs), exemplified by schemes such as Groth16 [17], Bulletproofs [6], and Stark [2],

K. Jee and A. Kate (Eds.): ACNS 2026, LNCS 16571, pp. 297–326, 2027.
https://doi.org/10.1007/978-3-032-32560-0_11

represent a remarkable cryptographic primitive for proving memberships in NP languages. These sophisticated cryptographic constructions enable a prover to assure a verifier of the validity of a given statement by presenting concise proofs while disclosing no additional information. With prominent applications in Zcash [21], zkRollups [7], zkBridge [30], and zkLogin [1], zkSNARKs have become crucial for enabling privacy-preserving and scalable applications, driving continued research towards improving their efficiency and applicability.

Despite their powerful asymptotic guarantees, modern zkSNARKs encounter a significant practical challenge: the computational burden on the prover. In real-world scenarios, this burden increases considerably with the complexity of the underlying computation. This growth is primarily governed by the number of constraints and the degree of the polynomials involved. As a result, enhancing the prover's efficiency remains a crucial objective for enabling wider adoption.

A recurring component in many IOP-based SNARKs is the sum-check protocol [19], which verifies that a multivariate polynomial sums to a claimed value over the Boolean hypercube. While sum-check enjoys low communication and verifier complexity, its prover complexity crucially depends on how polynomial evaluations are realized. In particular, when verifying identities involving high-degree polynomials, existing constructions such as HyperPlonk [9] require explicit computation of univariate polynomials during the sum-check protocol. This step relies on fast polynomial multiplication and introduces a quasi-linear $\log^2 d$ overhead in the polynomial degree d. Similar overheads arise in SuperSpartan [24] when extending polynomial IOPs from R1CS to Customizable Constraint Systems (CCS).

Although many SNARK constructions operate with low-degree polynomial constraints, higher-degree polynomials arise in more expressive settings. In particular, in HyperPlonk and CCS, higher-degree constraints result from the use of customized gates with elevated algebraic degree, whereas in lookup arguments [18,25], the use of rational functions (e.g., logarithmic derivatives) introduces polynomial identities of increased degree. In such settings, the effective polynomial degree may scale with the algebraic degree of customized gates or the arity of the constraints, making the $\log^2 d$ factor in existing sum-check protocols non-negligible in the prover complexity.

This work shows that the quasi-linear prover overhead in existing high-degree sum-check protocols is not inherent. At a high level, we demonstrate that this overhead can be eliminated by avoiding explicit polynomial multiplication, resulting in provers whose running time is linear in the effective degree of the polynomial.

1.1 The Contributions

We summarize our main contributions as follows.

A GKR-Based Sum-Check for High-Degree Polynomials. We introduce DESC PIOP, a new protocol for verifying sum-checks of high-degree virtual polynomials [9] over the Boolean hypercube, achieving linear prover time. Our key observation is that sum-check efficiency is not intrinsic to polynomial degree, but rather to how algebraic constraints are organized and exposed to the GKR framework. By encoding high-degree compositions as structured arithmetic circuits and applying a generalized GKR protocol [31] over aggregated constraints, DESC PIOP bypasses the polynomial multiplication bottleneck that arises in conventional sum-check, while preserving soundness and achieving linear prover time.

CCS with Linear Prover Time via Algebraic Constraint Re-encoding. We integrate DESC PIOP into the CCS, yielding a proof system with $O(qmd)$ prover complexity, where q denotes the number of constraint multisets, m the constraint system size, and d the maximum multiset cardinality. This improves upon the original CCS implementation, which required $O(qmd\log^2 d)$ prover time. The improvement follows from a re-encoding of CCS constraints as structured compositions of sparse matrix–vector products and Hadamard products, enabling their verification via linear-time GKR-style sum-checks rather than explicit high-degree polynomial expansions.

Optimized Sparse Polynomial Commitments. We propose SPARK PIOP, a polynomial IOP for sparse multilinear polynomial commitments that improves prover performance. By combining logarithmic-derivative-based lookup arguments with our DESC PIOP framework, we reduce the total commitment size from $(3c+1)\cdot \mathsf{pc}(n) + c\cdot \mathsf{pc}(m)$ in Lasso to $(2c+2)\cdot \mathsf{pc}(n) + c\cdot \mathsf{pc}(m)$, while preserving linear prover time. Here, n denotes the number of nonzero entries, m is the table size, c is the decomposition parameter, and $\mathsf{pc}(\cdot)$ is the polynomial commitment size of a multilinear polynomial. Moreover, SPARK PIOP supports efficient batch verification of multiple lookup checks and sparse matrix evaluations in parallel, without compromising soundness. For example, within the CCS framework, this enables the prover to generate proofs for multiple sparse polynomial evaluations simultaneously, aggregating them into a single sum-check instance and thereby reducing the total commitment size.

A Refined Perspective on GKR-Style Proofs. Finally, as a conceptual consolidation, we generalize the core insight behind DESC—that constraint organization dictates efficiency—to the GKR protocol itself. While DESC (Sect. 3) reorganizes constraints to solve the computational bottleneck of high degree polynomials, Sect. 6 extends this philosophy to address the communication bottleneck in general circuits.

By reorganizing circuit layers into low-degree polynomial relations, we show that the constraint reorganization is a universal tool for optimizing GKR-based proof systems. Specifically, for a circuit of depth d and width S, this approach reduces the total communication complexity from the standard $6d\log S$ to approximately $4.25d\log S$ ($\approx 29\%$ reduction), while preserving linear prover time and efficient verification.

1.2 Technical Overview

At a conceptual level, our work highlights a unifying principle: the efficiency of sum-check–based proof systems is determined by how algebraic constraints are organized before verification. Enforcing high-degree polynomial sum-checks directly leads to unnecessary prover overhead. By reorganizing these constraints into low-degree polynomial forms and applying a GKR-style proof framework, we preserve linear-time prover complexity and maintain efficient verification.

Based on this principle, we summarize our technical contributions in the following four points.

Sum-Check for High-Degree Polynomials. We first apply this framework to the problem of verifying sums of high-degree multivariate polynomials over the Boolean hypercube. Specifically, we consider polynomials of the form $f(x) = h(g_1(x), ..., g_c(x))$, where h is a degree-d polynomial represented by a general arithmetic circuit and each g_i is multilinear. A naive application of sum-check would require explicitly expanding h, which would lead to prohibitive prover complexity. We introduce DESC PIOP to avoid this bottleneck. Crucially, DESC reformulates the high-degree polynomial evaluation as a data-parallel circuit: it treats h as a low-depth arithmetic subcircuit and evaluates 2^μ independent, parallel copies of it over the Boolean hypercube. The sum-check protocol is first used to reduce the global sum $\sum_{x \in \{0,1\}^\mu} f(x)$ to a single evaluation of the multilinear extension $\tilde{f}$ at a random point. The resulting evaluation is then verified using the generalized GKR protocol, without performing explicit polynomial multiplications.

Optimizing Prover Time in CCS. We next apply DESC PIOP to the CCS framework. A CCS instance enforces polynomial constraints of the form

$$\sum_{i=0}^{q-1} c_i \cdot \prod_{j \in S_i} \widetilde{g}_j(\boldsymbol{x}) = 0, \quad \forall \boldsymbol{x} \in \{0,1\}^n,$$

where each g_j is a sparse linear combination of the witness, and $\widetilde{g}_j$ denotes its multilinear extension over the Boolean hypercube. The degree of the resulting polynomial is determined by the maximum cardinality of the multisets S_i, which can be large in practice.

By interpreting the CCS constraint as a high-degree polynomial identity over the Boolean hypercube, its verification can be reduced to a single sum-check instance. DESC PIOP executes this sum-check with linear-time prover complexity by evaluating the underlying computation as a data-parallel arithmetic circuit. Consequently, the prover time of CCS is reduced from $O(qmd \log^2 d)$ to $O(qmd)$, while preserving soundness and efficient verification.

SPARK PIOP and Batch Verification for Sparse Commitments. We further apply our techniques to sparse multilinear polynomial commitments. In the SPARK protocol [23], verifying a sparse polynomial evaluation is reduced to checking lookup relations. While originally implemented via product checks, we point out that these relations can also be naturally enforced via logarithmic-derivative arguments. The advantage of this approach is that it enables efficient batching: after clearing denominators, these checks give rise to high-degree polynomial identities. By integrating logarithmic-derivative arguments with DESC PIOP, our framework inherently optimizes the batching process, significantly reducing commitment overhead without compromising soundness.

Revisiting GKR through Constraint Organization. Rather than treating sum-check as an intrinsic component of GKR, we observe that the efficiency of GKR-style proofs is governed by how circuit constraints are algebraically organized before invoking sum-check. By encoding circuit layers using low-degree polynomial constraints expressed via summations, sparse matrix–vector multiplications, and Hadamard products, additive relations are absorbed and multiplicative dependencies are aggregated.

This reorganization reduces the effective circuit depth and the number of sum-check layers, while maintaining the doubly efficient nature of GKR for both the prover and the verifier. Furthermore, by analyzing the impact of bounded polynomial degrees on communication cost, we identify degree parameters that achieve an optimal communication trade-off within our protocol.

1.3 Related Work

Modern SNARKs generally compile information-theoretic proofs (e.g., Interactive Oracle Proofs (IOPs) [4]) into cryptographic proofs via polynomial commitments. While systems like STARK [2], Aurora [3], Sonic [20], Plonk [14], and Fractal [10] rely on univariate polynomial commitment schemes, a growing number of frameworks—including Libra [29], Spartan [23], Gemini [5], HyperPlonk [9], and Brakedown [16]—leverage multilinear polynomial commitment schemes. At the foundational core of multilinear SNARKs is the sum-check [19]. Despite its powerful capabilities, applying traditional sum-check (e.g., HyperPlonk [9]) to high-degree multivariate polynomials introduces a computational bottleneck: evaluating expressions of the form $v = \sum_{x\in\{0,1\}^\mu} \prod_{i=1}^{d} g_i(\boldsymbol{x})$ requires $O(2^\mu \cdot d\log^2 d)$ prover time and $O(d\mu)$ communication/verification. Our DESC framework (Sect. 3) resolves this inefficiency. By integrating the GKR protocol [15], DESC strictly improves the prover time to $O(2^\mu \cdot d)$ while maintaining highly efficient $O(\mu\log d + \log^2 d)$ communication and $O(\mu\log d + \log^2 d + d)$ verification.

While the proof systems like GKR, Plonk, and Spartan provide efficient verification for arithmetic circuits, they incur massive overheads when expressing non-arithmetic operations (e.g., range checks). Lookup arguments [13] circumvent this by enforcing relations against precomputed tables, with recent advancements achieving costs independent of table size [8,12]. Fundamentally, lookups serve as a powerful tool to enforce memory consistency. Spartan [23] introduced Memory-in-the-Head using 2-dimensional tensors, which Lasso subsequently generalized to c-dimensional tensors. While both rely on product checks, we observe the additive structure of logarithmic derivatives [18] excels in batch verification. Integrating this into DESC improves proving efficiency and reduces Lasso's commitment overhead from $4c + 1$ to $3c + 2$ polynomials (a $\sim 25\%$ reduction).

The foundational GKR protocol [15] and its extensions [29] established succinct interactive proofs with linear prover time. However, their standard evaluations are typically constrained to basic addition and multiplication operations, which significantly limits the optimization space for layer transitions. To overcome this, we optimize the GKR architecture via CCS [24] by employing custom gates. This approach explicitly balances the number of sum-checks against the per-round polynomial degrees, thereby providing a highly flexible trade-off between prover time and communication complexity while strictly maintaining the asymptotic linear prover overhead.

2 Preliminaries

2.1 Notation

Let $\mathbb{F}$ be a finite field. We define the Boolean hypercube of dimension μ as $B_\mu := \{0,1\}^\mu \subseteq \mathbb{F}^\mu$. For any positive integer n, we denote its binary representation by $\langle n \rangle = (a_1, \ldots, a_k)$, where $k = \lceil \log_2 n \rceil$. This representation satisfies $n = \sum_{i=1}^{k} a_i \cdot 2^{i-1}$, with coefficients $a_i \in \{0,1\}$ and $\lceil \cdot \rceil$ denoting the ceiling function. Furthermore, we let $\mathcal{F}_\mu^{\leq d}$ denote the family of μ-variate polynomials in $\mathbb{F}[X_1, \ldots, X_\mu]$ such that the individual degree of each variable is at most d. Any polynomial $f \in \mathcal{F}_\mu^{\leq d}$ can be accessed via a virtual oracle, denoted as $[[f]]$.

2.2 The Multivariate Polynomial

A multivariate polynomial involves more than one variable; otherwise, it's termed a univariate polynomial. If the degree of the multivariate polynomial in each variable is at most one, it's referred to as a multilinear polynomial.

Definition 1 (Low-degree polynomial). *A multivariate polynomial f over a finite field $\mathbb{F}$ is called low-degree polynomial if the degree of f in each variable is exponentially smaller than $|\mathbb{F}|$.*

Lemma 1 (Schwartz-Zippel Lemma [22,26]). *Let $\mathbb{F}$ be any field, and let $g : \mathbb{F}^\mu \to \mathbb{F}$ be a nonzero μ-variate polynomial of total degree at most d. Then on any finite set $S \subseteq \mathbb{F}$,*

$$\Pr_{x \leftarrow S^\mu}[g(\boldsymbol{x}) = 0] \leq d/|S|.$$

Definition 2 (Low-degree Extensions (LDEs)). *Suppose $g : \{0,1\}^\mu \to \mathbb{F}$ is a function that maps μ bit elements into an element of $\mathbb{F}$. A polynomial extension of g is a low-degree μ-variate polynomial $\widetilde{g}(\cdot)$ such that $\widetilde{g}(\boldsymbol{x}) = g(\boldsymbol{x})$ for all $\boldsymbol{x} \in \{0,1\}^\mu$.*

A multilinear polynomial extension (MLE), denoted as $\widetilde{g}(\cdot)$, is a low-degree polynomial where the degree of each variable is at most one. For a function $f : \{0,1\}^\mu \to \mathbb{F}$, its multilinear extension $\widetilde{f} : \mathbb{F}^\mu \to \mathbb{F}$ is the unique multilinear polynomial that extends f as follows

$$\begin{aligned}\widetilde{f}(x_1,\ldots,x_\mu) &= \sum_{e\in\{0,1\}^\mu} f(e)\cdot\prod_{i=1}^{\mu}(e_i\cdot x_i + (1-e_i)(1-x_i)) \\ &= \sum_{e\in\{0,1\}^\mu} f(\boldsymbol{e})\cdot eq(\boldsymbol{x},\boldsymbol{e}).\end{aligned}$$

Here, the function $eq(\boldsymbol{x},\boldsymbol{e})$ is defined as the multilinear extension of the Boolean equality function $eq(\boldsymbol{x},\boldsymbol{e})$. In the Boolean space, the equality function $eq(\boldsymbol{x},\boldsymbol{e})$ evaluates to:

$$eq(\boldsymbol{x},\boldsymbol{e}) = \begin{cases}1, & \text{if } \boldsymbol{x}=\boldsymbol{e},\\ 0, & \text{otherwise.}\end{cases}$$

The value $\widetilde{f}(\boldsymbol{r})$ for any $\boldsymbol{r}\in\mathbb{F}^\mu$ can be computed in $O(2^\mu)$ operations over $\mathbb{F}$.

2.3 The Logarithmic Derivative

The logarithmic derivative of a polynomial $p(X)$ over a field $\mathbb{F}$ is defined as the rational function $p'(X)/p(X)$. Crucially, applying the logarithmic derivative to a product of linear factors transforms it into a sum of simple fractions. This algebraic property allows us to elegantly reduce multiset equality checks to rational function identities.

Lemma 2 (Multiset Check). *The condition for two multisets $\{a_i\}_1^n$, $\{b_i\}_1^n$ $(a_i, b_i \in \mathbb{F}_p)$ to be equal is that $\prod_{i=1}^n (X+a_i) = \prod_{i=1}^n (X+b_i)$ holds in $\mathbb{F}(X)$, which is equivalent to:*

$$\sum_{i=1}^{n}\frac{1}{X+a_i} = \sum_{i=1}^{n}\frac{1}{X+b_i}.$$

The proof is given in [18].

This lemma is often used to construct lookup arguments [12]. The goal is for the prover to convince the verifier that, given committed polynomials $f(x)$ and $t(x)$, the set $f(\mathbb{D}) := \{f(u) : u\in\mathbb{D}\}$ is a subset of $t(\mathbb{H}) := \{t(h) : h\in\mathbb{H}\}$, where $\mathbb{D}$ and $\mathbb{H}$ are domains in $\mathbb{F}$. Here, $f(\mathbb{D})$ is the lookup vector, and $t(\mathbb{H})$ is the table, with $m := |\mathbb{D}|$ and $N := |\mathbb{H}|$. To prove $f(\mathbb{D})\subseteq t(\mathbb{H})$, the prover relies on the identity:

$$\sum_{u\in\mathbb{D}}\frac{1}{x+f(u)} = \sum_{h\in\mathbb{H}}\frac{m_h}{x+t(h)},$$

where m_h represents the multiplicity of $t(h)$ in $f(\mathbb{D})$, i.e., the number of times $t(h)$ appears in $f(u)$.

2.4 Argument of Knowledge

An argument of knowledge Π is a protocol involving two parties, a prover $\mathcal{P}$ and a verifier $\mathcal{V}$. In general, it consists of three algorithms, namely Setup, Prove and Verify, and allows the prover to convince the verifier that given a string x it knows a witness w such that (x, w) is in an NP relation.

Definition 3. *An argument of knowledge for an indexed family of NP relations* $\{\mathcal{R}_{ind}\}_{ind \in \mathcal{I}}$ *is a triple of algorithms* $\Pi = (\mathrm{Setup}, \mathcal{P}, \mathcal{V})$ *with the following syntax:*

- $(\mathrm{pp}, \mathrm{vp}) \leftarrow \mathrm{Setup}\left(ind, 1^\lambda\right)$*: in the offline phase,* Setup *is given the index* ind *and* 1^λ *outputs public parameters* pp*, and verifier public parameters* vp.
- $b \leftarrow \langle \mathcal{P}(\mathrm{pp}, x, w), \mathcal{V}(\mathrm{vp}, x)\rangle$*: in the online phase,* $\mathcal{P}$ *receives input* pp *and a pair of* $(x, w) \in \mathcal{R}_{ind}$*, and* $\mathcal{V}$ *receives input* vp *and* x*. The parties interact with each other. Finally,* $\mathcal{V}$ *outputs 0 or 1.*

The algorithms should satisfy the following security requirements.

- *Completeness. For any* $ind \in \mathcal{I}$ *and* $(x, w) \in \mathcal{R}_{ind}$*,*

$$\Pr\left[b = 1 \,\middle|\, \begin{array}{c} (\mathrm{pp}, \mathrm{vp}) \leftarrow \mathrm{Setup}\left(ind, 1^\lambda\right) \\ b \leftarrow \langle \mathcal{P}(\mathrm{pp}, x, w), \mathcal{V}(\mathrm{vp}, x)\rangle \end{array}\right] = 1.$$

- *Knowledge soundness. For any PPT algorithm* $\mathcal{P}^*$*, there exists a PPT extractor* E *such that for any* $ind \in \mathcal{I}$ *and auxiliary inputs* $z \in \{0,1\}^*$*,*

$$\Pr\left[b = 1 \wedge (x, w) \notin \mathcal{R}_{ind} \,\middle|\, \begin{array}{c} (\mathrm{pp}, \mathrm{vp}) \leftarrow \mathrm{Setup}\left(ind, 1^\lambda\right) \\ (x, \mathrm{st}) \leftarrow \mathcal{P}^*(\mathrm{pp}, z, \perp) \\ b \leftarrow \langle \mathcal{P}^*(\mathrm{pp}, z, \mathrm{st}; r), \mathcal{V}(\mathrm{vp}, x)\rangle \\ w \leftarrow \mathrm{E}(\mathrm{pp}, z; r) \end{array}\right] = negl\ .$$

SNARK. SNARKs can be constructed from information-theoretic proof systems that provide the verifier with oracle access to prover messages, such as Polynomial Interactive Oracle Proof (PIOP). The information-theoretic proof is then compiled using cryptographic tools, such as a polynomial commitment scheme.

2.5 Multilinear Polynomial Commitment

Definition 4 (Commitment scheme). *A commitment scheme* Γ *is a tuple* $\Gamma = (\mathrm{Setup}, \mathrm{Commit}, \mathrm{Open})$ *of PPT algorithms where:*

- $\mathrm{gp} \leftarrow \mathrm{Setup}(1^\lambda)$ *generates public parameters* gp*;*
- $(C, r) \leftarrow \mathrm{Commit}(\mathrm{gp}, x)$ *takes a secret message* x *and outputs a public commitment* C *and (optionally) a secret opening hint* r *(which might or might not be the randomness used in the computation);*

- $b \in \{0,1\} \leftarrow \text{Open}(\text{gp}, C, x, r)$ *verifies the opening of commitment* C *to the message* x *provided with the opening hint* r.

Definition 5 (Multilinear Polynomial Commitment). *A polynomial commitment scheme is a tuple of protocols* $\Gamma = (\text{Setup}, \text{Commit}, \text{Open}, \text{Eval})$ *where* (Setup, Commit, Open) *is a binding commitment scheme for a message space* $R[X]$ *of polynomials over some ring* R, *and*

- $b \in \{0,1\} \leftarrow \text{Eval}((\text{vp}, \text{pp}), C, \mathbf{z}, y, d, \mu; f)$ *is an interactive public-coin protocol between a PPT prover* $\mathcal{P}$ *and verifier* $\mathcal{V}$. *Both* $\mathcal{P}$ *and* $\mathcal{V}$ *have as input a commitment* C, *points* $\mathbf{z} \in \mathbb{F}^{\mu}$ *and* $y \in \mathbb{F}$. *The prover has prover parameters* pp, *and the verifier has verifier parameters* vp. *The prover additionally knows the opening of* C *to a secret multilinear polynomial* $f \in \mathcal{F}_{\mu}$. *The protocol convinces the verifier that* $f(\mathbf{z}) = y$.

A polynomial commitment scheme is correct if an honest committer can successfully convince the verifier of any evaluation. Specifically, if the prover is honest, then for all polynomials $f \in \mathcal{F}_{\mu}$ *and all points* $z \in \mathbb{F}^{\mu}$,

$$\Pr\left[b = 1 \,\middle|\, \begin{array}{l} \text{gp} \leftarrow \text{Setup}\left(1^{\lambda}, \mu\right) \\ (C, r) \leftarrow \text{Commit}(\text{gp}, f) \\ y \leftarrow f(\mathbf{z}) \\ b \leftarrow \text{Eval}(\text{gp}, c, z, y, d, \mu; f, r) \end{array} \right] = 1.$$

2.6 PIOP Compilation

PIOP compilation transforms the interactive oracle proof into an interactive argument of knowledge (without oracles) Π. The compilation replaces the oracles with polynomial commitments. Every query by the verifier is replaced with an invocation of the Eval protocol at the query point $\boldsymbol{z}$. The compiled verifier accepts if the PIOP verifier accepts and if the output of all Eval invocations is 1. If Π is public-coin, then it can further be compiled to a non-interactive argument of knowledge (or NARK) using the Fiat-Shamir transform.

Theorem 1 (PIOP Compilation). *If the polynomial commitment scheme* Γ *has witness-extended emulation, and if the* t*-round Polynomial IOP for* $\mathcal{R}$ *has negligible knowledge error, then* Π, *the output of the PIOP compilation, is a secure (non-oracle) argument of knowledge for* $\mathcal{R}$. *The compilation also preserves zero knowledge. If* Γ *is hiding and Eval is honest-verifier zero-knowledge, then* Π *is honest-verifier zero-knowledge. The efficiency of the resulting argument of knowledge* Π *depends on the efficiency of both the PIOP and* Γ:

- *Prover time The prover time is equal to the sum of (i) prover time of the PIOP, (ii) the oracle length times the commitment time, and (iii) the query complexity times the prover time of* Γ.
- *Verifier time The verifier time is equal to the sum of (i) the verifier time of the PIOP and (ii) the verifier time for* Γ *times the query complexity of the PIOP.*

- *Proof size The proof size is equal to the sum of (i) the message complexity of the PIOP times the commitment size and (ii) the query complexity times the proof size of Γ. If the proof size is $O\left(\log^c(|\boldsymbol{w}|)\right)$, then we say the proof is succinct.*

2.7 Sum-Check

[19] introduced the sum-check protocol, which allows a verifier $\mathcal{V}$ to delegate the computation of $v = \sum_{\boldsymbol{b}\in\{0,1\}^\mu} f(\boldsymbol{b})$ to an unbounded prover $\mathcal{P}$, who then establishes the correctness of the sum.

Definition 6 (Sum-check relation). *The relation $\mathcal{R}_{SUM}$ is the set of tuples $(x;\omega) = ((v,[[f]]);f)$, where f has u independent variables and a degree of d, and $\sum_{\boldsymbol{b}\in\{0,1\}^\mu} f(\boldsymbol{b}) = v$.*

Construction. Given a tuple $(v,[[f]];f)$, the sum-check is defined as follows.

- For $i = \mu, \mu-1, \ldots, 1$:
  - The prover computes $r_i(x_i) := \sum_{\boldsymbol{b}\in\{0,1\}^{i-1}} f\left(\boldsymbol{b}, x_i, \alpha_i, \ldots, \alpha_\mu\right)$ and sends r_i to the verifier. r_i is a univariate polynomial of degree at most d.
  - The verifier checks that $v = r_i(0) + r_i(1)$, samples $\alpha_i \leftarrow \mathbb{F}$, sends α_i to the prover, and sets $v \leftarrow r_i\left(\alpha_i\right)$.
- Finally, the verifier accepts if $f\left(\alpha_1, \ldots, \alpha_\mu\right) = v$.

Theorem 2 (Sum-check PIOP [9]). *The PIOP for $\mathcal{R}_{SUM}$ is perfectly complete and has knowledge error $\delta_{sum}^{d,\mu} := d\mu/|\mathbb{F}|$.*

We refer to [28] for the proof of the theorem.

Batching. Multiple sum-check instances, such as $(s,[[f]])$ and $(s',[[g]])$, can be efficiently batched together. This is achieved through a random-linear combination, demonstrating that $(s+\alpha s', [[f]]+\alpha[[g]]) \in \mathcal{L}\left(\mathcal{R}_{\mathrm{SUM}}\right)$, where α is a random challenge sent by verifier. The batching step has soundness $1/|\mathbb{F}|$.

Complexity. The verifier and communication costs amount to $O(d\mu)$. The prover time is $O(2^\mu \cdot d\log^2 d)$, primarily due to the application of fast polynomial multiplication techniques, as elaborated in [9].

2.8 GKR Protocol

We refer to Libra [29] for background of the GKR protocol [15]. Before describing the GKR protocol, we introduce some additional notations.

Let $C : \mathbb{F}^n \rightarrow \mathbb{F}^k$ be a layered arithmetic circuit with depth d. Without loss of generality, we assume n and k are powers of 2, padding the layers with dummy gates if necessary. Let S_i denote the number of gates in the i-th layer, and let $s_i = \lceil\log_2 S_i\rceil$. For simplicity, we assume S_i is a power of 2. We define a function $V_i : \{0,1\}^{s_i} \rightarrow \mathbb{F}$ that maps a binary string $\boldsymbol{b} \in \{0,1\}^{s_i}$ to the output of gate $\boldsymbol{b}$ in layer i, where $\boldsymbol{b}$ is the gate label. Specifically, V_0 represents the circuit's output, while V_d corresponds to the input layer.

We define two Boolean functions $add_i, mult_i : \{0,1\}^{s_{i-1}+2s_i} \to \{0,1\}$, known as wiring predicates. These functions take a gate label $\boldsymbol{z} \in \{0,1\}^{s_{i-1}}$ from layer $i-1$ and two gate labels $\boldsymbol{x}, \boldsymbol{y} \in \{0,1\}^{s_i}$ from layer i, and output 1 if and only if gate $\boldsymbol{z}$ is an addition (for add_i) or multiplication (for $mult_i$) gate with inputs from gates $\boldsymbol{x}$ and $\boldsymbol{y}$. Using these predicates, the value $V_i(\boldsymbol{z})$ can be expressed recursively as:

$$V_i(\boldsymbol{z}) = \sum_{\boldsymbol{x},\boldsymbol{y} \in \{0,1\}^{s_{i+1}}} add_{i+1}(\boldsymbol{z},\boldsymbol{x},\boldsymbol{y})\big(V_{i+1}(\boldsymbol{x}) + V_{i+1}(\boldsymbol{y})\big) + mult_{i+1}(\boldsymbol{z},\boldsymbol{x},\boldsymbol{y})\big(V_{i+1}(\boldsymbol{x})V_{i+1}(\boldsymbol{y})\big).$$

To apply the sum-check protocol, we utilize multilinear extensions (MLE). Let $\widetilde{V}$, $\widetilde{add}$, and $\widetilde{mult}$ be the MLEs of their respective functions over $\mathbb{F}$. The recursive relation is rewritten as:

$$\widetilde{V}_i(\boldsymbol{z}) = \sum_{\boldsymbol{x},\boldsymbol{y} \in \{0,1\}^{s_{i+1}}} \widetilde{add}_{i+1}(\boldsymbol{z},\boldsymbol{x},\boldsymbol{y})\big(\widetilde{V}_{i+1}(\boldsymbol{x}) + \widetilde{V}_{i+1}(\boldsymbol{y})\big) + \widetilde{mult}_{i+1}(\boldsymbol{z},\boldsymbol{x},\boldsymbol{y})\big(\widetilde{V}_{i+1}(\boldsymbol{x})\widetilde{V}_{i+1}(\boldsymbol{y})\big).$$

By iteratively invoking the sum-check protocol for each layer $i = 1, \ldots, d$, the verifier reduces a claim regarding the circuit's output $\widetilde{V}_0$ to a single evaluation of the input $\widetilde{V}_d$ at a random point.

Theorem 3. *[29] Let $C : \mathbb{F}^n \to \mathbb{F}^k$ be a depth-d layered arithmetic circuit. GKR protocol is an interactive proof for the function computed by C, achieving soundness $O(d \log |C|/|\mathbb{F}|)$. It employs $O(d \log |C|)$ rounds of interaction, and the running time of the prover $\mathcal{P}$ is $O(|C|)$. Let the optimal computation time for all $\widetilde{add}_i$ and $\widetilde{mult}_i$ operations be T; then the running time of $\mathcal{V}$ is $O(n + k + d \log |C| + T)$. Specifically, for log-space uniform circuits, T is polylogarithmic in $|C|$, i.e., $T = \text{polylog}\,|C|$.*

2.9 Customizable Constraint System

Customizable Constraint System (CCS) [24] generalizes Rank-1 Constraint Systems (R1CS) [23] without additional overhead as follows.

Definition 7. *A Customizable Constraint System is defined as follows:*

- *Size bounds $m, n, \ell, t, q, d \in \mathbb{N}$ with $n > \ell$;*
- *A sequence of matrices $M_0, \ldots, M_{t-1} \in \mathbb{F}^{m \times m}$, with at most $n = \Omega(m)$ non-zero entries in total;*
- *A sequence of q multisets $\{S_0, \ldots, S_{q-1}\}$, where each multiset has elements from $\{0, \ldots, t-1\}$ and cardinality at most d;*
- *A sequence of q constants $\{c_0, \ldots, c_{q-1}\}$, where each constant is from $\mathbb{F}$.*

- *A CCS instance consists of a public input* $\boldsymbol{x} \in \mathbb{F}^{\ell}$.
- *A CCS witness consists of a vector* $\boldsymbol{w} \in \mathbb{F}^{n-\ell-1}$.
- *A CCS structure-instance tuple* $(S, \boldsymbol{x})$ *is satisfied by a CCS witness* $\boldsymbol{w}$ *if:* $\sum_{i=0}^{q-1} c_i \cdot (\bigcirc_{j \in S_i} M_j \cdot \boldsymbol{z}) = \mathbf{0}$, *where* $\boldsymbol{z} = (\boldsymbol{w}, 1, \boldsymbol{x}) \in \mathbb{F}^m$, $M_j \cdot \boldsymbol{z}$ *denotes matrix-vector multiplication,* $\bigcirc$ *denotes the Hadamard product between vectors,* $\mathbf{0}$ *is an* m*-dimensional vector with all entries equal to the additive identity in* $\mathbb{F}$.

3 An Efficient Sum-Check for High-Degree Polynomials

In this section, we consider the scenario where a prover demonstrates to a verifier that the sum of a multivariate polynomial $f(\boldsymbol{x})$ over all $\boldsymbol{x} \in \{0,1\}^{\mu}$ equals a specific value v, where $f(\boldsymbol{x})$ is represented as

$$f(\boldsymbol{x}) := h\big(g_1(\boldsymbol{x}), \ldots, g_c(\boldsymbol{x})\big).$$

Here $g_1(\boldsymbol{x})$ is a multilinear polynomial. The polynomial h, which has degree d, can be computed by a general arithmetic circuit of depth $O(\log d)$, commonly referred to as a low-depth circuit.

In previous approaches, the sum-check protocol (in Subsect. 2.7) is directly employed for the high-degree polynomial. Specifically, in each round, the prover computes a universal polynomial $r_i(x_i)$. As detailed in [27,29], the computation of $r_i(x_i)$ involves two main steps: first, evaluating the function h at d distinct points, followed by performing interpolation to derive the polynomial $r_i(x_i)$. This approach exhibited a time complexity of $O(2^{\mu} d^2)$. In [9], the authors introduced an optimized method that reduces the complexity to $O(2^{\mu} \cdot d \log^2 d)$ for low-depth circuits, such as $f(\boldsymbol{x}) := \prod_c g_c(\boldsymbol{x})$. This improvement is achieved by using fast polynomial multiplication.

We optimize the prover runtime to $O(2^{\mu} \cdot d)$. This is done by embedding the generalized GKR protocol [31] into the sum-check protocol for high-degree polynomials. Specifically, we define $\widetilde{f}(\boldsymbol{x})$ implicitly as the multilinear extension of f based on its evaluations over the Boolean hypercube:

$$\widetilde{f}(\boldsymbol{x}) = \sum_{\boldsymbol{b} \in \{0,1\}^{\mu}} f(\boldsymbol{b}) \cdot eq(\boldsymbol{x}, \boldsymbol{b}) = \sum_{\boldsymbol{b} \in \{0,1\}^{\mu}} h\big(g_1(\boldsymbol{b}), \ldots, g_c(\boldsymbol{b})\big) \cdot eq(\boldsymbol{x}, \boldsymbol{b}).$$

By the standard properties of multilinear extensions (Definition 2), the target sum is preserved:

$$v = \sum_{\boldsymbol{b} \in \{0,1\}^{\mu}} f(\boldsymbol{b}) = \sum_{\boldsymbol{b} \in \{0,1\}^{\mu}} \widetilde{f}(\boldsymbol{b}).$$

To compute this sum efficiently without explicitly expanding the high-degree composite polynomial f, our protocol proceeds in two phases:

1. **Phase 1: Sum-check for** v**.** The prover and verifier execute a standard sum-check protocol on the low-degree multilinear polynomial $\widetilde{f}$ to verify the claim $\sum_{\boldsymbol{b} \in \{0,1\}^{\mu}} \widetilde{f}(\boldsymbol{b}) = v$. This phase reduces the global sum over the hypercube to a single claimed evaluation $\widetilde{f}(\boldsymbol{\alpha})$, where $\boldsymbol{\alpha} \in \mathbb{F}^{\mu}$ is a random challenge chosen by the verifier $\mathcal{V}$.

2. **Phase 2: Generalized GKR for $\widetilde{f}(\boldsymbol{\alpha})$.** Instead of evaluating $\widetilde{f}(\boldsymbol{\alpha})$ directly—which would require expanding h—we validate it using the generalized GKR protocol. Conceptually, the 2^μ evaluations of $f(\boldsymbol{b})$ correspond precisely to the outputs of a data-parallel circuit C comprising 2^μ independent copies of the subcircuit h. Consequently, $\widetilde{f}$ is exactly the multilinear extension of this circuit's output layer. The verification is thus elegantly delegated to the GKR protocol, where the input layer of C is encoded as:

$$\widetilde{V}_{\text{in}}(\boldsymbol{z}_1, \boldsymbol{z}_2) = \sum_{i \in [c]} eq(\boldsymbol{z}_1, \langle i \rangle) \cdot g_i(\boldsymbol{z}_2).$$

Here, $\boldsymbol{z}_1 \in \{0,1\}^{\lceil \log c \rceil}$ indexes the specific input polynomial g_i, and $\boldsymbol{z}_2 \in \{0,1\}^\mu$ specifies the evaluation point over the Boolean hypercube. Querying the oracles $[[g_i]]$ at this input layer inherently enforces the correct polynomial composition.

Next, we detail the implementation of the second-phase validation. For instance, consider $f(\boldsymbol{x}) := h\big(g_1(\boldsymbol{x}), \ldots, g_c(\boldsymbol{x})\big) = \prod_{k=1}^{4} g_k(\boldsymbol{x})$. The computation of $f(\boldsymbol{x})$ is compiled into a two-layer subcircuit structured as follows:

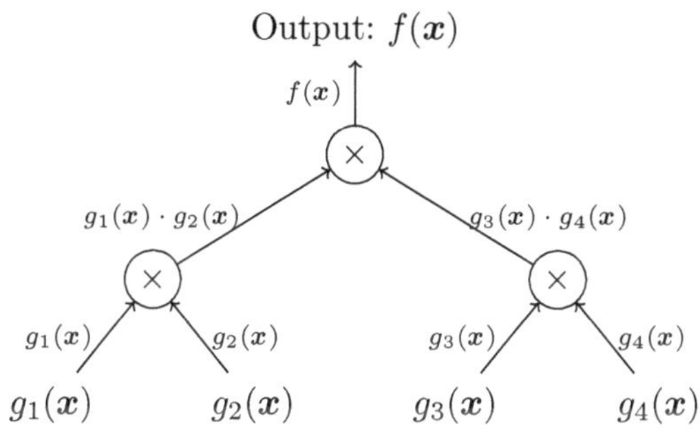

The circuit C comprises 2^μ identical subcircuits h arranged in parallel, with its input structured as 2^μ distinct tuples. Each tuple corresponds to the evaluations of polynomials g_1, g_2, g_3, g_4 at a specific point $\boldsymbol{x} \in \{0,1\}^\mu$, denoted as $(g_1(\boldsymbol{x}), g_2(\boldsymbol{x}), g_3(\boldsymbol{x}), g_4(\boldsymbol{x}))$. To formally capture the input structure, we define the multilinear extension of the input layer as

$$\widetilde{V}_2(z_1, z_2) := \sum_{i \in [c]} eq(z_1, \langle i \rangle) \cdot g_i(z_2),$$

where $\boldsymbol{z}_1 \in \{0,1\}^{\lceil \log c \rceil}$ and $\boldsymbol{z}_2 \in \{0,1\}^\mu$. One can verify that $\widetilde{V}_2(\langle i \rangle, \boldsymbol{x}) = g_i(\boldsymbol{x})$ holds as intended. According to the GKR protocol in Subsect. 2.8, the value of each gate at layer i can be expressed as a function of the values at layer $i+1$ through the following relation:

$$\begin{aligned}\widetilde{V}_i(\boldsymbol{z}) = & \sum_{\boldsymbol{x},\boldsymbol{y} \in \{0,1\}^{s_{i+1}}} \widetilde{\text{add}}_{i+1}(\boldsymbol{z}, \boldsymbol{x}, \boldsymbol{y}) \left(\widetilde{V}_{i+1}(\boldsymbol{x}) + \widetilde{V}_{i+1}(\boldsymbol{y})\right) \\ & + \widetilde{\text{mult}}_{i+1}(\boldsymbol{z}, \boldsymbol{x}, \boldsymbol{y}) \left(\widetilde{V}_{i+1}(\boldsymbol{x})\widetilde{V}_{i+1}(\boldsymbol{y})\right).\end{aligned}$$

This requires the verifier to evaluate both $\widetilde{\text{add}}_{i+1}$ and $\widetilde{\text{mult}}_{i+1}$ in the GKR protocol. To perform this computation efficiently, we next leverage the data-parallel structure of circuit C to represent $\widetilde{V}_i(\boldsymbol{z})$.

Let $\boldsymbol{z} = (\boldsymbol{z}_1, \boldsymbol{z}_2) \in \{0,1\}^{\mu} \times \{0,1\}^{k_i}$ be the label of a gate at layer i, where $\boldsymbol{z}_1$ indicates which sub-circuit of C the gate belongs to, and $\boldsymbol{z}_2$ specifies the label of the gate within that sub-circuit. Similarly, let $\boldsymbol{x} = (\boldsymbol{x}_1, \boldsymbol{x}_2) \in \{0,1\}^{\mu} \times \{0,1\}^{k_{i+1}}$ and $\boldsymbol{y} = (\boldsymbol{y}_1, \boldsymbol{y}_2) \in \{0,1\}^{\mu} \times \{0,1\}^{k_{i+1}}$ be the labels of two gates at layer $i+1$. For any $\boldsymbol{z} \in \{0,1\}^{\mu+k_i}$, the function V_i satisfies $V_i(\boldsymbol{z}_1, \boldsymbol{z}_2) = W_i(\boldsymbol{z}_1, \boldsymbol{z}_2)$, with W_i defined by:

$$
\begin{aligned}
W_i(\boldsymbol{z}_1, \boldsymbol{z}_2) = \sum_{\boldsymbol{x}_2, \boldsymbol{y}_2 \in \{0,1\}^{k_{i+1}}} & \widetilde{\text{add}}_{i+1}(\boldsymbol{z}_2, \boldsymbol{x}_2, \boldsymbol{y}_2) \left(\widetilde{V}_{i+1}(\boldsymbol{z}_1, \boldsymbol{x}_2) + \widetilde{V}_{i+1}(\boldsymbol{z}_1, \boldsymbol{y}_2) \right) \\
& + \widetilde{\text{mult}}_{i+1}(\boldsymbol{z}_2, \boldsymbol{x}_2, \boldsymbol{y}_2) \left(\widetilde{V}_{i+1}(\boldsymbol{z}_1, \boldsymbol{x}_2) \widetilde{V}_{i+1}(\boldsymbol{z}_1, \boldsymbol{y}_2) \right).
\end{aligned}
$$

This states that an addition (respectively, multiplication) gate $\boldsymbol{z} \in \{0,1\}^{\mu+k_i}$ of C is connected to gates $\boldsymbol{x}, \boldsymbol{y} \in \{0,1\}^{\mu+k_{i+1}}$ of C if and only if $\boldsymbol{z}, \boldsymbol{x}, \boldsymbol{y}$ all belong to the same sub-circuit of C (i.e., $\boldsymbol{z}_1 = \boldsymbol{x}_1 = \boldsymbol{y}_1$), and within that sub-circuit, gate $\boldsymbol{z}$ is connected to gates $\boldsymbol{x}$ and $\boldsymbol{y}$.

Finally, the polynomial $W_i(\boldsymbol{z}_1, \boldsymbol{z}_2)$ is of degree 2 in $\boldsymbol{z}_1$ and degree 1 in $\boldsymbol{z}_2$. Consequently, the (unique) multilinear extension $\widetilde{V}_i$ of V_i is:

$$
\widetilde{V}_i(\boldsymbol{z}_1, \boldsymbol{z}_2) = \sum_{\boldsymbol{e} \in \{0,1\}^{\mu}} eq(\boldsymbol{z}_1, \boldsymbol{e}) \cdot W_i(\boldsymbol{e}, \boldsymbol{z}_2).
$$

For a general circuit h, we refer to the generalized GKR protocol [31] with linear prover time. In this framework, gates at layer i may receive inputs from gates across multiple subsequent layers, specifically from layer $i+1$ through layer d. To accommodate this extended layered dependency, a key assumption is introduced: each gate at layer i must take at least one input directly from the immediately subsequent layer $i+1$, which is designated as its left operand. Under this assumption, the multilinear extension $\widetilde{V}_i$ of the circuit values at layer i can be reformulated in terms of values from deeper layers as follows:

$$
\begin{aligned}
\widetilde{V}_i(\boldsymbol{z}) = \sum_{j=i+1}^{d} \sum_{\substack{\boldsymbol{y}_j \in \{0,1\}^{s_j} \\ \boldsymbol{x}_{i+1} \in \{0,1\}^{s_{i+1}}}} & \widetilde{\text{add}}_{i+1,j}(\boldsymbol{z}, \boldsymbol{x}_{i+1}, \boldsymbol{y}_j)(\widetilde{V}_{i+1}(\boldsymbol{x}_{i+1}) + \widetilde{V}_j(\boldsymbol{y}_j)) \\
& + \widetilde{\text{mult}}_{i+1,j}(\boldsymbol{z}, \boldsymbol{x}_{i+1}, \boldsymbol{y}_j)(\widetilde{V}_{i+1}(\boldsymbol{x}_{i+1}) \widetilde{V}_j(\boldsymbol{y}_j)),
\end{aligned}
$$

where $\widetilde{\text{add}}_{i+1,j}(\boldsymbol{z}_i, \boldsymbol{x}_{i+1}, \boldsymbol{y}_j) = 1$ ($\widetilde{\text{mult}}_{i+1,j}(\boldsymbol{z}_i, \boldsymbol{x}_{i+1}, \boldsymbol{y}_j) = 1$) if and only if gate $\boldsymbol{z}_i$ in layer $i+1$ is the addition (multiplication) of values $\widetilde{V}_{i+1}(\boldsymbol{x}_{i+1})$ and $\widetilde{V}_j(\boldsymbol{y}_j)$.

Building on the data-parallel structure of circuit C, we now express $\widetilde{V}_i(\boldsymbol{z})$ in a similar manner. For $\boldsymbol{z} \in \{0,1\}^{\mu+k_i}$, we have $V_i(\boldsymbol{z}_1, \boldsymbol{z}_2) = W_i(\boldsymbol{z}_1, \boldsymbol{z}_2)$:

$$W_i(\boldsymbol{z}_1, \boldsymbol{z}_2) = \sum_{j=i+1}^{d} \sum_{\substack{\boldsymbol{y}_j \in \{0,1\}^{k_j} \\ \boldsymbol{x}_{i+1} \in \{0,1\}^{k_{i+1}}}} \widetilde{\text{add}}_{i+1,j}(\boldsymbol{z}_2, \boldsymbol{x}_{i+1}, \boldsymbol{y}_j)\big(\widetilde{V}_{i+1}(\boldsymbol{z}_1, \boldsymbol{x}_{i+1}) + \widetilde{V}_j(\boldsymbol{z}_1, \boldsymbol{y}_j)\big)$$
$$+ \widetilde{\text{mult}}_{i+1,j}(\boldsymbol{z}_2, \boldsymbol{x}_{i+1}, \boldsymbol{y}_j)\big(\widetilde{V}_{i+1}(\boldsymbol{z}_1, \boldsymbol{x}_{i+1})\widetilde{V}_j(\boldsymbol{z}_1, \boldsymbol{y}_j)\big),$$

From this, we conclude that the multilinear extension $\widetilde{V}_i$ of V_i is given by:

$$\widetilde{V}_i(\boldsymbol{z}_1, \boldsymbol{z}_2) = \sum_{\boldsymbol{e} \in \{0,1\}^{\mu}} eq(\boldsymbol{z}_1, \boldsymbol{e}) \cdot W_i(\boldsymbol{e}, \boldsymbol{z}_2).$$

Prover Cost. The key to achieving an $O(|h| \cdot 2^{\mu})$ runtime for an honest prover builds upon the GKR protocol with linear prover time.

Verifier Cost. To bound the verifier time, it is necessary to evaluate $\widetilde{\text{add}}$ and $\widetilde{\text{mult}}$ at random points. When a linear prover time generalized GKR protocol is applied to the subcircuit h, the prover can perform these evaluations in $O(|h|)$ time. Consequently, the verifier can also evaluate $\widetilde{\text{add}}$ and $\widetilde{\text{mult}}$ in $O(|h|)$ time, which remains independent of the number of subcircuit copies 2^{μ}.

Additionally, the verifier must evaluate the eq function at a random point in each layer i. Since this can be done using $O(\mu)$ field operations for any input, it does not affect the overall asymptotic time complexity.

Definition 8 (Doubly efficient sum-check (DESC) relation). *The relation $\mathcal{R}_{DESC}$ is defined as the set of tuples $(i; x; \omega) = \left(h; \left(v, \left[\left[\widetilde{V}_{in}\right]\right]\right); \widetilde{V}_{in}\right)$, where the input multilinear polynomial oracle $\widetilde{V}_{in}$ is given by*

$$\left[\left[\widetilde{V}_{in}(\boldsymbol{z})\right]\right] = \sum_{i \in [c]} eq(\langle i \rangle, \boldsymbol{z}_1) \cdot [[g_i(\boldsymbol{z}_2)]] .$$

Here, $\boldsymbol{z} = (\boldsymbol{z}_1, \boldsymbol{z}_2)$, $\boldsymbol{z}_1 \in \mathbb{F}^{|\log c|}$, and $\boldsymbol{z}_2 \in \mathbb{F}^{\mu}$. Each g_i is a multilinear polynomial. The function h is computable by a general arithmetic circuit of depth $O(\log d)$, and it satisfies $\sum_{\boldsymbol{x} \in \{0,1\}^{\mu}} h(g_1(\boldsymbol{x}), \ldots, g_c(\boldsymbol{x})) = v$.

Construction. Given a tuple $\left(h; (v, \{[[g_i]]\}_{i \in [c]}); \{g_i\}_{i \in [c]}\right)$ and a μ-variate polynomial f such that $f(\boldsymbol{x}) = h(g_1(\boldsymbol{x}), \ldots, g_c(\boldsymbol{x}))$, the DESC protocol is described as follows:

- Run a sum-check to convince $\mathcal{V}$ that $\left(\left(v, [[\widetilde{f}]]\right); \widetilde{f}\right) \in \mathcal{R}_{\text{SUM}}$, where in each round, the prover sends a univariate polynomial r_i of degree ≤ 1.
- The verifier $\mathcal{V}$ receives $\widetilde{f}(\alpha_1, \ldots, \alpha_{\mu}) = v$ and runs a generalized GKR for:

$$\left(C; \left(v, \left[\left[\widetilde{V}_{in}\right]\right]\right); \left(\widetilde{V}_{in}\right)\right) \in \mathcal{R}_{\text{GKR}}.$$

- Finally, $\mathcal{V}$ queries oracles $\{[[g_i]]\}_{i\in[c]}$ to verify the claim of the input $\widetilde{V}_{in}$.

Theorem 4 (DESC PIOP). *The PIOP for* $\mathcal{R}_{DESC}$ *is perfectly complete and has knowledge error* $\delta^{d,\mu}_{desc} := O\big(\log d \cdot (\mu + \log|h|)/|\mathbb{F}|\big)$.

Proof. **Completeness Error:** The completeness is straightforward by the completeness of the sum-check and the generalized GKR.

Knowledge Soundness: The first sum-check protocol exhibits knowledge error of $O(\mu/|\mathbb{F}|)$. Regarding the evaluation verification phase, Theorem 2 of [31] states that the generalized GKR protocol has a soundness error of $O(D \cdot \log S/|\mathbb{F}|)$, where D is the circuit depth and S is the circuit width. In our construction, the verification is performed over a data-parallel circuit consisting of 2^μ copies of the sub-circuit h, which has a depth of $D = O(\log d)$ and a width of $S = |h| \cdot 2^\mu$. Substituting these parameters, the error for this phase is $O(\log d \cdot (\mu + \log|h|)/|\mathbb{F}|)$. Consequently, the overall soundness error is dominated by the second phase and bounded by $O\left(\log d \cdot (\mu + \log|h|)/|\mathbb{F}|\right)$.

Complexity. Finally, building upon the efficiency results of the generalized GKR protocol, we summarize the complexity analysis. Let $C : \mathbb{F}^n \to \mathbb{F}^k$ be a general arithmetic circuit of depth D. The generalized GKR protocol (Protocol 3) achieves a prover time of $O(|C|)$, a proof size of $O(D\log|C| + D^2)$, and a verifier time of $O(D\log|C| + D^2 + T)$, where T represent the costs to evaluate the multilinear extensions of the wiring predicates at random points.

For the DESC PIOP, the verification circuit is structured as 2^μ parallel copies of a subcircuit h with depth $O(\log d)$. By substituting the circuit size $|C| = 2^\mu|h|$ and depth $D = O(\log d)$ into the general bounds, and leveraging the structural uniformity for efficient verifier evaluations, we obtain the following complexity:

- The prover time is $\mathrm{tp}^h_{\mathrm{desc}} = O\left(|h| \cdot 2^\mu\right)$.
- The verifier time is $\mathrm{tv}^h_{\mathrm{desc}} = O\big(|h| + \log^2 d + \log d \cdot (\mu + \log|h|)\big)$.
- The total proof size is $\mathrm{ps}^h_{\mathrm{desc}} = O\big(\log^2 d + \log d \cdot (\mu + \log|h|)\big)$.
- The query complexity is $\mathrm{q}^h_{\mathrm{desc}} = c$, with proof oracles $\{g_i\}_{i\in[c]}$.

4 CCS with Linear Prover Time

This section presents a PIOP for CCS (detailed in Subsect. 2.9) that achieves linear prover time. A CCS structure-instance pair $(S, \boldsymbol{x})$ is said to be satisfiable if there exists a witness vector $\boldsymbol{w}$ such that the following condition holds:

$$\sum_{i=0}^{q-1} c_i \cdot (\bigcirc_{j\in S_i} M_j \cdot \boldsymbol{z}) = \mathbf{0}.$$

Here, q is the number of multisets S_i, each satisfying $S_i \subset [t]$ and $|S_i| \le d$; each c_i is a constant in $\mathbb{F}$; $\boldsymbol{z} = (\boldsymbol{w}, 1, \boldsymbol{x})$ is a witness-instance pair; and

$M_0, \ldots, M_{t-1} \in \mathbb{F}^{m \times m}$ are matrices with at most $n = \Omega(m)$ non-zero entries in total. The protocol is initiated by running a sum-check protocol to check:

$$\sum_{\boldsymbol{x} \in \{0,1\}^{\log m}} eq(\boldsymbol{\alpha}, \boldsymbol{x}) f(\boldsymbol{x}) = 0, \tag{1}$$

where $\boldsymbol{\alpha}$ is a given random challenge vector, and the function $f(\boldsymbol{x})$ is defined as:

$$f(\boldsymbol{x}) := h\big(g_1(\boldsymbol{x}), \ldots, g_t(\boldsymbol{x})\big) = \sum_{i=0}^{q-1} c_i \cdot \prod_{j \in S_i} g_j(\boldsymbol{x}),$$

$$g_j(\boldsymbol{x}) := \sum_{\boldsymbol{y} \in \{0,1\}^{\log m}} \widetilde{M}_j(\boldsymbol{x}, \boldsymbol{y}) \cdot \widetilde{z}(\boldsymbol{y}).$$

Directly applying the sum-check protocol to Eq. (1) results in a prover time of $O(qmd \log^2 d)$. This complexity arises primarily from using FFTs to multiply d degree-1 polynomials. Although d is typically small (e.g., 2 or 5), it may take larger values in practice, potentially exceeding 100 in some instances.

To address the prover time in this setting, we design a PIOP for CCS that achieves a complexity of $O(qmd)$. Specifically, we reformulate the computation of h as a general subcircuit of size $O(qd)$. The circuit C is composed of m such subcircuits, and the multilinear extension of its input is defined as:

$$\widetilde{V}_{\text{in}}(\boldsymbol{x}_1, \boldsymbol{x}_2) = \sum_{j \in [t]} \widetilde{\mathsf{eq}}(\boldsymbol{x}_1, \langle j \rangle) \cdot \sum_{\boldsymbol{y} \in \{0,1\}^{\log m}} \widetilde{M}_j(\boldsymbol{x}_2, \boldsymbol{y}) \cdot \widetilde{z}(\boldsymbol{y}),$$

where $\langle j \rangle$ denotes the binary representation of j. By subsequently applying the sum-check PIOP in combination with a batched sum-check protocol, we achieve the prover complexity of $O(qmd)$.

Definition 9 (CCS Relation). *The relation $\mathcal{R}_{\mathsf{CCS}}$ is the set of all tuples*

$$\left(\left(q, \left\{c_i, S_i, \left[\left[\widetilde{M}_i\right]\right]\right\}_{i \in [t]}\right); (\boldsymbol{x}, [[\widetilde{\boldsymbol{w}}]]); \left(\widetilde{\boldsymbol{w}}, \left\{\widetilde{M}_i\right\}_{i \in [t]}\right)\right),$$

and satisfies the following condition. Let $\boldsymbol{z} = (\boldsymbol{w}, 1, \boldsymbol{x})$ with multilinear extension $\widetilde{\boldsymbol{z}}$, and define for each $j \in [t]$ the polynomial

$$g_j(\boldsymbol{x}) := \sum_{\boldsymbol{y} \in \{0,1\}^{\log m}} \widetilde{M}_j(\boldsymbol{x}, \boldsymbol{y}) \cdot \widetilde{z}(\boldsymbol{y}).$$

Then the constraint function

$$h(g_1(\boldsymbol{x}), \ldots, g_t(\boldsymbol{x})) = \sum_{i=0}^{q-1} c_i \cdot \prod_{j \in S_i} g_j(\boldsymbol{x}) = 0 \quad \textit{for all } \boldsymbol{x} \in \{0,1\}^{\log m}.$$

Construction. Given a tuple

$$\left(\left(q, \left\{c_i, S_i, \left[\left[\widetilde{M_i}\right]\right]\right\}_{i\in[t]}\right); (\boldsymbol{x}, [[\widetilde{\boldsymbol{w}}]]); \left(\widetilde{\boldsymbol{w}}, \left\{\widetilde{M_i}\right\}_{i\in[t]}\right)\right),$$

the CCS PIOP is described as follows:

- The verifier $\mathcal{V}$ selects a random challenge vector $\boldsymbol{\alpha}$ and sends it to prover $\mathcal{P}$.
- Let $\widetilde{f}(\boldsymbol{\alpha}) = \sum_{\boldsymbol{x}\in\{0,1\}^{\log m}} eq(\boldsymbol{\alpha}, \boldsymbol{x}) \cdot h(g_1(\boldsymbol{x}), \ldots, g_t(\boldsymbol{x})) = 0$.
- Run a generalized GKR for the relation:

$$\left(h; \left(0, \left[\left[\widetilde{V_{\text{in}}}\right]\right]\right); \left(\widetilde{V_{\text{in}}}\right)\right) \in \mathcal{R}_{\text{GKR}},$$

  where $\left[\left[\widetilde{V_{\text{in}}}(\boldsymbol{z})\right]\right] := \sum_{i\in[c]} \text{eq}(\langle i\rangle, \boldsymbol{z}_1) \cdot [[g_i(\boldsymbol{z}_2)]]$.
- $\mathcal{V}$ receives claims $v_i = \sum_{\boldsymbol{y}\in\{0,1\}^{\log m}} \widetilde{M_i}(\boldsymbol{\alpha}_2, \boldsymbol{y}) \cdot \widetilde{z}(\boldsymbol{y})$ for $i \in [t]$ and checks:

$$\widetilde{V_{\text{in}}}(\boldsymbol{\alpha}_1, \boldsymbol{\alpha}_2) = \sum_{i\in[c]} \text{eq}(\langle i\rangle, \boldsymbol{\alpha}_1) \cdot g_i(\boldsymbol{\alpha}_2).$$

  If yes, $\mathcal{V}$ sends challenges $\{e_i\}_{i\in[t]}$ and runs a sum-check on:

$$\sum_{\boldsymbol{y}\in\{0,1\}^{\log m}} \left(\sum_{i=1}^{t} e_i \cdot \widetilde{M_i}(\boldsymbol{\alpha}_2, \boldsymbol{y})\right) \cdot \widetilde{z}(\boldsymbol{y}) = \sum_{i=1}^{t} e_i \cdot v_i.$$

- Finally, verifier $\mathcal{V}$ queries oracles $\left\{\left[\left[\widetilde{M_i}\right]\right]\right\}_{i\in[t]}$ and $[[\widetilde{\boldsymbol{w}}]]$ to validate the correctness of the last message in the sum-check protocol.

Theorem 5 (CCS PIOP). *The PIOP for $\mathcal{R}_{CCS}$ is perfectly complete and has knowledge error* $\delta_{ccs}^{t,q,d,\mu} := O\left(t + \log d \cdot (\mu + \log(qd))\right)/|\mathbb{F}|$.

The proof builds upon the batched sum-check protocol and Theorem 4.

Complexity. With respect to the overhead of the DESC PIOP, we compare our protocol with the SuperSpartan PIOP for CCS [24], as detailed below (Table 1).

Table 1. As detailed in the table above, the comparison assumes a CCS instance parameterized by t sparse matrices, q multisets, and a maximum algebraic degree d, subject to the bound $t \leq qd$. The evaluated efficiency metrics are denoted as follows: tp_{ccs} represents the prover time, tv_{ccs} the verifier time, ps_{ccs} the total proof size, and q_{ccs} the verifier's oracle query complexity.

	tp_{ccs}	tv_{ccs}	ps_{ccs}	q_{ccs}
[24]	$O\left(n + qmd\log^2 d\right)$	$O(dq + d\log m)$	$O(d\log m)$	$t+1$
This work	$O\left(n + qmd\right)$	$O\left(dq + \log d \cdot \log(qdm)\right)$	$O\left(\log d \cdot \log(qdm)\right)$	$t+1$

5 Sparse Polynomial Commitments

This section introduces an efficient PIOP designed to construct sparse polynomial commitments (SPARK). The PIOP refines existing multilinear polynomial commitment schemes, originally developed for dense polynomials, into a framework capable of efficiently managing sparse multilinear polynomials.

5.1 SPARK PIOP

The SPARK was introduced by Setty et al. [23] for the sparse polynomial $\widetilde{M}(\mathbf{x}, \mathbf{y})$, where $\mathbf{x}, \mathbf{y} \in \{0,1\}^{\log m}$. In this framework, let n denote the number of non-zero coefficients in $\widetilde{M}$. Without loss of generality, assume m and n are powers of two. Building on the definition of the multilinear extension provided in Definition 2, the evaluation of $\widetilde{M}(\boldsymbol{\alpha}, \boldsymbol{\beta})$ can be expressed as:

$$\widetilde{M}(\boldsymbol{\alpha}, \boldsymbol{\beta}) = \sum_{\boldsymbol{x}, \boldsymbol{y} \in \{0,1\}^{\log m}} M(\boldsymbol{x}, \boldsymbol{y}) \cdot eq(\boldsymbol{x}, \boldsymbol{\alpha}) \cdot eq(\boldsymbol{y}, \boldsymbol{\beta}).$$

This formulation was later generalized by Setty et al. [25] to exploit the inherent tensor structure of the eq function. Specifically, they extended the original expression for $\widetilde{M}(\boldsymbol{\alpha}, \boldsymbol{\beta})$ as a sparse $2\log m$-variate multilinear polynomial to handle the evaluation of a sparse $c\log m$-variate multilinear polynomial $\widetilde{M}$ at random point $(\boldsymbol{\alpha}_1, \ldots, \boldsymbol{\alpha}_c)$. The generalized formulation is expressed as:

$$\begin{aligned}\widetilde{M}(\boldsymbol{\alpha}_1, \ldots, \boldsymbol{\alpha}_c) &= \sum_{\boldsymbol{x}_1, \ldots, \boldsymbol{x}_c \in \{0,1\}^{\log m}} M(\boldsymbol{x}_1, \ldots, \boldsymbol{x}_c) \cdot \prod_{i=1}^{c} eq(\boldsymbol{x}_i, \boldsymbol{\alpha}_i) \\ &= \sum_{\boldsymbol{k} \in \{0,1\}^{\log n}} val(\boldsymbol{k}) \cdot \prod_{i=1}^{c} E_i(\boldsymbol{k}),\end{aligned}$$

where for each $\boldsymbol{k} \in \{0,1\}^{\log n}$, the term $val(\boldsymbol{k})$ represents the $s_{id}(\boldsymbol{k})$-th nonzero entry of matrix M, and $E_i(\boldsymbol{k})$ is given by $E_i(\boldsymbol{k}) = eq(\phi_i(\boldsymbol{k}), \boldsymbol{\alpha}_i)$. Here, $\phi_i(\boldsymbol{k})$ corresponds to the i-th coordinate block $\boldsymbol{x}_i$ associated with this nonzero entry, and the index $s_{id}(\boldsymbol{k})$ is explicitly defined as the decimal representation of the binary coordinates: $s_{id}(\boldsymbol{k}) := \text{decimal}(\boldsymbol{k}) = \sum_{i=1}^{\log m} k_i \cdot 2^{i-1}$.

The "memory in the head" technique from [23] is used to verify the correctness of each E_i. In this chapter, we build upon the logarithmic derivative (in Subsect. 2.3) to achieve this. Our approach further enables efficient batch verification, yielding a polynomial commitment scheme with reduced overhead. The underlying idea of this methodology is detailed below.

First, we define the index $s_{\sigma,i}(\boldsymbol{k}) = s_{id}(\boldsymbol{x}_i)$ such that the condition $E_i(\boldsymbol{k}) = eq(\boldsymbol{x}_i, \boldsymbol{\alpha}_i)$ implies:

$$\big(E_i(\boldsymbol{k}), s_{\sigma,i}(\boldsymbol{k})\big) = \big(eq(\boldsymbol{x}_i, \boldsymbol{\alpha}_i), s_{id}(\boldsymbol{x}_i)\big) \tag{2}$$

A multiplicity counter polynomial $m_i(\boldsymbol{x}_i)$ is then defined to track the frequency of occurrences of $\big(eq(\boldsymbol{x}_i, \boldsymbol{\alpha}_i), s_{id}(\boldsymbol{x}_i)\big)$ across $\boldsymbol{k} \in \{0,1\}^{\log n}$, exactly recording how many times each specific coordinate block $\boldsymbol{x}_i$ appears among the non-zero entries. By Multiset Check Lemma 2, if Eq. (2) holds for all $\boldsymbol{k} \in \{0,1\}^{\log n}$, then for any randomly chosen challenges $e_{i,1}$ and $e_{i,2}$, we have:

$$\begin{aligned}\sum_{\boldsymbol{k}\in\{0,1\}^{\log n}} & \frac{1}{1+e_{i,1}\cdot E_i(\boldsymbol{k})+e_{i,2}\cdot s_{\sigma,i}(\boldsymbol{k})} \\ = \sum_{\boldsymbol{x}_i\in\{0,1\}^{\log m}} & \frac{m_i(\boldsymbol{x}_i)}{1+e_{i,1}\cdot eq(\boldsymbol{x}_i,\boldsymbol{\alpha}_i)+e_{i,2}\cdot s_{id}(\boldsymbol{x}_i)}.\end{aligned} \tag{3}$$

For each $i \in [c]$, we define the functions as follows:

$$\begin{aligned} f_{2i-1}(\boldsymbol{k}) &= 1+e_{i,1}\cdot E_i(\boldsymbol{k})+e_{i,2}\cdot s_{\sigma,i}(\boldsymbol{k}), \\ f_{2i}(\boldsymbol{k}_1,\boldsymbol{k}_2) &= 1+\left(e_{i,1}\cdot eq(\boldsymbol{k}_1,\boldsymbol{\alpha}_i)+e_{i,2}\cdot s_{\mathrm{id}}(\boldsymbol{k}_1)\right)\cdot t(\boldsymbol{k}_2), \\ m_i'(\boldsymbol{k}_1,\boldsymbol{k}_2) &= m_i(\boldsymbol{k}_1)\cdot t(\boldsymbol{k}_2), \quad t(\boldsymbol{k}_2) = \prod_{j\in[\log(n/m)]} k_{2,j}, \end{aligned}$$

where $\boldsymbol{k}_1 \in \{0,1\}^{\log m}$ and $\boldsymbol{k}_2 \in \{0,1\}^{\log(n/m)}$. To validate Eq. (3) for each $i \in [c]$, we reduce the problem to verifying that the following sum equals zero:

$$\sum_{\boldsymbol{k}\in\{0,1\}^{\log n}} \left(\frac{1}{f_{2i-1}(\boldsymbol{k})} - \frac{m_i'(\boldsymbol{k})}{f_{2i}(\boldsymbol{k})}\right) = 0.$$

And then, the verifier selects random challenges $\{e_{i,3} \in \mathbb{F}\}_{i\in[c]}$ and checks:

$$\sum_{\boldsymbol{k}\in\{0,1\}^{\log n}} \sum_{i=1}^{c} e_{i,3} \left(\frac{1}{f_{2i-1}(\boldsymbol{k})} - \frac{m_i'(\boldsymbol{k})}{f_{2i}(\boldsymbol{k})}\right) = 0. \tag{4}$$

By combining the rational function (4) over a common denominator, the problem reduces to verifying that a high-degree polynomial is zero everywhere on the Boolean hypercube. By integrating logarithmic-derivative arguments with DESC PIOP, our framework inherently optimizes this batching process. The DESC PIOP efficiently performs this verification as a data-parallel circuit with a linear-time prover. Crucially, this optimization allows the prover to merge multiple sparse matrix evaluations into a single sum-check instance, significantly reducing commitment overhead.

Definition 10 (SPARK relation). *The relation $\mathcal{R}_{SPARK}$ is defined as the set of tuples*

$$(i;x;\omega) = ((\delta,[[val]]);(\boldsymbol{\alpha}_1,\ldots,\boldsymbol{\alpha}_c,v);val),$$

where the parameter δ specifies the positions of non-zero entries in a sparse matrix M, and val represents $\log n$-variate degree-1 polynomials that determine the values of these non-zero entries, such that $M(\boldsymbol{\alpha}_1,\ldots,\boldsymbol{\alpha}_c) = v$.

Construction. The tuple $\big((\delta, [[val]]); (\boldsymbol{\alpha}_1, \ldots, \boldsymbol{\alpha}_c, v); val\big)$ defines a matrix structure where the parameter δ determines the placement of non-zero entries. This configuration generates $2c$ oracles: $[[s_{\sigma,i}]]$ and $[[m_i]]$ for $i \in [c]$. The index polynomials $s_{\sigma,i}(\boldsymbol{k})$ determine the positions of non-zero elements, while the counter polynomials $m_i(\boldsymbol{x})$ track the frequency of these non-zero element positions. The SPARK PIOP protocol is defined as follows:

- The prover $\mathcal{P}$ sends the oracles $\{[[E_i]]\}_{i \in [c]}$ to the verifier $\mathcal{V}$.
- $\mathcal{V}$ sends the challenges $e_{i,1}, e_{i,2}, e_{i,3}$ (for $i \in [c]$) to $\mathcal{P}$.
- $\mathcal{P}$ sends $[[\widetilde{h}]]$ to $\mathcal{V}$, where the multilinear extension $\widetilde{h}(\boldsymbol{k})$ is defined as:

$$\widetilde{h}(\boldsymbol{k}) = \sum_{i \in [c]} e_{i,3} \cdot \left(\frac{1}{f_{2i-1}(\boldsymbol{k})} - \frac{m_i'(\boldsymbol{k})}{f_{2i}(\boldsymbol{k})} \right) \quad \text{for } \boldsymbol{k} \in \{0,1\}^{\log n}, \tag{5}$$

  with the polynomials $f_i(\boldsymbol{k})$ and $m_i'(\boldsymbol{k})$ given by:

$$\begin{aligned} f_{2i-1}(\boldsymbol{k}) &= 1 + e_{i,1} \cdot E_i(\boldsymbol{k}) + e_{i,2} \cdot s_{\sigma,i}(\boldsymbol{k}), \\ f_{2i}(\boldsymbol{k}_1, \boldsymbol{k}_2) &= 1 + \big(e_{i,1} \cdot eq(\boldsymbol{k}_1, \boldsymbol{\alpha}_i) + e_{i,2} \cdot s_{\text{id}}(\boldsymbol{k}_1)\big) \cdot t(\boldsymbol{k}_2), \\ m_i'(\boldsymbol{k}_1, \boldsymbol{k}_2) &= m_i(\boldsymbol{k}_1) \cdot t(\boldsymbol{k}_2), \quad t(\boldsymbol{k}_2) = \prod_{i \in [\log(n/m)]} k_{2,i}. \end{aligned}$$

- $\mathcal{V}$ sends the challenges $e_4, e_5 \in \mathbb{F}$ and $\boldsymbol{\beta} \in \mathbb{F}^{\log n}$ to $\mathcal{P}$.
- Run a sum-check to check:

$$\sum_{\boldsymbol{k} \in \{0,1\}^{\log n}} val(\boldsymbol{k}) \cdot \widetilde{E}(\boldsymbol{k}) + e_4 \cdot \widetilde{h}(\boldsymbol{k}) + e_5 \cdot \text{eq}(\boldsymbol{\beta}, \boldsymbol{k}) \cdot \left(\widetilde{h}(\boldsymbol{k}) \cdot \widetilde{h}_1(\boldsymbol{k}) + \widetilde{h}_2(\boldsymbol{k})\right) = 0,$$

  where $\widetilde{E}$, $\widetilde{h}_1$, and $\widetilde{h}_2$ are the multilinear extensions of E, h_1, and h_2:

$$E(\boldsymbol{k}) := \prod_{i=1}^{c} E_i(\boldsymbol{k}), \quad h_1(\boldsymbol{k}) = \prod_{i=1}^{2c} f_i(\boldsymbol{k}), \quad h_2(\boldsymbol{k}) = \sum_{i=1}^{2c} m_i''(\boldsymbol{k}) \cdot \prod_{j \in [2c] \setminus \{i\}} f_j(\boldsymbol{k}),$$

  with

$$\text{for } i \in [2c], \; m_i''(\boldsymbol{k}) = \begin{cases} -e_{(i+1)/2,3} & \text{if } i \text{ is odd}, \\ e_{i/2,3} \cdot m_i'(\boldsymbol{k}) & \text{if } i \text{ is even}. \end{cases}$$

- The $\mathcal{V}$ receives $val(\boldsymbol{\gamma}), \widetilde{E}(\boldsymbol{\gamma}), \widetilde{h}(\boldsymbol{\gamma}), \widetilde{h}_1(\boldsymbol{\gamma}), \widetilde{h}_2(\boldsymbol{\gamma})$ to verify the consistency of the messages in the final round of the sum-check protocol, where $\boldsymbol{\gamma} \in \mathbb{F}^{\log n}$ is a randomly sampled challenge. The $\mathcal{V}$ then queries oracles $[[val]]$ and $[[\widetilde{h}]]$ to confirm the correctness of $val(\boldsymbol{\gamma})$ and $\widetilde{h}(\boldsymbol{\gamma})$.
- Run 3 GKR in parallel for:

$$\left(E; \left(\left[\left[\widetilde{V}_{E,\text{in}}\right]\right], \widetilde{E}(\boldsymbol{\gamma})\right); \widetilde{V}_{E,\text{in}}\right), \quad \left(h_1; \left(\left[\left[\widetilde{V}_{h_1,\text{in}}\right]\right], \widetilde{h}_1(\boldsymbol{\gamma})\right); \widetilde{V}_{h_1,\text{in}}\right),$$
$$\left(h_2; \left(\left[\left[\widetilde{V}_{h_2,\text{in}}\right]\right], \widetilde{h}_2(\boldsymbol{\gamma})\right); \widetilde{V}_{h_2,\text{in}}\right) \in \mathcal{R}_{\text{GKR}}.$$

As shown in Subsect. 5.2, the layered arithmetic subcircuits for h_1 and h_2 have size $O(c)$. We have also defined the input functions for the circuit composed of these subcircuits in parallel. The subcircuit E, which shares a similar structure to h_1, also has a size of $O(c)$.
- The $\mathcal{V}$ queries oracles $\{[[s_{\sigma,i}]], [[m_i]], [[E_i]]\}_{i\in[c]}$ to validate the correctness of the input layer's claim.

Theorem 6.
The PIOP for $\mathcal{R}_{SPARK}$ has completeness error $\delta_c = O(c \cdot \log n/|\mathbb{F}|)$ and has knowledge error $\delta^{c,n}_{spark} := O\left(c + \log^2 c + \log c \cdot \log n)/|\mathbb{F}|\right)$.

Proof. **Completeness Error:** The Eq. (5) exhibits a completeness error of $O(c \cdot \log n/|\mathbb{F}|)$, since the probability that $f_i = 0$ is at most $\log n/|\mathbb{F}|$ for each $i \in [2c]$. Notably, the PIOPs for sum-check exhibit perfect completeness. Consequently, the completeness error is upper bounded by $O(c \cdot \log n/|\mathbb{F}|)$.

Knowledge Error: The batch verification process, as demonstrated in Eq. (5), has a knowledge error of c. Specifically, the PIOP for $\mathcal{R}_{\mathrm{SUM}}$ has a knowledge error of $O(\log n/|\mathbb{F}|)$. Similarly, the PIOP for $\mathcal{R}_{\mathrm{GKR}}$ demonstrates a soundness error of $O(\log(c) \cdot \log(c \cdot n)/|\mathbb{F}|)$. Consequently, the overall soundness error is bounded by $O\left((c + \log^2 c + \log c \cdot \log n)/|\mathbb{F}|\right)$. □

Complexity. The layered arithmetic subcircuits for E, h_1, and h_2 are all of size $O(c)$. When we include the cost of the GKR protocol, the overall complexity of the SPARK PIOP for $\mathcal{R}_{\mathrm{SPARK}}$ is as follows:

- The prover time is $\mathrm{tp}_{\mathrm{spark}} = O(cn)$.
- The verifier time is $\mathrm{tv}_{\mathrm{spark}} = O(c + \log^2 c + \log c \cdot \log n)$.
- The total proof size is $\mathrm{r}_{\mathrm{spark}} = O(c + \log^2 c + \log c \cdot \log n)$.
- The query complexity and the number of proof oracles is $3c + 2$, with the oracles being $\{[[m_i]], [[s_{\sigma,i}]], [[E_i]]\}_{i\in[c]}$, $[[val]]$ and $[[\widetilde{h}]]$.

SPARK. SPARK PIOP is then instantiated using a polynomial commitment scheme to produce a sparse polynomial commitment, which requires commitments to $2c + 2$ dense multilinear polynomials over $\log n$ variables and c dense polynomials over $\log m$ variables.

Theorem 7. *Assuming the existence of a polynomial commitment scheme for $(\log m)$-variate multilinear polynomials characterized by the following parameters (with m being a positive integer and, without loss of generality, a power of 2):*

- *the size of the polynomial commitment is* $\mathsf{pc}(m)$*;*
- *the time of the commit algorithm is* $\mathsf{tc}(m)$*;*
- *the time of the prover to prove a polynomial evaluation is* $\mathsf{tp}(m)$*;*
- *the time of the verifier to verify a polynomial evaluation is* $\mathsf{tv}(m)$*;*
- *the proof size is* $\mathsf{p}(m)$*,*

there exists a polynomial commitment scheme for multilinear polynomials over $c \log m$ *variables that evaluate to a non-zero value at most* n *locations over the Boolean hypercube* $\{0,1\}^{c \log m}$*, with the following parameters:*

- *the size of the sparse polynomial commitment is* $(2c+2) \cdot \mathsf{pc}(n) + c \cdot \mathsf{pc}(m)$*;*
- *the time of the commit algorithm is* $O\left(c \cdot (\mathsf{tc}(n) + \mathsf{tc}(m))\right)$*;*
- *the prover time to prove a polynomial evaluation is* $O(c \cdot (\mathsf{tp}(n) + \mathsf{tp}(m)))$*;*
- *the verifier time to verify a polynomial evaluation is* $O(c \cdot (\mathsf{tv}(n) + \mathsf{tv}(m)))$*;*
- *the proof size is* $O(c \cdot (\mathsf{p}(n) + \mathsf{p}(m)))$*.*

5.2 Constructing Layered Circuits for h_1 and h_2

Without loss of generality, we assume c is a power of 2. If not, we extend the definitions of $f_{2i-1}(\boldsymbol{k})$, $f_{2i}(\boldsymbol{k})$, and $m'_i(\boldsymbol{k})$ for $i \in \{c+1, \ldots, 2^{\lceil \log c \rceil}\}$ as follows:

$$f_{2i-1}(\boldsymbol{k}) = f_{2i}(\boldsymbol{k}) = m'_i(\boldsymbol{k}) = 1 \quad \text{for all } \boldsymbol{k} \in \{0,1\}^{\log n}.$$

Finally, Eq. (4) can be transformed into the following equation:

$$\sum_{\boldsymbol{k} \in \{0,1\}^{\log n}} \sum_{i \in [2^{\lceil \log c \rceil}]} e_{i,3} \cdot \left(\frac{1}{f_{2i-1}(\boldsymbol{k})} - \frac{m'_i(\boldsymbol{k})}{f_{2i}(\boldsymbol{k})} \right) = 0.$$

To verify this relation, we define a multilinear polynomial $\widetilde{h}(\boldsymbol{k})$ and reduce the problem to verifying the following two conditions:

$$\sum_{\boldsymbol{k} \in \{0,1\}^{\log n}} \widetilde{h}(\boldsymbol{k}) = 0,$$

and

$$\widetilde{h}(\boldsymbol{k}) = \sum_{i \in [c]} e_{i,3} \cdot \left(\frac{1}{f_{2i-1}(\boldsymbol{k})} - \frac{m'_i(\boldsymbol{k})}{f_{2i}(\boldsymbol{k})} \right) \quad \text{for all } \boldsymbol{k} \in \{0,1\}^{\log n}.$$

We can directly apply the sum-check protocol to verify the first condition. For the second condition, we express it as a high-degree polynomial identity:

$$\widetilde{h}(\boldsymbol{k}) \cdot h_1(\boldsymbol{k}) + h_2(\boldsymbol{k}) = 0 \quad \text{for all } \boldsymbol{k} \in \{0,1\}^{\log n},$$

where

$$h_1(\boldsymbol{k}) := g_1\big(f_1(\boldsymbol{k}), \ldots, f_{2c}(\boldsymbol{k})\big) = \prod_{i=1}^{2c} f_i(\boldsymbol{k}),$$

$$\begin{aligned} h_2(\boldsymbol{k}) :=& g_2\big(m''_1(\boldsymbol{k}), \ldots, m''_{2c}(\boldsymbol{k}), f_1(\boldsymbol{k}), \ldots, f_{2c}(\boldsymbol{k})\big) \\ =& \sum_{i=1}^{2c} m''_i(\boldsymbol{k}) \cdot \prod_{j \in [2c] \setminus \{i\}} f_j(\boldsymbol{k}), \end{aligned}$$

with

$$m''_i(\boldsymbol{k}) = \begin{cases} -e_{(i+1)/2,3} & \text{when } i \text{ is odd,} \\ e_{i/2,3} \cdot m'_i(\boldsymbol{k}) & \text{when } i \text{ is even.} \end{cases}$$

Subsequently, a random challenge $\boldsymbol{\alpha} \in \mathbb{F}^{\log n}$ is selected, and a sum-check protocol is employed to confirm the relation:

$$\sum_{\boldsymbol{k} \in \{0,1\}^{\log n}} eq(\boldsymbol{\alpha}, \boldsymbol{k})\big(\widetilde{h}(\boldsymbol{k}) \cdot h_1(\boldsymbol{k}) + h_2(\boldsymbol{k})\big) = 0.$$

To validate the sum to 0, we can employ the DESC PIOP. Since h is a multilinear polynomial, we transform the computations of h_1 and h_2 into two arithmetic subcircuits C_1 and C_2, respectively. The verification reduces to checking whether the following relation holds:

$$\sum_{\boldsymbol{k} \in \{0,1\}^{\log n}} eq(\boldsymbol{\alpha}, \boldsymbol{k})\big(\widetilde{h}(\boldsymbol{k}) \cdot \widetilde{h}_1(\boldsymbol{k}) + \widetilde{h}_2(\boldsymbol{k})\big) = 0.$$

Here, $\widetilde{h}_1(\boldsymbol{k})$ and $\widetilde{h}_2(\boldsymbol{k})$ represent the multilinear extensions of the outputs from C_1 and C_2, respectively. Each of these circuits consists of n subcircuits h_1 and h_2 operating in parallel. The multilinear extensions of the inputs are defined as:

$$\widetilde{V}_{1,\log(2c)}(\boldsymbol{x}, \boldsymbol{k}) = \sum_{i \in [2c]} eq(\boldsymbol{x}, \langle i \rangle) \cdot f_i(\boldsymbol{k}),$$

$$\widetilde{V}_{2,\log(2c)}(\boldsymbol{x}, \boldsymbol{k}) = \sum_{i \in [2c]} eq(\boldsymbol{x}, \langle i \rangle) \cdot m_i''(\boldsymbol{k}),$$

where $\boldsymbol{x} \in \{0,1\}^{\log(2c)}$, $\boldsymbol{k} \in \{0,1\}^{\log n}$, and $\langle i \rangle$ denotes the binary representation of i. To illustrate the construction of C_1 and C_2, consider a simple case where $c = 2$. The computation of subcircuit h_1 is defined layer by layer as follows:

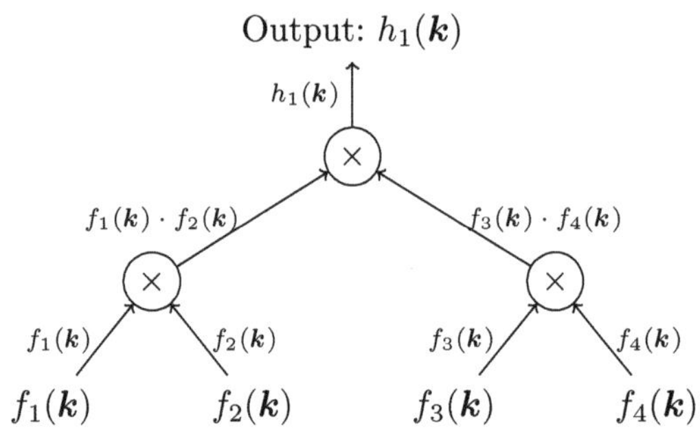

Subsequently, we can infer that for layer i ($i \in [2]$) in circuit C_1, the following holds for $\boldsymbol{z} \subset \{0,1\}^{i-1+\log n}$:

$$\widetilde{V}_{1,i-1}(\boldsymbol{z}) = \widetilde{V}_{1,i}(0, \boldsymbol{z}) \cdot \widetilde{V}_{1,i}(1, \boldsymbol{z}). \tag{6}$$

The computation of subcircuit h_2 is defined based on the computation trajectory of h_1. Specifically, we have:

$$\sum_{i=1}^{4} m_i''(\boldsymbol{k}) \cdot \prod_{j \in [4] \setminus \{i\}} f_j(\boldsymbol{k}) = (m_1''(\boldsymbol{k}) \cdot f_2(\boldsymbol{k}) + m_2''(\boldsymbol{k}) \cdot f_1(\boldsymbol{k})) \cdot f_3(\boldsymbol{k}) \cdot f_4(\boldsymbol{k})$$
$$+ (m_3''(\boldsymbol{k}) \cdot f_4(\boldsymbol{k}) + m_4''(\boldsymbol{k}) \cdot f_3(\boldsymbol{k})) \cdot f_1(\boldsymbol{k}) \cdot f_2(\boldsymbol{k}).$$

From this, we generalize the output at layer i (where $i \in [2]$) of C_2 as:

$$\widetilde{V}_{2,i-1}(\boldsymbol{x}) = \widetilde{V}_{2,i}(0, \boldsymbol{x}) \cdot \widetilde{V}_{1,i}(1, \boldsymbol{x}) + \widetilde{V}_{2,i}(1, \boldsymbol{x}) \cdot \widetilde{V}_{1,i}(0, \boldsymbol{x}). \tag{7}$$

For any $c > 2$, we can similarly deduce from Eqs. (6), (7) that the circuits C_1 and C_2 satisfy:

$$\widetilde{V}_{1,i-1}(\boldsymbol{x}) = \widetilde{V}_{1,i}(0, \boldsymbol{x}) \cdot \widetilde{V}_{1,i}(1, \boldsymbol{x}),$$
$$\widetilde{V}_{2,i-1}(\boldsymbol{x}) = \widetilde{V}_{2,i}(0, \boldsymbol{x}) \cdot \widetilde{V}_{1,i}(1, \boldsymbol{x}) + \widetilde{V}_{2,i}(1, \boldsymbol{x}) \cdot \widetilde{V}_{1,i}(0, \boldsymbol{x}).$$

From this structure, it follows that each layer i in C_1 and C_2 has a width of $2^i \cdot n$; and the subcircuits $\widetilde{h}_1$ and $\widetilde{h}_2$ have a size of $O(c)$, with the total depth being $\log(2c)$.

6 Doubly Efficient Interactive Proofs

In the previous sections, we demonstrated that the quasi-linear prover overhead in high-degree Sum-Checks is not inherent, but rather a byproduct of how polynomial constraints are represented. By reorganizing these constraints into data-parallel circuits, DESC PIOP achieved linear prover time. We explicitly define DESC as an optimized method for efficiently proving evaluations of high-degree virtual polynomials [11].

This success prompts a broader question: Can this "constraint-first" perspective optimize other aspects of GKR-based proofs? Here, we revisit the GKR protocol. Rather than claiming a unifying GKR framework, we focus on generalizing widely used structures—such as product circuits ($Y = \prod_{i=1}^{n} X_i$)—into a communication-efficient instantiation for arithmetic circuits. By incorporating CCS-style algebraic structure, we express each layer using matrix–vector multiplications, Hadamard products, and summations.

The key insight is that GKR efficiency depends on the algebraic organization of constraints, not on a strict nesting of sum-checks. Restructuring constraints in this way improves aggregation without changing the underlying proof paradigm, preserving linear prover time while reducing communication overhead.

6.1 An Improved GKR Protocol for Layered Circuits

The original GKR protocol verifies a depth-d layered arithmetic circuit $C : \mathbb{F}^n \to \mathbb{F}^k$ by recursively applying sum-checks to $\widetilde{V}_i$, the multilinear extension of the values at layer i.

Whereas the standard GKR layer reduction takes the form $\widetilde{V}_i(\boldsymbol{z}) = \sum_{\boldsymbol{x}} \mathrm{eq}(\boldsymbol{z}, \boldsymbol{x}) \cdot \widetilde{V}_{i+1}(0, \boldsymbol{x}) \cdot \widetilde{V}_{i+1}(1, \boldsymbol{x})$, we generalize this relation to efficiently capture structured constraints:

$$\widetilde{V}_i(\boldsymbol{z}) = \sum_{\boldsymbol{x} \in \{0,1\}^{s_i}} \mathrm{eq}(\boldsymbol{z}, \boldsymbol{x}) \cdot f_i(\boldsymbol{x}),$$

where $f_i(\boldsymbol{x})$ is defined as the Hadamard product of matrix-vector multiplications over layer $i+1$:

$$f_i(\boldsymbol{x}) = \left(\sum_{\boldsymbol{y} \in \{0,1\}^{s_{i+1}}} \widetilde{A}_{i+1}(\boldsymbol{x}, \boldsymbol{y}) \cdot \widetilde{V}_{i+1}(\boldsymbol{y}) \right) \cdot \left(\sum_{\boldsymbol{y} \in \{0,1\}^{s_{i+1}}} \widetilde{B}_{i+1}(\boldsymbol{x}, \boldsymbol{y}) \cdot \widetilde{V}_{i+1}(\boldsymbol{y}) \right).$$

Since the evaluations of $\sum \widetilde{A}\widetilde{V}_{i+1}$ and $\sum \widetilde{B}\widetilde{V}_{i+1}$ at $\boldsymbol{x}$ naturally substitute for $\widetilde{V}_{i+1}(0, \boldsymbol{x})$ and $\widetilde{V}_{i+1}(1, \boldsymbol{x})$, we can reduce them into a single evaluation claim for $\widetilde{V}_{i+1}$ via a random linear combination. This elegantly bypasses the need for an additional Sum-check protocol over $\boldsymbol{y}$, providing a framework that sufficiently covers various constraint representations. This reformulation is sound, since the R1CS naturally captures both additive and multiplicative relations between linear combinations of variables [28].

To optimize proof size while strictly guaranteeing a prover time linear in field operations, we further introduce CCS to support higher-degree compositions. For example, extending a layer reduction modeled as the product of multiple evaluation points (e.g., the product of four points $\widetilde{V}_{i+1}(0, 0, \boldsymbol{x})$, $\widetilde{V}_{i+1}(1, 0, \boldsymbol{x})$, $\widetilde{V}_{i+1}(0, 1, \boldsymbol{x})$, $\widetilde{V}_{i+1}(1, 1, \boldsymbol{x})$) allows $\widetilde{V}_i$ to be expressed as a degree-c composition:

$$\widetilde{V}_i(\boldsymbol{z}) = \sum_{\boldsymbol{x} \in \{0,1\}^{s_i}} \mathsf{eq}(\boldsymbol{z}, \boldsymbol{x}) \cdot \prod_{j=1}^{c} \left(\sum_{\boldsymbol{y} \in \{0,1\}^{s_{i+1}}} M_j(\boldsymbol{x}, \boldsymbol{y}) \cdot \widetilde{V}_{i+1}(\boldsymbol{y}) \right),$$

where $M_1, \ldots, M_c \in \mathbb{F}^{m \times m}$ are sparse matrices. When $c = 4$, this higher-degree grouping reduces the number of Sum-check invocations to $\log_4 n$. This structure naturally extends to the full CCS framework to support weighted sums of such products, decreasing communication complexity and providing a highly flexible prover-time/communication tradeoff.

The protocol implements the layer-to-layer reduction via two sum-check invocations. First, the claim $\widetilde{V}_i(\boldsymbol{u}_i) = \sum_{\boldsymbol{x}} \mathsf{eq}(\boldsymbol{u}_i, \boldsymbol{x}) \cdot f_i(\boldsymbol{x})$ is reduced to a single evaluation point $\boldsymbol{v}_i \in \mathbb{F}^{s_i}$, yielding $m_j(\boldsymbol{v}_i) = \sum_{\boldsymbol{y}_{i+1}} \widetilde{M}_j(\boldsymbol{v}_i, \boldsymbol{y}_{i+1}) \cdot \widetilde{V}_{i+1}(\boldsymbol{y}_{i+1})$ for $j \in [c]$.

Next, a random linear combination $\boldsymbol{e} \in \mathbb{F}^c$ aggregates these c equations into a single claim:

$$\sum_{j=1}^{c} e_j \cdot m_j(\boldsymbol{v}_i) = \sum_{\boldsymbol{y}_{i+1} \in \{0,1\}^{s_{i+1}}} \left(\sum_{j=1}^{c} e_j \cdot \widetilde{M}_j(\boldsymbol{v}_i, \boldsymbol{y}_{i+1}) \right) \widetilde{V}_{i+1}(\boldsymbol{y}_{i+1}).$$

A second sum-check reduces this aggregated sum to a single evaluation $\widetilde{V}_{i+1}(\boldsymbol{u}_{i+1})$ at a random point $\boldsymbol{u}_{i+1}$. This completes the transition to layer $i+1$, operating on structured algebraic constraints rather than individual gates.

Comparison with the Original GKR Protocol. In the original GKR protocol, a depth-d layered arithmetic circuit of width S is verified gate by gate. At each layer, sum-check is applied to a multivariate polynomial in $2 \log S$ variables, corresponding to the binary encodings of the two input wires of each gate.

Each variable appears with degree at most 2. Consequently, each round of the sum-check protocol communicates 3 field elements, resulting in a communication cost of $6 \log S$ per layer and $6d \log S$ overall, with prover time $O(dS)$. For uniform circuits, the verifier can evaluate the wiring predicates at each layer in time $O(\log S)$, yielding an overall verifier time of $O(d \log S)$.

Our formulation preserves the GKR proof paradigm but reorganizes how arithmetic constraints are encoded. Instead of explicit addition and multiplication gates, each layer is expressed using summations, sparse matrix–vector multiplications, and Hadamard products. Importantly, addition constraints are absorbed into linear combinations and do not contribute to circuit depth; only multiplicative dependencies induce new sum-check layers.

For example, consider a binary-tree summation computing $y = \sum_{i=1}^{n} x_i$ with $n = 2^k$. Under the standard GKR formulation, this computation is realized by a depth-$\log n$ circuit of addition gates, incurring $\log n$ layers of sum-check. In contrast, under an R1CS or CCS-style encoding, the same computation is represented as a single linear constraint, resulting in constant effective depth.

Similarly, consider a multiplication tree computing $y = \prod_{i=1}^{n} x_i$ with $n = 2^k$. In the standard GKR protocol, this requires a binary multiplication tree of depth $d = \log n$, leading to $\log n$ sum-check invocations. In our formulation, these multiplications are aggregated into bounded-degree algebraic constraints. By grouping at most d_1 multiplicative terms, the effective depth is reduced to $\log_{d_1}(n)$. Consequently, the first sum-check at each effective layer involves a polynomial of degree $d_1 + 1$, while subsequent aggregated claims have degree 2. The resulting total communication complexity is

$$(d_1 + 5) \log S \cdot \log_{d_1}(2^d),$$

which is minimized at $d_1 = 6$, yielding approximately $4.25\, d \log S$.

This improvement arises from a re-encoding of the circuit rather than the introduction of a new proof system. In particular, for uniform circuits, the sparse matrix predicates admit efficient evaluation by the verifier, analogous to the evaluation of the $\widetilde{add}$ and $\widetilde{mult}$ wiring predicates in the original GKR protocol. As a result, the protocol preserves linear prover time and efficient verification.

Comparison with Optimized Sum-Check Techniques. Since Sum-check and GKR serve as sub-protocols, existing state-of-the-art optimizations integrate seamlessly into our framework. These optimizations include utilizing binary-tree topologies, sending d evaluations per round, or alternatively, leveraging polynomial commitments (e.g., sending commitments to degree-d univariate polynomials for final batch verification). By combining these techniques with our CCS-based GKR, DESC achieves better proof size than standard Sum-check under identical optimizations, while consistently offering flexible trade-offs between communication and prover time.

6.2 DE-PIOP for General Arithmetic Circuits

In this section, we present a generalized DEIP protocol specifically designed for general arithmetic circuits, referred to as DE-PIOP. The protocol is designed to validate a claimed value v as the output of a general arithmetic circuit.

As demonstrated in [31], in a general arithmetic circuit, each gate within layer i can receive outputs from gates spanning layers $i+1$ through d. To accommodate this layered dependency, a key assumption is that every gate at layer i must receive at least one input from layer $i+1$, designated as the left operand. Under this assumption, the multilinear extension of the output $\widetilde{V}_i$ in layer $(i+1)$ can be re-expressed as:

$$\widetilde{V}_i(\boldsymbol{z}) = \sum_{j=i+1}^{d} \sum_{\substack{\boldsymbol{y}_j \in \{0,1\}^{s_j} \\ \boldsymbol{x}_{i+1} \in \{0,1\}^{s_{i+1}}}} \widetilde{add}_{i+1,j}(\boldsymbol{z}_i, \boldsymbol{x}_{i+1}, \boldsymbol{y}_j)\big(\widetilde{V}_{i+1}(\boldsymbol{x}_{i+1}) + \widetilde{V}_j(\boldsymbol{y}_j)\big)$$
$$+ \widetilde{mult}_{i+1,j}(\boldsymbol{z}_i, \boldsymbol{x}_{i+1}, \boldsymbol{y}_j)\big(\widetilde{V}_{i+1}(\boldsymbol{x}_{i+1})\widetilde{V}_j(\boldsymbol{y}_j)\big),$$

where $\widetilde{add}_{i+1,j}(\boldsymbol{z}_i, \boldsymbol{x}_{i+1}, \boldsymbol{y}_j) = 1$ ($\widetilde{mult}_{i+1,j}(\boldsymbol{z}_i, \boldsymbol{x}_{i+1}, \boldsymbol{y}_j) = 1$) if and only if gate $\boldsymbol{z}_i$ in layer $i+1$ is the addition (multiplication) of values $\widetilde{V}_{i+1}(\boldsymbol{x}_{i+1})$ and $\widetilde{V}_j(\boldsymbol{y}_j)$.

We generalize this formulation by assuming that the inputs to each gate in layer i are linear combinations of outputs from layers $i+1$ through d. Under this assumption, we redefine $V_i(\boldsymbol{z})$ as follows:

$$\widetilde{V}_i(\boldsymbol{z}) := \sum_{\boldsymbol{x}_i \in \{0,1\}^{s_i}} f_i(\boldsymbol{x}_i) = \sum_{\boldsymbol{x}_i \in \{0,1\}^{s_i}} eq(\boldsymbol{z}, \boldsymbol{x}_i) \cdot f_{i,a}(\boldsymbol{x}_i) \cdot f_{i,b}(\boldsymbol{x}_i),$$

where

$$f_{i,a}(\boldsymbol{x}_i) = \sum_{j=i+1}^{d} \sum_{\boldsymbol{y}_j \in \{0,1\}^{s_j}} \widetilde{A}_{i+1,j}(\boldsymbol{x}_i, \boldsymbol{y}_j)\widetilde{V}_j(\boldsymbol{y}_j),$$

$$f_{i,b}(\boldsymbol{x}_i) = \sum_{j=i+1}^{d} \sum_{\boldsymbol{y}_j \in \{0,1\}^{s_j}} \widetilde{B}_{i+1,j}(\boldsymbol{x}_i, \boldsymbol{y}_j)\widetilde{V}_j(\boldsymbol{y}_j).$$

By following the methodology of [31], it is straightforward to derive a corresponding doubly-efficient interactive protocol for this generalized construction.

7 Conclusion

Our work presents an efficient Sum-Check framework built upon the GKR protocol: efficiency is fundamentally determined by the algebraic organization of constraints. We validated this principle in two directions: first, through DESC PIOP (Sect. 3), which eliminates the prover bottleneck for high-degree polynomials by treating them as structured circuits; and second, through a refined GKR protocol (Sect. 6), which reduces communication overhead by aggregating circuit layers. Together, these results suggest that future optimizations should focus on the algebraic encoding of the computation rather than the proof protocol itself.

Acknowledgments. We thank the anonymous reviewers for their valuable comments. This work is supported by the National Natural Science Foundation of China (Grant No. 62272269) and the Scientific Research Innovation Capability Support Project for Young Faculty (Grant No. ZYGXQNJSKYCXNLZCXM-I21).

References

1. Baldimtsi, F., et al.: zklogin: privacy-preserving blockchain authentication with existing credentials. In: Proceedings of the 2024 on ACM SIGSAC Conference on Computer and Communications Security, pp. 3182–3196 (2024)
2. Ben-Sasson, E., Bentov, I., Horesh, Y., Riabzev, M.: Scalable zero knowledge with no trusted setup. In: Annual International Cryptology Conference, pp. 701–732. Springer (2019)
3. Ben-Sasson, E., Chiesa, A., Riabzev, M., Spooner, N., Virza, M., Ward, N.P.: Aurora: transparent succinct arguments for R1CS. In: Ishai, Y., Rijmen, V. (eds.) EUROCRYPT 2019. LNCS, vol. 11476, pp. 103–128. Springer, Cham (2019). https://doi.org/10.1007/978-3-030-17653-2_4
4. Ben-Sasson, E., Chiesa, A., Spooner, N.: Interactive oracle proofs. In: Hirt, M., Smith, A. (eds.) TCC 2016. LNCS, vol. 9986, pp. 31–60. Springer, Heidelberg (2016). https://doi.org/10.1007/978-3-662-53644-5_2
5. Bootle, J., Chiesa, A., Hu, Y., Orru, M.: Gemini: elastic snarks for diverse environments. In: Annual International Conference on the Theory and Applications of Cryptographic Techniques, pp. 427–457. Springer (2022)
6. Bünz, B., Bootle, J., Boneh, D., Poelstra, A., Wuille, P., Maxwell, G.: Bulletproofs: short proofs for confidential transactions and more. In: 2018 IEEE Symposium on Security and Privacy (SP), pp. 315–334. IEEE (2018)
7. Buterin, V.: An incomplete guide to rollups. Vitalik Buterin website (2021)
8. Campanelli, M., Faonio, A., Fiore, D., Li, T., Lipmaa, H.: Lookup arguments: improvements, extensions and applications to zero-knowledge decision trees. In: IACR International Conference on Public-Key Cryptography, pp. 337–369. Springer (2024)
9. Chen, B., Bünz, B., Boneh, D., Zhang, Z.: Hyperplonk: plonk with linear-time prover and high-degree custom gates. In: Annual International Conference on the Theory and Applications of Cryptographic Techniques, pp. 499–530. Springer (2023)
10. Chiesa, A., Ojha, D., Spooner, N.: Fractal: post-quantum and transparent recursive proofs from holography. In: Canteaut, A., Ishai, Y. (eds.) EUROCRYPT 2020. LNCS, vol. 12105, pp. 769–793. Springer, Cham (2020). https://doi.org/10.1007/978-3-030-45721-1_27
11. Diamond, B.E., Posen, J.: Succinct arguments over towers of binary fields. In: Annual International Conference on the Theory and Applications of Cryptographic Techniques, pp. 93–122. Springer (2025)
12. Eagen, L., Fiore, D., Gabizon, A.: CQ: cached quotients for fast lookups. Cryptology ePrint Archive (2022)
13. Gabizon, A., Williamson, Z.J.: Plookup: a simplified polynomial protocol for lookup tables. Cryptology ePrint Archive (2020)
14. Gabizon, A., Williamson, Z.J., Ciobotaru, O.: PLONK: permutations over lagrange-bases for oecumenical noninteractive arguments of knowledge. IACR Cryptol. ePrint Arch. 953 (2019)

15. Goldwasser, S., Kalai, Y.T., Rothblum, G.N.: Delegating computation: interactive proofs for muggles. J. ACM (JACM) **62**(4), 1–64 (2015)
16. Golovnev, A., Lee, J., Setty, S., Thaler, J., Wahby, R.S.: Brakedown: linear-time and field-agnostic snarks for R1CS. In: Annual International Cryptology Conference, pp. 193–226. Springer (2023)
17. Groth, J.: On the size of pairing-based non-interactive arguments. In: Annual International Conference on the Theory and Applications of Cryptographic Techniques, pp. 305–326. Springer (2016)
18. Haböck, U.: Multivariate lookups based on logarithmic derivatives. Cryptology ePrint Archive (2022)
19. Lund, C., Fortnow, L., Karloff, H., Nisan, N.: Algebraic methods for interactive proof systems. J. ACM (JACM) **39**(4), 859–868 (1992)
20. Maller, M., Bowe, S., Kohlweiss, M., Meiklejohn, S.: Sonic: zero-knowledge snarks from linear-size universal and updatable structured reference strings. In: Proceedings of the 2019 ACM SIGSAC Conference on Computer and Communications Security, pp. 2111–2128 (2019)
21. Sasson, E.B., et al.: Zerocash: decentralized anonymous payments from bitcoin. In: 2014 IEEE Symposium on Security and Privacy, pp. 459–474. IEEE (2014)
22. Schwartz, J.T.: Fast probabilistic algorithms for verification of polynomial identities. J. ACM **27**(4), 701–717 (1980)
23. Setty, S.: Spartan: efficient and general-purpose zksnarks without trusted setup. In: Annual International Cryptology Conference, pp. 704–737. Springer (2020)
24. Setty, S., Thaler, J., Wahby, R.: Customizable constraint systems for succinct arguments. Cryptology ePrint Archive (2023)
25. Setty, S., Thaler, J., Wahby, R.: Unlocking the lookup singularity with lasso. In: Annual International Conference on the Theory and Applications of Cryptographic Techniques, pp. 180–209. Springer (2024)
26. Shoup, V.: Lower bounds for discrete logatithms and related problems. In: EUROCRYPT 1997, pp. 256–266 (1997)
27. Thaler, J.: Time-optimal interactive proofs for circuit evaluation. In: Annual Cryptology Conference, pp. 71–89. Springer (2013)
28. Thaler, J.: Proofs, arguments, and zero-knowledge. Found. Trends® Priv. Secur. **4**(2–4), 117–660 (2022)
29. Xie, T., Zhang, J., Zhang, Y., Papamanthou, C., Song, D.: Libra: succinct zero-knowledge proofs with optimal prover computation. In: Boldyreva, A., Micciancio, D. (eds.) CRYPTO 2019. LNCS, vol. 11694, pp. 733–764. Springer, Cham (2019). https://doi.org/10.1007/978-3-030-26954-8_24
30. Xie, T., et al.: zkbridge: trustless cross-chain bridges made practical. In: Proceedings of the 2022 ACM SIGSAC Conference on Computer and Communications Security, pp. 3003–3017 (2022)
31. Zhang, J., et al.: Doubly efficient interactive proofs for general arithmetic circuits with linear prover time. In: Proceedings of the 2021 ACM SIGSAC Conference on Computer and Communications Security, pp. 159–177 (2021)

Practical Subvector Commitments with Optimal Opening Complexity

Matteo Campanelli(✉)

Offchain Labs and University of Tartu, Tartu, Estonia
binarywhalesinternaryseas@gmail.com

Abstract. We introduce a simple pairing-based vector commitment with subvector opening where, after a one-time preprocessing, the prover can open a subvector of size ℓ in *linear* time. Our focus is on practically relevant solutions compatible with already deployed setups—specifically, the powers-of-τ setup used by KZG and many popular SNARKs. We achieve substantial concrete speedups over aSVC (Tomescu et al., SCN 2020), the relevant state of the art in deployable subvector commitments with $O(\ell \log^2 \ell)$ prover and verifier time: our opening is over 60× faster on subvectors of any size; on large subvectors our opening and verification achieve ≈4000× and 170× speedups respectively (and four times as much with parallelism).

Our main result is a construction secure in the AGM and in which:

- A commitment is a single $\mathbb{G}_2$ element and a proof is a single $\mathbb{G}_1$ element;
- Opening requires ℓ point additions in $\mathbb{G}_1$;
- Verification is dominated by 2ℓ $\mathbb{G}_1$ operations.

We also describe two variants of our main design that are directly compatible with deployed applications and where the commitment is a $\mathbb{G}_1$ element; these two schemes show similar speedups over prior work. We additionally support cross-commitment and distributed aggregation, and provide an open-source implementation.

1 Introduction

Vector commitment schemes [LY10,CF13] are a cryptographic primitive that, in contrast to simple hashing, enable a form of fine-grained integrity: a weak client holding a short digest $\mathsf{cm}_{\boldsymbol{v}}$ to a vector $\boldsymbol{v}$, can ensure that position i in $\boldsymbol{v}$ has value y by checking a small proof π. What distinguishes this primitive from other commitment schemes is that both the commitment and the opening are of size independent of m, the length of the vector $\boldsymbol{v}$[1]. Vector

[1] This definition is sometimes extended to include constructions with a mild dependency on m, e.g., $\log m$. In this work we focus on *highly succinct* schemes—i.e., with commitments and proofs of constant-size.

K. Jee and A. Kate (Eds.): ACNS 2026, LNCS 16571, pp. 327–350, 2027.
https://doi.org/10.1007/978-3-032-32560-0_12

commitments—and their extensions with subvector-opening described below—have numerous applications, including "stateless" blockchains[2] [TAB+20], verifiable databases [BGV11], decentralized storage networks [CFG+20], revocation in group signatures [LPY12], and proofs of replication [Fis19, ABC+24].

Subvector Commitments. In some settings (including all of the example applications above) we are interested in opening a committed vector in multiple positions at the same time. That is, the client can request a set of positions $I \subset \{1, \ldots, m\}$ and receive a response $\boldsymbol{y}$ together with a proof π_I guaranteeing that $\boldsymbol{y} = (v_i)_{i \in I}$. Here we strengthen our requirements on the size of the proof π: it should not be only independent of $|\boldsymbol{v}|$, but also independent of ℓ, the size of the requested subvector $\boldsymbol{y}$. We refer to this type of opening as *subvector opening* and to the corresponding primitive as a *subvector commitment* (or SVC).

Fast Opening Through Preprocessing. Because in a vector commitment there exists only a limited number of possible individual openings (as many as the positions in the committed vector $\boldsymbol{v}$), it is possible in principle to *preprocess* the openings π_i for all the possible queries on single positions v_i. With the help of the right algebraic setting and cryptographic assumptions, we can sometimes exploit this fact to design an efficient SVC that works as follows. When the client requests a set of positions $I = \{i_1, \ldots, i_\ell\}$, the prover:

(i) retrieves from memory the relevant individual proofs $\pi_{i_1}, \ldots, \pi_{i_\ell}$;

(ii) uses a special *aggregation* procedure to combine them all into a single and constant-sized proof π^*, which it then sends to the client.

Through this approach, one can build SVCs where the opening time is independent of the vector size m, but instead grows only as a function of ℓ.[3] For this blueprint to be genuinely effective in practice, the resulting SVC should also satisfy two extra properties: aggregation should be more efficient than recomputing the proofs from scratch (else it would defy the point of the approach); both commitments and proofs should be *updatable*, that is we should be able to modify them efficiently whenever the vector $\boldsymbol{v}$ changes.

Limitations of the State of the Art. Prior work has shown that the aggregation-based approach is possible from different types of cryptographic assumptions, such as elliptic curves endowed with bilinear pairings [GRWZ20, TAB+20] and groups of unknown-order [CFG+20, BBF19]. Among these two families of designs, pairing-based ones are generally the most attractive from a practical point of view: compared to their counterparts based on unknown-order groups, they tend to feature more compact proofs, smaller constants in running times, homomorphic commitments and/or rely on trusted setups that are already widely deployed (see also discussion in Sect. 1.2)[4] Yet despite these advantages, even the most performant among deployable pairing-based SVCs—the aggregatable SVC (aSVC) of Tomescu et al. [TAB+20]—requires $O(\ell \log^2 \ell)$ time for

[2] This term usually refers to a chain design where validation is stateless and can be performed by just accessing a short digest of the current state.

[3] Notice that ℓ, the size of the requested subvector, can be much smaller than m.

[4] Pairing-based schemes have also proven practical through deployments at massive scale. E.g., KZG vector opening is at the heart of Ethereum's sharding [BFL+22].

both aggregation and verification (due to their reliance on polynomial division techniques). Designing a *deployable* SVC with linear-time openings and verification has remained an open problem (where by "deployable" we mean an SVC with the practically relevant characteristics outlined above).

1.1 This Work: Optimal Opening Time and Faster Verification from Existing Setups

Our main contribution is constructing a pairing-based SVC where, after a one-time preprocessing stage, opening runs in *linear* time (the theoretical optimal). Verification in our scheme is dominated by $\approx 2\ell$ group operations (specifically, ℓ $\mathbb{G}_1$ operations plus one multi-scalar multiplication of size ℓ), improving on the $O(\ell \log^2 \ell)$ field operations and size-ℓ $\mathbb{G}_2$ MSM required by Tomescu et al. [TAB+20] (see summary in Table 1). Our improvements are not only asymptotic, but translate to substantial concrete improvements. As we show in Sect. 7, our main scheme obtains the following speedups:

- *Opening:* 60× on subvectors of *any* size; 4000× on large subvectors ($\ell \approx$64K).
- *Verification:* 170× on large subvectors (over 750× when using parallelism).

In our main construction, a commitment is a single $\mathbb{G}_2$ element, in contrast to the scheme in Tomescu et al. where it lies in $\mathbb{G}_1$. We remove this limitation in two variants of our main scheme without sacrificing efficiency. Notably, both these schemes also show orders of magnitude speedups (see Sect. 7.2).

All our constructions support: homomorphism, efficient updatability of commitments and proofs, and aggregation of proofs across multiple commitments (cross-commitment aggregation). Being *associative* (same-commitment aggregation is a simple sum of proofs), our proofs are particularly suitable for settings where proof generation is distributed among nodes. We also show that all m individual proofs can be preprocessed in $O(m \log m)$ time. Although we rely on a different verification equation, we establish a connection between the proofs in our schemes and those in KZG commitments. This allows us to leverage techniques for preprocessing KZG openings, specifically Feist-Khovratovich [FK23]. We prove the security of our schemes in the Algebraic Group Model (AGM).

Additional contributions of this work include:

- The two aforementioned variants of our main construction—$\Pi_{\mathbb{G}_1}^{\mathsf{fastP}}$ (optimized for proving time) and $\Pi_{\mathbb{G}_1}^{\mathsf{fastV}}$ (optimized for verification time). These constructions feature a commitment cm consisting of a single $\mathbb{G}_1$ element. If cm is a commitment to vector $\boldsymbol{v}$, it corresponds to a KZG commitment [KZG10] to the (standard) Lagrange-basis encoding of $\boldsymbol{v}$. Thus our variants are fully compatible with already deployed trusted setups and other KZG-based applications, such as popular SNARKs [GWC19] and Ethereum's data availability sampling solutions [BFL+22].
- An open source Rust implementation built on arkworks [ark22], with a comprehensive experimental evaluation comparing our schemes against aSVC.

Table 1. Comparison of practical subvector commitments with sublinear opening. The table reports dominating costs for running times. For costs: $\mathbb{P}$ refers to one pairing; $\mathsf{MSM}_i(\ell)$ (for $i \in \{1,2\}$) refers to one multi-scalar multiplication of size ℓ in group $\mathbb{G}_i$. A star ($\star$) marks constructions from this work. Variants are described in Sect. 5. The efficiency profile for our verifier-optimized variant ($\Pi_{\mathbb{G}_1}^{\mathsf{fastV}}$) assumes the optimization of Remark 1. In Sect. 1.2 we compare to other solutions with superlinear opening time that rely on random oracles and that have bespoke setups or larger proof sizes.

Scheme	cm|	$\lvert\pi\rvert$	Preproc.	Open	Verify
aSVC [TAB+20]	$1\,\mathbb{G}_1$	$1\,\mathbb{G}_1$	$O(m\log m)$	$O(\ell\log^2\ell)\,\mathbb{F}$, $\mathsf{MSM}_1(\ell)$	$O(\ell\log^2\ell)\,\mathbb{F}$, $2\,\mathbb{P}, \mathsf{MSM}_2(\ell)$
Main constr. *(Fig. 1)	$1\,\mathbb{G}_2$	$1\,\mathbb{G}_1$	$O(m\log m)$	$\ell\,\mathbb{G}_1$	$\ell\,\mathbb{G}_1, 3\,\mathbb{P}$, $\mathsf{MSM}_1(\ell)$
Variant* $\Pi_{\mathbb{G}_1}^{\mathsf{fastP}}$	$1\,\mathbb{G}_1$	$1\,\mathbb{G}_1$	$O(m\log m)$	$\ell\,\mathbb{G}_1$	$\ell\,\mathbb{G}_2, 3\,\mathbb{P}$, $\mathsf{MSM}_1(\ell)$
Variant* $\Pi_{\mathbb{G}_1}^{\mathsf{fastV}}$	$1\,\mathbb{G}_1$	$1\,\mathbb{G}_1, 1\,\mathbb{G}_2$	$O(m\log m)$	$\ell\,\mathbb{G}_1, \ell\,\mathbb{G}_2$	$\ell\,\mathbb{G}_1, 3\,\mathbb{P}$, $\mathsf{MSM}_1(\ell)$

Application Highlight: Faster Proving in Verifiable Databases. Our constructions show immediate improvements to recent works adopting vector commitments in the bilinear settings for verifiable databases (or VDBs). At its essence, a VDB is a specialized proof system for database queries where the client holds only a short digest to the whole database. Recently, Botta et al. [BBC+25] proposed qedb, a VDB that supports a representative subset of SQL. At its heart, it combines accumulators and subvector commitments with specific features (including subvectors instantiated with aSVC by Tomescu et al. [TAB+20]) in order to obtain an expressive VDB that is provably secure and features high modularity and performance without relying on general-purpose proof systems.

Our construction $\Pi_{\mathbb{G}_1}^{\mathsf{fastP}}$ can be used as a drop-in replacement for the SVC in [BBC+25]. We now highlight how it can provide substantial speedups on a relevant subset of their supported queries and leave as future work a full-fledged analysis of the impact of this change. We consider queries of the following form (where C1 and C2 are columns in the table T and v is an arbitrary literal):

Q: SELECT C1 FROM T WHERE C2 = v

For simplicity here we focus on the implications for the cost of *proving* in this type of query; however, we remark that proving other queries and verification will also benefit from the speedups of $\Pi_{\mathbb{G}_1}^{\mathsf{fastP}}$ against aSVC (we do not discuss them here as they would be substantially more complex to analyze quantitatively). In qedb, the cost of proving a query like Q consists in simply providing an aSVC opening for a vector commitment encoding C (for this specific type of equality checks, the prover also provides an additional precomputed value—a commitment to an "inverted index"—to show the filtering was done on the right rows; this does not require any computation).

Examples of Our Improvements: Consider a table T with N ≈130K rows and where the result of Q is (three scenarios): *a)* 1% of the table T; *b)* 10% of T; *c)* 25% of T. Then, by using our scheme $\Pi_{\mathbb{G}_1}^{\mathsf{fastP}}$ as a replacement for the SVC in qedb, we can achieve 2–3 orders of magnitude speedups. Specifically, we obtain these ballpark improvements for the proving time for query Q[5]:

a) 0.2 s → 1ms; *b)* 5 s → 8ms; *c)* half a minute → 16ms.

Scenario Highlight: Broad Applicability within Ethereum's Ecosystem. Our scheme requires only a standard powers-of-τ setup—which also underlies Ethereum's blob commitments [BFL+22] and PLONK-based rollups—showing potential applicability in this setting. Ethereum uses SVC-like primitives in data availability sampling (DAS) and in the past has considered switching to Verkle Trees for stateless validation via compact state proofs [BFB+24]. The current DAS implementation opens over cosets [WZ24], partly for erasure coding compatibility; our arbitrary-position openings could benefit designs needing flexible access. For stateless validation, our distributed aggregation could let validators with partial witnesses combine proofs incrementally and without centralized coordination.

1.2 Related Work

The literature on vector commitments is vast and we refer the reader to two surveys on the topic, [Nit21] and [PRvdM25]. The notion of *subvector* commitment was introduced in [LM19].

Subvector Commitments from Bilinear Pairings. Tomescu et al. [TAB+20] proposed an aggregatable vector commitment (dubbed aSVC) with a setup compatible with the KZG commitment [KZG10] and other popular SNARK designs [CHM+20,CFF+21,GWC19]. Schemes satisfying this setup are substantially easier to deploy in practice because: they are reusable by different cryptographic constructions, they provide higher trust (they can be "updated" by different parties and their security holds as long as a *single* party performs the update honestly [GKM+18]), and they have already been generated and used at large scale [axi25,ale21,eth23]. Here we point out two differences between aSVC and our work, and refer the reader to the rest of the text for a comparison along different metrics (see specifically: Sect. 2 for a comparison of the techniques; Table 1 and Sect. 7 for an efficiency comparison). In contrast to our work, the aggregation in [TAB+20] cannot be performed incrementally or in a distributed manner but is *one-hop* only (in the sense of [CNR+22]); also, aSVC cannot perform aggregation *across commitments* (see comparison with Pointproofs below). A dimension in which aSVC offers a better tradeoff compared to our solution is the requirement for the client to store only a number of items of the setup linear

[5] These timings are derived from the relevant benchmarks in Sect. 7.

in the size of the opened subvector; our schemes, in contrast, require the client to keep a $O(m)$-sized portion of the parameters. We remark that this limitation can often be inconsequential for the verifier for at least two reasons: this storage overhead is mild (for $m \approx 10^5$ it requires storing $\approx$ 5MB for our main scheme and $\Pi_{\mathbb{G}_1}^{\mathsf{fastV}}$ and $\approx$ 10 MB for $\Pi_{\mathbb{G}_1}^{\mathsf{fastP}}$); in settings where we prove verification inside a SNARK[6] [BCC+17]the client can simply keep a succinct commitment to the setup parameters and obtain the guarantee that the correct subset of parameters were used as part of the SNARK proof.

Pointproofs [GRWZ20, LPR22] are a construction for SVC obtained as a variation of [LY10] and with constant-sized proof and commitments (all the observations in these paragraphs also generally apply to schemes based on [LY10]). Pointproofs satisfy a property called *cross-commitment aggregation* (see Sect. 4.2), which our constructions also satisfy (but that is not satisfied by aSVC). The parameters for Pointproofs require a larger and idiosyncratic setup that is not compatible with those already deployed or with those used by other SNARKs[7]—this reduces the opportunity for simple deployment of this scheme. Their single-commitment aggregation requires a multi-scalar multiplication with challenges from a random oracle, making it not strictly linear and concretely less efficient than ours[8]. Also, in contrast to Pointproofs, our aggregation is associative making it suitable for distributed settings [CFG+20].

The work in [CNR+22] proposes a construction of linear-map vector commitments (LVC), i.e. commitments to vectors that support proofs of evaluations for linear maps. The equation we obtain in our Lemma 1 is loosely related to the techniques used by the Lagrange-basis scheme in [CNR+22]. This scheme does support some forms of aggregation with preprocessing [CNR+22, §8.2] for *arbitrary* opening subsets—which, importantly, may apply to subvector openings—but these present a few caveats. Both types of aggregation in [CNR+22] have superlinear complexity—one is based on [TAB+20] (whose limitations we discuss throughout this paper), while the other is based on an MSM with random-oracle challenges (discussed in Footnote 8). Additionally, the proofs in [CNR+22] are larger and consist of three group elements. Overcoming these limitations is part of our contributions: we find techniques adjacent to those in [CNR+22] that lead to subvector proofs with a *single* group element (in our main construction

6 This practice is not uncommon and can be useful if the SVC is used in the context of proving a more complex computation or to make the verifier extremely efficient.

7 This setup consists of a special powers-of-τ sequence up to degree $2m$ (instead of m as in standard KZG), with a "hole"—the element $[\tau^{m+1}]_1$ must be absent (i.e., no party should know $[\tau^{m+1}]_1$).

8 Aggregation based on a random oracle $\mathcal{H}$ requires an MSM of size ℓ with high-entropy scalars derived from $\mathcal{H}$. An MSM of this type involves $\omega(\ell)$ (superlinear) cost because Pippenger's algorithm requires these many group operations for such an MSM (see discussion on page 3 in [GLS+21]). In contrast, our scheme requires ℓ plain group additions. This difference results in roughly 20–50× speedups in our favor—these can be inferred directly from our benchmarks by comparing aSVC commitment times (an MSM of comparable structure) against our aggregation times (see Tables 2 and 3 in the full version of this paper [Cam26]).

and in the variant $\Pi_{\mathbb{G}_1}^{\mathsf{fastP}}$) and provide an efficient and simple preprocessing for our schemes—one that can also reuse existing implementations—by observing a relation between the structure of our proofs and those in KZG-style schemes, despite them relying on different verification equations.

We finally cite other prominent works based on bilinear pairings: [LJGK25], which improves on batch updates in vector commitments based on KZG; [SCP+22], which proposes a tree-based construction on top of the PST commitment [PST13] (with proofs of logarithmic size); [LM19], which originally introduced the notion of subvector opening and proposed a pairing-based scheme with constant-sized proofs (not supporting aggregation and requiring quadratic opening time).

Other Works on Subvector Commitments. A number of works use the properties of hidden order groups, pairing-free elliptic curves and lattices to design schemes with attractive features, some of which support aggregation. In general, these schemes exhibit worse asymptotics than pairing-based constructions and/or are concretely less efficient (due to larger constants). A partial list of such works includes [BBF19, AR20, CFG+20, CEO22, CHAK23, WW23, TB23].

2 Technical Overview

Let $(\mathbb{G}_1, \mathbb{G}_2, \mathbb{G}_T)$ be a bilinear group of prime order p, along with a pairing $e : \mathbb{G}_1 \times \mathbb{G}_2 \to \mathbb{G}_T$ (see also Sect. 3.1 for reference on basic notation). A common approach for constructing vector commitments from pairings is to encode a vector $\mathbf{a} = (a_1, \ldots, a_m)$ as the polynomial $f_{\mathbf{a}}(X) = \sum_i a_i \lambda_i(X)$, where $\lambda_i(X)$ are the Lagrange basis polynomials over a multiplicative subgroup $\mathbb{H} = \{h_1, \ldots, h_m\}$ of roots of unity (used for FFT). The commitment is then simply a polynomial commitment to $f_{\mathbf{a}}(X)$, specifically a KZG polynomial commitment. The KZG scheme works as follows. At setup time a secret value τ is sampled (and then discarded—it should be known to no one after the setup phase); the parameters for KZG for polynomials up to degree m contain powers of the secret τ in the groups $\mathbb{G}_1$ and $\mathbb{G}_2$, i.e., $([\tau_i]_1, [\tau_i]_2)_{i=1}^{m}$. A commitment to $f_{\mathbf{a}}(X)$ is simply $[f_{\mathbf{a}}(\tau)]_1$ ($[f_{\mathbf{a}}(\tau)]_2$ for KZG commitments in $\mathbb{G}_2$) which can be computed as $\sum_{j=0}^{m-1} c_j [\tau^j]_1$ where the values c_j are the coefficients of the polynomial. In order to open a single position i with value a_i, a KZG evaluation proof π_i consists of a commitment to the quotient polynomial $q_i(X)$. The latter is the solution to the following polynomial equation, which is checked by the verifier through pairings[9]:

$$(f_{\mathbf{a}}(X) - a_i) = q_i(X)(X - h_i)$$

The challenge that aSVC [TAB+20] addresses is how to *aggregate* multiple individual proofs $\pi_i = [q_i(\tau)]_1$ into a single constant-sized subvector proof *efficiently*. Their approach leverages partial fraction decomposition: they observe

[9] For concreteness, the pairing analogue of this equation is:

$$e\left([f_{\mathbf{a}}(\tau)]_1 - [a_i]_1, [1]_2\right) = e\left([q_i(\tau)]_1, [\tau]_2 - [h_i]_2\right).$$

that the quotient polynomial for a batch opening can be written as a linear combination $q(X) = \sum_{i \in I} c_i \cdot q_i(X)$, where the coefficients c_i depend on the derivative A'_I of the accumulator polynomial $A_I(X) = \prod_{j \in I}(X - h_j)$. Computing these coefficients requires evaluating A'_I at all points in I, which takes $O(\ell \log^2 \ell)$ field operations using subproduct trees and DFT-based techniques. The aggregated proof is then $\pi_I = \sum_{i \in I} c_i \cdot \pi_i$.

If one wants to achieve *linear-time* aggregation, a natural approach would be to find a scheme where precomputed proofs could simply be summed, i.e., computing $\pi^* = \sum_{i \in I} \pi_i$. However, this is not possible with standard KZG proofs—the quotient polynomials $q_i(X)$ have different denominators $(X - h_i)$, so their commitments are not directly additive in a useful way. This is precisely why aSVC must develop its more complex aggregation machinery. In this work, in order to obtain *linear-time* aggregation, we need to find an altogether different verification equation.

We derive such an equation by working with the product $p(X) := f_{\mathbf{a}}(X)\lambda_j(X)$ rather than the difference $f_{\mathbf{a}}(X) - a_j$. We then consider the division of this polynomial p by $t(X)$, the vanishing polynomial of $\mathbb{H}$. The key insight is that this division yields a verification equation with a particularly nice structure. The remainder of $p(X)/t(X)$ is $a_j\lambda_j(X)$ and, denoting by $q'_j(X)$ the resulting quotient, we: *i)* use as opening proof for position j simply $\pi_j = [q'_j(\tau)]_1$; *(ii)* let the verifier check the following polynomial equation (via pairings):

$$f_{\mathbf{a}}(X)\lambda_j(X) = q'_j(X) \cdot t(X) + a_j\lambda_j(X)$$

To see that this approach enables linear-time aggregation, consider what happens for two positions i and j. We have that:

$$f_{\mathbf{a}}(X)\underbrace{(\lambda_i(X) + \lambda_j(X))}_{\Lambda_{\mathsf{LHS}}} \equiv \underbrace{a_i\lambda_i(X) + a_j\lambda_j(X)}_{\Lambda_{\mathsf{RHS}}} \pmod{t(X)}$$

meaning that the sum of quotients $q'_i(X) + q'_j(X)$ is exactly the quotient for the combined opening. Consequently, the aggregated proof is simply $\pi^* = \pi_i + \pi_j$, a single group addition. This extends immediately to any subset I.

In order to reduce the computational burden for the verifier—who needs to compute Λ_{LHS} and Λ_{RHS} above—a natural choice is to encode these two terms in $\mathbb{G}_1$ (where group operations are cheaper). A simple corollary of this choice, by inspection of the equation above, is that the commitment to the vector (which encodes $f_{\boldsymbol{a}}(X)$) will lie in $\mathbb{G}_2$. We will later describe two variants of our scheme where the commitment lies in the group $\mathbb{G}_1$ offering different efficiency tradeoffs.

We observe several properties satisfied by our design. Besides the obvious homomorphic features of its commitments and the associativity of its proofs, we also show that it enables aggregation of proofs *across different commitments*[10]. Finally, by an observation connecting the structure of our proofs to that of KZG, we leverage known techniques for efficient preprocessing and updates.

[10] Through which, a client verifying k subvectors for as many commitments and index sets *at the same time*, can simply receive a single proof instead of k separate ones.

Outline of the Remainder of the Paper. We provide general background in Sect. 3. Our main scheme and its core correctness and security properties are presented in Sect. 4; in that same section we discuss cross-commitment aggregation. Variants of our scheme with commitment in $\mathbb{G}_1$ are in Sect. 5. The observations required to show an efficient preprocessing and updatability are discussed in Sect. 6. We describe our experimental evaluation in Sect. 7.

3 Preliminaries

3.1 General Background and Notation

Bilinear Groups. A bilinear group is described by a tuple $\mathsf{gk} = (p, \mathbb{G}_1, \mathbb{G}_2, \mathbb{G}_T, e)$ such that $\mathbb{G}_1, \mathbb{G}_2$ are cyclic (additive) groups of prime order p. We use the notation $[a]_1, [b]_2, [c]_t$ for elements in $\mathbb{G}_1, \mathbb{G}_2$ and $\mathbb{G}_T$ respectively and use the convention that $[1]_i$ denotes the generator for $\mathbb{G}_i$ and $[v] := v[1]_i$ for $v \in \mathbb{F}, i \in \{1, 2\}$. $e : \mathbb{G}_1 \times \mathbb{G}_2 \to \mathbb{G}_T$ is a bilinear asymmetric map (pairing), which means that $\forall a, b \in \mathbb{F}$, $e([a]_1, [b]_2) := [ab]_t$. We implicitly have that $[1]_t := e([1]_1, [1]_2)$ generates $\mathbb{G}_T$. We use $[a]_{1,2}$ to refer to the two group elements $[a]_1 \in \mathbb{G}_1, [a]_2 \in \mathbb{G}_2$. We denote by gk the group description $\mathsf{gk} = (p, \mathbb{G}_1, \mathbb{G}_2, \mathbb{G}_T, e)$ and by BGen the algorithm generating it on input a security parameter.

Algebraic Group Model. The algebraic group model (AGM) [FKL18] is a security framework where we consider only so-called algebraic adversaries. Such adversaries have direct access to group elements and, in particular, can use their bit representation, like in the standard model. However, these adversaries are assumed to be able to "explain" new group elements, showing how to apply group operations to received group elements. This requirement is formalized as follows: Suppose an adversary $\mathcal{A}$ is given some group elements $[x_1]_1, \ldots, [x_n]_1 \in \mathbb{G}_1$. Then, for every new group element $[z]_1 \in \mathbb{G}_1$ that the adversary outputs, it must also output $z_1, \ldots, z_n \in \mathbb{F}$ such that $[z]_1 = \sum_{i=1}^{n} z_i [x_i]_1$. The analogous requirement holds for elements in $\mathbb{G}_2$.

Cryptographic Assumptions. We will use the following assumptions.

Definition 1 (m-DLOG Assumption). *The m-Discrete Logarithm assumption holds with respect to a bilinear group generator* BGen *if for all* PPT *adversaries $\mathcal{A}$, the following probability is negligible in λ:*

$$\Pr\left[\tau \leftarrow \mathcal{A}\left(\mathsf{gk}, \left\{[\tau^i]_1\right\}_{i=0}^{m}, \left\{[\tau^i]_2\right\}_{i=0}^{m}\right) \;\middle|\; \mathsf{gk} \leftarrow \mathsf{BGen}(1^\lambda);\ \tau \leftarrow\$\, \mathbb{F}\right]$$

Definition 2 (SDH Assumption [BB04]). *The strong Diffie-Hellman assumption (SDH) holds with respect to a bilinear group generator* BGen *if for all* PPT *adversaries $\mathcal{A}$ and degree bound $m > 0$, we have that the following is negligible for $b \in \{1, 2\}$:*

$$\Pr\left[T = \left[\frac{1}{\tau + c}\right]_b \mid \mathsf{gk} \leftarrow \mathsf{BGen}(1^\lambda); \tau \leftarrow\$\, \mathbb{F}; S := \left\{\left[\tau^i\right]_{1,2}\right\}_{i=0}^{m}; (T, c) \leftarrow \mathcal{A}(\mathsf{gk}, S)\right]$$

Algebraic Preliminaries. Let $\omega \in \mathbb{F}$ be a primitive m-th root of unity, so $\omega^m = 1$ and $\omega^k \neq 1$ for $0 < k < m$. Define the set of all m-th roots of unity:

$$\mathbb{H} = \{1, \omega, \omega^2, \dots, \omega^{m-1}\}$$

We write $h_i = \omega^{i-1}$ for $i \in [m]$, so $\mathbb{H} = \{h_1, h_2, \dots, h_m\}$. The vanishing polynomial of $\mathbb{H}$ is: $t(X) = \prod_{i=1}^{m}(X - h_i) = X^m - 1$. The Lagrange polynomial $\lambda_i(X)$ is the unique polynomial of degree $m - 1$ satisfying:

$$\lambda_i(h_j) = \delta_{ij} = \begin{cases} 1 & \text{if } i = j \\ 0 & \text{if } i \neq j \end{cases}$$

Two ways of expressing the standard Lagrange interpolation formula are:

$$\lambda_i(X) = \frac{t(X)}{t'(h_i)(X - h_i)} = \frac{h_i \cdot t(X)}{m(X - h_i)} = \frac{h_i(X^m - 1)}{m(X - h_i)} \qquad (\star)$$

$$\lambda_i(X) = \frac{1}{m}\sum_{k=0}^{m-1} \omega^{-(i-1)k} X^k.$$

It is easy to see that $\lambda_i(0) = \frac{1}{m}$ for all $i \in [m]$. We will also use two simple properties of Lagrange polynomials—that for any $i, j \in [m], i \neq j$:

$$\lambda_i(X)\lambda_j(X) \equiv 0 \pmod{t(X)} \qquad \lambda_i(X)^2 \equiv \lambda_i(X) \pmod{t(X)}.$$

DFT. The Lagrange and monomial bases are related by the Discrete Fourier Transform (DFT). If $A(X) = \sum_{j=1}^{m} a_j \lambda_j(X) = \sum_{k=0}^{m-1} \hat{a}_k X^k$, then the coefficient vectors are related by $\mathbf{a} = F \cdot \hat{\mathbf{a}}$ and $\hat{\mathbf{a}} = \frac{1}{m}\bar{F} \cdot \mathbf{a}$, where F is the DFT matrix with entries $F_{i,k} = \omega^{(i-1)k}$ and $\bar{F}$ has entries $\bar{F}_{k,i} = \omega^{-(i-1)k}$.

3.2 Vector Commitments (VC)

Definition 3 (Vector Commitment). *A vector commitment scheme for vectors of length m consists of the following algorithms:*

- $\mathsf{VC.Setup}(1^\lambda, 1^m) \to \mathsf{pp}$: *On input security parameter λ and vector length m, outputs public parameters* pp.
- $\mathsf{VC.Commit}(\mathsf{pp}, \mathbf{a}) \to (\mathsf{cm}, \mathsf{aux})$: *On input parameters* pp *and a vector* $\mathbf{a} = (a_1, \dots, a_m) \in \mathbb{F}^m$, *outputs a commitment* cm *and auxiliary information* aux.
- $\mathsf{VC.OpenSingle}(\mathsf{pp}, \mathsf{aux}, i, a_i) \to \pi$: *On input public parameters* pp, *auxiliary information* aux, *position $i \in [m]$, and value a_i, outputs a proof π.*
- $\mathsf{VC.VfySingle}(\mathsf{pp}, \mathsf{cm}, i, v, \pi) \to \{0, 1\}$: *On input parameters* pp, *commitment* cm, *position $i \in [m]$, value v, and proof π, outputs 1 (accept) or 0 (reject).*

Definition 4 (VC Correctness). *A vector commitment is correct if for any $\lambda, m \in \mathbb{N}$, any vector $\mathbf{a} \in \mathbb{F}^m$, and any $i \in [m]$:*

$$\Pr\left[\mathsf{VC.VfySingle}(\mathsf{pp}, \mathsf{cm}, i, a_i, \pi) = 1 \;\middle|\; \begin{array}{l} \mathsf{pp} \leftarrow \mathsf{VC.Setup}(1^\lambda, 1^m) \\ (\mathsf{cm}, \mathsf{aux}) \leftarrow \mathsf{VC.Commit}(\mathsf{pp}, \mathbf{a}) \\ \pi \leftarrow \mathsf{VC.OpenSingle}(\mathsf{pp}, \mathsf{aux}, i, a_i) \end{array}\right] = 1$$

Definition 5 (VC Position Binding). *A vector commitment is position binding if for any PPT adversary $\mathcal{A}$ and any $\lambda, m \in \mathbb{N}$:*

$$\Pr\left[\begin{array}{c} \mathsf{VfySingle}(\mathsf{pp}, \mathsf{cm}, i, v, \pi) = 1 \wedge \\ \mathsf{VfySingle}(\mathsf{pp}, \mathsf{cm}, i, v', \pi') = 1 \wedge \\ v \neq v' \end{array} \;\middle|\; \begin{array}{l} \mathsf{pp} \leftarrow \mathsf{Setup}(1^\lambda, 1^m) \\ (\mathsf{cm}, i, v, \pi, v', \pi') \leftarrow \mathcal{A}(\mathsf{pp}) \end{array}\right] \leq \mathsf{negl}(\lambda)$$

3.3 Subvector Commitments (SVC)

Definition 6 (Subvector Commitment). *A subvector commitment scheme extends a vector commitment with the ability to open multiple positions simultaneously. It consists of the following algorithms:*

- $\mathsf{SVC.Setup}(1^\lambda, 1^m) \to \mathsf{pp}$*: On input security parameter λ and vector length m, outputs public parameters* pp.
- $\mathsf{SVC.Commit}(\mathsf{pp}, \mathbf{a}) \to (\mathsf{cm}, \mathsf{aux})$*: On input parameters* pp *and a vector $\mathbf{a} = (a_1, \ldots, a_m) \in \mathbb{F}^m$, outputs a commitment* cm *and auxiliary information* aux.
- $\mathsf{SVC.Precompute}(\mathsf{pp}, \mathsf{aux}) \to \mathsf{aux}'$*: On input public parameters* pp *and auxiliary information* aux*, outputs extended auxiliary information* aux' *that enables efficient subvector opening.*
- $\mathsf{SVC.OpenMultiple}(\mathsf{pp}, \mathsf{aux}', I, (a_i)_{i \in I}) \to \pi$*: On input public parameters* pp*, extended auxiliary information* aux'*, a set of positions $I \subseteq [m]$, and values $(a_i)_{i \in I}$, outputs a proof π.*
- $\mathsf{SVC.VfyMultiple}(\mathsf{pp}, \mathsf{cm}, I, (v_i)_{i \in I}, \pi) \to \{0, 1\}$*: On input public parameters* pp*, commitment* cm*, a set of positions $I \subseteq [m]$, values $(v_i)_{i \in I}$, and proof π, outputs 1 (accept) or 0 (reject).*

Definition 7 (SVC Correctness). *A subvector commitment is correct if for any $\lambda, m \subset \mathbb{N}$, any vector $\mathbf{a} \in \mathbb{F}^m$, and any $I \subseteq [m]$:*

$$\Pr\left[\begin{array}{r} \mathsf{VfyMultiple}(\mathsf{pp}, \mathsf{cm}, I, \qquad \\ (a_i)_{i \in I}, \pi) = 1 \end{array} \;\middle|\; \begin{array}{l} \mathsf{pp} \leftarrow \mathsf{Setup}(1^\lambda, 1^m) \\ (\mathsf{cm}, \mathsf{aux}) \leftarrow \mathsf{Commit}(\mathsf{pp}, \mathbf{a}) \\ \mathsf{aux}' \leftarrow \mathsf{Precompute}(\mathsf{pp}, \mathsf{aux}) \\ \pi \leftarrow \mathsf{OpenMultiple}(\mathsf{pp}, \mathsf{aux}', I, (a_i)_{i \in I}) \end{array}\right] = 1$$

Definition 8 (SVC Position Binding). *A subvector commitment is position binding if for any PPT adversary $\mathcal{A}$ and any $\lambda, m \in \mathbb{N}$ the following is negligible:*

$$\Pr\left[\begin{array}{c} \mathsf{VfyMultiple}(\mathsf{pp}, \mathsf{cm}, I, (v_i)_{i \in I}, \pi) = 1 \wedge \\ \mathsf{VfyMultiple}(\mathsf{pp}, \mathsf{cm}, I', (v'_i)_{i \in I'}, \pi') = 1 \wedge \\ \exists i^* \in I \cap I' : v_{i^*} \neq v'_{i^*} \end{array} \;\middle|\; \begin{array}{l} \mathsf{pp} \leftarrow \mathsf{Setup}(1^\lambda, 1^m) \\ (\mathsf{cm}, I, (v_i)_{i \in I}, \pi, \\ \qquad I', (v'_i)_{i \in I'}, \pi') \leftarrow \mathcal{A}(\mathsf{pp}) \end{array}\right]$$

4 Our Construction

Our construction is presented in Fig. 1. In that figure we proceed by describing our construction "incrementally", providing first a vector commitment with single opening and then augmenting it as an SVC with preprocessing.

4.1 Analysis of the Construction

The properties of our scheme will rely on the following fact:

Lemma 1. *Let $p \in \mathbb{F}[X]$ with $p(X) = \sum_{i \in [m]} a_i \lambda_i(X)$ and let $\mathbb{H} \subset \mathbb{F}$ a multiplicative subgroup of $\mathbb{F}$ of order m. For any $j \in [m]$*

$$p(X)\lambda_j(X) = q'_j(X)t(X) + a_j\lambda_j(X)$$

where $q'_j(X) = \frac{(p(X)-a_j)\lambda_j(X)}{t(X)} = \frac{h_j}{m(X-h_j)}(p(X) - a_j)$.

Proof. Consider the division of $p(X)\lambda_j(X)$ by $t(X)$, the vanishing polynomial in $\mathbb{H}$. Its remainder is $a_j\lambda_j(X)$. Indeed:

$$p(X)\lambda_j(X) \equiv a_1\lambda_1(X)\lambda_j(X) + \cdots + a_m\lambda_m(X)\lambda_j(X) \equiv a_j\lambda_j(X) \pmod{t(X)}$$

where above we used the simple properties on Lagrange polynomials described in Section 3. Notice that the degree of $a_j\lambda_j(X)$ is strictly less than m (the degree of t). We can then check, that using $q'(X)$ as defined above, we have:

$$\begin{aligned}
&p(X)\lambda_j(X) - q'_j(X)t(X) - a_j\lambda_j(X)\\
&= p(X)\lambda_j(X) - \frac{h_j t(X)}{m(X-h_j)}(p(X) - a_j) - a_j\lambda_j(X)\\
&= p(X)\lambda_j(X) - \lambda_j(X)(p(X) - a_j) - a_j\lambda_j(X) = 0
\end{aligned}$$

where above we used the equivalent description of λ_j in ($\star$). □

Theorem 1. *The scheme* VC *(resp.* SVC*) in Fig. 1 is correct.*

Proof. This follows immediately by inspection and by applying Lemma 1. □

Theorem 2. *The scheme* VC *in Fig. 1 satisfies position binding for single opening under the SDH Assumption (Definition 2).*

Proof. Consider an adversary that provides commitment cm, two accepting proofs π, π' for respective claims (i, v), (i, v') with $v \neq v'$. We know that:

$$e([\lambda_i(\tau)]_1, \mathsf{cm}) = v \cdot e([\lambda_i(\tau)]_1, [1]_2) + e(\pi, [t(\tau)]_2) \quad (1)$$

$$e([\lambda_i(\tau)]_1, \mathsf{cm}) = v' \cdot e([\lambda_i(\tau)]_1, [1]_2) + e(\pi', [t(\tau)]_2) \quad (2)$$

$\mathsf{Setup}(1^\lambda, 1^m)$:

1. Generate bilinear group $\mathsf{gk} = (p, \mathbb{G}_1, \mathbb{G}_2, \mathbb{G}_T, e)$.
2. Sample $\tau \leftarrow \mathbb{F}$
3. Compute $[\lambda_i(\tau)]_1$, $[\lambda_i(\tau)]_2$ for $i \in [m]$ (see Section 6). Compute $[t(\tau)]_2$.
4. Output[a] $\mathsf{pp} = \left(\mathsf{gk}, \left([\tau^i]_{1,2}\right)_{i=1}^m, \left([\lambda_i(\tau)]_{1,2}\right)_{i=1}^m, [t(\tau)]_2\right)$.

$\mathsf{VC.Commit}(\mathsf{pp}, \boldsymbol{a})$:

1. Compute $\mathsf{cm} = \sum_{j=1}^{m} a_j [\lambda_j(\tau)]_2$
2. Output $(\mathsf{cm}, \mathsf{aux} = f_a)$ where $f_a(X) := \sum_i a_i \lambda_i(X)$.

$\mathsf{VC.OpenSingle}(\mathsf{pp}, \mathsf{aux}, i, a_i)$:

1. Compute[b] $q'_i(X) := \frac{f_a(X)\lambda_i(X) - a_i \lambda_i(X)}{t(X)}$.
2. Output $\pi_i = \sum_{j \in [m]} q'_i(h_j)[\lambda_j(\tau)]_1$ // i.e., $\pi_i = [q'_i(\tau)]_1$

$\mathsf{VC.VfySingle}(\mathsf{pp}, \mathsf{cm}, i, v, \pi)$: Accept iff this holds:

$$e\Big([\lambda_i(\tau)]_1, \mathsf{cm}\Big) = e\Big(v \cdot [\lambda_i(\tau)]_1, [1]_2\Big)) + e\Big(\pi, [t(\tau)]_2\Big)$$

$\mathsf{SVC.Commit}(\mathsf{pp}, \boldsymbol{a})$: // identical to VC.Commit

1. Compute $\mathsf{cm} = \sum_{j=1}^{m} a_j [\lambda_j(\tau)]_2$
2. Output $(\mathsf{cm}, \mathsf{aux} = f_a)$ where $f_a(X) := \sum_i a_i \lambda_i(X)$.

$\mathsf{SVC.Precompute}(\mathsf{pp}, \mathsf{aux})$:

1. Compute $\pi_i \leftarrow \mathsf{VC.OpenSingle}(\mathsf{pp}, \mathsf{aux})$ for all i (see also Section 6).
2. Output $\mathsf{aux}' = \mathsf{aux} || (\pi_i)_{i \in [m]}$

$\mathsf{SVC.OpenMultiple}(\mathsf{pp}, \mathsf{aux}, I = (i_1, \ldots, i_\ell), (a_i)_{i \in I})$:

1. Output $\pi^* = \sum_{i \in I} \pi_i$

$\mathsf{SVC.VfyMultiple}(\mathsf{pp}, I = (i_1, \ldots, i_\ell), (v_i)_{i \in I}, \pi^*)$:

1. Let $\Lambda^*_{\mathrm{LHS}} = \sum_{i \in I} [\lambda_i(\tau)]_1$ and $\Lambda^*_{\mathrm{RHS}} = \sum_{i \in I} v_i [\lambda_i(\tau)]_1$.
2. Accept iff this holds:

$$e\Big(\Lambda^*_{\mathrm{LHS}}, \mathsf{cm}\Big) = e\Big(\Lambda^*_{\mathrm{RHS}}, [1]_2\Big) + e\Big(\pi^*, [t(\tau)]_2\Big)$$

[a] Not all the elements in pp are necessary for this construction. Having redundant elements allows us to simply reuse these public parameters for the variants in Section 5. See also discussion in Remark 2.

[b] See also discussion in Section 6 for an efficient way of computing it.

Fig. 1. Our main construction of VC (single opening) and SVC (subvector opening).

Let us look at what the above implies for the discrete logarithms in $\mathbb{G}_1$. By subtracting Eq. (1) from Eq. (2), we can conclude:

$$
\begin{aligned}
(v - v')\,\lambda_i(\tau) = \mathsf{dlog}_{\mathbb{G}_1}(\pi' - \pi)t(\tau) &\Longrightarrow (v - v')\,\frac{h_i t(\tau)}{m\,(\tau - h_i)} = \mathsf{dlog}_{\mathbb{G}_1}(\pi' - \pi)t(\tau) \\
&\xrightarrow[\text{probability}]{\text{but with negligible}} (v - v')\,\frac{h_i}{m\,(\tau - h_i)} = \mathsf{dlog}_{\mathbb{G}_1}(\pi' - \pi) \\
&\Longrightarrow \frac{1}{\tau - h_i} = m\frac{\mathsf{dlog}_{\mathbb{G}_1}(\pi' - \pi)}{h_i(v - v')} \\
&\Longrightarrow \left[\frac{1}{\tau - h_i}\right]_1 = \frac{m}{h_i(v - v')}\,(\pi - \pi')
\end{aligned}
$$

This directly leads to a way to break SDH (Definition 2): the adversary can simply provide $\left(T = \frac{m}{h_i(v-v')}\,(\pi - \pi')\,, c = -h_i\right)$. Notice that the extra elements in pp do not give any extra power to the adversary as they can be computed in polynomial time by the input given in Definition 2. This concludes the proof. □

Theorem 3. *The scheme* SVC *in Fig. 1 satisfies position binding for multiple openings in the AGM under the Discrete Logarithm Assumption.*

A proof of Theorem 3 is in the full version of this paper [Cam26].

4.2 Additional Property: Cross-Commitment Aggregation

Our construction extends naturally to support cross-commitment aggregation as defined in [GRWZ20]. This property (informally) states that a prover can prove the opening of multiple commitments at the same time by providing a single proof. We describe the case of two commitments; the general case follows analogously. The blueprint below can be made non-interactive in the random oracle model (we stress that we rely on the random oracle only for the case of cross-commitment aggregation). A security argument is in the full version [Cam26].

Given commitments $\mathsf{cm}, \tilde{\mathsf{cm}}$ to vectors $\boldsymbol{a}, \tilde{\boldsymbol{a}}$ respectively, with corresponding subvector openings $(I, (a_i)_{i\in I})$ and $(\tilde{I}, (\tilde{a}_i)_{i\in\tilde{I}})$ and proofs $\pi^*, \tilde{\pi}^*$, we define the aggregated proof as $\pi := \alpha \cdot \pi^* + \tilde{\alpha} \cdot \tilde{\pi}^*$ where $\alpha, \tilde{\alpha} \leftarrow \mathbb{F}$ are random challenges. Then, the verifier: computes $\Lambda_{\mathsf{LHS}} = \sum_{i\in I}[\lambda_i(\tau)]_1$, $\tilde{\Lambda}_{\mathsf{LHS}} = \sum_{i\in\tilde{I}}[\lambda_i(\tau)]_1$, $\Lambda_{\mathsf{RHS}} = \sum_{i\in I} v_i[\lambda_i(\tau)]_1$, $\tilde{\Lambda}_{\mathsf{RHS}} = \sum_{i\in\tilde{I}} \tilde{v}_i[\lambda_i(\tau)]_1$ ($v_i, \tilde{v}_i$ are claimed values); it accepts iff:

$$
e\,(\alpha \cdot \Lambda_{\mathsf{LHS}}, \mathsf{cm}) + e\left(\tilde{\alpha} \cdot \tilde{\Lambda}_{\mathsf{LHS}}, \tilde{\mathsf{cm}}\right) = e\left(\alpha \cdot \Lambda_{\mathsf{RHS}} + \tilde{\alpha} \cdot \tilde{\Lambda}_{\mathsf{RHS}}, [1]_2\right) + e\,(\pi, [t(\tau)]_2)
$$

5 Constructions with Commitment in $\mathbb{G}_1$

It is possible to modify our construction in Sect. 4 to have a commitment in $\mathbb{G}_1$. However, this change requires the verifier to use terms $[\lambda_i(\tau)]_2$ in $\mathbb{G}_2$. When verifying subvector opening, this implies that either the prover or the verifier must perform such operations. We thus show two variants, both with commitment in $\mathbb{G}_1$, optimized respectively for proving and verification:

- $\Pi^{\mathsf{fastP}}_{\mathbb{G}_1}$, where the prover performs exclusively group operations in $\mathbb{G}_1$;
- $\Pi^{\mathsf{fastV}}_{\mathbb{G}_1}$, where the verifier performs exclusively[11] group operations in $\mathbb{G}_1$.

In both variants the commitment algorithm, on input a vector $\boldsymbol{a}$, computes $\mathsf{cm} = \sum_j a_j[\lambda_j(\tau)]_1$. The preprocessing stage works as in the main scheme.

We describe our constructions as we did in Fig. 1, i.e., proceeding incrementally the subvector case from the single opening setting. In both cases the security argument is essentially the same as the one provided for our main construction.

5.1 The Construction $\Pi^{\mathsf{fastP}}_{\mathbb{G}_1}$

Single Opening. The single opening prover is exactly as in Fig. 1. The single opening verifier accepts iff the following holds:

$$e\Big(\mathsf{cm}, [\lambda_i(\tau)]_2\Big) = e\Big(v \cdot [\lambda_i(\tau)]_1, [1]_2\Big)\Big) + e\Big(\pi, [t(\tau)]_2\Big)$$

The only change with the original construction above is in switching the terms in the pairing on the left-hand side.

Subvector opening. The prover proceeds exactly as in Fig. 1. The verifier, on input a proof π^* and a subvector $\boldsymbol{v} = \{v_i\}_{i \in I}$ with $I = \{i_1, \ldots, i_\ell\}$, computes:

$$\Lambda^*_{\mathrm{LHS}} = \sum_{i \in I} [\lambda_i(\tau)]_2 \qquad \Lambda^*_{\mathrm{RHS}} = \sum_{i \in I} v_i\,[\lambda_i(\tau)]_1$$

and checks: $e\Big(\mathsf{cm}, \Lambda^*_{\mathrm{LHS}}\Big) = e\Big(\Lambda^*_{\mathrm{RHS}}, [1]_2\Big) + e\Big(\pi^*, [t(\tau)]_2\Big)$.

5.2 The Construction $\Pi^{\mathsf{fastV}}_{\mathbb{G}_1}$

This variant essentially works by delegating the verifier's $\mathbb{G}_2$ operations in $\Pi^{\mathsf{fastP}}_{\mathbb{G}_1}$ to the prover. The verifier performs an additional check to ensure that the discrete logarithm of the $\mathbb{G}_2$ element provided by the prover is the expected one.

Single Opening. The single opening prover and verifier are the same as in $\Pi^{\mathsf{fastP}}_{\mathbb{G}_1}$.

Subvector Opening. On input a set of indices I, the prover outputs $(\pi^*, \Lambda^*_{\mathrm{LHS}})$ with $\pi^* = \sum_{i \in I} \pi_i$ (as in the main scheme) and $\Lambda^*_{\mathrm{LHS}} = \sum_{i \in I} [\lambda_i(\tau)]_2$.

The verifier, on input a proof π^* and a subvector $\boldsymbol{v} = \{v_i\}_{i \in I}$, computes:

$$\Lambda^{(\mathrm{check})}_{\mathrm{LHS}} = \sum_{i \in I} [\lambda_i(\tau)]_1 \qquad \Lambda^*_{\mathrm{RHS}} = \sum_{i \in I} v_i\,[\lambda_i(\tau)]_1$$

and checks the following two equations:

$$e\Big(\mathsf{cm}, \Lambda^*_{\mathrm{LHS}}\Big) = e\Big(\Lambda^*_{\mathrm{RHS}}, [1]_2\Big) + e\Big(\pi^*, [t(\tau)]_2\Big) \quad e\Big([1]_1, \Lambda^*_{\mathrm{LHS}}\Big) = e\Big(\Lambda^{(\mathrm{check})}_{\mathrm{LHS}}, [1]_2\Big)$$

Remark 1 (Optimizing the verifier in $\Pi^{\mathsf{fastV}}_{\mathbb{G}_1}$). We can exploit the special structure of the two pairing equations above and reduce them to a single one as follows. The verifier samples a random $\rho \leftarrow\!\$\, \mathbb{F}$ and then checks the equation:

$$e\Big(\mathsf{cm} + \rho[1]_1, \Lambda^*_{\mathrm{LHS}}\Big) = e\Big(\Lambda^*_{\mathrm{RHS}} + \rho\Lambda^{(\mathrm{check})}_{\mathrm{LHS}}, [1]_2\Big) + e\Big(\pi^*, [t(\tau)]_2\Big)$$

---

[11] In addition to 3 pairings.

6 Preprocessing in Quasi-Linear Time and Updatability

In this section we observe how the structure of our proofs and those in KZG are related (Sect. 6.1). This has three implications: computing our individual openings *only requires linear time*; for subvector opening, we can preprocess all individual proofs in $O(m \log m)$ time using techniques from [FK23] (Sect. 6.2); updating proofs can be performed efficiently following [TAB+20] (Sect. 6.3).

6.1 A First Observation on the Structure of Our Proofs

The proof π_i for position i is defined as $\pi_i = [q_i'(\tau)]_1$ where $q_i'(X) = \frac{(f_a(X)-a_i)\lambda_i(X)}{t(X)}$ and $f_a(X) = \sum_{j=1}^{m} a_j \lambda_j(X)$ is the polynomial encoding of the committed vector. Using the identity $\lambda_i(X) = \frac{h_i \cdot t(X)}{m(X-h_i)}$ from Eq. ($\star$), we can rewrite:

$$q_i'(X) = \frac{\lambda_i(X)}{t(X)} \cdot (f_a(X) - a_i) = \frac{h_i}{m} \cdot \frac{f_a(X) - a_i}{X - h_i} = \frac{h_i}{m} q_i(X)$$

where above we defined q_i as $q_i(X) := \frac{f_a(X)-a_i}{X-h_i}$. The polynomial $q_i(X)$ also corresponds to the quotient polynomial used in the KZG evaluation proof that $f_a(h_i) = a_i$. We can thus compute our openings by computing KZG proofs and the scaling them appropriately, i.e. we can compute $\pi_i = [q_i'(\tau)]_1 = \frac{h_i}{m} \cdot [q_i(\tau)]_1$. Moreover, as a consequence our individual opening proofs can be computed in linear time since computing the quotients $q_i(X)$ consists mainly of a simple shift of coefficients together with an appropriate rescaling[12]. In the next subsection we discuss how to compute all m quotients $[q_i(\tau)]_1$ efficiently.

6.2 Efficiently Computing All Individual Proofs π_i

Here we provide a self-contained description of the techniques from [FK23], which we can leverage in order to compute our proofs. In a nutshell: all quotients $[q_i(\tau)]_1$ can be expressed as evaluations of a single (formal) polynomial with coefficients in $\mathbb{G}_1$. Let $f_a(X) = \sum_{k=0}^{m-1} \hat{a}_k X^k$ be the *monomial* representation of the committed polynomial. We can compute $(\hat{a}_0, \ldots, \hat{a}_{m-1})$ by an inverse DFT from $(a_1, \ldots, a_m)$. We provide a proof of the following lemma in the full version of this paper [Cam26].

Lemma 2 (FK Lemma [FK23]**).** *For all $i \in [m]$, we have $[q_i(\tau)]_1 = P(h_i)$ where $P(X) = \sum_{j=1}^{m-1} P_j X^{j-1}$, and we define the coefficients $P_j \in \mathbb{G}_1$ as:*

$$P_j = \sum_{k=j}^{m-1} \hat{a}_k [\tau^{k-j}]_1 = \hat{a}_{m-1}[\tau^{m-1-j}]_1 + \hat{a}_{m-2}[\tau^{m-2-j}]_1 + \cdots + \hat{a}_j [1]_1$$

[12] This is fairly immediate to show and well known. See, e.g., [FK23, §1.2].

An implication of the statement above is that computing P at all points $\{h_1, \ldots, h_m\}$ gives us the values we were looking for. Since these points correspond to the m-th roots of unity, computing all $P(h_i)$ simultaneously is exactly an FFT of the coefficient vector $(P_1, \ldots, P_{m-1}, 0)$ over the group $\mathbb{G}_1$.

Computing the Coefficients of P via Toeplitz Multiplication. It remains to show how to compute the coefficients $(P_1, \ldots, P_{m-1})$ efficiently. Observe that:

$$\begin{pmatrix} P_1 \\ P_2 \\ P_3 \\ \vdots \\ P_{m-1} \end{pmatrix} = \begin{pmatrix} \hat{a}_{m-1} & \hat{a}_{m-2} & \hat{a}_{m-3} & \cdots & \hat{a}_1 \\ 0 & \hat{a}_{m-1} & \hat{a}_{m-2} & \cdots & \hat{a}_2 \\ 0 & 0 & \hat{a}_{m-1} & \cdots & \hat{a}_3 \\ \vdots & & & \ddots & \vdots \\ 0 & 0 & 0 & \cdots & \hat{a}_{m-1} \end{pmatrix} \begin{pmatrix} [\tau^{m-2}]_1 \\ [\tau^{m-3}]_1 \\ [\tau^{m-4}]_1 \\ \vdots \\ [1]_1 \end{pmatrix}$$

This is a multiplication of an upper-triangular Toeplitz matrix by a vector of group elements. A description of how to compute it in $O(m \log m)$ time by embedding into a circulant matrix and using FFT, together with the complete preprocessing algorithm, is in the full version of this paper [Cam26].

Remark 2 (Efficiently deriving the $[\lambda(\tau)]_{1,2}$ parameters without τ). Recall from Fig. 1 that the verifier in our scheme(s) requires some terms encoding the Lagrange polynomials in the group. These can be computed in time $O(m \log m)$ from a standard KZG-style setup even without having the secret point τ and can be carried out using techniques similar to those described above (we stress, however, that deriving these parameters is a once-and-for-all and vector-independent step). Recall that the Lagrange polynomials satisfy $\lambda_i(X) = \frac{1}{m}\sum_{k=0}^{m-1} \omega^{-(i-1)k} X^k$, so evaluating at τ and encoding in $\mathbb{G}_1$ gives $[\lambda_i(\tau)]_1 = \frac{1}{m}\sum_{k=0}^{m-1} \omega^{-(i-1)k}[\tau^k]_1$. This is precisely an inverse DFT over the group $\mathbb{G}_1$ of the vector $\left([\tau^j]_1\right)_{j=0}^{m-1}$. We can compute all $[\lambda_i(\tau)]_{1,2}$ via two inverse FFTs over $\mathbb{G}_1$ and $\mathbb{G}_2$ respectively. The overall running time for this parameter derivation step is in the same ballpark as that of precomputing all individual proofs.

6.3 Updatability of Our Construction

Our commitments are immediately updatable using standard techniques: when any entry a_k of the committed vector changes by δ we compute the updated commitment as $\mathsf{cm}' \leftarrow \mathsf{cm} + \delta \cdot [\lambda_k(\tau)]_i$ in the appropriate group $\mathbb{G}_i$. Since the proofs in our construction are scalar multiples of standard KZG evaluation proofs, we can directly apply the mechanism developed for aSVC [TAB+20] based on *update keys*. Update keys are small, position-dependent auxiliary data that enable efficient local proof maintenance: when a vector entry changes, any proof-holder can update their proof in constant time without access to the full vector. Each update key $\mathsf{upk}_j = (\alpha_j, u_j)$ consists of two group elements that can be precomputed during setup, and all m update keys can be computed in $O(m \log m)$ time using DFT-based techniques. Given these keys, when any entry

a_k of the committed vector changes by δ, a proof π_j for any j can be updated to a valid proof with respect to the new commitment in $O(1)$ time, using only upk_j and upk_k. A self-contained description of this mechanism is in the full version of this paper [Cam26].

7 Experimental Evaluation

Here we describe our implementation and our experimental results comparing our constructions to aSVC [TAB+20].

Experimental Setup. We implement aSVC [TAB+20], our main scheme and our two variants in Rust on top of the arkworks library [ark22]. The code is available at:

https://github.com/matteocam/linear-time-svc

As an instantiation for the bilinear setting we adopt the curve BLS12-381, which provides ≈128 bits of security. Unless stated otherwise, our benchmarks are run *single-threaded.* The machine we use for our experiments is a common laptop, specifically a Mac Book Air with Apple M2 CPU (8 cores) and 24 GB of RAM. We summarize the results for our main construction in Fig. 2.

7.1 Evaluating Our Main Construction

Preprocessing Time. The time to compute all proofs is essentially the same in both aSVC and our scheme (our preprocessing requires exactly m additional group operations but otherwise it is the same). It takes ≈20 min for $m = 2^{17}$.

Commitment Size and Commitment Time. Our main construction requires committing to the vector in $\mathbb{G}_2$. This implies that our commitment is twice as large in comparison to aSVC and our variants (96B instead of 48B). Also, this implies an additional overhead in our main scheme for computing the commitment (due to $\mathbb{G}_2$ operations being more expensive than their $\mathbb{G}_1$ counterparts). Our experiments show that this consistently yields a 3× slowdown compared to aSVC and our two variants. We believe that, in many settings, the additional costs for commitment times may not be significant because: *i)* committing is a one-off operation; *ii)* the actual commitment times are relatively low (our scheme can commit to a vector of size $\approx 1M$ in less than half a minute without using any special hardware). In settings where commitment size is crucial (or it is crucial to have compatibility with other schemes using the same type of $\mathbb{G}_1$ commitment to the vector), our two variants offer a viable alternative. As we show later in this section, they still provide substantial speedups compared to aSVC.

Opening Time. We measure opening time and verification (see below) on relevant opening sizes (up to $\ell \approx$ 64K) for a vector of size $m \approx 130K$. For the largest subvectors our construction achieves massive speedups (≈4000×) and can provide an opening within 30ms, in contrast to aSVC which requires approximately two minutes. We also observe large improvements at small vectors, in particular a 62× speedup for small subvectors (ℓ=4) and over 100× speedups from $\ell \approx 32$.

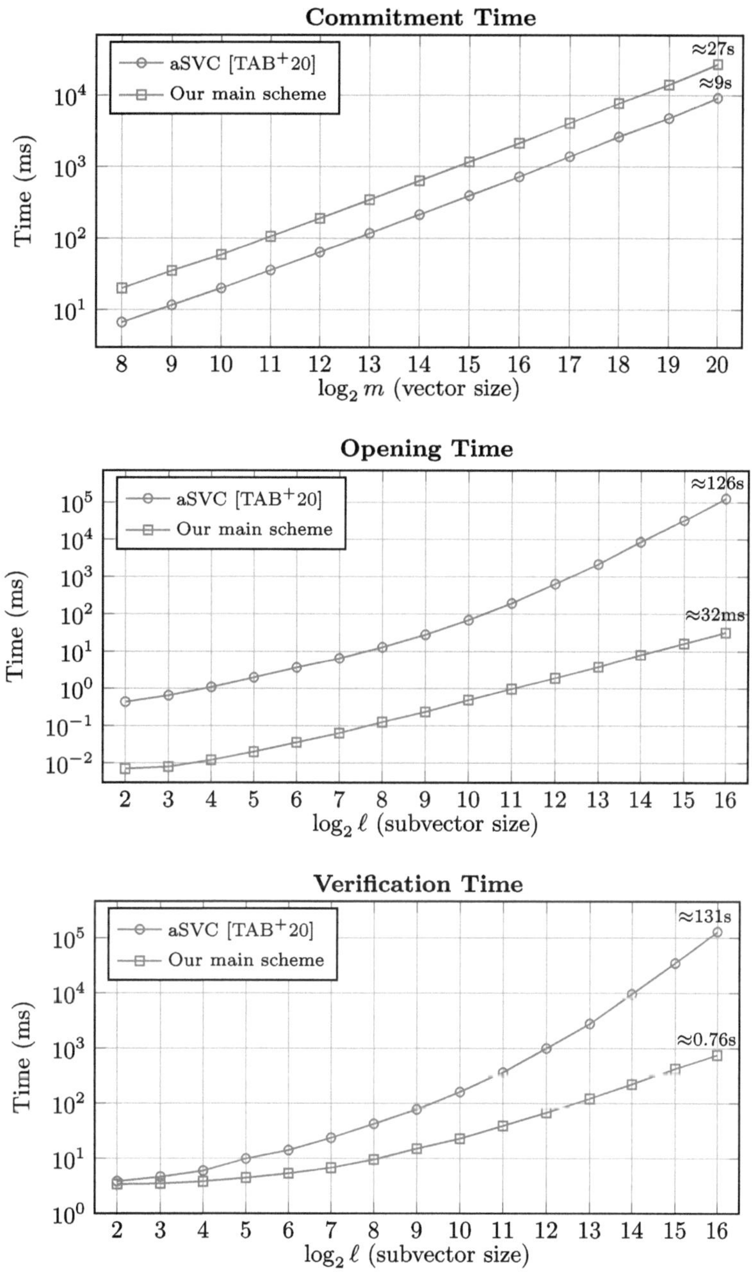

Fig. 2. Performance comparison of aSVC and our main scheme (single-threaded). Top: Commitment time as a function of vector size m (from 2^8 to 2^{20}). Middle and bottom: Opening and verification times for $m = 2^{17}$ as a function of subvector size ℓ (log-log scale).

Verification Time. For the large subvectors our construction achieves significant speedups (≈170×) and can verify an opening in ≈ 0.7s, in contrast to aSVC which requires more than two minutes. The speedups for the smallest subvector sizes ($\ell \leq 8$) are moderate (13%–57% faster than aSVC), but we start observing noticeable speedups starting from relatively small subvectors—over 2× for $\ell \approx 32$, with improvements growing consistently as subvector size increases. As we discuss later in this section, for verification, we can obtain even larger speedups when comparing the two constructions if we exploit parallelism.

7.2 Additional Discussion

The Effects of Parallelism on Verification Time. We also evaluate our main scheme against aSVC when running both of them using parallel features of the library arkworks. In general, parallelism has minor effects with the exception of our verifier. Our aggregation algorithm performs ℓ additions among group elements and its running times stay the same. For aSVC, the running times of both opening and verification see relatively minor improvements[13], plausibly due to the reliance on FFTs in both algorithms. Our verification algorithm consists of ℓ $\mathbb{G}_1$ operations and one multi-scalar multiplication in $\mathbb{G}_1$. The latter gets substantially optimized through parallelism and as a consequence we obtain a 10× speedup against aSVC already at $\ell = 256$ and over 750× speedup for $\ell \approx 64K$ (with a verification time of ≈ 170ms, 4× faster than single-threaded execution).

Evaluating Our Variants. Because of their efficiency profile (see Table 1), our variants show that one can obtain roughly the same large speedups of our main scheme while also having a commitment in $\mathbb{G}_1$. For our prover-optimized variant ($\Pi_{\mathbb{G}_1}^{\mathsf{fastP}}$), the improvements for opening times over aSVC are exactly the same as those of our main scheme. The verifier in $\Pi_{\mathbb{G}_1}^{\mathsf{fastP}}$ shows milder speedups over aSVC at the same opening sizes compared to our main construction. For example, it is 40% faster at $\ell = 64$ and ≈ 3× faster at $\ell \approx 1500$ than aSVC. Opening times for our verifier-optimized variant ($\Pi_{\mathbb{G}_1}^{\mathsf{fastV}}$) are generally 3–4× higher than in our main scheme; despite this, they still show large speedups over aSVC, e.g. ≈ 30× at $\ell = 16$ and ≈ 54× at $\ell = 2048$ (improving further with parallelism).

The Role of $\mathbb{G}_2$ Operations in the aSVC Verifier. The dominant costs in the aSVC verifier stem from the $O(\ell \log^2 \ell)$ field operations and the multi-scalar multiplication (MSM) in $\mathbb{G}_2$. There exist, however, standard techniques that allow delegating this MSM to the prover by replacing it with ≈ ℓ field operations and one additional pairing. This modification—which also adds one extra $\mathbb{G}_2$ element to the final aSVC proof—is described, e.g., in Appendix I of [BBC+25].

[13] This is especially true for opening, where the improvements are always below 10% compared to the times in Fig. 2. For verification, aSVC obtains a 10% (or less) speedup at most values of ℓ but we observe a more noticeable improvement (≈ 30%) for ℓ in the range 2^9–2^{12}.

As a sanity check around the *robustness* of our claimed speedups, we have also investigated whether they would hold against this optimized variant of the aSVC verifier. We find, however, that such a change in aSVC would have marginal consequences: from our measurements, this MSM contributes to approximately 30–50% of the time in the aSVC verifier for $\ell \leq 2048$, after which point an overwhelming fraction of the running time consists of field operations (e.g., the MSM takes less than a 4% fraction at $\ell = 32768$). This implies that, on any subvector size, *even if* we considered the MSM *completely free* in the aSVC verifier, we would obtain at most a 2× speedup in aSVC; yet, our construction would still be 10× faster on most subvector sizes. On small subvectors, e.g. $\ell \leq 16$—where the impact of the MSM in aSVC is relatively low—the benefits would not be sufficient to see any substantial change.

Acknowledgments. I am grateful to Ed Felten, Mahak Pancholi and Victor Shoup for the encouraging and insightful discussions, and to the anonymous reviewers, whose comments improved this work. Huge thanks to Dario Fiore for the knowledgeable and generous feedback. Finally, thanks to Domenico Campanelli and Rita Fumarola for (somewhat) tolerating academic writing at their place during the holiday season (and for all the food fueling it, of course).

This work was supported by the Estonian Research Council grant PRG2531.

References

ABC+24. Ateniese, G., Baldimtsi, F., Campanelli, M., Francati, D., Karantaidou, I.: Advancing scalability in decentralized storage: a novel approach to proof-of-replication via polynomial evaluation. In: Reyzin, L., Stebila, D. (eds.) CRYPTO 2024, Part II, vol. 14921. LNCS, pp. 3–39, Santa Barbara, CA, USA, August 18–22, 2024. Springer, Cham, Switzerland (2024). https://doi.org/10.1007/978-3-031-68379-4_1

ale21. ALEO trusted setup (2021). https://setup.aleo.org/

AR20. Agrawal, S., Raghuraman, S.: KVaC: key-value commitments for blockchains and beyond. In: Moriai, S., Wang, H. (eds.) ASIACRYPT 2020. LNCS, vol. 12493, pp. 839–869. Springer, Cham (2020). https://doi.org/10.1007/978-3-030-64840-4_28

ark22. Arkworks contributors: arkworks ZKSNARK ecosystem (2022). https://arkworks.rs

axi25. Axiom trusted ceremony (2025). https://web.archive.org/web/20250120135649/https://docs.axiom.xyz/docs/transparency-and-security/kzg-trusted-setup

BB04. Boneh, D., Boyen, X.: Efficient selective-ID secure identity based encryption without random oracles. In: Cachin, C., Camenisch, J.L. (eds.) EUROCRYPT 2004, vol. 3027. LNCS, pp. 223–238, Interlaken, Switzerland, May 2–6, 2004. Springer Berlin Heidelberg, Germany (2004). https://doi.org/10.1007/978-3-540-24676-3_14

BBC+25. Botta, V., Bottoni, S., Campanelli, M., Ragnoli, E., Trombetta, A.: QEDB: expressive and modular verifiable databases (without SNARKs). Cryptology ePrint Archive, Report 2025/1408 (2025)

BBF19. Boneh, D., Bünz, B., Fisch, B.: Batching techniques for accumulators with applications to IOPs and stateless blockchains. In: Boldyreva, A., Micciancio, D. (eds.) CRYPTO 2019. LNCS, vol. 11692, pp. 561–586. Springer, Cham (2019). https://doi.org/10.1007/978-3-030-26948-7_20

BCC+17. Bitansky, N., et al.: The hunting of the SNARK. J. Cryptol. **30**(4), 989–1066 (2017)

BFB+24. Buterin, V., Feist, D., Ballet, G., Merriam, P., Herold, G.: EIP-6800: Ethereum state using VERKLE trees (2024). https://eips.ethereum.org/EIPS/eip-6800

BFL+22. Buterin, V., et al.: EIP-4844: shard blob transactions. Ethereum Improvement Proposals, February (2022). Deployed on Ethereum mainnet March 13, 2024 (Dencun upgrade)

BGV11. Benabbas, S., Gennaro, R., Vahlis, Y.: Verifiable delegation of computation over large datasets. In: Rogaway, P. (ed.) CRYPTO 2011. LNCS, vol. 6841, pp. 111–131. Springer, Heidelberg (2011). https://doi.org/10.1007/978-3-642-22792-9_7

Cam26. Campanelli, M.: Practical subvector commitments with optimal opening complexity. Cryptology ePrint Archive, Paper 2026/118 (2026)

CEO22. Campanelli, M., Engelmann, F., Orlandi, C.: Zero-knowledge for homomorphic key-value commitments with applications to privacy-preserving ledgers. In: Galdi, C., Jarecki, S. (eds.) SCN 22, vol. 13409. LNCS, pp. 761–784, Amalfi, Italy, September 12–14, 2022. Springer, Cham, Switzerland (2022). https://doi.org/10.1007/978-3-031-14791-3_33

CF13. Catalano, D., Fiore, D.: Vector commitments and their applications. In: Kurosawa, K., Hanaoka, G. (eds.) PKC 2013. LNCS, vol. 7778, pp. 55–72. Springer, Heidelberg (2013). https://doi.org/10.1007/978-3-642-36362-7_5

CFF+21. Campanelli, M., Faonio, A., Fiore, D., Querol, A., Rodríguez, H.: Lunar: a toolbox for more efficient universal and updatable zkSNARKs and commit-and-prove extensions. In: Tibouchi, M., Wang, H. (eds.) ASIACRYPT 2021, Part III, vol. 13092. LNCS, pp. 3–33, Singapore, December 6–10, 2021. Springer, Cham, Switzerland (2021). https://doi.org/10.1007/978-3-030-92078-4_1

CFG+20. Campanelli, M., Fiore, D., Greco, N., Kolonelos, D., Nizzardo, L.: Incrementally aggregatable vector commitments and applications to verifiable decentralized storage. In: Moriai, S., Wang, H. (eds.) ASIACRYPT 2020. LNCS, vol. 12492, pp. 3–35. Springer, Cham (2020). https://doi.org/10.1007/978-3-030-64834-3_1

CHAK23. Campanelli, M., Hall-Andersen, M., Kamp, S.H.: Curve trees: practical and transparent zero-knowledge accumulators. In: Calandrino, J.A., Troncoso, C. (eds.) USENIX Security 2023, pp. 4391–4408, Anaheim, CA, USA, August 9–11, 2023 (2023) USENIX Association

CHM+20. Chiesa, A., Hu, Y., Maller, M., Mishra, P., Vesely, N., Ward, N.: Marlin: preprocessing zkSNARKs with universal and updatable SRS. In: Canteaut, A., Ishai, Y. (eds.) EUROCRYPT 2020. LNCS, vol. 12105, pp. 738–768. Springer, Cham (2020). https://doi.org/10.1007/978-3-030-45721-1_26

CNR+22. Campanelli, M., Nitulescu, A., Ràfols, C., Zacharakis, A., Zapico, A.: Linear-map vector commitments and their practical applications. In: Agrawal, S., Lin, D. (eds.) ASIACRYPT 2022, Part IV, vol. 13794. LNCS, pages 189–219, Taipei, Taiwan, December 5–9, 2022. Springer, Cham, Switzerland (2022). https://doi.org/10.1007/978-3-031-22972-5_7

eth23. Ethereum KZG ceremony (2023). https://github.com/ethereum/kzg-ceremony

Fis19. Fisch, B.: Tight proofs of space and replication. In: Ishai, Y., Rijmen, V. (eds.) EUROCRYPT 2019. LNCS, vol. 11477, pp. 324–348. Springer, Cham (2019). https://doi.org/10.1007/978-3-030-17656-3_12

FK23. Feist, D., Khovratovich, D.: Fast amortized KZG proofs. Cryptology ePrint Archive, Report 2023/033 (2023)

FKL18. Fuchsbauer, G., Kiltz, E., Loss, J.: The algebraic group model and its applications. In: Shacham, H., Boldyreva, A. (eds.) CRYPTO 2018. LNCS, vol. 10992, pp. 33–62. Springer, Cham (2018). https://doi.org/10.1007/978-3-319-96881-0_2

GKM+18. Groth, J., Kohlweiss, M., Maller, M., Meiklejohn, S., Miers, I.: Updatable and universal common reference strings with applications to zk-SNARKs. In: Shacham, H., Boldyreva, A. (eds.) CRYPTO 2018, Part III, vol. 10993. LNCS, pp. 698–728, Santa Barbara, CA, USA, August 19–23, 2018. Springer, Cham, Switzerland (2018). https://doi.org/10.1007/978-3-319-96878-0_24

GLS+21. Golovnev, A., Lee, J., Setty, S.T., Thaler, J. and Wahby, R.S.: Brakedown: linear-time and post-quantum SNARKs for R1CS. Cryptology ePrint Archive, Report 2021/1043 (2021)

GRWZ20. Gorbunov, S., Reyzin, L., Wee, H. and Zhang, Z.: PointProofs: aggregating proofs for multiple vector commitments. In: Ligatti, J., Ou, X., Katz, J., Vigna, G. (eds.) ACM CCS 2020, pp. 2007–2023, Virtual Event, USA, November 9–13 (2020). ACM Press

GWC19. Gabizon, A., Williamson, Z.J., Ciobotaru, O.: PLONK: permutations over Lagrange-bases for oecumenical noninteractive arguments of knowledge. Cryptology ePrint Archive, Report 2019/953 (2019)

KZG10. Kate, A., Zaverucha, G.M., Goldberg, I.: Constant-size commitments to polynomials and their applications. In: Abe, M. (ed.) ASIACRYPT 2010. LNCS, vol. 6477, pp. 177–194. Springer, Heidelberg (2010). https://doi.org/10.1007/978-3-642-17373-8_11

LJGK25. Luo, Z., Jia, Y., Gracia, A.V.O., Kate, A.: CauchyProofs: batch-updatable vector commitment with easy aggregation and application to stateless blockchains. In: Blanton, M., Enck, W., Nita-Rotaru, C., (eds.) 2025 IEEE Symposium on Security and Privacy, pp. 1947–1963, San Francisco, CA, USA, May 12–15 (2025). IEEE Computer Society Press

LM19. Lai, R.W.F., Malavolta, G.: Subvector commitments with application to succinct arguments. In: Boldyreva, A., Micciancio, D. (eds.) CRYPTO 2019. LNCS, vol. 11692, pp. 530–560. Springer, Cham (2019). https://doi.org/10.1007/978-3-030-26948-7_19

LPR22. Libert, B., Passelègue, A., Riahinia, M.: PointProofs, revisited. In: Agrawal, S., Lin, D. (eds). ASIACRYPT 2022, Part IV, vol. 13794. LNCS, pp. 220–246, Taipei, Taiwan, December 5–9, 2022. Springer, Cham, Switzerland. https://doi.org/10.1007/978-3-031-22972-5_8

LPY12. Libert, B., Peters, T., Yung, M.: Group signatures with almost-for-free revocation. In: Safavi-Naini, R., Canetti, R. (eds.) CRYPTO 2012. LNCS, vol. 7417, pp. 571–589. Springer, Heidelberg (2012). https://doi.org/10.1007/978-3-642-32009-5_34

LY10. Libert, B., Yung, M.: Concise mercurial vector commitments and independent zero-knowledge sets with short proofs. In: Micciancio, D. (ed.) TCC

2010. LNCS, vol. 5978, pp. 499–517. Springer, Heidelberg (2010). https://doi.org/10.1007/978-3-642-11799-2_30

Nit21. Nitulescu, A.: SOK: vector commitments (2021). https://www.di.ens.fr/nitulesc/files/vc-sok

PRvdM25. Pathak, V., Ruj, S., van der Meyden, R.: Vector commitment design, analysis, and applications: a survey. Cryptology ePrint Archive, Report 2025/667 (2025)

PST13. Papamanthou, C., Shi, E., Tamassia, R.: Signatures of correct computation. In: Sahai, A. (ed.) TCC 2013. LNCS, vol. 7785, pp. 222–242. Springer, Heidelberg (2013). https://doi.org/10.1007/978-3-642-36594-2_13

SCP+22. Srinivasan, S., Chepurnoy, A., Papamanthou, C., Tomescu, A., Zhang, Y.: Hyperproofs: aggregating and maintaining proofs in vector commitments. In: Kevin R.B., Kurt Thomas, B. (eds.) USENIX Security 2022, pp. 3001–3018, Boston, MA, USA, August 10–12, 2022. USENIX Association (2022)

TAB+20. Tomescu, A., Abraham, I., Buterin, V., Drake, J., Feist, D., Khovratovich, D.: Aggregatable subvector commitments for stateless cryptocurrencies. In: Galdi, C., Kolesnikov, V. (eds.) SCN 2020. LNCS, vol. 12238, pp. 45–64. Springer, Cham (2020). https://doi.org/10.1007/978-3-030-57990-6_3

TB23. Nusret Tas, E., Boneh, D.: Vector commitments with efficient updates. In: 5th Conference on Advances in Financial Technologies (2023)

WW23. Wee, H., Wu, D.J.: Succinct vector, polynomial, and functional commitments from lattices. In: Hazay, C., Stam, M. (eds) Advances in Cryptology – EUROCRYPT 2023. EUROCRYPT 2023, Part III. LNCS, vol. 14006. pp. 385–416, Lyon, France, April 23–27. Springer, Cham, Switzerland (2023). https://doi.org/10.1007/978-3-031-30620-4_13

WZ24. Wagner, B., Zapico, A.: A documentation of Ethereum's PeerDAS. Cryptology ePrint Archive, Paper 2024/1362 (2024)

The Cost of Fluidity: Communication Complexity Trade-Offs in Fluid MPC

Shancheng Zhang[1], Zongyang Zhang[1(✉)], and Bernardo Magri[2]

[1] Beihang University, Beijing, China
{zscbuaa,zongyangzhang}@buaa.edu.cn
[2] University of Manchester, Manchester, UK
bernardo.magri@manchester.ac.uk

Abstract. Secure multi-party computation (MPC) enables mutually distrustful parties to jointly evaluate a function on their private inputs. Classic MPC protocols, however, assume a *static* set of participants in which every party must remain online throughout the entire computation. Recent advances have introduced MPC models with *dynamic participation*, such as Fluid MPC, in which computation steps are delegated to a sequence of committees that change across epochs. This approach improves robustness, enabling parties to go offline once their roles are complete. Yet, this flexibility comes at a cost: the most efficient dynamic-participation MPC protocols still incur communication overheads exceeding traditional MPC by more than an order of magnitude. In this work, we formalize the communication complexity of (d, n)-threshold secret-sharing-based Fluid MPC. We prove a tight trade-off between communication cost and the adversary's corruption threshold, showing that linear communication complexity $O(n)$ is impossible when the corruption threshold t exceeds a proportion of d. Matching this bound, we construct a protocol with a communication cost of $9.3n$ elements per multiplication gate against a semi-honest adversary and $37.3n$ elements against a malicious adversary. A C++ implementation confirms that our approach brings the cost of fluidity within practical limits.

1 Introduction

Secure multiparty computation [27] enables a set of mutually distrusting parties to compute a function on their private inputs while revealing nothing beyond the prescribed output. Over the past decade, the community has dramatically improved MPC's efficiency in both honest and dishonest-majority settings [8, 9,22]. Yet all traditional protocols assume a fixed group of parties that remain online throughout the computation. This requirement is brittle for long-running tasks, such as training deep-learning models: a single network hiccup can stall the entire computation.

Recently, MPC models with *dynamic participation* have been introduced, in which the computation is carried out by committees that may change during execution. Notable examples include the YOSO model [19] and the Fluid MPC

K. Jee and A. Kate (Eds.): ACNS 2026, LNCS 16571, pp. 351–381, 2027.
https://doi.org/10.1007/978-3-032-32560-0_13

model [7], where the existing Fluid MPC protocols [1,2,7,24] are relatively efficient in practice. In the Fluid MPC model, the computation is divided into *epochs*, each executed by its own committee, with only a brief handoff phase between consecutive ones. This design allows parties to join or leave between epochs. When each epoch is restricted to a single communication round (that is, a committee may send messages only once to its successor), the protocol achieves what the authors call *maximal fluidity*.

The first Fluid MPC protocol incurred $O(n^2)$ field-element communication per gate in the honest majority setting, where n is the committee size [7]. Rachuri et al. [24] and Bienstock et al. [1] progressively extended this paradigm to the dishonest majority setting; notably, [1] achieves linear communication in the honest majority setting via a P_{king} mechanism. Subsequent works, such as [2,15,28], have reduced overhead further by adopting relaxed security models, including fluid participation or reduced corruption thresholds. However, while [1] remains the state-of-the-art regarding communication efficiency for the standard setting, its costs remain significantly higher than those of traditional MPC protocols like [8,20]. This gap currently limits the practical adoption of Fluid MPC. These observations prompt two natural questions:

(1) What is the inherent trade-off between communication cost and security settings for MPC with maximal fluidity?
(2) Can we design maximally Fluid MPC protocols that meet this bound while approaching the efficiency of the best traditional MPC schemes?

Addressing either question is challenging: no systematic study of Fluid MPC's communication complexity yet exists. In traditional MPC, the efficiency of deterministic protocols (without amortization) is fundamentally constrained by the Dolev-Reischuk bound [14], which establishes the impossibility of achieving Byzantine Agreement with a communication complexity of $o(n^2)$. However, this lower bound is specific to malicious adversaries within a static committee. It does not extend to the Fluid MPC setting, where committees are dynamic, nor does it apply when the adversary is restricted to semi-honest behavior. Bienstock *et al.* [1] observation, that transferring shares between committees under dishonest majority costs $O(n^2)$ communication in the preprocessing phase, hints that super-linear overhead may be unavoidable, but no formal lower bound for other settings is known, such as honest majority. Closing this gap by establishing theoretical limits and developing nearly optimal protocols would directly benefit large-scale privacy-preserving applications.

1.1 Our Contributions

We advance towards answering these questions by investigating the communication restriction of *secret-sharing-based* Fluid MPC in the *maximal-fluidity* setting.

In particular, we establish an identical communication *cost reduction* from the multiplication gate of Fluid MPC protocols to a secret-sharing scheme that transmits shares from one committee to the future, which is defined as $\mathcal{F}_{\text{reshare}}$ in [11]. We then show that achieving $\mathcal{F}_{\text{reshare}}$ with $O(n)$ communication complexity requires the corruption threshold t to be strictly limited relative to the security threshold d of the underlying secret-sharing (where d is one less than the reconstruction threshold). In particular, $t < d/2$ is necessary for optimal communication efficiency. This bound implies that sublinear communication is unattainable for any information-theoretically secure Fluid MPC protocol utilizing secret sharing for inter-committee transfers. Finally, we design a maximally fluid protocol for $t < n/4$ that achieves a concrete communication cost comparable to the most efficient traditional MPC protocols.

In more details, our contributions are:

1. *Reduction between Reshare and Fluid MPC.* We formalize the transfer gate intuition from [10], proving that $\mathcal{F}_{\text{reshare}}$ serves as a proxy for the communication bounds of any Fluid MPC protocol based on secret sharing. This result remains valid even for protocols that lack an explicit resharing phase [10,12], providing a generalized framework for evaluating inter-committee communication costs.
2. *Communication Framework & Complexity Trade-off.* Using $\mathcal{F}_{\text{reshare}}$ as a tool, we distinguish between the corruption threshold t and the security threshold d, introducing parameters to model inter-party communication. We show that any $O(n)$-communication protocol must exhibit a specific communication pattern with a cost of $\lambda\gamma(n-\mu)+T(\mu,n)$ field elements[1]. This allows us to formalize the trade-off between communication overhead and the corruption threshold (e.g., $t < (1-1/(\lambda+1))(d+2)$), proving that communication complexity is fundamentally restricted even under semi-honest security.
3. *Optimal protocol.* Under the bound, we propose an *optimal* reshare scheme expanded from [1] and based on Shamir sharing that applies when $t \leq d/2$ and $d < n/2$. Building on this scheme, we construct a maximally fluid MPC protocol that is maliciously secure with abort. The protocol communicates on average $9.3n$ field elements per multiplication in the semi-honest case and $37.3n$ in the malicious case, roughly a six-fold improvement over the current best result [1].
4. *Implementation and evaluation.* Our prototype, written in C++ and simulated in OMNeT++, confirms our results and shows only moderate overhead compared with traditional MPC protocols, such as ATLAS [20], underscoring the practicality of our approach.

1.2 Related Work

Our paper extends the recent line of Fluid MPC protocols [1,2,7,11,24], which aim to keep communication low even when committees change over time. A broader body of work addresses multiparty computation with dynamic or one-shot participants (which called Maximal fluidity). Furthermore, some works try to achieve high efficiency by relaxing the fluidity [28].

[1] $\lambda, \gamma > 0$ are constants, $\mu = o(n)$, and $T(\mu, n) = O(n)$.

One-Round Communication. The YOSO (You Only Speak Once) series of protocols, initiated by Gentry *et al.* [19] and expanded in follow-up papers [4,5,13], restricts every party to a single outgoing message. Although the adversary model differs from that of Fluid MPC, both frameworks share the goal of scaling to large, unstable networks. David *et al.* [10] bridge the two settings and propose a dynamic-participant MPC protocol that guarantees output delivery. Escudero et al. [15] recently proposed a computational YOSO MPC protocol using packed secret sharing that achieves sub-linear communication for large n. Our results show that while the $O(n)$ lower bound is strict in the information-theoretic setting, it only applies to computational protocols when t is large relative to d and n is below a certain threshold. Thus, the results in [15] circumvents these boundaries, providing an intuitive confirmation of the limits established in this work.

Application-Driven Variants. Fluid-style techniques have inspired several specialised protocols. Gama *et al.* [17] handle "Delayed Parties" in star-shaped networks, achieving robustness against nodes that come online late. Escudero *et al.* [16] develop locally repairable MPC, which shares the Fluid objective of maintaining progress despite participant churn.

Together, these results highlight the growing interest in MPC schemes that tolerate large, dynamic populations, a direction our work continues by clarifying the fundamental communication limits of Fluid MPC.

2 Technical Overview

This section sketches the core ideas behind our results. We begin by showing how the reshare functionality in [11] captures the communication bound of Fluid MPC. We then state a simplified communication cost bound theorem, illustrated through a concrete $n = 7$ example, highlighting the communication bottleneck. Finally, we outline our matching, efficient Fluid MPC construction.

Throughout this work, computations are performed over a finite field $\mathbb{F}$ of prime order p, and we denote the target circuit as C. The dynamic parties are partitioned into a sequence of committees $\mathcal{C}^1, \mathcal{C}^2, \ldots$ of sizes $n_1, n_2, \ldots$, respectively. Each committee $\mathcal{C}^j$ utilizes a (d_j, n_j) threshold secret-sharing scheme and is assumed to withstand up to t_j corruptions.[2] For ease of exposition, this section assumes a uniform setting where $n_j = n \geq 3$, $d_j = d$, and $t_j = t$ for all j.

2.1 Reshare: A Tool for Fluid MPC Analysis

In [1] it is shown that the only step absent between traditional MPC and Fluid MPC is transferring shares (generated Beaver triple) from $\mathcal{C}^1$ to $\mathcal{C}^3$. Following [1, 11], we call this transfer "reshare". In this work we use the functionality $\mathcal{F}_{\mathsf{reshare}}$ in [11], but with difference for permitting any distance between source and target committees; the secret can be sent by committee $\mathcal{C}^j$ to committee $\mathcal{C}^{j'}$ for $j < j'$.

[2] Specifically, any subset of at least $d_j + 1$ parties can reconstruct the shared secret.

A bit more formally, let $[v]^j_{d_j}$ denote the (d_j, n_j) threshold shares of v held by $\mathcal{C}^j$. The functionality moves these shares through the intervening committees so that $\mathcal{C}^{j'}$ ends with an independently randomised $(d_{j'}, n_{j'})$ share $[v]^{j'}_{d_{j'}}$; every party $P^{j'}_i \in \mathcal{C}^{j'}$ receives a fresh share $v^{j'}_i$, and security holds against a malicious adversary with abort.

Reshare as the Core of Secret Share-Based Fluid MPC. In this work, we demonstrate that the reshare functionality is more than a convenience; it is actually the *communication bottleneck* that separates Fluid MPC from classical MPC protocols. [10] notices that if a secret share-based Fluid MPC protocol is asked to evaluate one multiplication, the resulting transcript *is* a reshare protocol.[3] Inspired by it, we formally prove that any complexity restriction for $\mathcal{F}_{\mathsf{reshare}}$ therefore *strictly* transfers to Fluid MPC protocols of that kind, and any efficient reshare construction immediately yields an equally efficient Fluid protocol. Consequently, if a given communication bound and security setting makes reshare impossible, then any Fluid MPC protocol under the same constraints is also ruled out.

2.2 Treating t and d Separately

Recall that a (d, n) threshold secret sharing scheme tolerates any coalition of up to d colluding parties. Most Shamir-based MPC protocols simply set the corruption threshold t equal to d ($t = d$); additive schemes in a dishonest-majority setting push this to the extreme with $t = d = n - 1$. To analyse communication limits of Fluid MPC, we *decouple* these two parameters. We note that although our framework permits $d \geq t$ (i.e. the reconstruction threshold may exceed the privacy threshold), it *does not* rely on ramp secret-sharing [3]: we assume the adversary learns at most t shares in one parties' committee, so perfect privacy holds for t shares, and no information leaks in the region between t and d shares.

Next, we state a streamlined version of our reshare communication cost restriction under the simplifying assumption that every committee uses identical parameters (n, d, t). Informally, the result shows that "cheap" reshare (and hence a cheap Fluid MPC) forces a strict cap on t.

Simplified Theorem. Assume a reshare implementation is allowed only $O(n)$ field elements of communication. Label the final recipient committee $\mathcal{C}^{j'}$. Then, partition its parties into (1) at most $\mu = o(n)$ "heavy" parties that together receive no more than $T(\mu, n) = O(n)$ elements ($T(0, n) = 0$), and (2) $n - \mu$

[3] More specifically, a secret share based Fluid MPC protocol evaluating a circuit that contains a single multiplication gate that multiplies any shares of value $[x]_d$ by $[x]_d$ is equivalent to reshare the value $[x]_d$. Furthermore, since most existing dynamic-participant MPC protocols are based on secret sharing, we implicitly refer to secret-sharing-based Fluid MPC protocols whenever discussing Fluid MPC.

"light" parties, each of which can receive a single message from each of up to λ parties in $\mathcal{C}^{j'-1}$, with each message containing at most γ field elements, for $\mu \geq 0$ and fixed constants $\lambda, \gamma > 0$. Thus the entire hop from $\mathcal{C}^{j'-1}$ to $\mathcal{C}^{j'}$ costs at most $\lambda\gamma(n-\mu) + T(\mu, n)$ field elements. If, in addition,

$$t \geq \left(1 - \frac{1}{\lambda+1}\right)(d+2),$$

then, even against a *semi-honest* adversary,

- no information-theoretically secure reshare exists, and
- no PPT or statistically secure reshare exists whenever
  - $t \geq d$, or
  - $t < d$ and n is below a moderate threshold.[4]

We make a few remarks about the previous theorem statement. First, this theorem actually propose a trade-off between the communication and the adversary corruption threshold t. Intuitively speaking, if we consider schemes that can tolerate a larger proportion of adversary corruptions, the communication structure must be more complex, leading to increased communication overhead. Conversely, to achieve a more efficient communication scheme, the adversary's corruption threshold must not exceed a specific proportion, that is $t \geq \left(1 - \frac{1}{\lambda+1}\right)(d+2)$.

Second, traditionally, the security of MPC protocols with computational security is mainly measured based on the size of the finite field or ring used, and the number of parties n is not included in the security parameter. However, we observe that under certain conditions (especially for PPT or statistical adversaries), the security parameter κ must include information about the size of n. Furthermore, although this informal theorem restricts the number of parties in all committees to be the same, similar conclusions can still be drawn for settings where the number of parties is unrestricted, although the restrictions on inter-committee communication will be more complex. Finally, the proof relies solely on the abstraction $\mathcal{F}_{\mathsf{reshare}}$ and does not assume any particular sharing technique. Treating additive sharing as an $(n-1, n)$ share scheme therefore places the impossibility result in [1] as a special case of our theorem.

This theorem can be directly transferred to secret share based Fluid MPC according to the relationship between it and reshare. Next, we briefly illustrate the core of our proof technique for the special and weakened case where $t = d$ and reshare occurs between two contiguous committees, whereas our main restriction applies to $t < d$ and committees with *any distance*.

Informal and Weakened Lemma. Consider two disjoint committees $\mathcal{C}^1$ and $\mathcal{C}^2$ with the same parameter settings, no information-theoretically secure protocol can implement $\mathcal{F}_{\mathsf{reshare}}$ between them using only $O(n)$ field-element communication when $t = d$.

[4] As we will discuss later, at least $n \geq 72$ is required for 2^{64} field security.

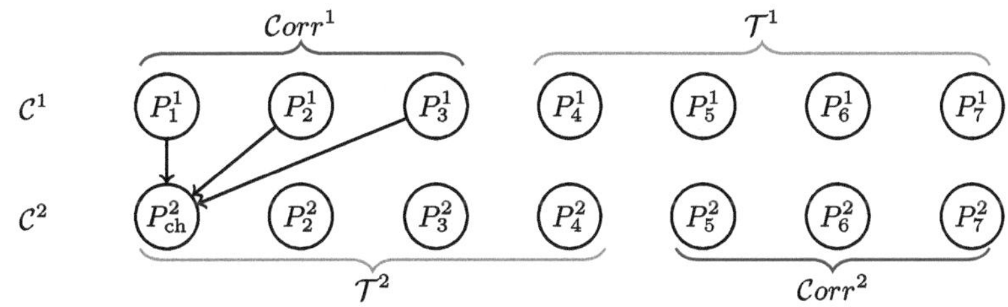

Fig. 1. Message transmission of resharing between two 7-party committees. Three shaded nodes in $\mathcal{C}^1$ send messages to a single light-blue receiver P_{ch} in $\mathcal{C}^2$. The adversary (red) first corrupts those three senders, then corrupts three additional parties in $\mathcal{C}^2$. With the three shares it now holds plus the computable share of P_{ch}, the adversary recovers v.

Proof Intuition. A reshare protocol that costs $O(n)$ field elements has room for only linear pass of messages from $\mathcal{C}^1$ to $\mathcal{C}^2$. Consequently, at least one party in the target committee, call it the chosen party P_{ch}, must receive inputs from *no more than* t senders in $\mathcal{C}^1$; otherwise the outgoing traffic from $\mathcal{C}^1$ alone already scales as $\Omega(n(t+1)) = \Omega(n^2)$.

The adversary proceeds in two phases: (1) It waits until the t senders $\mathcal{S}_{\text{ch}}^1 \subseteq \mathcal{C}^1$ have delivered their messages to P_{ch} and then checks if it just corrupted exactly those parties. This choice succeeds with probability $\varepsilon_t = 1/\binom{n}{t} > 0$ when corruption is random. (2) Then the adversary corrupts any t parties in $\mathcal{C}^2 \setminus \{P_{\text{ch}}\}$ with a probability of 1 because the adversary is adaptive. Privacy breaks because P_{ch} is honest, its output share v_{ch}^2 is a deterministic function f of the t incoming messages $\{\boldsymbol{m}_i\}_{P_i^1 \in \mathcal{S}_{\text{ch}}^1}$ and the local randomness $\boldsymbol{r}$ it generates. Notice that v_{ch}^2 is uniquely determined by the other $n-1$ shares, the randomness does not affect the result of f. The adversary, who now holds all the messages $\{\boldsymbol{m}_i\}$, can *compute* $v_{\text{ch}}^2 = f(\{\boldsymbol{m}_i\}, 0^*)$ without corrupting P_{ch}. Adding the t shares obtained in the second round of corruptions gives the adversary $t+1 = d+1$ shares in total, exactly the number needed to reconstruct the secret v. This violates perfect privacy and yields the desired contradiction. Figure 1 depicts the flow for a concrete example with $n = 7$ and $t = d = 3$.

The lemma above already rules out $O(n)$ communication when $t = d$, even against a semi-honest adversary. It therefore carries over *a fortiori* to the malicious R-adaptive setting used elsewhere in the paper.

2.3 Efficient Fluid MPC Based on Optimal Reshare

Once an $O(n)$ reshare is available (Sect. 2.1), a fully Maximally-Fluid MPC over Shamir sharing follows almost verbatim: each multiplication consists of one reshare plus $O(n)$ communication [1]. The informal bound, however, shows that such efficiency forces a tight relation between the privacy and reconstruction thresholds: with inter-committee bandwidth capped at $\lambda\gamma\,(n-\mu)+T(\mu,n)$, PPT security for all committee size becomes impossible whenever $t \geq \left(1-\frac{1}{\lambda+1}\right)(d+2)$.

Choosing Optimal Parameters. For optimal efficiency, we set $\lambda = \gamma = 1,\ \mu = 0$, so the hop from one committee to the next costs *at most* n field elements. Under the bound above, this forces $t \leq d/2$, which we adopt from here on. Our reshare scheme expends the work of [1] and supports every linear (d, n) scheme with $t \leq d/2$ and therefore applies far beyond Shamir secret sharing.

Building the Full Protocol. With the optimal reshare in place, we construct a Maximally-Fluid MPC that uses Shamir sharing together with the double-random- sharing technique, avoiding the complicated generation of Beaver triple. We re-engineer the random-share generators $\mathcal{F}_{\textsf{double-rand}}$ and $\mathcal{F}_{\textsf{zero}}$ from traditional MPC so that each is produced in batches by linearly combining one random share from every party and is suitable for Fluid setting.

Performance. Against a semi-honest adversary, one multiplication gate completes in three rounds, compared with seven in [1]. The average bandwidth per gate drops to $9.3n$ field elements (semi-honest) and $37.3n$ field elements (malicious). These figures approach the best traditional MPC protocols. A prototype written in `C++` and simulated in OMNeT++ [26] confirms that the overhead remains modest when compared with ATLAS [20].

3 Security Model and Preliminaries

In this section, we introduce some preliminaries needed for our work. We will first present the definition of Fluid MPC, as well as some definitions that we need. Finally, we provide some cryptographic concepts used in this paper.

3.1 Fluid MPC and Security Model

Next, we give a brief introduction on the Fluid MPC concepts from [7]. We discuss it in more details in Appendix A.

We consider a client-server model within a universe $\mathcal{U}$ of all clients and servers, formalizing the concept of dynamic parties. Roughly speaking, clients remain unchanged, while servers are allowed to change continuously during the computation. The entire computation process can be divided into the input stage, execution stage, and output stage. The input stage and output stage are similar to static party MPC, where fixed clients provide inputs during the input stage and receive computation results during the output stage. The execution stage in Fluid MPC is divided into epochs, each executed by a static set of parties, and further divided into the computation phase and hand-off phase. According to the epoch number, we refer to the set of parties executing $epoch_j$ as $\mathcal{C}^j$ and the set of clients as $\mathcal{C}^{\text{clnt}}$. The size for committee $\mathcal{C}^j$ is denoted as n_j while the corruption threshold is denoted as t_j ($t_j = \Theta(n_j)$).

The computing idea mainly follows the 'layered circuit' similar to [7], which constructs the whole arithmetic circuit C by layers. Each layer consists of multiple arithmetic gates. The maximum number of arithmetic gates contained in each layer is called the width of the circuit. In this paper, we set the width w to be at least $\Omega(n)$.

3.2 Preliminaries

Linear (d, n)-threshold secret sharing scheme [25]. The linear (d, n)-threshold secret sharing scheme supports linear combination calculation. Similar with setting of t_j, we set (d_j, n_j)-threshold secret sharing scheme is used in committee $\mathcal{C}^j$, $d_j = \Theta(n_j)$. The algorithms are listed below:

- $\Pi_{\mathrm{LSS}}.\mathrm{Share}(x) \rightarrow [x]_d$: A dealer shares the secret value $x \in \mathbb{F}$ and, to be concise, generates n secret shares $\{x^1, \ldots, x^n\}$, denoted as $[x]_d$.
- $\Pi_{\mathrm{LSS}}.\mathrm{Rec}([x]_d, i) \rightarrow x$: One party P_i is allowed to obtain the original secret x after receiving at least $d + 1$ shares.
- $\Pi_{\mathrm{LSS}}.\mathrm{Open}([x]_d) \rightarrow x$: This procedure allows every party to obtain the original secret x with at least $d + 1$ shares as input.

Moreover, we denote shares of x held by parties in set S as $[x]_S$, and denote shares of x held by committee $\mathcal{C}^j$ as $[x]^j$. Set of trusted honest parties in committee $\mathcal{C}^j$ is denoted as $\mathcal{T}^j$, and the set of corrupted parties is denoted as $\mathcal{C}orr^j$. Furthermore, we denote $\bigcup S$ as the union set of all elements in the set S.

4 Complexity Limitation of the Fluid MPC Based on Threshold Secret Share

First, we recall the definition of the reshare functionality $\mathcal{F}_{\mathsf{reshare}}$ in [11]. The relationship between it and the secret share based Fluid MPC protocol will then be illustrated. Furthermore, with the tool $\mathcal{F}_{\mathsf{reshare}}$, the restriction for Fluid MPC based on threshold secret sharing will be proved under different settings.

4.1 Existential Relationship Between Reshare and Fluid MPC

Firstly, we recall the functionality $\mathcal{F}_{\mathsf{reshare}}$ here, which slightly extends the definition in [11]. In $\mathcal{F}_{\mathsf{reshare}}$, we consider reshare from committee $\mathcal{C}^j$ to $\mathcal{C}j'$ for any $j < j'$. This extension is necessary for restriction theorems about the complexity of Fluid MPC (like the Lemma 1).

Furthermore, considering reshare from one committee to the next defined in [11] is useful for the construction of Fluid MPC protocol, we denotes $\mathcal{F}_{\mathsf{reshare}}$ of two-layers as $\mathcal{F}_{\mathsf{rs-two}}$. Here we only present the functionality of $\mathcal{F}_{\mathsf{rs-two}}$.

Inspired from the transfer gate idea in [10], we present Lemma 1 here to demonstrate the relationship between $\mathcal{F}_{\mathsf{reshare}}$ and Fluid MPC, which illustrates why we use $\mathcal{F}_{\mathsf{reshare}}$ as a tool to analyze Fluid MPC.

Lemma 1. *Let Π_{MPC} be a secret share-based Fluid MPC protocol with maximum-fluidity that computes a multiplication gate in $j' - j + 1$ rounds and has the total communication cost of $F(n)$ field elements, i.e., $\mathcal{C}^j$ has shares of inputs and each party in $\mathcal{C}^{j'}$ receives a share of the computation result. Then, under the same committee setting and adversary capabilities, there exists a protocol π_{reshare} that implements $\mathcal{F}_{\mathsf{reshare}}$ among $\mathcal{C}^j$ to $\mathcal{C}^{j'}$ and has $F(n)$ field elements communication cost.*

Functionality 1: $\mathcal{F}_{\text{reshare}}$

Functionality: $\mathcal{C}^j$ reshares a re-randomised (d_j, n_j)-threshold sharing $[v]^j_{d_j}$ to committee $\mathcal{C}^{j'}, j' > j$.

1. In epoch j, $\mathcal{F}_{\text{reshare}}$ receives $v^j_i, P^j_i \in \mathcal{T}^j$ and reconstructs v. $\mathcal{F}_{\text{reshare}}$ further computes the shares of $[v]^j_{d_j}$ held by corrupted parties in $\mathcal{C}^j$, and sends these shares to the adversary.
2. In epoch j', $\mathcal{F}_{\text{reshare}}$ randomly generates shares of $[v]^{j'}_{d_{j'}}$. $\mathcal{F}_{\text{reshare}}$ firstly sends shares of corrupted parties in $\mathcal{C}^{j'}$ to the adversary and waits for its response.
   - If the adversary replies continue, $\mathcal{F}_{\text{reshare}}$ sends other shares to honest parties in $\mathcal{C}^{j'}$.
   - If the adversary replies abort, $\mathcal{F}_{\text{reshare}}$ sends abort to honest parties.

Functionality 2: $\mathcal{F}_{\text{rs-two}}$ [11]

Functionality: $\mathcal{C}^j$ reshares a re-randomised (d_j, n_j)-threshold sharing $[v]^j_{d_j}$ to committee $\mathcal{C}^{j+1}$.

Proof. To show this, we can construct a protocol π_{reshare} that implements $\mathcal{F}_{\text{reshare}}$ using the existing Π_{MPC} protocol as described next.

1. $\mathcal{C}^j$ invokes Π_{MPC} to compute one multiplication gate Multiply$([v]^j_{d_j}, [1]^j_{d_j})$.
2. $\mathcal{C}^{j'}$ receives computing result $[v]^{j'}_{d_{j'}}$ as the reshare result.

Note that in addition to invoking Π_{MPC}, it is necessary to generate random shares of 1, which can be introduced via input gate or collaboratively produced by all parties, which will introduce n field elements communication cost. However, we argue that the generated shares of 1 can be reused. So if we consider at least $\Omega(n)$ reshare operations, then the evenly distributed consumption for generating shares of 1 will be negligible. Thus, the built π_{reshare} has the same communication cost of $F(n)$ field elements. ■

Therefore, directly from Lemma 1, we obtain the following Corollary 1 that conditions the existence of Fluid MPC on the existence of reshare.

Corollary 1. *Under any fixed execution model, if there exists no protocol π_{reshare} that securely realizes $\mathcal{F}_{\text{reshare}}$ with communication cost at most $F(n)$ (field elements), then no secret-sharing-based Fluid MPC protocol Π_{MPC} can securely evaluate a multiplication gate with communication cost at most $F(n)$.*

4.2 Linear Protocol for $d = t$ Is Impossible

Given Corollary 1, the existence of linear protocols can be discussed. We begin with the setting that $d = t$, which is widely used in traditional MPC based on Shamir secret share [20] or repeated secret share [22]. Firstly, we present Lemma 2 to discuss the situation where every committee has the same settings. The proof mainly follows the idea demonstrated in Sect. 2.2, which focuses on the last layer of communication between $\mathcal{C}^{j'}$ and $\mathcal{C}^{j'-1}$. According to the information controlled by the adversary, the contradiction will be constructed.

Without loss of generality, we simplify the notation by analyzing an instance of $\mathcal{F}_{\mathsf{reshare}}$ that concludes at committee $\mathcal{C}^2$. This transformation re-indexes the final two committees, replacing $\mathcal{C}^{j'-1}$ and $\mathcal{C}^{j'}$ with $\mathcal{C}^1$ and $\mathcal{C}^2$, respectively.

Lemma 2. *Assume a uniform setting where every committee $\mathcal{C}^j$ with size n, corruption threshold t, and (d,n)-threshold secret sharing of $d = \Theta(n)$. If $t \geq d$, then there exists no protocol π_{reshare} that securely realizes $\mathcal{F}_{\mathsf{reshare}}$ with $O(n)$ communication complexity against a PPT adversary.*

Due to space constraints, the proof of Lemma 2 is deferred to Appendix B.2.

Consequently, we have established that realizing $\mathcal{F}_{\mathsf{reshare}}$ with $O(n)$ communication is impossible when $d = t$ for fixed-size committees. Since the constant-size setting is a special case of the variable-size setting, this impossibility result extends immediately to the general case. We formalize this general impossibility in Corollary 2. Furthermore, building on Claim 2 in the proof of Lemma 2, Corollary 3 characterizes the required communication structure for any valid $O(n)$ reshare protocol.

Corollary 2. *Let each $\mathcal{C}^j$ be a committee using (d_j, n_j)-threshold secret sharing scheme and $d_j = \Theta(n)$. If the corruption threshold satisfies $t_j \geq d_j$, then there exists no protocol π_{reshare} that securely realizes $\mathcal{F}_{\mathsf{reshare}}$ with $O(n)$ communication complexity against a semi-honest PPT adversary.*

Proof. Assuming that there exists a π_{reshare} realizing $\mathcal{F}_{\mathsf{reshare}}$ from $\mathcal{C}^{2-(j'-j)}$ to $\mathcal{C}^2$ with a communication complexity of $O(n)$ field elements. The setting of $t_j > d_j$ is obviously impossible. As for the $t_j = d_j$ situation, similar to the Part 3 in the proof for Lemma 2, we denote the event that $\mathcal{S}_i^1$ is a subset of $\mathcal{C}orr^1$ as A_i. The probability can be computed as $p_i = \Pr[A_i] = \binom{n_1-\lambda}{t_1-\lambda}/\binom{n_1}{t_1}$. This means that the *adaptive* adversary can compromise the security of π_{reshare} with at least $\epsilon_{\mathrm{ad}} \geq p_i$ probability. Moreover, the probability that the *static* adversary compromises the security of π_{reshare} is at least

$$\epsilon_{\mathrm{st}} \geq p_i \cdot p_{\mathrm{st}} = p_i \cdot \frac{\binom{n_1}{t_2}}{\binom{n_2}{t_2}} = \frac{\binom{n_1-\lambda}{t_1-\lambda}\binom{n_1}{t_2}}{\binom{n_1}{t_1}\binom{n_2}{t_2}}.$$

Noting that p_i and ϵ_{st} are both polynomial functions of n_1 and n_2, the attack strategy is suitable for PPT adversaries. ■

Corollary 3. *Assume a $\mathcal{F}_{\mathsf{reshare}}$ implementation is allowed only $O(n)$ field elements of communication. Then, parties in $\mathcal{C}^{j'}$ can be divided into (1) at most $\mu = o(n)$ parties that together receive no more than $T(\mu, n) = O(n)$ elements ($T(0,n) = 0$), and (2) $n - \mu$ parties, each of which can receive a single message* *from each of up to* λ *parties in* $\mathcal{C}^{j'-1}$*, with each message containing at most* γ *field elements, for* $\mu = o(n) \geq 0$ *and fixed constants* $\lambda, \gamma > 0$*. Thus the costs of the last communication round (from* $\mathcal{C}^{j'-1}$ *to* $\mathcal{C}^{j'}$*) are at most* $\lambda\gamma(n-\mu)+T(\mu, n)$ *field elements.*

4.3 $t < d$ Is Not Enough

As demonstrated in Corollary 1, Lemma 2 and Corollary 2, the setting of traditional MPC protocols [6,18,20], which have $t = d$, is impossible for $O(n)$ Fluid MPC. Moreover, we will illustrate in this section that there are limitations even when $t < d$. We will still begin with the setting where every committee has the same size, n, and show the conclusion for the variable situation later. For the sake of notational simplicity, in this section, we still consider the $\mathcal{F}_{\mathsf{reshare}}$ from the committee $\mathcal{C}^{2-j'+j}$ to $\mathcal{C}^2$

Information-Theoretic Adversary. Recalling previous proof for Lemma 2, when we consider $d-t > 0$, the adversary must corrupts $\mathcal{C}^1$ in an appropriate manner, ensuring that $Corr^1$ encompasses at least $d-t+1$ of the $\mathcal{S}_i^1 \in \mathcal{S}^1$, where $\mathcal{S}_i^1$ means the set of parties in $\mathcal{C}^1$ who send message to P_i^2. This allows the adversary to acquire shares held by $d-t+1$ parties in $\mathcal{C}^2$ without corruption. Subsequently, by corrupting other t honest parties in $\mathcal{C}^2$, the adversary can obtain $d+1 = d-t+1+t$ shares, thus compromising the privacy of the protocol. Given that λ represents the number of parties included in $\mathcal{S}_i^1$, it is important to consider the possibility of an adversary successfully controlling them. Consequently, we will discuss different value ranges for t and λ separately:

-*When* $\lfloor \frac{t}{\lambda} \rfloor \leq n-\mu$, we assert that for any constant $\lambda < t$ (it always holds considering $\lambda = O(1)$ while $t = \Theta(n)$), regardless of the communication arrangement generated by π_{reshare} which realizes $\mathcal{F}_{\mathsf{reshare}}$, there exists at least one strategy for the adversary to have non-zero probability to corrupt $\mathcal{C}^1$ such that $Corr^1$ encompasses at least $\lfloor \frac{t}{\lambda} \rfloor$ of the $\mathcal{S}_i^1 \in \mathcal{S}^1$. To achieve this, considering that $\forall i, |\mathcal{S}_i^1| \leq \lambda$, it suffices to arbitrarily select $\lfloor \frac{t}{\lambda} \rfloor$ $\mathcal{S}_i^1$ from $\mathcal{S}^1$, and ensure that $Corr^1$ contains the union of these selected $\{\mathcal{S}_i^1\}$, which totally has $\lfloor \frac{t}{\lambda} \rfloor \cdot \lambda \leq t$ parties need to be corrupted.

Based on the previous discussion, when $\lfloor \frac{t}{\lambda} \rfloor \geq d-t+1$, the adversary will have the capability to compromise the protocol's privacy. Since $\lfloor \frac{t}{\lambda} \rfloor > \frac{t}{\lambda} - 1$, it suffices to ensure that $\frac{t}{\lambda} - 1 \geq d-t+1$, which is equivalent to:

$$t \geq \frac{d+2}{1+\frac{1}{\lambda}} = \left(1 - \frac{1}{\lambda+1}\right)(d+2) = \left(1 - \frac{1}{\lambda+1}\right)d + 2\left(1 - \frac{1}{\lambda+1}\right) \tag{1}$$

It is worth noting that this section requires $t < d$, so we need to check whether the above condition can be satisfied. We point out that the condition becomes unsatisfiable, leading to $d \leq \left(1 - \frac{1}{\lambda+1}\right)(d+2)$, if and only if $2\lambda \geq d$, which is clearly impossible. Thus, in this situation (including the setting about the value of λ and μ), an information-theoretical security protocol π_{reshare} to realize $\mathcal{F}_{\mathsf{reshare}}$ is impossible. In particular, when $\lambda = 1$, meaning that parties in $\mathcal{L}$ receive message inputs from at most one party in $\mathcal{C}^1$, we have $t \geq \frac{d}{2}+1$. Considering t is an integer, the constraint condition will be $t > \frac{d}{2}$.

-When $n-\mu < \lfloor \frac{t}{\lambda} \rfloor$, this situation can only arise when $\lambda = 1$ and $n-\mu < t$. Specifically, there will be $n-\mu$ parties in $\mathcal{C}^2$ can only receive single message from single party in $\mathcal{C}^1$. The adversary can just randomly corrupt t parties in each committee. Then it has $\binom{n-\mu}{t-\mu}/\binom{n}{t}$ probability to get all shares hold by parties in $\mathcal{C}^2 \backslash \mathcal{L}$ and $t-\mu$ more shares, only has no idea of $n-t<\mu$ parties' shares. Notice each of these $n-t<\mu$ parties can only receive single message from single party in $\mathcal{C}^1$. However, adversary also do random corruption in $\mathcal{C}^1$, it has $\binom{n-(n-t)}{t-(n-t)}/\binom{n}{t} > \binom{n-\mu}{t-\mu}/\binom{n}{t}$ probability to just control all inputs of these $n-t$ parties and gets there shares. So, overall, even static PPT adversary can get all shares hold by $\mathcal{C}^2$ with at least $\left(\binom{n-\mu}{t-\mu}/\binom{n}{t}\right)^2$ probability, which is obviously unsafe. For the sake of simplicity, the following discussions in this paper will *no longer consider* the analysis for the case when $n-\mu < \lfloor \frac{t}{\lambda} \rfloor$.

PPT adversary. Moreover, if we take the PPT adversary into consideration, we need to further determine the probability of the adversary successfully executing the attack when $t \geq \left(1-\frac{1}{\lambda+1}\right)(d+2)$. As mentioned in footnote 8, the message transfer strategy of π_{reshare} to realize $\mathcal{F}_{\mathsf{reshare}}$ will influence the best corruption strategy of the adversary. Thus, we have to construct the proof by adversary's knowledge of π_{reshare}'s strategy.

Specifically, we consider three types of adversary's knowledge for 'no information', 'fully deterministic' and 'completely random'. For brevity, illustrations of the adversary successfully attacking with information of these strategies are provided in the full version [29].

Finally, based on the given attack success probabilities for PPT adversaries under different settings, we can list the minimum number of parties n required to achieve different security levels. These are shown in Table 1. In which we consider settings of $\lambda = 1$, $\mu = 0$ and $d = n/2$ (or $d = (n-1)/2$ with odd n) for $t \geq \left(1-\frac{1}{\lambda+1}\right)(d+2)$, which implies $t = d/2$ under *static* adversary. Considering that as the adversary's capability increases with the proportion of t to n increases, the scheme will become increasingly difficult to resist the adversary's attacks, requiring a larger n to achieve the same security level. Therefore, the values of n in Table 1 are representative. It is worth noting that the 'fully deterministic' strategy used by existing schemes [1,2,7,24], where the adversary knows all parties' transmission targets during the hand-off phase, *cannot* resist PPT adversaries for arbitrary values of n.

4.4 Restriction for $O(n)$ Complexity $\mathcal{F}_{\mathsf{reshare}}$ and Fluid MPC

We have fully demonstrated the limitations for designing $\mathcal{F}_{\mathsf{reshare}}$. In this section, we will conclude the discussion shown before and further illustrate the situation of Fluid MPC protocol.

Table 1. Minimal n to realize $O(n)$ costs $\mathcal{F}_{\mathsf{reshare}}$ against PPT R-*static* adversary

Adversary's knowledge of realising $\mathcal{F}_{\mathsf{reshare}}$	Security levels		
	64-bit	128-bit	256-bit
No information	72	142	280
Fully deterministic	No security		
Completely random	> 1000	-	-

Note: This table shows the minimal committee size to realize O(n) costs Freshare against PPT R-static adversary with different communication information known by adversary for the last round when $t \geq (1 - \frac{1}{\lambda+1})d + 2$, specially for $\lambda = 1$, $\mu = 0$ and d = n/2. 'No information' refers to the restriction regardless of the strategy used. And adversary has no information of that. 'Fully deterministic' means that the communication strategy between two committees is completely determined and public. Note that this is the strategy employed by all existing Fluid MPC schemes, and under this strategy, no level of security can be achieved. 'Completely random' means that each party selects the recipient of their message randomly. Adversary can know this random strategy but has no idea of the exact transmit ways. In this case, until n = 1000, the adversary's success rate remains above 0.4, making it extremely difficult to achieve even the most basic level of security.

Restriction for $O(n)$ Complexity $\mathcal{F}_{\mathsf{reshare}}$. Assuming that π_{reshare} is a procedure to realize $\mathcal{F}_{\mathsf{reshare}}$, we give the Theorem 1 of limitations for designing π_{reshare}. We assume the number of parties to a linear arrange of a constant number n, i.e., $\forall j \in [D], an \leq n_j \leq bn$, where a and b are two constant numbers. The proof is shown in Appendix B.1.

Theorem 1. *If the communication cost of realizing $\mathcal{F}_{\mathsf{reshare}}$ is required to be $O(n)$. Then, the parties in the last transmitted committee $C^{j'}$ can be divided into two categories. One category consists of $\mu = o(n) \geq 0$ parties. These parties can receive, without restriction, a total of no more than $T(\mu, n_{j'-1}, n_{j'}) = O(n)$ field elements from any parties in the $C^{j'-1}$, and $T(0, n_{j'-1}, n_{j'}) = 0$. The other category consists of the remaining $n_{j'} - \mu$ parties, and each party can receive at most γ field elements from each of up to λ parties in the $C^{j'-1}$, for fixed constants $\lambda, \gamma > 0$.*

Thus the entire communication from $C^{j'-1}$ to $C^{j'}$ costs at most $\lambda\gamma(bn - \mu) + T(\mu, n_{j'-1}, n_{j'})$ field elements. If, in addition, $t_{j'} + \frac{t_{j'-1}}{\lambda} \geq d_{j'} + 2$ (equivalent to $t \geq (1 - \frac{1}{\lambda+1})(d_{j'} + 2)$ when $t_{j'} = t_{j'-1} = t$), then, even against a static semi-honest adversary,

- *no information-theoretically secure $\mathcal{F}_{\mathsf{reshare}}$ implementation exists, and*
- *no PPT secure $\mathcal{F}_{\mathsf{reshare}}$ implementation exists whenever 1.$t_{j'} \geq d_{j'}$, or 2.$t_{j'} < d_{j'}$ and n is below a moderate threshold.*

Restriction for $O(n)$ Fluid MPC. Now, using Corollary 1 along with Theorem 1, we can derive Theorem 2 that provides conditional constraints for designing Fluid MPC with $O(n)$ complexity.

Theorem 2. *If the communication cost of secret share based protocol Π_{MPC} to realize multiplication gate of $\mathcal{F}_{\text{DABB}}$ is required to be $O(n)$. Without loss of generality, we consider that committee $\mathcal{C}^j$ has the input of the multiplication gate and executes the protocol to let $\mathcal{C}^{j'}$ gain the result shares. Then, the parties in $\mathcal{C}^{j'}$ can be divided into two categories. One category consists of $\mu = o(n) \geq 0$ parties. These parties can receive, without restriction, a total of no more than $T(\mu, n_{j'-1}, n_{j'}) = O(n)$ field elements from any parties in the $\mathcal{C}^{j'-1}$, and $T(0, n_{j'-1}, n_{j'}) = 0$. The other category consists of the remaining $n_{j'} - \mu$ parties, and each party can receive at most γ field elements from each of up to λ parties in the $\mathcal{C}^{j'-1}$, for fixed constants $\lambda, \gamma > 0$.*

Thus the entire communication from $\mathcal{C}^{j'-1}$ to $\mathcal{C}^{j'}$ costs at most $\lambda\gamma(bn - \mu) + T(\mu, n_{j'-1}, n_{j'})$ field elements. If, in addition, $t_{j'} + \frac{t_{j'-1}}{\lambda} \geq d_{j'} + 2$ (equivalent to $t \geq (1 - \frac{1}{\lambda+1})(d_{j'} + 2)$ when $t_{j'} = t_{j'-1} = t$), then, even against a static semi-honest adversary,

- *no information-theoretically secure Π_{MPC} exists, and*
- *no PPT secure Π_{MPC} exists whenever 1. $t_{j'} \geq d_{j'}$, or 2. $t_{j'} < d_{j'}$ and n is below a moderate threshold.*

proof. As illustrated in Corollary 1, if we consider the multiply computation of Π_{MPC}, then it can be constructed to a procedure π_{reshare} that can realize $\mathcal{F}_{\text{reshare}}$ with same communication cost between each layer from committee $\mathcal{C}^j$ to $\mathcal{C}^{j'}$. According to the restrictions in Theorem 1 for π_{reshare}, these conditions are also applicable to Π_{MPC}. ∎

5 Efficient Fluid MPC Protocol Based on Random Double Sharings

Recall the idea presented in the introduction: we want to design a Fluid MPC protocol meets the bound while approaching the efficiency of the best traditional MPC schemes. We design an efficient Fluid MPC based on Shamir secret share and random double sharing. It can be seen that the protocol is optimal when $\lambda = 1, \mu = 0$ and $\gamma = 1$, considering that $\lambda \geq 1$ and $\mu \geq 0$. In these conditions, $t < d/2 + 1$ must be meet to avoid the bound for realizing $\mathcal{F}_{\text{DABB}}$. Therefore, to realize the efficiency, we propose a Fluid MPC protocol for $\lambda = 1, \mu = 0, \gamma = 1$, and $t \leq d/2$. This protocol achieves maximal Fluidity with the constant number of parties in each committee. We assume that $\forall j, |\mathcal{C}^j| = n$ and use (d, n)-Shamir secret sharing, where $d < n/2$. We will begin with basic constructions and then demonstrate the final protocol later.

5.1 Random Sharings Generation

At first, in the Fluid MPC protocol and reshare scheme proposed in this paper, random double sharings $[r]_d, [r]_{2d}$ are needed for the multiplication scheme. At the same time, the random zero sharings $[0]_d$ are also needed for the construction of the $\mathcal{F}_{\mathsf{reshare}}$. Therefore, to be rigorous, we first present the implementations of two functionalities $\mathcal{F}_{\mathsf{double-rand}}$ and $\mathcal{F}_{\mathsf{zero}}$. These concepts draw parallels with those presented in [1]. Thus, we only briefly demonstrate usages without detailed definitions, and we refer readers to their work for formal definitions. Procedures that implement these two functionalities are shown in the full version [29].

Functionality 3: $\mathcal{F}_{\mathsf{double-rand}}$ [1]

Functionality: Distribute degree-d and degree-$2d$ random shares of the same random value r to $\mathcal{C}^j$.

Functionality 4: $\mathcal{F}_{\mathsf{zero}}$ [1]

Functionality: Distribute degree $2d$ random shares of $o = 0$ to $\mathcal{C}^j$.

5.2 Efficient Reshare for Shamir Secret Sharing

Given limitations in Sect. 4 and Theorem 1, we propose a procedure π_{reshare} for resharing $[r]_d$ using a (d, n)-Shamir threshold secret sharing, under the optimal conditions $t \leq \frac{d}{2}$ and $\lambda = 1, \gamma = 1, \mu = 0$. According to the Corollary 3 and Theorem 1, these settings contribute to the theoretically optimal communication cost for the implementations of $\mathcal{F}_{\mathsf{reshare}}$. In brief, to realize reshare, we add a random sharing of zero $[0]_d$ to $[r]_d$ and let the parties transfer their shares one-to-one. Since $t \leq d/2$, the adversary can get at most d shares, which ensures the security of reshare. We first propose the $\pi_{\mathsf{rs-two}}$ for the two-layers situation[5]. Then, π_{reshare} is built by repeating execute $\pi_{\mathsf{rs-two}}$. We give the Lemma 3 to demonstrate the proposed procedure can securely compute functionality $\mathcal{F}_{\mathsf{reshare}}$ without checking the correct of output, which actually achieves *weak privacy.*

Lemma 3. *The procedure π_{reshare} can securely compute the functionality $\mathcal{F}_{\mathsf{reshare}}$ with Weak Privacy in the $\mathcal{F}_{\mathsf{zero}}$-hybrid model in the presence of a malicious R-adaptive adversary and committees have same settings of t, d, n and $t \leq d/2$.*

[5] It is worth noting that $\pi_{\mathsf{rs-two}}$ bears some similarities to the work in [1]. However, the scheme proposed in this paper applies to all linear secret sharing schemes and is proven to be theoretically optimal.

Procedure 1: $\pi_{\mathsf{rs-two}}$

Usage: $\mathcal{C}^j$ reshare a re-randomized (d,n)-threshold share $[v]_d^j$ to committee $\mathcal{C}^{j+1}$.

1. $\mathcal{C}^j$ invoke $\mathcal{F}_{\mathsf{zero}}$ to get a random zero sharing $[0]_d^j$.
2. The parties of $\rfloor^j$ locally compute $[v']_d^j = [v]_d^j + [0]_d^j$.
3. $\forall P_i^{j-1} \in \mathcal{C}^{j-1}$, each party sends $v_i'^j$ to $P_i^{j+1} \in \mathcal{C}^{j+1}$.
4. $\mathcal{C}^{j+1}$ output $[v']_d^{j+1}$.

Procedure 2: π_{reshare}

Usage: $,j$ reshare a re-randomized (d,n)-threshold share $[v]_d^j$ to committee $\mathcal{C}^{j'}$.

1. For k in $[j, j'-1]$, $\mathcal{C}^k$ invokes $\pi_{\mathsf{rs-two}}$ to reshare the $[v]_d^k$ to $[v]_d^{k+1}$
2. $\mathcal{C}^{j'}$ outputs $[v]_d^{j'}$.

The proof of Lemma 3 is shown in the full version [29]. Furthermore, a correctness verification stage must be considered to achieve the *secure with abort.* We use the robust circuit idea designed in [7], which is informally described below.

1. All parties in $\mathcal{C}^j$ have random share $[r]_d^j$ and inputs $\{[v]_d^j, [rv]_d^j\}$.
2. All parties in $\mathcal{C}^j$ use π_{reshare} to reshare $[v]_d^j, [rv]_d^j$ and $[r]_d$ separately.
3. Open the random number r, then all parties open share $[dis]_d = [rv]_d^{j'} - r \cdot [v]_d^{j'}$ and check if $dis = 0$.

Consider that the r is not known to the adversary before it is opened, the probability of the adversary cheating successfully is statistically negligible. Moreover, although the stages described before can defeat a malicious adversary, we do not need to do the checking for every reshare implementation separately. The check for all gates and reshares can be done together with the robust circuit idea before the output stage of the Fluid MPC protocol.

5.3 Secure Multiplication Based on Shamir Secret Sharing

Using the procedures we presented before, in this section, we propose an efficient multiplication procedure π_{mult} for Fluid MPC. Overall, this procedure originates from a series of Shamir MPC multiplication protocols [8,20,21] based on P_{king} and random double sharings. However, in the Fluid MPC settings, random double sharings $[r]_d^j, [r]_{2d}^j$ are generated in real time and used to mask multiplication results in $\mathcal{C}^j$. After masking, degree-d sharings $[r]_d^j$ used for unmasking need to be reshared to $\mathcal{C}^{j+2}$.

Procedure 3: π_{mult}

Usage: $\mathcal{C}^j$ hold $[x]_d^j, [y]_d^j$, and $\mathcal{C}^{j+2}$ output $[x \cdot y]_d^{j+2}$.

1. $\mathcal{C}^j$ invokes $\pi_{\mathsf{double-rand}}$ to obtain $[r]_d^j, [r]_{2d}^j$.
2. The parties of $\mathcal{C}^j$ locally compute

$$[e]_{2d}^j = [x]_d^j \cdot [y]_d^j + [r]_{2d}^j.$$

   Then, all parties in $\mathcal{C}^j$ jointly select a special party P_{king} in $\mathcal{C}^{j+1}$. Parties send $[e]_{2d}^j$ to P_{king} and invoke π_{reshare} so that $\mathcal{C}^{j+2}$ get $[r]_d^{j+2}$.
3. $P_{king} \in \mathcal{C}^{j+1}$ locally runs $\Pi_{\mathrm{LSS}}.\mathrm{Rec}([e]_{2d}^j)$ to obtain $e = x \cdot y + r$ and broadcasts e to $\mathcal{C}^{j+2}$.
4. All parties in $\mathcal{C}^{j+2}$ locally compute $[x \cdot y]_d^{j+2} = e - [r]_d^{j+2}$.

It is worth noting that π_{mult} operates with maximal Fluidity, and all communications can be completed in a one-way manner. The computations of the committees are independent of each other and can be performed simultaneously.

5.4 Efficient Fluid MPC Protocol

With all the preparation, we present our efficient Fluid MPC protocol in this section, which achieves maximal fluidity and is secure against the *malicious R-adaptive* adversary. The proposed protocol assumes that all committees have the same number of parties and use the same (d, n)-threshold secret sharing scheme. Similar to the idea of [7], we will first present the *weak privacy* protocol and then modify it to the malicious security. The *weak privacy* conception for Fluid MPC was defined in [7], which protects privacy in a malicious R-adaptive adversary environment without guaranteeing the correctness of the output.

Weak Privacy Scheme The Protocol Π_{wpmain} presented here achieves *Weak Privacy* against a *malicious R-adaptive adversary.* The proof of Theorem 3 is deferred to the full version [29].

Theorem 3. *Let $\mathcal{A}$ be a malicious R-adaptive adversary, protocol Π_{wpmain} can compute $\mathcal{F}_{\mathsf{DABB}}$ with Weak Privacy in the presence of $\mathcal{A}$ in the $\mathcal{F}_{\mathsf{commit}}$-hybrid model, controlling at most t servers in each epoch and d clients.*

Malicious Security With Abort. Finally, considering that Π_{wpmain} is a linear-based Fluid MPC protocol, according to the *Malicious Security Compiler* and Theorem 2 proposed in CGG[+]21 [7], Π_{wpmain} can achieve **Malicious R-Adaptive Security With Abort** under the same fluidity conditions by computing a robust version circuit $\widetilde{C}$ of the layered arithmetic circuit C, in which $\widetilde{C}$ has one more layer than C and mostly with its width increasing to at most $4w + 4$ compared to the width w of C.

Protocol 4: Π_{wpmain}

Input: $\forall P_i \in \mathcal{C}^{\mathsf{clnt}}$, if P_i wants to generate a Shamir sharing of input x_i, then it executes $\Pi_{\mathrm{LSS}}.\mathsf{Share}(x_i)$ to get $[x_i]_d^{\mathsf{clnt}}$.

Computing: Each committee will sequentially compute the arithmetic gates contained in the corresponding layer of circuit C. Each layer of the circuit will involve three committees, executing the following for different arithmetic gates:

Linear combination: To compute linear combination of $([x_1]_d^j, \cdots, [x_\ell]_d^j)$ and $\boldsymbol{a}^T$, all parties in committee $\mathcal{C}^j$ locally obtain $[z]_d^j = [a_1x_1 + \cdots + a_\ell x_\ell]_d^j = ([x_1]_d^j, \cdots, [x_\ell]_d^j) \cdot \boldsymbol{a}^T$. Then, all parties in committee $\mathcal{C}^j$ invoke π_{reshare} to let committee $\mathcal{C}^{j+2}$ get $[z]_d^{j+2}$.

Multiplication: To compute multiplication of $[x]_d^j$ and $[y]_d^j$, committee $\mathcal{C}^j$ invokes π_{mult} on them to let committee $\mathcal{C}^{j+2}$ get the result $[z]_d^{j+2} = [x \cdot y]_d^j$.

Output: Parties in the last committee $\mathcal{C}^{last}$ open the circuit result shares $[\boldsymbol{z}]_d^{last} = ([z_1]_d^{last}, \cdots)$ to the clients. Clients then reconstruct them and output $\boldsymbol{z}$.

5.5 Efficiency Analysis and Implementation Comparison

We primarily consider the communication complexity (measured in the number of field elements) required to compute a single multiplication gate under both semi-honest and malicious R-adaptive adversary settings for these three protocols. It is worth noting that BEP23 [1] does not provide specific implementations for functionalities such as $\mathcal{F}_{\mathsf{double-rand}}$ and $\mathcal{F}_{\mathsf{zero}}$. In the following comparison, we assume that their implementation is similar to what is proposed in this work.

Table 2. Average Communication Cost for Single Multiplication Gate Evaluation

Protocols	Types	Threshold	Semi-honest	Malicious
CGG$^+$21 [7]	Fluid	$t < n/2$	n^2	$4n^2$
BEP23 [1]		$t < n/2$	$60n$	$232n$
BEP24 [2]*		$t < n/3$	-	$O(n)$
Our Work		$t < n/4$	$9.3n(9\frac{1}{3}n)$	$37.3n(37\frac{1}{3}n)$
ATLAS [20]	Traditional	$t < n/2$	$4n$	$4n$

* Notice the work BEP24 [2] with $t < n/3$ threshold aims for high security (perfectly secure) and uses similar computation technic with BEP23 [1], we omit the specific communication cost.

As shown in Table 2, both our work and CGG$^+$21 [7] utilize robust arithmetic circuits to achieve malicious security with abort. The size of the robust circuit $\widetilde{C}$ scales proportionally to the original circuit C, depending on the specific structure of C. To compare the efficiency of our protocol, we consider the worst-case scenario, where a multiplication gate, when converted to a robust arithmetic circuit, results in a computational load equivalent to 4 multiplication gates. Even in this scenario, and ignoring constant-level communication costs (which are significantly higher in [1] than in our protocol), our protocol demonstrates a significant efficiency advantage. Compared to BEP23 [1], our protocol incurs only 1/6 of its communication overhead for both semi-honest and malicious security.

To emphasize the efficiency advantages of the protocol proposed in this paper, we further conduct a simulation comparison with ATLAS [20], the state-of-the-art traditional MPC scheme. Interested readers are referred to Appendix C for details.

6 Conclusion

In this work, we studied the communication complexity of Fluid MPC in the maximally fluid setting and identified resharing as the key abstraction governing its cost. By formalizing the reduction from Fluid MPC multiplication to reshare, we obtained a communication resilience trade-off with security settings. Motivated by this bound, we then present concrete Fluid MPC constructions with linear communication per multiplication gate, obtaining improvements over prior work in both the semi honest and malicious with abort settings.

Acknowledgments.. This work was supported by the National Cryptologic Science Fund of China (2025NCSF02022), the National Natural Science Foundation of China (62372020).

Appendix

A Fluid MPC and Security Model

Here, we separately introduce conceptions of fluid MPC and various dimensional definitions of the adversary $\mathcal{A}$ and corruption, referring readers to [1,7,24] for complete definitions.

A.1 Fluid MPC Model

Fluidity. This is defined as the minimum number of synchronous communication rounds in any epoch during the execution stage. We refer to a protocol as achieving maximal Fluidity if each epoch j lasts only one communication round, i.e., no interaction exists in the computation phase. In this paper, consistent with [1,7,24], we focus exclusively on maximal Fluidity.
Committee Formation. We consider that every committee is determined 'On-the-fly', which means that committee $\mathcal{C}^{j+1}$ is somehow determined and known to every party $P_i^j \in \mathcal{C}^j$ at the start of the hand-off phase of epoch j. Taking inspiration from [1], we assume that the environment $\mathcal{E}$ informs $\mathcal{C}^j$ about the

committee $\mathcal{C}^{j+1}$ at the start of the hand-off phase of epoch j. We denote the number of parties in committee $\mathcal{C}^j$ as n_j. Finally, we denote the number of committees or epochs as D.

A.2 Security Model

Semi-honest or Malicious. Adversary $\mathcal{A}$ receives the corrupted parties' local state determined by environment $\mathcal{E}$. As in the traditional MPC setting, for a semi-honest adversary, $\mathcal{A}$ only knows the local state, while a malicious adversary $\mathcal{A}$ can take full control of the corrupted parties.
Corruption Threshold. Different from previous works [1,7,24], we consider a more refined corruption threshold. We denote t_j as the number of parties in committee $\mathcal{C}^j$ that can be adversary corrupt. We mainly consider the *retroactive effect* adversary, which means if a party is corrupted, then it will be counted to meet every corruption threshold of the committee that includes this party. To simplify, we can assume that every committee has different parties. Specifically, without loss of generality, we assume that for every committee $\mathcal{C}^j$, $t_j = \Theta(n_j)$ or, in other words, $n_j > t_j \geq \sigma n_j$, where σ is a constant positive number according to the security parameter.
Point of Corruption. As demonstrated before, the committee $\mathcal{C}^j$ is determined at the start of the hand-off phase of epoch $j-1$. Similar to the definition in [7], in a *static* manner, an adversary can only corrupt the parties when $\mathcal{C}^j$ is determined. An *adaptive* adversary, however, can corrupt parties at any time when $\mathcal{C}^j$ is alive.
Effect on Prior Epochs. Similar to [7], we consider a *retroactive effect* adversary. Consider that a party may be alive in multiple committees, *retroactive effect* means when a party in $\mathcal{C}^j$ is corrupted, then committees before $\mathcal{C}^j$ who include this party have to count it to meet the corruption threshold. For simplicity, we can consider a party that only lives in one committee.
Dynamic Arithmetic Black Box. While we discuss the limitation of communication cost in the weakest setting, even with a *semi-honest R-static adversary*, the protocol we proposed can defend against a *malicious R-adaptive adversary* with abort. Security with abort is general for designing MPC protocols, ensuring that honest clients can all receive the output or all of the parties abort. That is the same as in previous works [1,7,24]. Moreover, we adapt the dynamic arithmetic black box (DABB) ideal functionality $\mathcal{F}_{\mathsf{DABB}}$ shown in [1,24], which is based on the finite field $\mathbb{F}_p$ and includes 'Parameters, Init, Input, Next-Committee, Linear Combination, Multiply and Output'. Furthermore, to formally define communication and committee management, we use the functionality $\mathcal{F}_{\mathsf{commit}}$, which is also used in [1]. The formal definitions of $\mathcal{F}_{\mathsf{DABB}}$ and $\mathcal{F}_{\mathsf{commit}}$ are shown in Appendix A.3.
Weak Privacy. In our work, we adopt the idea of *Weak Privacy* and *Malicious Security Compiler* proposed in [7]. In brief, *Weak privacy* describes a Fluid MPC scheme that can protect privacy in a *malicious R-adaptive adversary* environment without guaranteeing the correctness of the output. The *Malicious Security Compiler*, on the other hand, provides a method to transform a linear-based

Fluid MPC scheme with Weak privacy into one with security with abort, where a linear protocol means every operation of the protocol is linear.

A.3 Dynamic Arithmetic Black Box (DABB)

We adapt the dynamic arithmetic black box (DABB) ideal functionality $\mathcal{F}_{\mathsf{DABB}}$ shown in [1,24], which is based on finite field $\mathbb{F}_p$. To further enhance the generality of $\mathcal{F}_{\mathsf{DABB}}$, we modify the $\mathcal{F}_{\mathsf{DABB}}$ definition from the works of [1,24] by revising 'Add' to 'Linear Combination'. This addresses the issue of vague definitions for scalar multiplication and scalar addition in previous works. It is worth noting that the 'relay gate', which transmits computed values to a later layer, can be implemented using a 'Linear combination gate' by simply setting $\boldsymbol{a} = (1, \cdots, 1)$. The $\mathcal{F}_{\mathsf{DABB}}$ we present includes 'Parameters, Init, Input, Next-Committee, Linear Combination, Multiply and Output', which is suitable for more common situations than the Fluid MPC model proposed in [7]. Similar to the traditional MPC, the designing of realizing Multiply will be the key part of the protocol. The formal definition of $\mathcal{F}_{\mathsf{DABB}}$ is shown following.

Functionality 5: $\mathcal{F}_{\mathsf{DABB}}$

Parameters: Finite field $\mathbb{F}_p$, universe $\mathcal{U}$ of parties, and set of clients $\mathcal{C}_{\mathrm{clnt}} \subseteq \mathcal{U}$. The functionality assumes that all parties have agreed upon public identifiers id_x, for each variable x used in the computation.
Init: On input $(\mathsf{Init}, \mathcal{C})$ from every party $P_i \in \mathcal{C}^{\mathrm{clnt}}$, where each P_i sends the same set $\mathcal{C} \subseteq \mathcal{U}$, initialize $j = 1, \mathcal{C}^1 = \mathcal{C}$ as the first active committee.
Input: On input $(\mathsf{Input}, \mathrm{id}_x, x)$ from some $P_i \in \mathcal{T}^{\mathrm{clnt}}$, and $(\mathsf{Input}, \mathrm{id}_x)$ from all other parties in $\mathcal{C}orr^{\mathrm{clnt}}$, store the pair (id_x, x).
Next-Committee: On input $(\mathsf{Next-Committee}, \mathcal{C})$ from every party $P_i \in \mathcal{C}^j$, where each P_i sends the same set $\mathcal{C} \subseteq \mathcal{U}$, update $j = j+1, \mathcal{C}^j = \mathcal{C}$.
Linear Combination: On input $(\mathsf{LC}, \mathrm{id}_z, \mathbf{id}_x, \boldsymbol{a})$ from every party $P_i \in \mathcal{C}^j$, where $\mathbf{id}_x$ is a vector of $(\mathrm{id}_{x_1}, \cdots \mathrm{id}_{x_\ell})$ and $\boldsymbol{a}$ is a ℓ-dimensional coefficient vector, compute $z = (x_1, \cdots, x_\ell) \cdot \boldsymbol{a}^T$ and store (id_z, z).
Multiply: On input $(\mathsf{Mult}, \mathrm{id}_z, \mathrm{id}_x, \mathrm{id}_y)$ from every party $P_i \in \mathcal{C}^j$, compute $z = x \cdot y$ and store (id_z, z).
Output: On input $(\mathsf{Output}, \{\mathrm{id}_{z_m}\})$ from every party $P_i \in \mathcal{C}^{\mathrm{clnt}} \cup \mathcal{C}^j$, where a value z_m for each id_{z_m} has been stored previously, retrieve $\{(\mathrm{id}_{z_m}, z_m)\}$ and them to adversary. Wait for input from the adversary, if it is Deliver, send the output to every $P_i \in \mathcal{C}^{\mathrm{clnt}}$. Otherwise, abort.

Furthermore, we use the functionality $\mathcal{F}_{\mathsf{commit}}$ to determine the communication between parties, which is also used and shown in [1].

B Constructions and Proofs Omitted from Main Text

B.1 Proof of Theorem 1

Proof. Firstly, we prove the situation when the settings of each committee are pairwise equal. The situation for $t \geq d$ is proved by Lemma 2 and the communication costs are proved in Corollary 3. When we consider $d > t \geq (1 - \frac{1}{\lambda+1})(d+2)$ and $\lfloor \frac{t}{\lambda} \rfloor \leq n - \mu$[6]. There exists a feasible corruption method for the adversary that allows it to compromise the privacy protection security of π_{reshare} with a non-zero probability. As described in Sect. 4.3, for adversaries with different capabilities, there exists a non-zero lower bound on the success rate of this attack.

For an adversary with information-theoretic capabilities, as shown in Eq. 1, the adversary can always find a corruption method. For an adversary with PPT capabilities. If the adversary has *adaptive* capabilities, then according to Sect. 4.3, a lower bound for its attack success probability can be given as $\epsilon_{\mathrm{ad}} \geq 1/\binom{n}{t}$. If the adversary has *static* capabilities, then according to the full version [29], a lower bound for its attack success probability can be given as $\epsilon_{\mathrm{st}} \geq \frac{\binom{n - \lfloor \frac{t}{\lambda} \rfloor}{d - \lfloor \frac{t}{\lambda} \rfloor + 1}}{\binom{n}{t}\binom{n}{d - \lfloor \frac{t}{\lambda} \rfloor + 1}}$. For the exact choice of n, t, λ, the values of ϵ_{ad} and ϵ_{st} are both nonzero constants.

However, considering that ϵ_{ad} and ϵ_{st} are both exponentially small in terms of n. As n increases, these two probabilities will rapidly decrease and can break through the adversary's attack success probability of $1/p$ commonly seen in existing MPC schemes [21,23]. Therefore, it is necessary for us to take the size of n into consideration. As shown in Table 1, there does not exist a procedure π_{reshare} that is secure for any number of parties n against a PPT adversary.

Secondly, for situation that committees have different setting. As mentioned in the information-theoretic adversary situation of Sect. 4.3, the adversary can corrupt $t_{j'-1}$ parties that denoted as $\mathcal{C}orr^{j'-1} \subset \mathcal{C}^{j'-1}$, which have none zero opportunity to encompass at least $\left\lfloor \frac{t_{j'-1}}{\lambda} \right\rfloor$ $\mathcal{S}_i^{j'-1} \in \mathcal{S}^{j'-1}$. Therefore, the adversary can gain $\left\lfloor \frac{t_{j'-1}}{\lambda} \right\rfloor$ parties' shares of secret v in committee $\mathcal{C}^{j'}$ without corruption. And corrupting $d_{j'} - \left\lfloor \frac{t_{j'-1}}{\lambda} \right\rfloor + 1$ more parties in $\mathcal{C}^{j'}$ will be enough for the adversary to obtain the secret v. To ensure this attack, $t_{j'-1}, t_{j'}$ and $d_{j'}$ have to meet the condition $t_{j'} \geq d_{j'} - \left\lfloor \frac{t_{j'-1}}{\lambda} \right\rfloor + 1$. Considering that $\left\lfloor \frac{t_{j'-1}}{\lambda} \right\rfloor > \frac{t_{j'-1}}{\lambda} - 1$, $t_{j'} + \frac{t_{j'-1}}{\lambda} \geq d_{j'} + 2$ is sufficient.

[6] The first condition can be satisfied because $2\lambda < d$. For the second condition, the opposite case $\lfloor \frac{t}{\lambda} \rfloor > n - \mu$ is demonstrated in Sect. 4.3. For the sake of brevity, it will not be elaborated upon in this proof.

B.2 Proof of Lemma 2

Proof. Assuming that there exists a π_{reshare} that can securely compute $\mathcal{F}_{\mathsf{reshare}}$ with at most $O(n)$ field elements communication cost, as shown in Table 3, we separate the proof into three parts.

Table 3. Proof strategy for Lemma 2

Steps	Situation	Adversary ability	Proof strategy
Part 1	$t > d$	PPT	Adversary can easily compute the secret with $t > d$ shares
Part 2	$t = d$	Information-theoretic	The state of a special party $P^2_{\text{ch}} \in \mathcal{C}^2$ can be controlled by the adversary without corruption.
Part 3	$t = d$	PPT/Statistical	Introducing three parameters μ, λ, γ to find more parties in $\mathcal{C}^2$ whose state can be controlled by the adversary without corruption.

Part 1. When $t > d$, the adversary can easily reconstruct the secret v based on shares held by corrupted parties, which means no π_{reshare} can securely compute $\mathcal{F}_{\mathsf{reshare}}$.
Part 2. As for $t = d$, we begin with an *information-theoretic adversary*, then we have the following claim:

Claim 1. There must exist a party $P^2_{\text{ch}} \in \mathcal{C}^2$, which can receive messages from at most t parties in committee $\mathcal{C}^1$. Otherwise, π_{reshare} will have at least $\Omega(n \cdot (t+1)) = \Omega(n^2)$ communication cost.

Adaptive Adversary. For the situation of the *adaptive* adversary, denote the set of parties in $\mathcal{C}^1$ who send messages to P^2_{ch} as $\mathcal{S}^1_{\text{ch}}$, $|\mathcal{S}^1_{\text{ch}}| = t$ (If $|\mathcal{S}^1_{\text{ch}}| < t$, add a sufficient amount of random parties from $\mathcal{S}^1_{\text{ch}}$ to make up for it). Then, the adversary will have probability of ϵ_{base} to corrupt all parties in $\mathcal{S}^1_{\text{ch}}$ exactly right, which means $\mathcal{C}orr^1 = \mathcal{S}^1_{\text{ch}}$. The probability is at least:

$$\epsilon_{\text{base}} = \Pr[\mathcal{C}orr^1 = \mathcal{S}^1_{\text{ch}}] = 1/\binom{n}{t} > 0.$$

Here $1/\binom{n}{t}$ is computed in a completely random situation in which the adversary has no information about the transmission strategy.[7]

When the adversary corrupts all parties in $\mathcal{S}^1_{\text{ch}}$ with non-zero probability ϵ_{base}, denote the messages received by P^2_{ch} from $P^1_i \in \mathcal{S}^1_{\text{ch}}$ as $\boldsymbol{m}_i = \{m_i^{(1)}, m_i^{(2)}, \cdots\}$.

[7] This situation is suitable with the *adaptive* adversary when the strategy is like that every $P^1_i \in \mathcal{C}^1$ randomly sends a message to a party in $\mathcal{C}^2$. In this strategy, before sending the message, there is no way to acquire the exact transmission choice. After sending the message, the parties in $\mathcal{C}^1$ will be permanently inactive.

According to the Fluid model, the share v^2_{ch} held by P^2_{ch} will be determined by the messages received from parties in $\mathcal{S}^1_{\text{ch}}$ and the random vector $\boldsymbol{z}$ generated by itself. That is, there exists a function f such that $v^2_{\text{ch}} = f(\bigcup_{P^1_i \in \mathcal{S}^1_{\text{ch}}} \boldsymbol{m}_i, \boldsymbol{z})$. Moreover, we point out that $v^2_{\text{ch}} = f(\bigcup_{P^1_i \in \mathcal{S}^1_{\text{ch}}} \boldsymbol{m}_i, \boldsymbol{z}) = f(\bigcup_{P^1_i \in \mathcal{S}^1_{\text{ch}}} \boldsymbol{m}_i, \boldsymbol{0})$.

Considering that shares $\{v^2_i\}$ held by $P^2_i \notin \mathcal{C}^2 \backslash P^2_{\text{ch}}$ is uniquely determined. Therefore, regardless of the value of the random vector $\boldsymbol{z}$, the calculated v^2_{ch} will be the same. As a result, the adversary can acquire v^2_{ch} by calculating $f(\bigcup_{P^1_i \in \mathcal{S}^1_{\text{ch}}} \boldsymbol{m}_i, \boldsymbol{0})$. It is worth noting that the *adaptive* adversary can do the corruption at any time during the committee's lifetime. Thus, it can corrupt other $t = d$ parties in $\mathcal{C}^2$, know $t+1 = d+1$ shares $\{v^2_{\text{ch}}\} \cup [v]_{\mathcal{C}orr^2}$ of v, and break the privacy of the protocol.
Static Adversary. As discussed before, adversary has to corrupt other t parties in $\mathcal{C}^2$ except P^2_{ch}. However, the *static* adversary can only decide the corruption at the beginning of the hand-off phase, when $\mathcal{C}^2$ is determined by the environment $\mathcal{E}$. At this point, the adversary may have no idea of the specific transfer methods that will be used during the hand-off phase. Thus, the *static* adversary needs to design the corruption strategy according to the transfer strategy of $\pi_{\textsf{reshare}}$[8]. Note that no matter how $\pi_{\textsf{reshare}}$ is designed, the adversary can choose corrupted set $\mathcal{C}orr^2$ randomly, which has at least a p_{st} probability to meet $\mathcal{C}orr^2 \subset \mathcal{C}^2 \backslash P^2_{\text{ch}}$. In which p_{st} is:

$$p_{\text{st}} = \Pr\left[\mathcal{C}orr^2 \subset \mathcal{C}^2 \backslash P^2_{\text{ch}}\right] = \frac{\binom{n-1}{t}}{\binom{n}{t}} = 1 - \frac{t}{n} \geq 1 - \sigma,$$

which is greater than a non-zero constant. Therefore, the *static* adversary has at least

$$\epsilon_{\text{st\_loose}} \geq \epsilon_{\text{base}} \cdot p_{\text{st}} = \frac{\binom{n-1}{t}}{\binom{n}{t}^2} > 0$$

probability to successfully compromise the privacy security of $\pi_{\textsf{reshare}}$, which means informational security is impossible.
Part 3. As for a PPT or statistical adversary (For the sake of simplicity, we will only mention PPT adversary later), if we consider that the parameter n is a constant number, then $\epsilon_{\text{st\_loose}}$ will be a non-zero constant probability, and the proof before is enough.

Nevertheless, in the Fluid MPC setting, n is a variable number. This means n is included in the security parameter σ and contributes to the success rate of the adversary. In this situation, the success rate $\epsilon_{\text{base}}, \epsilon_{\text{st\_loose}}$ of the adversary is inversely proportional to the n-th power, which is secure with the PPT adversary. As far as we know, this is the *first* work to connect the number of parties with the security probability in the MPC with dynamic parties.

Considering that p_{st} is greater than a non-zero constant, we have to enhance the ϵ_{base} to be a polynomial function of n. Recall the claim in Part 2, the t

[8] This is meaning that every strategy of $\pi_{\textsf{reshare}}$ will have a 'Best Strategy' for adversary, which is not needed in the proof of lemma 2. However, this will be discussed in a later section, especially for the situation of the PPT adversary and $t < d$.

restriction is much more than needed. We have a tighter claim. Assuming that there exists a π_{reshare} that can securely compute $\mathcal{F}_{\mathsf{reshare}}$ with at most $O(n)$ field elements communication cost, we have:

Claim 2. Committee $\mathcal{C}^2$ can be divided into two sets $\mathcal{H}$ and $\mathcal{L}$ according to the received data volume measured in field elements. In which $|\mathcal{H}| = \mu = o(n)$ is asymptotically negligible to n and $|\mathcal{L}| = |\mathcal{C}^2| - \mu = n - \mu$. And, $\forall P_i^2 \in \mathcal{L}$, P_i^2 can receive single message from no more than λ parties separately in the committee $\mathcal{C}^1$ and every message has at most γ field elements, where $\lambda > 0, \gamma > 0$ are constant integers.

Here, we firstly show why this separation exists. As shown in Fig. 2, we let any party that receives $\omega(1)$ field elements belong to 'heavy' set $\mathcal{H}$. Then $|\mathcal{H}| = \mu$ must be asymptotically negligible to n (i.e., $o(n)$), otherwise communication costs of $\mathcal{H}$ will be $\omega(1) \cdot \Omega(n) = \omega(n)$. We use $T(\mu, n) = O(n)$ to describe the total communication costs of $\mathcal{H}$, notes that $T(0, n) = 0$. The last $n - \mu$ parties are denoted as 'light' set $\mathcal{L}$. Considering that $\mu = o(n)$, thus $|\mathcal{L}| \sim n$. Every party in $\mathcal{L}$ must be restricted to constant communication costs (i.e., $\lambda \cdot \gamma$), otherwise communication costs of $\mathcal{L}$ will be $\omega(1) \cdot \Omega(n) = \omega(n)$.

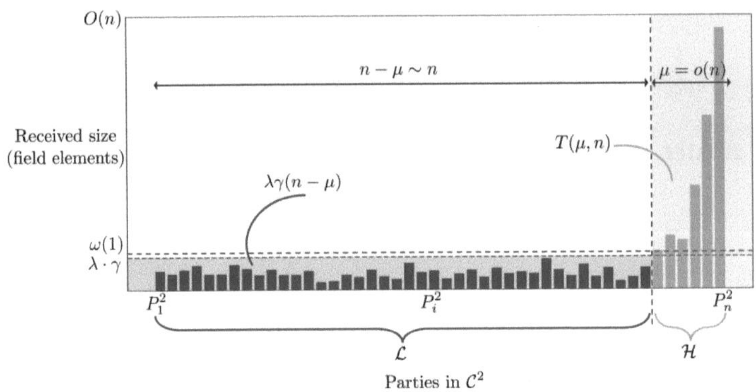

Fig. 2. Data received by committee $\mathcal{C}^2$ under an $O(n)$ communication bound. If a protocol implements the functionality $\mathcal{F}_{\mathsf{reshare}}$ to transmit a share to $\mathcal{C}^2$ with total communication cost $O(n)$, then the final-round communication pattern must follow the structure illustrated in the figure. Without loss of generality, let the last $\mu = o(n)$ *heavy* parties (denoted by $\mathcal{H}$) each receive up to $O(n)$ field elements, yielding a total communication cost $T(\mu, n) = O(n)$ (with $T(0, n) = 0$). The remaining $n - \mu \approx n$ *light* parties, denoted by $\mathcal{L}$, each receive at most $\lambda \cdot \gamma$ field elements, where $\lambda \geq 0$ and $\gamma \geq 0$ are fixed constants. Hence, the total data received by all parties in $\mathcal{L}$ is $\lambda\gamma(n - \mu)$.

Furthermore, if $\lambda = 0$ or $\gamma = 0$, all $n - \mu$ parties in $\mathcal{L}$ would not receive any input. Consequently, the shares held by these parties could only be random values or 0 without loss of generality. Which is unacceptable to recover the secret v. To sum up, we have $\mu = o(n) \geq 0, \gamma \geq 1$ and $\lambda \geq 1$.

Denote the set of parties in $\mathcal{C}^1$ who send messages to $P_i^2 \in \mathcal{L}$ as $\mathcal{S}_i^1$(without loss of generality, we assume $\mathcal{L} = \{P_1^2, \cdots, P_{n-\mu}^2\}$). We set $|\mathcal{S}_i^1| = \lambda$, which will be filled up with other parties when $\mathcal{S}_i^1$ does not have enough parties. Furthermore, we denote that $\mathcal{S}^1 = \{\mathcal{S}_i^1 | P_i^2 \in \mathcal{L}\}$. The adversary-controlled set of parties $\mathcal{C}orr^1$ only needs to contain any $\mathcal{S}_i^1 \in \mathcal{S}^1$ to gain all input messages for party $P_i^2 \in \mathcal{C}^2$. This enables the computation of the share held by P_i^2. Subsequently, by selecting $\mathcal{C}orr^2 \subset \mathcal{C}^2 \backslash P_i^2$, the adversary can obtain $t + 1 = d + 1$ shares, ultimately compromising the privacy of the secret.

Adaptive Adversary. Thus, we consider the probability of the adversary having $\mathcal{C}orr^1$ contain at least one $\mathcal{S}_i^1 \in \mathcal{S}^1$, which is $\epsilon_{\text{ad}} = \Pr\left[\exists \mathcal{S}_i^1 \in \mathcal{S}^1, \mathcal{S}_i^1 \subset \mathcal{C}orr^1\right]$

However, ϵ_{ad} is a variable according to the distribution of $\mathcal{S}^1$. Thus, it is hard to compute an exact value of ϵ_{ad}. Fortunately, we can give a sufficiently large lower bound of ϵ_{ad}. The worst strategy for adversary is choosing the corruption $\mathcal{C}orr^1$ randomly. Then, let event A_i denote $\mathcal{S}_i^1 \subset \mathcal{C}orr^1$, whose probability can be computed as: $p_i = \Pr[A_i] = \binom{n-\lambda}{t-\lambda} / \binom{n}{t}$. It is worth noting that p_i is a polynomial function of n. At the same time,

$$\epsilon_{\text{ad}} = \Pr\left[\bigcup_{i=1}^{n-\mu} A_i\right] \geq p_i.$$

Therefore, ϵ_{ad} is none-negligible for a PPT adversary. As mentioned before, ϵ_{ad} is the success probability of the *adaptive* adversary executing the attack.

Static Adversary. The *static* adversary additionally needs to meet the condition $\mathcal{C}orr^2 \subset \mathcal{C}^2 \backslash P_i^2$ to execute the attack while having $\exists\ \mathcal{S}_i^1 \in \mathcal{S}^1, \quad \mathcal{S}_i^1 \subset \mathcal{C}orr^1$. Therefore, considering that the choices of $\mathcal{C}orr^1$ and $\mathcal{C}orr^2$ are uncorrelated when corruption is random, we can also give a lower bound for the success probability of *static* adversary to execute the attack as follows

$$\epsilon_{\text{st}} \geq p_i \cdot p_{\text{st}} = \frac{\binom{n-\lambda}{t-\lambda}\binom{n-1}{t}}{\binom{n}{t}^2}.$$

This is computed by only considering the inputs of one party $P_i^{j'}$ controlled by the adversary. Noting that $\binom{n-\lambda}{t-\lambda}\binom{n-1}{t} / \binom{n}{t}^2$ is a polynomial function of n, the attack strategy is feasible for PPT adversaries. ■

C Efficiency Comparison with Traditional MPC

To emphasize the efficiency advantages of the protocol proposed in this paper, we conduct a simulation comparison with ATLAS [20], the state-of-the-art traditional MPC scheme, within a local area network (LAN) environment under a semi-honest adversary[9]. The results, shown in Table 4, are expressed in seconds. These simulations are performed using the event simulator OMNeT++ [26].

[9] The code for our protocol is publicly accessible at https://github.com/stillalive-HaHaHa/Fluid-protocol.

We assume each pair of participants communicates over channels with latency ranging from 0.4 ms to 0.5 ms and a channel rate of 100 Mbps. Computations are based on a finite field of size $2^{31} - 1$, with each field element represented using 32 bits for convenience. We evaluate the communication time required to compute a circuit consisting of $1,000,000$ multiplication gates at various circuit depths. Additionally, since our protocol does not consider on-the-fly committee establishment, we assume that committee formation is completed instantly for simulation purposes.

Table 4. Comparison of communication time cost for one million multiplication gates between our protocol and state-of-art traditional protocol

Protocol	Depth	Number of parties				
		5	9	13	17	21
Ours	1k	2.5307	2.3412	2.3945	2.3465	2.3219
	5k	6.2470	6.0429	6.3347	6.2161	6.1634
	10k	11.2083	10.9456	11.2602	11.0487	11.0017
ATLAS [20]	1k	1.5807	1.6117	1.6199	1.6293	1.6330
	5k	5.2721	5.4500	5.5021	5.5556	5.5784
	10k	9.8868	10.2480	10.3551	10.4639	10.5104

Note: One million multiplication gates are computed on a LAN and measured in seconds.

In practical computing environments, the time required for a single message transmission is composed of communication delay and data transfer time. The communication delay is determined solely by network conditions and remains unaffected by the communication complexity of the protocol. Therefore, it can be observed that the actual communication overhead of our proposed Fluid MPC protocol is only marginally greater than that of ATLAS. This demonstrates that the functionality of Fluid MPC can be achieved with relatively low cost, underscoring its practical applicability and value.

References

1. Bienstock, A., Escudero, D., Polychroniadou, A.: On linear communication complexity for (maximally) fluid MPC. In: Handschuh, H., Lysyanskaya, A. (eds.) Advances in Cryptology – CRYPTO 2023, Part I. Lecture Notes in Computer Science, vol. 14081, pp. 263–294. Springer, Cham, Switzerland, Santa Barbara, CA, USA (Aug 20–24, 2023). https://doi.org/10.1007/978-3-031-38557-5_9
2. Bienstock, A., Escudero, D., Polychroniadou, A.: Perfectly secure fluid MPC with abort and linear communication complexity. IACR Commun. Cryptol. **1**(4) (2025). https://doi.org/10.62056/aesg89n4e
3. Blakley, G.R., Meadows, C.: Security of ramp schemes. In: Blakley, G.R., Chaum, D. (eds.) Advances in Cryptology – CRYPTO'84. Lecture Notes in Computer Science, vol. 196, pp. 242–268. Springer Berlin Heidelberg, Germany, Santa Barbara, CA, USA (Aug 19–23, 1984). https://doi.org/10.1007/3-540-39568-7_20

4. Campanelli, M., David, B., Khoshakhlagh, H., Konring, A., Nielsen, J.B.: Encryption to the future - a paradigm for sending secret messages to future (anonymous) committees. In: Agrawal, S., Lin, D. (eds.) Advances in Cryptology – ASIACRYPT 2022, Part III. Lecture Notes in Computer Science, vol. 13793, pp. 151–180. Springer, Cham, Switzerland, Taipei, Taiwan (Dec 5–9, 2022). https://doi.org/10.1007/978-3-031-22969-5_6
5. Cascudo, I., David, B., Garms, L., Konring, A.: YOLO YOSO: fast and simple encryption and secret sharing in the YOSO model. In: Agrawal, S., Lin, D. (eds.) Advances in Cryptology – ASIACRYPT 2022, Part I. Lecture Notes in Computer Science, vol. 13791, pp. 651–680. Springer, Cham, Switzerland, Taipei, Taiwan (Dec 5–9, 2022). https://doi.org/10.1007/978-3-031-22963-3_22
6. Chida, K., et al.: Fast large-scale honest-majority MPC for malicious adversaries. In: Shacham, H., Boldyreva, A. (eds.) Advances in Cryptology – CRYPTO 2018, Part III. Lecture Notes in Computer Science, vol. 10993, pp. 34–64. Springer, Cham, Switzerland, Santa Barbara, CA, USA (Aug 19–23, 2018). https://doi.org/10.1007/978-3-319-96878-0_2
7. Choudhuri, A.R., Goel, A., Green, M., Jain, A., Kaptchuk, G.: Fluid MPC: secure multiparty computation with dynamic participants. In: Malkin, T., Peikert, C. (eds.) Advances in Cryptology – CRYPTO 2021, Part II. Lecture Notes in Computer Science, vol. 12826, pp. 94–123. Springer, Cham, Switzerland, Virtual Event (Aug 16–20, 2021). https://doi.org/10.1007/978-3-030-84245-1_4
8. Damgård, I., Nielsen, J.B.: Scalable and unconditionally secure multiparty computation. In: Menezes, A. (ed.) Advances in Cryptology – CRYPTO 2007. Lecture Notes in Computer Science, vol. 4622, pp. 572–590. Springer Berlin Heidelberg, Germany, Santa Barbara, CA, USA (Aug 19–23, 2007). https://doi.org/10.1007/978-3-540-74143-5_32
9. Damgård, I., Pastro, V., Smart, N.P., Zakarias, S.: Multiparty computation from somewhat homomorphic encryption. In: Safavi-Naini, R., Canetti, R. (eds.) Advances in Cryptology – CRYPTO 2012. Lecture Notes in Computer Science, vol. 7417, pp. 643–662. Springer Berlin Heidelberg, Germany, Santa Barbara, CA, USA (Aug 19–23, 2012). https://doi.org/10.1007/978-3-642-32009-5_38
10. David, B., et al.: Perfect MPC over layered graphs. In: Handschuh, H., Lysyanskaya, A. (eds.) Advances in Cryptology – CRYPTO 2023, Part I. Lecture Notes in Computer Science, vol. 14081, pp. 360–392. Springer, Cham, Switzerland, Santa Barbara, CA, USA (Aug 20–24, 2023). https://doi.org/10.1007/978-3-031-38557-5_12
11. David, B., Mondal, A., Satish, R.: Rumors MPC: GOD for dynamic committees, low communication via constant-round chat. In: Hanaoka, G., Yang, B. (eds.) Advances in Cryptology - ASIACRYPT 2025 - 31st International Conference on the Theory and Application of Cryptology and Information Security, Melbourne, VIC, Australia, December 8-12, 2025, Proceedings, Part V. Lecture Notes in Computer Science, vol. 16249, pp. 102–132. Springer (2025). https://doi.org/10.1007/978-981-95-5116-3_4
12. Deligios, G., Konring, A., Liu-Zhang, C., Narayanan, V.: Statistical layered MPC. In: Boyle, E., Mahmoody, M. (eds.) Theory of Cryptography - 22nd International Conference, TCC 2024, Milan, Italy, December 2–6, 2024, Proceedings, Part IV, pp. 362–394. Lecture Notes in Computer Science, Springer (2024). https://doi.org/10.1007/978-3-031-78023-3_12

13. Dettling, G., Liu-Zhang, C., Masserova, E., Rambaud, M., Urban, A.: Broadcast for dynamic committees without trusted setup. IACR Cryptol. ePrint Arch. **2025**, 2078 (2025)
14. Dolev, D., Reischuk, R.: Bounds on information exchange for byzantine agreement. J. ACM **32**(1), 191–204 (1985). https://doi.org/10.1145/2455.214112
15. Escudero, D., Masserova, E., Polychroniadou, A.: Towards scalable YOSO MPC via packed secret-sharing. In: Hanaoka, G., Yang, B. (eds.) Advances in Cryptology - ASIACRYPT 2025 - 31st International Conference on the Theory and Application of Cryptology and Information Security, Melbourne, VIC, Australia, December 8-12, 2025, Proceedings, Part V, pp. 68–101. Lecture Notes in Computer Science, Springer (2025). https://doi.org/10.1007/978-981-95-5116-3_3
16. Escudero, D., Tjuawinata, I., Xing, C.: On information-theoretic secure multiparty computation with local repairability. In: Tang, Q., Teague, V. (eds.) Public-Key Cryptography - PKC 2024 - 27th IACR International Conference on Practice and Theory of Public-Key Cryptography, Sydney, NSW, Australia, April 15-17, 2024, Proceedings, Part II. Lecture Notes in Computer Science, vol. 14602, pp. 205–239. Springer (2024). https://doi.org/10.1007/978-3-031-57722-2_7
17. Gama, M., Beni, E.H., Orsini, E., Smart, N.P., Zajonc, O.: MPC with delayed parties over star-like networks. In: Guo, J., Steinfeld, R. (eds.) Advances in Cryptology – ASIACRYPT 2023, Part I. Lecture Notes in Computer Science, vol. 14438, pp. 172–203. Springer, Singapore, Singapore, Guangzhou, China (Dec 4–8, 2023). https://doi.org/10.1007/978-981-99-8721-4_6
18. Gennaro, R., Rabin, M.O., Rabin, T.: Simplified VSS and fast-track multiparty computations with applications to threshold cryptography. In: Proceedings of the Seventeenth Annual ACM Symposium on Principles of Distributed Computing, pp. 101–111. PODC '98, Association for Computing Machinery, New York, NY, USA (1998). https://doi.org/10.1145/277697.277716
19. Gentry, C., et al.: YOSO: You only speak once - secure MPC with stateless ephemeral roles. In: Malkin, T., Peikert, C. (eds.) Advances in Cryptology – CRYPTO 2021, Part II. Lecture Notes in Computer Science, vol. 12826, pp. 64–93. Springer, Cham, Switzerland, Virtual Event (Aug 16–20, 2021). https://doi.org/10.1007/978-3-030-84245-1_3
20. Goyal, V., Li, H., Ostrovsky, R., Polychroniadou, A., Song, Y.: ATLAS: efficient and scalable MPC in the honest majority setting. In: Malkin, T., Peikert, C. (eds.) Advances in Cryptology – CRYPTO 2021, Part II. Lecture Notes in Computer Science, vol. 12826, pp. 244–274. Springer, Cham, Switzerland, Virtual Event (Aug 16–20, 2021). https://doi.org/10.1007/978-3-030-84245-1_9
21. Goyal, V., Song, Y., Zhu, C.: Guaranteed output delivery comes free in honest majority MPC. In: Micciancio, D., Ristenpart, T. (eds.) Advances in Cryptology – CRYPTO 2020, Part II. Lecture Notes in Computer Science, vol. 12171, pp. 618–646. Springer, Cham, Switzerland, Santa Barbara, CA, USA (Aug 17–21, 2020). https://doi.org/10.1007/978-3-030-56880-1_22
22. Mohassel, P., Rindal, P.: ABY^3: A mixed protocol framework for machine learning. In: Lie, D., Mannan, M., Backes, M., Wang, X. (eds.) ACM CCS 2018: 25th Conference on Computer and Communications Security, pp. 35–52. ACM Press, Toronto, ON, Canada (Oct 15–19, 2018). https://doi.org/10.1145/3243734.3243760
23. Nordholt, P.S., Veeningen, M.: Minimising communication in honest-majority MPC by batchwise multiplication verification. In: Preneel, B., Vercauteren, F. (eds.) ACNS 2018: 16th International Conference on Applied Cryptography and Network Security. Lecture Notes in Computer Science, vol. 10892, pp. 321–339.

Springer, Cham, Switzerland, Leuven, Belgium (Jul 2–4, 2018). https://doi.org/10.1007/978-3-319-93387-0_17
24. Rachuri, R., Scholl, P.: Le mans: dynamic and fluid MPC for dishonest majority. In: Dodis, Y., Shrimpton, T. (eds.) Advances in Cryptology – CRYPTO 2022, Part I. Lecture Notes in Computer Science, vol. 13507, pp. 719–749. Springer, Cham, Switzerland, Santa Barbara, CA, USA (Aug 15–18, 2022). https://doi.org/10.1007/978-3-031-15802-5_25
25. Shamir, A.: How to share a secret. Commun. ACM **22**(11), 612–613 (1979). https://doi.org/10.1145/359168.359176
26. Varga, A.: OMNeT++, pp. 35–59. Springer Berlin Heidelberg, Berlin, Heidelberg (2010). https://doi.org/10.1007/978-3-642-12331-3_3
27. Yao, A.C.: How to generate and exchange secrets (extended abstract). In: 27th Annual Symposium on Foundations of Computer Science, pp. 162–167. IEEE Computer Society, Los Alamitos, CA, USA (1986). https://doi.org/10.1109/SFCS.1986.25
28. Zeng, Y., Yang, K., Feng, D., Zhang, M.: Ion: Concretely efficient submaximal-fluid MPC with linear communication. IACR Cryptol. ePrint Arch. **2025**, 1508 (2025). https://eprint.iacr.org/2025/1508
29. Zhang, S., Zhang, Z., Magri, B.: The cost of fluidity: Communication complexity trade-offs in fluid MPC. Cryptology ePrint Archive, Paper 2026/725 (2026). https://eprint.iacr.org/2026/725

Practice-Oriented Instances of Deterministic LPN

Carlos Cid[1,3], Alex Davidson[2], and Atharva Phanse[1(✉)]

[1] Simula UiB, Bergen, Norway
{carlos,atharva}@simula.no
[2] LASIGE, Faculdade de Ciências, Universidade de Lisboa, Lisbon, Portugal
aadavidson@ciencias.ulisboa.pt
[3] Okinawa Institute of Science and Technology Graduate University, Onna, Japan

Abstract. We develop a framework for instantiating and implementing the Learning Parity with Noise (LPN) assumption, via a deterministic noise paradigm. Our approach allows high flexibility in the choice of error rate (τ), mirroring the functionality of Bernoulli sampling in the standard LPN. This improves upon previous deterministic frameworks which are fairly rigid in the choice of τ, or depend on non-cryptographic sources of physical noise. We give a number of theoretical relations between existing deterministic frameworks and our new design. In addition, we build new instantiations of τ-Unbalanced Weak Pseudorandom Functions, based on novel compositions and designs of diffusion and folding functions. Our choices of building blocks take from both symmetric cryptographic primitives and low-depth Boolean formulae. Finally, we implement our framework with a selection of diffusion tools, and show that native hardware instructions in common CPUs give rise to instantiations that are highly efficient. All in all, we provide a firm basis for real-world deployment of recent LPN-based applications—such as those related to VOLE proof systems and MPC—even in scenarios where high-quality randomness sources do not exist, e.g. resource-constrained devices.

Keywords: LPN · Weak Pseudorandom Functions · Deterministic Noise

1 Introduction

The Learning Parity with Noise (LPN) problem [15] is a widely studied topic in complexity theory and has a rich history in cryptography. Given a uniform distribution $\mathcal{U}$ over $\mathbb{Z}_2$, and a Bernoulli distribution Ber_τ with parameter $\tau < 1/2$, the decisional variant of LPN asks one to distinguish samples of the form $(\boldsymbol{a}, \langle \boldsymbol{a}, \boldsymbol{s} \rangle + e) \in \mathbb{Z}_2^\ell \times \mathbb{Z}_2$ given that $\boldsymbol{a}, \boldsymbol{s} \leftarrow\$ \mathcal{U}^\ell$, and $e \leftarrow \mathsf{Ber}_\tau$, from $(\boldsymbol{a}, u) \leftarrow\$ (\mathcal{U}^\ell, \mathcal{U})$. The problem is known to be NP-hard in the worst case [46], while Blum, Kalai, and Wasserman [16] showed that random instances could be solved with subexponential $O(2^{\ell/\log \ell})$ data and time complexity.[1] Importantly,

[1] Recently, so-called *linear test* frameworks have arisen aiming to capture this attack and subsequent cryptanalytic advances in a unified adversarial strategy [4,22,27].

K. Jee and A. Kate (Eds.): ACNS 2026, LNCS 16571, pp. 382–412, 2027.
https://doi.org/10.1007/978-3-032-32560-0_14

meaningful quantum speed-ups for LPN are not known to exist, which makes it a potential building block for post-quantum cryptography.

Since 2001, LPN has been used to instantiate secure identification protocols [50,52], public-key encryption [39], PRNGs [15], and more [60]. More recently, several new applications of LPN have been proposed, including vector oblivious linear evaluation (VOLE) protocols [4], multi-party computation protocols [13], post-quantum signatures [9] and multi-party homomorphic secret sharing [28]. From a theoretical perspective, certain low-depth pseudorandom functions (PRF) are intrinsically linked to instances of the LPN assumption [2,19,23], and by extension, enjoy various practical use-cases. Alongside this *renaissance*, a variety of related problems have emerged that aid the building of new constructions. These include a ring-based variant (Ring-LPN) [48], as well as variants of the problem instance, such as variable-density [22] and sparse LPN [32], that are still conjectured to remain hard.

Motivation for Studying Determinism in LPN. Beyond the applications mentioned, the simplicity of the LPN assumption can make it very attractive for lightweight applications, particularly for authentication in resource-constrained environments. This is exemplified by the *HB family* of protocols [50], with follow-up variations including [38,44,52,58] (see Appendix A for an overview). However, prior work [5] has noted that a main drawback of LPN-based protocols is that Bernoulli sampling requires significant computational resources, which can be, in general, monetarily expensive. In addition, when considering authentication protocols, the cost of the Bernoulli sampling is often on the prover (*tag*) device, which is typically weaker. Despite such drawbacks, the strong security guarantees of the LPN assumption have motivated researchers to investigate ways to overcome its practical limitations. To address the limitations associated with the Bernoulli sampling in real-world applications, the following question arises:

> *Can we devise alternative interpretations of LPN that do not require native sources of entropy and randomness for producing secure instances?*

Derandomization is a standard approach in cryptography to mitigate reliance on randomness and address these limitations. In the case of LWE, the Learning with Rounding (LWR) problem [6] provides a counterpart that allows producing LWE-like samples, but effectively with deterministic errors. Various works have shown the equivalence of LWR to LWE, for a variety of parameter selections [3,20], meaning that many LWE-based cryptographic applications may be redesigned in the LWR paradigm, and deployed where access to random sampling from LWE error distributions is not possible.

Inflexibility in Deterministic Noise Generation. In the case of LPN, various works have shown this to be also possible. Recent literature on weak PRFs has already made connections between constructions and deterministic instances of LPN (which we will refer to as *DLPN*) with specific noise rates. For example, the weak PRF candidate defined as:

$$\mathsf{PRF}(\boldsymbol{k}, \boldsymbol{x}) = (\langle \boldsymbol{k}, \boldsymbol{x} \rangle \pmod 2 + \langle \boldsymbol{k}, \boldsymbol{x} \rangle \pmod 3) \pmod 2,$$

proposed in [19] is equivalent to a deterministic LPN instance with noise rate $\tau = 1/3$. However, modifying such candidates to cater for different noise rates appears difficult.[2]. A formal framework called LPN with *simple* deterministic noise was proposed [23], where LPN samples are constructed as $b = \langle \boldsymbol{a}, \boldsymbol{s} \rangle + g(k, \boldsymbol{a})$, for a secret $k \leftarrow_\$ \{0,1\}^\lambda$. While such a framework would appear to provide more flexibility, the presence of an additional secret k is cumbersome: it requires additional storage on the part of small devices, and running of a secure process for embedding such secrets onto chips. From a more theoretical angle, the function g does not appear to admit simple configuration of the *error parameter* $\tau < 1/2$ (without modifying the effective *security parameter* λ), which means that a new function effectively has to be configured for any given choice of noise rate. We believe this provides a practical barrier to use them for instantiating practical and meaningful LPN applications, where variable noise rates may be required for maintaining functionality and security.

On the other hand, a recent line of literature has shown links between deterministic creation of LPN samples, with a paradigm known as Learning Parity with Physical Noise (LPPN) [55]. In LPPN, the noise is sampled from physical phenomena, such as via inexact implementations of inner-products that can arise during the engineering process of seemingly identical hardware chips. Although the approach offers a promising way to avoid random error sampling in LPN, hardware-based cryptanalysis has revealed effective attacks, suggesting that achieving strong cryptographic security remains challenging [11,12,53].

Practical, Deterministic Instances for Configurable Noise. In summary, to migrate a range of LPN-based schemes to real-world applications implemented in environments with constrained entropy sources, we need the following:

- to design and instantiate a deterministic noise framework for LPN, with the ability to configure the noise rate flexibly, ideally for any $0 < \tau < 1/2$;
- to provide concrete realisations of deterministic noise sampling functions $g_\tau(\boldsymbol{a}, \boldsymbol{s})$ that enable producing LPN samples that satisfy cryptographic guarantees of security, while producing noise rates very close to τ; and,
- that such functions must be efficient to execute, even in constrained environments.

In principle, DLPN instances that satisfy these constraints would allow deploying advanced cryptographic primitives across a range of computing scenarios. Note that it is important to provide a distinction between theoretical low-complexity techniques, and those that are very efficient in practice in hardware and software. In particular, while recent developments in low-depth pseudorandom functions appear to provide promising avenues forward for efficient implementations, equally as interesting are PRF constructions that rely heavily on real-world optimisations (such as embedded hardware-level instructions).

[2] In the case of [19], modifying the moduli produces noise rates that converge to $1/2$.

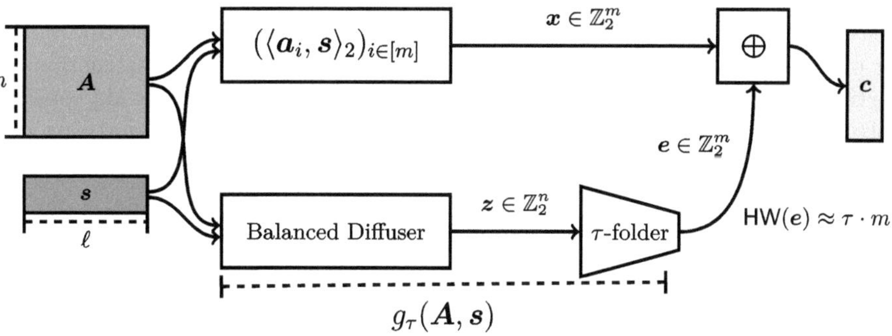

Fig. 1. Diagrammatic representation of DLPN instance generation.

Overview and Contributions. In this work, we first develop a modified deterministic noise framework (Sect. 3) for LPN samples of the form:

$$c_i = \langle a_i, s\rangle + g_\tau(a_i, s) \pmod 2$$

where $g_\tau : \mathbb{Z}_2^{m\times\ell} \times \mathbb{Z}_2^\ell \to \{0,1\}^m$. When $m = 1$, we construct g_τ such that $\Pr\left[1 \leftarrow g_\tau(a, s : a, s \leftarrow_\$ \mathbb{Z}_2^\ell)\right] \approx \tau$. For general m, we consider $A \leftarrow_\$ \mathbb{Z}_2^{m\times\ell}$, and construct g_τ such that $\mathsf{HW}(g_\tau(A, s)) \approx \tau \cdot m$. We do so by composing a *balanced diffuser* function with a τ-dependent *folding* function (Fig. 1).

Secondly, we demonstrate a possible construction for τ-folder (F_τ) that accepts balanced binary strings of length n (Sect. 4), and produces binary strings of length m with hamming weight $\tau \cdot m$. Our formulation of F_τ follows similar ideas to those used in the development of the Tribes [2] and SIPSER [23] functions used at the heart of low-depth pseudorandom functions. However, our approach, which we refer to as *universal* Tribes, allows configuring the function flexibly, dependent on the desired value of the parameter τ.

For instantiating the balanced diffuser function ($\mathsf{Diffuse} : \mathbb{Z}_2^{\ell\times m} \times \mathbb{Z}_2^\ell \to \mathbb{Z}_2^\lambda$) we consider several approaches ranging from full pseudorandom functions, to more streamlined approaches that conjecture security based on the "full diffusion" property of a sufficiently non-linear permutation. In principle, we note that algebraic attacks that expose the insecurity of the original Tribes function stemmed from the fact that Diffuse was essentially implemented as a linear function [18]. We argue that non-linear balanced functions can serve to instantiate this paradigm, and we discuss relevant cryptanalysis accordingly. Bringing the previous two results together, in Lemma 3, we show that implementing $g_\tau = \mathsf{F}_\tau \circ \mathsf{Diffuse}$ directly from a PRF constructs DLPN samples that are indistinguishable from standard LPN samples with error-rate τ.

To highlight performance variability in our approach to building DLPN instances, we provide experimental analysis (Sect. 6) that compares several ways of implementing Diffuse on two different platforms. We observe that, in general, all Diffuse instantiations that we devise outperform constructions based on linear maps (such as WPRF candidates in **AC0**[**MOD2**]), while availability of AES-hardware acceleration has a significant positive impact on AES-round based instantiations of Diffuse. As an aside, we see our results as informative for ongoing research into developing practical low-depth PRF constructions. In particular, we demonstrate that low-depth constructions of wPRFs lag considerably behind well-known symmetric primitives that are already offer strong PRF guarantees.

1.1 Related Work

Learning with Rounding. The Learning with Rounding (LWR) assumption [6] is a deterministic variant of the Learning with Errors (LWE) assumption, in which the 'errors' are sampled deterministically based on the choices of $\boldsymbol{a}, \boldsymbol{s} \in \mathbb{Z}_q^n$. In particular, it has been shown that an effective way for demonstrating secure instances of LWR is to compute $\lfloor p/q \cdot \langle \boldsymbol{a}, \boldsymbol{s} \rangle \rceil$, where the choice of p indicates that errors are sampled deterministically in the range $[-q/4p, q/4p)$. Such an approach clearly cannot be adapted to the LPN setting, as $q = 2$.

Learning Parity with Physical Noise. The work of [55] shows that LPN-based schemes can be instantiated with 'noise' terms generated by utilising the inexact computation of the inner product. This is formalised as a new assumption called *Learning Parity with Physical-Noise* (see Sect. 3.1). The effective error rate can be controlled by changing the frequency and voltage overscaling. Due to the practicality of the approach, an LPPN processor has been demonstrated in subsequent works [53,54]. However, cryptanalysis has shown that the errors generated are not always cryptographically secure, which can lead to attacks on the assumption (and subsequent fixes) [11,12]. Note that [55] already postulates the existence of a *deterministic* variant of LPN, but stops short of defining it.

LPN and Low-Depth WPRFs. LPN has been studied in relation to construction of weak Pseudorandom Functions (PRFs) in low complexity classes [2,19, 23]. A weak PRF relaxes the notion of the standard or "strong" PRFs by having the inputs to the PRF sampled uniformly at random.

Motivated by analogous constructions of weak PRFs based on the Learning with Rounding assumption, [2] considers candidate PRF families of the form $F_A(x) = g(Ax)$ where A is a public matrix and g is essentially a *rounding function*, which adds a "deterministic-noise" to the samples Ax. It constructs g (the so-called Tribes function of Ajtai and Linial [1]) as a specific DNF formula:

$$g(K, x) = \bigvee_{i=1}^{\lambda} \bigwedge_{j=1}^{\log \lambda} x_{ij}. \tag{1}$$

On the negative side, the same work proves that the LPN assumption is not sufficient for proving existence of weak PRFs of the above form in **AC0**[**MOD2**] (constant-depth, with access to MOD2 gates). This candidate was broken in [18].

Boyle et al. in [22] propose a WPRF and a new variant of LPN assumption in relation to it, named *Variable Density-LPN* (or *VDLPN*, for short). For input

$x \in \{0,1\}^n$ and key $k \in \{0,1\}^n$, the WPRF is defined as:

$$f_k(x) = \bigoplus_{i=1}^{D} \bigoplus_{j=1}^{w} \bigwedge_{h=1}^{i} (x_{i,j,h} \oplus k_{i,j,h})$$

where D, ω are set to the security parameter λ and $n = w \cdot D \cdot (D-1)/2$. Informally, this candidate weak PRF can be seen as a finite sum of LPN samples with different secret vectors, where each parity term is twice as dense as the previous term ([22], Sect. 1.3)

Motivated by the previous approaches, [23] proposes a weak and strong PRF candidate in **AC0**[**MOD2**], improving on the design principle of [2]. In particular, they show that generic constructions of strong PRFs can be built from weak PRFs using the formulation $f_{s,K}(x) = \langle x, s\rangle \oplus g(K, x)$, where $s \in \{0,1\}^n$, $K \in \{0,1\}^{(n-1)\times n}$ and $g(K, x)$ is a weak PRF. In [23], the Tribes function is replaced with $g(x) = \bigvee_{i=1}^{\lambda} \bigwedge_{j=1}^{\lambda} \bigvee_{i=1}^{w} x_{ijk}$, which corresponds to a degree-3 representation of the SIPSER function [45,62]. Using this construction, it is possible to evade the attacks shown against Tribes, thanks to higher non-linearity of g. The work also considers a deterministic interpretation of LPN, on which they base their construction of strong PRFs, named *Learning Parity with Simple Deterministic Noise*—we discuss this assumption in Sect. 3.1.

In [19] the authors propose a construction of low-depth weak PRFs, that is equivalent to a deterministic formulation of LPN, with noise rate 1/3. Their alternative binary weak PRF, $F(k, x) = (\langle k, x\rangle \pmod 2 + \langle k, x\rangle \pmod 3) \pmod 2$, where both key k and input x are binary vectors of length n. The noise term is determined by the value of the inner product $\langle k, x\rangle$ computed over the integers.

PRFs from Symmetric Encryption. In contrast to the constructions discussed above, block ciphers are very well-understood primitives, that may be modelled as a *pseudorandom permutation* (PRP) to define other cryptographic functionality, e.g. MAC, stream ciphers, etc. Several ways of using a PRP to construct a PRF have also been proposed, some of which discussed in [59], the simplest being truncation of the n-bit PRP output by $m < n$ bits, resulting on a PRF with $(n-m)$-bit outputs. This has been shown in [40] to be secure up to $\approx 2^{\frac{n+m}{2}}$ queries.[3] However, secure instances applying this simple approach will typically result in low-rate PRF constructions. A few more efficient alternatives are discussed in [59], e.g. based on the XOR of PRPs, their sequential computation, input feed-forwarding, as well as combinations of these. The authors then propose a construction with heuristic security – FastPRF – and its instantiation with the AES block cipher, AES-PRF. The choice of AES to instantiate PRF-from-PRP constructions makes sense if targetting real-world deployment in software: as noted in [63], AES-NI instructions can improve performance by up to 10 times when compared with standard AES software implementations.

The *heuristic* approach of FastPRF also features in [7], where the low-latency PRF called Orthros is proposed, as the XOR of two keyed permutations. While

[3] In the case where there is no truncation, i.e. $m = 0$, this gives the standard birthday bound for the well-known PRP-PRF switch technique.

each permutation is not claimed to be strong enough as stand-alone block ciphers (i.e. they do not claim to behave like a PRP), they may however be combined to define a secure PRF. Other proposals of low-latency PRF based on keyed permutations include the Kirby construction [56], and its instantiation KOALA [34].

In this work, we employ some of these approaches to define our deterministic noise functions. We may use AES-based keyed permutations, of which we may not be able to claim PRP-security, but when combined with truncation and folding operations, appear to lead to secure DLPN constructions.

1.2 Paper Outline

This work is organised as follows. We begin in Sect. 2 by specifying the notation and necessary definitions. In Sect. 3 we define the Deterministic LPN problem, and consider the relation with standard LPN and its main variants. We discuss in Sect. 4 how to instantiate the noise function and provide concrete instantiations that are expected to have good software performance. We provide arguments for the security of our proposed constructions in Sect. 5, and report the experimental results for their benchmarks in Sect. 6.

2 Preliminaries

2.1 Notation

Matrices (e.g. $\boldsymbol{M}$) and vectors (e.g. $\boldsymbol{v}$) will be denoted by upper- and lower-case bold font, respectively. We may interchangeably refer to ℓ-bit strings by their counterpart vectors in $\mathbb{Z}_2^\ell$. We will denote by $[n]$ the set $\{1, \ldots, n\}$.

We denote by Ber_τ an efficient Bernoulli sampler with probability parameter τ. We use PPT to refer to polynomial probabilistic time, in the context of discussing the efficiency of some algorithm A. For a set X, we use $x \leftarrow\$ X$ to denote sampling uniformly from it.

We use λ to denote a security parameter, and let $\mathsf{negl}(\lambda)$ denote a negligible function. We say that some problem P is computationally hard to solve, if for all PPT algorithms $\mathcal{A}$, we have that $\Pr[\mathcal{A} \text{ succeeds in solving } P] < \mathsf{negl}(\lambda)$.

2.2 Learning Parity with Noise

The Learning Parity with Noise (LPN) problem is one of the most prominent hard learning problems with application in cryptography [15]. Informally, it asks one to distinguish noisy inner products in $\mathbb{Z}_2$ from uniformly sampled bits.

Definition 1 (Decisional/Search LPN problem). *Let $\boldsymbol{A} \leftarrow\$ \mathbb{Z}_2^{m\times\ell}$, for polynomials $m = m(\lambda)$ and $\ell = \ell(\lambda)$. Then, for $0 < \tau < 1/2$, consider the following distributions: (i) D_0: sample $\boldsymbol{s} \leftarrow\$ \mathbb{Z}_2^\ell$ and $\boldsymbol{e} \leftarrow\$ (\mathsf{Ber}_\tau)^m$; output $(\boldsymbol{A}\cdot\boldsymbol{s}+\boldsymbol{e})$; and (ii) D_1: output $\boldsymbol{u} \leftarrow\$ \mathbb{Z}_2^m$. The* decisional Learning Parity with Noise *(LPN) problem considers a PPT algorithm $\mathcal{A}$, which is given the input $(\boldsymbol{A}, D_b)$ for $b \leftarrow\$ \mathbb{Z}_2$, outputs $b' \in \{0,1\}$, and succeeds if $b' = b$. Likewise, the* search LPN *problem requires a PPT algorithm $\mathcal{A}'$ to, given an output from D_0, recover the vector $\boldsymbol{s}$.*

The success probability for the algorithm $\mathcal{A}$, is given by:

$$p^{\mathsf{LPN}}_{\mathcal{A},m,\ell,\tau}(\lambda) = \Pr\left[b' = b \middle| \substack{b \leftarrow\$ \{0,1\} \\ b' \leftarrow \mathcal{A}((\boldsymbol{A}, D_b))}\right],$$

and corresponding advantage by: $a^{\mathsf{LPN}}_{\mathcal{A}}(\lambda) = \mathsf{Adv}^{\mathsf{LPN}}_{\mathcal{A},m,\ell,\tau}\lambda = |p^{\mathsf{LPN}}_{\mathcal{A},m,\ell,\tau}(\lambda) - 1/2|$. The *decisional LPN assumption* states that solving $\mathsf{LPN}_{m,\ell,\tau}$ is hard (i.e. $a^{\mathsf{LPN}}_{\mathcal{A}}(\lambda) < \mathsf{negl}(\lambda)$) for any PPT adversary algorithm $\mathcal{A}$. The hardness of search LPN is defined equivalently. In this work we will refer always to the decisional variant of LPN, which is known to be equivalent to the search variant [15].

2.3 Pseudorandom and Unbalanced Functions

Definition 2 (Weak/Strong PRFs). *Let $\mathcal{K}, \mathcal{X}, \mathcal{Y}$ be the key, input, and output spaces, respectively, parameterised by a security parameter λ. Let $\mathcal{F} = \{f_k \mid f_k : \mathcal{X} \to \mathcal{Y}\}$ be a family of functions indexed by $k \in \mathcal{K}$, and $\mathcal{RF}$ be the set of all functions from $\mathcal{X}$ to $\mathcal{Y}$.*
Then, for $\{x_i\}_{i\in[m]}$ (for some $m = \mathsf{poly}(\lambda)$), let D_0 be the distribution that samples $k \leftarrow\$ \mathcal{K}$, and outputs $\{f_k(x_i)\}_{i\in[m]}$, and let D_1 be a distribution that samples $f \leftarrow\$ \mathcal{RF}$, and outputs $\{f(x_i)\}_{i\in[m]}$.

- *We say that $\mathcal{F} : \mathcal{K} \times \mathcal{X} \to \mathcal{Y}$ is a (strong)* pseudorandom function *(PRF) family, if all PPT algorithms $\mathcal{A}$ attempting to distinguish between D_0 and D_1, where $\{x_i\} \leftarrow \mathcal{A}$, have advantage bounded by $\mathsf{negl}(\lambda)$.*
- *We say that $\mathcal{F} : \mathcal{K} \times \mathcal{X} \to \mathcal{Y}$ is a* weak pseudorandom function *(WPRF) family, if all PPT algorithms $\mathcal{A}$ attempting to distinguish between D_0 and D_1, where $\{x_i\} \leftarrow\$ \mathcal{X}$, have advantage bounded by $\mathsf{negl}(\lambda)$.*

We state the notion of τ-unbalanced function families, defined in [23].

Definition 3 (τ-Unbalanced Function Families [23]). *We say that $\mathcal{F}_\tau = \{f \mid f : \mathcal{X} \to \{0,1\}\}$ is a τ-Unbalanced Function Family if for $f \leftarrow\$ \mathcal{F}_\tau$, we have $\Pr_x[f(x) = 1] = \tau$.*

While the notion of τ-unbalanced function families is sufficiently generic, we will also work with a more concrete definition that explicitly takes into account indistinguishability from sources of randomness. In particular, we consider the notion of an unbalanced weak pseudorandom function in Definition 4.

Definition 4 (τ-Unbalanced Weak Pseudorandom Function). *Let $\ell = \ell(\lambda)$, $m = m(\lambda)$, $n = n(\lambda) \in \mathbb{N}$, let $\mathcal{F}_\tau$ be a τ-unbalanced function family (Definition 3), and let $g_\tau : \{0,1\}^\ell \times \{0,1\}^n \to \{0,1\}$.*
Now, let $\{\boldsymbol{x}_i\}_{i\in[m]} \leftarrow\$ (\{0,1\}^\ell)^m$ be a set of m independently sampled binary vectors of length n. If D_0 denotes the distribution that samples $\boldsymbol{s} \leftarrow\$ \{0,1\}^n$, and then outputs $\{g_\tau(\boldsymbol{x}_i, \boldsymbol{s})\}_{i\in[m]}$, and D_1 the distribution that samples $f \leftarrow\$ F_\tau$, and outputs $\{f(\boldsymbol{x}_i)\}_{i\in[m]}$. We say that g is a τ-unbalanced weak pseudorandom function (τ-UWPRF) for $\mathcal{X}$ if, for all PPT algorithms $\mathcal{A}$, we have

$$\Pr\left[b' = b \middle| \substack{b \leftarrow\$ \{0,1\} \\ b' \leftarrow \mathcal{A}((\{x_i\}_{i\in[m]}, D_b))}\right] = 1/2 + \mathsf{negl}(\lambda).$$

Finally we restate in Lemma 1 a result that was implied in [23], but only proven in the paper's (non-public) full version [24].

Lemma 1 (τ-UWPRF to WPRF [24]). *Let g_τ be a τ-UWPRF. Then, under the assumption that decisional $\mathsf{LPN}_{m,\ell,\tau}$ is hard, we can obtain a standard WPRF (Definition 2).*

Proof. Assume that $\ell = n$, and thus $g_\tau : \{0,1\}^\ell \times \{0,1\}^\ell \rightarrow \{0,1\}$, and let $f : \{0,1\}^\ell \times \{0,1\}^\ell \rightarrow \{0,1\}$ be defined as $L(\boldsymbol{x}, \boldsymbol{s}) = (\langle \boldsymbol{x}, \boldsymbol{s} \rangle + g_\tau(\boldsymbol{x}, \boldsymbol{s}))$. We now construct an adversary $\mathcal{B}$ that attempts to distinguish between $(\{\boldsymbol{x}_i\}_{i \in [m]}, L(\boldsymbol{x}_i))$ and $(\boldsymbol{x}_i, u \leftarrow\$ \{0,1\})$. If no such $\mathcal{B}$ exists with advantage greater than $\mathsf{negl}(\lambda)$, then we conclude that L is a WPRF.

- h_1: We replace g_τ with a randomly sampled function $f : \{0,1\}^\ell \mapsto \{0,1\}$ from a τ-unbalanced function family F_τ. This follows directly from Definition 4.
- h_2: We replace outputs of F_τ with independent samples from a Bernoulli distribution with parameter τ (Ber_τ). These games are statistically indistinguishable, since the only chance of distinguishing the two arises when we have a collision $x_i = x_j$ for $i \neq j$ and $i, j \in [m]$ for the input samples.
- h_3 We now replace the entire output of L, with $u \leftarrow\$ \{0,1\}$. Note that this follows because $L(\boldsymbol{x}_i, \boldsymbol{s}) = \langle \boldsymbol{x}_i, \boldsymbol{s} \rangle + \mathsf{Ber}_\tau$, which is exactly the form of $\mathsf{LPN}_{m,\ell,\tau}$.

After transitioning to h_3, we have completed the proof.

3 Deterministic Variants of LPN

In order to use instances of LPN in applications, we must consider the following necessary computation. Given a uniformly sampled secret $\boldsymbol{s} \in \mathbb{Z}_2^\ell$ and m samples of random vectors $\boldsymbol{a}_i \in \mathbb{Z}_2^\ell$, we will compute $(\langle \boldsymbol{a}_i, \boldsymbol{s} \rangle + e_i)_{i=1}^m$ for error bits $\{e_i\}_{i \in [m]}$ sampled independently from Ber_τ. As noted, sampling of randomness is a non-trivial task for many real-world devices.

The same may also apply for the parameters a_i (public) and s (secret) above, but for example in LPN-based cryptographic schemes, s can be viewed as a secret key, while a_i's can be provided from public sources of randomness (such as randomness beacons), or by a Verifier device in identification schemes like the HB protocol [50] and follow up works.

In the case of LWE [61], deterministic variants that allow "sampling" errors based alone on the long-term public and secret data have been developed and studied. Similar observations have been made for LPN [11,19,23,55], but the exact nature of the assumption has often been left implicit, or only concretely specified for specific parameterisations. In the following sequence of definitions, we give a new asymptotic formulation of (decisional) deterministic LPN that unifies prior art, and upon which we can then use to postulate hard variants of the problem. Note that the search variant of deterministic LPN follows naturally, and deterministic Ring LPN [48] may also be defined using the same framework.

Definition 5 (Decisional Deterministic LPN). *Let $m = m(\lambda)$, $\ell = \ell(\lambda) \in \mathbb{N}$, and $0 < \tau < 1/2$. Let $g_\tau : \mathbb{Z}_2^{m\times\ell} \times \mathbb{Z}_2^\ell \mapsto \mathbb{Z}_2^m$ be a function. Let $\boldsymbol{A} \leftarrow\$ \mathbb{Z}_2^{m\times\ell}$, and consider the following distributions: (i) D_0: sample $\boldsymbol{s} \leftarrow\$ \mathbb{Z}_2^\ell$; output $(\boldsymbol{A}\cdot\boldsymbol{s} + g_\tau(\boldsymbol{A},\boldsymbol{s}))$; and (ii) D_1: output $\boldsymbol{u} \leftarrow\$ \mathbb{Z}_2^m$. Then, the* determinsitic LPN *problem (denoted $\mathsf{DLPN}_{m,\ell,g_\tau}$) considers a PPT algorithm $\mathcal{A}$, that is given the input $(\boldsymbol{A}, D_b)$ for $b \leftarrow\$ \mathbb{Z}_2$, outputs $b' \leftarrow\$ \mathbb{Z}_2$, and succeeds if $b' = b$.*

For the adversary algorithm $\mathcal{A}$, we denote their success probability by:

$$p^{\mathsf{DLPN}}_{\mathcal{A},m,\ell,g_\tau}(\lambda) = \Pr\left[b' = b \middle| \substack{b \leftarrow\$ \{0,1\} \\ b' \leftarrow \mathcal{A}((\boldsymbol{A},D_b))}\right],$$

and corresponding advantage by: $a^{\mathsf{DLPN}}_{\mathcal{A}}(\lambda) = \mathsf{Adv}^{\mathsf{DLPN}}_{\mathcal{A},m,\ell,g_\tau}\lambda = |p^{\mathsf{DLPN}}_{\mathcal{A},m,\ell,g_\tau}(\lambda) - 1/2|$. The *deterministic LPN assumption* states that solving $\mathsf{DLPN}_{m,\ell,g_\tau}$ is hard (i.e. $a^{\mathsf{DLPN}}_{\mathcal{A}}(\lambda) < \mathsf{negl}(\lambda)$) for any PPT adversary algorithm $\mathcal{A}$.

Remark 1 (Number of samples). Note that the parameter m defines the number of samples that the adversary sees. Therefore, we may abuse notation and simply write $\mathsf{DLPN}_{\ell,g_\tau}$, when we consider m to be arbitrary.

Remark 2 (On families of functions). We could write Definition 5 with respect to a function family $G_\tau = G_\tau(\lambda)$, from which g_τ is then sampled. We could then demonstrate hard instances of DLPN corresponding to different function families G_τ. However, in the following we will focus on specific instances of the function g_τ, and therefore prefer to consider this formulation.

3.1 Relationships with LPN and Variants

Below, we state Lemma 2 which shows the equivalence of $\mathsf{LPN}_{m,\ell,\tau}$ and $\mathsf{DLPN}_{m,\ell,g_\tau}$ under the assumption that τ-UWPRF exist. We note that the result is valid for both the search and decisional variants.

Lemma 2 ($\mathsf{LPN} \approx_c \mathsf{DLPN}$). *Let $\mathsf{LPN}_{m,\ell,\tau}$ be the decisional LPN problem. For some function, let $g_\tau : \{0,1\}^{m\times\ell} \times \{0,1\}^\ell \to \{0,1\}^m$ be an unbalanced weak pseudorandom function, and let $\mathsf{DLPN}_{m,\ell,g_\tau}$ be the decisional deterministic LPN problem, as given in Definition 5. Then, if g_τ is an unbalanced weak pseudorandom function (Definition 4), the two problems are computationally equivalent.*

Proof. The proof follows almost trivially from the proof of Lemma 1. Consider an instance of the LPN problem $\boldsymbol{A}\cdot\boldsymbol{s}+\boldsymbol{e}$ for $\boldsymbol{e} \leftarrow\$ \{0,1\}^m_\tau$. Then, we can apply the hybrid arguments in reverse to transition from h_3 to h_1, where $\boldsymbol{e} \leftarrow g_\tau(\boldsymbol{A},\boldsymbol{s})$ is generated as the result of the τ-UWPRF, g_τ. Note that in h_1, we have exactly an instance of $\mathsf{DLPN}_{m,\ell,g_\tau}$. We can perform the reverse transformation to guarantee computational equivalence.

Learning Parity with Physical Noise. This LPN variant was proposed in [55], where the LPN function is replaced by the a physical device (modelled by a function $\mathsf{PF} : \mathbb{Z}_2^\ell \times \mathbb{Z}_2^\ell \to \mathbb{Z}_2$), that outputs inexact inner products with some probability ϵ.

Definition 6 (Learning Parity with Physical Noise (LPPN) [11,55]). *Let* $\mathsf{PF}_\epsilon : \mathbb{Z}_2^\ell \times \mathbb{Z}_2^\ell \times \{0,1\}^* \rightarrow \mathbb{Z}_2$ *be a function such that* $\mathsf{PF}_\epsilon(\boldsymbol{a}, \boldsymbol{b}; r) = \langle \boldsymbol{a}, \boldsymbol{b} \rangle + e_r$ *for some* $\boldsymbol{a}, \boldsymbol{b} \in \mathbb{Z}_2^\ell$*, randomness* $r \leftarrow\$ \{0,1\}^*$*, and* $e_r \leftarrow\$ \{0,1\}$ *such that* $\Pr_r[e_r = 1] = \epsilon \in [0, 1/2)$*. Then we say that the* $\mathsf{LPPN}_{1,\ell,\epsilon}$ *is hard if the output of* PF_ϵ *(on uniformly distributed randomness r) is indistinguishable from a uniformly random value in* $\mathbb{Z}_2$*.*

Note that the LPPN problem is equivalent to the standard LPN problem in the general case. However, typically the inner product function PF_ϵ [11,12] is implemented as a physical circuit, where noise is introduced through natural perturbations that occur in the evaluation of the function. In particular, we cannot guarantee that the probability density function associated with $\Pr_r[e_r = 1]$ outputs errors with sufficient frequency or unpredictably to generate secure LPN samples. Therefore, the security guarantee is conjectured on the specific physical function used, and does not guarantee LPN-hard noise rates. Furthermore, the initial noise rate itself depends on the physical phenomena that is occurring, and thus the distribution of e_r is somewhat unpredictable and independent of the computation performed. As such, we cannot use this approach to directly generate LPN samples where noise rates need to be sampled with specific values.

Learning Parity with Simple Deterministic Noise. In [23], a variant of DLPN is briefly discussed, known as *Learning Parity with Simple Deterministic Noise.* We detail the form of this problem in Definition 7 below.

Definition 7 (Learning Parity with Simple Deterministic Noise (LPSDN)). *Let* ℓ, τ *all be defined as in Definition 5. Let* $f : \mathcal{K} \times \mathbb{Z}_2^{m \times \ell} \mapsto \mathbb{Z}_2^m$ *be a* τ*-UWPRF, where* $\mathcal{K}$ *is some arbitrary key space (e.g.* $\{0,1\}^\lambda$*). Let* $\boldsymbol{A} \leftarrow\$ \mathbb{Z}_2^{m \times \ell}$*,* $k \leftarrow\$ \mathcal{K}$*, and consider the following distributions:*

1. D_0*: sample* $\boldsymbol{s} \leftarrow\$ \mathbb{Z}_2^\ell$*; output* $(\boldsymbol{A} \cdot \boldsymbol{s} + f(k, \boldsymbol{A}))$*;*
2. D_1*: output* $\boldsymbol{u} \leftarrow\$ \mathbb{Z}_2^m$*.*

Then, solving the $\mathsf{LPSDN}_{m,\ell,\tau}$ *problem requires distinguishing between* D_0 *and* D_1 *with non-negligible probability.*

It is clear that $\mathsf{LPSDN}_{m,\ell,\tau}$ and $\mathsf{DLPN}_{m,\ell,g_\tau}$ are almost equivalent. The main difference is that in the latter, we require that $\mathcal{K} = \mathbb{Z}_2^\ell$, and $k = \boldsymbol{s}$. This ensures a true deterministic link between the error vector, and the choices of $\boldsymbol{A}$ and $\boldsymbol{s}$, and simplifies the exposition of the problem – in practical applications, it also means that we only have a single secret to store, instead of a secret and a key.

4 Concrete Constructions of Unbalanced Functions

The recent surge in the number of practical protocols and constructions built from LPN [13,21,27] illustrates the potential for using the problem as a security basis in various applications. In particular, LPN's role in building practical zero-knowledge proof systems with low prover overheads (based on VOLE) provides motivation for instantiating such primitives in low-power settings, where sampling secure randomness may not be guaranteed.

In Sect. 3, we showed that $\mathsf{DLPN}_{m,\ell,g_\tau}$ is essentially equivalent to $\mathsf{LPN}_{m,\ell,\tau}$, when g_τ is a τ-UWPRF. Therefore, our primary question is: how to construct g_τ in a secure manner? To address this question, we will consider two functions $\mathsf{Diffuse} : \mathbb{Z}_2^{m\times\ell} \times \mathbb{Z}_2^{\ell} \rightarrow \mathbb{Z}_2^{n}$ and $\mathsf{Folder}_\tau : \mathbb{Z}_2^{n} \rightarrow \mathbb{Z}_2^{m}$, for some polynomial $n = n(\lambda)$ and $\tau \in (0, 1/2)$. We will denote these functions by D and F_τ, respectively. Then, we will build g_τ as the composition $g_\tau = \mathsf{F}_\tau \circ \mathsf{D}$. Concretely, this approach will allow us to separate the pieces of the function that manage the *pseudorandomness* of the WPRF, from those that ensure that the output is *τ-unbalanced.*

To illustrate our approach, we start with a simple example based on well-known cryptographic primitives. We then discuss general Boolean formulae that appear amenable to building τ-unbalanced functions (Folder_τ), and end the discussion by focusing on the pseudorandomness of $\mathsf{Diffuse}$. In particular, we discuss alternative, practical approaches for providing security in the LPN setting. In some cases, such constructions are *conjectured* secure, based on the supposed hardness of less-standard cryptographic objects (such as prior work on WPRFs [19,23], or low-depth symmetric primitives). In the case where we specify new constructions, we provide justification for their hardness in Sect. 5.

Simple, Secure Candidate from PRFs. Let $\mathsf{PRF} : \mathcal{K} \times \mathcal{X} \rightarrow \mathbb{Z}_2^n$ be a pseudorandom function for $\mathcal{K} = \mathbb{Z}_2^{m\times\ell}$ and $\mathcal{X} = \mathbb{Z}_2^{\ell}$. Then, we can instantiate a secure instance of g_τ for any $\tau = 2^{-\mu}$ for $\mu \leq n/m$. To see this, consider the function $\mathsf{D} = \mathsf{PRF}$, and F_τ defined as (where $\mu = n/m$, for simplicity):

$$\mathsf{F}_\tau(y \in \mathbb{Z}_2^n) = \bigwedge_{i=1}^{\mu} y_i \| \ldots \| \bigwedge_{i=1}^{\mu} y_{((m-1)\cdot n/m)+i}. \tag{2}$$

Function F_τ simply computes a sequential AND of the first μ bits. Considering $g_\tau = \mathsf{F}_\tau \circ \mathsf{D}$, Lemma 3 shows that it achieves the necessary security guarantee.

Lemma 3. *Let D and F_τ be defined as above, then $g_\tau = \mathsf{F}_\tau \circ \mathsf{D}$ is a τ-unbalanced function.*

Proof. The proof proceeds as a series of hybrid steps, as detailed below.

h_1: Replace D with a random function $D : \mathcal{X} \mapsto \mathbb{Z}_2^n$. This follows directly from the fact that D is a PRF.

h_2: Treating the output of $D(x)$ as a sequence of random bits $y \in \{0, 1\}^n$, consider the first bit output by $g_\tau(y) = \mathsf{F}_\tau(D(x)) = \bigwedge_{i=1}^{\mu} y_i$. If any of the μ bits of y in question are set to 0, then $F(y) = 0$, and otherwise the first bit of $F(y)$ is 1. The probability that the first bit is 1 is therefore exactly equal to $2^{-\mu}$. Therefore, we can transition to a game where we replace the first bit of the output of g_τ with the output of Ber_{2^μ}. In general, we can make m hybrid transitions, one for each bit of the desired output of g_τ, to eventually replace g_τ with m independent samples from Ber_τ. Therefore, for any choice of $\mu \leq n/m$, then g_τ represents a $(2^{-\mu})$-unbalanced PRF.

Remark 3. Recall that, for establishing computational equivalence of DLPN and LPN (Lemma 2) we require that g_τ be τ-UWPRF (Definition 4). While Definition 4 is a rather bespoke notion, concrete instantiations of such a function remain elusive. We provide one possible concrete instantiation, which is the composition $g_\tau = \mathsf{F}_\tau \circ \mathsf{D}$. Now, if we were to choose D as a (strong) PRF in this formulation, then this would clearly allow us to prove that this composition is a τ-UWPRF in Lemma 3. However, such strong PRFs are typically onerous from a performance perspective. Therefore, one must rely on the principle that secure instantiations of DLPN arise as long as g_τ is a τ-UWPRF. This would then enable us to obtain computational equivalence of DLPN with LPN. In summary, our approach provides a flexible framework for DLPN instantiations, where one can replace D with a suitable function, and suitability is determined as an application-specific metric. In our experimental evaluation in Sect. 6, our focus is on instantiating D with as high software performance as possible. This leads us naturally to τ-UWPRF candidates that perform well in this context.

With this simple candidate, there is a temptation to suggest that the problem is solved. However, many applications of LPN require careful management of the noise rate reaching specific capabilities, while ensuring meaningful security. In particular, it is common to configure LPN noise rates to all values of 2 decimal places in precision, between 0.49 and 0.01 (see [35] for various parameterisations and their effective security). Therefore we would like to be able to devise instantiations of τ-UWPRFs with arbitrary choices of $\tau \in (0, 1/2)$.

4.1 Folding for Arbitrary Noise Rates

Before constructing Folder_τ for arbitrary τ, we highlight recent work towards the building low-depth WPRFs from Boolean formulae. We will eventually build our own configurable Boolean formulae that allows us to simulate τ-UWPRFs for arbitrary τ, where previous instantiations provide suitable parameterisations for only fixed values. For now, we continue to assume that $\mathsf{Diffuse}$ is instantiated as a pseudorandom function, which is important for establishing security and functionality. We note that our constructions and previous attempts mentioned in this section fall into the case of $m = 1$ in Definition 4.

Recall, the Tribes and SIPSER constructions discussed in Sect. 1.1. It can be shown that $\Pr_{x \in \{0,1\}^n}[g(x) = 1] = 1 - (1 - \frac{1}{2^{\log \lambda}})^\lambda$ and $1 - \left[1 - (\frac{1}{2^w})^\lambda\right]^\lambda$ when g is either the Tribes or the SIPSER function. We note that, for a desired security parameter, it is not possible to configure the unbalancedness of this function (if we consider the function as a τ-UWPRF). In other words, a concrete choice of τ is implied by the concrete choice of λ. We address this problem by providing a construction of Folder_τ that can be instantiated for any value of $\tau \in (0, 1/2)$.

Constructing Configurable Instances. Essentially we are dealing with problem of constructing *unbalanced* Boolean function. The problem of constructing Boolean functions with various desired properties has been widely studied, but the focus is mostly on balanced Boolean functions (for instance, see [25]). To the best of our knowledge, there is limited literature for construction of unbalanced Boolean functions for given value of n and $\tau \in (0, 1/2)$.

In the truth-table representation of the function, we would like to construct a τ-UWPRF for any $\tau \in (0, 1/2)$ with corresponding truth table of hamming weight $\approx \lfloor \tau 2^n \rfloor$. However, we would like an algebraic representation of the function for theoretical analysis and also for large values of n, representing the function as a truth table would appear to be impractical. With this in mind, we present a more flexible approach of constructing depth-2 unbalanced functions in DNF formula using a function description that follows a similar format to that of the Tribes function [2]. Here, the advantage of lies in high efficiency, for example due to parallelizable ANDs. when instantiating the function for use in real-world applications. This was also the primary goal of prior work of [2,23]

Arbitrary Noise Rates from *Universal* Tribes. Consider the Tribes Boolean function [1] as the folding function. As in its original form, we can interpret the Tribes function differently from [2] for parameters ω, s such that:

$$\mathsf{Tribes}_{\omega,s}(x_1, \ldots, x_n) = \bigvee_{i=1}^{s} \bigwedge_{j=1}^{\omega} x_{i,\omega}$$

where $n = \omega \times s$.[4] Here we view n-bit inputs as divided into s blocks or "tribes" where each tribe consists of ω bits. The function then is the OR of s ANDs of ω bits. We have $\Pr_{x \in \{0,1\}^n}[\mathsf{Tribes}_{\omega,s}(x) = 1] = 1 - (1 - \frac{1}{2^\omega})^s$, the "unbalancedness".

We can generalise this formulation more, by choosing variable tribe sizes to get the desired unbalancedness, while using only the first few bits of the input. The reader may wonder how it is we plan to guarantee security in this regime, given the aforementioned attacks [18]. For now, we assume that the n bits we receive as input from the function Diffuse are pseudorandom and are complex functions of input LPN samples. This is a departure from the original Tribes map, that received inputs from a linear map. However, we highlight later (in Sect. 4.2) how we can produce pseudorandom (or at least non-linear, balanced) output very efficiently in practice. We define this general formulation as *universal* description for Tribes (which we denote UTribes), and describe it below. The idea is that, we sequentially choose the 'next' best tribe size, until sufficiently low approximation of τ is reached, or we run out of available bits to define the tribe sizes. Formally, we denote out construction by $\mathsf{UTribes}_{\omega_1,\ldots,\omega_m}$, where $\omega_1, \ldots, \omega_t$ are the respective Tribes sizes, and the formal statement of the construction in Definition 8.

Definition 8. *For $\tau \in (0, 1/2)$, and let $\omega_0, \ldots, \omega_t \in \mathbb{N}$. Then $\mathsf{UTribes}_{\omega_1,\ldots,\omega_t}$: $\{0,1\}^n \to \{0,1\}$ is a function defined as follows:*

$$\mathsf{UTribes}_{\omega_1,\ldots,\omega_t}(x_1, \ldots, x_n) = \bigvee_{i=1}^{t} \bigwedge_{j=1}^{\omega_i} x_{\omega_i}.$$

[4] This is sometimes known as a generalised form of Tribes [42].

Proposition 1. *Let $\tau \in (0, 1/2)$, and let $\omega_0 \in \mathbb{N}$ be the smallest positive integer such that $\frac{1}{2^{\omega_0}} < \tau$. Define the Boolean function $\mathsf{UTribes}_{\omega_1,\ldots,\omega_t}$ as in Definition 8. First, define $f^0 : \{0,1\}^n \to \{0,1\}$ as follows:*

$$f^0(x_1, \ldots, x_n) = x_1 \wedge \ldots \wedge x_{\omega_0}$$

Inductively define ω_t for $t > 0$ as follows. Suppose we have $\omega_0, \ldots, \omega_t$ and let

$$\Omega_t = \sum_{i=0}^{t} \omega_i, \quad \tau_t = \Pr_{x \in \mathbb{F}_2^n} [f^t(x) = 1]$$

Then define $\omega_{t+1} \in \mathbb{N}$ as the smallest positive integer larger than ω_t such that $\frac{1}{2^{\omega_{t+1}}} < (\tau - \tau_t)$ and $\Omega_{t+1} < n$. Define

$$f^{t+1}(x) = f^t(x_1, \ldots, x_n) \bigvee (x_{\Omega_t+1} \wedge \ldots \wedge x_{\Omega_t+\omega_{t+1}})$$

Then for $t \in \mathbb{N}$, if $\epsilon_t = \tau - \tau_t$ is the approximation error, we have that $\epsilon_0 > \epsilon_1 > \ldots \epsilon_t$ and $\epsilon_t < 2^{-(\omega_{t+1}-1)}$. In other words, with increasing t, $NR(f_t)$ gives an increasingly better approximation of τ.

Proof. Since f_{m+1} is an OR between two terms, f^t and the next 'tribe' terms $(x_{\Omega_t+1} \wedge \ldots \wedge x_{\Omega_t+\omega_{t+1}})$, we have that

$$\begin{aligned}
\Pr[f^{t+1}(x) = 1] &= \Pr[f^t(x) \vee (x_{\Omega_t+1} \wedge \ldots \wedge x_{\Omega_t+\omega_{t+1}}) = 1] \\
&= \Pr[f^t(x) = 1] + \Pr[(x_{\Omega_t+1} \wedge \ldots \wedge x_{\Omega_t+\omega_{t+1}}) = 1] \\
&- \Pr[f^t(x) = 1, (x_{\Omega_t+1} \wedge \ldots \wedge x_{\Omega_t+\omega_{t+1}}) = 1] \\
&= \Pr[f^t(x) = 1] + \Pr[(x_{\Omega_t+1} \wedge \ldots \wedge x_{\Omega_t+\omega_{t+1}}) = 1] \\
&- \Pr[f^t(x) = 1] \times \Pr[(x_{\Omega_t+1} \wedge \ldots \wedge x_{\Omega_t+\omega_{t+1}}) = 1] \\
&= \tau_t + \frac{1}{2^{\omega_{t+1}}}(1 - \tau_t) \\
\Pr[f^{t+1}(x) = 1] &< \tau_t + \frac{1}{2^{\omega_{t+1}}} \qquad (3)
\end{aligned}$$

Since ω_{t+1} was chosen such that $\frac{1}{2^{\omega_{t+1}}} < (\tau - \tau_t)$ we have, $\Pr[f^{t+1}(x) = 1] = \tau_{t+1} < \tau$. Similarly we have that $\tau_{t+1} = \Pr[f^{t+1}(x) = 1] = \tau_t + \frac{1}{2^{\omega_{t+1}}}(1 - \tau_t)$, which implies $\tau_{t+1} > \tau_t$.

We have therefore shown that starting with $\tau_0 < \tau$ we have a strictly increasing sequence of $\tau_0 < \tau_1 < \ldots < \tau_t < \tau_{t+1} < \tau$ and hence a decreasing sequence $\epsilon_0 > \epsilon_1 > \ldots \epsilon_t$ where $\epsilon_t = \tau - \tau_t$ is the approximation error.

Finally, recall that ω_{t+1} was chosen such that $\frac{1}{2^k} > (\tau - \tau_t)$ for all positive integers $k < \omega_{t+1}$ and $\frac{1}{2^{\omega_{t+1}}} < (\tau - \tau_t)$, So, we have that

$$\epsilon_t = (\tau - \tau_t) < \frac{1}{2^{\omega_{t+1}-1}} \qquad (4)$$

We give examples on how to realise g_τ, for different values of τ in Appendix B.

4.2 Instantiating the Diffuse Function

We discuss in this section the instantiation of the function Diffuse (D), whose output is provided as input to the folding function (F_τ). From a security point of view, to allow us to apply the guarantees from Lemma 3, we need D to provide *pseudorandomness*. Thus, any pseudorandom function that can process long enough inputs, and with enough output bits, could be viable for this use-case. Recall, however, that the D function need only satisfy weak pseudorandomness, since the input to D is assumed to be randomly sampled; moreover an adversary does not see the output of D, but only the one bit output of $\mathsf{F}_\tau \circ \mathsf{D}$.

Given our motivation of sampling LPN error in low-capability devices, we also require that such functions are highly efficient. Thus, rather than relying on low-depth theoretical complexity classes, we will consider performance benchmarking as a metric of efficiency instead. We recall, as stated in Remark 3, that D can be replaced with any other function suitable according to the metric for application in question. Here, our metric is software performance, not low depth. In the following, we discuss our suggested constructions to be used in place of D, and to be evaluated in our experiments in Sect. 6.

ASCON. Ascon-PRF [30] is a cryptographic primitive from the Ascon v1.2 family [29], designed to provide efficient pseudorandom functionality for resource-constrained devices. It uses the same Ascon permutation as selected by NIST as the standard for lightweight cryptography [66]. We will use the AsconPRFs with arbitrary input size and 16/32 byte output.

Candidate Low-Depth Weak PRFs. As discussed early, the literature on low-depth WPRF constructions has advanced over the past few years. In particular, the candidates from [19,23] appear to have avoided polynomial-time attacks [26]. However, given that the construction of [19] only allows realising error rates of 1/3 (or converging to 1/2 in the general case, by altering the moduli), we will consider the SIPSER-based construction of [23]. This assumes that we can achieve approximations of arbitrary τ, which is not a given due to the lack of flexibility in defining the noise rate in the standard SIPSER formulation. That said, we may define for now $\mathsf{D}_{\boldsymbol{M}}(\boldsymbol{x}) = \boldsymbol{M} \cdot \boldsymbol{x}$, where $\boldsymbol{M} \leftarrow\!\$\ \mathbb{Z}_2^{\ell \times \ell}$.

A problem with the above construction, when interpreted within our deterministic LPN framework is that $\boldsymbol{M}$ is an extra secret parameter. To get around this and make the formulation compatible, we can instead sample $\boldsymbol{M} \leftarrow \mathsf{PRG}(\boldsymbol{A}\|\boldsymbol{s})$. We note that if we define $g_\tau = \mathsf{UTribes}_{\omega_1,\ldots,\omega_t}(\mathsf{PRG}(\boldsymbol{A}\|\boldsymbol{s}) \cdot \boldsymbol{x})$, then we may fall foul of the same cryptanalysis that impacted the construction of [2]; see [18]. While the construction of [2] used a public matrix, and our matrix can be kept secret, we note that our universal Tribes formulation is not meaningfully different from the original Tribes function, from a cryptanalytic perspective. Therefore, while SIPSER does not maintain the same level of configurability as UTribes, we believe that using SIPSER here may be necessary from a security perspective. However, we also note that defining g_τ as above at least maintains a performance lower bound for this approach, since UTribes is a more efficient DNF formula than SIPSER.

Simpira. While PRFs in $\mathbf{AC0}[\mathbf{MOD2}]$ may lead to fast implementations by their very nature, this ignores the fact that modern computing architectures are equipped with specific hardware instructions for computing AES rounds, leading to very efficient implementations of AES-based designs. From a practical perspective, this corresponds to considering low-depth PRFs in $\mathbf{AC0}[\mathbf{AES}]$, i.e. constant-depth circuits with gates for computing AES rounds. Note that this question has already motivated research on constructing various symmetric key primitives based on the AES-round function, making use of AES-NI for efficient implementation [8,17,33,51]. Our first candidate based on this approach is Simpira (version 2) [43], a family of permutations using the AES round function as a building block, supporting inputs of $128 \times b$ bits, where b is a positive integer.

LightMAC. Following this approach even further, we propose a second candidate construction based on LightMAC [57]. LightMAC is a parallelisable MAC construction based on a block cipher mode of operation, with proof of security based on the underlying PRP. The original work instantiates LightMAC with PRESENT and AES [57]. In our case, to build D aiming for higher efficiency, we do not use the full AES, but rather instantiate it with **AES4**, a reduced-round version of AES with 4 rounds. **AES4** is obviously not a PRP-secure, but *may* be used securely as a building block of a mode of operation when not aiming for the standard block cipher functionality. **AES4** has already been used in the AE scheme AEZ [49], and in fact in EliMAC [31], a very similar construction to LightMAC. However, to prevent length-extension attacks in the MAC setting, EliMAC finishes the tag computation with a full 10-round AES operation. We conjecture that this is an overkill in our setting, where we only require pseudorandom output bits, and the attacker doesn't see the entire output of Diffuse. Thus our choice to use LightMAC instantiated with **AES4**.

5 Security Analysis

From the symmetric-key cryptanalysis point of view, an instance of the determinist LPN construction is essentially a Boolean function defined as the sum of a secret linear function (the inner product by $\boldsymbol{s}$) and a secret non-linear function $g_{\mathcal{T}}$ with *known* structure. This Boolean function takes as input known, but randomly sampled vectors $\boldsymbol{x}_i$, and produces as output $b_i \in \mathbb{Z}_2$.

$$b_i = \langle \boldsymbol{s}, \boldsymbol{x}_i \rangle + g_{\mathcal{T}}(\boldsymbol{s}, \boldsymbol{x}_i).$$

The adversary has access to $(\boldsymbol{x}_i, b_i)$ and wishes to recover $\boldsymbol{s}$ (in the search variant of DLPN). In view of the results presented concerning the relationship between the LPN and DLPN problems (Sect. 3.1), it is clear that the security of the DLPN construction fundamentally relies on the non-linear properties of $g_{\mathcal{T}}$.

In this case the most viable cryptanalytic approach is to attempt an *algebraic attack*. This may be possible if the degree and/or complexity of the non-linear component is not sufficiently high. And indeed this was the attack method used against the DLPN versions proposed in [2]. We also refer to Sect. 4.1 of [23] for a discussion on the resistance of DLPN constructions against algebraic attacks.

Regarding the instances introduced in this paper, we confidently assert that an algebraic attack is infeasible against two of our instantiations, namely when using ASCON and Simpira (even if followed by no folding). This follows straightforwardly from the security assurances provided by the two ciphers. For the case of LightMAC, we are not able to infer this directly based on the provable properties of the MAC construction – since we do not use a PRP, but rather the **AES4**. However, even after a single folding, the polynomial expression of the noise function will be highly complex and of large degree – as far as we are aware, **AES4** is not susceptible to algebraic attacks. Therefore we feel again confident to claim that our LightMAC-based construction is also resistant to algebraic attacks. These arguments are of course heuristic, but explicitly describing the output bits of cryptographic algorithms such as **AES4** or ASCON is not feasible in practice. In comparison, the security assessment of the construction based on the secret matrix operation followed by UTribes/SIPSER requires a careful analysis of specific parameter choices (as illustrated by the attack in [2]). Based on this discussion, we are confident that our DLPN constructions are resistant to algebraic attacks.

DLPN instantiations must also to be assessed against the standard attacks against LPN, for example based on the BKW algorithm. In turn, such an analysis leads to the selection of suitable parameters ℓ and τ. In this context, we note the assumption made in our constructions that the non-linear component g is a τ-unbalanced weak pseudorandom function. This will be the case for the Folder_τ functions defined in Sect. 4.1 under the assumption that their input – the output bits of the function Diffuse – are independent and uniformly random. Again, we are confident in claiming that our instantiations with ASCON, Simpira and LightMAC[**AES4**] satisfy these assumptions.

In conclusion, we are highly confident that our DLPN construction and instantiations are secure against algebraic and BKW-based attacks. In our analysis, we did not identify any additional attack avenues against our construction in the weak PRF setting.

6 Experimental Results

In this section we describe the implementation of our deterministic LPN framework using the functions discussed in Sect. 4. We implement $g_\tau = \mathsf{F}_\tau \circ \mathsf{D}$, for various values of τ, ℓ where $\mathsf{F}_\tau = \mathsf{UTribes}$, and D is one of the candidate functions from Sect. 4.2. The source code is available at this link.

6.1 Platform Choices

The different options for Diffuse are chosen so that they are expected to perform well in software. However, performance is of course platform-dependent and affected by many factors. For instance Ascon-PRF has optimised implementations for different platforms, while performance of AES-round based Diffuse function is directly dependent on availability of AES-round hardware support.

Most modern processors have hardware acceleration for AES round, most notably AES-NI on processors with x86 architecture. But many IoT and embedded devices (where LPN based protocols are highly relevant) use processors with ARM-based architecture. Hence we are interested in learning the performance of AES on such processors. AES hardware support is available for some ARM-based processors, as part of *Cryptographic Extensions* instruction set. However, it is not present on the chip by default and is up to manufacturers whether to include the license for this support. Most mobile phones with ARM processors include this but SoC devices, like Raspberry Pi 3, 4, don't [36]. When explicit AES hardware support is lacking, the polynomial instruction may still be used for efficient AES implementations if ARM NEON is available [41]. Finally, although matrix multiplication is a simple linear operation in theory, its implementation – particularly for large dimensions – can be cumbersome. To the best of our knowledge, no optimised implementation exists that is both portable across devices and competitive with complex cryptographic functions at large scales.

With this in mind, we ran our experiments on two devices to obtain diverse benchmarks. On a AMD EPYC server with 24-core processor and `x86_64` architecture, a server-grade processor with AES-NI that demonstrates the benefit of hardware AES acceleration. The second platform is a Raspberry Pi 3B with ARM Cortex-A53 processor, running in 32 bit mode. This device was chosen to test our results on a setup resembling IoT devices. While the device does not have any hardware acceleration, we note the availability of AES optimisation across processors. Moreover, using a pure C implementation on a platform without AES support actually showcases the huge effect of AES hardware support.

6.2 Implementation Details

Overall Benchmarks. To measure the CPU cycle count, we use `__rdtscp()` on the x86 platform and `perf_event_open()` on the Raspberry Pi. For each candidate D, we keep the vector length ℓ and the LPN secret s constant. By one evaluation of DLPN we mean that we sample a binary vector a of length ℓ uniformly at random and compute the $g_\tau(s,a) = \mathsf{D} \circ \mathsf{UTribes}$, for different choices of D. We run a quarter of evaluations of DLPN in the cache warm-up phase. Then start the CPU cycle counter and run the evaluations for all samples and calculate the average number of CPU cycles, This experiment is repeated five times and the lowest average CPU cycle count is reported. We also measure the total experiment time (in ms) using `clock_gettime` and memory (in MB) using `getrusage`. More details are provided in the linked GitHub repository. We repeat the experiment for $\ell \in \{512, 1024, 2048, 4096\}$ and $\tau \in \{0.01, 0.05, 0.1, 0.33\}$. We report partial results in Table 1, and in full Tables 3 and 4 in Appendix E. The exact description of $\mathsf{UTribes}$ for the selected values of τ can be found in Sect. 4.

Implementation Choices. For the AMD server, we use the reference implementation of AsconPRF[5]. We wrote our own implementation for LightMAC

[5] https://github.com/ascon/ascon-c/tree/main/crypto_auth/asconprfv13/ref.

Table 1. Experimental results for x86-64 and RPi3

$\ell = 1024$	$\tau = 0.33$ (x86)			$\tau = 0.05$ (x86)			$\tau = 0.33$ (RPi3)			$\tau = 0.05$ (RPi3)		
	Cycles	Time (ms)	Memory (MB)	Cycles	Time (ms)	Memory (MB)	Cycles	Time (ms)	Memory (MB)	Cycles	Time (ms)	Memory (MB)
Simpira	607	26.4	13	644	28	13	42559	353	2	42742	372	2
Ascon	1439	62.3	13	1480	64.5	13	6854	87	2	7037	84	2
LightMAC[**AES4**]	713	31	101	757	32.9	101	38016	282	2	38199	347	2
Matrix	7574	329	161	7793	339	161	488474	3668	2	488655	3497	2
$\ell = 2048$	$\tau = 0.33$ (x86)			$\tau = 0.05$ (x86)			$\tau = 0.33$ (RPi3)			$\tau = 0.05$ (RPi3)		
	Cycles	Time (ms)	Memory (MB)	Cycles	Time (ms)	Memory (MB)	Cycles	Time (ms)	Memory (MB)	Cycles	Time (ms)	Memory (MB)
Simpira	1132	49	26	1171	51	26	87695	694	3	87878	696	3
Ascon	2220	96.7	26	2275	99.1	26	10782	108	3	10965	116	3
LightMAC[**AES4**]	1253	54.6	201	1295	56.4	201	71367	416	3	71550	513	3
Matrix	15253	664	230	15671	682	230	1963057	14096	4	1963241	14103	4

using AES-NI intrinsics in C, whereas the reference implementation of Simpira[6] also utilises these. For Raspberry Pi, due to lack of AES support, we use TinyAES to write our own implementations for Simpira and LightMAC. For Ascon on the other hand, we use the relevant optimised implementation. For the case where Diffuse is a linear map, i.e. multiplication by a fixed $\ell \times \ell$ matrix, we use the M4RI library for matrix multiplication, which appears to be one of the most well-known libraries supporting optimised matrix operations.[7]. However, we could not find a similar optimised library for binary matrix-vector multiplication on Raspberry Pi. Hence, we used our own C implementation, with ARM NEON intrinsic in C for bitwise XOR. Exact specification of how we instantiate each Diffuse is given in Appendix C.

6.3 Results and Discussion

Comparison of Diffuse Instantiations. Across the benchmarks in Table 1, Table 2, and Appendix E, we observe that implementing D with Simpira and LightMAC[**AES4**] incurs the least computation costs for producing deterministic LPN instances. This is clearly due to their use of AES-NI. Simpira is slightly more efficient, which is somewhat surprising given that we instantiate LightMAC with AES4. However, as Simpira was designed for processing large block lengths in mind, this potentially explains the high performance. Furthermore, Simpira's reference implementation may benefit from optimisations that are lacking in our LightMAC implementation. The performances drop drastically with Raspberry Pi 3, which demonstrated the benefit of having AES support. A factor may also be that we wrote our own implementation using TinyAES, and several optimisations could still be possible. Finally, we also note the availability of optimised AES implementations (both with and without AES hardware support) as discussed in Sect. 6.1 and optimised Simpira for low-end devices [65].

Ascon-PRF remains competitive across both platforms, and as a NIST standard, it offers stronger security guarantees. Ascon is a solid, conservative

---

6 https://mouha.be/simpira/.

7 https://github.com/malb/m4ri/.

Table 2. Experimental results for [23] WPRF

	$\ell = 512$, $\tau = 0.077$			$\ell = 1024$, $\tau = 0.019$			$\ell = 2048$, $\tau = 0.001$		
	Cycles	Time (ms)	Mem. (MB)	Cycles	Time (ms)	Mem. (MB)	Cycles	Time (ms)	Mem. (MB)
Matrix + SIPSER	5848	254	119	11107	483	141	20896	910	185

choice for instantiating DLPN. Furthermore, using the platform-specific optimised implementations of Ascon-PRF (instead of the reference implementation), may lead to improved performances and portability on large range of platforms.

Considering the matrix-based low-depth WPRF constructions, our implementation of the UTribes variant is much less efficient than all other choices. Our M4RI-based implementation incurs an order of magnitude performance slow-down in CPU cycles, when compared with the AES-NI-based constructions. From a memory perspective, while Simpira, LightMAC[**AES4**], and Ascon-PRF are essentially equivalent, the memory costs of the WPRF constructions appear to be around an order of magnitude higher. Overall, it is possible that our M4RI-based implementation is not optimal; the same can be said about our ARM NEON implementation. However, it is unlikely that any optimisation would reduce the gap in performance for matrix multiplication. Moreover, the lack of optimised implementation of linear maps for different platforms demonstrates the difficulty of using D as matrix, when we are interested in instantiating DLPN in practice. Overall, we believe these numbers give an accurate representation of the overall performance and how it compares to other Diffuse.

Note that, for a fixed ℓ, changing the value of τ affects the measurements only slightly for all choices of Diffuse. The memory usage remains the same, while CPU cycles and time incur only slight variations. We believe this is because UTribes is instantiated with different tribe-lengths and number of tribes for different τ. For example, the number of tribes and total tribe length for $\tau = 0.1$ is $4, 26$ and for $\tau = 0.05$ is $5, 41$, resp. Thus UTribes $_{0.05}$ is slightly slower than UTribes $_{0.1}$. Optimisations could potentially be introduced to improve the performance of UTribes further. However, since we implement Diffuse and UTribes separately and sequentially, the gain will be equal across all Diffuse instantiations.

WPRF Comparison. For completeness, given that our UTribes formulation of g_τ for processing linear maps outputs may be susceptible to cryptanalysis, we also produced an implementation of SIPSER-based WPRF from [23]. Results are shown in Table 2. As noted previously, our UTribes is indeed a lower bound for performance, and the SIPSER-based construction is indeed much slower. Furthermore, the configurability of τ is less fine-grained, and it is harder to achieve higher values. Our results indicate that instantiating WPRFs from τ-UWPRFs, using the transformation detailed in Lemma 1, is better served using the function compositions built from symmetric primitives (as opposed to current candidate low-depth WPRFs).

Acknowledgments. This work was supported by FCT and the CMU Portugal program through the project "Fully-Homomorphic Encryption from Post-Quantum Code-Based Assumptions", ref. 2024.12595.CMU (DOI: 10.54499/2024.12595.cmu), and the LASIGE Research Unit, ref. UID/00408/2025 - LASIGE. Initial drafts of this work were also supported by NOVA.ID.FCT through the CertiCoLab project, funded by the EEA Grants Bilateral Fund (FBR_OC2_103-CertiCoLab).

A Overview of HB-family protocols

The HB family of protocols, which include a series of work starting with Hopper and Blum [50] are authentication protocols specifically designed for resource-constrained devices such as RFID tags. These protocols typically contain a challenge-response sequence that resembles an LPN instance, thus allowing them to leverage the simplicity of LPN and security of the LPN problem. In these protocols, a prover device (referred to as *tag*) proves the knowledge of a shared key $s \in \mathbb{Z}_2^n$ to the verifier device (referred to as reader *reader*). In the first and the simplest protocol (HB) [50], the reader sends challenges $a_i \in \mathbb{Z}_2^n$ and the tag responds with the bit $r_i = \langle a_i, s\rangle + e_i$, where $e_i \leftarrow \mathsf{Ber}_\tau$. This is repeated for m samples $a_1, \ldots, a_m$ and the verifier, using the shared secret s, then checks if $r_i = \langle a_i, s\rangle$. Taking into account the noise rate τ, the tag has authenticated successfully if the check fails at most $\lfloor \tau m \rfloor$ many times. It is clear that this challenge-response resembles an LPN instance, leading to security against *passive* adversaries. However, an *active* adversary can repeatedly query the same challenge vector v, and naively guess the value $\langle s, v\rangle$ by majority rule, as the error is only added with probability $\tau < 1/2$. Repeating this for n linearly independent vectors $v_1, \ldots, v_n$ leads to easily recovering the n-bit secret s.

The follow up work of HB+ [52] protocol set up a similar protocol as HB but with two shared secret bit-strings, instead of one. The work claimed security against active adversaries, again by reduction to the hardness of LPN, but the proof was shown to be flawed [37] through a Man-in-the-Middle (MITM) attack. There have been several other variants of similar authentication protocols. We refer to [5, Appendix A] for a summary.

B Folding Function Example Parametrisations

Given the $\mathsf{UTribes}$ function described in Section 4.1, we provide examples of instantiations of F_τ in DNF formula, that allow us to realise the function g_τ, for various values of τ. Note that the function formulations are derived explicitly from the construction in Section 4.1, and vary with the value of τ sought.

$\tau = 0.33$**:** Number of tribes $= 5$, and tribe sizes $\omega_0 = 2, \omega_1 = 4, \omega_2 = 5, \omega_3 = 6, \omega_4 = 11$.

$$g_{\frac{1}{3}}(x_1, \ldots, x_n) = \left(\bigwedge_{i=1}^{2} x_i\right) \vee \left(\bigwedge_{i=3}^{6} x_i\right) \vee \left(\bigwedge_{i=7}^{11} x_i\right) \vee \left(\bigwedge_{i=12}^{17} x_i\right) \vee \left(\bigwedge_{i=18}^{28} x_i\right)$$

Given that the next tribe length would be $\omega_6 = 12$, this gives an approximation error of $\epsilon_5 < 2^{-11}$ (Equation (4)). Total number of bits used $= 28$.

$\tau = 0.1$: Number of tribes $= 4$, and tribe sizes $\omega_0 = 4, \omega_1 = 5, \omega_2 = 7, \omega_3 = 10$.

$$g_{\frac{1}{10}}(x_1, \ldots, x_n) = \left(\bigwedge_{i=1}^{4} x_i\right) \vee \left(\bigwedge_{i=5}^{9} x_i\right) \vee \left(\bigwedge_{i=10}^{16} x_i\right) \vee \left(\bigwedge_{i=17}^{26} x_i\right)$$

Given that the next tribe length would be $\omega_5 = 12$, this gives an approximation error of $\epsilon_4 < 2^{-11}$. Total number of bits used $= 26$.

$\tau = 0.05$: Number of tribes $= 5$, with sizes $\omega_0 = 5, \omega_1 = 6, \omega_2 = 9, \omega_3 = 10, \omega_4 = 11$

$$g_{\frac{1}{20}}(x_1, \ldots, x_n) = \left(\bigwedge_{i=1}^{5} x_i\right) \vee \left(\bigwedge_{i=6}^{11} x_i\right) \vee \left(\bigwedge_{i=12}^{20} x_i\right) \vee \left(\bigwedge_{i=21}^{30} x_i\right) \bigvee \left(\bigwedge_{i=31}^{41} x_i\right)$$

Given that the next tribe length would be $\omega_6 = 12$, this gives an approximation error of $\epsilon_5 < 2^{-11}$. Total number of bits used $= 41$.

$\tau = 0.01$: Number of tribes $= 4$, with sizes $\omega_0 = 7, \omega_1 = 9, \omega_2 = 12, \omega_3 = 17$

$$g_{\frac{1}{100}}(x_1, \ldots, x_n) = \left(\bigwedge_{i=1}^{7} x_i\right) \vee \left(\bigwedge_{i=8}^{16} x_i\right) \vee \left(\bigwedge_{i=17}^{28} x_i\right) \vee \left(\bigwedge_{i=29}^{45} x_i\right)$$

Given that the next tribe length would be $\omega_6 = 22$, this gives an approximation error of $\epsilon_4 < 2^{-21}$. Total number of bits used $= 41$.

C Implementation specifications for Diffuse

Simpira. We generate a vector $s \in \{0,1\}^\ell$ which is cast as an `_m128i` variable. This is the LPN secret and is fixed. For each iteration, we generate LPN sample $a_i \in \{0,1\}^\ell$ (again as `_m128i` variable) and is mix with the LPN secret by bitwise XOR of both, and then apply the Simpira permutation as Diffuse. For this, use the reference implementation of Simpira [8]. The file `Permutations_Ref.c` contains reference implementations for all values of B (here B is the number of 128-bit word in the input vector), which utilize the `aesenc` native instruction (hence the need for generating inputs as `_m128i`). The n-bit output vector (which is in `_m128i` format) is the unpacked and we apply UTribes to get the noise bit. Specifically, for each LPN sample of length n we apply the corresponding Simpira permutation S_B where $B = \ell/128$ then compute the noise term as

$$e_i = \mathsf{UTribes}(S_B(s \oplus a_i))$$

[8] https://mouha.be/simpira/.

Ascon-PRF. We use the reference implementation of Ascon-PRF, but do not use any platform-specific optimisations.[9] We generate a vector $s \in \{0,1\}^\ell$ as a byte array. This is the LPN secret and is fixed. For each iteration, we generate LPN sample $a_i \in \{0,1\}^\ell$ as a byte array. Then we apply the Ascon-PRF with input a_i, key s, input-length and key-length (in bytes) is ℓ in bytes and output length is 16 bytes. Then we convert the output in an array of bits and apply UTribes to the first few bits (≤ 64) to get the noise bit. Specifically, the noise bit e_i is given as:

$$e_i = \mathsf{UTribes}(F(s, a_i, \text{inlen} = \ell, \text{outlen} = 128)).$$

We note that we experiment also with outlen = 256, and show the results in the first table shown. However the results indicate that the performance degrades expectably, and so we do not repeat the results for other dimensions.

LightMAC. We use the LightMAC construction as described in Section 4.2 (i.e. with a similar design philosophy to that of EliMAC [31]), but we note that UTribes only uses an initial sequence of bits (≤ 64) of the final output, thus we do not need to specifically perform the truncation that occurs in the final round. Furthermore, for the block cipher encryption function, E, we use **AES4** as described in [49]. That is, for sub-keys $K = (K_0, K_1, K_2, K_3, K_4)$ and input $X \in \{0,1\}^{128}$

$$\mathbf{AES4}(K, X) = \mathtt{aesenc}(\mathtt{aesenc}(\mathtt{aesenc}(\mathtt{aesenc}(X \oplus K_0, K_1), K_2), K_3), K_4)$$

where `aesenc` is one AES round (where we use the native instruction). We generate a 128-bit master key s (this can be derived from the LPN secret), and use the AES-key expansion to get 10 sub-keys $(K_0, \ldots, K_9)$, and use the first 4 sub-keys during E_{k_1} and last 5 sub-keys during E_{k_2} in LightMAC

We make two choices for cleaner implementations. In the original construction, the user has a choice of how this s-bit vector i_s is determined based on i. For instance, it could be the s bit representation of i (Section 2, [57]). Additionally, s should be chosen such that the input message M is of length at most $2^s(n_1 - s)$ bits. We choose $s = 8$ and i_8 to be the 8-bit representation of i. This choice is made for simplicity's sake, so that, for every index i, we can then cast the integer value of i as an unsigned byte and concatenate with 15 bytes taken from the message stream and encrypt the 16 bytes with **AES4**. Since we choose $E = \mathbf{AES4}$, then $n_1 = 128$ and the maximum message length is $2^8 \times 120$, which is suitable for our choices of LPN dimensions.

9 https://github.com/ascon/ascon-c/tree/main/crypto_auth/asconprfv13/ref.

Matrix-based Diffusewith UTribes. For the case where Diffuse is a linear map i.e. multiplication by a fixed $\ell \times \ell$ matrix. We use the M4RI library for fast matrix multiplication, which appears to be one of the most well-known libraries supporting optimised matrix multiplication operations.[10] We generate an $\ell \times \ell$ matrix M (in the `mzd_t` datatype native to the M4RI library), and keep it fixed. For each iteration, we generate the LPN vectors $\boldsymbol{a}_i \in \{0,1\}^\ell$ by casting the random bytes in an array and pointing an `mzd_t` vector `v` to it. Then we multiply M with `v` using `_mzd_mul_va` function from the library. For Raspberry Pi, we could not find such a library for optimized linear maps. We wrote our own implementation where we utilized ARM NEON intrinsics for performing bitwise XOR between each matrix row and $\boldsymbol{a}_i$, and to get the parity of the number of 1's in the resulting vector, we use `libpopcount.h`, a portable library for population count. We read the bits from the resulting output `mzd_t`-type vector, and apply UTribes to the first few bits (≤ 64, see example parametrisations in Section 4).

Matrix-based Diffusewith SIPSER. While the case above should lower bound the performance of the WPRF from [23], we test a full implementation that uses the SIPSER function applied after linear map for x86 platform. Note that the SIPSER formulation is the one that would appear to maintain security against known cryptanalysis. This variant is determined by a parameter λ which relates to the input length ℓ, and as discussed previously, the error rate τ is a function of λ. For LPN vector length $\ell \in \{512, 1024, 2048\}$, the closest we get is $\lambda \in \{16, 22, 32\}$ respectively, and this implies that the approximate τ that is used in our experiments is $\{0.077, 0.019, 0.001\}$ respectively.

D Applications of DLPN

Relationship with VOLE. LPN has become a vital building block in the construction of primitives based on vector oblivious linear evaluation (VOLE) [22]. VOLE itself lends itself to practical instantiations of signatures schemes [9], zero-knowledge proofs [10], oblivious pseudorandom functions [47], and oblivious transfer [64], amongst many other use-cases. With VOLE seeing increased practical usage, this requires sampling secure instances of LPN for building similarly secure instances of VOLE. One of the appealing aspects of VOLE-based protocols is that their computational load is fairly low, and this leads to zero-knowledge proofs with lower prover overheads (as opposed to zkSNARKs [14], for example). This motivates incorporating such applications with lower powered clients. As a result, we see a potentially important application of our DLPN framework in instantiating VOLE-based applications, where constrained clients may be asked to sample many LPN instances that each require valuable sources of randomness. This would allow clients to build VOLE instances, with security dependent on the parameterisation and construction of DLPN that is used.

[10] https://github.com/malb/m4ri/.

Large-scale MPC. The work of [13] demonstrates how to build generic multi-party computation from LPN, noting that specific error rates (e.g. 1/8 or 1/16) are required to ensure that the computation remains correct. Such secure computation frameworks appear to be efficient at large-scale, and also ensure active security, which is preferable for higher-risk applications. DLPN here would allow specifically configuring error rates to the required values, while permitting that such computation systems can be built without sampling sources of randomness. Such an instantiation could be useful for building federated learning platforms, requiring computation over private data by large numbers of constrained clients.

E Full experimental results

Table 3. Experimental results for x86-64.

$\ell = 512$	$\tau = 0.33$			$\tau = 0.1$			$\tau = 0.05$			$\tau = 0.01$		
	Cycles	Time (ms)	Memory (MB)	Cycles	Time (ms)	Memory (MB)	Cycles	Time (ms)	Memory (MB)	Cycles	Time (ms)	Memory (MB)
Simpira	430	18.7	7	437	19	7	465	20.2	7	472	20.5	7
Ascon-128	1018	44.3	7	1025	44.7	7	1053	45.8	7	1078	46.9	7
Ascon-256	1196	52.1	7	1200	52.3	7	1237	53.8	7	1240	54.9	7
LightMAC[**AES4**]	477	20.8	7	470	22.4	7	513	22.3	7	517	22.5	7
Matrix	5104	222	128	5002	217	128	5011	218	128	5049	219	128

$\ell = 1024$	$\tau = 0.33$			$\tau = 0.1$			$\tau = 0.05$			$\tau = 0.01$		
	Cycles	Time (ms)	Memory (MB)	Cycles	Time (ms)	Memory (MB)	Cycles	Time (ms)	Memory (MB)	Cycles	Time (ms)	Memory (MB)
Simpira	607	26.4	13	627	27	13	644	28	13	656	28.5	13
Ascon	1439	62.3	13	1433	62.4	12	1480	64.5	13	1488	64.8	13
LightMAC[**AES4**]	713	31	101	724	31	101	757	32.9	101	762	33.2	101
Matrix	7574	329	161	7569	329	161	7793	339	161	7566	329	161

$\ell = 2048$	$\tau = 0.33$			$\tau = 0.1$			$\tau = 0.05$			$\tau = 0.01$		
	Cycles	Time (ms)	Memory (MB)	Cycles	Time (ms)	Memory (MB)	Cycles	Time (ms)	Memory (MB)	Cycles	Time (ms)	Memory (MB)
Simpira	1132	49	26	1148	50	26	1171	51	26	1179	51	26
Ascon	2220	96.7	26	229	97	26	2275	99.1	26	2285	99.5	26
LightMAC[**AES4**]	1253	54.6	201	1265	55.1	201	1295	56.4	201	1305	56.8	201
Matrix	15253	664	230	15174	661	230	15671	682	230	15043	655	230

$\ell = 4096$	$\tau = 0.33$			$\tau = 0.1$			$\tau = 0.05$			$\tau = 0.01$		
	Cycles	Time (ms)	Memory (MB)	Cycles	Time (ms)	Memory (MB)	Cycles	Time (ms)	Memory (MB)	Cycles	Time (ms)	Memory (MB)
Simpira	2057	89.6	51	2063	90	51	2098	91	51	2116	92	51
Ascon	3855	167	51	3858	168	51	3914	170	51	3916	170	51
LightMAC[**AES4**]	2287	99.3	51	2265	98.6	51	2328	101	51	2323	101	51
Matrix	67391	2935	369	66292	2887	369	67515	2940	369	67683	2948	369

Table 4. Experimental results for Raspberry Pi 3.

$\ell = 512$	$\tau = 0.33$			$\tau = 0.1$			$\tau = 0.05$			$\tau = 0.01$		
	Cycles	Time (ms)	Memory (MB)	Cycles	Time (ms)	Memory (MB)	Cycles	Time (ms)	Memory (MB)	Cycles	Time (ms)	Memory (MB)
Simpira	17674	192	1	17674	174	1	17857	173	1	17913	172	1
Ascon-128	4889	72	1	4862	73	1	5072	75	1	5128	88	1
Ascon-256	5804	80	1	5777	82	1	5987	74	1	6043	96	1
LightMAC[**AES4**]	23182	209	1	23155	219	1	23364	192	1	23421	207	1
Matrix-ℓ	125188	994	1	125160	959	1	125369	936	1	125427	940	1
Matrix-128	32039	294	1	32011	295	1	32222	282	1	32277	296	1

$\ell = 1024$	$\tau = 0.33$			$\tau = 0.1$			$\tau = 0.05$			$\tau = 0.01$		
	Cycles	Time (ms)	Memory (MB)	Cycles	Time (ms)	Memory (MB)	Cycles	Time (ms)	Memory (MB)	Cycles	Time (ms)	Memory (MB)
Simpira	42559	353	2	42532	355	2	42742	372	2	42798	379	2
Ascon-128	6854	87	2	6827	97	2	7037	84	2	7093	98	2
Ascon-256	7769	82	2	7742	87	2	7952	90	2	8008	94	2
LightMAC[**AES4**]	38016	282	2	37989	268	2	38199	347	2	38255	265	2
Matrix-ℓ	488474	3668	2	488445	3692	2	488655	3497	2	488717	3533	2
Matrix-128	61934	509	2	61907	503	2	62116	480	2	62173	5066	2

$\ell = 2048$	$\tau = 0.33$			$\tau = 0.1$			$\tau = 0.05$			$\tau = 0.01$		
	Cycles	Time (ms)	Memory (MB)	Cycles	Time (ms)	Memory (MB)	Cycles	Time (ms)	Memory (MB)	Cycles	Time (ms)	Memory (MB)
Simpira	87695	694	3	87669	700	3	87878	696	3	87934	688	3
Ascon-128	10782	108	3	10755	117	3	10965	116	3	11021	101	3
Ascon-256	11697	94	3	11670	113	3	11880	112	3	11936	114	3
LightMAC[**AES4**]	71367	416	3	71340	490	3	71550	513	3	71606	479	3
Matrix-ℓ	1963057	14096	4	1963030	14102	4	1963241	14103	4	1963329	14232	4
Matrix-128	123647	927	3	123619	974	3	123828	947	3	123885	950	3

$\ell = 4096$	$\tau = 0.33$			$\tau = 0.1$			$\tau = 0.05$			$\tau = 0.01$		
	Cycles	Time (ms)	Memory (MB)	Cycles	Time (ms)	Memory (MB)	Cycles	Time (ms)	Memory (MB)	Cycles	Time (ms)	Memory (MB)
Simpira	183386	1376	6	183359	1388	6	183569	1396	6	183628	1375	6
Ascon-128	18641	128	6	18641	148	6	18824	127	6	18880	130	6
Ascon-256	19556	124	6	19529	132	6	19739	128	6	19795	150	6
LightMAC[**AES4**]	134369	866	6	134344	919	6	134552	933	6	134608	964	6
Matrix-ℓ	7390247	55704	8	7390223	52778	8	7390435	52342	8	7390486	52326	8
Matrix-128	231908	1645	6	231880	1643	6	232091	1607	6	232146	1603	6

References

1. Ajtai, M., Linial, N.: The influence of large coalitions. Comb. **13**(2), 129–145 (1993)
2. Akavia, A., Bogdanov, A., Guo, S., Kamath, A., Rosen, A.: Candidate weak pseudorandom functions in AC0. MOD2. In: Proceedings of the 5th Conference on Innovations in Theoretical Computer Science, ITCS 2014, pp. 251–260. Association for Computing Machinery, New York, NY, USA (2014)
3. Alwen, J., Krenn, S., Pietrzak, K., Wichs, D.: Learning with rounding, revisited. In: Canetti, R., Garay, J.A. (eds.) CRYPTO 2013. LNCS, vol. 8042, pp. 57–74. Springer, Heidelberg (2013). https://doi.org/10.1007/978-3-642-40041-4_4
4. Applebaum, B., Damgård, I., Ishai, Y., Nielsen, M., Zichron, L.: Secure arithmetic computation with constant computational overhead. In: Katz, J., Shacham, H. (eds.) CRYPTO 2017. LNCS, vol. 10401, pp. 223–254. Springer, Cham (2017). https://doi.org/10.1007/978-3-319-63688-7_8
5. Armknecht, F., Hamann, M., Mikhalev, V.: Lightweight authentication protocols on ultra-constrained RFIDs - myths and facts. In: Saxena, N., Sadeghi, A.-R. (eds.) Radio Frequency Identification: Security and Privacy Issues, pp. 1–18. Springer International Publishing, Cham (2014)

6. Banerjee, A., Peikert, C., Rosen, A.: Pseudorandom functions and lattices. In: Pointcheval, D., Johansson, T. (eds.) EUROCRYPT 2012. LNCS, vol. 7237, pp. 719–737. Springer, Heidelberg (2012). https://doi.org/10.1007/978-3-642-29011-4_42
7. Banik, S., Isobe, T., Liu, F., Minematsu, K., Sakamoto, K.: Orthros: a low-latency PRF. IACR Trans. Symmetric Cryptol. **2021**(1), 37–77 (2021)
8. Bariant, A., Baudrin, J., Leurent, G., Pernot, C., Perrin, L., Peyrin, T.: Fast AES-based universal hash functions and macs: Featuring LeMac and PetitMac. IACR Trans. Symmetric Cryptol. **2024**(2), 35–67 (2024)
9. Baum, C., et al.: FAEST: algorithm specifications. Technical report, National Institute of Standards and Technology (2023)
10. Baum, C., Dittmer, S., Scholl, P., Wang, X.: SOK: vector OLE-based zero-knowledge protocols. Des. Codes Cryptogr. **91**(11), 3527–3561 (2023)
11. Bellizia, D., et al.: Learning parity with physical noise: imperfections, reductions and FPGA prototype. IACR Trans. Cryptogr. Hardw. Embed. Syst. **2021**(3), 390–417 (2021)
12. Bellizia, D., Hoffmann, C., Kamel, D., Méaux, P., Standaert, F.: When bad news become good news towards usable instances of learning with physical errors. IACR Trans. Cryptogr. Hardw. Embed. Syst. **2022**(4), 1–24 (2022)
13. Ben-Efraim, A., Cong, K., Omri, E., Orsini, E., Smart, N.P., Soria-Vazquez, E.: Large scale, actively secure computation from LPN and free-XOR garbled circuits. In: Canteaut, A., Standaert, F.-X. (eds.) EUROCRYPT 2021. LNCS, vol. 12698, pp. 33–63. Springer, Cham (2021). https://doi.org/10.1007/978-3-030-77883-5_2
14. Bitansky, N., Canetti, R., Chiesa, A., Tromer, E.: From extractable collision resistance to succinct non-interactive arguments of knowledge, and back again. In: Goldwasser, S. (ed.) Innovations in Theoretical Computer Science 2012, Cambridge, MA, USA, 8–10 January 2012, pp. 326–349. ACM (2012)
15. Blum, A., Furst, M., Kearns, M., Lipton, R.J.: Cryptographic primitives based on hard learning problems. In: Stinson, D.R. (ed.) CRYPTO 1993. LNCS, vol. 773, pp. 278–291. Springer, Heidelberg (1994). https://doi.org/10.1007/3-540-48329-2_24
16. Blum, A., Kalai, A., Wasserman, H.: Noise-tolerant learning, the parity problem, and the statistical query model. In: Yao, F.F., Luks, E.M. (eds.) Proceedings of the Thirty-Second Annual ACM Symposium on Theory of Computing, 21–23 May 2000, Portland, OR, USA, pp. 435–440. ACM (2000)
17. Bogdanov, A., Lauridsen, M.M., Tischhauser, E.: AES-based authenticated encryption modes in parallel high-performance software. IACR Cryptology ePrint Archive, p. 186 (2014)
18. Bogdanov, A., Rosen, A.: Pseudorandom functions: three decades later. Cryptology ePrint Archive, Paper 2017/652 (2017). https://eprint.iacr.org/2017/652
19. Boneh, D., Ishai, Y., Passelègue, A., Sahai, A., Wu, D.J.: Exploring Crypto Dark Matter:- new simple PRF candidates and their applications. In: Beimel, A., Dziembowski, S. (eds.) TCC 2018. LNCS, vol. 11240, pp. 699–729. Springer, Cham (2018). https://doi.org/10.1007/978-3-030-03810-6_25
20. Boneh, D., Lewi, K., Montgomery, H., Raghunathan, A.: Key homomorphic PRFs and their applications. In: Canetti, R., Garay, J.A. (eds.) CRYPTO 2013. LNCS, vol. 8042, pp. 410–428. Springer, Heidelberg (2013). https://doi.org/10.1007/978-3-642-40041-4_23
21. Boyle, E., Couteau, G., Gilboa, N., Ishai, Y.: Compressing vector OLE. In: Lie, D., Mannan, M., Backes, M., Wang, X. (eds.) Proceedings of the 2018 ACM SIGSAC Conference on Computer and Communications Security, CCS 2018, Toronto, ON, Canada, 15–19 October 2018, pp. 896–912. ACM (2018)

22. Boyle, E., Couteau, G., Gilboa, N., Ishai, Y., Kohl, L., Scholl, P.: Correlated pseudorandom functions from variable-density LPN. In: Irani, S. (ed.) 61st IEEE Annual Symposium on Foundations of Computer Science, FOCS 2020, Durham, NC, USA, 16–19 November 2020, pp. 1069–1080. IEEE (2020)
23. Boyle, E., Couteau, G., Gilboa, N., Ishai, Y., Kohl, L., Scholl, P.: Low-complexity weak pseudorandom functions in AC0[MOD2]. In: Malkin, T., Peikert, C. (eds.) CRYPTO 2021. LNCS, vol. 12828, pp. 487–516. Springer, Cham (2021). https://doi.org/10.1007/978-3-030-84259-8_17
24. Boyle, E., Couteau, G., Gilboa, N., Ishai, Y., Kohl, L., Scholl, P.: Low-complexity weak pseudorandom functions in AC0[MOD2] (2021). Full version, made available privately by the authors
25. Carlet, C., Sarkar, P.: Use of simple arithmetic operations to construct efficiently implementable Boolean functions possessing high nonlinearity and good resistance to algebraic attacks. Cryptology ePrint Archive, Paper 2024/1305 (2024)
26. Cheon, J.H., Cho, W., Kim, J.H., Kim, J.: Adventures in crypto dark matter: attacks and fixes for weak pseudorandom functions. In: Garay, J.A. (ed.) PKC 2021. LNCS, vol. 12711, pp. 739–760. Springer, Cham (2021). https://doi.org/10.1007/978-3-030-75248-4_26
27. Couteau, G., Rindal, P., Raghuraman, S.: Silver: silent VOLE and oblivious transfer from hardness of decoding structured LDPC codes. In: Malkin, T., Peikert, C. (eds.) CRYPTO 2021. LNCS, vol. 12827, pp. 502–534. Springer, Cham (2021). https://doi.org/10.1007/978-3-030-84252-9_17
28. Dao, Q., Ishai, Y., Jain, A., Lin, H.: Multi-party homomorphic secret sharing and sublinear MPC from sparse LPN. In: Handschuh, H., Lysyanskaya, A. (eds.) Advances in Cryptology - CRYPTO 2023 - 43rd Annual International Cryptology Conference, CRYPTO 2023, Santa Barbara, CA, USA, 20–24 August 2023, Proceedings, Part II. LNCS, vol. 14082, pp. 315–348. Springer (2023)
29. Dobraunig, C., Eichlseder, M., Mendel, F., Schläffer, M.: Ascon v1.2: lightweight authenticated encryption and hashing. J. Cryptol. **34**(3), 33 (2021)
30. Dobraunig, C., Eichlseder, M., Mendel, F., Schläffer, M.: Ascon MAC, PRF, and Short-Input PRF - Lightweight, Fast, and Efficient Pseudorandom Functions (2024)
31. Dobraunig, C., Mennink, B., Neves, S.: EliMAC: speeding up LightMAC by around 20%. IACR Trans. Symmetric Cryptol. **2023**(2), 69–93 (2023)
32. Döttling, N., Müller-Quade, J., Nascimento, A.C.A.: IND-CCA secure cryptography based on a variant of the LPN problem. In: Wang, X., Sako, K. (eds.) ASIACRYPT 2012. LNCS, vol. 7658, pp. 485–503. Springer, Heidelberg (2012). https://doi.org/10.1007/978-3-642-34961-4_30
33. Drucker, N., Gueron, S., Krasnov, V.: Making AES great again: the forthcoming vectorized AES instruction. Cryptology ePrint Archive, Paper 2018/392 (2018)
34. Eliasi, P.A., et al.: Koala: a low-latency pseudorandom function. Cryptology ePrint Archive, Paper 2024/1249 (2024)
35. Esser, A., Kübler, R., May, A.: LPN decoded. In: Katz, J., Shacham, H. (eds.) CRYPTO 2017. LNCS, vol. 10402, pp. 486–514. Springer, Cham (2017). https://doi.org/10.1007/978-3-319-63715-0_17
36. Fujii, H., Rodrigues, F.C., López, J.: Fast AES implementation using ARMv8 ASIMD without cryptography extension. In: Seo, J.H. (ed.) ICISC 2019. LNCS, vol. 11975, pp. 84–101. Springer, Cham (2020). https://doi.org/10.1007/978-3-030-40921-0_5
37. Gilbert, H., Robshaw, M., Sibert, H.: Active attack against HB+: a provably secure lightweight authentication protocol. Electron. Lett. **41**, 1169–1170 (2005)

38. Gilbert, H., Robshaw, M.J.B., Seurin, Y.: HB#: increasing the security and efficiency of HB+. In: Smart, N. (ed.) EUROCRYPT 2008. LNCS, vol. 4965, pp. 361–378. Springer, Heidelberg (2008). https://doi.org/10.1007/978-3-540-78967-3_21
39. Gilbert, H., Robshaw, M.J.B., Seurin, Y.: How to encrypt with the LPN problem. In: Aceto, L., Damgård, I., Goldberg, L.A., Halldórsson, M.M., Ingólfsdóttir, A., Walukiewicz, I. (eds.) ICALP 2008. LNCS, vol. 5126, pp. 679–690. Springer, Heidelberg (2008). https://doi.org/10.1007/978-3-540-70583-3_55
40. Gilboa, S., Gueron, S.: The advantage of truncated permutations. Discret. Appl. Math. **294**, 214–223 (2021)
41. Gouvêa, C.P.L., López, J.: Implementing GCM on ARMv8. In: Nyberg, K. (ed.) CT-RSA 2015. LNCS, vol. 9048, pp. 167–180. Springer, Cham (2015). https://doi.org/10.1007/978-3-319-16715-2_9
42. Gross, R.: Generalized tribes. Boolean Zoo, Weizmann Institute (2019)
43. Gueron, S., Mouha, N.: Simpira v2: a family of efficient permutations using the AES round function. In: Cheon, J.H., Takagi, T. (eds.) ASIACRYPT 2016. LNCS, vol. 10031, pp. 95–125. Springer, Heidelberg (2016). https://doi.org/10.1007/978-3-662-53887-6_4
44. Hammouri, G., Sunar, B.: PUF-HB: a tamper-resilient HB based authentication protocol. In: Bellovin, S.M., Gennaro, R., Keromytis, A., Yung, M. (eds.) ACNS 2008. LNCS, vol. 5037, pp. 346–365. Springer, Heidelberg (2008). https://doi.org/10.1007/978-3-540-68914-0_21
45. Håstad, J.: Almost optimal lower bounds for small depth circuits. In: Hartmanis, J. (ed.) Proceedings of the 18th Annual ACM Symposium on Theory of Computing, 28–30 May 1986, Berkeley, California, USA, pp. 6–20. ACM (1986)
46. Håstad, J.: Some optimal inapproximability results. In: Leighton, F.T., Shor, P.W. (eds.) Proceedings of the 29th Annual ACM Symposium on the Theory of Computing, El Paso, Texas, USA, 4–6 May 1997, pp. 1–10. ACM (1997)
47. Heimberger, L., Kales, D., Lolato, R., Mir, O., Ramacher, S., Rechberger, C.: Leap: a fast, lattice-based OPRF with application to private set intersection. In: Fehr, S., Fouque, P. (eds.) Advances in Cryptology - EUROCRYPT 2025 - 44th Annual International Conference on the Theory and Applications of Cryptographic Techniques, Madrid, Spain, 4–8 May 2025, Proceedings, Part VII. LNCS, vol. 15607, pp. 254–283. Springer (2025)
48. Heyse, S., Kiltz, E., Lyubashevsky, V., Paar, C., Pietrzak, K.: Lapin: an efficient authentication protocol based on ring-LPN. In: Canteaut, A. (ed.) FSE 2012. LNCS, vol. 7549, pp. 346–365. Springer, Heidelberg (2012). https://doi.org/10.1007/978-3-642-34047-5_20
49. Hoang, V.T., Krovetz, T., Rogaway, P.: Robust authenticated-encryption AEZ and the problem that it solves. In: Oswald, E., Fischlin, M. (eds.) EUROCRYPT 2015. LNCS, vol. 9056, pp. 15–44. Springer, Heidelberg (2015). https://doi.org/10.1007/978-3-662-46800-5_2
50. Hopper, N.J., Blum, M.: Secure human identification protocols. In: Boyd, C. (ed.) ASIACRYPT 2001. LNCS, vol. 2248, pp. 52–66. Springer, Heidelberg (2001). https://doi.org/10.1007/3-540-45682-1_4
51. Jean, J., Nikolić, I.: Efficient design strategies based on the AES round function. In: Peyrin, T. (ed.) FSE 2016. LNCS, vol. 9783, pp. 334–353. Springer, Heidelberg (2016). https://doi.org/10.1007/978-3-662-52993-5_17
52. Juels, A., Weis, S.A.: Authenticating pervasive devices with human protocols. In: Shoup, V. (ed.) CRYPTO 2005. LNCS, vol. 3621, pp. 293–308. Springer, Heidelberg (2005). https://doi.org/10.1007/11535218_18

53. Kamel, D., Bellizia, D., Bronchain, O., Standaert, F.: Side-channel analysis of a learning parity with physical noise processor. J. Cryptogr. Eng. **11**(2), 171–179 (2021)
54. Kamel, D., Bellizia, D., Standaert, F.-X., Flandre, D., Bol, D.: Demonstrating an LPPN processor. In: Proceedings of the 2018 Workshop on Attacks and Solutions in Hardware Security, ASHES 2018, pp. 18–23. ACM, New York, NY, USA (2018)
55. Kamel, D., Standaert, F., Duc, A., Flandre, D., Berti, F.: Learning with physical noise or errors. IEEE Trans. Dependable Secur. Comput. **17**(5), 957–971 (2020)
56. Lefevre, C., Belkheyar, Y., Daemen, J.: Kirby: a robust permutation-based PRF construction. Cryptology ePrint Archive, Paper 2023/1520 (2023)
57. Luykx, A., Preneel, B., Tischhauser, E., Yasuda, K.: A MAC mode for lightweight block ciphers. In: Peyrin, T. (ed.) FSE 2016. LNCS, vol. 9783, pp. 43–59. Springer, Heidelberg (2016). https://doi.org/10.1007/978-3-662-52993-5_3
58. Madhavan, M., Thangaraj, A., Sankarasubramanian, Y., Viswanathan, K.: NLHB: a non-linear Hopper-Blum protocol. In: 2010 IEEE International Symposium on Information Theory, pp. 2498–2502 (2010)
59. Mennink, B., Neves, S.: Optimal PRFs from blockcipher designs. IACR Trans. Symmetric Cryptol. **2017**(3), 228–252 (2017)
60. Pietrzak, K.: Cryptography from learning parity with noise. In: Bieliková, M., Friedrich, G., Gottlob, G., Katzenbeisser, S., Turán, G. (eds.) SOFSEM 2012. LNCS, vol. 7147, pp. 99–114. Springer, Heidelberg (2012). https://doi.org/10.1007/978-3-642-27660-6_9
61. Regev, O.: On lattices, learning with errors, random linear codes, and cryptography. In: Gabow, H.N., Fagin, R. (eds.) Proceedings of the 37th Annual ACM Symposium on Theory of Computing, Baltimore, MD, USA, 22–24 May 2005, pp. 84–93. ACM (2005)
62. Rossman, B., Servedio, R.A., Tan, L.: An average-case depth hierarchy theorem for Boolean circuits. In: Guruswami, V. (ed.) IEEE 56th Annual Symposium on Foundations of Computer Science, FOCS 2015, Berkeley, CA, USA, 17–20 October, 2015, pp. 1030–1048. IEEE Computer Society (2015)
63. Rott, J.K.: Intel advanced encryption standard instructions (AES-NI). Blog (2012)
64. Roy, L.: SoftSpokenOT: quieter OT extension from small-field silent VOLE in the Minicrypt model. In: Dodis, Y., Shrimpton, T. (eds.) Advances in Cryptology - CRYPTO 2022 - 42nd Annual International Cryptology Conference, CRYPTO 2022, Santa Barbara, CA, USA, 15–18 August 2022, Proceedings, Part I. LNCS, vol. 13507, pp. 657–687. Springer (2022)
65. Sim, M., et al.: Optimized implementation of Simpira on microcontrollers for secure massive learning. Symmetry **14**(11) (2022)
66. Sönmez Turan, M., McKay, K., Chang, D., Kang, J., Kelsey, J.: Ascon-based lightweight cryptography standards for constrained devices: authenticated encryption, hash, and extendable output functions. Technical report, National Institute of Standards and Technology, NIST SP 800-232 (2024)

Secure Protocols and Multi-Party Computation

How to Kickstart $\mathcal{F}_{\text{SMT}}^{S\to R}$ with Short Authentication Strings and Out-of-Band Communication

Wasilij Beskorovajnov[3(✉)] and Jörn Müller-Quade[1,2,3]

[1] Karlsruhe Institute of Technology (KIT), Karlsruhe, Germany
mueller-quade@kit.edu
[2] KASTEL Security Research Labs, Karlsruhe, Germany
[3] FZI Research Center for Information Technology, Karlsruhe, Germany
Beskorovajnov@fzi.de

Abstract. We study "send this data to that device now" exchanges under an active network adversary without PKI or pre-shared secrets. We model a human-verifiable out-of-band channel for comparing short codes as a first-class UC functionality $\mathcal{F}_{\text{OOB}}^{\text{SAS}}$. Building on this, we give two commitment-style protocols, π_{SAS} (one-sided) and $\pi_{\text{SAS}}^{\times}$ (mutual), that are new variations of MANA IV and prove that they realize $\mathcal{F}_{\text{AUTH}}^{S\to R}(\varepsilon)$ and $\mathcal{F}_{\text{AUTH}}^{S\leftrightarrow R}(\varepsilon)$ with explicit misbinding parameter $\varepsilon = 2^{-t}$. We then compose SAS-based authentication with standard KEM/DEM encryption to obtain a UC-secure message-transfer functionality $\mathcal{F}_{\text{SMT}}^{S\to R}(\varepsilon)$, preserving the explicit ε under composition, and we detail practical instantiations over signatures or MACs. Complementing the theory, we systematize real-world tooling: popular file-transfer utilities either form unauthenticated WebRTC/DTLS channels or use PAKE "one-code" designs that couple rendezvous and a long shared secre, but none deploy a session-bound SAS. Our approach decouples rendezvous from authentication and reduces the out-of-band burden to comparing a short t-bit string. We also sketch an RO-free variant (coin-flip plus non-malleable commitments) with the same user interface.

1 Introduction

There is a small but active ecosystem of "send this to that device now" tools: PAKE/one-code utilities such as Magic Wormhole[1], WebWormhole[2], and croc[3]; browser-based WebRTC/DTLS tools like PairDrop[4] and FilePizza[5]. Despite different plumbing, all must answer the same question: is this the intended peer under an active network adversary?

[1] https://github.com/magic-wormhole/magic-wormhole.
[2] https://github.com/saljam/webwormhole.
[3] https://github.com/schollz/croc.
[4] https://github.com/schlagmichdoch/PairDrop.
[5] https://github.com/kern/filepizza.

K. Jee and A. Kate (Eds.): ACNS 2026, LNCS 16571, pp. 415–443, 2027.
https://doi.org/10.1007/978-3-032-32560-0_15

A first observation is that today's file-transfer tools do not deploy a session-bound, human comparison step. Instead we see two dominant patterns. (i) Unauthenticated DTLS over WebRTC: the browser checks a DTLS certificate against a fingerprint delivered by signaling, but there is no user-verifiable bind, so a malicious signaling service can splice two DTLS associations and sit in the middle; (ii) PAKE "one-code" designs: a single human-readable code carries both a rendezvous reference and a PAKE password. This yields smooth UX but requires moving a comparatively long codes out of band and shifts security to the secrecy and integrity of that code.

We revisit a different, well-studied bind: the *short authentication string* (SAS). Here each endpoint derives a short t-bit value from the live run (e.g., via a commitment-style transcript hash or a coin-flip bound to the transcript) and the user compares the two values over an auxiliary authenticated channel. Vaudenay showed that when users compare correctly, an active man-in-the-middle succeeds with probability at most 2^{-t} [34]. This paper treats that human-verifiable step as a first-class component, models it in UC, and shows how SAS-based authentication composes to secure message transfer while keeping the out-of-band burden to comparing only a short t-bit string.

Threat Model and Scope. Following the standard SAS and device-pairing literature, we work in a two-party setting with honest endpoints S and R, while the adversary has full control over the network and the rendezvous/service infrastructure. We therefore focus on the case of a channel/service adversary with honest endpoints, and make this explicit in our UC functionalities. Modeling endpoint compromise (e.g., malicious devices or UIs) is orthogonal to our goals here and is discussed as a limitation and direction for future work.

Contributions

1. **Ideal OOB/SAS functionality.** We introduce $\mathcal{F}_{\mathrm{OOB}}^{\mathrm{SAS}}$, a UC ideal functionality for a hybrid, human-verifiable out-of-band channel that authenticates short strings. The current version handles synchronous comparisons.
2. **PISAS and PISAS$^{\times}$ as UC secure variants of MANA IV.** We give protocols π_{SAS} (one-sided) and π_{SAS}^{X} (mutual) that follow the MANA IV commit–challenge–open mechanics [25,28] (both parties confirm the SAS) while binding arbitrary messages (e.g., KEM public keys/encapsulations or context) with two differences.
   - First, we add session identifiers to the protocol description, which are crucial for UC security.
   - Second, we omit the initial plaintext message from the first network flow. This change is not required for UC, nor does sending the message inside the first flow compromise UC security. Our justification is that (A) the message is already included in the commitment, and the final flow (which also authenticates all flows) contains the opening information needed to recover it, and (B) we find it more sensible to reveal the actual message at the end, where it is immediately followed by authentication. In fact,

some commitment implementations might be more efficient if the message is not included.

We prove they UC-realize $\mathcal{F}_{\mathrm{AUTH}}^{S\to R}(\varepsilon)$ and $\mathcal{F}_{\mathrm{AUTH}}^{S\leftrightarrow R}(\varepsilon)$, respectively. We also present a sketch of a variant of π_{SAS}^{X} without random oracles in the full version.

3. **Composable secure message transfer.** We show how composing SAS-based authentication with standard encryption primitives (KEM/DEM) yields a UC realization of secure message transfer $\mathcal{F}_{\mathrm{SMT}}^{S\to R}(\varepsilon)$, preserving the explicit misbinding parameter under composition. We detail two practical instantiations: an SMT variant over signatures and an SMT variant over MACs in the Appendix B.
4. **Systematization of practice.** We systematize real-world tooling along the axes "how peers meet," "what the human binds," and "what the service learns" under a malicious-server assumption.

   In Sect. 6.1 we analyze deployed one-shot file transfer tools and show that many DTLS-/WebRTC-based designs provide no end-to-end authentication at all, and can be straightforwardly upgraded to our UC-secure pattern by adding a single SAS check.

   In Sect. 6.2 we survey deployed SAS usage and make explicit a separation between *session-bound SAS* (e.g., ZRTP, Matrix SAS, BLE Numeric Comparison) and *identity-key fingerprints* (e.g., Signal, WhatsApp, iMessage, Wire, Threema, Telegram), and use this to classify which deployed protocols are already subsumed by our analysis and which would require additional mechanisms.

The code and the reference application of the protocols π_{SAS}^{X} are available on Github[6].

2 Related Work

A well-known and widely adopted paradigm for establishing a session key, that can be used for secure file transfer, is an Authenticated Key-Agreement (AKA). These protocols, however, tend to be complex, both in terms of their design and their target guarantees. They are typically built for environments with multiple parties that may act interchangeably as sender or receiver, and with corruption that can be static or adaptive. This complexity is not itself a showstopper. The core challenge, however, lies in the authentication component of most AKA protocols, which usually relies on a public-key infrastructure (PKI), an assumption that is not viable in our setting.

It is worth noting that there is a line of AKA protocols where authentication is achieved via Short Authentication Strings (SAS), which can be seen—roughly speaking—as fingerprints of the communication transcript. As shown by Vaudenay [34], such mechanisms can securely realize the authentication step of an

[6] https://github.com/collapsinghierarchy/noisytransfer-protocol.

AKA under a weak, human-verifiable out-of-band (OOB) channel. We will return to SAS-based approaches below.

Another nearby alternative is Password-Authenticated Key Exchange (PAKE), which requires a password distribution phase. This phase is often avoided in discussions, but it implicitly assumes the existence of some secure channel, oftentimes an OOB channel with confidentiality and authenticity, for the safe transmission or registration of the password. This is precisely the kind of assumption we wish to avoid. Instead, we assume only an authenticated OOB channel for "short strings", which removes the need for confidentiality guarantees that PAKE's registration phase relies on.

A closely related device-onboarding scenario appears with low-power/IoT devices, where unassociated devices share no state and PKI setup may be costly or infeasible. To address this, works in the *Message Recognition Protocol* (MRP) family introduce a weaker primitive that authenticates message origin without providing full identity authentication or confidentiality. MRPs can bootstrap secure links in such constrained settings [11,19,21,29]. These are adjacent to our goal but target a different abstraction and guarantee set.

SAS and Out-Of-Band (OOB) Channels. Authenticating a session by comparing a short authenticated string (SAS) over an auxiliary, human-verifiable channel originates with Vaudenay [34], who formalized SAS-based authentication and gave commitment-style protocols that remain secure against attackers who may delay, drop, or replay the OOB message but can only cause a misbinding with probability at most 2^{-t} for t-bit SAS. Subsequent work optimized and generalized SAS for pairing and key agreement: Laur–Nyberg's MANA/MA-DH and MANA-IV families [25], Pasini–Vaudenay's non-interactive message authentication [31], and group extensions of SAS-based AKE [27]. In particular, Laur and Pasini's consolidated treatment [28] describes the MANA IV pattern, i.e., commitment, challenge, and opening, followed by a bidirectional SAS comparison, for mutual data authentication.

Formal Security for SAS Protocols. Most of the SAS literature proves security in bespoke, game-based models tailored to pairing/AKE (typically commitment-based, sometimes in the random-oracle model), including SAS-based message authentication and AKE with key-reuse constraints [22,26,31,32]. These works bound an active attacker's success by 2^{-t} for a t-bit display and provide concrete, protocol-specific guarantees. However, to the best of our knowledge there is no treatment that (i) defines a UC authenticated-channel ideal functionality with an explicit misbinding parameter ε, (ii) shows that an SAS-based protocol realizes such a functionality in a modern UC framework, and (iii) composes this into higher-level secure message transfer while preserving the explicit ε under composition. A related line (e.g., [28]) studies user-aided security outside the modern UC framework and does not expose the OOB/SAS channel as a first-class ideal functionality with parameter ε. Closer to modern UC, Benin–Toledo–Tromer [11] model message-recognition protocols in UC using an ideal comparison primitive and focus on authentication bootstrapping (one human check, then continue) without confidentiality (termed"privacy" there). They also do not parameterize the residual MitM guess probability as an explicit ε carried through composition. This is the gap our $\mathcal{F}_{\text{OOB}}^{\text{SAS}}$, $\mathcal{F}_{\text{AUTH}}^{S\to R}/\mathcal{F}_{\text{AUTH}}^{S\leftrightarrow R}$, and $\mathcal{F}_{\text{SMT}}^{S\to R}$ treatment fills.

3 Preliminaries

3.1 Notation

We model $H : \{0,1\}^* \to \{0,1\}^n$ as a random oracle; for $t \le n$ let $\mathsf{Trunc}_t : \{0,1\}^n \to \{0,1\}^t$ be fixed-bit truncation. We write $\text{sas}_t(x) = \mathsf{Trunc}_t(H(x))$. $\mathsf{Ber}(\varepsilon)$ denotes a Bernoulli random variable with success probability ε. For a finite set S, we write $x \leftarrow\$ S$ to denote that x is sampled uniformly at random from S.

3.2 Cryptographic Primitives

- $\mathsf{KEM} = (\mathsf{KeyGen}, \mathsf{Encaps}, \mathsf{Decaps})$ is an **IND-CPA–secure** key-encapsulation mechanism.
- $\mathsf{DEM} = (\mathsf{Enc}, \mathsf{Dec})$ is an **OT-CPA–secure** data-encapsulation (symmetric) cipher.
- $\mathsf{SIG} = (\mathsf{KeyGen}, \mathsf{Sign}, \mathsf{Ver})$ is an **EUF-CMA–secure** digital-signature scheme.

One-Time IND-CPA Security for a DEM. Let $\mathsf{DEM} = (\mathsf{ENC}, \mathsf{DEC})$ be a symmetric encryption scheme with keyspace $\mathcal{K}$. We define the one-time indistinguishability experiment against an adversary $\mathcal{A}$:

Definition 1 (OT-CPA for randomized DEM [23]). *In experiment* $\mathsf{Exp}_{\mathsf{DEM}}^{\mathsf{OT\text{-}CPA}}(\mathcal{A})$*:*

1. *The challenger samples* $K \leftarrow\$ \mathcal{K}$ *and* $b \leftarrow\$ \{0,1\}$*.*
2. $\mathcal{A}$ *outputs two equal-length messages* (m_0, m_1)
3. *The challenger samples fresh internal randomness* r *for* ENC *and returns* $c \leftarrow \mathsf{ENC}_K(m_b; r)$ *to* $\mathcal{A}$*.*
4. $\mathcal{A}$ *outputs a bit* b'*.*

The advantage is

$$\mathsf{Adv}_{\mathsf{DEM}}^{\mathsf{OT\text{-}CPA}}(\kappa) \;:=\; \max_{\mathcal{A}} \left| \Pr[\mathsf{Exp}_{\mathsf{DEM}}^{\mathsf{OT\text{-}CPA}}(\mathcal{A}){=}1] - \tfrac{1}{2} \right|,$$

where $\mathsf{Exp}_{\mathsf{DEM}}^{\mathsf{OT\text{-}CPA}}(\mathcal{A}){=}1$ *iff* $b'{=}b$*. Security requires* $\mathsf{Adv}_{\mathsf{DEM}}^{\mathsf{OT\text{-}CPA}}(\kappa) = \mathsf{negl}(\kappa)$*.*

Commitments

Definition 2 (Commitment scheme). *A commitment scheme is a tuple of PPT algorithms* (Commit, Verify) *with message space* $\mathcal{M}$ *and randomness space* $\mathcal{R}$, *where*

$$(C, d) \leftarrow \mathsf{Commit}(m; r)$$

on input $m \in \mathcal{M}$ *and randomness* $r \leftarrow\$ \mathcal{R}$ *produces a commitment* C *and decommitment witness* d. *The deterministic* $\mathsf{Verify}(C, m, d)$ *outputs a bit in* $\{0, 1\}$, *accepting valid openings.*

Correctness. *For all* $m \in \mathcal{M}$,

$$\Pr_{r \leftarrow\$ \mathcal{R}}\left[\mathsf{Verify}(C, m, d) = 1 \;\middle|\; (C, d) \leftarrow \mathsf{Commit}(m; r)\right] \geq 1 - \mathsf{negl}(\lambda),$$

i.e., honestly generated commitments open successfully except with negligible probability.

Computational Binding. *For every PPT adversary* $\mathcal{A}$,

$$\Pr\left[\begin{array}{c}(C, m, m', d, d') \leftarrow \mathcal{A}(1^\lambda) : \; m \neq m' \\ \mathsf{Verify}(C, m, d) = 1 \wedge \mathsf{Verify}(C, m', d') = 1\end{array}\right] \leq \mathsf{negl}(\lambda).$$

That is, no efficient adversary can produce a single commitment along with two different valid openings.

Computational Hiding. *For every PPT adversary* $\mathcal{A}$, *the advantage in the following experiment is negligible:*

1. $\mathcal{A}$ *outputs two messages* $m_0, m_1 \in \mathcal{M}$ *of equal length.*
2. *A random bit* $b \leftarrow\$ \{0, 1\}$ *and randomness* $r \leftarrow\$ \mathcal{R}$ *are chosen, and* $C \leftarrow \mathsf{Commit}(m_b; r)$ *is computed.*
3. $\mathcal{A}$ *is given* C *and outputs a guess* b'.

The hiding advantage is

$$\left|\Pr[b' = b] - \tfrac{1}{2}\right| \leq \mathsf{negl}(\lambda).$$

Thus, commitments to m_0 *and* m_1 *are computationally indistinguishable.*

In our main constructions we instantiate Commit as hash-then-open in the random-oracle model (binding and computationally hiding under [10]).

3.3 Universal Composability Framework

The UC framework [13, 14] additionally introduces an interactive Turing machine $\mathcal{Z}$, called the environment, which has to distinguish the real world execution from the ideal world simulation by actively communicating with the adversary during the function computation. Additionally, we define the environment's view with an adversary and a function as the input, the exchanged messages between the corrupted parties and adversary together with the outputs. This restricts the simulation-based proof since rewinding of the adversary is not possible in this case. For a formal statement, we recite the simulation paradigm of the UC framework by Canetti.

Definition 3 ([14]). *Let π be a protocol on inputs $\mathbf{x} = (x_1, \ldots, x_n) \in X^n$ for n parties and $\mathcal{F}$ a functionality. We say that π UC-securely realizes $\mathcal{F}$ if for all polynomially bounded adversaries $\mathcal{A}$ a simulator $\mathcal{S}$ exists such that for every polynomially bounded environment $\mathcal{Z}$:*

$$IDEAL_{\mathcal{F},\mathcal{S},\mathcal{Z}}(\lambda, \mathbf{x})_{\lambda\in\mathbb{N},\mathbf{x}\in X^n} \overset{c}{\approx} REAL_{\pi,\mathcal{A},\mathcal{Z}}(\lambda, \mathbf{x})_{\lambda\in\mathbb{N},\mathbf{x}\in X^n},$$

where $REAL_{\pi,\mathcal{A},\mathcal{Z}}(\lambda, \mathbf{x})_{\lambda\in\mathbb{N},\mathbf{x}\in X^n}$ is the environment's view when interacting with $P_1, \ldots, P_n$ and $\mathcal{A}$ and $IDEAL_{\mathcal{F},\mathcal{S},\mathcal{Z}}(\lambda, \mathbf{x})_{\lambda\in\mathbb{N},\mathbf{x}\in X^n}$ is $\mathcal{Z}$'s view when interacting with $\mathcal{F}$ and $\mathcal{S}$.

Additionally, the Universal Composition framework has the property that any UC-secure protocol can be securely (concurrently) composed with any other UC-secure protocol. This is the universal composition theorem, which is rephrased here without proof.

Theorem 1 (UC composition theorem, see [14]). *Let $\mathcal{F}$ and $\mathcal{G}$ be two ideal functionalities. Further let ρ be a protocol that securely UC-realizes $\mathcal{G}$ and let π be a protocol that securely UC-realizes $\mathcal{F}$. Then the composed protocol ρ^π securely UC-realizes $\mathcal{G}$.*

We refer the proof to [14].

3.4 Ideal Functionalities

The following authenticated channel is included only as a warm-up: it motivates the first step in proving a simplified variant of our SAS-based authentication protocol. It is the standard $\mathcal{F}_{\mathrm{AUTH}}^{S\to R}$ from Canetti [14], extended with a bounded active-forgery hook to capture the residual success probability from random guessing a short authentication string. Concretely, in $\mathcal{F}_{\mathrm{AUTH}}^{S\to R}(\varepsilon)$ we let the adversary (i) schedule delivery and (ii) make a single online forgery attempt per session that succeeds with probability ε (e.g., $\varepsilon = 2^{-t}$ for a t-bit SAS). This abstraction serves as a stepping stone toward our cross-authentication functionality and the full SAS-based secure channel.

Compromise of Endpoints. We ignore party corruptions in our two-party setting. Some works, such as [32], explicitly incorporate corruption of one endpoint in their models of authentication protocols and prove security as long as at least one endpoint remains honest and the corrupted endpoint continues to behave honestly. In our main protocols π_{SAS} and π_{SAS}^X, which realize the authentication functionalities $\mathcal{F}_{\mathrm{AUTH}}^{S\to R}$ and $\mathcal{F}_{\mathrm{AUTH}}^{S\leftrightarrow R}$, an adversary who corrupts a party gains at most its internal state. Since we do not store any long-term secrets in the state, our results are compatible with those works even without an explicit corruption model. The situation is different for protocols realizing $\mathcal{F}_{\mathrm{SMT}}^{S\to R}$, where learning the internal state also reveals the secret keys corresponding to public keys previously authenticated by π_{SAS}^X, which trivially breaks confidentiality. We argue, however, that this honest-endpoint threat model is still in accordance with SAS-related work such as [32], which use the classical Bellare–Rogaway model [9], where security is defined for sessions between honest endpoints and full endpoint compromise is not within the scope of the guarantees. Extending our modeling to capture post-compromise security is an interesting direction for future work.[7]

Ideal Functionality $\mathcal{F}^{S\to R}_{\text{AUTH}}(\varepsilon)$

Parameters. Forgery bound $\varepsilon \in [0,1]$.
Parties. A sender S, a receiver R, and the adversary $\mathcal{A}$. We assume S and R remain honest.
State per sid**:** $m \leftarrow \perp$; $R \leftarrow \perp$; $\mathit{forged}_{\mathsf{sid}} \in \{\perp, \mathsf{false}, \mathsf{true}\}$ (init $\perp$).

- **Delayed Send.** Upon input $(\mathsf{Send}, \mathsf{sid}, R, m)$ from S, record (m, R), set $\mathit{forged}_{\mathsf{sid}} \leftarrow \perp$, and send back-door $(\mathsf{Sent}, \mathsf{sid}, S, R, m)$ to $\mathcal{A}$.
- **Active Forgery (one online attempt).** Upon back-door $(\mathsf{Forge}, \mathsf{sid}, m', R)$ from $\mathcal{A}$ (at most once per sid): sample $b \leftarrow \mathsf{Ber}(\varepsilon)$; send $(\mathsf{ForgeResult}, \mathsf{sid}, b)$ to $\mathcal{A}$; set $\mathit{forged}_{\mathsf{sid}} \leftarrow$ (true if $b{=}1$ else false); if $b{=}1$, also record (m', R) for this sid.
- **Release.** Upon back-door $(\mathsf{ok}, \mathsf{sid})$ from $\mathcal{A}$:
  - If $\mathit{forged}_{\mathsf{sid}} = \mathsf{true}$, output $(\mathsf{Sent}, \mathsf{sid}, S, m')$ to R.
  - Else if $\mathit{forged}_{\mathsf{sid}} = \perp$ (no attempt), output $(\mathsf{Sent}, \mathsf{sid}, S, m)$ to R.
  - Else ($\mathit{forged}_{\mathsf{sid}} = \mathsf{false}$; attempted and failed), **output nothing**.
- **Ignore** all other inputs and back-door messages.

Cross-Authentication with a Bernoulli Forgery-Gate. In the next step we lift $\mathcal{F}^{S\to R}_{\text{AUTH}}(\varepsilon)$ to a two-sided, user-aided cross-authentication functionality $\mathcal{F}^{S\leftrightarrow R}_{\text{AUTH}}(\varepsilon)$ in the sense of Laur–Pasini [28]: each party contributes a short context string (e.g., ephemeral identifiers or public parameters), the adversary receives the prescribed leakage and may schedule delivery, and is granted a single online misbinding attempt that succeeds with probability ε (capturing random SAS guessing). On acceptance, both parties obtain the peer's authenticated contribution, which we later use as input to the SAS-based secure channel.

Ideal Functionality $\mathcal{F}^{S\leftrightarrow R}_{\text{AUTH}}(\varepsilon)$

Parameters. Forgery bound $\varepsilon \in [0,1]$.
Parties. Honest S and R, and the adversary $\mathcal{A}$.
State per sid**.** $m_S \leftarrow \perp$, $m_R \leftarrow \perp$; $\mathsf{forged} \in \{\perp, \mathsf{true}, \mathsf{false}\}$ (init $\perp$); $m^{\mathsf{fg}}_S, m^{\mathsf{fg}}_R \leftarrow \perp$; $\mathsf{delivered} \leftarrow \mathsf{false}$.

- **Propose (from S).** On $(\mathsf{Propose}, \mathsf{sid}, R, m_S)$: record m_S; send back-door $(\mathsf{Seen}, \mathsf{sid}, S, m_S)$ to $\mathcal{A}$.

[7] See, for example, recent analyses of post-compromise security for secure messaging protocols [17].

• **Respond (from R).** On $(\mathsf{Respond}, \mathsf{sid}, S, m_R)$: record m_R; send back-door $(\mathsf{Seen}, \mathsf{sid}, R, m_R)$ to $\mathcal{A}$.

• **Active Forgery (one online attempt).** At any time *before* delivery, upon back-door $(\mathsf{Forge}, \mathsf{sid}, m'_S, m'_R)$ (at most once per sid): sample $b \leftarrow \mathsf{Ber}(\varepsilon)$; send $(\mathsf{ForgeResult}, \mathsf{sid}, b)$ to $\mathcal{A}$. If $b = 1$, set $(m_S^{\text{fg}}, m_R^{\text{fg}}) \leftarrow (m'_S, m'_R)$ and $\mathsf{forged} \leftarrow \mathsf{true}$; else set $\mathsf{forged} \leftarrow \mathsf{false}$.

• **Release.** Upon back-door $(\mathsf{ok}, \mathsf{sid})$ from $\mathcal{A}$, if $\mathsf{delivered} = \mathsf{false}$ and $m_S \neq \perp$ and $m_R \neq \perp$ then:
- If $\mathsf{forged} = \mathsf{true}$, output $(\mathsf{XAuth}, \mathsf{sid}, S, m_S^{\text{fg}})$ to R and $(\mathsf{XAuth}, \mathsf{sid}, R, m_R^{\text{fg}})$ to S; set $\mathsf{delivered} \leftarrow \mathsf{true}$.
- Else if $\mathsf{forged} = \perp$ (no attempt), output $(\mathsf{XAuth}, \mathsf{sid}, S, m_S)$ to R and $(\mathsf{XAuth}, \mathsf{sid}, R, m_R)$ to S; set $\mathsf{delivered} \leftarrow \mathsf{true}$.
- Else ($\mathsf{forged} = \mathsf{false}$; attempted and failed), **output nothing** and set $\mathsf{delivered} \leftarrow \mathsf{true}$.

• **Ignore** all other inputs/back-door messages.

Secure Message Transfer with a Bernoulli MitM-Gate. The next functionality refines secure message transmission to account for the non-negligible online success of an active adversary under SAS/PAKE-style human authentication, in the same spirit as our authenticated-channel variants. We constrain leakage to message length only, i.e., $\ell(m) = |m|$. Classical UC $\mathcal{F}_{\text{SMT}}^{S\to R}$ delivers the sender's message intact once the adversary schedules delivery, which over-idealizes SAS/PAKE-backed channels: an attacker may achieve a *MitM misbinding* with probability essentially $\varepsilon \approx 2^{-t}$ for a t-bit SAS (up to standard concurrency factors), or roughly $1/|\mathcal{D}|$ per online guess in the PAKE setting [18,32,34]. Following Canetti–Halevi–Katz's UC treatment of low-entropy secrets [18], we adopt the "explicit guessing power" modeling and build a single Bernoulli(ε) gate into the functionality. Concretely, the adversary gets exactly one online misbinding attempt per session, reflecting a single SAS comparison; if it succeeds, confidentiality and authenticity fail for that session (the original m is learned) and the adversary may substitute the delivered message, with delivery still gated by $(\mathsf{ok}, \mathsf{sid})$.

Functionality $\mathcal{F}_{\text{SMT}}^{S\to R}(\varepsilon)$

Parameters. Misbinding success bound $\varepsilon \in [0, 1]$; leakage $\ell(m) = |m|$.
Parties. Honest S and R, and the adversary $\mathcal{A}$.
State per sid**:** $m \leftarrow \perp$; $R \leftarrow \perp$; $\mathsf{auth} \in \{\perp, \mathsf{true}, \mathsf{false}\}$ (init $\perp$); $m^{\text{mitm}} \leftarrow \perp$; $\mathsf{delivered} \leftarrow \mathsf{false}$.

• **Send.** On $(\mathsf{Send}, \mathsf{sid}, R, m)$ from S: record m and R; set $\mathsf{auth} \leftarrow \perp$ and $m^{\text{mitm}} \leftarrow \perp$; send back-door $(\mathsf{Sent}, \mathsf{sid}, S, R, \ell(m))$ to $\mathcal{A}$.

• **Active MitM.** Before delivery and at most once per sid, upon back-door $(\mathsf{MisbindTry}, \mathsf{sid})$: sample $b \leftarrow \mathsf{Ber}(\varepsilon)$; send $(\mathsf{MisbindResult}, \mathsf{sid}, b)$ to $\mathcal{A}$.

– If $b = 1$, set auth ← true and send back-door (Reveal, sid, m) to $\mathcal{A}$.
– Else set auth ← false.

- **Set substituted payload.** At any time before delivery, upon back-door (SetMitmPayload, sid, m'): if auth $\neq$ true then ignore; else require $|m'| = |m|$ (else ignore); if $m^{\text{mitm}} = \perp$ then set $m^{\text{mitm}} \leftarrow m'$.
- **Delivery (gated by ok).** Upon back-door (ok, sid) from $\mathcal{A}$, if delivered = false then:
  – If auth = true **and** $m^{\text{mitm}} \neq \perp$, output (Sent, sid, S, m^{mitm}) to R and set delivered ← true.
  – Else if auth = false (attempted and failed), **output nothing** and set delivered ← true.
  – Else (auth = $\perp$; no attempt), output (Sent, sid, S, m) to R and set delivered ← true.
- **Ignore** all other inputs and back-door messages.

4 Universally Composable Authentication from SAS

This section puts SAS-based authentication on a UC footing. We expose a hybrid $\mathcal{F}_{\text{OOB}}^{\text{SAS}}$ channel for short, human-verifiable comparison and give two compact protocols, π_{SAS} and π_{SAS}^{X}, that follow a commit–respond–open pattern with a single SAS check. We prove they UC-realize $\mathcal{F}_{\text{AUTH}}^{S\rightarrow R}(\varepsilon)$ and $\mathcal{F}_{\text{AUTH}}^{S\leftrightarrow R}(\varepsilon)$ with $\varepsilon = 2^{-t}$ in the ROM.

4.1 Out-of-Band SAS Confirmation

One crucial component of our protocol is the authenticated *out-of-band channel* (OOB), which we model as a hybrid functionality and follow the modelling from [11]. Our abstraction captures the synchronous user interaction between the Sender and Receiver required to verify the SAS.

Ideal Functionality $\mathcal{F}_{\text{OOB}}^{\text{SAS}}$

Parties: R (receiver) and S (sender) and the adversary $\mathcal{A}$.

- **SAS Comparison:** Upon input (SAS, sid, s) from S or R, store the SAS and send (SAS, sid, s) to $\mathcal{A}$. If the SAS from the other party was already received, i.e. s', compute the flag $b := (s == s')$ then return to the sender and receiver (SAS, sid, b) (immediate delivery).
- **Ignore** all other inputs and back-door messages.

This channel differs from the usual model of data transmission over untrusted networks, where an adversary can arbitrarily drop messages. In our $\mathcal{F}_{\text{OOB}}^{\text{SAS}}$ hybrid, we assume the SAS is displayed to honest users on uncompromised hardware and software, so message delivery cannot be suppressed. Addressing a compromised display or denial-of-service attack on the OOB channel is an interesting direction for future work, but we leave it outside the scope of this paper. In the full version, we also discuss how human error and asynchronicity relate to our modeling choices.

4.2 Universally Composable SAS and OOB Based One-Sided Authentication

We begin with a minimal, user-aided authentication primitive: a three-move SAS protocol that binds a sender's short context string to a receiver, using a single human comparison. The hash H is modeled as a random oracle and the displayed short authentication string (SAS) is the t-bit truncation of H on the session transcript. We will argue that the adversary's best active success is $\varepsilon = 2^{-t}$, up to standard concurrency factors [28,32,34]. The human check is abstracted by the ideal functionality $\mathcal{F}_{\text{OOB}}^{\text{SAS}}$, and we keep the network parties honest.

Real Protocol π_{SAS} (hybrid $\mathcal{F}_{\text{OOB}}^{\text{SAS}}$)

Parties. S, R, the adversary $\mathcal{A}$, and hybrid $\mathcal{F}_{\text{OOB}}^{\text{SAS}}$.
Parameters. Output length $t \in \mathbb{N}$. Let H be a random oracle and $\mathsf{SAS}(x) := \text{Trunc}_t(H(x))$.

0. Session setup (SID).
Either receive a session identifier sid from the calling environment, or (if not provided) have S sample a fresh $\mathsf{sid} \leftarrow\$ \{0,1\}^\kappa$ and notify R over the main channel. All local state and every call to subroutines/functionalities in this session is tagged with the same sid.

1. Commitment. $S \to R: \quad (C, d) \leftarrow \mathsf{Commit}(\mathsf{sid} \parallel \mathsf{m}_S; \mathsf{r}_S)$, where r_S are the sender's random coins (contained in d); send C.

2. Receiver's Contribution. $R \to S: \quad$ sample $\mathsf{r}_R \leftarrow\$ \{0,1\}^\kappa$.

3. Reveal & SAS. $S \to R: \quad$ send $\mathsf{Open}(C, d)$.
If R rejects the opening, abort. Otherwise both compute

$$s := \mathsf{SAS}(\mathsf{sid} \parallel \mathsf{m}_S \parallel \mathsf{r}_S \parallel \mathsf{r}_R)$$

and each party sends $(\mathsf{SAS}, \mathsf{sid}, s)$ to $\mathcal{F}_{\text{OOB}}^{\text{SAS}}$.

4. Confirmation. $\mathcal{F}_{\text{OOB}}^{\text{SAS}} \to \{S, R\}: \quad (\mathsf{SAS}, \mathsf{sid}, b)$.
R outputs m_S iff $b = 1$; otherwise abort.

Theorem 2 (UC security of π_{SAS} toward $\mathcal{F}_{\text{AUTH}}^{S \to R}(\varepsilon)$). *Let $t \in \mathbb{N}$ and define $\varepsilon := 2^{-t}$. Assume: (i) $\mathsf{Com} = (\mathsf{Commit}, \mathsf{Open})$ is computationally hiding and binding; (ii) H is modeled as a random oracle and $\mathsf{SAS}(x) = \text{Trunc}_t(H(x))$; (iii) the hybrid functionality $\mathcal{F}_{\text{OOB}}^{\text{SAS}}$ (SAS comparison with leakage to the adversary) is available. Then for every PPT adversary $\mathcal{A}$ there exists a PPT simulator $\mathcal{S}$ such that for every PPT environment $\mathcal{Z}$,*

$$\mathsf{EXEC}_{\mathcal{Z}, \mathcal{A}, \Pi_{\mathsf{SAS}}}^{\mathcal{F}_{\text{OOB}}^{\text{SAS}}} \approx \mathsf{IDEAL}_{\mathcal{Z}, \mathcal{S}, \mathcal{F}_{\text{AUTH}}^{S \to R}(\varepsilon)}.$$

Hence, in the $\mathcal{F}_{\mathrm{OOB}}^{\mathrm{SAS}}$-hybrid, Π_{SAS} UC-realizes the authenticated one-way channel with a single online active-forgery attempt that succeeds with probability ε.

Note that committing to the message, and thus hiding it in the first flow, is not strictly required. If the commitment scheme is more efficient when the committed values are small (and the message may be rather large), then it is perfectly fine to instead commit to some small random string and send the message bits in plaintext.

We nevertheless justify our choice by arguing that revealing the message in the last step is a more sensible approach: we follow the reveal step directly with the out-of-band comparison and thus authenticate the message immediately. In contrast, revealing the (still unauthenticated) message in the first flow may leave some time before it is authenticated, since two network flows are still missing, and it might tempt security laypersons to pre-process the unauthenticated message.

The full proof can be found in Appendix A. Unfortunately, $\mathcal{F}_{\mathrm{AUTH}}^{S\to R}$ is yet not sufficient for our requirements of a user-friendly protocol (albeit theoretically we can now effectively compose multiple instances and provide "virtual" bi-directional authentication), which is the same argument that [11] used in order to define the functionality $\mathcal{F}_{\mathrm{AUTH}}^{S\leftrightarrow R}(k)$, which is a straight forward extension of $\mathcal{F}_{\mathrm{AUTH}}^{S\to R}$ in order to allow bi-directional "back-and-forth" communication of k authenticate messages between S and R.

4.3 Universally Composable Cross-Authentication from SAS

In this section we extend π_{SAS} to support *bi-directional* delivery of one application message per party. The change is minimal: the receiver R now *piggybacks* its message m_R alongside its fresh nonce r_R in Step 2. The SAS then commits to the full transcript $(\mathsf{sid}, \mathsf{m}_S, \mathsf{m}_R, \mathsf{r}_S, \mathsf{r}_R)$, so any tampering that alters what either party sees requires a collision on the truncated random-oracle output. The session identifier sid is carried throughout to ensure subroutine-respecting composition. In the following we show that this change does not contradict the security.

Real Protocol π_{SAS}^{X} (hybrid $\mathcal{F}_{\mathrm{OOB}}^{\mathrm{SAS}}$)

Parties. S, R, the adversary $\mathcal{A}$, and hybrid $\mathcal{F}_{\mathrm{OOB}}^{\mathrm{SAS}}$.
Parameters. Output length $t \in \mathbb{N}$. Let H be a random oracle and $\mathsf{SAS}(x) := \mathrm{Trunc}_t(H(x))$. Let sid be the session identifier of this instance.

1. Commitment. $S \to R:\quad (C, d) \leftarrow \mathsf{Commit}(\mathsf{sid} \parallel \mathsf{m}_S; \mathsf{r}_S)$, where r_S are the commitment coins (contained in d); send C.

2. Receiver's Contribution.

$R \to S:\quad$ choose m_R and sample $\mathsf{r}_R \leftarrow\$ \{0,1\}^\kappa$; send $(\mathsf{m}_R, \mathsf{r}_R)$.

3. Reveal & SAS. $S \to R:$ send $\mathsf{Open}(C, d)$.
If R rejects the opening, abort. Else both compute

$$s := \mathsf{SAS}(\mathsf{sid} \parallel \mathsf{m}_S \parallel \mathsf{m}_R \parallel \mathsf{r}_S \parallel \mathsf{r}_R).$$

and send $(\mathsf{SAS}, \mathsf{sid}, s)$ to $\mathcal{F}_{\text{OOB}}^{\text{SAS}}$.

4. Confirmation. $\mathcal{F}_{\text{OOB}}^{\text{SAS}} \to \{S, R\}:$ $(\mathsf{SAS}, \mathsf{sid}, b)$.
R outputs m_S and S outputs m_R iff $b = 1$; otherwise both abort.

Theorem 3 (UC security of π_{SAS}^X toward $\mathcal{F}_{\text{AUTH}}^{S \leftrightarrow R}(\varepsilon)$). *Let $t \in \mathbb{N}$ and set $\varepsilon := 2^{-t}$. Assume: (i) $\mathsf{Com} = (\mathsf{Commit}, \mathsf{Open})$ is computationally hiding and binding; (ii) H is modeled as a random oracle and $\mathsf{SAS}(x) = \mathrm{Trunc}_t(H(x))$; (iii) the hybrid functionality $\mathcal{F}_{\text{OOB}}^{\text{SAS}}$ is available. Then for every PPT adversary $\mathcal{A}$ there exists a PPT simulator $\mathcal{S}$ such that for every PPT environment $\mathcal{Z}$,*

$$\mathsf{EXEC}_{\mathcal{Z}, \mathcal{A}, \pi_{\text{SAS}}^X}^{\mathcal{F}_{\text{OOB}}^{\text{SAS}}} \approx \mathsf{IDEAL}_{\mathcal{Z}, \mathcal{S}, \mathcal{F}_{\text{AUTH}}^{S \leftrightarrow R}(\varepsilon)}.$$

Hence, in the $\mathcal{F}_{\text{OOB}}^{\text{SAS}}$-hybrid, π_{SAS}^X UC-realizes cross-authentication $\mathcal{F}_{\text{AUTH}}^{S \leftrightarrow R}(\varepsilon)$ with a single online active-forgery attempt of success probability ε.

Proof. For the sake of brevity we only provide the most important differences to the previous proof.

- **SAS inputs (pair-aware).** At compare time use

$$x_R := (\mathsf{sid} \parallel \mathsf{m}'_S \parallel m_R \parallel \mathsf{r}'_S \parallel \mathsf{r}_R), \qquad x_S := (\mathsf{sid} \parallel \mathsf{m}_S \parallel \tilde{m}_R \parallel \mathsf{r}_S \parallel \tilde{\mathsf{r}}_R).$$

  Tampering is the semantic event $x_R \neq x_S$ (covers flips of m_R and/or r_R in transit in addition to commitment tamper).
- **Pre-hit hybrid.** $\mathsf{preHit}_{\mathsf{sid}} := [x_R \in T \vee x_S \in T]$ remains negligible; proof unchanged (requires guessing hidden r_S).
- **Tamper lemma.** Conditioned on binding and $x_R \neq x_S$, the RO outputs are independent uniform strings; hence $\Pr[\mathrm{Trunc}_t(H(x_R)) = \mathrm{Trunc}_t(H(x_S)) \mid x_R \neq x_S] = 2^{-t} \pm \mathsf{negl}(\kappa)$.
- **Coupling.** If $x_R = x_S$ (no tamper), emulate $\mathcal{F}_{\text{OOB}}^{\text{SAS}}$ with b=1 and, on $(\mathsf{ok}, \mathsf{sid})$, let $\mathcal{F}_{\text{AUTH}}^{S \leftrightarrow R}$ output the honest pair. If $x_R \neq x_S$ (tamper), query the forgery gate with $(\mathsf{Forge}, \mathsf{sid}, m'_S, m'_R)$ in $\mathcal{F}_{\text{AUTH}}^{S \leftrightarrow R}(\varepsilon)$, get b, and prefix-program the RO so equality of the two t-bit SAS values holds iff b=1; return the same b from the emulated $\mathcal{F}_{\text{OOB}}^{\text{SAS}}$.

Final Distinguishing Bound. Let $\Delta(\kappa)$ be the UC advantage between $\mathsf{EXEC}_{\mathcal{Z},\mathcal{A},\pi_{\text{SAS}}^X}^{\mathcal{F}_{\text{OOB}}^{\text{SAS}}}$ and $\mathsf{IDEAL}_{\mathcal{Z},\mathcal{S},\mathcal{F}_{\text{AUTH}}^{S \leftrightarrow R}(\varepsilon)}$. Then

$$\Delta(\kappa) \leq \mathcal{A}_{\mathsf{Com}}^{\text{hide}}(\kappa) + \mathcal{A}_{\mathsf{Com}}^{\text{bind}}(\kappa) + 2\, q_H(\kappa)\, 2^{-\kappa} + \left| \Pr_{\text{real}}[\text{accept} \mid x_R \neq x_S] - \varepsilon \right| = \mathsf{negl}(\kappa),$$

since $\Pr_{\text{real}}[\text{accept} \mid x_R \neq x_S] = 2^{-t} \pm \mathsf{negl}(\kappa)$ by the tamper lemma, and $\varepsilon = 2^{-t}$.

Final Simulator (Differences vs. Prior). The full simulator is included in the full version.

- **Ordering fix.** Matches the real-world message order $C \to (m_R, \mathsf{r}_R) \to$ reveal; the receiver's contribution is buffered until the commitment C is observed (no premature receiver start).
- **Other mechanisms unchanged.** Forge-gate invocation (single call on tamper, cached bit b), prefix-constrained lazy RO programming, and ok-coupled delivery remain as in the previous simulator.
- **Attempt-conditioned gate.** The $\mathcal{F}_{\text{AUTH}}^{S \leftrightarrow R}$ forge gate is invoked *iff* $x_R \neq x_S$.

□

5 Canonical Secure Message Transfer

We now move beyond mere authenticity to confidential and authenticated communication. That is, we aim to realize a standard secure–message–transmission functionality $\mathcal{F}_{\text{SMT}}^{S \to R}$ with the addition of a forge-gate attack vector, thus we will use $\mathcal{F}_{\text{SMT}}^{S \to R}(\varepsilon)$ from Fig. 3.4. In the previous section we proved that π_{SAS}^{X} UC-realizes $\mathcal{F}_{\text{AUTH}}^{S \leftrightarrow R}(\varepsilon)$ (Theorem 3). Our first construction leverages π_{SAS}^{X} to authenticate public-key material (a KEM public key and a digital-signature verification key), after which payloads are sent via a KEM–DEM channel with signed ciphertexts. Our second construction minimizes asymmetric cryptography by replacing digital signatures with a MAC, whose key is contributed and bound through π_{SAS}^{X}. The second construction is presented in Appendix B. Our target in this section is the canonical realization of $\mathcal{F}_{\text{SMT}}^{S \to R}$ of Fig. 3.4. Following Canetti's recipe [14][8], we combine

- a KEM/DEM channel with a CPA-secure KEM and an OT-CPA-secure DEM for semantic confidentiality,
- an EUF-CMA digital signature to authenticate ciphertexts (and bind sender identity), and
- the cross-authentication functionality $\mathcal{F}_{\text{AUTH}}^{S \leftrightarrow R}$ (Sect. 3.4) to distribute the KEM public key and the signature verification key.
- a Session identifier sid to denote the SID of this protocol instance. We invoke the subroutine π_{SAS}^{X} with the same sid (subroutine-respecting).

and obtain the following protocol.

Real Protocol $\pi_{\text{SAS+KEM+DEM+Sig}}$ (hybrid $\mathcal{F}_{\text{OOB}}^{\text{SAS}}$)

Primitives and model.

- **KEM** $(\mathsf{Gen}, \mathsf{Encap}, \mathsf{Decap})$ IND-CPA.
- **DEM** $(\mathsf{ENC}, \mathsf{DEC})$ one-time IND-CPA (fresh key per session).
- **Sig** $(\mathsf{KGen}, \mathsf{Sign}, \mathsf{Vfy})$ EUF-CMA.

[8] See pp. 79 ff. and Claim 27 in the journal version.

– Cross-authentication subroutine π_{SAS}^{X} in the $\mathcal{F}_{\mathrm{OOB}}^{\mathrm{SAS}}$ hybrid.
– Signed context

$$\mathsf{ctx} := \text{“}\pi_{\mathrm{SAS+KEM+DEM+Sig}}\text{”} \,\|\, \mathsf{sid} \,\|\, \text{“S}\to\text{R”}.$$

Parties. Sender S and Receiver R.

Phase 1 — Cross-authentication via π_{SAS}^{X}.

S: $(\mathsf{vk}_S, \mathsf{sk}_S) \leftarrow \mathsf{Sig.KGen}$; set $m_S \leftarrow \mathsf{vk}_S$.
R: $(\mathsf{pk}_R, \mathsf{sk}_R) \leftarrow \mathsf{KEM.Gen}$; set $m_R \leftarrow \mathsf{pk}_R$.
Run π_{SAS}^{X} under the *same* sid on inputs (m_S, m_R).
Abort iff π_{SAS}^{X} outputs $b = 0$ (SAS mismatch).

Phase 2 — One-shot KEM–DEM (Enc-Then-Sign).

(2a) Sender S with payload m:
$(K, c_{\mathsf{KEM}}) \leftarrow \mathsf{Encap}(\mathsf{pk}_R)$; $\quad c_{\mathsf{DEM}} \leftarrow \mathsf{DEM.ENC}(K, m)$
$\sigma \leftarrow \mathsf{Sig.Sign}_{\mathsf{sk}_S}(\mathsf{ctx}, c_{\mathsf{KEM}}, c_{\mathsf{DEM}})$
$S \to R$: $(\mathsf{sid}, c_{\mathsf{KEM}}, c_{\mathsf{DEM}}, \sigma)$
(2b) Receiver R:
Abort if $\mathsf{Sig.Vfy}_{\mathsf{vk}_S}(\sigma; \mathsf{ctx}, c_{\mathsf{KEM}}, c_{\mathsf{DEM}}) = 0$
$K \leftarrow \mathsf{Decap}(\mathsf{sk}_R, c_{\mathsf{KEM}})$; $\quad m \leftarrow \mathsf{DEM.DEC}(K, c_{\mathsf{DEM}})$
Output $(\mathsf{Sent}, \mathsf{sid}, S, \mathsf{m})$ to the environment.

Theorem 4 (UC realization of $\mathcal{F}_{\mathrm{SMT}}^{S \to R}(\varepsilon)$ in the $\mathcal{F}_{\mathrm{AUTH}}^{S \leftrightarrow R}(\varepsilon)$-hybrid). *Assume:*

(i) KEM *is* IND-CPA*;*
(ii) DEM *is one-time* OT-CPA*;*
(iii) Sig *is* EUF-CMA*;*
(iv) π_{SAS}^{X} *UC-realizes* $\mathcal{F}_{\mathrm{AUTH}}^{S \leftrightarrow R}(\varepsilon)$ *(one online misbinding with success* ε*).*

Protocol $\pi_{SAS+KEM+DEM+Sig}$ *is subroutine-respecting (same* sid *in* π_{SAS}^{X} *and in* ctx*) and uses fresh* $(\mathsf{vk}_S, \mathsf{pk}_R)$ *per session. Then, in the* $\mathcal{F}_{\mathrm{AUTH}}^{S \leftrightarrow R}(\varepsilon)$*-hybrid,* $\pi_{SAS+KEM+DEM+Sig}$ *UC-realizes* $\mathcal{F}_{\mathrm{SMT}}^{S \to R}(\varepsilon)$ *with length-only leakage. For any PPT environment,*

$$\mathcal{A}^{\mathrm{UC}} \le \varepsilon + \mathcal{A}_{\mathsf{Sig}}^{\mathsf{EUF\text{-}CMA}} + \mathcal{A}_{\mathsf{KEM}}^{\mathsf{IND\text{-}CPA}} + \mathcal{A}_{\mathsf{DEM}}^{\mathsf{OT\text{-}CPA}} + \mathsf{negl}(\kappa).$$

The full proof is presented in the full version.

6 Systematization of the Real-World Tooling Landscape

This section surveys how popular tools handle rendezvous, authentication, and transport when two endpoints want to “connect now” with minimal setup. Our goal is to extract the architectural patterns that matter for security and not to audit implementations. We read public docs and code as of 03 Sep 2025 and place each tool along a few common axes: (i) how peers meet (discovery/rendezvous), (ii) what—if anything—the human binds out of band (none/PAKE password/short SAS), (iii) which transport is used (and where encryption terminates), and (iv) what the back-end service learns under an active, malicious-server assumption.

We then look at two slices. First, Sect. 6.1 systematizes one-shot file-transfer tools and contrasts self-signed DTLS data channels with PAKE-based "one code" designs, and with our SAS-based alternative. Second, Sect. 6.2 reviews SAS-style checks in deployed systems and separates true *session-bound SAS* from longer, identity-fingerprint comparisons. Throughout, we connect these mechanisms to our modeling ($\mathcal{F}_{\text{OOB}}^{\text{SAS}}$, $\mathcal{F}_{\text{AUTH}}^{S\to R}/\mathcal{F}_{\text{AUTH}}^{S\leftrightarrow R}$) to clarify what each pattern actually guarantees when the service operator is adversarial.

6.1 File Transfer in the Real World

We now narrow the scope to one-shot device–to–device transfers between co-located devices owned by the same person. We retain the adversarial-service threat model stated above: signaling/rendezvous infrastructure may be malicious, while on-the-wire transports provide confidentiality and integrity. Under this model the residual question is what the service learns and whether any human out-of-band bind (if any) defeats MitM. We begin with tools that form WebRTC data channels without a user-verifiable bind, then cover PAKE-based "one-code" designs, and finally contrast both with our SAS-based alternative. An asynchronous variant, where comparison occurs later or across users, entails different UX/trust trade-offs and is left for future work.

Unauthenticated DTLS. PairDrop[9], *ShareDrop*[10], *FilePizza*[11], and *Snapdrop*[12] establish WebRTC data channels without exposing any user-verifiable binding (no SAS, no Password, no fingerprint UI). Technically, browsers set up an SCTP association over DTLS over UDP. Each peer's self-signed DTLS certificate fingerprint is conveyed inside SDP via the signaling channel (see WebRTC security architecture RFC 8826/8827). If signaling is malicious, it can substitute SDPs and fingerprints and terminate two DTLS associations, achieving a full MitM despite DTLS on the wire. This is not a flaw in DTLS or SCTP but a missing *identity bind*: the browser or app verifies that the DTLS cert matches the fingerprint it received, but there are no additional checks that this fingerprint corresponds to the intended peer.

A clean mitigation is to add a user-verifiable bind. Our framework provides exactly that: a cross-authentication functionality $\mathcal{F}_{\text{AUTH}}^{S\leftrightarrow R}(\varepsilon)$ realized from a short-authentication-string (SAS) over an authenticated OOB channel. Concretely, one can display a short fingerprint/SAS derived from the agreed transcript and ask both sides to compare it over an auxiliary authenticated channel

[9] https://github.com/schlagmichdoch/PairDrop.
[10] https://github.com/ShareDropio/sharedrop.
[11] https://github.com/kern/filepizza.
[12] https://github.com/SnapDrop/snapdrop.

and if it matches, the session is user-bound and MitM is defeated under the stated $\varepsilon = 2^{-t}$ budget. The noisytransfer protocol implementation[13] and the companion `noisyauth` npm package[14] are available for this purpose. It is also worthwhile mentioning that at PairDrop it is already being discussed about adding similar protections[15].

PAKE-Based. Tools like Magic Wormhole[16], WebWormhole[17], and croc[18] follow the same architectural pattern. The sender locally creates a single human-readable code and shares it out of band with the receiver. Codes have usually the form `N-word-word...` (e.g., `7-crossover-clockwork`). That code combines two roles: a rendezvous reference (e.g., a mailbox nameplate or a server slot) and a PAKE password. The receiver inputs the code, which lets both sides attach to the same rendezvous and then run a PAKE to authenticate and derive keys. Two integration styles are common: (i) PAKE directly yields application-layer channel keys for encrypted streaming (e.g., SPAKE2 [24] in Magic Wormhole and croc), or (ii) PAKE authenticates[19] the signaling metadata before the data channel forms (e.g., CPace protects the SDP carrying DTLS certificate fingerprints in WebWormhole [20]). Under a malicious-server assumption, the service learns the rendezvous identifier and sees the PAKE transcript but not the password. Security then hinges on online-guess resistance and careful client-side handling. This pattern delivers a strong user experience: one code, typed once. It also defines a practical ceiling for PAKE-based UX because the out-of-band message must carry a sufficiently long shared secret alongside rendezvous data.

Our SAS-based approach decouples these concerns: use a short, non-secret rendezvous code purely for meeting, then display and compare a short SAS for binding. No long secret needs to be carried out of band, and the residual misbinding risk is explicit via the $\varepsilon = 2^{-t}$ budget, assuming a synchronous $\mathcal{F}_{\text{OOB}}^{\text{SAS}}$ is available as in our model. It is an interesting open question which of the paradigms provide the best usability/security tradefoff.

6.2 SAS Handling in the Real World

Beyond file transfer, many deployed systems ask users to compare short strings or longer fingerprints to detect MitM. The items below use *identity-key fingerprints* (often with a QR fallback), not a short, session-bound SAS in the formal sense. They are excellent for long-term identity verification in persistent conversations or ecosystems, but they do not authenticate a fresh one-shot transcript and their displayed values are much larger (e.g., 60 decimal digits) and change only when long-term keys rotate. Longer fingerprints are not primarily about limiting online

13 https://github.com/collapsinghierarchy/noisytransfer-protocol.
14 https://www.npmjs.com/package/@noisytransfer/noisyauth.
15 https://github.com/schlagmichdoch/PairDrop/issues/180.
16 https://github.com/magic-wormhole/magic-wormhole.
17 https://github.com/saljam/webwormhole.
18 https://github.com/schollz/croc.
19 and unnecessarily encrypts.

guessing (as in SAS), but rather about making it infeasible to find alternative keys that yield the same displayed value. The relevant bound is given by the collision resistance (or, depending on the comparison model, second-preimage resistance) of the fingerprinting function.

From our understanding, a similar $\mathcal{F}_{\mathrm{OOB}}^{\mathrm{SAS}}$ could be used, for example, with a simple exchange of public-key material of a KEM and a digital signature, where the received public keys' fingerprints are compared. In that setting, however, there would be no human in the loop: the $\mathcal{F}_{\mathrm{OOB}}^{\mathrm{SAS}}$ would instead be a QR code that performs the comparison automatically. A proper treatment of this approach would require formal modeling of fingerprinting, which would greatly expand the scope of this work. We therefore exclude such approaches from our SAS-focused analysis, but we acknowledge that a formal analysis would be insightful and would enable rigorous comparisons.

- **Signal.** Each 1:1 chat shows a safety number (numeric and QR) that fingerprints the parties' identity keys; when keys change, the app forces re-verification [33]. This is an identity fingerprint, not a per-session SAS.
- **WhatsApp.** Each chat exposes a security code (60 digits and QR) that users compare/scan to verify the chat's long-term keys [35]; again a fingerprint rather than a live SAS.
- **Apple iMessage (Contact Key Verification).** Users compare short verification codes (or rely on posted public verification codes) to detect key substitution on Apple's servers; the check binds directory-backed identity keys, not a transient handshake [1,2,4].
- **Wire.** Conversations/devices expose key fingerprints (with QR) for out-of-band comparison, targeting identity/device trust establishment rather than per-run SAS binding [3,8].
- **Threema.** Contacts are verified by scanning a QR code or comparing the public-key fingerprint to prevent MitM; this is a stable identity fingerprint, not recomputed per session [6,7].
- **Telegram Secret Chats.** Clients display a key visualization derived from the chat's keys for users to compare; functionally this is a human-verifiable fingerprint for the chat, not a short SAS of a fresh run [5].

The following real-world examples constitute SAS-based authentication protocols for exchanged key material in various forms. We summarize the following analysis in Table 1.

ZRTP SAS Derivation. ZRTP derives a human-verifiable SAS during its DH key agreement ([36], §4–§7).

- **Handshake setup.** After Hello/HelloAck ([36], §4–§7), the initiator A fixes its DH payload by sending Commit with a standard hash commitment $\mathsf{hvi} = \mathsf{Hash}(\mathsf{DHPart2}_A \,\|\, \mathsf{Hello}_B)$.
- **DH exchange and check.** Peers exchange DHPart1/DHPart2; verify $\mathsf{hvi} \stackrel{?}{=} \mathsf{Hash}(\mathsf{DHPart2}_A \,\|\, \mathsf{Hello}_B)$. Compute the shared DH value and derive the master secret s_0.

- **Context for SAS.** Set $\mathsf{KDF\_Context} := \mathsf{ZID}_i \,\|\, \mathsf{ZID}_r \,\|\, \mathsf{total\_hash}$, where ZID_* are the 96-bit ZRTP identifiers and $\mathsf{total\_hash}$ is the running hash of all ZRTP messages in this run.
- **Derive SAS bits.** Using the spec's HMAC-based KDF (NIST SP 800-108 style; not necessarily HKDF), compute

$$\mathsf{sashash} := \mathsf{KDF}(s_0, "SAS", \mathsf{KDF\_Context}, 256)$$

  and take $v := \text{MSB}_{32}(\mathsf{sashash})$.
- **Render to users.** If $\mathsf{B32}$ was negotiated, show the MSB 20 bits of v as four Base32 characters; if $\mathsf{B256}$, show the MSB 16 bits as two PGP-word-list words ([36], §5.1.6). Users compare the display verbally/visually.

This is a classical SAS-derivation protocol in the Vaudenay/MANA sense: the commitment caps active attacker adaptivity, the SAS is bound to the live transcript via $\mathsf{KDF\_Context}$, and a successful MitM requires guessing the t-bit display. In our terminology, ZRTP aligns with π_{SAS}^{X} when we view the protocol messages as $m_S := \mathsf{DHPart2}_A$ and $m_R := \mathsf{DHPart1}_B$, and the verbal/visual code comparison as the $\mathcal{F}_{\text{OOB}}^{\text{SAS}}$ step. If the used KDF is modeled as a Random Oracle the universal composability from π_{SAS}^{X} thus also translates to ZRTP SAS-derivation.

Matrix/Element: Matrix implements a SAS verification (`m.sas.v1`) that follows the same Vaudenay/MANA commit, reveal, compare pattern as ZRTP: the acceptor first commits to its ephemeral key (hash over key and other information), both sides run ECDH, and the SAS is derived via HKDF-SHA256 from the shared secret and an info string binding user IDs, device IDs, both ephemeral keys, and a transaction id, then rendered as three 4-digit numbers or seven emoji [30]. After users confirm a match, Matrix additionally MAC-authenticates each device's long-term keys under a key from the same ECDH output, tying the human check to concrete device identities. At a high level this is the same session-bound SAS approach as ZRTP/MANA-IV/MA-DH. The small differences are the commitment target and the identity-binding step that follows the SAS.

Bluetooth LE Secure Connections (Numeric Comparison) SAS. In LE Secure Connections, both sides exchange ECDH public keys (PK_A, PK_B), commit to fresh nonces via `Pairing Confirm`, reveal the nonces via `Pairing Random`, and then display a 6-digit value for human comparison (the "SAS"). This follows the MANA-IV commit, reveal and compare pattern, with the difference that both endpoints commit (each sends a confirm) rather than only the initiator. Concretely, the commitment values and the final SAS are:

$$\begin{aligned} C_A &= f4(\text{PK}_{Ax}, \text{PK}_{Bx}, N_A, 0) \\ C_B &= f4(\text{PK}_{Bx}, \text{PK}_{Ax}, N_B, 0) \\ \text{SAS} &= g2(\text{PK}_{Ax}, \text{PK}_{Bx}, N_A, N_B) \bmod 10^6 \end{aligned}$$

where $f4$ and $g2$ are defined as AES-CMAC keyed by the (pre-reveal and thus still-secret) nonce N_A, with $g2$ first reduced $\bmod 2^{32}$ before rendering as six decimal digits. Security thus hinges on two CMAC-based components: (i) $f4$ as a computational "commitment" to the nonce bound to both public keys, and (ii) $g2$ as a PRF-derived short value over $(\mathrm{PK}_{Ax}, \mathrm{PK}_{Bx}, N_A, N_B)$. Under standard PRF/MAC assumptions for AES-CMAC and fresh, uniform nonces, $f4$ is *hiding* (the tag leaks nothing about the nonce prior to reveal) and *binding* (after sending C on a fixed input, opening to a different nonce would require finding a new CMAC key that reproduces C), and $g2$ yields a value computationally indistinguishable from uniform on $\{0,1\}^{32}$ (hence $\approx 10^{-6}$ success after decimal reduction).

However, unlike our π^X_{SAS} protocol, BLE's $g2$ is not modeled as a random oracle. Our UC simulator for π^X_{SAS} relies on a programmable random oracle to (A) guarantee exact uniformity under truncation and (B) program equal/different t-bit prefixes at the forge-gate. A fixed PRF such as CMAC does not provide that programmability. Thus, while BLE's Numeric Comparison is sound in the usual game-based sense, the UC simulation strategy we use for π^X_{SAS} does not carry over verbatim to BLE's SAS derivation. In the full version we also sketch an RO-free alternative (coin-flip c and commit-then-bind) that attains the same user interface while allowing a clean UC proof with standard UC commitments and a UC coin-flip [12,15,16]. It is, however, conceptually different from the BLE handshake.

Table 1. Session-bound SAS mechanisms and their relation to our UC analysis.

Protocol	Subsumed by our analysis?	Commitment primitive	SAS derivation primitive
π^X_{SAS} (this work)	Yes (reference UC-realizing SAS protocol).	Generic hiding and binding commitment $C = \mathsf{Commit}(\mathsf{sid} \parallel m_S; \mathsf{r}_S)$ with opening d (coins r_S).	$s := \mathrm{Trunc}_t(H(\mathsf{sid} \parallel m_S \parallel m_R \parallel \mathsf{r}_S \parallel \mathsf{r}_R))$, where H is modelled as a random oracle and r_R is sampled by R.
ZRTP	Yes (under RO-style modeling of the KDF).	Hash-based commitment to the DH-transcript $\mathsf{Hash}(\mathsf{DHPart2}_A \parallel \mathsf{Hello}_B)$.	$\mathsf{KDF}(s_0, \text{'}sas\text{'}, \mathsf{context}, 256)$; SAS is the MSB t bits, rendered as Base32 / PGP words.
Matrix/Element (`m.sas.v1`)	Yes, up to HKDF modeling and the additional identity-MAC step.	Hash-based commitment to the acceptor's ephemeral key.	SAS from HKDF-SHA256 over the ECDH output and an info string; rendered as numbers or emoji.
BLE Secure Connections (Numeric Comparison)	Not directly: AES-CMAC-based SAS; our UC proof relies on RO programmability.	AES-CMAC tags $f4$.	$g2(\mathrm{PK}_{Ax}, \mathrm{PK}_{Bx}, N_A, N_B) \bmod 10^6$, where $g2$ is an AES-CMAC; displayed as six decimal digits;

7 Conclusion

We studied instant, one-shot device–to–device exchanges under an active network adversary without PKI or pre-shared secrets. Our main result is that a short, human-verifiable comparison can be treated as a first-class resource with a precise, composable failure budget $\varepsilon = 2^{-t}$. We modeled this via $\mathcal{F}_{\mathrm{OOB}}^{\mathrm{SAS}}$, gave simple commitment-style protocols π_{SAS} and $\pi_{\mathrm{SAS}}^{\times}$ that are new variations of MANA IV, proved they realize $\mathcal{F}_{\mathrm{AUTH}}^{S \to R}(\varepsilon)$ and $\mathcal{F}_{\mathrm{AUTH}}^{S \leftrightarrow R}(\varepsilon)$, and showed how to compose them with standard KEM/DEM into $\mathcal{F}_{\mathrm{SMT}}^{S \to R}(\varepsilon)$ while preserving the explicit ε. Practically, this decouples rendezvous from authentication: the out-of-band step shrinks to comparing a short t-bit string instead of transporting a long shared secret.

Our systematization clarifies where today's tools stand. Browser WebRTC data channels commonly lack a user-verifiable bind and are thus vulnerable to adversarial signaling. PAKE "one-code" designs deliver strong usability but couple rendezvous codes with out-of-band secrets. Session-bound SAS fixes the missing bind with an explicit risk budget (identical to PAKEs) and can be retrofitted to existing stacks by hashing the negotiated transcript and showing a short code to both sides. We released reference code[20] to make this easy to integrate.

Limitations and Future Work. Our mainline proofs use a random-oracle instantiation for hashing and commitments. We sketched an RO-free variant based on a UC coin-flip and non-malleable commitments, but the full proof is left for future work and we need to rely upon a Common Reference String setup. We assumed synchronous, co-present users and set the human-error parameter $\varepsilon_{\mathrm{human}} = 0$ to isolate cryptographic guarantees. A calibrated treatment of human fallibility and asynchronous comparisons is also left to future work. Additional directions include group extensions, a stronger treatment of compromised UIs and denial-of-service (DoS) against the OOB channel, and analyzing SAS-based protocols within a deniability framework. Last but not least, extending our UC model to capture endpoint compromise and to provide some form of post-compromise security is outside the scope of this work and left for future research.

A Simulation Proof of π_{SAS}

Theorem 5 (UC security of π_{SAS} toward $\mathcal{F}_{\mathrm{AUTH}}^{S \to R}(\varepsilon)$). *Let $t \in \mathbb{N}$ and define $\varepsilon := 2^{-t}$. Assume: (i)* $\mathsf{Com} = (\mathsf{Commit}, \mathsf{Open})$ *is computationally hiding and binding; (ii) H is modeled as a random oracle and* $\mathsf{SAS}(x) = \mathrm{Trunc}_t(H(x))$*; (iii) the hybrid functionality $\mathcal{F}_{\mathrm{OOB}}^{\mathrm{SAS}}$ (SAS comparison with leakage to the adversary) is available. Then for every PPT adversary $\mathcal{A}$ there exists a PPT simulator $\mathcal{S}$ such that for every PPT environment $\mathcal{Z}$,*

$$\mathsf{EXEC}_{\mathcal{Z}, \mathcal{A}, \Pi_{\mathsf{SAS}}}^{\mathcal{F}_{\mathrm{OOB}}^{\mathrm{SAS}}} \approx \mathsf{IDEAL}_{\mathcal{Z}, \mathcal{S}, \mathcal{F}_{\mathrm{AUTH}}^{S \to R}(\varepsilon)}.$$

[20] https://github.com/collapsinghierarchy/noisytransfer-protocol.

Hence, in the $\mathcal{F}_{\mathrm{OOB}}^{\mathrm{SAS}}$-hybrid, Π_{SAS} UC-realizes the authenticated one-way channel with a single online active-forgery attempt that succeeds with probability ε.

At a high level, in the ideal world the simulator receives the sender's input m_S from $\mathcal{F}_{\mathrm{AUTH}}^{S\to R}(\varepsilon)$ via the back-door tape. Using this, it precomputes the honest transcript (including the t-bit SAS) and emulates the network and $\mathcal{F}_{\mathrm{OOB}}^{\mathrm{SAS}}$ leakage exactly, preserving the real execution's scheduling. The only remaining distinguishing avenue is an active forgery/misbinding. Via a short hybrid sequence (commitment hiding/binding and RO unpredictability and programming) we bound its success by $\varepsilon = 2^{-t}$ and couple it to the Bernoulli(ε) gate of $\mathcal{F}_{\mathrm{AUTH}}^{S\to R}(\varepsilon)$.

Hybrid Argument. We work with the standard dummy-adversary reduction and indistinguishability of hybrids in the UC sense (cf. Canetti [14]). We keep S, R honest throughout; the adversary controls network scheduling and sees the $\mathcal{F}_{\mathrm{OOB}}^{\mathrm{SAS}}$ leakage.

Notation. Fix a session identifier sid chosen by the environment. The sender's payload is m_S; the receiver samples $\mathsf{r}_R \leftarrow\$ \{0,1\}^\kappa$; the sender's commitment coins are $\mathsf{r}_S \leftarrow\$ \{0,1\}^\kappa$. We model H as a random oracle with output length $n = n(\kappa)$ and write $\mathrm{Trunc}_t : \{0,1\}^n \to \{0,1\}^t$. Unless stated otherwise,

$$s \ := \ \mathrm{Trunc}_t\big(H(\mathsf{sid} \parallel m_S \parallel \mathsf{r}_S \parallel \mathsf{r}_R)\big).$$

Random-Oracle Table. We implement H via *lazy sampling* using a global partial map

$$T : \{0,1\}^* \rightharpoonup \{0,1\}^n,$$

initially empty and shared across all ITMs in the execution (parties, adversary, and simulator). On a query x to H: if $x \in \mathrm{dom}(T)$ return $T[x]$; otherwise sample $y \leftarrow\$ \{0,1\}^n$ uniformly, set $T[x] \leftarrow y$, and return y. We say "*program T at x*" to mean assigning $T[x]$ to some value (possibly under a t-bit prefix constraint in the coupling step), always without overwriting existing entries. Throughout, $x \in T$ abbreviates $x \in \mathrm{dom}(T)$.

For the SAS comparison we will form

$$x_R := (\mathsf{sid} \parallel \mathsf{m}'_S \parallel \mathsf{r}'_S \parallel \mathsf{r}_R) \quad \text{and} \quad x_S := (\mathsf{sid} \parallel \mathsf{m}_S \parallel \mathsf{r}_S \parallel \tilde{\mathsf{r}}_R),$$

taken from the values actually seen on R's and S's wires, respectively. We use the event $\mathsf{preHit}_{\mathsf{sid}} := [\, x_R \in T \ \vee \ x_S \in T \,]$ to denote a *pre-reveal RO hit* in session sid. The commitment's decommitment is denoted d.

Game H0 (Real). The real execution of Π_{SAS} in the $\mathcal{F}_{\mathrm{OOB}}^{\mathrm{SAS}}$-hybrid against $\mathcal{A}$.

H1 (Code lifting). We introduce an intermediate wrapper that internally runs *all* honest parties and the hybrid $\mathcal{F}_{\mathrm{OOB}}^{\mathrm{SAS}}$, and forwards wires to $\mathcal{A}$ and $\mathcal{Z}$ verbatim. This is the usual "all-powerful simulator shell" that only reorganizes code, not distributions.

Lemma 1. $\mathsf{EXEC}[\mathrm{H0}] \equiv \mathsf{EXEC}[\mathrm{H1}]$ *(perfectly indistinguishable).*

H2 (Hiding-based replacement of the commitment). In H2, the wrapper replaces the real $C \leftarrow \mathsf{Commit}(\mathsf{sid} \parallel m_S; \mathsf{r}_S)$ by a uniform string $C \leftarrow\$ \{0,1\}^{n(\kappa)}$, while still opening it later to $(\mathsf{sid} \parallel m_S, d)$ as in the real protocol (i.e., it stores a table to ensure a consistent decommitment). Collisions among sampled C are ruled out with overwhelming probability via the birthday bound.

Lemma 2 (Commitment hiding). *If* Com *is computationally hiding, then* $\mathsf{EXEC}[\mathrm{H1}] \approx \mathsf{EXEC}[\mathrm{H2}]$.

Sketch. A standard reduction: a distinguisher between H1 and H2 yields a PPT adversary that breaks hiding by telling apart a commitment to m_S from a random string placed on the same wire. □

H3 (Abort on BAD *double-opening).* From H2, define H3 that aborts and outputs a special symbol Bad if the adversary ever induces a valid *second* opening $(m', d') \neq (m_S, d)$ for the same C.

Lemma 3 (Commitment binding). *If* Com *is binding then* $\Pr[\mathsf{Bad}]$ *is negligible, hence* $\mathsf{EXEC}[\mathrm{H2}] \approx \mathsf{EXEC}[\mathrm{H3}]$.

H4^{pre} (Flag pre-reveal RO hits). H4^{pre} is identical to H3 except it sets a boolean flag $\mathsf{preHit}_{\mathsf{sid}} \leftarrow \mathsf{true}$ if, *before* the SAS comparison in session sid, the adversary has queried the RO at either x_R or x_S (as defined later in H4), i.e., if $x_R \in T$ or $x_S \in T$ holds at SAS time. Execution proceeds unchanged.

Lemma 4 (Pre-reveal RO hits are negligible). *Let* $\mathsf{r}_S \leftarrow\$ \{0,1\}^{\kappa}$ *be sampled and hidden inside the sender's commitment (so* $x_R := (\mathsf{sid} \parallel m'_S \parallel \mathsf{r}'_S \parallel \mathsf{r}_R)$ *and* $x_S := (\mathsf{sid} \parallel m_S \parallel \mathsf{r}_S \parallel \tilde{\mathsf{r}}_R)$ *contain* r_S*). Then for any PPT adversary making* $q_H(\kappa)$ *RO queries,*

$$\Pr[\mathsf{preHit}_{\mathsf{sid}}] \;\leq\; 2\, q_H(\kappa) \cdot 2^{-\kappa} \;=\; \mathsf{negl}(\kappa).$$

Consequently, $\mathsf{EXEC}[\mathrm{H3}] \approx \mathsf{EXEC}[\mathrm{H4}^{\mathrm{pre}}]$.

Proof. Before reveal, (m_S, r_S) is hidden; in particular r_S is uniform and unknown. Hitting x_R (or x_S) with an RO query requires guessing r_S, which succeeds with probability at most $q_H \cdot 2^{-\kappa}$ per input. A union bound over $\{x_R, x_S\}$ gives the claim. □

H4 (Flag tamper and identical-until-bad). H4 is identical to H3 except it sets a boolean flag $\mathsf{tampered}_{\mathsf{sid}} \leftarrow \mathsf{true}$ if, in session sid, the adversary alters either (i) the sender's first message (a valid commitment C' is placed on $S \to R$ that differs from the honest C), or (ii) the receiver's nonce in flight ($\tilde{\mathsf{r}}_R \neq \mathsf{r}_R$ is placed on $R \to S$). At the SAS comparison, define

$$s_R := \mathrm{Trunc}_t(H(\mathsf{sid} \parallel \mathsf{m}'_S \parallel \mathsf{r}'_S \parallel \mathsf{r}_R)), \qquad s_S := \mathrm{Trunc}_t(H(\mathsf{sid} \parallel \mathsf{m}_S \parallel \mathsf{r}_S \parallel \tilde{\mathsf{r}_R})),$$

where in the non-tampered case $\tilde{\mathsf{r}}_R = \mathsf{r}_R$, $\mathsf{m}'_S = \mathsf{m}_S$ and $\mathsf{r}'_S = \mathsf{r}_S$. Let the *bad* event be $\mathsf{bad}_{\mathsf{sid}} := [\mathsf{tampered}_{\mathsf{sid}} \wedge (s_R = s_S)]$. Execution proceeds unchanged (no abort); we only *record* $\mathsf{bad}_{\mathsf{sid}}$.

Lemma 5 (SAS equality under tampering). *Model H as a random oracle. Conditioned on* $\mathsf{tampered}_{\mathsf{sid}}$ *and on the commitment being binding to* m_S*, the two inputs* $(\mathsf{sid} \parallel \mathsf{m}'_S \parallel \mathsf{r}'_S \parallel \mathsf{r}_R)$ *and* $(\mathsf{sid} \parallel \mathsf{m}_S \parallel \mathsf{r}_S \parallel \tilde{\mathsf{r}}_R)$ *are distinct with overwhelming probability; hence* s_R *and* s_S *are independent uniform t-bit strings. Therefore,* $\Pr[\mathsf{bad}_{\mathsf{sid}}] \leq 2^{-t} + \mathsf{negl}(\kappa)$*, and by the fundamental lemma of game-playing,*

$$\Big|\Pr[\mathsf{EXEC}[\mathrm{H3}] \in \mathcal{V}] - \Pr[\mathsf{EXEC}[\mathrm{H4}] \in \mathcal{V}]\Big| \;\leq\; \Pr[\mathsf{bad}_{\mathsf{sid}}] \;\leq\; 2^{-t} + \mathsf{negl}(\kappa)$$

for any PPT test $\mathcal{V}$*.*

Proof. Binding fixes m_S (and r_S if included) from R's perspective once C is opened honestly. If the adversary injects a different commitment C', it must also provide a valid opening to make R proceed; except with negligible probability this opening yields $(\mathsf{m}'_S, \mathsf{r}'_S) \neq (\mathsf{m}_S, \mathsf{r}_S)$, thereby diverging from S's view. The only remaining effective tamper point is delivering $\tilde{\mathsf{r}}_R \neq \mathsf{r}_R$ to S, which then diverges from R's view that uses r_R.

In the random-oracle model, distinct inputs yield independent uniform outputs; after truncation, $\Pr[s_R = s_S] = 2^{-t}$. Any residual probability mass is due only to violating binding or forcing an RO collision on distinct inputs, both of which are negligible in κ. □

H5 (Coupling to the ideal Bernoulli gate and Prefix-constrained lazy RO). We define a simulator $\mathcal{S}$ that, on top of H4's code lifting, replaces the real network and $\mathcal{F}_{\mathrm{OOB}}^{\mathsf{SAS}}$ by a perfect emulation driven by the ideal functionality $\mathcal{F}_{\mathrm{AUTH}}^{S\to R}(\varepsilon)$, while maintaining a lazy-sampled RO table T.

- **On** $(\mathsf{Sent}, \mathsf{sid}, S, \mathsf{m}_S)$ **from** $\mathcal{F}_{\mathrm{AUTH}}^{S\to R}(\varepsilon)$**:** $\mathcal{S}$ starts a local simulation of the real transcript: sample $C \leftarrow\$ \{0,1\}^{n(\kappa)}$, $\mathsf{r}_R \leftarrow\$ \{0,1\}^{\kappa}$ (and any sender coins embedded in the commitment), relay C on $S{\to}R$, then (under adversarial scheduling) relay r_R on $R{\to}S$, then the opening $(\mathsf{m}_S, \mathsf{r}_S)$ on $S{\to}R$. No accept bit is returned yet; $\mathcal{S}$ only mirrors $\mathcal{F}_{\mathrm{OOB}}^{\mathsf{SAS}}$'s leakage interface later at SAS time.
- **At the SAS comparison (semantic tamper test):** Form

$$x_R := (\mathsf{m}'_S \parallel \mathsf{r}'_S \parallel \mathsf{r}_R), \qquad x_S := (\mathsf{m}_S \parallel \mathsf{r}_S \parallel \tilde{\mathsf{r}}_R),$$

  where x_R uses the actually received opening on R's side and x_S uses whatever $\tilde{\mathsf{r}}_R$ arrived at S.
  - *If* $x_R = x_S$ *(no tamper):* program T lazily at x_R (if needed), let both parties' SAS be $s := \mathrm{Trunc}_t(H(x_R))$, leak $(\mathsf{SAS}, \mathsf{sid}, s)$ to $\mathcal{A}$ for each party, and return $b{=}1$ from the emulated $\mathcal{F}_{\mathrm{OOB}}^{\mathsf{SAS}}$. Later, upon $(\mathsf{ok}, \mathsf{sid})$ from $\mathcal{A}$, forward it to $\mathcal{F}_{\mathrm{AUTH}}^{S\to R}(\varepsilon)$ so that it delivers $(\mathsf{Sent}, \mathsf{sid}, S, \mathsf{m}_S)$ to R.
  - *If* $x_R \neq x_S$ *(tamper):* invoke the ideal gate by sending $(\mathsf{Forge}, \mathsf{sid}, \mathsf{m}', R)$ to $\mathcal{F}_{\mathrm{AUTH}}^{S\to R}(\varepsilon)$ (where m' is the message determined by the adversarial flow) and receive $(\mathsf{ForgeResult}, \mathsf{sid}, b)$. Now program the RO lazily with a t-bit prefix constraint consistent with T:

* If neither x_R nor x_S is in T: sample $y_R, y_S \leftarrow\$ \{0,1\}^n$ uniformly subject to $\text{Trunc}_t(y_R) = \text{Trunc}_t(y_S)$ iff b=1; set $T[x_R] \leftarrow y_R$, $T[x_S] \leftarrow y_S$.
* If exactly one is in T: sample the other uniformly subject to the same t-bit relation to the existing one and add it to T.
* If both are already in T: if the existing t-bit relation contradicts b, this is precisely the negligible pre-reveal hit isolated in Lemma 4; otherwise proceed.

Let $s_R = \text{Trunc}_t(T[x_R])$, $s_S = \text{Trunc}_t(T[x_S])$; leak $(\mathsf{SAS}, \mathsf{sid}, s_R)$ and $(\mathsf{SAS}, \mathsf{sid}, s_S)$ to $\mathcal{A}$ as $\mathcal{F}_{\text{OOB}}^{\text{SAS}}$ would, and return that same bit b from the emulated $\mathcal{F}_{\text{OOB}}^{\text{SAS}}$ to both parties.

– **When $\mathcal{A}$ later sends** $(\mathsf{ok}, \mathsf{sid})$**:** If no successful forgery occurred (i.e., $b \neq 1$ in the tampered case), forward $(\mathsf{ok}, \mathsf{sid})$ to $\mathcal{F}_{\text{AUTH}}^{S\to R}(\varepsilon)$ to deliver $(\mathsf{Sent}, \mathsf{sid}, S, \mathsf{m}_S)$ to R.

Crucially, in the real world, any successful misbinding with honest parties requires that the two t-bit SAS values coincide on *distinct* RO inputs. By Lemma 5, this occurs with probability at most $\varepsilon + \mathsf{negl}(\kappa)$, where $\varepsilon = 2^{-t}$. The coupling above replaces this event by the Bernoulli(ε) gate of $\mathcal{F}_{\text{AUTH}}^{S\to R}(\varepsilon)$ and mirrors the same accept/reject outcome in the emulated $\mathcal{F}_{\text{OOB}}^{\text{SAS}}$, while preserving scheduling and leakage.

Lemma 6. $\mathsf{EXEC}[\text{H5}] \approx \mathsf{IDEAL}[\mathcal{F}_{\text{AUTH}}^{S\to R}(\varepsilon), \mathcal{S}]$.

Conclusion. By transitivity of indistinguishability across H0–H5, we obtain the claim of Theorem 5.

Final Distinguishing Bound. Let $\Delta(\kappa)$ denote the UC distinguishing advantage of any PPT $(\mathcal{A}, \mathcal{Z})$ pair between $\mathsf{EXEC}_{\mathcal{Z},\mathcal{A},\Pi_{\mathsf{SAS}}}^{\mathcal{F}_{\text{OOB}}^{\text{SAS}}}$ and $\mathsf{IDEAL}_{\mathcal{Z},\mathcal{S},\mathcal{F}_{\text{AUTH}}^{S\to R}(\varepsilon)}$. Then

$$\begin{aligned}\Delta(\kappa) \;\le\; & \underbrace{\mathcal{A}_{\mathsf{Com}}^{\text{hide}}(\kappa)}_{\text{H1}\to\text{H2}} \;+\; \underbrace{\mathcal{A}_{\mathsf{Com}}^{\text{bind}}(\kappa)}_{\text{H2}\to\text{H3}} \;+\; \underbrace{\Pr[\mathsf{preHit}_{\mathsf{sid}}]}_{\le\, 2\,q_H(\kappa)\,2^{-\kappa}} \\ & + \underbrace{\left|\,\Pr_{\text{real}}[\text{accept} \mid x_R \neq x_S] - \varepsilon\,\right|}_{\le\, \mathsf{negl}(\kappa)\ \text{by Lemma}5,\ \varepsilon=2^{-t}}\end{aligned}$$

and thus

$$\Delta(\kappa) \;\le\; \mathcal{A}_{\mathsf{Com}}^{\text{hide}}(\kappa) \;+\; \mathcal{A}_{\mathsf{Com}}^{\text{bind}}(\kappa) \;+\; 2\,q_H(\kappa)\,2^{-\kappa} \;+\; \mathsf{negl}(\kappa) \;=\; \mathsf{negl}(\kappa).$$

The full simulator is given in the full version. □

Attempt-Conditioned Gate. We sample the Bernoulli gate with parameter $\varepsilon = 2^{-t}$ *iff* the run reaches a genuine tamper point at SAS time, namely $x_R \neq x_S$. Let $I \in \{0,1\}$ indicate this event. In the real world, conditioned on I=1 the two RO inputs are distinct, so the accept probability is $\varepsilon \pm \mathsf{negl}(\kappa)$; hence

$$\Pr[\mathsf{accept}]_{\text{real}} \;=\; \Pr[I{=}1]\cdot\varepsilon \;\pm\; \mathsf{negl}(\kappa).$$

In the ideal world, the simulator triggers the gate exactly when $I=1$, and the functionality returns $\mathrm{Ber}(\varepsilon)$, yielding

$$\Pr[\mathsf{accept}]_{\mathrm{ideal}} = \Pr[I=1] \cdot \varepsilon.$$

Thus an adversary who "plays weak" (e.g., tampers rarely or avoids creating $x_R \neq x_S$) merely decreases $\Pr[I=1]$ in *both* worlds; it cannot alter the per-attempt success, which is fixed at ε. Consequently the overall success probabilities match up to the negligible terms already isolated in the hybrids (pre-hit and RO-collision events).

B MAC-Based SMT

Our next goal is to reduce the asymmetric footprint of the SMT stack by replacing the signature layer with symmetric authentication, while keeping the SAS-based cross-authentication as the only out-of-band (OOB) trust anchor. The main motivation is efficiency: asymmetric primitives are typically more costly than symmetric ones, as argued in [11]. This follows a common design line in SAS/PAKE-backed channels, where public-key signing can be traded for MACs keyed by ephemeral session material, but at the price of losing public verifiability and the "signature firewall" (i.e., verification before any decryption/long-term use). We note that the loss of public verifiability may, in some settings, support deniability goals, however a formal deniability analysis of our construction is out of scope. We retain the UC modelling of SAS via $\mathcal{F}_{\mathrm{OOB}}^{\mathrm{SAS}}$ and cross-authentication via π_{SAS}^{X}, and we continue to target the same ideal functionality $\mathcal{F}_{\mathrm{SMT}}^{S\to R}(\varepsilon)$ with length-only leakage and a single online misbinding event of success probability $\varepsilon = 2^{-t}$.

Real Protocol $\pi_{\mathrm{SAS+KEM+DEM+MAC}}$ (hybrid $\mathcal{F}_{\mathrm{OOB}}^{\mathrm{SAS}}$)

Primitives.

- Equivocable commitment $\mathsf{Com} = (\mathsf{Commit}, \mathsf{Open})$: hiding, binding, with trapdoor for equivocation (used only by the UC simulator).
- KEM $\mathsf{KEM} = (\mathsf{Gen}, \mathsf{Encap}, \mathsf{Decap})$: IND-CPA.
- DEM $\mathsf{DEM} = (\mathsf{ENC}, \mathsf{DEC})$: *one-time* IND-CPA (fresh KEM key per session).
- MAC (e.g. HMAC) with UF-CMA security.
- Random oracle H for SAS; $\mathrm{sas}(x) = \mathsf{Trunc}_t(H(x))$.

Parties. Sender S sends a single message m to receiver R.

Context string.

$$\mathsf{ctx} := \text{“}\pi_{\mathrm{SAS+KEM+DEM+MAC}}\text{”} \,\|\, \mathsf{sid} \,\|\, \text{“S}\to\text{R”}.$$

Phase 1 — Cross-authentication via π_{SAS}^{X} (SID reuse)

1: S: sample $K_{\mathsf{MAC}} \leftarrow\$ \{0,1\}^{\kappa}$ and commitment coins r_S; set $C_S \leftarrow \mathsf{Commit}(K_{\mathsf{MAC}}; r_S)$; define $m_S \leftarrow C_S$.

R: $(\mathsf{pk}_R, \mathsf{sk}_R) \leftarrow \mathsf{KEM.Gen}$; sample $\mathsf{r}_R \leftarrow\$ \{0,1\}^{\kappa}$; define $m_R \leftarrow \mathsf{pk}_R$.
Run π_{SAS}^{X} under the *same* sid with inputs (m_S, m_R).
Abort iff π_{SAS}^{X} outputs $(\mathsf{SAS}, \mathsf{sid}, 0)$.
(On success b=1: S learns $(\mathsf{pk}_R, \mathsf{r}_R)$ *and R learns C_S; SAS leakage flows via $\mathcal{F}_{\text{OOB}}^{\text{SAS}}$ as usual.)*

Phase 2 — One-shot transport with post-decrypt MAC check

(2a) Sender S with payload m:
$(K, c_{\mathsf{KEM}}) \leftarrow \mathsf{KEM.Encap}(\mathsf{pk}_R)$
$P \leftarrow (m, K_{\mathsf{MAC}}, r_S)$ *(carry MAC key & its opening inside the DEM payload)*
$c_{\mathsf{DEM}} \leftarrow \mathsf{DEM.ENC}(K, P)$
$\tau \leftarrow \mathsf{MAC}_{K_{\mathsf{MAC}}}(\mathsf{ctx} \,\|\, c_{\mathsf{KEM}} \,\|\, c_{\mathsf{DEM}})$
$S \to R$: $(\mathsf{sid}, c_{\mathsf{KEM}}, c_{\mathsf{DEM}}, \tau)$
(2b) Receiver R:
$K \leftarrow \mathsf{KEM.Decap}(\mathsf{sk}_R, c_{\mathsf{KEM}})$ *(abort on failure)*
$P \leftarrow \mathsf{DEM.DEC}(K, c_{\mathsf{DEM}})$; parse P as $(m, K_{\mathsf{MAC}}, r_S)$ *(abort on failure)*
Commitment check: accept only if $\mathsf{Open}(C_S; r_S, K_{\mathsf{MAC}})$ succeeds
Tag check: accept only if $\mathsf{MAC}_{K_{\mathsf{MAC}}}(\mathsf{ctx} \,\|\, c_{\mathsf{KEM}} \,\|\, c_{\mathsf{DEM}}) = \tau$
If both checks pass, output $(\mathsf{Sent}, \mathsf{sid}, S, m)$ to the environment; else abort.

References

1. About imessage contact key verification (2023). https://support.apple.com/en-us/118246
2. Advancing imessage security: contact key verification (2023). https://security.apple.com/blog/imessage-contact-key-verification/
3. How can i compare key fingerprints? (2024). https://support.wire.com/hc/en-us/articles/207692235-How-can-I-compare-key-fingerprints
4. Use contact key verification on iphone (2024). https://support.apple.com/guide/iphone/use-contact-key-verification-iph654dd8c53/ios
5. Telegram secret chats: end-to-end encryption (2025). https://core.telegram.org/api/end-to-end, key visualization and fingerprint details
6. Threema support: private FAQ (identity verification) (2025). https://threema.com/en/support/private
7. What is the QR code good for? (2025). https://threema.com/en/faq/qr-code-expl
8. Wire security & privacy (2025). https://wire.com/en/security
9. Bellare, M., Rogaway, P.: Entity authentication and key distribution. In: Annual International Cryptology Conference, pp. 232–249. Springer (1993)
10. Bellare, M., Rogaway, P.: Random oracles are practical: a paradigm for designing efficient protocols. In: ACM CCS, pp. 62–73 (1993). https://doi.org/10.1145/168588.168596
11. Benin, A., Toledo, S., Tromer, E.: Secure association for the internet of things. In: 2015 International Workshop on Secure Internet of Things (SIoT), pp. 25–34. IEEE (2015)
12. Blum, M.: Coin flipping by telephone. In: CRYPTO 1981 (reprinted in SIGACT News, 1983) (1983), commit-then-open coin tossing

13. Canetti, R.: Universally composable security: a new paradigm for cryptographic protocols. In: 42nd FOCS, pp. 136–145 (2001). https://doi.org/10.1109/SFCS.2001.959888
14. Canetti, R.: Universally composable security. J. ACM (JACM) **67**(5), 1–94 (2020)
15. Canetti, R., Fischlin, M.: Universally composable commitments. In: CRYPTO 2001. Springer (2001). UC commitments in CRS; enables UC coin-toss via commit⊕
16. Canetti, R., Lindell, Y., Ostrovsky, R., Sahai, A.: Universally composable two-party and multi-party secure computation. In: STOC 2002 (2002), general UC framework; CRS-hybrid feasibility and building blocks
17. Cremers, C., Medinger, N., Naska, A.: Impossibility results for post-compromise security in real-world communication systems. In: 2025 IEEE Symposium on Security and Privacy (SP), pp. 4391–4405. IEEE (2025)
18. Exchange, K.: Universally composable password-based. In: Advances in Cryptology-EUROCRYPT 2005: 24th Annual International Conference on the Theory and Applications of Cryptographic Techniques, Aarhus, Denmark, 22–26 May 2005, Proceedings, vol. 3494, p. 404. Springer (2005)
19. Goldberg, I., Mashatan, A., Stinson, D.R.: On message recognition protocols: recoverability and explicit confirmation. Int. J. Appl. Cryptogr. **2**(4), 331–346 (2010). https://doi.org/10.1504/IJACT.2010.038305. https://dl.acm.org/doi/10.1504/IJACT.2010.038305
20. Haase, B., et al.: Cpace, a balanced composable pake (2025). https://datatracker.ietf.org/doc/draft-irtf-cfrg-cpace/, internet-Draft, IRTF CFRG
21. Hammell, J., Weimerskirch, A., Girão, J., Westhoff, D.: Recognition in a low-power environment. In: Proceedings of the 25th IEEE International Conference on Distributed Computing Systems Workshops (ICDCSW'05) — Second International Workshop on Wireless Ad Hoc Networking (WWAN), pp. 933–938. IEEE Computer Society, Columbus, OH, USA (2005). https://doi.org/10.1109/ICDCSW.2005.119
22. Jarecki, S., Saxena, N.: Authenticated key agreement with key re-use in the short authenticated strings model. In: International Conference on Security and Cryptography for Networks. LNCS, vol. 6280, pp. 253–270. Springer, Springer (2010). https://nsaxena.engr.tamu.edu/wp-content/uploads/sites/238/2019/12/js-scn10.pdf
23. Katz, J., Lindell, Y.: Introduction to Modern Cryptography, 3rd edn. CRC Press (2020)
24. Ladd, W.: Spake2, a password-authenticated key exchange (2023). https://www.rfc-editor.org/rfc/rfc9382, iRTF RFC 9382
25. Laur, S., Nyberg, K.: Efficient mutual data authentication using manually authenticated strings. In: Cryptology and Network Security: 5th International Conference, CANS 2006, Suzhou, China, 8–10 December 2006, Proceedings, vol. 4301, pp. 90–107. Springer (2006)
26. Laur, S., Nyberg, K.: Efficient mutual data authentication using manually authenticated strings (extended version). Technical report 2005/424, IACR ePrint (2006). https://kodu.ut.ee/~swen/publications/articles/laur-nyberg-2006.pdf
27. Laur, S., Pasini, S.: SAS-based group authentication and key agreement protocols. In: PKC 2008. LNCS, vol. 4939, pp. 197–213. Springer (2008). https://doi.org/10.1007/978-3-540-78440-1_12. https://iacr.org/archive/pkc2008/49390198/49390198.pdf
28. Laur, S., Pasini, S.: User-aided data authentication. Int. J. Secure. Network. **4**(1–2), 69–86 (2009)

29. Mashatan, A., Vaudenay, S.: A message recognition protocol based on standard assumptions. In: ACNS 2010. LNCS, vol. 6123, pp. 384–401. Springer (2010). https://doi.org/10.1007/978-3-642-13708-2_23. https://infoscience.epfl.ch/record/148699/files/MRP_ACNS10.pdf
30. Matrix.org: Implementing more advanced E2EE features (SAS emoji/numbers) (2024). https://matrix.org/docs/guides/implementing-more-advanced-e-2-ee-features-such-as-cross-signing/. Accessed 03 Sept 2025
31. Pasini, S., Vaudenay, S.: An optimal non-interactive message authentication protocol. In: CT-RSA 2006. LNCS, vol. 3860, pp. 280–296. Springer (2006). https://doi.org/10.1007/11605805_18. https://link.springer.com/chapter/10.1007/11605805_18
32. Pasini, S., Vaudenay, S.: SAS-based authenticated key agreement. In: International Workshop on Public Key Cryptography, pp. 395–409. Springer (2006)
33. Signal Messenger: What is a safety number and why do i see that it changed? (2024). https://support.signal.org/hc/en-us/articles/360007060632. Accessed 03 Sept 2025
34. Vaudenay, S.: Secure communications over insecure channels based on short authenticated strings. In: Advances in Cryptology – CRYPTO 2005. Lecture Notes in Computer Science, vol. 3621, pp. 309–326. Springer (2005)
35. WhatsApp: About security code change notifications (2024). https://faq.whatsapp.com/1524220618005378. Accessed 03 Sept 2025
36. Zimmermann, P.R., Johnston, A., Callas, J.: ZRTP: media path key agreement for unicast secure RTP. RFC 6189 (2011). https://datatracker.ietf.org/doc/html/rfc6189

Sovereign Modal Signatures

Yingfei Yan[1], Khai Hanh Tang[2(✉)], Hien Chu[3,4(✉)], Sherman S. M. Chow[5], San Ling[2], Huaxiong Wang[2], and Kai Zhang[6]

[1] Université Clermont Auvergne, CNRS, LIMOS, Clermont-Ferrand, France
[2] Nanyang Technological University, 50 Nanyang Ave, Singapore, Singapore
khaihanh.tang@ntu.edu.sg
[3] TU Wien, Vienna, Austria
hien.chu@tuwien.ac.at
[4] Friedrich-Alexander-Universität Erlangen-Nürnberg, Erlangen, Germany
[5] Department of Information Engineering, Chinese University of Hong Kong, Sha Tin, Hong Kong
[6] School of Mathematics and Statistics, Shaanxi Normal University, Xi'an, China

Abstract. Signing anonymously under both hidden and public policies with per-signature accountability has only been studied piecemeal, as prior schemes address at most one dimension or restrict function classes. Here, we introduce sovereign modal signatures, the first scheme unifying both dimensions with support for hidden-circuit evaluation over bounded-size arithmetic circuits without universal circuits. Each signer holds a private attribute and a hidden policy F, certified by an authority and concealed from signatures. Resting on a public combiner P, the signing process maps the joint outputs of F and an ad hoc function G to a derived message and an opening tag governing per-signature traceability.

Modifying the effective policy at signing time requires no key reissuance, since G is chosen freshly against the fixed F. Achieving zero-knowledge evaluation of F without exposing its structure is our core challenge, resolved by treating F's PLONK description as witness rather than statement. No universal circuits are required: our reduction yields a fixed verification circuit of size linear in F's gate count; the resulting scheme is provably secure in the random oracle model.

Concretely, our generic construction needs only signatures, public-key encryption, and non-interactive zero-knowledge arguments of knowledge for arithmetic circuits. Hidden arithmetic circuits over any finite field are fully supported, subsuming the restricted Boolean and linear function classes of prior hidden-function schemes. Our post-quantum instantiation combines ZKBoo (Usenix Security '16) under the MPC-in-the-Head (MPCitH, STOC '07) paradigm with lattice-based primitives over $\mathbb{Z}_q$, achieving plausibly post-quantum security without pairings or the algebraic group model. With proof sizes quasilinear in F's gate count and linear in G and P's multiplications, the scheme also readily admits richer MPCitH instantiations.

Keywords: Accountable Anonymity · Functional Signatures · Lattices

K. Jee and A. Kate (Eds.): ACNS 2026, LNCS 16571, pp. 444–472, 2027.
https://doi.org/10.1007/978-3-032-32560-0_16

1 Introduction

Privacy-preserving signatures serve a fundamental purpose: a signer proves she satisfies a governing policy and belongs to an authorized group, without disclosing her identity. The design space is determined by two independent axes of control. The first axis is *signability* (signing eligibility control): what messages a signer may sign, and whether the governing policy is public knowledge or a hidden credential. The second axis is *accountability*: when, and how completely, a designated authority may recover the signer's identity from a signature. Three decades of work have advanced each axis in isolation, leaving a fragmented landscape in which no single scheme addresses both.

Signability. Ring signatures (RS) [9,61] and group signatures (GS) [19,45] impose no constraint: any enrolled member may sign any message freely. Attribute-based signatures (ABS) [57] and multimodal private signatures (MPS) [58] allow signing only when the message and the signer's attribute together satisfy a function chosen publicly at signing time. Functional signatures (FS) [12] and policy-based signatures (PBS) [8] go further: each signing key encodes a fixed *hidden* function, and a signature is valid only when this function approves the message. The hidden function cannot be updated without reissuing the key, and no existing construction supports it beyond restricted circuit classes, namely, linear systems over $\mathbb{Z}_2$ [20,68], quadratic Boolean functions [65], or functions left abstract [12,37]. This stands in sharp contrast to public-function schemes, which already support all bounded-size arithmetic circuits [52,63].

Accountability. Group signatures [19] expose the full signer identity to a tracing authority upon misuse; ring signatures [61] hide the signer unconditionally among n members. Bifurcated anonymous signatures (BiAS) [49] introduced per-signature accountability control, letting the signer choose at each signing between full traceability and unconditional anonymity. MPS [58] refines the traceable branch into distinct modes, such as role-level or group-membership linkability. A spectrum of intermediate mechanisms has been proposed along this axis, from linkable and accountable ring signatures to certified limited opening [23,25,26,48,67,71]; we survey these in Sect. 1.2. Throughout, accountability predicates are publicly known and chosen from a fixed set at signing time. Hidden policies and flexible accountability have not been jointly designed.

The Intersection Gap. Existing notions advance one line at a time; even MPS [58], which touches both, fixes a finite set of disclosure modes and restricts hidden policies to narrow function classes. No known scheme simultaneously enforces a hidden arithmetic signing policy, admits an ad hoc public policy overlaid at signing time, and grants per-signature control over how much identity the authority recovers. This gap is a deployment barrier. Consider corporate compliance. An auditor signs reports under a proprietary risk-scoring function F, hidden to protect business logic, composed with a publicly auditable eligibility check G; routine reports require only role-level accountability, while reports flagging systemic risk require full identity recovery. Specifying F, G, and the accountability rule as a single coherent system is beyond any existing primitive.

Expressiveness. Unifying the two axes requires proving in zero knowledge the correct evaluation of a hidden function F over a bounded-size arithmetic circuit, without exposing F's structure or computation trace. Universal circuits [66] offer a general approach: to evaluate a circuit $\mathsf{C}(\mathbf{x})$ with input $\mathbf{x}$, one proves the evaluation of a fixed universal program $\mathcal{U}$ on input the code of C and $\mathbf{x}$. Despite recent improvements [47,54,55,72], current universal circuits remain too large for practical use in privacy-preserving signatures. The best known construction [55] achieves quasilinear size using Boolean gates, still larger than a direct arithmetic-circuit proof by a $\log n_{\mathsf{gate}}$ factor of the number of gates n_{gate}.

Converting arithmetic operations to Boolean circuits is also unsatisfying. An addition over the finite field $\mathbb{F}_q$ requires $2 \log q$ bit multiplications and a single multiplication costs $\log^2 q$ bit multiplications under schoolbook arithmetic, with faster algorithms such as Karatsuba [41] and FFT reducing but not closing this gap. Arguments for bounded-size Boolean circuits exist [59] but do not extend to $\mathbb{Z}_q$ arithmetic at acceptable cost.

Prior schemes thus restrict hidden functions to narrow classes, bounded public families [58], or leave the function class open [12]. A recent MPS construction [65] supports quadratic Boolean functions and could extend to all Boolean circuits via techniques from [59], but arithmetic circuits over $\mathbb{Z}_q$ remain out of reach. This state of affairs motivates three research questions (RQs).

RQ 1. *Can a privacy-preserving signature scheme prove the correct evaluation of an arbitrary hidden bounded-size arithmetic circuit over* $\mathbb{F}_q$*, without universal circuits and the algebraic group model?*

RQ 2. *Is there a single signature notion that unifies hidden and public policy enforcement with flexible per-signature signability and accountability, subsuming FS, PBS, ABS, BiAS, and MPS as special cases?*

RQ 3. *Can the notion from* ***RQ 2*** *be instantiated generically from standard primitives and concretely from post-quantum lattice-based assumptions?*

1.1 Our Contributions

We answer RQ 1, RQ 2, and RQ 3 affirmatively. We first establish that hidden arithmetic-circuit evaluation is achievable (RQ 1), then define the notion that exploits this capability (RQ 2), and finally construct and instantiate it (RQ 3).

Efficient Hidden Arithmetic-Circuit Evaluation (RQ 1). The main technical challenge is proving in zero knowledge the evaluation of the function $P(F(M, \mathsf{attr}, w), G(M, \mathsf{attr}, w))$, concealing both the function F and its computation trace. Evaluating a hidden circuit requires concealing not only the inputs but also the circuit structure and all intermediate computation traces, making standard non-interactive zero-knowledge arguments of knowledge (NIZKAoK) techniques for public circuits not directly applicable. We resolve this by adapting PLONK's arithmetization [34]: PLONK encodes each arithmetic gate as a quadratic constraint via selector values and enforces wire consistency across gates via a permutation. Crucially, this encoding, which we call the *PLONK description* pd of C and which we refer to via PLONK's arithmetization throughout, is a vector of length linear in the total gate count of C. Treating this description as part of the *witness* rather than the statement reduces hidden-circuit satisfiability to verifying a fixed public circuit $\mathcal{U}^{\mathsf{plonk}}$ of the same linear size.

Concretely, to prove F's evaluation without revealing its structure, we fix F's PLONK description as part of the witness, derive random challenges α, β from the random oracle, and view the resulting constraint system as a fixed public verification circuit $\mathcal{U}_F^{\mathsf{plonk}}$ whose size is linear in the gate count of F. A NIZKAoK on $\mathcal{U}_F^{\mathsf{plonk}}$ then certifies F's evaluation in zero knowledge, as efficiently as if F's circuit structure were public. This yields the first efficient privacy-preserving signature scheme supporting hidden arithmetic-circuit evaluation without universal circuits [66] and without the algebraic group model [32], and consequently yields the first efficient privacy-preserving signature scheme supporting hidden arithmetic-circuit evaluation without universal circuits. See Sect. 4 for a detailed discussion.

Prior attempts either require non-standard assumptions [11, 22] or restrict to narrow circuit classes [51, 65]; our technical contribution here is this application of a PLONKish-based reduction, not general uses of zero-knowledge proofs.

A New Notion (RQ 2). We propose *Sovereign Modal Signatures* (SMS), a notion in which both axes are governed by a single unified mechanism. "*Sovereign*" names the per-signature autonomy of the signer, who governs the effective policy and accountability mode at each signing, unconstrained by a predefined menu of options. "*Modal*" names the mode-structured accountability output, generalizing the finite multimodal disclosure of MPS [58] to an open-ended spectrum governed by the signer's choice of G and the certified structure of F. "Sovereign modal" thus names a compound property: the signer exercises *sovereign* per-signature control over a *mode*-structured policy and accountability system.

In SMS, each signer holds a private attribute attr and a hidden policy F certified by a function-issuing authority FA. For each message M, the signer additionally chooses an *ad hoc* function $G \in \mathcal{G}$, freely selected at each signing without reissuing the certificate. G is *public*: any verifier can confirm that G approved the message, providing the publicly auditable policy component absent from FS and PBS. Hiding G would forfeit this auditability and double the proof cost; the flexibility of SMS lies in the per-signature choice of G, not its concealment. In practice, G's inputs or outputs may themselves carry private information, *e.g.*, as ciphertexts or commitments, even when G's structure is public. G does not override F's accountability encoding; a public combiner P composes their outputs so that both the signing policy and the accountability mode are jointly determined:

$$(\overline{M}, \mathsf{op}) = P\big(F(M, \mathsf{attr}, w), G(M, \mathsf{attr}, w)\big). \tag{1}$$

The output $\overline{M}$ determines what is signed, and op determines what the authority recovers. A special value $\mathsf{op} \notin \mathcal{OP}_{\mathsf{sgnbl}}$ blocks signing entirely; any $\mathsf{op} \in \mathcal{OP}_{\mathsf{sgnbl}}$ permits a signature and encodes the accountability mode, ranging from unconditional anonymity through partial disclosure to full identity recovery. The signer produces a signature on $\overline{M}$ in the manner of a functional signature [12], binding the output to the certified hidden policy, with op then encrypted for the tracing authority TA [58]. Tracing is triggered by TA running Open on any valid signature, recovering exactly the information encoded in op. Throughout, attr and F remain hidden from all signatures.

Crucially, even with F hidden, any verifier can confirm that the signature was produced under a policy certified by FA and a publicly known G, with P yielding a signable output, a form of policy compliance auditability absent from FS and PBS. The effective policy can be updated at each signing via G without reissuing the key or the certified hidden F. Existing primitives arise as special cases: PBS and FS correspond to P acting as the identity on F's output; ABS and BiAS correspond to P acting as the identity on G's output; MPS corresponds to G selecting an index into a public function family fed to P. SMS thus subsumes RS, GS, ABS, BiAS, MPS, FS, and PBS as special cases, and realizes the single-signer, function-bound slice of the functional credentials framework envisioned [24].

Table 1. Comparison of SMS with prior privacy-preserving signature schemes

Scheme	Public Policy		Hidden Policy		Accountability
	Scoped	Class	Scoped	Class	
RS [9,61]	—	—	—	—	—
GS [19,45]	—	—	—	—	Identity (ID)
PBS [8]	—	—	✓	Linear [20,68]	—
FS [12]	—	—	✓	NP	—
ABS [57]	✓	Arithmetic [63]	—	—	—
BiAS [49]	—	—	—	—	ID/None [49]
MPS [58]	✓	Arithmetic [58,65]	—	—	Finite Modal
SMS	✓	Arithmetic	✓	Arithmetic	Sovereign Modal

Scoped: whether this policy class determines signing eligibility.
Arithmetic: instantiations exist for all bounded-size arithmetic circuits over $\mathbb{F}_q$.
Linear: instantiations exist for linear functions over $\mathbb{Z}_2$.
Finite Modal: selection from a predefined, bounded set of disclosure modes.
Sovereign Modal: signer-governed control over an open-ended spectrum.

Table 1 situates SMS among prior privacy-preserving signatures; SMS is the unique one with public arithmetic functions, hidden arithmetic functions, sovereign per-signature policy control, and modal accountability simultaneously.

Generic Construction and Post-quantum Instantiation (RQ 3). Based on the paradigm of Nguyen *et al.* [58], we build SMS generically from four standard primitives: a secure signature scheme $\mathcal{S}$, a chosen-plaintext-secure (CPA-secure) public-key encryption scheme $\mathcal{E}$, a strongly unforgeable one-time signature scheme $\mathcal{OTS}$, and a NIZKAoK for arithmetic circuits satisfying simulation-sound extractability [18], where a valid proof always yields an extractable witness even in the presence of simulated proofs. The hidden-circuit evaluation of NIZKAoK is handled by the PLONK-based reduction established in RQ 1: fixing F's PLONK description as part of the witness reduces the proof obligation to a fixed public verification circuit, enabling the NIZKAoK to verify F's evaluation as efficiently as that of a public circuit of the same size. The NIZKAoK proves in zero knowledge that the signer holds a valid FA-issued certificate over (attr, F), that $P(F(\cdot,\cdot,\cdot), G(\cdot,\cdot,\cdot))$ evaluates correctly to a signable opening tag, and that the tag is honestly encrypted for TA and bound to a one-time verification key certified under the signer's attribute key. This avoids universal circuits [66], pairing-based assumptions, and idealized algebraic models.

Regarding our post-quantum instantiation, we employ ZKBoo [35] under the MPC-in-the-Head (MPCitH) paradigm [39]. ZKBoo's direct handling of arithmetic-circuit satisfiability makes it a natural fit for the NIZKAoK slot in the generic SMS construction, and this instantiation replaces the abstract NIZKAoK with ZKBoo without redesigning the signing protocol. The lattice-based primitives over $\mathbb{Z}_q$ include Lindner–Peikert (LP) public-key encryption (PKE) [50] ($\mathcal{E}_{\mathsf{lp}}$), Jeudy–Roux-Langlois–Sanders (JRS) signatures [40] ($\mathcal{S}_{\mathsf{jrs}}$), and Kawachi–Tanaka–Xagawa (KTX) commitments [43]. Since ZKBoo satisfies simulation-sound extractability with quasi-unique response [29], *i.e.*, any commitment and challenge admit at most one valid response up to negligible probability, it subsumes the anti-malleability role of $\mathcal{OTS}$ in the generic construction.

The PLONK's arithmetization induces a two-phase witness structure. Witnesses available before the random challenges α, β are committed first. Witnesses determined by α, β are committed in a second phase. This requires a targeted modification to ZKBoo's decomposition, detailed in Sect. 5. The resulting signature size is quasilinear in the gate count of F and linear in the number of multiplications of G and P, with a $\log q$ overhead arising from the binary decomposition required to parse field elements into the binary representation compatible with the lattice-based primitives. This framework also supports richer instantiations via advanced MPCitH techniques [3,4,7,16,17,30,42,62] and vector oblivious linear evaluation in the head (VOLEitH) techniques [6,13,27,60].

Benchmarking with concrete parameter selection is deferred to future work. See Sect. 5 and the full version [69] for details of these building blocks.

1.2 Related Work

Signability in Prior Notions. Table 1 summarizes the landscape. Here, we discuss the work most closely related to SMS in design goals. We classify MPS [58] as limited function composition: the signer evaluates a public function to obtain an index j, then selects the j-th member of a public family $\{P_i\}_{i=1}^{k}$ as the effective hidden policy. The hidden function is never directly composed with a public one; the family size is bounded ($k = 4$ in [58]); and the selection circuit evades, rather than solves, the challenge of proving hidden-circuit satisfiability. SMS replaces selection with genuine composition via the combiner P, supports an unbounded family $\mathcal{F}$ of hidden arithmetic circuits, and directly confronts hidden-circuit evaluation. Furthermore, MPS's selection-based approach costs $\mathcal{O}(k \cdot (n_{\mathsf{mlt}} + n_{\mathsf{add}}))$ constraints; the PLONK-based reduction developed here reduces this to $\mathcal{O}(n_{\mathsf{mlt}} + n_{\mathsf{add}})$, removing the multiplicative factor k. The original PBS construction [8], built on Groth–Sahai proofs [36] over structure-preserving signatures [2], is inherently restricted to functions expressible as bilinear maps. Subsequent lattice-based constructions [20,68] extend the reach only to linear systems over $\mathbb{Z}_2$. Bobolz *et al.* [10] introduced universal anonymous signatures to balance utility and privacy, but omit hidden signing functions and provide only a high-level framework without concrete instantiations. Nguyen *et al.* [59] defined bicameral and auditably private signatures, pairing a private signing policy with a public disclosure mechanism in a fixed two-state model; that binary structure is a special case of SMS, which supports arbitrary composition of hidden and public functions and a continuously variable accountability spectrum.

Accountability Mechanisms in Prior Notions. The accountability axis has a richer history than the binary GS model suggests. Linkable ring signatures, proposed by Liu, Wei, and Wong [56], allow linking two signatures by the same signer without revealing identity. Accountable ring signatures, introduced by Xu and Yung [67] and first realized in the standard model by Lai, Zhang, Chow, and Schröder [48], allow the signer to designate an opener who can later reveal the signer's identity, thereby combining the ad hoc group flexibility of ring signatures with the accountability of group signatures. Chow, Susilo, and Yuen [25] proposed escrowed linkability, where only a designated linking authority can decide whether two ring signatures share a signer. Traceable ring signatures, proposed by Fujisaki and Suzuki [33], publicly reveal any signer who signs two distinct messages under the same tag, without any designated opener.

Kiayias, Tsiounis, and Yung [44] introduced traceable signatures, where a tracing trapdoor tags a misbehaving user's signatures without opening others; Chow [23] improved this by enabling per-user tagging without first collecting all signatures. Abe, Chow, Haralambiev, and Ohkubo [1] introduced double-trapdoor anonymous tags for a modular construction of traceable signatures supporting authorship claiming and denial: the signer herself can selectively prove or disprove her authorship of a specific signature, a form of user-controlled accountability orthogonal to authority-initiated tracing. Kiayias and Zhou [46] proposed hidden identity-based signatures, where the opening authority needs only its secret key to reveal the signer's identity; Chow, Zhang, and Zhang [26] gave the first standard-model construction. Zhang, Wu, and Chow [71] introduced certified limited opening, delegating opening rights so that neither the master certifier nor unauthorized parties can revoke anonymity. Each of these offers a distinct tracing granularity; SMS's opening tag op can encode any of these levels as a special configuration of the combiner P; user-controlled accountability such as authorship claiming and denial points to a natural extension of the framework.

Proofs for Hidden Function Evaluations. Several recent works construct zero-knowledge proofs for the satisfiability of hidden circuits, but each either targets a different security model or a different problem class. Ling *et al.* [51] gave zero-knowledge proofs for committed symmetric Boolean functions, covering only a narrow subclass. Boneh, Nguyen, and Ozdemir [11] commit to a hidden circuit's PLONK's description via Marlin [21], yielding proofs of arithmetic-circuit satisfiability, but their construction relies on the algebraic group model (AGM) [32], which carries documented soundness concerns [70]. Di *et al.* [28] propose MUX-Proofs, layering Marlin over a univariate sum-check to verify RAM steps encoded as rank-1 constraint systems; Choudhuri *et al.* [22] introduced Sublonk, applying PLONK's arithmetization to arbitrary-degree polynomials for instruction-level proofs. Both also rely on the AGM.

Our construction operates in the random oracle model (ROM) for both the generic and the lattice-based instantiation, avoiding these concerns entirely. Tang, Pham, and Ngo [64] apply PLONK's arithmetization to prove correct execution of RAM programs, a problem structurally different from that of hidden-circuit evaluation for signatures; the treatment developed here, specifically treating the PLONK's description as a witness component to reduce hidden-circuit satisfiability to a fixed public verification circuit, is tailored to the NIZKAoK requirements of privacy-preserving signatures and is not addressed in that prior work. In short, no prior scheme achieves ROM-based proofs for arbitrary hidden bounded-size arithmetic circuits in a privacy-preserving signature setting.

Relationship to Anonymous Credentials. Anonymous credentials [5,14,15] and SMS share structural ancestry: both involve a certifying authority, a hidden user attribute, and a zero-knowledge proof of possession. The two paradigms are nonetheless orthogonal. The former focuses on selective disclosure of attribute *values* in a presentation token, where the predicate being proven is public to the verifier. SMS focuses on signing messages under a hidden function *structure* F, whose circuit topology is concealed from signatures, and adds per-signature accountability control absent from anonymous credentials, which typically target full unlinkability. Combining the two, producing an SMS signature while selectively disclosing which attributes the signer holds, is a natural direction for future work and is part of the broader functional credentials framework [24].

1.3 Notations, Conventions, and Paper Organization

Let $\emptyset$ and ϵ denote the empty set and empty string, respectively. We say a quantity p_λ (indexed by the security parameter λ) satisfies $p_\lambda \leq \mathsf{negl}(\lambda)$ if there is a negligible function $\epsilon(\lambda)$ and λ_0 such that $p_\lambda \leq \epsilon(\lambda)$ for all $\lambda \geq \lambda_0$. $x \leftarrow \mathcal{D}$ means x is drawn from distribution $\mathcal{D}$. $x \xleftarrow{\$} S$ means x is drawn uniformly from set S. Let $\mathbb{Z}$, $\mathbb{Z}_+$, and $\mathbb{N}$ denote the integers, positive integers, and natural numbers $\{0, 1, 2, \ldots\}$. For $a, b \in \mathbb{Z}$ with $a \leq b$, let $[a, b] = \{a, \ldots, b\}$. For $b \in \mathbb{Z}_+$, let $[b] = \{1, \ldots, b\}$. Bold lower/upper-case letters, *e.g.*, $\mathbf{x}/\mathbf{A}$, denote column vectors/matrices. $(\mathbf{x}\|\mathbf{y})$ denotes the concatenation of the vectors, $[\mathbf{x}^\top \mid \mathbf{y}^\top]^\top$.

Throughout, $\mathcal{M}$ denotes the *input* message space and $\overline{\mathcal{M}}$ denotes the *output* message space (the space of derived messages after applying the combiner P); elements are written $M \in \mathcal{M}$ and $\overline{M} \in \overline{\mathcal{M}}$. This distinction is maintained consistently across all definitions, constructions, and security experiments.

Paper Organization. The next section defines SMS: syntax, correctness, and security. Section 3 presents the generic construction. Section 4 develops the PLONK arithmetization framework for proving hidden function evaluations, supporting the generic construction. Section 5 overviews the post-quantum lattice-based instantiation via ZKBoo and the modified decomposition. Full details of the lattice-based instantiation, all primitives, proofs, parameter settings, and preliminaries are in the full version.

2 Definition of SMS

This section formalizes SMS by defining its syntax (Sect. 2.1) and security requirements (Sect. 2.2). The security experiments are collected in Fig. 1; the supporting oracles are defined in Sect. 2.2 and referenced throughout. SMS subsumes other notions via the combiner P, using F and G to encode policies.

2.1 Syntax

We adopt the partial-dynamic model [45], where users may join at any time but revocation is not supported; a fully dynamic model would additionally allow membership expiry.

Parties. The *function-issuing authority* FA holds master function key mfk and enrolls users by certifying each user's attribute and hidden policy. The *tracing authority* TA holds tracing key tsk and recovers signer identity or role from an opening tag when authorized. Each *user* holds a certified attribute–policy pair (attr, F) and chooses a public ad hoc function G at each signing. *Verifiers* check signatures publicly using pp and the declared G.

Signing Process. To sign a message $M \in \mathcal{M}$ with auxiliary witness $w \in \mathcal{W}$ supporting the computations of F and G, the signer computes

$$(\overline{M}, \mathsf{op}) = P\big(F(M, \mathsf{attr}, w),\ G(M, \mathsf{attr}, w)\big),$$

where P is the public combiner fixed in pp and $\overline{M} \in \overline{\mathcal{M}}$ is the derived message (equal to M when P returns the input message unchanged). If $\mathsf{op} \in \mathcal{OP}_{\mathsf{sgnbl}}$ the signer issues a signature Σ on $(\overline{M}, G)$, which also serves as a zero-knowledge proof of correct evaluation; if $\mathsf{op} \notin \mathcal{OP}_{\mathsf{sgnbl}}$ signing is blocked. The attribute attr and policy F remain hidden in Σ; only TA learns op via Open.

Definition 1 (SMS). *An SMS scheme is defined by the algorithms below.*

$\mathsf{Setup}(1^\lambda, N)$: *On input security parameter* 1^λ *and maximum user count* N, *run* $(\mathsf{vk}, \mathsf{mfk}) \leftarrow \mathcal{S}.\mathsf{KeyGen}(1^\lambda)$ *for* FA *and* $(\mathsf{ek}, \mathsf{tsk}) \leftarrow \mathcal{E}.\mathsf{KeyGen}(1^\lambda)$ *for* TA, *initialize* $\mathsf{State} := \emptyset$, *and publish the public parameter*

$$\mathsf{pp} = (\mathsf{gpk},\ \mathcal{M},\ \overline{\mathcal{M}},\ \mathcal{AS},\ \mathcal{W},\ \mathcal{F},\ \mathcal{G},\ P,\ \mathcal{OP},\ \mathcal{OP}_{\mathsf{sgnbl}}),$$

where gpk *incorporates* vk *and* ek, $\mathcal{M}$ *and* $\overline{\mathcal{M}}$ *are the input and derived message spaces,* $\mathcal{AS}$ *and* $\mathcal{W}$ *are the attribute and witness spaces,* $\mathcal{F}$ *and* $\mathcal{G}$ *are the hidden and ad hoc function families,* P *is the public combiner,* $\mathcal{OP}$ *is the set of all opening values, and* $\mathcal{OP}_{\mathsf{sgnbl}} \subsetneq \mathcal{OP}$ *is the signable subset. We write* $\mathsf{Setup}(1^\lambda)$ *for* $\mathsf{Setup}(1^\lambda, N)$ *when* N *is immaterial. Output* $(\mathsf{pp}, \mathsf{State}, \mathsf{mfk}, \mathsf{tsk})$. *The strict inclusion ensures that* $\mathcal{OP} \setminus \mathcal{OP}_{\mathsf{sgnbl}}$ *is non-empty, so the combiner* P *can block signing by outputting a value outside* $\mathcal{OP}_{\mathsf{sgnbl}}$, *encoding a policy rejection without producing a signature.*
The unified Setup *is retained here for notational convenience. In deployments where* FA *and* TA *are distinct,* Setup *can be split into two independent key generation algorithms:* $\mathsf{Setup}_{\mathsf{FA}}(1^\lambda)$ *outputting* $(\mathsf{vk}, \mathsf{mfk})$ *and* $\mathsf{Setup}_{\mathsf{TA}}(1^\lambda)$ *outputting* $(\mathsf{ek}, \mathsf{tsk})$, *with* pp *assembled from their public components, such that the two authority keys* mfk *and* tsk *are held by separate parties* FA *and* TA.

$\mathsf{Join}\langle \mathsf{U}(1^\lambda), \mathsf{FA}(\mathsf{mfk})\rangle(\mathsf{pp}, \mathsf{State}, \mathsf{attr}, F)$: FA *enrolls user* U *with attribute* $\mathsf{attr} \in \mathcal{AS}$ *and assigns function* $F \in \mathcal{F}$. *Upon successful completion:*

1. U *obtains* $(\mathsf{sec}_{\mathsf{attr}}, \mathsf{cert}_{\mathsf{attr}})$, *where* $\mathsf{sec}_{\mathsf{attr}}$ *is the user secret key and* $\mathsf{cert}_{\mathsf{attr}}$ *is a certificate binding* (attr, F);
2. FA *updates* $\mathsf{State}' := (\mathsf{State} \| (\mathsf{attr}, F, \mathsf{trans}))$, *where* trans *is the transcript. The updated state* State′ *replaces* State *in subsequent executions.*

If Join *fails,* U *receives* $\perp$, *and* State *is unchanged. By convention,* $\mathsf{cert}_{\mathsf{attr}}$ *encodes* (attr, F) *in the clear so that any party may read* (attr, F) *from* $\mathsf{cert}_{\mathsf{attr}}$; *the pair* (attr, F) *need only be concealed from signatures, not from certificates. We write* $\mathsf{sec}_{\mathsf{attr}} \leftrightharpoons_{\mathsf{pp}} \mathsf{cert}_{\mathsf{attr}}$ *to indicate that* $(\mathsf{sec}_{\mathsf{attr}}, \mathsf{cert}_{\mathsf{attr}})$ *was produced by an honest execution of* Join *under* pp, $\mathsf{sec}_{\mathsf{attr}} \not\leftrightharpoons_{\mathsf{pp}} \mathsf{cert}_{\mathsf{attr}}$ *otherwise.*

$\mathsf{Sign}(\mathsf{pp}, \mathsf{cert}_{\mathsf{attr}}, \mathsf{sec}_{\mathsf{attr}}, G, M, w)$: *Given* pp, *a certificate* $\mathsf{cert}_{\mathsf{attr}}$ *along with a secret* $\mathsf{sec}_{\mathsf{attr}}$, *a function* $G \in \mathcal{G}$, *a message* $M \in \mathcal{M}$, *and a witness* $w \in \mathcal{W}$, *output a derived message* $\overline{M} \in \overline{\mathcal{M}}$ *and a signature* Σ. *Return* $\perp$ *if it fails.*

$\mathsf{Verify}(\mathsf{pp}, G, \overline{M}, \Sigma)$: *Output* 1 *if* Σ *is a valid SMS signature on* $\overline{M} \in \overline{\mathcal{M}}$ *under function* $G \in \mathcal{G}$ *and parameters* pp; *output* 0 *otherwise.*

$\mathsf{Open}(\mathsf{pp}, \mathsf{tsk}, G, \overline{M}, \Sigma)$: *Using tracing key* tsk, *extract and return the opening value* $\mathsf{op} \in \mathcal{OP}$ *from a valid signature* Σ *on derived message* $\overline{M}$ *under function* G. *The information recoverable from* op *ranges from a role or partial identity to the full identity, depending on the configuration encoded in* P.

Illustration. A central bank issues digital currency (CBDC) to verified citizens. Each citizen's signing key encodes a certified hidden policy $F(M, \mathsf{attr}, w)$ that checks transaction validity against her know-your-customer compliance tier attr: whether the transaction amount is within her spending limit, the merchant category is permitted, and the note has not been spent before (via witness w). At each payment, the citizen additionally chooses a public function G encoding the transaction's public validity conditions, *e.g.*, that the amount is positive and the merchant is registered. The combiner P outputs the transaction record $\overline{M}$ and an opening tag op reflecting the transaction's risk level: routine payments yield $\mathsf{op} = \mathsf{pseudonym}$, exposing only a per-citizen unlinkable tag to the central bank; transactions flagged by F as anomalous yield $\mathsf{op} = \mathsf{id}$, exposing the citizen's full identity to the regulator. If F rejects the transaction outright, P outputs $\mathsf{op} \notin \mathcal{OP}_{\mathsf{sgnbl}}$, blocking the payment without producing a signature. The spending policy F remains hidden from merchants and the public; verifiers confirm only that G approved the transaction under some certified hidden policy.

2.2 Correctness and Security

The system maintains a public state State recording each enrolled user's attribute, assigned function, and enrollment transcript. State is *consistent* if every recorded transcript verifies under Join. A secure SMS scheme satisfies correctness, privacy, and unforgeability.

Correctness. Correctness requires that honest signatures verify and open correctly, that the system state remains consistent throughout, and that only enrolled users can produce valid signatures.

Definition 2 (Correctness). *For* $\mathsf{Setup}(1^\lambda)$ *returning* $(\mathsf{pp}, \mathsf{State}, \mathsf{mfk}, \mathsf{tsk})$, *an SMS scheme* $\mathcal{SMS}$ *is* correct *if the following conditions hold.*

1. $\mathcal{OP}_{\mathsf{sgnbl}} \subsetneq \mathcal{OP}$ *and all attributes in* State *are pairwise distinct.*
2. *If* $\mathsf{Join}\langle \mathsf{U}(1^\lambda), \mathsf{FA}(\mathsf{mfk})\rangle(\mathsf{pp}, \mathsf{State}, \mathsf{attr}, F)$ *is executed honestly, with transcript* trans*:* $\mathsf{cert}_{\mathsf{attr}} \leftrightharpoons_{\mathsf{pp}} \mathsf{sec}_{\mathsf{attr}}$*,* trans *is valid, with* $(\mathsf{attr}, F, \mathsf{trans})$ *inserted into* State.
3. *For* $(\mathsf{attr}, F, \cdot) \in \mathsf{State}$ *with* $\mathsf{cert}_{\mathsf{attr}} \leftrightharpoons_{\mathsf{pp}} \mathsf{sec}_{\mathsf{attr}}$*,* $G \in \mathcal{G}$*,* $M \in \mathcal{M}$*,* $w \in \mathcal{W}$*:*

$$\Pr\left[\begin{array}{l|l} b = 1 & (\overline{M}, \Sigma) \leftarrow \mathsf{Sign}(\mathsf{pp}, \mathsf{cert}_{\mathsf{attr}}, \mathsf{sec}_{\mathsf{attr}}, G, M, w), \\ \wedge\, \mathsf{op} \in \mathcal{OP}_{\mathsf{sgnbl}} & (M', \mathsf{op}) = P(F(M, \mathsf{attr}, w), G(M, \mathsf{attr}, w)), \\ \wedge\, \mathsf{op} = \mathsf{op}' & b := \mathsf{Verify}(\mathsf{pp}, G, \overline{M}, \Sigma), \\ \wedge\, \overline{M} = M' & \mathsf{op}' \leftarrow \mathsf{Open}(\mathsf{pp}, \mathsf{tsk}, G, \overline{M}, \Sigma) \end{array}\right] = 1. \tag{2}$$

Adversary model. The adversary $\mathcal{A}$ interacts with the system via oracles that model realistic attack capabilities, defined below, and the security properties are parameterized by which oracles $\mathcal{A}$ may access. We write $(\cdot)^{\mathsf{condition}}$ to denote that an oracle returns ϵ when $\mathsf{condition}$ holds.

Oracles OMfk, OTsk. OMfk returns mfk to $\mathcal{A}$ and sets flag amfk to True. OTsk returns tsk and sets flag atsk to True. Both flags are initialized to False.

Oracle OCU, set $\mathcal{L}_{\mathsf{cu}}$. On query (attr, F) with $(\mathsf{attr}, \cdot) \notin \mathcal{L}_{\mathsf{cu}}$, OCU acts as an honest FA, runs Join, sets $\mathcal{L}_{\mathsf{cu}} := \mathcal{L}_{\mathsf{cu}} \cup \{(\mathsf{attr}, F)\}$, updates State, and returns $(\mathsf{sec}_{\mathsf{attr}}, \mathsf{cert}_{\mathsf{attr}})$ to $\mathcal{A}$.

Oracle OHU, set $\mathcal{L}_{\mathsf{hu}}$. On query attr with $(\mathsf{attr},\cdot) \notin \mathcal{L}_{\mathsf{cu}}$, OHU acts as an honest FA, samples $F \in \mathcal{F}$, runs Join, and sets $\mathcal{L}_{\mathsf{hu}} := \mathcal{L}_{\mathsf{hu}} \cup \{(\mathsf{attr}, F)\}$ and updates State. The secrets of users in $\mathcal{L}_{\mathsf{hu}}$ are not given to $\mathcal{A}$. Both OCU and OHU guarantee that all attributes in State are distinct and $\mathcal{L}_{\mathsf{cu}} \cap \mathcal{L}_{\mathsf{hu}} = \emptyset$ on the attribute component.

Oracle OSign, set $\mathcal{L}_{\mathsf{sig}}$. On query (attr, G, M, w), if $\exists F$ such that $(\mathsf{attr}, F) \in \mathcal{L}_{\mathsf{hu}}$, $G \in \mathcal{G}$, $M \in \mathcal{M}$, $w \in \mathcal{W}$, and $\mathsf{op} \in \mathcal{OP}_{\mathsf{sgnbl}}$ where op is determined by P, F, G, M, attr, w, then OSign returns $(\overline{M}, \Sigma) \leftarrow \mathsf{Sign}(\mathsf{pp}, \mathsf{cert}_{\mathsf{attr}}, \mathsf{sec}_{\mathsf{attr}}, G, M, w)$ and inserts $(\mathsf{attr}, G, M, \Sigma)$ into $\mathcal{L}_{\mathsf{sig}}$.

Oracle OOpen. On query $(G, \overline{M}, \Sigma)$, return $\mathsf{op} \leftarrow \mathsf{Open}(\mathsf{pp}, \mathsf{tsk}, G, \overline{M}, \Sigma)$.

Privacy. Privacy guarantees that SMS signatures reveal no information about the signer's attribute attr or hidden policy F. $\mathcal{A}$ chooses G and two candidate signers, each with a valid certificate, secret, message, and witness, and attempts to identify which signer produced the challenge signature. Both candidate signers must use the same G, since G is public and a verifier could trivially distinguish signatures produced under different public functions.

$\mathcal{A}$ may access OCU, OHU, OMfk, and OSign, but not OTsk or OOpen: access to tsk trivially breaks privacy, and allowing OOpen access requires public-key encryption to be secure against chosen-ciphertext attacks, a conceptually straightforward extension (*e.g.*, [58]). To prevent trivial wins, both candidate signers must yield the same derived message $\overline{M}$ and a signable opening value.

Definition 3 (Privacy). *Let* $\mathsf{E}_{\mathcal{A}}^{\mathsf{priv}\text{-}b}(\lambda)$ *be defined as in Fig. 1.* $\mathcal{SMS}$ *is* private *if, for any probabilistic polynomial-time (PPT)* $\mathcal{A}$,

$$\left|\Pr\left[\mathsf{E}_{\mathcal{A}}^{\mathsf{priv}\text{-}0}(\lambda) = 1\right] - \Pr\left[\mathsf{E}_{\mathcal{A}}^{\mathsf{priv}\text{-}1}(\lambda) = 1\right]\right| \leq \mathsf{negl}(\lambda).$$

Unforgeability. Unforgeability prevents any PPT $\mathcal{A}$ from producing a valid SMS signature without a legitimate certificate–secret pair. It encompasses three nested properties, formalized jointly in $\mathsf{E}_{\mathcal{A}}^{\mathsf{unforge}}(\lambda)$ (Fig. 1).

- *Extractability.* Every valid forgery $(G, \overline{M}, \Sigma)$ must extract to a list of witnesses $(\mathsf{attr}', F', M', w')$ such that $\mathsf{op}' \in \mathcal{OP}_{\mathsf{sgnbl}}$, $\mathsf{op}' = \mathsf{op}$ as opened by Open, and $\widetilde{M} = \overline{M}$. No adversary can produce a signature whose extracted witness is inconsistent with its opening value or its derived message.
- *Type-1 unforgeability (traceability).* Extractability holds, and $\mathcal{A}$ cannot forge a signature whose extracted (attr', F') lies outside the corrupted set $\mathcal{L}_{\mathsf{cu}}$.
- *Type-2 unforgeability (non-frameability).* Extractability holds, and no coalition of users, FA, and TA can forge a signature whose extracted (attr', F') belongs to $\mathcal{L}_{\mathsf{hu}}$.

The two unforgeability types are independent, as the table below shows.

	Type-1 (Traceability)	Type-2 (Non-frameability)
Forgery target	$(\mathsf{attr}', F') \notin \mathcal{L}_{\mathsf{cu}}$	$(\mathsf{attr}', F') \in \mathcal{L}_{\mathsf{hu}}$
Covers	$\mathcal{L}_{\mathsf{hu}} \cup (\mathcal{AS} \setminus (\mathcal{L}_{\mathsf{cu}} \cup \mathcal{L}_{\mathsf{hu}}))$	$\mathcal{L}_{\mathsf{cu}} \cup (\mathcal{AS} \setminus (\mathcal{L}_{\mathsf{cu}} \cup \mathcal{L}_{\mathsf{hu}}))$
OMfk access	Restricted	Restricted

Neither type implies the other: Type-2 covers $\mathcal{L}_{\mathsf{cu}}$ but not $\mathcal{L}_{\mathsf{hu}}$; Type-1 covers $\mathcal{L}_{\mathsf{hu}}$ but not $\mathcal{L}_{\mathsf{cu}}$. A forgery is non-trivial only if $(G, \overline{M}, \Sigma)$ was not previously obtained via OSign, enforced by the $\mathcal{L}_{\mathsf{sig}}$ membership check in $\mathsf{E}^{\mathsf{unforge}}$.

Extractability permits OMfk access in $\mathsf{E}^{\mathsf{unforge}}$ because it only requires consistency of extracted components with the system prescription, independent of membership. Conversely, for Type-1 and Type-2 unforgeability, OMfk access is restricted, because possessing mfk would allow $\mathcal{A}$ to certify attributes outside both $\mathcal{L}_{\mathsf{cu}}$ and $\mathcal{L}_{\mathsf{hu}}$, trivially breaking the membership-based winning conditions; in particular, $\mathcal{A}$ could certify the same attribute as an honest user under a different hidden function (*e.g.*, $(\mathsf{attr}, F) \in \mathcal{L}_{\mathsf{hu}}$ but $(\mathsf{attr}, F') \notin \mathcal{L}_{\mathsf{hu}}$ where $F' \neq F$), producing a valid signature outside the honest-user record.

Simulated Setup for Extraction. We devise algorithms $\mathsf{SimSetup}$ and $\mathsf{Extract}$ to enable simulation-sound extractability [18]: a simulated setup indistinguishable from the real one, with a trapdoor for extracting the underlying witness.

Definition 4 (Simulated setup and extraction).

$\mathsf{SimSetup}(1^\lambda)$: *Identical to* Setup *but additionally outputs extraction trapdoor* τ_{ext}. *Output:* $(\mathsf{pp}, \mathsf{State}, \mathsf{mfk}, \mathsf{tsk}, \tau_{\mathsf{ext}})$.

$\mathsf{Extract}(\mathsf{pp}, \tau_{\mathsf{ext}}, G, \overline{M}, \Sigma)$: *Given* pp, *trapdoor* τ_{ext}, $G \in \mathcal{G}$, $\overline{M} \in \overline{\mathcal{M}}$, *and signature* Σ, *return* $(\mathsf{attr}, F, M, w) \in \mathcal{AS} \times \mathcal{F} \times \mathcal{M} \times \mathcal{W}$.

The correctness of SMS under $\mathsf{SimSetup}$ is defined identically to Definition 2 with Setup replaced by $\mathsf{SimSetup}$; additionally, the extracted components must match those used to create the signature. Setup indistinguishability implies this correctness against PPT adversaries, while correctness of the simulated setup holds unconditionally.

Definition 5 (Setup indistinguishability). $\mathcal{SMS}$ *satisfies* setup indistinguishability *if, for any PPT* $\mathcal{A}$,

$$\left|\Pr\left[\mathsf{E}_{\mathcal{A}}^{\mathsf{real}}(\lambda) = 1\right] - \Pr\left[\mathsf{E}_{\mathcal{A}}^{\mathsf{sim}}(\lambda) = 1\right]\right| \leq \mathsf{negl}(\lambda),$$

where $\mathsf{E}_{\mathcal{A}}^{\mathsf{real}}(\lambda)$ *and* $\mathsf{E}_{\mathcal{A}}^{\mathsf{sim}}(\lambda)$ *are defined in Fig. 1.*

Definition 6 (Unforgeability). $\mathcal{SMS}$ *is* unforgeable *if, for any PPT* $\mathcal{A}$,

$$\Pr\left[\mathsf{E}_{\mathcal{A}}^{\mathsf{unforge}}(\lambda) = 1\right] \leq \mathsf{negl}(\lambda),$$

where $\mathsf{E}_{\mathcal{A}}^{\mathsf{unforge}}(\lambda)$ *is defined in Fig. 1.*

Experiment $\mathsf{E}^{\mathsf{priv}\text{-}b}_{\mathcal{A}}(\lambda)$**:**
$(\mathsf{pp}, \mathsf{State}, \mathsf{mfk}, \mathsf{tsk}) \leftarrow \mathsf{Setup}(1^\lambda)$.
$\mathsf{amfk} := \mathrm{False}$, $\mathcal{L}_{\mathsf{cu}} := \emptyset$, $\mathcal{L}_{\mathsf{hu}} := \emptyset$, $\mathcal{L}_{\mathsf{sig}} := \emptyset$.
$(\mathsf{aux}, G, (\mathsf{cert}_{\mathsf{attr}_i}, \mathsf{sec}_{\mathsf{attr}_i}, M_i, w_i)_{i\in\{0,1\}}) \leftarrow \mathcal{A}^{\mathsf{OCU},\mathsf{OHU},\mathsf{OMfk},\mathsf{OSign}}(\mathsf{pp})$.
Obtain (attr_i, F_i) from $\mathsf{cert}_{\mathsf{attr}_i}$ for $i \in \{0,1\}$.
If $G \notin \mathcal{G}$ or $(\exists i \in \{0,1\}\colon M_i \notin \mathcal{M} \vee \mathsf{attr}_i \notin \mathcal{AS} \vee F_i \notin \mathcal{F} \vee \mathsf{sec}_{\mathsf{attr}_i} \not\leftrightarrow_{\mathsf{pp}} \mathsf{cert}_{\mathsf{attr}_i})$, return 0.
$(\overline{M}_i, \mathsf{op}_i) := P(F_i(M_i, \mathsf{attr}_i, w_i), G(M_i, \mathsf{attr}_i, w_i))$ for $i \in \{0,1\}$.
If $\overline{M}_0 \neq \overline{M}_1 \vee \mathsf{op}_0 \notin \mathcal{OP}_{\mathsf{sgnbl}} \vee \mathsf{op}_1 \notin \mathcal{OP}_{\mathsf{sgnbl}}$, return 0.
Set $(\overline{M}, \Sigma) \leftarrow \mathsf{Sign}(\mathsf{pp}, \mathsf{cert}_{\mathsf{attr}_b}, \mathsf{sec}_{\mathsf{attr}_b}, G, M_b, w_b)$.
$b' \leftarrow \mathcal{A}^{\mathsf{OCU},\mathsf{OHU},\mathsf{OMfk},\mathsf{OSign}}(\mathsf{pp}, \overline{M}, \Sigma, \mathsf{aux})$.
Return b'.

Experiment $\mathsf{E}^{\mathsf{real}}_{\mathcal{A}}(\lambda)$**:**
$(\mathsf{pp}, \mathsf{State}, \mathsf{mfk}, \mathsf{tsk}) \leftarrow \mathsf{Setup}(1^\lambda)$.
$\mathsf{amfk} := \mathrm{False}$, $\mathsf{atsk} := \mathrm{False}$, $\mathcal{L}_{\mathsf{cu}} := \emptyset$, $\mathcal{L}_{\mathsf{hu}} := \emptyset$, $\mathcal{L}_{\mathsf{sig}} := \emptyset$.
$b \leftarrow \mathcal{A}^{\mathsf{OCU},\mathsf{OHU},\mathsf{OMfk},\mathsf{OTsk},\mathsf{OSign},\mathsf{OOpen}}(\mathsf{pp})$.
Return b.

Experiment $\mathsf{E}^{\mathsf{sim}}_{\mathcal{A}}(\lambda)$**:**
$(\mathsf{pp}, \mathsf{State}, \mathsf{mfk}, \mathsf{tsk}, \tau_{\mathsf{ext}}) \leftarrow \mathsf{SimSetup}(1^\lambda)$. //Change $\mathsf{Setup}(1^\lambda)$ in $\mathsf{E}^{\mathsf{real}}_{\mathcal{A}}(\lambda)$ to $\mathsf{SimSetup}(1^\lambda)$
$\mathsf{amfk} := \mathrm{False}$, $\mathsf{atsk} := \mathrm{False}$, $\mathcal{L}_{\mathsf{cu}} := \emptyset$, $\mathcal{L}_{\mathsf{hu}} := \emptyset$, $\mathcal{L}_{\mathsf{sig}} := \emptyset$.
$b \leftarrow \mathcal{A}^{\mathsf{OCU},\mathsf{OHU},\mathsf{OMfk},\mathsf{OTsk},\mathsf{OSign},\mathsf{OOpen}}(\mathsf{pp})$.
Return b.

Experiment $\mathsf{E}^{\mathsf{unforge}}_{\mathcal{A}}(\lambda)$**:**
$(\mathsf{pp}, \mathsf{State}, \mathsf{mfk}, \mathsf{tsk}, \tau_{\mathsf{ext}}) \leftarrow \mathsf{SimSetup}(1^\lambda)$.
$\mathsf{amfk} := \mathrm{False}$, $\mathsf{atsk} := \mathrm{False}$, $\mathcal{L}_{\mathsf{cu}} := \emptyset$, $\mathcal{L}_{\mathsf{hu}} := \emptyset$, $\mathcal{L}_{\mathsf{sig}} := \emptyset$.
$(G, \overline{M}, \Sigma) \leftarrow \mathcal{A}^{\mathsf{OCU},\mathsf{OHU},\mathsf{OMfk},\mathsf{OTsk},\mathsf{OSign},\mathsf{OOpen}}(\mathsf{pp})$.
If $G \notin \mathcal{G} \vee \overline{M} \notin \overline{\mathcal{M}} \vee \mathsf{Verify}(\mathsf{pp}, G, \overline{M}, \Sigma) = 0$, return 0.
$(\mathsf{attr}', F', M', w') \leftarrow \mathsf{Extract}(\mathsf{pp}, \tau_{\mathsf{ext}}, G, \overline{M}, \Sigma)$.
If $\mathsf{attr}' \notin \mathcal{AS} \vee F' \notin \mathcal{F} \vee M' \notin \mathcal{M} \vee w' \notin \mathcal{W} \vee (\mathsf{attr}', G, M', \Sigma) \in \mathcal{L}_{\mathsf{sig}}$, return 0.
$\mathsf{op} \leftarrow \mathsf{Open}(\mathsf{pp}, \mathsf{tsk}, G, \overline{M}, \Sigma)$.
$(\widetilde{M}, \mathsf{op}') := P(F'(M', \mathsf{attr}', w'), G(M', \mathsf{attr}', w'))$.
Return 1 if (3) holds; otherwise return 0.

$$
\begin{aligned}
&(\mathsf{op}' \notin \mathcal{OP}_{\mathsf{sgnbl}} \vee \mathsf{op} \neq \mathsf{op}' \vee \overline{M} \neq \widetilde{M}) && \text{//extractability} \\
&\vee (\mathsf{amfk} = \mathrm{False} \wedge (\mathsf{attr}', F') \notin \mathcal{L}_{\mathsf{cu}}) && \text{//type-1 unforgeability} \\
&\vee (\mathsf{amfk} = \mathrm{False} \wedge (\mathsf{attr}', F') \in \mathcal{L}_{\mathsf{hu}}) && \text{//type-2 unforgeability}
\end{aligned} \tag{3}
$$

Fig. 1. Experiments for security of SMS

3 Generic Construction of SMS

With the SMS notion established, we build a generic scheme from standard primitives, treating the hidden-circuit NIZKAoK as an abstract component instantiated in Sect. 4. Following Nguyen *et al.* [58], each enrolled user holds an FA-issued certificate $\mathsf{cert}_{\mathsf{attr}} = (\mathsf{attr}, F, \mathsf{vk}_{\mathsf{attr}}, \sigma)$ binding their attribute, hidden policy, and a per-user verification key, where $\sigma \leftarrow \mathcal{S}.\mathsf{Sign}(\mathsf{mfk}, (\mathsf{attr}, F, \mathsf{vk}_{\mathsf{attr}}))$ and the global verification key vk is embedded in gpk.

At signing, the user encrypts the opening tag op under TA's public key ek, producing a ciphertext $\mathsf{ct}_{\mathsf{op}}$ that TA can later decrypt to recover op. A NIZKAoK proof $\Pi_{\mathsf{g\text{-}SMS}}$ certifies correct evaluation of $P(F(\cdot), G(\cdot))$, validity of the membership certificate, and correct encryption of op, without revealing attr, F, or any intermediate computation trace. How the NIZKAoK handles the hidden evaluation of F via PLONK's arithmetization is developed in Sect. 4; here, we treat the NIZKAoK as an abstract component for arithmetic circuit satisfiability. In the SMS instance for the CBDC example, F checks the spending limit, G validates the merchant, and P sets op to the pseudonym or identity tag.

Without further binding, an adversary could modify $(\mathsf{ct}_{\mathsf{op}}, \Pi_{\mathsf{g\text{-}SMS}})$ to produce a new valid SMS signature. The user generates a one-time key pair $(\mathsf{ovk}, \mathsf{osk})$ at the time of signing, certifies ovk under $\mathsf{sk}_{\mathsf{attr}}$, and computes a one-time signature $\sigma_{\mathsf{one\text{-}time}}$ over all signature components. The NIZKAoK then proves validity of $\sigma_{\mathsf{one\text{-}time}}$ under $\mathsf{vk}_{\mathsf{attr}}$ rather than proving the secret key $\mathsf{sk}_{\mathsf{attr}}$ directly, binding all components together against post hoc modification.

3.1 Construction

Suppose $\mathcal{S} = (\mathcal{S}.\mathsf{KeyGen}, \mathcal{S}.\mathsf{Sign}, \mathcal{S}.\mathsf{Verify})$ is a secure signature scheme, $\mathcal{OTS} = (\mathcal{OTS}.\mathsf{KeyGen}, \mathcal{OTS}.\mathsf{Sign}, \mathcal{OTS}.\mathsf{Verify})$ is a strongly unforgeable one-time signature scheme, $\mathcal{E} = (\mathcal{E}.\mathsf{KeyGen}, \mathcal{E}.\mathsf{Enc}, \mathcal{E}.\mathsf{Dec})$ is a CPA-secure PKE scheme with randomness space $\mathsf{R}_{\mathsf{encrypt}}$. We also use a NIZKAoK system $\mathcal{NIZKAoK}$ for arithmetic circuit satisfiability. The message space $\mathcal{M}$, derived message space $\overline{\mathcal{M}} = \mathbb{F}_{\mathsf{msg}}^{\ell}$, attribute space $\mathcal{AS}$, witness space $\mathcal{W}$, function families $\mathcal{F}$ and $\mathcal{G}$, combiner P, opening set $\mathcal{OP}$, and signable subset $\mathcal{OP}_{\mathsf{sgnbl}} \subsetneq \mathcal{OP}$ are determined as part of Setup.

All computations are over $\mathbb{F}$ (instantiated as $\mathbb{Z}_q$ for a prime q). Each $F \in \mathcal{F}$ and $G \in \mathcal{G}$ share output length n_{out}, so the combiner has type $P\colon \mathbb{F}^{2n_{\mathsf{out}}} \to \overline{\mathcal{M}} \times \mathcal{OP}$. The witness decomposes as $\mathbf{w} = (\mathbf{w}_F \| \mathbf{w}_G)$, where $\mathbf{w}_F$ and $\mathbf{w}_G$ support the computations of F and G, respectively.

$\mathsf{Setup}(1^\lambda, N) \to (\mathsf{pp}, \mathsf{State}, \mathsf{mfk}, \mathsf{tsk})$: Sample $(\mathsf{ek}, \mathsf{dk}) \leftarrow \mathcal{E}.\mathsf{KeyGen}(1^\lambda)$ for TA, $(\mathsf{vk}, \mathsf{sk}) \leftarrow \mathcal{S}.\mathsf{KeyGen}(1^\lambda)$ for FA, and lastly $\mathsf{pp}_{\mathsf{nizk}}$ as the public parameter of $\mathcal{NIZKAoK}$. Set $\mathsf{gpk} := (\mathsf{ek}, \mathsf{vk}, \mathsf{pp}_{\mathsf{nizk}})$, $\mathsf{mfk} := \mathsf{sk}$, $\mathsf{tsk} := \mathsf{dk}$, and $\mathsf{State} := \emptyset$. Determine $\mathcal{M}$, $\overline{\mathcal{M}}$, $\mathcal{AS}$, $\mathcal{W}$, $\mathcal{F}$, $\mathcal{G}$, P, $\mathcal{OP}$, $\mathcal{OP}_{\mathsf{sgnbl}}$. Return

$$\mathsf{pp} := (\mathsf{gpk}, \mathcal{M}, \overline{\mathcal{M}}, \mathcal{AS}, \mathcal{W}, \mathcal{F}, \mathcal{G}, P, \mathcal{OP}, \mathcal{OP}_{\mathsf{sgnbl}}),\ \mathsf{State},\ \mathsf{mfk},\ \mathsf{tsk}.$$

$\mathsf{Join}\langle \mathsf{U}(1^\lambda), \mathsf{FA}(\mathsf{mfk})\rangle(\mathsf{pp}, \mathsf{State}, \mathsf{attr}, F) \to (\mathsf{State}', (\mathsf{cert}_{\mathsf{attr}}, \mathsf{sec}_{\mathsf{attr}}))$: For user enrollment, user U and function-issuing authority FA proceed as follows.

1. U computes $\sigma_{\mathsf{enrl}} \leftarrow \mathcal{S}.\mathsf{Sign}(\mathsf{sk}_{\mathsf{attr}}, (\mathsf{attr}, F, \mathsf{vk}_{\mathsf{attr}}))$, where $(\mathsf{vk}_{\mathsf{attr}}, \mathsf{sk}_{\mathsf{attr}}) \leftarrow \mathcal{S}.\mathsf{KeyGen}(1^\lambda)$, and sends $(\mathsf{vk}_{\mathsf{attr}}, \sigma_{\mathsf{enrl}})$ to FA.

2. FA aborts if $\mathcal{S}.\mathsf{Verify}(\mathsf{vk_{attr}}, (\mathsf{attr}, F, \mathsf{vk_{attr}}), \sigma_{\mathsf{enrl}}) = 0$ or attr is already in State. Otherwise, FA computes $\sigma \leftarrow \mathcal{S}.\mathsf{Sign}(\mathsf{mfk}, (\mathsf{attr}, F, \mathsf{vk_{attr}}))$, sends σ to U, and updates $\mathsf{State}' := (\mathsf{State} \| (\mathsf{attr}, F, \mathsf{trans} := (\mathsf{vk_{attr}}, \sigma_{\mathsf{enrl}}, \sigma)))$. The updated state State$'$ replaces State in subsequent executions.
3. U proceeds if $\mathcal{S}.\mathsf{Verify}(\mathsf{vk}, (\mathsf{attr}, F, \mathsf{vk_{attr}}), \sigma) = 1$. Otherwise, U aborts.
4. U sets $\mathsf{cert_{attr}} := (\mathsf{attr}, F, \mathsf{vk_{attr}}, \sigma)$ and $\mathsf{sec_{attr}} := \mathsf{sk_{attr}}$.

$\mathsf{Sign}(\mathsf{pp}, \mathsf{cert_{attr}}, \mathsf{sec_{attr}}, G, M, w) \rightarrow (\overline{M}, \Sigma)$**:** To sign a message M,

1. Parse $\mathsf{gpk} = (\mathsf{ek}, \mathsf{vk}, \mathsf{pp_{nizk}})$, $\mathsf{cert_{attr}} = (\mathsf{attr}, F, \mathsf{vk_{attr}}, \sigma)$, $\mathsf{sec_{attr}} = \mathsf{sk_{attr}}$.
2. Compute $(\overline{M}, \mathsf{op}) := P(F(M, \mathsf{attr}, w), G(M, \mathsf{attr}, w))$.
3. Abort if $\mathsf{op} \notin \mathcal{OP}_{\mathsf{sgnbl}}$. Set $\mathsf{ct_{op}} := \mathcal{E}.\mathsf{Enc}(\mathsf{ek}, \mathsf{op}; r_{\mathsf{op}})$ with $r_{\mathsf{op}} \leftarrow \mathsf{R_{encrypt}}$.
4. Generate $(\mathsf{ovk}, \mathsf{osk}) \leftarrow \mathcal{OTS}.\mathsf{KeyGen}(1^\lambda)$ and $\sigma_{\mathsf{ovk}} \leftarrow \mathcal{S}.\mathsf{Sign}(\mathsf{sk_{attr}}, \mathsf{ovk})$.
5. Execute the prover of $\mathcal{NIZKAoK}$ to generate $\Pi_{\textsf{g-SMS}}$, for $\mathrm{R}_{\textsf{g-SMS}}$ (as in (4)) with the statement $(\mathsf{pp}, G, \overline{M}, \mathsf{ct_{op}}, \mathsf{ovk})$ and witness $(\mathsf{attr}, \mathsf{vk_{attr}}, F, \sigma, M, w, \mathsf{op}, r_{\mathsf{op}}, \sigma_{\mathsf{ovk}})$.
6. Compute $\sigma_{\textsf{one-time}} \leftarrow \mathcal{OTS}.\mathsf{Sign}(\mathsf{osk}, (G, \overline{M}, \mathsf{ct_{op}}, \Pi_{\textsf{g-SMS}}))$.
7. Return $(\overline{M}, \ \Sigma_{\textsf{g-SMS}}) = (\overline{M}, \ (\mathsf{ct_{op}}, \Pi_{\textsf{g-SMS}}, \mathsf{ovk}, \sigma_{\textsf{one-time}}))$.

The relation $\mathrm{R}_{\textsf{g-SMS}}$ certified by $\Pi_{\textsf{g-SMS}}$ is:

$$(\mathsf{pp}, G, \overline{M}, \mathsf{ct_{op}}, \mathsf{ovk};\ \mathsf{attr}, \mathsf{vk_{attr}}, F, \sigma, M, w, \mathsf{op}, r_{\mathsf{op}}, \sigma_{\mathsf{ovk}}) \in \mathrm{R}_{\textsf{g-SMS}} \tag{4}$$

$$\iff \begin{cases} \mathcal{S}.\mathsf{Verify}(\mathsf{vk}, (\mathsf{attr}, F, \mathsf{vk_{attr}}), \sigma) = 1, \\ (\overline{M}, \mathsf{op}) = P(F(M, \mathsf{attr}, w), G(M, \mathsf{attr}, w)) \ \wedge \ \mathsf{op} \in \mathcal{OP}_{\mathsf{sgnbl}}, \\ \mathsf{ct_{op}} = \mathcal{E}.\mathsf{Enc}(\mathsf{ek}, \mathsf{op};\ r_{\mathsf{op}}) \ \wedge \ \mathcal{S}.\mathsf{Verify}(\mathsf{vk_{attr}}, \mathsf{ovk}, \sigma_{\mathsf{ovk}}) = 1. \end{cases}$$

The relation captures three obligations simultaneously: the signer holds a valid FA-issued certificate over (attr, F); the combiner evaluation is correct and the resulting tag is signable; and op is honestly encrypted for TA under ek.

$\mathsf{Verify}(\mathsf{pp}, G, \overline{M}, \Sigma_{\textsf{g-SMS}}) \rightarrow \{0, 1\}$**:** To verify $\Sigma_{\textsf{g-SMS}}$:

1. Parse $\mathsf{gpk} = (\mathsf{ek}, \mathsf{vk}, \mathsf{pp_{nizk}})$ and $\Sigma_{\textsf{g-SMS}} = (\mathsf{ct_{op}}, \Pi_{\textsf{g-SMS}}, \mathsf{ovk}, \sigma_{\textsf{one-time}})$.
2. Return 1 if and only if $\mathcal{OTS}.\mathsf{Verify}(\mathsf{ovk}, (G, \overline{M}, \mathsf{ct_{op}}, \Pi_{\textsf{g-SMS}}), \sigma_{\textsf{one-time}}) = 1$ and $\Pi_{\textsf{g-SMS}}$ is valid for $\mathrm{R}_{\textsf{g-SMS}}$ with public parameter $\mathsf{pp_{nizk}}$ and statement $(\mathsf{pp}, G, \overline{M}, \mathsf{ct_{op}}, \mathsf{ovk})$.

$\mathsf{Open}(\mathsf{pp}, \mathsf{tsk}, G, \overline{M}, \Sigma_{\textsf{g-SMS}}) \rightarrow \mathcal{OP}$**:** Parse $\Sigma_{\textsf{g-SMS}} = (\mathsf{ct_{op}}, \Pi_{\textsf{g-SMS}}, \mathsf{ovk}, \sigma_{\textsf{one-time}})$ and $\mathsf{tsk} = \mathsf{dk}$. Return $\mathsf{op}' := \mathcal{E}.\mathsf{Dec}(\mathsf{dk}, \mathsf{ct_{op}})$.

3.2 Analysis

Theorem 1 (Security). *$\mathcal{SMS}_{\mathsf{generic}}$ satisfies correctness, privacy, setup indistinguishability, and unforgeability (Definitions 2, 3, 5, and 6), assuming that $\mathcal{NIZKAoK}$ is a simulation-sound extractable argument of knowledge, $\mathcal{S}$ is existentially unforgeable, $\mathcal{OTS}$ is strongly unforgeable, and $\mathcal{E}$ is CPA-secure.*

Proof (Sketch). Correctness follows directly from the correctness of the underlying primitives. We order the properties by logical dependency.

Privacy. The only signature-dependent information visible to the adversary is $\mathsf{ct}_{\mathsf{op}}$ and $\Pi_{\mathsf{g\text{-}SMS}}$. Since the two candidate signers produce the same $\overline{M}$ (enforced by the privacy experiment), the only differing public component is the ciphertext $\mathsf{ct}_{\mathsf{op}}$; CPA security of $\mathcal{E}$ ensures $\mathsf{ct}_{\mathsf{op}}$ is indistinguishable. The zero-knowledge property of the $\mathcal{NIZKA}o\mathcal{K}$ ensures $\Pi_{\mathsf{g\text{-}SMS}}$ reveals no information about the witness, including attr, F, and the computation trace. Together, the two components are jointly indistinguishable across the two signers.

Setup Indistinguishability. $\mathsf{SimSetup}$ is identical to Setup except that it additionally generates an extraction trapdoor τ_{ext} (deferred to the full version). All other components, namely, $\mathcal{S}$, $\mathcal{OTS}$, $\mathcal{E}$, are executed identically in the real and simulated setups. Setup indistinguishability follows from the simulation indistinguishability of $\mathcal{NIZKA}o\mathcal{K}$: any adversary distinguishing the two setups yields a distinguisher for $\mathcal{NIZKA}o\mathcal{K}$'s simulation indistinguishability.

Extractability. Given a valid forgery $(G, \overline{M}, \Sigma_{\mathsf{g\text{-}SMS}})$, $\mathsf{Extract}$ runs $\mathcal{NIZKA}o\mathcal{K}$'s extractor on $\Pi_{\mathsf{g\text{-}SMS}}$ using trapdoor τ_{ext} to recover $(\mathsf{attr}', F', M', w', \mathsf{op}', r'_{\mathsf{op}}, \sigma'_{\mathsf{ovk}})$. The simulation-sound extractability [18] guarantees that the extracted witness satisfies $\mathrm{R}_{\mathsf{g\text{-}SMS}}$, so $\mathsf{op}' \in \mathcal{OP}_{\mathsf{sgnbl}}$, $\mathsf{op}' = \mathsf{op}$, and $\widetilde{M} = \overline{M}$ hold.

Type-1 Unforgeability (Traceability). Suppose $\mathcal{A}$ forges a signature with extracted $(\mathsf{attr}', F') \notin \mathcal{L}_{\mathsf{cu}}$. By extractability, the extracted σ' verifies, meaning $\mathcal{S}.\mathsf{Verify}(\mathsf{vk}, (\mathsf{attr}', F', \mathsf{vk}'_{\mathsf{attr}}), \sigma') = 1$. Since (attr', F') was never enrolled by FA (not in $\mathcal{L}_{\mathsf{cu}}$), no honest Join execution produced σ', and $\mathcal{A}$ did not receive mfk (as OMfk is restricted). This yields a forgery against $\mathcal{S}$ under verification key vk.

Type-2 Unforgeability (Non-frameability). Suppose $\mathcal{A}$ forges a signature with extracted $(\mathsf{attr}', F') \in \mathcal{L}_{\mathsf{hu}}$. By extractability, $\mathcal{S}.\mathsf{Verify}(\mathsf{vk}'_{\mathsf{attr}}, \mathsf{ovk}', \sigma'_{\mathsf{ovk}}) = 1$, where $\mathsf{vk}'_{\mathsf{attr}}$ is the honest user's verification key recorded in State. The one-time signature $\sigma_{\mathsf{one\text{-}time}}$ on $(G, \overline{M}, \mathsf{ct}_{\mathsf{op}}, \Pi_{\mathsf{g\text{-}SMS}})$ verifies under ovk', which was never signed by the honest user's $\mathsf{sk}'_{\mathsf{attr}}$ (since the forgery is fresh relative to $\mathcal{L}_{\mathsf{sig}}$). This yields a forgery against the existential unforgeability of $\mathcal{S}$ under $\mathsf{vk}'_{\mathsf{attr}}$, the honest user's per-user verification key.

The role of $\mathcal{OTS}$ is distinct: strong unforgeability of $\mathcal{OTS}$ prevents an adversary from taking a legitimately obtained signature $(\mathsf{ct}_{\mathsf{op}}, \Pi_{\mathsf{g\text{-}SMS}}, \mathsf{ovk}, \sigma_{\mathsf{one\text{-}time}})$ and modifying any component to produce a new valid signature, since $\sigma_{\mathsf{one\text{-}time}}$ binds all components under ovk, which is itself certified under $\mathsf{vk}_{\mathsf{attr}}$.

Details (*e.g.*, $\mathsf{SimSetup}$ and $\mathsf{Extract}$) are deferred to the full version. □

4 Proving Hidden Function Evaluations via PLONK

The key observation is that PLONKish arithmetization encodes any arithmetic circuit C via a description vector pd of length linear in the gate count of C, and crucially, this encoding has the same algebraic structure for any two circuits of the same gate count, independent of circuit topology. Treating pd as part of the *witness* rather than the statement therefore reduces hidden-circuit satisfiability to verifying a single fixed public circuit of the same linear size, without universal circuits and without non-standard assumptions.

Section 4.1 introduces the PLONK constraint system and reduces it to a purely quadratic form compatible with standard NIZKAoK proof systems. Section 4.2 applies this framework to the SMS evaluation structure, merging the hidden-circuit proof for F with the public-circuit proofs for G and P into a single merged circuit $\mathsf{C}_{\mathsf{merge}}$. Throughout this section, let C be an arithmetic circuit over $\mathbb{F}$ with n_{in} inputs, n_{gate} gates, and $n_{\mathsf{w}} := n_{\mathsf{in}} + 3n_{\mathsf{gate}}$.

In the CBDC example, $\mathsf{C}_{\mathsf{merge}}$ coalesces F's limit checks, G's merchant validation, and P's risk scoring into a single verifiable statement.

4.1 Transforming PLONK's Constraints to Quadratic Constraints

PLONK's Constraint System. PLONK's arithmetization [34] encodes C via selectors $\{s_i^{\mathsf{lf}}, s_i^{\mathsf{rg}}, s_i^{\mathsf{mlt}}, s_i^{\mathsf{cnst}}\}_{i=1}^{n_{\mathsf{gate}}}$ and a permutation $\varphi\colon [n_{\mathsf{w}}] \to [n_{\mathsf{w}}]$ encoding wire-sharing. Let $\ell_{\mathsf{plonk}} := 4n_{\mathsf{gate}} + n_{\mathsf{w}}$. Following the formulation of Tang, Pham, and Ngo [64], these are collected into the *PLONK description*:

$$\mathsf{pd} = \left((s_i^{\mathsf{lf}})_{i=1}^{n_{\mathsf{gate}}} \parallel (s_i^{\mathsf{rg}})_{i=1}^{n_{\mathsf{gate}}} \parallel (s_i^{\mathsf{mlt}})_{i=1}^{n_{\mathsf{gate}}} \parallel (s_i^{\mathsf{cnst}})_{i=1}^{n_{\mathsf{gate}}} \parallel (\varphi(i))_{i=1}^{n_{\mathsf{w}}}\right) \in \mathbb{F}^{\ell_{\mathsf{plonk}}}. \tag{5}$$

This vector fully encodes the circuit's gate structure and wiring.

For any input $\mathbf{x} \in \mathbb{F}_{\mathsf{in}}^{n}$, evaluating C yields gate-value sequences $\mathbf{a} = (a_i)_{i=1}^{n_{\mathsf{gate}}}$, $\mathbf{b} = (b_i)_{i=1}^{n_{\mathsf{gate}}}$, $\mathbf{c} = (c_i)_{i=1}^{n_{\mathsf{gate}}}$, and output $\mathbf{c}_{\mathsf{out}} = (c_i)_{i=n_{\mathsf{gate}}-n_{\mathsf{out}}+1}^{n_{\mathsf{gate}}}$ for some $n_{\mathsf{out}} \leq n_{\mathsf{gate}}$. The *extended witness* is:

$$\widetilde{\mathbf{w}} = (\mathbf{x} \parallel \mathbf{a} \parallel \mathbf{b} \parallel \mathbf{c}) = (w_i)_{i=1}^{n_{\mathsf{w}}} \in \mathbb{F}^{n_{\mathsf{w}}}. \tag{6}$$

Together with pd, $\widetilde{\mathbf{w}}$ carries all information needed to verify C's evaluation.

For random challenges $\alpha, \beta \in \mathbb{F}$, the output $\mathbf{c}_{\mathsf{out}}$ is correct if and only if:

$$\begin{cases} s_i^{\mathsf{lf}} \cdot w_{n_{\mathsf{in}}+i} + s_i^{\mathsf{rg}} \cdot w_{n_{\mathsf{in}}+n_{\mathsf{gate}}+i} & \\ \quad + s_i^{\mathsf{mlt}} \cdot (w_{n_{\mathsf{in}}+i} \cdot w_{n_{\mathsf{in}}+n_{\mathsf{gate}}+i}) & \forall i \in [n_{\mathsf{gate}}], \\ \quad + s_i^{\mathsf{cnst}} - w_{n_{\mathsf{in}}+2n_{\mathsf{gate}}+i} = 0 & \\ \prod_{i=1}^{n_{\mathsf{w}}} (\alpha + \beta \cdot i + w_i) = \prod_{i=1}^{n_{\mathsf{w}}} (\alpha + \beta \cdot \varphi(i) + w_i), \quad \alpha, \beta \xleftarrow{\$} \mathbb{F}. & \end{cases} \tag{7}$$

The first equation encodes gate constraints; the second encodes wire consistency via a grand product check. This system can be viewed as a circuit $\mathcal{U}^{\mathsf{plonk}}$ taking $(\mathsf{pd}, \widetilde{\mathbf{w}}, \alpha, \beta)$ as inputs and verifying whether $\mathsf{C}(\mathbf{x}) = \mathbf{c}_{\mathsf{out}}$. The soundness error is at most $n_{\mathsf{w}}/|\mathbb{F}|$.

Reduction to Quadratic Constraints. The gate constraint in (7) contains the cubic term $s_i^{\mathsf{mlt}} \cdot (w_{n_{\mathsf{in}}+i} \cdot w_{n_{\mathsf{in}}+n_{\mathsf{gate}}+i})$. To reduce to purely quadratic constraints, introduce auxiliary variables: $\widehat{w}_i := w_{n_{\mathsf{in}}+i} \cdot w_{n_{\mathsf{in}}+n_{\mathsf{gate}}+i}$ for each $i \in [n_{\mathsf{gate}}]$. For the grand product, define running products:

$$\widetilde{w}_1 := \alpha + \beta + w_1, \qquad w'_1 := \alpha + \beta \cdot \varphi(1) + w_1,$$
$$\widetilde{w}_i := \widetilde{w}_{i-1} \cdot (\alpha + \beta \cdot i + w_i) \qquad w'_i := w'_{i-1} \cdot (\alpha + \beta \cdot \varphi(i) + w_i)$$

for all $i \in [2, n_{\mathsf{w}}]$. The grand product holds if and only if $\widetilde{w}_{n_{\mathsf{w}}} = w'_{n_{\mathsf{w}}}$. System (7) is therefore equivalent to the following purely quadratic system:

$$\begin{cases} \widehat{w}_i - w_{n_{\mathsf{in}}+i} \cdot w_{n_{\mathsf{in}}+n_{\mathsf{gate}}+i} = 0 & \forall i \in [n_{\mathsf{gate}}], \\ s_i^{\mathsf{lf}} \cdot w_{n_{\mathsf{in}}+i} + s_i^{\mathsf{rg}} \cdot w_{n_{\mathsf{in}}+n_{\mathsf{gate}}+i} + s_i^{\mathsf{mlt}} \cdot \widehat{w}_i + s_i^{\mathsf{cnst}} - w_{n_{\mathsf{in}}+2n_{\mathsf{gate}}+i} = 0 & \forall i \in [n_{\mathsf{gate}}], \\ \alpha + \beta + w_1 - \widetilde{w}_1 = 0, \alpha + \beta \cdot \varphi(1) + w_1 - w'_1 = 0, \widetilde{w}_{n_{\mathsf{w}}} = w'_{n_{\mathsf{w}}}, & \\ \widetilde{w}_{i-1} \cdot (\alpha + \beta \cdot i + w_i) - \widetilde{w}_i = 0 & \forall i \in [2, n_{\mathsf{w}}], \\ w'_{i-1} \cdot (\alpha + \beta \cdot \varphi(i) + w_i) - w'_i = 0 & \forall i \in [2, n_{\mathsf{w}}]. \end{cases} \tag{8}$$

System (8) has the same structure for any arithmetic circuit of the same gate count, independent of the specific circuit. This uniformity is what enables hidden-circuit satisfiability proofs: the constraints do not expose the circuit's topology.

All witnesses supporting verification of (8) are collected in:

$$\mathsf{wit} = \left(\mathsf{pd} \parallel \mathbf{x} \parallel \mathbf{a} \parallel \mathbf{b} \parallel \mathbf{c} \parallel (\widehat{w}_i)_{i=1}^{n_{\mathsf{gate}}} \parallel (\widetilde{w}_i)_{i=1}^{n_{\mathsf{w}}} \parallel (w'_i)_{i=1}^{n_{\mathsf{w}}}\right). \tag{9}$$

This vector is fully determined by α, β, and $(w_i)_{i=1}^{n_{\mathsf{w}}}$.

Two-Phase Witness Structure. The vector wit splits into two parts: $\mathsf{wit} = (\mathsf{wit}_{\mathsf{pre}} \parallel \mathsf{wit}_{\mathsf{suf}})$, where

$$\mathsf{wit}_{\mathsf{pre}} = \left(\mathsf{pd} \parallel \mathbf{x} \parallel \mathbf{a} \parallel \mathbf{b} \parallel \mathbf{c} \parallel (\widehat{w}_i)_{i=1}^{n_{\mathsf{gate}}}\right) \quad \text{is determined without knowing } \alpha, \beta;$$
$$\mathsf{wit}_{\mathsf{suf}} = \left((\widetilde{w}_i)_{i=1}^{n_{\mathsf{w}}} \parallel (w'_i)_{i=1}^{n_{\mathsf{w}}}\right) \quad \text{is determined only after } \alpha, \beta \text{ are known.}$$

This split is critical for the ZKBoo-based instantiation of Sect. 5: the prover first commits to $\mathsf{wit}_{\mathsf{pre}}$, derives α, β from a random oracle, then computes and commits to $\mathsf{wit}_{\mathsf{suf}}$.

In summary, any hidden arithmetic circuit F can now be verified via a fixed public system of quadratic constraints of size $\mathcal{O}(n_{\mathsf{in}} + n_{\mathsf{add}} + n_{\mathsf{mlt}})$, with the circuit's structure encoded entirely in the witness wit.

Sizes. Since $n_{\mathsf{w}} = \mathcal{O}(n_{\mathsf{in}} + n_{\mathsf{gate}}) = \mathcal{O}(n_{\mathsf{in}} + n_{\mathsf{add}} + n_{\mathsf{mlt}})$, the witness vector wit has $\mathcal{O}(n_{\mathsf{in}} + n_{\mathsf{add}} + n_{\mathsf{mlt}})$ field elements, and system (8) has $\mathcal{O}(n_{\mathsf{in}} + n_{\mathsf{add}} + n_{\mathsf{mlt}})$ multiplications and additions over $\mathbb{F}$.

4.2 Proving SMS Function Evaluations

This subsection applies the PLONK framework of Sect. 4.1 to the SMS evaluation structure, producing a single merged circuit $\mathsf{C}_{\mathsf{merge}}$ whose satisfiability the NIZKAoK in Sign proves.

Proving the Hidden Evaluation of F. Let F be the signer's hidden policy with $n_{\mathsf{in}}^{(F)}$ inputs, $n_{\mathsf{gate}}^{(F)}$ gates, and $n_{\mathsf{w}}^{(F)} := n_{\mathsf{in}}^{(F)} + 3n_{\mathsf{gate}}^{(F)}$. The signer evaluates F

on $\mathbf{x} = (M \| \mathsf{attr} \| w)$ and retains the full computation trace. Let pd_F denote F's PLONK description of the form (5). The signer then samples $\alpha, \beta \xleftarrow{\$} \mathbb{F}$ from a random oracle and assembles the witness vector:

$$\mathsf{wit}_F = \left(\mathsf{pd}_F \parallel \mathbf{x} \parallel \mathbf{a} \parallel \mathbf{b} \parallel \mathbf{c} \parallel (\widehat{w}_i)_{i=1}^{n_{\mathsf{gate}}^{(F)}} \parallel (\widetilde{w}_i)_{i=1}^{n_{\mathsf{w}}^{(F)}} \parallel (w_i')_{i=1}^{n_{\mathsf{w}}^{(F)}}\right), \tag{10}$$

where $\mathbf{x} = (M \| \mathsf{attr} \| w)$ and all remaining components follow the definitions of Sect. 4.1. Viewing system (8) instantiated with pd_F as a single verification circuit $\mathcal{U}_F^{\mathsf{plonk}}$, the signer must prove that wit_F satisfies $\mathcal{U}_F^{\mathsf{plonk}}$ with public output out_F. Since $\mathcal{U}_F^{\mathsf{plonk}}$ has $\mathcal{O}(n_{\mathsf{in}}^{(F)} + n_{\mathsf{gate}}^{(F)})$ multiplications, this proof is as efficient as proving the satisfiability of a public circuit of the same size.

For the NIZKAoK to be sound, α and β must be derived from a random oracle after the prover commits to $\mathsf{wit}_{\mathsf{pre}}$; allowing the prover to choose α, β in advance would permit a cheating prover to satisfy the grand product trivially. This commitment-then-challenge structure is precisely the two-phase split $(\mathsf{wit}_{\mathsf{pre}}, \mathsf{wit}_{\mathsf{suf}})$ of Sect. 4.1, and it drives the modification to ZKBoo in Sect. 5.

Treating G and P as Public Circuits. Since G and P are public, PLONK's arithmetization is not needed for them. They are treated directly as arithmetic circuits C_G and C_P, and their evaluations are proved as standard public-circuit satisfiability.

Merging into a Single Circuit. Given α, β, wit_F, M, attr, w, and intermediate outputs out_F and out_G, we merge $\mathcal{U}_F^{\mathsf{plonk}}$, C_G, and C_P into a single circuit $\mathsf{C}_{\mathsf{merge}}$ capturing: α, β, wit_F, and out_F satisfy $\mathcal{U}_F^{\mathsf{plonk}}$; and $G(M, \mathsf{attr}, w) = \mathsf{out}_G$ and $P(\mathsf{out}_F, \mathsf{out}_G) = (\overline{M}, \mathsf{op})$. A single NIZKAoK applied to $\mathsf{C}_{\mathsf{merge}}$ then certifies the full evaluation $P(F(M, \mathsf{attr}, w), G(M, \mathsf{attr}, w))$ with public inputs α, β, $(\overline{M}, \mathsf{ct}_{\mathsf{op}})$ and private witnesses M, attr, w, op, wit_F, out_F, out_G, without leaking F's circuit structure or computation trace.

After the Fiat–Shamir transform, α and β are derived from the random oracle and are publicly recomputable by the verifier; the remaining witnesses M, attr, w, wit_F, out_F, out_G are known only to the signer and hidden by the NIZKAoK.

Sizes. Let $n_{\mathsf{add}}^{(T)}$ and $n_{\mathsf{mlt}}^{(T)}$ denote the addition and multiplication gate counts of function $T \in \{F, G, P\}$. Circuit $\mathsf{C}_{\mathsf{merge}}$ has:

$$\begin{aligned} \text{additions:} \quad & \mathcal{O}\big(n_{\mathsf{in}}^{(F)} + n_{\mathsf{add}}^{(F)} + n_{\mathsf{mlt}}^{(F)}\big) + n_{\mathsf{add}}^{(G)} + n_{\mathsf{add}}^{(P)}; \\ \text{multiplications:} \quad & \mathcal{O}\big(n_{\mathsf{in}}^{(F)} + n_{\mathsf{add}}^{(F)} + n_{\mathsf{mlt}}^{(F)}\big) + n_{\mathsf{mlt}}^{(G)} + n_{\mathsf{mlt}}^{(P)}. \end{aligned}$$

For NIZKAoK systems whose proof size depends on the multiplication count, the dominant cost is $\mathcal{O}(n_{\mathsf{in}}^{(F)} + n_{\mathsf{add}}^{(F)} + n_{\mathsf{mlt}}^{(F)}) + n_{\mathsf{mlt}}^{(G)} + n_{\mathsf{mlt}}^{(P)}$, where $n_{\mathsf{in}}^{(F)} = |M| + |\mathsf{attr}| + |w|$, so the dominant multiplication count is $\mathcal{O}(|M| + |\mathsf{attr}| + |w| + n_{\mathsf{add}}^{(F)} + n_{\mathsf{mlt}}^{(F)}) + n_{\mathsf{mlt}}^{(G)} + n_{\mathsf{mlt}}^{(P)}$, which is quasilinear in the gate count of F and linear in the multiplications of G and P. This confirms the proof-size claim of Sect. 1.1. The ZKBoo-based instantiation exploits the two-phase split $(\mathsf{wit}_{\mathsf{pre}}, \mathsf{wit}_{\mathsf{suf}})$ from Sect. 4.1 to handle the random challenges α, β; details are in Sect. 5.

5 Lattice-Based Instantiation of SMS

This section instantiates the generic SMS construction of Sect. 3 in the post-quantum setting, combining lattice-based primitives over $\mathbb{Z}_q$ with ZKBoo [35], a zero-knowledge argument of knowledge following MPC-in-the-Head [39]. Two design choices drive the instantiation. First, ZKBoo's simulation-sound extractability with quasi-unique response [29] subsumes the anti-malleability role of the one-time signature $\mathcal{OTS}$ in the generic construction, simplifying the lattice scheme. Second, proving the hidden evaluation of F via PLONK's arithmetization (Sect. 4) requires random challenges α, β derived after committing to $\mathsf{wit}_{\mathsf{pre}}$; applying ZKBoo directly would allow a cheating prover to choose α, β in advance and satisfy the grand product check trivially. We therefore modify ZKBoo to interleave the pre-challenge and post-challenge commitment phases.

Section 5.1 describes the instantiation and the relation $\mathrm{R}_{\mathsf{l\text{-}SMS}}$. Section 5.2 presents the modified ZKBoo protocol. Section 5.3 analyzes the signature size. Full details of all primitives, proofs, and parameter settings are in the full version.

5.1 Instantiation Overview

Primitive Choices. The generic construction is instantiated with LP PKE [50] ($\mathcal{E}_{\mathsf{lp}}$) as $\mathcal{E}$, whose simple structure based on the learning-with-errors assumption is compatible with ZKBoo's arithmetic circuit proofs; JRS signatures [40] ($\mathcal{S}_{\mathsf{jrs}}$) as $\mathcal{S}$, whose lattice-based signing keys support efficient zero-knowledge membership proofs; and ZKBoo [35] as the NIZKAoK, with all computations over $\mathbb{Z}_q$ for a prime q. KTX commitments [43] replace the per-user key pair.

OTS Elimination. Because ZKBoo satisfies simulation-sound extractability with quasi-unique response [29], it subsumes the anti-malleability role of the one-time signature $\mathcal{OTS}$ required in the generic construction: any adversary modifying a ZKBoo proof cannot produce a second valid proof for a different statement without breaking the quasi-unique response property. Retaining $\mathcal{OTS}$ in the lattice setting would require a fresh key pair and an additional signature over all components per signing, increasing both signature size and signing cost; ZKBoo's quasi-unique response gives the same guarantee at no extra cost. Consequently, $(\mathsf{vk}_{\mathsf{attr}}, \mathsf{sk}_{\mathsf{attr}})$ no longer serves as a one-time signing key pair for ovk, but is still required for membership proofs.

Membership Key via KTX. Following the KTX commitment paradigm [43], we enforce the relationship $\mathsf{vk}_{\mathsf{attr}} = \mathsf{bin}(\mathbf{H} \cdot \mathsf{sk}_{\mathsf{attr}})$, where $\mathbf{H} \in \mathbb{Z}_q^{n \times m}$ is public and random, $\mathsf{bin}(\cdot)$ denotes binary decomposition, and $\mathsf{sk}_{\mathsf{attr}}$ is a uniformly random binary vector chosen by the enrolling user. By the security of the KTX commitment, $\mathsf{vk}_{\mathsf{attr}}$ computationally hides $\mathsf{sk}_{\mathsf{attr}}$; by the hardness of the short integer solution problem, no adversary seeing $\mathsf{vk}_{\mathsf{attr}}$ can recover a binary preimage.

Relation $\mathrm{R}_{\mathsf{l\text{-}SMS}}$. The NIZKAoK proves membership in a relation $\mathrm{R}_{\mathsf{l\text{-}SMS}}$ containing two classes of constraints.

1. *Lattice-based constraints.* These enforce binary-vector structure, small ℓ_∞-norm bounds, and linear relationships over $\mathbb{Z}_q$. Binary-vector structure is captured by $\langle \mathbf{v}, \mathbf{1} - \mathbf{v} \rangle = \mathbf{0}$. Small-norm bounds are handled via the following binary decomposition lemma.

Lemma 1 (Binary decomposition, [53] [38, Appendix A.1]). *Let $v \in \mathbb{N}$ and $k = \lfloor \log_2 v \rfloor + 1$. Define the basis $\mathcal{B}_v = \{B_i\}_{i=1}^{k} = \{2^i\}_{i=0}^{k-1} \cup \{v - (2^{k-1} - 1)\}$. Then $x \in [0, v]$ if and only if there exist bits $b_1, \ldots, b_k$ satisfying $x = \sum_{i=1}^{k} b_i B_i$.*

Using Lemma 1, each bound $\|\mathbf{a}\|_\infty \leq u$ is reduced to binary-vector and linear constraints, compatible with ZKBoo's arithmetic circuit satisfiability. The proof of Lemma 1 is deferred to the full version.

2. *Circuit satisfiability constraints.* These enforce $P(F(\cdot), G(\cdot))$ and any auxiliary public circuits are correctly evaluated, including the circuit checking $\mathsf{op} \in \mathcal{OP}_{\mathsf{sgnbl}}$. The hidden $F(\cdot)$ evaluation is handled by the PLONK reduction of Sect. 4.

The full relation $\mathrm{R}_{\mathsf{I\text{-}SMS}}$ is also deferred to the full version.

ZKBoo as the NIZKAoK. ZKBoo proves arithmetic circuit satisfiability and is plausibly post-quantum. Proving $\mathrm{R}_{\mathsf{I\text{-}SMS}}$ requires the hidden-circuit strategy of Sect. 4, which introduces additional challenges $\alpha, \beta \xleftarrow{\$} \mathbb{Z}_q$ that must be generated from the random oracle after the prover commits to $\mathsf{wit}_{\mathsf{pre}}$. The Fiat-Shamir transform [31] makes the protocol non-interactive; however, the standard ZKBoo decomposition must be modified to accommodate the two-phase witness structure $(\mathsf{wit}_{\mathsf{pre}}, \mathsf{wit}_{\mathsf{suf}})$. Section 5.2 describes this modification. The result is a plausibly post-quantum SMS scheme enforcing hidden arithmetic policies with per-signature modal accountability.

5.2 Modifying the ZKBoo Protocol

In the original ZKBoo protocol [35], the computation trace of a circuit C, treated as a witness W, is decomposed via a randomized function $\mathsf{decompose}(W)$, into three views $\{\mathsf{view}_j\}_{j=1}^{3}$, such that any two views reveal no information of W, then committed by the prover as $\{\mathsf{cview}_j\}_{j=1}^{3}$. The verifier challenges the prover to open two of the three commitments; consistency of the two opened views certifies correct evaluation. See the full version for more details.

Modified Decomposition. For proving $\mathrm{R}_{\mathsf{I\text{-}SMS}}$, the witness decomposes as W_{pre} and W_{suf} (the pre- and post-challenge components of Sect. 4.1): W_{pre} is determined before the challenges α, β are known, and W_{suf} is determined only after.

Specifically, we run $\mathsf{decompose}(W_{\mathsf{pre}})$ to obtain *pre-views* $\{\mathsf{preview}_j\}_{j=1}^{3}$ and treat each $\mathsf{preview}_j$ as the prefix of the full view: $\mathsf{view}_j = (\mathsf{preview}_j \| \mathsf{sufview}_j)$. The suffix views $\{\mathsf{sufview}_j\}_{j=1}^{3}$ are obtained by running $\mathsf{decompose}(\cdot)$ on the combined process of (i) computing all components of W_{suf} using entries of $\{\mathsf{preview}_j\}_{j=1}^{3}$ and (ii) checking system (8). The resulting full views $\{\mathsf{view}_j\}_{j=1}^{3}$ are thus a valid ZKBoo decomposition of the extended witness $(W_{\mathsf{pre}} \| W_{\mathsf{suf}})$.

Modified Protocol. The modified protocol proceeds in three phases.

1. The prover commits to $\{\mathsf{preview}_j\}_{j=1}^3$, sending commitments $\{\mathsf{cpreview}_j\}_{j=1}^3$ to the verifier.
2. The verifier sends $\alpha, \beta \xleftarrow{\$} \mathbb{Z}_q$ (derived from the random oracle in the non-interactive version). The prover computes $\{\mathsf{sufview}_j\}_{j=1}^3$ and sends commitments $\{\mathsf{csufview}_j\}_{j=1}^3$.
3. The commitment to view_j is the pair $(\mathsf{cpreview}_j, \mathsf{csufview}_j)$. The prover and verifier execute the original ZKBoo consistency check on the requested views.

This structure ensures that α, β are unknown to the prover when it commits to $\mathsf{wit}_{\mathsf{pre}}$, preventing the cheating-prover attack identified in Sect. 4.2. See the full version for the full protocol description and security analysis.

5.3 Signature Size

The final SMS signature is $\Sigma_{\mathsf{l\text{-}SMS}} = (\mathsf{ct}_{\mathsf{op}}, \Pi_{\mathsf{l\text{-}SMS}})$, where $\mathsf{ct}_{\mathsf{op}}$ encrypts op and $\Pi_{\mathsf{l\text{-}SMS}}$ is the non-interactive version of the modified ZKBoo for $\mathrm{R}_{\mathsf{l\text{-}SMS}}$. Thus $|\Sigma_{\mathsf{l\text{-}SMS}}| = |\mathsf{ct}_{\mathsf{op}}| + |\Pi_{\mathsf{l\text{-}SMS}}|$. Since $|\Pi_{\mathsf{l\text{-}SMS}}|$ dominates $|\mathsf{ct}_{\mathsf{op}}|$, we focus on the former. The full lattice parameter settings, including $|\mathsf{ct}_{\mathsf{op}}|$, are deferred to the full version.

Bounding $|\Pi_{\mathsf{l\text{-}SMS}}|$. The proof $\Pi_{\mathsf{l\text{-}SMS}}$ consists of κ repetitions of the modified ZKBoo, with a soundness error 2/3 of each repetition, where $\kappa = \lceil \lambda \cdot (\log_2 3 - 1)^{-1} \rceil$ achieves soundness error $2^{-\lambda}$. Each repetition contributes commitments $\mathsf{cpreview}_j$ and $\mathsf{csufview}_j$ (compressed via hashing) and a response rsp_j. Thus $|\Pi_{\mathsf{l\text{-}SMS}}| = \mathcal{O}(\kappa \cdot (|\mathsf{cpreview}| + |\mathsf{csufview}| + |\mathsf{rsp}|))$. The dominant term is $|\mathsf{rsp}|$. Addition-gate outputs in the views can be recomputed for free [17,42], so only multiplication-gate outputs need to be transmitted.

Response Size. The $\log q$ factor in the response arises because all lattice-based primitives operate over binary representations: every $\mathbb{Z}_q$ field element must be binary-decomposed before lattice arithmetic applies, multiplying each element's contribution to $|\mathsf{rsp}|$ by $\log q$. With this decomposition, $|\mathsf{rsp}|$ is bounded by

$$\begin{aligned}\mathcal{O}\Big(&\log q \cdot \big(|\mathsf{lparams}| + |M| + |\mathsf{attr}| + |w| + n_{\mathsf{add}}^{(F)} + n_{\mathsf{mlt}}^{(F)} + |\mathsf{op}| \cdot \log q\big)\\ &+ |\mathsf{lparams}'| + n_{\mathsf{mlt}}^{(G)} + n_{\mathsf{mlt}}^{(P)} + n_{\mathsf{mlt}}^{(\mathsf{op})}\Big)\end{aligned} \tag{11}$$

$\mathbb{Z}_q$-elements, where $|\mathsf{lparams}|$ and $|\mathsf{lparams}'|$ denote the parameter sizes of the PKE and signature primitives, instantiated as LP and JRS respectively; their exact values depend on choices deferred to the full version, while $n_{\mathsf{mlt}}^{(\mathsf{op})}$ counts the multiplication for the circuit checking of $\mathsf{op} \in \mathcal{OP}_{\mathsf{sgnbl}}$.

Asymptotic Summary. From (11), $|\Pi_{\mathsf{l\text{-}SMS}}|$ is quasilinear in the total gate count of F (due to the $\log q$ factor from binary decomposition) and linear in the multiplication counts of G and P. This matches the proof-size claim of Sect. 1.1 and confirms that the $\log q$ overhead is an unavoidable cost of working with lattice-based primitives, not an artifact of the construction. This framework admits richer instantiations via advanced MPCitH [3,4,7,16,17,30,42,62] and VOLEitH techniques [6,13,27,60].

6 Conclusion

Sovereign modal signatures (SMS) unify hidden and public policy enforcement with per-signature modal accountability, addressing a decade-old open problem in privacy-preserving signatures by treating a circuit's PLONK description as a witness rather than a statement, achieving the first efficient privacy-preserving signature scheme for hidden arithmetic-circuit evaluation without universal circuits or idealized algebraic models.

Multi-stakeholder deployments, *e.g.*, audit systems, regulatory compliance, and credential delegation, are the natural home for SMS: each participant operates under a certifying authority's hidden policy, overlays a publicly verifiable check at signing time, and exposes exactly as much identity as the configuration prescribes, realizing the functional credentials vision of prior work [24].

Concrete directions for future work include threshold and distributed issuance, revocation within the partial-dynamic model, and measured efficiency at the 128-bit post-quantum security level; more broadly, the PLONK-based hidden-circuit reduction developed here is a general tool applicable to any privacy primitive using hidden arithmetic-circuit proofs in the random oracle model.

Acknowledgments. The first four authors utilized AI tools for linguistic and stylistic refinement.

Research at Nanyang Technological University is supported by Singapore Ministry of Education Academic Research Fund Tier 2 Grant MOE-T2EP20223-0016, the National Research Foundation, Singapore and Infocomm Media Development Authority under its Trust Tech Funding Initiative. Any opinions, findings and conclusions or recommendations expressed in this material are those of the author(s) and do not reflect the views of National Research Foundation, Singapore and Infocomm Media Development Authority.

Yingfei Yan is supported by the European Astral Project ERASMUS-EDU 2024:101184483. She thanks Xidian University for its support and Nanyang Technological University (NTU) and The Chinese University of Hong Kong (CUHK) for their hospitality during her visits.

Sherman Chow is supported in part by the Research Grants Council of Hong Kong under the Collaborative Research Fund (C5097-25GF) and the General Research Fund (14210825).

Kai Zhang is supported in part by the Natural Science Foundation of Shaanxi Province (No. 2025JC-YBMS-748).

References

1. Abe, M., Chow, S.S.M., Haralambiev, K., Ohkubo, M.: Double-trapdoor anonymous tags for traceable signatures. Int. J. Inf. Secur. **12**(1), 19–31 (2013). https://doi.org/10.1007/s10207-012-0184-3
2. Abe, M., Fuchsbauer, G., Groth, J., Haralambiev, K., Ohkubo, M.: Structure-preserving signatures and commitments to group elements. In: CRYPTO 2010. LNCS, vol. 6223, pp. 209–236. Springer, Heidelberg (2010). https://doi.org/10.1007/978-3-642-14623-7_12

3. Aguilar-Melchor, C., Gama, N., Howe, J., Hülsing, A., Joseph, D., Yue, D.: The return of the SDitH. In: EUROCRYPT, Part V. LNCS, vol. 14008, pp. 564–596 (2023). https://doi.org/10.1007/978-3-031-30589-4_20
4. Aguilar-Melchor, C., Hülsing, A., Joseph, D., Majenz, C., Ronen, E., Yue, D.: SDitH in the QROM. In: ASIACRYPT, Part VII. LNCS, vol. 14444, pp. 317–350 (2023). https://doi.org/10.1007/978-981-99-8739-9_11
5. Au, M.H., Susilo, W., Mu, Y., Chow, S.S.M.: Constant-size dynamic k-times anonymous authentication. IEEE Syst. J. **7**(2), 249–261 (2013). https://doi.org/10.1109/JSYST.2012.2221931
6. Baum, C., et al.: Publicly verifiable zero-knowledge and post-quantum signatures from VOLE-in-the-head. In: CRYPTO, Part V. LNCS, vol. 14085, pp. 581–615 (2023). https://doi.org/10.1007/978-3-031-38554-4_19
7. Baum, C., Nof, A.: Concretely-efficient zero-knowledge arguments for arithmetic circuits and their application to lattice-based cryptography. In: PKC 2020, Part I. LNCS, vol. 12110, pp. 495–526. Springer, Cham (2020). https://doi.org/10.1007/978-3-030-45374-9_17
8. Bellare, M., Fuchsbauer, G.: Policy-based signatures. In: PKC 2014. LNCS, vol. 8383, pp. 520–537. Springer, Heidelberg (2014). https://doi.org/10.1007/978-3-642-54631-0_30
9. Bender, A., Katz, J., Morselli, R.: Ring signatures: stronger definitions, and constructions without random oracles. In: TCC 2006. LNCS, vol. 3876, pp. 60–79. Springer, Heidelberg (2006). https://doi.org/10.1007/11681878_4
10. Bobolz, J., Diaz, J., Kohlweiss, M.: Foundations of anonymous signatures: formal definitions, simplified requirements, and a construction based on general assumptions. In: FC. LNCS, vol. 14745, pp. 121–139 (2025). https://doi.org/10.1007/978-3-031-78679-2_7
11. Boneh, D., Nguyen, W., Ozdemir, A.: Efficient functional commitments: how to commit to a private function. Cryptology ePrint Archive, Paper 2021/1342 (2021). https://ia.cr/2021/1342
12. Boyle, E., Goldwasser, S., Ivan, I.: Functional signatures and pseudorandom functions. In: PKC 2014. LNCS, vol. 8383, pp. 501–519. Springer, Heidelberg (2014). https://doi.org/10.1007/978-3-642-54631-0_29
13. Bui, D.: Efficient multi-instance vector commitment and application to post-quantum signatures. In: ACISP, Part II. LNCS, vol. 15659, pp. 23–41 (2025). https://doi.org/10.1007/978-981-96-9098-5_2
14. Camenisch, J., Lysyanskaya, A.: An efficient system for non-transferable anonymous credentials with optional anonymity revocation. In: EUROCRYPT 2001. LNCS, vol. 2045, pp. 93–118. Springer, Heidelberg (2001). https://doi.org/10.1007/3-540-44987-6_7
15. Camenisch, J., Lysyanskaya, A.: Signature schemes and anonymous credentials from bilinear maps. In: CRYPTO 2004. LNCS, vol. 3152, pp. 56–72. Springer, Heidelberg (2004). https://doi.org/10.1007/978-3-540-28628-8_4
16. Carozza, E., Couteau, G., Joux, A.: Short signatures from regular syndrome decoding in the head. In: EUROCRYPT, Part V. LNCS, vol. 14008, pp. 532–563 (2023). https://doi.org/10.1007/978-3-031-30589-4_19
17. Chase, M., et al.: Post-quantum zero-knowledge and signatures from symmetric-key primitives. In: CCS, pp. 1825–1842 (2017). https://doi.org/10.1145/3133956.3133997
18. Chase, M., Lysyanskaya, A.: On signatures of knowledge. In: Dwork, C. (ed.) CRYPTO 2006. LNCS, vol. 4117, pp. 78–96. Springer, Heidelberg (2006). https://doi.org/10.1007/11818175_5

19. Chaum, D., van Heyst, E.: Group signatures. In: Davies, D.W. (ed.) EUROCRYPT 1991. LNCS, vol. 547, pp. 257–265. Springer, Heidelberg (1991). https://doi.org/10.1007/3-540-46416-6_22
20. Cheng, S., Nguyen, K., Wang, H.: Policy-based signature scheme from lattices. Des. Codes Cryptogr. **81**(1), 43–74 (2016). https://doi.org/10.1007/S10623-015-0126-Y
21. Chiesa, A., Hu, Y., Maller, M., Mishra, P., Vesely, N., Ward, N.: Marlin: preprocessing zkSNARKs with universal and updatable SRS. In: Canteaut, A., Ishai, Y. (eds.) EUROCRYPT 2020, Part I. LNCS, vol. 12105, pp. 738–768. Springer, Cham (2020). https://doi.org/10.1007/978-3-030-45721-1_26
22. Choudhuri, A.R., Garg, S., Goel, A., Sekar, S., Sinha, R.: SublonK: sublinear prover PlonK. In: PETS, vol. 2024, pp. 314–335 (2024). https://doi.org/10.56553/POPETS-2024-0080
23. Chow, S.S.M.: Real traceable signatures. In: Jacobson, M.J., Rijmen, V., Safavi-Naini, R. (eds.) SAC 2009. LNCS, vol. 5867, pp. 92–107. Springer, Heidelberg (2009). https://doi.org/10.1007/978-3-642-05445-7_6
24. Chow, S.S.M.: Functional credentials for Internet of Things. In: IoTPTS, p. 1 (2016). https://doi.org/10.1145/2899007.2899014
25. Chow, S.S.M., Susilo, W., Yuen, T.H.: Escrowed linkability of ring signatures and its applications. In: Nguyen, P.Q. (ed.) VIETCRYPT 2006. LNCS, vol. 4341, pp. 175–192. Springer, Heidelberg (2006). https://doi.org/10.1007/11958239_12
26. Chow, S.S.M., Zhang, H., Zhang, T.: Real hidden identity-based signatures. In: Kiayias, A. (ed.) FC 2017. LNCS, vol. 10322, pp. 21–38. Springer, Cham (2017). https://doi.org/10.1007/978-3-319-70972-7_2
27. Cui, H., Liu, H., Yan, D., Yang, K., Yu, Y., Zhang, K.: ReSolveD: shorter signatures from regular syndrome decoding and VOLE-in-the-head. In: PKC, Part I. LNCS, vol. 14601, pp. 229–258 (2024). https://doi.org/10.1007/978-3-031-57718-5_8
28. Di, Z., Xia, L., Nguyen, W., Tyagi, N.: MuxProofs: succinct arguments for machine computation from vector lookups. In: ASIACRYPT, Part V. LNCS, vol. 15488, pp. 236–265 (2025). https://doi.org/10.1007/978-981-96-0935-2_8
29. Faust, S., Kohlweiss, M., Marson, G.A., Venturi, D.: On the non-malleability of the Fiat-Shamir transform. In: Galbraith, S., Nandi, M. (eds.) INDOCRYPT 2012. LNCS, vol. 7668, pp. 60–79. Springer, Heidelberg (2012). https://doi.org/10.1007/978-3-642-34931-7_5
30. Feneuil, T., Joux, A., Rivain, M.: Syndrome decoding in the head: shorter signatures from zero-knowledge proofs. In: CRYPTO, Part II. LNCS, vol. 13508, pp. 541–572 (2022). https://doi.org/10.1007/978-3-031-15979-4_19
31. Fiat, A., Shamir, A.: How to prove yourself: practical solutions to identification and signature problems. In: Odlyzko, A.M. (ed.) CRYPTO 1986. LNCS, vol. 263, pp. 186–194. Springer, Heidelberg (1987). https://doi.org/10.1007/3-540-47721-7_12
32. Fuchsbauer, G., Kiltz, E., Loss, J.: The algebraic group model and its applications. In: Shacham, H., Boldyreva, A. (eds.) CRYPTO 2018, Part II. LNCS, vol. 10992, pp. 33–62. Springer, Cham (2018). https://doi.org/10.1007/978-3-319-96881-0_2
33. Fujisaki, E., Suzuki, K.: Traceable ring signature. In: Okamoto, T., Wang, X. (eds.) PKC 2007. LNCS, vol. 4450, pp. 181–200. Springer, Heidelberg (2007). https://doi.org/10.1007/978-3-540-71677-8_13
34. Gabizon, A., Williamson, Z.J., Ciobotaru, O.: PLONK: permutations over Lagrange-bases for oecumenical noninteractive arguments of knowledge. Cryptology ePrint Archive, Paper 2019/953 (2019). https://ia.cr/2019/953

35. Giacomelli, I., Madsen, J., Orlandi, C.: ZKBoo: faster zero-knowledge for boolean circuits. In: USENIX Security, pp. 1069–1083 (2016). https://www.usenix.org/conference/usenixsecurity16/technical-sessions/presentation/giacomelli
36. Groth, J., Sahai, A.: Efficient non-interactive proof systems for bilinear groups. In: Smart, N. (ed.) EUROCRYPT 2008. LNCS, vol. 4965, pp. 415–432. Springer, Heidelberg (2008). https://doi.org/10.1007/978-3-540-78967-3_24
37. Guo, Q., Huang, Q., Ma, S., Xiao, M., Yang, G., Susilo, W.: Functional signatures: new definition and constructions. Sci. China Inf. Sci. **64**(12) (2021). https://doi.org/10.1007/S11432-019-2855-3
38. He, Y., Ling, S., Tang, K.H., Wang, H.: Everlasting fully dynamic group signatures. In: ACNS, Part III. LNCS, vol. 15827, pp. 3–28 (2025). https://doi.org/10.1007/978-3-031-95767-3_1, ePrint Archive https://ia.cr/2025/627
39. Ishai, Y., Kushilevitz, E., Ostrovsky, R., Sahai, A.: Zero-knowledge from secure multiparty computation. In: STOC, pp. 21–30 (2007). https://doi.org/10.1145/1250790.1250794
40. Jeudy, C., Roux-Langlois, A., Sanders, O.: Lattice signature with efficient protocols, application to anonymous credentials. In: CRYPTO, Part II. LNCS, vol. 14082, pp. 351–383 (2023). https://doi.org/10.1007/978-3-031-38545-2_12
41. Karatsuba, A.A., Ofman, Y.P.: Multiplication of many-digital numbers by automatic computers. In: Doklady Akademii Nauk, vol. 145, pp. 293–294 (1962)
42. Katz, J., Kolesnikov, V., Wang, X.: Improved non-interactive zero knowledge with applications to post-quantum signatures. In: CCS, pp. 525–537 (2018). https://doi.org/10.1145/3243734.3243805
43. Kawachi, A., Tanaka, K., Xagawa, K.: Concurrently secure identification schemes based on the worst-case hardness of lattice problems. In: Pieprzyk, J. (ed.) ASIACRYPT 2008. LNCS, vol. 5350, pp. 372–389. Springer, Heidelberg (2008). https://doi.org/10.1007/978-3-540-89255-7_23
44. Kiayias, A., Tsiounis, Y., Yung, M.: Traceable signatures. In: Cachin, C., Camenisch, J.L. (eds.) EUROCRYPT 2004. LNCS, vol. 3027, pp. 571–589. Springer, Heidelberg (2004). https://doi.org/10.1007/978-3-540-24676-3_34
45. Kiayias, A., Yung, M.: Secure scalable group signature with dynamic joins and separable authorities. Int. J. Secur. Networks **1**(1/2), 24–45 (2006). https://doi.org/10.1504/IJSN.2006.010821
46. Kiayias, A., Zhou, H.-S.: Hidden identity-based signatures. In: Dietrich, S., Dhamija, R. (eds.) FC 2007. LNCS, vol. 4886, pp. 134–147. Springer, Heidelberg (2007). https://doi.org/10.1007/978-3-540-77366-5_14
47. Kiss, Á., Schneider, T.: Valiant's universal circuit is practical. In: Fischlin, M., Coron, J.-S. (eds.) EUROCRYPT 2016, Part III. LNCS, vol. 9665, pp. 699–728. Springer, Heidelberg (2016). https://doi.org/10.1007/978-3-662-49890-3_27
48. Lai, R.W.F., Zhang, T., Chow, S.S.M., Schröder, D.: Efficient sanitizable signatures without random oracles. In: Askoxylakis, I., Ioannidis, S., Katsikas, S., Meadows, C. (eds.) ESORICS 2016, Part I. LNCS, vol. 9878, pp. 363–380. Springer, Cham (2016). https://doi.org/10.1007/978-3-319-45744-4_18
49. Libert, B., Nguyen, K., Peters, T., Yung, M.: Bifurcated signatures: folding the accountability vs. anonymity dilemma into a single private signing scheme. In: Canteaut, A., Standaert, F.-X. (eds.) EUROCRYPT 2021, Part III. LNCS, vol. 12698, pp. 521–552. Springer, Cham (2021). https://doi.org/10.1007/978-3-030-77883-5_18
50. Lindner, R., Peikert, C.: Better key sizes (and attacks) for LWE-based encryption. In: Kiayias, A. (ed.) CT-RSA 2011. LNCS, vol. 6558, pp. 319–339. Springer, Heidelberg (2011). https://doi.org/10.1007/978-3-642-19074-2_21

51. Ling, S., Nguyen, K., Phan, D.H., Tang, H., Wang, H.: Zero-knowledge proofs for committed symmetric Boolean functions. In: Cheon, J.H., Tillich, J.-P. (eds.) PQCrypto 2021. LNCS, vol. 12841, pp. 339–359. Springer, Cham (2021). https://doi.org/10.1007/978-3-030-81293-5_18
52. Ling, S., Nguyen, K., Phan, D.H., Tang, K.H., Wang, H., Xu, Y.: Fully dynamic attribute-based signatures for circuits from codes. In: PKC, Part I. LNCS, vol. 14601, pp. 37–73 (2024). https://doi.org/10.1007/978-3-031-57718-5_2
53. Ling, S., Nguyen, K., Stehlé, D., Wang, H.: Improved zero-knowledge proofs of knowledge for the ISIS problem, and applications. In: Kurosawa, K., Hanaoka, G. (eds.) PKC 2013. LNCS, vol. 7778, pp. 107–124. Springer, Heidelberg (2013). https://doi.org/10.1007/978-3-642-36362-7_8
54. Lipmaa, H., Mohassel, P., Sadeghian, S.: Valiant's universal circuit: improvements, implementation, and applications. Cryptology ePrint Archive, Paper 2016/017 (2016). https://ia.cr/2016/017
55. Liu, H., Yu, Yu., Zhao, S., Zhang, J., Liu, W., Hu, Z.: Pushing the limits of Valiant's universal circuits: simpler, tighter and more compact. In: Malkin, T., Peikert, C. (eds.) CRYPTO 2021, Part II. LNCS, vol. 12826, pp. 365–394. Springer, Cham (2021). https://doi.org/10.1007/978-3-030-84245-1_13
56. Liu, J.K., Wei, V.K., Wong, D.S.: Linkable spontaneous anonymous group signature for Ad Hoc groups. In: Wang, H., Pieprzyk, J., Varadharajan, V. (eds.) ACISP 2004. LNCS, vol. 3108, pp. 325–335. Springer, Heidelberg (2004). https://doi.org/10.1007/978-3-540-27800-9_28
57. Maji, H.K., Prabhakaran, M., Rosulek, M.: Attribute-based signatures. In: Kiayias, A. (ed.) CT-RSA 2011. LNCS, vol. 6558, pp. 376–392. Springer, Heidelberg (2011). https://doi.org/10.1007/978-3-642-19074-2_24
58. Nguyen, K., Guo, F., Susilo, W., Yang, G.: Multimodal private signatures. In: CRYPTO, Part II. LNCS, vol. 13508, pp. 792–822 (2022). https://doi.org/10.1007/978-3-031-15979-4_27
59. Nguyen, K., Roy, P.S., Susilo, W., Xu, Y.: Bicameral and auditably private signatures. In: ASIACRYPT, Part II. LNCS, vol. 14439, pp. 313–347 (2023). https://doi.org/10.1007/978-981-99-8724-5_10
60. Ouyang, Y., Tang, D., Xu, Y.: Code-based zero-knowledge from VOLE-in-the-head and their applications: simpler, faster, and smaller. In: ASIACRYPT, Part V. LNCS, vol. 15488, pp. 436–470 (2025). https://doi.org/10.1007/978-981-96-0935-2_14
61. Rivest, R.L., Shamir, A., Tauman, Y.: How to leak a secret. In: Boyd, C. (ed.) ASIACRYPT 2001. LNCS, vol. 2248, pp. 552–565. Springer, Heidelberg (2001). https://doi.org/10.1007/3-540-45682-1_32
62. Delpech de Saint Guilhem, C., Orsini, E., Tanguy, T.: Limbo: efficient zero-knowledge MPCitH-based arguments. In: CCS, pp. 3022–3036 (2021). https://doi.org/10.1145/3460120.3484595
63. Sakai, Y.: Succinct attribute-based signatures for bounded-size circuits by combining algebraic and arithmetic proofs. In: SCN. LNCS, vol. 13409, pp. 711–734 (2022). https://doi.org/10.1007/978-3-031-14791-3_31
64. Tang, K.H., Pham, N.M., Ngo, C.N.: RAMenPaSTA: parallelizable scalable transparent arguments of knowledge for RAM programs. Cryptology ePrint Archive, Paper 2024/336 (2024). https://ia.cr/2024/336
65. Tran, N., Nguyen, K., Liu, D., Pieprzyk, J., Susilo, W.: Improved multimodal private signatures from lattices. In: ACISP. LNCS, vol. 14896, pp. 3–23 (2024). https://doi.org/10.1007/978-981-97-5028-3_1

66. Valiant, L.G.: Universal circuits (preliminary report). In: STOC, pp. 196–203 (1976). https://doi.org/10.1145/800113.803649
67. Xu, S., Yung, M.: Accountable ring signatures: a smart card approach. In: CARDIS. IFIP, vol. 153, pp. 271–286 (2004)
68. Xu, Y., Safavi-Naini, R., Nguyen, K., Wang, H.: Traceable policy-based signatures and instantiation from lattices. Inf. Sci. **607**, 1286–1310 (2022). https://doi.org/10.1016/j.ins.2022.06.031
69. Yan, Y., et al.: Sovereign modal signatures. Cryptology ePrint Archive (2026). Full version
70. Zhang, C., Zhou, H.S., Katz, J.: An analysis of the algebraic group model. In: ASIACRYPT, Part IV. LNCS, vol. 13794, pp. 310–322 (2022). https://doi.org/10.1007/978-3-031-22972-5_11
71. Zhang, T., Wu, H., Chow, S.S.M.: Structure-preserving certificateless encryption and its application. In: Matsui, M. (ed.) CT-RSA 2019. LNCS, vol. 11405, pp. 1–22. Springer, Cham (2019). https://doi.org/10.1007/978-3-030-12612-4_1
72. Zhao, S., Yu, Yu., Zhang, J., Liu, H.: Valiant's universal circuits revisited: an overall improvement and a lower bound. In: Galbraith, S.D., Moriai, S. (eds.) ASIACRYPT 2019, Part I. LNCS, vol. 11921, pp. 401–425. Springer, Cham (2019). https://doi.org/10.1007/978-3-030-34578-5_15

Practical Zero-Trust Threshold Signatures in Large-Scale Asynchronous Networks

Offir Friedman(✉), Avichai Marmor, Dolev Mutzari, Yehonatan C. Scaly, and Yuval Spiizer

dWallet Labs, Tel Aviv, Israel
{offir,avichai,dolev,yehonatan,yuval}@dwalletlabs.com

Abstract. Threshold signatures are a fundamental primitive in applied cryptography, primarily used to mitigate the custodial risk involved in managing keys. However, existing constructions rely on synchronous communication assumptions and fixed participant sets, limiting their applicability to real-world networks. In addition, as the committees managing those keys serve an ever-growing number of clients and assets, they become lucrative targets for attacks. This issue is often called the *Honeypot Problem.* A recent work proposed the *2PC-MPC* paradigm, in which a client and a decentralized network jointly generate signatures, aiming to mitigate this issue.

In this work, we present the first *asynchronous* 2PC-MPC protocol for ECDSA signatures, designed to operate over reliable broadcast channels as implemented in modern blockchains. Our protocol tolerates dynamic, post-determined quorums whose participants may change between rounds. This allows the protocol to align with asynchronous consensus layers while providing identifiable abort, public verifiability, guaranteed output delivery (assuming completeness of the broadcast channel) and censorship resistance for the client.

We introduce *global presigns*, which are generated autonomously by the network and remain client-agnostic until signing. This enables effective background preprocessing, and results in sub-second online signing network-side latency for dozens of concurrent clients.

From a technical perspective, our asynchronous design eliminates commitment rounds, yielding one-round client interaction for both key generation and signing. We also remove the need for zero-knowledge proofs toward the client. This results in a client complexity independent of network size, without proof aggregation (which is particularly challenging over asynchronous channels). Our constructions are proven UC-secure in the asynchronous setting. To achieve concrete security over 256-bit elliptic curves, we introduce the *Slightly-Enhanced ECDSA Unforgeability* assumption and provide a tight reduction in the EC-GGM model.

Beyond theoretical analysis, we implement our protocols and evaluate them in both a local benchmark and a live permissionless deployment with dozens of validators, demonstrating practical performance and robustness under heterogeneous execution speeds.

K. Jee and A. Kate (Eds.): ACNS 2026, LNCS 16571, pp. 473–500, 2027.
https://doi.org/10.1007/978-3-032-32560-0_17

1 Introduction

In recent years, there has been growing interest in thresholdizing digital signatures [4,11,33], distributing the signing process among multiple parties. This is primarily because digital signatures serve as an authentication mechanism in Bitcoin [60], Ethereum [14], and similar platforms where the digital signature on a transaction constitutes a proof of ownership of the funds. Specifically, much effort has been made for thresholdizing ECDSA [1,6,7,15–17,23,27,28,30,31,41–43,54,56,73,75,76] due to its widespread use in cryptocurrency.

Threshold signature based solutions have been widely deployed in the cryptocurrency industry and focus mainly on two use cases: decentralized bridges (e.g. THORChain [69], Keep Network [57], Near Network [48] and Internet Computer [68]) and distributed custody (e.g. Coinbase Wallet [55], Qredo [51], Zengo [50], Fireblocks [36], Copper [24], Web3 Auth [52] and Lit Protocol [21]).

Ultimately, in both applications, the signing key may be shared between the client and a *distributed permissionless network* in a way that requires the active consent of both to produce a signature. Currently, for ECDSA-based protocols only trusted (i.e. without client involvement) custodians are deployed.

Additionally, to the best of our knowledge, due to inherent limitations of existing threshold ECDSA signing protocols, all real-world networks for both use-cases are deployed with a rather small number of nodes (e.g. Internet Computer uses up to 30 [68]). This undermines the vision of decentralization as a smaller number of nodes can more easily collude. Nowadays, blockchains typically have hundreds to thousands of validators (e.g., Ethereum currently has 4,540 active nodes [34]). Recently, [39] has taken a pivotal step towards increasing the number of nodes, and we follow their approach in this work. Their main observation is that designing the protocol over a *broadcast channel* is more scalable with the number of parties. Indeed, prior to the work of [39], all practical threshold ECDSA schemes were designed to work over *unicast channels*, assuming secure point-to-point (P2P) channels between *every* pair of parties. While secure point-to-point channels can be constructed in theory (under an appropriate PKI setup), in practice, they inherently incur a high network load and a message complexity quadratic in the number of parties, as each party computes and sends a message to every other party. Instead, [39] opts to rely on a *broadcast channel*, and reduces the message complexity to linear. Moreover, by working over a broadcast channel, their protocol achieves *identifiable abort* (IA) and *public verifiability* (PV). When the broadcast channel is implemented over a blockchain, one also gets *immutability of messages*, which enables easy *recovery from failures*. It also provides *incentive mechanisms* for faithful participation. Blockchains also provide *censorship resistance* for the client, as opposed to trusted custodians.

Nevertheless, some key aspects remain unaddressed. Primarily, their choice of assuming a synchronous broadcast channel sidesteps many of the difficulties that arise when implementing the protocol over existing broadcast channel implementations. Existing networks typically work over an *asynchronous* or a *partially synchronous reliable broadcast communication channel*. In particular, the parties do not have synchronized clocks, cannot agree on which parties are online and which parties are unavailable. Therefore, parties who participate in one communication round may not be available for the next one. Section 2 discusses these gaps and places our approach in the context of prior work on threshold signatures. Building on [39], we address these critical challenges and provide an affirmative answer to the question below:

Can we design an asynchronous, permissionless, decentralized network, concurrently servicing numerous clients requesting digital signatures?

Zero Trust. Our protocol demands participation of a client in addition to the distributed network and thus maintains the *Zero Trust* principle [67], which has been foundational in blockchain ecosystems. Under this principle, no one is trusted, not even miners or validators, and every client calculates and verifies the state itself.

Currently, isolated networks that offer *interoperability* are compromising on Zero Trust principles in order to enable cross-network operations. Instead, they take a *Castle-and-Moat* approach, aiming to create a strong, fortified perimeter around their network. Unfortunately, *Castle-and-Moat Protocols* (CMPs) manage an ever-increasing amount of digital assets in cross-chain interactions, creating the *Honeypot Problem*: as a CMP gains higher *Total Value Locked* (TVL), the protocol becomes a more lucrative target for malicious players. For many years, we have witnessed attacks targeting CMPs. For instance, Wormhole [45] was exploited for over 320 million USD [74].

In order to resolve those issues and comply with the Zero Trust architecture, [39] proposed the *2PC-MPC* framework, which we follow in this work and briefly cover below. In this framework, both the client and a threshold of a decentralized network must collaborate in order to produce a signature. This ensures that even if the network is compromised, it cannot sign any transaction without client consent. In particular, on top of hacking the network, the adversary has to access the secret key share of each client individually, thereby addressing the honeypot problem. The only threat of an adversary controlling the network is Denial of Service (DoS), namely, preventing a client from using its wallet. Nevertheless, the requirement for the client to collaborate with the network to produce a signature raises many practical difficulties. First, the access structure is inherently hierarchical. Prior solutions that used a threshold access structure had to compromise on the size of the network, as the user must have the same weight as the whole network. Second, the client is typically lightweight, and does not have comparable computational power to parties in the decentralized network. Optimally, the computation complexity of the client should be independent of the network size. Third, the client typically does not have direct access to internal entities in the decentralized network, and might not even be aware of their identities. Exposing such communication channels may pose additional cybersecurity threat for parties in the network, and would also significantly increase the communication overhead of the client.

With the above issues in mind, [39] added to the 2PC-MPC *hierarchical access structure* an additional requirement that when met, allows for the system to scale with the number of parties in the decentralized network. Namely, the client experiences a *two-party computation* (2PC) protocol, wherein the network emulates the second party by participating in *multi-party computation* (MPC) protocol.[1] Hence the name: 2PC-MPC.

Another important aspect of a decentralized system is the number of clients it can concurrently service. Prior works on threshold signatures are typically focused on a single key, and do not consider the system as a whole. Therefore, each node in the decentralized network must hold a private share per each wallet of each client in the system. Instead, in [39], the *private storage* of each party in the decentralized network is independent of the number of clients as well as the number of nodes. This is achieved by utilizing a *threshold additively homomorphic encryption scheme* (TAHE) [25]. Essentially, the network share of each signing key is stored in public, encrypted under the TAHE public key, and only the underlying AHE secret decryption key is secretly shared.[2] In this work, we take a different approach, enabling the network to utilize a single *global key share* which will be used across all clients. This change also significantly simplifies any resharing or reconfiguration of the secret. Specifically, one does not need to reshare the secret key of the TAHE scheme but instead may only reshare elements in $\mathbb{Z}_q$ and generate a fresh TAHE key.

1.1 Our Contribution

Our primary contribution is the design and implementation of a 2PC-MPC protocol for an *asynchronous* decentralized network, servicing numerous clients concurrently to securely generate ECDSA signatures. The motivation behind this design is to be on par with implementation requirements of existing blockchains and their underlying communication channels, as we cover in Sect. 2. Additionally, Sect. 2 also provides extensive comparison with prior works, further highlighting the challenges addressed in this work and the advantage of our approach.

In addition, our protocol supports *global presigns*, which are generated autonomously by the network and are not bound to any particular client or request until the final signing step. This design allows the network to precompute presigns in the background whenever spare capacity is available and then serve signing requests with lower latency. Practically, global presigns (i) improve utilization as each presign generated is more likely to be used, (ii) simplify load management and rate limiting by maintaining a presign buffer, and (iii) reduce client interactivity requirements, since the client is only involved at signing time rather than throughout presign generation.

---

[1] The client can verify that it interacts with a decentralized network if the communication channel with the network is a blockchain. However, their design potentially allows hiding the size of the network, in case a future application might demand that.

[2] The idea of using TAHE and storing only the secret-key shares to minimize private storage was proposed in the YOSO line of work [44].

Technical Contributions. On top of that, this work introduces several contributions that might have independent interest. As a side-effect of complying with asynchronous networks, we improve the round complexity, compared to the 2PC-MPC protocol in [39]. This is because we may not use commitment rounds, as parties may not be available in the next round to open them. As a result, both DKG and signing consist of a one-round trip between the blockchain and the client. Our sign phase can be broken into a *presign* phase, and an *online-signing phase*. The presign phase is executed without client involvement in an *offline phase*, potentially before the message to be signed is decided. This preprocessing can reduce computation and latency during high-demand periods. When instantiated in the standard threshold access structure, that is, by removing the client and retaining only the committee of parties, DKG completes in a single round, presigning requires two rounds; and the online signing step is a single round. In this sense, our round complexity matches the best known constructions that allow the presigning and signing phases to involve different subsets of parties [23]. If, instead, one enforces that the same set of parties participates in both presign and sign, then recent two-round protocols are also known [26,58].

In addition, we alleviate the need for *zero-knowledge* (ZK) proofs towards the client, that were used in [39] to prove honest behavior. In order to admit the 2PC-MPC framework, [39] offered to aggregate the proofs from each party in the network. However, their aggregation approach is inherently synchronous and as such doesn't work for our purpose.

In terms of security, our protocol circumvents the *Enhanced-ECDSA unforgeability* assumption (proposed in [15]), even when allowing presigns. Enhanced ECDSA was proven secure in the EC-GGM model in [46], but the concrete parameters of the reduction are not sufficient when working over 256-bit elliptic curves commonly used nowadays (e.g., secp256k1 [5] used in both Bitcoin and Ethereum). We propose the *Slightly-Enhanced ECDSA unforgeability* assumption, and provide a reduction (also in EC-GGM) with a satisfying complexity. We believe other threshold ECDSA protocols can be adjusted to rely on this assumption instead.

Moreover, in this work we also consider *proactive aborts*, namely, the participating subset in each session and each communication round is not only post-determined, but is also adversarially chosen. This allows our protocol to tolerate an adversary that not only corrupts part of the network participants, but also has control over the network communication channel.

In Sect. 1.2 we delve deeper into the concrete design of our proposed system. In Appendix A, a range of applications that can be built upon it is listed.

1.2 System Overview

In this work, we design a blockchain-based massively decentralized cryptosystem for securely maintaining digital wallets on the bulk of deployed blockchains. Below we briefly describe the system as a whole.

The Blockchain. The blockchain is *permissionless*, and before the beginning of every *epoch*, *reconfiguration* allows *validators* to join or leave the network. The blockchain is based on *Proof of Stake* (PoS), and each *validator* has a *voting power* proportional to its stake [53]. In turn, during each reconfiguration, validators may also withdraw part of their stake, or increase their stake, which could change their voting power accordingly. The weighted access structure is implemented by giving each validator a number of secret shares of the TAHE secret key proportional to their voting power. This only affects performance during the sign phase of the protocol.

Communication. Clients can communicate with the blockchain by sending transactions and parsing blocks. The MPC party emulation sub-protocols can be implemented over the *consensus protocol* [9,10,37] used for producing blocks. The *block proposer* validator is responsible for aggregating the last MPC round, computing the message to send to the client, and including it in its proposed block. Oftentimes, such a communication channel is either asynchronous (as in Narwhal-Tusk [29]) or *partially synchronous* (as in Narwhal [66]-Bullshark).

Policies. Upon creation, wallets will specify policies, either by using *smart contracts* (see [59,71] and [47,70] for recent overviews and surveys) implemented on-chain, or using light-clients [19] in order to validate policies posted on another blockchain. Before validators participate in signing a transaction, they validate that it matches the policy of the corresponding wallet. Policies can specify, for instance, a *whitelist* or a *blacklist* of accounts, a *transaction limit*, a limit on the number of transactions per epoch, or anything else that can be specified in a smart contract. Compromising a client will not allow an adversary to bypass the policy of its wallet. Compromising the blockchain can only be exploited to bypass policies for wallets for which the client share was also compromised. This ensures security can only be enhanced by sharing the key with the blockchain. The only added risk for the client is DOS of the network.

With the above architecture, our cryptosystem supports a range of versatile applications across multiple blockchains. In Section A, we illustrate several key use-cases enabled by the flexibility, security, and scalability of the above design.

1.3 Paper Organization

Section 2 covers limitations of prior work, pinpointing the main technical challenges we address. Section 3 contains preliminaries and definitions. Our 2PC-MPC ECDSA protocols are presented in Sect. 4. In Sect. 5 we analyze security, and Sect. 6 provides implementation details and evaluation. Additional material appears in the appendices: applications (Appendix A), extended preliminaries (Appendix B), formal languages (Appendix C), full security proofs (Appendix D), raw performance data (Appendix E), TAHE instantiation via Class Groups (Appendix F), and adaptation to Schnorr signatures (Appendix G).

2 Related Work

This section discusses prior work, focusing on [39] whose 2PC-MPC framework we follow.

The work in [39] is described over an *ideal broadcast functionality*. In reality, consensus protocols implement a broadcast channel over P2P channels, e.g. via gossiping [2]. This distinction is crucial, since implementing an ideal broadcast channel over asynchronous networks is theoretically impossible [37]. This abstraction complicates using off-the-shelf broadcast implementations; we address these issues in this work.

In particular, they assume a *synchronous communication channel*, with a known bound on clock drift and message transmission delays, allowing parties to agree if a party does not broadcast a message. This also occurs in [63], an adaptation of [31] that achieves identifiable abort via a synchronous broadcast channel. Synchronous communication is a stringent requirement [72]; blockchains typically use partially-synchronous [32] or asynchronous channels. In this work, protocols are defined over an asynchronous channel, supporting existing broadcast implementations (e.g., Narwhal-Tusk [29], Narwhal-Bullshark [66], Mysticeti [3]) with significantly lower latency. In asynchronous communication, parties compute and broadcast messages for the next round as soon as a threshold from the previous round broadcasts, without coordinating on which parties failed to participate. While ROAST [63] adapts FROST1 [49] for asynchronous communication, it requires running multiple FROST sessions in parallel (up to the number of honest parties), making it asymptotically more expensive and consuming significant storage for managing parallel sessions.

In addition, prior works such as [39] often require the same subset of parties to participate in all rounds of a subprotocol (DKG, presign or sign). This is not on par with existing broadcast channel implementations [3,29,66], which only ensure that an arbitrary threshold of parties is online during each round. Our protocol allows participants to dynamically change between rounds, which aligns with existing broadcast implementations. While [63] also addresses this indirectly by ensuring one session where a fixed threshold participates in all rounds, our approach allows different subsets in each round, yielding better performance.

Finally, beyond practical challenges, we address theoretical concerns in securing ECDSA with presigns. Prior threshold ECDSA protocols enabling presigns (e.g., [15,17,27,31,39]) assumed the Enhanced ECDSA Unforgeability assumption [15], stating that forging signatures is hard even if the adversary queries nonce parts before deciding on messages. This was established in the EC-GGM model [46], but with cubic reduction complexity, insufficient for 256-bit curves. We propose Slightly-Enhanced (SE) ECDSA Unforgeability and achieve quadratic complexity. Our presign consists of a pair of nonces; at signing, they are combined based on the message, client input, presign, and public key, making SE-ECDSA compatible with 256-bit curves. Notably, in Appendix G.3, we prove security of an analogous SE-Schnorr oracle under the *Algebraic One-More Discrete Log* (AOMDL) assumption, which may simplify simulation of threshold Schnorr protocols with presigns such as FROST3 [22].

3 Preliminaries

Notation. Group elements and sets are denoted by capital letters (G, H), while field elements are typically denoted by small letters x, r. Algorithms are denoted by calligraphic big letters $(\mathcal{A}, \mathcal{F})$. Message identifiers are denoted in a sans-serif font $(\mathsf{sid}, \mathsf{ssid})$. Subscripts are usually reserved for descriptors and superscripts are used for indexing. In cases where only a descriptor is needed, it will be subscripted. For a finite set P the notation $x \leftarrow P$ implies that x is sampled uniformly at random from P. We also write $x \leftarrow \mathcal{A}(\cdot)$ for the output of an algorithm.

Entities. We consider two sets of parties, denoted by A and B. A is a collection of "centralized" entities identified by pid_A, which play the role of the clients in the system. The set B represents a single distributed entity identified by pid_B, which plays the role of the decentralized network, wherein each party $B_i \in B$ is a validator.

Communication Model. Parties in B do not communicate directly with the parties in A. Instead, an authorized subset of B agrees on a common message to send back to A. The receiving party in A is unaware of the identity of the individual parties comprising B or its internal structure. Typically, blockchains expose a distributed ledger that is publicly accessible to everyone, yet no individual is exposed to direct communication channels with the validators that maintain it. This is formalized in $\mathcal{F}_{\mathsf{global\text{-}broadcast}}$ (Functionality 2).

The internal communication channel between parties in B is an asynchronous reliable broadcast (ARB) channel, which is captured in $\mathcal{F}_{\mathsf{broadcast}}$ (Functionality 1). This is an abstraction of the communication channel used in blockchains to achieve agreement on transactions. Some of the potential instantiations can be found in [3,29,66]. Following [65], we note that the functionality only ensures *consistency*, and not *completeness*. Completeness suggests that if a single honest party generates an output, then every honest party eventually generates an output. Instead, this is viewed as a property of the broadcast protocol itself. In our context, completeness ensures guaranteed output delivery, but for security and correctness of our protocol, consistent broadcast suffices.

Typically, a consensus protocol is implemented on top of a reliable broadcast channel, so as to agree on an *order* for the transactions. However, in our context, a weaker notion may suffice. Recall that our system produces signatures to be posted on other blockchains, who may be responsible for ordering these transactions. Therefore, we only require a mechanism to agree upon a subset of messages corresponding to an authorized subset of parties from the previous MPC round of a given session sid. This is captured by $\mathcal{F}_{\mathsf{ACS}}$ (Functionality 3). A potential instantiation can be found in [65]. Another possibility, although relying on consensus, is to take the first set of blocks that contain an authorized subset.

For brevity, when we refer to the *Reliable Broadcast Model*, we mean that we are working in the $(\mathcal{F}_{\mathsf{broadcast}}, \mathcal{F}_{\mathsf{global\text{-}broadcast}}, \mathcal{F}_{\mathsf{ACS}})$-hybrid model. The broadcast functionalities are adapted from [65], while $\mathcal{F}_{\mathsf{ACS}}$ is a rephrasing from [64].

Adversarial Model. We work within the *static* adversarial model, meaning that the adversary selects the set of parties to corrupt before any protocol begins and cannot corrupt any parties afterward. The adversary is also a *rushing* adversary, that first sees the broadcast messages of all honest parties before sending any of its own. In addition, the adversary can *proactively* and *adaptively* block or delay messages. This is modeled by letting it choose a valid subset of parties to participate in each round. Indeed, while an attacker aims to corrupt parties as early as possible and maintain control when feasible, the adaptive blocking and delaying of messages can be viewed as a form of static corruption over the network infrastructure itself. The adversary also has access to the headers of any communication between honest parties and ideal functionalities, and for ease of exposition, we assume this implicitly throughout without explicitly stating it each time.

Due to our use of a reliable broadcast channel, we assume that the number of (static + adaptive) corruptions in B is at most $n/3$ throughout, and otherwise B is considered corrupt. Essentially, an adversary that corrupts more than a third of the network may fork the network into two disjoint components and break consistency. It may also stop participating, in which case guaranteed output delivery fails, breaking liveness and censorship resistance.

Ideal Functionality. The security of the 2PC-MPC architecture is defined by the ideal functionality $\mathcal{F}_{\mathsf{tsig}}^{\mathcal{G},\Gamma_D}$ (Functionality 1). This functionality incorporates a signing oracle $\mathcal{G}$. The functionality regulates access to the oracle in a straightforward manner: it permits any authorized subset to request key generation, presigning, and signing operations from the oracle. Any other type of query is controlled by the adversary.

Functionality 1: 2PC-MPC Signature Functionality $\mathcal{F}_{tsig}^{\mathcal{G},\Gamma_B}$

The functionality interacts with two disjoint sets of parties A and B along with an adversary $\mathcal{A}$ controlling a subset U. The functionality is parameterized by a signing oracle $\mathcal{G}$ and an access structure Γ_B.

1. **Key Generation**: Upon receiving $(\mathsf{keygen}, \mathsf{sid}, \mathsf{pid}_A)$ from A_{pid_A} along with $(\mathsf{keygen}, \mathsf{sid}, \mathsf{pid}_A, \mathsf{pid}_B)$ from a subset $S \in \Gamma_B$, do as follows:
   (a) Send $(\mathsf{keygen}, \mathsf{sid})$ to $\mathcal{G}$.
   (b) Act as a proxy between $\mathcal{A}$ and $\mathcal{G}$ until the oracle outputs $(\mathsf{keygen\text{-}output}, \mathsf{sid}, X)$ which it sends to all parties.
2. **Presign**: Upon receiving $(\mathsf{pres}, \mathsf{sid}, \mathsf{ssid}, \mathsf{pid}_B)$ from a subset $S \in \Gamma_B$, do as follows:
   (a) Send $(\mathsf{pres}, \mathsf{sid}, \mathsf{ssid})$ to $\mathcal{G}$.
   (b) Act as a proxy between $\mathcal{G}$ and $\mathcal{A}$ until the oracle outputs $(\mathsf{pres\text{-}output}, \mathsf{sid}, \mathsf{ssid}, \boldsymbol{K})$ which it sends to all parties.
3. **Sign**: Upon receiving $(\mathsf{sign}, X, \mathsf{msg}, \mathsf{sid}, \mathsf{ssid}, \mathsf{pid}_A)$ from $A_{\mathsf{pid}_A} \in A_X$ for which (X, A_X) is recorded, along with $(\mathsf{sign}, \mathsf{msg}, \mathsf{sid}, \mathsf{ssid}, \mathsf{pid}_A, \mathsf{pid}_B)$ from a subset $S \in \Gamma_B$, do as follows:
   (a) Send $(\mathsf{sign}, \mathsf{msg}, \mathsf{sid}, \mathsf{ssid})$ to $\mathcal{G}$.
   (b) Act as a proxy between $\mathcal{G}$ and $\mathcal{A}$ until the oracle outputs $(\mathsf{sign\text{-}output}, \mathsf{sid}, \mathsf{ssid}, \sigma)$ which it sends to all parties.

Zero-Knowledge Proofs (ZKPs). We recall the formal definition of *Zero-Knowledge Proofs* (ZKPs) and *Zero-Knowledge Proofs of Knowledge* (ZKPoK) in Appendix B.2. For a given ternary relation $R : \{0,1\}^* \times \{0,1\}^* \times \{0,1\}^* \mapsto \{0,1\}$, and every fixed $\mathsf{pp} \in \{0,1\}^*$, we define the following NP language $L[\mathsf{pp}] = \{x; w \mid R(\mathsf{pp}, x; w) = 1\}$. Namely, we require that for each $\mathsf{pp} \in \{0,1\}^*$, $R(\mathsf{pp}, \cdot; \cdot)$ is computable in polynomial time. In our context, pp consists of *public parameters* (e.g., a public encryption key or a specification of an elliptic curve), x is a *statement*, and w is a *witness.*

All of the ZKPs used are non-interactive, either by applying the Fiat-Shamir transform [35], or by applying Fischlin's transform [38] in case UC-extractable proofs are needed. A ZK protocol for the language L will be denoted as $\Pi_{\mathsf{zk}}^{L[\mathsf{pp}]}$ for the former case, and as $\Pi_{\mathsf{uc\text{-}zk}}^{L[\mathsf{pp}]}$ for the latter case. Formal definitions of the languages used in our protocol are provided in Appendix C.

Statement Aggregation. As all messages from B to parties in A must be aggregated, to this end we refer to a simple aggregation protocol. Given a language L and a binary operator $+ : L^2 \to L$, the aggregation protocol Π_{agg}^{L} works as follows. First, each party B_i sends to $\mathcal{F}_{\mathsf{broadcast}}$ a ZKP relative to L for $(\boldsymbol{Y}_i; \boldsymbol{w}_i)$ and validates the proofs of the other parties. Then, using $\mathcal{F}_{\mathsf{ACS}}$, the parties agree on a subset of the statements, and using $\mathcal{F}_{\mathsf{global\text{-}broadcast}}$, the statement $\sum_j \boldsymbol{Y}_j$ is sent to the client.

Homomorphic Commitments. For a commitment scheme with public parameters pp we denote the message space of the commitment as $\mathcal{M}_{\mathsf{pp}}$ and randomness space as $\mathcal{R}_{\mathsf{pp}}$. Unless specified otherwise $\mathsf{Com}_{\mathsf{pp}}$ refers to Pedersen Commitments [62] on the appropriate elliptic curve. Homomorphic Addition is denoted by $\oplus$ and scalar multiplication by $\odot$.

Threshold Additively Homomorphic Encryption (TAHE). Additively Homomorphic Encryption (AHE) is a public key encryption scheme that supports homomorphic addition of two ciphertexts. The scheme is parameterized by four abelian groups: the plaintext space $\mathcal{P}_{pk}$, the ciphertext space $\mathcal{C}_{pk}$, the randomness space $\mathcal{R}_{pk}$, and the key space $\mathcal{K}_{\kappa}$. We denote plaintext as pt, ciphertexts as ct, randomness as η, and public-secret key pairs as $(\mathsf{pk}; \mathsf{sk})$. We use $\oplus$ and $\odot$ for homomorphic addition and scalar multiplication respectively.

We utilize an AHE scheme with $\mathcal{P}_{pk} = \mathbb{Z}_q$, where q is the prime order of the elliptic curve used for the digital signature scheme. This can be achieved natively using class group-based AHE [18] or by interpreting the plaintext as a $\mathbb{Z}$-module using the Paillier scheme [61], as done in [39]. We require the AHE scheme to satisfy *circuit privacy* with respect to linear transformations. Specifically, the scheme admits *Secure Linear Evaluation* of two ciphertexts, ct_0 and ct_1, with coefficients a_0 and a_1, denoted as $\mathsf{AHE.Eval}(\mathsf{pk}, (\mathsf{ct}_0, \mathsf{ct}_1), (a_0, a_1); \eta)$. This evaluation should not reveal any information to an adversary holding sk and the randomness used for encrypting ct_0 and ct_1, other than the output of the linear evaluation on the messages. We denote by Scale the operation that multiplies a single ciphertext by a scalar while preserving the same guarantee. Note that we only demand that $\mathsf{ct}_0, \mathsf{ct}_1$ are elements of the ciphertext space and are not necessarily valid encryptions, see Appendix F for discussion.

In our protocols, we utilize Threshold Additively Homomorphic Encryption (TAHE), which allows any set of $t+1$ parties to decrypt while preventing any smaller subset from doing so. This is captured by an ideal functionality $\mathcal{F}_{\mathsf{TAHE}}$ (Functionality 5). We define an Additively Homomorphic Encryption (AHE) scheme and extend it to the threshold security model. This functionality can be emulated using class group-based TAHE [13] or Paillier-based TAHE with circuit privacy ([39], following [40]). Importantly, to obtain security against malicious adversaries, TAHE schemes often use *verification keys* which should be thought of as homomorphic commitments on the secret key shares. The verification keys are produced in the *Distributed Key Generation* (DKG) phase, and are then used during the threshold decryption phase in order to prove correctness of the decryption shares.

4 Protocols

Next, we describe our protocol, consisting of four sub-protocols: global distributed key generation 1, client key generation 2, presign 3, and sign 4.

4.1 Global Key Generation

In an asynchronous network, a standard commit and reveal approach is unusable: openings may be delayed indefinitely, blocking progress. However, simply removing commitments would let parties adapt their inputs and break security. Our approach is to run two, "insecure" asynchronous sub-protocols without commitments, resulting in two public key parts $X_{0,B}, X_{1,B}$, each of which may be biased by the adversary. We observe that taking a pseudorandom combination of the two that is determined after all parties send their inputs is sufficient for security. In our protocol, this randomization happens during the client key generation phase.

Concretely, the protocol proceeds in a single round. Each party B_i samples two secret key shares $x_0^i, x_1^i \leftarrow \mathbb{Z}_q$, computes the corresponding public shares $X_0^i = x_0^i G$ and $X_1^i = x_1^i G$, and encrypts the secret shares under the TAHE public key. Each party then proves, via a ZKP in the language L_{EncDL}, that the ciphertexts and public shares are consistent. Using the aggregation protocol Π_{agg}, the parties aggregate their individual contributions into the global outputs $X_{0,B} = \sum_i X_0^i$, $X_{1,B} = \sum_i X_1^i$, along with ciphertexts $\mathsf{ct}_{\mathsf{key},0}, \mathsf{ct}_{\mathsf{key},1}$ encrypting the corresponding summed secret key shares $x_0 = \sum_i x_0^i$ and $x_1 = \sum_i x_1^i$. These global outputs are then used by all subsequent client key generation instances.

Protocol 1: Global Key-Generation: $\Pi_{\mathsf{global\text{-}keygen}}$: $\mathsf{GlobalKeyGen}(\mathbb{G}, G, q, \Gamma_B, \mathsf{sid}, \mathsf{pk})$

1. **Each B_i does the following:**
   - **Round 1**:
   (a) Sample $x_0^i, x_1^i \leftarrow \mathbb{Z}_q$ and $\eta_0^i, \eta_1^i \leftarrow \mathcal{R}_{pk}$.
   (b) Compute $X_0^i = x_0^i G$, $X_1^i = x_1^i G$ and $\mathsf{ct}_0^i = \mathsf{AHE.Enc}(\mathsf{pk}, x_0^i; \eta_0^i)$, $\mathsf{ct}_1^i = \mathsf{AHE.Enc}(\mathsf{pk}, x_1^i; \eta_1^i)$.
   (c) Run $\Pi_{\mathsf{agg}}^{\Gamma_B, L_{\mathsf{EncDL}}[\mathsf{pk},(\mathbb{G},G,q)]}$ on inputs $(X_0^i, \mathsf{ct}_0^i; x_0^i, \eta_0^i)$ and $(X_1^i, \mathsf{ct}_1^i; x_1^i, \eta_1^i)$ to obtain $(X_{0,B}, X_{1,B}, \mathsf{ct}_{\mathsf{key},0}, \mathsf{ct}_{\mathsf{key},1})$.
   - **Output**: $X_{0,B}, X_{1,B}, \mathsf{ct}_{\mathsf{key},0}, \mathsf{ct}_{\mathsf{key},1}$.

4.2 Client Key Generation

On the client side of the DKG, all clients operate over the common global DKG output $X_{0,B}, X_{1,B}$. Each client A samples its additive share of the secret key $x_A \leftarrow \mathbb{Z}_q$ and broadcasts $X_A = x_A \cdot G$, alongside a corresponding UC extractable zk proof π_{DL}. The coefficients $\mu_x^0, \mu_x^1, \mu_x^G \in \mathbb{Z}_q$ are then derived by querying the random oracle on the tuple $(\mathsf{sid}, \mathbb{G}, G, q, X_A, X_{0,B}, X_{1,B}, \pi_{\mathsf{DL}})$. Notably, the random oracle input includes π_{DL}, a UC-extractable ZKP of x_A. This binds the coefficients not only to the client's public share X_A but also to a proof of knowledge of the underlying secret, which is essential for security (see the proof sketch of Theorem 2). The network part is then computed as $X_B = \mu_x^0 \cdot X_{0,B} + \mu_x^1 \cdot X_{1,B} + \mu_x^G \cdot G$, and the public key is set as $X = X_B + X_A$. The corresponding secret key satisfies $x = \mu_x^0 \cdot x_0 + \mu_x^1 \cdot x_1 + \mu_x^G + x_A$, where x_0, x_1 are the network's secret shares from the global DKG.

Essentially, we view $(X_{0,B}, X_{1,B})$ as a commitment to the network part. As such the client does not need to commit to X_A as it only observes a commitment of X_B. Then, the affine transformation defined by $\mu_x^0, \mu_x^1, \mu_x^G$, can be viewed as the opening of the network's part X_B. Since the coefficients depend on the client part X_A, X_B is "opened" only after the client decides on its input. Notably, the client cannot commit before because the network DKG is global and we may not assume all clients could commit before it is performed.

Protocol 2: Centralized Party Key-Generation: $\Pi_{\text{centralized-keygen}}$**:** $\mathsf{CentralizedKeyGen}(\mathbb{G}, G, q, \textbf{sid}, \textbf{pk}; \textbf{global-keygen}, A_{\textbf{pid}})$

1. A_{pid} **does the following:**
   - **Round 1**:
   (a) Verify that $X_{0,B}, X_{1,B} \in \mathbb{G}$ and $\mathsf{ct}_{\text{key},0}, \mathsf{ct}_{\text{key},1} \in \mathcal{C}_{pk}$. If any check fails, terminate and designate B as malicious; otherwise continue.
   (b) Sample $x_{A_{\text{pid}}} \leftarrow \mathbb{Z}_q$ and compute $X_{A_{\text{pid}}} = x_{A_{\text{pid}}} G$.
   (c) Run $\Pi_{\text{uc-zk}}^{L_{\text{DL}}[(\mathbb{G},G,q)]}(X_{A_{\text{pid}}}; x_{A_{\text{pid}}})$ to generate a proof π_{DL}.
   (d) Send $(\mathsf{broadcast}, \mathsf{sid}, \mathsf{pid}_A, X_{A_{\text{pid}}}, \pi_{\text{DL}})$ to $\mathcal{F}_{\text{broadcast}}$.
2. **Output**
   - Each B_i:
     (a) Receive $(\mathsf{sid}, \mathsf{pid}_A, X_{A_{\text{pid}}}, \pi_{\text{DL}})$.
     (b) Verify π_{DL}. If it fails, designate A_{pid} as malicious and abort; otherwise continue.
     (c) Query the random oracle $\mathcal{H}(\mathsf{sid}, \mathbb{G}, G, q, X_{A_{\text{pid}}}, X_{0,B}, X_{1,B}, \pi_{\text{DL}})$ to obtain $\mu_x^0, \mu_x^1, \mu_x^G$.
     (d) Output $X_{A_{\text{pid}}}$ and record $(\mathsf{keygen}, \mathsf{pid}_A, \mathsf{global\text{-}keygen}, X_{A_{\text{pid}}}, \mu_x^0, \mu_x^1, \mu_x^G)$.
   - A_{pid}:
     (a) Query the random oracle $\mathcal{H}(\mathsf{sid}, \mathbb{G}, G, q, X_{A_{\text{pid}}}, X_{0,B}, X_{1,B}, \pi_{\text{DL}})$ to obtain $\mu_x^0, \mu_x^1, \mu_x^G$.
     (b) Output $X_{A_{\text{pid}}}$ and record $(\mathsf{keygen}, \mathsf{pid}_A, \mathsf{global\text{-}keygen}, X_{A_{\text{pid}}}, \mu_x^0, \mu_x^1, \mu_x^G)$.

4.3 Global Presign

Global presigns may be consumed by any client to generate a signature in the online signing phase. As such, by the stage they are created the client nonce contribution is yet to be committed. Therefore, similarly to the technique used in the global DKG, the network will generate two public nonces $K_{0,B}, K_{1,B}$. During online signing, the final network part will be a-posteriori derived, as a pseudorandom linear combination of the two parts $\mu_k^0 K_{0,B} + \mu_k^1 K_{1,B} + \mu_k^G G$.

The protocol proceeds in two rounds and uses a random mask γ_B to blind the secret key shares. In the first round, each party B_i samples a random mask share $\gamma_B^i \leftarrow \mathbb{Z}_q$, encrypts it under pk, and homomorphically multiplies the global key ciphertexts $\mathsf{ct}_{\mathsf{key},0}, \mathsf{ct}_{\mathsf{key},1}$ by γ_B^i to obtain encryptions of $\gamma_B^i \cdot x_0$ and $\gamma_B^i \cdot x_1$. These are aggregated via Π_{agg} to produce ct_γ (encrypting the combined mask $\gamma_B = \sum_i \gamma_B^i$) and $\mathsf{ct}_{\gamma_B \cdot \mathsf{key},0}, \mathsf{ct}_{\gamma_B \cdot \mathsf{key},1}$ (encrypting $\gamma_B \cdot x_0$ and $\gamma_B \cdot x_1$). In the second round, each party samples nonce shares $k_0^i, k_1^i \leftarrow \mathbb{Z}_q$ and homomorphically scales ct_γ by each nonce share, yielding encryptions of $k_0^i \cdot \gamma_B$ and $k_1^i \cdot \gamma_B$. It also computes the public nonce parts $R_{B,0}^i = k_0^i G$ and $R_{B,1}^i = k_1^i G$. The parties again aggregate via Π_{agg} to obtain the final outputs. The mask γ_B will later cancel during the sign phase when the ciphertext ct_A is divided by $\mathsf{ct}_{\alpha,\beta}$, ensuring that the final signature is correctly formed.

Protocol 3: Global Presign: $\Pi^{\mathsf{ECDSA}}_{\mathsf{global\text{-}presign}}$: $\mathsf{GlobalPresign}(\mathbb{G}, G, q, \mathsf{sid}, \mathsf{pk}; \mathsf{global\text{-}keygen}, \mathsf{ct}_{\mathsf{key},0}, \mathsf{ct}_{\mathsf{key},1})$

The protocol outputs:

- ct_γ – an encryption of a randomizer γ_B.
- $\mathsf{ct}_{\gamma_B \cdot \mathsf{key},0}$, $\mathsf{ct}_{\gamma_B \cdot \mathsf{key},1}$ – encryptions of $\gamma_B \cdot x_0$ and $\gamma_B \cdot x_1$, respectively.
- $\mathsf{ct}_{\gamma \cdot k_0}$, $\mathsf{ct}_{\gamma \cdot k_1}$ – encryptions of $k_0 \cdot \gamma_B$ and $k_1 \cdot \gamma_B$, respectively.
- $R_{B,0}$, $R_{B,1}$ – curve points equal to $k_0 G$ and $k_1 G$, respectively.

1. **Each B_i does the following:**
   - **Round 1**:

   (a) Sample $\gamma_B^i \leftarrow \mathbb{Z}_q$ and $\eta_1^i, \eta_2^i, \eta_3^i \leftarrow \mathcal{R}_{pk}$, and compute:
      i. $\mathsf{ct}_\gamma^i = \mathsf{AHE.Enc}(\mathsf{pk}, \gamma_B^i; \eta_1^i)$,
      ii. $\mathsf{ct}^i_{\gamma_B \cdot \mathsf{key},0} = \mathsf{AHE.Scale}(\mathsf{pk}, \mathsf{ct}_{\mathsf{key},0}, \gamma_B^i; \eta_2^i)$,
      iii. $\mathsf{ct}^i_{\gamma_B \cdot \mathsf{key},1} = \mathsf{AHE.Scale}(\mathsf{pk}, \mathsf{ct}_{\mathsf{key},1}, \gamma_B^i; \eta_3^i)$.

   (b) Run $\Pi_{\mathsf{agg}}^{\Gamma_B, L_{\mathsf{EncDH}}[\mathsf{pk}, \mathsf{ct}_{\mathsf{key},0}, \mathsf{ct}_{\mathsf{key},1}]}$ on inputs $(\mathsf{ct}_\gamma^i, \mathsf{ct}^i_{\gamma_B \cdot \mathsf{key},0}, \mathsf{ct}^i_{\gamma_B \cdot \mathsf{key},1}; \gamma_B^i, \eta_1^i, \eta_2^i, \eta_3^i)$ to obtain $(\mathsf{ct}_\gamma, \mathsf{ct}_{\gamma_B \cdot \mathsf{key},0}, \mathsf{ct}_{\gamma_B \cdot \mathsf{key},1})$.
   - **Round 2**:

   (a) Sample $k_0^i, k_1^i \leftarrow \mathbb{Z}_q$ and $\eta_{4,0}^i, \eta_{4,1}^i \leftarrow \mathcal{R}_{pk}$, and compute:
      i. $\mathsf{ct}^i_{\gamma \cdot k_0} = \mathsf{AHE.Scale}(\mathsf{pk}, \mathsf{ct}_\gamma, k_0^i; \eta_{4,0}^i)$,
      ii. $\mathsf{ct}^i_{\gamma \cdot k_1} = \mathsf{AHE.Scale}(\mathsf{pk}, \mathsf{ct}_\gamma, k_1^i; \eta_{4,1}^i)$,
      iii. $R_{B,0}^i = k_0^i G$,
      iv. $R_{B,1}^i = k_1^i G$.

   (b) Run $\Pi_{\mathsf{agg}}^{\Gamma_B, L_{\mathsf{ScaleDL}}[\mathsf{pk}, (\mathbb{G}, G, q), \mathsf{ct}_\gamma]}$ on inputs $(\mathsf{ct}^i_{\gamma \cdot k_0}, R^i_{B,0}; k_0^i, \eta^i_{4,0})$ and $(\mathsf{ct}^i_{\gamma \cdot k_1}, R^i_{B,1}; k_1^i, \eta^i_{4,1})$ to obtain $(\mathsf{ct}_{\gamma \cdot k_0}, R_{B,0})$ and $(\mathsf{ct}_{\gamma \cdot k_1}, R_{B,1})$.

   (c) **Output**: Record $(\mathsf{sid}, \mathsf{global\text{-}presign}, \mathsf{ct}_\gamma, \mathsf{ct}_{\gamma_B \cdot \mathsf{key},0}, \mathsf{ct}_{\gamma_B \cdot \mathsf{key},1}, \mathsf{ct}_{\gamma \cdot k_0}, \mathsf{ct}_{\gamma \cdot k_1}, R_{B,0}, R_{B,1})$.

4.4 Online Sign

In the 2PC-MPC framework, the client runtime and communication overhead should be independent of network size. It turns out that the challenge lies in the ZKPs, as the statements sent by the network are always summed in our protocols. However, we find proof aggregation for the corresponding summed-up statements to be quite challenging over an asynchronous network.

Instead, we remove the proofs toward the client altogether. Conceptually, we want to view the client as a signing oracle. The unforgeability of the signing oracle will ensure the network will not be able to forge a signature regardless of what it sends to the client. While this concept somewhat works for EdDSA, it fails for ECDSA and allows non-trivial attacks, as explained below.

In our protocol, the client essentially gets the ingredients it needs to compute $R := k_A^{-1} \cdot R_B$ and an encryption of $\sigma_A := k_A \cdot (m + rx)$ under B's public key. One can think of (R, σ_A) as an ECDSA signature with respect to the group $(\mathbb{G}, R_B)$, signing key x, and nonce k_A. Party B can then translate it into an ECDSA signature over $(\mathbb{G}, G)$ by decrypting σ_A and dividing it by k_B, where $R_B = k_B \cdot G$. Therefore, intuitively, party A acts as an ECDSA signing oracle, with the key distinction that the adversary can pick the generator of the group R_B every time.

Nevertheless, the above protocol enables the following attack. Party B sends X instead of R_B, which becomes possible now that a ZKP for $R_B \leftarrow X$ is not required. It will get $k_A^{-1} \cdot X$ and (the encryption of) $\sigma_A = k_A(m + rx)$. It then multiplies $k_A^{-1}X$ by σ_A to get $(m + rx) \cdot X$, which gives away $x^2 \cdot G$. By repeating this, it can get $x^k \cdot G$, for any $k \in \mathsf{poly}(\kappa)$. This is an instance of the Strong Diffie-Hellman Problem which is known to be broken in certain settings [20].

In order to resolve this issue, we allow the client to apply an affine transformation to the nonce of B. In particular, it sends $\mathsf{Enc}(\alpha k_B + \beta)$. Notice that we could not fix α or β as a single degree of freedom would allow the adversary to extract them bringing us back to square one. This may seem to shift too much power to the client. However, as long as the derivation of the network nonce part R_B depends on α, β and k_A, this extra power is still captured by the slightly enhanced signing oracle. To this end, the client sends homomorphic commitments to α, β and k_A, and the network nonce part is computed as $R_B = \mu_k^0 \cdot R_{B,0} + \mu_k^1 \cdot R_{B,1} + \mu_k^G \cdot G$, where the coefficients $\mu_k^0, \mu_k^1, \mu_k^G$ are derived based on those commitments as well.

The sign protocol (Protocol 4) has the client first derive the combined encrypted key $\mathsf{ct}_{\gamma\cdot\mathsf{key}}$ from the presign outputs using the key-derivation coefficients $\mu_x^0, \mu_x^1, \mu_x^G$ and the public key X. The client then samples $k_A, \alpha, \beta \leftarrow \mathbb{Z}_q$ and publishes Pedersen commitments C_k, C_α, C_β along with ZKPs of well-formedness. The nonce-derivation coefficients $\mu_k^0, \mu_k^1, \mu_k^G$ are obtained from a random oracle query on the public data together with these commitments and proofs. Using $\mu_k^0, \mu_k^1, \mu_k^G$, the client combines the two presign nonces into the network nonce R'_B, applies the affine transformation to get $R_B = \alpha R'_B + \beta G$, and computes $R = k_A^{-1} \cdot R_B$. The client also homomorphically evaluates the ciphertexts to produce $\mathsf{ct}_{\alpha,\beta}$ (encrypting $\gamma_B \cdot k_B$) and ct_A (encrypting $\gamma_B \cdot k_A(m+rx)$), accompanied by ZKPs proving consistency with the commitments. The network verifies all proofs, decrypts ct_A and $\mathsf{ct}_{\alpha,\beta}$ via $\mathcal{F}_{\mathsf{TAHE}}$, and recovers $s = \mathsf{ct}_{\alpha,\beta}^{-1} \cdot \mathsf{ct}_A = k_B^{-1} \cdot k_A(m + rx) = k^{-1}(m + rx)$, yielding the final ECDSA signature (r, s).

5 Security

In this section, we introduce the *Slightly Enhanced* signing oracle 2 and prove its security in the EC-GGM model in Sect. 5.1. We then prove the security of our protocols in Sect. 5.2. Because our protocol has no commitments, a rushing adversary can introduce an *additive bias* into the public-key shares $X_{B,0}, X_{B,1}$ and into the public nonce shares $R_{B,0}, R_{B,1}$. We therefore model this explicitly by allowing an additive bias in the signing oracle. Moreover, the adversarial model permits *adaptive message delays*, which give the adversary additional control.

In the standalone setting, this can be handled by guessing a single honest party that participates in the round and rewinding if the adversary delays that party's message. In the UC setting, we instead proceed as follows. The simulator queries the signing oracle to obtain X, and then sends $X + x_i \cdot G$, where $x_i \leftarrow \mathbb{Z}_q$ is sampled uniformly at random (for each relevant party index i). Once the set of honest participants S_H is determined, the resulting final value becomes $|S_H| \cdot X + \sum_{i \in S_H} x_i + \beta$. Consequently, the signing oracle must allow not only an additive bias β, but also a *multiplicative bias* (of $|S_H|$). It remains to UC-extract β. We do so by extracting the secret key of the TAHE scheme and then decrypting the appropriate ciphertexts.

In addition to the aforementioned biases, our signing oracle supports global keys and global presigns. Namely, the adversary may derive polynomially many public keys from the same X_0, X_1 and presigns are connected to a specific key only upon a sign request. We call this new oracle *Slightly Enhanced* and it is presented in 2.

Functionality 2: Slightly Enhanced ECDSA Signing Oracle: $\mathcal{G}^*_{\mathsf{SE\text{-}ECDSA}}$

1. Generation of global keys: Sample $\tilde{x}_0, \tilde{x}_1 \leftarrow \mathbb{Z}_q$ and send $\tilde{X}_0 = \tilde{x}_0 \cdot G$ and $\tilde{X}_1 = \tilde{x}_1 \cdot G$.
2. On input $(\mathsf{biaskey}, \mathsf{sid}, \alpha_x^0, \beta_x^0, \alpha_x^1, \beta_x^1)$ set $x_0 \leftarrow \alpha_x^0 \cdot \tilde{x}_0 + \beta_x^0$ and $x_1 \leftarrow \alpha_x^1 \cdot \tilde{x}_1 + \beta_x^1$, together with $X_0 \leftarrow x_0 \cdot G$ and $X_1 \leftarrow x_1 \cdot G$. Then set $(\mu_x^0, \mu_x^1, \mu_x^G) = \mathcal{H}(\mathsf{sid}, X_0, X_1)$. Finally, set $x = \mu_x^0 \cdot x_0 + \mu_x^1 \cdot x_1 + \mu_x^G$ and $X = x \cdot G$, and record $(\mathsf{sid}, X; x)$.
3. On input $(\mathsf{pres}, \mathsf{ssid})$, sample $\tilde{k}_0, \tilde{k}_1 \leftarrow \mathbb{Z}_q$, compute $\tilde{R}_0 = \tilde{k}_0 \cdot G$ and $\tilde{R}_1 = \tilde{k}_1 \cdot G$, record $(\mathsf{ssid}, \tilde{R}_0, \tilde{R}_1; \tilde{k}_0, \tilde{k}_1)$ and send $(\mathsf{ssid}, \tilde{R}_0, \tilde{R}_1)$.
4. On input $(\mathsf{sign}, \mathsf{sid}, \mathsf{ssid}, \mathsf{msg}; \delta_x, \alpha_{\mathsf{pres},0}, \beta_{\mathsf{pres},0}, \alpha_{\mathsf{pres},1}, \beta_{\mathsf{pres},1})$ do:
   (a) Retrieve $(\mathsf{sid}, X; x)$ and $(\mathsf{ssid}, \tilde{R}_0, \tilde{R}_1; \tilde{k}_0, \tilde{k}_1)$. If no such ssid or sid exists, ignore.
   (b) Compute $k_0 \leftarrow \alpha_{\mathsf{pres},0} \cdot \tilde{k}_0 + \beta_{\mathsf{pres},0}$ and $k_1 \leftarrow \alpha_{\mathsf{pres},1} \cdot \tilde{k}_1 + \beta_{\mathsf{pres},1}$.
   (c) Set $R_0 = k_0 \cdot G$ and $R_1 = k_1 \cdot G$.
   (d) Set $(\mu_k^0, \mu_k^1, \mu_k^G) = \mathcal{H}(\mathsf{sid}, \mathsf{ssid}, X, \delta_x, R_0, R_1, \mathsf{msg})$, and set $k = \mu_k^0 \cdot k_0 + \mu_k^1 \cdot k_1 + \mu_k^G$ and $R = k \cdot G$.
   (e) Set $r = R_{x-axis}$ and compute $s = k^{-1} \cdot (\mathcal{H}(\mathsf{msg}) + r \cdot (x + \delta_x))$.
   (f) Erase $(\mathsf{ssid}, \tilde{R}_0, \tilde{R}_1; \tilde{k}_0, \tilde{k}_1)$ from memory and return $(\mathsf{sid}, \mathsf{ssid}, \mathsf{msg}; \alpha_{\mathsf{pres},0}, \beta_{\mathsf{pres},0}, \alpha_{\mathsf{pres},1}, \beta_{\mathsf{pres},1}; R, s, r)$.

Protocol 4: Sign $\Pi_{\mathsf{Sign}}^{\mathsf{ECDSA}}$

$\mathsf{Sign}(\mathbb{G}, G, H, q, \mathbf{sid}, \Gamma_B, \mathbf{pk}, X_A, \mu_x^0, \mu_x^1, \mu_x^G, \mathbf{global\text{-}keygen}, \mathbf{pres}, \mathbf{msg})$

1. A_{pid_A} **does as follows**:
   (a) Calculate $\mathsf{ct}_{\gamma\cdot\mathsf{key}} = \mu_x^0 \odot \mathsf{ct}_{\gamma_B\cdot\mathsf{key},0} \oplus \mu_x^1 \odot \mathsf{ct}_{\gamma_B\cdot\mathsf{key},1} \oplus \mu_x^G \odot \mathsf{ct}_\gamma$ and $X = X_A + \mu_x^0 X_{0,B} + \mu_x^1 \cdot X_{1,B} + \mu_x^G \cdot G$.
   (b) Call the random oracle $\mathcal{H}$ on msg and receive m.
   (c) Sample $k_A, \alpha, \beta \leftarrow \mathbb{Z}_q$ and $\rho_0, \rho_1, \rho_2, \rho_3 \leftarrow \mathcal{R}_{\mathsf{pp}}$, and computes:
      i. $C_k = \mathsf{Pedersen.Com}_{G,H}(k_A; \rho_0)$
      ii. $C_\alpha = \mathsf{Pedersen.Com}_{G,H}(\alpha; \rho_1)$
      iii. $C_\beta = \mathsf{Pedersen.Com}_{G,H}(\beta; \rho_2)$
      iv. $C_{kx} = \mathsf{Pedersen.Com}_{X_A,H}(k_A; \rho_3)$
   (d) Run the protocols $\Pi_{\mathsf{zk}}^{L_{\mathsf{Dcom}}[C_k,H]}(G; k_A^{-1}, -k_A^{-1}\rho_0)$, $\Pi_{\mathsf{zk}}^{L_{\mathsf{Dcom}}[C_\alpha,H]}(G; (\alpha^{-1}, -\alpha^{-1}\rho_1)$ and $\Pi_{\mathsf{zk\text{-}uc}}^{L_{\mathsf{Dcom}}[G,H]}(C_\beta; \beta, \rho_2)$ generating proofs π_k and π_α, π_β.
   (e) We denote $\mathsf{pubdata} = \mathsf{sid}, \mathsf{msg}, \mathbb{G}, G, q, H, X, \mathsf{pres}_{X,\mathsf{sid}}$. Call the random oracle on $\mathcal{H}(\mathsf{pubdata}, C_k, C_{kx}, X_A, C_\alpha, C_\beta, \pi_k, \pi_\alpha, \pi_\beta)$, and receives $\mu_k^0, \mu_k^1, \mu_k^G$. It then computes:
      – $\mathsf{ct}_{\gamma\cdot k} = (\mu_k^0 \odot \mathsf{ct}_{\gamma\cdot k_0}) \oplus (\mu_k^1 \odot \mathsf{ct}_{\gamma\cdot k_1}) \oplus (\mu_k^G \odot \mathsf{ct}_\gamma)$
      – $R_B' = (\mu_k^0 R_{B,0}) + (\mu_k^1 \cdot R_{B,1}) + \mu_k^G \cdot G$
   (f) Sample $\eta_0, \eta_1 \leftarrow \mathcal{R}_{pk}$ and computes:
      i. $\mathsf{ct}_{\alpha,\beta} = \mathsf{AHE.Eval}(\mathsf{pk}, (\mathsf{ct}_\gamma, \mathsf{ct}_{\gamma\cdot k}), (0, \beta, \alpha); \eta_0)$
      // In honest protocol encrypts $\gamma \cdot (\alpha \cdot (\mu_k^0 k_{B,0} + \mu_k^1 k_{B,1} + \mu_k^G) + \beta) := \gamma \cdot k_B$
      ii. $R_B = (\alpha \cdot R_B') + (\beta \cdot G)$
      iii. $R = k_A^{-1} \cdot R_B$ and $r = R_{x-axis}$
      iv. $a_1 = r \cdot k_A \cdot x_A + m \cdot k_A$ and $a_2 = r \cdot k_A$
      v. $\mathsf{ct}_A = \mathsf{AHE.Eval}(\mathsf{pk}, (\mathsf{ct}_\gamma, \mathsf{ct}_{\gamma\cdot\mathsf{key}}), (0, a_1, a_2); \eta_1)$
      // In honest protocol encrypts $\gamma \cdot k_A(m + rx)$
   (g) Generate the following proofs:
      i. $\pi_{kx} \leftarrow \Pi_{\mathsf{zk}}^{L_{\mathsf{DcomEq}}[(G,H),(X_A,H)]}(C_k, C_{kx}; k_A, \rho_0, \rho_3)$
      ii. $\pi_R \leftarrow \Pi_{\mathsf{zk}}^{L_{\mathsf{DComDL}}[G,H,(\mathbb{G},R,q)]}(C_k, R_B; k_A, \rho_0)$
      iii. $\pi_{R_B} \leftarrow \Pi_{\mathsf{zk}}^{L_{\mathsf{VecDComDL}}[(G,H),(\mathbb{G},(R_B',G),q)]}(C_\alpha, C_\beta), R_B; (\alpha, \beta), \rho_1, \rho_2)$
      iv. $\pi_{\mathsf{ct}_{\alpha,\beta}} \leftarrow \Pi_{\mathsf{zk}}^{L_{\mathsf{DComEval}}[G,H,\mathsf{pk},(\mathsf{ct}_\gamma,\mathsf{ct}_{\gamma\cdot k}),(\mathbb{G},G,q))]}(\mathsf{ct}_{\alpha,\beta}, (C_\beta, C_\alpha); (\beta, \alpha), \rho_0, \rho_1, \eta_0)$
      v. $\pi_{\mathsf{ct}_A} \leftarrow \Pi_{\mathsf{zk}}^{L_{\mathsf{DComEval}}[G,H,\mathsf{pk},(\mathsf{ct}_\gamma,\mathsf{ct}_{\gamma\cdot\mathsf{key}}),(\mathbb{G},G,q)]}(\mathsf{ct}_A, (C_1, C_2); (a_1, a_2), \rho_3 r + \rho_0 m, r\rho_0, \eta_1)$
   (h) Denote $T_A = (R, R_B, C_k, C_\alpha, C_\beta, C_{kx}, \mathsf{ct}_A, \mathsf{ct}_{\alpha,\beta}, \pi_k, \pi_\alpha, \pi_\beta, \pi_{kx}, \pi_R, \pi_{R_B}, \pi_{\mathsf{ct}_{\alpha,\beta}}, \pi_{\mathsf{ct}_A})$ and send $(\mathsf{broadcast}, \mathsf{sid}, T_B)$ to $\mathcal{F}_{\mathsf{broadcast}}$.
2. **Each** B_i **does as follows**:
   - **Round 1**:
   (a) Calculate $\mathsf{ct}_{\gamma\cdot\mathsf{key}} = \mu_x^0 \odot \mathsf{ct}_{\gamma_B\cdot\mathsf{key},0} \oplus \mu_x^1 \odot \mathsf{ct}_{\gamma_B\cdot\mathsf{key},1} \oplus \mu_x^G \odot \mathsf{ct}_\gamma$ and $X = X_A + \mu_x^0 X_{0,B} + \mu_x^1 \cdot X_{1,B} + \mu_x^G \cdot G$.
   (b) Call the random oracle $\mathcal{H}(\mathsf{msg})$ and receives m.
   (c) Receive $(\mathsf{broadcast}, \mathsf{sid}, (R, R_B, C_k, C_\alpha, C_\beta, C_{kx}, \mathsf{ct}_A, \mathsf{ct}_{\alpha,\beta}, \pi_k, \pi_\alpha, \pi_\beta, \pi_{kx}, \pi_R, \pi_{R_B}, \pi_{\mathsf{ct}_{\alpha,\beta}}, \pi_{\mathsf{ct}_A}))$ from $\mathcal{F}_{\mathsf{broadcast}}$.
   (d) Call the random oracle $\mathcal{H}(\mathsf{pubdata}, C_k, C_{kx}, X_A, C_\alpha, C_\beta, \pi_k, \pi_\alpha, \pi_\beta)$ and compute:
      i. $\mathsf{ct}_{\gamma\cdot k} = (\mu_k^0 \odot \mathsf{ct}_{\gamma\cdot k_0}) \oplus (\mu_k^1 \odot \mathsf{ct}_{\gamma\cdot k_1}) \oplus (\mu_k^G \odot \mathsf{ct}_\gamma)$
      ii. $R_B' = (\mu_k^0 R_{B,0}) + (\mu_k^1 \cdot R_{B,1}) + \mu_k^G \cdot G$
      iii. $C_1 = (r \odot C_{kx}) \oplus (m \odot C_k)$
      iv. $C_2 = r \odot C_k$
   (e) Verify the proofs. If fail abort and consider A_{pid_A} malicious.
   (f) Send $(\mathsf{decrypt}, \mathsf{pk}, \mathsf{ct}_A)$ and $(\mathsf{decrypt}, \mathsf{pk}, \mathsf{ct}_{\alpha,\beta})$ to $\mathcal{F}_{\mathsf{TAHE}}$.
   - **Broadcast Round**:
   (a) Receive $(\mathsf{decrypted}, \mathsf{pk}, \mathsf{ct}_A, \mathsf{pt}_A)$ and $(\mathsf{decrypted}, \mathsf{pk}, \mathsf{ct}_{\alpha,\beta}, \mathsf{pt}_4)$ from $\mathcal{F}_{\mathsf{TAHE}}$.
   (b) Compute $s' = \mathsf{pt}_4^{-1} \cdot \mathsf{pt}_A \mod q$ and $s = \min\{s', q - s'\}$.
   (c) Send $(\mathsf{global\text{-}broadcast}, \mathsf{sid}, i, (r, s))$ to $\mathcal{F}_{\mathsf{global\text{-}broadcast}}^{\Gamma_B}$
3. **Output**:
   (a) A_{pid_A} receives $(\mathsf{global\text{-}broadcast}, \mathsf{sid}, (r, s))$ from $\mathcal{F}_{\mathsf{global\text{-}broadcast}}^{\Gamma_B}$.
   (b) A_{pid_A} verifies that (r, s) is a valid ECDSA signature, if the verification fails it aborts and considers B malicious.
   (c) Both A_{pid_A} and B outputs (r, s).

5.1 Analyzing Slightly Enhanced ECDSA

In this section, we provide a sketch of the security proof of the existential unforgeability game 1 with respect to the signing oracle 2 in the EC-GGM model [46]. In this model, a *group oracle* essentially samples a random mapping π between $\mathbb{Z}_q$ and the curve $\mathbb{G}$. The adversary interacts with the group oracle in order to perform computations over $\mathbb{G}$.

Theorem 1 (10). *Let $\mathcal{A}$ be an adversary to the existential unforgeability game 1 with respect to the ECDSA oracle $\mathcal{G}^{*}_{\mathsf{SE\text{-}ECDSA}}$ (Functionality 2) in the EC-GGM model (Lazy Simulation 6), that makes at most N presignature, signing, hash, or group queries, where $\mathcal{H}_{\mathsf{key}}, \mathcal{H}_{\mathcal{M}}$ and all $\mathcal{H}_k$ are modeled as independent Random Oracles. Then $\mathsf{Adv}(\mathcal{A}, \mathsf{Exp}_{\mathsf{EU}}^{\mathcal{G}^{*}_{\mathsf{SE\text{-}ECDSA}}}, \textit{lazy-sim}) \leq \mathcal{O}(\frac{N^2}{q})$.*

Proof (sketch). Our proof follows the steps taken in [46], and we refer to Appendix D.2 for a detailed proof.

As in [46], the proof consists of three steps. First, the signing oracle is simulated with a *lazy simulation*, wherein group mapping and the random oracle outputs are sampled "on the fly", only upon queries of new values. Second, the lazy simulation is reduced to a *symbolic simulation*, where in particular, the private signing key and the random values of the signatures are replaced with combinations of symbolic variables. The main impact of using a slightly enhanced oracle is apparent in the symbolic simulation. In contrast to [46], we show that by using two nonces in the presign, it is possible to keep one of the two corresponding variables symbolic throughout the entire simulation. This is the main difference which leads to a better security bound. Specifically, we prove that any adversary to our protocol that can forge a signature in the EC-GGM model with non-negligible probability must use $\Omega(\sqrt{q})$ overall oracle queries.

The security proof of the symbolic simulation is based on the symbolic verification equation of the forged signature and the equality of symbolic polynomials. Following [46], we then split the proof into several cases, depending on the creation of R^* of the forged signature. We show that the probability of each case is negligible.

Experiment 1: $\mathcal{G}^*$-Existential Unforgeability Experiment $\mathsf{Exp}_{\mathsf{EU}}^{\mathcal{G}^*}(\mathcal{A}, 1^\kappa, n_\mathsf{s}, n_\mathsf{kg})$ following [6]

The experiment interacts with an adversary $\mathcal{A}$ and is parameterized with 1^κ.

1. Call $\mathcal{G}^*$ with (setup) and hand $(\mathbb{G}, G, q)$ to $\mathcal{A}$.
2. The adversary $\mathcal{A}$ makes at most $n_\mathsf{kg} = \mathsf{poly}(\kappa)$ adaptive keygen calls to $\mathcal{G}^*$ and at most $n_\mathsf{s} = \mathsf{poly}(\kappa)$ adaptive pres or sign calls to $\mathcal{G}^*$ in the following way:
   - Call $\mathcal{G}^*$ with $(\mathsf{keygen}, \mathsf{sid})$ and hand X to $\mathcal{A}$.
   - Call $\mathcal{G}^*$ with $(\mathsf{pres}, \mathsf{ssid})$ and hand K_0 and K_1 to $\mathcal{A}$.
   - Call $\mathcal{G}^*$ with $(\mathsf{sign}, \mathsf{sid}, \mathsf{ssid}, \mathsf{msg})$ and hand $(\mathsf{sid}, \mathsf{ssid}, \mathsf{msg}, \sigma)$ to $\mathcal{A}$.
3. $\mathcal{A}$ outputs $(\mathsf{sid}, \mathsf{msg}, \sigma)$.

The experiment's output is 1 iff $\mathsf{Verify}(\mathsf{sid}, \mathsf{msg}, \sigma) = 1$ and m was not queried to $\mathcal{G}^*$, otherwise output 0.

5.2 Protocol Simulations

Next, we describe the main security theorems satisfied by our protocols.

Signing Protocols. The ECDSA based protocols UC realize their corresponding threshold signing functionality (Functionality 1) with Oracle 2 in the *reliable broadcast model* and $\mathcal{F}_\mathsf{TAHE}$ (Functionality 5)-hybrid model.

Theorem 2. *The protocols Π_{keygen}, $\Pi_{presign}^{ECDSA}$, and Π_{sign}^{ECDSA} UC realize $\mathcal{F}_{tsig}^{\mathcal{G}^*_{SE\text{-}ECDSA}, \binom{[n]}{t+1}}$ in the* reliable broadcast model *and $\mathcal{F}_{TAHE}$-hybrid model.*

Proof. (sketch). We refer the reader to Appendix D.1 for the detailed proof. For the simulator to succeed in the emulation of the ideal functionality, it must land on the signing oracle's public key and public nonce. The general approach is as follows: each sub-protocol simulation forwards its query to $\mathcal{G}^*_{\mathsf{SE\text{-}ECDSA}}$, receiving a value. The simulator embeds the value sent by the signing oracle into the honest parties' messages additively, then extracts the adversary's secrets. The actual output of the protocol is then a known bias away from the real execution, and the simulator inputs $\mathcal{G}^*_{\mathsf{SE\text{-}ECDSA}}$ with the correct biases. While the protocol allows for different sources of biases on these values, they are all affine linear, and as such even a composition of them is still affine linear and captured by the allowed biases in $\mathcal{G}^*_{\mathsf{SE\text{-}ECDSA}}$. Thus the main difficulty becomes extracting the adversary's values without re-winding and in the correct timing in the protocol.

When A is honest, the simulator embeds the oracle's public key and nonce directly into X_A and R, which works since the client speaks second. The adversary's secrets are extracted via the TAHE secret key which is itself extracted in the $\mathcal{F}_\mathsf{TAHE}$ simulation; and the resulting signature is embedded into the $\mathcal{F}_\mathsf{TAHE}$ decryption outputs. When A is malicious, during DKG it can adaptively query the random oracle for $\mu_x^0, \mu_x^1, \mu_x^G$ on various X_A values after observing X_B^0, X_B^1, before deciding which to send. The simulator must answer these queries *before* knowing the final X_A. This is resolved by including π_{DL}, a UC-extractable ZKP of x_A, in the random oracle input: the simulator extracts x_A upon each query, interprets it as an additive bias, and forwards it to $\mathcal{G}^*_{\mathsf{SE\text{-}ECDSA}}$ which determines $\mu_x^0, \mu_x^1, \mu_x^G$. A similar challenge arises during sign: the random oracle input for $\mu_k^0, \mu_k^1, \mu_k^G$ includes UC-extractable ZKPs of k_A, α, and β, allowing the simulator to extract them and adjust the μ_k coefficients so that the resulting nonce aligns with the oracle's re-randomization.

Indistinguishability follows from circuit privacy and semantic security of the AHE scheme, the zero-knowledge property, and random oracle programming.

6 Performance

We implemented our ECDSA protocol in Rust; the code will be made publicly available upon publication. We instantiate our TAHE with Class Groups based on [12]. We also build upon [8] and implement the first constant-time Class-Group library. All times are reported for $\sigma = 64, \kappa = 128, t = \frac{2}{3}n$ and the secp256k1 curve. We report the raw data for our real-world deployment experiments in Tables 1, 2, and 3.

Local Benchmarks. We conduct controlled local experiments on a MacBook Pro Apple M2 Max with a 3.49 GHz CPU running single-threaded. Figure 1 shows the network performance scaling of our Presign and Sign protocols with increasing party count. We omit DKG data as it is negligible except for the TAHE key generation. The Sign protocol demonstrates log-linear scaling, growing from 0.38 s (12 parties) to 0.94 s (120 parties), while the Presign protocol exhibits higher computational overhead, ranging from 2.1 s to 5.2 s.

The centralized party computation time remains effectively constant across all party counts, averaging 1.93 s with a coefficient of variation below 1%.

Real-World Deployment. We report performance data from real-world usage of our protocol over the Narwhal consensus layer with $n = 85$ validators in a permissionless setting where participants may dynamically enter and leave. Validator nodes are required to have minimum hardware specifications of 16 physical CPU cores, 128 GB RAM, 4 TB NVMe storage, and 1 Gbps network connectivity. That said, this requirement cannot be enforced or verified. Figure 2 shows the total protocol time distribution across validators (i.e. including both computation and communication), with complete data provided in Tables 1 and 2. The Sign protocol achieves a mean time of 1.05 s with a standard deviation of 0.47 s, while the Presign protocol requires 17.3 s on average with 9.2 s standard deviation. The significant variance (CV $\approx$ 45–53%) demonstrates that asynchronous execution provides performance benefits beyond being merely a consensus necessity; validators complete computations at heterogeneous speeds without blocking protocol progress.

Table 1. Presign protocol computation times across validators on Narwhal consensus.

Validator	Presign (ms)	Validator	Presign (ms)
Validator 1	28,867	Validator 44	10,552
Validator 2	24,626	Validator 45	13,903
Validator 3	1,692	Validator 46	20,144
Validator 4	19,041	Validator 47	10,943
Validator 5	11,451	Validator 48	10,204
Validator 6	18,895	Validator 49	12,272
Validator 7	9,732	Validator 50	30,496
Validator 8	1,679	Validator 51	25,470
Validator 9	17,215	Validator 52	23,567
Validator 10	10,866	Validator 53	10,134
Validator 11	21,933	Validator 54	17,461
Validator 12	7,175	Validator 55	11,392
Validator 13	19,305	Validator 56	12,120
Validator 14	25,174	Validator 57	36,546
Validator 15	16,436	Validator 58	15,694
Validator 16	35,783	Validator 59	21,392
Validator 17	1,646	Validator 60	20,510
Validator 18	23,343	Validator 61	14,504
Validator 19	29,277	Validator 62	10,104
Validator 20	21,454	Validator 63	14,333
Validator 21	12,606	Validator 64	27,246
Validator 22	18,449	Validator 65	18,475
Validator 23	1,696	Validator 66	18,651
Validator 24	25,182	Validator 67	2,882
Validator 25	20,579	Validator 68	12,059
Validator 26	25,248	Validator 69	6,960
Validator 27	26,737	Validator 70	11,194
Validator 28	29,214	Validator 71	12,120
Validator 29	27,156	Validator 72	11,738
Validator 30	27,189	Validator 73	11,753
Validator 31	16,875	Validator 74	55,079
Validator 32	19,091	Validator 75	11,611
Validator 33	13,837	Validator 76	10,904
Validator 34	18,852	Validator 77	9,658
Validator 35	1,648	Validator 78	11,996
Validator 36	16,226	Validator 79	19,001
Validator 37	20,076	Validator 80	23,095

Table 2. Sign protocol computation times across validators on Narwhal consensus.

Validator	Sign (ms)	Validator	Sign (ms)
Validator 1	865	Validator 44	750
Validator 2	855	Validator 45	1,069
Validator 3	574	Validator 46	989
Validator 4	780	Validator 47	1,331
Validator 5	1,311	Validator 48	1,131
Validator 6	773	Validator 49	1,285
Validator 7	1,205	Validator 50	991
Validator 8	658	Validator 51	867
Validator 9	797	Validator 52	1,018
Validator 10	829	Validator 53	1,161
Validator 11	858	Validator 54	815
Validator 12	818	Validator 55	969
Validator 13	887	Validator 56	1,561
Validator 14	885	Validator 57	2,774
Validator 15	1,456	Validator 58	1,195
Validator 16	1,116	Validator 59	1,674
Validator 17	577	Validator 60	757
Validator 18	1,021	Validator 61	1,480
Validator 19	822	Validator 62	1,289
Validator 20	847	Validator 63	1,130
Validator 21	760	Validator 64	799
Validator 22	802	Validator 65	823
Validator 23	556	Validator 66	838
Validator 24	857	Validator 67	856
Validator 25	875	Validator 68	937
Validator 26	850	Validator 69	984
Validator 27	859	Validator 70	985
Validator 28	923	Validator 71	1,022
Validator 29	848	Validator 72	973
Validator 30	1,857	Validator 73	3,868
Validator 31	915	Validator 74	954
Validator 32	808	Validator 75	1,288
Validator 33	1,026	Validator 76	1,280
Validator 34	808	Validator 77	1,552
Validator 35	563	Validator 78	858
Validator 36	842	Validator 79	867
Validator 37	1,427		

We do not have direct access to a global breakdown of communication versus computation time across validators. That said an execution report was provided to us by a single participating validator. Based on this report, communication accounts for 88.3% of the Presign protocol execution time and 54.4% of the Sign protocol execution time, where communication includes all consensus layer overhead as well as data uploads and downloads. The full reported measurements are summarized in Table 3.

Table 3. Communication overhead analysis for ECDSA Secp256k1 protocols. Measurements from c4d-standard-32 hardware running two validators. Communication time computed as difference between total protocol time and computation time.

Protocol	Computation (s)	Total Time (s)	Communication (s)	Comm. %
Sign	0.939	2.059	1.121	54.4%
Presign	7.769	66.330	58.561	88.3%

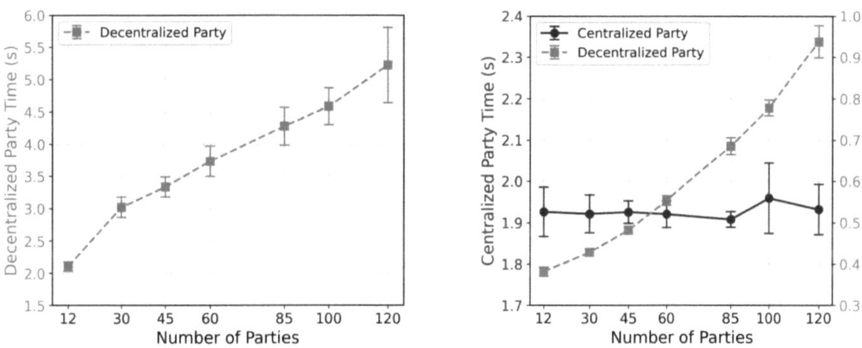

(a) Presign. (b) Sign.

Fig. 1. 2PC-MPC performance scaling with number of parties from local benchmarks.

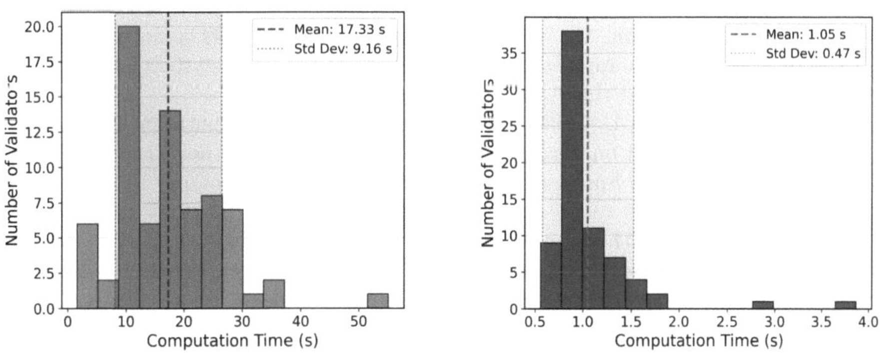

(a) Presign. (b) Sign.

Fig. 2. Protocol time distribution across validators. Performed over Narwhal consensus with $n = 85$ validators.

Disclosure of Interests. Offir Friedman, Avichai Marmor, Dolev Mutzari, Yehonatan C. Scaly, and Yuval Spiizer were employees of dWallet Labs Ltd. while working on this paper and may hold equity in the company. The authors declare that they have no other competing interests relevant to the content of this article.

References

1. Abram, D., Nof, A., Orlandi, C., Scholl, P., Shlomovits, O.: Low-bandwidth threshold ECDSA via pseudorandom correlation generators. In: SP, pp. 2554–2572. IEEE (2022)
2. Aysal, T.C., Yildiz, M.E., Sarwate, A.D., Scaglione, A.: Broadcast gossip algorithms for consensus. IEEE Trans. Signal Process. **57**(7), 2748–2761 (2009)
3. Babel, K., Chursin, A., Danezis, G., Kokoris-Kogias, L., Sonnino, A.: Mysticeti: low-latency dag consensus with fast commit path. arXiv preprint arXiv:2310.14821 (2023)
4. Bacho, R., Loss, J., Tessaro, S., Wagner, B., Zhu, C.: Twinkle: threshold signatures from DDH with full adaptive security. In: Annual International Conference on the Theory and Applications of Cryptographic Techniques, pp. 429–459. Springer, Heidelberg (2024). https://doi.org/10.1007/978-3-031-58716-0_15
5. Balasubramanian, K.: Security of the secp256k1 elliptic curve used in the bitcoin blockchain. Indian J. Cryptography Netw. Secur. (IJCNS) **4**(1), 1–5 (2024)
6. Blokh, C., Makriyannis, N., Peled, U.: Efficient asymmetric threshold ecdsa for mpc-based cold storage. Cryptology ePrint Archive (2022)
7. Boneh, D., Gennaro, R., Goldfeder, S.: Using level-1 homomorphic encryption to improve threshold DSA signatures for bitcoin wallet security. In: Lange, T., Dunkelman, O. (eds.) LATINCRYPT 2017. LNCS, vol. 11368, pp. 352–377. Springer, Cham (2019). https://doi.org/10.1007/978-3-030-25283-0_19
8. Bouvier, C., Castagnos, G., Imbert, L., Laguillaumie, F.: I want to ride my bicycl: bicycl implements cryptography in class groups. J. Cryptol. **36**(3), 17 (2023)
9. Bracha, G., Toueg, S.: Resilient consensus protocols. In: Proceedings of the Second Annual ACM Symposium on Principles of Distributed Computing, pp. 12–26 (1983)
10. Bracha, G., Toueg, S.: Asynchronous consensus and broadcast protocols. J. ACM (JACM) **32**(4), 824–840 (1985)
11. Brandão, L., Davidson, M.: Notes on threshold eddsa/schnorr signatures (2023)
12. Braun, L., et al.: An improved threshold homomorphic cryptosystem based on class groups. Cryptology ePrint Archive (2024)
13. Braun, L., Damgård, I., Orlandi, C.: Secure multiparty computation from threshold encryption based on class groups. In: Annual International Cryptology Conference, pp. 613–645. Springer, Heidelberg (2023). https://doi.org/10.1007/978-3-031-38557-5_20
14. Buterin, V., et al.: Ethereum white paper. GitHub Repository **1**, 22–23 (2013)
15. Canetti, R., Gennaro, R., Goldfeder, S., Makriyannis, N., Peled, U.: UC non-interactive, proactive, threshold ECDSA with identifiable aborts. In: CCS, pp. 1769–1787 (2020). https://eprint.iacr.org/2021/060.pdf
16. Castagnos, G., Catalano, D., Laguillaumie, F., Savasta, F., Tucker, I.: Bandwidth-efficient threshold EC-DSA. In: Kiayias, A., Kohlweiss, M., Wallden, P., Zikas, V. (eds.) PKC 2020. LNCS, vol. 12111, pp. 266–296. Springer, Cham (2020). https://doi.org/10.1007/978-3-030-45388-6_10

17. Castagnos, G., Catalano, D., Laguillaumie, F., Savasta, F., Tucker, I.: Bandwidth-efficient threshold ec-dsa revisited: online/offline extensions, identifiable aborts proactive and adaptive security. Theor. Comput. Sci. **939**, 78–104 (2023)
18. Castagnos, G., Laguillaumie, F.: Linearly homomorphic encryption from DDH. In: Nyberg, K. (ed.) CT-RSA 2015. LNCS, vol. 9048, pp. 487–505. Springer, Cham (2015). https://doi.org/10.1007/978-3-319-16715-2_26
19. Chatzigiannis, P., Baldimtsi, F., Chalkias, K.: Sok: blockchain light clients. In: International Conference on Financial Cryptography and Data Security, pp. 615–641. Springer, Heidelberg (2022). https://doi.org/10.1007/978-3-031-18283-9_31
20. Cheon, J.H.: Security analysis of the strong Diffie-Hellman problem. In: Vaudenay, S. (ed.) EUROCRYPT 2006. LNCS, vol. 4004, pp. 1–11. Springer, Heidelberg (2006). https://doi.org/10.1007/11761679_1
21. Chris, C., David, S.: Lit protocol whitepaper. Github Repository (2024). https://github.com/LIT-Protocol/whitepaper
22. Chu, H., Gerhart, P., Ruffing, T., Schröder, D.: Practical schnorr threshold signatures without the algebraic group model. In: Annual International Cryptology Conference, pp. 743–773. Springer, Heidelberg (2023). https://doi.org/10.1007/978-3-031-38557-5_24
23. Cohen, R., Doerner, J., Kondi, Y., Shelat, A.: Secure multiparty computation with identifiable abort via vindicating release. In: Annual International Cryptology Conference, pp. 36–73. Springer, Heidelberg (2024). https://doi.org/10.1007/978-3-031-68397-8_2
24. Copper: Wallets as a service. Whitepaper (2021). https://copper.co/en/products/wallets-as-a-service
25. Cramer, R., Damgård, I., Nielsen, J.B.: Multiparty computation from threshold homomorphic encryption. In: Pfitzmann, B. (ed.) EUROCRYPT 2001. LNCS, vol. 2045, pp. 280–300. Springer, Heidelberg (2001). https://doi.org/10.1007/3-540-44987-6_18
26. Dahari-Garbian, H., Nof, A., Parker, L.: Trout: Two-round threshold ecdsa from class groups. In: Proceedings of the 2025 ACM SIGSAC Conference on Computer and Communications Security, pp. 380–393 (2025)
27. Dalskov, A., Orlandi, C., Keller, M., Shrishak, K., Shulman, H.: Securing DNSSEC keys via threshold ECDSA from generic MPC. In: Chen, L., Li, N., Liang, K., Schneider, S. (eds.) ESORICS 2020. LNCS, vol. 12309, pp. 654–673. Springer, Cham (2020). https://doi.org/10.1007/978-3-030-59013-0_32
28. Damgård, I., Jakobsen, T.P., Nielsen, J.B., Pagter, J.I., Østergaard, M.B.: Fast threshold ECDSA with honest majority. In: Galdi, C., Kolesnikov, V. (eds.) SCN 2020. LNCS, vol. 12238, pp. 382–400. Springer, Cham (2020). https://doi.org/10.1007/978-3-030-57990-6_19
29. Danezis, G., Kokoris-Kogias, L., Sonnino, A., Spiegelman, A.: Narwhal and tusk: a dag-based mempool and efficient bft consensus. In: Proceedings of the Seventeenth European Conference on Computer Systems, pp. 34–50 (2022)
30. Doerner, J., Kondi, Y., Lee, E., Shelat, A.: Threshold ECDSA from ECDSA assumptions: the multiparty case. In: SP 2019, pp. 1051–1066. IEEE (2019)
31. Doerner, J., Kondi, Y., Lee, E., Shelat, A.: Threshold ECDSA in three rounds. IACR Cryptol. ePrint Arch. 765 (2023)
32. Dwork, C., Lynch, N., Stockmeyer, L.: Consensus in the presence of partial synchrony. J. ACM **35**(2), 288–323 (1988). https://doi.org/10.1145/42282.42283
33. Ergezer, S., Kinkelin, H., Rezabek, F.: A survey on threshold signature schemes. Network **49** (2020)

34. Etherscan: Ethereum node tracker. Etherscan (2024). https://etherscan.io/nodetracker
35. Fiat, A., Shamir, A.: How to prove yourself: practical solutions to identification and signature problems. In: Odlyzko, A.M. (ed.) CRYPTO 1986. LNCS, vol. 263, pp. 186–194. Springer, Heidelberg (1987). https://doi.org/10.1007/3-540-47721-7_12
36. Fireblocks: A guide to digital asset wallets and service providers. Whitepaper (2023). https://www.fireblocks.com/a-guide-to-digital-asset-wallets-and-service-providers/
37. Fischer, M.J., Lynch, N.A., Paterson, M.S.: Impossibility of distributed consensus with one faulty process. J. ACM (JACM) **32**(2), 374–382 (1985)
38. Fischlin, M.: Communication-efficient non-interactive proofs of knowledge with online extractors. In: Shoup, V. (ed.) CRYPTO 2005. LNCS, vol. 3621, pp. 152–168. Springer, Heidelberg (2005). https://doi.org/10.1007/11535218_10
39. Friedman, O., et al.: 2pc-mpc: Emulating two party ecdsa in large-scale mpc. Cryptology ePrint Archive (2024)
40. Friedman, O., Marmor, A., Mutzari, D., Scaly, Y.C., Spiizer, Y., Yanai, A.: Tiresias: large scale, maliciously secure threshold paillier. Cryptology ePrint Archive (2023)
41. Gagol, A., Kula, J., Straszak, D., Swietek, M.: Threshold ECDSA for decentralized asset custody. IACR Cryptol. ePrint Arch. 498 (2020)
42. Gennaro, R., Goldfeder, S.: Fast multiparty threshold ECDSA with fast trustless setup. IACR Cryptol. ePrint Arch. 114 (2019)
43. Gennaro, R., Goldfeder, S., Narayanan, A.: Threshold-optimal DSA/ECDSA signatures and an application to bitcoin wallet security. In: International Conference on Applied Cryptography and Network Security, pp. 156–174. Springer, Heidelberg (2016). https://eprint.iacr.org/2016/013.pdf
44. Gentry, C., et al.: YOSO: you only speak once. In: Malkin, T., Peikert, C. (eds.) CRYPTO 2021. LNCS, vol. 12826, pp. 64–93. Springer, Cham (2021). https://doi.org/10.1007/978-3-030-84245-1_3
45. Gray, E.: Governor. GitHub Repository (2022). https://github.com/wormhole-foundation/wormhole/blob/main/whitepapers/0007_governor.md
46. Groth, J., Shoup, V.: On the security of ecdsa with additive key derivation and presignatures. In: Annual International Conference on the Theory and Applications of Cryptographic Techniques, pp. 365–396. Springer, Heidelberg (2022). https://doi.org/10.1007/978-3-031-06944-4_13
47. Hu, B., et al.: A comprehensive survey on smart contract construction and execution: paradigms, tools, and systems. Patterns **2**(2) (2021)
48. Illia, P., Alexander, S.: The near white paper. Whitepaper (2021). https://pages.near.org/papers/the-official-near-white-paper/
49. Komlo, C., Goldberg, I.: FROST: flexible round-optimized schnorr threshold signatures. In: Dunkelman, O., Jacobson, Jr., M.J., O'Flynn, C. (eds.) SAC 2020. LNCS, vol. 12804, pp. 34–65. Springer, Cham (2021). https://doi.org/10.1007/978-3-030-81652-0_2
50. KZen, T.: Bitcoin wallet powered by two-party ecdsa - extended abstract. Whitepaper (2019). https://github.com/ZenGo-X/gotham-city/blob/master/white-paper/
51. KZen, T.: Radical new infrastructure for digital asset ownership and blockchain interoperability. Whitepaper (2019). https://www.qredo.com/qredo-white-paper.pdf
52. Labs, T.: Web3 auth. Github Repository (2024). https://github.com/web3auth

53. Leonardos, S., Reijsbergen, D., Piliouras, G.: Weighted voting on the blockchain: improving consensus in proof of stake protocols. Int. J. Network Manag. **30**(5), e2093 (2020)
54. Lindell, Y.: Fast secure two-party ECDSA signing. In: Annual International Cryptology Conference, pp. 613–644. Springer, Heidelberg (2017). https://eprint.iacr.org/2017/552.pdf)
55. Lindell, Y.: Digital asset management with mpc. Whitepaper (2023). https://www.coinbase.com/blog/digital-asset-management-with-mpc-whitepaper
56. Lindell, Y., Nof, A.: Fast secure multiparty ECDSA with practical distributed key generation and applications to cryptocurrency custody. In: CCS, pp. 1837–1854. ACM (2018)
57. Luongo, M., Pon, C.: The keep network: a privacy layer for public blockchains. Keep Netw., Rep (2018)
58. Lyu, Y., Li, Z., Zhou, H.S., Deng, X.: Threshold ecdsa in two rounds. In: Proceedings of the 2025 ACM SIGSAC Conference on Computer and Communications Security, pp. 2937–2950 (2025)
59. Mohanta, B.K., Panda, S.S., Jena, D.: An overview of smart contract and use cases in blockchain technology. In: 2018 9th International Conference on Computing, Communication and Networking Technologies (ICCCNT), pp. 1–4. IEEE(2018)
60. Nakamoto, S.: Bitcoin whitepaper, **9**, 15 (2008). https://bitcoin.org/bitcoin.pdf-(: 17.07.2019)
61. Paillier, P.: Public-key cryptosystems based on composite degree residuosity classes. In: Stern, J. (ed.) EUROCRYPT 1999. LNCS, vol. 1592, pp. 223–238. Springer, Heidelberg (1999). https://doi.org/10.1007/3-540-48910-X_16
62. Pedersen, T.P.: Non-interactive and information-theoretic secure verifiable secret sharing. In: Feigenbaum, J. (ed.) CRYPTO 1991. LNCS, vol. 576, pp. 129–140. Springer, Heidelberg (1992). https://doi.org/10.1007/3-540-46766-1_9
63. Ruffing, T., Ronge, V., Jin, E., Schneider-Bensch, J., Schröder, D.: Roast: robust asynchronous schnorr threshold signatures. In: Proceedings of the 2022 ACM SIGSAC Conference on Computer and Communications Security, pp. 2551–2564 (2022)
64. Shoup, V.: A theoretical take on a practical consensus protocol. Cryptology ePrint Archive (2024)
65. Shoup, V., Smart, N.P.: Lightweight asynchronous verifiable secret sharing with optimal resilience. J. Cryptol. **37**(3), 27 (2024)
66. Spiegelman, A., Giridharan, N., Sonnino, A., Kokoris-Kogias, L.: Bullshark: dag bft protocols made practical. In: Proceedings of the 2022 ACM SIGSAC Conference on Computer and Communications Security, pp. 2705–2718 (2022)
67. Stafford, V.: Zero trust architecture. NIST Special Publ. **800**, 207 (2020)
68. Team, D.: The internet computer for geeks. Cryptology ePrint Archive (2022)
69. Thorchain: Thorchain: A decentralised liquidity network. Whitepaper (2020). https://github.com/thorchain/Resources/blob/master/Whitepapers/THORChain-Whitepaper-May2020.pdf
70. Tolmach, P., Li, Y., Lin, S.W., Liu, Y., Li, Z.: A survey of smart contract formal specification and verification. ACM Comput. Surv. (CSUR) **54**(7), 1–38 (2021)
71. Wang, S., Yuan, Y., Wang, X., Li, J., Qin, R., Wang, F.Y.: An overview of smart contract: architecture, applications, and future trends. In: 2018 IEEE Intelligent Vehicles Symposium (IV), pp. 108–113. IEEE (2018)
72. Wilhelmi, F., Giupponi, L., Dini, P.: Analysis and evaluation of synchronous and asynchronous flchain. Comput. Netw. **218**, 109390 (2022)

73. Wong, H.W.H., Ma, J.P.K., Yin, H.H.F., Chow, S.S.M.: Real threshold ECDSA. In: NDSS. The Internet Society (2023)
74. Wormhole: Wormhole incident report – 02/02/22. Wormholecrypto Medium (2022). https://wormholecrypto.medium.com/wormhole-incident-report-02-02-22-ad9b8f21eec6
75. Xue, H., Au, M.H., Xie, X., Yuen, T.H., Cui, H.: Efficient online-friendly two-party ECDSA signature. IACR Cryptol. ePrint Arch. 318 (2022)
76. Zyskind, G., Yanai, A., Pentland, A.S.: Unstoppable wallets: chain-assisted threshold ECDSA and its applications. IACR Cryptol. ePrint Arch. 832 (2023)

SoK: Outsourced Private Set Intersection

Sophie Hawkes and Christian Weinert(✉)

Department of Information Security, Royal Holloway, University of London, Egham, UK
sophie.hawkes.2022@live.rhul.ac.uk, christian.weinert@rhul.ac.uk

Abstract. Private set intersection (PSI) protocols are an essential privacy-enhancing technology for many real-world use cases, ranging from mobile contact discovery to fraud detection. However, PSI executed directly between input parties can result in unreasonable performance overhead. This motivates the study of outsourced PSI, where clients delegate the heavy PSI operations to an untrusted (cloud) server. In this SoK, we introduce a framework of 12 distinct properties that characterize outsourced PSI protocols based on security, functionality, and efficiency. By analyzing 20 protocols through this framework, we provide a valuable resource and an interactive tool for researchers and practitioners to select the most suitable protocols for their specific requirements. Finally, we discuss research gaps between trends in regular PSI and the current state of outsourced PSI, identifying promising avenues for future work.

Keywords: Private Set Intersection · Cloud Computing · Outsourcing · MPC

1 Introduction

As modern life becomes increasingly digitized, the amount of data generated, collected, and stored is growing exponentially. This motivates the need for efficient and secure methods of processing and analyzing data to provide important insights. Many organizations are now realizing the potential benefits of sharing data with each other, for example, detecting financial fraud across multiple banks (e.g. [2]). However, strict privacy regulations and concerns about losing business advantage often prevent them from doing this. To address this challenge, the field of *secure multi-party computation (MPC)* has gained momentum, with the aim of allowing the joint computation on private data without revealing any sensitive information.

In particular, *private set intersection (PSI)* is an important cryptographic protocol that enables two (or more) parties, each with a private database, to compute the intersection of their sets without revealing any information about the non-matching items. PSI has many interesting real-world applications, such as privacy-preserving matchmaking [63] and integration of medical data [40]. Without such cryptographic techniques, parties wishing to compute on their

K. Jee and A. Kate (Eds.): ACNS 2026, LNCS 16571, pp. 501–527, 2027.
https://doi.org/10.1007/978-3-032-32560-0_18

joint data often create a data-sharing agreement (DSA) governing data usage to ensure privacy, security, and legal compliance. In practice, facilitating DSAs can be highly complex and time consuming. Even with a DSA in place, there is always the risk of malicious behaviour, collusion with another party, or a data breach. However, the main barrier preventing the use of PSI is often the high computation and communication costs involved, limiting its practical scalability.

As a general solution for scaling resource-intensive workloads in a cost-effective way, *cloud computing* has become widespread for the delegation of data storage and processing. Thus, organizations with limited resources can potentially outsource also tasks such as PSI to third-party cloud service providers (CSPs). Although outsourcing provides clear benefits in terms of efficiency and scalability, it raises significant concerns about the security and privacy of sensitive data. So, one may ask, is it possible to have the best of both worlds?

Consequently, researchers have proposed novel protocols for a new kind of PSI, known as *outsourced PSI*, in which clients outsource the heavy PSI computations to a third-party server or CSP. Other terms frequently used include *delegated*, *server-aided*, or *cloud-assisted PSI*, making this area of research particularly incomprehensible. Some outsourced PSI protocols completely outsource even the storage of datasets securely to a server (removing the need for a local copy), making them increasingly feasible even for memory-restricted clients.

Contributions. In this SoK, we present a comprehensive overview of the existing literature on outsourced PSI, the first to focus solely on the detailed exposition and discussion of such protocols. Papers were selected based on a focused search using the criteria ("outsourced" OR "server-aided" OR "cloud-assisted") AND "private set intersection", followed by a snowballing approach, then screening out works beyond the scope of this paper (e.g., PSI cardinality). Beginning with Kerschbaum in 2012 [30,31], numerous different outsourced PSI protocols have been designed, based on a range of underlying cryptographic building blocks, and with a variety of additional properties. With so many subtle variations in design and diverse real-world applications, it is difficult to determine what schemes are best suited to which use cases, hence the need for an in-depth analysis of the key considerations developers/researchers should consider when selecting an outsourced PSI protocol.

Motivated by this, we review 20 outsourced PSI protocols and develop a framework to characterize them according to key properties that define their functionality and security. We identify 12 distinct characteristics, such as whether the server learns the cardinality of the intersection, the verifiability of the server's computation, and the security model. We provide this framework as an interactive selection tool to researchers or practitioners wishing to implement a solution based on outsourced PSI, by provoking reflection on the requirements for their specific use case, and hence forming a criteria for which protocol they should select. Furthermore, we analyze the asymptotic complexity for both communication and computation costs, thereby providing insights into how the protocols scale, e.g., with increasing database size and number of participants. In addition, we synthesize existing benchmarks where available, giving an understanding of which schemes are best suited to practical deployment. These findings also form the basis for a performance estimator included in our interactive tool to further narrow down the protocol selection.

Finally, we discuss the insights gathered from our findings and identify research gaps to inspire future research directions in this area. With particular reference to current advances in traditional PSI such as unbalanced and fuzzy PSI, we look ahead to how this progress could translate to outsourced settings and the impact these new properties could have on real-world applications.

2 Related Work

2.1 Private Set Intersection

Private set intersection (PSI) enables two or more parties, each with a private dataset, to jointly compute the intersection of their datasets without revealing any information about non-matching elements. The first PSI protocols were introduced by Meadows [39], based on Diffie-Hellman key exchange, and by Freedman et al. [19], based on homomorphic encryption and oblivious transfer (OT). Significant breakthroughs for efficiency include the use of OT extension [7] and batching for oblivious pseudo-random function (OPRF) techniques [32], as well as improvements from oblivious key-value store (OKVS) and vector oblivious linear evaluation (VOLE) approaches [46,47].

Of the two existing surveys on PSI, Vos et al. [55] focus on collusion-resistant multi-party PSI in the semi-honest model and explicitly exclude server-assisted protocols. Morales et al. [42] do discuss outsourced PSI, but consider a smaller subset of protocols within the much broader scope of their paper, leaving an opportunity for a detailed, comparative analysis of the specific properties and nuances of these protocols and the outsourced setting.

Outsourced PSI-CA. Instead of learning the elements in the intersection of sets, sometimes it suffices to output only the size of the intersection, known as *PSI cardinality* or PSI-CA. Whilst, as we discuss in § 4, unintentionally leaking the intersection cardinality during standard PSI is not desirable, learning just the intersection cardinality is preferable in many real-world applications. For example, in secure mobile contact tracing for monitoring the spread of a disease [16] by comparing devices in close proximity, it is only necessary to output the number of matches to positive records, not the records themselves. Similar to regular PSI, there have been numerous works in the past decade on outsourced or cloud-assisted PSI-CA, such as [14,26,52,54]. These protocols are considered out of scope for this work, as it is not meaningful to directly compare PSI and PSI-CA protocols due to their inherent difference in functionality [14].

Third-Party PSI. Outsourced PSI is known by many names, such as cloud-assisted, server-assisted, and delegated PSI. However, the third-party PSI proposed by Yeo et al. [59] is in a markedly different setting. In these protocols, an inputless third-party receives the intersection result, whilst the two sending parties learn nothing about the other's set, differently to outsourced PSI in which the client(s) learn the result and the third party (server) learns nothing.

Arbiter PSI. The requirement that either both (or all) parties that contribute their sets for the PSI computation receive the result, or else none do, is known as *fairness*. One popular method for achieving this is to use a third-party called an *arbiter*, which may be trusted (e.g., Asokan et al. [8]) or semi-trusted (e.g., Dong et al. [15]), but either way merely steps in to ensure fairness to honest parties after a malicious abort, rather than aiding computation.

2.2 Outsourced Secure Computation

Whilst our work focuses solely on outsourcing PSI, we briefly discuss outsourcing both more general computations and other specific private set operations.

Outsourced MPC. PSI sits within the broader category of secure multi-party computation (MPC), in which arbitrary functions can be computed over the parties' private data, rather than specifically the intersection. In the outsourced MPC scenario [27,37,38], typically clients send secret shares of their private inputs to outsourcing servers, which run a two- or multi-party protocol and return shares of the output. Parties then jointly reconstruct the result from these secret shares. It is possible to compute the intersection with this outsourced MPC approach, however, not as efficiently as with a protocol optimized for PSI. Yet the main advantage of general outsourced MPC protocols is their flexibility, enabling the secure computation of arbitrary functions. Recent work by Liu et al. [36] provides a server-aided two-party protocol with malicious security, for heterogeneous networks of smart devices with limited and/or unequal computational resources.

Outsourced Private Database Operations. Beyond the intersection of sets, there exists research into privacy-preserving variants of other set operations in the outsourced setting. Two such operations are outsourced/delegated private set union (PSU) [13,33,51], and database join operations on, e.g., user IDs without revealing additional data [12,41]. More complex SQL-like queries or aggregates – both summary functions (e.g., sum, count, average) and exemplary functions (e.g., min/max, median) – may also be privately computed over outsourced datasets [33,41]. Asharov et al. [6] design a secure statistical analysis platform with several variants of join and group-by operations.

3 Preliminaries

3.1 Definitions and Notation

In the two-party case, we define two clients, A and B (Alice and Bob), and a cloud server S. Alice and Bob have datasets D_A and D_B, respectively. In the multi-party case, we define n clients $A_1, \ldots, A_{n-1}$, and B and a cloud server S. In both cases w.l.o.g. client B is often the party requesting the intersection computation. The computational security parameter λ determines the level of security against computationally bounded adversaries. A PPT (probabilistic polynomial time) algorithm is defined as having a running time polynomial in λ, and a function ϵ :

$\mathbb{N} \to \mathbb{R}$ is said to be negligible if for sufficiently large λ, $\epsilon(\lambda)$ approaches zero faster than the inverse of any polynomial in λ.

Security Model. The security of outsourced PSI protocols typically relies on *simulation-based* security [24]. As discussed further in § 4, adversaries may be either semi-honest (follows the protocol, but tries to learn extra information), or malicious (can arbitrarily deviate from the protocol).

Whilst existing works on outsourced PSI are proven solely in the stand-alone simulation framework (e.g., [3,18,63]), this implies that they are secure under sequential composition [34]. Future work is needed to design outsourced PSI protocols with security under the universal composability (UC) framework [11].

3.2 Advanced Encryption and Sharing Primitives

Beyond standard symmetric and asymmetric encryption schemes, including digital signatures [14], there are several more advanced encryption primitives that are involved in the existing outsourced PSI literature.

Homomorphic Encryption. One frequently used building block for PSI is homomorphic encryption (HE). It enables the computation of certain operations, such as addition and/or multiplication, on data encrypted under a key K, producing an encrypted result where the computation carries through to the original data once decrypted. Here the symbol $\star$ represents the operation on the ciphertexts, and the symbol $*$ the operations with the plaintexts: $\mathrm{Dec}_K(\mathrm{Enc}_K(x) \star \mathrm{Enc}_K(y)) = x * y$.

Additive HE. An additive HE (AHE) scheme on ciphertexts $\mathrm{Enc}_K(x)$, $\mathrm{Enc}_K(y)$ must be homomorphic in addition and scalar multiplication, such that multiplication (or more generally some operation $\star$) performed on the ciphertexts corresponds to the sum of the underlying plaintexts: $\mathrm{Dec}_K(\mathrm{Enc}_K(x)\cdot\mathrm{Enc}_K(y)) = x + y$, $\mathrm{Dec}_K(\mathrm{Enc}_K(x)^a) = x \cdot a$. The Paillier public key cryptosystem is a popular AHE scheme used in many outsourced PSI protocols [3–5,29]. Another example is exponential ElGamal (exElGamal), as used by Miyaji et al. [40].

Multiplicative HE. A multiplicative HE (MHE) scheme must satisfy: $\mathrm{Dec}_K(\mathrm{Enc}_K(x) \cdot \mathrm{Enc}_K(y)) = x \cdot y$, $\mathrm{Dec}_K(\mathrm{Enc}_K(x)^a) = x^a$. For outsourced PSI, both RSA [58] and ElGamal [14] schemes have been used in this way.

Fully HE. Fully HE (FHE) allows any number (subject to noise limitations) of both addition and multiparty operations. The noise limitations can be alleviated by a process called bootstrapping. Although bootstrapping is computationally intensive, fast bootstrapping is possible for FHE over the torus (TFHE), as used in CMPSI [18]. However, somewhat homomorphic encryption (SHE) permits both but only a finite number, e.g., the BGN scheme used by Kerschbaum [31] can take arbitrary additions but only one multiplication.

Secret Sharing. Secret sharing (SS) is a cryptographic method in which a party splits a secret into *shares* and distributes them among a group of participants such that no participant can reconstruct the secret on their own. This could be simple additive SS or Shamir's SS as in PRISM [33].

Threshold Cryptography. In threshold cryptography not all shares are necessarily required to reconstruct the secret, instead there is some minimum or threshold number of secret shares required to reconstruct the key and decrypt. In particular, parties can agree on a shared key without a dealer [33,40].

3.3 Efficient Data Structures and Representations

There are different strategies that outsourced PSI protocols use to represent their sets to improve their efficiency.

Polynomial Point-Value Set Representation. This technique was introduced as a novel representation for datasets in PSI by Abadi et al. in their initial outsourced PSI paper [3] and subsequently used in their later works [1,4,5,29]. Suppose we define the universe of all possible elements of a set D_A as a field $R_{D_A} = \mathbb{F}_p$, then we can let all the elements a_i of D_A be all the roots of a polynomial $\rho_{D_A}(x)$ in the polynomial ring $R_{D_A}[x]$. Thus, we get the following representation of the set D_A as a polynomial: $\rho_{D_A}(x) = \prod_{i=1}^{d}(x - a_i) \in R_{D_A}[x]$, $d = |D_A|$. Any polynomial $\rho(x)$ of degree strictly less than n can be defined by n point co-ordinate pairs (x_i, y_i) and recovered by polynomial interpolation. This representation reduces multiplication complexity from $O(d^2)$ to $O(d)$ and is achieved by publishing fixed x_i values, hence the point-value form consists of simply a vector of the y_i values.

Hash Tables. Computing over polynomials of high degree is costly. Hash tables in PSI provide a method for reducing computational complexity, by splitting large sets into smaller subsets called *hash bins*. A hash table tells you the *address* of an element, i.e., which bin it maps to [1,5,29]. If all clients use the same hash function, then elements in the intersection will be mapped to the same bin, allowing the PSI protocol to perform bin-wise operations, greatly reducing the number of comparisons required.

Bloom Filter. To efficiently check whether an element is a member of a specific set, many outsourced PSI schemes [1,14,31,40,63] utilize Bloom filters (BFs), a probabilistic data structure that allows false positives (at a controllable rate) but never false negatives. A BF is created with an empty m-bit string, set to all zeros, and k hash functions h_i. The bit positions corresponding to the hashes when applying the hash functions to every set element are set to 1. If all of the h_i value positions for a given element x are set to 1, then x is considered a member of the set.

Cuckoo Filter. More recently developed and with proven better performance [48], Cuckoo filters boast constant time lookups even in the worst case and, unlike Bloom filters, support deletion.

Elastic BF. An Elastic BF (EBF) [57] adds a cooperative array of m buckets at the index position of each standard m-bit Bloom filter. The output of the k

independent hash functions is separated into two parts (the quotient and remainder of division by m). The remainder becomes the BF index and the quotient is called the *elastic fingerprint* and stored in the corresponding bucket. Besides deletion, EBF supports expansion when buckets become too full.

Oblivious Key Value Store. As introduced by Garimella et al. [20], OKVS is an abstraction of data structures that map key-value pairs (k_i, v_i) [42]. A *key-value store* (KVS) consists of two algorithms: Encode outputs an object S from n key-value pairs and Decode outputs a value v from input object S and key k. We say a KVS is *oblivious* if the encodings of random values under two different key sets are computationally indistinguishable.

3.4 Permutations and Pseudorandomness

For many cryptographic primitives, permutations and pseudorandomness are key concepts that provide the basis for constructing secure and efficient protocols.

Permutation Function. A permutation function (PF) on a set $D_A = \{a_i\}$ is a bijective mapping from one permutation of D_A to another, rearranging the elements into a new order [33]: $\pi : D_A \mapsto D_A, \quad \pi(D_A) = \{a_{\pi(i)} : a_i \in D_A\}$.

Pseudorandom Number Generator. A PRG (or PRNG) takes an initial value (a *seed*) and generates a deterministic sequence of numbers that is indistinguishable in polynomial time from a uniform distribution [23,33].

Pseudorandom Function. A pseudorandom function (PRF) takes a specific bit-string input and outputs a value in the output space $\mathcal{U}$ that is deterministic given a key K of length λ, yet indistinguishable from random to any party that does not know the secret key $K \in \{0,1\}^\lambda$ [1]: $F_K : K \times \{0,1\}^* \mapsto \mathcal{U}$.

Pseudorandom Permutation. A pseudorandom permutation (PRP) is a PRF where the function is a permutation, hence bijective. It takes a key K of length λ and permutes the elements of a set D_A in a deterministic and pseudorandom manner [1]: $\pi_K : K \times D_A \mapsto D_A, \; \pi_K(D_A) = \{a_{\pi_K(i)} : a_i \in D_A\}$.

3.5 Oblivious Protocols

Obliviousness in protocols prevents parties from revealing their inputs to each other, whilst helping to enable secure computation and data sharing.

Oblivious Transfer. Oblivious transfer (OT) refers to a protocol where the sender Alice wishes to send a message to the receiver Bob, without learning what message he receives. In Rabin's original OT protocol [45], Bob either receives the message m or no message $\perp$, and Alice does not know which. In 1-out-of-2 OT [17], Alice has two messages, m_0 and m_1, and Bob receives only one message m_b ($b \in \{0,1\}$), with Alice remaining oblivious to his choice. In practice, *OT extension* is required to reduce the computational overhead by leveraging a few expensive base OTs to generate a large number of cheaper ones [48].

Oblivious Polynomial Evaluation. Oblivious polynomial evaluation (OPE) is the evaluation of a polynomial ρ (known by the sender) on an input value x (known by the receiver). The sender learns nothing, and the receiver learns $\rho(x)$ [42].

Oblivious Pseudorandom Functions. An oblivious pseudorandom function (OPRF) is a protocol where Bob receives the result $\text{OPRF}_K(y_1), \ldots,$ $\text{OPRF}_K(y_n)$ of his inputs under Alice's key K, yet Bob learns nothing about K and Alice learns nothing about Bob's inputs [48]: $F_{\text{OPRF}} : (K, y) \mapsto (\perp, F_K(y))$.

Proxy Re-Encryption. Proxy re-encryption (PRE) allows comparing the plaintexts of ciphertexts encrypted under different keys. The idea is that Alice and Bob generate a "re-key", which they send to a third-party or proxy. This re-key enables the proxy to transform Alice's ciphertext into a ciphertext under Bob's key, allowing him to decrypt "on behalf" of her, with the proxy remaining oblivious. In the server setting, both parties may send intermediary re-keyed ciphertexts to the server to test whether their plaintexts match [64]. PRE can be based on asymmetric or symmetric encryption schemes. A symmetric-key PRE (SKPRE) can be constructed using a key homomorphic PRF [61].

Zero-Knowledge Proofs. A zero-knowledge proof (ZKP) is a cryptographic method by which one party (prover P) can prove to another (verifier V) that some statement is true, without revealing any further information [23]. A ZKP of knowledge (ZKPoK) can specifically prove knowledge of some value [14].

4 Properties

In this section, we define the key characteristics observed across existing outsourced PSI protocols. Particularly when selecting a PSI protocol for a specific real-world application, there are nuances to carefully consider which properties are most important. Through comprehensive analysis of a wide range of protocols, summarized in Table 1, we derived the following properties.

(Intersection) Cardinality Hiding. One of the main objectives of PSI is to ensure that the server remains unaware of any information regarding the clients' datasets or their intersection. The size or *cardinality* of the intersection may reveal sensitive information if learned by the server, for example, simply knowing the cardinality is greater than zero discloses the existence of an intersection between datasets. If a protocol does not reveal the size of the intersection to the server or any unauthorized third party, we say it is *cardinality hiding.*

Input Cardinality Leakage. Similarly, in some applications it may be unacceptable for the server to learn the exact size of parties' private datasets, known as *input cardinality leakage*. In most applications, it is unlikely that all of the clients' datasets will have exactly the same number of elements. Therefore, an important design feature can be that clients' datasets can have different cardinalities, independent or even unknown from each other [40]. A trivial technique would be padding all set lengths to equal some upper bound, simultaneously providing an effective means of hiding the true size of parties' datasets and avoiding input cardinality leakage. However, in the unbalanced PSI setting, where one dataset is much smaller than the other, it may also be important that the computation and communication complexities avoid the inefficiency of trivially padding the smaller set to the larger set size.

Repeatability. When clients outsource the computation of PSI, they need to transfer their encrypted dataset to the server. If the client cannot reuse the outsourced data with a different client (or group of clients) without compromising security, and has to re-encrypt the data locally for each intersection, it is referred to as *one-off delegation*. This approach requires the client to either constantly download or maintain a local copy of their data, limiting their ability to fully benefit from outsourcing to reduce storage and communication costs. As a result, achieving *repeated delegation* becomes desirable, as it allows clients to outsource their dataset once and then perform multiple PSI computations, sometimes, but not always (e.g., Ruan and Zeng [48]), without a local copy.

Non-interactive Setup. In some settings, clients must communicate with each other during the setup phase, e.g., to establish a shared secret key. However, in the outsourced setting it is often the case that clients may only interact with each other via the server, perhaps asynchronously. A *non-interactive* setup phase is where clients are able to prepare and outsource their datasets to the server without any knowledge or interaction with the other clients.

Authorization. In a non-interactive protocol, clients may wish to have some control over who can perform intersections on their outsourced data, hence the desire for *authorization*. A protocol requires authorization if the client requesting the intersection must obtain permission from the other clients in order to receive the result. However, this stands in contrast to the ability to compute intersections with offline parties, which may be preferred in scenarios when a client perhaps has some trust in the other clients of the server and is happy to provide their outsourced data with no restrictions.

Multiple Clients. Another key property of PSI protocols is the number of clients whose intersection may be computed. In *two-party (2P-)PSI*, there are two clients, A and B. Client B initiates a request for the server to compute its intersection with A, i.e., $f(A, B) = A \cap B$. In *multi-party (MP-)PSI*, there are n clients, $A_1, ..., A_{n-1}$ and B. Client B requests its intersection with the sets of all the other clients $A_1, ..., A_{n-1}$, i.e., $f(A_1, ..., A_{n-1}, B) = \bigcap_1^{m-1} A_1, ..., A_{n-1} \cap B$.

Verifiability. The cloud server may not always be trusted not to tamper with the datasets or computation results, and therefore the clients want a method to *verify* the integrity of the data and the correctness of the result, with some proof that the server has behaved honestly and not deviated from the protocol.

Updatability. Many PSI protocols are designed for handling static sets, with a prohibitive cost of updating securely, despite many real-world environments that require frequent updates, such as stock market analysis and dynamic data systems. A protocol is considered *efficiently updatable* if it permits updates at sub-linear cost, i.e. eliminating the need to download the entire set.

Constant Client-side Storage. By *constant client-side storage*, we refer to the ability to fully outsource client datasets to storage in the cloud, to the point where no local copy of the dataset is required (for the computation and result), only some constant secret material.

Number of Servers. Although many of the existing outsourced PSI protocols consider the simple case of one cloud server, others are designed to share the delegated computation of the intersection between multiple cloud servers.

Table 1. Synthesis of 20 papers across our framework of characteristics. **Properties:** CH = (intersection) cardinality hiding , IC = input cardinality leakage (d=upper bound (*implicit), D=size of attribute domain), R = repeatability , NI = non-interactive setup , A = authorized (—=interactive), 2P = two-party , MP = multi-party , V = verifiability , U = updatability , CS = constant client-side storage , #S = number of cloud servers , AM = adversary model (○ =any party semi-honest, ◐ =malicious client, semi-honest (^{R}=rational) server, ◑ =semi-honest client, malicious server, ● =any party malicious), CR = collusion resistance (○ =server and clients may not collude, ● =server may collude with some (but not all) client(s)).

Paper	Properties												
	CH	IC	R	NI	A	2P	MP	V	U	CS	#S	AM	CR
Kerschbaum (SAC'12) [30]	✓	$\|A\|,\|B\|$			—	✓	✓				1	○	●
Kerschbaum (ASIACCS'12)[31]	✓	$\|A\|,d$		✓		✓					1	○	○
Kamara et al. (FC'14)[28]	✓	$\|A_i\|,\|B\|$			—	✓	✓				1	●	○
Liu et al. (IC2E'14) *ESIP* [35]		$\|A\|,\|B\|$	✓	✓	✓	✓	✓			✓	1	○	○
Abadi et al. (SEC'15) *O-PSI* [3]	✓	$\|A_i\| = \|B\|$	✓	✓	✓	✓	✓			✓	1	○	○
Zheng and Xu (IC2E'15) *VDSI* [64]		$\|A\|,\|B\|$	✓	✓	✓	✓	✓	✓		✓	≥ 1	◐	○
Abadi et al. (FC'16) *VD-PSI* [4]	✓	d	✓	✓	✓	✓	✓	✓		✓	1	◑	○
Zhang et al. (Inf. Sci.'17) [61]		$\|A_i\|,\|B\|$		✓	✓	✓	✓			✓	2	◐^{R}	○
Miyaji et al. (J. Medical Syst.'17) [40]	✓	d*			—	✓	✓				1	○	○
Yang et al. (CCPE'18) [58]	✓	$\|A\| = \|B\|$	✓	✓	✓	✓	✓	✓		✓	1	○	○
Zhao and Chow (WPES'18) [63]	✓	$\|A\|,\|B\|$			—	✓	✓				1	○	○
Abadi et al. (TDSC'19) *EO-PSI* [5]	✓	d	✓	✓	✓	✓	✓	✓		✓	1	○	○
Kavousi et al. (ICEE'20) [29]	✓	d	✓	✓	✓	✓	✓			✓	1	○	○
Debnath et al. (DSC'21) *OPSI* [14]	✓	$\|A_i\|,\|B\|$	✓	✓	✓	✓		✓		✓	1	●	○
Li et al. (SIGMOD'21) *PRISM* [33]	✓	D	✓	✓			✓	✓		✓	≥ 2	◑	○
Abadi et al. (FC'22) *Feather* [1]	✓	d	✓	✓	✓	✓	✓		✓	✓	1	○	○
Ruan and Zeng (ICCIR'22) [48]	✓	$\|A\| = \|B\|$	✓	✓		✓	✓				1	○	○
Fan et al. (Mathematics'23) *CMPSI*[18]	✓	$\|A\|,\|B\|$	✓	✓		✓	✓				1	○	●
Zhang et al. (WAIM'24) [62]	✓	d	✓	✓	✓	✓	✓		✓	✓	1	○	○
Wei and Hu (ePrint'25) *D-PSI* [56]	✓	d*			—	✓	✓				1	○	○

Adversary Model. The security of outsourced PSI protocols typically relies on *simulation-based* security [24]. We say a scheme has *semi-honest security* if it is secure against an adversary that follows the protocol exactly, but keeps a record of all messages they send and receive to try and learn extra information. In contrast, in the *malicious security* model, the adversary may deviate from the protocol, actively trying to compromise security.

Collusion-Resistance. It is very common in the existing outsourced PSI literature to include a non-collusion assumption, that is an assumption that the server does not collude with any of the clients. However, some protocols display so-called *collusion resistance* between clients, e.g., an honest majority of clients is required, or all but one client may collude without breaking security.

5 Protocols

Whilst all surveyed protocols have their differences in the way they execute outsourced PSI, in general they follow this structure:

1. **Outsourcing stage:** Security parameters and keys are generated, then clients Alice and Bob send an encrypted version of their sets to the server.
2. **Request:** Bob sends a request (either to the server or directly to Alice) to securely compute the intersection with Alice.
3. **PSI computation:** The server (obliviously) computes the intersection and sends the encoded result to Bob (and sometimes also Alice).
4. **Result retrieval:** Recipient(s) use their secret information to decode the result and reveal the intersection.

Much of this diversity between schemes stems from the choice of building blocks, hence we introduce the protocols below as categorized according to their underlying cryptographic primitives (e.g. homomorphic encryption, pseudorandom functions, secret sharing). We further evaluate the protocols against our framework of characteristics as defined above, and highlight key properties, including security and efficiency.

5.1 Public Key Encryption (PKE)

The first works on outsourcing intersection computations to untrusted cloud servers were two papers by Kerschbaum in 2012 [30,31]. In the former, bitwise XOR operations are used to construct protocols under two scenarios: both a public output setting (where the server learns the intersection and sends this to the parties in plaintext) via keyed hash functions, and an oblivious service provider setting (where the server learns neither the intersection nor its size) via RSA encryption. Notably, this scheme offers some collusion resistance, in that the server and one client may collude without compromising security. However, the setup does not support more than two clients, and is not non-interactive, since Alice and Bob must jointly choose the RSA modulus.

In 2014, Liu et al. introduced the Encrypted Set Intersection Protocol (ESIP) for Outsourced Datasets [35], which has a non-interactive setup and authorization functionality, but does not hide the cardinality of the intersection from the server. Clients independently outsource their sets by hashing their elements, adding randomness and encrypting under symmetric keys. After authorization of a query, clients exchange re-randomization information encrypted under public keys via the server, enabling the server to privately identify the underlying matches, which it then sends to the requester for decryption. While the non-interactive setup means no prior knowledge of other clients is required to outsource data, clients must compute and send some new values to the server whenever an intersection is requested, increasing communication costs. Nevertheless, the authorization within the request ensures that clients have control over who can perform PSI with their outsourced data. However, the scheme is not fully private because it is not cardinality hiding, so the server learns the size of the intersection. Furthermore, there have been several issues discovered that undermine the security of this scheme, such as one-time pad re-use [5], and the possibility of revealing information about other intersections through repeated use of the same set, i.e., if $A \cap B$ and $A \cap C$ are computed with the same A, then the server can learn information about $B \cap C$ without their permission [3].

5.2 Homomorphic Encryption

Kerschbaum's latter 2012 work [31] introduced the first outsourced PSI based on HE, which has become the most popular building block from which to construct outsourced PSI schemes. There are schemes based on all three types of HE introduced in § 3.2, as discussed in the following.

AHE. Research led by Abadi et al. has explored multiple protocols for outsourced PSI using AHE , beginning in with *O-PSI* [3]. This protocol uses Paillier AHE and introduces a novel way of representing the clients' datasets (of maximum size d) as polynomials in point-value form. During the setup phase, the server publishes parameters including a PRF and a vector $\tilde{v}$ of $2d + 1$ random points. Alice and Bob independently encode their datasets as polynomials and evaluate these at each point in $\tilde{v}$, resulting in vectors they blind under a random secret key for the PRF and send to the server. During the online phase, Bob requests to perform PSI with Alice by sending her his random blinding values encrypted with his public key. She authorizes the request by applying the inverses of her blinding values to Bob's encrypted values, and sending this with their IDs to the server, which uses HE to "switch" the blinding factors and compute the intersection. The result is sent to Bob, who decrypts with his private key and interpolates the resulting polynomial to learn the intersection values. Despite offering additional dataset integrity validation via homomorphic tags, the public key and HE operations of the overall approach have a "major impact on performance" [5]. Moreover, Oliaee et al. [43] show that O-PSI is vulnerable to man-in-the-middle (MITM) attacks.

The subsequent paper by Abadi et al. [4] follows on with Verifiable Delegated PSI on outsourced private datasets (VD-PSI), efficiently adding verifiability of correctness for the intersection result computation, with the extra cost only linear to the intersection size. Like O-PSI [3], clients send to the server vectors encoding their sets in point-value polynomial representation form, blinded with keyed pseudo-random values, then publish their Paillier public keys. Now, the requesting party Bob chooses a random value $\beta \in \mathbb{F}_p^*$, which he and Alice will both add to their sets in such a way that β will be in the intersection only if it has been computed honestly. This allows for verification with such a low overhead, as the only computation necessary is checking if β is included in the intersection. VD-PSI can be reused for unlimited computations, offering significant advantage over non-repeatable protocols that necessitate frequently re-encrypting and uploading the data.

Zhao and Chow [63] took a different approach, proposing privacy-preserving matchmaking using AHE-based OPE and BFs, in which most of the public-key operations are outsourced to a semi-honest server. Interestingly, they design a novel encrypted PSI cardinality (ePSI-CA) scheme, inspired by existential PSI (X-PSI), that underlies and unifies both their above-threshold and below-threshold PSI functionalities (called $t^{\geq}$-PSI and $t^{\leq}$-PSI). If we set $t = 0$ in $t^{\geq}$-PSI, then we get a general PSI scheme [63], however the communication costs are very large.

MHE. The first MHE-based scheme, and indeed the first HE scheme, was proposed by Kerschbaum [31]. It provides an initial semi-honest PSI protocol using Bloom filters, encrypted bit-wise using Goldwasser-Micali (GM) multiplicative homomorphic encryption [25] (based on quadratic residuosity), and the Sander-Young-Yung (SYY) technique [50] to achieve unbounded fan-in logical-AND on multiple encrypted bits in XOR-homomorphic schemes like GM. Thus, it is helpful for checking the presence of elements in a Bloom Filter. The PSI protocol is then extended to the malicious setting via client set certification. Finally there is a protocol for outsourced PSI in the semi-honest setting, incorporating a novel combination of the SYY technique and a simplification of the Boneh-Goh-Nissim (BGN) MHE scheme [10] modelled after the quadratic residues of GM. However, a local copy of the set must be kept in order to produce the result, hence this could be considered as not true outsourcing [3].

An improved variant of O-PSI [3] is given by Yang et al. [58] that contributes a large improvement in efficiency due to the use of RSA (multiplicatively homomorphic) instead of Paillier (additively homomorphic). Another advantage of their scheme is that it avoids the requirement that Bob must communicate with Alice directly to send his request, which is a barrier to true outsourcing in which all interactions between clients are delegated to the cloud.

Debnath et al. [14] devised an OPSI scheme using ElGamal MHE, ElGamal digital signatures, and Bloom filters. Their scheme achieves malicious security via ZKPs of discrete logarithms and they also extend their approach to a cardinality-only scheme OPSI-CA, through random permutation. They satisfy many attractive properties, like non-interactive setup, repeatability, and verifiable security against a malicious adversary. On the other hand, it should be noted that the design is only for two clients, a trusted third party is required to initialize identities and parameters, and particularly that the cardinalities of the private sets are made public, which might not be suitable for all use cases.

FHE. Fan et al. introduce CMPSI (Cloud-assisted Multi-party PSI) [18] using FHE over the torus (TFHE). They first give secure computation protocols for AND, OR and XNOR gates between multi-key LWE samples, and a secure comparison protocol (SCP) to test for equality between encrypted input data vectors. Similar to other schemes [14,33,64], public parameters are generated and shared by a Parameter Generation Centre (PGC), from which the clients generate a secret key and corresponding public key, bootstrapping key and key switching key. Both sending and receiving clients send their datasets (containing vectors of k Boolean values) encrypted under their secret key to the server, along with their public key set. The server performs SCP and secure OR on the ciphertexts, resulting in an encrypted Boolean vector of whether each element in the receiver's set was in the sender's, which is sent to the receiver who decrypts with the joint key. Unlike most schemes, CMPSI is secure even if the cloud server colludes with some of the clients since all keys are needed for decryption. Furthermore, it is secure against passive man-in-the-middle (MITM) attacks and has lower communication cost than Kamara et al. [28].

Similarly, Wei and Hu [56] use FHE, a privacy-preserving AND sub-protocol, and joint decryption. However, in this case each client set is represented by a Bloom filter where each encoded bit is encrypted under a jointly generated public key (a multi-key variant of BFV) and sent to the cloud server. The intersection of all Bloom filters is computed via a bitwise AND using only homomorphic additions. However, it requires a privacy-preserving zero-test to guarantee security against leakage of "differential" information about the intersection. The protocol does not meet its claim of repeatable and fully delegated outsourcing, since the jointly generated key material prevents repeated intersection computation with new clients, and at least the querier must maintain a local copy of their dataset.

5.3 Pseudorandom Protocols (PRP and/or PRF)

Kamara et al. [28] present four different server-aided PSI protocols based on PRPs to deliver varying security properties: semi-honest security, malicious (via dummy sets) and covert (via careful parameter setting) security, fairness, and cardinality hiding. These protocols all allow clients to jointly generate a key k under which they permute their sets, hence the setup is interactive. The fairness property is achieved by simply adding another layer of PRP, proving that the intersection computed and committed to by the server matches the intersection of clients' one-layered PRP values (revealed by applying the second PRP key). For the cardinality size-hiding variant, Alice and Bob share one keyed PRP, and Alice and the server share another; Bob obtains his set under both PRPs via the server and receives Alice's too and computes the intersection himself.

Importantly, the computational costs scale linearly, enabling efficient PSI on sets with billions of entries. Consequently, this scheme has been used as a point of comparison for implementation performance in several later works [4,18,33,44].

Abadi et al. improve upon their own O-PSI protocol [3] above by introducing a more efficient version called EO-PSI in [5]. This scheme is 10–100 times faster than O-PSI because it avoids any PKE or exponentiation by relying on PRFs, and it also utilizes hash tables , thus breaking down the polynomial into multiple polynomials of smaller degree. The protocol is extended to multiple clients, but does not scale well, with the polynomial evaluations becoming the limiting factor as the number of parties increases [1]. The need for secure channels between parties goes unmentioned in this work, hence Kavousi et al. [29] discuss passive attacks against EO-PSI and consequently amend the protocol in such a way as to remove the requirement that messages sent between parties are secret, furthermore reducing the computational complexity in the process.

Returning to another work by Abadi et al., they later proposed Feather [1], significantly improving the efficiency amongst multiple clients. Crucially, Feather was the first scheme allowing outsourced sets to be efficiently updatable, with 1000 times faster updates than EO-PSI [5] (for 2^{20} elements). Set elements are stored in bins within hash tables, hence clients need only to update, re-encode and send bins, instead of the entire set, thus the update complexity depends solely on the number of bins b, with $O(b)$ communication and $O(b^2)$ computation overhead. However, there is only semi-honest security, secure communication channels are assumed, and some leakage to the cloud (e.g., about query and access patterns) is permitted for the sake of efficiency. Further efficiency gains come from clients evaluating random polynomials locally instead of in the cloud, Horner's method for polynomial evaluation, and replacing the padding in EO-PSI [5] with blinded Bloom filters. Feather is shown to support up to 100 clients with 2^{20} set elements, resulting in twice as fast delegated PSI and 26 times faster cloud runtime than EO-PSI [5].

5.4 Proxy Re-Encryption (PRE)

Verifiable Delegated Set Intersection (VDSI) by Zheng and Xu [64] was the first outsourced PSI protocol to be verifiable, in the sense that the server generates a proof that it has executed the PSI operation correctly, which can be verified by the receiving client(s) before decrypting the result. The scheme is based on bilinear maps, where the server is able to compare ciphertexts encrypted under different keys by using proxy re-encryption : clients Alice and Bob send re-keys to the server as part of their authentication request. A novel aspect is the creation of a cryptographic multi-accumulator, which allows to privately test the set membership of $D_A \cap D_B \subseteq D_A (\subseteq D_B)$ in one go. However, similarly to ESIP [35], VDSI is not cardinality-hiding, and is vulnerable to the same leakage in repeated use of outsourced data to compute intersection with different sets. In addition, VDSI is subject to plaintext guess attacks from the server, requires a trusted third party (TTP) to initialize public parameters, and requires an authenticated private communication channel between each client and the cloud.

Zhang et al. [61] introduced a reputation-based two-server aided protocol, which combines a symmetric key proxy re-encryption (SKPRE) scheme, based on the learning with errors (LWE) problem, with a social game that assigns clients a reputation score based on previous behavior and penalizes them for defecting or colluding. If we assume that all parties are rational and choose the strategy that optimizes their reputation score, then it is always better for them to choose non-collusion, even if they do not receive the intersection, which avoids the typical PSI fairness impossibility results, allowing for collusion-free computation with complete fairness. Along with non-interactive setup and support for multiple clients, all clients have different keys, so not all information is compromised if one party's key is. Furthermore, there is no user-to-user interaction or costly public key infrastructure (PKI) operations.

5.5 Secret Sharing

Miyaji et al. [40] design an outsourced multi-party PSI protocol for integrating medical data using secret sharing. Their two main criteria are that dataset cardinalities can be independent, and that the client-side computational complexity is independent of the number of clients. To start, the clients initialize exponential ElGamal pairs and publish their public keys, and compute the (n, n)-threshold public key, then send the Bloom filter of their set encrypted under this key to the server. The server randomizes and broadcasts the result back to the clients, who jointly threshold decrypt the result and obtain the intersection by a Bloom filter check. Hence, the protocol is not repeatable for computing intersections with a new set of parties, and a local copy must be kept. They demonstrate practical performance of a maximum 450 s for up to 16,384 elements and 16 parties, at different bit security levels; whilst clearly infeasible for many real-world applications with millions or even billions of set elements [49], it may indeed be well-suited to its intended use on patient data between hospitals/clinics.

PRISM by Li et al. [33] extends secret sharing to not just PSI over multiple public outsourcing servers, but also PSU and aggregation functions, including PSI sum, average, maximum, median and cardinality, as well as PSI over multiple attributes. PRISM utilizes both additive and Shamir's SS, cyclic groups, permutation functions and a PRG. There is security for both semi-honest and malicious servers, including hiding access patterns from servers but they assume that no servers communicate with each other to collude, and a trusted initiator is required as in [14,64]. PRISM scales even better than Kamara et al. [28] for two clients and a billion values, and also scales nicely for up to 50 clients and 20 million values.

5.6 Oblivious Primitives

Ruan and Zeng [48] introduced an offline outsourced PSI based on OT, OPRFs, and Cuckoo filters to achieve computation and communication complexity linear in the set size. However, the offline nature of the scheme means that there is no authentication stage, and there is no concrete performance evaluation to compare it to its contemporaries. Moreover, as with some of the earlier protocols, clients must keep a local copy of their dataset to match the result of their Cuckoo filter look-ups to intersection elements, hence the outsourcing is not complete.

More recently, Zhang et al. [62] proposed a new updatable outsourced multi-party PSI scheme, joining Feather [1] as the only other efficiently updatable protocol (similarly achieved via hash tables), but it has up to 30% faster runtimes in comparison (for multiple parties). They achieve this speed-up by avoiding the large number of polynomial computations that slow down Feather's intersection computation, instead using an EBF and OKVS structure. The protocol has semi-honest security and a non-collusion assumption, but one of the main limitations is the communication complexity since the cost goes from 0.2 MB for two clients with 2^{10} elements to over 280 MB for 2^{20} elements.

6 Performance

Performance of outsourced PSI protocols must be considered from two perspectives – asymptotic complexity and concrete benchmarks. Note that our analysis of practical runtimes relies on self-reported benchmark data, from non-uniform implementations with differing software, hardware and network environments. Consequently, it is vital to bear in mind the limitations of this approach, as discussed further in Sects. 6.2 and 6.3.

6.1 Asymptotic Complexity

We summarize the asymptotic communication and computation complexity of all 20 outsourced PSI protocols in Table 2.

Communication Complexity. The communication complexity is the total amount of data sent between parties in a protocol. Several outsourced PSI protocols achieve linear communication complexity, proportional to the size of the clients' datasets. Where protocols experience quadratic communication complexity, e.g., in Kerschbaum [30], this poses challenges when dealing with large datasets or a vast amount of clients. On the other hand, VDSI [64] achieves even smaller communication than linear to dataset size, instead being proportional to the size of the intersection. For multi-party outsourced PSI, the number of clients can also influence the communication complexity, for example, Feather [1] is linear to both dataset cardinality and number of clients. However, other multi-party protocols may even be independent of the number of participants.

Computation Complexity. Computation complexity refers to the total computational resources required by the clients and server to execute a protocol. Similarly to communication, two of the main factors affecting the computation complexity are the size of the input datasets, and the number of clients in the multi-party case. This can be seen in Table 2, where the dependence

Table 2. Taxonomy of protocols categorized by underlying cryptographic primitive, along with their asymptotic complexities; u=size of dataset A, v=size of dataset B, d=maximum size of datasets, λ=security parameter, m=size of intersection, n=number of clients, k=number of hashes, b=hash bin capacity, w=EBF bucket capacity.

Type	Paper	Computation Complexity	Communication Complexity
PKE	Kerschbaum (SAC'12) [30]	$O(uv) \approx O(d^2)$	$O(u+v)+O(uv) \approx O(d^2)$
	Liu et al. (IC2E'14) *ESIP* [35]	$O(d^2)$	$O(d)$
AHE	Abadi et al. (SEC'15) *O-PSI* [3]	$O(d^2)$	$O(d)$
	Abadi et al. (FC'16) *VD-PSI* [4]	$O(d)$	$O(d)$
	Zhao and Chow (WPES'18) [63]	$O(\log(\lambda)(u+v))$	$O(\log(\lambda)(u+v))$
MHE	Kerschbaum (ASIACCS'12) [31]	$O(v(k\lambda+k+2\lambda))$	$O(ku+\lambda v)$
	Yang et al. (CCPE'18) [58]	$O(d)$	$O(d)$
	Debnath et al. (DSC'21) *OPSI* [14]	$O(d)$	$O(d)$
FHE	Fan et al. (Mathematics'23) *CMPSI* [18]	$O(d)$	$O(d)$
	Wei and Hu (ePrint'25) *D-PSI* [56]	$O(nd\log(n))$	$O(nd)$
PRE	Zheng and Xu (IC2E'15) *VDSI* [64]	$O(d)$	$O(m)$
	Zhang et al. (Inf. Sci.'17) [61]	$O(2(u+v+m))$	$O(2(u+v)+3m)$
SS	Miyaji et al. (J. Medical Syst.'17) [40]	$O(u_i+nu)$	$O(u+n+nu)$
	Li et al. (SIGMOD'21) *PRISM* [33]	$O(nd)$	$O(nd)$
PRF	Abadi et al. (TDSC'19) *EO-PSI* [5]	$O(d)$	$O(d)$
	Kavousi et al. (ICEE'20) [29]	$O(d)$	$O(d)$
PRP	Kamara et al. (FC'14) [28]	$O(d)$	$O(d)$
	Abadi et al. (FC'22) *Feather* [1]	$O(nd)$	$O((n-1)d)$
	Zhang et al. (WAIM'24) [62]	$O(nd)$	$O(nd(bw))$
OPRF	Ruan and Zeng (ICCIR'22) [48]	$O(d)$	$O(d)$

on these variables is clear. Evidently, the type of primitive(s) used in an outsourced PSI protocol significantly influences the computation complexity. Earlier protocols depending on public-key operations suffered from quadratic computational complexity, whereas using only symmetric key operations helped protocols to achieve linear computation. For example, while O-PSI [3] introduced the point-value polynomial representation, crucial for reducing computational cost, its use of Paillier homomorphic encryption is expensive. This compared to the subsequent EO-PSI [5] that was designed to avoid public-key operations, hence requires only modular additions and multiplications, and gains further computational efficiency via utilizing hash tables. Beyond the adoption of hash tables, other improvements in set representation have reduced the computational overheads, from the initial use of Bloom filters to advancements like Cuckoo and EBFs. In general, homomorphic encryption (particularly FHE) brings significant computational costs, whereas OPRF-based PSI protocols are known for their efficiency.

Verification/Malicious Security Overhead. To gain additional properties such as verification or malicious security, it is usually necessary to introduce some overhead. The first verifiable outsourced protocol VDSI [64] uses a novel multi-accumulator scheme based on bilinear maps on cyclic group $|G|$ of order p, which contributes $5p$ output size and computational overhead linear to the size of both clients' dataset sizes and the size of the intersection. In VD-PSI [4], the computation complexity of verification is linear to only the intersection size $O(m)$, compared to the malicious security in Kamara et al. [28], which is linear to the total number of inputs, i.e., the sum of dataset sizes. Notably, even in the multi-party context, the verification overhead of VD-PSI does not depend on the number of clients. The security against collusion in Zhang et al. [61] comes from the reputation system, where parties rate each other then compute new trust values. PRISM [33] enables PSI result verification by each client secret sharing the complement of each element with a second server, hence twice the computation and communication is needed server-side, in addition to the client-side preparation of complement values and verification calculations, which are both linear to the number of elements. Both ElGamal signatures and ZKPs are used for verification and to obtain malicious security in Debnath et al. [14], however, they still achieve linear complexity.

Update Complexity. Efficient updatability is a major limitation for many existing protocols, as most require clients to download their entire dataset, perform local updates, and then re-upload the entire dataset. This incurs high communication and computation costs that scale linearly with the set size. Feather [1] proposed the first efficiently updatable protocol via its use of hash tables, since the client must only retrieve and reupload one bin. Thus, Feather has an update complexity of $O(b)$ for communication and $O(b^2)$ for computation, where b is the bin size. Another efficiently updatable protocol is Zhang et al. [62], where like Feather its update complexity is independent of the set size, but rather depends on the selection of two parameters – bin size and EBF bucket capacity.

6.2 Practical Performance

Implementations. Whilst 14 out of 20 papers indicated to have implemented the proposed protocols, only 4 papers have open-source implementations available: Kamara et al. [28], O-PSI [3], EO-PSI [5], and Feather [1]; and 1 pending [56]. Despite reaching out to the remaining 9 authors, we were not able to gain access to additional implementations. Therefore, for these works, we have to rely on self-reported results. In terms of programming languages, C++ was by far the most frequently chosen, with 8 out of the 14 protocols [1,3,5,18,28,31,40,63], using libraries such as Crypto++, Paillier, PBC, NTL, GMP, and MKTFHE. There were also 2 implementations in Java [30,64], 1 Rust [56], and 3 did not specify [33,58,62].

Memory Usage. As discussed in Morales et al. [42], memory consumption tends to be poorly addressed in the PSI literature. This is also the case with outsourced PSI, perhaps as one of its main goals is to shift the burden to the cloud, which is assumed to have highly capable resources. The RAM required on the client side depends largely on the choice of data structure used to encode the dataset, and for probabilistic options like Bloom filters, the chosen error rate is also a factor.

Runtime. The lack of open-source implementations unfortunately prevented us from conducting benchmarks in a unified environment for a fair comparison. Therefore, in Table 3, we synthesize the available self-reported runtimes across varying client numbers and dataset sizes, for which we refer to Table 13 of [33], Table 6 of [1], and Tables 2, 3–4 of [62]. However, these tests were all run on different client hardware and cloud server environments – obviously, the technology available in 2014 will have been very different in capacity to that available 10 years later in 2024. The implementation of Feather for comparison in Zhang et al. [62] is already over 7 times faster, only two years later. Moreover, some papers only include graphical representations of their runtime data, making it impossible to retrieve accurate numbers for comparison. Nevertheless, from Table 3 we learn that for two clients [35] appears faster than any other scheme for smaller dataset sizes, as illustrated for 2^{10} elements in Fig. 1. Although quickest, ESIP [35] is not cardinality hiding or repeatable, highlighting that we must still consider performance in the context of the other properties defined in § 4. Their protocol is followed by Zhang et al. [62] and Feather, which satisfy several useful properties like efficient updates. Furthermore, by the time we get to $2^{20} \approx 1$ M elements, Fig. 1 shows that the fastest protocol is now Kamara et al. [28], almost three times faster than Zhang et al. [62].

For more than two clients, the winner for large sets is PRISM [33], which can handle 20M elements from 10 clients in 18 s. For smaller client numbers and set sizes, the slowest is consistently Miyaji et al. [40], taking 15 s for 2^{10} elements on 4 clients, compared to Zhang et al. [62] (0.22 s), which is always just slightly faster than Feather [1] (0.26 s).

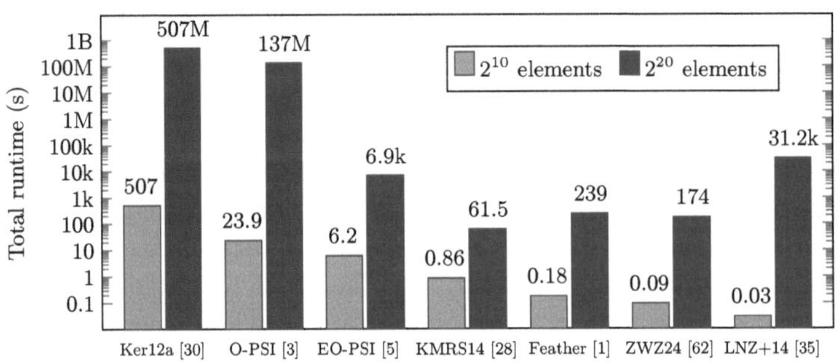

Fig. 1. Total (self-reported) runtime comparison for two clients and different set sizes. Results for Ker12a and O-PSI for 2^{20} elements extrapolated from original data.

6.3 Outsourced PSI Selection Tool

To provide a practical, data-driven resource to anyone choosing an outsourced PSI protocol, we develop an interactive selection tool. It enables easy filtering of protocols based on any combination of the 12 characteristics from

Table 3. Collation of self-reported runtimes across varying numbers of clients (#C), for the minimum and maximum set size in each case. Runtimes given to two decimal places where possible; -g- = graphical representation only, s^+ = encryption time only.

Type	Protocol	#C	Minimum		Maximum	
			set size	runtime	set size	runtime
PKE	Kerschbaum (SAC'12) [30]	2	100	5.15 s	1000	507.29 s
	Liu et al. (IC2E'14) *ESIP* [35]		2^{10}	0.03 s	2^{20}	31,186.40 s
AHE	Abadi et al. (SEC'15) *O-PSI* [3]	2	2^{10}	23.9 s	2^{15}	57,357.5 s
	Zhao and Chow (WPES'18) [63]		100	979.28 s	—	—
MHE	Kerschbaum (ASIACCS'12) [31]		2^4	336.72 s	2^7	20,667.76 s
	Yang et al. (CCPE'18) [58]		100	-g-	5000	-g-
FHE	Fan et al. (Mathematics'23) *CMPSI* [18]		2^8	0.01 s^+	2^{20}	47.99 s^+
	Wei and Hu (ePrint'25) *D-PSI* [56]		2^8	0.01 s^+	2^{20}	32.53 s^+
PRE	Zheng and Xu (IC2E'15) *VDSI* [64]	2	2^{10}	-g-	2^{15}	-g-
SS	Miyaji et al. (J. Medical Syst.'17) [40]	4	2^6	1.02 s	2^{14}	297 s
		8	2^6	1.5 s	2^{14}	355 s
		16	2^6	1.98 s	2^{14}	450 s
	Li et al. (SIGMOD'21) *PRISM* [33]	10	5 M	4.2 s	20 M	18 s
		20	5 M	8.6 s	20 M	≈ 33 s (-g-)
		50	5 M	20 s	20 M	≈ 71 s (-g-)
PRF	Abadi et al. (TDSC'19) *EO-PSI* [5]	2	2^{10}	6.2 s	2^{20}	6,864.20 s
PRP	Kamara et al. (FC'14) [28]		1000	0.86 s	1 M	61.54 s
	Abadi et al. (FC'22) *Feather* [1]		2^{10}	1.33 s	2^{20}	1,801.6 s
		4	2^{12}	5.43 s	2^{20}	1,835.51 s
		15	2^{12}	6.3 s	2^{20}	2,443.61 s
		16 K	2^{10}	328.85 s	2^{11}	909.46 s
	↑(*Feather* results reported in [62])	2	2^{10}	0.18 s	2^{20}	239.12 s
		4	2^{10}	0.26 s	—	—
		16	2^{10}	0.79 s	—	—
		1000	2^{10}	41.72 s	—	—
	Zhang et al. (WAIM'24) [62]	2	2^{10}	0.09 s	2^{20}	173.55 s
		4	2^{10}	0.22 s	—	—
		16	2^{10}	0.60 s	—	—
		1000	2^{10}	28.16 s	—	—

our framework. Existing open-source implementations are linked. A key innovation is the transformation of a static collection of benchmark data dispersed across papers into one dynamic, predictive model for protocol analysis tailored to the target scenario. Our tool is available at https://github.com/hawkesse/SoK-Outsourced-PSI and a scaled screenshot is provided in Fig. 2.

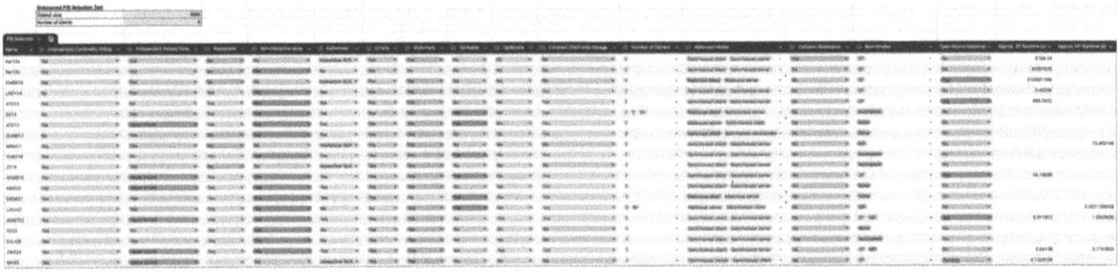

Fig. 2. Scaled screenshot of our interactive selection tool. Users can filter the individual properties based on their needs and obtain performance estimates based on the individually chosen input set sizes and number of parties.

Methodology. All available benchmark data was collated from the literature and evaluated, excluding any partial benchmarks, e.g., only encryption runtime. The result was 9 protocols benchmarked in the two-party setting, and 4 protocols benchmarked in the multi-party setting. The relationship between number of parties and runtime may be non-trivial, hence we only investigate multi-party runtimes for those protocols where multi-party benchmarks were provided.

The tool calculates an estimated runtime based on the dataset size input by the user and the extrapolation of collated benchmark data of the form (x =dataset size, y =runtime). All regression models are constrained to pass through the origin (since a dataset of zero items should result in zero runtime), and are determined by the scheme's known asymptotic computation cost. For quadratic time algorithms, we compute the quadratic regression equation through the origin, i.e., of the form $y = mx^2$. For linear time algorithms, we use $y = mx$. The slope m represents the per-item cost and is fixed for each protocol.

In the multi-party setting with more than two clients, the estimation is dependent on both a given choice of dataset size and given number of parties, i.e., (x =dataset size, y =number of parties, z =runtime). Two different methods were used, depending on the format of reported benchmark data. For protocols Miyaji et al. [40] and PRISM [33], where measurements for multiple dataset sizes were available for each number of parties, a two-stage 2D regression model ($z = (gy + c)x$) was chosen. Separate initial linear regression equations were computed as in the 2P setting for each number of parties benchmarked, with slopes m_n ($n = 4, 8, 16$ and $n = 10, 20, 50$ resp.), then a second linear regression was computed between the number of parties n and their slopes m_n to create the gradient equation $(gy + c)$. Here, c is the baseline per-item cost and g illustrates the rate at which, e.g., more parties make each item more expensive to process. For Feather [1] and Zhang et al. [62], where only one dataset size per party size was reported, a direct 3D regression through the origin ($z = ax + by$) was used instead, due to data sparsity. Thus, a and b express the per-item and per-party costs, respectively.

Limitations. The benchmark data was gathered from a range of academic papers published over more than a decade. While this approach ensures the most extensive list of protocols, the challenges to comparability due to both lack of uniform testing environments and increase in computing and networking speeds over time must be acknowledged. Therefore, our tool is not intended to predict exact runtimes but to capture the underlying trends, for example, the regression coefficients, as a meaningful complement to the paper's extensive qualitative analysis. We propose that the tool itself and the methodology behind it, could serve as a foundation for future, more standardized benchmarking efforts.

7 Discussion and Future Directions

One of the key properties that we identify is hiding the cardinality of the intersection from the server, but what about the cardinality of the input sets? In certain cases, the size of a dataset could reveal sensitive information, e.g., when computing the intersection between flight passengers and a government no-fly watch list [60]. It could be argued that a PSI protocol does not meet the goal of learning nothing about the other party's set if they can learn the set size.

In many scenarios, one party's set may be much larger than the other, known as *unbalanced* PSI. For example, in mobile contact discovery a client's small set of contacts is compared to a large database of registered users. Ideally, outsourced PSI protocols would allow for unbalanced set sizes with communication and computation complexities that scale linearly in the size of the smaller set. This has been achieved for the regular PSI (with pre-processing) [53], yet has not been explored in the outsourced setting – we leave this as future work.

Another area of PSI research currently receiving a lot of interest is *fuzzy PSI*. This is a specific case of *structurally-aware PSI* [21,22], in which the receiver has N balls of radius δ and dimension d, and the sender learns which of their points lie within one of receiver's balls [9]. There are many compelling use cases for private matching between inexact values within a certain threshold such as comparing biometric data or GPS locations. Whilst the algorithm by van Baarsen and Pu [9] has comparably good efficiency, outsourcing the computations could still bring benefits, thus outsourced fuzzy PSI is another promising direction of research.

Fairness in PSI ensures that either all honest parties receive the intersection result, or no one does (cf. § 2.1). Only two of the outsourced PSI protocols consider this property – Kamara et al. [28] via applying a second PRP layer, and Zhang et al. [61] via a reputation-based game under the assumption of rational servers. Fairness will be essential to consider if considering future applications of outsourced PSI to auctions and financial analysis, to ensure that no party is able to act on information ahead of the others and gain an unfair advantage.

As recommendations for future work, we would urge researchers to contribute open-source implementations of their protocols where possible, to encourage future benchmarking and adoption for real-world use cases. In a similar manner, we encourage sharing open access data on benchmark experiments, and to report results on concrete communication costs, not just runtimes. Another beneficial action is to provide asymptotic and concrete performance results for each individual party (e.g. client A_i, client B, server) and/or phase (e.g. encryption, computation, decryption) to more clearly convey the resource requirements.

8 Conclusion

In this SoK, we have carefully reviewed 20 existing outsourced PSI protocols. Our work includes a comparison of primitives, performance, and security models, and additionally provides a framework of 12 properties that characterize crucial yet overlooked nuances between different protocols. Furthermore we provide an interactive selection tool. Finally, we discuss the research gap between regular PSI and outsourced PSI, and identify trends such as fuzzy PSI, unbalanced PSI, and fairness for further study in the outsourced setting.

Acknowledgements. Sophie Hawkes was supported by the EPSRC and the UK government as part of the Centre for Doctoral Training in Cyber Security for the Everyday at Royal Holloway, University of London (EP/S021817/1).

References

1. Abadi, A., Dong, C., Murdoch, S.J., Terzis, S.: Multi-party Updatable Delegated Private Set Intersection. In: FC. LNCS, vol. 13411, pp. 100–119. Springer (2022)
2. Abadi, A., et al.: Starlit: privacy-preserving federated learning to enhance financial fraud detection. IACR ePrint https://ia.cr/2024/90
3. Abadi, A., Terzis, S., Dong, C.: O-PSI: delegated private set intersection on outsourced datasets. In: SEC. IFIP AICT, vol. 455, pp. 3–17. Springer (2015)
4. Abadi, A., Terzis, S., Dong, C.: VD-PSI: verifiable delegated private set intersection on outsourced private datasets. In: FC. LNCS, vol. 9603, pp. 149–168. Springer (2016)
5. Abadi, A., Terzis, S., Metere, R., Dong, C.: Efficient delegated private set intersection on outsourced private datasets. IEEE TDSC **16**(4), 608–624 (2019)
6. Asharov, G., Hamada, K., Kikuchi, R., Nof, A., Pinkas, B., Tomida, J.: Secure statistical analysis on multiple datasets: join and group-by. In: CCS, pp. 3298–3312. ACM (2023)
7. Asharov, G., Lindell, Y., Schneider, T., Zohner, M.: More efficient oblivious transfer and extensions for faster secure computation. In: CCS, pp. 535–548. ACM (2013)
8. Asokan, N., Schunter, M., Waidner, M.: Optimistic protocols for fair exchange. In: CCS, pp. 7–17. ACM (1997)
9. van Baarsen, A., Pu, S.: Fuzzy private set intersection with large hyperballs. In: EUROCRYPT. LNCS, vol. 14655, pp. 340–369. Springer (2024)
10. Boneh, D., Goh, E., Nissim, K.: Evaluating 2-DNF formulas on ciphertexts. In: TCC. LNCS, vol. 3378, pp. 325–341. Springer (2005)
11. Canetti, R.: Universally composable security: a new paradigm for cryptographic protocols. In: FOCS, pp. 136–145. IEEE (2001)
12. Chen, Y., Huang, K.: JEDI: Joint and effective privacy preserving outsourced set intersection and data integration protocols. IEEE TIFS **18**, 4504–4514 (2023)
13. Chung, H., Kim, M., Yang, P.C.: Multiparty delegated private set union with efficient updates on outsourced datasets. In: IEEE TDSC, pp. 1–16 (2024)
14. Debnath, S.K., Sakurai, K., Dey, K., Kundu, N.: Secure outsourced private set intersection with linear complexity. In: DSC, pp. 1–8. IEEE (2021)

15. Dong, C., Chen, L., Camenisch, J., Russello, G.: Fair private set intersection with a semi-trusted arbiter. In: Wang, L., Shafiq, B. (eds.) DBSec 2013. LNCS, vol. 7964, pp. 128–144. Springer, Heidelberg (2013). https://doi.org/10.1007/978-3-642-39256-6_9
16. Duong, T., Phan, D.H., Trieu, N.: Catalic: delegated PSI cardinality with applications to contact tracing. In: Moriai, S., Wang, H. (eds.) ASIACRYPT 2020. LNCS, vol. 12493, pp. 870–899. Springer, Cham (2020). https://doi.org/10.1007/978-3-030-64840-4_29
17. Even, S., Goldreich, O., Lempel, A.: A randomized protocol for signing contracts. CACM **28**(6), 637–647 (1985)
18. Fan, C., et al.: Cloud-assisted private set intersection via multi-key fully homomorphic encryption. Mathematics **11**(8) (2023)
19. Freedman, M.J., Nissim, K., Pinkas, B.: Efficient private matching and set intersection. In: Cachin, C., Camenisch, J.L. (eds.) EUROCRYPT 2004. LNCS, vol. 3027, pp. 1–19. Springer, Heidelberg (2004). https://doi.org/10.1007/978-3-540-24676-3_1
20. Garimella, G., Pinkas, B., Rosulek, M., Trieu, N., Yanai, A.: Oblivious key-value stores and amplification for private set intersection. In: Malkin, T., Peikert, C. (eds.) CRYPTO 2021. LNCS, vol. 12826, pp. 395–425. Springer, Cham (2021). https://doi.org/10.1007/978-3-030-84245-1_14
21. Garimella, G., Rosulek, M., Singh, J.: Structure-aware private set intersection, with applications to fuzzy matching. In: CRYPTO. LNCS, vol. 13507, pp. 323–352. Springer (2022)
22. Garimella, G., Rosulek, M., Singh, J.: Malicious secure, structure-aware private set intersection. In: CRYPTO. LNCS, vol. 14081, pp. 577–610. Springer (2023)
23. Goldreich, O.: The Foundations of Cryptography – Volume 1: Basic Tools. Cambridge University Press (2001)
24. Goldreich, O.: The Foundations of Cryptography – Volume 2: Basic Applications. Cambridge University Press (2004)
25. Goldwasser, S., Micali, S.: Probabilistic Encryption. J. Comput. Syst. Sci. **28**(2), 270–299 (1984)
26. Jolfaei, A.A., Mala, H., Zarezadeh, M.: EO-PSI-CA: efficient outsourced private set intersection cardinality. J. Inf. Secur. Appl. **65**, 102996 (2022)
27. Kamara, S., Mohassel, P., Raykova, M.: Outsourcing multi-party computation. IACR ePrint https://ia.cr/2011/272
28. Kamara, S., Mohassel, P., Raykova, M., Sadeghian, S.: Scaling private set intersection to billion-element sets. In: Christin, N., Safavi-Naini, R. (eds.) FC 2014. LNCS, vol. 8437, pp. 195–215. Springer, Heidelberg (2014). https://doi.org/10.1007/978-3-662-45472-5_13
29. Kavousi, A., Mohajeri, J., Salmasizadeh, M.: Improved secure efficient delegated private set intersection. In: ICEE, pp. 1–6. IEEE (2020)
30. Kerschbaum, F.: Collusion-resistant outsourcing of private set intersection. In: SAC, pp. 1451–1456. ACM (2012)
31. Kerschbaum, F.: Outsourced private set intersection using homomorphic encryption. In: ASIACCS, pp. 85–86. ACM (2012)
32. Kolesnikov, V., Kumaresan, R., Rosulek, M., Trieu, N.: Efficient batched oblivious PRF with applications to private set intersection. In: CCS, pp. 818–829. ACM (2016)
33. Li, Y., Ghosh, D., Gupta, P., Mehrotra, S., Panwar, N., Sharma, S.: PRISM: private verifiable set computation over multi-owner outsourced databases. In: SIGMOD, pp. 1116–1128. ACM (2021)

34. Lindell, Y.: How to simulate it - A tutorial on the simulation proof technique. In: Tutorials on the Foundations of Cryptography, pp. 277–346. Springer International Publishing (2017)
35. Liu, F., Ng, W.K., Zhang, W., Giang, D.H., Han, S.: Encrypted set intersection protocol for outsourced datasets. In: IC2E, pp. 135–140. IEEE (2014)
36. Liu, Z., Wang, L., Bao, H., Cao, Z., Zhou, L., Liu, Z.: Efficient and privacy-preserving cloud-assisted two-party computation scheme in heterogeneous networks. IEEE Trans. Ind. Informatics **20**(5), 8007–8018 (2024)
37. López-Alt, A., Tromer, E., Vaikuntanathan, V.: Cloud-Assisted Multiparty Computation from Fully Homomorphic Encryption. IACR ePrint https://ia.cr/2011/663
38. López-Alt, A., Tromer, E., Vaikuntanathan, V.: On-the-fly multiparty computation on the cloud via multikey fully homomorphic encryption. In: STOC, pp. 1219–1234. ACM (2012)
39. Meadows, C.: A more efficient cryptographic matchmaking protocol for use in the absence of a continuously available third party. In: S&P, pp. 134–137. IEEE (1986)
40. Miyaji, A., Nakasho, K., Nishida, S.: Privacy-preserving integration of medical data - a practical multiparty private set intersection. J. Medical Syst. **41**(3), 37:1–37:10 (2017)
41. Mohassel, P., Rindal, P., Rosulek, M.: Fast database joins and PSI for secret shared data. In: CCS, pp. 1271–1287. ACM (2020)
42. Morales Escalera, D., Agudo, I., López, J.: Private set intersection: a systematic literature review. Comput. Sci. Rev. **49**, 100567 (2023)
43. Oliaee, M.M., Delavar, M., Ameri, M.H., Mohajeri, J., Aref, M.R.: On the security of O-PSI: a delegated private set intersection on outsourced datasets. In: ISCISC, pp. 77–81. IEEE (2017)
44. Pinkas, B., Schneider, T., Zohner, M.: Scalable private set intersection based on OT extension. ACM TOPS **21**(2), 7:1–7:35 (2018)
45. Rabin, M.O.: How To Exchange Secrets with Oblivious Transfer. Technical Report TR-81, Aiken Computation Lab, Harvard University (1981)
46. Raghuraman, S., Rindal, P.: Blazing fast PSI from improved OKVS and subfield VOLE. In: CCS, pp. 2505–2517. ACM (2022)
47. Rindal, P., Schoppmann, P.: VOLE-PSI: fast OPRF and circuit-PSI from vector-OLE. In: Canteaut, A., Standaert, F.-X. (eds.) EUROCRYPT 2021. LNCS, vol. 12697, pp. 901–930. Springer, Cham (2021). https://doi.org/10.1007/978-3-030-77886-6_31
48. Ruan, O., Zeng, J.: A delegated offline private set intersection protocol for cloud computing environments. In: ICCIR, pp. 735–739. ACM (2022)
49. Sadat, M.N., Aziz, M.M.A., Mohammed, N., Pakhomov, S., Liu, H., Jiang, X.: A privacy-preserving distributed filtering framework for NLP artifacts. BMC Med. Inform. Decis. Mak. **19**(1), 183:1–183:10 (2019)
50. Sander, T., Young, A.L., Yung, M.: Non-Interactive CryptoComputing For NC^1. In: FOCS, pp. 554–567. IEEE (1999)
51. Shakya, R., Yasumura, Y., Suzuki, T., Ishimaki, Y., Yamana, H.: Outsourced private set union on multi-attribute datasets for search protocol using fully homomorphic encryption. In: iiWAS, pp. 55–62. ACM (2019)
52. Shi, Y., Yang, W., Xu, W., Li, Q.: Research on outsourced PSI protocols for privacy preserving data sharing. In: ICBDS. CCIS, vol. 1563, pp. 125–136. Springer (2021)
53. Son, Y., Jeong, J.: PSI with computation or circuit-PSI for unbalanced sets from homomorphic encryption. In: ASIACCS, pp. 342–356. ACM (2023)

54. Tajima, A., Sato, H., Yamana, H.: Outsourced private set intersection cardinality with fully homomorphic encryption. In: ICMCS, pp. 1–8. IEEE (2018)
55. Vos, J., Conti, M., Erkin, Z.: Sok: Collusion-resistant multi-party private set intersections in the semi-honest model. In: SP, pp. 465–483. IEEE (2024)
56. Wei, S., Hu, J.: Delegated PSI from homomorphic encryptions. IACR ePrint https://ia.cr/2025/868
57. Wu, Y., et al.: Elastic bloom filter: Deletable and expandable filter using elastic fingerprints. IEEE Trans. Computers **71**(4), 984–991 (2022)
58. Yang, X., Luo, X., Wang, X.A., Zhang, S.: Improved outsourced private set intersection protocol based on polynomial interpolation. CCPE **30**(1) (2018)
59. Yeo, F.Y., Ying, J.H.M.: Third-party private set intersection. In: ISIT, pp. 1633–1638. IEEE (2023)
60. Zhan, Y., Zhang, Z., Liu, Q., Wang, B.: Hiding the input-size in multi-party private set intersection. DESI **91**(9), 2893–2915 (2023)
61. Zhang, E., Li, F., Niu, B., Wang, Y.: Server-aided private set intersection based on reputation. Inf. Sci. **387**, 180–194 (2017)
62. Zhang, Y., Wang, L., Zhou, L.: efficient updateable private set intersection on outsourced datasets. In: APWeb/WAIM. LNCS, vol. 14964, pp. 84–99. Springer (2024)
63. Zhao, Y., Chow, S.S.M.: Can you find the one for me? In: WPES@CCS, pp. 54–65. ACM (2018)
64. Zheng, Q., Xu, S.: Verifiable delegated set intersection operations on outsourced encrypted data. In: IC2E, pp. 175–184. IEEE (2015)

Updatable Private Set Intersection and Beyond: Efficient Constructions via Circuit PSI

Ferran Alborch[1(✉)], Tom Chauvier[1], Antonio Faonio[1], Alexandre Fontaine[1], Ferhat Karakoç[2], Alptekin Küpçü[3], Camille Malek[1], and Melek Önen[1]

[1] EURECOM, Sophia Antipolis, Sophia Antipolis, France
{ferran.alborch,antonio.faonio,melek.onen}@eurecom.fr, akupcu@ku.edu.tr
[2] Ericsson Research, İstanbul, Turkey
ferhat.karakoc@ericsson.com
[3] Koç University, İstanbul, Turkey

Abstract. Private Set Intersection (PSI) has been widely studied, deployed, and demonstrated on static datasets. In this work, we investigate the problem of designing efficient and secure updatable PSIs in the honest-but-curious model by adopting the approach of executing a small number of PSIs over smaller sets instead of one PSI over the entire updated sets. We first identify that existing constructions suffer from privacy leakages and further propose to mitigate them thanks to the use of circuit PSIs, which are variants of PSI protocols that output the secret shares of the intersection instead of outputting the resulting intersection, combined with secure shuffling when needed. We construct a generic framework for PSI over updated sets and show that this framework can easily be extended to a protocol that outputs the cardinality of the intersection instead of the intersection itself.

Keywords: Private set intersection · Dynamic datasets · circuit-PSI

1 Introduction

Private Set Intersection (PSI) enables two mutually distrusting parties, each of them holding some private datasets, to compare these datasets and disclose only their common records, and nothing more. This functionality excels in various use cases, such as mobile private contact discovery [26,28,37], privacy-preserving contact tracing [8,50,52], online advertising measurement [22], and privacy breach detection [40]. Researchers have investigated various challenges such as scalability [29], balanced and unbalanced settings with respect to the size of the datasets or the resources of the actual parties [48], the extension to the multi-party setting [34], or additional features whereby instead of revealing the actual intersection, the protocol only reveals the output of a function over this intersection (cardinality for statistical analysis, for example) [27].

K. Jee and A. Kate (Eds.): ACNS 2026, LNCS 16571, pp. 528–558, 2027.
https://doi.org/10.1007/978-3-032-32560-0_19

One aspect that has not yet been investigated deeply is the case where datasets are not static, i.e. datasets are modified over time. Indeed, real datasets are frequently updated as new data is generated or collected and some data might become useless or have expired. In this context, the computed intersections or other further computations over these intersections can become obsolete rapidly. While there exist some solutions that tackle this problem by taking advantage of the existing output and therefore not re-executing the PSI or circuit-PSI protocol from scratch [2,4,5,35,51], we observe that these solutions still suffer from privacy leakages (we refer to Fig. 1 and Sect. 2 for more details).

Our Contributions. In this paper, we identify and study these leakages, which arise when one considers both additions of new elements and deletions of old elements in the datasets, and further propose new constructions for PSI and cardinality of PSI over updated sets in the honest-but-curious model. Inspired by Badrinarayanan et.al. [4], our constructions rely on the splitting of the datasets into smaller ones and performing some operations over them separately, before obliviously re-unifying the intermediate outputs. Apart from asymptotic efficiency, an important advantage of our solution is that it supports the (one-sided) client-server setting where only the client receives the ultimate output (the actual new intersection).

2 Problem Statement

PSI protocols are two-party protocols allowing parties P_1 and P_2, each owning (static) sets X, Y, respectively, to compute the intersection $X \cap Y$ without leaking any extra information besides the cardinality of at least one of the input sets.

For some applications, however, outputting the intersection itself might be too much. For example, if the use case requires computing the cardinality of the intersection only (e.g., when computing counting queries over shared data), outputting the elements of the intersection could be considered a leakage. In this case, we can use Cardinality-PSI protocols.

Other use cases require computing arbitrary statistics over the intersection. In general, the parties may want to compute an arbitrary function $f(X \cap Y)$. A particular kind of PSI is then used, called Circuit-PSI, where the parties obtain secret shares of the intersection. These shares can then be used within a two-party computation (2PC) protocol to obtain the intended output of f over the intersection.

Updatable PSI (uPSI). Updatable PSI, and its variants such as updatable cardinality-PSI, or updatable circuit-PSI, protocols deal with dynamic sets being updated through time, and their intersection (or an appropriate function over it) being updated along with it. The main goal of updatable PSI is to speed up the computation of PSI on updated sets by leveraging the knowledge of the intersection (or the cardinality, or the secret shares) from the previous sets. The underlying assumption is that the updates are orders of magnitude smaller than the full dataset. For a more detailed review of the related work we refer to Sect. 3.

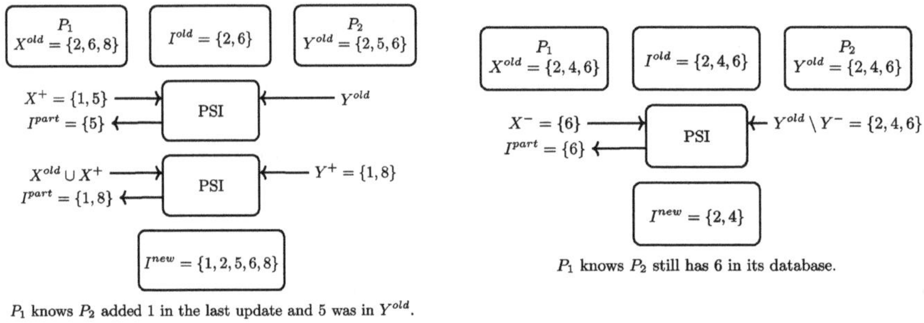

(a) Leakage from partial updates (we assume $X^- = Y^- = \emptyset$).

(b) Leakage from the size of the update (we assume $X^+ = Y^+ = Y^- = \emptyset$).

Fig. 1. Representation of leakages in updatable private set intersection.

Typical solutions to updatable PSI or updatable cardinality-PSI, including our solutions, split the sets into significantly smaller ones (such as the set of added or removed elements), and execute private set intersections and some other operations over these smaller sets [4,5,35,51]. The difference between the solutions in the related work and ours is how these sets are defined and used to implement the operations on them.

While with this approach (and similar approaches) there is a significant performance gain, we observe that the independent execution of multiple PSIs or cardinality-PSIs among smaller sets results in some unauthorized disclosure of either elements of the set or some information about the cardinality of sets.

Indeed, consider the example in Fig. 1. We denote the old sets with X^{old}, Y^{old}, the newly-added elements with X^+, Y^+, and the elements removed from the respective sets with X^-, Y^-. Thus we have new sets $X^{new} = (X^{old} \setminus X^-) \cup X^+$ and $Y^{new} = (Y^{old} \setminus Y^-) \cup Y^+$. I^{old} and I^{new} denote the old and new intersections. The protocol in Fig. 1a computes the new intersection by computing the union of $X^+ \cap Y^{old}$ and $X^{new} \cap Y^+$. For simplicity, the protocol works when we assume X^- and Y^- are empty. In the figure, we consider the case where both P_1 and P_2 are adding the same element (element 1 in the example) and P_1 is adding an element P_2 already had in its old set (element 5 in the example). By receiving the intermediate intersections in cleartext, P_1 discovers that P_2 added element 1, and element 5 was already in P_2's old dataset, whereas, in an ideal execution of the updated intersection, these should be hidden. In particular, P_1 can distinguish the case where P_2 starts with $\{2,1,6\}$ and adds $\{5,8\}$ from the case where P_2 starts with $\{2,5,6\}$ and adds $\{1,8\}$. This information, which is analogous in the case of deleted elements, then becomes an unauthorized leakage. The work in [51] suffers of this form of leakage.

To illustrate such a leakage with a real-life use case, we consider the use case of privacy-preserving contact tracing during the COVID-19 pandemic [8,50]. The list of users that a user is in contact with is always being updated with time. Hence, when using the naïve PSI with smaller sets, the application can leak the list of users infected *at the same time*, which adds the additional information of *when* the users were infected with respect to the intended leakage of *only the infected users*.

Therefore, the outputs of the intermediate operations executed on smaller sets need to be protected. The natural approach for this is to use Circuit-PSI, due to the inherent protection provided by its secret-shared output. This observation has already been made, either implicitly or explicitly, in prior work such as [2,4,35].

Nevertheless, we identify that this new proposal still suffers from two additional categories of leakages: Namely, (i) the leakage of the size of the input sets to (the smaller instances of) circuit-PSIs and (ii) the leakage of reconstructed outputs from (the smaller instances of) circuit-PSIs.

For the former form of leakage, consider the example in Fig. 1b. When P_1 removes an element of the old intersection from its database (element 6 in the example) while P_2 does not remove anything (i.e., $|Y^-| = 0$), P_1 can infer that this element is still in P_2's database due to the knowledge of that $|Y^{old}| = |Y^{old} \setminus Y^-|$. This information, which is analogous in the case of added elements, becomes an unauthorized leakage. For example, in the use case of private contact discovery in messaging applications, PSI helps new users discover other users in their contact list who employ the same messaging application. As the contact list is regularly updated, the previously described leakage (for example, the size of removed contacts) would allow a contact being blocked by a user to distinguish whether he/she was blocked or the user left the app. To address this leakage, we propose to pad the sets for the circuit-PSIs and obtain a fixed size of α elements for each of them.

For the latter form of leakage, we notice that to compute the new intersection, one of the parties needs to reconstruct using the output of the (smaller instances of) circuit-PSIs. As previously mentioned using Fig. 1a, such outputs result in some unauthorized leakage. In the context of cardinality-PSI, this does not pose a problem because only the final output is reconstructed (hence intermediate cardinalities are not leaked). In the context of updatable PSI though, the elements themselves need to be revealed. The party reconstructing intermediate outputs should not be able to discover which element is the output of which circuit-PSI. Note that the exact information leaked by the naïve reconstruction of shares is the same as when not using circuit-PSI. As such, the same previously described examples on the discovery of infected people apply here as well. To address this leakage, we propose to use an oblivious permutation, namely to randomly shuffle the secret shared values, before the reconstruction of the actual elements.

3 Related Work

Private Set Intersection. The first PSI construction was proposed by Meadows in [38], based on the Diffie-Hellman key exchange, and protocols have been since proposed based on a plethora of different cryptographic primitives, like Cuckoo hashing and oblivious transfer [33,41,43], polynomials over finite fields

[18,19,25], homomorphic encryption [15,16], or oblivious key-value stores and vector oblivious linear evaluation [42,44,45]. A PSI protocol is defined as *one-sided* if only one of the parties obtains the intersection, and *two-sided* if both of them obtain the output. It is clear that in the honest-but-curious setting one-sided protocols imply two-sided protocols but the inverse is not true. While PSI protocols usually assume both parties have similar computing power and set sizes, some PSI protocols [23,36,48] are *unbalanced* or *asymmetric*: a (potentially client P_1 with small set X and a powerful server P_2 with very large set Y. The objective is then to achieve computational or communication cost complexity linear with the size of X and sublinear with respect to the size of Y.

Circuit-Private Set Intersection. Circuit PSI, first introduced by Huang et al. in [27], is a variant of PSI where instead of outputting the intersection, it outputs the output of a circuit executed over this intersection (without leaking the intersection itself). Some of the most common circuits are *cardinality*, which outputs only the size of the intersection, *payload sum*, where each element has an associated payload and the protocol outputs the sum of those related to the elements of the intersection, and *threshold*, where the intersection is output only if its size is greater than some predetermined threshold.

Recent Circuit PSI constructions deliver a generic output of secret shares of the intersection [3,12,30,45,48,53] to be further used in any upcoming circuit, with linear computation and communication. The most generalized version encompassing the rest is that of [31], where the output given to P_1 is any strings d_i^0, d_i^1 where the first one is received if the element i is not in the intersection and otherwise the second is received.

Updatable Private Set Intersection. The study of private set intersection for updatable sets involves two parties computing the intersection on their respective dynamic private sets. The key problem to solve is to find a protocol that can be run over the updates of the respective sets to update the (previously computed) intersection of the old sets in such a way that it is more efficient than re-running a standard PSI protocol over the updated sets.

Updatable PSI was first explored by Kiss et al. [32] in the setting of mobile applications by developing a solution with costly pre-computation, which can be updated. Unfortunately, the paper does not provide any formal analysis of the leakage when the datasets are updated. Abadi et al. [1] propose a solution for the multi-party case by delegating the computation to a server, which becomes impractical in a setting considering only two parties.

The first work to formalize updatable PSI and give concrete security definitions as well as an analysis of the leakage is by Badrinayan et al. [5]. They propose two one-sided solutions based on the DDH assumption, one that supports arbitrary inserts, and one for arbitrary inserts along with "weak deletion". Here weak deletion implies that elements inserted in the latest t days can be deleted (where t is a parameter). Their constructions also leak the size of the updates per day and the size of intermediate intersections.

In a follow-up work [4], they give one-sided solutions for arbitrary deletions as well as tackling some extended functionalities like cardinality or payload sum

Table 1. Comparison of updatable PSI schemes with extended functionalities, where α denotes the size of the updates and n the size of the sets.

	Func.	Updates	Communication Complexity	Output
[5]	PSI	Add	$O(\alpha \cdot \log n)$	One-sided
[4]			$O(\alpha \cdot \log n)$	One-sided
[4]		Add & Del	$O(\alpha \cdot \log^2 n)$	One-sided
[51]			$O(\alpha \cdot \log n)^\dagger$	Two-sided
[2]			$O(\alpha \cdot \log n^2)$	Two-sided
[35]			$O(\alpha \cdot \log n + \sqrt{n})$	Two-sided
Section 5			$O(\alpha \cdot \log n + \alpha \cdot \log \alpha)$	One-sided
[4]	Card.	Add	$O(\alpha \cdot \log n)$	One-sided
[4]		Add & Del	$O(\alpha \cdot \log^2 n)$	One-sided
Section 6			$O(\alpha \cdot \log n)$	One-sided

†In [51] they claim their complexity to be $O(\log \alpha \cdot \log n)$ because they only execute their PIR over the added elements, but the number of added elements is $O(\alpha)$ rather than $O(\log \alpha)$.

PSI. To do so, they propose a new oblivious data structure inspired by path ORAM, through which each party sends their "encrypted" database to the other party and can perform oblivious updates as well as compute the intersection. This approach, however, has the drawback of high storage necessity. It also does not solve the leakage of the size of the updates.

Wang et al. [51] propose a construction based on sparse PIR that leaks both the intermediate intersections and the size of the updates. Agarwal et al. [2] construct an updatable PSI scheme based on a novel dynamic structured encryption scheme, leaking the size of the update. Ling et al. [35] give a very efficient generic construction based on unbalanced PSI (where one party has a small set) and private set union, leaking the size of the updates. All these constructions only consider two-sided outputs. Moreover, [2,35] seem to require non-trivial modifications for extended functionalities such as cardinality-PSI, because both schemes rely on using a Private Set Union (PSU) protocol after obtaining partial intersections. There is, therefore, a need for accessing the elements of the partial intersections which are basically the inputs to PSU. The knowledge of these elements already results in significant leakage for the extended functionalities. This makes [4] our closest related work, and this is why we chose to compare against them in Sect. 7.

A summary of our contributions with respect to the state of the art can be found in Table 1. Overall, we provide the asymptotically most efficient updatable PSI and updatable cardinality-PSI solutions that support additions and deletions freely, without leaking intermediate steps or sizes of updates.

4 Preliminaries

We define parties P_1 and P_2 holding sets X^{old}, Y^{old}, respectively, whereby $X^{old} = \{x_1, \ldots, x_{n_X}\}$ and $Y^{old} = \{y_1, \ldots, y_{n_Y}\}$ with size $|X^{old}| = n_X$ and $|Y^{old}| = n_Y$. (X^+, X^-) and (Y^+, Y^-) correspond to the sets of added and removed elements for P_1 and P_2, respectively. We naturally require the updates to be valid, meaning that $X^+ \cap X^{old} = \varnothing$ and $X^- \subseteq X^{old}$, and analogously for Y^{old}. Finally, $X^{new} = (X^{old} \setminus X^-) \cup X^+$, and analogously for Y^{new}.

Furthermore, we use $[m]$ to denote the set $\{1, 2, \ldots, m\}$ of integers between 1 and m. We denote by κ and λ the computational and statistical security parameters, respectively.

Hybrid Models. We identify the ideal functionality for a task F with $\mathcal{F}_{\mathrm{F}}$, and with Π_{F} we denote the corresponding protocol realizing such an ideal functionality. For two-party ideal functionalities (resp. protocols) we write $(O_1; O_2) \leftarrow \mathcal{F}_{\mathrm{F}}(I_1; I_2)$ (resp. $(O_1; O_2) \leftarrow \Pi_{\mathrm{F}}(I_1; I_2)$) to indicate the execution of the ideal functionality (resp. protocol) where I_i is the input and O_i is the output of party P_i for $i \in \{1, 2\}$. When the functionality receives a common input CI agreed upon by both parties, we write $\mathcal{F}_{\mathrm{F}}(CI; I_1; I_2)$ as shorthand for $\mathcal{F}_{\mathrm{F}}((CI, I_1); (CI, I_2))$. In this case, we assume that the common input is also leaked to the adversary.

We consider protocols defined in hybrid models. Specifically, a two-party protocol Π_{F} (realizing a functionality $\mathcal{F}_{\mathrm{F}}$) is in the $\mathcal{F}_{\mathrm{G}}$-hybrid model if the protocol is run between two parties that can interact with a trusted-third party that computes the functionality $\mathcal{F}_{\mathrm{G}}$.

We recall the composition theorem [21, Theorem 7.3.3]: if a protocol Π_{F} securely realizes $\mathcal{F}_{\mathrm{F}}$ in the $\mathcal{F}_{\mathrm{G}}$-hybrid model and a protocol Π_{G} securely realizes $\mathcal{F}_{\mathrm{G}}$, then we can construct a new composed protocol Π'_{F} that executes Π_{F}, and whenever Π_{F} invokes the trusted functionality $\mathcal{F}_{\mathrm{G}}$, the call is replaced by an execution of Π_{G}. The composed protocol Π'_{F} securely realizes $\mathcal{F}_{\mathrm{F}}$.

Secret Sharing. A *t-out-of-n* secret sharing scheme [47], shares the given secret information s among n parties and any t parties can recover it together. In this work, we consider *2-out-of-2* secret sharing schemes, as follows.

Definition 1 (*2-out-of-2* Secret Sharing Scheme). *Let $\kappa \in \mathbb{N}$ be a security parameter. We define a 2-out-of-2* secret sharing scheme *as the following tuple of probabilistic polynomial time (*PPT*) algorithms.*

- $\mathsf{SS.SetUp}(1^\kappa)$*: given the security parameter κ as input, it outputs some public parameters* $\mathsf{SS.param}$. *We will assume these public parameters are input to all the other algorithms.*
- $\mathsf{SS.Share}(x)$*: given an element x as input, it outputs two secret shares $s^{(1)}$ and $s^{(2)}$.*
- $\mathsf{SS.Combine}(s^{(1)}, s^{(2)})$*: given two compatible secret shares $s^{(1)}$ and $s^{(2)}$, it outputs a string* res.

Functionality 1 Combine and Permute $\mathcal{F}_{\text{CnP}}$

Parameters. The secret sharing scheme parameters SS.param.
Inputs. P_1 inputs $\{s_i^{(1)}\}_{i\in[m]}$, P_2 inputs $\{s_i^{(2)}\}_{i\in[m]}$ and permutation $\pi(\cdot)$ of m elements.
Outputs. P_1 receives $\pi(\{\mathsf{SS.Combine}(s_i^{(1)}, s_i^{(2)})\}_{i\in[m]})$, P_2 receives nothing. The adversary receives m.

Functionality 2 One-Sided Private Set Intersection $\mathcal{F}_{\text{PSI}}$

Inputs. P_1 inputs X, P_2 inputs Y.
Outputs. P_1 receives intersection $I = X \cap Y$, P_2 receives nothing. The adversary receives $|X|, |Y|$.

Secret sharing schemes have two main properties: *correctness* and *secrecy*, which are formally defined in Appendix C. Basically, correctness means when sharing and combining are done honestly, the correct secret would be recovered. Secrecy means that when less than t shares are combined, they do not reveal the secret s. In this work we will focus on arithmetic secret shares.

Combine and Permute. The Combine and Permute (CnP) [14,49] protocol is a cryptographic primitive that ensures the privacy of shuffling within secret sharing schemes. The main idea is that when shares are being reconstructed, there exists a link between the share and the reconstructed value, which, in larger protocols with shares being obtained from different subroutines, may leak unwanted information. CnP protocols can be used in reconstruction to obtain the shared values in a random order, thus breaking the link to the previously owned shares, as done in [11]. More concretely, P_1 (who will receive the combined shares) inputs a set of m secret shares $\{s_i^{(1)}\}_{i\in[m]}$ and P_2 inputs a set of m secret shares $\{s_i^{(2)}\}_{i\in[m]}$ as well as a permutation of m elements $\pi(\cdot)$. The protocol outputs the reconstructed shares shuffled under permutation π, $\pi(\{\mathsf{SS.Combine}(s_i^{(1)}, s_i^{(2)})\}_{i\in[m]})$ to P_1. The ideal functionality is given in Functionality 1.

Circuit PSI. Circuit PSI (cPSI) protocols are 2PC protocols that allow two parties to obtain secret shares of the intersection of their respective private sets without revealing any further information. These secret shares can be further used to compute any arbitrary circuit over the intersection by using some generic 2PC protocol. As such, depending on the specific generic 2PC protocol used afterwards, the shares can be set differently. For example, some protocols have secret shares of the value of elements, while others have secret shares of 1 with one of the parties having a correspondence to their dataset. In more details, when P_1 inputs set X of size n_X and P_2 inputs set Y, then the protocol outputs a set of n_X secret shares $\{s_i^{(1)}\}_{i\in[n_x]}$ to P_1 and a set of n_X secret shares $\{s_i^{(2)}\}_{i\in[n_x]}$ to

Functionality 3 Circuit Private Set Intersection $\mathcal{F}_{\text{cPSI}}$

Parameters. The secret sharing scheme parameters $\mathsf{SS.param}$,
Inputs. P_1 inputs X and P_2 inputs Y.
Common Inputs. Two flags, one string $\mathsf{mode} \in \{\mathsf{CA}, \mathsf{PSI}\}$, and an integer $\mathsf{side} \in \{1, 2\}$.
Outputs. P_1 and P_2 receive a set of n_X secret shares $\{s_i^{(1)}, s_i^{(2)}\}_{i \in [n_X]}$ where

$$\mathsf{SS.Combine}\left(s_i^{(1)}, s_i^{(2)}\right) = \begin{cases} 1 & \text{if } \mathsf{mode} = \mathsf{CA} \text{ and } z_i \in X \cap Y, \\ z_i & \text{if } \mathsf{mode} = \mathsf{PSI} \text{ and } z_i \in X \cap Y, \\ 0 & \text{otherwise.} \end{cases}$$

Where the functionality parses set $Z = \{z_1, \ldots, z_{|Z|}\}$ and the set is defined as:

$$Z := \begin{cases} X & \text{if } \mathsf{side} = 1 \\ Y & \text{if } \mathsf{side} = 2 \end{cases}$$

The adversary receives $|X|, |Y|$.

Functionality 4 One-sided Updatable Private Set Intersection $\mathcal{F}_{\text{uPSI}}$

Inputs. P_1 inputs X^{old}, X^+, X^- with $|X^+|, |X^-| \leq \alpha$ where X^+, X^- are valid updates for X^{old}, and $I^{old} = X^{old} \cap Y^{old}$, P_2 inputs Y^{old}, Y^+, Y^- with $|Y^+|, |Y^-| \leq \alpha$ where Y^+, Y^- are valid updates for Y^{old}.
Outputs. P_1 receives the new intersection $I^{new} = X^{new} \cap Y^{new}$, P_2 receives nothing.
The adversary receives $|X^{old}|, |Y^{old}|, |X^{new}|, |Y^{new}|$.

P_2. While the ideal functionality for PSI is given in Functionality 2, Functionality 3 represents Circuit PSI, where we have stated both types of shares that will be used by our constructions.

Unbalanced PSI. Unbalanced PSI [23,36,48] refers to private set intersection protocols tailored for scenarios where one party holds a significantly smaller dataset than the other. These protocols optimize for this asymmetry: the communication complexity depends only on the size of the smaller set, and the computational cost for each party is proportional to the size of its own input.

5 Updatable PSI

5.1 Definition

Functionality 4 defines the one-sided updatable PSI ideal functionality. The two parties input their previous sets X^{old}, Y^{old} as well as the sets of added and removed elements X^+, X^-, Y^+, Y^-. P_1 also inputs the previously computed intersection $I^{old} = X^{old} \cap Y^{old}$. With these inputs, $\mathcal{F}_{\text{upsi}}$ outputs the new intersection $I^{new} = X^{new} \cap Y^{new}$ to P_1 only, where $X^{new} := (X^{old} \setminus X^-) \cup X^+$ and analogously for Y^{new}. The leakage only includes the sizes of old and new sets (since new sets will be used as old sets in the next execution between the same parties). Note that since we are in the honest but curious setting, by chaining instantiations of this functionality we obtain a functionality for an arbitrary amount of updates. For a more detailed explanation, we refer to Appendix A.

5.2 Construction of Disjoint Sets

Let P_1 own X^{old}, X^+, X^- and P_2 own Y^{old}, Y^+, Y^-. In general, we assume $|X^+|, |X^-| \ll |X^{old}|$ (and analogously for Y). The goal is to compute intersection $I^{new} = X^{new} \cap Y^{new}$ of $X^{new} := (X^{old} \setminus X^-) \cup X^+$ and $Y^{new} := (Y^{old} \setminus Y^-) \cup Y^+$ leveraging the knowledge of the old intersection $I^{old} = X^{old} \cap Y^{old}$. For the sake of efficiency, instead of computing I^{new} from X^{new} and Y^{new}, we compute a constant number of intermediate intersections between one small set and one large set.

The main candidates for small sets are the four update sets X^+, X^-, Y^+, Y^-. The first intuition is to use each update set, individually. The added elements $X^+ \cap Y^{new}$ and $Y^+ \cap X^{new}$ as well as the deleted elements $X^- \cap Y^{old}$ and $Y^- \cap X^{old}$, and then compute I^{new} as:

$$(I^{old} \setminus ((X^- \cap Y^{old}) \cup (Y^- \cap X^{old}))) \cup (X^+ \cap Y^{new}) \cup (Y^+ \cap X^{new}). \quad (1)$$

However, we observe that there are elements appearing in more than one of these intermediate intersections. For example $X^+ \cap Y^+$ appears in both $X^+ \cap Y^{new}$ and $Y^+ \cap X^{new}$. There could be some issues with this solution. Firstly, if the union of the intermediate intersection is not performed obliviously, this setup clearly leaks the elements in $X^+ \cap Y^+$ and $X^- \cap Y^-$, which is an unauthorized leakage. Secondly, computing the cardinality by simply summing the secret-shared values would not work, because elements that appear more than once would be counted multiple times.

It is therefore more practical to compute four mutually disjoint intersections. To achieve this, we isolate the elements in $X^+ \cap Y^+$ and $X^- \cap Y^-$, ensuring that each element is included in exactly one of the four intersections. In Eq. (1), since $X^+ \cap Y^+$ is both in $X^+ \cap Y^{new}$ and $Y^+ \cap X^{new}$, we can replace X^{new} by $X^{new} \setminus X^+$ which corresponds to $Y^+ \cap X^{old} \setminus X^-$, and similarly since $X^- \cap Y^-$ is both in $Y^- \cap X^{old}$ and $X^- \cap Y^{old}$, we replace Y^{old} with $Y^{old} \setminus Y^-$ and obtain the intersection $X^- \cap Y^{old} \setminus Y^-$. Putting it all together we obtain:

$$\begin{aligned} I^{new} &= \left(I^{old} \setminus \left((X^- \cap Y^{old}) \uplus (Y^- \cap (X^{old} \setminus X^-))\right)\right) \\ &\quad \uplus \left((X^+ \cap Y^{new}) \uplus (Y^+ \cap (X^{old} \setminus X^-)\right) \end{aligned}$$

where $\uplus$ denotes the disjoint union of sets, namely, $A \uplus B = A \cup B$ if $A \cap B = \emptyset$, otherwise it defines their co-product. Appendix B provides a numerical example[1].

Lemma 1. *Let $X^{old}, X^+, X^-, Y^{old}, Y^+, Y^-$ be sets and X^+, X^- (respectively Y^+, Y^-) are valid updates for X^{old} (respectively Y^{old}) and let $I^{old} = X^{old} \cap Y^{old}$. Set*

$$I_1 := (X^{new} \cap Y^+) \qquad I_2 := X^+ \cap (Y^{old} \backslash Y^-)$$
$$I_3 := (X^{old} \cap Y^-) \qquad I_4 := (X^- \cap (Y^{old} \backslash Y^-))$$

Then

$$X^{new} \cap Y^{new} = (I^{old} \setminus (I_3 \cup I_4)) \cup (I_1 \cup I_2) \tag{2}$$
$$I_1 \cap I_2 = I_3 \cap I_4 = I^{old} \cap I_1 = I^{old} \cap I_2 = \emptyset \tag{3}$$

Moreover, $I^+ = I_1 \cup I_2, I^- = I_3 \cup I_4$ are valid updates for I^{old}.

We refer to Appendix C for a formal proof of the lemma.

Corollary 1. *Let $X^{old}, X^+, X^-, Y^{old}, Y^+, Y^-, I^{old}$, I_1, I_2, I_3, I_4 be sets defined as in Lemma 1. Then*

$$|X^{new} \cap Y^{new}| = |I^{old}| - (|I_3| + |I_4|) + (|I_1| + |I_2|).$$

5.3 Protocol Description

To compute the updated intersection while improving the performance with respect to the naive PSI solution, our protocol calls a protocol securely realizing the ideal functionality $\mathcal{F}_{cPSI}$ (Functionality 3) with the PSI mode four disjoint times with the sets X^+, X^-, Y^+, Y^-. Since the size of the updates are much smaller than the sizes of X and Y, performing four calls to an unbalanced PSI is more efficient than computing the intersection over the updated sets from scratch.

To address the leakage of the size of the updates, the first step of the protocol is for each party to locally add some dummy elements to these sets to reach a common threshold size set of α. Thus, leaking the size of the updates is no longer an issue, since it is known beforehand. We also discuss how to pick α later on in this section.

Secondly, to address the leakage regarding the reconstructed output from the cPSI executions, we take two different measures. First, when executing the four instances of cPSI, we make sure to define the big sets in such a way that the four resulting intersections are disjoint, to avoid the leakage, as explained in

[1] Note that this way of assembling the sets is only one of four possible ways we can achieve through this method (for both added and deleted elements, one may choose which party gets the larger set), which are, under most circumstances, interchangeable.

Sect. 5.2. The second measure is when reconstructing the shares: To avoid the party obtaining the intersections (and thus reconstructing the shares) to know which element came from which intersection, we reconstruct them by calling a protocol that securely realizes the ideal functionality $\mathcal{F}_{CnP}$ twice: one for added elements (X^+, Y^+) and one for removed elements (X^-, Y^-). Therefore, the reconstruction will not disclose the specific outputs of each intersection. Finally, the party obtaining the new added and deleted elements can update the old intersection. The description of this protocol is in Protocol 1.

Protocol 1 One-sided Updatable Private Set Intersection Π_{uPSI}

Parameters: Threshold set size α.
Inputs: P_1 inputs X^{old}, X^+, X^- with $|X^+|, |X^-| \leq \alpha$, and, $I^{old} = X^{old} \cap Y^{old}$, P_2 inputs Y^{old}, Y^+, Y^- with $|Y^+|, |Y^-| \leq \alpha$.
Outputs: P_1 outputs $I^{new} = X^{new} \cap Y^{new}$. P_2 outputs nothing.

1. P_1 and P_2 check locally the sets X^+, X^- and Y^+, Y^- valid updates for X^{old} and Y^{old} and add dummy elements until $|X^+| = |X^-| = |Y^+| = |Y^-| = \alpha$, as well as $|X^{old} \backslash X^-| = |X^{old}|$ and $|Y^{old} \backslash Y^-| = |Y^{old}|$.
2. P_1 and P_2 execute four circuit-PSIs as follows:
   - $(\boldsymbol{s}^{(1)}_{Y^+}; \boldsymbol{s}^{(2)}_{Y^+}) \leftarrow \mathcal{F}_{\text{cPSI}}(\mathsf{PSI}, 2;\ X^{new}; Y^+)$.
   - $(\boldsymbol{s}^{(1)}_{X^+}; \boldsymbol{s}^{(2)}_{X^+}) \leftarrow \mathcal{F}_{\text{cPSI}}(\mathsf{PSI}, 1;\ X^+; Y^{old} \backslash Y^-)$.
   - $(\boldsymbol{s}^{(1)}_{Y^-}; \boldsymbol{s}^{(2)}_{Y^-}) \leftarrow \mathcal{F}_{\text{cPSI}}(\mathsf{PSI}, 2;\ X^{old}; Y^-)$.
   - $(\boldsymbol{s}^{(1)}_{X^-}; \boldsymbol{s}^{(2)}_{X^-}) \leftarrow \mathcal{F}_{\text{cPSI}}(\mathsf{PSI}, 1;\ X^-; Y^{old} \backslash Y^-)$.
3. P_1 and P_2 run the following two CnPs where $||$ denotes concatenation:
   - $(I^-; \perp) \leftarrow \mathcal{F}_{\text{CnP}}(\boldsymbol{s}^{(1)}_{Y^-} \| \boldsymbol{s}^{(1)}_{X^-}; \boldsymbol{s}^{(2)}_{Y^-} \| \boldsymbol{s}^{(2)}_{X^-})$.
   - $(I^+; \perp) \leftarrow \mathcal{F}_{\text{CnP}}(\boldsymbol{s}^{(1)}_{Y^+} \| \boldsymbol{s}^{(1)}_{X^+}; \boldsymbol{s}^{(2)}_{Y^+} \| \boldsymbol{s}^{(2)}_{X^+})$.
4. P_1 outputs $I^{new} = (I^{old} \backslash I^-) \cup I^+$.

Fig. 2. Our generic protocol for standard updatable private set intersection.

On the Selection of α. For practical scenarios, we note that there is a trade-off in the choice of the parameter α. If α is small compared to the number of updates our protocol will propose a small overhead (linear in α) while a larger α will converge to regular cPSI. In particular, in our empirical evaluation (see Sect. 7), we chose $\alpha = O(log(n))$.

Construction of Dummy Elements. In order to avoid potential collisions in dummy elements added by both parties, prefixes specific to each party can be utilized. As a concrete example, the j-th dummy element of P_i can be the concatenation of the identifier of P_i, the index of the dummy element (e.g. j), and a specific fixed string such that is not in the domain of items of the set.

5.4 Complexity Analysis

For ease of notation, let us assume $n = |X^{old}| = |Y^{old}|$ (and therefore $|X^{new}|$, $|Y^{new}| \leq n + \alpha$). The complexity of our updatable PSI protocol depends on the complexity of the underlying building blocks, namely the protocols Π_{cPSI} and Π_{CnP} instantiating their respective ideal functionalities. Indeed, the communication cost is computed as 4 times the communication cost of Π_{cPSI} in step 2, and 2 times the cost of Π_{CnP} in step 3. Considering an asymmetric circuit PSI like [48] with a communication complexity of $O(\alpha \cdot \log(n/\alpha))$ and a CnP like [13] with a communication complexity of $O(\alpha \cdot \log \alpha)$, we get an asymptotic, communication complexity of $O(\alpha \cdot \log n/\alpha + \alpha \cdot \log \alpha)$. Analogously, for computation time we will have the 4 parallel independent executions of Π_{cPSI} in step 1 followed by the 2 parallel executions of Π_{CnP} and finished (for P_1) by the reconstruction of I^{new}. Using, for example, the cPSI from [23] leveraging the linear complexity in the update sets and sublinear in the big sets, we could get an asymptotic computation complexity of $O(\alpha \cdot \log n + \alpha \cdot \log \alpha)$.

Functionality 5 One-sided Updatable Cardinality-Private Set Intersection $\mathcal{F}_{\mathrm{uPSI\text{-}card}}$

Inputs. P_1 inputs X^{old}, X^+, X^- with $|X^+|, |X^-| \leq \alpha$ and $c^{old} = |X^{old} \cap Y^{old}|$, P_2 inputs Y^{old}, Y^+, Y^- with $|Y^+|, |Y^-| \leq \alpha$.
Outputs. P_1 receives the cardinal of the new intersection $c^{new} = |X^{new} \cap Y^{new}|$, P_2 receives nothing.
The adversary receives $|X^{old}|, |Y^{old}|, |X^{new}|, |Y^{new}|$.

5.5 Correctness and Security

Theorem 1. *Protocol Π_{uPSI} presented in Fig. 1 securely realizes the ideal functionality $\mathcal{F}_{uPSI}$ in the $(\mathcal{F}_{cPSI}, \mathcal{F}_{CnP})$-hybrid model against a semi-honest adversary, assuming the secret sharing scheme holds secrecy.*

Proof Sketch. For the complete proof we refer to Appendix C, here we provide a sketch. Lemma 1 ensures the correctness of the protocol, since the j-th execution of $\mathcal{F}_{\mathrm{cPSI}}$ in protocol Π_{uPSI} computes the secret shares of the elements in set I_j defined in the lemma. Regarding privacy, notice that the parties in the protocol only interact with the ideal functionalities. In particular, when invoking $\mathcal{F}_{\mathrm{cPSI}}$, the parties receive secret shares as output. By the secrecy of the secret-sharing scheme, no information about the underlying sets is revealed beyond their cardinalities, which the parties fix to α using dummy inputs. Therefore, even the cardinalities do not leak.

When invoking $\mathcal{F}_{\mathrm{CnP}}$, party P_1 obtains sets I^- and I^+. It is important to note that, thanks to Eq. (3) in Lemma 1, the outputs of these functionalities can indeed be interpreted as sets, since there are no repeated elements. We also note that sets I^- and I^+ can be efficiently derived from I^{old} and the output of the ideal functionality $\mathcal{F}_{\mathrm{uPSI}}$ realized by the protocol, since, by Lemma 1, they constitute valid updates for I^{old}. Thus, the outputs of $\mathcal{F}_{\mathrm{CnP}}$ can be simulated using the input and output of P_1 in the ideal world, only.

6 Updatable Cardinality-PSI

We present our new protocol for one-sided updatable cardinality-PSI and extend it to support the payload sum feature as well. Our protocol uses the cPSI functionality in CA mode and arithmetic secret sharing to address the two leakages identified in Sect. 2.

6.1 Definition

Functionality 5 defines the one-sided updatable cardinality-PSI ideal functionality. The two parties input their previous sets X^{old}, Y^{old} as well as the sets of added and removed elements X^+, X^-, Y^+, Y^-, and P_1 also inputs the previously computed cardinality result $c^{old} = |X^{old} \cap Y^{old}|$. With these inputs, $\mathcal{F}_{\text{uPSI-card}}$ (Functionality 5) outputs the cardinality of the new intersection $c^{new} = |X^{new} \cap Y^{new}|$ to P_1 only, where $X^{new} := (X^{old} \setminus X^-) \cup X^+$ and analogously for Y^{new}. Similarly to the previous section, by chaining instantiations of this functionality we obtain a functionality for an arbitrary amount of updates.

Protocol 2 One-sided Updatable Cardinality-Private Set Intersection $\Pi_{\text{uPSI-card}}$

Parameters: Threshold set size α.
Inputs: P_1 inputs X^{old}, X^+, X^-, as well as $c^{old} = |X^{old} \cap Y^{old}|$.
P_2 inputs Y^{old}, Y^+, Y^-.
Outputs: P_1 outputs $c^{new} = |X^{new} \cap Y^{new}|$. P_2 outputs nothing.

1. P_1 and P_2 check locally the sets X^+, X^- and Y^+, Y^- valid updates for X^{old} and Y^{old} and add dummy elements until $|X^+| = |X^-| = |Y^+| = |Y^-| = \alpha$, as well as $|X^{old} \backslash X^-| = |X^{old}|$ and $|Y^{old} \backslash Y^-| = |Y^{old}|$.
2. P_1 and P_2 four circuit-PSIs for cardinality as follows:
   - $\{(\mathbf{c}^{(1)}_{Y+,i}; \mathbf{c}^{(2)}_{Y+,i})\}_{i \in [\alpha]} \leftarrow \mathcal{F}_{\text{cPSI}}(\mathsf{CA}, 2;\ X^{new}; Y^+)$.
   - $\{(\mathbf{c}^{(1)}_{X+,i}; \mathbf{c}^{(2)}_{X+,i})\}_{i \in [\alpha]} \leftarrow \mathcal{F}_{\text{cPSI}}(\mathsf{CA}, 1;\ X^+; Y^{old} \backslash Y^-)$.
   - $\{(\mathbf{c}^{(1)}_{Y-,i}; \mathbf{c}^{(2)}_{Y-,i})\}_{i \in [\alpha]} \leftarrow \mathcal{F}_{\text{cPSI}}(\mathsf{CA}, 2;\ X^{old}; Y^-)$.
   - $\{(\mathbf{c}^{(1)}_{X-,i}; \mathbf{c}^{(2)}_{X-,i})\}_{i \in [\alpha]} \leftarrow \mathcal{F}_{\text{cPSI}}(\mathsf{CA}, 1;\ X^-; Y^{old} \backslash Y^-)$.
3. P_j, $j \in \{1, 2\}$, locally computes

$$c^{(j)} = \sum_{i \in [\alpha]} \mathbf{c}^{(j)}_{Y+,i} + \mathbf{c}^{(j)}_{X+,i} - \mathbf{c}^{(j)}_{Y-,i} - \mathbf{c}^{(j)}_{X-,i}.$$

   P_2 sends $c^{(2)}$ to P_1.
4. P_1 outputs $c^{new} = c^{old} + \mathsf{SS.Combine}(c^{(1)}, c^{(2)})$.

Fig. 3. Our generic protocol for updatable cardinality-private set intersection.

6.2 Protocol Description

Similar to the construction of Π_{uPSI} in Protocol 1, the protocol $\Pi_{\text{uPSI-card}}$ for cardinality in Protocol 2 executes four circuit-PSIs in CA mode, using the sets $I_1, \ldots, I_4$ defined in Lemma 1. Namely, the outputs of the cPSI sub-protocols are shares of binary vectors, where a 0 in the j-th position indicates that the j-th element is not in the intersection, and a 1 indicates that it is. Moreover, we assume a linear secret-sharing scheme (alternatively, additively homomorphic encryption can be employed, as in [31]) (Fig. 3).

Analogously to the construction in the previous section, to address the leakage of the size of the updates, each party locally adds dummy elements to the update sets to reach a common threshold set size of α. By using the CA mode of cPSI and the linearity of arithmetic secret shares, each party can locally add all the shares received from the added intersections and subtract all the shares received from the deleted intersections to obtain a secret share of the change in cardinal from the old to the new intersection. Then, this value can be reconstructed by P_1 and added to the old cardinal. Note that in the cardinality case, the fact that the four intersections computed are disjoint is a requirement to guarantee the correctness of the protocol. Moreover, since the shares of individual elements in the intersection are not reconstructed one by one, no leakage occurs about their position within the sets $I_1, \ldots, I_4$. Therefore, the CnP functionality is no longer required.

6.3 Complexity Analysis

For ease of notation, let us assume $n = |X^{old}| = |Y^{old}|$ (and therefore $|X^{new}|$, $|Y^{new}| \leq n+\alpha$). The communication cost and the computation cost is computed as 4 times that of Π_{cPSI}. The remaining operations consists of simple sum and reconstruction of one single secret share. Hence, as in the previous case, considering an asymmetric circuit PSI like [48], we get an asymptotic complexity for communication cost of $O(\alpha \cdot \log(n/\alpha))$, and considering the proposal in [23], we get a complexity of $O(\alpha \cdot \log n)$ for computation cost.

6.4 Security

Theorem 2. *Protocol $\Pi_{uPSI-card}$ presented in Fig. 2 securely and correctly realizes the ideal functionality $\mathcal{F}_{uPSI-card}$ described as Functionality 5 in the $\mathcal{F}_{cPSI}$-hybrid model against a semi-honest adversary, assuming the arithmetic secret sharing holds secrecy and correctness.*

Proof Sketch. Correctness follows directly from Corollary 1 and from the linearity of the secret sharing scheme.[2] The proof of privacy is almost trivial; nevertheless,

[2] As a caveat, linear secret-sharing schemes are usually defined over finite fields (or finite rings). Strictly speaking, this means our protocol computes the cardinality modulo the size of the underlying field. The common way to address this is simply to choose a field large enough to avoid wrap-around.

we describe the simulator. The simulator samples one secret share, for example $\mathbf{c}^{(1)}_{X^+,1}, \mathbf{c}^{(2)}_{X^+,1}$, to form a sharing of the value $\delta = c^{\text{new}} - c^{\text{old}}$, while sampling the remaining shares as sharings of 0. It then simulates the interactions with $\mathcal{F}_{\text{cPSI}}$ by setting the outputs of these interactions to the sampled shares. The proof follows by a standard hybrid argument relying on the secrecy of secret-shared values.

6.5 Updatable Payload-Sum-PSI

Private set intersection for payload sum is a variant of PSI, where each element in the sets has a related payload v_x and the objective is to output the sum of the payloads of the elements in the intersection, i.e., $\sum_{x \in X^{old} \cap Y^{old}} v_x$.

To modify $\Pi_{\text{uPSI-card}}$ into $\Pi_{\text{uPSI-sum}}$, we only need to slightly change the underlying base circuit-PSI protocol in PSI mode. This cPSI now will output secret shares of the value v_x rather than the actual element. Then, all the steps of the protocol described in Fig. 2 are executed identically and P_1 obtains the resulting payload sum.

Regarding the more generic functionality of circuit-PSI, designing an efficient updatable version from this architecture comes with impractical challenges. For a more detailed study of these, as well as some solutions to partially circumvent them we refer to Appendix D.

7 Performance Evaluation

7.1 Experimental Setting

We have implemented[3] our constructions for updatable PSI and updatable cardinality-PSI in Rust. Regarding the circuit-PSI protocol Π_{cPSI}, we use the proposal by Karakoç and Küpçü [31], since, on top of being very efficient due to its leveraging of oblivious programmable pseudo-random function and Cuckoo tables, it also offers flexibility for its output. Indeed, the output can either be secret shares of 1 or 0 and suit the computation of the cardinality, or secret shares of the value of the element or 0 and suit standard uPSI. Some additional optimizations to our protocol $\Pi_{\text{uPSI-card}}$ were made thanks to this use and are explained in Appendix E. To implement this scheme we have chosen to use the secure equality test by Ciampi and Orlandi in [17] with the `oblivious_transfer_protocols` library [24] for Oblivious Transfer extension and the `aes` library [46], as well as the Paillier encryption scheme [39] with the `kzen-paillier` library [7] for the homomorphic encryption scheme. The underlying additive arithmetic secret sharing scheme uses a simple addition in $\mathbb{Z}_L$ with L being an upper bound to the domain of the secret sharing. Finally, for the combine and permute protocol Π_{CnP}, we use the naïve approach described in [13, Appendix C] where P_1 encrypts its shares with an additively homomorphic encryption scheme, sends

[3] Implementation available at https://gitlab.eurecom.fr/project-spring-2025/PSI/.

them to P_2, who reconstructs the output while being encrypted, shuffles them, and finally sends them back to P_1 for decryption.

We believe that the most relevant work to compare against our solution is [4][4], since it is the only solution that implements cardinality-PSI, payload-sum-PSI, and the standard PSI when sets are updated. Nevertheless, in that solution, P_2 constructs an oblivious data structure of Y and preliminarily sends it to P_1, who further executes all queries locally. Hence, compared to our solution, the one in [4] requires a much larger amount of storage and a significant communication overhead before the query execution starts.

All benchmarks were obtained on an Intel Core i7-7800X (6C/12T, 3.5 GHz, AVX-512), with 128 GB of RAM running Ubuntu 20.04 operating system. The parties are executed in a different thread each, and communicate through localhost. As in the previous work [4], we use the Linux `tc` command to simulate different network settings, with LAN at 0.2ms network latency and 1 Gbps bandwidth, and WAN at 80ms network latency and testing several bandwidths of 200 Mbps, 50 Mbps, and 5 Mbps.

The size of the datasets n ranges from 2^{16} to 2^{17}. We had to stop at this size because the solution in [4] could not be executed with larger sizes (the authors also mentioned that they had to increase their RAM for larger datasets). For larger datasets, we only tested our own protocols. The size of updates α varies from 2^4 to 2^6. Note that the sizes of the new (updated) sets will be bounded by $n \pm \alpha$.

7.2 Performance Results

We evaluate our protocols Π_{uPSI} and $\Pi_{\text{card-uPSI}}$ in terms of communication and computation cost, and compare them with the performance of protocols proposed by Badrinarayan et al. [4] supporting both addition and deletion (i.e., Sect. 4, in [4]). Table 2 depicts the obtained measurements. We also evaluate the run-time and communication cost for larger sets frow which we were not able to run the code from [4] and these results are shown in Table 3.

Communication Cost. As expected, our solution for updatable cardinality-PSI is slightly more efficient than our standard updatable PSI due to the additional use of the combine and permute protocol in our updatable PSI. Compared to [4], in general, our solution incurs higher communication cost when the updates are smaller. The communication cost of our solutions grows linearly with the updates more slowly than the one in [4]. Therefore, we outperform [4] as the update size grows.

It is worth noting that our solutions and [4] follow very different approaches leading to very different architectures. [4] uses an oblivious data structure for each dataset that is stored by the other party and can be obliviously updated and queried, whereas our solutions compute these updates with each party only having access to its (updated) dataset as well as the old intersection (or cardinal

[4] Implementation available: https://github.com/ruidazeng/upsi-revisited.

Table 2. Comparison of our constructions with state-of-the-art constructions from [4]. Best performances are highlighted in **bold**, and when our protocol outperforms [4], the corresponding cells are emphasized in green, otherwise, i.e., when [4] performs better, the actual cells are highlighted in blue.

	n	α	Protocol	Comm. (MB)	Online Run Time (s)			
					LAN	200 Mbps	50 Mbps	5 Mbps
PSI	2^{16}	2^4	[4]	**54.11**	113.23	117.01	182.95	183.06
		2^5		107.11	218.05	229.42	368.42	367.27
		2^6		211.72	424.17	447.79	735.09	738.92
		2^4	Protocol 1	96.42	**6.00**	**11.99**	**22.22**	**159.16**
		2^5		**97.47**	**7.44**	**13.62**	**23.24**	**162.28**
		2^6		**99.6**	**10.46**	**16.29**	**27.38**	**167.58**
	2^{17}	2^4	[4]	**55.16**	114.89	119.29	185.95	**187.62**
		2^5		**108.90**	222.46	232.35	374.99	**375.51**
		2^6		217.65	438.58	462.03	762.45	764.81
		2^4	Protocol 1	191.69	**9.64**	**18.56**	**42.17**	311.89
		2^5		192.74	**11.44**	**19.8**	**40.63**	314.37
		2^6		**194.88**	**14.2**	**22.81**	**43.76**	**321.26**
Cardinality PSI	2^{16}	2^4	[4]	**53.47**	108.65	114.04	178.37	179.77
		2^5		106.20	211.80	223.37	360.40	362.58
		2^6		210.48	416.50	438.17	722.02	728.79
		2^4	Protocol 2	91.55	**3.88**	**8.89**	**18.95**	**150.06**
		2^5		**94.58**	**3.97**	**9.23**	**19.46**	**154.6**
		2^6		**97.37**	**3.86**	**9.73**	**19.81**	**158.42**
	2^{17}	2^4	[4]	**54.92**	112.32	116.89	183.10	**182.38**
		2^5		**109.07**	217.40	229.49	369.83	372.83
		2^6		216.69	429.72	451.35	749.89	751.44
		2^4	Protocol 2	182.17	**7.65**	**16.43**	**35.5**	294.69
		2^5		187.39	**7.88**	**15.29**	**36.68**	**302.56**
		2^6		**191.33**	**7.87**	**17.31**	**37.42**	**309.43**

Table 3. Run-time and communication cost for our constructions with big sets.

n	α	Protocol	Comm. (MB)	Online Run Time (s)			
				LAN	200 Mbps	50 Mbps	5 Mbps
2^{20}	2^4	Protocol 1	1525.53	96.52	150.50	319.10	2489.80
	2^5		1526.5	98.67	140.44	307.39	2492.97
	2^6		1528.72	100.66	157.01	309.14	2495.41
	2^4	Protocol 2	1451.6	90.54	140.11	305.08	2370.96
	2^5		1487	93.74	136.93	295.56	2432.86
	2^6		1506.98	96.32	147.65	302.41	2458.83

thereof). Therefore, [4] inherently requires a much larger local storage cost, while sending less information, in general. Furthermore, these oblivious data structures must be sent to the other party beforehand, adding communication cost.

With respect to the communication cost in larger sets ($n = 2^{20}$), we see that it becomes notably large. This is mostly due to the specific OT extension library in Rust that is used in our implementation, which is not as highly optimized as some other C libraries, and to not implementing the Silent OT extension [9].

Computation Time. Similar to the communication cost, as expected, the computation time is lower for the cardinality case than the standard PSI case. As for comparison results, our protocol outperforms [4], by 11× to 40× for updatable PSI and by 14× to 107× for updatable cardinality-PSI in the LAN setting, and almost all of the WAN settings. It is worth noting that our implementation seems to be more sensitive to bandwidth because, due to the design choice, our code incurs more latency than in the performance results of the implementation from [4]. Indeed, in our benchmarks, the running time increases more significantly when the bandwidth is smaller (for example, $5Mbps$). Future work can be done to mitigate this through code optimizations.

Regarding computation time in the scenario with the largest sets, we observe that our protocol with $n = 2^{20}$ elements even outperforms in the LAN setting than of [4] with $n = 2^{16}$ elements. The performance drops in the WAN settings, which is explainable because of the combination of the sensitivity of our implementation to bandwidth and the high communication cost.

Table 4. Benchmarking of our constructions with real-life data from the ENRON mail database.

α	Protocol	Comm. (MB)	Offline Runtime (s)	Online Runtime (s)			
				LAN	200 Mbps	50 Mbps	5 Mbps
2^6	Protocol 1	380.85	9.29	20.51	35.4	77.92	616.73
2^8		393.96	14.1	39.43	53.96	98.39	656.47
2^{10}		443.1	33.45	108.6	126.13	170.59	796.25
2^6	Protocol 2	374.23	9.29	14.27	26.93	70.12	601.85
2^8		387.85	14.1	14.31	32.12	71.52	624.39
2^{10}		426.48	33.45	14.67	32.35	76.97	686.11

7.3 Evaluation on Real Data

To empirically evaluate our constructions in a real-life use case, we consider a scenario of spam detection. In such a scenario, an entity puts into place a spam filter by setting up a blacklist (for example in relation to the email addresses), and computes a PSI with its clients' received emails (their senders) to remove the spam. To analyze our constructions' efficiency in this situation, we have opted to use real data from the Enron mail database.[5] We randomly extracted two separate datasets of the same size (around 2^{18}) from the Enron database, one for each party. The set of added elements are randomly sampled from the remaining data in the Enron database, and the set of removed elements are randomly selected from the parties datasets (with varying sizes). This setting corresponds to a worst-case scenario for our constructions because both original datasets are equally large.

We measured both the running time and the communication overhead. The results are shown in Table 4. From this table, we clearly observe that our protocols become the fastest when the difference of the size of the update and size of the old set is maximized. This is an expected behavior thanks to the asymmetric nature of the underlying circuit PSI.

8 Conclusion

We have proposed new constructions for updatable PSI and updatable cardinality-PSI, improving the current state-of-the-art [4] by 11× to 40× for updatable PSI, and by 14× to 107× for updatable cardinality-PSI in computation time in the LAN setting.

Our work may inspire several avenues of follow-up works. One of these would be to continue the path towards updatable circuit-PSI, even if this would need to come from a different architecture than ours (using four smaller circuit-PSI executions). It could also take shape of proposing schemes for other specific circuits (such as fuzzy PSI, or threshold PSI). Another avenue is to extend the security model and solution to the malicious case. The main hurdle in that direction consists of how to commit the sets of each individual execution of the intersection without incurring a linear communication and computation cost with respect to the large sets (thus being asymptotically equivalent to the naive solution of re-executing the full PSI). Finally, with respect to the concrete efficiency of our construction, the main bottleneck of our implementation (both in computation time and communication cost) is the execution of OT extension. To improve this concrete efficiency, a better OT extension library could be implemented or silent OT extension [9,10] can be employed to have an even better asymptotic growth. Also, with respect to the implementation, the code can be optimized to reduce the impact of low bandwidth on the protocol. Finally, the code can be further parallelized by using multiple threads per party, instead of only one.

Acknowledgments. This work was partially supported by the French National Research Agency (ANR) Project ANR-23-CE39-0009-06 TRUST, the Scientific and Technological Research Council of Türkiye (TÜBİTAK) projects 119E088, 123E462, and the 1515 Frontier Research and Development Laboratories Support Program project 5169902.

[5] https://www.kaggle.com/datasets/wcukierski/enron-email-dataset/code.

A A Reactive Functionality for Updatable PSI

Given the dynamic nature of updatable PSI, one could alternatively define its ideal functionality as a reactive functionality. That is, a stateful and interactive functionality where the parties can submit new inputs over time and receive updated outputs. We present a simple reactive ideal functionality for updatable PSI in Fig. 4. Similarly, one could consider a reactive ideal functionality for the cardinality version of PSI.

We can show that $\mathcal{F}'_{\text{uPSI}}$ and $\mathcal{F}_{\text{uPSI}}$ in section 4 are equivalent in the honest-but-curious setting, namely there is a (trivial) protocol in the $\mathcal{F}_{\text{uPSI}}$-hybrid world that realizes functionality $\mathcal{F}'_{\text{uPSI}}$ and vice versa.

We focus on one direction of the equivalence showing a protocol realizing $\mathcal{F}'_{\text{uPSI}}$. The protocol requires party P_1 to store set X^i and intersection I^i, and party P_2 to store Y^i. At each iteration, party P_1 (respectively, P_2) sets $X^{\text{old}} = X^i$ and sends the tuple $(X^{\text{old}}, X^+, X^-)$ and I^i (respectively, $(Y^{\text{old}}, Y^+, Y^-)$) to the ideal functionality $\mathcal{F}_{\text{uPSI}}$. The party P_1 updates the intersection I^{i+1} according to the output of the functionality.

The correctness of the protocol is straightforward to verify. The only point worth clarifying is the leakage received by the adversary: In the ideal functionality $\mathcal{F}_{\text{uPSI}}$, the adversary learns the cardinalities of both the old and the new sets at each update; in contrast, the reactive functionality $\mathcal{F}'_{\text{uPSI}}$ leaks the cardinality of the updated set, only. This difference, however, is not significant. The initial sets X^0 and Y^0 are trivially of size zero. Furthermore, at each iteration i, the adversary already knows the cardinality of the old set from iteration $i-1$. Therefore, the additional leakage in $\mathcal{F}_{\text{uPSI}}$ does not reveal any new information beyond what the adversary already learns during the protocol execution.

Finally, we note that this composition is only possible because we consider the honest-but-curious setting. In the malicious setting, a corrupted party P_1 may not maintain a consistent internal state. In particular, it can arbitrarily

---

Functionality 6 One-sided Reactive Updatable Private Set Intersection $\mathcal{F}'_{\text{uPSI}}$

At first activation the functionality initializes empty sets $X^0, Y^0 = \emptyset$ associated to P_1 and P_2 respectively and a counter $i = 0$.

Inputs. At each iteration the party P_1 sends input (X^+, X^-) with $|X^+|, |X^-| \leq \alpha$ where X^+, X^- are valid updates for X^i, and the party P_2 inputs (Y^+, Y^-) with $|Y^+|, |Y^-| \leq \alpha$ where Y^+, Y^- are valid updates for Y^i.
The ideal functionality sets $X^{i+1} \leftarrow (X^i \setminus X^-) \cup X^+$ and $Y^{i+1} \leftarrow (Y^i \setminus Y^-) \cup Y^+$.

Outputs. When both parties have sent their input for the current iteration, the ideal functionality sends to P_1 the new intersection $I^{i+1} = X^{i+1} \cap Y^{i+1}$, P_2 receives nothing. The ideal functionality increase its counter i. The adversary receives $|X^{i+1}|, |Y^{i+1}|$.

Fig. 4. A reactive Ideal functionality for updatable PSI.

modify I^i and X^i, or it may send invalid updates, because there is no guarantee that $X^- \subseteq X^{\text{old}}$ or that $X^+ \cap X^{\text{old}} = \emptyset$ will hold. Without these conditions, the integrity of the update process cannot be enforced, making the composition insecure in the presence of an actively malicious adversary.

B Numerical Example of Disjoint Sets

In this section we give a concrete numerical example of the disjoint sets we compute to facilitate its comprehension. Let P_1 own $X^{old} = \{2, 6, 8\}$, and P_2 own $Y^{old} = \{2, 5, 6\}$ and as such $I^{old} = \{2, 6\}$. Then let the update be $X^+ = \{1, 5\}$, $Y^+ = \{1, 8\}$, $X^- = \{2, 8\}$ and $Y^- = \{2, 6\}$. Adding it all together, then the partial intersections we compute will be $I_1 = Y^+ \cap ((X^{old} \backslash X^-) \cup X^+) = \{1\}$, $I_2 = X^+ \cap (Y^{old} \backslash Y^-) = \{5\}$, $I_3 = Y^- \cap X^{old} = \{2, 6\}$ and $I_4 = X^- \cap (Y^{old} \backslash Y^-) = \emptyset$. Which in turn give us $I^{new} = (I^{old} \setminus (I_3 \cup I_4)) \cup (I_1 \cup I_2) = \{1, 5\}$, noting that $X^{new} = \{1, 5, 6\}$ and $Y^{new} = \{1, 5, 8\}$.

Now consider a second update, in which P_1 adds $X^+ = \{3, 4\}$ and removes $X^- = \{1, 6\}$ while P_1 adds $Y^+ = \{2, 4\}$ and removes $Y^- = \{1, 5\}$. In this step, we will then have $X^{old} = \{1, 5, 6\}$, $Y^{old} = \{1, 5, 8\}$ and $I^{old} = \{1, 5\}$ (which are the new sets of the previous step), and the computed sets will be $I_1 = \{4\}$, $I_2 = \emptyset$, $I_3 = \{1, 5\}$ and $I_4 = \emptyset$. This will then give us $I^{new} = (I^{old} \backslash (I_3 \cup I_4)) \cup (I_1 \cup I_2) = \{4\}$, noting that $X^{new} = \{3, 4, 5\}$ and $Y^{new} = \{2, 4, 8\}$.

C Security Definitions and Proofs

C.1 Security Definitions

Definition 2 (Correctness and Secrecy of Secret Sharing). *Let* $\mathsf{SS} = (\mathsf{SS.SetUp}, \mathsf{SS.Share}, \mathsf{SS.Combine})$ *be a 2-out-of-2 secret sharing scheme.*

- *We say it is* correct *if for any element* x $\Pr[\mathsf{SS.Combine}(s^{(X)}, s^{(Y)}) \neq x] = \mathsf{negl}(\kappa)$, *where* $\mathsf{SS.param} \leftarrow \mathsf{SS.SetUp}(1^\kappa)$ *and* $(s^{(X)}, s^{(Y)}) \leftarrow \mathsf{SS.\ Share}(x)$.
- *We say it is* secret *if for any elements* x_0, x_1 *the following distributions are indistinguishable* $s_0^{(X)} \approx s_1^{(X)}$, $s_0^{(Y)} \approx s_1^{(Y)}$ *where* $(s_0^{(X)}, s_0^{(Y)}) \leftarrow \mathsf{SS.Share}(x_0)$ *and* $(s_1^{(X)}, s_1^{(Y)}) \leftarrow \mathsf{SS.Share}(x_1)$.

Definition 3 (Security of 2PC Protocol). *Let* Π *be a 2PC protocol, let* $View_i^{\Pi}(X; Y)$ *be the view of party* P_i *(including input, random tape and all received messages) of the protocol* Π *with inputs* X *by* P_X *and* Y *by* P_Y*, and let* $Out_i^{\Pi}(X; Y)$ *be the output of* P_i *in protocol* Π *on inputs* X *by* P_X *and* Y *by* P_Y*. Then,* Π *is said to securely compute an ideal functionality* $\mathcal{F}$ *in the semi-honest model if for any PPT adversary* $\mathcal{A}$ *there exist PPT simulators* Sim_X *and* Sim_Y *such that for all inputs* x *and* y

$$View_X^{\Pi}(X; Y), Out_X^{\Pi}(X; Y) \approx_c Sim_X(x, \mathcal{F}_X(X; Y)), \mathcal{F}_Y(X; Y),$$
$$View_Y^{\Pi}(X; Y), Out_Y^{\Pi}(X; Y) \approx_c Sim_Y(x, \mathcal{F}_Y(X; Y)), \mathcal{F}_X(X; Y),$$

where $F_i(X; Y)$ *denotes the output of* P_i *for the ideal functionality on inputs* X, Y

C.2 Proof of Lemma 1

Proof. First we get that:

$$I^{new} = (X^{new} \cap (Y^{old} \backslash Y^-)) \cup (X^{new} \cap Y^+) \tag{4}$$
$$= ((X^{old} \backslash X^-) \cap (Y^{old} \backslash Y^-)) \cup (X^+ \cap (Y^{old} \backslash Y^-)) \cup (X^{new} \cap Y^+), \tag{5}$$

where at steps 4, 5 we have applied the distributive property between set intersection and set union and the definition of $Y^{new} = (Y^{old} \backslash Y^-) \cup Y^+$, and simarly for X^{new}. We note that

$$((X^{old} \backslash X^-) \cap (Y^{old} \backslash Y^-)) = (X^{old} \backslash (X^- \cup Y^-)) \cap (Y^{old} \backslash (X^- \cup Y^-),$$

in fact, any element in $X^{old} \backslash X^-$ but not in $X^{old} \backslash (X^- \cup Y^-)$ is then in $X^{old} \cap Y^-$ (and in particular in Y^-) and therefore not in the intersection $(X^{old} \backslash X^-) \cap (Y^{old} \backslash Y^-)$ (and analogously for $Y^{old} \backslash Y^-$). Subbing the equation above into Eq. (5) and setting $I_1 := X^{new} \cap I^+$ we have:

$$I^{new} = ((X^{old} \backslash (X^- \cup Y^-)) \cap (Y^{old} \backslash (X^- \cup Y^-))) \cup (X^+ \cap (Y^{old} \backslash Y^-)) \cup I_1$$
$$= (I^{old} \backslash (X^- \cup Y^-)) \cup (X^+ \cap (Y^{old} \backslash Y^-)) \cup I_1 \tag{6}$$
$$= I^{old} \backslash ((X^- \cup Y^-) \cap (X^{old} \cap Y^{old})) \cup (X^+ \cap (Y^{old} \backslash Y^-)) \cup I_1 \tag{7}$$

At step 6 we have applied the right distributive property of set difference over set intersection and $I^{old} = X^{old} \cap Y^{old}$, at step 7 we have used the definition of set difference. For convenience, we set $I_2 := (X^+ \cap (Y^{old} \backslash Y^-))$ and $I^- := ((X^- \cup Y^-) \cap (X^{old} \cap Y^{old}))$. Thus

$$I^{new} = I^{old} \backslash I^- \cup (I_2 \cup I_1) \tag{8}$$

We focus now on I^-:

$$I^- = (X^- \cap (X^{old} \cap Y^{old})) \cup (Y^- \cap (X^{old} \cap Y^{old})) \tag{9}$$
$$= (X^- \cap Y^{old}) \cup (Y^- \cap X^{old}) \tag{10}$$
$$= (X^- \cap (Y^{old} \backslash Y^-)) \cup (Y^- \cap X^{old}) \tag{11}$$

Where at step 9 we have applied the distributive property between set intersection and set union, at step 10 we have used the associative property of set intersection as well as $X^- \subseteq X^{old}$ (and analogously $Y^- \subseteq Y^{old}$), and finally at step 11 we have used that any element in $X^- \cap Y^{old}$ not in $X^- \cap (Y^{old} \backslash X^-)$ must be in $Y^- \cap X^- \subseteq Y^{old} \cap Y^-$ since $Y^- \subseteq Y^{old}$. Setting $I_3 := (X^{old} \cap Y^-)$ and $I_4 := (X^- \cap (Y^{old} \backslash Y^-))$ and plugging the above derivation for I^- in Eq. (8), we obtain Eq. (2) in the statement of the lemma.

To finish the proof we only need to prove that the sets are disjoint. It is clear that $I_4 = X^- \cap (Y^{old} \backslash Y^-)$ and $I_3 = X^{old} \cap Y^-$ are disjoint because $Y^{old} \backslash Y^-$ and Y^- are disjoint. Then, I^{old} and $I_1 = (X^{new} \cap Y^+)$ are disjoint since $Y^{old} \cap Y^+ = \varnothing$ (analogously for $X^+ \cap (Y \backslash Y^-)$). Finally, $I_1 = (X^{new} \cap Y^+)$ and $I_2 = X^+ \cap (Y^{old} \backslash Y^-)$ are disjoint since $Y^{old} \cap Y^+ = \varnothing$.

C.3 Proof of Theorem 1

Proof. We first show that the protocol is correct. First we notice that the four call to $\mathcal{F}_{\text{cPSI}}$ compute the sets $I_1, \ldots, I_4$ in Lemma 1. Moreover, since I_1 and I_2 (resp. I_3 and I_4) are disjoint the output of the second call (resp. first call) to $\mathcal{F}_{\text{CnP}}$ can be indeed parsed as a set. Thus, by Eq. (2) of Lemma 1 the set I^{new} computed by P_1 is indeed equal to the intersection $X^{new} \cap Y^{new}$.

We now focus on privacy. Consider the following simulator $\mathcal{S}_1$ w.r.t. corrupted P_1:

1. Receive in input X^{old}, X^+, X^-, I^{old} and the output I^{new}.
2. Sample secret shares of vectors $\mathbf{0}$ of the size α, which is the public threshold parameter, let them be $\boldsymbol{s}^{(i)}_{Y+}, \boldsymbol{s}^{(i)}_{X+}, \boldsymbol{s}^{(i)}_{Y-}, \boldsymbol{s}^{(i)}_{X-}$ with $i \in \{1, 2\}$. The vectors of shares $\boldsymbol{s}^{(1)}_{Y+}, \boldsymbol{s}^{(1)}_{X+}, \boldsymbol{s}^{(1)}_{Y-}, \boldsymbol{s}^{(1)}_{X-}$ are considered in the simulated view of P_1 as result of the interaction with the (simulated) ideal functionality $\mathcal{F}_{cPSI}$.
3. Compute the set I^+, I^- from I^{old}, I^{new} and set a random permutation of the elements in I^+ (resp. in I^-) as the output of the interaction with the first call (resp. second call) of the ideal functionality $\mathcal{F}_{CnP}$.

The simulator $\mathcal{S}_2$ w.r.t. corrupted P_2 is identical but it does not run the step 3.

We can prove the indistinguishability between the simulated and real worlds in two step. First we perform a hybrid argument, using the secrecy property of the secret-sharing scheme. In each hybrid, we replace one secret-sharing instance of the dummy value 0 with one of the real value. We omit the details of the reduction to the secrecy property, since it follows a standard textbook argument. We then arrive at a hybrid in which the first part executes the real protocol running the functionality $\mathcal{F}_{\text{cPSI}}$, while the hybrid still simulates the output of $\mathcal{F}_{\text{CnP}}$ by setting I^-, I^+ as in Step 3. This hybrid would diverge from the real world only if the simulated sets I^+ or I^- differed from the values $\bar{I}^+$ and $\bar{I}^-$ obtained by reconstructing the shares. However, both $\bar{I}^-$ and $\bar{I}^+$ are valid updates of I^{old} (by Lemma 1), and by definition I^- and I^+ are also valid updates of I^{old}. Furthermore, by Eq. (3) it follows that $\bar{I}^- = I^-$ and $\bar{I}^+ = I^+$.

D Towards Updatable Circuit-PSI

In this section, we study the challenges of designing a generic updatable circuit PSI and identify some solutions that address these challenges, partially.

D.1 Challenges

Generic circuit PSI protocols, as mentioned in Sect. 2, allow computation of arbitrary circuits over the intersection of two private sets. To do so, especially for the case where one wants to evaluate different circuits over one same intersection, such protocols compute secret shares of the intersection, and further execute generic 2PC protocols [6,20,54] for the actual circuit to be executed.

In the particular case of updatable circuit PSI, where we propose to execute four intermediate and smaller intersections, deleting elements becomes a point of contention. Indeed, the existing shares of the deleted elements should be deleted/modified. As also noted in [4], this means that the parties will learn which of the existing shares are modified, unless all elements are updated, incurring a cost linear with the size of the large sets (which is undesirable since this would cost as a naive re-execution of circuit PSI).

While in [4], authors argue that this situation results in the leakage of the lifetime of the elements, only, (i.e. when each element being deleted was previously added), we argue that this leakage is much more important. To explain this greater leakage, we need to take a closer look on how circuit PSI applies the generic 2PC protocol to the secret shared intersection: The output of the circuit PSI is a set of secret shares of either some values corresponding to the existence of the elements in the intersection, or zero (for elements not in the intersection). For example, in an unbalanced circuit PSI, each share represents an element of the small set, with the share being one of 0 if the element is not in the intersection and of 1 (or the value of the element itself) if the element appears in the intersection. This means, in particular, that the owner of the small set knows the mapping between its elements and the secret shares. This mapping can be necessary for the actual circuit that is to be executed (such as in the case of PSI).

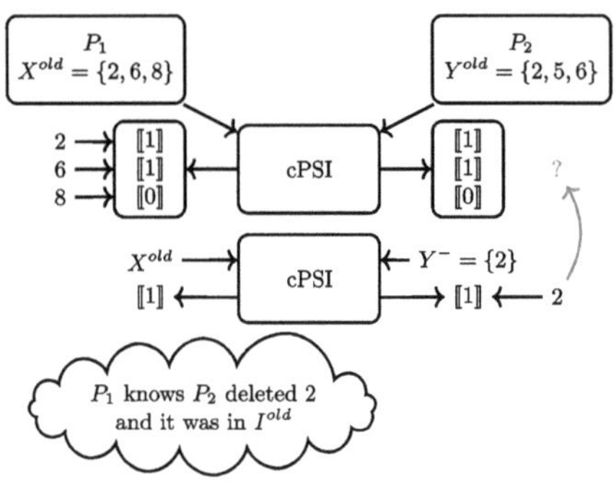

Fig. 5. Inherent leakage in updatable circuit PSI.

For ease of explanation, in Fig. 5, let us assume that both P_1, P_2 have shares of the old intersection $X^{old} \cap Y^{old}$ ($\{2, 6\}$ in the example), more concretely, they have $\{s^{(1)}_{old,i}, s^{(2)}_{old,i}\}_{i \in [n_X]}$ which are shares of 0 if the element x_i is not in $X^{old} \cap Y^{old}$ and shares of 1 (or shares of the x_i itself) otherwise. As such, P_1 knows the correspondence between the elements of its old dataset and these shares. Now, consider the execution of the intermediate intersection $Y^- \cap X^{old}$ ($\{2\}$ in the example). In this case, the parties obtain $s^{(1)}_{Y^-,i}, s^{(2)}_{Y^-,i}{}_{i \in [\alpha]}$. Moreover, we may assume that $|Y^-| \ll |X^{old}|$. To leverage this unbalance for an efficient protocol, P_2 (the owner of Y^-) should be given the mapping between the output shares and its set Y^-. Then, for every $s^{(1)}_{Y^-,i}, s^{(2)}_{Y^-,i}$ combining to 1, we know that there exist some j such that $s^{(1)}_{old,j}, s^{(2)}_{old,j}$ combine to 1 that needs to be modified (in the example, it would be the first row of the shares of I^{old}). However, linking these two shares together leaks too much information, since normally P_2 does not know the position of the deleted element in the old intersection and P_1 does not normally know the value of the deleted element. Indeed, if such a link is made, P_2 will learn when the removed element was added by P_1 (if we had several update processes before), but more importantly, P_1 recovers the exact value being removed by P_2 (through its correspondence).

D.2 Work Arounds

Previously Chosen Circuit. One of the ways to avoid the leakage is something we used throughout this work. Certain particular circuits, if known before-hand, may have their own way of circumventing this issue. For example, the identity circuit (i.e. standard PSI) avoids this since the leakage is already covered by the ideal functionality. Similarly, the cardinality circuit avoids matching shares by aggregating everything with the addition. However, having a fixed circuit to compute defeats the purpose of constructing *generic* updatable circuit PSI.

Only Addition. Another way, which was already explored in [4], would be to allow only addition of elements in the updates. Since the leakage comes from identifying the shares of the deleted elements in the old intersection, by forbidding deletions, the leakage is circumvented. Note that constructing an updatable circuit PSI with only addition is trivial from our construction of updatable PSI. By executing the steps of Protocol 1 without deletions, and only using $\mathcal{F}_{\text{cPSI}}$ over $X^+ \cap Y^{old}$ and $Y^+ \cap X^{new}$, we obtain a protocol that correctly and securely executes updatable circuit PSI only with addition (correctness comes directly from the underlying cPSI protocol and security is trivial from Theorem 1). For example, in the case of spam filters, the blacklist is only increased by adding new spam mails and the mails being received in the inbox can be considered to only increase (since deletions are not checked against the spam filter).

One Party Updates. A final alternative to sidestep the leakage is by only allowing one of the parties to update their dataset. Note that the leakage only appears when two different parties have access to (different) mappings; so if only one party has access to the mappings (i.e. only one party can make updates), the leakage is mostly avoided. The construction would work at a high level as follows. Assuming P_1 is the party allowed to update its dataset, the protocol would first run the intersections $X^+ \cap Y^{old}$ and $X^- \cap Y^{old}$, and then P_1 would tell P_2 which shares should be updated. Since P_2 never has access to any mapping, the only leakage is for P_2 knowing the lifetime of elements without knowing what exact values have this lifetime, which we argue is a reasonable leakage to allow. Such a situation can appear, for example, in the case of secure password breach alerts, where the credentials do not change, but the data found in the deep web is constantly updated.

E Implementation Optimization

In this section, we discuss the optimizations made our protocol $\Pi_{\text{uPSI-card}}$ on our implementation due to the fact of using the specific unbalanced circuit PSI protocol from [31] as our building block Π_{cPSI}.

Let us first give a high level overview of the construction in [31]. For ease of notation, let us assume that the party P_1 has the big dataset and P_2 has the small dataset. First of all, P_2 encodes its dataset into a cuckoo table and P_1 encodes its dataset into a hash table, both with the same hash functions. Note that every row of the cuckoo table has at most one element while each row of the hash table will have potentially many elements. Then, by using a batched Oblivious Programmable Pseudo-Random Function (OPPRF) based on garbled bloom filters and oblivious transfer proposed in [31] as well as the secure equality test proposed in [17], they output to P_2 for every row i of the cuckoo table $Enc_X(b)$, a (homomorphic) ciphertext encrypted by P_1 where $b = 0$ if the element in row i of the cuckoo table is not in row i of the hash table and $b = 1$ otherwise. Next, through homomorphic operations, P_2 computes $Enc_X(d_b)$ for some predefined d_0, d_1. Finally, all the ciphertexts are sent back to P_1, who decrypts them to obtain d_b for every row in the cuckoo table.

In the application to our updatable private set intersection protocols, we will have d_0, d_1 be secret shares, in the case of cardinality shares of either 0 or 1 and in the standard case shares of either 0 or the element in the intersection. The optimization comes from the realization that after the OPPRF and secure equality test, the amount of ciphertexts of 1 already reflects the cardinal. As such in our implementation first we add all the ciphertexts corresponding to the rows of the cuckoo table and then homomorphically add a random value to convert it to a share of the cardinal of the intersection. The improvement is then both in computation time, given that we perform less homomorphic operations as well as less decryptions, and in communication cost, since we send only one ciphertext instead of one per row of the cuckoo table.

References

1. Abadi, A., Dong, C., Murdoch, S.J., Terzis, S.: Multi-party updatable delegated private set intersection. In: Financial Cryptography and Data Security, pp. 100–119 (2022). https://doi.org/10.1007/978-3-031-18283-9_6
2. Agarwal, A., Cash, D., George, M., Kamara, S., Moataz, T., Singh, J.: Updatable private set intersection from structured encryption. IACR Commun. Cryptol. **2**(4) (2026). https://doi.org/10.62056/av4fsgbmo
3. van Baarsen, A., Stevens, M.: Amortizing circuit-PSI in the multiple sender/receiver setting. IACR Commun. Cryptol. **1**(3) (2024). https://doi.org/10.62056/a0fhsgvtw
4. Badrinarayanan, S., Miao, P., Shi, X., Tromanhauser, M., Zeng, R.: Updatable private set intersection revisited: Extended functionalities, deletion, and worst-case complexity. In: Advances in Cryptology – ASIACRYPT 2024, pp. 200–233 (2025). https://doi.org/10.1007/978-981-96-0938-3_7

5. Badrinarayanan, S., Miao, P., Xie, T.: Updatable private set intersection. Proc. Priv. Enhancing Technol. **2022**(2), 378–406 (2022). https://doi.org/10.2478/popets-2022-0051
6. Ben-Or, M., Goldwasser, S., Wigderson, A.: Completeness theorems for non-cryptographic fault-tolerant distributed computation. In: Proceedings of the Twentieth Annual ACM Symposium on Theory of Computing, STOC 1988, pp. 1–10 (1988). https://doi.org/10.1145/62212.62213
7. Benattar, G., Cornejo, M., Leontiadis, I., Poumeyrol, M., Shlomovits, O., Varlakov, D.: Paillier, 0.4.3 edn. (2022). https://crates.io/crates/kzen-paillier
8. Berke, A., Bakker, M., Vepakomma, P., Larson, K., Pentland, A.S.: Assessing disease exposure risk with location data: a proposal for cryptographic preservation of privacy (2020). https://arxiv.org/abs/2003.14412
9. Boyle, E., et al.: Efficient two-round OT extension and silent non-interactive secure computation. In: Proceedings of the 2019 ACM SIGSAC Conference on Computer and Communications Security, CCS 2019, pp. 291–308 (2019). https://doi.org/10.1145/3319535.3354255
10. Boyle, E., Couteau, G., Gilboa, N., Ishai, Y., Kohl, L., Scholl, P.: Efficient pseudorandom correlation generators: silent OT extension and more. In: Boldyreva, A., Micciancio, D. (eds.) CRYPTO 2019. LNCS, vol. 11694, pp. 489–518. Springer, Cham (2019). https://doi.org/10.1007/978-3-030-26954-8_16
11. Chandran, G.R., Schneider, T., Stillger, M., Weinert, C.: Concretely efficient private set union via circuit-based psi. In: Proceedings of the 20th ACM Asia Conference on Computer and Communications Security, ASIA CCS 2025, pp. 149–162 (2025). https://doi.org/10.1145/3708821.3710839
12. Chandran, N., Gupta, D., Shah, A.: Circuit-psi with linear complexity via relaxed batch OPPRF. Proc. Priv. Enhancing Technol. **2022**(1), 353–372 (2022). https://doi.org/10.2478/popets-2022-0018
13. Chase, M., Ghosh, E., Poburinnaya, O.: Secret-shared shuffle. In: Moriai, S., Wang, H. (eds.) ASIACRYPT 2020. LNCS, vol. 12493, pp. 342–372. Springer, Cham (2020). https://doi.org/10.1007/978-3-030-64840-4_12
14. Chase, M., Miao, P.: Private set intersection in the internet setting from lightweight oblivious PRF. In: Micciancio, D., Ristenpart, T. (eds.) CRYPTO 2020. LNCS, vol. 12172, pp. 34–63. Springer, Cham (2020). https://doi.org/10.1007/978-3-030-56877-1_2
15. Chen, H., Huang, Z., Laine, K., Rindal, P.: Labeled psi from fully homomorphic encryption with malicious security. In: Proceedings of the 2018 ACM SIGSAC Conference on Computer and Communications Security, CCS 2018, pp. 1223–1237 (2018). https://doi.org/10.1145/3243734.3243836
16. Chen, H., Laine, K., Rindal, P.: Fast private set intersection from homomorphic encryption. In: Proceedings of the 2017 ACM SIGSAC Conference on Computer and Communications Security, CCS 2017, pp. 1243–1255 (2017). https://doi.org/10.1145/3133956.3134061
17. Ciampi, M., Orlandi, C.: Combining private set-intersection with secure two-party computation. In: Catalano, D., De Prisco, R. (eds.) SCN 2018. LNCS, vol. 11035, pp. 464–482. Springer, Cham (2018). https://doi.org/10.1007/978-3-319-98113-0_25
18. Freedman, M.J., Nissim, K., Pinkas, B.: Efficient private matching and set intersection. In: Cachin, C., Camenisch, J.L. (eds.) EUROCRYPT 2004. LNCS, vol. 3027, pp. 1–19. Springer, Heidelberg (2004). https://doi.org/10.1007/978-3-540-24676-3_1

19. Ghosh, S., Nilges, T.: An algebraic approach to maliciously secure private set intersection. In: Ishai, Y., Rijmen, V. (eds.) EUROCRYPT 2019. LNCS, vol. 11478, pp. 154–185. Springer, Cham (2019). https://doi.org/10.1007/978-3-030-17659-4_6
20. Goldreich, O., Micali, S., Wigderson, A.: How to play any mental game. In: Proceedings of the Nineteenth Annual ACM Symposium on Theory of Computing, STOC 1987, pp. 218–229 (1987). https://doi.org/10.1145/28395.28420
21. Goldreich, O.: Foundations of Cryptography: Volume 2, Basic Applications, 1st edn. Cambridge University Press, USA (2009)
22. Google: Private intersection-sum protocols with applications to attributing aggregate ad conversions. https://research.google/pubs/pub51026/
23. Hao, M., et al.: Unbalanced Circuit-PSI from oblivious Key-Value retrieval. In: 33rd USENIX Security Symposium (USENIX Security 2024), pp. 6435–6451 (2024). https://www.usenix.org/conference/usenixsecurity24/presentation/hao-meng-unbalanced
24. Harchandani, L.: Oblivious Transfer (OT), Oblivious Transfer Extensions (OTE) and multi-party protocols based on that, 0.11.0 edn. (2025). https://crates.io/crates/oblivious_transfer_protocols
25. Hazay, C.: Oblivious polynomial evaluation and secure set-intersection from algebraic PRFs. In: Dodis, Y., Nielsen, J.B. (eds.) TCC 2015. LNCS, vol. 9015, pp. 90–120. Springer, Heidelberg (2015). https://doi.org/10.1007/978-3-662-46497-7_4
26. Hetz, L., Schneider, T., Weinert, C.: Scaling mobile private contact discovery to billions of users. In: Computer Security – ESORICS 2023: 28th European Symposium on Research in Computer Security, 2023, Proceedings, Part I, pp. 455–476 (2023). https://doi.org/10.1007/978-3-031-50594-2_23
27. Huang, Y., Evans, D., Katz, J.: Private set intersection: are garbled circuits better than custom protocols? In: 19th Annual Network and Distributed System Security Symposium, NDSS 2012. The Internet Society (2012). https://www.ndss-symposium.org/ndss2012/private-set-intersection-are-garbled-circuits-better-custom-protocols
28. Kales, D., Rechberger, C., Schneider, T., Senker, M., Weinert, C.: Mobile private contact discovery at scale. In: 28th USENIX Security Symposium (USENIX Security 2019), pp. 1447–1464 (2019). https://www.usenix.org/conference/usenixsecurity19/presentation/kales
29. Kamara, S., Mohassel, P., Raykova, M., Sadeghian, S.: Scaling private set intersection to billion-element sets. In: Christin, N., Safavi-Naini, R. (eds.) FC 2014. LNCS, vol. 8437, pp. 195–215. Springer, Heidelberg (2014). https://doi.org/10.1007/978-3-662-45472-5_13
30. Karakoç, F., Küpçü, A.: Linear complexity private set intersection for secure two-party protocols. In: Krenn, S., Shulman, H., Vaudenay, S. (eds.) CANS 2020. LNCS, vol. 12579, pp. 409–429. Springer, Cham (2020). https://doi.org/10.1007/978-3-030-65411-5_20
31. Karakoç, F., Küpçü, A.: Enabling two-party secure computation on set intersection. IEEE Trans. Dependable Secure Comput. 1–12 (2025). https://doi.org/10.1109/TDSC.2025.3561472
32. Kiss, Á., Liu, J., Schneider, T., Asokan, N., Pinkas, B.: Private set intersection for unequal set sizes with mobile applications. Proc. Priv. Enhancing Technol. **2017**(4), 177–197 (2017). https://doi.org/10.1515/popets-2017-0044
33. Kolesnikov, V., Kumaresan, R., Rosulek, M., Trieu, N.: Efficient batched oblivious PRF with applications to private set intersection. In: Proceedings of the 2016 ACM SIGSAC Conference on Computer and Communications Security, CCS 2016, pp. 818–829 (2016). https://doi.org/10.1145/2976749.2978381

34. Kolesnikov, V., Matania, N., Pinkas, B., Rosulek, M., Trieu, N.: Practical multi-party private set intersection from symmetric-key techniques. In: Proceedings of the 2017 ACM SIGSAC Conference on Computer and Communications Security, CCS 2017, pp. 1257–1272 (2017). https://doi.org/10.1145/3133956.3134065
35. Ling, G., Tang, P., Qiu, W.: Efficient updatable PSI from asymmetric PSI and PSU. Cryptology ePrint Archive, Paper 2024/1712 (2024). https://eprint.iacr.org/2024/1712
36. Mahdavi, R.A., et al.: Pepsi: practically efficient private set intersection in the unbalanced setting. In: Proceedings of the 33rd USENIX Conference on Security Symposium, SEC 2024 (2024). https://www.usenix.org/conference/usenixsecurity24/presentation/mahdavi
37. Marlinspike, M.: Technology preview: private contact discovery for signal. https://signal.org/blog/private-contact-discovery/
38. Meadows, C.: A more efficient cryptographic matchmaking protocol for use in the absence of a continuously available third party. In: 1986 IEEE Symposium on Security and Privacy, p. 134 (1986). https://doi.org/10.1109/SP.1986.10022
39. Paillier, P.: Public-key cryptosystems based on composite degree residuosity classes. In: Stern, J. (ed.) EUROCRYPT 1999. LNCS, vol. 1592, pp. 223–238. Springer, Heidelberg (1999). https://doi.org/10.1007/3-540-48910-X_16
40. Nepper, P., Nair, K.C., Sukhanov, V., Khaneja, V.: Better password protections in chrome. https://security.googleblog.com/2019/12/better-password-protections-in-chrome.html
41. Pinkas, B., Rosulek, M., Trieu, N., Yanai, A.: SpOT-light: lightweight private set intersection from sparse OT extension. In: Boldyreva, A., Micciancio, D. (eds.) CRYPTO 2019. LNCS, vol. 11694, pp. 401–431. Springer, Cham (2019). https://doi.org/10.1007/978-3-030-26954-8_13
42. Pinkas, B., Rosulek, M., Trieu, N., Yanai, A.: PSI from PaXoS: fast, malicious private set intersection. In: Canteaut, A., Ishai, Y. (eds.) EUROCRYPT 2020. LNCS, vol. 12106, pp. 739–767. Springer, Cham (2020). https://doi.org/10.1007/978-3-030-45724-2_25
43. Pinkas, B., Schneider, T., Zohner, M.: Faster private set intersection based on OT extension. In: 23rd USENIX Security Symposium (USENIX Security 2014), pp. 797–812 (2014). https://www.usenix.org/system/files/conference/usenixsecurity14/sec14-paper-pinkas.pdf
44. Raghuraman, S., Rindal, P.: Blazing fast PSI from improved OKVS and subfield vole. In: Proceedings of the 2022 ACM SIGSAC Conference on Computer and Communications Security, CCS 2022, pp. 2505–2517 (2022). https://doi.org/10.1145/3548606.3560658
45. Rindal, P., Schoppmann, P.: VOLE-PSI: fast OPRF and circuit-PSI from vector-OLE. In: Canteaut, A., Standaert, F.-X. (eds.) EUROCRYPT 2021. LNCS, vol. 12697, pp. 901–930. Springer, Cham (2021). https://doi.org/10.1007/978-3-030-77886-6_31
46. RustCrypto development team: RustCrypto: Advanced Encryption Standard (AES), 0.8.4 edn. (2024). https://crates.io/crates/aes
47. Shamir, A.: How to share a secret. Commun. ACM **22**(11), 612–613 (1979). https://doi.org/10.1145/359168.359176
48. Son, Y., Jeong, J.: PSI with computation or circuit-psi for unbalanced sets from homomorphic encryption. In: Proceedings of the 2023 ACM Asia Conference on Computer and Communications Security, ASIA CCS 2023, pp. 342–356 (2023). https://doi.org/10.1145/3579856.3582817

49. Song, X., Yin, D., Bai, J., Dong, C., Chang, E.C.: Secret-shared shuffle with malicious security. In: Network and Distributed System Security Symposium 2024 (NDSS 2024) (2024). https://doi.org/10.14722/ndss.2024.24021
50. Trieu, N., Shehata, K., Saxena, P., Shokri, R., Song, D.: Epione: lightweight contact tracing with strong privacy (2020). https://arxiv.org/abs/2004.13293
51. Wang, R., Zhou, J., Cao, Z., Dong, X., Raymond Choo, K.K.: Updatable private set intersection with forward privacy. IEEE Trans. Inf. Forensics Secur. **19**, 8573–8586 (2024). https://doi.org/10.1109/TIFS.2024.3461475
52. Wikipedia: Exposure notification. https://en.wikipedia.org/wiki/Exposure_Notification
53. Yang, Y., et al.: Maliciously secure circuit private set intersection via SPDZ-compatible oblivious PRF. Proc. Priv. Enhancing Technol. **2025**(2), 680–696 (2025). https://doi.org/10.56553/popets-2025-0082
54. Yao, A.C.C.: How to generate and exchange secrets. In: 27th Annual Symposium on Foundations of Computer Science (SFCS 1986), pp. 162–167 (1986). https://doi.org/10.1109/SFCS.1986.25

Round-Optimal Privacy Preserving Authenticated Key Exchange Even for Incomplete Sessions

Xavier Bultel and Khouredia Cisse(✉)

INSA Centre Val de Loire, Université d'Orléans, Inria, Bourges, France
{xavier.bultel,khouredia.cisse}@insa-cvl.fr

Abstract. Several modern applications, such as Signal or WireGuard, use efficient Noise-like *implicit* authentication key exchanges that require only a small number of exponentiations and two interactions. These protocols have been proven to be secure under the 'strong Diffie–Hellman' (SDH) assumption in the random oracle model (ROM). At ESORICS 2021, Ramacher, Slamanig and Weninger presented an extension to the implicit authenticated key exchange security model, which enables strong privacy properties to be captured in addition to key-secrecy, including man-in-the-middle privacy (ensuring privacy even if a session is interrupted) and forward privacy. They also proposed a protocol to instantiate their model. In this paper, we present an efficient Noise-like protocol that achieves privacy in this model. Our protocol is as efficient as Noise-like protocols that do not guarantee privacy in terms of exponentiations. Moreover, our protocol requires three interactions, which is optimal for this privacy model. It is also more efficient than the ESORICS 2021 protocol in terms of both exponentiations and interactions. Finally, we propose another round-optimal protocol, slightly less efficient in terms of exponentiations, but secure under the CDH assumption in the ROM.

Keywords: Authenticated Key Exchange · Privacy · Provable security

1 Introduction

End-to-end encryption and key exchange protocols are among the most fundamental tools in cryptography and have been widely used in practice for several decades. These protocols must be resistant to man-in-the-middle attacks, whereby an active attacker can alter communications. A standard method involves running a Diffie–Hellman key exchange, whereby Alice sends an ephemeral key $X = g^x$ and Bob sends $Y = g^y$, and the shared secret key is $K = g^{xy}$. Alice and Bob are also equipped with long-term signature keys generated a priori, which allows them to sign the transcript of the key exchange (i.e. the pair (X, Y)). As Bob already knows X when he sends Y, he can send his signature at the same time. However, Alice must send her signature after receiving Y. This method therefore requires three interactions. If any of these

K. Jee and A. Katc (Eds.): ACNS 2026, LNCS 16571, pp. 559–584, 2027.
https://doi.org/10.1007/978-3-032-32560-0_20

interactions are altered, Alice and Bob can detect this and abort the protocol, making active attacks ineffective. Under the impetus of the Noise framework[1], more efficient *implicit* authenticated key exchange protocols have been deployed in several real-world applications (e.g. Signal [11] or WireGuard [7]). In these protocols, authentication is implicit in the sense that users no longer sign the transcript, saving the last interaction, but instead use their long-term secret keys, in addition to g^{xy}, to generate the shared key. Therefore, even if an adversary can alter the interactions, they will not be able to share keys with Alice and Bob, meaning the attack will be ineffective for decrypting subsequent messages.

In [6], Cohn-Gordon *et al.* propose an optimised version of this type of protocol (and provide proof of optimal security in terms of reduction loss): Alice and Bob have long-term public keys $U = g^u$ and $V = g^v$, they exchange $X = g^x$ and $Y = g^y$, then compute the shared secret key $K = H(U\|V\|X\|Y\|g^{uy}\|g^{vx}\|g^{xy})$, where H is a hash function modeled as a random oracle. Knowledge of the long-term keys is necessary to compute Y^u for Alice and X^v for Bob, and knowledge of the ephemeral keys is necessary to compute, conversely, U^x for Alice and Y^v for Bob, which prevents the adversary from computing a key shared with Alice by impersonating Bob, and vice versa. Forward secrecy is ensured by g^{xy}; if the adversary finds the long-term keys a posteriori, the element g^{xy} does not depend on them, which prevents them from guessing K. Note that in this work, the authors implicitly assume that the responder, Bob, knows a priori that his interlocutor is Alice before receiving the first message containing X (otherwise he would not be able to computes U^y). In practice, Alice would have to send her identity to Bob in clear text before the protocol (since Alice and Bob do not have a shared key a priori). As a result, by its very nature, this protocol does not protect user identity.

In [13], Ramacher et al. propose to extend the model given by Cohn-Gordon et al. in order to capture two additional strong privacy properties: man-in-the-middle (MITM) privacy and forward privacy. However, this time the initiator must explicitly send their identity to the responder during the protocol, to prevent an adversary from deducing it. In their setup, Alice (the initiator) knows the long-term public key of the intended recipient (Bob). However, the responder does not initially know the identity of the party contacting them and only learns it during protocol execution. In MITM privacy, they consider an active adversary whose goal is to guess the identity of one of the two parties whose long-term keys are not corrupted during the execution of the protocol. Note that this model differs from other similar models in the literature in that it captures privacy even for incomplete sessions. In forward privacy, they consider an adversary attempting to guess the identity of the parties after the protocol has been successfully executed. The attacker is therefore not active during the interaction, but has access to the transcript and can corrupt the long-term keys of any user after the fact. The authors demonstrate that neither of these two privacy properties implies the other, and provide a protocol that verifies key-secrecy, MITM privacy, and forward privacy.

[1] See http://www.noiseprotocol.org/.

In this article, we propose efficient protocols (in terms of the number of exponentiations and interactions) that verify key-secrecy, MITM privacy, and forward privacy in the models of [6, 13]. We propose a first protocol based on the strong Diffie-Hellman assumption, which is similar to the computational Diffie-Hellman assumption (guessing g^{xy} from $X = g^x$ and $Y = g^y$ in a prime order group is difficult), except that the adversary also has an oracle $\mathsf{stDH}_x(A, Z)$ allowing them to test whether $Z = A^x$. Note that this assumption is required for the protocol proposed in [6]. Our protocol is more efficient than that of [13] and is also optimal in terms of the number of interactions. In terms of exponentiations, our protocol is similar to [6] (which does not have privacy). We also propose a variant of our protocol using Schnorr's signatures of knowledge that can be proven secure and private under the CDH assumption, which is weaker than SDH and is considered more standard. However, this protocol is slightly less computationally efficient, as it requires a few additional exponentiations.

1.1 Technical Overview of Our Contributions

Our SDH-based protocol Π_{SDH} is shown in Fig. 1, where g is the generator of a group of prime order p, H is a hash function modeled as a random oracle, $\mathsf{Enc}/\mathsf{Dec}$ are the encryption/decryption algorithms of an authenticated symmetric encryption scheme, and ctxt denotes the transcript (X, Y, C) of the protocol. This protocol is similar to Noise, except that Alice and Bob compute the key $K \leftarrow H(g^{vx} \| g^{yx} \| X \| Y)$, then Alice uses it to encrypt her public key (associated with her identity) and sends the ciphertext to Bob. Bob discovers Alice's identity by decrypting this public key (remember that before this, Bob does not know who he is communicating with). After verifying that the public key corresponds to a registered user (in practice, Bob verifies that the public key is certificated), Bob generates the shared key in an implicit authentication manner.

Alice (initiator) $\mathsf{sk_i} = u; \mathsf{pk_i} = U = g^u$		**Bob (responder)** $\mathsf{sk_r} = v; \mathsf{pk_r} = V = g^v$
$x \leftarrow \mathbb{Z}_p;\quad X \leftarrow g^x$	$\xrightarrow{X}$	$y \leftarrow \mathbb{Z}_p;\quad Y \leftarrow g^y$
$h_1 \leftarrow (V^x \| Y^x)$	$\xleftarrow{Y}$	$h_1 \leftarrow (X^v \| X^y)$
$\mathsf{K} \leftarrow \mathsf{H}(h_1 \| X \| Y)$		$\mathsf{K} \leftarrow \mathsf{H}(h_1 \| X \| Y)$
$\mathsf{C} \leftarrow \mathsf{Enc_K}(\mathsf{U})$	$\xrightarrow{C}$	$U \leftarrow \mathsf{Dec_K}(\mathsf{C})$
		If U is not a registered public key, Bob aborts the protocol.
$h_2 \leftarrow Y^u$		$h_2 \leftarrow U^y$
$\mathsf{K_i} \leftarrow \mathsf{H}(\mathsf{ctxt} \| h_1 \| h_2)$		$\mathsf{K_r} \leftarrow \mathsf{H}(\mathsf{ctxt} \| h_1 \| h_2)$

Fig. 1. Private authenticated key exchange protocol based on SDH (Π_{SDH}).

Key-secrecy can be proved in a similar way to [6]. Remember that an active adversary cannot re-compute the final keys K_i and K_r, so they cannot use them to determine Alice's or Bob's identity. To attack privacy, the ciphertext containing Alice's public key must therefore be exploited. As long as Bob remains uncorrupted, an adversary who intercepts messages sent by Alice cannot deduce $g^{xv} = V^x = X^v$, and therefore cannot deduce any information about the key K, which appears to be random. Thus, disguessing Alice's identity amounts to attacking the secure encryption, which ensures MITM privacy. On the other hand, for forward privacy, if the adversary accesses the transcript after the key exchange, they are unable to compute $X^y = Y^x = g^{xy}$ even if they know the long-term keys u and v. Once again, the key K seems random to them, and guessing Alice's identity is equivalent to attacking the encryption. In this protocol, each user performs four exponentiations, and the number of interactions is optimal for forward privacy: Alice cannot send her identity during the first interaction because she does not share any secrets with Bob. This would mean that Bob could discover Alice's identity solely using his long-term key, which is impossible if the protocol is forward private. There are therefore at least 3 interactions.

Furthermore, by adding Schnorr's Signature Of Knowledge (SOK) [16] of discrete logarithm on ephemeral keys (signing the user role) and public keys (signing the user identity), we construct a slightly less efficient protocol (three additional exponentiations per user during a session, and two additional exponentiations when verifying the public key certificate to also verify the SOK), but that can be proven under the CDH assumption instead of SDH. SDH allows, during a reduction, to artificially verify via an oracle whether, for a given CDH share $X = g^x$, the triplet (X, A, Z) verifies $Z = A^x$ or not for a chosen (A, Z). Our technique is to attach an extractable SOK to each element $A = g^a$, allowing a to be extracted to verify whether $Z = X^a$ instead.

In Fig. 2 we compare the efficiency, assumptions, and security of our protocols with those of [6,13]. For [13], we only consider the protocol achieving both (strong) MITM and forward privacy, which we instantiate with Diffie-Hellman key exchange, ElGamal encryption [9] and Shnorr signature [16]. We observe that our Π_{SDH} is more efficient in terms of both interactions and exponentiations than the only proven (strongly) private protocol in the literature [13].

Protocol	**Assump.**	**Privacy**	**Inter.**	**Exp.** (Alice)	**Exp.** (Bob)
Π [6]	SDH (ROM)	$\times$	2	4	4
Π_{Twin} [6]	CDH (ROM)	$\times$	2	8	7
Π_{Com} [6]	DDH (ROM)	$\times$	4	6	6
Π^4_{PKE} [13]	Generic (ROM)	✓	4	5	5
Π_{SDH}	SDH (ROM)	✓	3	4	4
Π_{CDH}	CDH (ROM)	✓	3	7*	7*

Fig. 2. Comparison of our work with [6] and [13]. $*$ Π_{CDH} also requires an additional exponentiation when generating long-term keys, and two additional exponentiations when verifying a certificate.

1.2 Related Work

As mentioned previously, our work is based on the privacy-preserving authenticated key exchange (PPAKE) model proposed by [13], but it should be noted that there are other competing PPAKE models. The earliest attempts to (informally) capture privacy in key agreement can be traced back to Aiello et al. [2], who introduced the idea of keeping a participant's identity hidden from unauthorised parties, including active attackers impersonating peers. Although they proposed two specific protocols, one for protecting the initiator's identity and the other for protecting the responder's, their notion of privacy was neither formally defined nor analysed. Prior to this, Canetti and Krawczyk [4] briefly mentioned the concept of identity concealment through encryption, albeit without providing a formal framework. Zhao [19] introduced the CAKE model, which formalises forward identity privacy, and limited MITM privacy. However, in this model, the MITM-privacy is only guaranteed if the key exchange is successful, which seems insufficient in practice, because even if the adversary who disrupted the exchange is unable to read the communication, they still learn the identities of the users who wish to communicate. To the best of our knowledge, comparing to prior models [15, 19] only the one proposed by [13] considers MITM attacks on incomplete sessions.

Another line of work involves studying how to add privacy to real-world protocols. Schäge et al. [15] proposed a tailored PPAKE model and applied it to real-world protocols such as IKEv2. However, their model also assumes prior knowledge of participants' identities and targets specific deployment contexts. On the other hand, the latest versions of TLS have been adapted to ensure certain (weak) privacy properties, which have been analysed in [3]. However, as the general structure of TLS has not been modified, it does not guarantee properties as strong as those of [15].

In a more recent article, Lyu et al. [10] propose another PPAKE model that differs from [13], and provide a protocol proven in the standard model requiring only 3 exchanges. The authors claim that their model is equivalent to the one in [13], and claim an attack on the forward-privacy of the protocol in [13]. However, as added in the 'follow-up work' section of the technical report [14] of [13], the two models differ because [10] assumes that messages are sent on broadcasting channels and that every potential receiver answers to every received message. Furthermore, the attack does not hold in the forward-privacy model of [13], since it considers an active attacker during the session, whereas [13] considers passive attackers only who can corrupt the long-term keys a posteriori. Furthermore, we remark that the protocol in [10] does not achieve the MITM-privacy definition given in [13]. In the MITM-privacy of [13], a user only reveals their identity to another user during a session if they are certain that they are communicating with the right person (formally, the attacker must guess the identity of a user in a session where they either do not yet know the identity of their interlocutor, or they know it and it is an uncorrupted user). In the protocol in [10], the first flow consists of Alice sending a MAC key to Bob encrypted with Bob's long-term key, then Bob uses this key to generate a MAC on they response. Thus, an adversary can verify whether a user is Bob or not by simply sending the first flow of the protocol, because only Bob will be able to respond, and then interrupt the session. In essence, once again, this paper does not consider MITM-privacy for interrupted sessions.

2 Preliminaries

In this section, we recall some cryptographic tools.

Definition 1 (Computational Diffie-Hellman assumptions). *Let λ be a security parameter, and let $\mathbb{G}$ be a cyclic group of prime order $p > 2^\lambda$ with generator g. Let $x, y \xleftarrow{\$} \mathbb{Z}_p$ be two scalars sampled uniformly at random.*

- *The* **Computational Diffie-Hellman** *(CDH) assumption in $\mathbb{G}$ states that for any Probabilistic Polynomial-Time (PPT) in λ algorithm $\mathcal{A}$, the advantage $\mathsf{Adv}_{\mathcal{A}}^{\mathsf{CDH}}(\lambda) = \Pr[\mathcal{A}(g^x, g^y) = g^{xy}]$ of $\mathcal{A}$ over CDH is negligible.*
- *The* **Strong Diffie-Hellman** *(SDH) assumption in $\mathbb{G}$ is defined as CDH except that $\mathcal{A}$ can access a test oracle $\mathsf{stDH}_x(A, Z)$ that returns 1 if $Z = A^x$, 0 otherwise: it states that for any PPT algorithm $\mathcal{A}$, the advantage $\mathsf{Adv}_{\mathcal{A}}^{\mathsf{SDH}}(\lambda) = \Pr\left[\mathcal{A}^{\mathsf{stDH}_x(\cdot,\cdot)}(g^x, g^y) = g^{xy}\right]$ of $\mathcal{A}$ over SDH is negligible. Note that, equivalently, the test oracle can be stDH_y, but the adversary cannot have access to both stDH_x and stDH_y.*

Theorem 7 in [1] proves that SDH holds in Shoup's generic group model. SDH trivially implies CDH.

Definition 2 (Authenticated Encryption [12]**).** *Let λ be a security parameter. A Symmetric Encryption scheme SE is a triplet $(\mathcal{K}, \mathsf{Enc}, \mathsf{Dec})$, where $\mathcal{K}$ is a secret key set verifying $|\mathcal{K}| > 2^\lambda$, $\mathsf{Enc}_k(m)$ is a an encryption algorithm that takes as input a secret key $k \in \mathcal{K}$ and a message m, and returns a ciphertext c, and $\mathsf{Dec}_k(c)$ is a decryption algorithm that takes as input a secret key $k \in \mathcal{K}$ and a ciphertext c, and returns a message m.*

We also define the authenticated encryption (AE) experiment $\mathsf{Exp}_{\mathsf{SE},b,\mathcal{A}}^{\mathsf{AE}}(\lambda)$ for the two-stage adversary $\mathcal{A} = (\mathcal{A}_1, \mathcal{A}_2)$ against SE as follows, where $\mathsf{Enc}_k(\cdot)$ and $\mathsf{Dec}_k(\cdot)$ are encryption/decryption oracles such that $\mathsf{Dec}_k(\cdot)$ returns $\perp$ on c, and returns $\perp$ on any query when $b = 1$:

$\mathsf{Exp}_{\mathsf{SE},b,\mathcal{A}}^{\mathsf{AE}}(\lambda)$:

$$
\begin{aligned}
&k \xleftarrow{\$} \mathcal{K};\ b \xleftarrow{\$} \{0,1\}\\
&(m_0, m_1) \leftarrow \mathcal{A}_1^{\mathsf{Enc}_k(.),\mathsf{Dec}_k(.)}(\lambda)\\
&c \leftarrow \mathsf{Enc}_k(m_b)\\
&\textit{returns } b' \leftarrow \mathcal{A}_2^{\mathsf{Enc}_k(.),\mathsf{Dec}_k(.)}(c)
\end{aligned}
$$

SE is said to be AE secure if for any PPT two-stage adversary $\mathcal{A}$, the advantage $\mathsf{Adv}_{\mathsf{SE},\mathcal{A}}^{\mathsf{AE}}(\lambda) = \left|\mathsf{Pr}\left[\mathsf{Exp}_{\mathsf{SE},0,\mathcal{A}}^{\mathsf{AE}}(\lambda) = 1\right] - \mathsf{Pr}\left[\mathsf{Exp}_{\mathsf{SE},1,\mathcal{A}}^{\mathsf{AE}}(\lambda) = 1\right]\right|$ is negligible.

For any of these assumptions/properties denoted X, we define the advantage over X as $\mathsf{Adv}^{\mathsf{X}}(\lambda) = \max_{\mathcal{A} \in \mathsf{Poly}(\lambda)} \mathsf{Adv}^{\mathsf{X}}_{\mathcal{A}}(\lambda)$, where $\mathsf{Poly}(\lambda)$ refers to the set of all the probabilistic polynomial-time (possibly two-stage) algorithms in lambda.

For any positive integer x, we write $[x] = \{1, 2, \ldots, x\}$ for the set of the first x positive integers.

3 Security Model

We rely on the authenticated key exchange (AKE) model of [6] for key-secrecy, and the extension of [13] for MITM and forward privacy. Note that in [13], a weak MITM-privacy is also proposed, which assumes that no user is ever corrupted. Since we do not use this weak property, we do not mention it here.

Execution Environment. We consider μ parties. Each party P_i is represented by a set of oracles $\{\pi_i^1, ..., \pi_i^\ell\}$, where each oracle corresponds to a session (a single execution of a protocol role), and where $\ell \in \mathbb{N}$ is the maximum number of protocol sessions per party. Each oracle π_i^s has access to the long-term key pair $(\mathsf{sk}_i, \mathsf{pk}_i)$ of the party P_i and the list L_{pk} containing the indices/public keys (i, pk_i) of all the parties. It also maintains a list of internal state variables that are described in the following. For each oracle π_i^s, the corresponding variables are initially set to the empty string $\perp$.

- Pid_i^s ("peer id") stores the identity of the intended communication partner. Note that in private key exchange protocols, a user may not know the identity of their partner at the start of a session. In this case, this variable will remain set to $\perp$ until the partner is identified.
- $\Psi_i^s \in \{\perp, \mathsf{Accept}, \mathsf{Reject}\}$ indicates if oracle π_i^s has successfully completed the protocol execution and "accepted" the resulting key, or aborted the protocol and "rejected" the key exchange. Until the protocol is complete or aborted, this value remains $\perp$. As a prerequisite, we stress that Pid_i^s must be instantiated (i.e. $\mathsf{Pid}_i^s \neq \perp$) for Ψ_i^s to be set to Accept.
- k_i^s stores the session key computed by π_i^s. Until the protocol is complete, this value remains $\perp$. It is assigned only if the oracle π_i^s reaches the Accept state. In other words: $k_i^s \neq \perp \Leftrightarrow \Psi_i^s = \text{accept}$.
- $\mathsf{esk}_i^s/\mathsf{epk}_i^s$: stores P_i's ephemeral secret/public keys specified by the protocol. These keys are generated specifically for each session by the parties involved and are renewed for each new session.
- $\overline{\mathsf{epk}}_i^s$: stores the ephemeral public key of the P_i's partner. This key is specific to the session and is received during an interaction specified in the protocol. Note that this key can be received before the partner's identity is learned by the oracle.
- $\mathsf{role}_i^s \in \{\perp, \mathsf{initiator}, \mathsf{responder}\}$ indicates π_i^s's role during the protocol.

Additionally, the environment keeps track of three initially empty lists: L_{corr}, containing all corrupted parties, L_{Send}, storing all sent messages, and L_{SessKey}, recording all established session keys.

Oracles and Attacker Model. Our attacker $\mathcal{A}$ has a full control over the communication network. Furthermore, the attacker knows the list of parties and their respective public keys. It interacts with the oracles through queries.

- $\mathsf{Send}(i, s, m)$: This allows $\mathcal{A}$ to send an arbitrary message m to oracle π_i^s if it exists. The oracle will respond according to the protocol specification and its current internal state. To start a new oracle, the message m takes a special form ($\mathbf{START} : \mathsf{role}, j$). If π_i^s was already initialized before, Send returns $\perp$. Otherwise, the oracle initializes π_i^s in the role role by setting $\mathsf{role}_i^s = \mathsf{role}$. If $\mathsf{role} = \mathsf{initiator}$, then it sets $\mathsf{Pid}_i^s = j$ and outputs the first message of the protocol. Else, if $\mathsf{role} = \mathsf{responder}$, the partner identity remains $\mathsf{Pid}_i^s = \perp$ (In this case, j is not used and can be set to the empty string $\perp$ in the query). Note that, in the case of the responder, the oracle does not receive the first message of the protocol during initialisation (it will receive it in the second query).
- $\mathsf{RevLTK}(i)$: For $i \leq \mu$, this returns the long-term private key sk_i of party P_i. After this query, P_i and all its oracles π_i^s (for any s) are said to be corrupted.
- $\mathsf{RegisterLTK}(i, \mathsf{pk}_i)$: For $i > \mu$, this allows the adversary to register a new party P_i with the public key pk_i. The adversary is not required to know the corresponding private key. After this query, the pair (i, pk_i) is added to L_{pk}. Parties registered by $\mathsf{RegisterLTK}(i, \mathsf{pk}_i)$ (and their oracles) are corrupted by definition.
- $\mathsf{RevSessKeySec}(i, s)$: This allows the adversary to learn the session key derived by an oracle. If $\Psi_i^s = \mathsf{accept}$, return k_i^s. Otherwise, return $\perp$. After this query, π_i^s is said to be revealed.

Furthermore, privacy properties require an alternative definition of the session key revelation oracle, which uses the definition of *matching conversations.*

Definition 3 (Matching Conversation). *Let Π be an N-message two-party protocol in which all messages are sent sequentially. If a session oracle π_i^s sent (resp. receive) the last message of the protocol, then π_j^t is said to have matching conversations to π_i^s if the first $N-1$ (resp. all N) messages of π_i^s transcript agrees with the first $N-1$ (resp. all) messages of π_j^t's transcript (excluding the initialisation messages received by both oracles).*

- $\mathsf{RevSessKeyPriv}(i, s)$: This is an alternative oracle to learn the session key. If there already is an entry (π_i^s, k^*) in L_{SessKey}, or if there is an entry (π_j^t, k^*) so that π_i^s and π_j^t have matching conversation, this oracle returns k^*. If $\Psi_i^s = \mathsf{accept}$, it sets $k^* \leftarrow k_i^s$, adds (π_i^s, k^*) to L_{SessKey}, and returns k^*, else if $\Psi_i^s = \mathsf{reject}$, it picks a random session key k^*, adds (π_i^s, k^*) to L_{SessKey}, and returns k^*. Otherwise (i.e. If $\Psi_i^s = \perp$), it returns $\perp$. After this query, π_i^s is said to be revealed.

Partnering. Here we recall the definitions used to formally determine whether a session key is corrupted or not, and whether two session oracles correspond to the execution of a protocol between the two corresponding parties.

Definition 4 (Origin-oracle). *An oracle π_j^t is an origin-oracle for an oracle π_i^s if $\Psi_j^t \neq \bot$, $\Psi_i^s = \mathsf{Accept}$ and the messages sent by π_j^t equal the messages received by π_i^s, except for the initialisation message received by π_i^s.*

Definition 5 (Partner oracles). *We say that two oracles π_i^s and π_j^t are partners if (i) each is an origin-oracle for the other; (ii) each one's identity is the other one's peer identity, i.e., $\mathsf{Pid}_i^s = j$ and $\mathsf{Pid}_j^t = i$; and (iii) they do not have the same role, i.e., $\mathsf{role}_i^s \neq \mathsf{role}_j^t$, $\mathsf{role}_i^s \neq \bot$, and $\mathsf{role}_j^t \neq \bot$.*

Security Experiment. The security model is formally defined as a game between an adversary, denoted by $\mathcal{A}$, and a challenger, denoted by $\mathcal{C}$. In this game, the adversary may issue the standard set of queries described earlier. Additionally, they are granted access to a special oracle $\mathsf{Test}(m)$ depending on a secret random bit b that the adversary has to guess in order to win. In key-secrecy, the oracle returns either the key for a given session or a random key. For privacy, this oracle initializes a session for one of two parties chosen by the adversary. Since our main focus is privacy, we defer the key-secrecy experiment in Appendix A.

Privacy. The oracle $\mathsf{Test}(m)$ is defined as follows: for $m = (X, i, j)$ such that $X \in \{\mathsf{MITM\text{-}privacy}, \mathsf{Forward\text{-}privacy}\}$ and $i, j \leq \mu$, it creates a new party $P_{i|j}$ with identifier $i|j$. This party has all the properties of P_i (if $b = 0$) or P_j (if $b = 1$), but no active sessions. The public key of $P_{i|j}$ is not announced to the adversary and the query $\mathsf{RevLTK}(i|j)$ always returns $\bot$. Furthermore it creates exactly one session $\pi_{i|j}^1$, and returns the new identifier $i|j$.

The experiment $\mathsf{Exp}_{\mathsf{PPAKE},\mathcal{A}}^X(\lambda)$, with X the label sent to the oracle Test, is defined as follows:

1. Let μ be the number of parties in the game and ℓ the number of sessions per user. $\mathcal{C}$ begins by drawing a random bit $b \xleftarrow{\$} \{0,1\}$ and generating key pairs $\{(\mathsf{sk}_i, \mathsf{pk}_i) \mid 1 \leq i \leq \mu\}$ as well as oracles $\{\pi_i^s \mid 1 \leq i \leq \mu, 1 \leq s \leq \ell\}$.
2. $\mathcal{C}$ now runs $\mathcal{A}$, providing all the public keys as input. During its execution, $\mathcal{A}$ may adaptively issue $\mathsf{Send}(i, s, m)$, $\mathsf{RevLTK}(i)$, $\mathsf{RevSessKeyPriv}(i, s)$ and $\mathsf{RegisterLTK}(i, \mathsf{pk}_i)$ queries any number of times and the $\mathsf{Test}(m)$ query once.
3. Depending on what argument X the $\mathsf{Test}(m)$ oracle was called with, we require the corresponding property below to hold through the entire game.
   (a) MITM-privacy: P_i and P_j are never corrupted. Furthermore, we require that $\mathsf{Pid}_{i|j}^1 = \bot$ or $\mathsf{Pid}_{i|j}^1 = k$ for some $k \leq \mu$, while P_k is never corrupted.
   (b) Forward-privacy: The returned oracle $\pi_{i|j}^1$ has a partner oracle π_k^r at the end of the game. Furthermore, no oracle besides π_k^r may be instructed to start a protocol run with intended partner $P_{i|j}$.
4. The game ends when $\mathcal{A}$ terminates with the output b' representing the guess of the secret bit b. If $b' = b$, it outputs 1. Otherwise, it outputs 0.

Definition 6. *Let* PPAKE *be a key exchange protocol. The advantage of an adversary $\mathcal{A}$ in breaking the $X \in \{\mathsf{MITM\text{-}privacy}, \mathsf{Forward\text{-}privacy}\}$ security of protocol* PPAKE *is defined as:*

$$\mathsf{Adv}_{\mathsf{PPAKE},\mathcal{A}}^X(\lambda) = \left| \Pr\left[\mathsf{Exp}_{\mathsf{PPAKE},\mathcal{A}}^X(\lambda) = 1\right] - \frac{1}{2} \right|.$$

4 Protocol Π_{SDH}

In this section, we prove that the protocol Π_{SDH} in Fig. 1, already presented informally in the introduction, has the three properties of our security model under the SDH assumption in the ROM.

In our proofs, during a session simulated by the oracle π_i^s where P_i is the initiator, $(\mathsf{pk}_i, \mathsf{sk}_i)$ corresponds to (U, u), $(\mathsf{pk}_{\mathsf{Pid}_i^s}, \mathsf{sk}_{\mathsf{Pid}_i^s})$ corresponds to (V, v) and $(\mathsf{epk}_i^s, \mathsf{esk}_i^s)$ corresponds to (X, x) in Fig. 1. When P_i is the responder, $(\mathsf{pk}_i, \mathsf{sk}_i)$ corresponds to (V, v), $(\mathsf{epk}_i^s, \mathsf{esk}_i^s)$ corresponds to (Y, y), and $(\mathsf{pk}_{\mathsf{Pid}_i^s}, \mathsf{sk}_{\mathsf{Pid}_i^s})$ corresponds to (U, u) when defined. Recall that when the oracle π_i^s is initialised for the role $\mathsf{responder}$, the value of Pid_i^s is set to $\perp$. In accordance with the protocol in Fig. 1, Pid_i^s is updated after the third query is received on the condition that the message received is well-formed, i.e., its decryption gives the public key of a registered user P_j. In this case, Pid_i^s will be set to j.

Theorem 1. *Our protocol Π_{SDH} instantiated with a secure AE scheme is MITM-private under the SDH assumption in the ROM.*

We prove MITM-privacy in two steps. First, we show that the adversary can never guess and send the Diffie-Hellman values of V^x and U^y to the RO instead of uncorrupted users (owners of V and U) under the SDH assumption in the random oracle. This result (Lemma 1) allows us to show that during the MITM-privacy experiment, the key K used by $P_{i\|j}$ is perfectly random, and therefore that the identity encrypted in C can only be recovered by attacking the secure authenticated encryption scheme.

Lemma 1. *Let E be the event: "at the end of the* MITM-privacy *experiment, for some tuple (s, i, j, R), P_i and P_j are never corrupted, $\mathsf{Pid}_i^s = j$, and the Rth query to the RO contains the value $g^{\mathsf{esk}_i^s \mathsf{sk}_j}$, where esk_i^s is the ephemeral key used in π_i^s". For any PPT adversary $\mathcal{A}$ playing the* MITM-privacy *experiment on Π_{SDH}, the probability that E occurs and $\mathcal{A}$ wins the experiment is negligible under the* SDH *assumption in the ROM.*

Proof. We show that $\mathsf{Pr}\left[\mathsf{Exp}_{\Pi_{\mathsf{SDH}},\mathcal{A}}^{\mathsf{MITM\text{-}privacy}}(\lambda) = 1 \wedge E\right]$ is negligible using the following sequence of games.

Game G_0: This is the experiment $\mathsf{Exp}_{\Pi_{\mathsf{SDH}},\mathcal{A}}^{\mathsf{MITM\text{-}privacy}}(\lambda)$ except that if E does not occur, the experiment returns 0. We have that:

$$\mathsf{Pr}\left[\mathsf{Exp}_{\Pi_{\mathsf{SDH}},\mathcal{A}}^{\mathsf{MITM\text{-}privacy}}(\lambda) = 1 \wedge E\right] = \mathsf{Pr}\left[G_0 \text{ returns } 1\right].$$

Game G_1: G_1 is the same as G_0 except that the challenger picks $(s_*, i_*, j_*) \xleftarrow{\$} [\ell] \times [\mu]^2$, and returns 0 if E does not occur on the tuple (s_*, i_*, j_*, R_*) for some query index R_*. We have that:

$$\mathsf{Pr}\left[G_0 \text{ returns } 1\right] \leq \ell\mu^2 \mathsf{Pr}\left[G_1 \text{ returns } 1\right].$$

We will show that $\Pr[G_1 \text{ returns } 1] \leq \mathsf{Adv}^{\mathsf{SDH}}(\lambda)$.

Let $\mathcal{A} \in \mathsf{Poly}(\lambda)$ be an adversary against G_1. We build the following algorithm $\mathcal{B} \in \mathsf{Poly}(\lambda)$ against SDH. $\mathcal{B}$(A,B) perfectly simulates G_1 to $\mathcal{A}$, except that:

- If at some stage $\mathsf{Pid}_{i_*}^{s_*} \neq \perp$ and $\mathsf{Pid}_{i_*}^{s_*} \neq j_*$, $\mathcal{B}$ aborts the game (G_1 will returns 0 anyway).
- $\mathcal{B}$ sets $\mathsf{pk}_{j_*} \leftarrow B$, and sets $\mathsf{epk}_{i_*}^{s_*} \leftarrow A$, where $\mathsf{epk}_{i_*}^{s_*}$ is the ephemeral public key used in $\pi_{i_*}^{s_*}$, noted X in the protocol (resp. Y) for the initiator (resp. responder). Note that $\mathcal{B}$ does not know the respective discrete logarithms sk_{j^*} and $\mathsf{esk}_{i_*}^{s_*}$ of pk_{j^*} and $\mathsf{epk}_{i_*}^{s_*}$. It is therefore necessary to specify how $\mathcal{B}$ simulates the oracles that would use these values, i.e. oracles $\pi_{j_*}^{s}$ for all s for sk_{j^*} and the oracle $\pi_{i_*}^{s_*}$ for $\mathsf{esk}_{i_*}^{s_*}$. These two cases are detailed in the two following items.
- **For simulating the oracles $\pi_{j_*}^{s}$ for all** s, each time that $\mathcal{B}$ should compute $(\overline{\mathsf{epk}_{j_*}^{s}})^{\mathsf{sk}_{j_*}}$, it sets a tuple $T_s \leftarrow (\overline{\mathsf{epk}_{j_*}^{s}}, \mathsf{pk}_{j_*})$. If, afterward, $\mathcal{B}$ needs to compute the hash of an element containing $(\overline{\mathsf{epk}_{j_*}^{s}})^{\mathsf{sk}_{j_*}}$ using the random oracle, it replaces $(\overline{\mathsf{epk}_{j_*}^{s}})^{\mathsf{sk}_{j_*}}$ with T_s and labels the query as *'incomplete'* when storing it in the list of random oracle queries (but still returns a random value corresponding to the query).
- **For simulating the oracles $\pi_{i_*}^{s_*}$**, we distinguish two cases:

There exists $(i, s) \neq (i_*, s_*)$ such that $\mathsf{epk}_i^s = \overline{\mathsf{epk}_{i_*}^{s_*}}$: In this case, the adversary $\mathcal{B}$ knows the secret key esk_i^s. Each time that $\mathcal{B}$ should compute $(\overline{\mathsf{epk}_{i_*}^{s_*}})^{\mathsf{esk}_{i_*}^{s_*}}$, it computes $(\mathsf{epk}_{i_*}^{s_*})^{\mathsf{esk}_i^s}$ instead. Each time that $\mathcal{B}$ should compute $\mathsf{pk}_{j_*}^{\mathsf{esk}_{i_*}^{s_*}}$, it sets the tuple $T \leftarrow (\mathsf{epk}_{i_*}^{s_*}, \mathsf{pk}_{j_*})$. If, afterward, $\mathcal{B}$ needs to compute the hash of an element containing $\mathsf{pk}_{j_*}^{\mathsf{esk}_{i_*}^{s_*}}$ using the random oracle, it replaces $\mathsf{pk}_{j_*}^{\mathsf{esk}_{i_*}^{s_*}}$ by T, and labels the query as *'incomplete'* when storing it in the list of random oracle queries (but still returns a random value corresponding to the query).

There is no $(i, s) \neq (i_*, s_*)$ such that $\mathsf{epk}_i^s = \overline{\mathsf{epk}_{i_*}^{s_*}}$: In this case, $\mathcal{B}$ does not know the discrete logarithm of $\overline{\mathsf{epk}_{i_*}^{s_*}}$. We distinguish two cases:

- If $\mathsf{role}_{i_*}^{s_*} = \mathsf{initiator}$, each time that $\mathcal{B}$ should compute $(\overline{\mathsf{epk}_{i_*}^{s_*}})^{\mathsf{esk}_{i_*}^{s_*}}$, it sets the result as $\perp$ instead. Each time that $\mathcal{B}$ should compute $\mathsf{pk}_{j_*}^{\mathsf{esk}_{i_*}^{s_*}}$, it sets the tuple $T \leftarrow (\mathsf{epk}_{i_*}^{s_*}, \mathsf{pk}_{j_*})$. If, afterward, $\mathcal{B}$ needs to compute the hash of an element containing both $(\overline{\mathsf{epk}_{i_*}^{s_*}})^{\mathsf{esk}_{i_*}^{s_*}}$ and $\mathsf{pk}_{j_*}^{\mathsf{esk}_{i_*}^{s_*}}$ using the random oracle, it replaces $(\overline{\mathsf{epk}_{i_*}^{s_*}})^{\mathsf{esk}_{i_*}^{s_*}}$ by $\perp$ and $\mathsf{pk}_{j_*}^{\mathsf{esk}_{i_*}^{s_*}}$ by T, and labels the query as *'$\perp$-incomplete'* when storing it in the list of random oracle queries (but still returns a random value corresponding to the query). For the sake of consistency with the random oracle, if at any time $\mathcal{B}$ generates an ephemeral key epk_i^s such that $\mathsf{epk}_i^s = \overline{\mathsf{epk}_{i_*}^{s_*}}$, then $\perp$ is replaced by $(\mathsf{epk}_{i_*}^{s_*})^{\mathsf{esk}_i^s}$ in the $\perp$-incomplete query, and the label is replaced by *'incomplete'*.

- Else if $\mathsf{role}_{i_*}^{s_*} = \mathsf{responder}$, $\mathcal{B}$ proceeds as in the previous case, except that it does not compute the key K and does not decrypt the ciphertext C it receives. Instead, it assumes that the decryption of C is pk_{j_*}. Recall that according to game G_1, the adversary must send to $\pi_{i_*}^{s_*}$ a ciphertext correctly formed of the key pk_{j_*} in order to keep a non-negligible advantage of winning. The game is therefore correctly simulated to $\mathcal{A}$ as long as the adversary keeps its advantage.

We note that in the two cases, $T = (A, B)$, and that there is at most one unique $\perp$-incomplete query.

- Each time $\mathcal{B}$ must process a query to the random oracle that matches the pattern of a previous query labelled *'incomplete'* (i.e. all elements that are not tuples match in the queries), it checks whether each group element Z corresponding to a tuple $T = (\mathsf{epk}, pk_{j_*})$ satisfies $\mathsf{stDH}_b(\mathsf{epk}, Z) = 1$. If so, it returns the value associated with the incomplete query; otherwise, it processes the query as usual. For instance, if $\mathcal{B}$ simulates the first response of P_{j_*} to the first message send by P_i in the session π_i^s, when generating K, it will replace the query $(X^v \| X^y \| X \| Y)$ with the incomplete query $((X, V) \| X^y \| X \| Y)$ to the random oracle H. If, subsequently, $\mathcal{A}$ sends a query $(Z \| X^y \| X \| Y)$, $\mathcal{B}$ will check whether $\mathsf{stDH}_v(X, Z) = 1$, and if so, it will return K (otherwise it will treat $(Z \| X^y \| X \| Y)$ as a standard query to a random oracle).
- Each time $\mathcal{B}$ must process a query to the random oracle that matches the pattern of the query labeled *'$\perp$-incomplete'* (i.e. all elements that are not tuples or $\perp$ match in the queries), it checks whether the group element Z of the query corresponding to the tuple $T = (A, B)$ in the incomplete query satisfies $\mathsf{stDH}_b(A, Z) = 1$. If so, it aborts the experiment and returns Z; otherwise, it processes the query as usual. As a result, it is never necessary to know the value replaced by $\perp$.
- To maintain consistency in responses, when $\mathcal{B}$ stores a new incomplete query, it must also check that no previous query matches this incomplete query in the same way; if so, it must return the corresponding hash of that previous query.
- In order to take into account all cases where the adversary sends a query containing $g^{\mathsf{esk}_{i_*}^{s_*} \mathsf{sk}_{j_*}}$ (possibly by chance) to the random oracle, $\mathcal{B}$ tests, for each element Z contained in each query, whether $\mathsf{stDH}_b(A, Z) = 1$.
- If, at any other point, $\mathcal{B}$ tests $\mathsf{stDH}_b(A, Z) = 1$, it aborts the experiment and returns Z.
- If $\mathcal{B}$ must process the query j_* to RevLTK, $\mathcal{B}$ aborts the game ($\mathcal{A}$ can no longer win G_1 because P_{j_*} must not be corrupted for event E to occur on j_*).

In this way, G_1 is perfectly simulated for $\mathcal{A}$ except for abortions when $\mathcal{A}$ can no longer win the game or when $\mathcal{B}$ is guaranteed to win their SDH experiment, and therefore:

$$\Pr[G_1 \text{ returns } 1] \leq \mathsf{Adv}^{\mathsf{SDH}}(\lambda).$$

Finally, the following concludes the proof:

$$\Pr\left[\mathsf{Exp}_{\Pi_{\mathsf{SDH}},\mathcal{A}}^{\mathsf{MITM\text{-}privacy}}(\lambda) = 1 \wedge E\right] \leq \ell\mu^2 \mathsf{Adv}^{\mathsf{SDH}}(\lambda).$$

Proof (Theorem 1). We use the following sequence of games.

Game G_0: This is the experiment $\mathsf{Exp}^{\mathsf{MITM\text{-}privacy}}_{\Pi_{\mathsf{SDH}},\mathcal{A}}(\lambda)$. We have that:

$$\Pr\left[\mathsf{Exp}^{\mathsf{MITM\text{-}privacy}}_{\Pi_{\mathsf{SDH}},\mathcal{A}}(\lambda) = 1\right] = \Pr\left[G_0 \text{ returns } 1\right].$$

Game G_1: Same as G_0 except that at the end of the game, if $\mathcal{A}$ wins according to the conditions of G_0, and if for some tuple (s, i_*, j_*, R), P_{i_*} and P_{j_*} are never corrupted, $\mathsf{Pid}^s_{i_*} = j_*$, and the Rth query to the RO contains the value $g^{\mathsf{esk}^s_{i_*}\mathsf{sk}_{j_*}}$ (where $\mathsf{esk}^s_{i_*}$ is the ephemeral key used in $\pi^s_{i_*}$), then G_1 sets $\mathsf{abort}_1 = \mathsf{true}$, aborts the game, and returns a random bit. According to Lemma 1, we have:

$$|\Pr\left[G_0 \text{ returns } 1\right] - \Pr\left[G_1 \text{ returns } 1\right]| \leq \Pr\left[\mathsf{abort}_1\right] \leq \ell\mu^2 \mathsf{Adv}^{\mathsf{SDH}}(\lambda).$$

Game G_2: G_2 is the same as G_1 except that if in two distinct sessions, the ephemeral public keys randomly chosen by the oracles are the same, then G_2 sets $\mathsf{abort}_2 = \mathsf{true}$, aborts and returns a random bit. At most, there is $\ell\mu$ sessions during the game, we deduce that:

$$|\Pr\left[G_1 \text{ returns } 1\right] - \Pr\left[G_2 \text{ returns } 1\right]| \leq \Pr[\mathsf{abort}_2] \leq (\mu\ell)^2/|\mathbb{G}|.$$

Game G_3: G_3 is the same as G_2 except that if the RO returns the same random element for two distinct queries, then G_3 sets $\mathsf{abort}_3 = \mathsf{true}$, aborts and returns a random bit. We set q as the number of queries to the random oracle during G_2, we have:

$$|\Pr\left[G_2 \text{ returns } 1\right] - \Pr\left[G_3 \text{ returns } 1\right]| \leq \Pr[\mathsf{abort}_3] \leq q^2/|\mathcal{K}|.$$

From this step, the abort conditions in games 2 and 3 ensure that the key K used in session $\pi^1_{i|j}$ if $P_{i|j}$ is the initiator is used only once for encryption (it can be used for decryption in the other session that matches the first two interactions and therefore uses the same ephemeral keys; this session is unique if it exists according to G_2). Furthermore, according to the condition of G_1, if the adversary submits the query to obtain K to the random oracle, then its winning probability drops to 1/2. K is therefore perfectly random from their point of view as long as they still have a non-zero advantage in winning the game.

Game G_4: G_4 is the same as G_3 except that if the role of $P_{i|j}$ in $\pi^1_{i|j}$ is initiator, then it computes $C \leftarrow \mathsf{Enc}_\mathsf{K}(\perp)$ instead of computing $C \leftarrow \mathsf{Enc}_\mathsf{K}(\mathsf{U})$ at the second interaction. If during the simulation of an oracle the challenger has to decrypt C with the key K, they do not decrypt C and act as if the decryption returned U. Furthermore, if during the simulation of an oracle the challenger has to decrypt a ciphertext $C' \neq C$ with the key K, they act as if the decryption had failed.

We claim that:

$$|\Pr\left[G_3 \text{ returns } 1\right] - \Pr\left[G_4 \text{ returns } 1\right]| \leq \mathsf{Adv}^{\mathsf{AE}}_{\mathsf{SE}}(\lambda).$$

We prove this claim by reduction. Assume that there exists an adversary $\mathcal{A}$ such that $|\Pr\left[G_3 \text{ returns } 1\right] - \Pr\left[G_4 \text{ returns } 1\right]|$ is non-negligible, we build the following AE adversary $\mathcal{B}$. $\mathcal{B}$ simulates the game G_3 to $\mathcal{A}$, except that:

- In $\pi^1_{i|j}$, if $P_{i|j}$ is the initiator, when $\mathcal{B}$ must determine K with the random oracle for the query $(V^x \| Y^x \| X \| Y)$, it associates the query with the label *'undefined'*. Then, instead of computing $C \leftarrow \mathsf{Enc}_K(U)$, it sends $(M_0, M_1) = (U, \bot)$ (where U is the public key of $P_{i|j}$ to its challenger and receives the challenge ciphertext ctxt. It sets $C \leftarrow \mathsf{ctxt}$.
- Each time that $\mathcal{B}$ should compute the hash of query labeled with *'undefined'* to determine the value of a key K, it uses its encryption/decryption oracles $\mathsf{Enc}_K(\cdot)$ and $\mathsf{Dec}_K(\cdot)$ instead of directly using the hash K (If $\mathcal{B}$ must decrypt C, it cannot use the decryption oracle; instead, it considers that the decryption of C is U).
- If at any point the adversary $\mathcal{A}$ requests or has requested a query labeled with *'undefined'* to the random oracle, $\mathcal{B}$ aborts the game and returns a random bit. Note that this behaviour is consistent with the condition introduced in game G_1.
- $\mathcal{B}$ returns 1 if and only if $\mathcal{A}$ wins the game.

In this way, if $b = 0$, G_3 is perfectly simulated at $\mathcal{A}$, else G_4 is perfectly simulated at $\mathcal{A}$, except for abortions when $\mathcal{A}$ has no longer advantage, and therefore, the following concludes the proof of the claim:

$$\mathsf{Pr}\left[G_3 \text{ returns } 1\right] = \mathsf{Pr}\left[\mathsf{Exp}^{\mathsf{AE}}_{\mathsf{SE},0,\mathcal{B}}(\lambda) = 1\right];$$

$$\mathsf{Pr}\left[G_4 \text{ returns } 1\right] = \mathsf{Pr}\left[\mathsf{Exp}^{\mathsf{AE}}_{\mathsf{SE},1,\mathcal{B}}(\lambda) = 1\right].$$

Game G_5: G_5 is the same as G_4 except that at the end of the game, if the oracle $\mathsf{RevSessKeyPriv}$ generated a random session key k^* equals to either another session key randomly generated by the same oracle or an output of the random oracle, then G_5 sets $\mathsf{abort}_5 = \mathsf{true}$, aborts and returns a random bit. We set q (resp. q_r) as the number of queries to the random oracle (resp. $\mathsf{RevSessKeyPriv}$) during G_4, we have:

$$|\mathsf{Pr}\left[G_4 \text{ returns } 1\right] - \mathsf{Pr}\left[G_5 \text{ returns } 1\right]| \leq \mathsf{Pr}[\mathsf{abort}_5] \leq q_r(q + q_r)/|\mathcal{K}|.$$

At this stage, we observe that:

- If $\pi^1_{i|j}$ is the initiator, the keys and the ciphertext produced by $\pi^1_{i|j}$ no longer contain any information about the real identity of $P_{i|j}$ according (the keys generated by the RO appear perfectly random to the adversary according to G_1, and the ciphertext contains $\bot$ according to G_4). If it is the responder, no exchanged message depends on the identity of $P_{i|j}$ anymore (according to G_1). It is therefore no longer possible to directly exploit messages exchanged by $\pi^1_{i|j}$ to deduce its identity. Furthermore, if another oracle (for an uncorrupted party) is initialized with $\mathsf{Pid} = i|j$ (i.e., with the initiator role), G_1 guarantees that the encryption and session keys used by this oracle appear to have been generated randomly from the adversary's point of view.

- If $\pi^1_{i|j}$ has a matching conversation, then it is with a unique partner oracle (because the ephemeral keys are all different according to G_2). In this case, according to the definition of the RevSessKeyPriv oracle, the revealing of the session key of the $\pi^1_{i|j}$ and the oracle that has a matching conversation with it will be the same (even if one of the parties reject the session). It will therefore not be possible to use RevSessKeyPriv as a distinguisher to learn information about $\pi^1_{i|j}$ identity. This prevents trivial attacks where the adversary engages an initiator oracle with partner P_i, and forwards messages from that oracle to $\pi^1_{i|j}$ (in this case, $\pi^1_{i|j}$ would accept the session if its identity is P_i, and fail if its identity is P_j).
- In all other cases, regardless of $P_{i|j}$ actual identity, if no oracle π^s_k has a matching conversation with $\pi^1_{i|j}$, then no oracle has the same context as $\pi^1_{i|j}$ and therefore no oracle shares the same session key, because the context is hashed to compute the session key, and all hash values are different according to G_3. It should also be noted that, by definition, even if a session oracle refuses the session after receiving the last message C, RevSessKeyPriv returns a random key that is different from those of the other oracles according to G_5. Thus, the key returned by RevSessKeyPriv on $\pi^1_{i|j}$ will be different from the key returned on any other session oracle. It is therefore not possible to use RevSessKeyPriv to distinguish the identity of $P_{i|j}$ in this case. This prevents attacks where the adversary would try to forge a end-of-session cipher C' containing the key of P_i in order to replace the real cipher C containing the key of $P_{i|j}$, in order to test whether the partner oracle of $\pi^1_{i|j}$ returns the same session key as $\pi^1_{i|j}$ (which would mean that $P_{i|j} = P_i$) or not.

Recall the winning conditions for the MITM-privacy experiment: P_i and P_j are never corrupted, and $\mathsf{Pid}^1_{i|j} = \bot$ or $\mathsf{Pid}^1_{i|j} = k$ while P_k is never corrupted. If $\mathsf{Pid}^1_{i|j} = \bot$, then the session key revealed by RevSessKeyPriv is random by definition. If $\mathsf{Pid}^1_{i|j} = k$ while P_k is never corrupted, then the session key of $\pi^1_{i|j}$ appears perfectly random to $\mathcal{A}$ according to G_1. As long as game G_5 has not been aborted, $\mathcal{A}$ has no further information that can be exploited to guess the identity of $P_{i|j}$, neither by exploiting messages sent/received by $\pi^1_{i|j}$, nor by comparing session keys, so its advantage is zero, and it cannot guess better than guessing at random:

$$\mathsf{Pr}\left[G_5 \text{ returns } 1\right] = 1/2.$$

By considering that $|\mathbb{G}| > 2^\lambda$ and $|\mathcal{K}| > 2^\lambda$, we can therefore conclude that:

$$\left|\mathsf{Pr}\left[\mathsf{Exp}^{\mathsf{MITM\text{-}privacy}}_{\Pi_{\mathsf{SDH}},\mathcal{A}}(\lambda) = 1\right] - 1/2\right| \leq \ell\mu^2 \mathsf{Adv}^{\mathsf{SDH}}(\lambda) + ((\mu\ell)^2 + q^2 + q_r(q+q_r))/2^\lambda + \mathsf{Adv}^{\mathsf{AE}}_{\mathsf{SE}}(\lambda).$$

Theorem 2. *Our protocol Π_{SDH}, instantiated with a secure AE scheme, is forward-private under the SDH assumption in the ROM.*

The proof of forward-privacy follows the same idea. Without interfering in the communications between two uncorrupted users, the adversary cannot deduce

g^{xy}, and the key K therefore appears to be completely random, perfectly hiding the identity U.

Proof (Theorem 2). We use the following sequence of games.

Game G_0: This is the experiment $\mathsf{Exp}^{\mathsf{Forward\text{-}privacy}}_{\Pi_{\mathsf{SDH}},\mathcal{A}}(\lambda)$. We have that:

$$\mathsf{Pr}\left[\mathsf{Exp}^{\mathsf{Forward\text{-}privacy}}_{\Pi_{\mathsf{SDH}},\mathcal{A}}(\lambda) = 1\right] = \mathsf{Pr}\left[G_0 \text{ returns } 1\right].$$

Game G_1: G_1 is the same as G_0 except that the challenger picks $(i_*, j_*, k_*, r_*) \xleftarrow{\$} [\mu]^3 \times [\ell]$, and if $i|j \neq i_*|j_*$ or if $\pi^{r_*}_{k_*}$ is not the partner oracle of $\pi^1_{i_*|j_*}$, then G_1 aborts and returns a random bit (note that according to the winning condition of the experiment, the returned oracle $\pi^1_{i|j}$ must have a partner oracle at the end of the game). We have that:

$$\mathsf{Pr}\left[G_0 \text{ returns } 1\right] \leq \ell\mu^3 \mathsf{Pr}\left[G_1 \text{ returns } 1\right].$$

Game G_2: This hop is identical to that from G_2 to G_3 in the previous proof.

Game G_3: G_3 is the same as G_2 except that if the adversary sends a query containing $g^{\mathsf{esk}^1_{i_*|j_*} \mathsf{esk}^{r_*}_{k_*}}$ (where $\mathsf{esk}^1_{i_*|j_*}$ and $\mathsf{esk}^{r_*}_{k_*}$ are the ephemeral keys x and y used in the two sessions) to the random oracle, then G_3 sets $\mathsf{abort}_3 = \mathsf{true}$, aborts and returns a random bit. We claim that:

$$\left|\mathsf{Pr}\left[G_2 \text{ returns } 1\right] - \mathsf{Pr}\left[G_3 \text{ returns } 1\right]\right| \leq \mathsf{Pr}[\mathsf{abort}_3] \leq \mathsf{Adv}^{\mathsf{SDH}}(\lambda)$$

We prove the claim by reduction. Let $\mathcal{A} \in \mathsf{Poly}(\lambda)$ be an adversary such that $\mathsf{Pr}[\mathsf{abort}_3]$ is non-negligible. We build the following algorithm $\mathcal{B} \in \mathsf{Poly}(\lambda)$ against SDH. $\mathcal{B}(A, B)$ simulates G_2 to $\mathcal{A}$, except that:

- $\mathcal{B}$ sets $\mathsf{epk}^1_{i_*|j_*} \leftarrow A$ and $\mathsf{epk}^{r_*}_{k_*} \leftarrow B$, where $\mathsf{epk}^1_{i_*|j_*}$ and $\mathsf{epk}^{r_*}_{k_*}$ are the ephemeral public keys used in $\pi^1_{i_*|j_*}$ and $\pi^{r_*}_{k_*}$, noted in the protocol X (resp. Y) for the initiator (resp. responder).
- Recall that $\mathcal{A}$ must ensure that $\pi^1_{i_*|j_*}$ and $\pi^{r_*}_{k_*}$ are partners (and so $\mathsf{Pid}^1_{i_*|j_*} = k_*$) in order to maintain a non-negligible advantage according to G_1. As soon as this condition can no longer be satisfied, $\mathcal{B}$ aborts the game by returning a random bit. When it simulates $\pi^1_{i_*|j_*}$, $\mathcal{B}$ computes $(\mathsf{epk}^1_{i_*|j_*})^{\mathsf{sk}_{k_*}}$ instead of $\mathsf{pk}_{k_*}^{\mathsf{esk}^1_{i_*|j_*}}$. Moreover, when $\mathcal{B}$ should compute $(\mathsf{epk}^{r_*}_{k_*})^{\mathsf{esk}^1_{i_*|j_*}}$, it replaces it with $T = (A, B)$. It then labels the queries to the random oracle containing T as *'incomplete'* when storing it in the list of random oracle queries (but still returns a random value corresponding to the query).
- In a similar way, when it simulates $\pi^{r_*}_{k_*}$, $\mathcal{B}$ computes $(\mathsf{epk}^{r_*}_{k_*})^{\mathsf{sk}_{i_*|j_*}}$ instead of $\mathsf{pk}_{i_*|j_*}^{\mathsf{esk}^{r_*}_{k_*}}$. Moreover, when $\mathcal{B}$ should compute $(\mathsf{epk}^1_{i_*|j_*})^{\mathsf{esk}^{r_*}_{k_*}}$, it replaces it with $T = (A, B)$. It then labels the queries to the random oracle containing T as *'incomplete'* when storing it in the list of random oracle queries (but still returns a random value corresponding to the query).

- Each time $\mathcal{B}$ must process a query to the random oracle that matches the pattern of a previous query labelled *'incomplete'*, it checks whether the group element Z of the query corresponding to the tuple $T = (A, B)$ in the incomplete query satisfies $\mathsf{stDH}_b(A, Z) = 1$. If so, it aborts the experiment and returns Z, otherwise, it processes the query as usual.
- To maintain consistency in responses, when $\mathcal{B}$ stores a new incomplete query, it must also check that no previous query matches this incomplete query; if so, it must return the corresponding hash of that previous query.

To keep an advantage in the game, the adversary must not interfere with communication between $\pi^1_{i_*|j_*}$ and $\pi^{r_*}_{k_*}$ (they must be exclusive partner oracles), and therefore cannot modify the ephemeral keys exchanged. In this way, G_2 is perfectly simulated at $\mathcal{A}$ except for abortions when $\mathcal{A}$ can no longer win the game or when $\mathcal{B}$ is guaranteed to win their SDH experiment, and therefore $\Pr[\mathsf{abort}_3] \leq \mathsf{Adv}^{\mathsf{SDH}}(\lambda)$, which concludes the proof of the claim.

From this step, the abort conditions in games 2 and 3 ensure that while the adversary keeps an advantage, the keys generated by the session seem to their fully random, and are never reused in another session (except the key shared with $\pi^{r_*}_{k_*}$). As a result, the latest information that the adversary can exploit about the identity of $P_{i|j}$ is the message encrypted with the key K, which contains its public key (if $P_{i|j}$ plays the role of initiator).

Game G_4 and G_5: These hops are identical to those from G_3 to G_4 and from G_4 to G_5 in the previous proof.

At this stage, we observe that:

- If $\pi^1_{i_*|j_*}$ is the initiator, the keys and the ciphertext produced by $\pi^1_{i_*|j_*}$ no longer contain any information about the real identity of $P_{i_*|j_*}$ (the keys generated by the RO appear perfectly random to the adversary according to G_3, and the ciphertext contains $\perp$ according to G_4). If it is the responder, no exchanged message with its partner oracle depends on the identity of $P_{i_*|j_*}$ anymore. It is therefore no longer possible to directly exploit messages exchanged by $\pi^1_{i_*|j_*}$ to deduce its identity. Furthermore, the winning conditions of the forward-privacy ensure that no oracle besides $\pi^{r_*}_{k_*}$ may be instructed to start a protocol run with intended partner $P_{i_*|j_*}$.
- As in the previous proof, if $\pi^1_{i_*|j_*}$ has a matching conversation, then the revealing of the session key of $\pi^1_{i_*|j_*}$ and the oracle that has a matching conversation with it will be the same. In all other cases, regardless of $P_{i_*|j_*}$ actual identity, if no oracle π^s_k has a matching conversation with $\pi^1_{i_*|j_*}$, then no oracle shares the same session key. It is therefore not possible to use $\mathsf{RevSessKeyPriv}$ to distinguish the identity of $P_{i_*|j_*}$.

Recall the winning conditions for the forward-privacy experiment: the returned oracle $\pi^1_{i|j}$ has a partner oracle π^r_k at the end of the game, and no oracle besides π^r_k may be instructed to start a protocol run with intended partner $P_{i|j}$. As long as game G_5 has not been aborted, $\mathcal{A}$ has no further information that can be exploited to guess the identity of $P_{i|j}$, neither by exploiting messages exchanged by $\pi^1_{i|j}$ and π^r_k, nor by comparing session keys, so its advantage is zero, and it cannot guess better than guessing at random:

$$\Pr[G_5 \text{ returns } 1] = 1/2.$$

By considering that $|\mathbb{G}| > 2^\lambda$ and $|\mathcal{K}| > 2^\lambda$, we can therefore conclude that:

$$\left|\Pr\left[\mathsf{Exp}^{\mathsf{Forward\text{-}privacy}}_{\Pi_{\mathsf{SDH}},\mathcal{A}}(\lambda) = 1\right] - 1/2\right| \leq \ell\mu^3 \left(\mathsf{Adv}^{\mathsf{SDH}}(\lambda) + (q + q^2 + q_r(q + q_r))/2^\lambda + \mathsf{Adv}^{\mathsf{AE}}_{\mathsf{SE}}(\lambda)\right).$$

Theorem 3. *Our protocol Π_{SDH} instantiated with a secure AE scheme is key secret under the SDH assumption in the ROM.*

Recall that a very similar protocol (Π) has already been proven key secret in [6], the only difference being the use of the key $K = \mathsf{H}(g^{xv}\|g^{xy}\|X\|Y)$ to encrypt the public key U (U is not a sensitive value for key-secrecy). Since the key K comes from the RO, it does not provide the adversary with any information about the values g^{xv} and g^{xy}, and is therefore of no use in guessing the session key. Since it essentially follows the same spirit as the proof of the protocol Π in [6], we have deferred it to the Appendix B.

5 Protocol Π_{CDH}

We are now building a variant of our protocol that can be proven under CDH, which is weaker than SDH and is generally considered more standard. This protocol uses signatures of knowledge of a discrete logarithm given a group element and a base. We first recall the formal definition of signature of knowledge.

Definition 7 (Signature Of Knowledge (SOK) [5]). *Let $\mathcal{R}$ be a binary relation and let $\mathcal{L}$ be a language such that $s \in \mathcal{L} \Leftrightarrow (\exists w, (s, w) \in \mathcal{R})$.* A signature of knowledge *for $\mathcal{L}$ is a couple of algorithms* (SOK, Verify) *such that the algorithm* $\mathsf{SOK}_m\{w : (s, w) \in \mathcal{R}\}$ *outputs a signature* sok *of a message m using w, and the algorithm* $\mathsf{Verify}(s, m, \mathsf{sok})$ *outputs a bit b such that* $\mathsf{Verify}(s, m, \mathsf{SOK}_m\{w : (s, w) \in \mathcal{R}\}) = 1$ *for any w such that $(s, w) \in \mathcal{R}$. A SOK must guarantee the following properties:*

- **Extractability.** *There exists a polynomial time knowledge extractor* Ext *and a negligible function* $\mathsf{Adv}^{\mathsf{ext}}_{\mathsf{SOK}}(\lambda)$ *such that for any algorithm* $\mathcal{A}^{\mathsf{Sim}(\cdot)}(\lambda)$ *having access to a simulator that forges signatures for chosen statement and that outputs a fresh tuple* (s, m, sok) *with* $\mathsf{Verify}(s, m, \mathsf{sok}) = 1$, *the extractor* $\mathsf{Ext}^{\mathcal{A}}(\lambda)$ *having access to $\mathcal{A}$ outputs w such that $(s, w) \in \mathcal{R}$ with probability at least* $1 - \mathsf{Adv}^{\mathsf{ext}}_{\mathsf{SOK}}(\lambda)$.
- **(Perfect) Zero-knowledge.** *A signature* sok leaks no information, *i.e., there exists a polynomial time algorithm* Sim *(called the* simulator*) such that* $\mathsf{SOK}_m\{w : (s, w) \in \mathcal{R}\}$ *and* $\mathsf{Sim}(m, s)$ *follow the same probability distribution for any (m, s) and any w such that $(s, w) \in \mathcal{R}$.*

Alice (initiator)		Bob (responder)
$\mathsf{sk_i} = u$; $\mathsf{pk_i} = U = g^u$		$\mathsf{sk_r} = v$; $\mathsf{pk_r} = V = g^v$
$\mathsf{sok}_i = \mathsf{SOK}_{P_i}\{u : U = g^u\}$		$\mathsf{sok}_j = \mathsf{SOK}_{P_j}\{v : V = g^v\}$
If sok_j is not a valid SOK, Alice aborts the protocol.		
$x \leftarrow \mathbb{Z}_p$; $X \leftarrow g^x$		
$\mathsf{sok}_X \leftarrow \mathsf{SOK}_0\{x : X = g^x\}$	$\xrightarrow{X, \mathsf{sok}_X}$	$y \leftarrow \mathbb{Z}_p$; $Y \leftarrow g^y$
		$\mathsf{sok}_Y \leftarrow \mathsf{SOK}_1\{y : Y = g^y\}$
		If sok_X is not a valid SOK, Bob aborts the protocol.
$h_1 \leftarrow (Y^x \Vert V^x)$	$\xleftarrow{Y, \mathsf{sok}_Y}$	$h_1 \leftarrow (X^y \Vert X^v)$
$\mathsf{K} \leftarrow \mathsf{H}(X \Vert Y \Vert h_1)$		$\mathsf{K} \leftarrow \mathsf{H}(X \Vert Y \Vert h_1)$
If sok_Y is not a valid SOK, Alice aborts the protocol.		
$\mathsf{C} \leftarrow \mathsf{Enc_K}(\mathsf{U})$	$\xrightarrow{C}$	$U \leftarrow \mathsf{Dec_K}(\mathsf{C})$
		If U is not a registered public key, or if sok_i is not a valid SOK, Bob aborts the protocol.
$h_2 \leftarrow Y^u$		$h_2 \leftarrow U^y$
$\mathsf{K_i} \leftarrow \mathsf{H}(\mathsf{ctxt} \Vert h_1 \Vert h_2)$		$\mathsf{K_r} \leftarrow \mathsf{H}(\mathsf{ctxt} \Vert h_1 \Vert h_2)$

Fig. 3. Private authenticated key exchange protocol based on CDH (Π_{CDH}).

The SOK of a discrete logarithm can be instantiated by the Schnorr protocol [17] rendered interactive with the Fiat-Shamir heuristic [8], and where the message is hashed with the rest of the elements. In this case, $\mathsf{SOK}_m\{w : W = g^w\}$ consists of choosing an r and returning $(R = g^r, \alpha = r + xH(g, W, R, m))$ (1 exponentiation), and $\mathsf{Verify}((g, W), m, \mathsf{sok})$ consists of verifying whether $g^\alpha = Ry^{H(g,W,R,m)}$ (2 exponentiations). Note that we implicitly consider in the SOK definition that any hash function will be simulated by a random oracle (RO). In particular, the Schnorr simulator Sim can program the random oracles (Sim picks (α, h), computes $R = y^h/y^\alpha$, and then programs the random oracle such that $h = H(g, W, R, m)$). However, the algorithm $\mathcal{A}$ in extractability only has black-box access to the random oracles, so it cannot program the random oracles and therefore cannot simulate valid proofs on its own on arbitrary statements to extract the witness.

Our Π_{CDH} protocol, shown in Fig. 3, is the same as the Π_{SDH} protocol, except that each user uses their long-term key to sign their identity, and uses their ephemeral key to sign their role (with `initiator` $= 0$ and `responder` $= 1$) at each session. Each user must therefore generate a SOK and verify a SOK at each session, which adds 3 exponentiations per user. Note that it is also necessary to verify the SOK of the long-term key, but this can be performed only once (when verifying the certificate of this key) and does not need to be repeated for other sessions with the same partner. The security of this protocol is given in the following theorem.

Theorem 4. *Our protocol Π_{CDH} instantiated with a secure AE scheme and the Schnorr SOK is MITM-private, forward-private and key-secret under the CDH assumption in the ROM.*

The detailed proof of this theorem is provided in the extended version of this work[2]. The proofs of the three properties follow essentially the same structure as those of the previous protocol, except for the CDH reductions. In the previous proofs, during these reductions, the SDH challenge (A, B) was used to instantiate a long-term key and an ephemeral key or two ephemeral keys. Since, before being hashed, these keys are used to compute Diffie-Hellman keys with several different key shares, and since it is sometimes impossible to compute these keys without knowing the discrete logarithm of A or B, we stored the key shares that would have had to be merged in the random oracle queries, then used the stDH oracle to check whether the attacker was sending the corresponding queries. For example, if an adversary's query corresponds to an incomplete query requiring the Diffie-Hellman key of key shares (X, B), we checked whether $\mathsf{stDH}_b(X, Z)$, where Z is the element sent by the adversary. In Π_{CDH}, in similar reductions, while (X, sok_X) is a fresh pair of ephemeral key and SOK (not already outputted by the challenger), we can instead use the knowledge extractor on sok_X to find x and compute $Z = B^x$. However, it should be noted that, since the discrete logarithm of A and B is unknown, the corresponding signatures must be simulated (these signatures are therefore non-extractable). Thus, the adversary could reuse these elements and signatures without knowing the corresponding discrete logarithms. However, since the signature signs the user's role (for ephemeral key) or the user's identity (for long-term key), they can only be reused in the same context. For example, if an oracle sends the ephemeral key A with a signature of the role `initiator`, the adversary cannot send the same ephemeral key back to the oracle, since they are supposed to play the role of the responder. For similar reasons, the adversary cannot register a user using such an ephemeral key as a public key. This prevents cases that cannot be simulated in the reductions.

6 Conclusion and Future Work

In this article, we have given two efficient round-optimal private key exchange protocols and proved their security in the ROM under SDH and CDH. There are many directions in which future research could go. Firstly, our privacy proofs are not tight, and it would be interesting to improve them and prove the optimal loss reduction that can be achieved for privacy. Secondly, it would be interesting to investigate whether a similar approach could be taken with quantum-resistant primitives, such as in key exchange based on key encapsulation mechanisms. Finally, since our protocols are very similar to Noise, which is used in real-world applications, it would be interesting to see what using our protocols would entail in practice (e.g. for Signal [11], WhatsApp [18] or Wireguard [7]).

[2] See https://hal.science/hal-05593610.

Acknowledgments. This work has been supported by the French National Research Agency through the PRIVASIQ project (ANR-23-CE39-0008).

A Key-Secrecy Experiment

Definition 8 (Freshness). *An oracle π_i^s is fresh if (i) $\Psi_i^s = \mathsf{Accept}$, (ii) $\mathsf{RevSessKey}(i, s)$ has not been issued; (iii) no query $\mathsf{RevSessKey}(j, t)$ has been issued, where π_j^t is a partner of π_i^s; and (iv) $P_{\mathsf{Pid}_i^s}$ was not corrupted before π_i^s accepted if π_i^s has an origin-oracle, and not corrupted at all if π_i^s has no origin-oracle.*

Key Secrecy. The oracle $\mathsf{Test}(i, s)$ is defined as follows: if $\Psi_i^s \neq \mathsf{Accept}$, return $\perp$. Else, return k_b where $k_0 = k_i^s$, and $k_1 \xleftarrow{\$} \mathcal{K}$ is a random key. After this query, oracle π_i^s is said to be tested. The experiment $\mathsf{Exp}_{\mathsf{PPAKE},\mathcal{A}}^{\text{key-secret}}(\lambda)$ is defined as follows:

1. Let μ be the number of parties in the game and ℓ the number of sessions per user. $\mathcal{C}$ begins by drawing a random bit $b \xleftarrow{\$} \{0, 1\}$ and generating key pairs $\{(\mathsf{sk}_i, \mathsf{pk}_i) \mid 1 \leq i \leq \mu\}$ as well as oracles $\{\pi_i^s \mid 1 \leq i \leq \mu, 1 \leq s \leq \ell\}$.
2. $\mathcal{C}$ now runs $\mathcal{A}$, providing all the public keys as input. During its execution, $\mathcal{A}$ may adaptively issue $\mathsf{Send}(i, s, m)$, $\mathsf{RevLTK}(i)$, $\mathsf{RevSessKeySec}(i, s)$ and $\mathsf{RegisterLTK}(i, \mathsf{pk}_i)$ queries any number of times and the $\mathsf{Test}(i, s)$ query once.
3. The game ends when $\mathcal{A}$ terminates with the output b' representing the guess of the secret bit b. If the tested oracle is not fresh, it outputs a random bit. Else, if the tested oracle remains fresh and $b' = b$, it outputs 1. Otherwise, it outputs 0.

We define the following three winning events in the game $\mathsf{Exp}_{\mathsf{PPAKE},\mathcal{A}}^{\text{key-secret}}(\lambda)$:

1. **Event** $\mathsf{breakSound}$**:** This event occurs if there exist two partner oracles π_i^s and π_j^t such that their session keys differ, i.e., $k_i^s \neq k_j^t$. In other words, two partner oracles compute different session keys.
2. **Event** $\mathsf{breakUnique}$**:** This event occurs if there exists an oracle π_i^s that has two distinct partner oracles π_j^t and $\pi_{j'}^{t'}$. That is, one oracle has more than one partner oracle.
3. Let $\mathsf{guessKE}$ be the output of the game $\mathsf{Exp}_{\mathsf{PPAKE},\mathcal{A}}^{\text{key-secret}}(\lambda)$. We define $\mathsf{breakKE}$ as the event where $\mathsf{guessKE} = 1$.

Definition 9. *Let* PPAKE *be a key exchange protocol. An adversary $\mathcal{A}$ breaks the key-secrecy of* PPAKE *if at least one of the events breakSound, breakUnique, or breakKE occurs during the game. The advantage of the adversary $\mathcal{A}$ in breaking the AKE security of protocol* PPAKE *is defined as:*

$$\mathsf{Adv}_{\mathsf{PPAKE},\mathcal{A}}^{\mathsf{AKE}}(\lambda) = \max \left\{ \Pr[\mathit{breakSound}], \Pr[\mathit{breakUnique}], \left| \Pr[\mathit{breakKE}] - \frac{1}{2} \right| \right\}.$$

B Proof of Key-Secrecy for Π_{SDH}

Lemma 2. *Let E be the event: "at the end of the* key-secrecy *experiment, for some tuple (s, i, j, R), P_j is never corrupted, $\mathsf{Pid}_i^s = j$, and the Rth query to the RO contains the value $g^{\mathsf{esk}_i^s \mathsf{sk}_j}$, where esk_i^s is the ephemeral key used in π_i^s". For any PPT adversary $\mathcal{A}$ playing the* key-secrecy *experiment on Π_{SDH}, the probability that E occurs and $\mathcal{A}$ wins the experiment is negligible under the* SDH *assumption in the ROM.*

Proof. This lemma can be proved in a manner similar to Lemma 1. The only notable difference is that in this lemma, we do not require that P_i be uncorrupted, which is never used in the proof of Lemma 1 (however, we do need P_j to be uncorrupted because in the reduction to SDH, the public key of P_j is replaced by one of the inputs of the SDH experiment and therefore the corresponding secret key is unknown).

Proof. We show that Π_{SDH} is key secret using the following sequences of games.

Game G_0. In this game, the adversary interacts with honestly behaving oracles according to the key-secrecy security experiment. Oracles derive session keys exactly as specified in the protocol. The adversary's goal is to distinguish a real session key from a random one. We define:

$$\Pr[\mathsf{break}_{\mathsf{KE}}] = \Pr[G_0 \text{ returns } 1].$$

Game G_1. This game is identical to G_0 except that the challenger aborts if at the end of the game, for some tuple (s, i, j, R), P_j is not corrupted, $\mathsf{Pid}_i^s = j$, and the Rth query to the RO contains the value $g^{\mathsf{esk}_i^s \mathsf{sk}_j}$, where esk_i^s is the ephemeral key used in π_i^s.

By Lemma 2, we have that:

$$|\Pr[G_0 \text{ returns } 1] - \Pr[G_1 \text{ returns } 1]| \leq \ell\mu^2 \mathsf{Adv}^{\mathsf{SDH}}(\lambda).$$

Game G_2. This game is identical to G_1 except that the challenger aborts the experiment if two oracles in the same role (either initiators or responders) generate identical session contexts. This implies a collision in their ephemeral exponents, which is highly unlikely. Given at most ℓ sessions per user and μ users, this collision occurs with probability at most:

$$|\Pr[G_1 \text{ returns } 1] - \Pr[G_2 \text{ returns } 1]| \leq \frac{(\mu\ell)^2}{|\mathbb{G}|}.$$

Game G_3. This game is identical to G_2 except that the challenger guesses a tuple (i_*, s_*, j_*, t_*) such that if the adversary $\mathcal{A}$ ever queries the Test oracle, it will be on $\pi_{i_*}^{s_*}$ and if that oracle has an origin oracle, it is $\pi_{j_*}^{t_*}$ (Note that t_* is unique, according to G_2). If the adversary $\mathcal{A}$ fails its guess, the game aborts. We have:

$$\Pr[G_2 \text{ returns }] \leq \mu^2\ell^2 \cdot \Pr[G_3 \text{ returns } 1].$$

Game G_4. This game is identical to G_3 except that the game sets $\mathsf{abort}_4 = \mathsf{true}$, aborts and returns a random bit if $\pi_{j_*}^{t_*}$ is the origin oracle of $\pi_{i_*}^{s_*}$, $\pi_{i_*}^{s_*}$ is fresh and the adversary has sent a query to the random oracle containing an element equal to $g^{\mathsf{esk}_{i_*}^{s_*}\mathsf{esk}_{j_*}^{t_*}}$ during the game. We claim that :

$$|\Pr[G_3 \text{ returns } 1] - \Pr[G_4 \text{ returns } 1]| \leq \mathsf{Pr}[\mathsf{abort}_4] \leq \mathsf{Adv}^{\mathsf{SDH}}(\lambda).$$

We prove this claim by reduction. Let $\mathcal{A} \in \mathsf{Poly}(\lambda)$ be an adversary such that $\mathsf{Pr}[\mathsf{abort}_4]$ is non-negligible. We build the following algorithm $\mathcal{B} \in \mathsf{Poly}(\lambda)$ against SDH. $\mathcal{B}$(A,B) simulates G_4 to $\mathcal{A}$, except that:

- $\mathcal{B}$ sets $\mathsf{epk}_{j_*}^{t_*} \leftarrow B$, and sets $\mathsf{epk}_{i_*}^{s_*} \leftarrow A$, where $\mathsf{epk}_{i_*}^{s_*}$ and $\mathsf{epk}_{j_*}^{t_*}$ are the ephemeral public keys, respectively, used in $\pi_{i_*}^{s_*}$ and $\pi_{j_*}^{t_*}$. If $\overline{\mathsf{epk}}_{i_*}^{s_*} \neq \mathsf{epk}_{j_*}^{t_*}$, then $\mathcal{B}$ aborts the game (in this case $\pi_{j_*}^{t_*}$ is not the origin oracle of $\pi_{i_*}^{s_*}$). Note that $\mathcal{B}$ does not know the respective discrete logarithms $\mathsf{esk}_{j_*}^{t_*}$ and $\mathsf{esk}_{i_*}^{s_*}$ of $\mathsf{epk}_{j_*}^{t_*}$ and $\mathsf{epk}_{i_*}^{s_*}$. It is therefore necessary to specify how $\mathcal{B}$ simulates the oracles that would use these values, i.e. oracle $\pi_{j_*}^{t_*}$ for $\mathsf{esk}_{j_*}^{t_*}$ and the oracle $\pi_{i_*}^{s_*}$ for $\mathsf{esk}_{i*}^{s_*}$.
- In $\pi_{i_*}^{s_*}$, when $\mathcal{B}$ should compute $(\mathsf{pk}_{\mathsf{Pid}_{i_*}^{s_*}}^{s_*})^{\mathsf{esk}_{i_*}^{s_*}}$, it computes $(\mathsf{epk}_{i_*}^{s_*})^{\mathsf{sk}_{\mathsf{Pid}_{i_*}^{s_*}}^{s_*}}$ instead. In the case where $\mathcal{B}$ does not know the secret key $\mathsf{sk}_{\mathsf{Pid}_{i_*}^{s_*}}^{s_*}$ (i.e. $\mathsf{pk}_{\mathsf{Pid}_{i_*}^{s_*}}^{s_*}$ has been chosen by $\mathcal{A}$), then $\mathcal{B}$ aborts the game. Recall that if $\pi_{i_*}^{s_*}$ is fresh and has an origin oracle, then $P_{\mathsf{Pid}_{i_*}^{s_*}}$ was not corrupted before $\pi_{i_*}^{s_*}$ accepts, so $\mathcal{B}$ knows the secret key of $P_{\mathsf{Pid}_{i_*}^{s_*}}$.
- In $\pi_{i_*}^{s_*}$, when $\mathcal{B}$ should compute $(\mathsf{epk}_{j_*}^{t_*})^{\mathsf{esk}_{i_*}^{s_*}}$, it sets a tuple $T \leftarrow (A, B)$. If, afterward, $\mathcal{B}$ needs to compute the hash of an element containing $(\mathsf{epk}_{j_*}^{t_*})^{\mathsf{esk}_{i_*}^{s_*}}$ using the random oracle, it replaces it with T and labels the query as *'incomplete'* when storing it in the list of random oracle queries (but still returns a random value corresponding to the query). Each time $\mathcal{B}$ must process a query to the random oracle that matches the pattern of a previous query labelled *'incomplete'* containing T, it checks whether the group element Z of the query corresponding to the tuple $T = (A, B)$ in the incomplete query satisfies $\mathsf{stDH}_b(A, Z) = 1$. If so, it aborts the experiment and returns Z, otherwise, it processes the query as usual.
- In $\pi_{j_*}^{t_*}$, when $\mathcal{B}$ should compute $(A')^{\mathsf{esk}_{j_*}^{t_*}}$ for some A', it sets a tuple $T' \leftarrow (A', B)$. If, afterward, $\mathcal{B}$ needs to compute the hash of an element containing $(A')^{\mathsf{esk}_{j_*}^{t_*}}$ using the random oracle, it replaces it with T' and labels the query as *'incomplete'* when storing it in the list of random oracle queries (but still returns a random value corresponding to the query). Each time $\mathcal{B}$ must process a query to the random oracle that matches the pattern of a previous query labelled *'incomplete'* containing T', it checks whether the group element Z' of the query corresponding to the tuple $T' = (A', B)$ in the incomplete query satisfies $\mathsf{stDH}_b(A', Z') = 1$. If so, it replaces T' by Z' in the stored query (note that a query can contains several tuples T').

- To maintain consistency in responses, when $\mathcal{B}$ stores a new incomplete query, it must also check that no previous query matches this incomplete query in the same way; if so, it must return the corresponding hash of that previous query.

In this way, G_4 is perfectly simulated at $\mathcal{A}$ except for abortions when $\mathcal{A}$ can no longer win the game or when $\mathcal{B}$ is guaranteed to win their SDH experiment, and therefore $\mathsf{Pr}\left[\mathsf{abort}_4\right] \leq \mathsf{Adv}^{\mathsf{SDH}}(\lambda)$,

Game G_5. This game is identical to G_4 except that the challenger aborts the game if the RO outputs two times the same value on two different queries, or outputs k_1. We set q as the number of queries to the RO, we have:

$$|\Pr[G_5 \text{ returns } 1] - \Pr[G_4 \text{ returns } 1]| \leq \mathsf{Pr}[\mathsf{abort}_5] \leq (q+1)^2/|\mathcal{K}|.$$

Remember that in order to have a significant probability of winning, the tested oracle ($\pi_{i_*}^{s_*}$ according to G_3) must remain fresh, which means that the session keys of the tested oracle's partner oracles must not have been revealed. Note that given the G_2 game, since session keys are always different, the tested oracle can only have one partner, and given the G_5 game, two oracles that are not partners have a different context and necessarily have different session keys. As a result, $\mathcal{A}$ cannot deduce the tested session key by revealing the session keys of other oracles. Finally, for the adversary to maintain a significant advantage, they must be in one of these two situations required by freshness of the tested session $\pi_{i_*}^{s_*}$:

- $P_{\mathsf{Pid}_{i_*}^{s_*}}$ was not corrupted before $\pi_{i_*}^{s_*}$ accepted if $\pi_{i_*}^{s_*}$ has an origin-oracle. In this case, the game G_4 ensures that the adversary must not have sent the key $(\overline{\mathsf{epk}_{i_*}^{s_*}})^{\mathsf{esk}_{i_*}^{s_*}}$ in a query to the RO, which is necessary to generate the oracle's session key.
- $P_{\mathsf{Pid}_{i_*}^{s_*}}$ was not corrupted at all if $\pi_{i_*}^{s_*}$ has no origin-oracle. In this case, the game G_1 ensures that the adversary must not have sent the key $(\mathsf{pk}_{\mathsf{Pid}_{i_*}^{s_*}})^{\mathsf{esk}_{i_*}^{s_*}}$ in a query to the RO, which is necessary to generate the oracle's session key.

In both cases, the session key of $\pi_{i_*}^{s_*}$ is therefore perfectly random from the point of view of $\mathcal{A}$. It therefore has no way of guessing whether the key returned by the test oracle is the real session key or a randomly chosen key. We deduce that:

$$\Pr[G_5 \text{ returns } 1] = 1/2.$$

Combining all bounds, we obtain:

$$\Pr[\mathsf{break}_{\mathsf{KE}}] \leq (\ell\mu)^2 \left(\frac{1}{|\mathbb{G}|} + 2 \cdot \mathsf{Adv}^{\mathsf{SDH}}(\lambda) + \frac{(q+1)^2}{|\mathcal{K}|}\right).$$

Furthermore, the probability of having two partner oracles at the same oracle is bounded by the probability that two oracles generate the same ephemeral key, and therefore:

$$\Pr[\mathsf{break}_{\mathsf{Unique}}] \leq \frac{(\mu\ell)^2}{|\mathbb{G}|}.$$

Finally, let us consider two partner oracles π_i^s and π_j^t, i.e., which share the same context and transcript, and satisfy $\mathsf{Pid}_i^s = j$ and $\mathsf{Pid}_j^t = i$. We will have:

$$k_i^s = H(\mathsf{ctxt}\|(\mathsf{pk}_j)^{\mathsf{esk}_i^s}\|(\mathsf{epk}_j^t)^{\mathsf{esk}_i^s}\|(\mathsf{epk}_j^t)^{\mathsf{sk}_i}) = H(\mathsf{ctxt}\|g^{\mathsf{sk}_j\mathsf{esk}_i^s}\|g^{\mathsf{esk}_j^t\mathsf{esk}_i^s}\|g^{\mathsf{esk}_j^t\mathsf{sk}_i});$$
$$k_j^t = H(\mathsf{ctxt}\|(\mathsf{epk}_i^s)^{\mathsf{sk}_j}\|(\mathsf{epk}_i^s)^{\mathsf{esk}_j^t}\|(\mathsf{pk}_i)^{\mathsf{esk}_j^t}) = H(\mathsf{ctxt}\|g^{\mathsf{sk}_j\mathsf{esk}_i^s}\|g^{\mathsf{esk}_j^t\mathsf{esk}_i^s}\|g^{\mathsf{esk}_j^t\mathsf{sk}_i}).$$

We deduce that $k_j^t = k_i^s$, then:

$$\Pr[\mathsf{breakSound}] \leq \Pr[k_i^s \neq k_j^t] = 0.$$

To conclude, we obtain the following bound for the AKE advantage:

$$\mathsf{Adv}_{\mathsf{PPAKE},\mathcal{A}}^{\mathsf{AKE}}(\lambda) \leq (\ell\mu)^2\left(\frac{1}{|\mathbb{G}|} + 2\cdot\mathsf{Adv}^{\mathsf{SDH}}(\lambda) + \frac{(q+1)^2}{|\mathcal{K}|}\right).$$

References

1. Abdalla, M., Bellare, M., Rogaway, P.: The oracle Diffie-Hellman assumptions and an analysis of DHIES. In: Naccache, D. (ed.) CT-RSA 2001. LNCS, vol. 2020, pp. 143–158. Springer, Heidelberg (2001). https://doi.org/10.1007/3-540-45353-9_12
2. Aiello, W., et al.: Just fast keying: key agreement in a hostile internet. ACM Trans. Inf. Syst. Secur. **7**(2), 242–273 (2004)
3. Arfaoui, G., Bultel, X., Fouque, P., Nedelcu, A., Onete, C.: The privacy of the TLS 1.3 protocol. IACR Cryptol. ePrint Arch. 749 (2019). https://eprint.iacr.org/2019/749
4. Canetti, R., Krawczyk, H.: Security analysis of IKE's signature-based key-exchange protocol. In: Yung, M. (ed.) CRYPTO 2002. LNCS, vol. 2442, pp. 143–161. Springer, Heidelberg (2002). https://doi.org/10.1007/3-540-45708-9_10
5. Chase, M., Lysyanskaya, A.: On signatures of knowledge. In: Dwork, C. (ed.) CRYPTO 2006. LNCS, vol. 4117, pp. 78–96. Springer, Heidelberg (2006). https://doi.org/10.1007/11818175_5
6. Cohn-Gordon, K., Cremers, C., Gjøsteen, K., Jacobsen, H., Jager, T.: Highly efficient key exchange protocols with optimal tightness - enabling real-world deployments with theoretically sound parameters. IACR Cryptol. ePrint Arch. 737 (2019). https://eprint.iacr.org/2019/737
7. Dowling, B., Paterson, K.G.: A cryptographic analysis of the wireguard protocol. IACR Cryptol. ePrint Arch. 80 (2018). http://eprint.iacr.org/2018/080
8. Fiat, A., Shamir, A.: How to prove yourself: practical solutions to identification and signature problems. In: Odlyzko, A.M. (ed.) CRYPTO 1986. LNCS, vol. 263, pp. 186–194. Springer, Heidelberg (1987). https://doi.org/10.1007/3-540-47721-7_12
9. Gamal, T.E.: A public key cryptosystem and a signature scheme based on discrete logarithms. IEEE Trans. Inf. Theory **31**(4), 469–472 (1985)
10. Lyu, Y., Liu, S., Han, S., Gu, D.: Privacy-preserving authenticated key exchange in the standard model. In: ASIACRYPT 2022, pp. 210–240. Springer (2022)

11. Marlinspike, M., Perrin, T.: The X3DH key agreement protocol (2016). https://signal.org/docs/specifications/x3dh/, signal Foundation Specification
12. Paterson, K.G., Ristenpart, T., Shrimpton, T.: Tag size *Does* matter: attacks and proofs for the TLS record protocol. In: Lee, D.H., Wang, X. (eds.) ASIACRYPT 2011. LNCS, vol. 7073, pp. 372–389. Springer, Heidelberg (2011). https://doi.org/10.1007/978-3-642-25385-0_20
13. Ramacher, S., Slamanig, D., Weninger, A.: Privacy-preserving authenticated key exchange: stronger privacy and generic constructions. In: Bertino, E., Shulman, H., Waidner, M. (eds.) ESORICS 2021. LNCS, vol. 12973, pp. 676–696. Springer, Cham (2021). https://doi.org/10.1007/978-3-030-88428-4_33
14. Ramacher, S., Slamanig, D., Weninger, A.: Privacy-preserving authenticated key exchange: stronger privacy and generic constructions. IACR Cryptol. ePrint Arch. 1338 (2022). https://eprint.iacr.org/2022/1338
15. Schäge, S., Schwenk, J., Lauer, S.: Privacy-preserving authenticated key exchange and the case of IKEv2. In: Kiayias, A., Kohlweiss, M., Wallden, P., Zikas, V. (eds.) PKC 2020. LNCS, vol. 12111, pp. 567–596. Springer, Cham (2020). https://doi.org/10.1007/978-3-030-45388-6_20
16. Schnorr, C.P.: Efficient identification and signatures for smart cards. In: Brassard, G. (ed.) CRYPTO 1989. LNCS, vol. 435, pp. 239–252. Springer, New York (1990). https://doi.org/10.1007/0-387-34805-0_22
17. Schnorr, C.P.: Efficient signature generation by smart cards. J. Cryptol. **4**(3), 161–174 (1991). https://doi.org/10.1007/BF00196725
18. WhatsApp Inc., Open Whisper Systems: Whatsapp encryption overview (2016). https://www.whatsapp.com/security/WhatsApp-Security-Whitepaper.pdf, technical Whitepaper
19. Zhao, Y.: Identity-concealed authenticated encryption and key exchange. In: Weippl, E.R., Katzenbeisser, S., Kruegel, C., Myers, A.C., Halevi, S. (eds.) Proceedings of the 2016 ACM SIGSAC Conference on Computer and Communications Security, Vienna, Austria, 24–28 October 2016, pp. 1464–1479. ACM (2016). https://doi.org/10.1145/2976749.2978350

Author Index

K. Jee and A. Kate (Eds.): ACNS 2026, LNCS 16571, pp. 585–586, 2027.
https://doi.org/10.1007/978-3-032-32560-0

MIX
Papier aus verantwortungsvollen Quellen
Paper from responsible sources
FSC® C105338

If you have any concerns about our products,
you can contact us on
ProductSafety@springernature.com

In case Publisher is established outside the EU,
the EU authorized representative is:
Springer Nature Customer Service Center GmbH
Europaplatz 3, 69115 Heidelberg, Germany

Printed by Libri Plureos GmbH
in Hamburg, Germany